DIMENSIONS
OF HUMAN
BEHAVIOR

FOURTH EDITION

Note From the Author: The Educational Policy and Accreditation Standards of the Council on Social Work Education, adopted in 2008 and revised on March 27, 2010, lays out 10 core social work competencies that should guide curriculum design in social work education programs. Competencies are practice behaviors that integrate knowledge, values, and skills. The seventh competency "Apply knowledge of human behavior and the social environment" is the explicit focus of this book and its companion volume *Dimensions of Human Behavior: Person and Environment.* That has been the focus of the books for all previous editions. In this 4th edition of the *Dimensions of Human Behavior* books, however, we have been more intentional about integrating all 10 core competencies while keeping the central focus on knowledge about human behavior and the social environment.

We have added material to assist the reader to engage in personal reflection related to social work's purpose and approach. Critical thinking questions have been added to each chapter to assist the reader in ongoing critical examination of personal biases, conceptual frameworks, and empirical research. The content on diversity and social and economic justice continues to be expanded in this 4th edition, with greater attention to issues of global social justice. New material on the changing social contexts of social work practice is introduced, most notably in terms of recent brain research, social policy initiatives, new technological developments, and global societal trends.

The ten core competencies and the related practice behaviors are presented below followed by a grid that indicates which of the core competencies are addressed in some fashion in each chapter. You might find it helpful to review these core competencies from to time to time as you are learning more and more about what it means to be a social worker.

COUNCIL ON SOCIAL WORK EDUCATION
EDUCATIONAL POLICY AND ACCREDITATION STANDARDS

Educational Policy 2.1 – Core Competencies

2.1.1—Identify as a professional social worker and conduct oneself accordingly. Social workers

- advocate for client access to the services of social work;

- practice personal reflection and self-correction to assure continual professional development;

- attend to professional roles and boundaries;

- demonstrate professional demeanor in behavior, appearance, and communication;

- engage in career-long learning; and

- use supervision and consultation.

2.1.2—Apply social work ethical principles to guide professional practice. Social workers

- recognize and manage personal values in a way that allows professional values to guide practice;

- make ethical decisions by applying standards of the National Association of Social Workers Code of Ethics and, as applicable, of the International Federation of Social Workers/International Association of Schools of Social Work Ethics in Social Work, Statement of Principles;

- tolerate ambiguity in resolving ethical conflicts; and

- apply strategies of ethical reasoning to arrive at principled decisions.

2.1.3—Apply critical thinking to inform and communicate professional judgments. Social workers

- distinguish, appraise, and integrate multiple sources of knowledge, including research-based knowledge, and practice wisdom;
- analyze models of assessment, prevention, intervention, and evaluation; and
- demonstrate effective oral and written communication in working with individuals, families, groups, organizations, communities, and colleagues.

2.1.4—Engage diversity and difference in practice. Social workers

- recognize the extent to which a culture's structures and values may oppress, marginalize, alienate, or create or enhance privilege and power;
- gain sufficient self-awareness to eliminate the influence of personal biases and values in working with diverse groups;
- recognize and communicate their understanding of the importance of difference in shaping life experiences; and
- view themselves as learners and engage those with whom they work as informants.

2.1.5—Advance human rights and social and economic justice. Social workers

- understand the forms and mechanisms of oppression and discrimination;
- advocate for human rights and social and economic justice; and
- engage in practices that advance social and economic justice.

2.1.6—Engage in research-informed practice and practice-informed research. Social workers

- use practice experience to inform scientific inquiry and
- use research evidence to inform practice.

2.1.7—Apply knowledge of human behavior and the social environment. Social workers

- utilize conceptual frameworks to guide the processes of assessment, intervention, and evaluation; and
- critique and apply knowledge to understand person and environment.

2.1.8—Engage in policy practice to advance social and economic well-being and to deliver effective social work services. Social workers

- analyze, formulate, and advocate for policies that advance social well-being; and
- collaborate with colleagues and clients for effective policy action.

2.1.9—Respond to contexts that shape practice. Social workers

- continuously discover, appraise, and attend to changing locales, populations, scientific and technological developments, and emerging societal trends to provide relevant services; and
- provide leadership in promoting sustainable changes in service delivery and practice to improve the quality of social services.

2.1.10(a)-(d)—Engage, assess, intervene, and evaluate with individuals, families, groups, organizations, and communities. Social workers

- substantively and effectively prepare for action with individuals, families, groups, organizations, and communities;
- use empathy and other interpersonal skills;
- develop a mutually agreed-on focus of work and desired outcomes;
- collect, organize, and interpret client data;
- assess client strengths and limitations;
- develop mutually agreed-on intervention goals and objectives;
- select appropriate intervention strategies;
- initiate actions to achieve organizational goals;
- implement prevention interventions that enhance client capacities;
- help clients resolve problems;
- negotiate, mediate, and advocate for clients;
- facilitate transitions and endings; and
- critically analyze, monitor, and evaluate interventions.

Chapter	Professional Identity	Ethical Practice	Critical Thinking	Engage Diversity	Human Rights & Justice	Research-Informed Practice	Human Behavior	Policy Practice	Practice Context	Engage, Assess, Intervene, & Evaluate
1	√	√	√	√	√	√	√		√	√
2	√	√	√	√	√	√	√	√	√	√
3	√	√	√	√	√	√	√	√	√	
4	√	√	√	√	√	√	√	√	√	√
5	√	√	√	√	√	√	√	√	√	√
6	√		√	√	√	√	√	√	√	√
7	√		√	√	√	√	√	√	√	√
8	√	√	√	√	√	√	√	√	√	√
9		√	√	√	√	√	√		√	√
10	√	√	√	√		√	√		√	√
Total Chapters	9	8	10	10	9	10	10	7	10	9

Dimensions of Human Behavior: The Changing Life Course and Social Work Core Competencies

DIMENSIONS OF HUMAN BEHAVIOR

THE CHANGING LIFE COURSE

FOURTH EDITION

ELIZABETH D. HUTCHISON
Virginia Commonwealth University

AND CONTRIBUTORS

Los Angeles | London | New Delhi
Singapore | Washington DC

For information:

SAGE Publications, Inc.
2455 Teller Road
Thousand Oaks, California 91320
E-mail: order@sagepub.com

SAGE Publications Ltd.
1 Oliver's Yard
55 City Road
London, EC1Y 1SP
United Kingdom

SAGE Publications India Pvt. Ltd.
B 1/I 1 Mohan Cooperative Industrial Area
Mathura Road, New Delhi 110 044
India

SAGE Publications Asia-Pacific Pte. Ltd.
33 Pekin Street #02–01
Far East Square
Singapore 048763

Printed in the United States of America

Library of Congress Cataloging-in-Publication Data

Dimensions of human behavior. The changing life course / [authored by] Elizabeth D. Hutchison and contributing authors. — 4th ed.
    p. cm.
Includes bibliographical references and index.
ISBN 978-1-4129-7641-1 (pbk.)
    1. Social psychology. 2. Human behavior. 3. Social structure. 4. Social service. I. Hutchison, Elizabeth D.
II. Title: Changing life course.

HM1033.D553 2011
302—dc22   2010018628

This book is printed on acid-free paper.

    11   12   13   14   10   9   8   7   6   5   4   3   2

Acquisitions Editor:	Kassie Graves
Associate Editor:	Leah Mori
Editorial Assistant:	Veronica Novak
Production Editor:	Karen Wiley
Copy Editor:	Amy Rosenstein
Typesetter:	C&M Digitals (P) Ltd.
Proofreader:	Dennis W. Webb
Indexer:	Rick Hurd
Cover Designer:	Edgar Abarca
Marketing Manager:	Stephanie Adams

Brief Contents

Detailed Contents

Case Studies

Chapter	Case	Case Information	Page
	9.3 Joseph and Elizabeth Menzel, a German Couple	79-year-old woman with dementia of the Alzheimer's type, living in small town in Bavaria, Germany, with 84-year-old husband, family caregiving issues, informal and formal caregiving integration	352
10 Very Late Adulthood	10.1 Margaret Davis Stays at Home	85-year-old Caucasian woman, rural southern West Virginia, hypertension, Type II diabetes, undiagnosed memory problems, family caregiving issues	400
	10.2 Bina Patel Outlives Her Son	90-year-old woman, immigrant from South Asia, mild stroke, 69-year-old son diagnosed with pancreatic cancer, family caregiving issues	401
	10.3 Pete Mullin Loses His Sister's Support	96-year-old second-generation Irish American Catholic, living in rural Florida retirement community with sister who is dying, loss and grief issues, care planning issues	402

Preface

Like many people, my life has been full of change since the first edition of this book was published in 1999. After a merger/acquisition, my husband took a new position in Washington, D.C., and we moved to the nation's capitol from Richmond, Virginia, where we had lived for 13 years. I changed my teaching affiliation from the Richmond campus of the Virginia Commonwealth University School of Social Work to the satellite program in northern Virginia. While I worked on the second edition of the book in 2002, my mother-in-law, for whom my husband and I had served as primary caregivers, began a fast decline and died rather quickly. A year later, my mother had a stroke, and my father died a month after that. Shortly after, my son relocated from Pennsylvania to North Carolina, and my daughter entered graduate school. In 2005, we celebrated the marriage of my daughter. Since the third edition was published, my husband started an encore career in California, I retired from teaching and joined my husband in California, my son was married, and we have welcomed two grandchildren into the family. Recently, my mother's health went into steep decline and she died. These events have all had an impact on my life course.

But, change has not been confined to change in my multigenerational family. Since the first edition of the book was published, we had a presidential election for which the outcome stayed in limbo for weeks. The economy has peaked, declined, revitalized, and then gone into the deepest recession since the Great Depression in the 1930s. Terrorists hijacked airplanes and forced them to be flown into the twin towers of the World Trade Center in New York City and into the Pentagon near my school. The United States entered military conflicts in Afghanistan and Iraq that continue to be waged at this writing. Thirty-three students at Virginia Tech University died in a mass murder/suicide rampage that shook the campus on a beautiful spring day. Natural disasters have killed and traumatized millions around the world. New communication technologies have continued to be developed at a fast clip, increasing our global interdependence. The United States elected its first African American president.

Since I was a child listening to my grandmother's stories about the challenges, joys, and dramatic as well as mundane events in her life, I have been captivated by people's stories. I have learned that a specific event can be understood only in the context of an ongoing life story. Social work has historically used the idea of person-in-environment to develop a multidimensional understanding of human behavior. This idea has become popular as well with most social and behavioral science disciplines. Recently, we have recognized the need to add the aspect of time to the person-environment construct, to capture the dynamic, changing nature of person-in-environment.

Organized around time, this book tries to help you understand the relationship between time and human behavior. The companion volume to this book, *Person and Environment*, analyzes relevant dimensions of person and environment and presents up-to-date reports on theory and research about each of these dimensions. The purpose of this volume is to show how these multiple dimensions of person and environment work together with dimensions of time to produce patterns in unique life course journeys.

LIFE COURSE PERSPECTIVE

As in the first edition, my colleagues and I have chosen a life course perspective to capture the dynamic, changing nature of person-environment transactions. In the life course perspective, human behavior is not a linear march through time, nor is it simply played out in recurring cycles. Rather, the life course journey is a moving spiral, with both continuity and change, marked by both predictable and unpredictable twists and turns. It is influenced by changes in the physical and social environment as well as by changes in the personal biological, psychological, and spiritual dimensions.

The life course perspective recognizes *patterns* in human behavior related to biological age, psychological age, and social age norms. In the first edition, we discussed theory and research about six age-graded periods of the life course, presenting both the continuity and the change in these patterns. Because mass longevity is leading to finer distinctions among life phases, nine age-graded periods were discussed in the second edition and continue to be discussed in the third and this fourth edition. The life course perspective also recognizes *diversity* in the life course related to historical time, gender, race, ethnicity, social class, and so forth, and we emphasize group-based diversity in our discussion of age-graded periods. Finally, the life course perspective recognizes the *unique life stories* of individuals—the unique configuration of specific life events and person-environment transactions over time.

GENERAL KNOWLEDGE AND UNIQUE SITUATIONS

The purpose of the social and behavioral sciences is to help us to understand *general patterns* in person-environment transactions over time. The purpose of social work assessment is to understand *unique configurations* of person and environment dimensions at a given time. Those who practice social work must weave what they know about unique situations with general knowledge. To assist you in this process, as we did in the first three editions, we begin each chapter with stories, which we then intertwine with contemporary theory and research. Most of the stories are composite cases and do not correspond to actual people known to the authors. We also call attention to the successes and failures of theory and research to accommodate human diversity related to gender, race, ethnicity, culture, sexual orientation, and disability.

In this fourth edition, we continue to use some special features that we hope will aid your learning process. As in the first three editions, key terms are presented in bold type in the chapters and defined in the Glossary. As in the second and third editions, we present orienting questions at the beginning of each chapter to help the reader to begin to think about why the content of the chapter is important for social workers. Key ideas are summarized at the beginning of each chapter to give readers an overview of what is to come. Active learning exercises and web resources are presented at the end of each chapter.

The bulk of this fourth edition will be familiar to instructors who used the third edition of *Dimensions of Human Behavior: The Changing Life Course*. Many of the changes that do occur came at the suggestion of instructors and students who have been using the third edition. To respond to the rapidity of changes in complex societies, all chapters have been comprehensively updated.

ALSO NEW IN THIS EDITION

The more substantial revisions for this edition include the following:

- Coverage of the global context of the human life course is expanded.

- Coverage of advances in neuroscience is greatly expanded.

- More content has been added on the effects of gender, race, ethnicity, social class, sexual orientation, and disability on life course trajectories.
- Greater attention has been given to the role of fathers.
- New exhibits have been added and others updated.
- Some new case studies have been added to reflect contemporary issues.
- Web resources have been updated.
- Critical thinking questions have been added to each chapter.

ONE LAST WORD

I hope that reading this book helps you to understand how people change from conception to death, and why different people react to the same stressful situations in different ways. I also hope that you will gain a greater appreciation for the ongoing life stories in which specific events are embedded. In addition, when you finish reading this book, I hope that you will have new ideas about how to reduce risk and increase protective factors during different age-graded periods and how to help clients find meaning and purpose in their own life stories.

You can help me in my learning process by letting me know what you liked or didn't like about the book.

—Elizabeth D. Hutchison
Rancho Mirage, California
ehutch@vcu.edu

Acknowledgments

A project like this book is never completed without the support and assistance of many people. A fourth edition stands on the back of the first, second, and third editions, and by now I have accumulated a large number of people to whom I am grateful.

Steve Rutter, former publisher and president of Pine Forge Press, shepherded every step of the first edition and provided ideas for many of the best features of the second edition that are carried forward in this book. Along with Paul O'Connell, Becky Smith, and Maria Zuniga, he helped to refine the outline for the second edition, and that outline continues to be used in this fourth edition.

The contributing authors and I are grateful for the assistance Dr. Maria E. Zuniga offered during the drafting of the second edition. She contributed the David Sanchez case study in Chapter 1 and provided many valuable suggestions of how to improve the coverage of cultural diversity in each chapter. Her suggestions improved the second edition immensely and have stayed with us as lasting lessons about human behavior in a multicultural society.

I am grateful once again to work with a fine group of contributing authors. They were gracious about timelines and incorporating feedback from reviewers. Most importantly, they were committed to providing a state-of-the-art knowledge base for understanding human behavior across the life course.

We were lucky to be working again with the folks at Sage. It has been wonderful to have the disciplined and creative editorial assistance of Kassie Graves again. In December 2009, I was lucky to have an invigorating day of meetings with Kassie and a host of other folks at Sage who manage the various stages of turning ideas into books and getting them into the hands of students and faculty. Associate Editor Leah Mori brought creative energy to some of the visual aspects of the book and did so in such a competent and pleasant way. Veronica Novak has been a steady assistant for the last three editions, managing the flow of work and responding to my many questions and requests. Once the drafting was done, Amy Rosenstein was a careful copy editor. As with the third edition, Karen Wiley served as the production editor and continued to work magic to develop reader-friendly design features.

I am grateful to my former faculty colleagues at Virginia Commonwealth University (VCU) who set a high standard for scientific inquiry and teaching excellence. They also provided love and encouragement through both good and hard times. My conversations about the human behavior curriculum with colleagues Rosemary Farmer, Marcia Harrigan, Holly Matto, and Mary Secret over many years have stimulated much thinking and resulted in many ideas found in this book.

My students over almost 30 years also deserve a special note of gratitude. They taught me all the time, and many things that I have learned in interaction with them show up in the pages of this book. They also provided a great deal of joy to my life journey. Those moments when I learn of former students doing informed, creative, and humane social work are special moments, indeed. I have also enjoyed receiving e-mail messages from students from other universities who are using the books and have found their insights to be very helpful.

My deepest gratitude goes to my husband, Hutch. Since the first edition of this book was published, we have weathered several challenging years and experienced many celebratory moments. He is constantly patient and supportive and often technically useful. But, more important, he makes sure that I don't forget that life can be great fun.

Finally, I am enormously grateful to a host of reviewers who thoughtfully evaluated the third edition and provided very useful feedback about how to improve upon it. Their ideas were very helpful in framing our work on this fourth edition:

Joanna Bettman
University of Utah

Kristina Hash
West Virginia University

Joan Digges
California State University, Bakersfield

Jan Ivery
Georgia State University

Mary Hart
Florida Gulf Coast University

Terri Combs-Orme
University of Tennessee

Irma Harrington
Tarleton State University

To Auggie and Ruby, two little people who are bringing much laughter and light to my life journey, and reminding me of how important it is to give all the little ones a good start on their life journeys.

CHAPTER

1

A Life Course Perspective

Elizabeth D. Hutchison

OPENING QUESTIONS

- Why do social workers need to understand how people change from conception to death?

- What do social workers need to know about biological, psychological, social, and spiritual changes over the life course?

- Why do different people react to the same type of stressful life event in different ways?

KEY IDEAS

As you read this chapter, take note of these central ideas:

1. The life course perspective attempts to understand the continuities as well as the twists and turns in the paths of individual lives.

2. The life course perspective recognizes the influence of historical changes on human behavior.

3. The life course perspective recognizes the importance of timing of lives not just in terms of chronological age, but also in terms of biological age, psychological age, social age, and spiritual age.

4. The life course perspective emphasizes the ways in which humans are interdependent and gives special attention to the family as the primary arena for experiencing and interpreting the wider social world.

5. The life course perspective sees humans as capable of making choices and constructing their own life journeys within systems of opportunities and constraints.

6. The life course perspective emphasizes diversity in life journeys and the many sources of that diversity.

7. The life course perspective recognizes the linkages between early life experiences and later experiences in adulthood.

Case Study 1.1

David Sanchez's Search for Connections

David Sanchez has a Hispanic name, but he explains to his social worker, as he is readied for discharge from the hospital, that he is a member of the Navajo tribe. He has spent most of his life in New Mexico but came to Los Angeles to visit his son Marco, age 29, and his grandchildren. While he was visiting them, he was brought to the emergency room and then hospitalized for what has turned out to be a diabetic coma. He had been aware of losing weight during the past year, and felt ill at times, but thought these symptoms were just signs of getting older, or perhaps, the vestiges of his alcoholism from the ages of 20 to 43. Now in his 50s, although he has been sober for seven years, he is not surprised when his body reminds him how he abused it.

The social worker suggests to Mr. Sanchez that he will need to follow up in the outpatient clinic, but he indicates that he needs to return to New Mexico. There he is eligible—because he is a Vietnam veteran—for health services at the local Veterans Administration (VA) hospital outpatient clinic. He also receives a disability check for a partial disability from the war. He has not been to the VA since his rehabilitation from alcohol abuse, but he is committed to seeing someone there as soon as he gets home.

During recent visits with Marco and his family, David started to recognize how much his years of alcohol abuse hurt his son. After Mrs. Sanchez divorced David, he could never be relied on to visit Marco or to provide child support. Now that Marco has his own family, David hopes that by teaching his grandchildren the ways of the Navajo, he will pay Marco back a little for neglecting him. During the frequent visits of this past year, Marco has asked David to teach him and his son how to speak Navajo. This gesture has broken down some of the bad feelings between them.

David has talked about his own childhood during recent visits, and Marco now realizes how much his father suffered as a child. David was raised by his maternal grandmother after his father was killed in a car accident when David was 7. His mother had been very ill since his birth and was too overwhelmed by her husband's death to take care of David.

Just as David became attached to his grandmother, the Bureau of Indian Affairs (BIA) moved him to a boarding school. His hair was cut short with a tuft left at his forehead, which gave the teachers something to pull when he was being reprimanded. Like most Native American/First Nations children, David suffered this harshness in silence. Now, he feels that it is important to break this silence. He has told his grandchildren about having his mouth washed out with soap for speaking Navajo. He jokes that he has been baptized in four different religions—Mormon, Catholic, Lutheran, and Episcopalian—because these were the religious groups running the boarding schools he attended. He also remembers the harsh beatings for not studying, or for committing other small infractions, before the BIA changed its policies for boarding homes and the harsh beatings diminished.

David often spent holidays at the school, because his grandmother had no money for transportation. He remembers feeling so alone. When David did visit his grandmother, he realized he was forgetting his Navajo and saw that she was aging quickly.

He joined the Marines when he was 18, like many high school graduates of that era, and his grandmother could not understand why he wanted to join the "White man's war." David now recognizes why his grandmother questioned his decision to go to war. During his alcohol treatments, especially during the use of the Native sweat lodge, he often relived the horrible memories of the bombings and killings in Vietnam; these were the memories he spent his adult life trying to silence with his alcohol abuse. Like many veterans, he ended up on the streets, homeless, seeking only the numbness his alcoholism provided. But the memories were always there. Sometimes his memories of the children in the Vietnam villages reminded him of the children from the boarding schools who had been so scared; some of the Vietnamese children even looked like his Native American friends.

(Continued)

(Continued)

It was through the Native American medicine retreats during David's rehabilitation that he began to touch a softer reality. He began to believe in a higher order again. Although his father's funeral had been painful, David experienced his grandmother's funeral in a more spiritual way. It was as if she was there guiding him to enter his new role. David now realizes this was a turning point in his life.

At his grandmother's funeral, David's great-uncle, a medicine man, asked him to come and live with him because he was getting too old to cut or carry wood. He also wanted to teach David age-old cures that would enable him to help others struggling with alcohol dependency, from Navajo as well as other tribes. Although David is still learning, his work with other alcoholics has been inspirational, and he finds he can make special connections to Vietnam veterans.

Recently, David attended a conference where one of the First Nations speakers talked about the transgenerational trauma that families experienced because of the horrible beatings children encountered at the boarding schools. David is thankful that his son has broken the cycle of alcoholism and did not face the physical abuse to which he was subjected. But he is sad that his son was depressed for many years as a teen and young man. Now, both he and Marco are working to heal their relationship. They draw on the meaning and strength of their cultural and spiritual rituals. David's new role as spiritual and cultural teacher in his family has provided him with respect he never anticipated. Finally he is able to use his grandmother's wise teachings and his healing apprenticeship with his great-uncle to help his immediate family and his tribe.

A social worker working a situation like this—helping Mr. Sanchez with his discharge plans—must be aware that discharge planning involves one life transition that is a part of a larger life trajectory.

—*Maria E. Zuniga*

Case Study 1.2

Mahdi Mahdi's Shared Journey

Social workers involved in refugee resettlement work are eager to learn all they can about the refugee experience. Social workers in these scenarios are learning from their clients, but they will also find it helpful to talk with other resettlement workers who have made a successful adjustment after entering the United States as refugees. In this particular case, the social worker has been particularly grateful for what she has learned from conversations with Mahdi Mahdi. Mahdi works as an immigration specialist at Catholic Social Services in Phoenix, providing the kind of services that he could have used when he came to Phoenix as a refugee in 1992.

Mahdi was born in Baghdad, Iraq, in 1957. His father was a teacher, and his mother stayed at home to raise Mahdi and his four brothers and two sisters. Mahdi remembers the Baghdad of his childhood as a mix of old and new architecture and traditional and modern ways of life. Life in Baghdad was "very good" for him until about 1974, when political unrest and military control changed the quality of life.

Mahdi and his wife were married after they graduated from Baghdad University with degrees in fine arts in 1982. Mahdi started teaching high school art when he graduated from college, but he was immediately drafted as an officer in the military to fight in the Iran-Iraq War. He was supposed to serve for only two years, but the war went on for eight years, and he was not able to leave the military until 1989. Mahdi recalls that many of his friends were killed in the war.

By the end of the war, Mahdi and his wife had two daughters, and after the war Mahdi went back to teaching. He began to think, however, of moving to the United States, where two of his brothers had already immigrated. He began saving money and was hoping to emigrate in November 1990.

But on August 2, 1990, Iraq invaded Kuwait, and war broke out once again. Mahdi was drafted again to fight in this war, but he refused to serve. According to the law in Iraq, anyone refusing the draft would be shot in front of his house. Mahdi had to go into hiding, and he remembers this as a very frightening time.

After a few months, Mahdi took his wife, two children, and brother in a car and escaped from Baghdad. He approached the American army on the border of Iraq and Kuwait. The Americans took Mahdi and his family to a camp at Rafha in northern Saudi Arabia and left them there with the Saudi Arabian soldiers. Mahdi's wife and children were very unhappy in the camp. The sun was hot, there was nothing green to be seen, and the wind storms were frightening. Mahdi also reports that the Saudi soldiers treated the Iraqi refugees like animals, beating them with sticks.

Mahdi and his family were in the refugee camp for about a year and a half. He was very frightened because he had heard that some members of the Saudi Arabian army had an unofficial agreement with the Iraqi army to drop any refugees that they wanted at the Iraq border. One day he asked a man who came into the camp to help him get a letter to one of his brothers. Mahdi also wrote to the U.S. embassy. Mahdi's brother petitioned to have him removed from the camp, and Mahdi and his family were taken to the U.S. embassy in Riyadh. Mahdi worked as a volunteer at the embassy for almost a month, and then he and his family flew to Switzerland, on to New York, and finally to Arizona. It was now September of 1992.

Mahdi and his family lived with one of his brothers for about a month and a half, and then they moved into their own apartment. Mahdi worked as a cashier in a convenience store and took English classes at night. He wanted to be able to help his daughters with their schoolwork. Mahdi reports that although the culture was very different from what he and his family were accustomed to, it did not all come as a surprise. Iraq was the first Middle Eastern country to get television, and Mahdi knew a lot about the United States from the programs he saw.

After a year and a half at the convenience store, Mahdi decided to open his own moving company, USA Moving Company. He also went to school half time to study physics and math. He kept the moving company for two years, but it was hard. Some customers didn't like his accent, and some of the people he hired didn't like to work for an Iraqi.

After he gave up the moving company, Mahdi taught seventh-grade fine arts in a public school for a couple of years. He did not enjoy this job, because the students were not respectful to him.

For the past several years, Mahdi has worked as an immigration specialist for Catholic Social Services. He enjoys this work very much and has assisted refugees and immigrants from many countries, including Somalia, Vietnam, and the Kosovo region of Yugoslavia. Mahdi has finished 20 credits toward a master's degree in art education, and he thinks he might go back to teaching someday.

Mahdi's father died in 1982 from a heart attack; Mahdi thinks that worrying about his sons' safety killed his father. Mahdi's mother immigrated to Arizona in 1996 and lives about a mile from Mahdi and his family, next door to one of Mahdi's brothers. (Three of Mahdi's brothers are in Phoenix and one is in Canada. One sister is in Norway and the other is in Ukraine.) Mahdi's mother loves being near the grandchildren, but she does not speak English and thus has a hard time meeting new people. In 1994, Mahdi and his wife had a third daughter. About 11 months ago, Mahdi's mother- and father-in-law immigrated to the United States and came to live with Mahdi and his family. His wife now stays home to take care of them. Mahdi is sensitive to how hard it is for them to move to a new culture at their age.

(Continued)

(Continued)

Mahdi and his family live in a neighborhood of Anglo Americans. His daughters' friends are mostly Anglo Americans and Hispanic Americans. Although Mahdi and his family are Muslim, Mahdi says that he is not a very religious person. They do not go to mosque, and his wife does not wear a veil—although his mother does. Mahdi says that his faith is a personal matter, and he does not like to draw attention to it. It is much better, he says, to keep it personal.

This part of the conversation brings Mahdi to mention the aftermath of September 11, 2001, and what it is like living in the United States as an Iraqi American since the terrorist attack. He says that, overall, people have been very good to him, although he has had some bad experiences on the street a few times, when people have stopped him and pointed their fingers angrily in his face. His neighbors and colleagues at work have offered their support.

Mahdi suggests that the social worker might want to talk with his daughter, Rusel, to get another view of the family's immigration experience. Rusel recently graduated from high school and is preparing to enroll at the University of Arizona to study civil engineering.

When Rusel thinks of Baghdad, it is mostly the war that she remembers. She remembers the trip in the car that took her family away from Baghdad, and she remembers being confused about what was happening. Her memories of the refugee camp in Rafha are not pleasant. The physical environment was strange and frightening to her: no trees, hot sand, flies everywhere, no water for a shower, no way to get cool, living in a tent with the sound of sandstorms.

When the Mahdi family left the camp, Rusel did not know where they were going, but she was glad to be leaving. Her memories of coming to the United States are very positive. She was happy to be living in a house instead of a tent and to be surrounded by uncles, aunts, and cousins. At first, it was very hard to communicate at school, but her teacher assigned another student, Nikki, to help Rusel adjust. Rusel is still grateful for the way that Nikki made her feel comfortable in her new surroundings. Rusel is also quick to add that she was in an English as a second language (ESL) program for three years, and she wants everybody to know how important ESL is for immigrant children. Certainly, she now speaks with remarkable English fluency. Rusel also is grateful that she had "Aunt Sue," an American woman married to one of her uncles, who helped her whole family adjust. She knows that many immigrant families come to the United States without that kind of built-in assistance, and she is proud of the work her father does at the Catholic Social Services.

Rusel is an exuberant young woman, full of excitement about her future. She turned somber, however, at the end of the conversation when she brought up the subject of September 11, 2001. She was very frightened then, and continues to be frightened, about how people in the United States view her and other Arabic people. She says, "I would not hurt a fly," but she fears that people will make other assumptions about her.

A social worker who will assist many refugee families has a lot to gain from learning stories like this—about Mahdi Mahdi's preimmigration experience, migration journey, and resettlement adjustments. We must realize, however, that each immigration journey is unique.

—Story told June 2002

The Suarez Family After September 11, 2001

Maria is a busy, active 11-year-old whose life was changed by the events of September 11, 2001. Her mother, Emma Suarez, worked at the World Trade Center and did not survive the attack.

Emma was born in Puerto Rico and came to the mainland to live in the South Bronx when she was 5, along with her parents, a younger brother, two sisters, and an older brother. Emma's father, Carlos, worked hard to make a living for his family, sometimes working as many as three jobs at once. After the children were all in school, Emma's mother, Rosa, began to work as a domestic worker in the homes of a few wealthy families in Manhattan.

Emma was a strong student from her first days in public school and was often at the top of her class. Her younger brother, Juan, and the sister closest to her in age, Carmen, also were good students, but they were never the star pupils that Emma was. The elder brother, Jesus, and sister, Aida, struggled in school from the time they came to the South Bronx, and both dropped out before they finished high school. Jesus has returned to Puerto Rico to live on the farm with his grandparents.

During her summer vacations from high school, Emma often cared for the children of some of the families for whom her mother worked. One employer was particularly impressed with Emma's quickness and pleasant temperament and took a special interest in her. She encouraged Emma to apply to colleges during her senior year in high school. Emma was accepted at City College and was planning to begin as a full-time student after high school graduation.

A month before Emma was to start school, however, her father had a stroke and was unable to return to work. Rosa and Aida rearranged their work schedules so that they could share the care of Carlos. Carmen had a husband and two young children of her own. Emma realized that she was now needed as an income earner. She took a position doing data entry in an office in the World Trade Center and took evening courses on a part-time basis. She was studying to be a teacher, because she loved learning and wanted to pass on that love to other students.

And then Emma found herself pregnant. She knew that Alejandro Padilla, a young man in one of her classes at school, was the father. Alejandro said that he was not ready to marry, however. Emma returned to work a month after Maria was born, but she did not return to school. At first, Rosa and Aida were not happy that Emma was pregnant with no plans to marry, but once Maria was born, they fell hopelessly in love with her. They were happy to share the care of Maria, along with Carlos, while Emma worked. Emma cared for Maria and Carlos in the evenings so that Rosa and Aida could work.

Maria was, indeed, an engaging baby, and she was thriving with the adoration of Rosa, Carlos, Aida, Juan, and Emma. Emma missed school, but she held on to her dreams to be a teacher someday.

On the morning of September 11, 2001, Emma left early for work at her job on the 84th floor of the south tower of the World Trade Center, because she was nearing a deadline on a big project. Aida was bathing Carlos when Carmen called about a plane hitting the World Trade Center. Aida called Emma's number, but did not get through to her.

(Continued)

(Continued)

The next few days, even weeks, are a blur to the Suarez family. Juan, Carmen, and Aida took turns going to the Family Assistance Center, but there was no news about Emma. At one point, because Juan was worried about Rosa, he brought her to the Red Cross Disaster Counseling Center where they met with a social worker who was specially trained for working in disaster situations. Rosa seemed to be near collapse.

Juan, Rosa, and Aida all missed a lot of work for a number of weeks, and the cash flow sometimes became problematic. They were blessed with the generosity of their Catholic parish, employers, neighbors, and a large extended family; however, financial worries are not their greatest concerns at the moment. They are relieved that Maria will have access to money for a college education, because children of parents who died in the World Trade Center catastrophe are eligible to receive death benefits until age 21, or 23 if they are full-time students. They continue to miss Emma terribly and struggle to understand the horrific thing that happened to her, but the pain is not as great as it once was. They all still have nightmares about planes hitting tall buildings, however.

Maria is lucky to have such a close loving family. She is sorry that she doesn't have clear memories of her mother and likes to look at photos of the beautiful young woman that she understands to be her mother. She feels sad when she hears people talk about the events of September 11, 2001, which happens in the South Bronx a lot.

A social worker doing disaster relief must be aware of the large impact that disasters have on the multigenerational family, both in the present and for years to come.

A DEFINITION OF THE LIFE COURSE PERSPECTIVE

One of the things that the stories of David Sanchez, Mahdi Mahdi, and the Suarez family have in common is that they unfolded over time, across multiple generations. We all have stories that unfold as we progress through life. A useful way to understand this relationship between time and human behavior is the **life course perspective,** which looks at how chronological age, relationships, common life transitions, and social change shape people's lives from birth to death. Of course, time is only one dimension of human behavior; characteristics of the person and the environment in which the person lives also play a part (see Exhibit 1.1). But it is common and sensible to try to understand a person by looking at the way that person has developed throughout different periods of life.

The purpose of this book and its companion volume *Dimensions of Human Behavior: Person and Environment* is to provide ways for you to think about the nature and complexities of the people and situations that are at the center of social work practice. To begin to do that, we must first clarify the purpose of social work and the approach it takes to individual and collective human behavior. This is laid out in the 2008 Educational Policy and Accreditation Standards of the Council on Social Work Education:

> The purpose of the social work profession is to promote human and community well-being. Guided by a person and environment construct, a global perspective, respect for human diversity, and knowledge based on scientific inquiry, social work's purpose is actualized through its quest for social and economic justice, the prevention of conditions that limit human rights, the elimination of poverty, and the enhancement of the quality of life for all persons. (Council on Social Work Education, 2008, p. 1)

Section 2.1.7 of the policy lays out the guidelines for the human behavior and the social environment curriculum, which includes knowledge about human behavior across the life course. That is the specific purpose of this book.

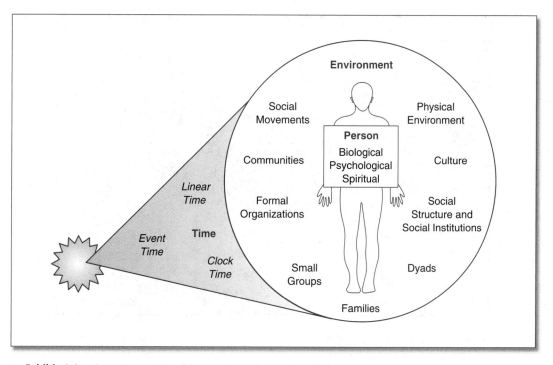

▲ **Exhibit 1.1**   The Relationship of Person, Environment, and Time

Social workers also have a well-defined value base to guide their efforts to promote individual and community well-being. Six core values of the profession have been set out in a preamble to the Code of Ethics established by the National Association for Social Workers (NASW) in 1996 and revised in 1999 (NASW, 1999). These values are service, social justice, dignity and worth of the person, importance of human relationships, integrity, and competence. Throughout the chapters, the contributing authors and I provide suggestions about needed social work services and how to provide those services in a trustworthy manner. We take social work's commitment to social justice seriously, and social justice issues are highlighted in every chapter. The life course perspective that forms the basis of this book puts equal value on individual agency and human connectedness; therefore, it serves as a good framework for social work's commitments to both the dignity and worth of the person as well as the importance of human relationships. The contributing authors and I draw on the best available evidence about the life course to assist the reader to develop and enhance expertise in serving people of all life stages.

You could think of the life course as a path. But note that it is not a straight path; it is a path with both continuities and twists and turns. Certainly, we see twists and turns in the life stories of David Sanchez, Mahdi Mahdi, and Emma Suarez. Think of your own life path. How straight has it been to date?

If you want to understand a person's life, you might begin with an **event history,** or the sequence of significant events, experiences, and transitions in a person's life from birth to death. An event history for David Sanchez might include suffering his father's death as a child, moving to live with his grandmother, being removed to a boarding school, fighting in the Vietnam War, getting married, becoming a father, divorcing, being treated for substance abuse, participating in medicine retreats, attending his grandmother's funeral, moving to live with his great-uncle, and reconnecting with Marco. Mahdi Mahdi's event history would most likely include the date he was drafted, the end of the Iran-Iraq War, escape from Baghdad, and resettlement in the United States. For young Maria Suarez, the events of September 11, 2001, will become a permanent part of her life story.

▲ **Photo 1.1**   The life course perspective emphasizes ways in which humans are interdependent and gives special emphasis to the family as the primary arena for experiencing the world.

You might also try to understand a person in terms of how that person's life has been synchronized with family members' lives across time. David Sanchez has begun to have a clearer understanding of his linkages to his great-uncle, father, son, and grandchildren. Mahdi Mahdi tells his story in terms of family connections, and Maria's story is thoroughly entwined with that of her multigenerational family.

Finally, you might view the life course in terms of how culture and social institutions shape the pattern of individual lives. David Sanchez's life course was shaped by cultural and institutional preferences for placing Native American children in boarding schools during middle childhood and adolescence and for recommending the military for youth and young adults. Mahdi Mahdi's life course was also heavily influenced by cultural expectations about soldiering. Maria Suarez's life course was changed forever by culture-related geopolitical conflict.

THEORETICAL ROOTS OF THE LIFE COURSE PERSPECTIVE

The life course perspective (LCP) is a theoretical model that has been emerging over the last 45 years, across several disciplines. Sociologists, anthropologists, social historians, demographers, and psychologists—working independently and, more recently, collaboratively—have all helped to give it shape.

Glen Elder Jr., a sociologist, was one of the early authors to write about a life course perspective, and he continues to be one of the driving forces behind its development. In the early 1960s, he began to analyze data from three pioneering longitudinal studies of children that had been undertaken by the University of California, Berkeley. As he examined several decades of data, he was struck with the enormous impact of the Great Depression of the 1930s on individual and family pathways (Elder, 1974). He began to call for developmental theory and research that looked at the influence of historical forces on family, education, and work roles.

At about the same time, social history emerged as a serious field. Social historians were particularly interested in retrieving the experiences of ordinary people, from their own vantage point, rather than telling the historical story from the vantage point of wealthy and powerful persons. Tamara Hareven (1978, 1982b, 1996, 2000) has played a key role in developing the subdiscipline of the history of the family. She is particularly interested in how families change and adapt under changing historical conditions and how individuals and families synchronize their lives to accommodate to changing social conditions.

As will become clearer later in the chapter, the life course perspective also draws on traditional theories of developmental psychology, which look at the events that typically occur in people's lives during different stages. The life course perspective differs from these psychological theories in one very important way, however. Developmental psychology looks for universal, predictable events and pathways, but the life course perspective calls attention to how historical time, social location, and culture affect the individual experience of each life stage.

The life course perspective is still relatively young, but its popularity is growing. In recent years, it has begun to be used to understand the pathways of families (Huinink & Feldhaus, 2009; MacMillan & Copher, 2005), organizations (King, 2009), and social movements (Della Porta & Diani, 2006). I suggest that it has potential for understanding patterns of stability and change in all types of social systems. Gerontologists increasingly use the perspective to understand how old age is shaped by events experienced earlier in life (Browne, Mokuau, & Braun, 2009; Ferraro & Shippee, 2009). The life course perspective has become a major theoretical framework in criminology (Chen, 2009; Haynie, Petts, Maimon, & Piquero, 2009) and the leading perspective driving longitudinal study of health behaviors and outcomes (Evans, Crogan, Belyea, & Coon, 2009; Osler, 2006). It has also been proposed as a useful perspective for understanding patterns of lifetime drug use (Hser, Longshore, & Anglin, 2007).

BASIC CONCEPTS OF THE LIFE COURSE PERSPECTIVE

Scholars who write from a life course perspective and social workers who apply the life course perspective in their work rely on a handful of staple concepts: cohorts, transitions, trajectories, life events, and turning points (see Exhibit 1.2 for concise definitions). As you read about each concept, imagine how it applies to the lives of David Sanchez, Mahdi Mahdi, and Maria Suarez as well as to your own life.

Cohorts

With their attention to the historical context of developmental pathways, life course scholars have found the concept of cohort to be very useful. In the life course perspective, a **cohort** is a group of persons who were born during the same time period and who experience particular social changes within a given culture in the same sequence and at the same age (Alwin & McCammon, 2003; Bjorklund & Bee, 2008; D. Newman, 2008; Settersten, 2003a). *Generation* is another term used to convey a similar meaning. Generation is usually used to refer to a period of about 20 years, but a cohort may be shorter than that, and life course scholars often make a distinction between the two terms, suggesting that a birth cohort becomes a generation only when it develops some shared sense of its social history and a shared identity (see Alwin, McCammon, & Hofer, 2006).

Cohorts differ in size, and these differences affect opportunities for education, work, and family life. For example, the baby boom that followed World War II (1946 to 1964) in the United States produced a large cohort. When this large cohort entered the labor force, surplus labor drove wages down and unemployment up (Pearlin & Skaff, 1996; Uhlenberg, 1996). Similarly, the large "baby boom echo" cohort, sometimes called Generation Y or the Millennium Generation (born 1980 to late 1990s), began competing for slots in prestigious universities at the beginning of the 21st century (Argetsinger, 2001).

> **Cohort:** Group of persons who were born during the same time period and who experience particular social changes within a given culture in the same sequence and at the same age
>
> **Transition:** Change in roles and statuses that represents a distinct departure from prior roles and statuses
>
> **Trajectory:** Long-term pattern of stability and change, which usually involves multiple transitions
>
> **Life Event:** Significant occurrence involving a relatively abrupt change that may produce serious and long-lasting effects
>
> **Turning Point:** Life event or transition that produces a lasting shift in the life course trajectory

▲ **Exhibit 1.2**   Basic Concepts of the Life Course Perspective

Some observers suggest that cohorts develop strategies for the special circumstances they face (K. Newman, 2008). They suggest that "boomers" responded to the economic challenges of their demographic bubble by delaying or avoiding marriage, postponing childbearing, having fewer children, and increasing the presence of mothers in the labor force. However, one study found that large cohorts in affluent countries have higher rates of suicide than smaller cohorts, suggesting that not all members of large cohorts can find positive strategies for coping with competition for limited resources (Stockard & O'Brien, 2002).

One way to visualize the configuration of cohorts in a given society is through the use of a **population pyramid**, a chart that depicts the proportion of the population in each age group. As Exhibit 1.3 demonstrates, different regions of the world have significantly different population pyramids. In nonindustrial and recently industrializing countries (in Africa, Southeast Asia, Latin America, and the Middle East), fertility rates are high and life expectancies are low, leading to a situation in which the majority of people are young. In these countries, young people tend to overwhelm labor markets and education systems, and national standards of living decline. Some of these countries, such as the Philippines, have developed policies that encourage out-migration while other countries, such as China, have developed policies to limit fertility. In affluent, late industrial countries (Europe, North America, Japan), fertility rates are low and life expectancy is high, resulting in large numbers of older adults and a declining youthful population. These countries are becoming increasingly dependent on immigration (typically more attractive to young adults) for a workforce and taxpayers to support the aging population. In the United States, migration of legal and illegal immigrants accounted for more than one fourth of the population growth in the 1980s and for about one third of the growth in the 1990s (McFalls, 1998). High rates of immigration and high fertility rates among immigrant families are continuing in the early part of the 21st century, and it is predicted that 82% of the projected U.S. population increase between 2005 and 2050 will be the result of immigration (Passel & Cohn, 2008). Despite the economic necessity of immigrants in societies with aging populations, in the United States, as in many other affluent countries, there are strong anti-immigrant sentiments and angry calls to close the borders.

Exhibit 1.3 also shows the ratio of males to females in each population. A cohort's **sex ratio** is the number of males per 100 females. Sex ratios affect a cohort's marriage rates, childbearing practices, crime rates, and family stability. Although there are many challenges to getting reliable sex ratio data, it is estimated that there are 105 males born for every 100 females in the world (Davis et al., 2007). In most parts of the world, 104 to 108 males are born for every 100 female births, but the sex ratio at birth has been declining in most industrial countries in recent years. The reasons are not clear, but exposure to environmental toxins is suspected, with male fetuses being more susceptible to such exposures than female fetuses (Davis et al.). However, in countries where there is a strong preference for male children, such

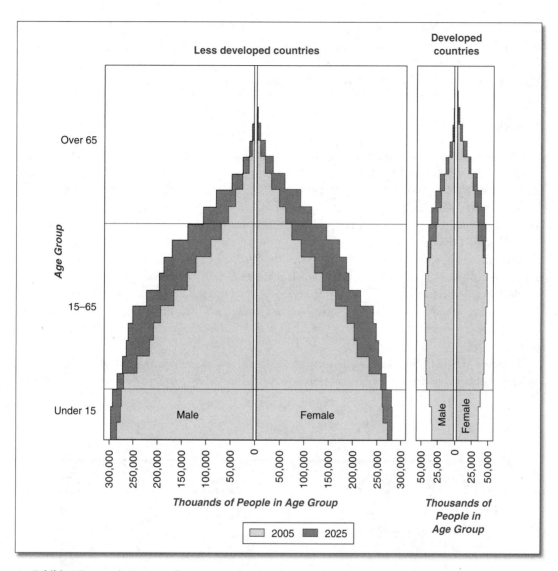

▲ **Exhibit 1.3**   Population Pyramids in Less Developed and Developed Countries

SOURCE: D. Newman, 2008. Reprinted with permission.

as China, India, Taiwan, and South Korea, female abortion and female infanticide have led to sex ratios of 110 or more at birth (Clarke & Craven, 2005). As you can see in Exhibit 1.3, sex ratios decline across adulthood because males die at higher rates at every age. Again, there are exceptions to this trend in impoverished countries with strong male preference, where female children may be abandoned, neglected, given less food, or given up for foreign adoption (D. Newman, 2008). Sex ratios can be further unbalanced by war (which leads to greater male mortality) or high rates of either male or female out-migration or in-migration.

For some time, sex ratios at birth have been lower for African Americans than for Whites in the United States, meaning that fewer African American boy babies are born per 100 girl babies than is the case in the White population.

However, recent research shows some narrowing in this disparity, with the sex ratio at birth declining among Whites and increasing slightly for African Americans. The racial disparity widens across the life course, however, with a 2005 estimated sex ratio of 86.5 men to 100 women among African American adults over age 18 compared with 96.4 men to 100 women among White adults (U.S. Bureau of the Census, 2008a).

Transitions

A life course perspective is stagelike because it proposes that each person experiences a number of **transitions,** or changes in roles and statuses that represent a distinct departure from prior roles and statuses (Elder & Kirkpatrick Johnson, 2003; Hagestad, 2003; Hser et al., 2007). Life is full of such transitions: starting school, entering puberty, leaving school, getting a first job, leaving home, retiring, and so on. Leaving his grandmother's home for boarding school and enrolling in the military were important transitions for David Sanchez. Rusel Mahdi is excited about the transition from high school to college.

Many transitions relate to family life: marriages, births, divorces, remarriages, deaths (Carter & McGoldrick, 2005a; Hagestad, 2003). Each transition changes family statuses and roles and generally is accompanied by family members' exits and entrances. We can see the dramatic effects of birth and death on the Suarez family as Maria entered and Emma exited the family circle. Nursing scholars have recently used the life course perspective, the concept of transitions in particular, to understand role changes that occur in family caregiving of older adults (Evans et al., 2009).

Transitions in collectivities other than the family, such as small groups, communities, and formal organizations, also involve exits and entrances of members as well as changes in statuses and roles. In college, for example, students

▲ **Photo 1.2**   The life course is full of transitions in roles and statuses; graduation from college or university is an important life transition that opens opportunities for future statuses and roles.

pass through in a steady stream. Some of them make the transition from undergraduate to graduate student, and in that new status they may take on the new role of teaching or research assistant.

Trajectories

The changes involved in transitions are discrete and bounded; when they happen, an old phase of life ends and a new phase begins. In contrast, **trajectories** involve a longer view of long-term patterns of stability and change in a person's life, involving multiple transitions (Elder & Kirkpatrick Johnson, 2003; George, 2003; Heinz, 2003). For example, getting married is a transition, but it is a transition that leads to a longer marital pathway that will have some stability but will probably involve other transitions along the way. Transitions are always embedded in trajectories. We do not necessarily expect trajectories to be a straight line, but we do expect them to have some continuity of direction. For example, we assume that once David Sanchez became addicted to alcohol, he set forth on a path of increased use of alcohol and deteriorating ability to uphold his responsibilities, with multiple transitions involving family disruption and job instability. Indeed, Hser et al. (2007) recommend the life course perspective for understanding drug use trajectories (or careers) that may include onset of use, acceleration of use, regular use, cessation of use, and relapse. Treatment may or may not be included in this trajectory.

Because individuals and families live their lives in multiple spheres, their lives are made up of multiple, intersecting trajectories—such as educational trajectories, family life trajectories, health trajectories, and work trajectories (George, 2003; Heinz, 2003). These interlocking trajectories can be presented visually on separate lifeline charts or as a single lifeline. See Exhibit 1.4 for instructions on completing a lifeline of interlocking trajectories.

Life Events

Specific events predominate in the stories of David Sanchez, Mahdi Mahdi, and Maria Suarez: death of a parent, escape from the homeland, terrorist attack. A **life event** is a significant occurrence involving a relatively abrupt change that may produce serious and long-lasting effects (Settersten, 2003a). The term refers to the happening itself and not to the transitions that will occur because of the happening. For example, participating in one's own wedding is a common life event in all societies. The wedding is the life event, but it precipitates a transition that involves changes in roles and statuses in relation to the family of origin as well as the marriage family.

One common method for evaluating the effect of life events is Thomas Holmes and Richard Rahe's Schedule of Recent Events, also called the Social Readjustment Rating Scale (Holmes, 1978; Holmes & Rahe, 1967). The Schedule of Recent Events, along with the rating of the stress associated with each event, appears in Exhibit 1.5. Holmes and Rahe constructed their schedule of events by asking respondents to rate the relative degree of adjustment required for different life events.

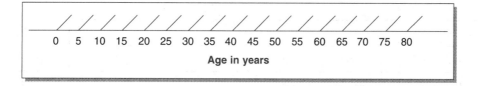

▲ **Exhibit 1.4**   My Lifeline (Interlocking Trajectories)

Assuming that you live until at least 80 years of age, chart how you think your life course trajectory will look. Write major events and transitions of your lifeline—you may want to write family events and transitions in one color, educational events and transitions in another, occupational events and transitions in another, and health events and transitional in another.

Life Event	Stress Rating
Death of a spouse	100
Divorce	73
Marital separation from mate	65
Detention in jail or other institutions	63
Death of a close family member	63
Major personal injury or illness	53
Marriage	50
Being fired at work	47
Marital reconciliation with mate	45
Retirement from work	45
Major change in the health or behavior of a family member	44
Pregnancy	40
Sexual difficulties	39
Gaining a new family member (e.g., through birth, adoption, elder moving in)	39
Major business readjustment (e.g., merger, reorganization, bankruptcy)	39
Major change in financial state (a lot worse off or a lot better off than usual)	38
Death of a close friend	37
Changing to a different line of work	36
Major change in the number of arguments with spouse (more or less)	35
Taking out a mortgage or loan for a major purchase	31
Foreclosure on a mortgage or loan	30
Major change in responsibilities at work (e.g., promotion, demotion, lateral transfer)	29
Son or daughter leaving home	29
Trouble with in-laws	29
Outstanding personal achievement	28
Wife beginning or ceasing work outside the home	26
Taking out a mortgage or loan for a lesser purchase (e.g., for a car, TV, freezer)	26
Major change in sleeping habits (a lot more or a lot less sleep, or change in part of day when asleep)	25

Life Event	Stress Rating
Major change in number of family get-togethers (e.g., a lot more or a lot less than usual)	24
Major change in eating habits (a lot less food intake or very different meal hours or surroundings)	23
Vacation	20
Christmas	20
Minor violations of the law (e.g., traffic tickets, jaywalking, disturbing the peace)	20
Beginning or ceasing formal schooling	19
Major change in living conditions (e.g., building a new home, remodeling, deterioration of home or neighborhood)	19
Revision of personal habits (e.g., dress, manners, associations)	18
Trouble with the boss	17
Major change in working hours or conditions	16
Change in residence	15
Major change in usual type and/or amount of recreation	13
Major change in church activities (e.g., a lot more or a lot less than usual)	12
Major change in social activities (e.g., clubs, dancing, movies, visiting)	11
Change to a new school	5

▲ **Exhibit 1.5**   Life Change Events From the Holmes and Rahe Schedule of Recent Events

SOURCE: Holmes, 1978, p. 747. Reprinted with permission.

Inventories like the Schedule of Recent Events can remind us of some of the life events that affect human behavior and life course trajectories, but they also have limitations:

Life events inventories are not finely tuned. One suggestion is to classify life events along several dimensions: "major versus minor, anticipated versus unanticipated, controllable versus uncontrollable, typical versus atypical, desirable versus undesirable, acute versus chronic. (Settersten & Mayer, 1997, p. 246)

Most existing inventories are biased toward undesirable, rather than desirable, events. Not all life events prompt harmful life changes. Indeed, researchers have begun to distinguish between positive and negative life events and to measure their different impacts on human behavior. For example, one research team explored the impact of recalled positive and negative life events on the psychological well-being of adolescents and found that the impact of recalled life events varies by personality type (Garcia & Siddiqui, 2009). Another research team investigated how positive and negative life events trigger weight loss and weight gain, finding that weight loss is more associated with positive life events and weight gain with negative life events (Ogden, Stavrinaki, & Stubbs, 2009). And, another research team examined the impact of positive and negative life events on oral health, finding that negative life events are associated with poor oral health but no association exists between oral health and positive life events (Brennan & Spencer, 2009). This later research project reflects the way that the life course perspective is influencing research on predictors of health, including greater focus on the effects of life events.

However, the preponderance of research on the impact of life events on human behavior focuses on the negative impact of negative life events. Some researchers are trying to understand the mechanisms that link stressful life events with immune system pathology (Herberth et al., 2008). Other often researched topics include the role of negative life events in depressive symptoms (Miklowitz & Johnson, 2009) and the impact of traumatic life events on mental health (Mongillo, Briggs-Gowan, Ford, & Carter, 2009).

Specific life events have different meanings to various individuals and to various collectivities. Those distinctive meanings have not been measured in most research on life events (Hareven, 2000). One example of a study that has taken different meanings into account found that women report more vivid memories of life events in relationships than men report (Ross & Holmberg, 1992). In an effort to capture the meanings that people make of life events, recent researchers have used the approach of asking respondents to recall life events rather than using existing life events' inventories (Garcia & Siddiqui, 2009).

Life events inventories are biased toward events more commonly experienced by certain groups of people: young adults, men, Whites, and the middle class (Settersten & Mayer, 1997). In one small exploratory study that used a life-line rather than an inventory of events in an attempt to correct for this bias, women reported a greater number of life events than men did (de Vries & Watt, 1996). Researchers have also developed a Children's Life Events Inventory, which has been used to study minority children and youth (Monaghan, Robinson, & Dodge, 1979) and an inventory to capture military events in the Chinese army (Hong-zheng, Zue-rong, & Mei-ying, 2004).

Turning Points

David Sanchez describes becoming an apprentice medicine man as a turning point in his life. For Mahdi Mahdi, the decision to refuse the draft was a turning point. Even though Maria Suarez was too young to think of September 11, 2001, as a turning point in her life, there is no doubt that the events of that day changed the course of her life. A **turning point** is a time when major change occurs in the life course trajectory. It may involve a transformation in how the person views the self in relation to the world and/or a transformation in how the person responds to risk and opportunity (Cappeliez, Beaupré, & Robitaille, 2008; Ferraro & Shippee, 2009). It serves as a lasting change and not just a temporary detour. As significant as they are to individuals' lives, turning points usually become obvious only as time passes (Rönkä, Oravala, & Pulkkinen, 2003). Yet in one Finnish study, 99% of respondents in their mid-30s reported that there had been at least one turning point in their lives; the average number of reported turning points was three (Rönkä et al.).

According to traditional developmental theory, the developmental trajectory is more or less continuous, proceeding steadily from one phase to another. But life course trajectories are seldom so smooth and predictable. They involve many discontinuities, or sudden breaks, and some special life events become turning points that produce a lasting shift in the life course trajectory. Inertia tends to keep us on a particular trajectory, but turning points add twists and turns or even reversals to the life course. For example, we expect someone who is addicted to alcohol to continue to organize his or her life around that substance unless some event becomes a turning point for recovery (Hser et al., 2007).

Transitions and life events do not always produce the major change that would constitute a turning point. However, either a transition or life event may be perceived as a turning point as time passes. Longitudinal research indicates that three types of life events can serve as turning points (Rutter, 1996):

1. Life events that either close or open opportunities

2. Life events that make a lasting change on the person's environment

3. Life events that change a person's self-concept, beliefs, or expectations

Some events, such as migration to a new country, are momentous because they qualify as all three types of events (Jasso, 2003). Migration, whether voluntary or involuntary, certainly makes a lasting change on the environment in which the person lives; it may also close and open opportunities and cause a change in self-concept and beliefs. Certainly, that seems to be the case with Mahdi Mahdi. Keep in mind, however, that individuals make subjective assessments of life events. The same type of life event may be a turning point for one individual, family, or other collectivity, but not for another. For example, one research team found that an HIV diagnosis was a turning point for 37% of their sample of HIV-positive people but was not reported as a turning point for 63% of the sample (Kremer, Ironson, & Kaplan, 2009). Less dramatic transitions may also become turning points, depending on the individual's assessment of their importance. An Australian study of women found a change in the nature of turning points in midlife—before midlife, turning points were likely to be related to role transitions; but after midlife, they were more likely to be related to personal growth (Leonard, 2006). A transition can become a turning point under five conditions (Hareven, 2000):

1. When the transition occurs simultaneously with a crisis or is followed by a crisis

2. When the transition involves family conflict over the needs and wants of individuals and the greater good of the family unit

3. When the transition is "off-time," meaning that it does not occur at the typical stage in life

4. When the transition is followed by unforeseen negative consequences

5. When the transition requires exceptional social adjustments

One research team interviewed older adults between the ages of 60 and 87 about perceived turning points in their lives and found that the most frequently reported turning points involved health and family. The perceived turning points occurred across the entire life course, but there was some clustering at midlife (ages 45–64), a period in which 32.2% of the reported turning points occurred (Cappeliez et al., 2008). Gender differences have been found in reported turning points in samples of young adults as well as samples of older adults, with women reporting more turning points in the family domain and men reporting more turning points in the work domain (Cappeliez et al.; Rönkä et al., 2003). It is not clear whether this gender difference will be manifested in future cohorts if women's work trajectories continue to become more similar to men's. Researchers have begun to study the turning points that lead women to leave abusive relationships (Khaw & Hardesty, 2007) and the turning points in the caregiving careers of Mexican American women who care for older family members (Evans et al., 2009). This later research identifies a "point of reckoning" turning point when the caregiver recognizes the need for extensive caregiving and reorganizes her life to accept responsibility for providing care.

Loss of a parent is not always a turning point, but when such a loss occurs off-time, as it did with David Sanchez and Maria Suarez, it is often a turning point. Emma Suarez may not have thought of her decision to take a job in the World Trade Center as a turning point, because she could not foresee the events of September 11, 2001.

Most life course pathways include multiple turning points, some that send life trajectories off track and others that bring life trajectories back on track. David Sanchez's Vietnam experience seems to have gotten him off track, and his grandmother's death seems to have gotten him back on track. In fact, we could say that the intent of many social work interventions is to get life course trajectories back on track. We do this when we plan interventions to precipitate a turning point toward recovery for a client with an addiction. Or, we may plan an intervention to help a deteriorating community reclaim its lost sense of community and spirit of pride. It is interesting to note that many social service organizations have taken "Turning Point" for their name.

Critical Thinking Questions 1.1

Consider the life course story of either David Sanchez or Mahdi Mahdi. Based on the information you have, what do you think would be the chapter titles if Mr. Sanchez or Mr. Mahdi wrote a book about his life? How about a book about your own life to date: what would be the chapter titles of that book? Which show up more in the chapter titles, life transitions (changes in roles in statuses) or life events (significant happenings)?

MAJOR THEMES OF THE LIFE COURSE PERSPECTIVE

Over a decade ago, Glen Elder Jr. (1994) identified four dominant, and interrelated, themes in the life course approach: interplay of human lives and historical time, timing of lives, linked or interdependent lives, and human agency in making choices. The meaning of these themes is discussed below, along with the meaning of two other related themes that Elder (1998) and Michael Shanahan (2000) have more recently identified as important: diversity in life course trajectories and developmental risk and protection. The meaning of these themes is summarized in Exhibit 1.6.

Interplay of Human Lives and Historical Time

As sociologists and social historians began to study individual and family life trajectories, they noted that persons born in different years face different historical worlds, with different options and constraints—especially in rapidly changing societies, such as the United States at the beginning of the 21st century. They suggested that historical time may produce **cohort effects** when distinctive formative experiences are shared at the same point in the life course and have a lasting impact on a birth cohort (Alwin & McCammon, 2003). The same historical events may affect different cohorts in different ways. For example, Elder's (1974) research on children and the Great Depression found that the life course trajectories of the cohort that were young children at the time of the economic downturn were more seriously affected by family hardship than the cohort that were in middle childhood and late adolescence at the time.

Analysis of large data sets by a number of researchers provides forceful evidence that changes in other social institutions impinge on family and individual life course trajectories (Vikat, Speder, Beets, Billari, & Buhler, 2007). Recently, researchers have examined the impact of globalization, declining labor market opportunities, and rising housing costs on young adult transitions (see K. Newman, 2008; Scherger, 2009). These researchers are finding that transitions associated with young adulthood (leaving the parental home, marriage, first parenthood) are occurring later for the current cohort of young adults than for their parents in many countries, particularly in countries with weak welfare states. No doubt, researchers will be studying the impact of the global economic recession that began in late 2007 on life course trajectories of different cohorts. Other aspects of the current historical era that will most likely generate life

Interplay of human lives and historical time: Individual and family development must be understood in historical context.

Timing of lives: Particular roles and behaviors are associated with particular age groups, based on biological age, psychological age, social age, and spiritual age.

Linked or interdependent lives: Human lives are interdependent, and the family is the primary arena for experiencing and interpreting wider historical, cultural, and social phenomena.

Human agency in making choices: The individual life course is constructed by the choices and actions individuals take within the opportunities and constraints of history and social circumstances.

Diversity in life course trajectories: There is much diversity in life course pathways as a result of cohort variations, social class, culture, gender, and individual agency.

Developmental risk and protection: Experiences with one life transition or life event have an impact on subsequent transitions and events and may either protect the life course trajectory or put it at risk.

▲ **Exhibit 1.6**   Major Themes of the Life Course Perspective

course research are the wars in Afghanistan and Iraq and the election of the first African American president in the United States.

Tamara Hareven's historical analysis of family life (2000) documents the lag between social change and the development of public policy to respond to the new circumstances and the needs that arise with social change. One such lag today in the United States is the lag between trends in employment among mothers and public policy regarding child care during infancy and early childhood. Social work planners and administrators confront the results of such a lag in their work. Thus, they have some responsibility to keep the public informed about the impact of changing social conditions on individuals, families, communities, and formal organizations.

Timing of Lives

"How old are you?" You have probably been asked that question many times, and no doubt you find yourself curious about the age of new acquaintances. Every society appears to use age as an important variable, and many social institutions in advanced industrial societies are organized, in part, around age—the age for starting school, the age of majority, retirement age, and so on (Settersten, 2003b). In the United States, our speech abounds with expressions related to age: "terrible 2s," "sweet 16," "20-something," "life begins at 40," "senior discounts," and lately "60 is the new 40."

Age is also a prominent attribute in efforts by social scientists to bring order and predictability to our understanding of human behavior. Life course scholars are interested in the age at which specific life events and transitions occur, which they refer to as the timing of lives. They may classify entrances and exits from particular statuses and roles as "off-time" or "on-time," based on social norms or shared expectations about the timing of such transitions (Settersten, 2003b). For example, child labor and childbearing in adolescence are considered off-time in late industrial and postindustrial countries, but in much of the world such timing of roles is seen as a part of the natural order (Dannefer, 2003a, 2003b). Likewise, death in early or middle adulthood is considered off-time in late industrial and postindustrial societies, but, because of the HIV/AIDS epidemic, has now become commonplace in much of Africa. Survivors' grief is probably deeper in cases of "premature loss" (Pearlin & Skaff, 1996), which is perhaps why Emma

Suarez's family keeps saying, "She was so young; she had so much life left." Certainly, David Sanchez reacted differently to his father's and his grandmother's deaths.

Dimensions of Age

Chronological age itself is not the only factor involved in timing of lives. Age-graded differences in roles and behaviors are the result of biological, psychological, social, and spiritual processes. Thus, age is often considered from each of the perspectives that make up the biopsychosocial framework (Solomon, Helvitz, & Zerach, 2009). Although life course scholars have not directly addressed the issue of spiritual age, it is an important perspective as well.

Biological age indicates a person's level of biological development and physical health, as measured by the functioning of the various organ systems. It is the present position of the biological person in relation to the potential life cycle. There is no simple, straightforward way to measure biological age. One method is to compare an individual's physical condition with the conditions of others; for example, bone density scans are compared with the scans of a healthy 20-year-old.

Psychological age has both behavioral and perceptual components. Behaviorally, psychological age refers to the capacities that people have and the skills they use to adapt to changing biological and environmental demands. Skills in memory, learning, intelligence, motivation, emotions, and so forth are all involved (Bjorklund & Bee, 2008). Perceptually, psychological age is based on how old people perceive themselves to be. Life course researchers have explored the perceptual aspect of psychological age since the 1960s; recent research has referred to this perceptual aspect of age as "subjective age" or "age identity" (Bowling, See-Tai, Ebrahim, Gabriel, & Solanki, 2005; Hubley & Russell, 2009; Solomon et al., 2009). The preponderance of research on subjective age has focused on older adults and found that older adults around the globe tend to report a subjective age that is 10–20 years younger than their chronological age (Hubley & Russell, 2009; Montepare, 2009). This research has also found that subjective age is a better predictor of mortality than chronological age (Uotinen, Rantanen, & Suutama, 2005). In addition, recent research has found subjective age to be a meaningful concept in adolescence, with younger adolescents feeling older than their chronological age and older adolescents feeling younger than their chronological age as they face the transition into adulthood (Galambos, Albrecht, & Jansson, 2009).

Social age refers to the age-graded roles and behaviors expected by society—in other words, the socially constructed meaning of various ages. The concept of **age norm** is used to indicate the behaviors that are expected of people of a specific age in a given society at a particular point in time. Age norms may be informal expectations, or they may be encoded as formal rules and laws. For example, cultures have an informal age norm about the appropriate age to leave the parental home. Conversely, many countries have developed formal rules about the appropriate age for driving, drinking alcohol, and voting. Life course scholars suggest that age norms vary not only across historical time and across societies, but also by gender, race, ethnicity, and social class within a given time and society (K. Newman, 2008; Scherger, 2009; Settersten, 2003b). They have paid particular attention to changes in age norms for the transitions of young adulthood (K. Newman, 2008; Scherger, 2009).

Although biological age and psychological age are recognized in the life course perspective, social age receives special emphasis. For instance, life course scholars use life phases such as middle childhood and middle adulthood, which are based in large part on social age, to conceptualize human lives from birth to death. In this book, we talk about nine phases, from conception to very late adulthood. Keep in mind, however, that the number and nature of these life phases are socially constructed and have changed over time, with modernization and mass longevity leading to finer gradations in life phases and consequently a greater number of them. Such fine gradations do not exist in most nonindustrial and newly industrializing countries (Dannefer, 2003a, 2003b).

Spiritual age indicates the current position of a person in the ongoing search for meaning, purpose, and moral relationships. David Sanchez is certainly at a different position in his search for life's meaning than he was when he came home from Vietnam. Although life course scholars have not paid much attention to spiritual age, it has been the subject of study by some developmental psychologists and other social scientists. In an exploration of the meaning of adulthood edited by Erik Erikson in 1978, several authors explored the markers of adulthood from the viewpoint of a number of spiritual and religious traditions, including Christianity, Hinduism, Islam, Buddhism, and Confucianism. Several themes emerged across the various traditions: contemplation, moral action, reason, self-discipline, character improvement, loving actions, and close community with others. All the authors noted that spirituality is typically seen as a process of growth, a process with no end.

James Fowler (1981) has presented a theory of faith development, based on 359 in-depth interviews, that strongly links it with chronological age. Ken Wilber's (2000, 2001) Integral Theory of Consciousness also proposes an association between age and spiritual development, but Wilber does not suggest that spiritual development is strictly linear. He notes, as do the contributors to the Erikson book, that there can be regressions, temporary leaps, and turning points in a person's spiritual development.

Standardization in the Timing of Lives

Life course scholars debate whether the trend is toward greater standardization in age-graded social roles and statuses or toward greater diversification (Brückner & Mayer, 2005; Scherger, 2009; Settersten, 2003b). Simone Scherger (2009) examined the timing of young adult transitions (moving out of parental home, marriage, becoming a parent) among 12 cohorts in West Germany. Cohorts of a five-year range (e.g., born 1920–1924) were used for the analysis, beginning with the cohort born in 1920–1924 and ending with the cohort born in 1975–1979. This research indicated a trend toward destandardization. There was greater variability in the timing of transitions (moving out of the parental home, marriage, and becoming a parent) among the younger cohorts than among the older cohorts. Scherger also found the transitions were influenced by gender (men made the transitions later than women) and education level (higher education was associated with delay in the transitions). It is important to note, however, that another research team found that young adult transitions have remained stable in the Nordic countries where strong welfare institutions provide generous supports for the young adult transitions (K. Newman, 2008). The implication for social workers is that we must pay attention to the uniqueness of each person's life course trajectory, but we can use research about regularities in the timing of lives to inform social policy.

Many societies engage in **age structuring,** or standardizing of the ages at which social role transitions occur, by developing policies and laws that regulate the timing of these transitions. For example, in the United States there are laws and regulations about the ages for compulsory education, working (child labor), driving, drinking, being tried as an adult, marrying, holding public office, and receiving pensions and social insurance. However, countries vary considerably in the degree to which age norms are formalized (K. Newman, 2008; Settersten, 2003b). It is often noted that formal age structuring becomes more prevalent as nations modernize. European life course scholars suggest that U.S.-based life course scholars have underplayed the role of government in age structuring, suggesting that, in Europe, strong centralized governments play a larger role than in the United States in structuring the life course (Leisering, 2003; Marshall & Mueller, 2003). Indeed, there is evidence that life course pathways in Germany and Switzerland are more standardized than in the United States and Britain (Perrig-Chiello & Perren, 2005). There is also evidence that events and transitions in childhood and adolescence are much more age-normed and structured than in adulthood (Perrig-Chiello & Perren).

Formalized age structuring has created a couple of difficulties that affect social workers. One is that cultural lags often lead to a mismatch between changing circumstances and the age structuring in society. Consider the trend for corporations to offer early retirement, before the age of 65, in a time when people are living longer and with better health. This mismatch has implications both for public budgets and for individual lives. Another problem with the institutionalization of age norms is increasing age segregation; people are spending more of their time in groups consisting entirely of people their own age. Social work services are increasingly organized around the settings of these age-segregated groups: schools, the workplace, long-term care, and so forth.

In spite of formal age structuring, as suggested earlier, there is much diversity in the sequencing and timing of adult life course markers, such as completing an education, beginning work, leaving home, marrying, and becoming a parent (K. Newman, 2008). Trajectories in the family domain may be more flexible than work and educational trajectories (Settersten, 2003b). However, the landscape of work is changing, with less opportunity for continuous and stable employment, and this is creating greater diversity in work trajectories (Heinz, 2003). Research in the future will, no doubt, capture the diverse work trajectories that were influenced by the economic recession that began in late 2007. In addition, although educational trajectories remain standardized for the most well-off, who move smoothly from secondary to higher education, they are less structured for other members of society (Pallas, 2003). Life course trajectories also vary in significant ways by gender, race, ethnicity, and social class (Scherger, 2009). This issue will be discussed further later in the chapter.

Linked or Interdependent Lives

The life course perspective emphasizes the interdependence of human lives and the ways in which people are reciprocally connected on several levels. It calls attention to how relationships both support and control an individual's behavior. **Social support,** which is defined as help rendered by others that benefits an individual or collectivity, is an obvious element of interdependent lives. Relationships also control behavior through expectations, rewards, and punishments.

In the United States, particular attention has been paid to the family as a source of support and control. In addition, the lives of family members are linked across generations, with both opportunity and misfortune having an intergenerational impact. The cases of David Sanchez, Mahdi Mahdi, and Maria Suarez are rich examples of lives linked across generations. But they are also rich examples of how people's lives are linked with those of people outside the family.

Links Between Family Members

Certainly, parents' and children's lives are linked. Elder's longitudinal research of children raised during the Great Depression found that as parents experienced greater economic pressures, they faced a greater risk of depressed feelings and marital discord. Consequently, their ability to nurture their children was compromised, and their children were more likely to exhibit emotional distress, academic trouble, and problem behavior (Elder, 1974). The connection between family hardship, family nurturance, and child behaviors and well-being is now well established (e.g., Barajas, Philipsen, & Brooks-Gunn, 2008; Conger & Conger, 2008; Elder, 1974; Werner & Smith, 2001). In addition to the economic connection between parents and children, parents provide social capital for their children, in terms of role models and networks of social support.

It should also be noted that parents' lives are influenced by the trajectories of their children's lives. For example, parents may need to alter their work trajectories to respond to the needs of a terminally ill child. Or parents may forgo early retirement to assist their young adult children with education expenses. Parents may be negatively affected by stressful situations that their children face. For instance, Mahdi Mahdi says that his father died from worrying about his sons. One research team found a relationship between the problems of adult children and the emotional and relational well-being of their parents. Research participants who reported having adult children with a greater accumulation of personal and social problems (e.g., chronic disease, mental health problems, substance abuse problems, work-related problems, relationship problems) also reported poorer levels of well-being than reported by participants whose children were reported to have fewer problems (Greenfield & Marks, 2006). Without longitudinal research, it is impossible to know which came first, reduced parental well-being or adult child problems, but this research does lend strong support for the idea that lives are linked across generations.

The pattern of mutual support between older adults and their adult children is formed by life events and transitions across the life course. It is also fundamentally changed when families go through historical disruptions such as

▲ **Photo 1.3**   Parents' and children's lives are linked—when parents experience stress or joy, so do children, and when children experience stress and joy, so do parents.

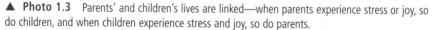

wars or major economic downturns. For example, the traditional pattern of intergenerational support—parents supporting children—is often disrupted when one generation migrates and another generation stays behind. It is also disrupted in immigrant families when the children pick up the new language and cultural norms faster than the adults in the family and take on the role of interpreter for their parents and grandparents (Clark, Glick, & Bures, 2009).

What complicates matters is that family roles must often be synchronized across three or more generations at once. Sometimes this synchronization does not go smoothly. Divorce, remarriage, and discontinuities in parents' work and educational trajectories may conflict with the needs of children. Similarly, the timing of adult children's educational, family, and work transitions often conflicts with the needs of aging parents (Huinink & Feldhaus, 2009). The "generation in the middle" may have to make uncomfortable choices when allocating scarce economic and emotional resources. When a significant life event in one generation (such as death of a grandparent) is juxtaposed with a significant life event in another generation (such as birth of a child), families and individual family members are especially vulnerable (Carter & McGoldrick, 2005a).

Links With the Wider World

Although the life course perspective has its origins in Elder's (1974) research on the ways that families and individuals are linked to situations in the economic institution, it seems that we know a lot more at this point about the ways that individuals and their multigenerational families are interdependent than about the interdependence between individuals and families and other groups and collectivities. However, in recent years life course researchers have been documenting the ways that individual and family life course trajectories are linked to situations in the labor market, the housing market, the education system, and the welfare system (K. Newman, 2008; Scherger, 2009). This line of research is well illustrated by one research project that examined young adult transitions in Western Europe and Japan (K. Newman). Katherine Newman (2008) reports that there are two divergent trends in the timing of young adult transitions in postindustrial societies. On the one hand, young adults are staying in the parental home for a prolonged period in Japan and the Southern European countries. For example, in Japan, the age of marriage has been rising, and more than 60% of unmarried men and 70% of unmarried women age 30–34 live with their parents. On the other hand, youth typically leave home at the age of 18 in the Nordic countries of Northern Europe (Denmark, Finland, Norway, and Sweden). This raises a question about the structural arrangements in these countries that are producing such divergent trends in life course trajectories.

First, changes in the labor market are driving the delayed departure of young adults from the parental home in Southern Europe and Japan (K. Newman, 2008). In the 1980s, when globalization began to produce higher unemployment, governments in Southern Europe and Japan began to loosen their commitment to lifetime employment. As a result, companies began to hire part-time and temporary workers; such tenuous connection to the labor market is associated with continued co-residence of young adults with their parents. Unemployment has always been higher in Southern Europe than in Northern Europe, but the divergence in young adult transitions in these two European regions is not fully explained by conditions in the labor market.

Second, timing of departure from the parental home is linked to situations in the housing market. In the United States, there are a number of housing options for marginally employed young adults, including pooling resources with a roommate or romantic partner or finding rental housing in a less desirable neighborhood. Such options are dependent on a strong rental housing market, however. In Southern European countries, great emphasis is put on owner-occupied housing and relatively little rental housing is available. For example, more than 85% of the population in Spain lives in homes they own. In addition, European banks typically are willing to lend only 50% of the cost of a house. In contrast, in the Nordic countries, there is a large rental sector in the housing market, with only 60% to 65% of the population living in homes that they own. Katherine Newman (2008) builds the case that these conditions in the housing market influence the timing of departure from the parental home.

Third, it is often suggested that there is a linkage between the education system and timing of departure from the parental home. More specifically, it is argued that young adults who participate in higher education leave the parental home later than those who do not participate in higher education, and that the trend toward greater participation in higher education is an important factor in the trend toward later departure from the parental home (see Scherger, 2009). This is not the whole story, however, because the Nordic countries have a higher proportion of emerging adults in higher education than countries in Southern Europe, and yet young adults in the Nordic countries depart the parental home earlier than those in Southern Europe (K. Newman, 2008).

And, finally, there is strong evidence of a linkage between the welfare system and the timing of departure from the parental home (K. Newman, 2008). More specifically, the early departure from the parental home in Nordic countries is subsidized by a generous welfare system that provides generous housing and educational benefits. The Nordic governments provide much of what families are expected to provide in the weaker welfare systems in Southern Europe and Japan.

Katherine Newman (2008) argues convincingly that it is a confluence of situations in different societal systems that impact individual and family life trajectories. In terms of linked lives, she found some evidence that young adults feel more closely linked to their families in Japan and Southern Europe than in Nordic countries—a situation that carried both positive and negative consequences. Nordic young adults, conversely, feel more closely linked to the government and the welfare institution than young adults in Japan and Southern Europe.

It is important for social workers to remember that lives are also linked in systems of institutionalized privilege and oppression. The life trajectories of members of minority groups in the United States are marked by discrimination and lack of opportunity, which are experienced pervasively as daily insults and pressures. However, various cultural groups have devised unique systems of social support to cope with the oppressive environments in which they live. Examples include the extensive and intensive natural support systems of Hispanic families like the Suarez family (Falicov, 2005) and the special role of the church for African Americans (Billingsley, 1999). Others construct lives of desperation or resistance in response to limited opportunities.

Dale Dannefer (2003a, 2003b) reminds us that, in the global economy, lives are linked around the world. The lifestyles of people in affluent countries depend on cheap labor and cheap raw products in Africa, South America, the Caribbean, parts of Asia, and other places. Children and women in impoverished countries labor long hours to make an increasing share of low-cost products consumed in affluent countries. Women migrate from impoverished countries to become the domestic laborers in affluent countries, allowing women in affluent countries to leave the home to take advantage of career opportunities, and allowing the domestic workers to send the money they make back home to support their own families (McMichael, 2008; Parrenas, 2001).

Human Agency in Making Choices

Mahdi Mahdi made a decision to refuse the draft, and this decision had a momentous impact on his own life course as well as the trajectory of members of his extended family. Like all of us, he made choices that fundamentally changed his life. In other words, he participated in constructing his life course through the exercise of **human agency,** or the use of personal power to achieve one's goals. The emphasis on human agency may be one of the most positive contributions of the life course perspective. Steven Hitlin and Glen Elder Jr. (2007) note that the concept of human agency is used by different theorists in different ways, but when used by life course theorists it refers to "attempts to exert influence to shape one's life trajectory" (p. 182). It involves acting with an orientation toward the future, with an eye for "possible selves" (Markus & Nurius, cited in Hitlin & Elder, 2007, p. 183).

A look at the discipline of social history might help to explain why considering human agency is so important to social workers. Social historians have attempted to correct the traditional focus on lives of elites by studying the lives of common people (Hareven, 2000). By doing so, they discovered that many groups once considered passive victims—for example, working-class people and slaves—actually took independent action to cope with the difficulties imposed by the rich and powerful. Historical research now shows that couples tried to limit the size of their families even in preindustrial societies (Wrigley, 1966), that slaves were often ingenious in their struggles to hold their families together (Gutman, 1976), and that factory workers used informal networks and kinship ties to manage, and sometimes resist, pressures for efficiency (Hareven, 1982a). These findings are consistent with social work approaches that focus on individual, family, and community strengths (Saleeby, 2008).

Emphasis on human agency in the life course perspective has been greatly aided by the work of psychologist Albert Bandura. Bandura proposes that humans are agentic, meaning they are capable of intentionally influencing their own functioning and life circumstances (Bandura, 2002, 2006). In his early work, he introduced the two concepts of *self-efficacy,* or sense of personal competence, and *efficacy expectation,* or expectation that one can personally accomplish a goal. More recently (Bandura, 2006), he has presented a psychological theory of human agency. This theory proposes that there are three modes of human agency:

1. *Personal agency* is exercised individually, using personal influence to shape environmental events or one's own behavior.

2. *Proxy agency* is exercised to influence others who have greater resources to act on one's behalf to meet needs and accomplish goals.

3. *Collective agency* is exercised on the group level when people act together to meet needs and accomplish goals.

Bandura argues that everyday life requires use of all three modes of agency. There are many circumstances, such as those discussed above, where individuals can exercise personal agency to shape situations. However, there are many situations over which individuals do not have direct control, and they must seek out others who have greater influence to act on their behalf. Other circumstances exist in which goals are only achievable or more easily and comprehensively achievable by working collectively with others.

Cultural psychology critics of the concept of human agency have argued that it is a culture-bound concept that does not apply as well in collectivist societies as in individualistic societies (see Markus & Kitayama, 2003). They argue that individualistic societies operate on a model of *disjoint agency*, where agency resides in the independent self. In contrast, collectivist societies operate on a model of *conjoint agency*, where agency resides in relationships between interdependent selves. Markus and Kitayama (2003) provide empirical support for their proposal that agency is experienced differently by members of individualistic and collectivist societies. They cite several studies that provide evidence that European American children perform better and are more confident if they are allowed to make choices (of tasks, objects, and so on), but Asian American children perform no better if allowed to make such choices. They also note that in U.S. coverage of the Olympics, athletes are typically asked about how they personally feel about their efforts and their success. In contrast, in Japanese coverage, athletes are typically asked "Who helped you achieve?" Markus and Kitayama do not deny that individuals from collectivist cultures sometimes think in terms of personal agency and individuals from individualistic cultures sometimes think in terms of collective agency. They argue, however, that there is a difference in the emphasis placed on these approaches to agency in different cultures.

Bandura (2002, 2006) agrees with this later statement. He argues that although people in all cultures must use all three modes of agency (personal, proxy, and collective), there are cultural variations in the relative emphasis put on the different modes. He also argues that there are individual variations of preferences within cultures and that globalization is producing some cultural sharing.

Clearly, however, human agency has limits. Individuals' choices are constrained by the structural and cultural arrangements of a given historical era. For example, Mahdi Mahdi's choices did not seem limitless to him; he faced the unfortunate choices of becoming a soldier again or refusing the draft. Unequal opportunities also give some members of society more options than others have. Hitlin and Elder (2007) suggest that there are both biological and social structural limits to agency. They note research that indicates that greater perceptions of personal control contribute to better health among older adults, but also propose that agency declines across the life course because of declining physical functioning.

The concepts of proxy agency and collective agency bring us back to linked and interdependent lives. These concepts add important dimensions to the discussion of human agency and can serve to counterbalance the extreme individualism of U.S. society. The modes of agency also raise important issues for social workers. When do we encourage clients to use personal individual agency, when do we use our own influence as proxy agents for clients, and when is collective agency called for?

Diversity in Life Course Trajectories

Life course researchers have long had strong evidence of diversity in individuals' life patterns. Early research emphasized differences between cohorts, but increasing attention is being paid to variability within cohort groups. However, the life course research to date has been based on samples from affluent societies and fails to account for global diversity, particularly for the life course trajectories of the great majority of the world's people who live in nonindustrial or early industrializing countries (Dannefer, 2003a, 2003b). Consequently, the life course perspective has the potential to accommodate global diversity but has not adequately done so to date.

We also want to interject a word here about terminology and human diversity. As we attempted to uncover what is known about human diversity in life course trajectories, we struggled with terminology to define identity groups. We searched for consistent language to describe different groups, and we were dedicated to using language that identity groups would use to describe themselves. However, we ran into challenges endemic to our time related to the language of diversity. First, it is not the case that all members of a given identity group at any given time embrace the same terminology for their group. Second, as we reviewed literature from different historical moments, we recognized the shifting nature of terminology. In addition, even within a given historical era, we found that different researchers used different terms and had different decision rules about who comprises the membership of identity groups. So, in the end, you will find that we have not settled on fixed terminology that is used consistently to describe identity groups. Rather, we use the language of individual researchers when reporting their studies, because we want to avoid distorting their work. We hope that you will recognize that the ever-changing language of diversity has both constructive potential to find creative ways to affirm diversity and destructive potential to dichotomize diversity into *the norm* and *the other.*

As we strive to provide a global context, we encounter current controversies about appropriate language to describe different sectors of the world. Following World War II, a distinction was made between First World, Second World, and Third World nations, with First World referring to the Western capitalist nations, Second World referring to the countries belonging to the socialist bloc led by the Soviet Union, and Third World referring to a set of countries that were primarily former colonies of the First World. More recently, many scholars have used the language of First World, Second World, and Third World to define global sectors in a slightly different way. *First World* has been used to describe the nations that were the first to industrialize, urbanize, and modernize. *Second World* has been used to describe nations that have industrialized but have not yet become central to the world economy. *Third World* has been used to refer to nonindustrialized nations that have few resources and are considered expendable in the global economy. This approach has lost favor in recent years (Leeder, 2004). Immanuel Wallerstein (1974, 1979) uses different language but makes a similar distinction; he refers to wealthy *core* countries, newly industrialized *semiperiphery* countries, and the poorest *periphery* countries. Other writers divide the world into *developed* and *developing* countries (McMichael, 2008), referring to the level of industrialization, urbanization, and modernization. Still others divide the world into the *Global North* and the *Global South,* calling attention to a history in which the Global North colonized and exploited the resources of the Global South. And, finally some writers talk about the *West* versus the *East,* where the distinctions are largely cultural. We recognize that such categories carry great symbolic meaning and can mask systems of power and exploitation. As with diversity, we attempted to find a respectful language that could be used consistently throughout the book. Again, we found that different researchers have used different language and different characteristics to describe categories of nations, and when reporting on their findings, we have used their own language to avoid misrepresenting their findings.

It seems, in any case, that Elder's four themes of the life course perspective can be used to more completely recognize diversity in its many forms:

1. *Interplay of human lives and historical time.* Cohorts tend to have different life trajectories because of the unique historical events each cohort encounters. Mahdi Mahdi wanted his daughter to tell her story because he knew that he and she had experienced the war, escape, and resettlement very differently. But, the same birth cohort in different parts of the world face very different historical events. For example, the post–World War II era was very different for young adults in Japan than it was in the United States (K. Newman, 2008). And, the children of Darfur in 2010 face very different historical events from the children in Australia.

2. *Timing of lives.* Age norms change with time, place, and culture. The life course perspective, developed in late industrial affluent countries, has paid little attention to such age norms as childhood marriage in Bangladesh, but it can be extended to accommodate a more global perspective (Chowdhury, 2004). Age norms also vary by social location or place in the social structure of a given society, most notably by gender, race, ethnicity, level of education, and social class (Scherger, 2009; Settersten, 2003a). These variables create differences from one cohort to another as well as differences among the individuals within a cohort.

3. *Linked or independent lives.* The differing patterns of social networks in which persons are embedded produce differences in life course experiences. Likewise, the different locations in the global economy produce very different

life course trajectories. The intersection of multiple trajectories—for example, the family lifeline, the educational lifeline, and the work lifeline—introduces new possibilities for diversity in life course patterns. Like many midlife adults, Mahdi Mahdi must find a way to balance his family lifeline, educational lifeline, and work lifeline.

4. *Human agency in making choices.* Human agency, particularly personal agency, allows for extensive individual differences in life course trajectories as individuals plan and make choices between options. It is not surprising, given these possibilities for unique experience that the stories of individuals vary so much. It is also important to remember that proxy agency and collective agency can produce both individual and group-based differences in life course trajectories.

A good indication of the diversity of life course trajectories is found in an often cited study by Ronald Rindfuss and colleagues (Rindfuss, Swicegood, & Rosenfeld, 1987). They examined the sequencing of five roles—work, education, homemaking, military, and other—among 6,700 U.S. men and 7,000 U.S. women for the eight years following their high school graduation in 1972. The researchers found 1,100 different sequences of these five roles among the men and 1,800 different sequences among the women. This and other research on sequencing of life course transitions has called increasing attention to the heterogeneity of life course trajectories (Scherger, 2009; Settersten, 2003a).

These research results indicate that men's life course trajectories are more rigidly structured, with fewer discontinuities, than women's. One explanation for this gender difference is that women's lives have been more strongly interwoven with the family domain than men's, and the family domain operates on nonlinear time, with many irregularities (Settersten & Lovegreen, 1998). Men's lives are still more firmly rooted in domains outside the family, such as the paid work world, and these domains operate in linear time. Men's and women's life trajectories have started to become more similar, and it has been suggested that this convergence is primarily because women's schooling and employment patterns are moving closer to men's, and not because men have become more involved in the family domain (Settersten & Lovegreen, 1998). However, the recent decline in employment stability is also leading to greater discontinuity in the life course trajectories of men (Heinz, 2003).

Life course trajectories also vary by social class. In impoverished societies, and in neighborhoods in affluent societies that are characterized by concentrated poverty, large numbers of youth drop out of school by the ninth grade (Dannefer, 2003a, 2003b; Kliman & Madsen, 2005). This was the case for Jesus and Aida Suarez. In contrast, youth in upper middle-class and upper class families expect an extended period of education with parental subsidies. These social class differences in educational trajectories are associated with differences in family and work trajectories. Affluent youth go to school and postpone their entry into adult roles of work and family. Less affluent youth, however, often enter earlier into marriage, parenting, and employment.

Another source of diversity in a country with considerable immigration is the individual experience leading to the decision to immigrate, the journey itself, and the resettlement period (Clark et al., 2009). The decision to immigrate may involve social, religious, or political persecution, and it increasingly involves a search for economic gain. Or, as in Mahdi Mahdi's case, it may involve war and a dangerous political environment. The transit experience is sometimes traumatic, and Mahdi Mahdi does not like to recall his escape in the middle of the night. The resettlement experience requires establishment of new social networks, may involve changes in socioeconomic status, and presents serious demands for acculturating to a new physical and social environment. Mahdi Mahdi speaks of the struggles in being a convenience store clerk with a college education. Gender, race, social class, and age all add layers of complexity to the migration experience. Family roles often have to be renegotiated as children outstrip older family members in learning the new language. Tensions can also develop over conflicting approaches to the acculturation process (Fabelo-Alcover, 2001). Just as they should investigate their clients' educational trajectories, work trajectories, and family trajectories, social workers should be interested in the migration trajectories of their immigrant clients.

Developmental Risk and Protection

As the life course perspective has continued to evolve, it has more clearly emphasized the links between the life events and transitions of childhood, adolescence, and adulthood (McLeod & Almazan, 2003; O'Rand, 2009). Studies indicate that childhood events sometimes shape people's lives 40 or 50 years later (Ferraro & Shippee, 2009). Indeed, recent biomedical research has suggested that we should look at factors that occur earlier than childhood, focusing on fetal undernutrition as a contributing factor in late life health conditions such as coronary heart disease, type 2 diabetes, and hypertension (see Joss-Moore & Lane, 2009).

It is quite an old idea that what happens at one point in the life journey influences what happens at later points. No doubt, you have heard some version of this idea for most of your life. However, the idea of earlier life experience affecting later development has taken on new energy since the explosion of longitudinal research a few decades ago (Elder & Giele, 2009). In longitudinal research, the researchers follow a group of people over a period of time, rather than comparing different groups at one point in time. This allows them to study individual lives over time, noting the factors that influence individual life trajectories.

Two different research traditions have examined how early life experiences affect later outcomes, one based in sociology and the other based in ecological developmental psychology. The sociological tradition is interested in cumulative advantage/cumulative disadvantage. The ecological developmental tradition is interested in risk, protection, and resilience. As you can see, we are borrowing language from the ecological developmental tradition. For the most part, there has been little cross-flow of ideas between these two disciplinary traditions, but there has been some recent attempt to integrate them, as we will discuss later.

Let's look first at research that focuses on **cumulative advantage/cumulative disadvantage.** Life course scholars have borrowed these concepts from sociologist Robert Merton to explain inequality within cohorts across the life course (Ferraro & Shippee, 2009). Merton (1968) found that in scientific careers, large inequalities in productivity and recognition had accumulated. Scholarly productivity brings recognition, and recognition brings resources for further productivity, which of course brings further recognition and so on. Merton proposed that, in this way, scientists who are productive early in their careers accumulate advantage over time whereas other scientists accumulate disadvantage. Sociologists propose that cumulative advantage and cumulative disadvantage are socially constructed; social institutions and societal structures develop mechanisms that ensure increasing advantage for those who succeed early in life and increasing disadvantage for those who struggle (Ferraro & Shippee). Recently, researchers have applied the concepts of cumulative advantage/cumulative disadvantage to study racial health disparities across the life trajectory (see Shuey & Willson, 2008).

Consider the effect of advantages in schooling. Young children with affluent parents attend enriched early childhood programs and well-resourced primary and secondary schools, which position them for successful college careers, which position them for occupations that pay well, which provide opportunities for good health maintenance, which position them for healthy, secure old age. This trajectory of unearned advantage is sometimes referred to as **privilege** (McIntosh, 1988). Children who do not come from affluent families are more likely to attend underequipped schools, experience school failure or dropout, begin work in low-paying sectors of the labor market, experience unemployment, and arrive at old age with compromised health and limited economic resources.

Now, let's look at the other research tradition. Longitudinal research has also led researchers across several disciplines to study human lives through the lens of ecological developmental risk protection. They have attempted, with much success, to identify multidimensional risk factors, or factors at one stage of development that increase the probability of developing and maintaining problem conditions at later stages. They have also been interested in individuals who have adapted successfully in the face of risk and have identified protective factors, or factors (resources) that decrease the probability of developing and maintaining problem conditions (Fraser, 2004; Hutchison, Matto, Harrigan, Charlesworth, & Viggiani, 2007).

Recently, gerontologists in the life course tradition have tried to integrate the cumulative advantage/disadvantage and the ecological developmental risk and protection streams of inquiry. Kenneth Ferraro and Tetyana Shippee (2009) present a cumulative inequality (CI) theory. They propose that advantage and disadvantage are created across multiple levels of systems, an idea that is similar to the multidimensional aspect of the ecological risk and protection approach. They also propose that "disadvantage increases exposure to risk but advantage increases exposure to opportunity" (p. 335). They further submit that "life course trajectories are shaped by the accumulation of risk, available resources, and human agency" (p. 335).

It is important to note that neither cumulative advantage/disadvantage theory nor the ecological developmental risk and protection approach argue that early deprivations and traumas inevitably lead to a trajectory of failure. Research on cumulative advantage/disadvantage is finding that cumulative processes are reversible under some conditions, particularly when human agency is exercised, resources are mobilized, and environmental conditions open opportunities (Ferraro & Shippee, 2009; O'Rand, 2009). For example, it has been found that when resources are mobilized to create governmental safety nets for vulnerable families at key life transitions, the effects of deprivation and trauma on health are reduced (Bartley, Blane, & Montgomery, 1997).

In the ecological developmental risk and protection stream of inquiry, protective factors provide the antidote to risk factors and minimize the inevitability of a trajectory of failure. Researchers in this tradition have begun to recognize the power of humans to use protective factors to assist in a self-righting process over the life course to fare well in the face of adversity, a process known as **resilience** (Vaillant, 2002; Werner & Smith, 2001). For example, researchers have found that home nurse visitation during the first two years of a child's life can reduce the risk of child abuse and criminal behavior among low-income mothers (Olds et al., 1997). Werner and Smith (2001) found that relationship with one supportive adult can be a strong protective factor across the life course.

The life course perspective and the concept of cumulative disadvantage are beginning to influence community epidemiology, which studies the prevalence of disease across communities (e.g., Kuh & Ben-Sholomo, 2004). Researchers in this tradition are interested in social and geographical inequalities in the distribution of chronic disease. They suggest that risk for chronic disease gradually accumulates over a life course through episodes of illness, exposure to unfavorable environments, and unsafe behaviors. They are also interested in how some experiences in the life course can break the chain of risk. Exhibit 1.7 shows how phases of life are interwoven with various risks and protective factors.

STRENGTHS AND LIMITATIONS OF THE LIFE COURSE PERSPECTIVE

As a framework for thinking about the aspect of time in human behavior, the life course perspective has several advantages over traditional theories of human development. It encourages greater attention to the impact of historical and social change on human behavior, which seems particularly important in rapidly changing global societies. Because it attends to biological, psychological, and social processes in the timing of lives, it is a good fit with a biopsychosocial perspective. Its emphasis on linked lives shines a spotlight on intergenerational relationships and the interdependence of lives. At the same time, with its attention to human agency, the life course perspective is not as deterministic as some earlier theories, and acknowledges people's strengths and capacity for change. Life course researchers are also finding strong evidence for the malleability of risk factors and the possibilities for preventive

Life Course Phase	Risk Factors	Protective Factors
Infancy	Poverty Child abuse/neglect Parental mental illness Teenage motherhood	Active, alert, high vigor Sociability Small family size
Infancy–Childhood	Poverty Child abuse/neglect Divorce Parental substance abuse	"Easy," engaging temperament
Infancy–Adolescence	Poverty Child abuse/neglect Parental mental illness Parental substance abuse Teenage motherhood Divorce	Maternal competence Close bond with primary caregiver (not necessarily biological parent) Supportive grandparents
Infancy–Adulthood	Poverty Child abuse/neglect Teenage motherhood	Low distress/low emotionality Mother's education
Early Childhood	Poverty	Advanced self-help skills
Preschool–Adulthood	Poverty Parental mental illness Parental substance abuse Divorce	Supportive teachers Successful school experiences
Childhood–Adolescence	Poverty Child abuse/neglect Parental mental illness Parental substance abuse Divorce Teenage parenthood	Internal locus of control Strong achievement motivation Special talents, hobbies Positive self-concept For girls: emphasis on autonomy with emotional support from primary caregiver For boys: structure and rules in household For both boys and girls: assigned chores Close, competent peer friends who are confidants

▲ **Exhibit 1.7** Risk and Protective Factors for Specific Life Course Phases   *(Continued)*

Life Course Phase	Risk Factors	Protective Factors
Childhood–Adulthood	Poverty Child abuse/neglect Parental mental illness Parental substance abuse Divorce Teenage parenthood	Average/above-average intelligence Ability to distance oneself Impulse control Strong religious faith Supportive siblings Mentors
Adolescence–Adulthood	Poverty	Planning, foresight

▲ **Exhibit 1.7**   (Continued)

SOURCE: Based on Werner, 2000, pp. 118–119.

interventions. With attention to the diversity in life course trajectories, the life course perspective provides a good conceptual framework for culturally sensitive practice. And finally, the life course perspective lends itself well to research that looks at cumulative advantage and cumulative disadvantage, adding to our knowledge about the impact of power and privilege, and subsequently suggesting strategies for social justice.

To answer questions about how people change and how they stay the same across a life course is no simple task, however. Take, for example, the question of whether there is an increased sense of generativity, or concern for others, in middle adulthood. Should the researcher study different groups of people at different ages (perhaps a group of 20-year-olds, a group of 30-year-olds, a group of 40-year-olds, a group of 50-year-olds, and a group of 60-year-olds) and compare their responses, in what is known as a cross-sectional design? Or should the researcher study the same people over time (perhaps at 10-year intervals from age 20 to age 60) and observe whether their responses stay the same or change over time, in what is known as a longitudinal design? I hope you are already raising the question, what happens to the cohort effect in a cross-sectional study? This question is, indeed, always a problem with studying change over time with a cross-sectional design. Suppose we find that 50-year-olds report a greater sense of generativity than those in younger age groups. Can we then say that generativity does, indeed, increase in middle adulthood? Or do we have to wonder if there was something in the social and historical contexts of this particular cohort of 50-year-olds that encouraged a greater sense of generativity? Because of the possibility of cohort effects, it is important to know whether research was based on a cross-sectional or longitudinal design.

Although attention to diversity and heterogeneity may be the greatest strength of the life course perspective, heterogeneity may also be its biggest challenge. The life course perspective, like other behavioral science perspectives, searches for patterns of human behavior. But the current level of heterogeneity in countries such as the United States may well make discerning patterns impossible. Perhaps, instead of thinking in terms of patterns, we can think in terms of processes and mechanisms. Another challenge related to diversity—perhaps a larger challenge—is that the life course perspective has not been used to consider diversity of experiences on a global level. This failure has led some scholars to suggest that the life course perspective, as it currently stands, is a perspective that only applies to affluent, late industrial societies (Dannefer, 2003a, 2003b; Fry, 2003). I would suggest, however, that there is nothing inherent in either the basic conceptions or the major themes of the life course perspective that make it inappropriate for use to understand human behavior at a global level. This is particularly true if human agency is understood to include proxy agency and collective agency.

Another possible limitation of the life course perspective is a failure to adequately link the micro world of individual and family lives to the macro world of social institutions and formal organizations (Dannefer, 2003a, 2003b;

Leisering, 2003). Social and behavioral sciences have, historically, divided the social world up into micro and macro and studied them in isolation. The life course perspective was developed by scholars like Glen Elder Jr. and Tamara Hareven, who were trying to bring those worlds together. Sometimes, however, this effort is more successful than at other times, and this remains a challenge for the future.

INTEGRATION WITH A MULTIDIMENSIONAL, MULTITHEORETICAL APPROACH

A companion volume to this book, *Dimensions of Human Behavior: Person and Environment,* recommends a multidimensional, multitheoretical approach for understanding human behavior. This recommendation is completely compatible with the life course perspective presented in this volume. The life course perspective clearly recognizes the biological and psychological dimensions of the person and can accommodate the spiritual dimension. The life course emphasis on linked or interdependent lives is consistent with the idea of the unity of person and environment presented in *Dimensions of Human Behavior: Person and Environment.* It can also easily accommodate the multidimensional environment (physical environment, culture, social institutions and social structure, families, small groups, formal organizations, communities, and social movements) discussed in the companion volume.

Likewise, the life course perspective is consistent with the multitheoretical approach presented in *Person and Environment.* The life course perspective has been developed by scholars across several disciplines, and they have increasingly engaged in cross-fertilization of ideas from a variety of theoretical perspectives. Because the life course can be approached from the perspective of the individual or from the perspective of the family or other collectivities, or seen as a property of cultures and social institutions that shape the pattern of individual lives, it builds on both psychological and sociological theories. Exhibit 1.8 demonstrates the overlap between the life course perspective and the eight theoretical perspectives presented in Chapter 2 of *Dimensions of Human Behavior: Person and Environment.*

Theoretical Perspective	Life Course Themes and Concepts
Systems Perspective: Human behavior is the outcome of reciprocal interactions of persons operating within organized and integrated social systems.	*Themes:* Timing of Lives; Linked or Interdependent Lives *Concepts:* Biological Age, Psychological Age, Social Age, Spiritual Age
Conflict Perspective: Human behavior is driven by conflict, dominance, and oppression in social life.	*Theme:* Developmental Risk and Protection *Concepts:* Cumulative Advantage; Cumulative Disadvantage
Rational Choice Perspective: Human behavior is based on self-interest and rational choices about effective ways to accomplish goals.	*Theme:* Human Agency in Making Choices *Concepts:* Choices; Opportunities; Constraints
Social Constructionist Perspective: Social reality is created when actors, in social interaction, develop a common understanding of their world.	*Themes:* Timing of Lives; Diversity in Life Course Trajectories; Developmental Risk and Protection *Concepts:* Making Meaning of Life Events; Social Age; Age Norms; Age Structuring; Acculturation; Cumulative Advantage and Disadvantage

▲ **Exhibit 1.8**   Overlap of the Life Course Perspective and Eight Theoretical Perspectives on Human Behavior   *(Continued)*

Theoretical Perspective	Life Course Themes and Concepts
Psychodynamic Perspective: Internal processes such as needs, drives, and emotions motivate human behavior; early childhood experiences are central to problems of living throughout life.	*Themes:* Timing of Lives; Developmental Risk and Protection *Concepts:* Psychological Age; Capacities; Skills
Developmental Perspective: Human behavior both changes and stays the same across the life cycle.	*Themes:* Interplay of Human Lives and Historical Times; Timing of Lives; Developmental Risk and Protection *Concepts:* Life Transitions; Biological Age, Psychological Age, Social Age, Spiritual Age; Sequencing
Social Behavioral Perspective: Human behavior is learned when individuals interact with the environment; human behavior is influenced by personal expectations and meanings.	*Themes:* Interplay of Human Lives and Historical Time; Human Agency in Making Choices; Diversity in Life Course Trajectories; Developmental Risk and Protection *Concepts:* Life Events; Human Agency
Humanistic Perspective: Human behavior can be understood only from the internal frame of reference of the individual; human behavior is driven by a desire for growth and competence.	*Themes:* Timing of Lives; Human Agency in Making Choices *Concepts:* Spiritual Age; Meaning of Life Events and Turning Points; Individual, Family, and Community Strengths

▲ **Exhibit 1.8**   (Continued)

Critical Thinking Questions 1.2

What are the age norms for adolescence in your family system? For young adulthood? For middle adulthood? For late adulthood? Does gender play a factor in age norms in your family? How do you think the age norms in your family might affect your social work practice with families that have different age norms?

IMPLICATIONS FOR SOCIAL WORK PRACTICE

The life course perspective has many implications for social work practice, including the following:

- Help clients make sense of their unique life's journeys and to use that understanding to improve their current situations. Where appropriate, help them to construct a lifeline of interlocking trajectories.

- Try to understand the historical contexts of clients' lives and the ways that important historical events have influenced their behavior.

- Where appropriate, use life event inventories to get a sense of the level of stress in a client's life.

- Be aware of the potential to develop social work interventions that can serve as turning points that help individuals, families, communities, and organizations to get back on track.

- Work with the media to keep the public informed about the impact of changing social conditions on individuals, families, communities, and formal organizations.

- Recognize the ways that the lives of family members are linked across generations and the impact of circumstances in one generation on other generations.

- Recognize the ways lives are linked in the global economy.

- Use existing research on risk, protection, and resilience to develop prevention programs.

- When working with recent immigrant and refugee families, be aware of the age norms in their countries of origin.

- Be aware of the unique systems of support developed by members of various cultural groups, and encourage the use of those supports in times of crisis.

- Support and help to develop clients' sense of personal competence for making life choices.

KEY TERMS

age norm	human agency	social age
age structuring	life course perspective	social support
biological age	life event	spiritual age
cohort	population pyramid	trajectories
cohort effects	privilege	transitions
cumulative advantage	psychological age	turning point
cumulative disadvantage	resilience	
event history	sex ratio	

ACTIVE LEARNING

1. Prepare your own lifeline of interlocking trajectories (see Exhibit 1.4 for instructions). What patterns do you see? What shifts? How important are the different sectors of your life—for example, family, education, work, health?

2. One research team found that 99% of young adult respondents to a survey on turning points reported that there had been turning points in their lives. Interview five adults and ask whether there have been turning points in their lives. If they answer no, ask about whether they see their life as a straight path or a path with twists and turns. If they answer yes, ask about the nature of the turning point(s). Compare the events of your interviewees as well as the events in the lives of David Sanchez, Mahdi Mahdi, and Emma Suarez, with Rutter's three types of life events that can serve as turning points and Hareven's five conditions under which a transition can become a turning point.

3. Think of someone whom you think of as resilient, someone who has been successful against the odds. This may be you, a friend, coworker, family member, or a character from a book or movie. If the person is someone you know and to whom you have access, ask them to what they owe their success. If it is you or someone to whom you do not have access, speculate about the reasons for the success. How do their life journeys compare with the common risk and protective factors summarized in Exhibit 1.7?

WEB RESOURCES

Each chapter of this textbook contains a list of Internet resources and websites that may be useful to readers in their search for further information. Each site listing includes the address and a brief description of the contents of the site. Readers should be aware that the information contained in websites may not be truthful or reliable and should be confirmed before being used as a reference. Readers should also be aware that Internet addresses, or URLs, are constantly changing; therefore, the addresses listed may no longer be active or accurate. Many of the Internet sites listed in each chapter contain links to other Internet sites containing more information on the topic. Readers may use these links for further investigation.

Information not included in the Web Resources sections of each chapter can be found by using one of the many Internet search engines provided free of charge on the Internet. These search engines enable you to search using keywords or phrases, or you can use the search engines' topical listings. You should use several search engines when researching a topic, as each will retrieve different Internet sites.

ASK
www.ask.com

BING
www.bing.com

EXCITE
www.excite.com

GOOGLE
www.google.com

LYCOS
www.lycos.com

YAHOO
www.yahoo.com

A number of Internet sites provide information on theory and research on the life course:

Bronfenbrenner Life Course Center (BLCC)
www.blc.cornell.edu

Site presented by the Bronfenbrenner Life Course Center at Cornell University contains information on the Center, current research, working papers, and links to work/family websites, demography websites, and gerontology websites.

The German Life History Study (GLHS)
www.mpib-berlin.mpg.de/en/forschung/bag

Site presented by the Max Planck Institute for Human Development in Berlin, Germany, contains information

on comprehensive research on social structure and the institutional contexts of the life course.

Life Course Project
http://lifecourse.anu.edu.au/

Site presented by the Life Course Project of the Australian National University contains information on a longitudinal study of gender roles.

Michigan Study of Adolescent and Adult Life Transitions (MSALT)
www.rcgd.isr.umich.edu/msalt/home.htm

Site presented by the Michigan Study of Adolescent and Adult Life Transitions project contains information about the longitudinal study begun in 1983, publications on the project, and family-oriented web resources.

Project Resilience
www.projectresilience.com

Site presented by Project Resilience, a private organization based in Washington, D.C., contains information on teaching materials, products, and training for professionals working in education, treatment, and prevention.

Twin Study at University of Helsinki
www.twinstudy.helsinki.fi/

Site presented by the Department of Public Health at the University of Helsinki contains information on an ongoing project begun in 1974 to study environmental and genetic factors in selected chronic diseases with links to other related resources.

CHAPTER

2

Conception, Pregnancy, and Childbirth

Marcia P. Harrigan and Suzanne M. Baldwin

(Continued)

OPENING QUESTIONS

- What biological, psychological, social, and spiritual factors influence the beginning of the life course?

- What recent technological advances related to conception, pregnancy, and childbirth are important to social work intervention?

- What unique knowledge do social workers bring to multidisciplinary teams working with issues of conception, pregnancy, and childbirth?

KEY IDEAS

As you read this chapter, take note of these central ideas:

1. Conception, pregnancy, and childbirth should be viewed as normative life transitions that require family or family-like supportive relationships to maximize favorable outcomes.

2. Conception, pregnancy, and childbirth are influenced by changing family structures and gender roles.

3. Variations in human behavior at this life stage related to social class, race and ethnicity, and religion—and their interplay—must be considered in assessment and intervention.

4. Assessment and intervention with women and their families at this life stage must reflect the most current scientific and technological developments and emerging societal trends.

5. Women who are poor or lack social support—and therefore experience greater stress than other women—are most at risk for poor pregnancy outcomes.

6. Prenatal care, including childbirth education, ensures the most positive pregnancy outcome possible. Universal access to prenatal care, then, should be a social work priority.

7. Although we are increasingly learning about the role of genetics in human development, 80% to 90% of fertilized ova with a genetic anomaly will abort spontaneously, resulting in 94% to 96% of all births occurring without genetic anomaly.

8. The incidence of low-birth-weight infants continues to be high, particularly for neonates born to poor and minority women and those exposed to teratogens such as nicotine, illegal drugs, and alcohol.

Jennifer Bradshaw's Experience With Infertility

Jennifer Bradshaw always knew that she would be a mom. She remembers being a little girl and wrapping up her favorite doll in her baby blanket. She would rock the doll and dream about the day when she would have a real baby of her own. Now, at 36, the dream of having her own baby is still just a dream as she struggles with infertility.

Like many women in her age group, Jennifer spent her late teens and 20s trying not to get pregnant. She focused on education, finding the right relationship, finances, and a career. As an African American woman, and the first person in her family to earn a PhD, she wanted to prove that she could be a successful clinical psychologist. She thought that when she wanted to get pregnant, it would just happen; that it would be as easy as scheduling anything else on her calendar. When the time finally was right and she and her husband, Allan, decided to get pregnant, they couldn't.

With every passing month and every negative pregnancy test, Jennifer's frustration grew. First, she was frustrated with herself and had thoughts like, "What is wrong with me?," "Why is this happening to us?," and "We don't deserve this." She would look around and see pregnant teens and think, "Why them and not me?" She also was frustrated with her husband for not understanding how devastating this was to her and wondered to herself, "Could it be him with the problem?" In addition, she was frustrated with her family and friends and started avoiding them to escape the comments and the next baby shower. Now, she is baby-less and lonely. She thinks having an infertility problem is even worse for African American women because of the "Black fertility" myth. She gets so tired of hearing, "No one else in the family has had a problem getting pregnant," "When my husband just breathed on me, I got pregnant," and "Just relax, and you will get pregnant." It has also been hard for Allan. For many men, masculinity is connected to virility; Allan would not even consider that he might be the one with the fertility problem, even though it is a male-factor issue in about 50% of infertility cases.

After months of struggling to get pregnant, multiple visits to the obstetrician/gynecologist a laparoscopic surgery, a semen analysis, timed intercourse (which began to feel like a chore), and after taking Clomid, a fertility drug that made her feel horrible, she and Allan finally accepted that they might need to see a specialist. She will never forget the first visit with the reproductive endocrinologist (RE). She was expecting a "quick fix," thinking that the RE would give her some special pills and then she would get pregnant. But, instead, he casually said to her, "I think your only option is *in vitro* fertilization [IVF], which runs about $16,000 per cycle, including medications." The RE also told her that for someone in her age range the success rate would be about 35% to 40%.

From her clinical practice and her friendship circle, Jennifer knows that many women think of *in vitro* as being a backup plan when they delay pregnancy. But she is learning that *in vitro* is a big deal. First, it is expensive. The $16,000 per cycle does not include the preliminary diagnostic testing, and in Jennifer's age group, the majority of women pursuing IVF will need at least two IVF cycles, $32,000 for two tries; three tries brings the bill up to $48,000. Jennifer has heard of couples spending close to $100,000 for infertility treatments.

Although about 15 states mandate insurance companies to cover fertility treatments, in the state where Jennifer lives, there is no fertility coverage mandate; consequently, her insurance company does not cover any infertility treatments. So at the very least, Jennifer and Allan would need to come up with $16,000 to give one IVF cycle a try. It's heartbreaking for them because they don't have $16,000 and their parents can't help them

(Continued)

(Continued)

out. So to give IVF even one try, they need to borrow the money. They are considering taking out a home equity loan to pay for the needed IVF cycles and know that they are lucky to be in a position to do that. They have heard of people packing up and moving to states with mandated fertility coverage and/or quitting their jobs and finding jobs that carry specific insurance that will cover fertility treatments. Some couples are even traveling abroad for fertility treatments that can be had for much less than in the United States.

Jennifer has heard that IVF is physically and emotionally exhausting. First the *in vitro* patient is forced into menopause, then the ovaries are hyperstimulated to release numerous eggs (up to 15 to 17 instead of 1), which can be painful. The eggs are surgically extracted, and finally the fertilized embryos are introduced to the IVF patient's body. Throughout this process, various hormone treatments are given via daily injections, multiple blood tests are taken, and at any point during the procedure something could go wrong and the IVF cycle called off. If all goes well, the IVF patient is left to keep her fingers crossed for the next two weeks waiting for a positive pregnancy test. If the test is negative, the treatment starts over again. She has heard that most women are an emotional wreck during the entire process because of the high stakes and the artificial hormones.

Jennifer and Allan decided to go the IVF route seven months after visiting the R.E. Before they made this decision, however, Jennifer carefully tracked her BBT (basal body temperature), purchased a high-tech electronic fertility monitor, used an ovulation microscope, took multiple fertility supplements, and used sperm-friendly lubricant during intercourse. Still nothing helped. When she heard that acupuncture has been found to increase the success rate of IVF, she started seeing a fertility acupuncturist on a weekly basis for both herbal formulas and acupuncture treatments. The acupuncture treatments/herbs are averaging about $100 per week, also not covered by insurance in her state.

Jennifer and Allan have decided to give IVF three tries and after that they will move on to the next plan, adoption. They adore each other and want more than anything to have their own little one, but if they cannot have that, they will adopt, and Jennifer will realize her dream of being a mom.

—*Nicole Footen Bromfield*

Case Study 2.2

The Thompsons' Premature Birth

The movement of her growing fetus drew Felicia into an entrancing world of hope and fantasy. Within days of discovering she was pregnant, her husband Will was suddenly deployed to a conflict zone. Through e-mails and occasional cellular phone calls, Felicia told Will details about the changes she experienced with the pregnancy but more and more, it seemed as if she and her baby were inhabiting a different world than that of her husband. His world was filled with smoke, dirt, bombs, and danger, punctuated with periods of boredom. Although she was only six months into the pregnancy, she had selected muted colors for the nursery and soft clothing in anticipation of the birth. Her changing figure was eliciting comments from her coworkers in the office where she worked part time as a secretary. With weeks of nausea and fatigue behind her, a general sense of well-being pervaded Felicia's mind and body. She avoided all news media as well as "war talk" at the office to protect her from worry and anxiety. Yet, even the sound of an unexpected car pulling up to the front of her home produced chills of panic. Was this the time when the officers would come to tell her that Will had been killed or wounded in combat? Her best friend only recently had experienced what every military wife fears may happen. The growing life within her and the constant threat of death filled her waking and sleeping hours.

Then, with dawn hours away, Felicia woke to cramping and blood. With 14 more weeks before her delivery date, Felicia was seized with fear. Wishing that Will were there, Felicia fervently prayed for herself and her fetus. The ambulance ride to the hospital became a blur of pain mixed with feelings of unreality. When she arrived in the labor and delivery suite, masked individuals in scrubs took control of her body while demanding answers to a seemingly endless number of questions. Felicia knew everything would be fine if only she could feel her son kick. Why didn't he kick?

As the pediatrician spoke of the risks of early delivery, the torrent of words and images threatened to engulf her. Suddenly, the doctors were telling her to push her son into the world—her fragile son who was too small and vulnerable to come out of his cocoon so soon. Then the pain stopped. Oblivious to the relief, Felicia listened for her baby's cry. It didn't come. Just a few hours earlier, she had fallen asleep while the fetus danced inside her. Now there was only emptiness. Her arms ached for the weight of her infant, and her heart broke with what she believed was her failure as a mother.

In the newborn intensive care unit (NICU), a flurry of activity revolved around baby boy Thompson. Born weighing only 1 pound 3 ounces, this tiny red baby's immature systems were unprepared for the demands of the extrauterine world. He was immediately connected to a ventilator, intravenous lines were placed in his umbilicus and arm, and monitor leads were placed on all available surfaces. Nameless to his caregivers, the baby, whose parents had already named Paul, was now the recipient of some of the most advanced technological interventions available in modern medicine.

About an hour after giving birth, Felicia saw Paul for the first time. Lying on a stretcher, she counted 10 miniature toes and fingers. Through a film of tears, trying to find resemblance to Will, who is of Anglo heritage, or herself, a light-skinned Latina, in this tiny form, Felicia's breathing synchronized to Paul's as she willed him to keep fighting.

Alone in her room, she was flooded with fear, grief, and guilt. What had she done wrong? Could Paul's premature birth have been caused by paint fumes from decorating his room? From her anxiety and worry about Will?

The Red Cross sent the standard message to Will. Was he in the field? Was he at headquarters? It mattered because Paul may not even be alive by the time Will found out he was born. How would he receive the news? Who would be nearby to comfort him? Would the command allow him to come home on emergency leave? If he were granted permission for emergency leave, it could be days of arduous travel, waiting for space on any military plane, before he landed somewhere in the United States. Felicia knew that Will would be given priority on any plane available; even admirals and generals step aside for men and women returning home to meet a family crisis. But, then again, the command may consider his mission so essential that only official notification of

(Continued)

(Continued)

Paul's death would allow him to return home. Although Felicia told herself she was being unreasonable, she was angry that Will was not here to comfort her. After all, she had supported his decision to join the military and had accepted that she would deliver her child alone. Then, why was this so overwhelming?

Thirteen days after his arrival, Paul took his first breath by himself. His hoarse, faint cry provoked both ecstasy and terror in his mother. A few days earlier Felicia had been notified by the Red Cross that her husband was on his way home, but information was not available regarding his arrival date. Now that he was off the ventilator, she watched Paul periodically miss a breath, which would lead to a decreased heart rate, then monitors flashing and beeping. She longed for Will's physical presence and support.

Will arrived home 2 days later. He walked into the NICU 72 hours after riding in an armed convoy to the airport. Although Paul would spend the next 10 weeks in the hospital, Will had 14 days before starting the journey back to his job, a very different battlefield than the one on which Paul was fighting.

Paul's struggle to survive was the most exhilarating yet terrifying roller-coaster ride of his parents' lives. Shattered hopes were mended, only to be reshattered with the next telephone call from the NICU. Now Felicia dreaded the phone as well as the sound of an unfamiliar car. For Felicia, each visit to Paul was followed by the long trip home to the empty nursery. For Will, stationed thousands of miles away, there was uncertainty, guilt, helplessness, and sometimes an overwhelming sense of inadequacy. Felicia feared the arrival of a car with officers in it, and Will dreaded a Red Cross message that his son had died.

Great joy and equally intense anxiety pervaded Paul's homecoming day. After spending 53 days in the NICU and still weighing only 4 pounds, 13 ounces, Paul was handed to his mother. She made sure that a video was made so that Will could share in this moment. How she wished he could participate, but she also knew that his heart and thoughts spanned the distance between war on the other side of the world and Paul's quiet victory at home. With more questions than answers about her son's future and her ability to take care of him, Felicia took their baby to his new home.

As the NICU social worker at a military hospital, the major goal must be to support the family as they face this challenging transition to parenthood. In the past 53 days, the social worker has helped Felicia answer her questions, understand the unfamiliar medical language of the health care providers, and understand and cope with the strong emotions she is experiencing. The social worker also helped during the transition of Will's arrival from war and his departure back to war. Understanding the dynamics of a NICU, families in crisis, and the needs of the military family separated by an international conflict is critical to providing this family the level of support needed to manage the multifaceted role transitions.

Case Study 2.3

Hazel Gereke's and Cecelia Kin's Experiences With the Options

Forty years ago, at age 44, Hazel Gereke gave birth to her fifth child, Terry. At the time of his birth, Terry's siblings ranged in age from 2 to 25, and his father was 48. Terry's mother tells the following story.

I menstruated regularly when I carried Terry and had long, heavy bleeding at first. I went to the doctor who said I was four-and-a-half months pregnant! I was too far along to do anything. You see, back then you had to have three doctors go before the hospital board to say the pregnancy jeopardized the mother's health. Well, my doctor was Catholic, so I knew that would not happen. I cried. My husband said, "Hazel, we'll love it!" I did not have an easy pregnancy with poor sleep, pains everywhere, and extended family demands on top of my other four kids.

Terry was hard to bottle feed but the doctor said he was only a "little slow." After his first birthday, he sat, began to walk, and said "Mama," "Daddy," "bye-bye," and "eat"—about seven to 10 words. He was beginning to dress and potty train. But when he was 15 to 18 months old, he had terrible seizures all summer long. When I enrolled him in school and saw on the record "Down child," I went right away to the doctor, who said the test would cost $75. Well, I said, "There's no need for a test—it won't change what he is." I worried because my son, Mike, was teased by the other kids when the county bus came for Terry—they called it "the dummy bus." I always knew who had compassion, because if they did, Terry stayed around. Otherwise, he went to his room.

When asked if she thinks anything should have happened differently over the years, Hazel reluctantly but honestly replies that "the pregnancy should have been stopped." Then asked "What has Terry contributed to your family?" she replies, "He has kept the family together and taught us not to take things for granted." Hazel Gereke has reminded us about the ambivalences and ambiguities that social workers need to keep in mind when working with pregnancy issues or at various points of decision-making across the life course. Let's hear from another woman, Cecelia Kin, who faces the same genetic challenge 40 years later. Here are selected notes from her journal written during her pregnancy.

June 9th: Maybe we just were not meant to have another baby . . . WHAT we have been through is all too amazing: three miscarriages before we had our darling 18-month-old Meridy, plus two more miscarriages since then. Well, at least I know I can get pregnant and we did have a healthy kid so why not again?

August 20th: YEH! This pregnancy is going soooo well: 10 weeks along ALREADY! I am tired, but I've thrown up only once and feel sooo much different from the pregnancies I lost . . . Looking back, I knew that each one was not right . . . I felt AWFUL ALL the time . . . But not this time. . . . What a relief. . . . . or is it a reward?

September 1st: It's been more than a week since my last journal entry . . . Today we went for the ultrasound, both of us thinking it would be so perfect. It wasn't. How could this happen to us? What have we done or not done? Haven't I done everything I could possibly do? I eat right, steered clear of drugs and hate any kind of alcohol . . . I exercise regularly . . . I am in perfect health!! Wham! I can't believe what we were told. I can't cry like this any longer. Writing about it may help; it usually does. So, here's how it went. We just sat there staring at each other after hearing: "A 1:25 chance of a baby with Down Syndrome." And they told us, "Don't worry"! You have to be kidding! We both insisted that the next step be done right away . . . so in three (LONG) days, we go back again, this time for something called chorionic villus testing . . . never heard of it.

September 16th: I can't believe this is happening; I feel so angry, so out of control. Then I think of Meridy and that we should just be thankful we have her and believe that our lives can be full, totally complete with just one kid. But, this is not what we want! How can I hold it all together? I don't want to cry all the time,

(Continued)

(Continued)

especially at work . . . I feel like such a wuss . . . and, I can't really tell anyone, just my husband . . . Worse yet, I don't think that we agree that we will terminate the pregnancy. I feel so guilty, so alone, so empty. How can HE say, "Oh, we can handle that"? I'M the one who arranges child care, I'M the one who stays home if Meridy is sick, takes her to the doctor, buys her clothes, her food. He comes home to dinner and a smiling kid racing to jump in his arms. What would a child with Down Syndrome be like? I can't bear to think of standing there holding this child while HE plays with Meridy. Bills. . . . I haven't even thought about that! Our life is great now but I work to provide extras . . . I love my job. I love my kid. I love my husband. I HATE what is happening. If I don't work, our lives are drastically changed. . . . Not an option: I carry the health insurance; he is self-employed. Perhaps this is all a mistake, . . . you know, one of those "false positives" where I will get a call that all is just fine or they reported someone else's test. . . . Right! Wishful thinking . . . Who could begin to understand where I AM COMING FROM? I know my family . . . they would never "get it"; I would be SOOOO-judged if the word "abort" passed my lips . . . even by my mom, and we are soooo close. . . but not on this . . . and, in this small, small town EVEERYONE would know what I DID. . . . Who can possibly help me—help us—with this mess?

Over the last 40 years, many things have changed: new technologies as well as changes in family norms and the decisions faced by those becoming parents. With new technologies, parents are faced with new, but still very difficult, decisions.

SOCIOCULTURAL ORGANIZATION OF CHILDBEARING

These four stories tell us that conception, pregnancy, and childbirth are experienced in different ways by different people. They also tell us about some of the possible variations, which reflect the complex interplay of person, environment, and time. The biological processes vary little for the vast majority of women and their families, but researchers continue to study the psychological, social, and spiritual dimensions of childbearing. This chapter presents a multidimensional overview of current knowledge about conception, pregnancy, and childbirth gleaned from the literatures of anthropology, genetics, medicine, nursing, psychology, social work, and sociology.

As you read, keep in mind that all elements of childbearing have deep meaning for a society. Procreation allows a culture to persist, as children are raised to follow the ways of their predecessors. Procreation may also allow a culture to expand if the birthrate exceeds the rate at which the society loses members. As Valsiner (1989) reminds us, "Human procreation is socially organized in all its aspects. In any cultural group around the world, society regulates the conditions under which a woman is to become pregnant, how she and her husband [family] should conduct themselves during the pregnancy, how labor and delivery take place, and how the newborn child is introduced into society" (p. 117). Pregnancy and childbearing practices are changing with ever-increasing globalization, demographic changes in immigration patterns, and refugees seeking asylum from war-torn countries. Unfortunately, health caregivers, including social workers, in the United States are often ill-prepared to provide culturally sensitive services (Davis, 2001; Gagnon et al., 2004; Ito & Sharts-Hopko, 2002; Yeo & Maeda, 2000). As this is being written, we are in the midst of a major political debate about the U.S. health care delivery system. If changes occur, will they promote or deter the health and well-being of women and their families?

> In what other ways might culture affect the childbearing experience?

In the United States, the social meaning of childbearing has changed rather dramatically over the past 30 years, in several ways (Carter & McGoldrick, 2005a; Walsh, 2006):

- Marriage and childbirth are more commonly delayed.

- Most people want smaller families.

- There are approximately 80 million involuntarily childless persons in the world (Bos, van Balan, & Visser, 2005).

- Various options for controlling reproduction are more available and accessible but oftentimes only to the economically advantaged.

- Sexual freedom has increased alongside more couples seeking infertility treatment.

- Over one third of pregnancies worldwide are unplanned, and one fourth are unwanted (Ahman & Shah, 2006).

- Single women of all ages get pregnant and keep the baby; after a decade-long decline in adolescent pregnancy, teen pregnancy began to incline again in 2006.

- Family values and sexual mores vary more compared with previous generations.

- Parents are less subject to traditional gender-role stereotyping—which prescribed that mom takes care of the baby while dad earns a paycheck, and so on.

- Fathers have been found to be more important in the baby's life, beyond their genetic contributions.

- Spouses return home unexpectedly from a war zone more often due to wives experiencing problematic pregnancies than due to other family crises (Schumm, Bell, & Knott, 2000).

- Medical advances and cultural globalization are raising new ethical issues.

These trends have prompted considerable debate over how our society should define *family.* The family operates at the intersection of society and the individual. For most people it serves as a safe haven and a cradle of emotional relationships. It is both the stage and partial script for the unfolding of the individual life course.

Family Diversity

We continue to witness what family historians call **family pluralism,** or recognition of the many viable types of family structures. Such pluralism is nothing new, but our tolerance for all types of families has grown over the past few decades. The definition of family must reflect this pluralism. Yet, unresolved moral, political, and economic issues abound (LePoire, 2006). These debates influence which family research proposals are funded (Udry, 1993); how abortion and family policy is constructed (Figueira-McDonough, 1990), particularly at the national level; and who gets access to such family resources as infertility treatment, birth control methods, and prenatal care.

We know that many children are born into a family comprising a married couple and their offspring all living together. We are well aware that some children are born to single women with and without significant others, and some are relinquished at birth. In addition, recent global conflicts have also affected children who have lost a parent in war. Other infants come into the world in the midst of natural disasters, as evidenced during Hurricane Katrina where women gave birth in alleys while waiting for rescue (Buekens, Xiong, & Harville, 2006). Many neglected, abused, and abandoned infants are placed in foster care. Yet, all these children live, formally or informally, for better or for worse, with a family of some type: foster, adoptive, extended, fictive kin, blended, and reunited are examples. Rarely does a child live without some type of family configuration, even those who live in arrangements such as group homes; thus, almost all children still experience the life course through a family lens.

Consider your own family beliefs about favorable and unfavorable circumstances of conception, pregnancy, and childbirth. Perhaps these views vary across the generations, but the views, forged by experiences of past generations, can still create an expectation for certain circumstances and behaviors. Consider the decision made by the Gereke family and the long-term impact on everyone in that immediate family. Also, consider Cecelia Kin's dilemma about abortion in contrast to the views of her parents as well as those of her husband and his family, all who live in a rural community. Why do you think that Jennifer Bradshaw's quest is so intense?

In the absence of a biological family "history," individuals tend to seek a substitute history. The literature is replete with accounts of the quest to find one's birth family to discover the past and predict the future. Yet, other children who were separated from their birth parents decide to accept their surrogate parents and the accompanying family network as sufficient for support of the necessary tasks of parenthood and other family roles over the life course.

For families separated by major cultural differences and great geographical distances, as is the situation for most immigrant families, the response to multigenerational family expectations, rituals, and themes related to conception, pregnancy, and childbirth may be difficult or problematic. Such experiences pressure families to adapt and change. Still, responses to conception, pregnancy, and childbirth continue to resonate with the themes, myths, legacies, and secrets that bind families across many generations.

Conception and Pregnancy in Context

The four case studies at the beginning of this chapter remind us that the emotional reaction to conception may vary widely. The Thompsons' conception brought joy, in contrast to Jennifer Bradshaw's frustration and lost dreams followed by her rising hopefulness; Mr. Gereke voiced confidence in contrast to his wife's apprehension; Cecelia Kin feels caught between her own values and wishes and those of important people in her life. The conception experience is influenced by expectations the parents learned growing up in their own families of birth as well as by many other factors: the parents' ages, health, marital status, social status, cultural expectations, peer expectations, school or employment circumstances, the social-political-economic context, and prior experiences with conception and childbearing, as well as the interplay of these factors with those of other people significant to the mother and father.

The conception experience may also be influenced by organized religion. The policies of religious groups reflect different views about the purpose of human sexual expression: pleasure, procreation, or perhaps both. Many mainstream religions, in their denominational policy statements, specify acceptable sexual behaviors (Bullis & Harrigan, 1992). Unwanted conception may be seen as an act of carelessness, promiscuity, or merely God's will—perhaps even punishment for wrongdoing. These beliefs are usually strongly held and have become powerful fodder for numerous social, political, economic, and religious debates related to conception, such as the continued debates about abortion legislation in the United States and around the globe.

Even the mechanisms of conception are socially constructed. Some traditional cultures, such as the Telefomin of New Guinea, believe that repeated intercourse is necessary to conceive, but they forbid intercourse after conception so that multiple births will not occur. In contrast, the Dusan of Borneo believe that conception occurs when the body heat created between males and females causes the woman's blood to boil, forming the child drop by drop; consequently, intercourse must occur throughout pregnancy for the child to develop fully (Valsiner, 1989). In the United States, conception is believed to be a complex biological event.

Just as the experience of conception has varied over time and across cultures, so has the experience of pregnancy. It too is influenced by religious orientations, social customs, changing values, economics, and even political ideologies. For example, societal expectations of pregnant women in the United States have changed, from simply waiting for birth to actively seeking to maintain the mother's—and hence the baby's—health, preparing for the birth process, and sometimes even trying to influence the baby's cognitive and emotional development while the baby is in the uterus.

Childbirth in Context

Throughout history, families—and particularly women—have passed on to young girls the traditions of childbirth practices. These traditions have been shaped by cultural and institutional changes. At the same time, the social function of childbirth has been institutionalized, changing the historical dynamics of pregnancy and childbirth dramatically.

Place of Childbirth

Until the early 20th century, 95% of births in the United States occurred at home with a midwife (a trained birthing specialist). Most U.S. presidents were born at home; Jimmy Carter (the 39th president) was the first to be born in a hospital (Rothman, 1991). The family was intimately involved. During the "lying-in month" following birth, the mother was sheltered from outside influences, often lying in a darkened room while being taught by family members how to care for her newborn (Devitt, 1977). Yet, home births faced some danger: in 1900, 8 of every 1,000 women who labored at home died (Achievements in Public Health, 1999). Hospital births also presented great risk at this time: 1 in 6 who delivered in a hospital also died, primarily from sepsis (Vellery-Rodot, 1926). As formalized medical training developed, so did the medicalization of childbirth. By 1940, more than 50% of deliveries occurred in hospitals (Campbell & MacFarlane, 1986), structuring the birthing process and ending the traditional lying-in month. Reflecting this trend, Hazel Gereke's first child was born at home, but her later children were

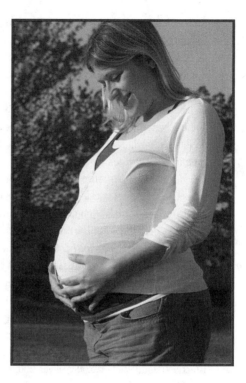

▲ **Photo 2.1**   Societal views of pregnancy in the United States have changed from simply waiting to being actively involved in nurturing the mother's and baby's health.

born in a hospital. To further the trend away from home births, the American Congress of Obstetricians and Gynecologists (ACOG) issued a policy statement in 1975 that protested in-home births and asserted that acceptable levels of safety were only available in the hospital. This policy statement was affirmed in 1999 and again in 2007; it was supported in 2008 by the American Medical Association (ACOG, 2008; American Medical Association House of Delegates, 2008). In fact, a former president of ACOG labeled home births as child abuse (Hosmer, 2001). In contrast, the American College of Nurse Midwives and the American Public Health Association (APHA) support planned home births (American College of Nurse-Midwives, 2005, APHA, 2001). One recent study that used a small randomized sample in the Netherlands, where home births are endorsed, showed no statistical difference in maternal and neonatal outcomes between home births with trained midwives and hospital births. This study has been criticized for its methodology, however (Jansen et al., 2009; McLachlan & Forster, 2009). Recent studies in the United States have shown that home births for identified low-risk women offer no increased risks for mortality and morbidity if there are adequate support structures such as trained midwives and referral sources available (de Jonge et al., 2009; Johnson & Davis, 2005).

The feminist movement advocated for less invasive deliveries in more friendly environments (Johanson, Newburn, & Macfarlane, 2002). However, by 1998, a study of 26,000 births in the United States found that only 1% occurred at home (Ventura, Martin, Curtin, & Mathews, 1998), despite an approximately 75% cost savings for home births over hospital births (Anderson & Anderson, 1999). This rate is declining, with less than 1% (0.59%) of all births in the United States in 2006 ($n = 38,568$) occurring in the home. Most mothers who report participating in planned home births are more than 30 years old, married, have at least one other child, live in less populated areas (small town or rural area), are nonsmokers and nondrinkers, and have comparable or higher educational levels compared with women who deliver at the hospital (Boucher, Bennett, McFarlin, & Freeze, 2009; Declercq, Paine, & Winter, 1995; Martin, Hamilton, et al., 2009). Different geographical regions demonstrate varying rates of home births, primarily related to the availability of hospital beds and health care preferences (Silveria, Copeland, & Feudtner, 2006). In one study, approximately 12.1% of those women who intended to deliver at home were transferred to the hospital (Johnson & Davis, 2005).

Today there are more than 6,500 certified nurse-midwives practicing in all 50 states, mostly in hospitals (American College of Nurse-Midwives, 2008). A current debate centers on the credentialing and supervision of nurse-midwives in home deliveries. The American Medical Association recently proposed several resolutions to promote the utilization of hospitals or birthing centers within hospitals rather than in-home births and recommended that all midwives should submit to supervision by physicians rather than practice autonomously (American Medical Association House of Delegates, 2008). In response, there has been an outcry by members of the American College of Nurse-Midwives to maintain a distinct professional identity (American College of Nurse-Midwives, 2009).

Two other major developments have occurred during the last 30 years (Bain, Gau, & Reed, 1995; Hodnett, Downe, Edwards, & Walsh, 2005). The first is the use of doulas (laywomen who are employed to stay with the woman through the entire labor, encouraging her and providing comfort measures). Studies have shown that women who use doulas (a word from the Greek that means "woman caregiver of a woman" or "woman servant") experience shorter labors, less pain, fewer medical interventions, higher rates of initiation of breastfeeding, and decreased postpartum depression (American Pregnancy Association, 2009; DONA International, n.d.; Scott, Klaus, & Klaus, 1999). The second development is the recent growth of birthing centers located close to a major hospital or within the hospital itself. Birthing centers offer an alternative to home delivery in a "homelike" freestanding facility with medical support. Recent research reveals that birthing centers reduce the number of medical interventions and increase maternal satisfaction (Hodnett et al., 2005; Oliver, 2005). Births at free-standing birthing centers occur with midwives in attendance 64.7% of the time (Martin, Hamilton, et al., 2009). Other studies have found that increased use of technology is linked to a decrease in the mother's satisfaction regarding the birthing process (Kornelsen, 2005; van der Hulst, van Teijlingen, & Bonsel, 2004). Birthing centers de-emphasize technology and model the dynamics of a home birth while allowing for rapid medical intervention if needed. Conflicting data exist regarding potential cost savings of birthing centers versus hospital delivery (American Association of Birth Centers, 2007; Anderson & Anderson, 1999; Henderson & Petrou, 2008; Stone, Zwanziger, Hinton, & Buenting, 2000). With the growing impetus to consider national health reform, balancing the safety and economic efficacy of alternative birthing plans, sites, and professionals should receive heightened attention (Bak, 2004; Bak 2009; Cooper, 2004).

A major change over time is the role of fathers in childbirth. During the 16th century, law and custom excluded men from observing deliveries, because labor was viewed as "something to be endured by women under the control of other experienced and knowledgeable women" (Johnson, 2002, p. 165). During the 1960s, when childbirth moved out of the home, hospitals still excluded fathers from participating in the labor process (Kayne, Greulich, & Albers, 2001) and some continue to do so if there are complications (Koppel & Kaiser, 2001). This became accepted practice but began to change in the 1970s. As more women were subjected to episiotomies (incisions to enlarge the opening for the baby during birth), enemas, and anesthesia in a male-dominated arena, often without their full knowledge or consent (Ashford, LeCroy, & Lortie, 2001), fathers were first invited in by physicians to serve as witnesses to avoid litigation (Odent, 1998, 1999). A 1995 survey in the United Kingdom found that fathers were present at 80% of all births, often serving as a "coach" (Woollett et al., 1995). There is still resistance to fathers' presence in the delivery room in some cultures but, when agreed upon by the couple, it has been shown that the father's involvement in the birthing process increases attachment, paternal satisfaction, nurturing behaviors, and positive feelings about the process (Pestvenidze & Bohrer, 2007; Reed, 2005), outcomes that are further enhanced if the father has attended childbirth classes (Wockel, Schafer, Beggel, & Abou-Dakn, 2007). Father-supported childbirth has also been found to increase mother's satisfaction with the birth process and decrease the amount of pain medication needed (Smith et al., 1991). Increasing attention is being given to restrictive policies of some hospitals that will not allow the father to be present if the baby is being delivered by Caesarian birth or if the mother has general anesthesia (Koppel & Kaiser, 2001).

Reflect on the Thompsons' situation with Will in Afghanistan, unaware of the pending birth of his first child, and Felicia in premature labor without any family present.

Childbirth Education

Childbirth education was not formalized until the early 1900s, when the Red Cross set up hygiene and health care classes for women as a public health initiative. In 1912, the U.S. Children's Bureau, created as a new federal agency to inform women about personal hygiene and birth, published a handbook titled *Prenatal Care,* emphasizing the need for medical supervision during pregnancy (Barker, 1998). When Dr. Grantley Dick-Read published *Childbirth Without Fear* in 1944, the medical establishment rejected the idea that women who were educated about childbirth would have less fear and therefore less need for pain medication (Lindell, 1988).

> How does childbirth education support human agency in making choices?

Not until the 1950s did the idea of childbirth education gain credibility. A French obstetrician, Dr. Fernand Lamaze, followed Dick-Read's work with the publication of his book *Painless Childbirth* (1958). Lamaze learned of Pavlov, a Russian psychologist (Lindell, 1988), and incorporated his patterns of hypnosis, which the Russians had learned to use to reduce childbirth pain. This book became the foundation for contemporary childbirth education and led to both social and political changes as women began to educate each other (Lindell, p. 10; Zwelling, 1996). Lamaze proposed that women could use their intellect to control pain if they had information about their bodies and relaxation techniques (DeHart, Sroufe, & Cooper, 2000; Lindell; Novak & Broom, 1995).

Childbirth education changed again in the 1980s as more women went back to work soon after birth and juggled multiple roles; technological interventions also increased at this time. The role of childbirth educator began to be filled by a professional from within the health care system (Zwelling, 1996). Childbirth education became a governmental priority as the gap widened between African Americans and other ethnic groups regarding the incidence of low birth weights and infant mortality (Armstrong, 2000). Significant socioeconomic and racial disparities exist in the utilization of childbirth classes, with one study finding that 76% of Caucasian women attended a childbirth class compared with 44% of African American women. Racial differences also exist in the utilization of prenatal care, with 89% of Caucasian women receiving first trimester prenatal care compared with 75% of African American women (Lu et al., 2003). With increased racial and ethnic diversity in births, childbirth educators must engage more, and a broader range of, minority women (Morton & Hsu, 2007). Research has demonstrated that lower minority participation in childbirth classes is most effected by lack of transportation and childcare problems (Berman, 2006), both of which can be addressed by social workers.

Efforts have been made to improve access to childbirthing resources, as illustrated with the Maternity Care Access Act of 1989, which created a means-tested program called First Steps to provide parenting and childbirth classes to women who previously could not afford them (Rabkin, Balassone, & Bell, 1995). Healthy People 2000 and 2010, the federal government's national health goals, also support prenatal education as a way to alter individual women's behavior, thereby improving pregnancy outcomes (Armstrong, 2000; Magill-Cuerden, 2006; U.S. Department of Health and Human Services, 2009c).

Childbirth classes do seem to help. Some outcome studies have shown that childbirth classes result in decreased pain and anxiety (Dickason, Schult, & Silverman, 1990; Goldberg, Cohen, & Lieberman, 1999), shorter labor, decreased use of forceps, improved infant outcome, increased maternal self-confidence (Koehn, 2008), and an overall positive experience (Riedmann, 1996). Recent research has also suggested that emotional support during labor can be more effective than childbirth classes (Waldenstrom, Hildingsson, Rubertsson, & Radestad, 2004). Meditation and psychological insight into the dynamics of labor and delivery may augment the traditional information offered in childbirth classes (Newman, 2005). Childbirth educators are also using the Internet to provide prenatal education and support (Bradley, 1995; Wang, Chung, Sung, & Wu, 2006), which provides enriched

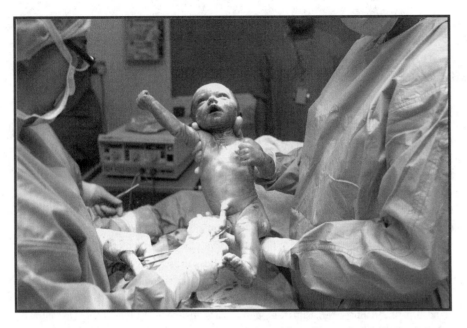

▲ **Photo 2.2**   A typical delivery—here a newborn baby is delivered by medical professionals in a hospital delivery room.

opportunities for those in rural areas or when face-to-face instruction is unavailable because of incarceration, lack of transportation, or disability.

Childbirth classes must address the needs of all involved in this major life event. The impact of childbirth classes on fathers is still being debated. It appears that the father's increased information leads to a more positive experience as well as his ability to adjust during the first postpartum year (Johnson & Baker, 2004), but some studies conclude that there is no relationship between the father's attendance and attachment to the infant at 6 weeks (Tiedje, 2001). At any rate, it appears that classes do not have the same level of positive influence for fathers as they do for mothers (Premberg & Lundgren, 2006), but women report that their relationship with the father is strengthened by his class attendance (Koehn, 2008). One study has shown that if adolescent fathers are provided support, including childbirth education, 82% of these fathers have daily contact with their children at the end of 2 years (Stengel, 2005). The adolescent father is typically 2 to 3 years older than the mother (Hollman & Alderman, 2008), potentially providing a level of maturity to the adolescent relationship that maximizes the educational intervention. Clearly, more information is needed to understand how prenatal education can meet the father's needs as well as the mother's needs—and not just the obstetrician's needs.

Hospital Stay

What historical trends are related to these changes in the view of childbirth?

Pregnancy and childbirth accounts for almost 25% of all hospital admissions in the United States, and in the 18 to 44 age group, three times as many women are admitted for inpatient stays as are men, primarily because of childbearing (Nursing, 2005).

We are living in an era that values cost-effective, innovative, comprehensive health services. Thus, policies regarding the length of the new mother's stay in the hospital are also changing. Forty years ago, women remained hospitalized for seven to 10 days following birth. By the early 1990s, the norm was two to three days. During the mid-1990s, however, controversial managed-care policies pushed for women with uncomplicated deliveries to be discharged within 24 hours, a savings of 2 hospital days. During the period following delivery, both the mother and infant undergo rapid transitions. The infant must adjust to a new environment, learn to nurse, and begin the process of bonding with parents. Life-threatening problems, such as heart problems, jaundice, or infections, may not be detected until the second or third day of life. Some research has shown, however, that early discharge of the mother and baby does not increase negative outcomes, and many women prefer to leave the hospital shortly after giving birth. Yet, many women appreciate continued assistance of health care workers and midwives after birth (Baker, 2006). Over a 10-year period, there has been a 50% increase in cesarean births, from 20.7% in 1996 to 31.1% in 2006 (Macdorman, Menacker, & Declercq, 2008; Menacker & Martin, 2008). Women who have had a cesarean birth have a higher rate of readmission with early discharge. With the increased incidence of cesarean birth, there also are increased hospital costs (Liu et al., 2002). A more recent trend is that employer-sponsored health care policies can require higher deductibles and co-pays (Wilde-Mathews, 2009), a trend that transfers even more of the cost of the necessary longer hospitalization to the parent(s).

REPRODUCTIVE GENETICS

Recognition of the need for genetics knowledge is not new to social work. In fact, Mary Richmond (1917) advocated that a social worker "get the facts of heredity" in the face of marriage between close relatives, miscarriage, tuberculosis, alcoholism, mental disorder, nervousness, epilepsy, cancer, deformities or abnormalities, or an exceptional ability.

Almost 50 years later, James Watson and Francis Crick (1953) first described the mechanisms of genetic inheritance. But it was not until 1970 that our knowledge of genetics began to explode. In 1990, the Human Genome Project (HGP) was funded by the U.S. Department of Energy and the National Institutes of Health as an international effort to map all the human genes by 2003. By June 2000, the first working draft of the human genome was completed, and in 2003 this project ended. The knowledge that resulted from the HGP has altered social work practice in many areas, primarily in working with persons of reproductive age. Genetic research continues around the world, with future findings that will continue to impact social work practice.

Genetic Mechanisms

Chromosomes and genes are the essential components of the hereditary process. Genetic instructions are coded in **chromosomes** found in each cell; each chromosome carries **genes,** or segments of deoxyribonucleic acid (DNA), that contain the codes producing particular traits and dispositions. Each mature **germ cell**—ovum or sperm—contains 23 chromosomes, half of the set of 46 present in each parent's cells. As you can see in Exhibit 2.1, when the sperm penetrates the ovum (**fertilization**), the parents' chromosomes combine to make a total of 46 chromosomes arrayed in 23 pairs.

The Human Genome Project (1990–2003) genetic researchers estimated that there are 20,000 to 25,000 genes in human DNA, with an average of 3,000 to 5,000 genes per chromosome, slightly more than the number mice have (Human Genome Project, 2009a). The goal now is to determine the complete sequencing of the three billion subunits of the human genome, an effort of global proportions involving both public and privately funded projects in more than 18 countries, including some developing countries (Human Genome Project, 2009a).

The genes constitute a "map" that guides the protein and enzyme reactions for every subsequent cell in the developing person and across the life course. Thus, every physical trait and many behavioral traits are influenced by the combined genes from the ovum and sperm.

Every person has a unique **genotype,** or array of genes, unless the person is an identical twin. Yet, the environment may influence how each gene pilots the growth of cells. The result is a **phenotype** (observable trait) that differs somewhat from the genotype. Thus, even a person who is an identical twin has some unique characteristics. On initial observation, you may not be able to distinguish between identical twins, but if you look closely enough, you will probably find some variation, such as differences in the size of an ear, hair thickness, or temperament.

A chromosome and its pair have the same types of genes at the same location. The exception is the last pair of chromosomes, the **sex chromosomes,** which, among other things, determine sex. The ovum can contribute only an X chromosome to the 23rd pair, but the sperm can contribute either an X or a Y and therefore determines the sex of the developing person. A person with XX sex chromosomes is female; a person with XY sex chromosomes is male (refer to Exhibit 2.1).

Genes on one sex chromosome that do not have a counterpart on the other sex chromosome create **sex-linked traits.** A gene for red/green color blindness, for example, is carried only on the X chromosome. When an X chromosome that carries this gene is paired with a Y chromosome, which could not carry the gene, red/green color blindness is manifested. So, almost all red/green color blindness is found in males. This gene for color blindness does not manifest if paired with an X chromosome unless the gene is inherited from both parents, which is rare. However, if a woman inherits the gene from either parent, she can unknowingly pass it on to her sons.

Whether genes express certain traits depends on their being either dominant or recessive. Traits governed by **recessive genes** (e.g., hemophilia, baldness, thin lips) will only be expressed if the responsible gene is present on each chromosome of the relevant pair. In contrast, traits governed by **dominant genes** (e.g., normal blood clotting, curly hair, thick lips) will be expressed if one or both paired chromosomes have the gene. When the genes on a chromosome pair give competing, yet controlling, messages, they are called **interactive genes,** meaning that both messages may be followed to varying degrees. Hair, eye, and skin color often depend on such interactivity. For example, a light-skinned person with red hair and hazel eyes may mate with a person having dark skin, brown hair, and blue eyes and produce a child with a dark complexion, red hair, and blue eyes.

Genetic Counseling

Although Mary Richmond noted in 1917 that many physical traits, medical problems, and mental health problems have a genetic basis, only recently has technology allowed us to identify the specific genes governing many of these traits. Now that the initial mapping of the human genome is complete, as further research is done, the goal is to develop genetic interventions to prevent or cure various diseases or disorders as well as affect conception, pregnancy, and childbirth in other ways. More than 1,000 genetic tests are available, ranging in costs from $200 to $3,000; they are seldom covered by insurance, and there is no federal regulation (Human Genome Project, 2009b). At present, research is underway to genetically alter sperm, leading to male contraception (Herdiman, Nakash, & Beedham, 2006).

Our quickly increasing ability to read a person's genetic code and understand the impact it could have on the person's life oftentimes demands the expertise of a genetic counselor to provide information and advice to guide decisions for persons concerned about hereditary abnormalities. Social workers, with their biopsychosocial perspective, are well positioned to assess the need and in some circumstances provide such services (Bishop, 1993; Schild & Black, 1984; Takahashi & Turnbull, 1994). The interdisciplinary field of genetic counseling acknowledges social work as one of its essential disciplines, thereby making at least a rudimentary understanding of genetics and related bioethical issues essential for social work practice (Garver, 1995; Human Genome Project, 2009b; Rauch, 1988; Reed, 1996). For example, researchers recently reported that a genetic variation has been identified that may explain why there is a higher rate of premature delivery for African American women compared with European American women. This is information that a social worker could use to encourage pregnant African American clients to seek medical consultation related to possible genetically based premature birth risks (Wang et al., 2006).

Social workers need to understand the rising bioethical concerns that genetic research fosters and to use such knowledge to help clients faced with genetically related reproductive decisions. The U.S. government has the largest

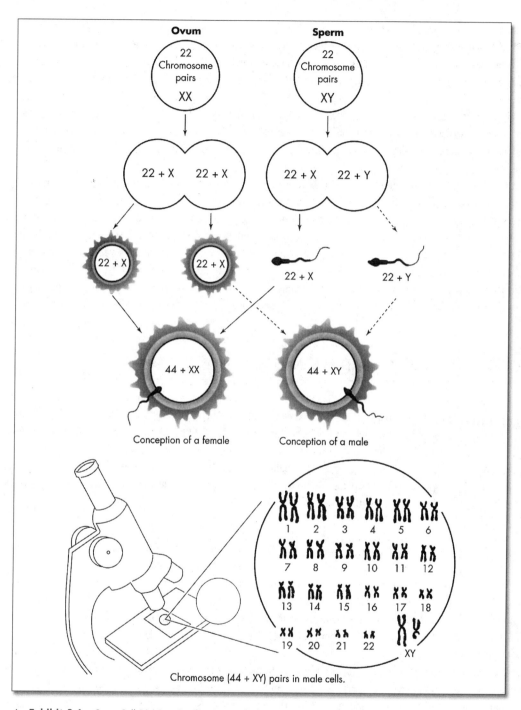

▲ **Exhibit 2.1** Germ Cell Division, Fertilization, and Chromosome Pairs

bioethics program in the world to address questions such as the following: Who should have access to genetic information? Do adoptive parents have the right to know the genetic background of an adoptee? Will genetic maps be used to make decisions about a pregnancy? Which genes should be selected for reproduction? Will persons who are poor be economically disadvantaged in the use of genetic information?

A major concern of genetic counseling is whether all genetic information should be shared with a client. Some information may only cause distress, because the technology for altering genes is in its infancy and applicable to only a few situations. But recent advances allow for earlier diagnosis, which reduces or prevents the effects of some rare diseases as well as gives some clients more decision options. Today, for example, a late-life pregnancy such as Hazel Gereke's could be evaluated genetically using amniocentesis in the third trimester, or earlier in the first trimester using chorionic villus testing, which allowed Cecelia Kin to know that her unborn child had Down syndrome. Such evaluation could lead to decisions ranging from abortion to preparation for parenting a child with a disability. However, these options typically are laced with economic, political, legal, ethical, moral, and religious considerations (Andrews, 1994; Chadwick, Levitt, & Shickle, 1997).

Ethical issues related to genetic engineering have an impact not only at the individual and family levels but also at the societal level. For example, when we are able to manipulate genes at will, we must be on guard against genetic elitism. It is one thing to use genetic engineering to eliminate such inherited diseases as sickle-cell anemia but quite another to use it to select the sex, body type, or coloring of a child. We are living in a time of tremendous ethical complexity, involving the interplay of new reproductive technologies; changing family structures, values, and mores; political and religious debate; and economic considerations. This ethical complexity extends to issues of social justice; as increasing numbers of persons gain the ability to control conception, plan pregnancy, and control pregnancy outcomes, social workers need to protect the interests of those who lack the knowledge and other resources to do so.

CONTROL OVER CONCEPTION AND PREGNANCY

> How are decisions about timing of childbearing related to biological age, psychological age, social age, and spiritual age?

The desire to plan the timing of childbearing is an ancient one, as is the desire to stimulate pregnancy in the event of infertility. Contraception and induced abortion have probably always existed in every culture. Effective solutions for infertility are more recent. But it is important to remember that not all methods of controlling conception and pregnancy are equally acceptable to all people. Cultural and religious beliefs, as well as personal circumstances, make some people more accepting of some methods than others.

Contraception

The range of birth control options available today provides women and men with the ability to plan pregnancy and childbirth more than ever before. In 2000, the World Health Organization (WHO) increased medical restrictions on contraception, decreasing the number of women who are eligible for oral contraceptives and intrauterine device (IUD) insertion, citing health concerns. Of the approximately 120 million women who become pregnant worldwide each year, approximately 38% of these are unplanned because of contraceptive failure or lack of pregnancy planning, and about 25% are unwanted (Ahman & Shah, 2006). It has been demonstrated that the rate of abortion increases as the availability of contraceptive use decreases, and abortion is often illegal and unsafe in nonindustrialized countries (Ahman & Shah; World Health Organization, 2004). However, it must also be recognized that the risk of pregnancy, with over half a million dying each year in pregnancy, childbirth, or the immediate postpartum period, is generally higher than the risk of adverse reactions to contraceptives (Belizan, 2008; Best, 2002). In Eastern, Western, and Middle Africa, there is a minimal use of contraceptives and abortion, resulting in high fertility rates (e.g., about six children per woman). However, in South America and Southeastern Asia, where there is limited access to contraceptives, abortion is often used as the primary regulator of fertility (Ahman & Shah). Therefore, the availability and acceptability of contraceptives in impoverished countries reduces the number of abortions (legal and illegal) and maternal mortality, in addition to regulating family size (Aitken et al., 2008). With the projected 7.4 to 10.6 billion people in the world by 2050, mostly born in countries with poor access to contraceptives, there is an urgent need to provide inexpensive, safe, convenient, and appropriate contraceptive devices to women and men worldwide. A need also exists to increase knowledge of these contraceptives (Goldenberg & Jobe, 2001; Prata, 2009). Overall, the cost of contraception is small in comparison to unwanted pregnancies. A recent review showed that half of all averted pregnancies were stopped by oral contraceptives, about 20% by injectable methods, and 10% by barrier and patch methods (Foster et al., 2009, p. 446), with the implant and intrauterine devices the most cost effective.

Complete sexual abstinence is the only certain form of contraception. Without any contraception, an estimated 85% of heterosexual couples who engage in regular intercourse will conceive within one year (Dirubbo, 2006; Trussell, 2004). There has been a push to encourage adolescents to engage in total abstinence, with educational systems being required, in some situations, to teach abstinence as the only form of birth control. Federal monies for abstinence-only education rose 74% under President Bush and during the last decade, a billion and a half dollars has been spent for abstinence-only programs (McFarlane, 2007).

Approximately 50% of pregnancies in the United States are unintended (Miller & Holman, 2006; Van der Wijden, Kleijnen, & Van den Berk, 2003). The reasons for this is uncertain because contraceptive failure rate data vary across studies. As research and development of various methods of contraceptives continues, information is evolving. It is important for social workers to be familiar with the choices women have and the potential impact of their choices as well as how women of various cultural, racial, and ethnic groups may vary in their use of such options, if available. Each birth control option needs to be considered in light of its cost, failure rate, potential health risks, and probability of use, given the user's sociocultural circumstances. Female and male contraception options include the following:

- *Breastfeeding.* Women who are exclusively breastfeeding and are amenorrhoeic are less likely than other women to conceive during the first 6 months postpartum (Hale, 2007). Breastfeeding without the use of other contraceptives carries a pregnancy risk of less than 2% during the first 6 months after giving birth. For breastfeeding to be an effective contraceptive during the first 6 months after delivery, a woman must be amenorrhoeic, nurse at least every 4 hours during the day and every 6 hours at night, and not introduce the infant to other foods, a practice known as the lactational amenorrhea method (LAM) (Tilley, Shaaban, Wilson, Glasier, & Mishell, 2009; Van der Wijden et al., 2003).

- *Coitus interruptus.* Primarily seen as a male form of contraception, premature withdrawal of the penis from the vagina before ejaculation is probably the oldest form of birth control (Costantino et al., 2007). However, the failure rate is approximately 19% to 27% a year (4% if used perfectly) (Bachmann, 2007; Freundl, Sivin, & Batár, 2010). Coitus interruptus offers no protection from sexually transmitted infections (STIs) and HIV, and may be unsatisfying (Fu, Darroch, Haas, & Ranjit, 1999; Hatecher et al., 1994; Mahendru, Putran, & Khaled, 2009).

- *Periodic abstinence.* Natural family planning, or the rhythm method, is a term used for birth control that does not employ drugs or devices (Freundl et al., 2010) and involves daily tracking of changes in the woman's body associated with the menstrual cycle and an avoidance of intercourse during fertile periods. The effectiveness rate is 90% to 98% if used perfectly, but if not practiced diligently, the failure rate rises to between 20% and 30% (American Academy of Family Physicians, 2005; Bachmann, 2007; Freundl et al., 2010).

- *Barrier methods.* The male condom (failure rate 2% when used correctly, 15% when used incorrectly or inconsistently over a 12-month period), the diaphragm (6%–20% failure rate), and the cervical cap (20%–36% failure rate) provide increased protection against STIs, with the male condom having the highest protection rate against HIV and hepatitis B (Freundl et al., 2010; Mahendru et al., 2009). Dissatisfaction with condom use is lower than for any other form of birth control, leading to a lower rate of discontinuance (12%) (Moreau, Cleland, & Trussell, 2007). The female condom that was introduced in 1992 either consists of two flexible rings, a soft sponge, or dissolvable capsule (Rowlands, 2009) and also provides some protection against STIs (Freundl et al., 2010). It has approximately a 5% failure rate when used correctly, 21% when used incorrectly or inconsistently (Family Health International, 2006), and costs between $2.50 and $5 per use. The female condom is visible after insertion (some women are requesting colored condoms), and may cause crackling or popping sounds. Originally thought to provide protection for low-income women internationally, it has not been well accepted (Severy & Spieler, 2000). Approximately 52% of women discontinue use of the diaphragm and cervical cap because they are dissatisfied (Moreau et al., 2007). Both male and female condoms are used with a spermicide that provides a chemical barrier against pregnancy but not STIs (Freundl et al., 2010). Spermicides can damage the skin of the male and increase the risk of infections, including HIV. Research is underway to develop spermicides that both kill sperm and lower the risk of STIs. Vaginal gels have also been found to have a wide variance in failure rates; many women are reluctant to use them, and often discontinue their use (Grimes et al., 2005).

- *Oral contraceptives.* The introduction of birth control pills in the United States in 1960 precipitated major changes in reproduction. With a failure rate of only about 0.3% to 8.0%, they revolutionized family planning (Alan Guttmacher Institute, 2005; Freundl, 2010). Approximately 29% of women who start an oral contraceptive discontinue it because of dissatisfaction (Moreau et al., 2007). The progesterone-only pill is safe for women who are breastfeeding (Mahendru et al., 2009). Using a combined estrogen and progesterone pill continuously (versus three out of four weeks to induce menstruation), most women will cease menstruation (amenorrhea) after several months. Using oral contraceptives that have estrogen can increase the risk of breast cancer, but the new regime that does not include the use of estrogen may actually reduce this risk (Rowlands, 2009). Smoking while using oral contraceptives is contraindicated because there is a higher risk of serious cardiovascular problems, and smoking can lower the levels of estrogen, affecting the efficiency of the contraceptive (Kroon, 2007; Ruger, Moser, & Frisch, 2000). The use of oral contraceptives can lead to the development of inflammatory bowel disease (Cornish et al., 2008) and may be contraindicated in women who are obese (e.g., body mass index greater than 35) (Mahendru et al., 2009).

- *Intramuscular injections.* In 1992, the introduction in the United States of depo-medroxyprogesterone acetate (Depo-Provera), a drug used for many years in Europe, allowed women protection against pregnancy for three months. There have been concerns that Depo-Provera leads to irregular bleeding, decreased bone density, headaches, dizziness, significant weight gain, and breast tenderness (Clark, Dillon, Sowers, & Nichols, 2005; Haider & Darney, 2007; Upadhyay, 2005). In addition, some research has shown that Depo-Provera negatively affects a woman's sense of well-being and sleep cycle (Brown, Morrison, Larkspur, Marsh, & Nicolaisen, 2008). There is a 0.05% to 3.0% failure rate over 12 months (Alan Guttmacher Institute, 2005; Upadhyay, 2005). The drug Lunelle is given by injection every month compared with the every-three-month injection of Depo-Provera (Freeman, 2004). New research is underway to develop a self-injectable form that will counteract the high discontinuance rates and make it more accessible for those without access to a clinic (Prabhakaran, 2008). This may increase access for rural populations as well as for low-income women but also will require increased education about proper administration.

- *Implants and patches.* Implants are tiny capsules inserted under the skin by a physician; they have a higher effectiveness rate than vasectomy. Older systems consisted of six capsules that made insertion and removal difficult and increased the likelihood of complications (Rowlands, 2009). Implanon, a new single-rod implant, has been shown to be highly effective (i.e., a failure rate of less than 0.05%) and does not carry the risks of multiple rod implants (Freundl et al., 2010; "Single-Rod Etonogestrel Implant Safe and Efficacious," 2009). In addition, women are given the option to select a transdermal patch, which is changed weekly for three weeks per monthly cycle (Hale, 2007; Rowlands, 2009). The patch has the same effectiveness as oral contraceptives in women who are not obese, but about 3% of women discontinue it because of skin irritation (Rowlands, 2009). In populations that are high risk for unintended pregnancies and abortions, the patch has lower continuation and effectiveness rates than do oral contraceptives, but in low-risk populations, women are more compliant using the patch than oral contraceptives (Bakhru & Stanwood, 2006; Miller & Holman, 2006).

- *Vaginal rings.* The vaginal ring remains in place for 3 weeks and then is removed for 1 week. The continuous release of hormones is similar to oral contraceptives, but there are steadier levels of the contraceptive hormones in the blood (Serrant-Green, 2008). The vaginal ring can be removed up to 2 hours before intercourse (Rowlands, 2009). Recent studies have shown that women are more satisfied with the vaginal ring than oral contraceptives (Schafer, Osborne, Davis, & Westhoff, 2006). They report less depression and irritability (Hollander, 2008) and experience less bleeding than with the pill (Roumen, Op Ten Berg, & Hoomans, 2006), but some women report problems with vaginal discomfort, coital problems, and expulsion (Rowlands, 2009). One study has shown that the vaginal ring can be used as emergency contraception because 87.5% of women who inserted the ring and maintained use for 7 days after intercourse experienced either no ovulation or disrupted ovulation (Croxatto et al., 2005). Another study showed that it was the most effective form of birth control for obese women (Gordon, Thakur, & Atlas, 2007).

- *Intrauterine devices (IUDs).* The use of IUDs has been marked by controversy and legal disputes for a number of years. They were introduced in the early 1900s, but high rates of infection and tissue damage discouraged their use until the 1960s. Most manufacturers discontinued production in the 1980s following expensive legal settlements. However, newer IUDs are widely used and are considered safe and reliable. No discernable difference exists in efficacy or side effects related to the copper levels in the IUDs or to the type of insertion used by the physician. Research is currently underway to develop an IUD whose insertion is easier and can be used in women who are not anatomically suited for insertion of current types (Rowlands, 2009). Approximately 15% of women discontinue use of the IUD within 1 year because of complications, but they have a contraceptive failure rate over 1 year of only between 0.6% and 0.8% for IUDs made of copper and 1.5% to 2% for hormonal IUDs (Freundl, 2010; Population Reports, 2005). The copper IUD does not protect against STIs. Approximately 2% to 10% are expelled during the first year, but if there are no complications, they can be worn for up to 10 years (Bachmann, 2007). Although IUDs are chosen as a contraceptive by only 2% of women (Alan Guttmacher Institute, 2005), conception after discontinuing for the first 3 months is higher than after stopping the pill (71%–80% for the IUD and 60% for women stopping the pill) (Kaplan et al., 2005). The IUD has been found to be the optimal contraceptive for women approaching menopause (Bhathena & Guillebaud, 2006) and can be used by women who are breastfeeding (Hale, 2007).

- *Voluntary surgical sterilization.* Tubal ligation, surgical sterilization for women, is considered permanent and has an effectiveness rate of approximately 99.5% (Alan Guttmacher Institute, 2005). A relatively new approach, which allows for a device to be inserted in the fallopian tubes, provides a barrier to the fertilized egg traveling to the uterus, but there is about a 6% failure rate and a risk of tubular rupture; it also requires verification of placement 3 months after placement (Rowlands, 2009). A hysterectomy, the removal of the uterus, is only done if there is a medical need and may involve the removal of the ovaries and fallopian tubes as well (Tan & Loth, 2010). For women who want to reverse the tubal ligation, there are new methods, including robotic surgery, that reduce the hospital and recovery time significantly from the traditional surgical procedure (Patel, Patel, Steinkampf, Whitten, & Malizia, 2008). In one study, the success rate for robotic surgery was 62.5% compared with the traditional pregnancy rate of 50% (Patel et al., 2008). Vasectomy, or male sterilization, likewise, is considered the most reliable method of contraception, with a failure rate of 0.08% to 0.015% in the first year (Hepp & Meuleman, 2006). Both surgeries require expertise with appropriate preoperative counseling, which may not be available in nonindustrial countries (Awsare, Krishnan, Boustead, Hanbury, & McNicholas, 2005). Recent advances in microsurgery have increased the success rates for reversal procedures, especially if the vasectomy was performed by a urologist less than 10 years ago. The resultant pregnancy rates within 2 years of reversal are approximately 50% (Busato & Wilson, 2009; Simon & Zieve, 2008).

- *Emergency contraception (EC).* In August 2006, the U.S. Food and Drug Administration (FDA) approved the "morning-after pill," otherwise known as "Plan B," to be available to women 18 years and older who have a government-issued identification card. It may be purchased without a prescription, but the drug is behind the pharmacist's counter and must be requested (Allen & Goldberg, 2007; Kavanaugh & Schwarz, 2008; Krisberg, 2006). A two-dose regime and a one-dose administration have been shown to be equally effective (Hansen, Saseen, & Teal, 2007), with an 89% effectiveness rate (Melby, 2009). Plan B contains the same ingredients as oral contraceptives, but higher doses are taken. Significant controversy exists regarding this medication, and some pharmacists have refused to provide it to women (Karpa, 2006). Advocates who oppose Plan B call for women under the age of 18 to have a prescription and for all women to talk to a pharmacist to obtain the contraceptive (Krisberg, 2006). The U.S. Agency for International Development (USAID) has recommended EC for women who have been raped, whose partner's condom breaks, who run out of other forms of contraceptives, who have forgotten to take several consecutive oral contraceptives doses, and who did not expect to have sexual relations (Severy & Spieler, 2000). The American Academy of Pediatrics has also supported the over-the-counter availability of EC (American Academy of Pediatrics-Committee on Adolescence, 2005). However, concerns have been expressed that women may rely on EC as a routine method of contraception rather than as an emergency form, leading to increased risk behaviors, and it offers no protection from STIs (Harvey, Beckman, Sherman, & Petitti, 1999). The cost is low, but there may be side effects, including nausea, vomiting, and bleeding (American Medical Association, 2002). In addition, the Copper T380A, an intrauterine contraceptive, has been used effectively for emergency contraception (Allen & Goldberg; Hale, 2007). It is important for the social worker to be familiar with these forms of birth control, especially if they work with populations who have a high rate of undesired fertility and low rates of contraceptive use.

• *New contraceptive methods.* Numerous clinical trials exist that are focused on providing contraceptives to those most in need, using easily delivered methods. Steroidal compounds are in clinical trials, and it is expected that they will help to prevent pregnancy even when women miss doses of their oral contraceptives. Mirena is one new intrauterine device that may reduce the negative effects found with Depo-Provera. In addition, a weekly hormonal injection for men (testosterone enanthate), which suppresses sperm production, has been found to reduce pregnancy rates, but the frequency of injection is problematic. Contraceptive vaccines continue to be tested, but the focus is moving from vaccinations for women and toward developing a vaccine for men. Other studies are focusing on the proteins in the sperm, changing the cervical mucus to make it less hospitable to sperm, and new implants. The uses of vaginal or transdermal gels, nasal sprays, and oral medications are being explored.

• Generally it takes 10 to 15 years for development of a new contraceptive (Aitken et al., 2008), but hopefully with new research techniques, the demands of affordable, accessible, effective, low-risk, and culturally acceptable contraceptive availability will be met. In addition, emphasis on providing services to special populations—such as women who suffer from a seizure disorder, developmental disability, movement limitations, or mental disorders—must receive attention. As women with disabilities are living longer, this is an area of interest to social workers (Diekema, 2003; Kaplan, 2006; Welner, 1997).

Medical Abortion

Abortion may be the most politicized, hotly debated social issue related to pregnancy today. But it was not always so controversial. Prior to the mid-1800s, abortion was practiced in the United States but was not considered a crime if performed before the fetus quickened (or showed signs of life). After 1860, however, physicians advocated banning abortion because of maternal harm caused by the use of dangerous poisons and practices (Figueira-McDonough, 1990). Legislators also wanted to see growth in the U.S. population. By 1900, all states had legislation prohibiting abortion except in extreme circumstances, typically medically related. Over the years, moral issues increasingly became the basis for debate. Hazel Gereke recounted that as late as 1966, legal abortion had to be "medically related," which did not cover the difficulty of another child for older parents or the difficulty of raising a child with Down syndrome, a condition that at that time could not be ascertained prenatally. Hazel's situation was also influenced by the moral or religious stance of the physician and perhaps the hospital. Consider Cecelia Kin's situation: Abortion is available to her, but familial beliefs and ethics contribute to her indecision and anguish.

Despite laws controlling abortion, it has remained an option for those with economic means. Poor women around the world have been the ones whose access to abortion services is limited, particularly in nonindustrialized countries. In 1973, in *Roe v. Wade,* the U.S. Supreme Court legalized abortion in the first trimester and left it to the discretion of the woman and her physician. Three years later, in 1976, the Hyde Amendment limited federal funding for abortion, and the Supreme Court ruled in 1989, in *Webster v. Reproductive Health Services,* that Medicaid could no longer fund abortions, except in cases of rape, incest, or life endangerment (Kaiser Family Foundation, 2008) and that much of the decision making related to abortion should return to the states. Today, states vary considerably in who has access to abortion, when, how, and at what cost. In some states, new rules are effectively decreasing access, particularly for poor and minority populations. Some poor African American women have no greater access to abortion now than they did more than 100 years ago (Ross, 1992), a situation that extends to any group of women who are economically and educationally disadvantaged. Eighty-seven percent of U.S. counties have no abortion provider, and more than one third of women aged 15 to 44 live in these counties (Kaiser Family Foundation), resulting in rural disparities in access to abortion.

It is estimated that 42% of unintended pregnancies end in abortion (Finer & Henshaw, 2006; Kaiser Family Foundation, 2008). Globally, abortion incidence fell from 45.5 million in 1995 to 41.6 million in 2003, a change attributed to increased contraception availability and use. The most dramatic decrease (from 90 to 44 per 1,000 women aged 15 to 44) was in Eastern Europe. In 2003, Western Europe had the lowest abortion rate in the world (12 per 1,000 women, aged 15 to 44) (Guttmacher Institute, 2009a). In spite of technological advances and improved accessibility, in 2003, there were an estimated 70,000 maternal deaths because of unsafe abortions worldwide; these were found most prevalently in nonindustrialized countries (Guttmacher Institute).

During the first trimester and until **fetal viability** (the point at which the baby could survive outside the womb) in the second trimester, U.S. federal law allows for a pregnant woman to legally choose an abortion, although states can narrow this option. Approximately 89% of abortions in the United States are performed during the first 12 weeks of pregnancy, 9.9% from 13 to 20 weeks, and 1% after 21 weeks (Kaiser Family Foundation, 2008; Strauss et al., 2002). Recent controversy regarding procedures for terminating a pregnancy after fetal viability has called attention to ethical and legal dilemmas that are being addressed in the legal system, by most religions, and in other parts of U.S. culture. Opinion polls continually reveal, however, that like Hazel Gereke, the vast majority of Americans favor abortion as an option under specified conditions. A January 2006 CBS News poll revealed that only 5% of respondents said that abortion should "never" be permitted (PollingReport.com, 2006). Global comparisons suggest that there is little to no relationship between legal restrictions on abortion and incidence (Guttmacher Institute, 2009a). For example, abortion rates are about the same in Africa (29%) as in Europe (28%), while there are vast differences in legality. African nations seldom allow abortions in contrast to European countries, where abortion is generally permitted. What is vastly different in these comparisons is the safety of abortion, which is largely ensured when it is legal.

The 25% decline in the rate of induced abortion in the United States between 1990 and 2005 is attributed to better education and increased use of birth control, including abstinence (Centers for Disease Control and Prevention [CDC], 2000; Kaiser Family Foundation, 2008). But, economic disparities continue to increase, with poorer women having a greater proportion of unwanted pregnancies compared with more affluent women. Between 1994 and 2001, the rate of unintended pregnancy among poor women increased by 29%, and the rate of unintended births increased by 44%. During this same period, the rate of unintended pregnancy among women at or above twice the poverty level declined by 20%, and the rate of unintended births declined as well. The social class disparity in abortion rates also increased during this period (Finer & Henshaw, 2006). Because of these combined factors, poor women are five times as likely as their affluent age counterparts to have unintended births. This disparity may be due, in large part, to the fact that poor women are twice as likely as affluent women to have no health insurance (Finer & Henshaw; Sonfield, 2003).

Abortion procedures fall into three categories:

1. *Chemical abortion,* also known as medical or nonsurgical abortion, uses the drugs methotrexate, misoprostol, and/or mifepristone (Mifeprex or RU-486, "abortion pill"), followed by prostaglandin. This procedure was used

in 13% of all U.S. abortions in 2005 and rose to 25% by 2008, with 98.5% effectiveness for Mifeprex (Fjerstad, Truissell, Sivin, Lichtenberg, & Cullins, 2009). The combined regimen has 92% efficacy if used within 49 days of gestation. Prostaglandin can be used alone but has lower efficacy (Spitz, Bardin, Benton, & Robbins, 1998).

2. *Instrumental or surgical evacuation.* One of two types of procedures was used in 87% of all U.S. surgical abortions as of 2005 (Jones, Zolna, Henshaw & Finer, 2008). The standard first-trimester vacuum curettage, also called manual vacuum aspiration or MVA, is the one most frequently performed in an outpatient clinic. A suction device is threaded through the cervix to remove the contents of the uterus. It is fairly safe, but because it is invasive, it introduces greater risks than the use of prostaglandin. The second-trimester curettage abortion, accounting for 2.4% of U.S. abortions in 2002 (Strauss et al., 2002), requires even greater dilation of the cervix to allow passage of a surgical instrument to scrape the walls of the uterus. If curettage abortion is performed on an outpatient basis, a second visit is required. With both types of instrumental evacuation, the woman faces risks of bleeding, infection, and subsequent infertility. Abortion between 18 to 26 weeks' gestation is referred to as "late-term abortion" and continues to be hotly debated. The Partial-Birth Abortion Ban Act was introduced in the United States in 1995, passed in 2003, and reaffirmed in Federal Court in 2007. This legislation does not prohibit abortion, as sometimes thought, but bans a procedure called intact dilation and extraction, with no health exceptions (Gosten, 2007). Since its passage, 31 states have banned partial-birth abortion, and the debate continues (Kaiser Family Foundation, 2008).

3. *Amnioinfusion.* In the second trimester, a saline solution can be infused into the uterus to end the pregnancy. Amnioinfusion is used in only 0.4% of abortions and requires the greatest medical expertise and follow-up care.

Regardless of the timing or type of abortion, all women should be carefully counseled before and after the procedure. Unplanned pregnancies typically create considerable psychological stress, and social workers can help pregnant women consider all alternatives to an unwanted pregnancy—including abortion—consistent with the client's personal values and beliefs. Following an abortion, most women experience only mild feelings of guilt, sadness, or regret that abate fairly soon, followed by relief that the crisis is resolved (David, 1996). Nevertheless, some women may have a more severe response and may require ongoing counseling, particularly those women who had faced pre-abortion trauma such as sexual abuse and intimate violence (Charles, Polis, Sridhara, & Blum, 2008; Robinson, Stotland, Russo, Lang, & Occhiogrosso, 2009). Some researchers have found that as many as 40% of women undergoing abortion have prior unwanted sexual experiences (Rue, Coleman, Rue, & Reardon, 2004). Two recently published reviews of studies that examined the relationship between abortion and subsequent emotional trauma concluded that the studies with the most methodological flaws reported the greatest trauma outcomes. This was in sharp contrast to those studies that were of higher quality, providing evidence that emotional trauma was related to preexisting disorders associated with sexual violence (Charles et al., 2008; Robinson et al., 2009). Counseling is also particularly important from a prevention perspective, because women receiving counseling following a first abortion have been found to practice contraception with greater frequency and success (David, 1996). Social workers need to be mindful of their personal views about abortion in order to help a client make an informed decision that reflects the client's values, religious beliefs, and available options. In addition, it is important to assess for prior traumatic experiences.

Infertility Treatment

Infertility, the inability to create a viable embryo after 1 year of intercourse without contraception (Clark, 2009; Jordon & Ferguson, 2006), is often a life crisis. There are more than 80 million "childless persons" in the world (Bos et al., 2005), but not all by choice. About 5 million women in the United States are impacted by infertility (approximately 1 in 6 couples) and about 10% to 15% are candidates for assisted reproductive technology (ART), including IVF. In 2007, the Centers for Disease Control and Prevention (CDC) reported that 430 registered fertility clinics in the United

States performed a total of 142,415 ART cycles. The ART treatment resulted in 43,408 deliveries and 57,564 infants born (CDC, 2009a). Forty percent of infertility problems reside with the female, 40% with the male, and the remaining 20% are either both the male and female or are unknown (Clark, 2009; Taylor, 2003). The costs of infertility treatment can be staggering, ranging from approximately $17 million spent in 2000 for

> How does infertility affect the multigenerational family?

male infertility surgery to about $18 billion the same year for assisted reproduction technology cycles (Meacham, Joyce, Wise, Kparker, & Niederberger, 2007). Jennifer and Allan Bradshaw are struggling to find a way to afford infertility treatment.

Social workers must be aware that the mind-body connection is clearly seen in the psychological consequences of infertility (Watkins & Baldo, 2004), as Jennfier Bradshaw so poignantly conveys. Information about the impact of infertility on the emotional health of couples is limited, and even less is known about counseling strategies for this specialized at-risk population (Lykeridou, Gourounti, Deltsidou, Loutradis, & Vaslamatzis, 2009; Wischmann, Scherg, Strowitzki, & Verres, 2009). Social workers can give increased attention to building resilience in this population with action-focused coping skills, an area that is significantly underexplored (Sexton, Byrd, & Von Kluge, 2010). Studies have shown that women experiencing infertility have a 69.2% risk of lifetime depression compared with 30% for women who do not experience infertility, and this peaks during the second or third year of treatment (Cwikel, Gidron, & Sheiner, 2004; Karjane, Stovall, Berger, & Svikis, 2008; Noble, 2005). Some infertility medications exacerbate depression (Baxter & Warnock, 2007). Anxiety, social stress, isolation, and marital dissatisfaction also have been shown to increase with infertility problems (Clayton, 2004; Cwikel et al.; Newton, Sherrard, & Glavac, 1999; Verhaak et al., 2005; Wilson & Kopitzke, 2002), exacerbating the higher levels of generalized anxiety disorder, panic disorder, and simple phobias that are present before the struggle with infertility begins (Karjane et al., 2008). However, social support, specifically a positive marital relationship, more than any other factor, modifies the psychological distress both during treatment and following failure of IVF (Gibson & Myers, 2002; Verhaak et al., 2005). Women who have experienced childhood or adult sexual abuse and domestic violence have higher rates of gynecological problems, including pelvic inflammatory disease (PID), which contribute to an increase in infertility (Champion, Piper, Holden, Korte, & Shain, 2004; Champion et al., 2005; Cwikel et al.). Chlamydia trachomatis, an STI, is one of the most common causes of infertility and may be transmitted through an involuntary sexual encounter (Cappello, de Macario, Di Felice, Zummo, & Macario, 2009).

The causes of infertility are many. Recent studies have shown that obesity in both men and women (Al-Hasani & Zohni, 2008; Pasquali, 2006; Sallmen, Sandler, Hoppin, Blair, & Baird, 2006; Wilkes & Murdoch, 2009), Polycystic ovary syndrome (PCOS) with associated insulin resistance (Hahn et al., 2006; McGovern, et al., 2007; Pasquali, Gambineri, & Pagotto, 2006), high exposure to lead (Chang et al., 2005), ovulation disorders (which sometimes can be modified by a change in diet and lifestyle), blocked fallopian tubes, endometriosis (Taylor, 2003), chromosomal abnormalities, and cervical and uterine congenital defects all affect fertility (Chavarro, Rich-Edwards, Rosner, & Willett, 2007; Kelly-Weeder & O'Connor, 2006; Khawaja et al., 2009). Women who are exposed to pesticides and pollutants (e.g., women who eat fish with high levels of mercury) and women who have high levels of exposure to lead and cadmium also have reduced fertility (Al-Saleh et al., 2008; Mendola, Messer, & Rappazzo, 2008). Black women have been shown to have twice the rate of infertility of White women, even when risk factors such as smoking and obesity are controlled for, but educational and economic disparities contribute to the higher rate of infertility and less utilization of IVF (Jain, 2006; Seifer, Frazier, & Grainger, 2008; Wellons et al., 2008).

Defective sperm function is a leading cause of infertility (Altken, Wingate, De Iullis, Koppers, & McLaughlin, 2006; Bloom et al., 2009), and approximately 67% of men undergoing surgery for infertility had a diagnosis of varicocele, an operable condition (Meacham et al., 2007). Occupational factors—including exposure to leads, pesticides, estrogens, oxidants, plastics, radiation, and heat—have been found to affect male fertility (Aitken, Skakkebaek, & Roman, 2006; Giudice, 2006; Kefer, Agarwal, & Sabenegh, 2009; Phillips & Tanphaichitr, 2008; Sheiner, Sheiner, Hammei, Potashnik, & Carel, 2003). Other factors have been implicated in male infertility, including sitting for extended periods of time (Boggia et al., 2009; Figa-Talamanca et al., 1996) and advanced age (Sloter et al., 2006). About 10% to 15% of male

Male Infertility		Female Infertility	
Problem	Treatment	Problem	Treatment
Low sperm count	Change of environment; antibiotics; surgery; hormonal therapy; artificial insemination	Vaginal structural problem Abnormal cervical mucus	Surgery Hormonal therapy
Physical defect affecting transport of sperm	Microsurgery	Abnormal absence of ovulation	Antibiotics for infection; hormonal therapy
Genetic disorder	Artificial insemination	Blocked or scarred fallopian tubes	Surgery; IVF
Exposure to work environment substances	Early detection and changes in work environment	Uterine lining unfavorable to implantation	Hormone therapy; antibiotics; surgery
Alcohol and caffeine use and cigarette smoking	Reduction or abstinence preconception	Obesity	Weight reduction
Advancing age	Sperm banking at younger age; artificial insemination	Alcohol and caffeine use and cigarette smoking	Abstinence preconception (and post to maximize pregnancy outcome)

▲ **Exhibit 2.2**   Causes and Cures for Infertility

infertility is due to genetic problems (an important issue when IVF is considered) (Ferlin, Arredi, & Foresta, 2006). Some studies seemed to indicate that cigarette smoking reduces the volume of semen in men (Kalyani, Basavaraj, & Kumar, 2007; Pasqualotto, Sobreiro, Hallak, Pasqualotto, & Lucon, 2006; Sepaniak et al., 2006), but other studies do not support this finding (Aziz, Agarwal, Nallella, & Thomas, 2006; Gaur, Talekar, & Pathak, 2007). Smoking has been shown to affect circulation levels of estrogen in women and reduces sperm quality (Gaur et al.; Grainger, Frazier, & Rowland, 2006; Kelly-Weeder & O'Connor, 2006), contributing to both male and female infertility. Caffeine and alcohol have been cited as contributors to infertility in men and women, but more recent evidence does not support this (Chavarro, Rich-Edwards, Rosner, & Willett, 2009; Derbyshire & Abdula. 2008; Papachristou Ornoy, 2006; Papachristou et al., 2006).

In the past, infertile couples could keep trying and hope for the best, but medical technology has given today's couples a variety of options, summarized in Exhibit 2.2. The primary treatment for male infertility, diagnosed by a sperm analysis, is artificial insemination, using fresh or frozen donor sperm injected into the uterus. This was used by the Arabs in the 14th century for horse breeding, but it was not until 1780 that a British surgeon demonstrated its effectiveness with humans (Bullough, 2005). Artificial insemination is also a treatment choice for lesbian couples and single parents (De Brucker et al., 2009). The success rate varies with age of both the male and female (Kdous et al., 2007), the duration of infertility, previous pregnancy history (Pandian, Bhattacharya, Vale, & Templeton, 2005), and the number of cycles. Overall, it is expected that a woman would become pregnant after one cycle 14% of the time and after 12 cycles 77% of the time, but this drops to 52% in 12 cycles for women between the ages of 40 and 45 (De Brucker et al.). The cost is approximately $300 to $500 per cycle. Ethical and legal questions have been raised regarding the legal status of the sperm donor (what parental rights does he have?) and the psychosocial impact on the mother. Sperm donors are routinely screened for genetic defects and physical suitability, but psychological screening remains controversial—in large part because it is nonstandardized and thus easily misinterpreted.

The birth of the first "test tube baby" in 1978, demonstrating the first of many **assisted reproductive technologies (ART)**, initiated a new era in infertility management and research. The first test tube baby was conceived in the United States in 1983, and by 2006 more than 1% of all babies born in the United States were a result of ART (Van Voorhis, 2006). The Fertility Clinical Success Rate and Certification Act, passed in 1992, requires all clinics performing ART to report success rates. Society for Assisted Reproductive Technology (SART) member clinics have developed embryo transfer guidelines that led participating clinics to reduce the number of transferred embryos, and these rates are published (Stern et al., 2007). ART involves the recovery of eggs following hormonal treatment to induce ovulation. Previously frozen eggs may be used, a less expensive and less invasive technique because it does not require removal or hyperstimulation, but the rates of success decrease (Davis & Jocoy, 2008). Donor eggs are often used for women over the age of 40 because the rate of live births using ART decreases with age, from more than 40% for a woman in her late 20s, to 30% at age of 38, and 10% at the age of 40 (Davis & Jocoy). However, recent research shows that the use of luteinizing hormone (LH), growth hormones, and gonadotrophic hormones may support successful later pregnancies (Alviggi, Humaidan, Howles, Tredway, & Hillier, 2009; Derman & Seifer, 2003).

By the time a couple considers the use of ART, they have often struggled with infertility for a long time, emotionally and physically, and may be desperate. But the high cost and limited success rates deter some prospective candidates. Some ART centers require a psychological evaluation of the couple to assess competency to parent, often focusing on issues of stress, guilt, anxiety, depression, and isolation (Hart, 2002). Treatment focuses on decreasing psychological denial and disengagement (van den Akker, 2005), and when conception occurs, treatment centers on decreasing anxiety in order to increase self-esteem and parenting efficacy (Cox, Glazebrook, Sheard, Ndukwe, & Oates, 2006). Infertile women seeking ART have more education and are less likely to have a child than surrogate or adoptive parents (van den Akker). There is current controversy about the use of ART with women who have HIV, although the current rate of transfer of the virus to the fetus is less than 2% (Zutlevics, 2006).

The most common types of ART include the following:

- *IVF.* Many clinics now inject the sperm directly into the egg(s) that is surgically retrieved (known as intracytoplasmic sperm injection), especially when there is low sperm motility. This has been found to increase success rates, but coverage of this procedure varies among states and so utilization of this procedure is often dictated by insurance plans (Check, 2007; Jain & Gupta, 2007). Treatment costs may vary among clinics, with one cycle of IVF costing approximately $10,000. Some clinics allow partial or complete refunds if pregnancy does not occur with higher priced multiple cycle plans, a practice that is sometimes referred to as "shared risk" (Advanced Fertility Center of Chicago, 2009). Success rates vary, but most clinics suggest that with a single cycle of IVF, there is a 30% to 40% success rate for women under the age of 34, with a live birth rate of 28.3% per cycle (Davis & Jocoy, 2008; Toner, 2002), odds slightly lower than what Jennifer Bradshaw was told. Obviously, in impoverished countries where childlessness is a "crippling social taboo," this procedure is beyond the reach of most of the population ("Cheap IVF Needed," 2006; Inhorn, 2003).

- *Gamete intrafallopian tube transfer (GIFT).* At one time, GIFT was used in about 25% of infertility cases, but now that IVF has the same success rate, it only represents 1% of ART procedures (CDC, 2009a; Jain & Gupta, 2007). Success rates are not well documented because this procedure is used so infrequently (Davis & Jocoy, 2008), but some estimate a 25% to 30% success rate with many GIFT treatments, resulting in multiple pregnancies (Wilson, 2009). GIFT requires the same procedure as IVF, except that the fertilized ova are surgically returned to the woman's fallopian tubes (Jain & Gupta, 2007).

- *Intrauterine insemination (IUI).* IUI involves bypassing the cervix (usually altered by antibodies or infection) and surgically implanting the ovum and spermatozoa into the uterus. It is a costly procedure, often used during the early stages of endometriosis. Pregnancy success rates are less than with GIFT (Lodhi et al., 2004).

- *Preservation and gestational surrogacy.* This procedure is the harvesting of embryos to preserve for future use. It is often used when women face surgery because of cancer and will not be able to conceive in the future (Plante, 2000). In 2007, there were 10,321 transfers of fresh donor embryos and 5,632 of frozen donor embryos in the United States, resulting in success rates of 55.1% and 31.9% of live births, respectively (CDC, 2009a). Cervical cancer is the fourth most frequent cancer diagnosed in women between 15 and 39 years old, and it directly affects fertility. Recent surgical procedures that avoid hysterectomy have led to increased fertility, but women have a 33% rate of miscarriage in the first two trimesters (Plante, 2006).

Each procedure carries risks. These include multiple gestations, which carry higher risks of maternal and neonate complications. There is a 50 times greater likelihood of having three or more babies with a pregnancy resulting from ART. Multiple births from ART represent about 50% of all multiple-birth pregnancies (Allen, Wilson, & Cheung, 2006; Gurgan & Demiro, 2007; Jain & Gupta, 2007). An increased rate of birth defects also exists; 6.2% of IVF-conceived children have major birth defects compared with 4.4% of naturally conceived children (Van Voorhis, 2006, p. 193). Sometimes IVF-conceived children have rare genetic malformations (Ceelen, van Weissenbruch, Vermeiden, van Leeuwen, Delemarre-van de Waal, 2008). Genetic counseling is strongly encouraged for this population (Geary & Moon, 2006). For men and women with HIV, infertility can be a result of the infection or caused by a separate issue. ART is being used to help women with HIV conceive, and sperm washing is being used to reduce the risk of transferring the virus from the male (Bostan et al., 2008; Semprini, Hollander, Vucetich, & Gilling-Smith, 2008).

All of these procedures except preservation and gestational surrogacy may use donated ova, but that practice has raised further legal and ethical questions, especially regarding parental rights and responsibilities. There are now an estimated 500,000 spare embryos frozen with about 20,000 added yearly. They can be thawed and destroyed, preserved indefinitely, used for stem cell research, or donated (Clark, 2009), but each option is potentially fraught with ethical and political dilemmas. Psychological and emotional issues may also arise, related to the introduction of third-party genetic material, secrecy, and confidentiality.

Although ART was originally limited to married couples, unattached females in increasing numbers are using this method of conception. A growing population of older women is delaying childbirth for a number of reasons: not having a partner (50%); wanting financial security (32%); a career (19%); being unaware of the impact of age on fertility (18%); and only becoming interested in having children later in life (26%) (Hammarberg & Clarke, 2005). Jennifer Bradshaw is among the 19% who delayed childbirth to establish a career. Whatever the reason, when women try to conceive later in life, they often end up using ART. Surrogate mothers have increasingly volunteered to provide the opportunity for gay couples to bear children, also utilizing ART techniques (Ross, Steele, & Epstein, 2006).

Uterine transplant is on the frontier of infertility treatment. This was first done in 2000 but did not lead to a successful pregnancy. It has been successful in animals and is being explored, especially to assist younger women who have had a hysterectomy (Nair, Stega, Smith, & Del Priore, 2008).

Adoption is another alternative for the infertile couple. In 2002, 2% of adults aged 18 to 44 adopted children while the percentage of infants relinquished by never-married mothers declined to only 1% (Jones, 2009). Adoption is not much less daunting than infertility treatment, however. Infertility coupled with exposure to adoptive relationships are the primary motivations for considering adoption (Bausch, 2006). A time-consuming multiphase evaluation, which includes a home study, is required before finalization of custody. The idea of parenting an infant with an unknown genetic heritage may be a challenge for some people, particularly because an increasing number of problems previously thought to be environmentally induced are being linked—at least in part—to genetics. On the positive side, however, some individuals and couples prefer adoption to the demands and uncertainties of ART, and some adoptive parents are also committed to giving a home to children in need of care.

> **Critical Thinking Questions 2.1**
>
> In recent years, there has been much controversy about sex education in public schools. Some people argue that there should be no sex education in public schools. What is your opinion on this topic? If you think there should be sex education in public schools, at what age do you think it should start? What arguments can you give for abstinence-only sex education? What arguments can you give for comprehensive sex education?

NORMAL FETAL DEVELOPMENT

The 40 weeks of **gestation,** during which the fertilized ovum becomes a fully developed infant, are a remarkable time. **Gestational age** is calculated from the date of the beginning of the woman's last menstrual period, a fairly easy time for the woman to identify. In contrast, **fertilization age** is measured from the time of fertilization, approximately 14 days after the beginning of the last menstrual period. The average pregnancy lasts 280 days when calculated from gestational age and 266 days from the time of fertilization. Conventionally, the gestation period is organized by trimesters of about three months each. This is a convenient system, but note that these divisions are not supported by clearly demarcated events.

First Trimester

In some ways, the first 12 weeks of pregnancy are the most remarkable. In an amazingly short time, sperm and ovum unite and are transformed into a being with identifiable body parts. The mother's body also undergoes dramatic changes.

Fertilization and the Embryonic Period

Sexual intercourse results in the release of an average of 200 million to 300 million sperm. Their life span is relatively short, and their journey through the female reproductive tract is fraught with hazards. Thus, only about one or two in 1,000 of the original sperm reach the fallopian tubes, which lead from the ovaries to the uterus. Typically, only one sperm penetrates the ripened ovum, triggering a biochemical reaction that prevents entry of any other sperm. The **zygote** (fertilized egg) continues to divide and begins about a seven-day journey to the uterus.

Following implantation in the uterine wall, the zygote matures into an **embryo.** The placenta, which acts like a filter between the mother and the growing embryo, also forms. The umbilical cord connects the fetus to the placenta. Oxygen, water, and glucose, as well as many drugs, viruses, bacteria, vitamins, and hormones, pass through the placenta to the embryo. Amniotic fluid in the uterus protects the embryo throughout the pregnancy.

By the third week, tissue begins differentiating into organs. During this period, the embryo is vulnerable to **teratogens**—substances that may harm the developing organism—but most women do not know they are pregnant. Exhibit 2.3 shows how some relatively common drugs may have a teratogenic effect in the earliest stage of fetal development. Research is also showing that maternal diet has an influence on brain development. Studies have found that nutritional deficiency in the first trimester results in an increase in brain abnormalities. High fat

Substance	Effects on Fetal Development
Acetaminophen (Tylenol)	None
Amphetamines	Cardiac defects, cleft palate
Antacids	Increase in anomalies
Antianxiety medications	Increase in anomalies
Antiepileptic medications	Neural tube defects, esp. facial
Antihistamines	None
Barbiturates	Increase in anomalies
Gentamycin (antibiotic)	Cranial nerve damage
Glucocorticoids (steroids)	Cleft palate, cardiac defects
Haloperidol	Limb malformations
Insulin	Skeletal malformations
Lithium	Goiter, eye anomalies, cleft palate
LSD	Chromosomal abnormalities
Penicillin	None
Phenobarbital	Multiple anomalies
Podophyllin (in laxatives)	Multiple anomalies
Tetracycline (antibiotic)	Inhibition of bone growth, discoloration of teeth
Tricyclic antidepressants	Central nervous system and limb malformations

▲ **Exhibit 2.3**   Potential Teratogens During the First Trimester

diets negatively affect the development of the hippocampus, which helps control long-term memory and spatial navigation. Protein deficiency causes global deficits and problems in the hippocampus and cortex. Iron deficiencies affect processing speed, recognition memory, and motor development and can cause irreversible behavioral and learning deficits. Zinc deficiency affects cognitive development, cerebella development, and attention (Georgieff, 2007; Massaro, Rothbaum, & Aly, 2006; Niculescu & Lupu, 2009). Nutritional deficiencies also are thought to be a potential risk for later development of schizophrenia (Rifas-Shiman et al., 2006). Research has also shown that thyroid hormones play an important role in brain development and that deficiencies, such as iodine deficiency, during the first and third trimesters may lead to later learning disabilities (de Escobar, 2004; de Escobar, Ares, Berbel, Obregon, & del Rey, 2008; Rifas-Shiman et al.; Sethi, 2004).

The Fetal Period

After the eighth week, the embryo is mature enough to be called a **fetus** (meaning "young one") (Novak & Broom, 1995), and the mother is experiencing signs of her pregnancy. Usually the mother has now missed one menstrual period, but if her cycle was irregular, this may not be a reliable sign. Approximately 50% of women experience nausea and vomiting (morning sickness) during the first trimester, as was the case for Felicia Thompson. A few experience vomiting so severe that it causes dehydration and metabolic changes requiring hospitalization. **Multigravidas,** women who have had a previous pregnancy, often recognize the signs of excessive fatigue and soreness in their breasts as a sign of pregnancy.

Between the seventh and 12th week, the fetal heart rate can be heard using a Doppler device that affords a three- or four-dimensional view leading to early diagnosis of maternal and fetal problems (Kurjak et al., 2005; Merce, Barco, Alcazar, Sabatel, & Trojano, 2009). At 12 weeks, the gender of the fetus can be detected, and the face is fully formed. The fetus is moving within the mother, but it is still too early for her to feel the movement.

Newly pregnant women often feel ambivalence. Because of hormonal changes, they may experience mood swings and become less outgoing. Concerns about the changes in their bodies, finances, the impact on their life goals, lifestyle adjustments, and interpersonal inter-

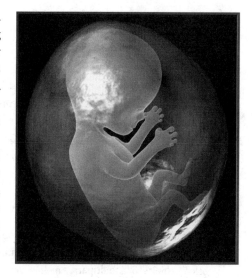

▲ **Photo 2.3**   After week eight, the embryo is mature enough to be called a fetus.

actions may cause anxiety. Often the father experiences similar ambivalence, and he may be distressed by his partner's mood swings. Parents who have previously miscarried may have a heightened concern for the well-being of this fetus.

Second Trimester

By the 16th week, the fetus is approximately 19 centimeters (7.5 inches) long and weighs 100 grams (3.3 ounces). The most rapid period of brain development is during the second trimester (van de Beek, Thijssen, Cohen-Kettenis, van Goozen, & Buitelaar, 2004). Recent evidence cautions pregnant women to monitor the eating of fish with higher levels of mercury to avoid negative impact on the infant's cognitive skills (McDiarmid, Gardiner, & Jack, 2008; Oken et al., 2005). The second trimester is generally a period of contentment and planning for most women, as it seems to have been for Felicia Thompson. For problem pregnancies, or in troubled environments, quite the opposite may occur. However, the fatigue, nausea and vomiting, and mood swings that often accompany the first few weeks usually disappear in the second trimester.

Hearing the heartbeat and seeing the fetus via ultrasound often bring the reality of the pregnancy home. As seen in the story of the Thompsons, *quickening*—the experience of feeling fetal movement—usually occurs around this time, further validating the personhood of the fetus. *Fetal differentiation,* whereby the mother separates the individuality of the fetus from her own personhood, is usually completed by the end of this trimester. Many fathers too begin to relate to the fetus as a developing offspring.

Some fathers enjoy the changing shape of the woman's body, but others may struggle with the changes. Unless there are specific contraindications, sexual relations may continue throughout the pregnancy, and some men find the second trimester a period of great sexual satisfaction. Often during the second trimester the pregnant woman also experiences a return of her prepregnancy level of sexual desire.

Third Trimester

By 24 weeks, the fetus is considered viable in many hospitals. Today, neurosonography can visualize the fetal brain anatomy when central nervous system (CNS) anomalies are suspected (Malinger, Lev, & Lerman-Sagie, 2006). In spite of fetal viability, parents are not usually prepared for childbirth early in the third trimester. Felicia Thompson, for instance, was not prepared for the birth of her son, Paul, who at 26 weeks' gestation, struggled to survive. Not only are parents not prepared, but the risks to newborns are very great if birth occurs prior to the 26th week of pregnancy. Recent research indicates another caution for mothers during the third trimester: Smoking during this period can affect critical brain development, lead to higher rates of preterm delivery and low-birth-weight infants, and contribute to subsequent behavioral problems (Baler, Vakow, Fowler, & Benveniste, 2008; Huang & Winzer-Serhan, 2006; Jaddoe et al., 2008).

The tasks of the fetus during the third trimester are to gain weight and mature in preparation for delivery. As delivery nears, the increased weight of the fetus can cause discomfort for the mother, and often she looks forward to delivery with increasing anticipation. Completion of preparations for the new arrival consume much of her attention.

Labor and Delivery of the Neonate

Predicting when labor will begin is impossible. However, one indication of imminent labor is *lightening* (the descent of the fetus into the mother's pelvis). For a **primipara**—a first-time mother—lightening occurs approximately two weeks before delivery. For a **multipara,** a mother who has previously given birth—lightening typically occurs at the beginning of labor. Often the mother experiences Braxton Hicks contractions, brief contractions that prepare the mother and fetus for labor—what Hazel Gereke referred to as "false labor." Usually, true labor begins with a show or release of the mucous plug that covered the cervical opening.

Labor is divided into three stages:

1.   In the first stage, the cervix thins and dilates. The amniotic fluid is usually released during this stage ("water breaking"), and the mother feels regular contractions that intensify in frequency and strength as labor progresses. Many factors determine the length of this stage, including the number of pregnancies the mother has experienced, the weight of the fetus, the anatomy of the mother, the strength of the contractions, and the relaxation of the mother in the process. Despite the stories that abound, most mothers have plenty of time to prepare for the upcoming birth. Near the end of this phase, "transition" occurs, marked by a significant increase in the intensity and frequency of the contractions and heightened emotionalism. The head crowns (is visible at the vulva) at the end of this stage.

2.   The second stage is delivery, when the **neonate** (newborn) is expelled from the mother. If the newborn is born breech (feet or buttocks first) or is transverse (positioned horizontally in the birth canal) and cannot be turned prior to birth, the mother may require a cesarean section.

3.   Typically, within one hour after delivery, the placenta, the remaining amniotic fluid, and the membrane that separated the fetus from the uterine wall are delivered with a few contractions. If the newborn breastfeeds immediately, the hormone oxytocin is released to stimulate these contractions.

Following birth, the neonate undergoes rapid physiological changes, particularly in its respiratory and cardiac systems. Prior to birth, oxygen is delivered to the fetus through the umbilical vein, and carbon dioxide is eliminated by the two umbilical arteries. Although the fetus begins to breathe prior to birth, breathing serves no purpose until after delivery. The neonate's first breath, typically in the form of a cry, creates tremendous pressure within the lungs, which clears amniotic fluid and triggers the opening and closing of several shunts and vessels in the heart. The blood flow is rerouted to the lungs.

Many factors, such as maternal exposure to narcotics during pregnancy or labor, can adversely affect the neonate's attempts to breathe—as can prematurity, congenital anomalies, and neonatal infections. Drugs and other interventions may be administered to maintain adequate respiration. To measure the neonate's adjustment to extrauterine life, Apgar scores—rather simple measurements of physiological health—are assessed at one, five, and 10 minutes after birth. Apgar scores determine the need for resuscitation and indicate the effectiveness of resuscitation efforts and long-term problems that might arise. The other immediate challenge to the newborn is to establish a stable temperature. Inadequately maintained body temperature creates neonatal stress and thus increased respiratory and cardiac effort, which can result in respiratory failure. Close monitoring of the neonate during the first four hours after birth is critical to detect any such problems in adapting to extrauterine life.

PREGNANCY AND THE LIFE COURSE

As the case studies at the beginning of the chapter indicate, pregnancy is a period of transition. Each family member faces changes in role identification and prescribed tasks. Regardless of the age of the parents or number of previous births, the pregnant woman, and the father when involved, must complete four different developmental tasks:

> Under what conditions might the transition to parenthood become a turning point?

1. The parent(s) must provide for the mother's safety and that of the neonate throughout pregnancy, labor, and delivery.

2. The parent(s) must help people in her/their social support system to accept this event.

3. The parent(s) must bond with her/their unborn child.

4. The parent(s) must come to terms with the inequality inherent in a parent/neonate relationship (based on Rubin, 1995).

Although the tasks were the same for Felicia Thompson, Hazel Gereke, Cecelia Kin, and their partners, each had very different resources for negotiating the tasks. To some extent, those resources were specific to their position in the life course. Remember, however, that the tasks are the same regardless of maternal age.

Teen Pregnancy

Fifty percent of adolescents in the United States are sexually active, resulting in approximately 700,000 pregnancies per year in women ages 15 to 19, more than 80% of which are unintended (Speidel, Harper, & Shields, 2008). One third are ended by abortion, another 33% result in miscarriage, and the remaining 33% deliver a live infant (Strasburger, 2007). Between 1991 and 2004, when there was a drop in teen pregnancy rates across all categories, overall pregnancy rates for 15- to 19-year-olds declined by 38% (Anderson, 2008; Contraceptive Technology Update, 2005, 2007; Potera, 2007), and abortion rates for adolescents decreased by 50% (CDC, 2008a, 2008b; 2009b). These declines primarily are attributed to abstinence and increased use of contraceptives (Potera, 2007). However, geographical, racial, and ethnic differences abound. Women in New England states demonstrate 19 births per 1,000 adolescent women while in Mississippi the rate soars to 68 births per 1,000 adolescent women, 60% higher than the national average of 42 births per 1,000 adolescent women (CDC, 2009b). Between 1991 and 2004, the pregnancy rates dropped 45% for Black adolescents and 48% for non-Hispanic White teenagers (Moffett, 2007). However, the birth rate among Hispanic and non-Hispanic Black teens remained three times higher than among Whites (Hamilton, Martin, & Ventura, 2007; Ventura, Abma, Mosher, & Henshaw, 2008). This trend was reversed between 2005 and 2007 as teen birth rates rose 1% between 2006 and 2007 (Landau, 2008).

> How important is the multigenerational family in social work practice with pregnant teens?

Nevertheless, the United States has the third highest teenage birth rate in industrialized countries, 52.1 per 1,000 adolescent women ages 15 to 19 compared with fewer than seven per 1,000 in Korea, Switzerland, Denmark, the

Netherlands, and Sweden (OECD, 2008; UNICEF, 2001). The social costs are high: An estimated $7 billion is spent each year on adolescent pregnancy, and only one third of the teen mothers are able to earn a high school diploma (Kaplan et al., 2001; Koshar, 2001). Approximately 38% of teens live in poverty, but 83% of adolescents who give birth are from low-income or impoverished families (Klein, 2005). In addition, daughters of teenage mothers are 66% more likely to become teen mothers themselves (Meade, Kershaw, & Ickovics, 2008). Long-term commitment and financial support from the father of the pregnant teen's child are unusual, further contributing to the isolation and impoverishment of the young adolescent mother.

Intimate Partner Violence and Teen Pregnancy

Adolescents are at significant risk for forced sexual intercourse, with an overall rate of 8% of high school adolescents reporting rape, females at twice the rate of males (Howard, Wang, & Yan, 2007). Although it is difficult to accurately determine the number of adolescent pregnancies that are a result of statutory rape, it appears that as many as 66% of the birth fathers are adult males and at least half of the birth mothers in these situations are under the age of 16 (Kandakai & Smith, 2007). Studies have shown that between 45% and 62% of girls who become pregnant had been sexually abused prior to the pregnancy, and the younger the teen is, the more likely the pregnancy resulted from sexual abuse (Kandakai & Smith; Noll, Shenk, & Putnam, 2009). In addition, adolescent males who have been sexually abused have a greater risk of fathering a child than those who have not (Francisco et al., 2008). There is an increased risk of complications among pregnant women who have experienced intimate partner violence (IPV), including low-birth-weight infants, premature delivery, and neonatal death. Moreover, the rate of homicide, the most common form of maternal death, is increased when women are exposed to IPV (Chambliss, 2008). In addition, the success of breastfeeding postpartum is compromised by IPV (Kendall-Tackett, 2007; Mohler et al., 2008; Sarkar, 2008). Finally, women who have a past history of abuse have an increased risk of depression and posttraumatic stress disorder and higher risk of postpartum depression (Kendall-Tackett). Witnessing domestic violence has been shown to be a risk factor for teen pregnancy, but the violence often does not stop in the teen's home. Approximately 25% of teens report violence in their dating relationships, and about half of pregnant teens have been physically abused during their pregnancy (Raphael, 2005; Shadigian & Bauer, 2004). In addition, for teens who live in highly stressful familial environments where there are uncontrollable anger issues and serious familial problems, including sexual and physical abuse, there is a higher pregnancy rate, impacted most specifically by the length of time of the family dysfunction (Hillis et al., 2004). Social workers are often on the front line helping these teens as they struggle with emotional and physical suffering.

Teen Pregnancy Outcomes

Teen pregnancy carries medical risks also. Pregnant teens have higher incidences of toxemia (pregnancy-induced high blood pressure), infections, and anemia than adult women, and their neonates are at greater risk for low birth weight, prematurity, and infant mortality than neonates born to adult women (Chedraui, 2008). The rate of prematurity and low birth weight among African American adolescents is twice as high as the rate for Hispanic and European American adolescents. New research is showing that obese pregnant teens experience an even higher risk of cesarean delivery, failure to progress in labor, preeclampsia, pregnancy-induced hypertension, gestational diabetes, low-birth-weight infants, and infants whose weight is greater than the 90th percentile at birth (Sukalich, Mingione, & Glantz, 2006). Although pregnancy-related complications are not limited to teen mothers, it is important for social workers to note that Black women are three times as likely to die from such complications as Caucasian women are (a rate that has risen 33% in the past 100 years) (Population Council, Inc., 1999). Teen abortions comprise 19% of all 1.21 million U.S. abortions (Kaiser Family Foundation, 2008).

Limited financial resources, the inadequate and fragmented facilities often found in impoverished communities, and the normal adolescent avoidance of problems frequently contribute to a delayed diagnosis of pregnancy for disadvantaged young women. Of course, delayed diagnosis hampers timely prenatal care and limits pregnancy options, increasing the risks of both mortality and morbidity (sickness) for fetus, newborn, and mother.

The experience of pregnancy varies somewhat with stage of adolescence:

- *Young adolescents, ages 10 to 14.* Following years of increases, the pregnancy rate for this group is remaining unchanged at 0.7 pregnancies per 1,000 women ages 10 to 14 (Hamilton et al., 2007, Klein, 2005). Adolescents in this age group are more likely than older teens to delay obtaining prenatal care (East, Khoo, & Reyes, 2006; Hueston, Geesey, & Diaz, 2008). A higher rate of pregnancy complications exists with this age group than with older teens, including higher infant mortality rates (Gilbert, Jandial, Field, Bigelow, & Danielsen, 2004; Markovitz, Cook, Flick, & Leet, 2005). Having a cohesive family, with parents who are actively engaged with the teen and monitor her activities, and positive peer choices are factors that protects against pregnancy at this age (Manlove, Logan, Moore, & Ikramullah, 2008). As the average age of first menstruation decreases, it is not uncommon for girls as young as 10 years old to ovulate. At the same time, the interval between the onset of menstruation and the completion of the educational process has lengthened, increasing the possibility of disrupting pregnant teens' education and thus predisposing them to a lifetime of poverty. Premature birth is 3.4 times more common for young adolescents than for nonadolescent women, possibly because of the difficulty of meeting the nutritional demands of both the growing fetus and the growing adolescent (DuPlessis, Bell, & Richards, 1997).

- *Middle adolescents, ages 15 to 17.* The rate of teen pregnancies in this age group dropped 46% between 1990 and 2004, from 77.1 per 1,000 in 1990 to 41.5 per 1,000 in 2004 (Moore, 2008). It increased 1% between 2006 and 2007, however (CDC, 2009c). This age group experiences more preterm deliveries and low-birth-weight babies than older teens (Gilbert et al., 2004). Young women at this age have completed most of their physical growth but are still emotionally immature. They may engage in sexual activity to demonstrate independence, maintain status in their peer group, explore self-identity, or experiment with new behaviors. The sense of invulnerability that permeates adolescence often provides a false sense of security.

- *Late adolescents, ages 18 to 19.* This group accounts for two thirds of all births to mothers under age 20. The highest birth rate is among non-Hispanic Black adolescents, followed closely by Native American adolescents (Education Daily, 2008). Interesting differences exist in birth outcomes among the different ethnic groups. Comparatively, White adolescents have the highest overall rate of negative outcomes of any ethnic group when compared with birth outcomes of women in the same racial group ages 20 to 29. African American teens have the highest rate of pregnancy complications, and this has been a historical pattern, but when compared with Black pregnant women ages 20 to 29, the differential is less than that of White women. Asian American women have the best pregnancy outcomes of any ethnic group (Gilbert et al., 2004). The relatively recent phenomenon of "adolescence" has redefined pregnancy for this age group. Until the 20th century, marriage and childbearing were normative during this life stage. Late adolescents who become pregnant tend to be more mature than younger teens and often have a positive relationship with the infant's father. They are more focused on the future and may have more social supports. However, if the teen's education is disrupted, the pregnancy may be viewed as a major impediment to achieving career goals.

One significant feature of teen pregnancy is the fact that there is a 66% greater chance of a teen giving birth if her mother also bore a child during adolescence (Meade, Kershaw, & Ickovis, 2008). From a family systems perspective, the pregnant teen may be repeating her mother's behaviors. Research also suggests that younger sisters of pregnant teens, compared with younger sisters without a pregnant older sister, show more acceptance of at-risk behaviors for pregnancy, engage in more problem behaviors, and have more interaction with the older sibling's social network (East, 1996; East & Shi, 1997). The family's response to the pregnancy and the teen mother's emotional stability will significantly influence her parenting behaviors. Positive role modeling of family dynamics and social support are especially important.

Prevention and the Costs of Teen Pregnancy

Many initiatives have focused on pregnancy prevention. In 2004, teen pregnancy in the United States cost at least $9.1 billion for health care, $2.3 billion for child welfare, and $2.9 billion in lower tax revenues (Koch, 2006); and public-supported Medicaid pays for more than 66% of adolescent deliveries (Gavin, Kuo, Adams, Ayadi, & Gilbert, 2005). Prenatal care for adolescents saves between $2,369 and $3,242 per delivery, with variations because of the time of initiation of care (Hueston, Quattlebaum, & Benich, 2008). The role of sex education is controversial in the United States and reached a fevered pitch during the Bush administration's promotion of abstinence-only programs. Although there are conflicting studies, most research shows that comprehensive sex education reduces the likelihood of teen pregnancy more than abstinence-only programs (Kohler, Manhart, & Lafferty, 2008; Santelli, Lindberg, Finer, & Singh, 2007). It is important for social workers to be aware of the various prevention models, policies, and funding that provide prevention programs to this high-risk group. Effective prevention programs must also consider issues outside the pregnancy, such as violence and substance abuse.

The role and needs of the adolescent father have been woefully neglected in the research on adolescent pregnancy. Almost 50% of all high school males have sexual intercourse, and they are likely to have four or more sexual partners during this life phase. Approximately 71% report using a condom during their first sexual encounter (Troccoli, 2006). Approximately 17.4 males per 1,000 between the ages of 15 and 19 become fathers in the United States (Kimball, 2004). An extensive study has shown that teen fathers who remain connected with their children enjoy the interactions with their children and are more invested in their children than older fathers (Fitzgerald & McKelvey, 2005). Often teen fathers have fewer financial resources, limited education, and fewer opportunities to juggle the demands of adolescence and fatherhood, and although they want to remain involved with their baby, the challenges sometimes prove to be too great (Kimball). It is important to engage the fathers in coparenting (Fagan, 2008) and provide supportive interventions (Dallas, 2009). For these reasons, many programs targeting teen mothers also provide services to engage teen fathers.

Early Adulthood Pregnancy

Physiologically, a young woman in her 20s and 30s is at the optimal age for pregnancy. Psychologically, young adults are involved in establishing life goals, and these often involve parenthood. Thus, pregnancy during this period of the life course is a normative event in most cultures. Research suggests that even during the prime childbearing years, women who have appropriate social support are healthier psychologically and physically during their pregnancies, especially among women who have a high-risk pregnancy (Cannella, 2006; Giurgescu, Penckofer, Maurer, & Bryant, 2006).

Often a woman in her second or third decade of life is actively employed. Legal, physical, and social considerations exist related to maintaining employment during pregnancy. Pregnant women are protected by two federal laws, the Pregnancy Discrimination Act (PDA), which amended Title VII of the Civil Rights Act of 1964 (Habig, 2008, p. 1215) and the United States Family and Medical Leave Act (FMLA), which directs employers on how to comply with the PDA (HR Specialist, 2009). The PDA states that a pregnant woman cannot be denied a job or be fired because of her pregnancy, nor can she be forced out of the workplace as long as she can complete her job requirements (HR Specialist). Pregnancy is not considered a disability, so it is not covered under the American with Disabilities Act (Habig). However, at times, some employers consider all women of childbearing age in the "flight-risk category" (Williams, 2000, p. 2169), and the PDA was developed to protect all women in their childbearing years from discrimination (Habig). In 2007, the Equal Employment Opportunity Commission (EEOC) experienced a 14% increase in pregnancy-based work complaints, and in 2008 there were 5,587 complaints (up 40% from the previous year) and 20,400 inquiries about pregnancy discrimination (Shellenbarger, 2008).

There have been numerous challenges to the PDA, and courts have interpreted the law in multiple ways (Piedra, 2008); this remains an area requiring social work advocacy. Employers are not required to provide insurance coverage for contraceptives (Habig, 2008; Pugh, 2007), or to pay for maternity leave (HR Specialist, 2009). It is expected that the number of complaints against employers will rise as more women are aware of their rights and they attempt to juggle careers and pregnancy.

Delayed Pregnancy

An increasing number of women are delaying childbirth until their late 30s and 40s, even into their 50s and 60s; the average age of first-time mothers has increased from 21.4 in 1970 to 25 in 2006 (Mathews & Hamilton, 2009). The percentage of women giving birth after 35 has increased from 1 in 100 births in 1970 to 1 in 12 in 2006 for married women (Mathews & Hamilton), and 1 in 6 births for single women over the age of 30 (Ventura, 2009). Differences exist across racial groups, with first births to women over 35 occurring in 5.6% of non-Hispanic Whites, 3.2% of African Americans, 1.9% of Puerto Ricans, and 1.4% of Mexican Americans (Khoshnood, Wall, & Lee, 2005). One specialist posits that delayed childbearing is primarily the result of men building their careers rather than women making the choice (Ryan, 2009). Many have been struggling with infertility for several years; others, like Jennifer Bradshaw, deliberately have chosen to wait until their careers are established. Other women are choosing to have children with a new partner. Some single women, driven by the ticking of the so-called biological clock, finally choose to go ahead and have a child on their own, often using artificial insemination (Hammarberg & Clarke, 2005).

> What cohort effects can you recognize in attitudes toward delayed pregnancy?

As a result of the increasing success rate of infertility treatment, there are reports of women bearing their own child or their grandchild(ren) at an elderly age. One single woman reportedly misrepresented her age when she sought infertility treatment, and with the assistance of IVF delivered twin boys at the age of 66. The toddler boys were orphaned in 2009 when their mother died of the cancer diagnosed shortly after she gave birth (Pykett, 2009). In recent years, there have been news reports of a woman who gave birth to her triplet grandchildren after IVF (Weingartner, 2008), and another woman, who was a surrogate mother for her daughter-in-law, delivering twin girls (Medical News Today, 2004).

Waiting until later in the life cycle to reproduce increases pregnancy risks. Although most women acknowledge that they may encounter fertility issues if pregnancy is delayed, approximately 85% of women who know they have fertility problems and are over the age of 30 believe that IVF will overcome the effects of age. As with Jennifer and Allan Bradshaw, they may be faced with a rude awakening when they start the process. If pregnancy is successful, the risks are substantial for prematurity and genetic anomalies. Although non-Hispanic Whites make up the largest proportion of women who deliver after the age of 35, 10.6% of older African American women deliver low-birth-weight babies (compared with 4.9% for non-Hispanic Whites, 7.6% for Puerto Ricans, and 5.3% for Mexican Americans (Khoshnood, Wall, & Lee, 2005). Women over 30 have increased risk of caesarean delivery and preterm labor, with women who have already had a delivery having fewer complications than women with their first pregnancy at this time of life (Brunner, Larisswa, & Huber, 2009; Chan & Lao, 2008). An increased chance of maternal and infant mortality exists as the maternal age increases (Joseph et al., 2005). Finally, advanced paternal age has been shown to increase the risk of prematurity, with fathers over the age of 34 more likely to have a premature baby than a teenaged father, when controlled for maternal age. No race or ethnicity differences were found in risk for the fathers (Reichman & Teitler, 2006).

Women who choose later pregnancy have increased challenges. They have higher incidences of preconceptual complications such as diabetes, hypertension, and high cholesterol, but this may be counterbalanced by healthier behaviors, fewer gynecological infections, and fewer psychosocial stressors than experienced by younger women (Weisman et al., 2006). For women in their early 30s, there is a 15% chance of pregnancy each month with a miscarriage risk of 20%; for women older than 35, there is a 10% chance of pregnancy each cycle with a 25% chance of miscarriage and 1/350 chance of Down syndrome. For women over 40, the rates of pregnancy per month drop to less than 5% naturally (about 10% with IVF), the rate of miscarriage is about 33%, and 1 in 38 babies is born with genetic anomalies. It is expected that all of the eggs of women over 45 are abnormal, and there is less than a 1% chance of pregnancy in one month, with a miscarriage rate of more than 50% and genetic problems in about 1 in 12 pregnancies (Southern California Center for Reproductive Medicine, 2009).

RISK AND PROTECTIVE FACTORS IN CONCEPTION, PREGNANCY, AND CHILDBIRTH

Despite significant advances in the medical management of pregnancy and childbirth, the United States ranks 30th in the world in infant mortality, worse than most industrialized nations (MacDorman & Mathews, 2009). In 2003, there were 12.1 maternal deaths per 100,000 live births in the United States (Hoyert, 2007). Thus, the understanding and prevention of **risk factors,** the characteristics that increase the likelihood of a problem, are of particular concern. Risk factors include biological, psychological, social, familial, environmental, and societal dimensions. Like risk factors, **protective factors,** which help reduce or protect against risk, also range from biological to societal dimensions. Exhibit 2.4 presents selected risk and protective factors for conception, pregnancy, and childbirth.

Social workers must be knowledgeable about the risk and protective factors that are associated with the most commonly occurring problems they address with individuals and families. It is also critical that social workers remember that the presence of a risk or protective factor cannot totally predict any one outcome. Even when a risk factor is present, it may not be sufficient to result in the related outcome, or the effect may have a rather broad range of impact. For example, pregnant women's prenatal heroin use is known as a risk factor for their children's intelligence, but children exposed to heroin in the womb have had IQ scores ranging from 50 to 124 (Wachs, 2000). Another consideration is timing. One child with a defective gene may experience the onset of a genetic illness much earlier or later than another child with the same gene.

> What do social workers need to know about the effects that different aspects of fetal development can have on subsequent development?

And finally, most outcomes are determined by several factors. Seldom is one environmental, social, or biological risk factor solely responsible for an outcome (Epps & Jackson, 2000). We are unlikely to ever be able to predict all the developmental patterns that might result from a given set of risks (Vallacher & Nowak, 1998; Wachs, 2000).

One explanation for the great variability in individual outcomes when risk factors are present is the concept of resiliency, or the ability to cope and adapt (Garmezy, 1993; Werner, 2000). Both individuals and families are faced with stressful situations, chronic or crisis, over the life course (Walsh, 2006). And both the individual and family may possess characteristics that have been identified as the ability to bounce back, respond, adapt, or successfully cope with these life events. Certain family characteristics related to resiliency—such as good communication and problem-solving processes—can serve as protective factors for individual development (Walsh). Family risk factors with individual impact may include marital discord and inadequate parenting skills. Throughout this chapter risk and protection themes emerge. Financial stability, available health care resources, and social support are recurring protective factors that relate to better outcomes. Major risk factors include maternal age (younger and older), nutritional deficiencies, parental genetic makeup, prematurity, and poverty.

Critical Thinking Questions 2.2

Pregnancy is a powerful experience for the pregnant woman as well as for her partner. What are the biological needs of the pregnant woman? The psychological needs? The social needs? Where there is an involved father, what are the biological needs of the father? The psychological needs? The social needs?

	Risk Factor	Protective Factors
Conception	Low sperm count	Father drug abstinence (marijuana)
	Fallopian tubal factors	Gynecological care
	Genetic abnormality	Genetic counseling
	Adolescent promiscuity	Family life education; contraception; abstinence
	Endometriosis	Hormone therapy; surgery
	Inadequate nutrition for sexually active women of childbearing age	Folic acid supplement
Pregnancy	Obesity	Normal weight maintenance
	Sexually transmitted diseases	Barrier birth control methods
	Female age (<18 or >35)	Family life education; birth control
	Delivery before 38 weeks	Women, Infants, and Children program
	Gestation, toxemia, diabetes	Prenatal care
	Stress because of inadequate resources	Social and economic support
	Trauma	Accident prevention (falls, fire, car)
	Smoking	Smoking cessation program
Birth	Venereal diseases such as gonorrhea and positive Group B Strep	Prenatal care; antibiotic eye drops for neonate; maternal testing
	Meconium aspiration; anoxia	C-section delivery; drugs during pregnancy; well-managed labor and delivery
	Prolonged and painful labor	Birthing classes; social support; father's presence at birth; adequate pain control

▲ **Exhibit 2.4**   Selected Risk and Protective Factors for Conception, Pregnancy, and Birth

SOCIAL WORK AND CHALLENGES IN CHILDBEARING

The events related to childbearing are affected by economic, political, and social forces. Social workers are well equipped to address the needs of all persons of reproductive age that derive from these forces. Although most pregnancies result in favorable outcomes, for those that do not social workers can play an important role. Moreover, many negative outcomes can be prevented through social work interventions, prenatal care, childbirth education, introduction to new medical technologies, and genetic counseling. The social worker who participates in these interventions requires knowledge of, and collaboration with, a range of other professionals.

Problem Pregnancies

In some sense, each of the pregnancies described at the beginning of this chapter is a problem pregnancy. Pregnancy can become problematic for a variety of reasons, but only four types of problem pregnancies are discussed here: undesired pregnancy, ectopic pregnancy, miscarriage and stillbirth, and maternal brain death.

Undesired Pregnancy

Approximately three million unplanned pregnancies per year in the United States result in a live birth (Afable-Munsuz & Braveman, 2008). This number has increased in recent years, especially among women 15 to 24 (18.6% of births) (Kissin, Anderson, Kraft, Warner, & Jamison, 2008). More than two thirds of these women are not married (National Campaign to Prevent Teen and Unplanned Pregnancy, 2008). It is estimated that 1.94 million unintended pregnancies are prevented each year through publically funded family services (Guttmacher Institute, 2009b). Clearly the women who find themselves pregnant or who are at risk for unintended pregnancies face many challenges, including a higher risk of pathological anger and rejection of the infant after birth (Brockinton, Aucamp, & Fraser, 2006). Pregnancies that are unplanned are a problem because they are associated with increased stress. A higher incidence of intimate partner violence exists both during the pregnancy and after delivery among women in this situation (Charles & Perreira, 2007). In addition, women experiencing an undesired pregnancy have a higher rate of smoking and using illicit drugs during pregnancy, and often wait until the third trimester to initiate care (Orr, James, & Reiter, 2008). The rates of unintended pregnancies are higher among Black and Latina women (35 and 40 per 1,000, respectively, compared with 22 per 1,000 among all women in the United States), those without a college education, unmarried women, and women who are poor (Afable-Munsuz & Braveman; Matteson, Peipert, Allsworth, Phipps, & Redding, 2006). Often women in unplanned pregnancies experience higher risk for inadequate prenatal care, health problems late in the pregnancy and right after birth, and significant postnatal problems. A higher risk of preterm birth also exists (Afable-Munsuz & Braveman). Of particular concern for social workers is the growing disparity of unwanted pregnancy related to income.

Ectopic Pregnancy

An ectopic pregnancy occurs if the zygote implants outside the uterus, 93% of the time in the fallopian tubes (Murano & Cocuzza, 2009). The incidence of ectopic pregnancy rose sixfold in the United States between 1970 and 1992, the last year that the CDC collected data. During, and since, this same time period, morbidity and mortality have substantially decreased (Kdous, 2006). Each year more than 100,000 pregnancies are terminated because of ectopic implantation, and it accounts for more than 9% of the maternal deaths in the first trimester (Ehrenberg-Buchner, Sandadi, Moawad, Pinkerton, & Hurd, 2009; Murano & Cocuzza; Walling, 2001). Although more than 50% of women presented with an ectopic pregnancy have no known risk factors (Brown-Guttovz, 2006), women who have had previous ectopic pregnancies, tubal damage from surgeries or infection (especially Chlamydia trachomatis, a major cause of pelvic inflammatory disease), a history of infertility, a previous abortion, IVF, IUD use, or a maternal age over 35 or under 25 are at greater risk for an ectopic pregnancy (Ankum, 2000; Blandford & Gift, 2006; Jaffe, 2006).

Ultrasound, or transvaginal sonography (TVS), is now a common obstetrical procedure used in early pregnancy in the United States and can detect an ectopic pregnancy within the first trimester (Bourne, 2009). Early diagnosis has resulted in innovative surgical and nonsurgical options (Ehrenberg-Buchner et al., 2009; McLaren et al., 2009). When found within the first 6 weeks of pregnancy, ectopic pregnancy is typically treated with medication (methotrexate), which has been found to be 89% effective (Ehrenberg-Buchner et al.); otherwise, abdominal surgery is necessary (Api et al., 2006; Cooper, 2000). Without early diagnosis, abdominal pain and vaginal bleeding are nonspecific and only occur in 50% of the patients with an ectopic pregnancy (Brown-Guttovz, 2006). If tubal rupture occurs, the situation is life threatening and requires a visit to the emergency clinic. TVS, coupled with the measurement of pregnancy hormonal levels, decreases maternal mortality (Bourne; Guvendag, 2006; Splete, 2002). However, because the diagnosis of ectopic pregnancy cannot be made without sophisticated medical equipment, all sexually active women with lower abdominal pain and vaginal bleeding should be evaluated (Tay, Moore, & Walker, 2000). Only 30% of women with an ectopic pregnancy will have difficulty with subsequent conception (Brown-Guttovz).

Miscarriage and Stillbirth

Miscarriage is the naturally occurring loss of a fetus prior to 20 weeks of gestation—a **spontaneous abortion.** Approximately 10% to 20% of all clinically recognized pregnancies end in spontaneous abortion, often without a discernible cause and often unrecognized by the mother (Neugebauer et al., 2006). Recurrent miscarriage, three or more consecutive miscarriages, occur in 2% to 3% of women and are usually caused by chromosomal abnormalities, metabolic disorders, immune factors, problems with the woman's reproductive anatomy, or metabolic disorders (Horn & Alexander, 2005). Approximately 70% of these women ultimately are able to conceive (Kiwi, 2006; "New Concepts on the Causes of Recurrent Miscarriages," 2006). Recent research focusing on the causes of miscarriage point to multiple potential factors, including fetal chromosomal anomalies (Christiansen, Nielsen, & Kolte, 2006), sickle cell trait (Taylor et al., 2006), uterine cancer (Critchley & Wallace, 2005), polycystic ovary syndrome (PCOS) (van der Spuy & Dyer, 2004), rubella (Edlich, Winters, Long, & Gubler, 2005), number of members in a household, coffee consumption, number of pregnancies, history of abortion (Nojomi, Akbarian, & Ashory-Moghadam 2006), stress (Nepomnaschy et al., 2006), and obesity (Yu, Teoh, & Robinson, 2006). At greater risk are those women who are African American, have less education, and of lower socioeconomic status, especially with income below the poverty level (Price, 2006).

An estimated 20.9% of threatened spontaneous abortions become complete abortions (Buss et al., 2006). If the abortion is incomplete, any placenta or fetus that is not expelled must be surgically removed or the mother risks hemorrhage and infection. Counseling of women who struggle with miscarriages focuses on genetics and the biopsychological needs of the woman and her family (Laurino et al., 2005; Neugebauer et al., 2006).

Stillbirth is defined as the fetal loss at 20 weeks or later and accounts for 60% of all perinatal mortality. Each year, more than 4 million stillbirths occur annually, most in impoverished countries (McClure, Nalubamba-Phiri, & Goldenberg, 2006; Nhu et al., 2006). In the United States approximately 25,000 stillbirths occur annually, 37.9 per 10,000 births with 3.2 per 1,000 occurring between 20 and 27 weeks and 4.3 per 1,000 after 28 weeks (Ananth, Liu, Joseph, Kramer, & Fetal and Infant Health Study Group of the Canadian Perinatal Surveillance System, 2008; Barclay, 2009). Approximately 8% to 13% of fetal deaths at this gestational period are caused by chromosomal and genetic abnormalities, with other risks including obesity, advanced maternal age, and women with no previous pregnancies. African American women experience 2.2 times greater chance of stillbirth than non-Hispanic White women, with higher education reducing the hazard for stillbirth more for Caucasian women than for Black women (Willinger, Ko, & Reddy, 2009). Women who had a preexisting mental illness prior to pregnancy have a greater rate of fetal loss (Gold, Dalton, Schwenk, & Hayward, 2007), and women who have been victims of domestic violence are also at greater risk. There is a greater chance of subsequent pregnancies ending in stillbirth once this has occurred (Barclay). In cases of stillbirth, labor generally proceeds immediately and is allowed to occur naturally. But the pregnancy may continue for several days following cessation of movement. Although this wait can be distressing for the mother, cesarean sections are usually avoided because of the high number of complications for the mother (Barclay). Stillbirths are often unexpected, resulting in great stress and anguish for parents, who blame themselves and struggle with unresolved guilt. Social workers can help parents to understand and cope with the strong emotions they are experiencing.

Maternal Brain Death (Postmortem Pregnancy)

Until recently, if a pregnant woman suffered irreversible brain death, the death of the fetus was almost inevitable. Today recent technological advances can maintain the woman on life support for up to five months, allowing for the maturation of the fetus before delivery (Catlin & Volat, 2009). To date there are reports of 22 postmortem pregnancies worldwide, and all but two have resulted in the delivery of a live infant. Although the ability to support a woman who is brain dead physiologically until the fetus is more mature is relatively new, Julius Caesar was born by cesarean section after his mother died (Sperling, 2004). Factors that promote successful fetal outcomes include appropriate resuscitation, prompt diagnosis of brain death, and adequate maternal nutrition (Hussein, 2004; Mallampalli & Guy, 2005; Souza et al., 2006). Legal and ethical issues are also raised by supporting a mother until delivery of the fetus, including organ harvesting, the rights of the fetus and the mother, and consideration of family member's decisions (Hussein; Hussein, Govenden, Grant, & Said, 2006; Lane et al., 2004; Sperling). It is common law that the fetus is denied the right of legal protection, and this was supported in *Roe v Wade*, where the 14th amendment was cited as not including the unborn as a person (Sperling, 2006). Social workers often participate as members of medical ethics teams where such issues are deliberated.

At-Risk Newborns

Not all pregnancies proceed smoothly and end in routine deliveries. There are more than 540,000 babies born too early in the United States and 13 million worldwide. In the United States, the rate of premature birth rose 31% between 1981 and 2007, and in 2007 12.7% of all births were early (Cantor, 2007; Gaylord, Greer, & Botti, 2008; Johnson & Chavkin, 2007; Kent, 2009; March of Dimes, 2010). This is one of the highest rates in industrialized countries (Johnson & Chavkin) and much higher than the targeted rate of 7.6% proposed in the Healthy People's Initiative goal for 2010 (Rabin, 2009). In 2007 Mississippi led the country with a premature birth rate of 18.3%, and Puerto Rico's rate was 19.4% (March of Dimes; Rabin). There is a disparity in the rates of prematurity among different ethnic groups. One in five of births to African American women is premature, compared with 1 in 8 for non-Hispanic White women. The African American infant has a mortality rate two to three times higher than non-Hispanic White women (Kent; MacDorman & Mathews, 2009), but there is some question as to whether the number of Black deaths is accurately reported (Wingate & Alexander, 2006). The rates for American Indian, Alaskan natives, and Puerto Rican premature births are also higher than those for the non-Hispanic White woman, but Asian, Pacific-Islander, Central and South American, Mexican, and Cuban rates are lower than for non-Hispanic White women (Damus, 2008; Grady, 2009; Reedy, 2007). Increased research attention is being given to the interplay between biological determinants and social patterns that may contribute to prematurity (Kramer & Hogue, 2009).

In 2005, the cost of preterm birth in the United States was $26.2 billion or $51,600 per infant during the initial hospitalization (Cantor, 2007). Costs for the first year of life for an infant born at fewer than 28 weeks' gestation soar to $181,000, and to $85,000 for the infant born between 28 and 31 weeks (Silber et al., 2009). Prematurity is the leading cause of death in infancy, with two thirds of infant deaths linked to prematurity (Callaghan, MacDorman, Rasmussen, Cheng, & Lackritz, 2006).

Several policy initiatives in the United States address the issue of prematurity. Passage of the Prematurity Research Expansion and Education for Mothers who Deliver Infants Early ([PREEMIE] PL 109-450) Act in 2006 mandated interagency coordination, improved data collection, and education for healthcare professionals (Cantor, 2007; Damus, 2008; GovTrack.us, 2006; Spong, 2009). The March of Dimes National Prematurity Campaign and the 2008 Surgeon General's Conference on prematurity also have brought increased attention to this serious health problem (Damus).

Prematurity and Low Birth Weight

A radical shift has occurred in our culture over the past 20 years: at first glance the desire for a positive pregnancy outcome has been replaced by the assumption that the pregnancy will be flawless and the baby will be perfect; yet, there is parental anxiety about maternal health and that of the baby (Tiran & Chummun, 2004). Prematurity is the leading cause for illness and death in obstetrics (Reedy, 2008) and can have a profound long-term effect on the family (Carvalho, Linhares, Padovani, & Martinez, 2009).

Approximately 70% of preterm births occur at 34 to 36 weeks' gestation (40 weeks is full gestation) and are referred to as **late-preterm births** (March of Dimes, 2009). These babies may weigh more than 2,500 grams but are still premature. Between 1990 and 2006, the rate of late preterm births rose 20%, with about 900 late preterm babies born each day in the United States. There appears to be minimal difference in this rate based on race or maternal age (Martin, Kirmeyer, Osterman, & Shepherd, 2009). Previously it was considered that babies born closer to their due date had fewer complications, but new evidence shows that they are at risk for possible neurodevelopmental problems, feeding and respiratory difficulties, and poor temperature regulation (Darcy, 2009; Reedy, 2008). These infants have increased rates of readmission to the hospital during their first year of life, higher health costs, and greater morbidity than full-term infants (McLaurin, Hall, Jackson, Owens, & Mahadevia, 2009).

Low-birth-weight (LBW) infants—infants weighing less than 2,500 grams (5 pounds 8 ounces) at birth—account for 65% of all premature births (Darcy, 2009). Infants under 2,500 grams account for 7.9% of births, those between 2,000 grams (4.4 pounds) and 2,499 grams (5.5 pounds) account for 4.9% of births, and those between 1,500 grams (3.3 pounds) and 1,999 grams (4.4 pounds) account for 1.4% of births (CDC, 2009d). In the past it was postulated that LBW infants had fewer long-term complications than more immature infants, but there may be more risk than expected (Reedy, 2007). LBW infants are six times more likely to die in the first week of life compared with a full-term infant and have a mortality rate in the first year three times greater (March of Dimes, 2009).

The rate of **very low-birth-weight (VLBW)** infants—infants weighing less than 1,500 grams (3 pounds 3 ounces)—has increased from 1.15% of all births in 1980 to 1.4% in 2007, primarily as a result of multiple births (often a complication of ART) (CDC, 2009d; Hoyert, Matthews, Menacker, Strobino, & Guyer, 2006; Lucille Packard Children's Hospital, 2010). Children born at this weight have a greater risk for poor physical growth (Datar & Jacknowitz, 2009), learning disabilities, and behavioral problems (March of Dimes, 2009). Infants born in rural areas have lower success rates than those born in urban areas, possibly as a result of less access to neonatal intensive care units (NICUs) (Abdel-Latif et al., 2006). There are significant racial differences in the number of VLBW infants born, with African American women having a higher premature delivery rate (Reedy, 2008).

Extremely low-birth-weight (ELBW) infants—infants weighing less than 1,000 grams (2.2 pounds)—experience approximately a 50% to 80% survival rate (Gargus et al., 2009). Delivery rates decrease as the neonate's weight decreases, with those between 500 grams (1.1 pounds) and 999 grams (2.2 pounds) representing 0.6% of those born prematurely and those under 500 grams (less than 1.1 pounds) only representing 0.2% (CDC, 2009d). One large study found that 18 months after birth, 40% of ELBW infants had died, 16% were unimpaired, 22% had mild impairments, and the same percentage had moderate to severe neurodevelopmental impairments. Less than 1% of infants born weighing less than 500 grams survived free of impairments (Gargus et al.). Paul Thompson is considered an ELBW newborn, and at approximately 540 grams, he has a 50% chance of survival.

About 30% of LBW births can be attributed to perinatal environmental factors, such as maternal illness (e.g., stress and genital infections), some maternal working conditions, smoking, poor maternal weight gain during pregnancy along with being underweight before the pregnancy, intrauterine infections, and maternal short stature (Goldenberg, Hauth, & Andrews, 2000; Heck, Schoendorf, & Chavez, 2002; Spencer & Logan, 2002). More than 50% of children are born to mothers who work during their pregnancy, and some work conditions pose risk of prematurity. Women who have high job stress, moderate or low social support, a demanding posture for 3 hours per day, and whole-body vibrations have an increased risk of premature delivery (Croteau, Marcoux, & Brisson, 2007).

One of the greatest risk factors for the infant's decreased birth weight (LBW, VLBW, ELBW, or intrauterine growth retardation) is maternal smoking. Women who smoke have smaller babies, with female neonates more negatively affected than males (Ling, Lian, Ho, & Yeo, 2009; Suzuki et al., 2008; Volgt, Hermanussen, Wittwer-Backofen, Fusch, & Hesse, 2006). Other risk factors for prematurity, LBW, and VLBW include alcohol and other drug use (especially polydrug and cocaine use) (Bada et al., 2005; Sokol et al., 2007). Also, advanced maternal age (greater than 30), high blood pressure, and a nontechnical/nonprofessional paternal occupation (perhaps a measure of socioeconomic status) are associated with repetitive premature deliveries (Sclowitz & Santos, 2006). Obesity, adolescent pregnancy, diabetes, late or inadequate prenatal care, a male infant or a multiple pregnancy, or a previous cesarean section also increase the risk of prematurity (Guillory, Cai, & Hoff, 2008). Finally, mothers enrolled in Medicaid have increased rates of prematurity and infant death compared with mothers enrolled in nonpublic insurance plans (Brandon et al., 2009). The mother's adequate nutrition prior to conception, as well as during pregnancy, is another important factor in fetal health. Risk is decreased by gaining between 20 and 35 pounds with a singleton pregnancy if the mother's prepregnancy weight was normal. If the mother was underweight, a gain of 28 to 40 pounds is recommended compared with 11 and 20 pounds if the mother was obese (Hitti, 2009; Institute of Medicine, 2009). Children born prematurely are at risk for lower IQ scores (Narberhaus et al., 2007; Weisglas-Kuperus et al., 2009), and more impairments in language and visual motor skills (Ortiz-Mantilla, Chourdhury, Leevers, & Benasich, 2008). Prematurity also contributes to developmental delays (Delgado, Vagi, & Scott, 2007; Kalia, Visintainer, Brumberg, Pici, & Kase, 2009) and cognitive disabilities (Petrini et al., 2009) as well as higher attention problems and self-regulatory problems (Aarnoudse-Moens, Weisglas-Kuperus, van Goudoever, & Oosterlaan, 2009). Preterm birth accounts for one third of all cases of cerebral palsy (Wenstrom, 2009) and carries a higher risk of neonatal seizures (Petrini et al.). Thus, the Thompsons have reason to wonder what the future holds for their baby. In spite of the risks associated with preterm birth, the first cohort of survivors is now reaching early adulthood, and early studies are heartening because their high school graduation rates are equal to their normal birth weight peers (Saigal et al., 2006).

The survival rates of premature infants have improved largely because of explosive growth in the field of neonatal medicine and the establishment of regional NICUs. Studying the long-term effects of prematurity is difficult because today's 5-year-old who was LBW received significantly less sophisticated care than the current patients in the NICU. It is proposed that the vulnerability of the premature brain during this critical period of fetal development is negatively affected by the stressful neonatal environmental conditions (Elley, 2001; Perlman, 2001). Therefore, neonatal environmental conditions may be as much of a risk factor for negative pregnancy outcomes as simple prematurity (Als, Heidelise, & Butler, 2008).

Newborn Intensive Care

As the Thompsons know all too well, parents' expectations for a healthy newborn are shattered when their child is admitted to an NICU. Their fear and anxiety often make it hard for them to form a strong emotional bond with their newborn. About 90% of mothers and 80% of fathers report that they develop an attachment to the infant during the third trimester of pregnancy. But when an infant is premature, the parents have not had the same opportunity. In addition, the fear that a sickly newborn may die inhibits some parents from risking attachment. Mothers of VLBW infants visit the newborn significantly less than do mothers of infants who weigh more; for fathers, visitation is influenced by geographical distance and the number of other children in the home (Latva, Lehtonen, Salmelin, & Tamminen, 2007). Some parents are consumed with guilt about their baby's condition and believe that they will only harm the newborn by their presence. The NICU experience places the mother at risk of depression, but it also has been found that short-term psychotherapy can reduce stress and promote visitation (Friedman, Kessler, & Martin, 2009). Felicia and Will Thompson had to work hard to contain their anxiety about Paul's frailties.

Early disruption in bonding may have a larger long-term impact on the child than the infant's actual medical condition (Wigert, Johannson, Berg, & Hellstrom, 2006). The response has been a movement toward family-centered NICU environments, which are structured to promote interaction between the infant and the parents, siblings, and others in the family's support system. Mothers seem to more readily engage in caring for their infants in this environment than fathers (Johnson, 2008). Ample opportunity to interact with Paul facilitated Felicia and Will Thompson's attempts to bond with him.

Neuroscientists have recently called attention to the physical environment needs of prematurely born babies, noting the competing needs of these vulnerable babies and the medical staff that care for them in NICUs. The medical staff needs lights, noisy equipment, and alarms to signal physiological distress. The vulnerable baby needs a physical environment that more nearly approximates the uterus, without bright lights and stressful noise stimulation (Brandon, Ryan, & Barnes, 2008; Zeisel, 2006). With this discrepancy in mind, NICUs are being modified to accommodate the neurological needs of the vulnerable newborns.

Neonatology, the care of critically ill newborns, has only recently been recognized as a medical specialty. It is a much-needed specialty, however. Since the advent of the NICU in the 1970s, the survival rate of critically ill neonates has continued to increase. It is highly unlikely that Paul Thompson would have survived in 1970. Social workers in a NICU must negotiate a complex technological environment requiring specialized skill and knowledge while attempting to respond with compassion, understanding, and appropriate advocacy. Research has clearly shown the need for social work intervention that enables the parents to bond with their children and decrease the level of stress (Spielman & Taubman-Ben-Ari 2009). It helps to remember that the effort could affect a neonate's life course.

Major Congenital Anomalies

Overall, only 2% to 4% of all surviving newborns have a birth defect. However, the number of neonates born with anomalies caused by genetics, exposure to teratogens, or nonhereditary factors that affect development of the fetus does not reflect the number of abnormal embryos. Fewer than half of all fertilized ova result in a live birth; the rest are spontaneously aborted. The probability that a fertilized ovum with a genetic anomaly will abort spontaneously ranges from 80% to 90% (Opitz, 1996). Social workers need to be mindful of the low probability that a child will be born with a genetic disorder or congenital anomaly when responding to parental fears. The American College of Medical Genetics with the March of Dimes has established a recommended list of 28 metabolic, endocrine, and hemoglobin disorders for which newborns should be screened because early intervention for these hereditary yet rare diseases is essential. As of March 2006, only five U.S. states met all of these recommendations. Each state health department or the National Newborn Screening and Genetics Resource Center (www.nccrcg.org/about.asp) provides the list of mandatory screenings by a specific state. Visit www.ornl.gov/sci/techresources/Human_Genome/medicine/genetest .shtml#testsavailable to obtain a list of diseases for which genetic tests are available.

Preventing, diagnosing, and predicting the outcome of genetic disorders are very difficult because of the complexities of genetic processes:

- *Variable expressivity.* Genes manifest differently in different people. For example, persons with cystic fibrosis, caused by a recessive gene, display wide variability in the severity of symptoms. The expression of the disorder appears to be influenced by the interplay of psychological, social, political, economic, and other environmental factors. The effects can be exacerbated by maternal substance abuse, inadequate maternal nutrition, and birth trauma. Children with cystic fibrosis born into poverty may not have benefited from early diagnosis, may live in an inner city that exposes them to increased levels of pollution, or may lack adequate home medical care because the primary caregiver is also responsible for meeting the family's economic needs.

- *Genetic heterogeneity.* The same characteristic may be a consequence of one of a number of genetic anomalies. For example, neural tube defects may result either from gene mutations or from exposure to specific teratogens (Motamedi & Meador, 2006; Ornoy, 2006).

- *Pleiotropy principle.* The same gene may influence seemingly unrelated systems (Rauch, 1988). Hair color, for example, is typically linked to a particular skin color (such as blonde hair with light complexion, black hair with olive complexion).

- *Epigenetics.* More recently, researchers have focused on another dimension of heritability that points to environmental factors that influence gene expression (phenotype) without changing the genetic makeup of a person (genotype). These factors influence the chemicals that trigger (methyl groups) or inhibit (acetyl groups) genetic expression. Furthermore, these chemicals appear to have a generational influence without genetic alterations. Examples of these epigenetic environmental influences include nutrition, trauma such as childhood abuse, and teratogens (Lederberg, 2001). The epigenetic influences in many cases are preventable and treatable, especially if identified early in development.

Genetic anomalies fall into four categories, summarized in Exhibit 2.5 (Opitz, 1996; Rauch, 1988; Reed, 1996; Vekemans, 1996):

1. *Inheritance of a single abnormal gene.* An inherited anomaly in a single gene may lead to a serious disorder. The gene may be recessive, meaning that both parents must pass it along, or it may be dominant, in which case only one parent needs to have the gene in order for it to be expressed in the child. A third possibility is that the disorder is sex-linked, meaning that it is passed along by either the father or the mother.

2. *Multifactorial inheritance.* Some genetic traits, such as height and intelligence, are influenced by environmental factors such as nutrition. Their expression varies because of **multifactorial inheritance,** meaning that they are controlled by multiple genes. Multifactorial inheritance is implicated in traits that predispose a person to mental illnesses, such as depression. However, these traits are merely predisposing factors, creating what is called **genetic liability.** Siblings born with the same genetic traits thus may vary in the likelihood of developing a specific genetically based disorder, such as alcoholism or mental illness (Rauch, 1988; Takahashi & Turnbull, 1994).

3. *Chromosomal aberration.* Some genetic abnormalities are not hereditary but rather are caused by a genetic mishap during development of the ovum or sperm cells. Sometimes the cells end up missing chromosomes or having too many. When the ovum or sperm cell has fewer than 23 chromosomes, the probability of conception and survival is minimal. But in the presence of too many chromosomes in the ovum or the sperm, various anomalies occur. Down syndrome, or trisomy 21, the most common chromosomal aberration, is the presence of 47 chromosomes—specifically, an extra chromosome in the 21st pair. Its prevalence is 1 in 600 to 1,000 live births overall as with Cecelia Kin, but as seen in Hazel Gereke's story, it increases to 1 in 350 for women over age 35 (Vekemans, 1996). Other chromosome anomalies include Turner syndrome (a single sex chromosome, X) and Klinefelter syndrome (an extra sex chromosome, XXY).

4. *Exposure to teratogens.* Teratogens can be divided into four categories: radiation, infections, maternal metabolic imbalance, and drugs and environmental chemicals. In the Thompson story, Felicia wondered if Paul's premature birth was a result of prenatal exposure to paint fumes. It may have been, depending on what specific chemicals were involved, when exposure occurred, and to what degree. Parents who, like the Thompsons, are experiencing considerable guilt over their possible responsibility for their baby's problems may take comfort from the knowledge that the impact of exposure to teratogens can vary greatly. Much depends on the timing of exposure. The various organ systems have different critical or **sensitive periods,** summarized in Exhibit 2.6.

Parents who have reason to fear these congenital anomalies often opt for diagnosis during pregnancy. Chorionic villi testing (CVT) involves the insertion of a catheter through the cervix into the uterus to obtain a sample of the developing placenta; it can be done as early as eight weeks but carries a slightly higher risk of causing spontaneous abortion (miscarriage) compared with amniocentesis. *Amniocentesis* is the extraction of amniotic fluid for chromosomal analysis; it involves inserting a hollow needle through the abdominal wall during the second trimester. A frequent procedure is ultrasonography (ultrasound), which produces a visual image of the developing fetus, typically done during 18 to 22 weeks of pregnancy. Risk factors for any prebirth genetic testing includes mothers over the age of 35, carriers of sex-linked genetic disorders and single gene defects, parents with chromosomal disorders, and women who have had previous and recurring pregnancy loss (American Pregnancy Association, 2009).

If an anomaly is detected, the decisions that need to be made are not easy ones. The possibility of false readings on these tests makes the decisions even more complicated. Should the fetus be aborted? Should fetal surgery be undertaken? Could gene replacement therapy, implantation of genetic material to alter the genotype—still a costly experimental procedure—prevent an anomaly or limit its manifestation? Do the parents have the financial and psychological means to care for a neonate with a disability? This was a question that the Gerekes and Cecelia Kin asked of themselves. What is the potential impact on the marriage and extended family system? What is the potential long-term impact of

Inheritance of Single Abnormal Gene		
Recessive	**Dominant**	**Sex-Linked**
Sickle-cell anemia Tay-Sachs disease Cystic fibrosis	Neurofibromatosis Huntington's disease	Hemophilia Duchenne muscular dystrophy
Multifactorial Inheritance		
Possible mental illness	Alcoholism	
Chromosomal Aberration		
Down syndrome (additional 21st chromosome)	Turner syndrome (X)	Klinefelter syndrome (XXY)

Exposure to Teratogens			
Radiation	**Infections**	**Maternal Metabolic Imbalance**	**Drugs and Environmental Chemicals**
Neural tube defects	Rubella: deafness, glaucoma Syphilis: neurological, ocular, and skeletal defects	Diabetes: neural tube defects Folic acid deficiency: brain and neural tube defects Hyperthermia (at 14–28 days): neural tube defects	Alcohol: mental retardation Heroin: attention deficit disorder Amphetamine: congenital defects

▲ **Exhibit 2.5**   Four Categories of Genetic Anomalies

knowing one's genetic makeup? For example, the 2008 Genetic Information Nondiscrimantion Act (GINA) prohibits insurance companies and employers from using genetic information in discriminatory ways (Human Genome Project, 2009b). However, as the U.S. health care system undergoes change and new knowledge about genetic engineering emerges, this is an issue that should be considered by social workers. We do know that nonurgent decisions should be postponed until parents have an opportunity to adjust to the crisis and acquire the necessary information (Fost, 1981).

Special Parent Populations

Social workers should recognize the risks involved for some special parent populations. Six of these special populations are discussed here.

Pregnant Substance Abusers

Our knowledge of the developmental impact of maternal use of illegal and legal substances is rapidly increasing. The good news is that health care professionals are increasingly able to avoid prescribing legal drugs that might harm

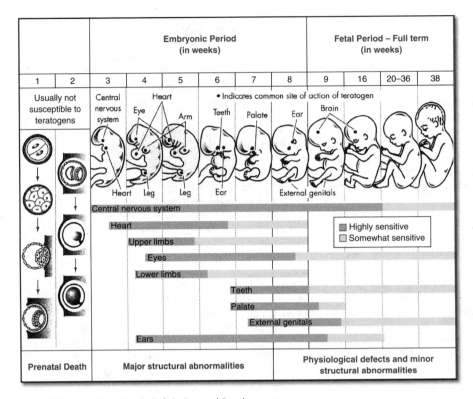

▲ **Exhibit 2.6**   Sensitive Periods in Prenatal Development

SOURCE: Moore & Persaud, 1998. Reprinted with permission from Elsevier.

the developing fetus, once pregnancy is confirmed. The bad news is that too many pregnant women are still harming their babies through use of illegal drugs or abuse of legal substances. And, unfortunately, many women do not know they are pregnant during the first trimester, a period when the fetus is very vulnerable to teratogens.

Although it is difficult to obtain reliable statistics, an estimated 22% of females of childbearing age abuse substances. Moreover, approximately 25% of pregnant women use two or more teratogenic substances. Among pregnant substance abusers, 91% use heroin, methadone, or other opiates, 35% use stimulants, 25% cannabis, 22% benzodiazepines, and 7% hallucinogens—with 38% injecting their main drug (McElhatton, 2000).

Possible effects of commonly abused legal and illegal substances are presented in Exhibit 2.7. Fetal alcohol spectrum disorders (FASD) include fetal alcohol effects (FAE) and fetal alcohol syndrome (FAS), which are caused by alcohol consumption during pregnancy. FASD results in cognitive disability, malformations of the skeletal system and major organ systems, central nervous system defects, and social and learning disabilities in the child. FASD are 100% preventable with alcohol abstinence (American Pregnancy Association, 2010). Cocaine and crack use is connected with increased chances of the placenta separating from the uterine wall, which can lead to maternal and fetal death, intracranial hemorrhage for both mother and newborn, urinary and genital defects in the neonate, and increased risk of sudden infant death syndrome as well as neonatal withdrawal that can last for several weeks. Amphetamines are associated with increased rates of spontaneous abortions and possible heart defects. Ecstasy seems to increase the likelihood of cardiovascular and musculoskeletal anomalies in the fetus (McElhatton, 2000). Pregnant substance abusers in general have a higher incidence of miscarriages, prematurity, and LBW, as well as STIs, tuberculosis, and HIV, than other pregnant women (Kesmodel, Wisborg, Olsen, Henriksen, & Secher, 2002; March of Dimes, 2006).

	Alcohol	Cocaine	Amphetamines	Cigarettes	Heroin
Abortion	X	X	X		X
Stillbirth	X	X	X		X
Prematurity	X	X	X	X	X
Intrauterine growth retardation	X	X	X	X	X
Respiratory distress	X	X			X
Withdrawal	X	X	X		X
Fine motor problems	X				X
Malformations	X	X	X		X
Developmental delays	X	X	X		X

▲ **Exhibit 2.7**   Commonly Abused Drugs and Fetal Effects

Furthermore, the neonate who was exposed prenatally to substances like alcohol, tobacco, and illegal drugs is 46 times more likely than normal to die in the first month of life (Larson, 1995).

Interestingly, some individuals appear to be "resistant" to teratogens like alcohol, and no teratogen causes defects all the time (Opitz, 1996). In fact, about 60% of babies born to alcoholic mothers show no signs of being affected by their mother's drinking (Opitz). Still, teratogenic substances should be avoided during pregnancy to increase the chances of a healthy outcome. Social workers are collaborating with other professionals to provide public education to women in the childbearing years about the teratogenic effects of alcohol, tobacco, and other drugs. Because fathers are known to influence the substance use by mothers, and there is increasing evidence that paternal use impacts sperm, fathers increasingly are included in preventive efforts (Bertrand, Floyd, & Weber, 2005; Chang, McNamara, Orav, & Wilkins-Haug, 2006).

Mothers With Eating Disorders

There was an increase in eating disorders, primarily anorexia nervosa (self-imposed starvation) and bulimia (binging and purging), among U.S. teenagers and women in the United States during the past century, but the rate has stabilized in recent years (Hoek, 2006). More common is obesity; more than half of women of childbearing age are overweight or obese, which poses risk of infertility and can impact postnatal recovery as well as the health of the baby (Allison, Lavery & Sarwer, 2009). Because eating disorders frequently result in menstrual disorders, reduced sex drive, and infertility, pregnancy is frequently overlooked in this population (Bonne, Rubinoff, & Berry, 1996). One study of almost 1,000 Fellows of the American College of Obstetricians and Gynecologists revealed that less than half of the obstetrics/gynecological fellows assess for an eating disorder (Leddy, Jones, Morgan, & Schulkin, 2009).

An eating disorder is likely to result in poor pregnancy outcomes, such as fetuses **small for gestational age** (SGA), LBW infants, and increased neonatal mortality (Bulik et al., 2009; National Eating Disorders Association, 2005). Premature delivery occurs at twice the expected rate, and perinatal mortality is six times the expected rate. The length of time the mother is able to breastfeed her infant has not been found to be affected by eating disorders, however (Brinch,

Isager, & Tolstrup, 1988). Social workers who work regularly with women with eating disorders or with pregnant women need to be knowledgeable about the possibilities for poor pregnancy outcomes in pregnant women with eating disorders.

Lesbian Mothers

In recent years, the number of lesbians who are or who desire to be mothers has increased, but these women continue to face many obstacles and dilemmas leading to disparities in family health when compared with heterosexual women and couples (Gartrell et al., 1996; O'Hanlon, 2009). More than one third of lesbians are estimated to be mothers, and it is reasonable to assume that more would choose motherhood if the larger society offered greater support.

Perhaps the major risk factor for lesbian mothers is the potential for rejection or disapproval by the members of a society with negative views of homosexuality (King, 2001; Laird & Green, 1996). Conception, pregnancy, and childbirth demand role realignments for heterosexual couples and create stress. These same dynamics occur in lesbian couples, but they often face a greater challenge because of society's reluctance to recognize lesbian relationships.

Lesbian mothers face other challenges. Despite increased availability of alternative fertilization methods, many health care providers remain insensitive to issues that lesbian women may face when using them and may limit access to fertility treatment (The Ethics Committee of the American Society for Reproductive Medicine, 2006). Lesbian women who become pregnant may lack the support of family and friends, and birthing facilities may not allow female partners to be involved with the birth process. In addition, employers may limit access to, or reluctantly provide, resources such as medical benefits for pregnancy and childbirth (Laird & Green, 1996). The lesbian partner of a childbearing or adopting lesbian mother may not be recognized as the child's parent in many states.

Yet, lesbian mothers have advantages that some other special parent populations do not have. A study of 27 lesbian mothers indicated that these family households are strong, individual functioning is good, and a variety of parenting skills are common (Dundas & Kaufman, 2000). Other studies of lesbian mothers report that all respondents sought prenatal care and that 89% to 100% attended childbirth education classes (Gartrell et al., 1996). Social workers can help health care providers recognize both the strengths of and the special challenges facing lesbian mothers.

Mothers and Fathers With Disabilities

One in five persons reports a physical or mental disability, and more than half of these people are female (Jans & Stoddard, 1999). People with physical or mental disabilities may be perceived as "asexual," and thus conception, pregnancy, and childbirth frequently are not considered relevant issues for them (Cole & Cole, 1993; Sawin, 1998). This is not the case. For one thing, not all disabilities negatively affect reproduction. For example, 75% of women with rheumatoid arthritis experience remission of disease during pregnancy (Connie, 1988; Corbin, 1987). Other interesting data come from a four-year national study funded by the National Institutes of Health (NIH), which compared 506 women with physical disabilities with 444 women without a disability (Nosek, 1995).

The NIH study found a remarkable difference between the two populations in the use of contraception, because women with disabilities have more limited options. For example, the use of barrier methods may be compromised by limited use of hands. Overall, women with disabilities were less likely to use oral contraception, possibly because their access to it was limited. Disabled and nondisabled women did not differ in their rates of tubal ligation and partner vasectomy, but women with disabilities were much more likely to have had a hysterectomy (22% vs. 12%), the most invasive and risky surgical sterilization option (Nosek, 1995).

Perhaps one of the most striking findings of the NIH study was that 10% of women with disabilities reported abuse—such as coerced sterilization—by health care providers, compared with only 3% of nondisabled women. In addition, for the women who had access to medical care, 37% of women with disabilities perceived their physician as uninformed about the effect of their disability on reproductive health (Nosek, 1995). This is an issue that exists worldwide and is perhaps even more pervasive in nonindustrialized countries (Emmett & Alant, 2006).

Women with disabilities who do decide to become pregnant must be monitored more closely than nondisabled women to offset the increased risks associated with the disability. Although women with disabilities have higher rates of complications during pregnancy (Nosek, Howland, Rintal, Young, & Chanpong, 1997), with careful planning they can make the adaptations needed to care for newborns. For a summary of the effects of selected disabilities on conception, pregnancy, and childbirth, see Sawin (1998).

Despite public distaste for the practice, some persons with disabilities continue to be targets of involuntary sterilization (Disabled Women's Network Ontario, 2006; International Federation of Persons with Physical Disability, 2008). Professionals do not agree about how to handle the reproductive rights of individuals with severe inheritable disorders or with limited capacity to care for a child. Many do agree, however, that physical, environmental, interpersonal, informational, and policy barriers leave people with disabilities disenfranchised from both the reproductive health system and other reproductive options.

Not surprisingly, a 1997 study identified reproductive health as one of the four top research priorities for disabled persons (Berkeley Planning Associates, 1996). For some populations such research is only recently emerging. Women with spinal bifida is a population that only recently is living beyond sexual maturity because of medical advances (Jackson & Mott, 2007). In addition, new models of psychosocial intervention with women with disabilities are emerging (Miller & Marini, 2004; Sheppard-Jones, Kleinert, Paulding, & Espinosa, 2008). As society slowly begins to recognize persons with disabilities as full members of society, some of the negative implications of conception, pregnancy, and childbirth with this population may be dispelled.

Incarcerated Pregnant Women

An estimated one out of four women inmates are pregnant when they are incarcerated or have delivered a baby within the preceding year, and about 90% have substance abuse problems (Eliason & Arndt, 2004; Wooldredge & Masters, 1993). These women and their babies are at particular risk because most of the mothers are poor; many abuse drugs prior to, during, and after incarceration; many have severe physical and mental health problems; and most lack education and skills related to pregnancy, childbirth, and prenatal care (Kaplan & Sasser, 1996). An analysis of research findings from 10 studies, all that reported a comparison group, revealed that prematurity and low birth weight occurred more frequently for imprisoned women if the comparison group was not disadvantaged. Otherwise, birth outcomes were more favorable for imprisoned women (Knight & Plugge, 2005).

Although the U.S. prison population grew at a slower rate between 2000 and 2008 compared with the previous decade, by the end of 2008 11,978 inmates were women (6.7%). Of these women in prison, 7,226 (60%) were between the childbearing ages of 19 and 40 (Bureau of Justice Statistics, 2009). For all jailed women, an estimated 80% are of childbearing age (Kyei-Aboagye, Vragovic, & Chong, 2000). Based on Bloom's (1995) analysis that 8% to 10% of women are pregnant when they enter prison, a rough estimate of the number of pregnant new prison inmates in 2008 would be 578 to 722. Over the past 10 to 15 years, this population has been the focus of some, albeit limited, research and development of services because of the high-risk pregnancy potential (Eliason & Arndt, 2004; Schulte-Day, 2006; Siefert & Pimlott, 2001; U.S. Federal Bureau of Prisons, 1998; Wismont, 2000). In general, birth outcomes in terms of weight are acceptable (Martin, Kim, Kupper, Meyer, & Hays, 1997), but there are variations. For example, one study of 360 infants revealed differences by race whereby Whites incarcerated during weeks 14 to 20 had lower birth weight infants compared with those incarcerated during weeks 1 to 13, but this was not found for Hispanics (Howard, Strobino, Sherman, & Crum, 2009). Another study of 147 infants found better birth weight if women had prenatal care that started in the first trimester and birth weight increased with each additional prenatal visit (Howard et al.). However, good prenatal care is typically found only in larger prisons associated with academic medical centers (Cordero, Hines, Shibley, & Landon, 1992; Gabel & Johnston, 1995).

Regardless of the type of facility, prison life can pose incredible stress because of illegal drug access, anger and hostility, lack of social support, concern/jealously about alternative caregivers, and impaired mother-child relationships (Hutchinson, Moore, Propper, & Mariaskin, 2008). Alternative living environments that provide adequate services are a possible means of improving pregnancy outcomes for this group of women (Blinn, 1997; Bloom & Steinhart, 1993; Siefert & Pimlott, 2001; Stevens & Patton, 1998). Social workers working in prisons and jails can advocate for conditions to improve birth outcomes for the infants and pregnancy consequences for the mothers as well as their extended families.

HIV-Infected Mothers

Women comprise nearly half of the 33.2 million HIV infections worldwide (Gable, Gostin, & Hodge, 2008); 68% of all HIV patients live in sub-Saharan Africa (Guidozzi & Black, 2009). The United Nations program on HIV and AIDS (UNAIDS) estimates that more than 600,000 mother-to-newborn HIV transmissions occur each year, with the numbers increasing rapidly, especially in Africa and Southeast Asia (UNAIDS, 2006). Transmission from mother to infant is estimated at 20% to 45% if the mother breastfeeds and takes no preventive drugs (Kanabus). However, 2005 data revealed that with the use of antiretroviral drugs for treatment and prophylaxis, no breastfeeding, and elected caesarian birth when appropriate, the risk of transmission is reduced to less than 2% (Mofenson, 2006). However, the stigma of HIV/AIDS paired with low status of women denies access to reproductive and sexual health services in many countries (Gable et al., 2008).

Elective cesarean sections reduce the risk of mother-to-infant transmission by 50%, and the use of highly active antiretroviral therapy (HAART) has reduced the rate of transmission to less than 5% (Kanabus, 2006; McIntyre & Gray, 2002). Recent studies are suggesting that AZT is a teratogen, causing mutations of the DNA if taken in the first trimester, but the risks must be weighed against the transmission of a potentially fatal viral infection (Kanabus, 2006). However, the cost of any treatment is prohibitive to women in impoverished countries and it is not widely available to them.

Breastfeeding is an area of special concern when there is no antiretroviral treatment. HIV can be transmitted through breast milk and is significant in the high rates of this disease in Africa, where, without HAART, breastfeeding may account for 40% of HIV transmissions from mothers to infants (Nduati et al., 2000). To further complicate the issue, infant mortality rates have increased in poor countries where formula feeding has been implemented—partially because of contaminated water supplies used to make the formula. The United Nations suggests that in poorer countries, breastfeeding is a better option because it does help prevent infectious disease and malnutrition (Kanabus, 2006; Kent, 2002). However, it also recommends that women be informed about their choices for infant feeding.

The standard protocol for neonates born to HIV-positive mothers is to treat them with the drug zidovudine (ZDV) for 6 weeks (Cotter & O'Sullivan, 2004). However, this medication is not widely available in poorer countries, increasing the number of children who will die from AIDS.

The news is encouraging in other ways. In 1994, the American Society for Reproductive Medicine (ASRM) discouraged women who were HIV positive from having children because transmission of the virus could not be prevented. In 2002, the same group said that the recent advances in therapies greatly reduce the rate of transmission and withdrew their recommendations to avoid childbearing. The Society (2002) suggested cesarean sections, bottle feeding, special sperm washing and testing if the father is HIV positive, and counseling if both mother and father are HIV positive, because of the possibility of orphaning the baby (ASRM, 2002).

Social workers must be aware of the complexities of this issue as well as societal prejudices against women with HIV infections. Working to increase HIV awareness and promote clear notification of HIV status will continue to be important social work roles in the next decade.

Critical Thinking Questions 2.3

What factors might be contributing to the increase in premature births in the United States? Why do you think the rate of prematurity is higher in the United States than in most other industrialized countries? How could you go about learning more about the answers to these questions?

IMPLICATIONS FOR SOCIAL WORK PRACTICE

Social workers practicing with persons at the stage of life concerned with conception, pregnancy, and childbirth should follow these principles:

- Respond to the complex interplay of biopsychosocial and spiritual factors related to conception, pregnancy, and childbirth.

- When working with clients, both females and males, of childbearing age, always consider the possibility of conception, pregnancy, and childbirth; their potential outcomes; and their impact on the changing person/environment configuration.

- Identify the needs of vulnerable or at-risk groups, and work to provide services for them. For example, structure birth education classes to include not only family but family-like persons, and provide interpreters for the hearing impaired or use appropriate technology to deliver content.

- Actively pursue information about particular disabilities and their impact on conception, pregnancy, and childbirth and include this topic in client assessment.

- Acquire and apply skills in advocacy, education about reproductive options, consumer guidance in accessing services, and case management.

- Assume a proactive stance when working with at-risk populations to limit undesirable reproductive outcomes and to help meet their reproductive needs. At-risk groups include adolescents, low-income women, women involved with substance abuse, women with eating disorders, and women with disabilities who lack access to financial, physical, psychological, and social services.

- Assist parents faced with a potential genetic anomaly to gain access to genetic screenings, prenatal diagnosis, postnatal diagnosis, treatment, and genetic counseling.

- Involve parents in decision making to the greatest extent possible by delaying nonurgent decisions until parents have had a chance to adjust to any crisis and acquire the necessary information to make an informed decision.

- Establish collaborative relationships with other professionals to enhance and guide assessment and intervention.

- Identify and use existing programs that provide education and prenatal services to women, particularly for those most at risk of undesirable outcomes.

KEY TERMS

assisted reproductive technologies (ART)
chromosomes
dominant genes
embryo
extremely low birth weight
family pluralism

fertilization
fertilization age
fetal viability
fetus
genes
genetic liability
genotype

germ cell
gestation
gestational age
infertility
interactive genes
late-preterm birth
low birth weight (LBW)

miscarriage	primipara	sex-linked trait
multifactorial inheritance	protective factors	small for gestational age (SGA)
multigravida	recessive genes	spontaneous abortion
multipara	risk factors	teratogen
neonate	sensitive period	very low birth weight (VLBW)
phenotype	sex chromosome	zygote

ACTIVE LEARNING

1. Select one topic from the chapter outline. Identify a community service setting that addresses the chosen topic. Interview a professional from that setting, preferably a social worker, to solicit the following information:

   • Services provided

   • The role of the social worker

   • The roles of the other disciplines

   • The mechanisms used to acquire new knowledge on the topic

   • The challenges and rewards of social work practice in that setting

2. Locate the National Association of Social Workers Code of Ethics on the organization's website at www.naswdc.org. Choose an ethical issue from the list below. Using the Code of Ethics as a guide, what values and principles can you identify to guide decision making related to the issue you have chosen?

   • Should all women and men, regardless of marital status or income, be provided with the most current technologies to conceive when they are unable to do so?

   • What are the potential issues of preservation and gestational surrogacy in terms of social justice and diversity?

   • Should pregnant women who abuse substances be incarcerated to protect the developing fetus?

   • Do adoptive parents have the right to know the genetic background of an adoptee?

   • Which genes should be selected for reproduction?

   • Will persons who are poor be economically disadvantaged in the use of genetic information?

3. Select one of the four life journeys that introduced this chapter: Jennifer Bradshaw's, the Thompsons', the Gerekes', or Cecelia Kin's. Identify the risk and protective factors related to their conception, pregnancy, and childbirth experience. Then change one factor in the story; for example, assume that Cecelia Kin lived in a metropolitan area and her income was not needed. How might that alter her life course? Then try changing one factor in another story; for example, assume Jennifer had only a 10th-grade education. How does that change the trajectory of her story? Try again; for example, assume Felicia Thompson was being treated for depression when she became pregnant. Again, how does that factor alter her life course and that of her child?

4. In student groups of three or four, review the list of contraception options presented in this chapter. With each group representing a different three- to five-year age range of the child-bearing age spectrum (ages 15 to 44), discuss the potential access and use or misuse of each form of contraception. Also, consider the role of a social worker in various social welfare settings in helping women (who represent different age, religious, and ethnic groups) select a form of birth control.

WEB RESOURCES

The American Pregnancy Association
www.americanpregnancy.org

Site presented by the American Pregnancy Association contains information on a number of pregnancy-related topics, including infertility, adopting, pregnancy options, multiples pregnancy, and the developing baby.

Center for Research on Women with Disabilities (CROWD)
www.bcm.edu/crowd

Site presented by the Center for Research on Women with Disabilities contains reports on sexual and reproductive health for women with disabilities, educational materials, and links to other related research.

Centers for Disease Control and Prevention
www.cdc.gov

U.S. government site contains public health information, current research, and health census data that include diseases and conditions related to conception, pregnancy, and childbirth with a focus on prevention. Available in both English and Spanish.

Childbirth.org
www.childbirth.org

Award-winning site maintained by Robin Elise Weiss contains information on conception, pregnancy, and birth, including recommended pregnancy books and access to a free online childbirth class.

Genetic Alliance
www.geneticalliance.org

Site presented by the Genetic Alliance, an information and advocacy organization, contains information about training, programs, public policy, publications, and events.

Human Genome Project
www.ornl.gov/hgmis

Site of the Human Genome Program of the U.S. Department of Energy that has sequenced the genes present in human DNA provides quick access to recent news, including related legislation. Available in both English and Spanish.

Planned Parenthood
www.plannedparenthood.org

Official site of the Planned Parenthood Federation of America Inc. contains information about Planned Parenthood, health and pregnancy, birth control, abortion, STDs, prochoice advocacy, and a guide for parents.

U.S. Bureau of Census
www.census.gov

Site presented by the U.S. Census Bureau provides current census data related to the family and social context of conception, pregnancy, and childbirth.

Women's-Health.com
www.womens-health.com

Free, membership site presented by Women's Health Interactive contains information on pregnancy and childbirth and provides links to partnership sites to access print, video, and audio media on human reproduction.

CHAPTER

Infancy and Toddlerhood

Debra J. Woody

Acknowledgment: The author wishes to thank Suzanne Baldwin, PhD, for her contributions to the discussion of breastfeeding.

OPENING QUESTIONS

- Why is it important for social workers to know about brain development?

- Why is it important for social workers to understand attachment issues between infants and toddler and their parents?

- How do child care provisions in the United States compare with those in other countries?

KEY IDEAS

As you read this chapter, take note of these central ideas::

1. Although growth and development in young children have some predictability and logic, the timing and expression of many developmental skills vary from child to child and depend in part on the environment and culture in which the child is raised.

2. Physical growth, brain development, and the development of sensory abilities and motor skills are all important aspects of physical development in infants and toddlers.

3. According to Piaget, infants and toddlers are in the sensorimotor stage of cognitive development, responding to what they hear, see, taste, touch, smell, and feel.

4. Erikson describes two stages of psychosocial development relevant to infants and toddlers, each with its own central task: trust versus mistrust (birth to age 1½) and autonomy versus shame and doubt (1½ to 3 years).

5. The attachment relationship between infants and toddlers and their caregivers can affect brain development.

6. Researchers have found that children who live in poor economic conditions face serious risks to development in all dimensions.

7. Results from a major study indicate that childhood adversities have a negative effect on health later in adulthood.

8. Prenatal care, diet, parental education, and social support are thought to influence infant mortality rates in the United States.

9. Polices and programs that promote early intervention may be the key to increasing positive developmental outcomes for infants and toddlers.

Case Study 3.1

Holly's Early Arrival

Although Marilyn Hicks had been very careful with her diet, exercise, and prenatal care during pregnancy, Holly arrived at 26 weeks' gestation, around 6 months into the pregnancy. Initially she weighed 3 pounds, 11 ounces, but she quickly lost the 11 ounces. Immediately after birth, Holly was whisked away to the neonatal unit in the hospital, and her parents had just a quick peek at her. The assigned social worker's first contact

(Continued)

(Continued)

with Marilyn and Martin Hicks, an Anglo couple, was in the neonatal unit. Although Marilyn Hicks began to cry when the social worker first spoke with her, overall both parents seemed to be coping well and had all their basic needs met at that time. The social worker left his business card with them and instructed them to call if they needed anything.

Despite her early arrival, Holly did not show any signs of medical problems, and after 6 weeks in the neonatal unit, her parents were able to take her home. The social worker wisely allowed the newly formed Hicks family time to adjust, and in keeping with the policy of the neonatal program, scheduled a follow-up home visit within a few weeks.

When the social worker arrives at the house, Marilyn Hicks is at the door in tears. She states that taking care of Holly is much more than she imagined. Holly cries "constantly" and does not seem to respond to Mrs. Hicks's attempts to comfort her. In fact, Mrs. Hicks thinks that Holly cries even louder when her mother picks her up or tries to cuddle with her. Mrs. Hicks is very disappointed, because she considers herself to be a nurturing person. She is unsure how to respond to Holly's "rejection of her." The only time Holly seems to respond positively is when Mrs. Hicks breastfeeds her.

Mrs. Hicks has taken Holly to the pediatrician on several occasions and has discussed her concerns. The doctor told her that nothing is physically wrong with Holly and that Mrs. Hicks has to be more patient.

Mrs. Hicks confides during this meeting that she read some horrifying material on the Internet about premature infants. According to the information she read, premature infants often have difficulty bonding with their caretaker, which in some children may ultimately result in mental health and emotional problems. Mrs. Hicks is concerned that this is the case with Holly.

This social worker must take into consideration that in addition to her fears, Mrs. Hicks must be exhausted. Her husband returned to work shortly after the baby came home, and Mrs. Hicks has not left the house since then. She tried taking a break once when her aunt came for a visit, but Holly cried so intensely during this time that her aunt refused to be left alone with Holly again. The social worker must now help Mrs. Hicks cope with the powerful feelings that have been aroused by Holly's premature birth, get any needed clarification on Holly's medical condition, and find ways to get Mrs. Hicks a break from caregiving. He will also want to help her to begin to feel more confident about her ability to parent Holly.

Case Study 3.2

Sarah's Teen Dad

Chris Johnson, the only dad in the teen fathers group facilitated by the social worker at a local high school, has sole custody of his infant daughter. Initially Sarah, Chris's daughter, lived with her mom and maternal grandparents. Chris was contacted by the social worker from Child Protective Services (CPS), who informed him that Sarah was removed from the mom's care because of physical neglect. The referral to CPS was made when Sarah was seen in a pediatric clinic and the medical staff noticed that she had not gained weight since the last visit, and was generally unresponsive in the examination. Further investigation by the CPS worker revealed that Sarah was left in her crib for most of the day, and few of Sarah's basic daily care needs were being fulfilled. Although Chris's contact with Sarah had been sporadic since her birth, he did not hesitate to pursue custody, especially given that the only other alternative was Sarah's placement in foster care. Chris's parents were also supportive of Chris's desire to have Sarah live with all of them. However, although they were willing to help, they were adamant that the responsibility for Sarah's care belonged to Chris, not them. They were unwilling to raise Sarah themselves and in fact required Chris to sign a written statement indicating that he, not them, would assume primary responsibility for Sarah's care. Chris's parents also insisted that he remain in school and earn his high school diploma.

Thus far the situation seems to be working well. At the last medical appointment, Sarah's weight had increased significantly and she responded to the nurse's attempts to play and communicate with her. Chris is continuing his education at the alternative high school, which also has a day care for Sarah. Chris admits that it is much more difficult than he anticipated. He attends school for half the day, works a part-time job the other half, and then has to care for Sarah in the evenings. Chris has shared several times in the group that it is a lot for him to juggle. He still mourns the loss of his freedom and "carefree" lifestyle. Like most of the other teen dads in the group, whether they physically live with the child or not, Chris is concerned about doing the best he can for Sarah; he states that he just wants to be a good dad.

Case Study 3.3

Overprotecting Henry

Irma Velasquez is still mourning the death of her little girl Angel, who was 2 years old when she was killed by a stray bullet that came into their home through the living room window. Although it has been about a year since the incident, no one has been arrested. The police do know, however, that neither Ms. Velasquez's daughter nor her family was the intended victim. The stray bullet was the result of a shoot-out between two rival drug dealers in the family's neighborhood.

Ms. Velasquez is just glad, now, that 14-month-old Henry was in his crib in the back of the house instead of in the living room on that horrible evening. He had fallen asleep in her lap a few minutes before but she had just returned from laying him in his crib when the shooting occurred. Irma Velasquez confides in her social worker at Victim Services that her family has not been the same since the incident. For one, she and her husband barely speak. His method of dealing with the tragedy is to stay away from home. She admits that she is angry with her husband because he does not make enough money for them to live in a safer neighborhood. She thinks that he blames her because she did not protect Angel in some way.

Ms. Velasquez admits that she is afraid that something bad will also happen to Henry. She has limited their area in the home to the back bedroom, and they seldom leave the house. She does not allow anyone, even her sister, to take care of him, and confesses that she has not left his side since the shooting. Even with these restrictions, Ms. Velasquez worries. She is concerned that Henry will choke on a toy or food, or become ill. She still does not allow him to feed himself, even dry cereal. He has just begun walking, and she severely limits his space for movement. Ms. Velasquez looks worn and exhausted. Although she knows these behaviors are somewhat irrational she states that she is determined to protect Henry. She further states that she just could not live through losing another child.

HEALTHY DEVELOPMENT IN INFANTS AND TODDLERS

What happens during the prenatal period and the earliest months and years of a child's life has lasting impact on the life course journey. In the earliest moments, months, and years, interactions with parents, family members, and other adults and children influence the way the brain develops, as do such factors as nutrition and environmental safety. Although it is never too late to improve health and well-being, what happens during infancy and toddlerhood sets the stage for the journey through childhood, adolescence, and adulthood. We were all infants and toddlers once, but sometimes, in our work as social workers, we may find it hard to understand the experience of someone 2 years old or younger. (Young children are typically referred to as **infants** in the first year, but as they enter the second year of life and become more mobile, they are usually called **toddlers,** from about 12 to 36 months of age.) As adults, we have become accustomed to communicating with words, and we are not always sure how to read the behaviors of the very young child. And we are not always sure how we are to behave with them. The best way to overcome these limitations, of course, is to learn what we can about the lives of infants and toddlers.

> What must social workers know about biological age, psychological age, and social age to understand whether an infant's or toddler's behavior is healthy or problematic?

In all three of the case studies at the beginning of this chapter, factors can be identified that may adversely affect the children's development. However, we must begin by understanding what is traditionally referred to as "normal" development. But because *normal* is a relative term with some judgmental overtones, we will use the term *healthy* instead.

Social workers employed in schools, hospitals, community mental health centers, and other public health settings are often approached by parents and teachers with questions about development in young children. To assess whether any of the children they bring to your attention require intervention, you must be able to distinguish between healthy

▲ **Photo 3.1**   Babies depend on others for basic physical and emotional needs. Family support and affection are important factors in healthy development.

and problematic development in three areas: physical, cognitive, and socioemotional development. As you will see, young children go through a multitude of changes in all three areas simultaneously. Inadequate development in any one of them—or in multiple areas—may have long-lasting consequences for the individual.

Keep in mind, however, that what is considered to be healthy is relative to environment and culture. Every newborn enters a world with distinctive features structured by the social setting that he or she encounters (Gardiner & Kosmitzki, 2008; Rogoff, 2003; Valsiner, 2000). Therefore, all aspects of development must be considered in cultural context. Each newborn enters a **developmental niche,** in which culture guides every aspect of the developmental process (Harkness & Super, 2003, 2006). Parents get their ideas about parenting and about the nature of children from the cultural milieu, and parents' ideas are the dominant force in how the infant and toddler develop. Harry Gardiner and Corinne Kosmitzki (2008) identify three interrelated components of the developmental niche: physical and social settings of everyday life, childrearing customs, and caretaker psychology. Exhibit 3.1 provides an overview of these three important components of the developmental niche encountered by every newborn. As you review this exhibit, think about the developmental niches encountered by Holly Hicks, Sarah Johnson, and Henry Velasquez as they begin their life journeys.

In the United States and other wealthy postindustrial societies, many newborns enter a developmental niche in which families have become smaller than in earlier eras. This results in a great deal of attention being paid to each child. Parents take courses and read books about how to provide the best possible care for their infants and toddlers. Infant safety is stressed, with laws about car seats, guidelines about the position in which the baby should sleep, and a "baby industry" that provides a broad range of safety equipment (baby monitors, baby gates, and so on) and toys, books, and electronics to provide sensory stimulation. Of course this developmental niche requires considerable resources, and many families in wealthy nations cannot afford the regulation car seat or the baby monitor. Chris Johnson is attending school, working, and caring for Sarah; he probably would be hard-pressed to find time to read parenting books, but he does find time to attend a group for teen fathers. Irma Velasquez's concern for Henry's safety focuses on protecting him from stray bullets rather than on baby monitors and baby gates. And, of course, the developmental niches in nonindustrial and newly industrializing countries are very different from the niche described above. For example, African pygmy newborns will be introduced to multiple caregivers who will help protect them from danger and prepare them to live an intensely social life (Gardiner & Kosmitzki, 2008). Unfortunately, many infants of the world live in developmental niches characterized by infection and malnutrition. Please keep these variations in mind as you read about infant and toddler development.

To make the presentation of ideas about infancy and toddlerhood manageable, this chapter follows a traditional method of organizing the discussion by type of development: physical development, cognitive development, emotional development, and social development. In this chapter, emotional development and social development are combined under the heading Socioemotional Development. Of course, all these types of development and behavior are interdependent, and often the distinctions blur.

Physical Development

Newborns depend on others for basic physical needs. They must be fed, cleaned, and kept safe and comfortable until they develop the ability to do these things for themselves. At the same time, however, newborns have an amazing set of physical abilities and potentials right from the beginning.

In Case Study 3.2, the pediatrician and CPS social worker were concerned that Sarah Johnson was not gaining weight. With adequate nourishment and care, the physical growth of the infant is quite predictable. Infants grow very rapidly throughout the first two years of life, but the pace of growth slows a bit in toddlerhood. The World Health Organization (WHO) undertook a project, called the Multicentre Growth Reference Study (MGRS), to construct standards for evaluating children from birth through 5 years of age. One part of that project was to construct growth standards to propose how

PHYSICAL AND SOCIAL SETTINGS OF DAILY LIFE
Size, shape, and location of living space
Objects, toys, reading materials
Ecological setting and climate
Nutritional status of children
Family structure (e.g., nuclear, extended, single parent, blended)
Presence of multiple generations (e.g., parents, grandparents, other relatives)
Presence or absence of mother or father
Presence of multiple caretakers
Role of siblings as caretakers
Presence and influence of peer group members

CUSTOMS OF CHILD CARE AND CHILD REARING
Sleeping patterns (e.g., co-sleeping vs. sleeping alone)
Dependence versus independence training
Feeding and eating schedules
Handling and carrying practices
Play and work patterns
Imitation rites
Formal versus informal learning

PSYCHOLOGY OF THE CARETAKERS
Parenting styles (e.g., authoritarian, authoritative, laissez-faire)
Value systems (e.g., dependence, independence, interdependence)
Parental cultural belief systems or ethnotheories
Developmental expectations

▲ **Exhibit 3.1** Components of Developmental Niche

SOURCE: Gardiner & Kosmitzki, 2008. Reproduced by permission of Pearson Education, Inc.

children *should* grow in *all* countries, of interest because of WHO's commitment to eliminate global health disparities. MGRS collected growth data from 8,440 affluent children from diverse geographical and cultural settings, including Brazil, Ghana, India, Norway, Oman, and the United States. To be eligible for the study, mothers needed to be breastfeeding and not smoking, and the environment needed to be adequate to support unconstrained growth.

The researchers found that there were no differences in growth patterns across sites, even though there were some differences in parental stature. Given the striking similarity in growth patterns across sites, they concluded that the data could be used to develop an international standard. Across sites, the average length at birth was 19.5 inches (49.5 cm), 26.3 inches (66.7 cm) at 6 months, 29.5 inches (75.0 cm) at 12 months, and 34.4 inches (87.4 cm) at 24 months (WHO Multicentre Growth Reference Study Group, 2006a). By 1 year of age, infant height was about 1.5 times birth height, and by 2 years, the toddler had nearly doubled the birth height.

In terms of weight, most newborns weigh between 5 and 10 pounds at birth. Infants triple their weight in the first year, and by age 2 most infants are quadruple their original weight. Thus, the average 2-year-old weighs between 20 and 40 pounds. Evidently, the size of individual infants and toddlers can vary quite a bit. Some of the difference is the result of nutrition, exposure to disease, and other environmental factors; much of it is the result of genetics. Some ethnic differences in physical development have also been observed. For example, Asian American children tend to be smaller than average, and African American children tend to be larger than average (Tate, Dezateux, Cole, and the Millennium Cohort Study Child Health Group, 2006). In recent years, there has been a great deal of concern about rapid weight gain during the first 6 months, which has been connected to overweight by age 4 and to several chronic diseases in adulthood. Researchers have found Latino American infants to be twice as likely as other infants in the United States to have this pattern of early rapid weight gain (Dennison, Edmunds, & Stratton, 2006). The WHO child growth standards, calculated by different methods, can be found at www.who.int/childgrowth/standards.

The importance of nutrition in infancy cannot be overstated. Nutrition affects physical stature, motor skill development, brain development, and most every other aspect of development. A recent report by UNICEF (2009) indicated that approximately 200 million children under the age of 5 in the developing world suffer from stunted growth because of chronic maternal and child undernutrition. Undernutrition accounts for more than a third of the deaths of children under the age of 5. Nutritional deficiencies during the first 1,000 days of the child's life can result in damage to the immune system and impair social and cognitive capacities (UNICEF, 2009).

Self-Regulation

Before birth, the bodily functions of the fetus are regulated by the mother's body. After birth, the infant must develop the capacity to engage in self-regulation (Davies, 2004; Shonkoff & Phillips, 2000). At first, the challenge is to regulate bodily functions, such as temperature control, sleeping, eating, and eliminating. That challenge is heightened for the premature or medically fragile infant, as Holly Hicks' mother is finding. Growing evidence indicates that some self-regulatory functions that allow self-calming and organize the wake-sleep cycles get integrated and coordinated during the third trimester, between 30 and 34 weeks' gestation (Institute of Medicine of the National Academies, 2006). Born at 26 weeks' gestation, Holly Hicks did not have the benefit of the uterine environment to support the development of these self-regulatory functions.

As any new parent will attest, however, infants are not born with regular patterns of sleeping, eating, and eliminating. With maturation of the central nervous system in the first 3 months, and with lots of help from parents or other caregivers, the infant's rhythms of sleeping, eating, and eliminating become much more regular (Davies, 2004). A newborn usually sleeps about 16 hours a day, dividing that time evenly between day and night. Of course, this is not a good fit with the way adults organize their sleep lives. At the end of 3 months, most infants are sleeping 14 to 15 hours per day, primarily at night, with some well-defined nap times during the day. Parents also gradually shape infants' eating schedules so that they are eating mainly during the day.

There are cultural variations in, and controversies about, the way caregivers shape the sleeping and eating behaviors of infants. The management of sleep is one of the earliest culturally influenced parenting behaviors. In some cultures, infants sleep with parents, and in other cultures, infants are put to sleep in their own beds and often in their own rooms. In some cultures, putting an infant to sleep alone in a room is considered to be neglectful (Gardiner & Kosmitzki, 2008). Co-sleeping, the child sleeping with the parents, is routine in most of the world's cultures (McKenna, 2002). Japanese and Chinese children often sleep with their parents throughout infancy and early childhood (Liu, Liu, Owens, & Kaplan, 2005). There are also cultural variations and controversies about breastfeeding versus bottle feeding. It is interesting to note that both breastfeeding and sleeping with parents induce shorter bouts of sleep and less sound sleep than the alternatives (Shonkoff & Phillips, 2000). Some researchers have speculated that the infant's lighter and shorter sleep pattern may protect against

> What have you observed about how culture influences the parenting of infants and toddlers?

sudden infant death syndrome (SIDS). Of course, parents sleeping with infants must be aware of the hazard of rolling over and suffocating the infant. Luckily, parents have also been found to sleep less soundly when they sleep with infants (Shonkoff & Phillips, 2000).

Parents become less anxious as the infant's rhythms become more regular and predictable. At the same time, if the caregiver is responsive and dependable, the infant becomes less anxious and begins to develop the ability to wait to have needs met.

Cultural variations exist in beliefs about how to respond when infants cry and fuss, whether to soothe them, or leave them to learn to soothe themselves. When parents do attempt to soothe infants, interestingly, they seem to use the same methods across cultures: "They say something, touch, pick up, search for sources of discomfort, and then feed" (Shonkoff & Phillips, 2000, p. 100). Infants who have been consistently soothed usually begin to develop the ability to soothe themselves after three or four months. This ability is the precursor to struggles for self-control and mastery over powerful emotions that occur in toddlerhood. More will be said about emotion self-regulation in a later section.

Sensory Abilities

Full-term infants are born with a functioning **sensory system**—the senses of hearing, sight, taste, smell, touch, and sensitivity to pain—and these abilities continue to develop rapidly in the first few months. Indeed, in the early months the sensory system seems to function at a higher level than the motor system, which allows movement. The sensory system allows infants, from the time of birth, to participate in and adapt to their environments. A lot of their learning happens through listening and watching (Newman & Newman, 2009; Novak & Pelaez, 2004). The sensory system is an interconnected system, with various sensory abilities working together to give the infant multiple sources of information about the world.

Hearing is the earliest link to the environment; the fetus is sensitive to auditory stimulation in the uterus (Porcaro et al., 2006). The fetus hears the mother's heartbeat, and this sound is soothing to the infant in the early days and weeks after birth. Newborns show a preference for their mother's voice over unfamiliar voices (Reis, 2006). Young infants can also distinguish changes in loudness, pitch, and location of sounds, and they can use auditory information to differentiate one object from another and to track the location of an object (Bahrick, Lickliter, & Flom, 2006; Wilcox, Woods, Tuggy, & Napoli, 2006). These capacities grow increasingly sensitive across the first 6 months after birth. Infants appear to be particularly sensitive to language sounds, and the earliest infant smiles are evoked by the sound of the human voice (Benasich & Leevers, 2003).

The newborn's vision improves rapidly during the first few months of life. By about the age of 4 months, the infant sees objects the same way that an adult would. Of course, infants do not have cognitive associations with objects as adults do. Infants respond to a number of visual dimensions, including depth, brightness, movement, color, and distance. Human faces have particular appeal for newborns. One to 2 days after birth, infants are able to discriminate among—and even imitate—happy, sad, and surprised expressions, but this ability wanes after a few weeks (Field, Woodson, Greenberg, & Cohen, 1982). Between 4 and 7 months, however, infants have been found to be able to recognize some expressions, particularly happiness, fear, and anger (McClure, 2000). Infants show preference for faces, and by 3 months, most infants are able to distinguish a parent's face from the face of a stranger (Nelson, 2001). Some researchers have found that infants are distressed by a lack of facial movement in the people they look at, showing that they prefer caregivers to have expressive faces (Muir & Lee, 2003).

Taste and smell begin to function in the uterus, and newborns can differentiate sweet, bitter, sour, and salty tastes. Sweet tastes seem to have a calming effect on both preterm and full-term newborns (Blass & Ciaramitaro, 1994; Smith & Blass, 1996). Recent research suggests that the first few minutes after birth is a particularly sensitive period for learning to distinguish smells (Delaunay-El Allam, Marlier, & Schaal, 2006). Breastfed babies are particularly sensitive to their mother's body odors. One research team found that newborns undergoing a heel prick were soothed by the smell of breast milk, but only if the milk came from the mother's breast (Nishitani et al., 2009).

Both animal and human research tells us that touch plays a very important role in infant development. In many cultures, swaddling, or wrapping a baby snugly in a blanket, is used to soothe a fussy newborn. We also know that gentle handling, rocking, stroking, and cuddling are all soothing to an infant. Regular gentle rocking and stroking are very effective in soothing low-birth-weight (LBW) babies, who may have underdeveloped central nervous systems. Skin-to-skin contact between parents and their newborns has been found to have benefit for both infants and their parents. Preterm babies who have lots of skin contact with their parents, including gentle touching and massage, gain weight faster, have better temperature regulation, and are more alert compared with preterm babies who do not receive extensive skin contact (Feldman, 2004; Feldman & Edelman, 2003). Infants also use touch to learn about their world and their own bodies. Young infants use their mouths for exploring their worlds, but by 5 or 6 months of age, infants can make controlled use of their hands to explore objects in their environment. They learn about the world and keep themselves entertained by exploring small details, transferring objects from one hand to the other, and examining the differences in surfaces and other features of the object (Streri, 2005).

Clear evidence exists that from the first days of life, babies feel pain. Recently, pediatric researchers have been studying newborn reactions to medical procedures such as heel sticks, the sticks used to draw blood for lab analysis. One researcher found that newborns who undergo repeated heel sticks learn to anticipate pain and develop a stronger reaction to pain than other infants (Taddio, Shah, Gilbert-Macleod, & Katz, 2002). These findings are leading pediatricians to reconsider their stance on the use of pain medications with newborns (Mathew & Mathew, 2003).

Reflexes

Although dependent on others, newborns are equipped from the start with tools for survival that are involuntary responses to simple stimuli, called **reflexes.** Reflexes aid the infant in adapting to the environment outside the womb. The presence and strength of a reflex is an important sign of neurological development, and the absence of reflexes can indicate a serious developmental disorder (Lee, 2009). Given Holly Hicks' early arrival, her reflex responses were thoroughly evaluated.

Newborns have two critical reflexes:

1. *Rooting reflex.* When infants' cheeks or the corners of their mouths are gently stroked with a finger, they will turn their head in the direction of the touch and open their mouths in an attempt to suck the finger. This reflex aids in feeding, because it guides the infants to the nipple.

2. *Sucking reflex.* When a nipple or some other suckable object is presented to the infant, the infant sucks it. This reflex is another important tool for feeding.

Many infants would probably perish without the rooting and sucking reflexes. Imagine the time and effort it would require for one feeding if they did not have them. Instead, infants are born with the ability to take in nutriment.

A number of reflexes disappear at identified times during infancy (see Exhibit 3.2) but others persist throughout adulthood (Lee, 2009). Both the rooting reflex and sucking reflex disappear between 2 and 4 months. By this time, the infant has mastered the voluntary act of sucking and is therefore no longer in need of the reflexive response. Several other infant reflexes appear to have little use now, but probably had some specific survival purposes in earlier times. The presence of an infant reflex after the age at which it typically disappears can be a sign of brain damage or stroke (Lee).

Reflex	Description	Visible
Sucking	The infant instinctively sucks any object of appropriate size that is presented to it.	First 2 to 4 months
Rooting	The head turns in the direction of a stimulus when the cheek is touched. The infant's mouth opens in an attempt to suck.	First 3 months
Moro/Startle	The arms thrust outward when the infant is released in midair, as if attempting to regain support.	First 5 months
Swimming	When placed facedown in water, the infant makes paddling, swimlike motions.	First 3 months
Stepping	When the infant is held in an upright position with the feet placed on a firm surface, the infant moves the feet in a walking motion.	First 3 months
Grasping	The infant grasps objects placed in its hand.	First 4 months
Babinski	The toes spread when the soles of the feet are stroked.	First year
Blinking	The eyes blink when they are touched or when sudden bright light appears.	Lifetime
Cough	Cough occurs when airway is stimulated.	Lifetime
Gag	Gagging occurs when the throat or back of mouth is stimulated.	Lifetime
Sneeze	Sneezing occurs when the nasal passages are irritated.	Lifetime
Yawn	Yawning occurs when the body needs additional oxygen.	Lifetime

▲ **Exhibit 3.2**   Infant Reflexes

Motor Skills

The infant gradually advances from reflex functioning to motor functioning. The development of **motor skills**—the ability to move and manipulate—occurs in a more or less orderly, logical sequence. It begins with simple actions such as lifting the chin and progresses to more complex acts such as walking, running, and throwing. Infants usually crawl before they walk.

> How do these motor skills help to promote a sense of human agency in making choices?

Motor development is somewhat predictable, in that children tend to reach milestones at about the same age and in the same sequence. As a part of the MGRS, WHO undertook a project to construct standards for evaluating the motor development of children from birth through 5 years of age. MGRS collected longitudinal data on six gross motor milestones of children ages 4 to 24 months in Ghana, India, Norway, Oman, and the United States. The milestones studied were sitting without support, standing with assistance, hands-and-knees crawling, walking with assistance, standing alone, and walking alone. Because WHO was trying to establish standards for evaluating child development, healthy children were studied in all five study sites. The researchers found that 90% of the children achieved five of the six milestones in the same sequence, but 4.3% of the sample never engaged in hands-and-knees crawling (WHO Multicentre Growth Reference Study Group, 2006b).

Based on the data collected, MGRS developed "windows of milestone achievement" for each of the six motor skills, with achievement at the 1st and 99th percentiles as the window boundaries. All motor achievement within the windows is considered normal variation in ages of achievement for healthy children. The windows of achievement for the six motor skills studied are reported in Exhibit 3.3. The results reveal that the windows vary from 5.4 months for sitting without support to 10.0 months for standing alone. This is quite a wide range for normal development and should be reassuring to parents who become anxious if their child is not at the low end of the window. Many parents, for example, become concerned if their child has not attempted to walk unassisted by age 1. However, some children walk alone at age 9 months; others do not even attempt to walk until almost 18 months.

Culture and ethnicity appear to have some influence on motor development in infants and toddlers. MGRS found that girls were slightly ahead of boys in gross motor development but the differences were not statistically significant. They did find small, but statistically significant, difference between sites of the study, however. The researchers speculate that these differences probably reflect culture-based child care behaviors, but the cause cannot be determined from the data, and a genetic component is possible. The earliest mean age of achievement for four of the six milestones occurred in the Ghanaian sample, and the latest mean age of achievement for all six milestones occurred in the Norwegian sample (WHO Multicentre Growth Reference Study Group, 2006c). The U.S. sample mean was in the middle range on all milestones except for hands-and-knees crawling, where it had the lowest mean achievement.

A longitudinal study of almost 16,000 infants in the United Kingdom took up this issue of cultural differences in developmental motor milestones. In this study, Black Caribbean infants, Black African infants, and Indian infants were, on average, more advanced in motor development than White infants. Pakistani and Bangladeshi infants were more likely than White infants to show motor delays. Although the delays among Pakistani and Bangladeshi infants appear to be explained by factors associated with poverty, the earlier development of Black Caribbean, Black African, and Indian infants could not be explained by economic advantage. The researchers suggest that parental expectations and parenting practices play a role in cultural differences in motor development (Kelly, Sacker, Schoon, & Nazroo, 2006).

▲ **Photo 3.2** Fine motor skills, the ability to move and manipulate objects, develop in a logical sequence.

Motor Milestone	Window of Milestone Achievement
Sitting without support	3.8–9.2 months
Standing with assistance	4.8–11.4 months
Hands-and-knees crawling	5.2–13.5 months
Walking with assistance	5.9–13.7 months
Standing alone	6.9–16.9 months
Walking alone	8.2–17.6 months

▲ **Exhibit 3.3**   Windows of Milestone Achievement in Months

SOURCE: Taken from WHO Multicentre Growth Reference Study Group, 2006b.

The development of motor skills (and most other types of skills, for that matter) is a continuous process. Children progress from broad capacities to more specific refined abilities. For example, toddlers progress from eating cereal with their fingers to eating with a spoon.

Parents are usually quite patient with their child's motor development. However, toilet training (potty training) is often a source of stress and uncertainty for new parents. Every human culture has mechanisms for disposing of human waste and socializes infants and toddlers to that method. One of the basic issues in this socialization is whether it should be in the hands of the child or the caregiver (Valsiner, 2000). In the United States until recently, many child development experts recommended that babies be potty trained during the first year of life. Consequently, many parents exercised strong measures, including scolding and punishment, to ensure timely toilet training. Even now, many grandparents proudly report that they tied their infants to the potty chair at times of predicted elimination (after eating, for example) until the child was able to master the skill. T. Berry Brazelton (1983), one of the best known pediatricians in the United States, endeavored to change this negative perspective. He advocated that parents begin potty training during the second year of life, during the lull time after standing and walking have been accomplished. Only then, he says, is the infant physiologically and psychologically ready to master this skill. That is the current position of the American Academy of Pediatrics (1999), who recommends waiting until the child is ready and guiding toilet training in a systematic way, beginning with bowel training. By age 3, most children have mastered toilet training, but even 5-year-olds are still prone to soiling accidents. It should be noted, however, that in some parts of the world there is a perception of readiness at a much earlier age (Valsiner, 2000).

The Growing Brain

We are living in the midst of a neuroscientific revolution that is clarifying the important role of the brain in helping to shape human behavior (Farmer, 2009; Garrett, 2009). Like the brains of other primates, human brains contain **neurons,** or specialized nerve cells that store and transmit information; they carry sensory information to the brain, and they carry out the processes involved in thought, emotion, and action. Between the neurons are **synapses,** or gaps that function as the site of information exchange from one neuron to another. During the prenatal period, the brain overproduces neurons in massive numbers. In fact, the human newborn has more synapses than the human adult. During infancy and toddlerhood, each neuron joins with thousands of other neurons to form a colossal number of synapses or connections. During the first three years of life, the human brain triples in weight and creates about 1,000 trillion new connections among neurons (Newman & Newman, 2009). The period of overproduction of synapses, or **blooming,** is followed by a period of **pruning,** or reduction, of the synapses to improve the efficiency of brain functioning. It is through this process of creating elaborate communication systems between the connecting neurons that more and more complex skills and abilities become possible. Thus, during these early years of life, children are capable of rapid new learning. The blooming and pruning of synapses process continues well into childhood and adolescence at different timetables in different regions of the brain. For example, overproduction of synapses in the visual cortex of the brain peaks in the fourth month after birth, and pruning in that region continues until sometime toward the end of the early childhood period (Huttenlocher & Kabholkar, 1997). By contrast, in the medial prefrontal cortex part of the brain, where higher-level cognition and self-regulation take place, synaptic blooming peaks at about 1 year of age, and pruning continues until middle to late adolescence.

The available evidence suggests that both genetic processes and early experiences with the environment influence the timing of brain development (Thompson & Nelson, 2001). Brain plasticity has been a major finding of neuroscientific research of the past few decades. There are two elements of **brain plasticity:** first, research indicates that the brain changes throughout life; and second, the brain changes in response to what it experiences—it is shaped by experience (Farmer, 2009). The human brain is genetically designed to accommodate an incredibly wide range of human experiences, and the environmental context helps to shape the brain for life in a particular developmental niche. What is used gets strengthened, and what is not used gets pruned. The infant and toddler contribute to their own brain development by repeating certain actions, attending to certain stimuli, and responding in particular ways to caregivers (Shonkoff & Phillips, 2000).

Exposure to speech in the first year expedites the discrimination of speech sounds; exposure to patterned visual information in the first few years of life is necessary for normal development of some aspects of vision. Some suggest that the entire infancy period is a crucial and sensitive time for brain development, given the quantity and speed at which the neurons develop and connect (Zigler, Finn-Stevenson, & Hall, 2002). Positive physical experiences (feeding, safety, and so on) and positive psychological experiences (touching, cooing, and playing) activate and simulate brain activity (Shonkoff & Phillips, 2000). So good nutrition and infant stimulation are essential for brain development, and exposure to environmental toxins, abuse, emotional trauma, and deprivation is hazardous (Shonkoff & Phillips; Teicher, 2002; Zigler et al.). Persistent stress for the infant or toddler has been found to result in overdevelopment of areas of the brain that process anxiety and fear and underdevelopment of other brain areas, particularly the frontal cortex (Schore, 2002).

Certain risks to brain development are associated with prematurity. Premature infants, like Holly Hicks, born at 24 to 28 weeks' gestation, have high rates of serious intracranial hemorrhage, which can lead to problems in cognitive and motor development, including cerebral palsy and mental retardation. Less serious intracranial hemorrhage can lead to later behavioral, attentional, and memory problems (Shonkoff & Phillips, 2000). Also, the premature infant faces the challenging environment of the neonatal intensive care unit (NICU) at a time when the brain is developing rapidly. With this in mind, architects and neonatalists have been working together in recent years to make the NICU a more nurturing environment for this rapid brain development (Zeisel, 2006). It is not yet clear whether Holly Hicks suffered any type of brain hemorrhage and what impact it will have on her future development if she did.

Recent research has focused on the relationship between infant/parent attachment and brain development. One of the most popular perspectives on this issue is presented in a book titled, *Why Love Matters: How Affection Shapes a Baby's Brain,* by Sue Gerhardt (2004). The premise here is that without affection and bonding, the frontal cortex of the brain cannot develop. The connection between attachment and brain development is discussed in more detail in the attachment section of this chapter.

Cognitive Development

How do the drives to learn and be in interaction with the environment promote interdependence?

As the brain develops, so does its ability to process and store information and to solve problems. These abilities are known as **cognition.** When we talk about how fast a child is learning, we are talking about cognitive development. Researchers now describe the infant as "wired to learn," and agree that infants have an intrinsic drive to learn and to be in interaction with their environments (Shonkoff & Phillips, 2000). A central element of cognition is language, which facilitates both thinking and communicating. Exhibit 3.4 lists some milestones in cognitive development.

Milestone	Age of Onset
Coos responsively	Birth–3 months
Smiles responsively	3–4 months
Smiles at self in mirror	3–4 months
Laughs out loud	3–4 months
Plays peek-a-boo	3–4 months
Shows displeasure	5–6 months
Babbles	6–8 months
Understands simple commands	12 months
Follows directions	2 years
Puts two to three words together	2 years
Uses sentences	2–3 years

▲ **Exhibit 3.4**   Selected Milestones in Cognitive Development

Piaget's Stages of Cognitive Development

To assess children's cognitive progress, many people use the concepts developed by the best-known cognitive development theorist, Jean Piaget (1952). Piaget believed that cognitive development occurs in successive stages, determined by the age of the child. His overall contention was that as a child grows and develops, cognition changes not only in quantity but also in quality.

Piaget used the metaphor of a slow-motion movie to explain his theory, which is summarized in Exhibit 3.5 as follows:

1. **Sensorimotor stage** (ages birth to 2 years). Infants at this stage of development can look at only one frame of the movie at a time. When the next picture appears on the screen, infants focus on it and cannot go back to the previous frame.

2. **Preoperational stage** (ages 2 to 7). Preschool children and children in early grades can remember (recall) the sequence of the pictures in the movie. They also develop **symbolic functioning**—the ability to use symbols to represent what is not present. However, they do not necessarily understand what has happened in the movie or how the pictures fit together.

3. **Concrete operations stage** (ages 7 to 11). Not until this stage can children run the pictures in the movie backward and forward to better understand how they blend to form a specific meaning.

4. **Formal operations stage** (ages 11 and beyond). Children gain the capacity to apply logic to various situations and to use symbols to solve problems. Adding to Piaget's metaphor, one cognitive scientist describes formal operations as the ability of the adolescent not only to understand the observed movie but also to add or change characters and create an additional plot or staging plan (Edwards, 1992).

The first of Piaget's stages applies to infants and toddlers. During the sensorimotor period, they respond to immediate stimuli—what they see, hear, taste, touch, and smell—and learning takes place through the senses and motor activities. Piaget suggests that infant and toddler cognitive development occurs in six substages during the sensorimotor period.

Substage 1: *Reflex Activity (birth to 1 month).* Because reflexes are what the infant can "do," they become the foundation to future learning. Reflexes are what infants build on.

Substage 2: *Primary Circular Reactions (1 to 4 months).* During this stage, infants repeat (thus the term circular) behaviors that bring them a positive response and pleasure. The infant's body is the focus of the response, thus the term primary. If, for example, infants by chance hold their head erect or lift their chest, they will continue to repeat these acts because they are pleasurable. Infants also have limited anticipation abilities.

Substage 3: *Secondary Circular Reactions (4 to 8 months).* As in the second substage, the focus is on performing acts and behaviors that bring about a response. In this stage, however, the infant reacts to responses from the environment. If, for example, 5-month-old infants cause the rattle to sound inadvertently as their arms move, they will continue attempts to repeat this occurrence.

Substage 4: *Coordination of Secondary Circular Reactions (8 to 12 months).* The mastery of **object permanence** is a significant task during this stage. Piaget contended that around 9 months of age, infants develop the ability to understand that an object or a person exists even when they don't see it. Piaget demonstrated this ability by hiding a favored toy under a blanket. Infants are able to move the blanket and retrieve the toy. Object permanence is related to the rapid development of memory abilities during this period (Rovee-Collier, 1999). Two other phenomena are related to this advance in memory. **Stranger anxiety,** in which the infant reacts with fear and withdrawal to unfamiliar persons, has been found to occur at about 9 months across cultures. Many first-time parents comment, "I don't know what has gotten into her; she has always been so outgoing." Babies vary in how intensely they react to the strange situation and in how they express their anxiety (Rieser-Danner, 2003). **Separation anxiety** also becomes prominent in this period. The infant is able to remember previous separations and becomes anxious at the signs of an impending separation from parents. With time, the infant also learns that the parent always returns.

Substage 5: *Tertiary Circular Reactions (12 to 18 months).* During this stage, toddlers become more creative in eliciting responses and are better problem solvers. For example, if the first button on the talking telephone does not make it talk, they will continue to press other buttons on the phone until they find the correct one.

Substage 6: *Mental Representation (18 months to 2 years).* Piaget described toddlers in this stage as actually able to use thinking skills in that they retain mental images of what is not immediately in front of them. For example, the toddler will look in a toy box for a desired toy and move other toys aside that prohibit recovery of the desired toy. Toddlers can also remember and imitate observed behavior. For example, toddlers roll their toy lawn mower over the lawn, imitating their parents' lawn mowing.

Stage	Characteristics
Sensorimotor (birth–2 years)	Infant is egocentric; he or she gradually learns to coordinate sensory and motor activities and develops a beginning sense of objects existing apart from the self.
Preoperational (2–7 years)	The child remains primarily egocentric but discovers rules (regularities) that can be applied to new incoming information. The child tends to overgeneralize rules, however, and thus makes many cognitive errors.
Concrete operations (7–11 years)	The child can solve concrete problems through the application of logical problem-solving strategies.
Formal operations (11 years and beyond)	The person becomes able to solve real and hypothetical problems using abstract concepts.

▲ **Exhibit 3.5**   Piaget's Stages of Cognitive Development

As much as Piaget's work has been praised, it has also been questioned and criticized. Piaget constructed his theory based on his observations of his own three children. Thus, one question has been how objective he was and whether the concepts can really be generalized to all children. Also, Piaget has been criticized for not addressing the influence of environmental factors—such as culture, family, and significant relationships and friendships—on cognitive development. However, for the past 30 years, researchers around the world have put Piaget's theory to test. This research literature is immense but has been summarized by several reviewers (see, for example, Bronfenbrenner, 1993; Rogof & Chavajay, 1995; Segall, Dasen, Berry, & Poortinga, 1999). Piaget's sensorimotor stage has been studied less than his other cognitive stages, but the existing research tends to support Piaget's theory, even though some minor cultural differences are noted (Gardiner & Kosmitzki, 2008). For example, some research has found that African infants receive more social stimulation and emotional support than European and American infants, while European and American infants get more experience with handling objects. This leads to African infants and toddlers developing more social intelligence and European and American children developing more technological intelligence (cited in Gardiner & Kosmitzki, 2008). This supports the idea of the importance of the developmental niche, but, overall, suggests much more similarity than difference in cognitive development across developmental niches during infancy and toddlerhood.

Research findings have called into question some aspects of Piaget's theory. For example, Piaget described young children as being incapable of object permanence until at least 9 months of age. However, infants as young as 3½ and 4½ months of age have been observed who are already proficient at object permanence (Baillargeon, 1987; Ruffman, Slade, & Redman, 2005). Other researchers (Munakata, McClelland, Johnson, & Siegler, 1997) have found that although infants seem aware of hidden objects at 3½ months, they fail to retrieve those objects until about 8 months of age. These researchers suggest that cognitive skills such as object permanence may be multifaceted and gradually developed (Baillargeon, 2004). Cognitive researchers have been interested in the development of object permanence in children with very low birth weight and in children with a range of intellectual and physical disabilities. One research team found that toddlers born full-term were more than six times more likely to have developed object permanence than children born prematurely with very low birth weight (Lowe, Erickson, MacLean, & Duvall, 2009). Susan Bruce and Zayyad Muhammad (2009) reviewed the research on the development of object permanence in children with intellectual disability, physical disability, autism, and blindness. They concluded that this research indicates that children with these disabilities develop object permanence in a similar sequence as children without disabilities, but at a slower rate. They also found evidence that children with severe disability benefit from systematic instruction in object permanence. It is interesting to note that much of the recent research on object permanence studies nonhuman animals. For example, one research team who studied Piagetian object permanence in Eurasian jays found support for Piagetian stages of cognitive development in this avian species (Zucca, Milos, & Vallortigara, 2007).

Categorization is a cognitive skill that begins to develop in the first year of life. Categorization, or recognizing similarities in groups of objects, is a fundamental element of information processing. There is evidence that by 6 months, infants begin to see patterns in and make distinctions about human faces (Nelson, 2001; Ramsey, Langlois, Hoss, Rubenstein, & Griffin, 2004). There is also evidence that by 3 months of age, infants can make a distinction between people and inanimate objects. They have been observed to smile and vocalize more and become more active when they are interacting with people than when interacting with inanimate objects (Rakison & Poulin-Dubois, 2001). Research has also found that 4½-month-old babies indicate recognition when two objects are different from each other (Needham, 2001). As toddlers develop language skills, they use language as well as visual cues to categorize objects (Nazzi & Gopnik, 2001).

Prelanguage Skills

Some of the developmental milestones for language development are listed in Exhibit 3.4. Although infants communicate with their caretakers from the beginning (primarily by crying), language development truly begins around 2 months of age. The first sounds, cooing, are pleasing to most parents. By age 4 months, infants babble. Initially, these babbles are unrecognizable. Eventually, between 8 and 12 months, infants make gestures to indicate their desires. The babble sounds and gestures together, along with caretakers' growing familiarity with the infant's "vocabulary," make it easier for infants to communicate their desires. For example, 12-month-old infants may point to their bottle located on the kitchen cabinet and babble "baba." The caretaker soon learns that "baba" means "bottle."

By the age of 18 to 24 months, the toddler can speak between 50 and 200 words. Piaget asserts that children develop language in direct correlation to their cognitive skills. Thus, most of the words spoken at this age relate to people and significant objects in the toddler's environment. These include words such as "mama," "dada," "cat," and "sissy" (sister), for example. There is an overall bias in infancy to use nouns (Gardiner & Kosmitzki, 2008). Toddlers' first words also include situational words such as "hot," "no," and "bye." Between 20 and 26 months, toddlers begin to combine two words together, also in tandem with growing cognitive abilities. For example, children can say "all gone" as they develop an understanding of object permanence (Berk, 2005).

Even with these skills, toddlers may be difficult to understand on occasion. Cindy, the mom of 24-month-old Steven, describes collecting her son from day care. During the trip home, Steven initiated conversation with Cindy by calling out "Mama." He began to "tell" her about something that Cindy assumes must have occurred during the day. Steven continued to babble to his mother with animation and laughs and giggles during the story. Although Cindy laughed at the appropriate moments, she was unable to understand most of what Steven was sharing with her.

The most important thing that adults can do to assist with language development is to provide opportunity for interactions. Adults can answer questions, provide information, explain plans and actions, and offer feedback about behavior. Adults can also read to infants and toddlers and play language games. The opportunity for interaction is important for deaf children as well as hearing children, but deaf children need interaction that involves hand and eye, as with sign language (Shonkoff & Phillips, 2000). Researchers have found that when talking with infants and toddlers, adults and even older children will engage in behaviors that facilitate language development; they tend to speak in a high pitch, use shorter sentences, and speak slowly (Singh, Morgan, & Best, 2002). However, there appear to be cultural differences in how adults communicate with infants and toddlers, and it is not clear how these differences affect language acquisition (Sabbagh & Baldwin, 2001).

Research indicates that all early infants are capable of recognizing and making sounds from a wide range of languages. However, as they have repeated interactions with caregivers and family members, they strengthen the neural connections for the sounds of the language(s) spoken in the home environment, and the neural connections for sounds from other languages are lost (Hoff, 2009). Miraculously, infants and toddlers who are bilingual from birth learn two languages as fast as monolingual infants learn one (Kovács & Mehler, 2009). Of course, language ability in any language is not retained unless the environment provides an opportunity for using the language.

Socioemotional Development

Infants and toddlers face vital developmental tasks in the emotional arena (some of which are listed in Exhibit 3.6), as well as in the social arena. Development during these early ages may set the stage for socioemotional development during all other developmental ages. This section addresses these tasks.

Milestone	Age
Emotional life centered on physical states. Exhibits distress, fear, and rage.	Newborn
Emotional life begins to be centered on relationships. Exhibits pleasure and delight.	3 months
Emotional life continues to be relational, but distinctions are made between those relationships, as in stranger anxiety and separation anxiety. Exhibits joy, fear, anxiety, and anger.	9 months
Emotional life becomes sensitive to emotional cues from other people. Exhibits a range of emotion from joy to rage.	End of first year
Emotional life becomes centered on regulation of emotional states.	Second and third year

▲ **Exhibit 3.6**   Selected Milestones in Emotional Development

SOURCES: Based on Davies, 2004, and Shonkoff & Phillips, 2000.

Erikson's Theory of Psychosocial Development

Erik Erikson's (1950) theory explains socioemotional development in terms of eight consecutive, age-defined stages of emotional development. Each stage requires the mastery of a developmental task. Mastery at each stage depends on mastery in the previous stages. If the "task facilitating factors" for a stage are absent, the individual will become stuck in that stage of development.

Each of Erikson's stages is overviewed in Exhibit 3.7 and discussed in the chapter about the part of the life course to which it applies. The following two stages are relevant to infants and toddlers:

How does the development of trust during infancy affect future relationships?

1. *Trust versus mistrust* (ages birth–1½). The overall task of this stage is for infants to develop a sense that their needs will be met by the outside world and that the outside world is an okay place to be. In addition, the infant develops an emotional bond with an adult, which Erikson believes becomes the foundation for being able to form intimate, loving relationships in the future. Erikson argues the need for

one consistent mother figure. The most important factor facilitating growth in this stage is consistency in having physical and emotional needs met: being fed when hungry, being kept warm and dry, and being allowed undisturbed sleep. In addition, the infant has to be protected from injury, disease, and so on, and receive adequate stimulation. Infants who develop mistrust at this stage become suspicious of the world and withdraw, react with rage, and have deep-seated feelings of dependency. These infants lack drive, hope, and motivation for continued growth. They cannot trust their environment and are unable to form intimate relationships with others. Given Ms. Velasquez's view that the outside world is not a safe place, described at the beginning of the chapter, her young son, Henry, is at risk of developing feelings of mistrust.

Life Stage	Psychosocial Challenge	Characteristic
Infancy (birth to about 1 year)	Basic trust versus basic mistrust	Infants must form trusting relationships with caregivers or they will learn to distrust the world.
Toddlerhood (about 1–3 years)	Autonomy versus shame and doubt	Toddlers must develop self-confidence and a sense of mastery over themselves and their worlds and they must use newly developed motor skills, or they will develop shame and doubt about their inability to develop control.
Early childhood (3–5 years)	Initiative versus guilt	Young children must develop a growing capacity to plan and initiate actions or they may feel guilt about their taking initiative.
Middle childhood (6–11 years)	Industry versus inferiority	School-aged children must develop a sense of competence to master and complete tasks or they learn to feel inferior or incompetent.
Adolescence (11–20 years)	Identity versus role diffusion	Adolescents must develop a sense of who they are and where they are going in life or they become confused about their identity.
Young adulthood (21–40 years)	Intimacy versus isolation	Young adults must develop the capacity to commit to deep associations with others or they feel a sense of isolation.
Middle adulthood (40–65 years)	Generativity versus stagnation	Midlife adults must develop the capacity to transcend self-interest to guide the next generation or they feel stagnated.
Late adulthood (over 65 years)	Ego integrity versus despair	Older adults must find integrity and contentment in their final years by accepting their life as it has been or they feel a sense of despair.

▲ **Exhibit 3.7**   Erikson's Stages of Psychosocial Development

SOURCE: Based on Erikson, 1950, 1978.

How does the toddler's experience with autonomy contribute to the capacity for human agency?

2. *Autonomy versus shame and doubt* (ages 1½–3). A child with autonomy has a growing sense of self-awareness and begins to strive for independence and self-control. These children feel proud that they can perform tasks and exercise control over bodily functions. They relate well with close people in the environment and begin to exercise self-control in response to parental limits. To develop autonomy, children need firm limits for controlling impulses and managing anxieties, but at the same time still need the freedom to explore their environment. Exhibit 3.8 summarizes possible sources of anxiety for toddlers (Davies, 2004). Toddlers also need an environment rich with stimulating and interesting objects and with opportunities for freedom of choice. Adults must accept the child's bodily functions as normal and good and offer praise and encouragement to enhance the child's mastery of self-control. At the other end of the spectrum are children who doubt themselves. They fear a loss of love and are overly concerned about their parents' approval. These children are ashamed of their abilities and develop an unhealthy kind of self-consciousness.

Erikson does not address whether tasks that should be mastered in one stage can be mastered later if the facilitating factors—such as a dependable, nurturing caregiver—are introduced. For example, we know that Sarah suffered some neglect until Chris Johnson and his parents provided a dependable, nurturing environment for her. At what point is it too late to undo psychosocial damage? Critics also question Erikson's emphasis on the process of individualization, through which children develop a strong identity separate from that of their family. Many believe this to be a North American, Western value and therefore not applicable to collectivistic societies such as many African, Latin, and Asian societies or to collectivistic subcultures in the United States.

Emotional Control

Researchers have paid a lot of attention to the strategies infants develop to cope with intense emotions, both positive and negative ones. They have noted that infants use a range of techniques to cope with intense emotions, including turning the head away, sucking on hands or lips, and closing their eyes. By the middle of the second year, toddlers have built a repertoire of ways to manage strong emotions. They make active efforts to avoid or disregard situations that arouse strong emotions; they move away or they distract themselves with objects. They soothe themselves by thumb sucking, rocking, or stroking; they also engage in reassuring self-talk. In addition, they develop substitute goals if they become thwarted in goal-directed behavior (Shonkoff & Phillips, 2000). However, researchers who do experimental infant research note that a number of infants must be discontinued from the research process because they cannot be calmed

Difficulty understanding what is happening

Difficulty communicating

Frustration over not being able to do what others can do or what they imagine others can do

Conflicts between wanting to be independent and wanting their parents' help

Separation or threat of separation from caregivers

Fears of losing parental approval and love

Reactions to losing self-control

Anxieties about the body

▲ **Exhibit 3.8**   Some Possible Sources of Anxiety for Toddlers

SOURCE: Adapted from Davies, 2004.

enough to participate (Newman & Newman, 2009). The ability to control the intensity of emotional states has important implications for early childhood school performance and social relationships (Calkins, 2004).

You may not be surprised to learn that researchers have found that one of the most important elements in how an infant learns to manage strong emotions is the assistance provided by the caregiver for emotion management (Siegel, 1999). Caregivers may offer food or a pacifier, or they may swaddle, cuddle, hug, or rock the infant. By the time the infant is 6 months old, caregivers often provide distraction and use vocalization to soothe. One research team found that for all levels of infant distress, the most effective methods of soothing were holding, rocking, and vocalizing. Feeding and offering a pacifier were effective when the infant was moderately distressed but not at times of extreme distress (Jahromi, Putnam, & Stifter, 2004). The child's temperament also makes a difference, as you will see in the next section.

Finally, there are cultural differences in expectations for management of emotions in infants. For example, Japanese parents try to shield their infants from the frustrations that would invite anger. In other words, some emotions are regulated by protecting the child from situations that would

▲ **Photo 3.3**   Toddlers begin to build a repertoire of ways to manage strong emotions. The ability to control the intensity of emotional states has important implications for early childhood school performance and social relationships.

arouse them (Kitayama, Karasaw, & Mesquita, 2004; Miyake, Campos, Kagan, & Bradshaw, 1986). Cultural differences also exist in how much independence infants and toddlers are expected to exercise in managing emotions. In one study comparing Anglo and Puerto Rican mothers, Harwood (1992) found that Anglo mothers expected their infants to manage their stranger anxiety and separation anxiety without clinging to the mother. The Puerto Rican mothers, conversely, expected their infants to rely on the mother for solace.

Temperament

Another way to look at emotional development is by evaluating **temperament**—the individual's innate disposition. The best-known study of temperament in infants and young children was conducted by Alexander Thomas, Stella Chess, and Herbert Birch (1968, 1970). They studied nine components of temperament: activity level, regularity of biological functions, initial reaction to any new stimulus, adaptability, intensity of reaction, level of stimulation needed to evoke a discernible response, quality of mood, distractibility, and attention span or persistence. From their observations, the researchers identified three types of temperament: easy, slow to warm up, and difficult. The *easy* baby is characterized by good mood, regular patterns of eating and sleeping, and general calmness. The *slow to warm up* baby has few intense reactions, either positive or negative, and tends to be low in activity level. The *difficult* baby is characterized by negative mood, irregular sleeping and eating patterns, and difficulty adapting to new experiences and people. There is a tendency for recent researchers to focus on two clusters of temperamental traits, negative emotions (irritability, fear, sadness, shyness, frustration, and discomfort) and regulatory capacity (ability to self-regulate behavior and engage in self-soothing), as important to parent-infant relationships as well as to future personality and behavior development (see Bridgett et al., 2009).

For an idea of the differences in infant temperament, consider the range of reactions you might see at a baptism service. One infant might scream when passed from one person to the other and when water is placed on his or her forehead. The mother might have difficulty calming the infant for the remainder of the baptism service. At the other extreme, one infant might make cooing noises throughout the entire service and seem unbothered by the rituals. The slow-to-warm-up infant might cautiously check out the clergy administering the baptism and begin to relax by the time the ritual is completed.

Thomas and his colleagues believed that a child's temperament appears shortly after birth and is set, or remains unchanged, throughout life. Recent research indicates, however, that a stable pattern of temperament is not evident until about 4 months, when the central nervous system is further developed (Shonkoff & Phillips, 2000). Whether temperament is permanent or not is still unresolved. There is growing agreement, however, about two aspects of temperament: (1) there is some stability to a child's positive or negative reactions to environmental events, and (2) this stability of reaction leads to patterned reactions from others (Vaughn & Bost, 1999).

Thomas, Chess, and Birch cautioned that a difficult temperament does not necessarily indicate future childhood behavior problems, as one might logically assume. More significant than an infant's temperament type is the "goodness of fit" between the infant and the expectations, temperament, and needs of those in the child's environment (Thomas & Chess, 1986). In other words, how well the infant's temperament matches with that of parents, caregivers, and siblings is crucial to the infant's emotional development. For example, there appears to be a "problematic fit" between Holly Hicks and her mother. Although Mrs. Hicks is able to meet Holly's basic needs, she feels rejected and overwhelmed by Holly's "difficult" temperament. Holly seems to get irritated with Mrs. Hicks's nurturing style. Thomas and Chess suggest that regardless of a child's temperament, caregivers and others in the child's environment can learn to work with a child's temperament. Thus, helping Mrs. Hicks develop a better fit between herself and Holly will help Holly develop toward healthy functioning.

Recent research provides some insight about what could happen between Holly and Mrs. Hicks, as well as between Mr. and Mrs. Hicks, over time. Researchers are finding that negative emotion in the first 3 months is related to decreases in regulatory capacity between 4 and 12 months. And, decreases in regulatory capacity in the infant between the ages of 4 and 12 months predicts poor parent-child relationships when the child is 18 months old (Bridgett et al., 2009). Another research team found a relationship between infant regulatory capacity and marital satisfaction. Following a group of infants and their families from the time the infants were 7 months old until they were 14 months, these researchers found that marital satisfaction increased as infants developed greater regulatory capacity and decreased when infants failed to gain in regulatory capacity (Mehall, Spinrad, Eisenberg, & Gaertner, 2009). As parents discipline infants and toddlers to help them gain self-control, different methods of discipline are indicated for children of different temperaments. Infants and toddlers who are fearful and inhibited respond best to gentle, low-power discipline techniques, but these techniques do not work well with fearless infants and toddlers who do best when positive feelings between the mother and child are emphasized (Kochanska, Aksan, & Joy, 2007).

Researchers have also been interested in whether there are cultural and socioeconomic differences in infant temperament. Several studies have found small to moderate cross-cultural differences in infant temperament and have attributed these differences mainly to genetics (see Gartstein, Knyazev, & Slobodskaya, 2005; Gartstein et al., 2006). To begin to examine the contributions of the role of genetics and environment to temperament, one research team compared three groups of Russian infants between the ages of 3 and 12 months: infants living in Russia, infants of parents who immigrated to Israel, and infants of parents who immigrated to the United States. They found some differences in temperament across these three situations, and concluded that the differences in temperament between the Russian-Israeli infants and the Russian-American immigrants probably reflect the different acculturation strategies used to adapt to different host societies (Gartstein, Peleg, Young, & Slobodskaya, 2009). Findings about the relationship between socioeconomic status and temperature are contradictory. Some researchers find no socioeconomic differences (Bridgett et al., 2009) while other researchers find that infants in more economically disadvantaged families have more difficult temperaments and conclude that this difference is largely explained by family stress (Jansen et al., 2009). The difference in findings about socioeconomic status and temperament could be caused by different samples, with socioeconomic variations in temperament more likely to show up when the sample includes greater income variability. Recent research indicates that temperament is a more complex concept than once thought and that it is influenced by both genetics and the developmental niche. Another implication is that families like the Hicks family who have an infant with negative emotion and poor regulatory capacity may be in special need of social work interventions to prevent a troubling developmental trajectory for the infant and the relationship between the parents.

Bowlby's Theory of Attachment

Another key component of emotional development is **attachment**—the ability to form emotional bonds with other people. Many child development scholars have suggested that attachment is one of the most important issues in infant development, mainly because attachment is the foundation for emotional development and a predictor of later functioning. Note that this view of attachment is similar to Erikson's first stage of psychosocial development. This perspective is similar to the one Mrs. Hicks found on the Internet, which raised issues of concern for her.

> How important is the early attachment relationship for the quality of future relationships?

The two most popular theories of attachment were developed by John Bowlby (1969) and Mary Ainsworth and colleagues (Ainsworth, Blehar, Waters, & Wall, 1978). Bowlby, who initially studied attachment in animals, concluded that attachment is natural, a result of the infant's instinct for survival and consequent need to be protected. Attachment between infant and mother ensures that the infant will be adequately nurtured and protected from attack or, in the case of human infants, from a harsh environment. The infant is innately programmed to emit stimuli (smiling, clinging, and so on) to which the mother responds. This exchange between infant and mother creates a bond of attachment. The infant initiates the attachment process, but later the mother's behavior is what strengthens the bond.

Bowlby hypothesized that attachment advances through four stages: preattachment, attachment in the making, clear-cut attachment, and goal-corrected attachment. This process begins in the first month of life, with the infant's ability to discriminate the mother's voice. Attachment becomes fully developed during the second year of life, when the mother and toddler develop a partnership. During this later phase of attachment, the child is able to manipulate the mother into desired outcomes, but the child also has the capacity to understand the mother's point of view. The mother and the child reach a mutually acceptable compromise.

Bowlby contends that infants can demonstrate attachment behavior to others; however, attachment to the mother occurs earlier than attachment to others and is stronger and more consistent. It is thought that the earliest attachment becomes the child's **working model** for subsequent relationships (Bowlby, 1982).

Attachment explains the child's anxiety when the parents leave. However, children eventually learn to cope with separation. Toddlers often make use of **transitional objects,** or comfort objects, to help them cope with separations from parents and to handle other stressful situations. During such times, they may cuddle with a blanket, teddy bear, or other stuffed animal. The transitional object is seen as a symbol of the relationship with the caregiver, but toddlers also see it as having magic powers to soothe and protect them (Davies, 2004).

Ainsworth's Theory of Attachment

One of the most widely used methods to investigate infant attachment, known as the strange situation procedure, was developed by Ainsworth and colleagues (Ainsworth et al., 1978). The Ainsworth group believed that the level of infant attachment to the mother could be assessed through the infant's response to a series of "strange" episodes. Basically, the child is exposed over a period of 25 minutes to eight constructed episodes involving separation and reunion with the mother. The type of child attachment to the mother is measured by how the child responds to the mother following the "distressing" separation.

Ainsworth and her colleagues identified three types of attachment:

1. *Secure attachment.* The child uses the mother as a home base and feels comfortable leaving this base to explore the playroom. The child returns to the mother every so often to ensure that she is still present. When the mother leaves the room (act of separation), the securely attached child will cry and seek comfort from the mother when she returns. But this child is easily reassured and soothed by the mother's return.

2. *Anxious attachment.* The child is reluctant to explore the playroom and clings to the mother. When the mother leaves the room, the child cries for a long time. When the mother returns, this child seeks solace from the mother but continues to cry and may swat at or pull away from the mother. Ainsworth and colleagues described these infants as somewhat insecure and doubted that their mothers would ever be able to provide the security and safety they need.

3. *Avoidant attachment.* Some infants seem indifferent to the presence of their mother. Whether the mother is present or absent from the room, these children's responses are the same.

More recent scholars have added a fourth response, known as the *insecure disorganized/disoriented* response (Belsky, Campbell, Cohn, & Moore, 1996; Main & Hesse, 1990). These children display contradictory behavior: They attempt physical closeness, but retreat with acts of avoidance. These infants often have mothers who are depressed, have a history of being abused, or continue to struggle with a traumatic experience in their own lives. Observations of mothers of infants with disorganized attachment style reveal two patterns of parenting. Some mothers are negative and intrusive and frighten their babies with intense bursts of hostility. Other mothers are passive or helpless; they rarely comfort their babies and may actually appear afraid of their babies (Lyons-Ruth, Lyubchik, Wolfe, & Bronfman, 2002). As a result, the infants become confused in the "strange" situation. They fear the unknown figure and seek solace from the mother, but retreat because they are also fearful of the mother. Some authors have suggested that the behavior associated with the disorganized style is actually an adaptive response to harsh caregiving (Stovall & Dozier, 1998). However, research suggests a link between disorganized attachment and serious mental health problems in later childhood and beyond (Lyons-Ruth et al.; Fonagy, 2003).

According to Ainsworth's attachment theory, children whose mothers are consistently present and responsive to their needs and whose mothers exhibit a warm, caring relationship develop an appropriate attachment. Findings from studies indicate that this is true, even when there are negative family issues such as alcoholism by the father (Edwards, Eiden, & Leonard, 2006). However, the implication is that only mother-infant attachment exists or is relevant to healthy infant development. This assumption probably seemed unquestionable when these theories were constructed. Today, however, many fathers have prominent, equal, and/or primary responsibilities in childrearing and child care, sometimes by choice, and other times because of necessity. Sarah Johnson's dad for example became the primary caretaker for Sarah out of necessity. The gender of the parent is irrelevant in the development of secure infant attachment. Rather, it is the behavior of the primary caregiver, regardless of whether it is mother or father, which has the most influence on infant attachment (Geiger, 1996). When fathers who are the primary caregivers are able to provide infants with the warmth and affection they need, the infants develop secure attachments to their fathers. In fact, under stress, the fathers become a greater source of comfort to their infants than the mothers who are the secondary caregivers (Geiger). Perhaps the best scenario is when infants develop secure attachments to both parents. In one study, infants with secure attachments to both parents demonstrated less behavioral difficulties as toddlers, even less problems than toddlers with only secure mother infant attachment (Volling, Blandon, & Kolak, 2006).

In addition to a more prominent role by fathers over the past 20 to 30 years, more women have entered the workforce, and many more children experience alternative forms of child care, including day care. The effect day care has on the development of attachment in young children continues to be a hotly debated topic. Some argue that day care has a negative effect on infant attachment and increases the risk of the infant's developing insecure and avoidant forms of attachment (see, e.g., Belsky, 1987; Belsky & Braungart, 1991). The risks are thought to be especially high if the infant attends day care during the first year of life. Others argue that day care does not have a negative effect on infant and early childhood attachment (Griffith, 1996; Shonkoff & Phillips, 2000). A study in the Netherlands found that professional caregivers may be alternative attachment figures for children when their parents are not available, but it is the professional caregivers' group-related sensitivity, rather than the child's individual relationship with one professional caregiver, that promotes a sense of security and safety in children. Girls were found to be more securely attached to their professional caregivers than boys, however (De Schipper, Tavecchio, & Van IJzendoorn, 2008). In one study in the United States, day care was found to mitigate the adverse effects of insecure mother-infant attachment (Spieker, Nelson, & Petras, 2003).

The question of how day care attendance affects attachment is probably not as simplistic as either side contends. Many factors appear to be associated with the development of attachment for children in day care. The overriding factor is the quality of the relationship between the infant and parents, regardless of the child's care arrangements. For example, mothers who have a positive attitude toward their infant, are emotionally available to their infant, and encourage age-appropriate levels of independence produce infants with secure attachment (Clarke-Stewart, 1988; Shonkoff & Phillips, 2000). Also, infants whose parents have a stable and loving marriage and whose father is significantly involved in their nurturing and care tend to develop secure attachment, even if they spend a significant portion of the day in child care (Schachere, 1990).

Recently, researchers have begun to study attachment among children in foster care. More than a half million children are in foster care in the United States (Children's Defense Fund, 2000). Most of these children come into foster care without secure attachments. Once in foster care, many children are subjected to frequent changes in their foster homes (Smith, Stormshak, Chamberlain, & Whaley, 2001). Problems with attachment may contribute to foster home disruptions, but foster home disruptions also contribute to attachment problems. Others conclude that institutional care can also have the same devastating effects on attachment (Johnson, Browne, & Hamilton-Giachritsis, 2006). Regardless, the child welfare system has historically paid too little attention to issues of attachment.

Let's look at one other issue concerning attachment. The manner in which infant attachment is measured raises some concerns. Most studies of attachment have used the Ainsworth group's strange situation method. However, this measure may not yield valid results with some groups or under certain conditions. For example, the avoidant pattern of attachment some investigators have noted among children in day care may not indicate lack of attachment, as some have concluded (Clarke-Stewart, 1989). These children may be securely attached but seem indifferent to the exit and return of the mother simply because they have become accustomed to routine separations and reunions with their mother.

The appropriateness of using the strange situation method with certain ethnic groups has also been questioned. In many parts of Asia, Africa, and South America, infants sleep with their parents and are carried on their mother's back or side throughout the day, and how well these infants tolerate separation from the mother may not be a good measure of their emotional health (Greenfield, Keller, Fuligni, & Maynard, 2003). One researcher found that Japanese mothers leave their babies in the care of others an average of 2.2 times in a given month, and only in the care of an immediate family relative such as the father or grandmother. They also keep their infants in close proximity; they often sleep in the same room and infants are carried on the mother's back (Takahashi, 1990). As a result, Japanese infants tend to be highly anxious when their mothers leave the room. The response to the mother leaving is so intense that these infants are not easily comforted when the mother returns. Some might label the response by these infants as a sign of insecure attachment, although the response is consistent with the environment they have experienced. Quite likely, the infants in fact have a secure and appropriate attachment to their mother (Takahashi).

> In what other ways does culture affect infant and toddler development?

Conversely, in many cultures, infants are cared for by a collective of mothers, older siblings, cousins, fathers, aunts, uncles, and grandparents. The level of sense of security in these infants depends on coordinated care of a number of caregivers. The strange situation does not capture the fluid nature of caregiving and the degree to which it supports infants' feelings of security and safety (Lewis, 2005). One study found that in Israeli kibbutz-reared children, one negative caregiving relationship could negatively affect other attachment relationships (Sagi, Koren-Karie, Gini, Ziv, & Joels, 2002). In spite of these concerns, findings from a large number of studies using the strange situation in Europe, Africa, Asia, and the Middle East as well as North America indicate that the attachment patterns identified by Ainsworth occur in many cultures (Gardiner & Kosmitzki, 2008). It is important to remember that attachment theory was developed by Euro-American theorists who conceptualized attachment as the basis for developing subsequent independence. However, in more collectivist cultures, attachment is seen as the basis for developing obedience and harmony (Weisner, 2005).

Attachment and Brain Development

Attachment directly affects brain development (Gerhardt, 2004; Perry, 2002a; Zigler et al., 2002). Gerhardt concludes that without emotional bonding with an adult, the orbitofrontal cortex in the brain of infants (the part of the brain that allows social relationships to develop) cannot develop well. During the first year of life, the infant must develop the capacity to tolerate higher and higher levels of emotional arousal. The caregiver helps the infant with this by managing the amount of stimulation that the infant receives. As the right orbitofrontal cortex develops, the infant is able to tolerate higher levels of arousal and stimulation. However, when the caregiver is not attuned to the needs of the infant in regards to managing stimulation during the first year of life, negative emotions result and growth of the right orbitofrontal cortex is inhibited (Farmer, 2009). This process has been called the social brain. Supporters of this perspective cite several studies to support these conclusions, including a recent investigation of infants reared in orphanages in Romania conducted by Chugani et al. (2001). The infants had little contact with an adult, were left in their cots for most of the day, fed with propped-up bottles, and were never smiled at or hugged. Research with these infants found that their brain development was severely impaired.

One question of concern is whether these deficiencies in brain development are permanent. Some suggest that the brain impairments can be reversed if changes in care and attachment occur early enough (Zigler et al., 2002). They highlight the strides in brain development made by the Romanian orphans who were adopted into caring homes before they were 6 months of age. Perhaps Sarah Johnson's improvement was the result of early intervention and moving her quickly to live with her dad. Others suggest that the brain impairments caused by lack of attachment with a primary caregiver are permanent (Perry, 2002a). Regardless, the implication is that future brain growth is seriously jeopardized if brain development is not adequately nurtured in the first 2 to 3 years. We have clear evidence that the human brain is plastic and changes over time with new experiences, but we also know that it is not completely plastic; brain vulnerabilities in early childhood predispose one to difficulties in managing social relationships, and social relationship problems affect ongoing brain development (Farmer, 2009). Gerhardt concludes that the best advice we can offer parents of newborns is to forget about holding flashcards in front of the baby, but, instead, hold and cuddle the infants and simply enjoy them.

The Role of Play

Historically, play was thought to be insignificant to development, especially for infants and toddlers. However, we now know that play allows infants and toddlers to enhance motor, cognitive, emotional, and social development.

Because of their differences in development in all areas, infants and toddlers play in different ways. Exhibit 3.9 describes four types of infant play and three types of play observed in very young children. These later types of play begin in toddlerhood and develop in union with cognitive and motor development. For example, young toddlers will play with a mound of clay by hitting and perhaps squishing it. More developed toddlers will mold the clay into a ball, and older toddlers will try to roll or throw the molded ball.

One zealous mother describes joining the "toy of the month club" in which she received developmental toys through the mail each month for the first 2 years of her child's life. This mother wanted to be sure that her child had every opportunity to advance in terms of motor and cognitive skills. Although this mother's efforts are to be applauded, she admits that these toys were very costly and that perhaps she could have achieved the same outcome with other less costly objects. For example, there is no evidence that a store-bought infant mobile is any more effective

	Types of Infant Play
Vocal play	Playful vocalizing with grunts, squeals, trills, vowels, and so on to experiment with sound and have fun with it
Interactive play	Initiating interactions with caregivers (at about 4–5 months), by smiling and vocalizing, to communicate and make connection
Exploratory play with objects	Exploring objects with eyes, mouth, and hands to learn about their shape, color, texture, movement, and sounds and to experience pleasure
Baby games	Participating in parent-initiated ritualized, repetitive games, such as peek-a-boo, that contain humor, suspense, and excitement and build an emotional bond
	Types of Toddler Play
Functional play	Engaging in simple, repetitive motor movements
Constructive play	Creating and constructing objects
Make-believe play	Acting out everyday functions and tasks and playing with an imaginary friend

▲ **Exhibit 3.9**   Types of Play in Infancy and Toddlerhood

SOURCES: Types of Infant Play based on Davies, 2004; Types of Toddler Play based on Rubin, Fein, & Vandenberg, 1983.

than a homemade paper one hung on a clothes hanger. The objective is to provide stimulation and opportunities for play. Fergus Hughes (2010, p. 68) makes the following suggestions about the appropriate toys for infants and toddlers during the first two years of life:

- Birth to 3 months: toys for sensory stimulation, such as rattles, bells, colorful pictures and wallpaper, crib ornaments, mobiles, music boxes, and other musical toys

- 3–6 months: toys for grasping, squeezing, feeling, and mouthing, such as cloth balls, soft blocks, and teething toys

- 6–12 months: colorful picture books, stacking toys, nesting toys, sponges for water play, mirrors, toy telephones, toys that react to the child's activity

- 12–18 months: push toys; pull toys; balls; plain and interlocking blocks; simple puzzles with large, easy-to-handle pieces; stacking toys; riding toys with wheels close to the ground

- 18–24 months: toys for the sandbox and water play; spoons, shovels, and pails; storybooks; blocks; dolls; stuffed animals, and puppets

Another important aspect of play is parent/child interaction. Parent/infant play may increase the likelihood of secure attachment between the parent and child (Davies, 2004; Hughes, 2010; Scarlett, Naudeau, Salonius-Pasternak, & Ponte, 2005). The act of play at least provides the opportunity for infants and parents to feel good about themselves by enjoying each other and by being enjoyed. Even before infants can speak or understand language spoken to them, play provides a mechanism of communication between the parent and infants. Infants receive messages about themselves through play, which promotes their sense of self (Scarlett et al.).

Many similarities exist in the way that mothers and fathers play with infants and toddlers, but also some differences. Both mothers and fathers are teachers and sensitive communicators, and both enjoy rough and tumble play with their babies (Roggman, Boyce, Cook, Christiansen, & Jones, 2004). But research has also noted some differences in the ways that mothers and fathers play with infants and toddlers. Fathers engage in more rough and tumble play; they are more likely to lift their babies, bounce them, and move their legs and arms. Mothers are more likely to offer toys, play conventional games of peek-a-boo and pat-a-cake, and engage in constructive play. However, mothers have been found to play differently with infant sons than with infant daughters, engaging in more conversation with daughters and making more statements about the baby's feelings when talking with daughters; conversely, they engage in more direction with sons and make more comments to call the baby's attention to his surroundings (Clearfield & Nelson, 2006). Mothers have also been found to be more likely to follow the child's lead, while fathers are more likely to steer play activity according to their preferences. It is important to note, however, that these mother/father differences have not been found in Sweden and Israel, both societies with more egalitarian gender roles than found in the United States (Hughes, 2010).

Play also is a vehicle for developing peer relations. A few decades ago, it was thought that babies really weren't interested in each other and could not form relationships with each other. Recent research challenges this view (Hughes, 2010; Shonkoff & Phillips, 2000). The peer group becomes more important at earlier ages as family size decreases and siblings are no longer available for daily social interaction. Researchers have found that very young infants, as young as 2 months after birth, get excited by the sight of other infants; by 6 to 9 months, infants appear to try to get the attention of other infants; and by 9 to 12 months infants imitate each other (Hughes). Although toddlers are capable of establishing relationships, their social play is a struggle, and a toddler play session is quite a fragile experience. Toddlers need help in structuring their play with each other. And yet, researchers have found that groups of toddlers in preschool settings develop play routines that they return to again and again over periods of months (Corsaro, 2005). These toddler play routines are primarily nonverbal, with a set of ritualized actions. For example, Corsaro notes a play routine in one Italian preschool in which a group of toddlers would rearrange the chairs in the room and work together to move them around in patterns. They returned to this routine fairly regularly over the course of a year, modifying it slightly over time. Peer relations are being built by "doing things together."

Developmental Disruptions

Providing interventions to infants and toddlers with disabilities is mandated by the Developmental Disabilities Assistance and Bill of Rights Act. However, accurately assessing **developmental delays** in young children is difficult (Zipper & Simeonsson, 2004). One reason is that although we have loose guidelines for healthy development in infants and toddlers, development varies by individual child. Young children walk, master potty training, and develop language skills on different time tables. It is therefore difficult to assess whether a particular child has a case of delayed development—and if so, which faculties are delayed. Premature infants like Holly Hicks, for example, often need time to catch up in terms of physical, cognitive, and emotional development. At what point does Holly's social worker decide that she is not developing fast enough, and label her developmentally delayed?

The other reason that accurate assessment of developmental difficulties in infants and toddlers is hard is that although many physical and cognitive disabilities have been found to be genetic and others to be associated with environmental factors, the cause of most disabilities is unknown. Anticipating what the risk factors might be for a particular child and how they might influence developmental delays is therefore difficult. Assessment should be multidimensional, including the child, the family, and the broader environment (Zipper & Simeonsson, 2004).

Autism Spectrum Disorders (also known as ASDs; pervasive developmental disorders, PDDs; or autism), for example, are a group of developmental disorders in which the main features are pervasive impairment in the nature and quality of social and communication development and the presence of restricted and repetitive behaviors (specific criteria are described in the *Diagnostic and Statistical Manual of Mental Disorders: DSM-IV-TR* and presented in the next chapter of this book). However, autism is often difficult to detect because children with the disorder exhibit a wide range of symptoms. Crane and Winsler (2008) observe for example that some children with autism are very verbal and interactive with family and friends but exhibit peculiar repetitive behaviors while other children with the disorder never develop verbal skills, prefer social isolation, and have moderate to severe mental retardation.

Usually autism is not diagnosed until age 3 or 4, but results from recent research indicate that signs of autism are detectable at birth and increase throughout the first two years of life. For example, results from retrospective interviews of parents with children diagnosed with autism indicate the presence of symptoms within the first 2 years of life (Wimpory, Hobson, Williams & Nash, 2000). In another study, infants between ages 8 to 10 months diagnosed with autism were unable to orient when their name was called and were less likely to look at another person while smiling (Werner, Dawson, Osterling & Dinno, 2000). From their research, Wetherby et al. (2004) identify the following additional warning signs of autism in children at age 2: a delay in verbal skills; lack of response to instructions; delay in using conventional toys in play; display of repetitive movements; and delay in social behaviors such as eye contact, sharing affect, pointing, and facial expression.

Because early detection and diagnosis is associated with improved outcomes for infants and toddlers with developmental delays in general (Shonkoff, Hauser-Cram, Krauss, & Upshur, 1992) the Centers for Disease Control and Prevention (CDC) recommends screening for all types of developmental delays and disabilities at 9, 18, and 24 or 30 months of age, and the CDC along with the American Academy of Pediatrics recommends the universal screening for autism specifically at 18 and 24 months of age (CDC, 2009e). Interventions for autism include behavior modification techniques, interventions to improve communication skills, dietary approaches, and use of medications.

Critical Thinking Questions 3.1

Revisit Exhibit 3.1 that lays out the components of the developmental niche. What do we know about the developmental niches involved in the three case studies at the beginning of the chapter, Holly, Sarah, and Henry? What strengths do you see in each of these developmental niches? What potential problems do you see?

CHILD CARE ARRANGEMENTS IN INFANCY AND TODDLERHOOD

Human infants start life in a remarkably dependent state, in need of constant care and protection. On their own, they would die. Toddlers are full of life and are making great strides in development in all areas, but they are also "not ready to set out for life alone in the big city" (Newman & Newman, 2009, p. 187). Societal health is dependent on finding good solutions to the question, who will care for infants and toddlers?

With large numbers of mothers of infants and toddlers in the paid workforce and not at home, this question becomes a challenging one. The United States seems to be responding to this challenge more reluctantly than other highly industrialized countries are. This difference becomes clear in comparative analysis of two solutions for early child care: family leave and paid child care.

Family Leave

> What impact might this trend have over time on the current cohort of infants and toddlers?

Because of changes in the economic institution in the United States between 1975 and 1999, the proportion of infants with mothers in paid employment increased from 24% to 54% (Shonkoff & Phillips, 2000). A similar trend is occurring around the world.

In response, most industrialized countries have instituted social policies that provide for job-protected leaves for parents to allow them to take off from work to care for their young children. Sweden was the first country to develop such a policy in 1974. The Swedish policy guaranteed paid leave.

By the early 1990s, the United States was the only industrialized country without a family leave policy (Kamerman, 1996). But in 1993, the U.S. Congress passed the Family and Medical Leave Act (FMLA) of 1993 (PL 103–3). FMLA requires businesses with 50 or more employees to provide up to 12 weeks of unpaid, job-protected leave during a 12-month period for workers to manage childbirth, adoption, or personal or family illness. Eligible workers are entitled to continued health insurance coverage during the leave period, if such coverage is a part of their compensation package.

Exhibit 3.10 highlights the family leave policies in selected countries. In 2002, the United States and Australia were the only affluent countries of the world that did not offer some paid parental leave at the time of birth and adoption. Australia does, however, provide families with a universal, flat rate maternity grant of $5,000 for each new child to assist with the costs of birth or adoption (Australian Government: Department of Family and Community Services: Office for Women, 2006). European countries also provide birth or maternity grants and family allowances. This is an area for social work advocacy in the United States.

Paid Child Care

Historically in the United States, mothers were expected to provide full-time care for infants and toddlers at home. If mothers were not available, it was expected that children would be cared for by domestic help or a close relative but still in their home setting (Kamerman & Kahn, 1995). Even in the 1960s, with the development of Head Start programs, the focus was on preschool age children; infants and toddlers were still expected to be cared for at home (Kamerman & Kahn, 1995). Thus, historically there was very little provision of alternative child care for most children below school age.

This phenomenon has changed dramatically, however, over the last 30 years. In 1999, about 61% of women in the United States with children age 6 and under worked outside the home, and 54% with children age 1 year and younger worked outside the home (Shonkoff & Phillips, 2000). Therefore, alternative child care has become a necessity in the United States. In 2005, 74% of U.S. children under the age of 6 were involved in some type of nonparental care (Newman & Newman, 2009).

Many advocates for day care refer to the European model as an ideal for the United States. Countries in Europe provide "universal" child care for all children, regardless of the parents' income, employment status, race, age, and so forth. These programs are supported through national policy and funded through public funds. If they pay at all, parents pay no more than a quarter of the monies needed. Parents in Europe thus pay far less than parents in the United States typically pay.

Currently, there are some innovative programs in Europe in which the focus is on providing alternative group care for toddlers in group settings outside the home (Kamerman & Kahn, 1995). The thought is that the cognitive and social skills of children age 2 and older can be enhanced in a group setting. This care is also funded and regulated through public funds. Workers who provide this care are well trained in child development and are paid well (by United States' standards) for their services. Most important, this care is available to all families and children.

As suggested earlier, there are controversies about whether child day care centers are harmful to infants and toddlers, but there is growing consensus that day care in general is not harmful to infants and toddlers (Shonkoff & Phillips, 2000). The primary concern is the quality of the day care provided. Researchers conclude that quality day care

Country	Duration of Leave	Percentage of Wage Replaced
Afganistán	3 months	100%
Australia	1 year	Unpaid
Belgium	15 weeks	75%–80%
Canada	1 year	55%
Denmark	1 year	60%
Greece	2 weeks' paternity	60%
Italy	16 weeks	50%
Mexico	5 months	80%
Norway	12 weeks	100%
Peru	52 weeks (or 42 weeks at 100%)	80%
Sweden	First 3 months	100%
	Subsequent 1 year	80%
United States	12 weeks	Unpaid

▲ **Exhibit 3.10**   Family Leave Policies in Selected Countries, 1999–2002

SOURCE: Based on Clearinghouse on International Developments in Child, Youth and Family Policies at Columbia University, 2002.

can even enhance cognitive development among 9-month-old infants (Schuetze, Lewis, & DiMartino, 1999). The National Research Council (1990) has identified three factors essential to quality day care, described in Exhibit 3.11. The Canadian Council on Learning (2006) suggests that a staff/child ratio of 1:6 qualifies as quality child care among children 2 and 3 years old (compared with 1:4 specified by the National Research Council). They also propose that quality group child care must include well-defined spaces, well-planned curriculum, and significant parental involvement.

Staff/child ratio	1:3 for infants, 1:4 for toddlers, and 1:8 for preschoolers
Group size	No larger than 6 for infants, 8 for toddlers, and 16 for preschoolers
Staff training	On child development and age-appropriate child care

▲ **Exhibit 3.11**   Identified Factors of Quality Day Care

SOURCE: National Research Council, 1990.

INFANTS AND TODDLERS IN THE MULTIGENERATIONAL FAMILY

Maria, a new mom, describes the first visit her mother and father made to her home after the birth of Maria's new infant. "Mom and Dad walked right past me as if I was not there, even though we had not seen each other for 6 months. I quickly realized that my status as their 'princess' was now replaced with a new little princess. During their visit, my husband and I had to fight to see our own child. When she cried, they immediately ran to her. And my mother criticized everything I did—she didn't like the

> What have you observed about how family relationships change when a baby is born?

brand of diapers I used, she thought the color of the room was too dreary for an infant—and she even scolded my husband at one point for waking the baby when he went to check on her. I appreciated their visit, but I must admit that I was glad when it was time for them to leave." Maria's description is not unique. The involvement of grandparents and other extended family members in the care of infants and toddlers may be experienced either as a great source of support or as interference and intrusion (and sometimes as a little of each). And, of course, cultures of the world have different norms about who is involved, and in what ways, in the care of infants and toddlers.

Yet, the specific roles of grandparents and other extended family members is rarely discussed within the family, which is why conflicts often occur (Hines, Preto, McGoldrick, Almeida, & Weltman, 2005). When these roles are clearly articulated and agreed upon, extended family members can provide support that enhances infant and toddler development (Hines et al.). Family involvement as a form of social support is further discussed as a "protective factor" later in this chapter.

The birth of a child, especially of a first child, brings about a major transition not only for parents but also for the entire kin network. Partners become parents; sons and daughters become fathers and mothers; fathers and mothers become grandfathers and grandmothers; and brothers and sisters become aunts and uncles. The social status of the extended family serves as the basis of the social status of the child, and the values and beliefs of the extended family will shape the way they care for and socialize the child (Carter & McGoldrick, 2005b; Newman & Newman, 2009). In addition, many children's names and child-rearing rituals, decisions, and behaviors are passed from past generations to the next.

To illustrate this point, there is an old joke about a mother who prepared a roast beef for most Sunday family dinners. She would always cut the roast in half and place it in two pans before cooking it in the oven. Observing this behavior, her young daughter asked her why she cut the roast in half. After some thought she told her daughter that she did not know for sure; she remembered that her mother had always cut her roast in half. Later the mother asked her mother why she had cut her roast in half before cooking it. The senior mother explained that she did not have a pan large enough for the size roast she needed to feed her family. Thus, she would cut the roast in half in order to fit it into the two pans that she did own.

Similar behavior affects decisions regarding infants and toddlers. One mother reports giving her infant daughter herb tea in addition to an ointment provided by her physician for a skin rash. It seems that this skin rash was common among infant girls in each generation in this family. A specific herb tea was traditionally used to treat the rash. This mother confesses that she did not tell her mother or grandmother that she used the ointment prescribed by her doctor. It is interesting for us to note that although the mother did not have complete faith in the tea, she also did not have complete faith in the ointment. The mother states that she is not sure which one actually cured the rash. Violation of family and cultural rituals and norms can be a source of conflict between new parents and other family members (Hines et al., 1999). For example, differences of opinion about baptism, male circumcision, and even child care arrangements can create family disharmony. One decision that often involves the multigenerational family is the decision whether to breastfeed or bottle feed the infant.

The Breastfeeding Versus Bottle Feeding Decision

Throughout history, most infants have been breastfed. However, alternatives to breastfeeding by the mother have always existed, sometimes in the form of a wet nurse (a woman employed to breastfeed someone else's infant) or in the form of animal milks. Following World War II, breastfeeding ceased to be the primary nutritional source for infants because of the promotion of manufactured formula in industrialized and nonindustrialized countries. Since the 1980s, cultural attitudes have shifted again in favor of breastfeeding. However, in the United States, only 39% of infants are breastfed at 6 months, 40% less than the Healthy People 2010 goal (CDC, 2006a). Employer support, including on-site day care centers, is needed to expand breastfeeding among working mothers, especially for women at risk of discontinuing breastfeeding early (Pascoe, Pletta, Beasley, & Schellpfeffer, 2002). It is important to note that in many impoverished countries, it is hazardous to use formula because of the lack of access to a safe water supply for mixing with the formula.

In European American and Mexican American families, the mother often seeks the opinion of the baby's father and maternal and paternal grandparents, whereas in African American families, the maternal grandmother and peers tend to be most influential in the decision to breastfeed (Baranowski, 1983). Korean mothers-in-law care for the new mother and are a powerful influence in choices about breastfeeding. In Saudi Arabia, a woman may breastfeed her infant openly and receive no notice, although otherwise she is fully veiled. In France, topless swimming is culturally acceptable, but breastfeeding in public is not (Riordan & Auerbach, 1999).

Most women decide to nurse primarily for infant health benefits. One benefit is increased immunity—which begins in the third trimester of pregnancy—to viruses such as mumps, chicken pox, and influenza (Jackson & Nazar, 2006). Breastfeeding has also been demonstrated to decrease the risk of obesity during childhood and adolescence, especially if infants are exclusively breastfed for 6 months (Weyermann, Beermann, Brenner, & Rothenbacher, 2006). Contraindications to breastfeeding are few, but they include maternal medical conditions such as untreated tuberculosis, leukemia, breast cancer diagnosed during lactation, drug abuse, and sexually transmitted diseases (Dickason, Silverman, & Kaplan, 1998). Mothers who are positive for HIV are often advised to avoid breastfeeding because breastfeeding is a risk factor for mother-to-infant transmission (Mbori-Ngacha et al., 2001). However, in poor countries the contaminated water supply may pose more risk than breastfeeding (Piwoz, Ross, & Humphrey, 2004).

Postpartum Depression

Family dynamics are often altered when mothers are depressed following childbirth. There is evidence that, around the world, between 10% and 15% of mothers will have postpartum depression in the first year of the infant's life (Posmontier & Horowitz, 2004; Wisner, Chambers, & Sit, 2006). Although social factors no doubt contribute to postpartum depression, it is generally accepted that the precipitous hormonal changes at birth, to which some women seem especially sensitive, play a large role. Postpartum depression often goes undiagnosed and untreated across cultural groups (Dennis & Chung-Lee, 2006), but it is more likely to receive attention in societies that have regular postpartum visits from midwives or nurses. For example, in the United Kingdom, new parents receive seven visits from midwives in the first two weeks' postpartum (Posmontier & Horowitz). Postpartum depression can be very disruptive to the early mother-infant relationship and, as discussed below, increases risk of impaired cognitive, emotional, and motor development (Wisner et al.). Both social support and pharmacological interventions have been found to be helpful (Sword, Watt, & Krueger, 2006). Different cultures have different expectations for maternal adaptation, and it is important for health providers to recognize these cultural influences (Posmontier & Horowitz).

Very little research exists on psychosocial and mental health issues for new fathers, but the Australian First Time Fathers Study has attempted to address this gap in knowledge (Condon, 2006). This study finds no evidence of male postnatal depression, but it does find that male partners of women with postpartum depression are at risk of depression, anxiety, and abusing alcohol. At first, most men are confused by their wives' depression, but supportive. If the depression lasts for months, which it often does, support is usually gradually withdrawn. Men report that they find their wives' irritability and lack of physical affection more troubling than the sadness and tearfulness. This study also found that male partners and other family members of depressed mothers often take on more and more of the care of the infant over time, which reinforces the mother's sense of incompetence. Communication breakdowns are very common in these situations.

Critical Thinking Questions 3.2

Why do you think that the United States was slower than other advanced industrial countries to develop family leave policies? Why do you think the United States' policy does not include paid family leave as is the case in almost all other advanced industrial societies? Do you think the United States should have "universal" child care for all children, regardless of parents' income, as they do in Europe? Why or why not?

RISKS TO HEALTHY INFANT AND TODDLER DEVELOPMENT

Unfortunately, not all infants and toddlers get the start they need in life. Millions of infants and toddlers around the world are impoverished, abandoned, neglected, and endangered. Collectively, the adults of the world have not ensured that every child has the opportunity for a good start in life. Not only do these adversities have consequences to the infant's or toddler's immediate development, research indicates that adversities experienced in childhood can have negative consequences throughout the individual's life span. In a large, well-known study referred to as the adverse childhood experience (ACE), study investigators examined the consequences of adverse childhood experiences, including abuse, family violence, and parental substance abuse, mental illness, or imprisonment on the infant's later adult physical and mental health outcomes (Felitti et al., 1998). Not only did they find a relationship between the two, they concluded that exposure to adversities during childhood, especially abuse and household dysfunction, increased the likelihood of developing a potentially fatal disease in adulthood. You have probably already surmised what some of the environmental factors are that inhibit healthy growth and development in infants and toddlers. This section addresses a few of those factors that social workers are especially likely to encounter: poverty, inadequate caregiving, and child abuse.

Poverty

Examining the social science evidence about the effects of family life on physical and mental health, Repetti, Taylor, and Seeman (2002, p. 359) made the following observation "The adverse effects of low SES [socioeconomic status] on mental and physical health outcomes are as close to a universal truth as social science has offered." When a family is impoverished, the youngest are the most vulnerable, and, indeed, children birth to age 3 have the highest rates of impoverishment around the world (UNICEF, 2005). Bellamy (2004) reports that 1 billion children across the world live in poverty, representing 1 in 2 children. Although children living in the poorest countries are much more likely than children living in wealthy countries to be poor (UNICEF, 2005), the proportion of children living in poverty in 17 of the 24 wealthiest nations has been rising (UNICEF Innocenti Research Centre, 2005). Using a relative measure of poverty as income below 50% of the national median income, the UNICEF researchers found that the percent of children living in poverty in 26 industrialized countries ranged from 2.4% in Denmark to 27.7% in Mexico. The United States had the second highest rate, 21.9%. All of the Scandinavian countries had child poverty rates less than 5%. Most European countries had rates between 5% and 10%.

> In what ways does social class affect the development of infants and toddlers?

In the United States, the National Center for Children in Poverty (NCCP) (Wight, Chau, & Aratani, 2010) estimates that families need an income about two times the U.S. federal poverty level to meet basic needs, and they refer to families below this level as low income. NCCP (2008) reports that of the more than 12 million infants and toddlers in the United States, 5.4 million (43%) live in low-income families, and 2.7 million (21%) live in families below the poverty level. There are racial and ethnic differences in the rates: 65% of Native American infants and toddlers live in low-income families, compared with 65% of Black infants and toddlers, 64% of Latino infants and toddlers, 27% of Asian infants and toddlers, and 30% of White infants and toddlers. Infants and toddlers with immigrant parents are more likely than infants and toddlers with native-born parents to live in low-income families, 61% compared with 40%. Geographical differences also exist in the rates of infants and toddlers in low-income families: 52% of infants and toddlers living in rural areas live in low-income families, compared with 49% of infants and toddlers in urban areas, and 35% of infants and toddlers in suburban areas. Half (49%) of infants and toddlers living in low-income families have at least one parent who works full-time, year-round.

Although some young children who live in poverty flourish, poverty presents considerable risks to children's growth and development. (That risk continues from infancy and toddlerhood into early and middle childhood, as Chapters 4 and 5 explain.) Children living in poverty often suffer the consequences of poor nutrition and inadequate health care. Many of these children do not receive proper immunizations, and many minor illnesses go untreated, increasing the potential for serious health problems. This phenomenon is particularly disturbing because many of these minor illnesses are easily treated. Most childhood ear infections, for example, are easily treated with antibiotics; left untreated, they can result in hearing loss.

In addition to inadequate health care and nutrition, children living in poverty often experience overcrowded living conditions. Overcrowding restricts opportunities for play, and thus, because most learning and development in young children takes place in the context of play, restricts healthy development. A study of development among 12-month-old Haitian American children found that the poorer children experienced more overcrowded conditions than those not living in poverty and consequently had less play time, fewer toys, a smaller number of safe areas to play, and less private time with parents (Widmayer, Peterson, & Larner, 1990). The living conditions of the children who were poor were associated with delayed motor development and lower cognitive functioning.

Negative associations between family poverty and children's cognitive development begin to emerge by the end of the second year of life. By age 2, poor toddlers score 4.4 points lower on IQ tests than nonpoor toddlers. In addition, poor infants and toddlers are more likely to demonstrate emotional and behavioral problems than nonpoor infants and toddlers. Three-year-olds who live in deep poverty have been found to display more internationalizing behavior symptoms, such as anxiety, withdrawal, and depression, than other children of the same age (Barajas, Philipsen, & Brooks-Gunn, 2008). Children are affected not only by the direct consequences of poverty but also by indirect factors such as family stress, parental depression, and inadequate or nonsupportive parenting (UNICEF, 2005). Irma Velasquez's depression and anxiety will affect her relationship with Henry. Poor children are also more likely to be exposed to environmental toxins (Song & Lu, 2002).

Most disturbing is the link between poverty and **infant mortality**—the death of a child before his or her first birthday. In general, infant mortality rates are the highest in the poorest countries (United Nations Development Program, 2005). Infant mortality rates in the United States are high compared with other industrialized nations (UNICEF, 2005), but Malaysia, a country with one quarter the average income of the United States, has achieved the same infant mortality rate as the United States (United Nations Development Program). Within the United States, mortality rates for infants are higher among the poor, and the rate among African Americans is twice that of European Americans (United Nations Development Program). As discussed in Chapter 2, low birth weight (LBW) as a result of inadequate prenatal care is the primary factor that contributes to the high infant mortality rate (United Nations Development Program).

Interestingly, the infant mortality rate for Hispanic women is lower than that of European American women (Hessol & Fuentes-Afflick, 2005), even though inadequate prenatal care is prominent among Hispanic women. This fact suggests that differences in prenatal care explain only part of the disparity in infant mortality rates. The mother's diet and social support network have been suggested as other factors that may affect birth weight and infant mortality rates (Gonzalez-Quintero et al., 2006; McGlade, Saha, & Dahlstrom, 2004). One comparative study found lower rates of alcohol and tobacco use among Hispanic women than among women of other racial/ethnic groups and the presence of stronger family, cultural, and social ties (McGlade et al.). These findings suggest that social support may offset the consequences of inadequate prenatal care.

Inadequate Caregiving

The most pervasive response to inadequate caregiving is nonorganic failure to thrive (NOFTT). This diagnosis is used to describe infants, usually between ages 3 to 12 months, who show poor development, primarily in terms of weight gain. These infants weigh less than 80% of the ideal weight for their age. The "nonorganic" feature refers to the lack of medical causes for the poor development, and is thought to be a consequence of environmental neglect (lack of food) and stimulus deprivation (Bassali & Benjamin, 2002). Overall, NOFTT is a consequence of the infant's basic needs going unmet, primarily the needs for feeding and nurturing.

A review of the literature identified several parental factors that appear to increase the likelihood of the development of NOFTT (Bassali & Benjamin, 2002; Marino, Weinman, & Soudelier, 2001). These include maternal depression, maternal malnutrition during pregnancy, marital problems between parents, and mental illness and/or substance abuse in the primary caretaker.

Parental mental illness and depression are associated with other problems among infants and toddlers as well. For example, infants of depressed mothers demonstrate less positive expressions of mood and personality and are less attentive in play (Gomez, 2001). Overall, they demonstrate less joy, even when they were securely attached to the mother. One analysis of the literature on parental mental illness and infant development concluded the following (Seifer & Dickstein, 2000):

- Parental mental illness increases the likelihood of mental health problems among their children.

- Mothers who are depressed are more negative in interaction with their infants.

- Similarly, infants with depressed mothers are more negative in their exchange with their mothers.

- There is an association between parental mental illness and insecure attachment between parents and infants.

- Depressed mothers view their infant's behavior as more negative than nondepressed mothers.

Child Maltreatment

National data indicate that in 2007, 794,000 children in the United States were assessed to be victims of abuse or neglect. (It is important to note that it is generally assumed that many abused and neglected children never come to the attention of government authorities.) The national data also indicate that 31.9% of all known victims of child maltreatment are younger than 4 years of age. Infants from birth to 1 year of age have the highest rate of victimization, 21.9 per 1,000 infants age birth to 1 year (U.S. Department of Health and Human Services, 2009a). For all age groups, 60% of confirmed cases of child maltreatment involved neglect, 10.8% involved physical abuse, 7.6% involved sexual abuse, and 4.2% involved psychological abuse.

How might child abuse or neglect experienced as an infant or toddler affect later development?

The effect of child maltreatment and other trauma on the brain during the first three years of life has been the subject of considerable study in recent years (see Rosemary Farmer's excellent discussion of this topic in Chapter 5 of her book *Neuroscience and Social Work Practice: The Missing Link*, 2009). Remember that neuroscientific research has clearly demonstrated that the brain is plastic throughout life, which means that it is shaped by experiences across the life course. Research indicates that several brain parts involved in responses to stress are especially disrupted and changed by traumatic events during the first three years of life. They include the brain parts that regulate homeostasis (brain stem and locus ceruleus), brain parts which form memory systems and are involved in emotion regulation (hippocampus, amygdala, and frontal cortex), and brain parts that regulate the executive functions of planning, working memory, and impulse control (orbito-frontal cortex, cingulate and dorsolateral prefrontal cortex). In addition, the major neuroendocrine stress response system, the hypothalamic-pituitary-adrenal (HPA) axis is also impacted by trauma. Research indicates that early life stress, such as child maltreatment, can lead to disruptions in HPA axis functioning and result in anxiety disorders and depression in adulthood (see Mello, Mello, Carpenter, & Price, 2003; Van Voorhees & Scarpa, 2004).

The child who experiences child maltreatment or other trauma at the ages of 2, 3, or 4 is at risk of developing memory problems, difficulty regulating emotions, and problems integrating sensory experiences. Research shows that people who experience childhood trauma are more likely to develop decreased volume in the hippocampus, a brain characteristic also found with adults experiencing posttraumatic stress disorder (PTSD). Injuries to the hippocampus have been found to be associated with cognitive impairments, memory deficits, poor coping responses, and dissociation (Farmer, 2009). When a child is exposed to extreme stress or trauma, the autonomic nervous system is activated, resulting in increased heart rate, respiration, and blood pressure. The child may freeze in place before beginning to fight. In the case of child sexual abuse, the child may dissociate, or detach from what is happening, becoming compliant and emotionally numb (Perry, 2002b).

As noted above, 60% of all confirmed cases of child maltreatment involve neglect. Child neglect is thought to occur when caregivers are ignorant of child development, overwhelmed by life stresses, or struggling with mental health or substance abuse problems. Children who experience neglect in the early years of life often do not thrive. Much of the early human research on child neglect focused on Romanian children who were placed in state-run institutions with few staff (staff-child ratio of 1:60) and very little sensory and emotional stimulation. At 3 years of age, these children were found to have delays in physical growth as well as in motor, cognitive, and language skills; they also had poor social skills. Preliminary research suggests that neglect leads to deficits in prefrontal cortex functioning (attention and social deficits) and executive functioning (planning, working memory, and impulse control). Working memory is key to learning. Early evidence suggests that these changes in brain functioning are related to difficulties managing emotions, problem solving, and social relationships. Most troubling is the finding that children who are neglected early in life have smaller brains than other children; they have fewer neurons and fewer connections between neurons. Exhibit 3.12 shows the brains of 3-year-old "normal" children alongside the brains of 3-year-old children who have faced extreme neglect.

An association has been found between infant temperament and abuse (Thomlison, 2004). Infants who have "difficult" temperament are more likely to be abused and neglected. Others suggest that the combination of difficult temperament and environmental stress interact (Thomlison). Similarly, infants and toddlers with mental, physical, or behavioral abnormalities are also at a higher risk for abuse (Guterman & Embry, 2004).

Social workers need to keep abreast of the developing neuroscience research on the effects of child maltreatment on brain development, but we must also remember to put the brain in context. We must advocate for policy that ensures that parents have the best available resources to provide the type of parenting that infants and toddlers need. We must also encourage research that examines how to heal the disrupted brain.

PROTECTIVE FACTORS IN INFANCY AND TODDLERHOOD

Many young children experience healthy growth and development despite the presence of risk factors. They are said to have resilience. Several factors have been identified as mediating between the risks children experience and their growth and development (Fraser, Kirby, & Smokowski, 2004; Werner, 2000). These factors are "protective" in the sense that they shield the child from the consequences of potential hazards (Fraser et al.). Following are some protective factors that help diminish the potential risks to infants and toddlers.

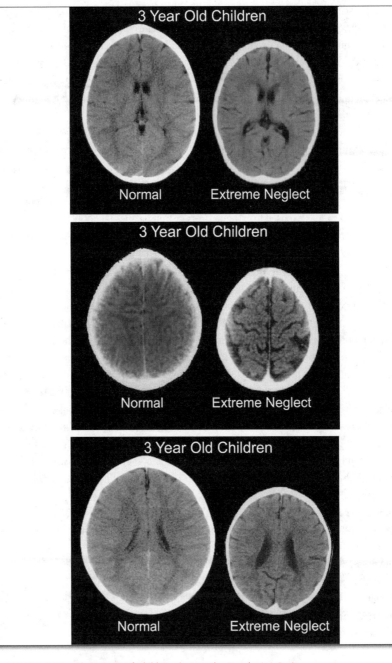

▲ **Exhibit 3.12**   The Impact of Child Neglect on the Developing Brain

SOURCE: Farmer, 2009.

Education

Research indicates that the education of the mother directly affects the outcome for infants and toddlers. This effect was found even in the devastating poverty that exists in Nicaragua (Pena & Wall, 2000). The infant mortality rate is predictably high in this country. However, investigators found that the higher the mother's level of formal education, the lower the infant mortality rate. Investigators hypothesize that mothers with higher levels of formal education provide better quality of care to their infants by feeding them more conscientiously, using available health care, keeping the household cleaner, and generally satisfying the overall needs of the infant. These mothers simply possessed better coping skills.

Similar results were found in a study of mothers and infants with two strikes against them—they were living in poverty and the infants were born premature (Bradley et al., 1994). Infants whose mothers had higher intellectual abilities demonstrated higher levels of cognitive and social development and were more likely to be in the normal range of physical development.

Social Support

Social support is often found in informal networks, such as friends and extended family members, or in formal support systems, such as the church, community agencies, day care centers, social workers, and other professions. The availability of social support seems to buffer many risk factors, such as stress experienced by parents (Werner & Smith, 2001). For example, Mrs. Hicks could truly benefit from having the opportunity to take a break from the stresses of caring for Holly. Both formal and informal social support can fill this gap for her. Even child abuse is reduced in the presence of positive social support networks (Coohey, 1996).

Extended family members often serve as alternative caregivers when parents cannot provide care because of physical or mental illness or job demands. Reliance on an extended family is particularly important in some cultural and socioeconomic groups. Sarah's dad, Chris Johnson, probably would not have been able to care for her without the support of his family. And, it is through the support of his family that he has been able to continue his education.

Easy Temperament

Infants with a positive temperament are less likely to be affected by risk factors (Fraser et al., 2004). The association between easy temperament and "protection" is both direct and indirect. Infants with a positive temperament may simply perceive their world more positively. Infants with a positive temperament may also induce more constructive and affirming responses from those in their environment.

National and State Policy

Many social workers and others advocate for better national and state policies that will enhance good health among infants and toddlers, build and support strong families, promote positive early learning experiences, and create systems that advance the development and well-being of infants and toddlers (Zero to Three, n.d.). This includes legislation and financial support to ensure things such as adequate health coverage for infants and toddlers, improved polices and programs that prevent child abuse, and development of programs and policies that promote parental and infant mental health. Also, continued support of national programs like the Women, Infants, & Children (WIC) program and the Child and Adult Care Food Program (CACFP) are considered crucial to promoting healthy physical development in infants and toddlers. Other advocates promote improving existing social and educational programs. Knitzer (2007) for example identifies what she wittingly refers to as legislation to improve the odds for young children. She suggests investing more federal and state financial resources to extend programs such as early head start to incorporate home visiting, center-based instruction, and family support for all low-income babies and toddlers through (instead of up to) age 3.

Critical Thinking Questions 3.3

Why do you think that researchers consistently find a negative association between family poverty and children's cognitive development? What biological, psychological, and social factors might be involved in that association? There is growing evidence that child maltreatment has a negative impact on brain development. What role can social workers play in informing the public about the impact of the environment on brain development?

IMPLICATIONS FOR SOCIAL WORK PRACTICE

In summary, knowledge about infants and toddlers has several implications for social work practice:

- Become well acquainted with theories and empirical research about growth and development among infants and toddlers.

- Assess infants and toddlers in the context of their environment, culture included.

- Promote continued use of formal and informal social support networks for parents with infants and toddlers.

- Continue to promote the elimination of poverty and the advancement of social justice.

- Advocate for compulsory health insurance and quality health care.

- Advocate for more affordable, quality child care.

- Collaborate with news media and other organizations to educate the public about the impact of poverty and inequality on early child development.

- Learn intervention methods to prevent and reduce substance abuse.

- Help parents understand the potential effects of inadequate caregiving on their infants, including the effects on brain development.

- Help parents and others understand the association between child development and consequential outcomes during adulthood.

- Provide support and appropriate intervention to parents to facilitate effective caregiving for infants and toddlers.

KEY TERMS

attachment	developmental niche	object permanence
blooming	formal operations stage	preoperational stage
brain plasticity	infant	pruning
cognition	infant mortality	reflex
concrete operations stage	motor skills	sensorimotor stage
developmental delays	neurons	sensory system

separation anxiety   synapses   transitional object
stranger anxiety   temperament   working model
symbolic functioning   toddler

1. Spend some time at a mall or other public place where parents and infants frequent. List behaviors that you observe that indicate attachment between the infant and caretaker. Note any evidence you observe that may indicate a lack of attachment.

2. Ask to tour a day care facility. Describe the things you observe that may have a positive influence on cognitive development for the infants and toddlers who are placed there. List those things that you think are missing from that setting that are needed to create a more stimulating environment.

3. Social support is considered to be a protective factor for individuals throughout the life course. List the forms of social support that are available to Marilyn Hicks, Chris Johnson, and Irma Velasquez. How do they help them with their parenting? In what ways could they be more helpful? How do they add to the level of stress?

The Clearinghouse on International Developments on Child, Youth and Family Policies
www.childpolicyintl.org

Site maintained at Columbia University contains international comparisons of child and family policies.

The Jean Piaget Society
www.piaget.org/index.html

Site presented by The Jean Piaget Society, an international interdisciplinary society of scholars, teachers, and researchers, contains information on the society, a student page, a brief biography of Piaget, and Internet links.

National Center for Children in Poverty (NCCP)
www.nccp.org

Site presented by the NCCP of the Mailman School of Public Health of Columbia University contains media resources and child poverty facts as well as information on child care and early education, family support, and welfare reform.

National Network for Child Care
www.nncc.org

Site presented by the Cooperative Extension System's National Network for Child Care contains a list of more than 1,000 publications and resources related to child care, an electronic mailing list, and a newsletter.

Zero to Three
www.zerotothree.org

Site presented by Zero to Three: National Center for Infants, Toddlers & Families, a national nonprofit charitable organization with the aim to strengthen and support families, contains Parents' Tip of the Week, Parenting A–Z, BrainWonders, a glossary, and links to the Erikson Institute and other Internet sites.

Early Childhood

Debra J. Woody and David Woody III

OPENING QUESTIONS

- Why do social workers need to know about the ability of young children (ages 3 to 6) to express emotions and feelings?

- What is the process of gender and ethnic recognition and development among young children?

- What do social workers need to know about play among young children?

KEY IDEAS

As you read this chapter, take note of these central ideas:

1. Healthy development is in many ways defined by the environment and culture in which the child is raised. In addition, although growth and development in young children have some predictability and logic, the timing and expression of many developmental skills vary from child to child.

2. According to Piaget, preschoolers are in the preoperational stage of cognitive development and become capable of cognitive recall and symbolic functioning.

3. Erikson describes the task of children ages 3 to 6 as being the development of initiative versus guilt.

4. As young children struggle to discover stability and regularity in the environment, they are often rigid in their use of rules and stereotypes.

5. Regardless of country of residence or culture, all children ages 3 to 6 engage in spontaneous play.

6. Three types of parenting styles have been described: authoritarian, authoritative, and permissive. Parenting styles are prescribed to some extent by the community and culture in which the parent resides, and researchers are beginning to examine the appropriateness of using this parenting style typology across cultural groups.

7. Poverty, ineffective discipline, divorce, and exposure to violence all pose special challenges for early childhood development.

Case Study 4.1

Terri's Terrible Temper

Terri's mother and father, Mr. and Mrs. Smith, really seem at a loss about what to do. They adopted Terri, age 3, when she was an infant. They describe to their social worker how happy they were to finally have a child. They had tried for many years, spent a lot of money on fertility procedures, and had almost given up on the adoption process when Terri seemed to be "sent from heaven." Their lives were going well until a year ago, when Terri turned 2. Mrs. Smith describes an overnight change in Terri's behavior. Terri has become a total terror at home and at preschool. In fact, the preschool has threatened to dismiss Terri if her behavior does not improve soon. Terri hits and takes toys from other children, she refuses to cooperate with the teacher, and does "what she wants to do."

(Continued)

(Continued)

Mr. and Mrs. Smith admit that Terri runs their household. They spend most evenings after work coaxing Terri into eating her dinner, taking a bath, and going to bed. Any attempt at a routine is nonexistent. When the Smiths try to discipline Terri, she screams, hits them, and throws things. They have not been able to use time-outs to discipline her because Terri refuses to stay in the bathroom, the designated time-out place. She runs out of the bathroom and hides. When they attempt to hold her in the bathroom, she screams until Mr. Smith gets too tired to continue to hold her or until she falls asleep. Mr. and Mrs. Smith admit that they frequently let Terri have her way because it is easier than saying no or trying to discipline her.

The "straw that broke the camel's back" came during a family vacation. Mrs. Smith's sister and family joined the Smiths at the beach. Mr. Smith describes the vacation as a total disaster. Terri refused to cooperate the "entire" vacation. They were unable to eat at restaurants because of her tantrums, and they were unable to participate in family activities because Terri would not let them get her ready to go. They tried allowing her to choose the activities for the day, which worked until other family members tired of doing only the things that Terri wanted to do. Terri would scream and throw objects if the family refused to eat when and where she wanted or go to the park or the beach when she wanted. Mrs. Smith's sister became so frustrated with the situation that she vowed never to vacation with them again. In fact, it was the sister who insisted that they get professional help for Terri.

Case Study 4.2

Jack's Name Change

Until last month, Jack Lewis, age 4, lived with his mother, Joyce Lewis, and father, Charles Jackson Lewis, in what Joyce describes as a happy home. She was shocked when she discovered that her husband was having an affair with a woman at work. She immediately asked him to leave and has filed for divorce. Charles moved in with his girlfriend and has not contacted Joyce or Jack at this point. Joyce just can't believe that this is happening to her. Her mother had the same experience with Joyce's father but had kept the marriage going for the sake of Joyce and her siblings. Joyce, conversely, is determined to live a different life from the life her mother chose. She saw how depressed her mother was until her death at age 54. Joyce states that her mother died of a broken heart.

Although Joyce is determined to live without Charles, she is concerned about how she and Jack will live on her income alone. They had a comfortable life before the separation, but it took both incomes. Although she plans to seek child support, she knows she will need to move, because she cannot afford the mortgage on her own.

Joyce would prefer for Jack not to have contact with his father. In fact, she is seriously considering changing Jack's name because he was named after his father. Joyce has tried to explain the situation to Jack as best she can. However, in the social worker's presence, she told Jack that she hopes he does not grow up to be like his father. She also told Jack that his father is the devil and is now living with a witch.

Joyce also shares that Jack has had difficulty sleeping and continues to ask when his father is coming home. Joyce simply responds to Jack by telling him that they probably will never see Charles again.

Case Study 4.3

A New Role for Ron and Rosiland's Grandmother

Ron, age 3, and Rosiland, age 5, have lived with Ms. Johnson, their grandmother, for the last year. Their mother, Shirley, was sent to prison a year ago after conviction of drug trafficking. Shirley's boyfriend is a known drug dealer and had asked Shirley to make a "delivery" for him. Shirley was arrested as she stepped off the bus in another state where she had taken the drugs for delivery. Ron and Rosiland were with her when she was arrested, because she had taken them with her. Her boyfriend thought that a woman traveling with two young children would never be suspected of delivering drugs.

Ron and Rosiland were put into foster care by Child Protective Services until Ms. Johnson arrived to pick them up. It had taken her two weeks to save enough money to get to the children and fly them all home. Ms. Johnson shares with the social worker how angry she was that Shirley's boyfriend refused to help her get the children home. Shirley calls the children when she can, but because her crime was a federal offense, she has been sent to a prison far away from home. The children ask about her often and miss her terribly. Ms. Johnson has told the children that their mom is away but has not told them that she will be away for some time. She is also unsure how much they understand about what happened, even though they were present when their mom was arrested.

Ms. Johnson shares that she has no choice but to care for the children, although this is definitely not the life she has planned. She was looking forward to living alone; her husband died several years ago. With her small savings, she was planning to visit her sister in another state for an extended visit. But that money is gone now, because these funds were used to get the children home. She seems to love both of the children but confides that the children "drive her crazy." She is not accustomed to all the noise, and they seem to need so much attention from her. Getting into the habit of having a scheduled day is also difficult for Ms. Johnson. Both children attend preschool, an arrangement Shirley made before her incarceration. Ms. Johnson describes the fact that the children attend preschool as a blessing, because it gives her some relief. Her social worker suspects that preschool is a blessing for the children as well.

HEALTHY DEVELOPMENT IN EARLY CHILDHOOD

As children like Terri Smith, Jack Lewis, and Ron and Rosiland Johnson emerge from toddlerhood, they turn their attention more and more to the external environment. Just as in infancy and toddlerhood they worked at developing some regularity in their body rhythms, attachment relationships, and emotional states, they now work to discover some stability and regularity in the external world. That is not always an easy task, given their limitations in cognitive and language development. Some children emerge from toddlerhood with a sense of confidence in the availability of support and a beginning sense of confidence in themselves. Other children, unfortunately, leave toddlerhood more challenged than when they entered that stage (Sroufe, Egeland, Carolson, & Collins, 2005). Much happens in all interrelated dimensions of development between ages 3 and 6, however, and most children emerge from early childhood with a much more sophisticated ability to understand the world and their relationships to it. They work out this understanding in an increasingly wider world, with major influences coming from family, school, peer groups, neighborhood, and the media.

Some child development scholars still refer to the period between ages 3 and 6 as the preschool age, but others have recently begun to refer to this period as early school age, reflecting the fact that a large number of children are enrolled in some form of group-based experience during this period. In 2007, 55% of 3- and 4-year-olds in the United States were enrolled in school, at least part time, compared with 20% in 1970 (U.S. Bureau of the Census, 2009). We will simply refer to this period between 3 and 6 years of age as early childhood. Remember as you read that the various types of development discussed in this chapter under separate headings actually are interdependent, and sometimes the distinctions between the dimensions blur.

> What historical trends are influencing our understanding of social age in early childhood?

International literature criticizes the notion that there is a universal early childhood. It suggests, instead, that there are multiple and diverse early childhoods, based on class, race, gender, geography, and time (see Dahlberg, Moss, & Pence, 2007; Penn, 2005; Waller, 2009). One critic notes that more than 95% of the literature on child development comes from the United States, and is, for the most part, written by men (Fawcett, 2000). There are growing criticisms that all children of the world are evaluated against Western developmental psychology science, which is a mix of statistical averages and historically and culturally specific value judgments (Dahlberg et al.; Nybell, Shook, & Finn, 2009; Penn). In this chapter, we have tried to broaden the view of early childhood, where the literature allows, but please keep the above criticism in mind as you read. Also keep these data about the world's children in mind (UNICEF, n.d.). Of 100 children born in the world in 2000:

- Thirty would suffer malnutrition in their first five years of life

- Twenty-six would not be immunized against basic childhood diseases

- Nineteen would lack access to safe drinking water

- Forty would lack adequate sanitation

- Seventeen would never go to school

Physical Development in Early Childhood

As Chapter 3 explained, infants and toddlers grow rapidly. From ages 3 to 6, physical growth slows significantly. On average, height during this stage increases about 2 to 3 inches per year, and the young child adds about 5 pounds of weight per year. As a result, young children look leaner. However, there is growing global concern about increasing obesity beginning in early childhood (Keenan & Evans, 2009). At the same time, by age 4, some children in Africa and Asia weigh as much as 13 pounds less than children of the same age in Europe and America (Hendrick, 1990). Two forms of malnutrition exist: Malnutrition caused by sedentary lifestyle and eating too much processed food, and malnutrition caused by having too little to eat (McMichael, 2008). As suggested in the previous chapter, the importance of adequate nutrition cannot be overemphasized; poor nutrition is involved in at least half of the 10.9 million child deaths in the world each year. It magnifies the effect of every disease (Hunger Notes, 2009).

Great variation exists in the height and weight of young children, and racial and ethnic differences in height and weight are still evident in the early childhood years. For example, in the United States, African American children in early childhood on average are taller than White and Hispanic children of the same age, and there is some evidence that Hispanic American children weigh more on average than other young children (Dennison et al., 2006; Overpeck et al., 2000). Children of low economic status are more likely than other children to be overweight during early child-hood, but severe food insecurity may lead to growth inhibition (Wang & Zhang, 2006).

As noted in Chapter 3, the brain continues to be shaped by experience throughout early childhood and beyond. By age 5, the child's brain is 90% of its adult size. Motor and cognitive abilities increase by leaps and bounds because of increased interconnections between brain cells, which allow for more complex cognitive and motor capability. In addition, through a process called **lateralization,** the two hemispheres of the brain begin to operate slightly differently, allowing for a wider range of activity. Simply stated, brain functioning becomes more specialized. The left hemisphere is activated during tasks that require analytical skills, including speaking and reading. Tasks that involve emotional expression and spatial skills, such as visual imagery, require response from the right hemisphere. With the development of the right hemisphere and the social-emotional components there, young children develop the ability to reflect on the feelings and thoughts of others (Beatson & Taryan, 2003). Note that this reflective function is a critical component of attachment. Brain lateralization was identified early in neuroscientific research, but current thinking is that we should avoid applying the right hemisphere/left hemisphere paradigm too rigidly. The hemispheres are in constant communication, and the tasks performed by each hemisphere are much more complex than once thought (Fogarty, 2009).

Because of other developments in the brain, children also obtain and refine some advanced motor skills during this time, such as running, jumping, and hopping, but less is known about motor development in early childhood compared with infancy and toddlerhood (Keenan & Evans, 2009). Early interven-tion specialists suggest the gross motor milestones presented in Exhibit 4.1. In addition to these **gross motor skills**—skills that require use of the large muscle groups—young children develop **fine motor skills**, including the ability to scribble and draw, and cut with scissors. Suggested fine motor milestones are also presented in Exhibit 4.1. As you review these suggested milestones, remember that there is much variability in motor development in early childhood. For example, one child may be advanced in gross motor skills and lag in fine motor skills, or the opposite. In addition, different motor skills are valued in different developmental niches, and the expression of motor skills will depend on the tools available to the child. With these cautions, parents and other adults who spend time with young children will find the milestones pre-sented in Exhibit 4.1 to be helpful to keep in mind as they interact with young children.

Increases in fine motor skills also allow young children to become more self-sufficient. However, allowing the extra time needed for young children to perform self-care tasks can be frustrating to adults. Ms. Johnson, for example, has lived alone for some time now and may need to readjust to allowing extra time for the children to "do it themselves." Spills and messes, which are a part of this developmental process, are also often difficult for adults to tolerate.

▲ **Photo 4.1**   During early childhood, young children make advancement in the development of fine motor skills, including the ability to draw.

Cognitive and Language Development

A few years ago, the first author of this chapter was at a doctor's office when a mother walked into the waiting area with her son, about age 3. The waiting area was very quiet, and the young child's voice seemed loud in the silence. The mother immediately began to "shh" her son. He responded by saying, "I don't want to shh, I want to talk." Of course,

	Gross Motor Skills	Fine Motor Skills
Most 3-year-olds can	Run forward Jump in place Stand on one foot with support Walk on tiptoe Avoid obstacles in path Catch an 8-inch ball Climb and walk up stairs with alternating feet	Turn single pages Snip with scissors Hold crayons with thumb and finger Use one hand consistently Imitate circular, vertical, and horizontal strokes Paint with some wrist action Make dots, lines, and circular strokes Roll, pound, squeeze, and pull clay Build tower of up to nine cubes String ½-inch beads Cut along a line Use a fork Manage large buttons Dress self with supervision
Most 4-year-olds can	Run around obstacles Walk on a line Balance on one foot for 5–10 seconds Hop on one foot Push, pull, and steer wheeled toys Ride a tricycle Use a slide independently Jump over 6–inch-high object and land on both feet Throw a ball overhead Catch a bouncing ball	Build a tower of nine small blocks Drive nails and pegs Copy a circle Manipulate clay material Hold a pencil with appropriate grasp
Most 5-year-olds can	Walk backwards toe-heel Jump forward 10 times without falling Walk up and down stairs independently with alternating feet Turn a somersault	Cut on a line Copy a cross Copy a square Print some capital letters

▲ **Exhibit 4.1**   Gross Motor and Fine Motor Skills in Early Childhood

SOURCE: Based on Early Intervention Support, 2009.

everyone laughed, which made the child talk even louder. The mother moved immediately to some chairs in the corner and attempted to get her son to sit. He refused, stating that he wanted to stand on one foot. The mother at once attempted to engage him with the toys she had with her. They played with an electronic game in which the child selects pieces to add to a face to make a complete face. This game kept the child's attention for a while until he became bored. The mother told him to "make the game stop." The child responded by yelling at the game, demanding that it stop making the face. The mother, understanding that her son had taken a literal interpretation of her comments, rephrased her directions and showed her son how to push the stop button on the game.

Next, the two decided to read a book about the Lion King. The child became very confused, because in the book, different from his memory of the movie, the main character, Simba, was already an adult at the beginning of the book. The child, looking at the pictures, argued that the adult lion was not Simba but instead was Simba's father. The mother attempted to explain that this book begins with Simba as an adult. She stated that just as her son will grow, Simba grew from a cub to an adult lion. The son looked at his mother bewildered, responding with, "I am not a cub; I am a little boy." The mother then tried to make the connection that just like the son's daddy was once a boy, Simba grew up to be a lion. The boy responded by saying that men and lions are not the same. Needless to say, the mother seemed relieved when her name was called to see the doctor.

This scene encapsulates many of the themes of cognitive and moral development in early childhood. As memory improves, and the store of information expands, young children begin to think much more in terms of categories, as the little boy in the doctor's office was doing (Davies, 2004; Newman & Newman, 2009). He was now thinking in terms of cubs, boys, lions, and men. They also begin to recognize some surprising connections between things. No doubt, in a short time, the little boy will recognize a connection between boys and cubs, men and lions, boys and men, as well as cubs and lions. Young children are full of big questions such as where do babies come from, what happens to people when they die, where does the night come from, and so on. They can think about themselves and about other people. They engage in creative and imaginative thought and begin to develop humor, empathy, and altruism (Marti, 2003). They make great strides in language development and the ability to communicate. And they make gradual progress in the ability to judge right and wrong and to regulate behavior in relation to that reasoning.

Piaget's Stages of Cognitive Development

In early childhood, children fit into the second stage of cognitive development described by Piaget, the preoperational stage. This stage is in turn divided into two substages:

Substage 1: Preconceptual stage (ages 2 to 3). The most important aspect of the preoperational stage is the development of symbolic representation, which occurs in the preconceptual stage. Through play, children learn to use symbols and actively engage in what Piaget labeled deferred imitation. Deferred imitation refers to the child's ability to view an image and then, significantly later, recall and imitate the image. For example, 3-year-old Ella, who watches the *Dora the Explorer* cartoon on TV, fills her backpack with a pretend map and other items she might need, such as a blanket and a flashlight, puts it on, creates a pretend monkey companion named Boots, and sets off on an adventure, using the kitchen as a barn, the space under the dining table as the woods, and keeping her eyes open all the while for the "mean" Swiper the Fox. Ella's cousin, Zachery, who is enthralled with the *Bob the Builder* cartoon, often pretends that he is Bob the Builder when he is playing with his toy trucks and tractors. Whenever Zachery encounters a problem, he will sing Bob's theme song, which is "Bob the Builder, can we fix it, yes we can!!"

Substage 2: Intuitive stage (ages 4 to 7). During the second part of the preoperational stage, children use language to represent objects. During the preconceptual stage, any object with long ears may be called "bunny." However, during the intuitive stage, children begin to understand that the term bunny represents the entire animal, not just a property of it. However, although young children are able to classify objects, their classifications are based on only one attribute at a time. For example, given a set of stuffed animals with various sizes and colors, the young child will group the animals either by color or by size. In contrast, an older child who has reached the intuitive stage may sort them by both size and color.

In early childhood, children also engage in what Piaget termed **transductive reasoning**, or a way of thinking about two or more experiences without using abstract logic. This can be explained best with an illustration. Imagine that 5-year-old Sam immediately smells chicken when he enters his grandmother's home. He comments that she must be having a party and asks who is coming over for dinner. When the grandmother replies that no one is coming over and that a party is not planned, Sam shakes his head in disbelief and states that he will just wait to see when the guests arrive. Sam recalls that the last time his grandmother cooked chicken was for a party. Because grandmother is cooking chicken again, Sam thinks another party is going to occur. This type of reasoning is also evident in the example of the mother and child in the doctor's office. Because the child saw Simba as a cub in the movie version of the *Lion King*, he reasons that the adult lion in the picture at the beginning of the book cannot possibly be Simba.

One last related preoperational concept described by Piaget is **egocentrism.** According to Piaget, in early childhood, children perceive reality only from their own experience and believe themselves to be at the center of existence. They are unable to recognize the possibility of other perspectives on a situation. For example, a 3-year-old girl who stands between her sister and the television to watch a program believes that her sister can see the television because she can. This aspect of cognitive reasoning could be problematic for most of the children described in the case examples. Jack may believe that it is his fault that his father left the family. Likewise, Ron and Rosiland may attribute their mother's absence to their behavior, especially given that they were present when she was arrested. Some researchers have found that children are less egocentric than Piaget suggested (Borke, 1975; Wimmer & Perner, 1983).

Language Skills

Language development is included under cognitive development because it is the mechanism by which cognitive interpretations are communicated to others. Note that for language to exist, children must be able to "organize" their experiences.

At the end of toddlerhood, young children have a vocabulary of about 1,000 words, and they are increasing that store by about seven or eight words per day (Bloom, 1998a; Davies, 2004). They can speak in two-word sentences, and they have learned the question form of language. They are asking "why" questions, persistently and often assertively, to learn about the world. Three-year-old speech is generally clear and easy to understand.

By the fourth year of life, language development is remarkably sophisticated. The vocabulary is becoming more and more adequate for communicating ideas, and 4-year-olds are usually speaking in sentences of 8 to 10 words. They have mastered language well enough to tell a story mostly in words, rather than relying heavily on gestures, as toddlers must do. But perhaps the most remarkable aspect of language development in early childhood is the understanding of grammar rules. By age 4, young children in all cultures understand the basic grammar rules of their language (Gardiner & Kosmitzki, 2008). They accomplish this mostly by a figuring out process. As they figure out new grammar rules, as with other aspects of their learning, they are overly regular in using those rules, because they have not yet learned the exceptions (Santrock, 2003). So we often hear young children make statements such as "she goed to the store," or perhaps "she wented to the store."

> How does language development in early childhood promote human agency in making choices?

There has been a long-standing debate about how language is acquired. How much of language ability is a result of genetic processes, and how much of it is learned? B. F. Skinner (1957) argued that children learn language by imitating what they hear in the environment and then being reinforced for correct usage. When children utter sounds heard in their environment, Skinner contended, parents respond in a manner (smiling, laughing, clapping) that encourages young children to repeat the sounds. As children grow older, they are often corrected by caregivers and preschool teachers in the misuse of words or phrases. At the other end of the spectrum, Noam Chomsky (1968) contended that language ability is primarily a function of genetics. Although somewhat influenced by the environment, children develop language skills as long as the appropriate genetic material is in place.

There is increasing consensus that both perspectives have merit. Although the physiology of language development is still poorly understood, it is thought that humans inherit, to a much higher degree than other organisms, a genetic capacity for flexible communication skills, including language and speech (Novak & Pelaez, 2004). But, many scholars also argue that language is "inherently social because it has to be learned from other persons" (Bloom, 1998b, p. 332). Children learn language by listening to others speak and by asking questions. Past toddlerhood, children increasingly take charge of their own language acquisition by asking questions and initiating dialogues (Bloom). Parents can assist children by asking questions, eliciting details, and encouraging children to reflect on their experiences (Haden, Hayne, & Fivush, 1997). One longitudinal study found that the size of vocabulary among 3-year-olds is correlated with the size of the vocabulary spoken to them from the age of 9 months and the amount of positive feedback provided for language development (Hart & Risley, 1995).

It appears that the developmental niche has an impact on the development of language skills. From observation of their environment—physical and social surroundings, childrearing customs, and caregiver personality—children learn a set of regulations, or rules for communication, that shape their developing language skills. Children have an innate capacity for language, but the structuring of the environment through culture is what allows language development to occur. Here are three examples of the importance of developmental niche for language development. In the first example, children whose parents ask them lots of questions and initiate frequent verbal interactions with them recognize more letters and numbers by age 5 or 6 and score higher on language proficiency tests in second grade than children whose parents do less verbal interaction with them (Mayes & Cohen, 2003). The second example involves different cultural valuing of silence. In the Colombian *mestizo* community and among Apache Native Americans, young children are expected to keep a respectful silence while interacting with others.

> How do social class, culture, and gender affect the "developmental niche" during early childhood?

Refraining from speaking is a form of communication, and the "useless habit" of talking too much is discouraged (Valsiner, 2000). The third example is not as straightforward. One research team found that by 5 years of age, Portuguese- and Mandarin Chinese–speaking children could distinguish the difference between the qualifiers "all" and "each," both conceptually and linguistically. English-speaking 5-year-olds do not make this distinction (Brooks, Jia, Braine, & Da Graca Dias, 1998). The researchers suggest that cultural values may play a role in this difference in language learning. They note that Portugal and China have collectivist-oriented cultures, and speculate that children in those cultures may begin to learn words and concepts that focus on the relationship between the individual and the collectivity earlier than children from more individualistic societies.

Moral Development

During early childhood, children move from a moral sense that is based on outside approval to a more internalized moral sense, with a rudimentary moral code. They engage in a process of taking society's values and standards as their own. They begin to integrate these values and standards into both their worldview and their self-concept. There are three components of moral development during early childhood (Newman & Newman, 2009):

1. *Knowledge* of the moral code of the community and how to use that knowledge to make moral judgments

2. *Emotions* that produce both the capacity to care about others and the capacity to feel guilt and remorse

3. *Actions* to inhibit negative impulses as well as to behave in a **prosocial,** or helpful and empathic manner

Understanding Moral Development

Moral development has been explored from several different theoretical perspectives that have been found to have merit. Three of these approaches to moral development are explored here:

1. *Psychodynamic approach.* Sigmund Freud's psychoanalytic theory proposed that there are three distinct structures of the personality: id, ego, and superego. According to Freud, the superego is the personality structure that guides moral development. There are two aspects to the superego: the *conscience,* which is the basis of a moral code, and the *ego ideal,* which is a set of ideals expected in a moral person. Freud (1927) thought that the superego is formed between the ages of 4 and 7, but more recent psychodynamic formulations suggest that infancy is the critical time for the beginning of moral development (Kohut, 1971). Freud thought that children would have more highly developed superegos when their parents used strict methods to inhibit the children's impulses. Contemporary research indicates the opposite, however, finding that moral behavior is associated with parental warmth, democratic decision making, and modeling of temptation resistance (Kochanska, Forman, Aksan, & Dunbar, 2005). New psychodynamic models emphasize a close, affectionate bond with the caregiver as the cornerstone of moral development. Freud also believed that males would develop stronger superegos than females, but research has not supported this idea.

2. *Social learning approach.* From the perspective of social learning theory, moral behavior is shaped by environmental reinforcements and punishments. Children are likely to repeat behaviors that are rewarded, and they are also likely to feel tension when they think about doing something that they have been punished for in the past. From this perspective, parental consistency in response to their children's behavior is important. Social learning theory also suggests that children learn moral conduct by observing models. Albert Bandura (1977) found that children are likely to engage in behaviors for which they see a model rewarded and to avoid behaviors that they see punished. This can be problematic for children who watch a lot of television, because they may come to view violence as an acceptable way to solve interactional conflict if they see violence go unpunished.

3. *Cognitive developmental approach.* Piaget's theory of cognitive development has been the basis for stage models of moral reasoning, which assume that children's moral judgments change as their cognitive development allows them to examine the logical and abstract aspects of moral dilemmas. Moral development is assisted by opportunities to encounter new situations and different perspectives. The most frequently researched stage model is the one presented by Lawrence Kohlberg (1969, 1976) and summarized in Exhibit 4.2. Kohlberg described three levels of moral reasoning, with two stages in each level. It was expected that in early childhood, children will operate at the **preconventional level,** with their reasoning about moral issues based, first, on what gets them rewarded or punished. This type of moral reasoning is thought to be common among toddlers. In the second stage, moral reasoning is based on what benefits either the child or someone the child cares about. This is consistent with the child's growing capacity for attachments. There is some empirical evidence that children between the ages of 3 and 6 do, indeed, begin to use the type of moral reasoning described in stage 2 (Walker, 1989). The idea of a hierarchical sequence of stages of moral development has been challenged as being based on a Western cultural orientation, but longitudinal studies in a variety of countries have produced support for the idea of evolution of moral reasoning (Gielen & Markoulis, 2001).

All of the above approaches to moral development in early childhood have been criticized for leaving out two key ingredients for moral development: **empathy,** or the ability to understand another person's emotional condition, and **perspective taking,** or the ability to see a situation from another person's point of view (Eisenberg, 2000). Neuroscientific research is currently suggesting that a special type of brain cell, called *mirror neuron,* is key to the development of empathy. Have you ever noticed how you instinctively smile when you see someone else smiling? Mirror neurons allow us to sense the move another person is about to make and the emotions he or she is experiencing. Emotion is contagious, because mirror neurons allow us to feel what the other person feels through a brain-to-brain connection.

> Why is the development of empathy important for future capacity for relationships?

Daniel Goleman (2006) calls this primal empathy; it is based on feelings, not thoughts. He has coined the phrase *social intelligence* to refer to this ability to be attuned to another person. It appears that humans have multiple systems of mirror neurons, and scientists are in the early stages of learning about them. Studies have found that people with autism have a dysfunctional mirror neuron system (Goleman).

There is growing agreement that empathy begins in infancy and grows throughout early childhood (Meltzoff, 2002). By age 3 or 4, children across cultures have been found to be able to recognize the type of emotional reaction that other children might have to different situations. Perspective taking, which is a thinking rather than feeling activity, has been found to grow gradually, beginning at about the age of 4 or 5 (Iannotti, 1985). Longitudinal research has found that children who show empathy and perspective taking at 4 and 5 years of age are more likely to exhibit prosocial behavior and sympathy during adolescence and early adulthood (Eisenberg et al., 1999).

In addition, there has been considerable examination of the degree to which Kohlberg's model is responsive to gender and cultural experience, in view of the study population upon which his theory is based—Harvard male undergraduates (Donleavy, 2007; Sherblom, 2008). Gilligan (1982) notes that gender, in American society, plays a significant role in how one experiences and acts on themes of ethical thinking, justice, and notions of individuality and connectedness. She suggests that there is strong gender bias in Kohlberg's theory, and her research indicated that women's moral thought is guided by caring and maintaining the welfare of others while men use more abstract principles of justice. As you can see from Exhibit 4.2, caring for others and maintaining harmony in relationships would

Level I:	Preconventional
	Stage 1: Moral reasoning is based on whether behavior is rewarded or punished.
	Stage 2: Moral reasoning is based on what will benefit the self or loved others.
Level II:	Conventional
	Stage 3: Moral reasoning is based on the approval of significant others.
	Stage 4: Moral reasoning is based on upholding societal standards.
Level III:	Postconventional
	Stage 5: Moral reasoning is based on social contracts and cooperation.
	Stage 6: Moral reasoning is based on universal ethical principles.

▲ **Exhibit 4.2**   Kohlberg's Stages of Moral Development

SOURCE: Based on Kohlberg, 1969, 1976.

put women in stage 3, at the highest. A similar criticism has been lodged about the poor fit of Kohlberg's theory with many non-European cultures that are more collectivist oriented than European and North American societies. Indeed, studies of Buddhist monks find that older monks barely reach Kohlberg's stage 4, indicating that their moral reasoning is not as well developed as Western male adolescents, by Kohlberg's model (Huebner & Garrod, 1993). The researchers suggest that the moral ideal in Western cultures is an autonomous individual with strong convictions who sticks up for those convictions. In contrast, the Buddhist moral ideal is guided by compassion and detachment from one's own individuality. How such themes are transmitted to young children can be indelible guideposts for managing and participating in interpersonal relationships (Seigfried, 1989).

One aspect of moral reasoning is *distributive justice,* or the belief about what constitutes a fair distribution of goods and resources in a society. Cross-cultural studies suggest that cultures hold different views on what constitutes a "fair" distribution of resources. Some societies, such as Sweden and Indonesia, see fairness in terms of need while other societies, such as the United States and Hong Kong, see fairness in terms of merit (Gardiner & Kosmitzki, 2008; Murphy-Berman & Berman, 2002). Reasoning about distributive justice starts in early childhood but is not well articulated until middle childhood (Gardiner & Kosmitzki, 2008).

Helping Young Children to Develop Morally

Growing evidence indicates that some methods work better than others for helping children develop moral reasoning and conduct. Activities that are particularly helpful are those that help children control their own behavior, help them understand how their behavior affects others, show them models of positive behavior, and get them to discuss moral issues (Arsenio & Gold, 2006; Walker & Taylor, 1991). It is important, however, to consider a child's temperament when undertaking disciplinary actions. Some children are more sensitive to messages of disapproval than others; sensitive children require a small dose of criticism, and less sensitive children usually require more focused and directive discipline (Kochanska, 1997).

Although religious beliefs play a central role in most societies in clarifying moral behavior, little research has been done to explore the role of religion in moral development in young children. Research (Roof, 1999) has indicated that adults often become affiliated with a religious organization when their children are in early childhood, even if the parents become "religious dropouts" after the children are out of the home. Religious rituals link young children to specific actions and images of the world as well as to a community that can support and facilitate their moral development. The major world religions also teach parents about how to be parents. Young children, with their comfortable embrace of magic, easily absorb religious stories on topics that may be difficult for adults to explain. Religion that emphasizes love, concern, and social justice can enrich the young child's moral development. Conversely, religion that is harsh and judgmental may produce guilt and a sense of worthlessness, which do not facilitate higher levels of moral reasoning.

Personality and Emotional Development

The key concern for Jack Lewis and for Ms. Johnson's grandchildren—Ron and Rosiland—is their emotional development. Specifically, will they grow into happy, loving, well-adjusted people despite the disruptions in their lives? Writing about the early childhood years, Sroufe and colleagues (2005) suggest that this is the period of life when a coherent personality emerges: "[I]t is no exaggeration to say that the person emerges at this time" (p. 121). Based on longitudinal study of 180 children born into poverty, they conclude that behavior and adaptation during early childhood predict later behavior and adaptation, something that they did not find to be the case with the predictive power of behavior and adaptation in infancy and toddlerhood. They suggest that the important themes of development during this period are self-direction, agency, self-management, and self-regulation. Young children do face important developmental tasks in the emotional arena. This section addresses these tasks, drawing on Erikson's theory of psychosocial development.

Erikson's Theory of Psychosocial Development

Erikson labeled the stage of emotional development that takes place during the early childhood years as *initiative versus guilt* (ages 3 to 6). (Refer back to Exhibit 3.7 for the complete list of Erikson's stages.) Children who pass successfully through this stage learn to get satisfaction from completing tasks. They develop imagination and fantasies, and learn to handle guilt about their fantasies.

At the beginning of this stage, children's focus is on family relationships. They learn what roles are appropriate for various family members, and they learn to accept parental limits. In addition, they develop gender identity through identification with the parent of the same sex. Age and sex boundaries must be appropriately defined at this stage, and parents must be secure enough to set limits and resist the child's possessiveness.

By the end of this stage, the child's focus turns to friendships outside the family. Children engage in cooperative play and enjoy both sharing and competing with peers. Children must also have the opportunity to establish peer relationships outside the family. This is one of the functions the preschool program serves for Ms. Johnson's grandchildren.

Children who become stuck in this stage are plagued with guilt about their goals and fantasies. They become confused about their gender identity and about family roles. These children are overly anxious and self-centered.

Emotions

Growing cognitive and language skills give young children the ability to understand and express their feelings and emotions. Children between the ages of 3 and 5 can recognize and label simple emotions, and they learn about themselves when they talk about their anxieties and fears (Hansen & Zambo, 2007). Children in early childhood can also identify feelings expressed by others—as the earlier discussion of empathy illustrated—and use creative ways to comfort others when they are upset. A friend describes the response of her 5-year-old son Marcus when he saw her crying about the sudden death of her brother in a car accident. Marcus hugged his mom and told her not to cry, because, although she was sad about Uncle Johnny, she still had Marcus. Marcus promised his mother to never drive a car so she would not have to worry about the same thing happening to him. This attempt to reduce his mother's sadness is a typical response from a child of this age (Findlay, Girardi, & Coplan, 2006).

The ability to understand emotion continues to develop as young children have more opportunity to practice these skills. Children reared in homes in which emotions and feelings are openly discussed are better able to understand and express feelings (Bradley, 2000). Early childhood educators Cory Cooper Hansen and Debby Zambo (2007) recommend the use of children's literature to help children understand and manage emotions. Here are some of their recommendations for how to do that (p. 277):

- Respect all responses to talks about emotions.
- Ask children to describe the emotions of story characters.
- Talk about your own emotions about story characters.
- Encourage children to draw, write, or paint about the emotions of story characters as well as their own emotional reactions.
- Sing or chant about emotions and how to handle them.
- Brainstorm ways that story characters can handle their emotions.

- Practice reading emotions from pictures in books.

- Use stuffed animals to "listen" to children's stories.

Most child development scholars agree that all emotions, including those that have been labeled "negative" (anger, sadness, guilt, disgust), are adaptive, but more needs to be learned about how the "negative" emotions can become problematic for children (Cole, Luby, & Sullivan, 2008). We know that by the first grade, most children can regulate their emotions well enough to learn, obey classroom rules, and develop friendships (Calkins & Hill, 2007; Shonkoff & Phillips, 2000). But, we also know that emotional receptivity makes young children vulnerable to environmental stress, and early exposure to adverse situations can have a negative effect on the brain, cardiovascular, and endocrine processes that support emotional development (Gunnar & Quevedo, 2007). It is important to recognize when emotional development is getting off course, and researchers are at work to develop understanding of that issue. For example, we know that most young children have tantrums. For most children, anger and distress are expressed in quick peaks in anger intensity that declines into whining and comfort-seeking behavior. Researchers are finding, however, that the tantrums of depressed young children are more violent, destructive, verbally aggressive, and self-injurious; they also have a longer recovery time (Belden, Thompson, & Luby, 2008). It is important to avoid both overreacting and underreacting to children's difficulties in regulating their emotions, and the guidelines are getting clearer.

> What are our societal expectations for regulation of emotions during early childhood?

Aggression

One behavior that increases during the early childhood years is aggression. Two types of aggression are observed in young children: **instrumental aggression,** which occurs while fighting over toys and space, and **hostile aggression,** which is an attack meant to hurt another individual. Recently, researchers have studied another typology of aggression: physical aggression and relational aggression. **Physical aggression,** as the name suggests, involves using physical force against another person. **Relational aggression** involves behaviors that damage relationships without physical force, behaviors such as threatening to leave a relationship unless a friend complies with demands, or using social exclusion or the silent treatment to get one's way. Researchers are finding that boys make greater use of physical aggression than girls, and girls make greater use of relational aggression (Ostrov, Crick, & Stauffacher, 2006).

Although some children continue high levels of aggression into middle childhood, usually physical aggression peaks early in the early childhood years (Alink, Mesmon, & van Zeijl, 2006). By the end of the early childhood years, children learn better negotiation skills and become better at asking for what they want and using words to express feelings. Terri Smith, in the first case study in this chapter, obviously has not developed these moderating skills.

Attachment

In early childhood, children still depend on their attachment relationships for feelings of security. In particularly stressful times, the attachment behavior of the young child may look very much like the clinging behavior of the 2-year-old. For the most part, however, securely attached children will handle their anxieties by verbalizing their needs. For example, at bedtime, the 4-year-old child may say, "I would like you to read one more story before you go." This increased ability to verbalize wants is a source of security. In addition, many young children continue to use transitional objects, such as blankets or a favorite teddy bear, to soothe themselves when they are anxious (Davies, 2004).

In their longitudinal study of 180 children born into poor families, Sroufe et al. (2005) examined, among other things, how attachment style in infancy and toddlerhood affected the developmental trajectory into early childhood. Here are some of the findings:

- Anxiously attached infants and toddlers were more dependent on their mothers, but performed more poorly on teaching tasks at age 3½ than either securely or avoidant attached toddlers.

- Securely attached infants and toddlers rated higher on curiosity, agency, activity, self-esteem, and positive emotions at age 4½ than either anxiously or avoidant attached toddlers.

- Securely attached infants and toddlers had better emotion regulation in early childhood than anxiously attached toddlers.

Sroufe and colleagues also found that temperament was not a powerful predictor of early childhood behavior.

Critical Thinking Questions 4.1

What types of children's literature might be particularly useful to help Terri Smith, Jack Lewis, and Ron and Rosiland Johnson in their emotional development? What types of stories would you look for if you were to work with these children? How concerned should we be about Terri Smith's tantrums? Do you think her emotional development is getting off course?

Social Development

In early childhood, children become more socially adept than they were as toddlers, but they are still learning how to be social and how to understand the perspectives of other people. The many young children who enter group care face increasing demands for social competence.

Peer Relations

In early childhood, children form friendships with other children of the same age and gender; boys gravitate toward male playmates and girls choose girls. Across cultures, young children's friendship groups are likely to be segregated by sex (Barbu, Le Maner-Idrissi, & Jouanjean, 2000; Maccoby, 2002a). When asked about the definition of a friend, most children in this age group think of a friend as someone with whom you play (Corsaro, 2005). Our neighbor children, for example, made their initial approach to our young son by saying, "Let's be friends; let's play" and "I'll be your friend if you will be mine." Young children do not view friendship as a trusting, lasting relationship, but even this limited view of friendship is important for this age group. For example, children who enter kindergarten with identified friends adjust better to school (Johnson, Ironsmith, Snow, & Poteat, 2000).

Research indicates that young children are at a higher risk of being rejected by their peers if they are aggressive and comparatively more active, demonstrate a difficult temperament, are easily distracted, and demonstrate lower perseverance (Campbell, 2002; Johnson et al., 2000; Walker, Berthelsen, & Irving, 2001). One would wonder, then, how young peers respond to Terri Smith. The rejection of some children is long lasting; even when they change their behavior and fit better with the norm, often they continue to be rejected (Walker et al.). It is important, therefore, to intervene early to help children like Terri Smith learn more prosocial behavior.

Self-Concept

In early childhood, the child seems to vacillate between grandiose and realistic views of the self (Davies, 2004). Conversely, children are aware of their growing competence, but at the same time, they have normal doubts about the self, based on realistic comparisons of their competence with the competence of adults. In early childhood, children begin to develop a self-concept, which includes a perception of oneself as a person who has desires, attributes, preferences, and abilities.

Some investigators have suggested that during early childhood, the child's ever-increasing understanding of the self in relation to the world begins to become organized into a **self-theory** (Epstein, 1973, 1991, 1998; Epstein, Lipson, Holstein, & Huh, 1993). As children develop the cognitive ability to categorize, they use categorization to think about the self. By age 2 or 3, children can identify their gender and race (discussed in greater detail shortly) as factors in understanding who they are. Between the ages of 4 and 6, young children become more aware that different people have different perspectives on situations (Ziv & Frye, 2003). This helps them to begin to understand cultural expectations and sensitizes them to the expectations that others have for them.

This growing capacity to understand the self in relation to others leads to self-evaluation, or **self-esteem**. Very early interpersonal experiences provide information that becomes incorporated into self-esteem. Messages of love, admiration, and approval lead to a positive view of the self (Brown, Dutton, & Cook, 2001). Messages of rejection or scorn lead to a negative view of the self (Heimpel, Wood, Marshall, & Brown, 2002). In addition to these interpersonal messages, young children observe their own competencies and attributes, and compare them with the competencies of other children as well as adults. And they are very aware of being evaluated by others, their peers as well as important adults (Newman & Newman, 2009).

Of course, a young child may develop a positive view of the self in one dimension, such as cognitive abilities, and a negative view of the self in another dimension, such as physical abilities (Harter, 1998). Children also learn that some abilities are more valued than others in the various environments in which they operate. For example, in individualistic-oriented societies, self-reliance, independence, autonomy, and distinctiveness are valued while interdependence and harmony are valued in most collectivistic-oriented societies. Self-esteem is based on different values in these different types of cultures (Brown, 2003; Sedikides, Gaertner, & Toguchi, 2003). It is probably the case that every culture includes both individualistic and collectivistic beliefs (Turiel, 2004), but the balance of these two belief systems vary greatly from culture to culture. An example of the way that these beliefs play out and influence self-development from an early age was described by Markus and Kitayama (2003), who noted that in U.S. coverage of the Olympics, athletes are typically asked about how they personally feel about their efforts and their success. In contrast, in Japanese coverage, athletes are typically asked "Who helped you achieve?" This idea of an interdependent self is consistent with cultural relational theory as well as feminist and Afro-centric perspectives on relationships.

Recently, cognitive neuroscientists have been exploring the ways that the brain gives rise to development of a sense of self. They have found that a right fronto-parietal network, which overlaps with mirror neurons, is activated during tasks involving self-recognition and discrimination between the self and the other (Kaplan, Aziz-Zadeh, Uddin, & Iacaboni, 2008; Uddin, Iacoboni, Lange, & Keenan, 2007). Viewing one's own face leads to greater signal changes in the inferior frontal gyrus (IFG), the inferior occipital gyrus, and the inferior parietal lobe. In addition, there is greater signal change in the right IFG when hearing one's own voice compared with hearing a friend's voice (Kaplan et al., 2008). Beginning evidence also indicates that the cortical midline structures (CMS) of the brain are involved in self-evaluation and in understanding of other's emotional states. In addition, there is beginning evidence of at least one pathway that connects the mirror neurons and the CMS, allowing for integration of self and other understanding (Uddin et al., 2007).

Gender Identity and Sexual Interests

During early childhood, gender becomes an important dimension of how children understand themselves and others. There are four components to gender identity during early childhood (Newman & Newman, 2009):

1. *Making correct use of the gender label.* By age 2, children can usually accurately identify others as either male or female, based on appearance.

2. *Understanding gender as stable.* Later, children understand that gender is stable, that boys grow up to be men and girls to be women.

> How does gender influence early childhood development?

3. *Understanding gender constancy.* Even with this understanding of gender stability, young children, with their imaginative thinking, continue to think that girls can turn into boys and boys into girls by changing appearance. For example, a 3-year-old given a picture of a girl is able to identify the person as a girl. But if the same girl is shown in another picture dressed as a boy, the 3-year-old will label the girl a boy. It is not until sometime between age 4 and 7 that children understand *gender constancy,* the understanding that one's gender does not change, that the girl dressed as a boy is still a girl.

4. *Understanding the genital basis of gender.* Gender constancy has been found to be associated with an understanding of the relationship between gender and genitals (Bem, 1998).

Before going further, it is important to differentiate among four concepts: sex, gender, gender identity, and sexual orientation. *Sex* refers to biologically linked distinctions that are determined by chromosomal information. An infant's external genitalia are usually used as the determinant of sex. In most humans, chromosomes, hormones, and genitalia are consistent, and determining sex is considered unambiguous. However, this is not always the case. Chromosomal, genetic, anatomical, and hormonal aspects of sex are sometimes not aligned (Rudacille, 2005). *Gender* is the cognitive, emotional, and social schemes that are associated with being female or male. *Gender identity* refers to one's sense of being male or female. *Sexual orientation* refers to one's preference for sexually intimate partners.

There is evidence of gender differences in multiple dimensions of human behavior, but also much debate about just how pervasive these differences are and, if they exist, how to explain them. In terms of the pervasiveness of gender differences, the findings are not at all consistent. In 1974, Eleanor Maccoby and Carol Jacklin reviewed more than 2,000 studies that included sex differences and concluded that there was evidence of four sex differences: (1) girls have greater verbal abilities than boys, (2) boys excel in visual-spatial ability, (3) boys excel in mathematical ability, and (4) boys are more aggressive. Thirty years later, Janet Hyde (2005) reviewed a large number of studies and found that in 78% of them, gender differences were close to zero or quite small and that there was evidence of much within-group difference. In other words, the differences among girls were as great or greater than the differences between boys and girls. There were substantial gender differences in a few areas, however: some aspects of motor performance, some sexual attitudes and behaviors, and physical aggression. Indeed, the research subsequent to the Maccoby and Jacklin review has found that the cognitive differences that they reported are very limited. Females do seem to have an advantage in verbal fluency and writing, but not in reading comprehension. Males' visual-spatial advantage seems to occur only in tasks requiring mental rotation of a three-dimensional object. Although males perform better on tests of broad mathematical ability, females score better on computation (Garrett, 2009).

In terms of the debate about the causes of gender differences, there are two competing perspectives: the biological determination perspective and the socially constructed perspective. There is some evidence to support each of these perspectives, suggesting, not surprisingly, that behavior is multiple determined. In terms of verbal ability, there is some evidence that females use both hemispheres of the brain for solving verbal problems while males use mostly the left hemispheres, but the findings in this regard are not consistent. Relatively strong evidence indicates that estrogen probably does contribute to women's verbal advantage. Men who take estrogen in their transsexual treatments to become female score higher on verbal learning than men who do not take estrogen as part of their transsexual transformation. Testosterone appears to play a role in spatial ability. Males who produce low levels of testosterone during the developmental years have less well-developed spatial ability; in addition, testosterone replacement therapy in older men improves their spatial functioning. Interestingly, there is only a small sex difference in aggression when behavior is studied in the laboratory, but a very large difference outside the laboratory. That is not convincing evidence for a biological basis for the gender differences in aggression (Garrett, 2009).

In terms of the socially constructed perspective, we know that human societies use gender as an important category for organizing social life. There are some rather large cultural and subcultural variations in gender role definitions, however. Existing cultural standards about gender are pervasively built into adult interactions with young children and into the reward systems that are developed for shaping child behavior. Much research evidence indicates that parents begin to use gender stereotypes to respond to their children from the time of birth (Gardiner & Kosmitzki, 2008). They cuddle more with infant girls and play more actively with infant boys. Later, they talk more with young girls and expect young boys to be more independent. Recent studies have found that the nature of parental influence on children's gender role development is more complex than this. Parents may hold to stereotypical gender expectations in some domains but not in others. For example, parents may have similar expectations for boys and girls in terms of sharing or being polite (McHale, Crouter, & Whiteman, 2003).

Once toddlers understand their gender, they begin to imitate and identify with the same-sex parent, if he or she is available. Once young children begin to understand gender role standards, they become quite rigid in their playing out of gender roles—only girls cook, only men drive trucks, only girls wear pink flowers, only boys wear shirts with footballs. This gender understanding also accounts for the preference of same-sex playmates and sex-typed toys (Davies, 2004). Remember, though, that the exaggeration of gender stereotypes in early childhood is in keeping with the struggle during this period to discover stability and regularity in the environment.

Evidence that gender differences in verbal, visual, and mathematical skills are at least partially socially constructed can be found in data that indicate that differences in all three areas have decreased over the same time period that gender roles have changed toward greater similarity. The dramatic difference in murder rates across societies suggests that there is a strong cultural influence on aggression (Garrett, 2009).

During early childhood, children become increasingly interested in their genitals. They are interested, in general, in how their bodies work, but the genitals seem to hold a special interest as the young child learns through experimentation that the genitals can be a source of pleasure. Between 3 and 5, children may have some worries and questions about genital difference; little girls may think they once had a penis and wonder what happened to it. Little boys may fear that their penises will disappear, like their sister's did. During early childhood, masturbation is used both as a method of self-soothing and for pleasure. Young children also "play doctor" with each other, and often want to see and touch their parents' genitals. Many parents and other caregivers are confused about how to handle this behavior, particularly in our era of heightened awareness of childhood sexual abuse. In general, parents should not worry about genital curiosity or about children experimenting with touching their own genitals. They should remember, however, that at this age children may be overstimulated by seeing their parents' genitals. And we should always be concerned when children want to engage in more explicit adultlike sexual play that involves stimulation of each other's genitals (Davies, 2004; Newman & Newman, 2009).

Racial and Ethnic Identity

Findings from research suggest that children first learn their own racial identity before they are able to identify the race of others (Kowalski, 1996). Elements of racial/ethnic identity awareness have been found to occur as early as the age of 3. Most children begin to self-identify as a member of a racial group by age 3 to 4, but identification with an ethnic group does not usually occur until later in childhood, between 5 and 8 years of age (Blackmon & Vera, 2008). Early identification of others by race is limited to skin color, which is more easily recognized than ethnic origin. Young children may label a Latino/Latina individual, for example, as either African American or White, depending on the individual's skin color. Young children

How important is racial and ethnic identity in early childhood?

also show a preference for members of their own race over another (Katz, 1976). Perhaps this choice is similar to the preference for same-sex playmates, a result of young children attempting to learn their own identity. In a study of children in a preschool setting, the children were observed to use race and ethnicity to define themselves and others, to include peers in play, and to exclude peers from stigmatized racial and ethnic groups (Van Ausdal & Feagin, 1996).

Social scientists concerned about the development of self-esteem in children of color have investigated racial bias and preference using children in early childhood as subjects. The most famous of these studies was conducted by Kenneth Clark and Mamie Clark in 1939. They presented African American children with Black dolls and White dolls and concluded that African American children responded more favorably to the White dolls and had more negative reactions to the Black dolls. A similar study 40 years later, observing young African American children in New York and Trinidad, reported similar results (Gopaul-McNicol, 1988). The young children from both New York and Trinidad preferred and identified with the White dolls. Interestingly, the same results have been reported more recently in studies of Taiwanese young children (Chang, 2001). Most of the Taiwanese children in the study indicated a preference for the White dolls and demonstrated a "pro-white attitude."

It is questionable, however, whether these preferences and biases are equated with self-concept and low self-esteem for children of color. Most argue that they are not. For example, racial bias and self-concept were not related among the young Taiwanese children (Chang, 2001). Likewise, findings from studies about young African

▲ **Photo 4.2**   Play is one of the few elements in the development of children that is universal—regardless of culture.

American children indicate high levels of self-concept despite the children's bias in favor of the White culture and values (Crain, 1996; Spencer, 1985). Spencer concludes, "Racial stereotyping in black children should be viewed as objectively held information about the environment and not as a manifestation of personal identity" (p. 220).

The Role of Play

The young child loves to play, and play is essential to all aspects of early child development. We think of the play of young children as fun-filled and lively. And yet it serves a serious purpose. Through play, children develop the motor skills essential for physical development, learn the problem-solving skills and communication skills fundamental to cognitive development, express the feelings and gain the self-confidence needed for emotional growth, and learn to cooperate and resolve social conflicts. Essentially, play is what young children are all about; it is their work.

As children develop in all areas during early childhood, their play activities and preferences for play materials change over time. Hughes (2010) makes the following recommendations about the preferred play materials at different ages during early childhood:

- Three-year-olds: props for imaginative play, such as dress-up clothes, doctor kits, and makeup; miniature toys that represent adult models, such as toy trucks, gas stations, dolls, doll houses, and airplanes; art materials, such as paint brushes, easels, marker pens, and crayons.

▲ **Photo 4.3** During early childhood, children engage in cooperative play and enjoy sharing and competing with peers.

- Four-year-olds: vehicles, such as tricycles and wagons; play materials to develop fine motor skills, such as materials for sewing, stringing beads, coloring, painting, and drawing; books that involve adventure.

- Five-year-olds: play materials to develop precision in fine motor skills, such as coloring books, paints and brushes, crayons, marker pens, glue, scissors, stencils, sequins and glitter, clay, and Play-Doh; play materials that develop cognitive skills, such as workbenches, play cards, table games, and board games.

In recent years, there has been a dramatic increase in the availability of computers and other instructional technology. These technologies have made their way into early childhood education programs, but there is controversy among early childhood educators about the positive and negative aspects of these technologies for early childhood development. There is evidence of benefits of instructional technologies in the preschool classroom. For example, 4- and 5-year-old children can use technology to develop language, art, mathematics, and science skills. Conversely, some early childhood educators are concerned that computers and other instructional technologies contribute to social isolation and limit children's creative play (Hughes, 2010). Adults must give serious consideration to how to balance the positive and negative aspects of these technologies.

The predominant type of play in early childhood, beginning around the age of 2, is **symbolic play**, otherwise known as fantasy play, pretend play, or imaginary play (Hughes, 2010; Pelligrini & Galda, 2000). Children continue to use vivid imaginations in their play, as they did as toddlers, but they also begin to put more structure into their play. Thus, their play is intermediate between the fantasy play of toddlers and the structured, rules-oriented play of middle childhood. Although toddler play is primarily nonverbal, the play of young children often involves highly sophisticated verbal productions. There is some indication that this preference for symbolic play during early childhood exists across cultures, but the themes of the play reflect the culture in which it is enacted (Roopnarine, Shin, Donovan, & Suppal, 2000).

Symbolic play during early childhood has four primary functions: providing an opportunity to explore reality, contributing to cognitive development, allowing young children to gain control over their lives, and serving as a shared experience and opportunity for development of peer culture. These functions are explained in more detail below.

Play as an Opportunity to Explore Reality

Young children imitate adult behavior and try out social roles in their play (Davies, 2004; Hughes, 2010). They play house, school, doctor, police, firefighter, and so on. As they "dress up" in various guises of adult roles, or even as spiders and rabbits, they are using fantasy to explore what they might become. Their riding toys allow them to play with the experience of having greater mobility in the world.

Play's Contribution to Cognitive Development

The young child uses play to think about the world, to understand cause and effect (Roskos & Christie, 2000). Throughout early childhood, young children show increasing sophistication in using words in their dramatic play.

Some researchers have asked the question, does symbolic play facilitate cognitive development, or does symbolic play require mature cognitive abilities? The question is unresolved; the available evidence indicates only that cognitive development is connected with play in early childhood (Roopnarine et al., 2000). Childhood sociologists have found that children create sophisticated language games for group play that facilitate the development of language and logical thinking (Corsaro, 2005). A number of researchers have studied how young children build literacy skills through play, particularly play with books (Roskos & Christie, 2000). Play that is focused on language and thinking skills has been described as **learning play** (Meek, 2000).

Play as an Opportunity to Gain Control

In his cross-cultural study of play, William Corsaro (2005), a childhood sociologist, demonstrates that young children typically use dramatic play to cope with fears. They incorporate their fears into their group play and thus develop some mastery over stress and anxiety.

▲ **Photo 4.4**   Young children use play to think about the world and to understand cause and effect.

This perspective on young children's play is the cornerstone of play therapy (Chethik, 2000). Anyone who has spent much time in a child care center has probably seen a group of 4-year-olds engaged in superhero play, their flowing capes improvised with towels pinned on their shirts. Such play helps the child compensate for inadequacy and fear that comes from recognizing that one is a small person in a big world (Davies, 2004). Corsaro suggests that the love for climbing toys that bring small children high over the heads of others serves the same purpose.

Children in preschool settings have also been observed trying to get control over their lives by subverting some of the control of adults. Corsaro (2005) describes a preschool where the children had been told that they could not bring any play items from home. The preschool teachers were trying to avoid the kinds of conflicts that can occur over toys brought from home. The children in this preschool found a way to subvert this rule, however; they began to bring in very small toys, such as matchbox cars, that would fit in their pockets out of sight when teachers were nearby. Corsaro provides a number of other examples from his cross-cultural research of ways that young children use play to take some control of their lives away from adults.

> How does play develop skills for human agency in making choices?

Play as a Shared Experience

Increasing emphasis is placed on the way that play in early childhood contributes to the development of peer culture. Many researchers who study the play of young children suggest that **sociodramatic play,** or group fantasy play in which children coordinate their fantasy, is the most important form of play during this time. Indeed, one researcher has reported that two thirds of the play among North American young children is sociodramatic play (Rubin, 1986). Young children are able to develop more elaborate fantasy play and sustain it by forming friendship groups, which in turn gives them experience with group conflict and group problem solving that carries over into the adult world (Corsaro, 2005).

As young children play in groups, they attempt to protect the opportunity to keep the play going by restricting who may enter the play field (Corsaro, 2005). Young children can often be heard making such comments as, "We're friends; we're playing, right?" Or perhaps, "You're not our friend, you can't play with us." The other side of the coin is that young children must learn how to gain access to play in progress (Garvey, 1984). An important social skill is being able to demonstrate that they can play without messing the game up. Young children learn a set of do's and don'ts to accomplish that goal (see Exhibit 4.3) and develop complex strategies for gaining access to play.

Conflict often occurs in young children's play groups, and researchers have found gender and cultural variations in how these conflicts get resolved. Young girls have been found to prefer dyadic (two-person) play interactions, and young boys enjoy larger groups (Benenson, 1993). These preferences may not hold across cultures, however. For example, White middle-class young girls in the United States are less direct and assertive in challenging each other in play situations than either African American girls in the United States or young girls in an Italian preschool (Corsaro, 2005). Greater assertiveness may allow for more comfortable play in larger groups.

Play as the Route to Attachment to Fathers

Most of the efforts to understand attachment focus on the link between mothers and children, and the effect of the maternal relationship. More recently, though, there has been growing concern about and interest in the importance of fathers in the development of attachment for young children. Some suggest that father-child attachment may be promoted mainly through play, much like mother-child relationship may be the result of caregiving activities (Laflamme, Pomerleau, & Malcuit, 2002; Roggman, 2004). Differences in play style noted for mothers versus that seen in fathers is of particular interest. Investigators conclude that more physical play is seen between fathers and young children compared with more object play and conventional play interaction between mothers and children (Goldberg, Clarke-Stewart, Rice, & Dellis, 2002). Both forms of play can involve the display of affection by the parent. Thus, both forms of play contribute to the development of parent-child attachment. This research broadens the notion that only certain kinds of play have the potential to effect positive attachment and affirms the notion that there is developmental value for children in father-child physical play. In fact, physical play stimulates, arouses, and takes children out of their comfort zone. Roggman further notes that the style of play often ascribed to fathers provides opportunity for young children to overcome their limits and to experience taking chances in a context where there is some degree of confidence that they will be protected.

Developmental Disruptions

Children develop at different rates. Most developmental problems in infants and young children are more accurately described as developmental delays, offering the hope that early intervention, or even natural processes, will

Do's
Watch what's going on.
Figure out the play theme.
Enter the area.
Plug into the action.
Hold off making suggestions about how to change the action.
Don'ts
Don't ask questions for information (if you can't tell what's going on, you'll mess it up).
Don't mention yourself or your reactions to what is going on.
Don't disagree or criticize what is happening.

▲ **Exhibit 4.3**   Do's and Don'ts of Getting Access to Play in Progress

SOURCE: Based on Garvey, 1984.

mitigate the long-term effects. Developmental delays may exist in cognitive skills, communication skills, social skills, emotion regulation, behavior, and fine and gross motor skills. Developmental problems in school-age children are typically labeled disabilities and classified into groups, such as cognitive disability, learning disabilities, and motor impairment (Zipper & Simeonsson, 2004).

Many young children with developmental difficulties, including emotional and behavioral concerns, are inaccurately assessed and misdiagnosed—often because young children are assessed independently of their environment (Freeman & Dyer, 1993; Sameroff, Bartko, Baldwin, Baldwin, & Seifer, 1998). After interviewing professionals who work with children age 6 and under, one research team compiled a list of traits observed in young children that indicate emotional and behavioral problems: extreme aggressive behavior, difficulty with change, invasion of others' personal space, compulsive or impulsive behavior, low ability to trust others, lack of empathy or remorse, and cruelty to animals (Schmitz & Hilton, 1996). Parents and teachers often handle these behaviors with firmer limits and more discipline. However, environmental risk factors, such as emotional abuse or neglect and domestic violence, may be the actual cause.

Given the difficulty of accurate assessment, assessment in young children should include many disciplines to gain as broad an understanding as possible (Zipper & Simeonsson, 2004). Assessment and service delivery should also be culturally relevant (Parette, 1995). In other words, culture and other related issues—such as family interaction patterns and stress, the social environment, ethnicity, acculturation, social influences, and developmental expectations— should all be considered when evaluating a child's developmental abilities.

For those children who have been labeled developmentally delayed, the main remedy has been social skill development. In one such program, two types of preschool classrooms were evaluated (Roberts, Burchinal, & Bailey, 1994). In one classroom, young developmentally delayed children were matched with nondelayed children of the same age; in another classroom, some of the "normal" children were the same age as the developmentally delayed children and some were older. Social exchange between the children with delays and those without delays was greater in the mixed-aged classroom. Another study evaluated the usefulness of providing social skills training to children with mild developmental disabilities (Lewis, 1994). In a preschool setting, developmentally delayed children were put in situations requiring social interaction and were praised for successful interaction. This method increased social interaction between the young children.

It is also important to recognize the parental stress that often accompanies care of children with developmental disabilities. Researchers have found that an educational intervention with parents that teaches behavioral management and how to plan activities that minimize disruptive behavior results in improved child behavior, improved parent-child relationship, and less parental stress (Clare, Mazzucchelli, Studman, & Sanders, 2006).

In the 1980s, concern about the quality of education in the United States led to upgrades in the elementary school curriculum. Many skills previously introduced in the first grade became part of the kindergarten curriculum. This has led to increased concern about kindergarten readiness, the skills that the young child should have acquired before entering kindergarten, as well as how to provide for the needs of developmentally delayed children in the kindergarten classroom. It has also led to controversies about when to begin to think of developmental delays as disabilities. A growing concern is that children with developmental problems should not be placed in kindergarten classrooms that do not provide support for their particular developmental needs (Litty & Hatch, 2006). States vary in how much support they provide to children with developmental delays to allow them to participate in fully inclusive classrooms (classrooms where they are mainstreamed with children without developmental delays), but a growing small minority of children with developmental delays in the United States are participating as full citizens in inclusive classrooms during preschool and kindergarten (Guralnick, Neville, Hammond, & Connor, 2008). Before leaving this discussion, we would like to emphasize one important point. When working with young children, we want to recognize and respect the variability of developmental trajectories. At the same time, however, we want to be attentive to any aspects of a child's development that may be lagging behind expected milestones so that we can provide extra support to young children in specific areas of development.

> ## Critical Thinking Questions 4.2
>
> What challenges might Terri Smith, Jack Lewis, and Ron and Rosalind Johnson face in developing self-esteem? How might a social worker help each of these children to develop a positive self-evaluation? How can play be used with each of these children to foster their social development?

EARLY CHILDHOOD EDUCATION

Universal early childhood enrollment, defined as a 90% enrollment rate, begins later in the United States than in several other countries: age 5 in the United States, compared with age 3 in France and Italy, and age 4 in Japan and the United Kingdom. In France, a large number of children below the age of 3 are enrolled in formal education (Sen, Partelow, & Miller, 2005).

Much evidence indicates that low-income and racial minority students in the United States have less access to quality early childhood education than their age peers (Education Trust, 2006). Many poorer school districts do not provide prekindergarten programs, and there was a 13% cut in funding to Head Start between 2002 and 2008. Those cuts, along with rising unemployment, led to a growing waiting list for low-income children to get into Head Start. New funds were appropriated for Head Start programs in 2009 and 2010, but many children remain on waiting lists (National Head Start Association, 2010). With tightening budgets, some low- to middle-income districts are canceling full-day kindergarten, and some public school districts have begun to provide for-pay preschool and full-day kindergarten, a practice that clearly disadvantages low-income children. Wealthy families are competing for slots for their young children in expensive preschool programs, called the "baby ivies," that provide highly enriched early learning environments, further advancing opportunities for children in privileged families (Kozol, 2005). Middle-class families, as well as impoverished families, are increasingly unable to access quality early childhood education; 78% of families who earned more than $100,000 per year in 2004 sent their young children to early childhood educational programs compared with less than half of families earning less than $50,000 per year (Calman & Tarr-Whelan, 2005).

In recent years, a coalition of business leaders, economists, and child development scholars has called for universal quality early childhood education in the United States, arguing that it is a wise investment (see Calman & Tarr-Whelan, 2005). Empirical evidence is mounting to support this argument. One longitudinal study has followed a group of children who attended the High/Scope Perry Preschool Program in Ypsilanti, Michigan, until they reached the age of 40 (Schweinhart et al., 2005). Between 1962 and 1967, the researchers identified a sample of 123 low-income African American children who had been assessed to be at high risk of school failure. They randomly assigned 58 of these children to attend a high-quality two-year preschool program for 2- and 3-year-olds, while the other 65 attended no preschool program. The program met for 2½ hours per day, 5 days a week, and teachers made home visits every 2 weeks. The teachers in the preschool program had bachelor's degrees and education certification. No more than eight children were assigned to a teacher, and the curriculum emphasized giving children the opportunity to plan and carry out their own activities. By age 40, the preschool participants, on average, were doing better than the nonparticipants in several important ways:

- They were more likely to have graduated from high school (65% vs. 45%).

- They were more likely to be employed (76% vs. 62%).

- They had higher median annual earnings ($20,800 vs. $15,300).

- They were more likely to own their own home (37% vs. 28%).

- They were more likely to have a savings account (76% vs. 50%).

- They had fewer lifetime arrests (36% vs. 55% arrested five or more times).

- They were less likely to have spent time in prison or jail (28% vs. 52% never sentenced).

The researchers report that the preschool program cost $15,166 per child and the public gained $12.90 for every dollar spent on the program by the time the participants were 40 years old. The savings came from reduced special education costs, increased taxes derived from higher earnings, reduced public assistance costs, and reduced costs to the criminal justice system.

Another longitudinal study began in North Carolina in 1972, when 112 low-income infants were randomly assigned to either a quality preschool program or to no program (Masse & Barnett, 2002). The group assigned to the preschool program was enrolled in the program for 5 years instead of the 2 years as in the High/Scope Perry study. The participants in this study were followed to the age of 21. The children who participated in the preschool program were less likely to repeat grades, less likely to be placed in special education classes, and more likely to complete high school. It is important to note that the researchers in this study also investigated the impact of the preschool program on the mothers. They found that the preschool program mothers earned $3,750 more per year than the mothers whose children did not attend the program, for a total of $78,750 more over 21 years.

The above two longitudinal studies investigated the impact of quality preschool education on low-income children, but there is also preliminary evidence of the benefit of early childhood education on all children. A study conducted at Georgetown University has examined the effect of prekindergarten (PK) programs in Tulsa, Oklahoma (Gromley, Gayer, Phillips, & Dawson, 2004). These programs are considered high quality because teachers are required to have a bachelor's degree, there are no more than 10 children per teacher, and teachers are paid on the same scale as public school teachers. The researchers found that children who attended PK scored better on letter-word identification, spelling, and applied problems than children of the same age who had not attended PK. This was true regardless of race or socioeconomic status.

These studies suggest that early childhood education programs are good for children, for families, for communities, and for the society. With such evidence in hand, social workers can join with other child advocates to build broad coalitions to educate the public about the multilevel benefits and to push for public policy that guarantees universal quality early childhood education.

EARLY CHILDHOOD IN THE MULTIGENERATIONAL FAMILY

Curiosity and experimentation are the hallmarks of early childhood. Young children are sponges, soaking up information about themselves, their worlds, and their relationships. They use their families as primary sources of information and as models for relationships. Where there are older siblings, they serve as important figures of identification and imitation. Aunts, uncles, cousins, and grandparents may also serve this role, but parents are, in most families, the most important sources of information, support, and modeling for young children.

Parents play two very important roles for their age-3 to age-6 child: educator and advocate (Newman & Newman, 2009). As educators, they answer children's big and little questions, ask questions to stimulate thinking and growth in communication skills, provide explanations, and help children figure things out. They teach children about morality and human connectedness by modeling honest, kind, thoughtful behavior, and by reading to their children about moral dilemmas and moral action. They help children develop emotional intelligence by modeling how to handle strong feelings and by talking with children about the children's strong feelings. They take young children on excursions in their real physical worlds as well as in the fantasy worlds found in books. They give children opportunities to perform tasks that develop a sense of mastery.

Not all parents have the same resources for the educator role or the same beliefs about how children learn. And some parents take their role as educators too seriously, pushing their young children into more and more structured time with higher and higher expectations of performance (Elkind, 2001). Many of these parents are pushing their own frustrated dreams onto their young children. The concern is that these children are deprived of time for exploration, experimentation, and fantasy.

In the contemporary era, children are moving into organized child care settings at earlier ages. As they do so, parents become more important as advocates who understand their children's needs. The advocate role is particularly important for parents of young children with disabilities. These parents may need to advocate to ensure that all aspects of early childhood education programs are accessible to their children.

For some children, like Ron and Rosiland Johnson, it is the grandparent and not the parent who serves as the central figure. Estimates are that 5.8 million children live in homes headed by a grandparent or other relative, with 4.4 million in homes headed by grandparents (Children's Defense Fund, 2008). In about 50% of these families, no biological parent is present in the home. Substance abuse, divorce, teen pregnancy, the AIDS epidemic, and imprisoned mothers such as Shirley account for the large number of children living in grandparent-headed homes. Some custodial grandparents describe an increased purpose for living, but others describe increased isolation, worry, physical and emotional exhaustion, and financial concerns (Clarke, 2008). These are some of the same concerns expressed by Ms. Johnson. In addition, grandparents caring for children with psychological and physical problems experience high levels of stress (Sands & Goldberg, 2000).

The literature indicates that young children often do better under the care of grandparents than in other types of homes. However, children parented by their grandparents must often overcome many difficult emotions (Smith, Dannison, & Vach-Hasse, 1998). These children struggle with issues of grief and loss related to loss of their parent(s) and feelings of guilt, fear, embarrassment, and anger. These feelings may be especially strong for young children who feel they are somehow responsible for the loss of their parent(s). Although children in this age group are capable of labeling their feelings, their ability to discuss these feelings with any amount of depth is very limited. In addition, grandparents may feel unsure about how to talk about the situation with their young grandchildren. Professional intervention for the children is often recommended (Smith et al.). Some mental health practitioners have had success providing group sessions that help grandparents gain control over their grandchildren's behavior, resolve clashes in values between themselves and their grandchildren, and help grandparents avoid overindulgence and set firm limits.

Grandparents are often important figures in the lives of young children even when they do not serve as primary caregivers; they provide practical support, financial support, and emotional support. They may offer different types of practical support, coming to the aid of the family when needs arise. Or, they may serve as the child care provider while parents work or provide baby-sitting services in the evening. They also provide financial support, depending on their financial circumstances. They may provide cash assistance or buy things such as clothes and toys for the children; it is distressing to some grandparents if they lack the financial resources to buy things for their grandchildren. Grandparents may also provide emotional support and advice to parents of young children; this is something that can be done at a distance by a variety of electronic technologies when grandparents live at some distance from the children (Clarke, 2008).

RISKS TO HEALTHY DEVELOPMENT IN EARLY CHILDHOOD

This section addresses a few risk factors that social workers are likely to encounter in work with young children and their families: poverty, ineffective discipline, divorce, and violence (including child abuse). In addition, the section outlines the protective factors that ameliorate the risks.

> Why is it important to recognize risk factors and protective factors in early childhood?

Poverty

As reported in Chapter 3, there are one billion children around the world living in poverty. Over 14 million children live in poverty in the United States—including 22% of children age 6 and younger. About 44% of U.S. children under 6 live in low-income families, with incomes below 200% of the poverty level. Sixty-nine percent of Native American children under age 6 live in low-income families, compared with 64% of African American and Latino children, 30% of White children, and 28% of Asian children (Wight & Chau, 2009a). Poverty—in the form of food insecurity, inadequate health care, and overcrowded living conditions—presents considerable risks to children's growth and development. In 2008, 22.3% of households with children under 6 years of age were food insecure. The research indicates that families with food insecurity usually attempt to provide adequate nutrition to the youngest children, with parents and older children making sacrifices to feed younger children (Nord, Andrews, & Carlson, 2009). A recent study of the Northern Cheyenne Indian reservation in southeastern Montana found that 70% of all households were food insecure (Whiting & Ward, 2008). Inadequate nutrition is a serious threat to all aspects of early childhood development. Inadequate health care means that many acute conditions become chronic. Overcrowding is problematic to young children in that it restricts opportunities for play, the means through which most development occurs.

Research indicates that young children reared in poverty are significantly delayed in language and other cognitive skills (Locke, Ginsborg, & Peers, 2002). The effects of poverty on children in early childhood appear to be long lasting. Children who experience poverty during their early years are less likely to complete school than children whose initial exposure to poverty occurred in the middle childhood years or during adolescence. Researchers have also found that children who live in poverty are at high risk for low self-esteem, peer conflict, depression, and childhood psychological disorders. Poverty is often associated with other risk factors such as overwhelmed parents, living in a violent setting or in deteriorated housing, and instability of frequent changes in residence and schools (Bartholomae & Fox, 2010).

Not all young children who live in poverty fare poorly, however. In their longitudinal study of 180 children born into poverty, Sroufe et al. (2005) report that four groups emerged by early childhood: They grouped 70 children into a very competent cluster who were high in enthusiasm, persistence, compliance, and affection for the mother. They grouped another 25 children into a very incompetent cluster characterized by high negativity and low compliance and affection. The other almost half of the children were grouped into two clusters that fell between very competent and very incompetent.

Homelessness

Families with children make up one third of the homeless population, and families became more and more vulnerable to home foreclosures and unemployment during the deep recession that started in late 2007. It is estimated that 42% of homeless families have children under the age of 6. Homeless children are sick more often, are exposed to more violence, and experience more emotional and behavioral problems and more delayed development than low-income housed children. Their school attendance is often disrupted because they need to change schools, but often because of transportation problems as well (Paquette & Bassuk, 2009).

Kristen Paquette and Ellen Bassuk (2009) note that parents' identities are often closely tied to relationships they maintain, especially with their children, and that homelessness undermines their ability to protect those they have a responsibility to protect. Like all parents, homeless parents want to provide their children with basic necessities. Being homeless presents dramatic barriers and challenges for parents, who too often lose the ability to provide essentials for their children, including shelter, food, and access to education. They must look for jobs and housing while also adhering to shelter rules. Their parenting is public, easily observed, and monitored by others. What they need is to be involved with a meaningful social support system that links them to organizations and professionals in the community who might offer resources and options that support them to engage in effective parenting.

Ineffective Discipline

A popular guidebook for parents declares, "Under no circumstances should you ever punish your child!!" (Moyer, 1974, p. 40). Punishment implies an attempt to get even with the child, whereas **discipline** involves helping the child overcome a problem. Parents often struggle with how forceful to be in response to undesired behavior. The Smiths are a good example of this struggle. And, indeed, the research on parental styles of discipline is finding that the question of appropriate style of parenting young children is a very complex question, indeed.

A good place to begin this discussion is with the work of Diana Baumrind (1971), who, after extensive research, described three parenting styles, authoritarian, authoritative, and permissive, which use different combinations of two factors: warmth and control (see Exhibit 4.4). The **authoritarian parenting** style uses low warmth and high control. These parents favor punishment and negative reinforcement, and children are treated as submissive. Children reared under an authoritarian parenting style have been found to become hostile and moody and have difficulty managing stress (Carey, 1994; Welsh, 1985). Baumrind considered the **authoritative parenting** style, in which parents consider the child's viewpoints but remain in control, to be the most desirable approach to discipline and behavior management. The authoritative parenting style has been found to be associated with academic achievement, self-esteem, and social competence (see Domenech Rodriguez, Donovick, & Crowley, 2009). The **permissive parenting** style accepts children's behavior without attempting to modify it. Baumrind suggested that children reared from the permissive parenting orientation are cheerful but demonstrate little if any impulse control. In addition, these children are overly dependent and have low levels of self-reliance. The Smiths' style of parenting probably fits here. Certainly, Terri Smith's behavior mirrors behavior exhibited by children reared with the permissive style. Some researchers have presented a fourth parenting style, **disengaged parenting,** parents who are aloof, withdrawn, and unresponsive (Novak & Pelaez, 2004). Baumrind's typology of parenting styles has been the building block of much theorizing and research on parenting styles and child outcomes.

Stephen Greenspan (2006) questions Baumrind's suggestion that authoritative parenting is the best parenting. He suggests that Baumrind paid too little attention to the context in which parental discipline occurs, arguing that there are times to exercise control and times to tolerate a certain level of behavioral deviance, and that a wise parent knows the difference between these types of situations. Greenspan proposes that another dimension of parenting should be added to Baumrind's two dimensions of warmth and control. He calls this dimension "tolerance," and he recommends a style of parenting called "harmonious." He suggests that harmonious parents are warm and set limits when they feel they are called for, and overlook some child behaviors in the interests of facilitating child autonomy and family harmony. It seems that many parents, like Terri Smith's parents, struggle with knowing which situations call for firm control and which ones call for tolerating some defiance.

Parenting styles are prescribed in part by the community and the culture; therefore, it is not surprising that there is growing sentiment that Baumrind's parenting typology may be a good model for understanding parenting in White, middle-class families, but may not work as well for understanding parenting in other cultural groups. We will examine two streams of research that have explored racial and ethnic variations in parenting styles: research on Latino families and research on African American families.

Strong support has not been found for Baumrind's parenting typology in research on Latino parenting styles. Some researchers have described Latino parenting as permissive and others have described it as authoritarian. One research team (Domenech Rodriguez et al., 2009), like Greenspan, suggests that another dimension of parenting should be added to Baumrind's two-dimension model of warmth and control. They call this dimension "autonomy granting," which they describe as allowing children autonomy of individual expression in the family. This seems to be very close to what Greenspan meant by "tolerance," because he writes of tolerance of emotional expression in the spirit of autonomy. Domenech Rodriguez and colleagues suggest that these three dimensions—warmth, control, and autonomy granting—can be configured in different ways to produce eight different parenting styles:

Authoritative: high warmth, high control, high autonomy granting

Authoritarian: low warmth, high control, low autonomy granting

Permissive: high warmth, low control, high autonomy granting

Neglectful: low warmth, low control, low autonomy granting

Protective: high warmth, high control, low autonomy granting

Cold: low warmth, high control, high autonomy granting

Affiliative: high warmth, low control, low autonomy granting

Neglectful II: low warmth, low control, high autonomy granting

Parenting Style	Description	Type of Discipline
Authoritarian	Parents who use this type of parenting are rigid and controlling. Rules are narrow and specific, with little room for negotiation, and children are expected to follow the rules without explanation.	Cold and harsh Physical force No explanation of rules provided
Authoritative	These parents are more flexible than authoritarian parents. Their rules are more reasonable, and they leave opportunities for compromises and negotiation.	Warm and nurturing Positive reinforcement Set firm limits and provide rationale behind rules and decisions
Permissive	The parents' rules are unclear, and children are left to make their own decisions.	Warm and friendly toward their children No direction given

▲ **Exhibit 4.4**   Three Parenting Styles

SOURCE: Adapted from Baumrind, 1971.

In their preliminary research, which involved direct observation of 56 first-generation Latino American families, they found that the majority (61%) used a protective parenting style but had different expectations for male and female children. There seems to be merit in adding the dimension of autonomy granting, because it may help to capture the parenting styles of cultural groups that are less individualistic than European American culture.

There is a relatively long line of research that has questioned the appropriateness of applying Baumrind's model to understand African American parenting, and the issues are proving to be complex. Much of this research has looked at the use of physical discipline, with the finding that physical discipline causes disruptive behaviors in White families but not Black families (see Lau, Litrownki, Newton, Black, & Everson, 2006, for a review of this research). Researchers have suggested that Black children may regard physical discipline as a legitimate parenting behavior because there is a culture of using physical discipline out of "concern for the child": high levels of firm control are used along with high levels of warmth and affection. Conversely, it is argued that White children may regard physical discipline as an act of aggression because it is often used when parents are angry and out of control (Lansford, Deater-Deckard, Dodge, Bates, & Pettit, 2004). The idea is that the context of the physical discipline and the meaning made of it will influence its impact. However, research by Lau et al. (2006) did not replicate earlier research that found that the effects of physical discipline differed by race. They found that for both Black and White children, physical discipline exacerbated impulsive, aggressive, and noncompliant behaviors for children who had exhibited behavioral problems at an early age. However, they also found that parental warmth protected against later problems in White children but seemed to exacerbate early problems in Black children. The researchers concluded that professionals must recognize that parenting may need to take different forms in different communities. Clearly, this is an issue that needs further investigation.

Research has also indicated that there are differences in parenting style based on the socioeconomic environment in which parenting occurs. Low-income parents have been noted to be more authoritarian than more economically advantaged parents. Using observation methods, one research team found that the socioeconomic differences in parenting styles is not that straightforward, however. They found that middle-class parents routinely use subtle forms of control while, at the same time, trying to instill autonomy in their children. Their children spend a large portion of their time under adult supervision, in one activity or another. The researchers also found that low-income parents tend to value conformity but allow their school-aged children to spend considerable leisure time in settings where they do not have adult supervision, consequently affording them considerable autonomy (Weininger & Lareau, 2009).

Findings from studies about punishment and young children indicate that punishment is often used in response to early childhood behavior that is age appropriate. So rather than encouraging the independence that is otherwise expected for a child, such age-appropriate behavior is discouraged (Culp, McDonald Culp, Dengler, & Maisano, 1999). In addition, recent evidence indicates that brain development can be affected by the stress created by punishment or physical discipline (Glaser, 2000). Harsh punishment and physical discipline interfere with the neural connection process that begins in infancy and continues throughout early childhood. But for many low-income parents, harsh punishment may be less an issue of control or "bad parenting" than an effort to cope with a desperate situation.

As you can see, there are many current controversies about effective parenting for young children, and this is an issue about which parents and professionals often have strong feelings. Research is beginning to recognize that different parenting styles may work well in different developmental niches. To make the issue even more complicated, scholars such as Judith Rich Harris (1998) and Steven Pinker (2002) argue that behavioral traits have such a strong genetic component that we should avoid overemphasizing the role of parenting style in behavioral outcomes. In fact, they argue that we have overemphasized the role of families in shaping behavior, other than by providing genetic heritage. Harris also argues that the peer group and community have more impact on child identity and behavior than parents. No doubt, Harris and Pinker would argue that the inconsistent findings about the impact of parenting styles are evidence that parenting style is not a supremely important variable in child development. Of course, we are learning more about the genetic component of human behavior, but we are also learning about the plasticity of the brain to be affected by experience. Parents are a very large part of that experience throughout life, but in early childhood, other people come to be a part of the context of ongoing brain development.

Divorce

The divorce rate in the United States increased steadily from the mid-19th century through the 1970s, except for a steep drop in the 1950s; it stabilized in the 1980s and has declined slightly since then (Fine, Ganong, & Demo, 2010). It is estimated that more than half of the children born in the 1990s spent some of their childhood in a single-parent household (Anderson, 2005). These single-parent families often live in poverty, and as we have already mentioned, poverty can have a negative effect on children's development. Following divorce, about two thirds of children live with their mother, and most women and children experience a sharp and, unfortunately, long-term decline in economic well-being after divorce (Fine et al.).

> How are young children affected by this historical trend toward high rates of divorce?

Researchers have come to very different conclusions about the effects of divorce on children. Some have found that children have severe and long-term problems following divorce (Wallerstein & Blakeslee, 1989). Others, using larger and more representative samples, have found less severe and more short-term effects of divorce on children (Barber & Demo, 2006). It has been suggested that the negative effects children experience may actually be the result of parents' responses to divorce rather than of the divorce itself (Hetherington & Kelly, 2002). After reviewing the disparate findings, Emery (1999) came to the following conclusions:

- Divorce is stressful for children.

- Divorce leads to higher levels of adjustment and mental health problems for children.

- Most children are resilient and adjust well to divorce.

- Children report considerable pain, unhappy memories, and continued distress about their parents' divorce.

- Postdivorce family interaction has a great influence on children's adjustment after divorce.

Several factors may protect children from long-term adjustment problems when their parents divorce. One significant parental issue is the relationship that the parents maintain during and after the divorce. With minimal conflict between the parents about custody, visitation, and child-rearing issues, and with parents' positive attitude toward each other, children experience fewer negative consequences (Hetherington & Kelly, 2002). Unfortunately, many children, like Jack Lewis in the case study, end up as noncombatants in the middle of a war, trying to avoid or defuse raging anger and disagreement between the two parents. Other protective factors are higher levels of predivorce adjustment, adequate provision of economic resource, and nurturing relationships with both parents (Fine et al., 2010).

Children who live in families where divorce results in economic hardship are at special risk. Chronic financial stress takes its toll on the mental and physical health of the residential parent, who is usually the mother. The parent often becomes less supportive and engages in inconsistent and harsh discipline. In these situations, children become distressed, often developing difficulties in cognitive and social development (Fine et al., 2010).

In early childhood, children are more vulnerable than older children to the emotional and psychological consequences of separation and divorce (Wallerstein & Blakeslee, 1989; Wallerstein & Corbin, 1991; Wallerstein, Corbin, & Lewis, 1988). One reason may be that young children have difficulty understanding divorce and often believe that the absent parent is no longer a member of the family and will never be seen again. In addition, because of young children's egocentrism, they often feel that the divorce is a result of their behavior and experience the absent parent's leaving as a rejection of them. One wonders if Jack Lewis thinks he not only caused his father to leave but also caused him to become the devil.

Violence

Many parents complain that keeping violence away from children requires tremendous work even in the best of circumstances. Children witness violence on television and through video and computer games and hear about it through many other sources. In the worst of circumstances, young children not only are exposed to violence but become victims of it as well. This section discusses three types of violence experienced by many young children: community violence, domestic violence, and child abuse.

Community Violence

In some neighborhoods, acts of violence are so common that the communities are labeled "war zones." However, most residents prefer not to be combatants. When surveyed, mothers in a Chicago housing project ranked neighborhood violence as their number one concern and as the condition that most negatively affects the quality of their life and the lives of their children (Dubrow & Garbarino, 1989). Unfortunately, neighborhood violence has become a major health issue for children (Krug, Dahlberg, Mercy, Zwi, & Lozano, 2002; Pennekamp, 1995).

A number of years ago, the first author (Debra) had the opportunity to observe the effects of community violence up close when she took her daughter to get her hair braided by someone who lived in a housing project, an acquaintance of a friend. Because the hair-braiding procedure takes several hours, she and her daughter were in the home for an extended period. While they were there, the news was released that Tupac Shakur (a popular rap singer) had died from gunshot injuries received earlier. An impromptu gathering of friends and relatives of the woman who was doing the braiding ensued. Ten men and women in their early 20s, along with their young children, gathered to discuss the shooting and to pay tribute to Tupac, who had been one of their favorite artists. As Tupac's music played in the background, Debra was struck by several themes:

- Many in the room told of a close relative who had died as a result of neighborhood violence. Debra noticed on the wall of the apartment three framed programs from funerals of young men. She later learned that these dead men were a brother and two cousins of the woman who lived in the apartment. All three had been killed in separate violent incidents in their neighborhood.

- A sense of hopelessness permeated the conversation. The men especially had little hope of a future, and most thought they would be dead by age 40. Clinicians who work with young children living in neighborhoods in which violence is prevalent relate similar comments from children (National Center for Clinical Infant Programs, 1992). When asked if he had decided what he wanted to be when he grew up, one child is quoted as saying, "Why should I? I might not grow up" (p. 25).

- Perhaps related to the sense of hopelessness was an embracing of violence. Debra observed that during lighter moments in the conversation, the guests would chuckle about physical confrontations between common acquaintances.

Ironically, as Debra and her daughter were about to leave, gunshots sounded and the evening get-together was temporarily interrupted. Everyone, including the children, ran out of the apartment to see what had happened. For Debra, the significance of the evening was summarized in one of the last comments she heard before leaving. One of the men stated, "If all that money didn't save Tupac, what chance do we have?" It is interesting to note that Tupac's music and poetry continue to be idolized. Many still identify with his descriptions of hopelessness.

These sorts of conditions are not favorable for adequate child development (Dubrow & Garbarino, 1989; Krug et al., 2002). Investigations into the effects of living in violent neighborhoods support this claim. Children who grow up in a violent environment are reported to demonstrate low self-esteem, deficient social skills, and difficulty coping with and managing conflict (MacLennan, 1994). When Debra and her daughter visited the housing project, for example, they witnessed a 3-year-old telling her mother to "shut up." The mother and child then began hitting each other. Yes, some of this behavior is a result of parenting style, but one cannot help wondering about the influence of living in a violent community.

For many children living in violent neighborhoods, the death of a close friend or family member is commonplace. When the second author (David) was employed at a community child guidance center, he found that appointments were often canceled so the parents could attend funerals.

Living so intimately with death has grave effects on young children. In one study of young children whose older siblings had been victims of homicide, the surviving siblings showed symptoms of depression, anxiety, psychosocial impairment, and posttraumatic stress disorder (Freeman, Shaffer, & Smith, 1996). These symptoms are similar to those observed in young children in situations of political and military violence—for example, in Palestinian children in the occupied West Bank (Baker, 1990) and in children in South African townships during apartheid (Magwaza, Kilian, Peterson, & Pillay, 1993). Perhaps the label "war zone" is an appropriate one for violent communities. However, positive, affectionate, caregiving relationships—whether by parents or other family members or individuals in the community—can play an important mediating role in how violence is managed by very young children (Glaser, 2000).

Domestic Violence

The family is the social group from whom we expect to receive our greatest love, support, nurturance, and acceptance. And yet, family relationships are some of the most violent relationships in many societies. It is estimated that wife beating occurs in about 85% of the world's societies, and husband beating occurs in about 27% (Newman, 2008). Some suggest that physical violence between siblings may be the most common form of family violence (Gelles, 2010). Domestic violence may take the form of verbal, psychological, or physical abuse, although physical abuse is the form most often implied. It is difficult to produce accurate statistics about the amount of family violence because what happens in families is usually "behind closed doors." An estimated 3.3 million children are exposed each year to violence against their mothers by family members (American Psychological Association, 1996).

> How does psychological age affect children's responses to domestic violence?

In early childhood, children respond in a number of ways during violent episodes (Smith, O'Connor, & Berthelsen, 1996). Some children display fright—that is, they cry and scream. Others attempt to stop the violence by ordering the abuser to stop, by physically placing themselves between the mother and the abuser, or by hitting the abuser. Many children attempt to flee by retreating to a different room, turning up the volume on the TV, or trying to ignore the violence.

The effects of domestic violence on children's development are well-documented. Distress, problems with adjustment, characteristics of trauma, and increased behavior problems have all been observed in children exposed to domestic violence (Hughes, 1988; Perloff & Buckner, 1996; Shepard, 1992; Turner, Finkelhor, & Ormrod, 2006). In addition, these children develop either aggressive behaviors or passive responses, both of which make them potential targets for abuse as teens and adults (Suh & Abel, 1990; Tutty & Wagar, 1994). Unfortunately, researchers are finding that children who witness intimate partner violence at home are also more likely to be victimized in other ways, including being victims of child maltreatment and community violence. The accumulation of victimization produces great risk for a variety of mental health problems in children (Turner et al.).

In early childhood, children are more vulnerable than school-age children to the effects of living with domestic violence (O'Keefe, 1994; Smith et al., 1996). Younger children simply have fewer internal resources to help them cope with the experience. In addition, older children have friendships outside the family for support, whereas younger children rely primarily on the family. Many parents who are victims of domestic violence become emotionally unavailable to their young children. Battered mothers, for example, often become depressed and preoccupied with the abuse and their personal safety, leaving little time and energy for the attention and nurturing needed by young children. Another reason that young children are more vulnerable to the effects of domestic violence is that children between the ages of 3 and 6 lack the skills to verbalize their feelings and thoughts. As a result, thoughts and feelings about the violence get trapped inside and continually infringe upon the child's thoughts and emotions. Finally, as in the case of divorce, because of their egocentrism, young children often blame themselves for the domestic abuse.

Domestic violence does not always affect children's long-term development, however. In one study, one third of the children seemed unaffected by the domestic violence they witnessed at home; these children were well adjusted and showed no signs of distress, anxiety, or behavior problems (Smith et al., 1996). Two factors may buffer the effect domestic violence has on children (O'Keefe, 1994):

1. *Amount of domestic violence witnessed by the child.* The more violent episodes children witness, the more likely they are to develop problematic behavior.

2. *Relationship between the child and the mother,* assuming the mother is the victim. If the mother-child relationship remains stable and secure, the probability of the child developing behavioral difficulties decreases significantly—even when the amount of violence witnessed by the child is relatively high.

Interestingly, the father-child relationship in cases of domestic abuse was not found to be related to the child's emotional or psychological development (O'Keefe, 1994). However, this finding should be reviewed with caution because it is often difficult to find fathers to include in this type of research and then to accurately measure the quality of attachment a younger child in such a circumstance experiences with the father or father figure (Mackey, 2001).

Child Maltreatment

It is difficult to estimate the rate of **child maltreatment,** because many incidences are never reported and much that is reported is not determined to be child maltreatment. The most prevalent forms of child maltreatment described by the U.S. Children's Bureau included neglect, physical abuse, sexual abuse, and emotional maltreatment (U.S. Department of Health and Human Services, 2009a). Child abuse may take the form of verbal, emotional, physical, or sexual abuse or child neglect. About three children die from maltreatment in the United States every day, and 86% of the children who die from child maltreatment are under 6 years of age (Thomlison, 2004). Girls are most likely to be victimized overall, but boys have a higher incidence of fatal injuries than girls (Sedlak & Broadhurst, 1996). National incidence data indicate no race or ethnicity differences in maltreatment incidence, but official reports of child maltreatment include an overrepresentation of African American and American Indian/Alaska Natives (Sedlak & Broadhurst, 1996). Poverty and the lack of economic resources are correlated with abuse, especially physical abuse and neglect (Sedlak & Broadhurst). In addition, family isolation and lack of a support system, parental drug and alcohol abuse, lack of knowledge regarding child rearing, and parental difficulty in expressing feelings are all related to child abuse (Gelles, 1989; Veltkamp & Miller, 1994; Wolfner & Gelles, 1993). An association has also been noted between abuse of young children and the overload of responsibilities that women often encounter. Mothers who work outside the home and are also responsible for most or all of the domestic responsibilities, and mothers with unemployed husbands, are more prone to abuse their young children than other groups of mothers are (Gelles & Hargreaves, 1981).

Child abuse creates risks to all aspects of growth and development, as shown in Exhibit 4.5, but children ages birth to 6 are at highest risk of having long-lasting damage (Thomlison, 2004). In their longitudinal research of 180 children born into poverty, Sroufe et al. (2005) found that young children who had been physically abused as toddlers had higher levels of negativity, noncompliance, and distractibility than other children. Those whose mothers were psychologically unavailable demonstrated more avoidance of and anger toward the mother. Children with a history all types of maltreatment had lower self-esteem and agency and demonstrated more behavior problems than other children. Children with a history of neglect were more passive than other children.

Physical Impairments	Cognitive Impairments	Emotional Impairments
Physical Abuse and Neglect		
Burns, scars, fractures, broken bones, damage to vital organs and limbs Malnourishment Physical exposure Poor skin hygiene Poor (if any) medical care Poor (if any) dental care Serious medical problems Serious dental problems Failure-to-thrive syndrome Death	Delayed cognitive skills Delayed language skills Mental retardation Delayed reality testing Overall disruption of thought processes	Negative self-concept Increased aggressiveness Poor peer relations Poor impulse control Anxiety Inattentiveness Avoidant behavior
Sexual Abuse		
Trauma to mouth, anus, vaginal area Genital and rectal pain Genital and rectal bleeding Genital and rectal tearing Sexually transmitted disease	Hyperactivity Bizarre sexual behavior	Overly adaptive behaviour Overly compliant behaviour Habit disorders (nail biting) Anxiety Depression Sleep disturbances Night terrors Self-mutilation
Psychological/emotional abuse	Pessimistic view of life Anxiety and fear Distorted perception of world Deficits in moral development	Alienation Intimacy problems Low self-esteem Depression

▲ **Exhibit 4.5**   Some Potential Effects of Child Abuse on Growth and Development

PROTECTIVE FACTORS IN EARLY CHILDHOOD

Many of the factors listed in Chapter 3 that promote resiliency during the infant and toddler years are equally relevant during the early childhood years. Other protective factors also come into play (Fraser et al., 2004):

- *Social support.* Social support mediates many potential risks to the development of young children. The presence of social support increases the likelihood of a positive outcome for children whose parents divorce (Garvin, Kalter, & Hansell, 1993), moderates the effects for children who experience violence (Nettles, Mucherah, & Jones, 2000), facilitates better outcomes for children of mothers with mental illness (Oyserman, Bybee, Mowbray, & MacFarlane, 2002), and is even thought to reduce the continuation of abuse for 2- and 3-year-olds who have experienced parental abuse during the first year of life (Kotch et al., 1997). Social support aids young children in several ways (Fraser et al., 2004). Having a consistent and supportive aunt or uncle or preschool teacher who can set firm but loving limits, for example, may buffer the effects of a parent with ineffective skills. At the community level, preschools, religious programs, and the like may help to enhance physical and cognitive skills, self-esteem, and social development. Through social support from family and nonfamily relationships, young children can receive care and support, another identified protective factor.

- *Positive parent-child relationship.* A positive relationship with at least one parent helps children to feel secure and nurtured (Fraser et al., 2004). Remember from Chapter 3 that a sense of security is the foundation on which young children build initiative during the early childhood years. Even if Jack Lewis never has contact with his father, Charles, a positive relationship with Joyce, his mother, can mediate this loss.

- *Effective parenting.* In early childhood, children need the opportunity to take initiative but also need firm limits, whether they are established by parents or grandparents or someone else who adopts the parent role. Terri Smith, for example, has not been able to establish self-control because her boundaries are not well defined. Effective parenting promotes self-efficacy and self-esteem and provides young children with a model of how they can take initiative within boundaries (Fraser et al., 2004).

- *Self-esteem.* A high level of self-worth may allow young children to persist in mastery of skills despite adverse conditions. Perhaps a high level of self-esteem can enhance Ron's, Rosiland's, and Jack's development despite the disruptions in their lives. In addition, research indicates that self-esteem is a protective factor against the effects of child abuse (Fraser et al., 2004).

- *Intelligence.* Even in young children, a high IQ serves as a protective factor. For example, young children with high IQs were less likely to be affected by maternal psychopathology (Tiet et al., 2001). Others suggest that intelligence results in success, which leads to higher levels of self-esteem (Fraser, 2004). For young children, then, intelligence may contribute to mastery of skills and independence, which may enhance self-esteem. Intelligence may also protect children through increased problem-solving skills, which allow for more effective responses to adverse situations.

Critical Thinking Questions 4.3

What type of parenting style do you think your parents used when you were a child? Did both parents use the same parenting style? Do you think the parenting style(s) used by your parents was effective? How do you think your parents' parenting style was affected by culture? Would you want to use the same parenting style that your parents used if you were a parent? Why or why not?

IMPLICATIONS FOR SOCIAL WORK PRACTICE

In summary, knowledge about early childhood has several implications for social work practice with young children:

- Become well acquainted with theories and empirical research about growth and development among young children.

- Continue to promote the elimination of poverty and the advancement of social justice.

- Collaborate with other professionals in the creation of laws, interventions, and programs that assist in the elimination of violence.

- Create and support easy access to services for young children and their parents.

- Assess younger children in the context of their environment.

- Become familiar with the physical and emotional signs of child abuse.

- Directly engage younger children in an age-appropriate intervention process.

- Provide support to parents and help facilitate positive parent-child relationships.

- Encourage and engage both mothers and fathers in the intervention process.

- Provide opportunities for children to increase self-efficacy and self-esteem.

- Help parents understand the potential effects of negative environmental factors on their children.

KEY TERMS

authoritarian parenting
authoritative parenting
child maltreatment
disengaged parenting
discipline
egocentrism
empathy
fine motor skills
gross motor skills

hostile aggression
instrumental aggression
lateralization
learning play
permissive parenting
perspective taking
physical aggression
preconventional level of moral
   reasoning

prosocial
relational aggression
self-esteem
self-theory
sociodramatic play
symbolic play
transductive reasoning

ACTIVE LEARNING

1. Watch any child-oriented cartoon on television. Describe the apparent and implied messages (both positive and negative) available in the cartoon about race and ethnicity, and gender differences. Consider how these messages might affect gender and ethnic development in young children.

2. Observe preschool-age children at play. Record the types of play that you observe. How well do your observations fit with what is described about play in this chapter?

3. The case studies at the beginning of this chapter (Terri, Jack, and Ron and Rosiland) do not specify race or ethnicity of the families. How important an omission did that appear to you? What assumptions did you make about the racial and/or ethnic background of the families? On what basis did you make those assumptions?

WEB RESOURCES

American Academy of Child & Adolescent Psychiatry
www.aacap.org

Site presented by American Academy of Child & Adolescent Psychiatry contains concise and up-to-date information on a variety of issues facing children and their families, including day care, discipline, children and divorce, child abuse, children and TV violence, and children and grief.

Children's Defense Fund
www.childrensdefense.org

Site presented by the Children's Defense Fund, a private nonprofit child advocacy organization, contains information on issues, the Black Community Crusade for Children, the Child Watch Visitation Program, and a parent resource network.

International Society for Child and Play Therapy
www.playtherapy.org

Site presented by the International Society for Child and Play Therapy contains reading lists, articles and research, recommended resources, and other related organizations.

National Family Resiliency Center, Inc. (NFSC)
www.divorceabc.com

Site presented by the NFSC contains information about support groups, resources for professionals, library of articles, news and events, KIDS Newsletter, and Frequently Asked Questions.

The Office for Studies in Moral Development and Education
www.uic.edu/~1nucci/MoralEd/office.html

Site presented by the Office for Studies in Moral Development and Education at the College of Education at the University of Illinois at Chicago contains an overview of Piaget's, Kohlberg's, and Gilligan's theories of moral development and the domain theory of moral development.

U.S. Department of Health & Human Services
www.dhhs.gov

Site maintained by the U.S. Department of Health & Human Services contains information on child care, child support enforcement, and children's health insurance.

CHAPTER

5

Middle Childhood

Leanne Charlesworth, Jim Wood, and Pamela Viggiani

OPENING QUESTIONS

- How have our conceptions of middle childhood changed through time?

- What types of individual, family, school, community, and other systemic qualities are most conducive to positive development during middle childhood?

- During middle childhood, what factors heighten developmental risk for children, and what supports resilience?

KEY IDEAS

As you read this chapter, take note of these central ideas:

1. Values and beliefs regarding childhood in general, and middle childhood specifically, are shaped by historical and sociocultural context.

2. During middle childhood, a wide variety of bio/psycho/social/spiritual changes take place across the developmental domains.

3. As children progress through middle childhood, the family environment remains extremely important, while the community environment—including the school—also becomes a significant factor shaping development.

4. During middle childhood, peers have an increasingly strong impact on development; peer acceptance becomes very important to well-being.

5. Poverty, family or community violence, special needs, and family disruption create developmental risk for many children.

Case Study 5.1

Anthony Bryant's Impending Assessment

Anthony is a 6-year-old boy living in an impoverished section of a large city. Anthony's mother, Melissa, was 14 when Anthony was born. Anthony's father—James, 15 when Anthony was born—has always spent a great deal of time with Anthony. Although James now also has a 2-year-old daughter from another relationship, he has told Melissa that Anthony and Melissa are the most important people in his life. Once Anthony was out of diapers, James began spending even more time with him, taking Anthony along to visit friends and occasionally, on overnight outings.

James's father was murdered when James was a toddler and he rarely sees his mother, who struggles with a serious substance addiction and is known in the neighborhood as a prostitute. James lived with his paternal grandparents until he was in his early teens, when he began to stay with a favorite uncle. Many members of James's large extended family have been incarcerated on charges related to their involvement in the local drug trade. James's favorite uncle is a well-known and widely respected dealer. James himself has been arrested a few times and is currently on probation.

Melissa and Anthony live with her mother. Melissa obtained her general equivalency diploma after Anthony's birth, and she has held a variety of jobs for local fast food chains. Melissa's mother, Cynthia, receives Supplemental Social Security Income/Disability because she has been unable to work for several years because of her advanced rheumatoid arthritis, which was diagnosed when she was a teenager. Melissa remembers her father only as a loud man who often yelled at her when she made noise. He left Cynthia and Melissa when Melissa was 4 years old, and neither has seen him since. Cynthia seemed pleased when Anthony was born and she has been a second mother to him, caring for him while Melissa attends school, works, and socializes with James and her other friends.

Anthony has always been very active and energetic, frequently breaking things and creating "messes" throughout the apartment. To punish Anthony, Cynthia spanks him with a belt or other object—and she sometimes resorts to locking him in his room until he falls asleep. Melissa and James are proud of Anthony's wiry physique and rough and tough play; they have encouraged him to be fearless and not to cry when he is hurt. Both Melissa and James use physical punishment as their main discipline strategy with Anthony, but he usually obeys them before it is needed.

Anthony entered kindergarten at the local public school last fall. When he started school, his teacher told Melissa that he seemed to be a very smart boy, one of the only boys in the class who already knew how to write his name and how to count to 20. It is now spring, however, and Melissa is tired of dealing with Anthony's teacher and other school staff. She has been called at work a number of times, and recently the school social worker requested a meeting with her. Anthony's teacher reports that Anthony will not listen to her and frequently starts fights with the other children in the classroom. Anthony's teacher also states that Anthony constantly violates school rules, like waiting in line and being quiet in the hallways, and he doesn't seem bothered by threats of punishment. Most recently, Anthony's teacher has told Melissa that she would like Anthony assessed by the school psychologist.

Case Study 5.2

Brianna Shaw's New Self-Image

When Brianna was born, her mother Deborah was 31 years old with a 13-year-old daughter (Stacy) from a prior, short-lived marriage. Deborah and Michael's relationship was relatively new when Deborah became pregnant with Brianna. Shortly after Deborah announced the pregnancy, Michael moved into her mobile home. Michael and Deborah initially talked about setting a wedding date and pursuing Michael's legal adoption of Stacy, whose father had remarried and was no longer in close contact.

Michael made it clear throughout Deborah's pregnancy that he wanted a son. He seemed very content and supportive of Deborah until around the time the couple found out the baby was a girl. In Stacy's view, Michael became mean and bossy in the months that followed. He started telling Stacy what to do, criticizing Deborah's appearance, and complaining constantly that Deborah wasn't any fun anymore since she stopped drinking and smoking while she was pregnant.

(Continued)

(Continued)

During Brianna's infancy, the couple's relationship began to change even more rapidly. Michael was rarely home and instead spent most of his free time hanging out with old friends. When he did come by, he'd encourage Deborah to leave Brianna with Stacy so the two of them could go out like "old times." Even though her parents were Deborah's full-time day care providers and both Brianna and Stacy were thriving, Deborah was chronically exhausted from balancing parenting and her full-time job as a nursing assistant. Soon, whenever Michael came by, the couple frequently argued and their shouting matches gradually escalated to Michael threatening to take Brianna away. Michael was soon dating another woman and his relationship with Deborah and Stacy became increasingly hostile during the following four years.

The summer that Brianna turned 5, the local hospital closed down and Deborah lost her job. After talking with her parents, Deborah made the decision to move her daughters to Fairfield, a city 4 hours away from home. An old high school friend had once told Deborah that if she ever needed a job, the large hospital her friend worked for had regular openings and even offered tuition assistance. Within two months, Deborah had sold her mobile home, obtained a full-time position with her friend's employer, and signed a lease for a small townhouse in a suburb known for its high-quality school system.

When Brianna started kindergarten in their new town, her teacher described her to Deborah as shy and withdrawn. Deborah remembered reading something in the school newsletter about a social skills group run by a school social worker, and she asked if Brianna could be enrolled. Gradually, the group seemed to make a difference and Brianna began to act more like her old self, forming several friendships during the following two years.

Today, Brianna is 8 years old and has just entered third grade. Brianna usually leaves for school on the bus at 8:00 a.m., and Deborah picks her up from an afterschool program at 5:45 p.m. When possible, Stacy picks Brianna up earlier, after her own classes at a local community college are over. Brianna still spends summers with her grandparents in the rural area where she was born. Academically, she has thus far excelled in school but a new concern is Brianna's weight. Brianna is 49 inches tall and weighs 72 pounds. Until the last year or so, Brianna seemed unaware of the fact that many people viewed her as overweight. In the last several months, however, Brianna has told Stacy and Deborah various stories about other children calling her "fat" and making other comments about her size. Deborah feels that Brianna is increasingly moody and angry when she is home. Brianna recently asked Deborah why she is "fat" and told Stacy that she just wishes she were dead.

Case Study 5.3

Manuel Vega's Difficult Transition

A slightly built 11-year-old Manuel is in sixth grade in Greenville, Mississippi. He speaks English moderately well. He was born in Texas where his mother, Maria, and father, Estaban, met. For Estaban, it has been an interesting journey from his hometown in Mexico to Mississippi. For generations, Estaban's family lived and worked near Izucar de Matamoros, a small city in Mexico on the inter-American highway. During their teen years in Izucar de Matamoros, Estaban and his four younger brothers worked on the local sugarcane farms and in the sugar refineries. By the time he was in his early 20s, Estaban began to look for better paying work and was able to get his license to haul products from Izucar de Matamoros to larger cities, including Mexico City. Estaban and one brother eventually moved to a medium-sized city where his employer, the owner of a small trucking company, provided an apartment for several of his single truckers.

After three productive years in the trucking industry, the company went bankrupt. With his meager savings, Estaban made arrangements to travel to Arizona to pursue his dream of owning his own trucking company. Working as a day laborer, he eventually made his way to Laredo, Texas, where he met and married Maria. Although both Maria and Estaban's formal schooling ended relatively early, both acquired a basic command of English while living in Laredo. During the late 1970s, Maria and Estaban requested documentation for Estaban and after a lengthy process, they were successful.

Estaban and Maria began their family while Estaban continued to work at day labor construction jobs in and around Laredo. At home and with their relatives and neighbors, Maria and Estaban spoke Spanish exclusively. In their neighborhood, Maria's many relatives not only provided social support, but also helped Maria sell tamales and other traditional Mexican foods to locals and occasional tourists. Eventually, the family saved enough money for the purchase of a small truck that Estaban used to make deliveries of Maria's specialties to more distant restaurants. However, the family faced many competitors in the local Mexican food industry. Maria's Uncle Arturo urged the family to move to the Mississippi Delta where he owns Mi Casa, a Mexican restaurant and wholesale business. Uncle Arturo was hopeful that Maria would enrich his menu with her mastery of Mexican cuisine. He promised employment for Estaban, hauling Mexican specialty food staples to the growing number of Mexican restaurants in the Delta, ranging from Memphis to Biloxi.

Almost 3 years ago, Estaban and Maria decided to take Arturo up on his offer and together with their two sons, they moved to Greenville. Their older son Carlos never adjusted to school life in Mississippi. Now 16, Carlos did not return to school this fall. Instead, he began working full-time for his father loading and unloading the truck and providing his more advanced English language capacity to open up new markets for the business. At first Maria and Estaban resisted the idea of Carlos dropping out of school, but he was insistent. Carlos always struggled in school; he repeated a grade early on in his education and found most of his other subjects challenging. The family's new business, after initially thriving, has struggled financially. Carlos knows the family finances have been in peril and that he is needed.

Carlos and his younger brother Manuel have always been close. Manuel yearns to be like his older brother, and Carlos has always considered it his job to protect and care for his younger brother. Carlos sees in Manuel the potential for school success that he never had. He tells Manuel that he must stay in school to acquire the "book learning" that he could never grasp. But leaving the warm embrace of their former neighborhood in Texas for the Mississippi Delta has been hard for Manuel. Their tight knit family bonds are still intact, but they are still struggling to understand how Delta culture operates. In Manuel's old school, most students and teachers spoke or knew how to speak Spanish, and Manuel always felt he fit in. Now, Manuel is one of a small percentage of Spanish-speaking students in his new school, where the vast majority of students and staff are African American and speak only English.

In the school setting, Manuel's new English as a second language (ESL) teacher, Ms. Jones, is concerned about him. His teacher reports that he struggles academically and shows little interest in classroom activities or peers, often seeming sullen. Ms. Jones has observed that Manuel frequently appears to be daydreaming and when teachers try to talk with him, he seems to withdraw further. Ms. Jones knows that Manuel's records from Texas indicate that he was an outgoing, socially adjusted primary-school student. However, his records also show that his reading and writing performance was below grade level starting in first grade. Ms. Jones has found that if she speaks with Manuel in Spanish while taking a walk around the school, he will share stories about his family and his old neighborhood and friends. To date, no educational or psychological assessments have taken place. When Manuel meets his social worker, he avoids eye contact and appears extremely uncomfortable.

HISTORICAL PERSPECTIVE ON MIDDLE CHILDHOOD

Until the beginning of the 20th century, children were viewed primarily in economic terms within most European countries and the United States (Fass & Mason, 2000). Emphasis was often placed on the child's productivity and ability to contribute to the family's financial well-being. Middle childhood represented a period during which children became increasingly able to play a role in maintaining or improving the economic status of the family and community. Beginning in the early 20th century, however, a radical shift occurred in the Western world's perceptions of children. Children passing through middle childhood became categorized as "school age," and their education became a societal priority. Child labor and compulsory education laws supported and reinforced this shift in societal values. In many parts of the nonindustrialized world, however, children continue to play important economic roles for families. In Latin America, Africa, and some parts of Asia, childhood is relatively short. Many children from the most impoverished families live and work on the streets (called "street children"). There is no time for the luxury of an indulged childhood. In rapidly industrializing countries striving toward universal primary school education, children must balance their economic productivity with time spent in school (Leeder, 2004).

The shift toward the universal public education of children is intended to be an equalizer, enabling children from a variety of economic backgrounds to become successful citizens. Historically in the United States, public schools were to be free and open to all. Instead, however, they reflected traditional public ambiguity toward poverty and diversity, and they embodied particular value systems and excluded certain groups (Allen-Meares, Washington, & Walsh, 1996). The first public schools in the United States were, in effect, open to European Americans only, and children from marginalized or nondominant groups rarely received advanced education. Today, in the United States and around the globe, schools continue to play a pivotal role in reinforcing segregation and **deculturalizing** various groups of children (Kozol, 2005; Spring, 2004). In essence, as schools pressure children from nondominant groups to assimilate or direct unequal resources toward their development (Darling-Hammond, 2007), they play a role in intentionally or unintentionally destroying or severely limiting a culture's ability to sustain itself. Most children from marginalized groups consistently achieve more poorly than the rest of the student population, a situation often referred to as the "achievement gap."

The evolution of our perceptions of middle childhood continues. Although there is incredible diversity among children, families, and communities, middle childhood has generally come to be viewed in the United States as a time when education, play, leisure, and social activities should dominate daily life (Fass & Mason, 2000). Sigmund Freud perceived middle childhood as a relatively uneventful phase of development. But in the 21st century, middle childhood is recognized as a potentially turbulent time in children's lives.

The age range classified as middle childhood is subject to debate. In the United States, it is most often defined as the period beginning at approximately ages 5 or 6 and ending at approximately ages 10 to 12 (Broderick & Blewitt, 2006; Craig & Baucum, 2002). However, some assert that middle childhood begins a bit later than 6 (Allen & Marotz, 2003) and ends at the onset of puberty (Davies, 2004), which ranges tremendously among children.

Images of middle childhood often include children who are physically active and intellectually curious, making new friends and learning new things. But as Anthony Bryant, Brianna Shaw, and Manuel Vega demonstrate, middle childhood is filled with both opportunities and challenges. For some children, it is a period of particular vulnerability. In fact, when we think of school-age children, images of child poverty and related school inequities, family and community violence, sexual victimization or **precociousness** (early development), learning challenges and physical and emotional ailments such as depression, asthma, and attention deficit/hyperactivity disorder (ADHD) may dominate our thoughts. In some parts of the world, children between the ages of 6 and 12 are vulnerable to war, land mines, and forced enlistment as soldiers. They are also vulnerable to slavelike labor and being sold as sex workers in an international child trafficking economy (Human Rights Watch, 2006).

MIDDLE CHILDHOOD IN THE MULTIGENERATIONAL FAMILY

During middle childhood, the child's social world expands dramatically. Although the family is not the only relevant force in a child's life, it remains an extremely significant influence on development. Families are often in a constant state of change and so the child's relationships with family members and the environment that the family inhabits are likely to be different from the child's first experiences of family. For example, consider the changes in Anthony Bryant's, Brianna Shaw's, and Manuel Vega's families over time and the ways in which family relationships have been continually evolving.

Despite the geographical distances that often exist between family members today, nuclear families are still emotional subsystems of extended, multigenerational family systems. The child's nuclear family is significantly shaped by past, present, and anticipated future experiences, events, and relationships (Carter & McGoldrick, 2005a). Profoundly important factors such as historical events, culture, and social structure often influence children through their family systems. And family members' experiences and characteristics trickle through families via generational ties. These experiences or characteristics may be biological in nature and therefore fairly obvious, or they may include more nebulous qualities such as acquired emotional strengths or wounds. For example, consider Brianna's maternal grandfather, who is African American and grew up with the legacy of slavery under Jim Crow laws and legal segregation in the United States, or Anthony's maternal grandmother, who as a child was repeatedly victimized sexually. Children become connected to events or phenomena such as a familial history of child abuse or a group history of discrimination and **oppression** (restrictions and exploitation), even in the absence of direct experiences in the present generation (see Crawford, Nobles, & Leary, 2003; McGoldrick, 2004).

> How are Anthony, Brianna, and Manuel affected by their multigenerational families?

Thus, the developing school-age child is shaped not only by events and individuals explicitly evident in present time and physical space but also by those events and individuals who have more directly influenced the lives of their parents, grandparents, great-grandparents, and beyond. These influences—familial, cultural, and historical in nature—shape all aspects of each child's development in an abstract and complex fashion.

DEVELOPMENT IN MIDDLE CHILDHOOD

New developmental tasks are undertaken in middle childhood, and development occurs within the physical, cognitive, emotional, and social dimensions. Although each developmental domain is considered separately for our analytical purposes, changes in the developing child reflect the dynamic interaction continuously occurring across these dimensions.

Physical Development

During middle childhood, physical development typically continues steadily, but children of the same chronological age may vary greatly in stature, weight, and sexual development. For most children, height and weight begin to advance less rapidly than during prior developmental phases, but steady growth continues. The nature and pace of physical growth during this period are shaped by both genetic and environmental influences in interaction (Craig & Baucum, 2002).

▲ **Photo 5.1**   New developmental tasks are undertaken in middle childhood, and development occurs within physical, cognitive, emotional, and social dimensions.

As children progress from kindergarten to early adolescence, their fine and gross motor skills typically advance. In the United States today, children in this age range are often encouraged to gain a high level of mastery over physical skills associated with a particular interest such as dance, sports, or music. However, medical professionals caution that school-age children continue to possess unique physical vulnerabilities related to the growth process and thus are susceptible to injuries associated with excessive physical activity or training (Craig & Baucum, 2002).

Middle childhood is a developmental phase of entrenchment or eradication of many potent risk or protective factors manifesting in this developmental domain. Focusing on risk, for children residing in chronically impoverished countries and communities, issues such as malnutrition and disease threaten physical health. Seemingly innocuous issues such as poor dental hygiene or mild visual impairment may become more serious as they begin to impact other areas of development such as cognitive, emotional, or social well-being. In the United States, health issues such as asthma and obesity are of contemporary concern and often either improve or become severe during middle childhood. Susceptibility to risk varies across socioeconomic and ethnic groups. In general, unintentional death and physical injury (for example, motor vehicle injuries, drowning, playground accidents, and sports-related traumatic brain injury) represent a major threat to well-being among school-age children (Borse et al., 2008). Moreover, as children move into middle childhood they gain other new risks: approximately one third of rapes occur before age 12, homicide risk increases, and among children ages 10 to 14, suicide is a leading cause of death (Centers for Disease Control and Prevention, 2008c). Some of the physical injuries unique to middle childhood may be indirectly facilitated by declines in adult supervision and adult overestimation of children's safety-related knowledge and ability to implement safety practices. In addition, children's continued physical and cognitive (specifically, judgment and decision-making processes) vulnerabilities combine, potentially, with an increasing propensity to engage in risk-taking activities and behaviors (Berk, 2002b).

Middle childhood is the developmental phase that leads from *prepubescence* (the period prior to commencement of the physiological processes and changes associated with puberty) to *pubescence* (the period during which the child begins to experience diverse and gradual physical processes associated with puberty). Pubescence includes the growth of pubic hair for boys and girls, breast development for girls, and genitalia development for boys. Many of us may not think of middle childhood as the developmental phase during which puberty becomes relevant. Precocious puberty has traditionally been defined as puberty beginning at an age that is more than 2.5 standard deviations below the population's mean age of pubertal onset. In the United States, this is approximately below age 8 in girls and below age 9 in boys (National Institute of Child Health and Human Development, 2007; Nield, Cakan, & Kamat, 2007). Ongoing consultation with a child's pediatrician or other health care provider is always recommended, but research suggests that many "early-maturing" children are simply at the early end of the normal age distribution for pubertal onset (Kaplowitz, 2006).

Focusing on racial differences, many studies have found that in the United States, non-Hispanic African American girls begin puberty earlier than other children (Adair & Gordon-Larsen, 2001; Benefice, Caius, & Garnier, 2004; Chumlea et al., 2003; National Institute of Child Health and Human Development, 2007). However, Sun et al. (2002) point out that across gender and racial groups, children continue to *complete* their **secondary sexual development,** or development of secondary sex characteristics, at approximately the same age. This issue will receive further attention in Chapter 6.

A trend toward earlier age of puberty onset, particularly among girls, has brought much attention to the potential causes. A wide variety of multidisciplinary researchers across the globe are examining available data regarding the causes of puberty onset. It is evident that a complex range of interacting factors, crossing the biopsychosocial spectrum, are relevant to understanding puberty onset. Wang, Needham, and Barr (2005) identify nutritional status; genetic predisposition, including race/ethnicity; and environmental chemical exposure as associated with age of puberty onset. It should be noted that careful examination of puberty onset trends suggests that the "trend toward earlier onset of puberty in U.S. girls over the past 50 years is not as strong as some reports suggested" (Kaplowitz, 2006, p. 487). Specifically, the average age of menarche decreased from approximately 14.8 years in 1877 to about 12.8 years in the mid-1960s (Kaplowitz). Most researchers have concluded that the general trend observed during this broad historical time period is the result of health and nutrition improvement within the population as a whole. A recent examination of available data concludes that there is little evidence to support a significant continued decline in more recent years. Nevertheless, some have suggested that our public education and health systems should reconsider the timing and nature of health education for children because the onset of puberty may impact social and emotional development and has traditionally been associated with a variety of "risky and unhealthy behaviors" (Wang et al., p. 1101) among children and adolescents. Indeed a relationship, albeit complex, appears to exist between puberty and social development for both boys and girls (Felson, 2002; Kaltiala-Heino, Kosunen, & Rimpela, 2003; McCabe & Ricciardelli, 2003). During middle childhood, girls experiencing early onset puberty may be at particular risk (American Association of University Women, 1995; Mendle, Turkheimer, & Emery, 2007). Intervention focused on self-protection and individual rights and responsibilities may be beneficial, and schools committed to the safety of their students must diligently educate staff and students about sexual development and risk.

> What impact do these differences in biological age have on psychological and social development during middle childhood?

Middle childhood is the developmental phase when increased public attention and self-awareness is directed toward various aspects of physical growth, skill, or activity patterns and levels deemed outside the normal range. Because physical development is outwardly visible, it affects perceptions of self and the way a child is viewed and treated by peers and adults. Physical development can also affect children's peer relationships. School-age children constantly compare themselves with others, and physical differences are often the topic of discussion. Whereas "late" developers may feel inferior about their size or lack of sexual development, "early" developers may feel awkward and out of place among their peers. Many children worry about being "normal." Reassurance by adults that physical development varies among people and that all development is "normal" is crucial.

Cognitive Development

For most children, the acquisition of cognitive abilities that occurs early in middle childhood allows the communication of thoughts with increasing complexity. Public education plays a major role in the cognitive development of children in the United States, if only because children attend school throughout the formative years of such development. When Anthony Bryant, Brianna Shaw, and Manuel Vega first entered school, their readiness to confront the challenges and opportunities that school presents was shaped by prior experiences. Anthony, for example, entered school generally prepared for the academic emphases associated with kindergarten. He was perhaps less prepared for the social expectations present in the school environment.

In Jean Piaget's (1936/1952) terms, children start school during the second stage (preoperational thought) and finish school when they are completing the fourth and final stage of cognitive development (formal operations). In the third stage (concrete operations), children are able to solve concrete problems using logical problem-solving strategies. By the end of middle childhood, they enter the formal operations stage and become able to solve hypothetical

▲ **Photo 5.2**   Middle childhood is a critical time for children to acquire a sense of self-confidence and develop conceptual thought.

problems using abstract concepts (refer back to Exhibit 3.5 for an overview of Piaget's stages of cognitive development). School children rapidly develop conceptual thought, enhanced ability to categorize complicated systems of objects, and the ability to solve problems. Bergen and Coscia (2001) point out that as you observe children moving into and through middle childhood, you will note these rapid gains in intellectual processes and memory. These brain-produced shifts in the child's understanding of him- or herself and the surrounding world are consistent with the transition into Piaget's concrete operational stage of cognitive development. Potential gains in cognitive development enable new learning in a variety of environments. For example, children gain enhanced ability to understand people, situations, and events within their surrounding environments. The task for caregivers and others within the child's environment is to recognize and respond to this ability sensitively by nurturing and supporting the child's expanding cognitive abilities.

Beyond Piaget's ideas, brain development and cognitive functioning during middle childhood have received relatively little attention when compared with research devoted to brain development in prior developmental phases. However, our ever-expanding general understanding of the human brain illuminates opportunities and vulnerabilities present throughout childhood. For example, professionals working with children are increasingly aware of the meaning and implications of brain plasticity. As pointed out in Chapter 3, infancy, toddlerhood, and early childhood appear to represent "sensitive periods" in brain development. By middle childhood, a child's brain development and functioning have been profoundly shaped by the nature of earlier experiences and development. And yet, remarkable brain plasticity continues, with brain structure and functioning capable of growth and refinement throughout life (Fogarty, 2009; Shonkoff & Phillips, 2000). The conceptual framework perhaps most useful to understanding this potential and the processes at play is nonlinear dynamic systems theory, also known as complexity or chaos theory (Applegate & Shapiro, 2005). Applied to this context, this theoretical perspective proposes that changes in one area or aspect of the neurological system may stimulate or interact with other neurological or broader physiological system components in an unpredictable fashion, potentially leading to unanticipated outcomes. Brain development follows a coherent developmental process, but brain plasticity in particular demonstrates the role of complex nonlinear neurological system dynamics and processes.

At least two aspects of brain development are of particular interest when we focus on middle childhood. The first is the idea that different brain regions appear to develop according to different timelines. In other words, middle childhood may be a "sensitive period" for certain aspects of brain development not yet clearly understood. The second important idea is the notion that brain synapses (connections between cells in the nervous system) that are initially present as children enter this developmental phase may be gradually eliminated if they are not used. As reported in Chapter 3, there seems to be a pattern of *synaptogenesis,* or creation and fine-tuning of brain synapses, in the human cerebral cortex during early childhood, which appears to be followed by a gradual pruning process that eventually reduces the overall number of synapses to their adult levels (Fogarty, 2009; Shonkoff & Phillips, 2000). The **cerebral cortex** is the outer layer of gray matter in the human brain thought to be responsible for complex, high-level intellectual functions such as memory, language, and reasoning. Ongoing positive and diverse learning opportunities during middle childhood may help facilitate continued brain growth and optimal refinement of existing structures. The National Research Council of Medicine (Shonkoff & Phillips) argues that it is essential to recognize that although genetic factors and the nature and timing of early experiences matter, "more often than not, the developing child remains vulnerable to risk and open to protective influences throughout the early years of life and into adulthood" (p. 31).

Variations in brain development and functioning appear to play a critical role in learning abilities and disabilities as well as patterns of behavior (Bergen & Coscia, 2001). During middle childhood, identification and potential diagnosis of special needs, including issues such as ADHD and autism spectrum disorders, typically peak. In recent years, an area of public interest is gender or sex-based differences in brain functioning and, possibly, learning styles. This interest has been stimulated in part by evidence suggesting that in some countries such as the United States, boys are currently at higher risk than girls for poor literacy performance, special education placement, and school dropout (Weaver-Hightower, 2003).

It has been suggested that brain-based cognitive processing, behavior, and learning style differences may be responsible for the somewhat stable trends observed in gender differences in educational achievement (Fogarty, 2009; King & Gurian, 2006; Sax, 2005). The importance of sex, or gender, in shaping the human experience cannot be overstated. Gender is a profoundly important organizing factor shaping human development, and its biological correlates may impact behavior and learning processes in ways we do not clearly understand. In particular, the nature and causes of educational achievement differences among girls and boys are "complex and the interconnections of the causes are poorly understood" (Weaver-Hightower, 2003, p. 487). Also, it is critically important to remember that among children, gender is but one of several personal and group characteristics relevant to understanding educational privilege specifically as well as risk and protection generally. Careful analysis of contemporary data and their shortcomings indicates that the differences between boys and girls are complex, and there simply is not clear evidence of exclusively one-sided educational advantage or disadvantage (Bailey, 2002).

Several developmental theorists, including those listed in Exhibit 5.1, have described the changes and developmental tasks associated with middle childhood. According to these traditional theorists, thinking typically becomes more complex, reasoning becomes more logical, the child's sense of morality expands and develops into a more internally based system, and the ability to understand the perspectives of others emerges. However, much developmental research historically lacked rigor and did not devote sufficient attention to females and children belonging to non-dominant groups. A number of contemporary developmental theorists have focused on assessing the relevance and applicability of these developmental tasks to all children. Most agree that the central ideas of the theorists summarized in Exhibit 5.1 continue to be meaningful. For example, Erikson's thoughts remain widely recognized as relevant to our understanding of school-age children. In some areas, however, these developmental theories have been critiqued and subsequently expanded. This is particularly true in the area of moral development.

The best-known theory of moral development is Lawrence Kohlberg's stage theory (for an overview of this theory, refer back to Exhibit 4.1). Kohlberg's research on moral reasoning found that children do not enter the second level of *conventional moral reasoning,* or morality based on approval of authorities or upon upholding societal standards, until about age 9 or 10, sometime after they have the cognitive skills for such reasoning. Robert Coles (1987, 1997) expanded upon Kohlberg's work and emphasized the distinction between moral imagination—the gradually developed capacity to reflect on what is right and wrong—and moral conduct, pointing out that a "well-developed conscience does not translate, necessarily, into a morally courageous life" (p. 3). To Coles, *moral behavior* is shaped by daily experiences, developing in response to the way the child is treated in his or her various environments such as home and school. The school-age child often pays close attention to the discrepancies between the "moral voices" and actions of the adults in his or her world, including parents, friends' parents, relatives, teachers, and coaches. Each new and significant adult sets an example for the child, sometimes complementing and sometimes contradicting the values emphasized in the child's home environment.

Also, Carol Gilligan (1982) has extensively criticized Kohlberg's theory of moral development as paying inadequate attention to girls' "ethic of care" and the keen emphasis girls often place on relationships and the emotions of others. Consistent with Gilligan's ideas, a number of developmental theorists have argued that girls possess heightened **interrelational intelligence,** which is based on emotional and social intelligence and is similar to Howard Gardner's concept of interpersonal intelligence (Borysenko, 1996, p. 41). Such developmentalists, drawing upon feminist scholarship, point out that both girls and boys advance rapidly in the cognitive and moral developmental

Theorist	Phase or Task	Description
Freud (1938/1973)	Latency	Sexual instincts become less dominant; superego develops further.
Erikson (1950)	Industry versus inferiority	Capacity to cooperate and create develops; result is sense of either mastery or incompetence.
Piaget (1936/1952)	Concrete operational	Reasoning becomes more logical but remains at concrete level; principle of conservation is learned.
Piaget (1932/1965)	Moral realism and autonomous morality	Conception of morality changes from absolute and external to relative and internal.
Kohlberg (1969)	Preconventional and conventional morality	Reasoning based on punishment and reward is replaced by reasoning based on formal law and external opinion.
Selman (1976)	Self-reflective perspective taking	Ability develops to view own actions, thoughts, and emotions from another's perspective.

▲ **Exhibit 5.1**   Phases and Tasks of Middle Childhood

domains during middle childhood, but the genders may be distinct in their approaches to social relationships and interactions, and such differences may shape the nature of development in all domains (Borysensko, 1996; Gilligan, 1982; Taylor, Gilligan & Sullivan, 1995). It is also important to note that collectivist-oriented societies put a high value on connectedness, and research with groups from collectivist societies indicates that they do not score well on Kohlberg's model of moral development. Gardiner and Kosmitzki (2008) argue that moral thought and development must be understood in cultural context.

Developmentalists have examined the implications of advancing cognitive abilities for children's understanding of their group identities. Children become much more aware of ethnic identities and other aspects of diversity (such as socioeconomic status and gender identities) during their middle childhood years. Cultural awareness and related beliefs are shaped by the nature of experiences such as exposure to diversity within the family and community, including school, contexts. Unlike the preschoolers' attraction to "black-and-white" classifications, children progressing through middle childhood are increasingly capable of understanding the complexities of group memberships; in other words, they are cognitively capable of rejecting oversimplistic stereotypes and recognizing the complexities present within all individuals and groups (Davies, 2004). McAdoo (2001) asserts that, compared with children who identify with the majority group, children from nondominant groups are much more likely to possess awareness of both their own group identity or identities as well as majority group characteristics. Thus, a now widely recognized developmental task associated with middle childhood is the acquisition of positive group identity or identities (Davies, 2004; Verkuyten, 2005). The terms *bicultural* or *multicultural competence* are used to refer to the skills children from nondominant groups must acquire in order to survive and thrive developmentally (Chestang, 1972; Lum, 2004, 2007; Norton, 1993).

Manuel speaks English as a second language and in some ways is representative of many school-age children. In the United States, approximately 20% of all children ages 5 through 17 enrolled in school speak a language other than English at home; this figure is expected to continue to increase steadily in the future (Kominski, Shin, & Marotz, 2008). Multi- and bilingual children in the United States were traditionally thought to be at risk of developmental deficits. However, significant research evidence demonstrates that bilingualism may have a positive impact on cognitive development. When controlling for socioeconomic status, bilingual children often perform better than monolingual children on tests of analytical reasoning, concept formation, and cognitive flexibility (Akbulut, 2007; Hakuta, Ferdman, & Diaz, 1987). Also, bilingual children may be more likely to acquire capacities and skills that enhance their reading achievement (Campbell & Sais, 1995). With growing evidence of brain plasticity and the way that environmental demands change brain structures, researchers have begun to explore the relationship between bilingualism and the brain. They have found that learning a second language increases the density of gray matter in the left inferior parietal cortex. The earlier a second language is learned and the more proficient the person becomes, the more benefit to brain development (Mechelli et al., 2004). Despite such findings, however, too often bilingual children receive little support for their native language and culture in the school context.

Cultural Identity Development

For many European American children, ethnicity does not lead to comparison with others or exploration of identity (Rotheram-Borus, 1993; Tatum, 2000). But for most children who are members of nondominant groups, ethnicity or race may be a central part of the quest for identity that begins in middle childhood and continues well into adolescence and young adulthood. By around age 7, cognitive advances allow children to view themselves and others as capable of belonging to more than one "category" at once, as capable of possessing two or more heritages simultaneously (Morrison & Bordere, 2001). As children mature, they may become more aware of not only dual or multiple aspects of identity but also of the discrimination and inequality to which they may be subjected. Such issues may in fact present overwhelming challenges for the school-age child belonging to a nondominant group. At a time when development of a sense of belonging is critical, these issues set some children apart from members of dominant groups and may increase the challenges they experience.

> How can cultural identity serve as a protective factor for children from nondominant groups?

Segregation based on ethnicity/race and social class is common in friendships at all ages, including middle childhood. Like adults, children are more likely to hold negative attitudes toward groups to which they do not belong (Haidt, 2007). However, children, like adults, vary in the extent to which they hold ethnic and social class biases. Verbalized prejudice declines during middle childhood as children learn to obey social norms against overt prejudice. However, children belonging to nondominant groups continue to face institutional discrimination and other significant challenges throughout this period of the life course (Gutierrez, 2004; Harps, 2005).

A particular challenge for children such as Manuel Vega may be blending contradictory values, standards, or traditions. Some children respond to cultural contradictions by identifying with the mainstream American culture (*assimilation*) in which they are immersed or by developing negative attitudes about their subcultural group memberships either consciously or subconsciously (*stereotype vulnerability*). Individual reactions, such as those of Manuel, will be shaped by the child's unique experiences and social influences. It is a major developmental task to integrate dual or multiple identities into a consistent personal identity as well as a positive ethnic or racial identity (Gibbs & Huang, 1989; Lomsky-Feder & Leibovitz, 2010). Many models of identity exist for children of mixed ethnicity, with new ideas and theories constantly emerging. It is clear that identity development for such children is diverse, extremely complex, and not well understood. As always, however, parents and professionals must start where the child is, with a focus on facilitating understanding and appreciation of heritage to promote development of an integrated identity and positive self-regard (Kopola, Esquivel, & Baptiste, 1994). Children should be provided with opportunities to explore their dual or multiple heritages and to select their own terms for identifying and describing themselves (Morrison & Bordere, 2001). Although studies have produced diverse findings, positive outcomes seem to be associated with supportive family systems and involvement in social and recreational activities that expose children to their heritage and lead to self-affirmation (Fuligni, 1997; Gibbs & Huang; Guarnaccia & Lopez, 1998; Herring, 1995).

Key tasks for adults, then, include educating children about family histories and supporting the creation of an integrated sense of self. Individuals and organizations within the child's social system can provide support by being sensitive to issues related to ethnic/racial origin and ethnic/racial distinctions; they can also help by celebrating cultural diversity and trying to increase the cultural sensitivity of all children. Such interventions appear to encourage fewer negative stereotypes of peers belonging to nondominant groups (Rotheram-Borus, 1993).

In general, it is critical to the positive identity development of all children, but particularly those from nondominant groups, that schools value diversity and offer a variety of experiences that focus on positive identity development (Morrison & Bordere, 2001). Ensuring that schools respect nondominant cultures and diverse learning styles is an important step. For schools to do this, all school staff must develop self-awareness. A variety of materials have been designed to facilitate this process among educators (see Lee, Menkart, & Okazawa-Rae, 1998; Matsumoto-Grah, 1992; Seefeldt, 1993) and other professionals (Fong, 2003; Lum, 2007; Sue & McGoldrick, 2005).

The family environment of course plays a critical role in shaping all aspects of development, and the family is typically the vehicle through which cultural identity is transmitted. Children typically learn, through their families, how to view their own ethnicity/race and that of others as well as coping strategies to respond to potential or direct exclusion, discrimination, or racism (Barbarin, McCandies, Coleman, & Atkinson, 2004).

Emotional Development

As most children move from early childhood into and through middle childhood, they experience significant gains in their ability to identify and articulate their own emotions as well as the emotions of others. Exhibit 5.2 summarizes several gains school-age children often make in the area of emotional functioning. It is important to recognize, however, that culture and other aspects of group identity may shape emotional development. For example, cultures vary in their acceptance of expressive displays of emotion.

> What are our societal expectations for emotional intelligence during middle childhood?

Many children in this age range develop more advanced coping skills that help them when encountering upsetting, stressful, or traumatic situations. As defined by Daniel Goleman (1995), **emotional intelligence** refers to the ability to "motivate oneself and persist in the face of frustrations, to control impulse and delay gratification, to regulate one's moods and keep distress from swamping the ability to think, to empathize and to hope" (p. 34). To Goleman (2006), emotional and social intelligence are inextricably linked, and many other developmentalists agree. As a result, interventions used with children experiencing social difficulties often focus upon enhancing some aspect of emotional intelligence.

Goleman also asserts that social and emotional intelligence are key aspects of both moral reasoning and moral conduct. In other words, although often it may seem that advancing capacities in the moral domain occurs naturally for children, positive conditions and interactions must exist in a child's life in order for optimal emotional and social competencies to develop. Thus, a child like Anthony Bryant, with seemingly great academic promise, may not realize his potential without timely intervention targeting the development of critical emotional competencies. These competencies include, for example, self-awareness, impulse control, and the ability to identify, express, and manage feelings, including love, jealousy, anxiety, and anger. Healthy emotional development can be threatened by a number of issues, including challenges such as significant loss and trauma. We increasingly recognize the vulnerability of school-age children to serious emotional and mental health issues. Assessment approaches that incorporate awareness of and attention to the possible existence of such issues are critical.

Fortunately, a substantial knowledge base regarding the promotion of positive emotional development exists. Many intervention strategies appear effective, particularly when they are preventive in nature and provided during or before middle childhood (see Hyson, 2004).

For example, Brianna Shaw, like too many children—particularly girls her age—is at risk of developing depression and could benefit from intervention focusing on the development of appropriate coping strategies. A number of interacting, complex biopsychosocial-spiritual factors shape vulnerability to ailments such as depression. Goleman (1995) argues that many cases of depression arise from deficits in two key areas of emotional competence: relationship skills and cognitive, or interpretive, style. In short, many children suffering from—or at risk of developing—depression likely possess a depression-promoting way of interpreting setbacks. Children with a potentially harmful outlook attribute setbacks in their lives to internal, personal flaws. Appropriate preventive intervention, based on a cognitive behavioral approach, teaches children that their emotions are linked to the way they think and facilitates productive, healthy ways of interpreting events and viewing themselves. For Brianna, such cognitive-behavioral oriented intervention may be helpful. Brianna also may benefit from a gender-specific intervention, perhaps with a particular focus upon relational resilience. Potter (2004) argues that gender-specific interventions are often most appropriate when the social problem is experienced primarily by one gender. She identifies eating disorders and depression as two examples of issues disproportionately impacting girls. Identifying the relevance of gender issues to Brianna's current emotional state and considering a gender-specific intervention strategy therefore may be appropriate. The concept of "relational resilience" is built upon relational-cultural theory's belief that "all psychological growth occurs in relationships": the building blocks of relational resilience are "mutual empathy, empowerment, and the development of courage" (Jordan, 2005, p. 79).

Many school-age girls and boys also experience depression and other types of emotional distress because of a variety of factors, including **trauma** (severe physical or psychological injury) or significant loss. Children with close ties to extended family are particularly likely to experience loss of a close relative at a young age and therefore are more prone to this sort of depression. Loss, trauma, and violence may present serious obstacles to healthy emotional development. Research demonstrates the remarkable potential resilience of children (see Garmezy, 1994; Goldstein & Brooks, 2005; Fraser, Kirby, & Smokowski, 2004; Luthar, 2003; Werner & Smith, 2001), but both personal and environmental attributes play a critical role in processes of resilience. To support the healthy emotional development of children at risk, appropriate multilevel prevention and intervention efforts are crucial.

Social Development

Perhaps the most widely recognized developmental task of this period is the acquisition of feelings of *self-competence.* Traditional developmentalists have pointed out that the school-age child searches for opportunities to demonstrate personal skills, abilities, and achievements. This is what Erik Erikson (1963) was referring to when he described the developmental task of middle childhood as industry versus inferiority (refer back to Exhibit 3.7 for a description of all eight of Erikson's psychosocial stages). *Industry* refers to a drive to acquire new skills and do meaningful "work." The experiences of middle childhood may foster or thwart the child's attempts to acquire an enhanced sense of *mastery* and self-efficacy. Family, peer, and community support may enhance the child's growing sense of competence; lack of such support undermines this sense. The child's definitions of self and accomplishment vary greatly according to interpretations in the surrounding environment. But superficial, external bolstering of self-esteem is not all that children of this age group require. External appraisal must be supportive and encouraging but also genuine for children to value such feedback.

> How does a growing sense of competence promote the capacity for human agency in making choices?

Some theorists argue that children of this age must learn the value of perseverance and develop an internal drive to succeed (Kindlon, 2003; Seligman, Reivich, Jaycox, & Gillham, 1995). Thus, opportunities to both fail and succeed must be provided, along with sincere feedback and support. Ideally, the developing school-age child acquires the sense of personal competence and tenacity that will serve as a protective factor during adolescence and young adulthood.

Families play a critical role in supporting development of this sense. For example, as the child learns to ride a bike or play a sport or musical instrument, adults can provide specific feedback and praise. They can counter the child's frustration by identifying and complimenting specific improvements and emphasizing the role of practice and per-severance in producing improvements. Failures and setbacks can be labeled as temporary and surmountable rather than attributed to personal flaws or deficits. The presence of such feedback loops is a key feature of high-quality adult-child relationships, in the family, school, and beyond. Middle childhood is a critical time for children to acquire a sense of competence. Each child experiences events and daily interactions that enhance or diminish feelings of self-competence.

Children are not equally positioned as they enter this developmental phase, as Anthony Bryant's, Brianna Shaw's, and Manuel Vega's stories suggest. Developmental pathways preceding entry into middle childhood are extremely diverse. Children experience this phase of life differently based not only on differences in the surrounding environment—such as family structure and socioeconomic status—but also on their personality differences. A particular personality and learning style may be valued or devalued, problematic or nonproblematic, in each of the child's expanding social settings (Berk, 2002a, 2002b). Thus, although Anthony, Brianna, and Manuel are moving through the same develop-mental period and facing many common tasks, they experience these tasks differently and will emerge into adoles-cence as unique individuals. Each individual child's identity development is highly dependent upon social networks of privilege and exclusion. A direct relationship exists between the level of control and power a child experiences and the degree of balance that is achieved in the child's emerging identity between feelings of power (privilege) and pow-erlessness (exclusion) (Johnson, 2005; Tatum, 1992). As children move toward adolescence and early adulthood, the amount of emotional, social, spiritual, and economic **capital,** or resources, acquired determines the likelihood of socioeconomic and other types of success as well as feelings of competence to succeed. Experiencing economically and socially just support systems is critical to optimum development.

Middle childhood is an important time in moral development, a time when most children become intensely inter-ested in moral issues. Advancing language capability serves not only as a communication tool but also as a vehicle for more sophisticated introspection. Language is also a tool for positive assertion of self and personal opinions as the child's social world expands (Coles, 1987, 1997). In recent years, many elementary schools have added **character**

- Ability to mentally organize and articulate emotional experiences
- Cognitive control of emotional arousal
- Use of emotions as internal monitoring and guidance systems
- Ability to remain focused on goal-directed actions
- Ability to delay gratification based on cognitive evaluation
- Ability to understand and use the concept of planning
- Ability to view tasks incrementally
- Use of social comparison
- Influence of internalized feelings (e.g., self-pride, shame) on behavior
- Capacity to tolerate conflicting feelings
- Increasingly effective defense mechanisms

▲ **Exhibit 5.2** Common Emotional Gains During Middle Childhood

SOURCE: Davies, 2004, pp. 369–372.

education to their curricula. Such education often consists of direct teaching and curriculum inclusion of mainstream moral and social values thought to be universal in a community (e.g., kindness, respect, honesty). Renewed focus on children's character education is in part related to waves of school violence and bullying. Survey research with children suggests that, compared with children in middle and high school settings, children in elementary school settings are at highest risk of experiencing bullying, either as a perpetrator or victim (Astor, Benbenishty, Pitner, & Meyer, 2004).

At a broader level, federal and state legislative initiatives have encouraged school personnel to confront bullying and harassment in the school setting (Limber & Small, 2003). Schools have been particularly responsive to these initiatives in the wake of well-publicized incidents of school violence. Today, most schools have policies in place designed to facilitate efficient and effective responses to aberrant behavior, including bullying and violence. The content and implementation details of such policies, of course, vary widely.

There is plentiful evidence to suggest that "the bully" or "bullying" has existed throughout modern human history (Astor et al., 2004). During the late 20th century, changes occurred within our views of and knowledge regarding bullying. In general, the public has become less tolerant of bullying, perhaps because of a fairly widespread belief that school shootings (such as the Columbine High School massacre) can be linked to bullying. Bullying is today recognized as a complex phenomenon, with both **direct bullying** (physical) and indirect bullying viewed as cause for concern (Astor et al.). **Indirect bullying** is conceptualized as including verbal, psychological, and social or "relational" bullying tactics.

In recent years, new interest has centered on the ways in which technology influences social relationships among children and youth as well as gender differences in relationships and bullying. Initially, attention was drawn to the previously underrecognized phenomenon of girls experiencing direct bullying, or physical aggression and violence, at the hands of other girls (Garbarino, 2006). Although both direct and indirect bullying crosses genders, more recent attention has centered on the widespread existence of indirect, or relational, bullying particularly among girls, and its potentially devastating consequences (Simmons, 2003; Underwood, 2003).

A positive outcome of recent attention to bullying is interest in establishing "best practices" in bullying prevention and intervention. Astor and colleagues (2004) argue that the United States is lagging behind other countries such as Norway, the United Kingdom, and Australia in implementing and evaluating comprehensive bullying prevention and intervention strategies; a benefit of our delayed status is our ability to learn from this international knowledge base. This knowledge base suggests that the most effective approaches to reducing bullying within a school is implementation of a comprehensive, school-wide prevention and intervention plan that addresses the contributing factors within all levels of the school environment (Espelage & Swearer, 2003; Plaford, 2006). In recent years, many school districts in the United States have implemented such initiatives and have experienced positive results (Beaudoin & Taylor, 2004).

Communities possess great potential to provide important support and structure for children. Today, however, many communities provide as many challenges as opportunities for development. Communities in which challenges outweigh opportunities have been labeled as "socially toxic," meaning that they threaten positive development (Garbarino, 1995). In contrast, within a socially supportive environment, children have access to peers and adults who can lead them toward more advanced moral and social thinking. This development occurs in part through the modeling of *prosocial behavior,* which injects moral reasoning and social sensitivity into the child's accustomed manner of reasoning and behaving. Thus, cognitive and moral development is a social issue. The failure of adults to take on moral and spiritual mentoring roles contributes significantly to the development of socially toxic environments.

This type of moral mentoring takes place in the **zone of proximal development**—the theoretical space between the child's current developmental level and the child's potential level if given access to appropriate models and developmental experiences in the social environment (Vygotsky, 1986). Thus, the child's competence alone interacts dynamically with the child's competence in the company of others. The result is developmental progress.

The Peer Group

Nearly as influential as family members during middle childhood are *peer groups:* collections of children with unique values and goals. As children progress through middle childhood, peers have an increasingly important impact on such everyday matters as social behavior, activities, and dress. By this phase of development, a desire for group belongingness is especially strong. Within peer groups, children potentially learn three important lessons. First, they learn to appreciate different points of view. Second, they learn to recognize the norms and demands of their peer group. And, third, they learn to have closeness to a same-sex peer (Newman & Newman, 2009). Whereas individual friendships facilitate the development of critical capacities such as trust and intimacy, peer groups foster learning about cooperation and leadership.

> What role do peer groups play in developing the capacity for meaningful relationships in middle childhood?

Throughout middle childhood, the importance of *group norms* is highly evident (von Salisch, 2001). Children are sensitive, sometimes exceedingly so, to their peers' standards for behavior, appearance, and attitudes. Brianna Shaw, for instance, is beginning to devalue herself because she recognizes the discrepancy between her appearance and group norms. Often it is not until adolescence that group norms may become more flexible, allowing for more individuality. This shift reflects the complex relationship among the developmental domains. In this case, the association between social and cognitive development is illustrated by simultaneous changes in social relationships and cognitive capacities.

Gains in cognitive abilities promote more complex communication skills and greater social awareness. These developments, in turn, facilitate more complex peer interaction, which is a vital resource for the development of **social competence**—the ability to engage in sustained, positive, and mutually satisfactory peer interactions. Positive peer relationships reflect and support social competence, as they potentially discourage egocentrism, promote positive coping, and ultimately serve as a protective factor during the transition to adolescence (Spencer, Harpalani, Fegley, Dell'Angelo, & Seaton, 2003).

Gender and culture influence the quantity and nature of peer interactions observed among school-age children (Potter, 2004). Sociability, intimacy, social expectations and rules, and the value placed on various types of play and other social activities are all phenomena shaped by both gender and culture.

Spencer et al. (2003) point out that children from nondominant groups are more likely to experience dissonance across school, family, and peer settings; for example, such children may experience language differences, misunderstandings of cultural traditions or expressions, and distinct norms, or rules, regarding dating behavior, peer intimacy, or cross-gender friendships. These authors also assert that although many youth experiencing dissonance across school, family, and peer systems may suffer from negative outcomes such as peer rejection or school failure, some may learn important coping skills that will serve them well later in life. In fact, the authors argue that given the clear trend toward increasing cultural diversity around the globe, "experiences of cultural dissonance and the coping skills they allow youth to develop should not be viewed as aberrant; instead, privilege should be explored as having a 'downside' that potentially compromises the development of coping and character" (p. 137).

A persistent finding is that, across gender and culture, peer acceptance is a powerful predictor of psychological adjustment. One well-known study asked children to fit other children into particular categories. From the results, the researchers developed five general categories of social acceptance: popular, rejected, controversial, neglected, and average (Coie, Dodge, & Coppotelli, 1982). Common predictors of popular status include physical appearance and prosocial behaviors in the social setting (Rotenberg et al., 2004). Rejected children are those who are actively disliked by their peers. They are particularly likely to be unhappy and to experience achievement and self-esteem issues. Rejected status is strongly associated with poor school performance, antisocial behavior, and delinquency in adolescence (DeRosier, Kupersmidt, & Patterson, 1994; Greenman & Schneider, 2009; Ollendick, Weist, Borden, & Greene, 1992). For this reason, we should be concerned about Brianna Shaw's growing sense of peer rejection.

Support for rejected children may include interventions to improve peer relations and psychological adjustment. Most of these interventions are based on social learning theory and involve modeling and reinforcing positive social behavior—for example, initiating interaction and responding to others positively. Several such programs have indeed helped children develop social competence and gain peer approval (Lochman, Coie, Underwood, & Terry, 1993; Wyman, Cross, & Barry, 2004; Young, Marchant, & Wilder, 2004).

Friendship and Intimacy

Throughout middle childhood, children develop their ability to look at things from others' perspectives. In turn, their capacity to develop more complex friendships—based on awareness of others' thoughts, feelings, and needs—emerges (Selman, 1976; von Salisch, 2001). Thus, complex and fairly stable friendship networks begin to form for the first time in middle childhood (Wojslawowicz-Bowker, Rubin, Burgess, Booth-Laforce, & Rose-Krasnor, 2006). Although skills such as cooperation and problem-solving are learned in the peer group, close friendships facilitate understanding and promote trust and reciprocity. Most socially competent children maintain and nurture both close friendships and effective peer-group interaction.

As children move through middle childhood, friendship begins to entail mutual trust and assistance and thus becomes more emotionally rather than behaviorally based (Asher & Paquette, 2003). In other words, school-age children may possess close friendships based on the emotional support provided for one another as much as, if not more than, common interests and activities. The concept of friend is transformed from the playmate of early childhood to the confidant of middle childhood. Violations of trust during this period are often perceived as serious violations of the friendship bond. As children move out of middle childhood and into adolescence, the role of intimacy and loyalty in friendship becomes even more pronounced. Moreover, children increasingly value mutual understanding and loyalty in the face of conflict among peers (Berndt, 1988).

Team Play

The overall incidence of aggression during peer activities decreases during middle childhood, and friendly rule-based play increases. This transition is due in part to the continuing development of a perspective-taking ability, the ability to see a situation from another person's point of view. In addition, most school-age children are exposed to peers who differ in a variety of ways, including personality, ethnicity, and interests.

School-age children are able to take their new understanding of others' needs and desires into account in various types of peer interaction. Thus, their communication and interaction reflects an enhanced ability to understand the role of multiple participants in activities. These developments facilitate the transition to many rule-based activities, such as team sports. Despite occasional arguments or fights with peers, involvement with team sports may provide great enjoyment and satisfaction. Participation in team sports during middle childhood may also have long-term benefits. One research team found a link between voluntary participation in team sports during middle childhood and level of physical activity in adulthood (Taylor, Blair, Cummings, Wun, & Malina, 1999). While participating in team sports, children also develop the capacity for interdependence, cooperation, division of labor, and competition (Van der Vegt, Eman, & Van De Vliert, 2001). In addition, participation in team sports raises issues of moral judgment and behaviors (Lee, Whitehead, & Ntoumanis, 2007).

Gender Identity and Gender Roles

Although most children in middle childhood have a great deal in common based upon their shared developmental phase, girls and boys differ significantly in areas ranging from their self-understanding and social relationships to school performance, interests, and life aspirations (Potter, 2004). Among most school-age children, gender identity, or an "internalized psychological experience of being male or female," is quite well-established (Diamond & Savin-Williams, 2003, p. 105).

Our understanding of the structure of gender roles is derived from various theoretical perspectives. An anthropological or social constructionist orientation illuminates the ways in which, throughout history, gender has shaped familial and societal systems and inevitably impacts individual development in an intangible yet profound fashion (Gardiner & Kosmitzki, 2008; Wertsch, del Rio, & Alvarez, 1995). Cognitive theory suggests that at the individual level, self-perceptions emerge. Gender, as one component of self-perception, joins related *cognitions* to guide children's gender-linked behaviors. A behavioral perspective suggests that gender-related *behaviors* precede self-perception in the development of gender role identity; in other words, at a very young age, girls start imitating feminine behavior and *later* begin thinking of themselves as distinctly female, and boys go through the same sequence in developing a masculine identity. Gender schema theory (see Bem, 1993, 1998), an information-processing approach to gender, combines behavioral and cognitive theories, suggesting that social pressures and children's cognition work together to perpetuate gender-linked perceptions and behaviors.

Feminist psychodynamic theorists such as Nancy Chodorow (1978, 1989) have proposed that while boys typically begin to separate psychologically from their female caregivers in early childhood, most girls deepen their connection to and identification with their female caregivers throughout childhood. Such theorists propose, then, that as girls and boys transition into adolescence and face a new level of individuation, they confront this challenge from very different psychological places, and girls are more likely to find the task emotionally confusing if not deeply overwhelming. This feminist, psychoanalytic theoretical orientation has been used to explain not only gender identity and role development, but also differences between boys and girls in their approaches to relationships and emotional expressiveness throughout childhood.

A related issue is a disturbing trend noted among girls transitioning from middle childhood to adolescence. Women's studies experts have pointed out that school-age girls often seem to possess a "confident understanding of self," which gradually disintegrates as they increasingly "discredit their feelings and understandings, experiencing increased self-doubt" during early adolescence and subsequently becoming susceptible to a host of internalizing and externalizing disorders linked to poor self-esteem (Potter, 2004, p. 60). A number of studies and theories attempt to explain this shift in girls' self-image and mental health as they transition to adolescence (see Pipher, 1994; Simmons, 2003), but Potter (2004) cautions against overgeneralization of the phenomena and in particular suggests that the trend may not apply widely across girls from differing ethnic groups, socioeconomic statuses, and sexual orientations.

During middle childhood, often boys' identification with "masculine" role attributes increases while girls' identification with "feminine" role attributes decreases (Archer, 1992; Levy, Taylor, & Gelman, 1995; Potter, 2004). For instance, boys are more likely than girls to label a chore as a "girl's job" or a "boy's job." As adults, females are the more androgynous of the two genders, and this movement toward androgyny appears to begin in middle childhood (Diamond & Savin-Williams, 2003; Serbin, Powlishta, & Gulko, 1993).

These differences have multiple causes, from social to cognitive forces. In the United States, during middle childhood and beyond, cross-gender behavior in girls is more socially acceptable than such behavior among boys. Diamond and Savin-Williams (2003) use the term "gender typicality," or the "degree to which one's appearance, behavior, interests, and subjective self-concept conform to conventional gender norms" (p. 105). Research to date suggests that for both genders, a traditionally "masculine" identity is associated with a higher sense of overall competence and better academic performance (Boldizar, 1991; Newcomb & Dubas, 1992). Diamond and Savin-Williams also emphasize the role of culture in this relationship, pointing out that this is likely because of the fact that traits associated with male, or for girls, "tomboy" status are those traits most valued in many communities. These traits include qualities such as athleticism, confidence, and assertiveness. Indeed, local communities with "more entrenched sexist ideologies" regarding male versus female traits are those in which boys exhibiting feminine or "sissy" behaviors are likely to suffer (p. 107).

In general, because of expanding cognitive capacities, as children leave early childhood and progress through middle childhood, their gender stereotypes gradually become more flexible, and most school-age children begin to accept that males and females can engage in the same activities (Carter & Patterson, 1982; Sagara, 2000). The relationships between gender identity, gender stereotyping, and individual gender role adoption are not clear cut. Even children well aware of community gender norms and role expectations may not conform to gender role stereotypes in their actual behavior (Diamond & Savin-Williams, 2003; Downs & Langlois, 1988; Serbin et al., 1993). Perhaps children acquire personal gender role preferences before acquiring knowledge of gender role stereotypes or perhaps they learn and interpret gender role stereotypes in very diverse ways. Our understanding of the complexities of gender and sexual identity development—and the relationships between the two during the life course—is in its infancy.

Spiritual Development

During the past few decades, interest in exploring the importance of spiritual development and spirituality across the life course has grown. Interdisciplinary study of spiritual development indicates that spirituality plays an important role in many if not most individuals' lives. Children are increasingly recognized as possessing awareness of spirituality and of utilizing that awareness to create meaning in their lives (Hyde, 2008a). Thus, spirituality in children is increasingly seen as an important dimension of development (Mercer, 2006). Early work on children's spiritual development viewed spirituality in the context of religious development (Hyde). For instance, Robert Coles argued that religion and spirituality overlapped in children and that even children with no religious affiliation utilized religious language to describe their spiritual lives (Coles, 1990). It has been suggested that during this early work on the spiritual development of children, children's utilization of religious language to describe their spirituality simply mirrored the language of the researchers. Simply put, the researchers posed questions to the children in their studies utilizing religious terminology (Hyde).

Subsequent research explored children's spirituality in the context of how children's spirituality provided a way for them to conceptualize the meaning of life. Further, this research has examined how children's understanding of spirituality relates to an awareness of something greater at play in the course of everyday happenings (Hyde, 2008a). Researchers have explored the themes of transcendence and spirituality as human experience (Champagne, 2001; Hay & Nye, 2006). Hart (2006) argues that children's spirituality encompasses the dimensions of wonder, wisdom, and interconnectedness. He suggests that these aspects of spirituality provide a sense of hope and perspective, allow for reflection, and help shape morality. Despite the varying views regarding how children understand and utilize their spirituality, researchers agree that children in middle childhood (and younger) do have a spiritual life and that spirituality can be a protective factor in the lives of children.

Spiritual development in middle childhood has been described in a variety of ways. Some researchers have identified children in middle childhood as in the "mythic-literal" stage of spiritual development (Fowler & Dell, 2006). The mythic-literal stage coincides with the cognitive and emotional developmental levels of children in middle childhood. Children in the mythic-literal stage of spiritual development utilize storytelling to make sense of the world, "often along the lines of simple fairness and moral reciprocity . . . (t)he child believes that goodness is rewarded and badness is punished" (Fowler & Dell, p. 39). This stage marks the beginning of ponderings and feelings about spirituality and faith (Fowler & Dell). A child at this stage of development may view getting a physical illness such as the stomach flu with having done something wrong, such as hitting a sibling.

However, children in middle childhood are also capable of going beyond a simple good versus evil conception of spirituality, "weave(ing) the threads of meaning" together to create a complex worldview that is meaningful to them (Hyde, 2008b, p. 244). For instance, when children are asked about heaven, they understand it differently; it has a unique meaning to each child. One interviewed child viewed heaven as "a thought. It's in your heart if you believe it's there" (Hyde, p. 239). Another interviewed child thought of heaven as different for everyone based on the people, places, and things they loved or valued in life. This child explained heaven as unique, so "if a person liked painting, then they'd go to a place where you can paint all you want" (Hyde, p. 239). It is apparent that children take an active role in constructing spiritual beliefs that help them make sense of their worlds (Mercer, 2006). Utilizing spirituality to create threads of meaning may help children cope with difficult environmental factors such as poverty, and may facilitate successful coping with challenges such as familial illness or death.

The spiritual education of children occurs in families, faith congregations/communities (e.g., churches, synagogues, mosques, temples), and schools. Families provide spiritual education in the form of family religious traditions and belief systems (Alexander & Carr, 2006). Faith congregations provide a community of members that share a common vision and tradition of spirituality as well as a space to express that spirituality (Alexander & Carr, 2006). And, many schools are returning to an emphasis on fostering spirituality in all of its manifestations. In secular democratic countries, the teaching of spirituality is fraught with concern regarding the separation of church and state. However, many school personnel believe it is possible that general cultivation of spirituality in schools especially as it relates to the development of a life with meaning, purpose, and hope as well as character development could foster the development of caring children with a sense of interconnectedness.

> ### Critical Thinking Questions 5.1
>
> How would you describe the physical development, cognitive development, cultural identity development, emotional development, social development, and spiritual development of Anthony Bryant, Brianna Shaw, and Manuel Vega? In what areas do they each show particular strengths? In what areas do they each show particular challenges? How could a social worker help each child to enhance development in areas where they are particularly challenged?

MIDDLE CHILDHOOD AND FORMAL SCHOOLING

Before discussing the role of formal schooling in the life of the school-age child in the United States and other relatively affluent societies, it is important to note that, in an era of a knowledge-based global economy, there continue to be large global gaps in opportunities for education. Although educational participation is almost universal between the age of 5 and 14 in affluent countries, 115 million of the world's children, most residing in Africa or South Asia, do not receive even a primary education and are particularly susceptible to economic downturns and environmental crises (United Nations Development Program, 2005; World Bank, 2009). A widening gap exists in average years of education between rich and poor countries (McMichael, 2008). The average child born in Mozambique in 2005 will receive four years of formal education, compared with eight years in South Asia, and 15 years in France (United Nations Development Program). Females will receive 1 year less of education, on average, than males in African and Arab countries and two years less in South Asia (United Nations Development Program). In sub-Saharan, Middle-Eastern/North African, and South Asian countries, primary school completion rates continue well below the United Nation's Millennium Education goals (World Bank) and while females in most affluent industrialized countries receive higher levels of education than males, on average, females in the three mentioned geographical areas fall well below that of males (Sen, Partelow, & Miller, 2005).

The current importance of formal schooling during middle childhood in advanced industrial countries cannot be overstated. Children entering school must learn to navigate a new environment quite different from the family. In school, they are evaluated on the basis of how well they perform tasks; people outside the family—teachers and other school staff as well as peers—begin shaping the child's personality, dreams, and aspirations (Good & Nichols, 2001). For children such as Manuel Vega, the environmental adjustment can be even more profound since the educational attainment of family members may be limited and high-stakes tests place a premature burden on English language learners (Solórzano, 2008). At the same time, the school environment has the potential to serve as an important resource for the physical, cognitive, emotional, social, and spiritual tasks of middle childhood for all children regardless of the previous schooling available to their parents. This role for schools is particularly important to help immigrant children deal with the culture shock that many experience transitioning to their adoptive countries. In addition, schools must be aware of conditions prevalent among such children, such as traumatic stress associated with events that have occurred in their home countries or in transit to their new homes (Vaage, Garløv, Hauff, & Thomsen, 2007).

Success in the school environment is very important to the development of self-esteem. Anthony Bryant, Brianna Shaw, and Manuel Vega illustrate the potentially positive as well as painful aspects of schooling. Manuel and Brianna seem increasingly distressed by their interactions within the school environment. Often, difficulties with peers create or compound academic challenges. Brianna's school experience is becoming threatening enough that she may begin to withdraw from the environment, which would represent a serious risk to her continued cognitive, emotional, and social development.

As children move through the middle years, they become increasingly aware that they are evaluated on the basis of what they are able to do. In turn, they begin to evaluate themselves based on treatment by teachers and peers and on self-assessments of what they can and cannot do well (Skaalvik & Skaalvik, 2004). School-age children consistently rate parents, classmates, other friends, and teachers as the most important influences in their lives (Harter, 1988). Thus, children are likely to evaluate themselves in a positive manner if they receive encouraging feedback from these individuals in their academic and social environments.

▲ **Photo 5.3** As children get older, schools are the primary context for development in middle childhood.

Formal Schooling and Cognitive Development

In the past few decades, school-age children have benefited from new research and theory focusing on the concept of intelligence. Traditional views of intelligence and approaches to intelligence testing benefited European American children born in the United States. Howard Gardner's work, however, represented a paradigm shift in the field of education. He proposed that intelligence is neither unitary nor fixed, and argued that intelligence is not adequately or fully measured by IQ tests. More broadly, in his theory of **multiple intelligences,** intelligence is "the ability to solve problems or fashion products that are of consequence in a particular cultural setting or community" (Gardner, 1993, p. 15). Challenging the idea that individuals can be described, or categorized, by a single, quantifiable measure of intelligence, Gardner proposed that at least eight critical intelligences exist: verbal/linguistic, logical/mathematical, visual/spatial, musical/rhythmic, bodily/kinesthetic, naturalist, interpersonal, and intrapersonal. This paradigm shift in the education field encouraged a culturally sensitive approach to students (Campbell, Campbell, & Dickinson, 1999) and a diminished role for standardized testing.

In its practical application, multiple intelligence theory calls for the use of a wide range of instructional strategies that engage the range of strengths and intelligences of each student (Kagan & Kagan, 1998). Gardner (2006) specifically calls for matching instructional strategies to the needs and strengths of students, stretching the intelligences—or maximizing development of each intelligence—by transforming education curricula, and celebrating or (at a minimum) understanding the unique pattern of intelligences of each student.

> How might this increased emphasis on cognitive diversity alter the life course of students such as Anthony, Brianna, and Manuel?

This last point is critical. Such understanding can facilitate self-knowledge and self-acceptance. Understanding and celebration of cognitive diversity, Gardner believes, will come from a transformation not only of curricula, or instructional methods, but also of the fundamental way in which adults view students and students view themselves and one another. Schools help children develop a positive self-evaluation by providing a variety of activities that allow children with different strengths to succeed. For example, schools that assess children in many areas, including those described by Gardner, may help children who have a deficit in one area experience success in another realm. Children can also be encouraged to evaluate themselves positively through the creation of individual student portfolios and through school initiatives that promote new skill development. Classroom and extracurricular activities can build on children's abilities and interests and help them develop or maintain self-confidence (Barr & Parrett, 1995, Littky & Grabelle, 2004).

For example, most children benefit from diverse educational materials and varied activities that appeal to visual, auditory, and experiential learning styles. Such activities can include group work, student presentations, field trips, audiovisual presentations, written and oral skill activities, discussion, and lectures (Roueche & Baker, 1986). In recent years, *flexible grouping* is frequently employed. It draws on both heterogeneous and homogenous grouping and recognizes that each method is useful to achieve distinct objectives. Grouping strategies include pairing students, forming cooperative and collaborative groups, modeling lessons for students, conducting guided practice, and setting up subject-based learning laboratories. A teacher may draw on any appropriate technique during a class period, day, or week. These approaches represent an attempt to adapt instruction to meet diverse student needs. Students such as Anthony Bryant, with more academic skill, may model effective methods of mastering academic material for less advanced students. Meanwhile, Anthony simultaneously learns more appropriate school behavior from his socially adept peers. Furthermore, this teaching method may help Anthony strengthen peer friendships—an important potential source of support as he confronts family transitions or conflict in the future.

Thus, in addition to calling for changes in instructional strategies, multiple intelligence theory calls for movement toward more comprehensive assessments of diverse areas of student performance. Such assessment includes naturalistic, across-time observation and development of self-appraisal materials such as student portfolios. This call, however, has occurred in tandem with the standards movement within the United States. Most schools and states have moved away from norm-referenced testing and toward *criterion-referenced testing,* which requires all graduating students to meet certain absolute scores and requirements. At present, all states have established some form of learning standards that all students must achieve in order to graduate from high school.

Formal Schooling and Diversity

Students such as Manuel Vega face considerable challenges in the school setting. Manuel's ability to engage in the school environment is compromised, and many schools are ill equipped to respond to the issues confronting children such as him. If Manuel is not supported and assisted by his school system, his educational experience may assault his healthy development. But if Manuel's personal and familial support systems can be tapped and mobilized, they may help him overcome his feelings of isolation in his new school environment. Carefully constructed and implemented interventions must be used to help Manuel. These interventions could include a focus on bridging the gap between his command of the rules of the informal register of English and the acquisition of formal standard English, without destroying his Spanish language base and his Mexican cultural heritage.

Today in the United States, Manuel's situation is not rare. About 1 in 4 elementary and high school students have at least one foreign-born parent (U.S. Department of Health and Human Services, 2009b) and, in general, students are more diverse than ever before. Many challenges face children who have recently arrived in the United States, particularly those fleeing war-torn countries. Research suggests that immigrant and refugee children are at heightened risk of experiencing mental health challenges and school failure (Coughlan & Owens-Manley, 2006; Vaage, Garløv, Hauff, & Thomsen, 2007).

Language difficulties and their consequences among such children are increasingly recognized. It has been established that children are best served when they are able to speak both their native language and the language of their host country (Moon, Kang, & An, 2008; Vuorenkoski, Kuure, Moilanen, Penninkilampi, & Myhrman, 2000). The mental health status among immigrant populations, however, appears to be dependent on a wide number of factors.

In general, **acculturation,** or a process by which two or more cultures remain distinct but exchange cultural features (such as foods, music, clothing), is easier on children than **assimilation,** or a process by which the minority culture must adapt and become incorporated into the majority culture, particularly in the school environment. Communication and interaction between families and schools is always important (Bhattacharya, 2000; U.S. Department of Health and Human Services, 2000).

It is essential for schools and professionals to recognize the importance of language to learning. Children acquire an informal language that contains the communication rules needed to survive in the familial and cultural group to which the child belongs. Schools often ignore the potency of these informal registers as they work toward their mission of teaching the "formal register" of the dominant middle class, deemed necessary to survive in the world of work and school. The need for specific strategies to acknowledge and honor the "informal register," while teaching the formal, has been identified by several literacy researchers (see Gee, 1996; Knapp, 1995). These researchers emphasize the importance of teaching children to recognize their internal, or natural, "speech" and the "register" they use in the school environment. Identifying and mediating these processes is best accomplished in the context of a caring relationship (Noddings, 1984). By sensitively promoting an awareness of such differences in the home and school, teachers, social workers, and other adults can help children experience less confusion and alienation.

Formal Schooling: Home and School

Indeed, parental involvement in school is associated with better school performance (Domina, 2005). Schools serving diverse populations are becoming increasingly creative in their approaches to encouraging parent involvement, including the development of sophisticated interpretation and translation infrastructures (Pardington, 2002). Unfortunately, many schools lag behind, suffering from either inadequate resources or the consequences of exclusive and racist attitudes within the school and larger community environments (see Jones, 2001).

The link between school and home is important in poor and affluent neighborhoods alike, because school and home are the two major spheres in which children exist. The more similar these two environments are, the more successful the child will be at school and at home. Students who experience vastly different cultures at home and at school are likely to have difficulty accommodating the two worlds (Ryan & Adams, 1995). A great deal of learning goes on before a child enters school. By the time Anthony Bryant, Brianna Shaw, and Manuel Vega began school, they had acquired routines, habits, and cognitive, social, emotional, and physical styles and skills (Kellaghan, Sloane, Alvarez, & Bloom, 1993). School is a "next step" in the educational process.

The transition is relatively easy for many students because schools typically present a mainstream model for behavior and learning. As most parents interact with their children, they model and promote the behavior that will be acceptable in school. Children from such backgrounds are often well prepared for the school environment because, quite simply, they understand the rules; as a result, the school is accepting of them (Payne, 2005). Furthermore, the school environment helps reinforce rules and skills taught in the home environment, just as the home environment helps reinforce rules and skills taught in the school environment. Research indicates that this type of home-school continuity often predicts school success (Ameta & Sherrard, 1995; Comer, 1994; Epstein & Lee, 1995; Kellaghan et al., 1993; Ryan & Adams, 1995).

In contrast, children with a distinct background may not be fluent in mainstream speech patterns and may not have been extensively exposed to school rules or materials such as scissors and books. These children, although possessing skills and curiosity, are often viewed as inferior in some way by school personnel (Comer, 1994; Solórzano, 2008). Children viewed in this manner may begin to feel inferior and either act out or disengage from the school process (Finn, 1989). Because the school environment does not support the home environment and the home environment does not support the school environment, these children face an increased risk of poor school outcomes.

Schools that recognize the contribution of home to school success typically seek family involvement. Parents and other family members can help establish the motivation for learning and provide learning opportunities within the home environment (Constable & Walberg, 1996; Jones, 2001). Children whose parents are involved in their education typically succeed academically (Fan, 2001; Fan & Chen, 2001; Houtenville & Conway, 2008; Zellman & Waterman, 1998). Unfortunately, poor communication between parents, children, and schools may short-circuit parental involvement. Traditionally, schools asked parents only to participate in Parent Teacher Association meetings, to attend parent-teacher meetings, to act as helpers in the classroom, and to review notes and written communications sent home with the schoolchild. This sort of parental participation does not always facilitate meaningful, open communication. Schools can establish more meaningful relationships with parents by reaching out to them, involving them as partners in decision making and school governance, treating parents and other caregivers (and their children) with authentic respect, providing support and coordination to implement and sustain parental involvement, and connecting parents with resources (see Dupper & Poertner, 1997; Patrikakou, Weisberg, Redding, & Walberg, 2005; Swap, 1993).

Formal Schooling: Schools Mirror Community

As microcosms of the larger U.S. society, schools mirror its institutional structures. Thus, schools often uphold racism, classism, and sexism (Bowles & Gintis, 1976; Harry, 2006; Keating, 1994; Ogbu, 1994). As discussed, cognitive development can be impacted by cultural factors specific to second-language usage and gender socialization as well as racial and class identities. Students belonging to nondominant groups have often been viewed as inherently less capable and thus failed to receive the cognitive stimulation needed for optimal growth and development. This problem has led to lowered expectations, segregation, and institutionalized mistreatment throughout the history of schooling. At the federal and state levels, from the mid-1960s through 1980, specific legislation was developed to attempt to rectify the effects of the unequal treatment of a variety of groups.

> How do racism, classism, and sexism affect middle childhood development?

In most parts of the country, however, members of historically mistreated groups (e.g., children with mental and physical challenges, children belonging to ethnic and racial minority groups) did not receive equal treatment, and they were forced to attend segregated and inferior schools throughout most of the 20th century. Over time, various court rulings, most prominently the 1954 *Brown v. Board of Education* decision (347 U.S. 483), made equal, integrated education the right of all U.S. citizens, ruling that "separate but equal" has no place in public education. However, in the past 15 years, courts at both the state and federal levels have been lifting desegregation orders, arguing that separate can be equal or at least "good enough." As a result, today the school systems in the United States are more segregated by race than they were 30 years ago (Boger & Orfield, 2005; Kozol, 2005). These court rulings as well as housing patterns and social traditions work against integrated public schooling. Schools continue to mirror the social systems with which they interact and thus often fall short of their democratic ideals (Darling-Hammond, 2007). Informal segregation often persists in schools, and poor children still suffer in schools that frequently do not provide enough books, supplies, teachers, or curricula challenging enough to facilitate success in U.S. society. That has led to the achievement gap between historically underrepresented groups and the more advantaged. Gloria Ladson-Billings in her presidential address to the 2006 American Educational Research Association identified a major cause of the gap as the nation's *education debt* for our current and past educational and political policies toward these groups of students (Kozol, 1991, 2005; Ladson-Billings, 2006).

The juxtaposition of inner-city, rural, and suburban schools continues to point to substantial divisions between economically rich and impoverished communities. For example, although less well documented, a consistent difficulty for rural schools throughout much of the world is access to a consistent supply of teachers, especially in math and science. Many countries in the developing world offer a range of incentives (Ladd, 2007) to attract teachers in subject shortage areas. Chronic teacher shortages inhibit rural children from receiving access to consistent high-quality teaching. In the United States, the challenges of rural education are compounded by the historic inability of American educational practice to provide consistent educational expertise and resources in low-wealth school districts. Often set in communities with agricultural economies, rural schools struggle to meet the language needs of migrant populations (Gutiérrez, 2008), to overcome the legacy of historical and re-constituted segregated schooling in many southern states (Ladson-Billings, 2004), and to compensate for the isolation of remote Indigenous populations throughout the Native-American reservation lands of the west. They also struggle to overcome the effects of rural poverty that has stayed close to 20% for several decades and has remained 5% more than the percentage for urban children in poverty since the late 1990s (O'Hare, 2009). Lack of access to high-quality schooling and health care combined with high poverty rates make rural children particularly vulnerable to reduced opportunity.

During all phases of childhood, children benefit from equal treatment and attention and suffer when **institutional discrimination**—the systemic denial of access to assets, economic opportunities, associations, and organizations based on minority status—is in place. Indeed even when African American and poor children, and children from predominantly Spanish-speaking populations, were integrated into public school systems in the 20th century, the process of *tracking* students assured that the vast majority of students of color and low socioeconomic status were relegated to less rigorous course sequences (Oakes, 1985; Owens, 1985). In addition, such division of students has often been based on standardized tests, which research suggests may be culturally and class biased. Students have also been divided based on school personnel reports. Such reports are often subjective and may inadvertently be based on assessments of students' dress, language, and behavior (Oakes; Oakes & Lipton, 1992). Throughout the history of public schooling, most teachers and other school staff have belonged to dominant groups, and consciously or unconsciously, they may have awarded privilege and preference to learning styles, language, and dress that they found familiar.

In short, post desegregation, tracking has traditionally served as a two-tiered system of ongoing educational inequality. Although it is necessary to understand the complexities of tracking, including both advantages and disadvantages (see Brunello & Checchi, 2007; Loveless, 1999; Wang, Walberg, & Reynolds, 2004), it is equally important to recognize that special education, non-college-bound, and nonaccelerated classes have been disproportionately populated by historically excluded students. These classes too often prepared students to work only in low-skilled, low-paying jobs. Conversely, regular education, college-bound, and accelerated classes have been disproportionately White and middle or upper class. These classes typically prepare their members for college and leadership roles. Thus, the traditional structure of public education often both reflected and supported ethnic and class divisions within U.S. society (Kozol, 2005; Oakes & Lipton, 1992; Winters, 1993).

> What impact have these historical trends in public education had on middle childhood development?

For an example of the dangers of tracking, consider Anthony Bryant. His behavior puts him at risk for eventual placement in specialized classes for emotionally disturbed children, even though his behavior may be a normal part of his developmental process (Hosp & Reschly, 2003). Currently, his fairly infrequent aggressive behavior seems to be dealt with by school personnel appropriately, which may prevent an escalation of the problem. Intervention with Anthony's family members may also facilitate a consistent, positive family response to Anthony's behavior. However, the professionals making decisions at Anthony's school and in his community could begin to interpret his behavior as serious and threatening. Thus, Anthony faces an increased risk of placement outside the "regular" track. What could follow, through a series of steps intended by the school system to provide special programming for Anthony, is his miseducation based on a set of faulty cultural lenses that diagnose his needs and prescribe deficient remedies. The potential miseducation of Anthony is compounded by social patterns that have persisted for years and work against the success of African American males and immigrant youth in particular.

Many school systems have now recognized their historically unequal treatment of students and taken steps to reduce discrimination. One approach is *mainstreaming,* or *inclusion,* the practice of placing all children who could be assigned to special education classrooms into regular education classrooms (Connor, Gabel, Gallagher, & Morton, 2008; Sleeter, 1995). An increasingly common and innovative approach in the disability arena is the *collaborative classroom.* Children with and without disabilities are team-taught by both a "regular" and a "special" education teacher. Heterogeneous grouping helps prevent students of different races, socioeconomic classes, and genders from being separated and treated unequally. Different approaches to teaching academic content are used in the hopes of accommodating a variety of learning styles and social backgrounds. Teachers, students, and other school personnel receive training on diversity. And sexual harassment policies have slowly been implemented and enforced in public schools. The policies are enforced by the requirement that all schools receiving federal funds designate a Title IX hearing officer to inquire about and, if warranted, respond to all allegations of harassment in its many forms.

Schools have also begun to include, in their curricula, content that reflects the diversity of their students. As the topic of diversity has become prominent in academic and popular discourse, educational materials are increasingly likely to include the perspectives of traditionally nondominant groups. As a result, more literature and history lessons represent females and minorities who have contributed to U.S. life.

In the last decade, clear and consistent educational research in the fields of literacy education and educational theory has also begun to detail effective instructional strategies and methodological approaches. Implementation of such research findings has disrupted the "stand and deliver," or lecture format, as the dominant approach to teaching and knowledge acquisition.

Schools located in areas with high rates of poverty have also been targeted for extra attention. *Full-service schools* attempt to provide school-based or school-linked health and social services for school children and their families (Dryfoos, 1994; Rubenstein, 2008). Similarly, school-based family resource centers attempt to provide children, families, and communities with needed supports (Adler, 1993, Smith & Brun, 2006). Such provision of holistic family services illustrates public education's continuing effort to meet the ideal of equal and comprehensive education, allowing all U.S. children equal opportunity to achieve economic and social success.

In addition, the U.S. Department of Education launched a major initiative to close the achievement gap of historically excluded populations with the passage by Congress of the No Child Left Behind Education (NCLB) Act of 2001 as an extension of the Elementary and Secondary Education Act. Increasingly, schools have been refocused on English Language Arts and math skill development training by the national standards movement and advanced by the requirements of NCLB and its accountability arm, but to the potential detriment of educating the whole child (Guisbond & Neill, 2004).

The NCLB shifted federal focus to school and teacher accountability for higher achievement, which is monitored by annual "high stakes" tests. All children must take such standardized assessments, and schools are required to disaggregate their results for each of five subpopulations including gender and students with disabilities, limited English proficiency, low socioeconomic status as well as students who are Black, Hispanic, American Indian/Alaskan

Native, Asian/Pacific Islander, or White. Under the provisions of the law, school districts must meet annual yearly progress (AYP) goals for both aggregated and disaggregated data sets. Districts failing to meet such goals face consequences ranging from providing extra funding for parents to acquire support services to having a school closed down for consistently missing AYP targets. As a result, educational research has been given higher status to influence educational policy than it has received in the past.

This push for educational accountability and its impact on the lives of children is complex and highly controversial. The application of the NCLB standards spurred a number of organizations and states (e.g., the National Educational Association, Michigan, Connecticut, and Utah) to either sue the federal government or sharply criticize the act for raising state achievement requirements without adequate supporting funds or as a violation of states' rights.

Nonetheless, many schools have adopted innovative practices designed to raise achievement of basic skills while attempting to meet the educational needs of all students (Sherer, 2009). However, only 10 reform programs received the highest grade (defined as moderate or limited success) by the Comprehensive School Reform Quality Center and American Institutes for Research (2006) in their federally funded three-year study of school reform programs. Two initiatives examined within this study serve as prime examples of the variety of philosophies that drive such schools. The Knowledge Is Power Program (KIPP) follows a prescription that demands that its students strictly adhere to a regimen of social behavior development coupled with long hours dedicated to mastering content-based curricula (Carter, 2000). Conversely, Expeditionary Learning Schools (a consortium of 140 schools) immerse their students in problem-based learning that is linked to authentic experiences often consummated outside the walls of the school (Cousins, 2000; Levy, 2000). As this report suggests, most schools are struggling to balance a number of competing demands while meeting the standards of the NCLB Act. Evidence regarding the effectiveness of the NCLB Act was to be examined during congressional hearings in 2007, when the act was up for reauthorization. In 2009, the Obama administration laid out an ambitious plan to provide the financial backing to carry out several new initiatives as well to encourage innovative ways to meet the goals of NCLB. Money was allocated as part of the stimulus funding process to reverse the underfunding trends of the Bush administration (Obama, 2009), and optimistic idea generation began anew.

Critical Thinking Questions 5.2

Think about your own middle childhood years, between the ages of 6 and 12. What are some examples of school experiences that helped you to feel competent and confident? What are some examples of school experiences that led you to feel incompetent and inferior? What biological, family, cultural, and other environmental factors lead to success and failure in school?

SPECIAL CHALLENGES IN MIDDLE CHILDHOOD

In the last several decades in the United States, family structures have become more diverse than ever (Amato, 2003; Fields, 2004; Parke, 2003). The percentage of children living with both parents has steadily declined during the last four to five decades. According to the U.S. Census Bureau data, in 2007 67.8% of children lived with married parents, 2.9% lived with two unmarried parents, 25.8% lived with one parent, and 3.5% lived with no parent present (Kreider & Elliott, 2009).

Social and economic trends have placed more parents of young children into the workforce in order to make ends meet. Legislation requires single parents who receive public assistance to remain engaged in or to re-enter the workforce (Parham, Quadagno, & Brown, 2009). The school day often does not coincide with parents' work schedules, and recent research suggests that as a result of parental employment, more than half of school-age children regularly need additional forms of supervision when school is not in session. Most of these children either participate in a before- or afterschool program (also known as wrap-around programs) or receive care from a relative (Lerner, Castellino, Lolli, & Wan, 2003). Many low- and middle-income families struggle to find affordable child care and often are forced to sacrifice quality child care for economic reasons (National Association of Child Care Resource and Referral Agencies, 2006; Wertheimer, 2003).

Unfortunately, available data suggest that the quality of child care experienced by the average child in the United States is less than ideal (Helburn & Bergmann, 2002; Vandell & Wolfe, 2000). This fact is particularly troubling because child care quality has been linked to children's physical health as well as cognitive, emotional, and social development (Tout & Zaslow, 2003; Vandell & Wolfe, 2000). These findings apply not only to early childhood programs but also to before- and afterschool programs for older children. Moreover, as children move from the early (ages 5 to 9) to later (10 to 12) middle childhood years, they are increasingly likely to take care of themselves during the before- and afterschool hours (Lerner et al., 2003). Regular participation in a high-quality before- and afterschool program is positively associated with academic performance, and a significant body of research suggests that how school-age children spend their afterschool hours is strongly associated with the likelihood of engaging in risky behaviors (Lerner et al.).

Inadequate and low-quality child care is just one of the challenges facing school-age children—along with their families and communities—in the 21st century. Other challenges include poverty, family and community violence, mental and physical challenges, and family disruption.

Poverty

A growing international consensus indicates that poverty is the most significant human rights challenge facing the world community (Grinspun, 2004). Indeed, foremost among threats to children's healthy development is poverty, which potentially threatens positive development in all domains (Duncan, Kalil, & Ziol-Guest, 2008; Gordon, Nandy, Pantazis, Pemberton, & Townsend, 2003; Harper, 2004; United Nations Children's Fund, 2000a, 2000b; Vandivere, Moore, & Brown, 2000). Unfortunately, it is estimated that half of the children of the world live in poverty, many in extreme poverty (Bellamy, 2004). That children should be protected from poverty is not disputed; in the United States, this societal value dates back to the colonial period (Trattner, 1998). The nature of policies and programs targeted at ensuring the minimal daily needs of children are met, however, has shifted over time, as has our success in meeting this goal (Chase-Lansdale & Vinovskis, 1995; United Nations Children's Fund, 2000a).

> How does poverty serve as a risk factor in middle childhood?

In the United States, the late 20th century brought a dramatic rise in the child poverty rate, which peaked in the early 1990s, declined for approximately a decade, and has gradually increased again during the first several years of the 21st century (Koball & Douglas-Hall, 2006). In 2007, the national poverty rate for the population as a whole was approximately 12.5%, and approximately 18% of children lived in poverty. In other words, approximately one in five children live in a family with an income below the federal poverty level (National Center for Children in Poverty, 2008).

As illustrated in Exhibit 5.3, children in the middle childhood age range are less likely to live in low-income or poor families than their younger counterparts, and this trend continues as children grow toward adulthood. Caucasian children comprise the majority of poor children in the United States. Young children and children from minority groups, however, are statistically overrepresented among the population of poor children (Linver, Fuligni, Hernandez, & Brooks-Gunn, 2004; National Center for Children in Poverty, 2008). This is a persistent contemporary trend; in other words, although in absolute numbers Caucasian children consistently compose the majority of poor

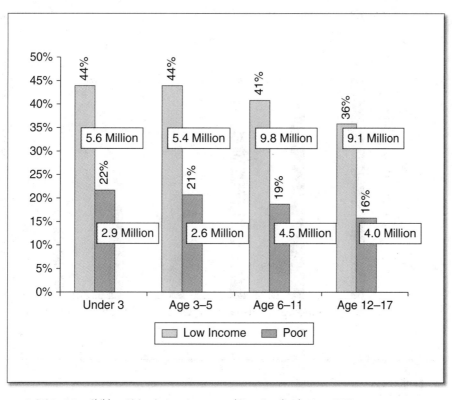

▲ **Exhibit 5.3**   Children Living in Low-Income and Poor Families by Age, 2008

SOURCE: Wight & Chau, 2009b. Reprinted with permission of the National Center for Children in Poverty.

children, children from Latino and African American families are consistently significantly overrepresented among all children in poverty. Currently, the percentage of African American (61%) or Latino (62%) children living in low-income families is twice as high as the percentage of Caucasian (27%) children (National Center for Children Living in Poverty, 2008; Linver et al., 2004; Wight & Chau, 2009b). The child poverty rates for different racial and ethnic groups in 2008 are presented in Exhibit 5.4.

In general, the risk factors associated with child poverty are numerous, especially when poverty is sustained. Children who grow up in poverty are more likely to be born with low birth weight, to experience serious and chronic health problems, to receive poorer health care and nutrition, to be homeless or live in substandard and overcrowded housing, to live in violent communities, and to experience family turmoil than children who grow up in better financial circumstances (Evans & English, 2002; Linver et al., 2004; United Nations Children's Fund, 2000b). Homeless children represent a small percentage of all children living in poverty, and yet it is estimated that more than one million children experience homelessness in the United States each year (Varney & van Vliet, 2008).

A number of perspectives attempt to explain the ways in which poverty impacts child development. Limited income constrains a family's ability to obtain or invest in resources that promote positive development. Poverty detrimentally impacts caregivers' emotional health and parenting practices. Individual poverty is correlated with inadequate family, school, and neighborhood resources, and, thus, children experiencing family poverty are likely experiencing additional, cumulative risk factors. Each of these perspectives is valid and sheds light on the complex and synergistic ways in which poverty threatens optimal child development (Linver et al., 2004).

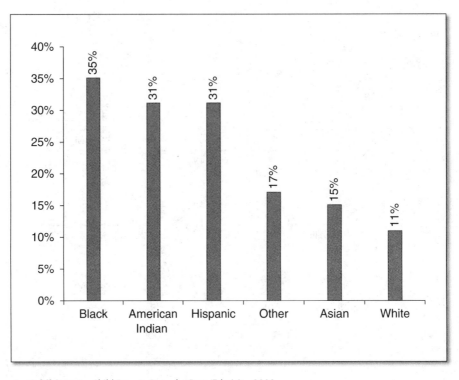

▲ **Exhibit 5.4**   Child Poverty Rates by Race/Ethnicity, 2008

SOURCE: Wight, Chau, & Aratani, 2010. Reprinted with permission of the National Center for Children in Poverty.

Children who have spent any part of their prenatal period, infancy, or early childhood in poverty have often already encountered several developmental challenges by the time middle childhood begins. Children who enter, progress through, and leave middle childhood in poverty are at much greater risk of negative developmental outcomes than those who briefly enter and then exit poverty while still in middle childhood (Moore, Redd, Burkhauser, Mbwana, & Collins, 2009).

Evidence suggests that persistent and "deep," or extreme, poverty poses the most significant threat to healthy child development (Linver et al., 2004; United Nations Children's Fund, 2000a). For example, extreme family poverty is correlated with homelessness, and poverty and homelessness combined increase a child's risk of abrupt family separation and experiencing or witnessing forms of trauma such as physical or sexual assault (Bassuk & Friedman, 2005).

But what does it actually mean, to a child, to be poor? Being poor is a relative concept, the meaning of which is defined by perceptions of and real exclusion (Dinitto & Cummins, 2006; Kozol, 2005). In most communities, one must be *not* poor in order to be fully engaged and included. Lack of income and certain goods deprive poor people of what is expected among those who belong; thus, poverty results in perceived and real inabilities and inadequacies. For example, children often participate in extracurricular activities such as sports, music, or art. These programs often involve registration, program, and equipment fees that are prohibitive to impoverished families. This is the essence of **relative poverty,** or the tendency to define one's poverty status in relation to others within one's social environment. Fundamentally, then, poverty is as much a social as an economic phenomenon. The social aspect of poverty has been extended by Payne (2005) to include emotional, spiritual, and support system impoverishment in addition to economic poverty. Such deficits in the developing child's background accumulate and result in impediments to the development of critical capacities including coping strategies. Unfortunately, income disparity—or the gap between the rich and the poor—has only continued to widen in recent years, both within and across countries around the globe (United Nations Children's Fund, 2000b, 2009).

The meaning of relative poverty for the school-age child is particularly profound. As evidence, James Garbarino (1995) points to an innocent question once asked of him by a child: "When you were growing up, were you poor or regular?" (p. 137). As the child struggles with the normal developmental tasks of feeling included and socially competent, relative poverty sends a persistent message of social exclusion and incompetence.

Family and Community Violence

Children are increasingly witness or subject to violence in their homes, schools, and neighborhoods (Hutchison, 2007). Although child maltreatment and domestic violence have always existed, they have been recognized as social problems only recently. Community violence is slowly becoming recognized as a social problem of equal magnitude, affecting a tremendous number of children and families. Exposure to violence is a particular problem in areas where a lack of economic and social resources already produces significant challenges for children (Maluccio, 2006). Among children from war-torn countries, the atrocities witnessed or experienced are often unimaginable to children and adults who have resided in the United States all of their lives (Office of the Special Representative of the Secretary-General for Children and Armed Conflict [OSRSG-CAAC] & United Nations Children's Fund, 2009).

> What protective factors can buffer the effects of neighborhood violence on school-age children?

Witnessing violence deeply affects children, particularly when the perpetrator or victim of violence is a family member. In the United States, experts estimate that anywhere between 3 and 10 million children may be impacted each year, but no consistent, valid data source exists regarding children witnessing or otherwise exposed to domestic violence (Children's Defense Fund, 2000; Fantuzzo, Mohr, & Noone, 2000).

In the United States, children appear most susceptible to nonfatal physical abuse between the ages of 6 and 12. Some speculate that in the United States, at least, this association may be due to increased likelihood of public detection through school contact during these years. The number of children reported to child protective services (CPS) agencies annually is staggering. In 2007, an estimated 3.2 million referrals or reports (involving approximately 5.8 million children) were made to CPS agencies. An estimated 794,000 children were determined to be victims of at least one type of abuse or neglect, with neglect accounting for approximately 60% of confirmed maltreatment cases in 2007 (U.S. Department of Health and Human Services, Administration on Children, Youth, and Families, 2009a). Child neglect is consistently the most common form of documented maltreatment, but it is important to note that victims typically experience more than one type of abuse or neglect simultaneously and therefore are appropriately included in more than one category. Maltreatment subtype trends are relatively stable over time; victims of child neglect consistently account for more than half of all child maltreatment victims (see Exhibit 5.5)

African American and Native American children are consistently overrepresented among confirmed maltreatment victims. Careful examination of this issue, however, has concluded that although children of color are disproportionately represented within the child welfare population, studies that are cognizant of the relationship between culture and parenting practices, that control for the role of poverty, and that examine child maltreatment in the general population find no association between a child's race or ethnicity and likelihood of child maltreatment. Thus, it is likely that the disproportionate representation of children of color within the child welfare system is caused by the underlying relationship between poverty and race or ethnicity (Thomlison, 2004).

A variety of factors contribute to child maltreatment and family violence (Charlesworth, 2007; Choi & Tittle, 2002; Freisthler, Merritt, & LaScala, 2006). These factors include parental, child, family, community, and cultural characteristics. Typically, the dynamic interplay of such characteristics leads to maltreatment, with the most relevant factors varying significantly depending upon the type of maltreatment examined. Thus, multiple theoretical

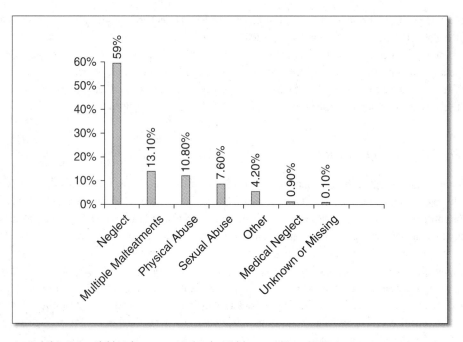

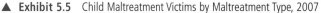

▲ **Exhibit 5.5**   Child Maltreatment Victims by Maltreatment Type, 2007

SOURCE: Figure 3-4 Victims by Maltreatment Type, 2007, U.S. Department of Health & Human Services
Administration for Children, Youth, and Families, 2009.

perspectives, particularly the life course, ecological, systems, and stress and coping perspectives, are helpful for
understanding situations of child maltreatment.

Not surprisingly, children who experience abuse have been found to report more unhappiness and troubled
behavior than children who only witness abuse (Maschi, Morgen, Hatcher, Rosato, & Violette, 2009). Witnesses, in
turn, report more adjustment difficulties than children who have neither been abused nor witnessed domestic violence. Because of the strong association between domestic violence and child maltreatment, however, many children
are likely to experience these challenges to healthy development simultaneously (Crozier & Barth, 2005; Lee &
Hoaken, 2007).

The impact of child maltreatment varies based on a number of factors, including but certainly not limited to, the
type of maltreatment, the age of the child, and many other child, family, and community characteristics. The Centers
for Disease Control and Prevention (CDC) (2005a) has published a helpful overview of child maltreatment consequences, pointing out that experiencing maltreatment as a child is associated with an overwhelming number of negative health outcomes as an adult. These outcomes include an increased likelihood of using or abusing alcohol and
other substances, disordered eating, depression, and susceptibility to certain chronic diseases.

Children who experience trauma, induced by either indirect or direct exposure to violence, may experience *posttraumatic stress disorder* (PTSD)—a set of symptoms that include feelings of fear and helplessness, reliving of the
traumatic experience, and attempts to avoid reminders of the traumatic experience (Balaban, 2008; Farkas, 2004;
Farmer, 2009). Researchers have also found changes in the brain chemistry of children exposed to chronic violence
(Kowalik, 2004; Perry, 2006). Clearly, witnessing or experiencing violence adversely affects children in a number of
areas, including the ability to function in school and the ability to establish stable social, including peer, relationships

(Guterman & Embry, 2004). Children who directly experience violence are at high risk of negative outcomes, but secondary exposure to violence and trauma—such as when a child's parents are suffering from PTSD—also may lead to negative outcomes for children (Hamblen, 2002). In general, the intergenerational nature of family violence has been established (Herrenkohl et al., 2004). Childhood exposure to violence significantly increases the likelihood of mental health difficulties and violence perpetration or revictimization. Currently, the focus is on understanding the specific pathways of intergenerational processes (Coid et al., 2001; Heyman & Smith Slep, 2002; Lang, Stein, Kennedy, & Foy, 2004). It is clear that prolonged exposure to violence has multiple implications for child development. Children are forced to learn lessons about loss and death, perhaps before they have acquired the cognitive ability to understand. They may therefore come to believe that the world is unpredictable and violent, a belief that threatens children's natural curiosity and desire to explore the social environment. Multiple experiences in which adults are unable to protect them often lead children to conclude that they must take on such responsibility for themselves, a prospect that can easily overwhelm the resources of a school-age child.

Experiencing such helplessness may also lead to feelings of incompetence and hopelessness, to which children who experience chronic violence react in diverse ways. Responses may be passive, including withdrawal symptoms and signs of depression; or they may be active, including the use of aggression as a means of coping with and transforming the overwhelming feelings of vulnerability (Charlesworth, 2007).

The emotional availability of a parent or other caretaker who can support the child's need to process traumatic events is critical. However, in situations of crisis stimulated by child maltreatment, domestic violence, and national or international violence, families are often unable to support their children psychologically. Even with the best of parental resources, moreover, children developing in violent and chronically dangerous communities continue to experience numerous challenges to development. The child's need for autonomy and independence is directly confronted by the parent's need to protect the child's physical safety. For example, hours spent indoors to avoid danger do not promote the much-needed peer relationships and sense of accomplishment, purpose, and self-efficacy so critical during this phase of development (Hutchison, 2007).

Mental and Physical Challenges

Although the term "disability" is still widely used in academic discourse and government policy, many are actively seeking to change popular discourse to reflect the need to see all children as possessing a range of physical and mental abilities. The use of the term disability establishes a norm within that range and labels those with abilities outside the norm as "disabled," which implies that group of individuals is "abnormal" and the group of individuals within the norm is "normal." In 2005, government data suggested that 6.7% of 5- to 20-year-olds, 12.7% of 21- to 64-year-olds, and 40.5% of those people 65 and older in the United States have some form of mental or physical "disability" (U.S. Bureau of the Census, 2005). Such a label, however, confines "normal" and "abnormal" to fixed categories that are not helpful to realizing a vision of a just and equal society. Slightly more than one in 10 children in the United States has difficulty performing one or more everyday activities, including for example, learning and self-care (Emmons, 2005; Hauser-Cram & Howell, 2003). Some of these difficulties are discussed below.

Attention Deficit Hyperactivity Disorder

ADHD is a commonly diagnosed childhood behavioral disorder impacting learning in the school environment. ADHD includes predominately inattentive, predominately impulsive-hyperactive, and combined inattentive-hyperactivity (American Psychiatric Association, 2000a) (see Exhibit 5.6 for diagnostic criteria for ADHD). Estimates of the prevalence of ADHD among school-age children range from 3% to 12%, with highest incidence of ADHD diagnosis occurring between ages 5 and 10; compared with girls, boys are significantly more likely to receive a diagnosis of

A. Either (1) or (2):

1. Six (or more) of the following symptoms of inattention have persisted for at least 6 months to a degree that is maladaptive and inconsistent with developmental level:

Inattention

    a. often fails to give close attention to details or makes careless mistakes in schoolwork, work, or other activities

    b. often has difficulty sustaining attention in tasks or play activities

    c. often does not seem to listen when spoken to directly

    d. often does not follow through on instructions and fails to finish schoolwork, chores, or duties in the workplace (not due to oppositional behavior or failure to understand instruction)

    e. often has difficulty organizing tasks and activities

    f. often avoids, dislikes, or is reluctant to engage in tasks that require sustained mental effort (such as schoolwork or homework)

    g. often loses things necessary for tasks or activities (toys, school assignments, pencils, books, or tools)

    h. is often easily distracted by extraneous stimuli

    i. is often forgetful in daily activities

2. Six (or more) of the following symptoms of *hyperactivity-impulsivity* have persisted for at least 6 months to a degree that it is maladaptive and inconsistent with developmental level:

Hyperactivity

    a. often fidgets with hands or feet or squirms in seat

    b. often leaves seat in classroom or in other situations in which remaining seated is expected

    c. often runs about or climbs excessively in situations in which it is inappropriate (in adolescents or adults, may be limited to subjective feelings of restlessness)

    d. often has difficulty playing or engaging in leisure activities quietly

    e. is often "on the go" or often acts as if "driven by a motor"

    f. often talks excessively

Impulsivity

    a. often blurts out answers to questions before they have been completed

    b. often has difficulty awaiting turn

    c. often interrupts or intrudes on others (e.g., butts into conversations or games)

B. Some hyperactive-impulsive or inattentive symptoms that caused impairment were present before age 7

C. Some impairment from the symptoms is present in two or more settings (e.g., at school [or work] and at home)

D. There must be clear evidence of clinically significant impairment in social, academic, or occupational functioning

E. The symptoms do not occur exclusively during the course of a pervasive developmental disorder, schizophrenia, or other psychotic disorder and are not better accounted for by another mental disorder (e.g., mood disorder, anxiety disorder, dissociated disorder, or a personality disorder)

▲ **Exhibit 5.6** Diagnostic Criteria for Attention Deficit/Hyperactivity Disorder

SOURCE: American Psychiatric Association, 2000a. Reprinted with permission.

ADHD (Schneider & Eisenberg, 2006; Strock, 2006). ADHD is associated with school failure or academic under-achievement, but the relationship is complex in part because of the strong relationship between ADHD and a number of other factors also associated with school difficulties (Barry, Lyman & Klinger, 2002; LeFever, Villers, Morrow, & Vaughn, 2002; Schneider & Eisenberg). Also, several studies suggest that the interpretation and evaluation of ADHD behaviors is significantly influenced by culturally linked beliefs (Glass & Wegar, 2000; Kakouros, Maniadaki, & Papaeliou, 2004). In other words, the extent to which ADHD-linked behaviors are perceived as problematic varies according to individual and group values and norms.

Autistic Spectrum Disorders

In recent years, growing public attention and concern have focused upon autistic spectrum disorders. Among children ages 3 to 10, slightly more than 3 per 1,000 children are diagnosed with autistic spectrum disorders; compared with girls, boys are three times as likely to receive such a diagnosis (Strock, 2004). Autism typically manifests and is diagnosed within the first 2 years of life; however, some children may not receive formal assessment or diagnosis until their early or middle childhood years. Like children with any special need or disability, children diagnosed with autistic spectrum disorders are extremely diverse; in particular, such children vary widely in terms of their intellectual and communicative abilities as well as the nature and severity of behavioral challenges (Volkmar, Paul, Klin, & Cohen, 2005). In general, autism consists of impairment within three major domains: reciprocal social interaction, verbal and nonverbal communication, and range of activities and interests (Holter, 2004) (see diagnostic criteria in Exhibit 5.7).

Emotional/Behavioral Disorder

In many schools, the children perhaps presenting the greatest challenge to educators and administrators are those who consistently exhibit disruptive or alarming behavior yet do not clearly fit the criteria for a disability diagnosis. Although the U.S. Individuals with Disabilities Education Act (IDEA) includes a definition for "seriously emotionally disturbed" children, not all school professionals and government education agencies consistently agree with or use this definition (Brauner & Stephens, 2006; Young et al., 2004). In fact, the National Mental Health and Special Education Coalition has publicized a definition of "emotionally/behaviorally disordered" children, suggesting that this term and a set of diagnostic criteria could be used in place of the IDEA definition (see Exhibit 5.8). Because of these definitional inconsistencies, it is extremely difficult to accurately estimate the number of school-age children falling within this population. Such estimates range from 0.05% to 6% of students.

Early identification and intervention, or provision of appropriate supportive services, are key protective factors for a child with special needs. In addition, the social environment more generally may serve as either a risk or protective factor, depending on its response to the child with a special need. Although difference of any sort is often noticed by children and adults, students with special needs or chronic illness are at particular risk for being singled out by their peers, and middle childhood is a critical time for such children. For children to acquire a clear and positive sense of self, they need positive self-regard. The positive development of all children is facilitated by support at multiple levels to promote feelings of self-competence and independence (Goldstein, Kaczmarek, & English, 2002). Educating all children and adults about special needs and encouraging the support of all students may help to minimize negative attitudes and incidents (Gargiulo, 2005; Garrett, 2006).

> What educational initiatives could minimize the risks associated with ADHD, autistic spectrum disorders, and other emotional/behavioral disorders?

A. A total of six (or more) items from (1), (2), and (3), with at least two from (1), and one each from (2) and (3):

  (1) qualitative impairment in social interaction, as manifested by at least two of the following:

  (a) marked impairment in the use of multiple nonverbal behaviors such as eye-to-eye gaze, facial expression, body postures, and gestures to regulate social interaction
  (b) failure to develop peer relationships appropriate to developmental level
  (c) a lack of spontaneous seeking to share enjoyment, interests, or achievements with other people (e.g., by a lack of showing, bringing, or pointing out objects of interest)
  (d) lack of social or emotional reciprocity

  (2) qualitative impairments in communication as manifested by at least one of the following:

  (a) delay in, or total lack of, the development of spoken language (not accompanied by an attempt to compensate through alternative modes of communication such as gesture or mime)
  (b) in individuals with adequate speech, marked impairment in the ability to initiate or sustain a conversation with others
  (c) stereotyped and repetitive use of language or idiosyncratic language
  (d) lack of varied, spontaneous make-believe play or social imitative play appropriate to developmental level

  (3) restricted repetitive and stereotyped patterns of behavior, interests, and activities, as manifested by at least one of the following:

  (a) encompassing preoccupation with one or more stereotyped and restricted patterns of interest that is abnormal either in intensity or focus
  (b) apparently inflexible adherence to specific, nonfunctional routines or rituals
  (c) stereotyped and repetitive motor mannerisms (e.g., hand or finger flapping or twisting, or complex whole-body movements)
  (d) persistent preoccupation with parts of objects

B. Delays or abnormal functioning in at least one of the following areas, with onset prior to age 3 years: (1) social interaction, (2) language as used in social communication, or (3) symbolic or imaginative play.

C. The disturbance is not better accounted for by Rett's Disorder or Childhood Disintegrative Disorder.

▲ **Exhibit 5.7**   Diagnostic Criteria for Autistic Disorder

SOURCE: American Psychiatric Association, 2000a, p. 75. Reprinted with permission.

Students who feel misunderstood by their peers are particularly likely to feel alone or isolated in the school setting. Students who are socially excluded by their peers often develop a dislike of school. Some students who are teased, isolated, or harassed on a regular basis may begin to withdraw or act out in order to cope with unpleasant experiences. Teachers, parents, and other school personnel who pay special attention to, and intervene with, students in this situation may prevent the escalation of such problems.

Children's adjustment to special needs is highly dependent on the adjustment of those around them. Families may respond in a number of ways to a diagnosis of a disability or serious illness. Often caregivers experience loss or grief stages; these stages may include the following: denial, withdrawal, rejection, fear, frustration, anger, sadness, adjustment, and acceptance (Boushey, 2001; Bruce & Schultz, 2002; Pejlert, 2001; Ziolko, 1993). The loss and grief stages are not linear but can be experienced repeatedly as parents interface with educational, social, and medical

Emotionally Disturbed	1. A condition exhibiting one or more of the following characteristics over a long period of time and to a marked degree, which adversely affects educational performance:
	
	  a. An inability to learn which cannot be explained by intellectual, sensory, or health factors;
	  b. An inability to build or maintain satisfactory interpersonal relationships with peers and teachers;
	  c. Inappropriate types of behavior or feelings under normal circumstances;
	  d. A general, pervasive mood of unhappiness or depression;
	  e. A tendency to develop physical symptoms or fears associated with personal or school problems.
	
	2. Includes children who are schizophrenic (or autistic). The term does not include children who are socially maladjusted, unless it is determined that they are seriously emotionally disturbed.

Emotional/Behavioral Disorder	1. A disability characterized by behavioral or emotional responses in school programs so different from appropriate age, culture, or ethnic norms that they adversely affect educational performance, including academic, social, vocational, or personal skills, and which:
	
	  a. Is more than a temporary, expected response to stressful events in the environment;
	  b. Is consistently exhibited in two different settings, at least one of which is school-related; and
	  c. Persists despite individualized interventions within the education program, unless, in the judgment of the team, the child or youth's history indicates that such interventions would not be effective.
	
	2. May include children or youth with schizophrenia disorders, affective disorders, anxiety disorders, or other sustained disturbances of conduct or adjustment when they adversely affect educational performance in accordance with Section I.

▲ **Exhibit 5.8** Diagnostic Criteria for Emotional/Behavioral Disorder or Disturbance

SOURCE: Young, Marchant, & Wilder, 2004, pp. 177–178. Reprinted with permission.

institutions throughout their child's life (Bruce & Schultz; Pejlert). Awareness of and sensitivity to these stages and the ongoing nature of grief and loss is critical for those assessing the need for intervention. Typically, parents are helped by advocacy and support groups and access to information and resources.

Families of children with special needs also typically desire independence and self-determination for their children. Family empowerment was an explicit focus of the Education for All Handicapped Children Act (PL 94–142) of 1975, which stresses parental participation in the development of an **individual education plan** (IEP) for each child. The IEP charts a course for ensuring that each child achieves as much as possible in the academic realm. The need to include the family in decision making and planning is also embodied in the IDEA of 1990 (reauthorized in 1997 and 2004), which replaced the Education for All Handicapped Children Act (Hauser-Cram & Howell, 2003). The IDEA requires that the IEP includes specific educational goals for each student classified as in need of special educational services. In addition, the IDEA assures all children the right to a free and appropriate public education and supports the placement of children with disabilities into integrated settings.

Prior to this act, the education of children with disabilities was left to individual states. As a result, the population labeled "disabled" and the services provided varied greatly. Today, however, through various pieces of legislation and several court decisions, society has stated its clear preference to educate children with special needs in integrated settings (*least restrictive environment*) to the maximum extent possible.

A recent examination of the nature of inclusion nationwide concluded that during the last two decades, students with special needs (including learning disabilities) were much more likely to be formally identified, but only approximately 15 states clearly moved toward educating students with special needs in less restrictive settings (McLeskey, Hoppey, Williamson, & Rentz, 2004). Evaluations of the impact of inclusive settings on children's school success suggest positive academic gains for children with special needs and neutral impact on academic performance for children without identified special needs (McDonnell et al., 2003).

However, some caution is in order against a "one size fits all" model of inclusion for all students with special needs, arguing that assessment of the optimal educational setting must be thorough and individualized. For example, some within the deaf community have argued that current full inclusion programs are unable "to meet the unique communication and social development needs of solitary deaf students" (Hehir, 2003, p. 36).

Hehir (2003) explains that while inclusion in statewide assessments has been shown to improve educational opportunities and achievement for some students with disabilities, "high-stakes" testing negatively impacts such progress if it alone is used as the basis for preventing students from being promoted a grade or graduating. In other words, standards-based reforms can positively impact students with disabilities if they improve the educational opportunities for all students. If such reforms, however, shift practice toward a system in which standardized testing is the only format through which student knowledge and capabilities are assessed, then many students, particularly those with special needs, are likely to suffer (Hehir, p. 40).

Family Disruption

Throughout history, most nuclear and extended families have succeeded in their endeavor to adequately protect and socialize their young. For too many children, however, the family serves as both a protective and risk factor because of unhealthy family attributes and dynamics. In the specific realm of family disruption, divorce was traditionally viewed as a developmental risk factor for children. Today, among U.S. children with married parents, approximately one half experience the divorce of their parents (Amato, 2003). Many parents marry a second time, thus "in 2001, 5.4 million children lived with one biological parent and either a stepparent or adoptive parent"; such children represent 11% of all children living with two parents (Kreider & Fields, 2005, p. 2). The likelihood of divorce is even greater for second marriages, and approximately half of these children experience the end of a parent's second marriage (Bramlett & Mosher, 2002). Many children experience the dissolution of their parents' nonmarital romantic relationships, and related attachments, without being counted in official "children of divorce" statistics or research. Although no reliable data on similar nonmarital relationship patterns exist, we can assume that similar trends exist among children's nonmarried parents and other caregivers.

Divorce and other types of family disruption lead to situations, including the introduction of new people, new housing and income arrangements, and new family roles and responsibilities (Hetherington & Jodl, 1994). Family disruption may also immerse the child in poverty (Zagorsky, 2005). As the body of research on children and divorce grows in depth and breadth, it has become apparent that divorce and other types of family disruption may detrimentally or positively impact children depending on the circumstances preceding and following the divorce (Adam & Chase-Lansdale, 2002; Amato, 2003; Fine, Ganong, & Demo, 2010; Gilman, Kawachi, & Fitzmaurice, 2003). For example, if divorce brings an end to seriously dysfunctional spousal tension or violence and results in positive changes within the home environment, child outcomes may be positive. Alternatively, if the divorce disrupted a healthy, nurturing family system and led to declines in the emotional and financial health of the child's primary caregiver(s), child outcomes may be negative.

Historically, many children experienced family disruption because of the death of one or both parents (Amato, 2003). Although improvements in public health have significantly reduced the likelihood of parental death, a substantial number of children continue to experience the death of a primary caregiver. Compared with adults, children have less cognitive and other resources to cope with death and loss (Saldinger, Cain, Kalter, & Lohnes, 1999). For children coping with the death of a parent, the circumstances of the death and the adjustment of the remaining caregivers are critical variables impacting child outcomes (Hope & Hodge, 2006; Kwok et al., 2005). Also, in recent years, a number of studies have focused upon "children of suicide." This literature notes the potential long-term impacts of parental suicide on surviving children and identifies the ways in which outcomes may be carried through generations (Cain, 2006).

Many school-age children experience disruption of attachment relationships through other means. For example, approximately 800,000 children spend some amount of time in foster care each year (Child Welfare League of America, 2005). Some of these children spend lengthy periods of time in some type of foster care setting, while some children enter and leave foster care rapidly and only once during their childhoods, and still other children cycle in and out of their home and foster care settings repeatedly. Approximately one third of the children in foster care at any time have been in substitute care for three years or more; approximately one fifth of children in foster care are identified as unlikely to ever return home and are awaiting a permanent plan (Downs, Moore, McFadden, Michaud, & Costin, 2004).

Family disruption is stressful for all children. Great variation exists, however, in the circumstances preceding and following the family disruption, the nature of the changes involved, and how children respond to this type of stress. Critical factors in outcomes for children include social supports within the family and surrounding community, the child's characteristics, the emotional well-being of caregivers, and in general the quality of care received following the family disruption. In addition, because middle childhood spans a wide age range, school-age children exhibit a wide range of cognitive, emotional, and behavioral responses to divorce and other types of family disruption. They may blame themselves and experience anxiety or other difficult emotions, or they may demonstrate a relatively mature understanding of the reasons behind the events.

Children experiencing family disruption without supports or those who have experienced difficulties preceding the disruption are most likely to experience long-term emotional and behavioral problems. Children placed in foster care or otherwise exposed to traumatic or multiple losses are more likely to fall into this group (Webb & Dumpson, 2006). These children are likely to face additional stress associated with the loss of familiar space, belongings, and social networks (Groves, 1997). However, with appropriate support and intervention as well as the presence of other protective factors, many children experiencing family disruption adjust over time.

RISK FACTORS AND PROTECTIVE FACTORS IN MIDDLE CHILDHOOD

School-age children face a variety of risks that undermine their struggles to develop a sense of purpose and self-worth. These risks include poverty, prejudice, and violence (Garbarino, 1995). More generally, risk factors are anything that increases the probability of a problem condition, its progression into a more severe state, or its maintenance (Fraser, 2004). Risk factors are moderated, however, by protective factors, either internal or external, which help children resist risk (Fraser; Garmezy, 1993, 1994; Werner & Smith, 2001). Risk and protective factors can be biological, psychological, social, and spiritual in nature, and like all influences on development, they span the micro to macro continuum (Bronfenbrenner, 1979). Dynamic, always evolving, interaction occurs among risk and protective factors present in each dimension of the individual child and his or her environment.

Resilience—or "survival against the odds"—arises from an interplay of risk and protective factors and manifests as adaptive behavior producing positive outcomes (Fraser, 2004). A variety of factors influence resilience during middle childhood. Whether a factor presents risk or protection often depends on its interaction with other factors influencing the individual child. For example, a highly structured classroom environment run by a "strict" teacher may function as a protective factor for one child while simultaneously functioning as a risk factor for another child.

The life course and systems perspectives provide tools for understanding positive development during middle childhood. These perspectives also facilitate assessment and intervention efforts. As social workers, we must recognize that resilience is rarely an innate characteristic. Rather, it is a process (Egeland, Carlson, & Sroufe, 1993; Fraser, 2004) that may be facilitated by influences within the child's surrounding environment. Indeed, research suggests that high-risk behavior among children increases when they perceive declining family involvement and community support (Benson, 1990; Blyth & Roehlkepartian, 1993). A primary goal of the professions dedicated to child well-being must be facilitation of positive external supports for children and enhancement of the person/environment fit so as to maximize protective factors and minimize risk factors. Exhibit 5.9 summarizes major risk and protective factors identified as most relevant to childhood.

Risk	Protective
Child/Individual	**Child/Individual**
Prematurity, birth anomalies	Good health
Exposure to toxins in utero	
Chronic or serious illness	
Temperament: for example, difficult or slow to warm up	Personality factors: easy temperament; positive disposition; active coping style; positive self-esteem, good social skills; internal locus of control; balance between help seeking and autonomy
Mental retardation, cognitive delays, low intelligence	Above-average intelligence
Childhood trauma	History of adequate development
Antisocial peer group	Hobbies and interests
Gender	Good peer relationships
Parental/Family	**Parental/Family**
Insecure attachment	Secure attachment; positive and warm parent-child relationship
Parent: insecure adult attachment pattern	Parent: secure adult attachment pattern
Single parenthood (with lack of support)	Parent(s) supports child in times of stress
Harsh parenting, maltreatment	Effective/positive (authoritative) parenting
Family disorganization; low parental monitoring	Household rules and structure, parental monitoring of child
Social isolation, lack of support, domestic violence	Support/involvement of extended family, including help with caregiving
High parental/interparental conflict	Positive, stable relationship between parents

Risk	Protective
Separation/divorce, especially high-conflict divorce	
Parental psychopathology	Stable parental mental health; Parent(s) model competence and good coping skills
Parental substance abuse	High parental expectations; Family models and aspects of prosocial behavior
Parental illness Death of a parent or sibling Foster care placement	Family residential stability; Stable parental physical health
Social/Environmental Risk Factors	**Social/Environmental Risk Factors**
Poverty/collective poverty	Middle-class or above socioeconomic status
Lack of access to adequate medical care, health insurance, and social services	Access to adequate health care and social services
Parental/community unemployment	Consistent parental/community employment
Inadequate child care	Adequate child care
Inadequate housing	Adequate housing
Exposure to racism, discrimination, injustice	Family religious faith/participation
Low-quality schools	High-quality schools
Frequent change of residence and schools/ transient community	Presence of caring adult(s); Supportive adults outside family who serve as role models/mentors to child
Exposure to environmental toxins	Healthy physical environment
Exposure to dangerous neighborhood(s), community violence, media violence	Collective efficacy Competence in normative roles
Few opportunities for education or employment	Many opportunities for education and employment

▲ **Exhibit 5.9**　Potential Childhood Risk and Protective Factors

SOURCES: Based on Davies, 2004, pp. 106–108; Fraser et al., 2004, pp. 36–49.

Critical Thinking Questions 5.3

There is general agreement that poverty and child maltreatment are among the most serious threats to healthy child development. How does poverty threaten physical, cognitive, emotional, social, and spiritual development during middle childhood? How does child maltreatment threaten physical, cognitive, emotional, social, and spiritual development during middle childhood?

IMPLICATIONS FOR SOCIAL WORK PRACTICE

This discussion of middle childhood suggests several practice principles for social workers and other professionals working with children:

- Development is multidimensional and dynamic; recognize the complex ways in which developmental influences interact, and incorporate this understanding into your work with children.

- Support parents and other family members as critically important social, emotional, and spiritual resources for their children.

- Support family, school, and community attempts to stabilize environments for children.

- Incorporate identification of multilevel risk and protective factors into assessment and intervention efforts.

- Recognize and support resilience in children and families. Support the strengths of children and families and their efforts to cope with adversity.

- Recognize the critical influence of the school environment on growth and development, and encourage attempts by school personnel to be responsive to all children and families.

- Understand the important role of peer groups in social and emotional growth and development; facilitate the development and maintenance of positive peer and other social relationships.

- Understand the ways in which the organization of schools reflects and supports the inequalities present in society. Support schools in their efforts to end practices and policies, intended or unintended, that sustain or reinforce inequalities based on differences such as race, ethnicity, gender, disability, and socioeconomic status.

- Facilitate meaningful teacher-family-child communication and school responsiveness to children experiencing difficulties in the school environment.

- Understand the effects of family, community, and societal violence on children, and establish prosocial, nurturing, nonviolent environments whenever possible; provide opportunities for positive nurturing and mentoring of children in the school and community environments.

- Become familiar with and implement best practices in areas such as trauma, loss and grief, social skill development, and character education.

- Promote cultural competency, and help children and other adults recognize and respect all forms of diversity and difference.

KEY TERMS

acculturation	emotional intelligence	precociousness
assimilation (culture)	indirect bullying	relative poverty
capital	individual education plan (IEP)	secondary sexual development
cerebral cortex	institutional discrimination	social competence
character education	interrelational intelligence	trauma
deculturalizing	multiple intelligences	zone of proximal development
direct bullying	oppression	

ACTIVE LEARNING

1. In small groups, compare and contrast the risk and protective factors present for Anthony Bryant, Brianna Shaw, and Manuel Vega. Brainstorm multilevel interventions you would consider if you were working with each child.

2. Assign pairs of students to the story of Anthony Bryant, Brianna Shaw, or Manuel Vega. Each pair should identify the relevance of the various developmental theorists, discussed in the chapter, to the assigned child, focusing on the theorist(s) whose idea(s) seem particularly relevant to the selected child. After approximately 20 minutes, form three small groups consisting of the pairs focusing on the same child. After comparing the similarities and differences in their assessments of the different theories, each group should report back to the full class.

3. Create a list of debate topics raised directly or indirectly in the chapter (e.g., school tracking, expansion of bilingual school curricula, educational assessment/standardized testing, federal spending or programs to address child poverty, gun control to reduce violence against children, family structure and family disruption, inclusion for children with special needs). Debates can take place between teams or individuals. Topics and "pro" or "con" designation can be assigned or chosen depending on the instructor's desired learning outcomes for the debate. Suggested times are two minutes to present a case for each side. Each team will also have one minute for rebuttal.

4. Use task rotation for important chapter issues such as *family and community violence:* (1) How does child maltreatment or trauma impact childhood development? (2) How are child witnesses impacted by acts of violence? (3) What programs might schools employ to support students impacted by violence? (4) What interventions might a social worker pursue to help families impacted by violence? *Task rotation description:* Questions are posted on chart paper around the room. Each group starts at a question, discusses it, writes ideas in response on the chart paper, and then after a short time (fewer than 3 minutes) is stopped and rotated to the next chart. At the next chart, they are given a brief period of time to review the work of the previous group and add any ideas the first group missed. The groups are stopped and rotated until all groups read and add to all issues listed on the charts. Whole group review follows.

WEB RESOURCES

American Association of University Women
www.aauw.org

Site maintained by the American Association of University Women contains information on education and equity for women and girls, including a report card on Title IX, a law that banned sex discrimination in education.

Child Trauma Academy
www.childtraumaacademy.com

Site presented by the Child Trauma Academy contains information on the impact of child maltreatment on the brain and the physiological and psychological effects of trauma on children.

Child Welfare Information Gateway
www.childwelfare.gov

Site presented by the Administration for Children and Families contains information and resources to protect children and strengthen families, including statistics, prevention information, state statutes, family-centered practice, and publications.

Forum on Child and Family Statistics
www.childstats.gov

Official website of the Federal Interagency Forum on Child and Family Statistics offers easy access to federal and state statistics and reports on children and families, including international comparisons.

Search Institute
www.search-institute.org

Site presented by Search Institute, an independent, non-profit, nonsectarian organization with the goal of advancing the well-being of adolescents and children, contains information on 40 developmental assets and methods for building assets for child and youth development.

CHAPTER

6

Adolescence

Susan Ainsley McCarter

OPENING QUESTIONS

- How do biological, psychological, social, and spiritual dimensions affect the adolescent phase of the life course?
- Why do social workers need to understand theories of identity formation when working with adolescents?
- What unique challenges do adolescents face when confronted with issues of sexuality, violence, and substance use and abuse?

KEY IDEAS

As you read this chapter, take note of these central ideas:

1. Adolescence is characterized by significant physical change, increased hormone production, sexual maturation, improved cognitive functioning, formative identity development, and increased independence.

2. During adolescence, increased hormone production results in a period called puberty, during which persons become capable of reproduction. Other visible physical changes during this period include skeletal, musculature, and fat distribution changes as well as development of primary and secondary sex characteristics.

3. Unseen growth and pruning occurs in the adolescent brain.

4. Psychological changes during this period include reactions to physical, social, and cultural changes confronting the adolescent as well as cognitive development, in which most individuals develop the abilities to contemplate the future, to comprehend the nature of human relationships, to consolidate specific knowledge into a coherent system, and to envision possible consequences from a hypothetical list of actions.

5. The greatest task of adolescence is identity formation—determining who one is and where one is going.

6. Adolescents in the United States spend nearly a third of their waking hours at school, where they should receive skills and knowledge for their next step in life, but a school that follows a Eurocentric educational model without regard for other cultures may damage the self-esteem of students from minority ethnic groups.

7. Among the physical and mental health risks to today's adolescents are violence; substance abuse; juvenile delinquency; poverty; low educational attainment; poor nutrition, obesity, and eating disorders; and depression and suicide.

Case Study 6.1

David's Coming-Out Process

The social worker at Jefferson High School sees many facets of adolescent life. Nothing much surprises her—especially not the way some of the kids hem and haw when they're trying to share what's really on their mind. Take David Costa, for instance. When he shows up for his first appointment, he is simply asked to tell a bit about himself.

- "Let's see, I'm 17," he begins. "I'm a centerfielder on the varsity baseball team. What else do you want to know? My parents are from Bolivia and are as traditional as you can imagine. My dad, David Sr., teaches history and is the varsity soccer coach here at Jefferson. My mom is a geriatric nurse. I have a younger sister, Patti. Patti Perfect. She goes to the magnet school and is in the ninth grade."
- "How are things at home?" his social worker asks.
- "Whatever. Patti is perfect, and I'm a 'freak.' They think I'm 'different, arrogant, stubborn.' I don't know what they want me to be. But I don't think that's what I am. That may be because . . . because I'm gay. I haven't come out to my parents. That's all I need!"

This is obviously a difficult confession for David to make to an adult, but with a little encouragement he continues: "There are a few other athletes who are gay, and then we have some friends outside of sports. Thank God! But basically when the whole team is together or when I'm with other friends, I just act straight. I talk about girls' bodies just like the other guys. I think that is the hardest. Not being able to be yourself. I'm at least glad that I've met other gay guys. It was really hard when I was about 13. I was so confused. I knew that men were supposed to be with women, not other men. What I was feeling was not 'normal,' and I thought I was the only one. I wanted to kill myself. That was a bad time."

David's tone changes. "Let's talk about something good. Let me tell you about Theo. I find Theo very attractive. I hope he likes my athletic build. I wonder if he would like to hang out together—get to know one another. He's a junior, and if we got together, the other guys I know would razz me about seeing a younger guy. But I keep thinking about him. And looking at him during school. I just need to say something to him. Some guys from the team are going out Thursday night after practice. He hasn't been invited in the past. Maybe if I invite him, he'll come."

Case Study 6.2

Carl's Struggle for Identity

Whereas David seeks out the social worker, Carl Fleischer, another 17-year-old, is sent to the social work office at the high school. He matter-of-factly shares that he is "an underachiever." He used to get an occasional B in his classes, but now it's mostly Cs with an occasional D.

When Carl is asked what he likes to do in his spare time, he replies, "I get high and surf the Net." Further probing elicits one-word answers until the social worker asks Carl about girlfriends. His face contorts as he slaps his ample belly: "I'm not exactly a sex symbol. According to my doctor, I'm a fatso. He says normal boys my age and height weigh at least 50 pounds less than I do. He also tells me to quit smoking and get some exercise. Whatever. My mom says I'm big-boned. She says my dad was the same way. I wouldn't know. I never met the scumbag. He left when my mom was pregnant. But you probably don't want to hear about that."

Carl won't say more on that topic, but with more prodding, he finally talks about his job, delivering pizzas two nights a week and on the weekends. "So if you need pizzas, call me at Antonio's. I always bring pies home for my mom on Tuesday and Friday nights. She works late those nights, and so we usually eat pizza and catch the Tuesday and Friday night lineups on TV. She lets me smoke in the house—cigarettes, not weed. Although I have gotten high in the house a couple times. Anyway, I am not what you would call popular. I am just a fat, slow geek and a pizza guy. But there are some heads who come into Antonio's. I exchange pies for dope. Works out pretty well: they get the munchies, and the pies keep me in with the heads."

Case Study 6.3

Monica's Quest for Mastery

Monica Golden, one of the peer counselors at Jefferson High, hangs around to chat after a meeting of the peer counselors. Monica is the eldest and tallest daughter in a family of five kids. Monica's mother is the assistant principal at Grover Middle School and her father works for the Internal Revenue Service. This year Monica is the vice president of the senior class, the treasurer for the Young Republicans, a starter on the track team, a teacher at Sunday school, and a Jefferson peer counselor.

When the social worker comments on the scope of these activities, Monica replies: "I really do stay busy. I worked at the mall last year, but it was hard to keep my grades up. I'm trying to get into college, so my family and I decided I shouldn't work this year. So I just babysit sometimes. A lot of my aunts and uncles have me watch their kids, but they don't pay me. They consider it a family favor. Anyway, I am waiting to hear back from colleges. They should be sending out the letters this week. You know, the fatter the envelope the better. It doesn't take many words to say, 'No. We reject you.' And I need to either get into a state school or get a scholarship so that I can use my savings for tuition."

Next they talk a little about Monica's options, and she shares that her first choice is Howard University. "I want to surround myself with Black scholars and role models and my dream is to be a pediatrician, you know. I love kids," Monica says. "I tried tons of jobs—that's where I got the savings. And, well, those with kids I enjoyed the most. Like I said, I've worked retail at the mall. I've worked at the supermarket as a cashier. I've worked at the snack bar at the pool. And I've been babysitting since I was 12. That's what I like the most."

"I'd love to have kids someday. But I don't even have a boyfriend. I wear glasses. My parents say I don't need contacts; they think I'm being vain. Not that I don't have a boyfriend because I wear glasses. Guys think I'm an overachiever. They think I'm driven and demanding and incapable of having fun. That's what I've been told. I think I'm just ambitious and extroverted. But really, I just haven't had much time to date in high school. I've been so busy. Well, gotta run."

THE SOCIAL CONSTRUCTION OF ADOLESCENCE ACROSS TIME AND SPACE

If we were asked to describe David Costa, Carl Fleischer, and Monica Golden, attention would probably be drawn to their status as adolescents. The importance of that status has changed across time and cultures, however. Adolescence was invented as a psychosocial concept in the late 19th and early 20th centuries as the United States made the transition from an agrarian to an urban-industrial society (Fass & Mason, 2000). Prior to this time, adolescents worked beside adults, doing what adults did for the most part (Leeder, 2004). This is still the case for adolescents in many nonindustrial societies today. As the United States and other societies became urbanized and industrialized, child labor legislation and compulsory education policies were passed, and adolescents were moved from the workplace to the school and became economically dependent on parents. The juvenile justice system was developed because juvenile offenders were seen as different from adult offenders, with less culpability for their crime because of their immaturity.

In 1904, G. Stanley Hall, an American psychologist, published *Adolescence: Its Psychology and Its Relations to Physiology, Anthropology, Sociology, Sex, Crime, Religion, and Education.* Hall proposed that adolescence is a period of "storm and stress," a period when hormones cause many psychological and social difficulties. Hall was later involved in the eugenics movement, and there is some hint of racist and classist bias in his work on adolescence, which was not

How have our views on
adolescence changed
over time?

unusual in his time. His discussion seemed to indicate that poor youth are at risk of trouble because of their heredity while middle-class youth are at risk of being corrupted by the world around them (Finn, 2009). Janet Finn (2009) argues that the public, professional, and scholarly conversations about adolescence in the 20th and beginning of the 21st century have focused on adolescents as trouble. Jane Kroger (2007) suggests that many societies are clear about what they want their adolescents to avoid (alcohol and other drugs, delinquency, and pregnancy), but not as clear about what positive things they would like their youth to achieve. There is growing agreement that the societal context in which adolescence is lived out in the United States and other wealthy nations is becoming increasingly less supportive for adolescent development (Fass & Mason, 2000). This concern has led, in recent years, to the construction of a positive youth development movement, which has focused on youth "as resources to be developed, and not as problems to be managed" (Silbereisen & Lerner, 2007a, p. 7).

Sociologists caution against thinking of a monolithic adolescence. They suggest that, unfortunately, many adults dichotomize children and adolescents as "our own" children and "other people's" children (Graff, 1995). Our own children are expected to have "an innocent and secure childhood and dependent, prolonged adolescence" (Graff, 1995, p. 332). Other people's children are expected to be resilient in their childhood and accountable for their own behavior at increasingly younger ages, as we see in the declining ages for being treated as an adult in the criminal justice system. Sociologists conclude that there are multiple adolescences, with gender, race, and class as major influences on the ways they are constructed and their realities.

Perhaps no life course phase has been the subject of more recent empirical research than adolescence. Most prominently, The National Longitudinal Study of Adolescent Health (Add Health) was initiated at the Carolina Population Center in 1994. It is a study of a representative sample of adolescents in grades 7–12 during the 1994–1995 school year. This cohort has been followed into young adulthood in 2008, when the sample was between 24 and 32 years of age. The Add Health study includes measures of social, economic, psychological, and physical well-being as well as contextual information on the family, neighborhood, community, school, friendships, peer groups, and romantic relationships. Add Health data are now generating large numbers of research reports. A partial listing of those reports can be found at http://www.cpc.unc.edu/projects/addhealth/pubs/published.

THE TRANSITION FROM CHILDHOOD TO ADULTHOOD

In industrialized countries, adolescence is described as the transitional period between childhood and adulthood. It is more than that, of course. It is a very rich period of the life course in its own right. For many, it is a thrilling time of life full of new experiences. The word *adolescence* originates from the Latin verb *adolescere,* which means "to grow into maturity." It is a period of life filled with transitional themes in every dimension of the configuration of person and environment: biological, psychological, social, and spiritual. These themes do not occur independently or without affecting one another. For example, David Costa's experience may be complicated because he is gay and because his family relationships are strained, but it is also strengthened by his supportive friendships and his participation in sports. Carl Fleischer's transition is marked by several challenges—his weight, his substance use, his lack of a relationship with his father, his academic performance—but also by the promise of his developing computer expertise and entrepreneurial skills. Monica Golden's movement through adolescence may be eased by her academic, athletic, and social success, but it also could be taxed by her busy schedule and high expectations for herself.

Many cultures have specific **rites of passage**—ceremonies that demarcate the transition from childhood to adulthood. Often these rites include sexual themes, marriage themes, themes of becoming a man or a woman, themes of added responsibility, or themes of increased insight or understanding. Such rites of passage are found in most nonindustrialized societies (Gardiner & Kosmitzki, 2008). For example, among the Massai ethnic group in Kenya and

▲ **Photo 6.1**   Adolescence is a period of life filled with transitional themes in every dimension of life: biological, psychological, social, and spiritual.

Tanzania, males and females are both circumcised at about age 13, and males are considered junior warriors and sent to live with other junior warriors (Leeder, 2004). For the most part, the transition from adolescence to adulthood is not marked by such clearly defined rituals in North America and many other Western countries (Gardiner & Kosmitzki). Some scholars who study adolescence have suggested that where there are no clear-cut puberty rituals, adolescents will devise their own rituals, such as "hazing, tattooing, dieting, dress, and beautification rituals" (Kroger, 2007, p. 41).

Some groups in North America continue to practice rites of passage, however. In the United States, some Jews celebrate the bar mitzvah for boys and bat mitzvah for girls at the age of 13 to observe their transition to adulthood and to mark their assumption of religious responsibility. Many Latino families, especially of Mexican heritage, celebrate *quincea era,* during which families attend Mass with their 15-year-old daughter, who is dressed in white and then presented to the community as a young woman. Traditionally, she is accompanied by a set of Padrinos, or godparents, who agree to support her parents in guiding her during this time. The ceremony is followed by a reception at which her father dances with her and presents her to the family's community of friends (Garcia, 2001; Zuniga, 1992). Among many First Nations/Native American tribes in North America, boys participate in a Vision Quest at age 14 or 15. The boy is taken into a "sweat lodge," where his body and spirit are purified by the heat. He is assisted by a medicine man who advises him and assists with ritual prayers. Later he is taken to another place where he is left alone to fast for 4 days. Similarly, some First Nations/Native American girls take part in a ritual of morning running and baking a ceremonial cake (see Gardiner & Kosmitzki, 2008).

Mainstream culture in the United States, however, has few such rites. Many young adolescents go through confirmation ceremonies in Protestant and Catholic churches. Otherwise, the closest thing to a rite of passage may be getting a driver's license, graduating from high school, registering to vote, graduating from college, or getting married. But these events all occur at different times and thus do not provide a discrete point of transition. Moreover, not all youth participate in these rites of passage.

Even without a cultural rite of passage, all adolescents experience profound biological, psychological, psychosocial, social, and spiritual changes. In advanced industrial societies, these changes have been divided into three phases: early adolescence (ages 11 to 14), middle adolescence (ages 15 to 17), and late adolescence (ages 18 to 20). Exhibit 6.1 summarizes the typical biological, psychological, and social developments in these three phases. Of course, adolescent development varies from person to person and with time, culture, and other aspects of the environment. Yet, deviations from the normative patterns of adolescent change may have psychological ramifications, because adolescents are so quick to compare their own development with that of their peers, and because of the cultural messages they receive about acceptable appearance and behavior.

BIOLOGICAL ASPECTS OF ADOLESCENCE

Adolescence is a period of great physical change, marked by a rapid growth spurt in the early years, maturation of the reproductive system, redistribution of body weight, and continuing brain development. Adequate care of the body during this exciting time is of paramount importance.

Puberty

Puberty is the period of the life course in which the reproductive system matures. It is a process that begins before any biological changes are visible and occurs through interrelated neurological and endocrinological changes that affect brain development, sexual maturation, levels and cycles of hormones, and physical growth. The hypothalamus, pituitary gland, adrenal glands, and **gonads** (ovaries and testes) begin to interact and stimulate increased hormone production. It is the increase of these hormones that leads to the biological changes. Although androgens are typically referred to as male hormones and estrogens as female hormones, males and females in fact produce all three major **sex hormones:** androgens, progestins, and estrogens. Sex hormones affect the development and functioning of the gonads (including sperm production and ova maturation), and mating and child-caring behavior.

> What is the impact of biological age on psychological age, social age, and spiritual age during adolescence?

During puberty, increased levels of androgens in males stimulate the development and functioning of the male reproductive system; increased levels of progestins and estrogens in females stimulate the development and functioning of the female reproductive system. Specifically, the androgen testosterone, which is produced in males by the testes, affects the maturation and functioning of the penis, prostate gland, and other male genitals; the secondary sex characteristics; and the sex drive. The estrogen estradiol, which is produced in females by the ovaries, affects the maturation and functioning of the ovaries, uterus, and other female genitals; the secondary sex characteristics; and child-caring behaviors.

Primary sex characteristics are those directly related to the reproductive organs and external genitalia. For boys, these include growth of the penis and scrotum. During adolescence, the penis typically doubles or triples in length. Girls' primary sex characteristics are not so visible but include growth of the ovaries, uterus, vagina, clitoris, and labia.

Secondary sex characteristics are those not directly related to the reproductive organs and external genitalia. Secondary sex characteristics are enlarged breasts and hips for girls, facial hair and deeper voices for boys, and hair and sweat gland changes for both sexes. Female breast development is distinguished by growth of the mammary glands, nipples, and areola. The tone of the male voice lowers as the larynx enlarges and the vocal cords lengthen. Both boys and girls begin to grow hair around their genitals and then under their arms. This hair begins with a finer texture and lighter color and then becomes curlier, coarser, and darker. During this period, the sweat glands also begin to produce noticeable odors.

Stage of Adolescence	Biological Changes	Psychological Changes	Social Changes
Early (11–14)	Hormonal changes Beginning of puberty Physical appearance changes Possible experimentation with sex and substances	Reactions to physical changes, including early maturation Concrete/present-oriented thought Body modesty Moodiness	Changes in relationships with parents and peers Less school structure Distancing from culture/tradition Seeking sameness
Middle (15–17)	Completion of puberty and physical appearance changes Possible experimentation with sex and substances	Reactions to physical changes, including late maturation Increased autonomy Increased abstract thought Beginning of identity development Preparation for college or career	Heightened social situation decision making Continue to renegotiate family relationships More focus on peer group Beginning of one-to-one romantic relationships Moving toward greater community participation
Late (18–22)	Slowing of physical changes Possible experimentation with sex and substances	Formal operational thought Continuation of identity development Moral reasoning	Very little school/life structure Beginning of intimate relationships Renewed interest in culture/tradition

▲ **Exhibit 6.1**   Typical Adolescent Development

Puberty is often described as beginning with the onset of menstruation in girls and production of sperm in boys, but these are not the first events in the puberty process. Menstruation is the periodic sloughing off of the lining of the uterus. This lining provides nutrients for the fertilized egg. If the egg is not fertilized, the lining sloughs off and is discharged through the vagina. However, for a female to become capable of reproduction, she must not only menstruate but also ovulate. Ovulation, the release of an egg from an ovary, usually does not begin until several months after **menarche,** the onset of menstruation. For males to reproduce, **spermarche**—the onset of the ability to ejaculate mobile sperm—must occur. Spermarche does not occur until after several ejaculations.

Females typically first notice breast growth, then growth of pubic hair, then body growth, especially hips; they then experience menarche, then growth of underarm hair, and finally an increase in production of glandular oil and sweat, possibly with body odor and acne. Males typically follow a similar pattern, first noticing growth of the testes, then growth of pubic hair, body growth, growth of penis, change in voice, growth of facial and underarm hair, and finally an increase in the production of glandular oil and sweat, possibly with body odor and acne. Girls experience the growth spurt before they have the capacity for reproduction but the opposite is the case for boys (Kroger, 2007).

Pubertal timing varies greatly. Generally, females begin puberty about two years earlier than males. Normal pubertal rates (meaning they are experienced by 95% of the population) are for girls to begin menstruating between the ages of 9 and 17 and for boys to produce sperm between the ages of 11 and 16 (Rew, 2005). The age at which puberty begins has been declining in this century, but there is some controversy about the extent of this shift (Newman & Newman, 2009).

In addition to changes instigated by sex hormones, adolescents experience growth spurts. Bones are augmented by cartilage during adolescence, and the cartilage calcifies later, during the transition to adulthood. Typically, boys develop broader shoulders, straighter hips, and longer forearms and legs; girls typically develop narrower shoulders and broader hips. These skeletal differences are then enhanced by the development of additional upper body musculature for boys and the development of additional fat deposits on thighs, hips, and buttocks for girls. These changes account for differences in male and female weight and strength.

The Adolescent Brain

Recent magnetic resonance imaging (MRI) studies are revealing new findings regarding adolescent brain development (Giedd, 2008; Gogtay et al., 2004; Johnson, Blum, & Giedd, 2009). Contrary to earlier belief, adolescence is a time of continued brain growth and change. As discussed in earlier chapters, researchers have known for some time that the early brain overproduces gray matter from development in the womb to about 3 years old, is highly plastic and thus shaped by experience, and goes through a pruning process. The neural connections or synapses that get exercised are retained, whereas the ones that are not exercised are eliminated. New brain research suggests that the adolescent brain undergoes another period of overproduction of gray matter just prior to puberty, peaking at about 11 years of age for girls and 12 years for boys, followed by another round of pruning. This process, like the infant's, is also affected by the individual's interactions with the outside world (Johnson et al.; Sowell, Trauner, Gamst, & Jernigan, 2002).

Currently, much interest surrounds recent findings about frontal lobe development during adolescence. The pruning process described above allows the brain to be more efficient to change in response to environmental demands and also facilitates improved integration of brain activities. Recent research indicates that pruning occurs in some parts of the brain earlier than in others, in general progressing from the back to the front part of brain, with the frontal lobes among the latest to show the structural changes. The frontal lobes, are key players in the "executive functions" of planning, working memory, and impulse control, and the latest research indicates that they may not be fully developed until about age 25 (Johnson et al., 2009). Because of the relatively late development of the frontal lobes, particularly the prefrontal cortex, different neuronal circuits are involved in the adolescent brain under different emotional conditions. The researchers make a distinction between "cold cognition" problem solving and "hot cognition" problem solving during adolescence. "Cold cognition" problem solving occurs when the adolescent is alone and calm, as they typically are in the laboratory. Conversely, "hot cognition" problem solving occurs in situations when teens are with peers, emotions are running high, they are feeling sexual tension, and so on. The research indicates that in situations of "cold cognition," teens even as young as 12 or 13 can reason and problem-solve as well as adults. But, in situations of "hot cognition," adolescent problem solving is more impulsive (Johnson et al.).

Similar to all social mammals, human adolescents tend to demonstrate three behavior changes: increased novelty seeking, increased risk taking, and greater affiliation with peers (Giedd, 2009). Brain research does not yet allow researchers to make definitive statements about the relationship between these adolescent behavior changes and changes in the brain, but these connections are being studied.

The emerging research on the adolescent brain is raising issues about social policy related to adolescents and is being used in ways that may be both helpful and hurtful to adolescent development. This is illustrated by two recent examples. In 2005, the U.S. Supreme Court heard the case of *Roper v. Simmons* (543 U.S. 551, 2005), involving 17-year-old Christopher Simmons who had been convicted of murdering a woman during a robbery. He had been sentenced to death for his crime. His defense team argued that his still developing adolescent brain made him less culpable for his crime than an adult and therefore he should not be subject to the death penalty. It is thought that the neuroscience evidence carried weight in the Court's decision to overturn the death penalty for juveniles (Haider, 2006). In another example, the state of Kansas used some interpretation of neuroscience research to label any consensual touching by youth under the age of 16 years as child abuse (Johnson et al., 2009).

The question that is being raised is what is the extent of human agency, the capacity for decision making, among adolescents? The answer to that question will vary from adolescent to adolescent. There is great risk that neuroscience research will be overgeneralized to the detriment of adolescents. Johnson et al. (2009) caution that it is important to put the adolescent brain in context, remembering that there are complex interactions of the brain with other biological systems as well as with "multiple interactive influences including experience, parenting, socioeconomic status, individual agency and self-efficacy, nutrition, culture, psychological well-being, the physical and built environments, and social relationships and interactions" (p. 219). Johnson and colleagues also recommend that we should avoid focusing on pathology and deficits in adolescent development and use neuroscience to examine the unique strengths and potentials of the adolescent brain. That is in keeping with the increasing focus on positive psychology and the related positive youth development movement.

> How do changes in the brain during adolescence affect the capacity to exercise human agency in making choices?

Researchers at Duke University have created an interdisciplinary team whose mission is to educate society, especially young people, about the brain—how to use it effectively and how to keep it healthy (a link to DukeLearn appears with the Web Resources at the end of this chapter). Knowing more about the neurodevelopment of their own bodies may change the behaviors of some adolescents.

Nutrition, Exercise, and Sleep

At any stage along the life course, the right balance of nutrition, exercise, and sleep is important. As the transition from childhood to adulthood begins, early adolescent bodies undergo significant biological changes from their brains to the hair follicles on their legs and everywhere in between. Yet it appears that few adolescents maintain a healthy balance during their time in adolescent flux.

The U.S. Department of Health and Human Services and the Department of Agriculture have begun several campaigns aimed at adolescent nutrition. They outline some of their recommendations in the Dietary Guidelines for Americans 2005 (U.S. Department of Health and Human Services/U.S. Department of Agriculture, 2005). For adolescents, they recommend consuming 2 cups of fruit and 2.5 cups of vegetables a day (for a 2,000 calorie intake); choosing a variety of fruits and vegetables each day selecting from all five vegetable subgroups—dark green, orange, legumes, starchy vegetables, and other vegetables—several times a week; consuming 3 or more ounce equivalents of whole-grain products per day; consuming 3 cups per day of fat-free or low-fat milk or equivalent milk products; limiting fat intake to between 25% to 35% of calories, with most fats coming from sources of polyunsaturated and monounsaturated fatty acids, such as fish, nuts, and vegetable oils; and consuming fewer than 2,300 mg (approximately one teaspoon of salt) of sodium per day.

Yet, the National Youth Risk Behavior Survey for 2007 (Centers for Disease Control and Prevention [CDC], 2008d) suggests that nationwide only 21.4% of young people in grades 9 to 12 had eaten at least five fruits and vegetables a day in the past 7 days. This is unfortunate, given the need for well-balanced diets and increased caloric intake during a period of rapid growth. Many U.S. youth say they don't have time to eat breakfast or that they aren't hungry in the morning. Yet the research is rather convincing, indicating that students who eat breakfast obtain higher test scores and are less likely to be tardy or absent from school (Lonzano & Ballesteros, 2006).

In terms of activity, the recommendation is for most people of every age to engage in regular physical activity and reduce sedentary activities to promote health, psychological well-being, and a healthy body weight. Physical fitness should be achieved by including cardiovascular conditioning, stretching exercises for flexibility, and resistance exercises or calisthenics for muscle strength and endurance. And the specific recommendation for adolescents is to engage in at least 60 minutes of physical activity on most, preferably all, days of the week (U.S. Department of Health and Human Services/U.S. Department of Agriculture, 2005).

Again, the data are not promising. Nationwide, 34.7% of high school students reported being physically active for a total of at least 60 minutes a day on at least 5 of the 7 days preceding the survey. Conversely, 24.9% of students played video or computer games or used the computer in some way for 3 hours or more on an average school day, and 35.4% watched television for 3 hours or more on an average school day (CDC, 2008d).

Along with other changes of puberty, there are marked changes in sleep patterns (Giedd, 2009; National Sleep Foundation, 2006). Changes in circadian rhythms create a tendency to be more alert late at night and to wake later in the morning. Given the mismatch of these sleep patterns with the timing of the school day, adolescents are often asleep during the school day. Sleep researchers suggest that adolescents require 8.5 to 9.25 hours of sleep each night (National Sleep Foundation).

Researchers assert that adolescents in the United States are the most sleep-deprived segment of a very sleep-deprived society (National Institutes of Health, 2001). Survey data show that only 20% of U.S. adolescents get at least nine hours of sleep on school nights. U.S. sixth-graders get an average of 8.4 hours of sleep on school nights, and U.S. high school seniors get an average of only 6.9 hours on school nights, which gives them 12 hours of sleep deficit over the course of a week (National Sleep Foundation, 2006). School performance is affected by insufficient sleep. More than a quarter of high school students fall asleep at school at least once a week, and students who get sufficient sleep have higher grades on average than students with sleep deficit. Mood is also affected by insufficient sleep; teens who get 9 or more hours of sleep per night report more positive moods than students who get insufficient sleep (National Sleep Foundation, 2006). Indeed, sleep deprivation is associated with depression in adolescents (Holm et al., 2009).

As suggested above, the risks of sleep deprivation are varied, and they can be serious. Drowsiness or fatigue is a principle cause of at least 100,000 police-reported traffic collisions annually, killing more than 1,500 Americans and injuring 71,000 more. Drivers 25 and younger cause more than half of the crashes attributed to drowsiness (National Sleep Foundation, 2005). Sleep deficit contributes to acne, aggressive behavior, eating too much or unhealthy foods, and to illness. It also heightens the effects of alcohol and can lead to increased use of caffeine and nicotine. Sleep-deprived youth may also present with symptoms that are similar to attention deficit hyperactivity disorder and thus run the risk of misdiagnosis (Marks & Rothbart, 2003).

PSYCHOLOGICAL ASPECTS OF ADOLESCENCE

Psychological development in adolescence is multifaceted. Adolescents have psychological reactions, sometimes dramatic, to the biological, social, and cultural dimensions of their lives. They become capable of and interested in discovering and forming their psychological selves. They may show heightened creativity as well as interest in humanitarian issues, ethics, religion, and reflection and record keeping, as in a diary (Rew, 2005). Evidence exists that adolescence is a time of increased emotional complexity and a growing capacity to understand and express a wider range of emotions and to gain insight into one's own emotions (Weissberg & O'Brien, 2004). Three areas of psychological development are particularly noteworthy: reactions to biological changes, changes in cognition, and identity development.

Psychological Reactions to Biological Changes

"Will my body ever start changing? Will my body ever stop changing? Is this normal? Am I normal? Why am I suddenly interested in girls? And why are the girls all taller (and stronger) than me? How can I ask mom if I can shave my legs?" These are some of the questions mentioned when Jane Kroger (2007, pp. 33–34) asked a class of 12- and 13-year-old adolescents what type of questions they think most about. As you can see, themes of biological changes were pervasive. If you can remember your own puberty process, you probably are not surprised that researchers have found that pubertal adolescents are preoccupied with physical changes and appearances (McCabe & Riccardelli, 2003). Young adolescents are able to reflect upon and give meaning to their biological transformations. Of course, responses to puberty are influenced by the way other people, including parents, siblings, teachers, and peers, respond to the adolescent's changing body. In addition, reactions to puberty are influenced by other events in the adolescent's life, such as school transition, family conflict, and peer relationships.

It appears that puberty is usually viewed more positively by males than by females, with boys focused on increased muscle mass and physical strength and girls focused on increased body weight and fat deposits (Phillips, 2003). Pubescent boys tend to report an improved body image, whereas pubescent girls are more prone to depression (Benjet & Hernandez-Guzman, 2002). These reactions are rooted in European culture that values muscular males and petite shapely females. For girls, body dissatisfaction and self-consciousness peaks between the ages of 13 and 15. There is evidence that African American adolescent girls are more satisfied with their body image and less inclined to eating disorders than Caucasian American girls, most likely related to a different cultural valuing of thinness in females (Franko & Streigel-Moore, 2002). Reactions to menstruation are often mixed. One study of Chinese American adolescent girls found that 85% reported that they were annoyed and embarrassed by their first menstruation, but 66% also reported positive feelings (Tang, Yeung, & Lee, 2003). Reactions to menarche are greatly affected by the type of information and level of support that young women receive from parents, teachers, peers, and health advisors (Brooks-Gunn & Paikoff, 1993). Research shows that pubescent females talk with parents and friends about their first menstruation, but pubescent males do not discuss their first ejaculation, an event sometimes seen as the closest male equivalent to first menstruation, with anyone (Kroger, 2007). Pubescent boys may receive less information from adults about nocturnal ejaculations than their sisters receive about menarche.

Because the onset and experience of puberty vary greatly, adolescents need reassurance regarding their own growth patterns. Some adolescents will be considered early maturers, and some will be considered late maturers. Timing and tempo of puberty are influenced by genetics, and there are ethnic differences. On average, African American adolescents enter puberty earlier than Mexican American adolescents, who enter puberty earlier than Caucasian Americans (Chumlea et al, 2003). There are psychological and social consequences of early and late maturing for both males and females, but the research findings are not always consistent. Early research indicated that the impact of pubertal timing varied by gender, but more recent research is indicating similar negative outcomes of early puberty for both males and females. Early puberty has been found to be associated with more involvement in high-risk behaviors, such as smoking, experimenting with drugs, early sex, and other unhealthy behaviors in both males and females (Biehl, Natsuaki, & Ge, 2007; Cota-Robles, Neiss, & Rowe, 2002; Ge, Conger, & Elder, 2001; Richter, 2006; Wichstrom, 2001). For females, but not males, early puberty has been linked with depression, not only at puberty but across the life course (Archibald, Graber, & Brooks-Gunn, 2003). Data from the Add Health research have produced similar findings for the connection between early puberty and alcohol use, with early maturing males and females engaging in more heavy drinking than later maturing youth and early puberty serving as a risk factor for alcohol-related problems across the life course (Biehl et al., 2007).

Changes in Cognition

During adolescence, most individuals develop cognitive abilities beyond those of childhood (Keating, 2004), including the following:

- Contemplation of the future
- Comprehension of the nature of human relationships

- Consolidation of specific knowledge into a coherent system
- Ability to envision possible consequences from a hypothetical list of actions (foresight)
- Abstract thought
- Empathy
- Internal control

Many of these abilities are components of Jean Piaget's fourth stage of cognitive development called formal operational thought (see Exhibit 3.5 for an overview of Piaget's stages of moral development). *Formal operational thought* suggests the capacity to apply hypothetical reasoning to various situations and the ability to use symbols to solve problems. David Costa, for example, demonstrated formal operational thought when he considered the possibility of getting to know Theo. He considered the reactions from his other friends if he were to get together with Theo; he examined his thoughts, and he formulated a strategy based on the possibilities and on his thoughts.

Whereas younger children focus on the here-and-now world in front of them, the adolescent brain is capable of retaining larger amounts of information. Thus, adolescents are capable of hypothesizing beyond the present objects. This ability also allows adolescents to engage in decision making based on a cost-benefit analysis. As noted above, brain research indicates that adolescent problem solving is as good as adult problem solving in "cold cognition" situations but is not equally sound in "hot cognition" situations. Furthermore, brain development alone does not result in formal operational thinking. The developing brain needs social environments that encourage hypothetical, abstract reasoning, and opportunities to investigate the world (Cohen & Sandy, 2007; Gehlbach, 2006). Formal operational thinking is more imperative in some cultures than in others but is most imperative in many fields in the changing economic base of postindustrialized societies. Although contemporary education is organized to facilitate formal operational thinking, students do not have equal access to sound curriculum and instruction.

Adolescent cognition, however, mirrors adolescence in the sense that it is multifaceted. In addition to the increased capacity for thought, adolescents also bring with them experience, culture, personality, intelligence, family values, identity, and so on. If we conceptualize adolescent cognitive development along a linear continuum from simple intuitive reasoning to advanced, computational, rational, and objective reasoning (Case, 1998; Moshman, 1998), we miss many other facets of individuals and the influences on their cognition. For example, research suggests that older adolescents may not be more objective than younger adolescents, perhaps because irrational cognitive tendencies and biases increase with age (Klaczynski, 2000; Klaczynski & Fauth, 1997). Older adolescents have more stereotypes, intuitions, memories, and self-evident truths that they may employ in processing information.

Identity Development

There is growing agreement that identity is a complex concept. From a psychological perspective, **psychological identity** is a "person's self-definition as a separate and distinct individual" (Gardiner & Kosmitzki, 2008, p. 154). From a sociological perspective, **social identity** is the part of the self-concept that comes from knowledge of one's membership in a social group and the emotional significance of that membership (Gardiner & Kosmitzki). Lene Arnett Jensen (2003) suggests that adolescents increasingly develop multicultural identities as they are exposed to diverse cultural beliefs, either through first-hand experience or through the media. She argues that the process of developing identity presents new challenges to adolescents in a global society. Jensen gives the example of arranged marriage in India, noting that on the one hand, Indian adolescents grow up with cultural values favoring arranged marriage, but at the same time, they are increasingly exposed to values that emphasize freedom of choice.

Theories of Self and Identity

Psychological identity is thought to have five common functions (Adams & Marshall, 1996, p. 433):

1. To provide a structure for understanding who one is

2. To provide meaning and direction through commitments, values, and goals

3. To provide a sense of personal control and free will

4. To enable one to strive for consistency, coherence, and harmony between values, beliefs, and commitments

5. To enable one to recognize one's potential through a sense of future possibilities and alternative choices

> How do factors such as gender, race, ethnicity, and social class affect identity development?

A number of prominent psychologists have put forward theories that address self or psychological identity development in adolescence. Exhibit 6.2 provides an overview of six theorists: Freud, Erikson, Kegan, Marcia, Piaget, and Kohlberg. All six help to explain how a concept of self or identity develops, and all six suggest that it cannot develop fully before adolescence. Piaget and Kohlberg suggest that some individuals may not reach these higher levels of identity development at all.

Sigmund Freud (1905/1953) thought of human development as a series of five psychosexual stages in the expression of libido (sensual pleasure). The fifth stage, the genital stage, occurs in adolescence, when reproduction and sexual intimacy become possible.

Theorist	Developmental Stage	Major Task or Processes
Freud	Genital stage	To develop libido capable of reproduction and sexual intimacy
Erikson	Identity versus role diffusion	To find one's place in the world through self-certainty versus apathy, role experimentation versus negative identity, and anticipation of achievement versus work paralysis
Kegan	Affiliation versus abandonment (Early Adolescence)	To search for membership, acceptance, and group identity, versus a sense of being left behind, rejected, and abandoned
Marcia	Ego identity statuses	To develop one of these identity statuses: identity diffusion, foreclosure, moratorium, or identity achievement
Piaget	Formal operational thought	To develop the capacity for abstract problem formulation, hypothesis development, and solution testing
Kohlberg	Postconventional morality	To develop moral principles that transcend one's own society: individual ethics, societal rights, and universal principles of right and wrong

▲ **Exhibit 6.2** Theories of Self or Identity in Adolescence

Building on Freud's work, Erik Erikson (1950, 1959, 1963, 1968) proposed eight stages of psychosocial development (refer back to Exhibit 3.7). He viewed psychosocial crisis as an opportunity and challenge. Each Eriksonian stage requires the mastery of a particular developmental task related to identity. His fifth stage, identity versus role diffusion, is relevant to adolescence. The developmental task is to establish a coherent sense of identity; failure to complete this task successfully leaves the adolescent without a solid sense of identity.

Robert Kegan (1982, 1994) suggests that there should be another stage between middle childhood and adolescence in Erikson's model. He suggests that before working on psychological identity, early adolescents face the psychosocial conflict of affiliation versus abandonment. The main concern is being accepted by a group, and the fear is being left behind or rejected. Successful accomplishment of group membership allows the young person to turn to the question of "Who am I?" in mid- and late adolescence.

James Marcia (1966, 1980) expounded upon Erikson's notion that adolescents struggle with the issue of identity versus role diffusion. Marcia proposed that adolescents vary in how easily they go about developing personal identity, and described four styles of identity development in adolescents:

1. *Identity diffusion.* No exploration of, or commitment to, roles and values

2. *Foreclosure.* Commitment made to roles and values without exploration

3. *Moratorium.* Exploration of roles and values without commitment

4. *Identity achievement.* Exploration of roles and values followed by commitment

Jean Piaget proposed four major stages leading to adult thought (refer back to Exhibit 3.4 for an overview of Piaget's stages). He expected the last stage, the stage of formal operations, to occur in adolescence, enabling the adolescent to engage in more abstract thinking about "who I am." Piaget (1972) also thought that adolescents begin to use formal operational skills to think in terms of what is best for society.

Lawrence Kohlberg (1976, 1984) expanded on Piaget's ideas about moral thinking to describe three major levels of moral development (refer back to Exhibit 4.2 for an overview of Kohlberg's stage theory). Kohlberg thought that adolescents become capable of **postconventional moral reasoning,** or morality based on moral principles that transcend social rules, but that many never go beyond conventional morality, or morality based on social rules.

These theories have been influential in conceptualizations of identity development. On perhaps a more practical level, however, Morris Rosenberg, in his book *Conceiving the Self* (1986), provides a very useful model of identity to keep in mind while working with adolescents—or perhaps to share with adolescents who are in the process of identity formation. Rosenberg suggests that identity comprises three major parts, outlined in Exhibit 6.3:

- *Social identity* is made up of several elements derived from interaction with other people and social systems.

- *Dispositions* are self-ascribed aspects of identity.

- *Physical characteristics* are simply one's physical traits, which all contribute a great deal to sense of self.

Exhibit 6.4 uses Rosenberg's model to analyze the identities of David Costa, Carl Fleischer, and Monica Golden. Notice that disposition is an element of identity based on self-definition. In contrast, a label is determined by others, and physical characteristics are genetically influenced. David has an athletic body and thinks of himself as athletic, but his parents—and perhaps others—label him as a freak. He is working to incorporate the fact that he is different into his identity. Carl has been labeled as a fatso, an underachiever, and a smoker. He seems to have incorporated these negative labels into his identity. Monica has been labeled as an overachiever, but she does not absorb the negative label, reframing it instead as ambitious.

Social Identity	Dispositions	Physical Characteristics
Social statuses: Basic classifications or demographic characteristics, such as sex, age, and socioeconomic status Membership groups: Groups with which the individual shares an interest, belief, origin, or physical or regional continuity (e.g., groups based on religion, political party, or race) Labels: Identifiers that result from social labeling (as when the boy who skips school becomes a delinquent) Derived statuses: Identities based on the individual's role history (e.g., veteran, high school athlete, or Harvard alumnus) Social types: Interests, attitudes, habits, or general characteristics (e.g., jock, geek, head, playboy, or go-getter) Personal identities: Unique labels attached to individuals (e.g., first name, first and last names, social security number, fingerprints, or DNA)	Attitudes (e.g., conservatism, liberalism) Traits (e.g., generosity, bravery) Abilities (e.g., musical talent, athletic skill) Values (e.g., efficiency, equality) Personality traits (e.g., introversion, extroversion) Habits (e.g., making lists, getting up early) Tendencies (e.g., to arrive late, to exaggerate) Likes or preferences (e.g., romance novels, pizzas)	Height Weight Body build Facial features

▲ **Exhibit 6.3**   Rosenberg's Model of Identity

SOURCE: Based on Rosenberg, 1986.

Scholars generally agree that identity formation is structured by the sociocultural context (see Gardiner & Kosmitzki, 2008; Kroger, 2007). Thus, the options offered to adolescents vary across cultures. Societies such as North American and other Western societies that put a high value on autonomy offer more options for adolescents than more collectivist-oriented societies. Some writers suggest that having a large number of options increases stress for adolescents (Gardiner & Kosmitzki). Think about David, Carl, and Monica. What is the sociocultural context of their identity struggles? What choices do they have, given their sociocultural contexts?

For those aspects of identity that we shape ourselves, individuals have four ways of trying on and developing a preference for certain identities:

1. *Future orientation.* By adolescence, youth have developed two important cognitive skills: They are able to consider the future, and they are able to construct abstract thoughts. These skills allow them to choose from a list of hypothetical behaviors based on the potential outcomes resulting from those behaviors. David Costa demonstrates future orientation in his contemplation regarding Theo. Adolescents also contemplate potential future selves.

2. *Role experimentation.* According to Erikson (1963), adolescence provides a psychosocial moratorium—a period during which youth have the latitude to experiment with social roles. Thus, adolescents typically sample membership in different cliques, build relationships with various mentors, take various academic electives, and join assorted groups and organizations—all in an attempt to further define themselves. Monica Golden, for example, sampled various potential career paths before deciding on becoming a pediatrician.

Element of Identity	David	Carl	Monica
Social Identity			
Social statuses	Male, 17, middle class	Male, 17, working class	Female, 17, upper middle class
Membership groups	Bolivian American, gay	European American, heads	African American, Christian, Young Republicans
Labels	Freak	Fatso, underachiever, smoker	Overachiever, brain
Derived statuses	Baseball player	Pizza deliverer	Senior class vice president, baby-sitter, track athlete
Social types	Jock	Geek, head (affiliate)	Brain, go-getter
Personal identity	David Costa	Carl Fleischer	Monica Golden
Disposition	Athletic	Underachiever, not popular, fat, slow, likes to get high, likes to surf the Internet	Athletic, ambitious, extroverted, likes children
Physical characteristics	Athletic build	Overweight	Tall

▲ **Exhibit 6.4**   Examples of Adolescent Identity

3. *Exploration.* Whereas role experimentation is specific to trying new roles, exploration refers to the comfort an adolescent has with trying new things. The more comfortable the individual is with exploration, the easier identity formation will be.

4. *Self-evaluation.* During the quest for identity, adolescents are constantly sizing themselves up against their peers. Erikson (1968) suggested that the development of identity is a process of personal reflection and observation of oneself in relation to others. George Herbert Mead (1934) suggested that individuals create a **generalized other** to represent how others are likely to view and respond to them. The role of the generalized other in adolescents' identity formation is evident when adolescents act on the assumed reactions of their families or peers. For example, what Monica Golden wears to school may be based not on what she thinks would be most comfortable or look the best but rather on what she thinks her peers expect her to wear. Thus, she does not wear miniskirts to school because "everyone" (generalized other) will think she is "loose."

Gender Identity

Adolescence, like early childhood in Chapter 4, is a time of significant gender identification, and much has been written lately in the United States about the specific experiences of either adolescent boys or adolescent girls (Garbarino, 1999, 2006; Kindlon & Thompson, 1999; Pipher, 1994; Pollack, 1999; Rimm, 1999; Wiseman, 2002). Exercise caution, however, with these types of works as some may present an exaggerated perspective for either gender experience. The general theme of these analyses is that female adolescents are sexualized in the media and overfocused on their bodies, and that male adolescents are steered away from their emotional lives and not provided the tools to negotiate them.

Gender identity, understanding of oneself as a man or woman, is elaborated and revised during late adolescence (Newman & Newman, 2009). Efforts are made to integrate the biological, psychological, and social dimensions of sex and gender. Culture plays a large role in this process. All cultures have norms about gender roles, and social institutions incorporate expectations about how females and males are to behave. Gender roles are learned in many social systems, beginning with the provision of gender scripts in families. Evidence shows that mainstream U.S. culture, as well as the cultures of many other societies, is moving toward more flexible standards for gendered behavior. There is much public conversation about gender roles and considerable revision is underway, allowing for increasing diversity in the enactment of gender roles. But in many cultures of the world, very distinct gender roles are prescribed, and gender is a major category for distributing power, with males receiving more power than females. Gender roles can be a source of painful culture clash for some immigrant groups who are migrating to North America and Europe, harder for some ethnic groups than for others. But, there is evidence that many immigrant families and individuals learn to be bicultural in terms of gender expectations, holding on to some traditional expectations while also innovating some new ways of doing gender roles (see Denner & Dunbar, 2004).

In most cultures, the concepts of gender and sexuality are closely related, and gender is divided into only two categories: female and male (Gardiner & Kosmitzki, 2008). Some groups have historically ascribed more than two genders, however, and there is growing recognition that chromosomal, genetic, anatomical, and hormonal aspects of sex are sometimes not aligned (Rudacille, 2005). For example, transgendered people develop a gender identity that is opposite to their biological sex. They are acutely uncomfortable with the gender assigned to them at birth, and feel certain that they were not born into the "right body." One possibility they have is to engage in sex change through hormone treatment and surgery. One study followed the adjustment of 20 adolescent transsexuals who had sex-reassignment surgery. In the one to four years of follow-up, the adolescents were doing well, and none of them had regrets about their decision to engage in sex change (Smith, van Goozen, & Cohen-Kettenis, 2001).

As we work with adolescents and strive to be responsive to their stories, we need to begin to consider what role being female or being male may play in who they are and what may be happening in their lives. How would David Costa's situation be different if he were a lesbian versus a gay male? What if Carl Fleischer was Carol? How are weight issues different for women and men? Are they different? And do successful Black men have different experiences or expectations from successful Black women? What if Monica Golden were male?

Identity and Ethnicity

Research indicates that ethnic origin is not likely to be a key ingredient of identity for Caucasian North American adolescents, but it is often central to identity in adolescents of ethnic minority groups (Branch, Tayal, & Triplett, 2000). Considerable research indicates that adolescence is a time when young people evaluate their ethnic background and explore ethnic identity (see French, Seidman, Allen, & Aber, 2006; Phinney, 2006). The development of ethnic identity in adolescence has been the focus of research across Canada, the United States, and Europe in recent years as ethnic diversity increases in all of these countries (e.g., Costigan, Su, & Hua, 2009; Hughes, Hagelskamp, Way, & Foust, 2009; Lam & Smith, 2009; Rivas-Drake, 2008; Street, Harris-Britt, & Walker-Barnes, 2009). Ethnic minority youth are challenged to develop a sense of themselves as members of an ethnic minority group while also coming to terms with their national identity (Lam & Smith). Adolescents tend to have wider experience with multicultural groups than when they were younger and may be exposed to ethnic discrimination, which can complicate the development of cultural pride and belonging (Costigan et al.).

Evidence in the research indicates that ethnic minority adolescents tend to develop strong ethnic identity, but there is also evidence of variability within ethnic groups in terms of extent of ethnic identity. Costigan and colleagues

> How can social workers use research like this to understand risk and protection in minority youth?

(2009) reviewed the literature on ethnic identity among Chinese Canadian youth and concluded that the evidence indicates a strong ethnic identity among these youth. Conversely, there was much variability in the extent to which these youth reported a Canadian identity. Adolescents negotiated ethnic identity in diverse ways across different settings, with different approaches being used at home versus in public settings. Lam and Smith (2009) studied how African and Caribbean adolescents (ages 11 to 16) in Britain negotiate ethnic identity and national identity and had similar findings to those for Chinese Canadian youth. They found that both groups, African and Caribbean, of adolescents rated their ethnic identity higher than their national identity and reported more pride in their ethnic heritage than in being British. They found, however, that girls reported stronger ethnic identity than boys. Using in-depth interviews rather than standardized instruments, Rivas-Drake (2008) found three different styles of ethnic identity among Latinos in one public university in the United States. One group reported high individualistic achievement motivation and alienation from other Latinos. A second group reported strong identification with Latinos and were motivated to remove perceived barriers for the group. A third group reported strong connection to Latinos but were not motivated to work to remove barriers for the group.

Ethnic identity develops within the context of the family, and there has been a general belief that children of immigrant parents acculturate more quickly than their parents, leaving parents with a stronger ethnic identity than their children. Some research in Canada questions that belief. Costigan and Dokis (2006) found that Chinese Canadian mothers and children indicated stronger ethnic identity than the fathers, and mothers and children did not differ from each other. Interestingly, they found that the adolescents tended to report stronger ethnic identity than their parents in families characterized by high levels of warmth. This finding may reflect the Canadian cultural context: Canada has an official policy of multiculturalism, which promotes the maintenance of one's cultural heritage. Conversely, researchers in the United States have found that African American parents are more likely than parents in other ethnic groups to feel the need to prepare their adolescents for racial bias as a part of their racial/ethnic socialization (Hughes et al., 2009). This most likely reflects a more hostile environment for African American youth in the United States than for the Chinese Canadian youth.

There are certainly added complexities for the identity formation process of minority youth. Arthur Jones (1992) suggests that "the usual rifts between young adolescents (ages 13 to 15) and their parents are sometimes more intense in middle-class African American families, especially those in which middle-class economic status is new for the parents. This is because the generation gap is more exaggerated" (p. 29). Consider Monica Golden, who is an upper middle-class, African American teenager in a predominantly White high school. What are some of the potential added challenges of Monica's adolescent identity formation? Is it any wonder that she is hoping to attend Howard University, a historically Black college, where she could surround herself with African American role models and professional support networks?

The available research on ethnic identity among ethnic minority youth indicates that most of these youth cope by becoming bicultural, developing skills to operate within at least two cultures. This research should alert social workers to tune into the process of ethnic identity development when they work with ethnic minority youth. It appears that ethnic identity is a theme for both David Costa and Monica Golden. They both appear to be developing some comfort with being bicultural, but they are negotiating their bicultural status in different ways. Discussion about their ethnic identity might reveal more struggle than we expected. Some youth may be more likely to withdraw from the challenges of accessing mainstream culture rather than confronting these challenges and seeking workable solutions. We must be alert to this possibility.

Critical Thinking Questions 6.1

What are the implications of recent research findings about the adolescent brain for social policy? This research is leading to a number of policy discussions about several issues, including the timing of the school day; regulations for adolescent driving, including the legal age of driving, whether evening driving should be allowed, whether other adolescents can be present in the car of an adolescent driver and so on; and age when a juvenile can be tried as an adult. What opinions do you hold about these issues? How are those opinions shaped by recent brain research?

SOCIAL ASPECTS OF ADOLESCENCE

The social environment—family, peers, organizations, communities, institutions, and so on—is a significant element of adolescent life. For one thing, as already noted, identity develops through social transactions. For another, as adolescents become more independent and move into the world, they develop their own relationships with more elements of the social environment.

Relationships With Family

Answering the question, "Who am I?" includes a consideration of the question, "How am I different from my brothers and sisters, my parents, and other family members?" For many adolescents, this question begins the process of **individuation**—the development of a self or identity that is unique and separate. David Costa seems to have started the process of individuation; he recognizes that he may not want to be what his parents want him to be. He does not yet seem comfortable with this idea, however. Carl Fleischer is not sure how he is similar to and different from his absent father. Monica Golden has begun to recognize some ways that she is different from her siblings, and she is involved in her own personal exploration of career options that fit her dispositions. It would appear that she is the furthest along in the individuation process.

Separation from parents has four components (Moore, 1987):

1. *Functional independence.* Literally being able to function with little assistance or independently from one's parents. An example would be getting ready for school: selecting an appropriate outfit, getting dressed, compiling school supplies, and feeding oneself.

2. *Attitudinal independence.* Not merely having a different attitude from parents, but developing one's own set of values and beliefs. An example might be choosing a presidential candidate based not on your parents' choice but on your values and beliefs.

3. *Emotional independence.* Not being dependent on parents for approval, intimacy, and emotional support. Emotional independence might mean discovering your own way to overcome emotional turmoil—for example, listening to your favorite CD after a fight with your girlfriend or boyfriend rather than relying on support from your parents.

4. *Conflictual independence.* Being able to recognize one's separateness from parents without guilt, resentment, anger, or other negative emotions. Conflictual independence is being comfortable with being different. Thus, instead of ridiculing your dad for wearing those shorts to the picnic, you are able to go to the picnic realizing that you would not wear those shorts but that your father's taste in shorts is not a reflection on you.

The concept of independence is largely influenced by culture. And mainstream culture in the United States places a high value on independence. However, as social workers, we need to recognize that the notion of pushing the adolescent to develop an identity separate from family is not acceptable to all cultural groups in the United States (Gardiner & Kosmitzki, 2008). Many Asian Indian families may view adolescent struggles for independence as a disloyal cutting off of family and culture (Hines et al., 2005). Peter Nguyen (2008; Nguyen & Cheung, 2009) has studied the relationships between Vietnamese American adolescents and their parents and found that a majority of the adolescents perceived their fathers as using a traditional authoritarian parenting style, which poses problems for their mental health in the context of the multicultural society in the United States. Our assessments of adolescent individuation should be culturally sensitive. Likewise, we must be realistic in our assessments of the functional independence of adolescents with cognitive, emotional, and physical disabilities.

Even when it is consistent with their cultural values, not all adolescents are able to achieve functional independence, attitudinal independence, emotional independence, and conflictual independence. Instead, many maintain a high level of conflict. Conflict is particularly evident in families experiencing additional stressors, such as divorce and economic difficulties (Fine, Ganong, & Demo, 2010). Conflict also plays out differently at different points in adolescence. Research suggests that conflicts with parents increase around the time of puberty but begin to decrease after that. Conflicts typically involve disagreements about chores, dress, and other daily issues (Allison & Schultz, 2004; Granic, Dishion, & Hollenstein, 2003).

> How can families stay connected to their adolescents while also honoring their struggle for independence and increased agency in making choices?

Adolescent struggles for independence can be especially potent in multigenerational contexts (Preto, 2005). These struggles typically come at a time when parents are in midlife and grandparents are entering late adulthood and both are facing stressors of their own. Adolescent demands for independence may reignite unresolved conflicts between the parents and the grandparents and stir the pot of family discord. The challenge for the family is to stay connected while also allowing the adolescent to widen contact with the world. Most families make this adjustment well, but often after an initial period of confusion and disruption.

The Society for Research on Adolescence prepared an international perspective on adolescence in the 21st century and reached three conclusions regarding adolescents and their relationships with their families:

- Families are and will remain a central source of support to adolescents in most parts of the world. Cultural traditions that support family cohesion, such as those in the Middle East, South Asia, and China, remain particularly strong, despite rapid change. A great majority of teenagers around the world experience close and functional relationships with their parents.

- Adolescents are living in a wider array of diverse and fluid family situations than was true a generation ago. These include divorced, single-parent, remarried, gay and lesbian, and multilocal families. More adolescents live in households without men. As a result of AIDS, regional conflicts, and migratory labor, many adolescents do not live with their parents.

- Many families are becoming better positioned to support their adolescents' preparation for adulthood. Smaller family sizes result in adults devoting more resources and attention to each child. Parents in many parts of the world are adopting a more responsive and communicative parenting style, which facilitates development of interpersonal skills and enhances mental health (Larson, Wilson, & Mortimer, 2002).

Relationships With Peers

In the quest for autonomy and identity, adolescents begin to differentiate themselves from their parents and associate with their peers. Early adolescents are likely to select friends that are similar to them in gender and interests, but by middle adolescence, the peer group often includes opposite-sex friends as well as same-sex friends (Kroger, 2007). Most early adolescents have one close friend, but the stability of these friendships is not high. In early adolescence the peer group tends to be larger than in middle childhood; these larger peer groups are known as *cliques.* By mid-adolescence, the peer group is organized around common interests; these groups tend to be even larger than cliques and are generally known as *crowds* (Brown & Klute, 2003). David Costa hangs out with the athletic crowd and appears to get support from other gay peers. Carl Fleischer is making contact with the "heads" crowd. Peer relationships contribute to adolescents' identities, behaviors, and personal and social competence.

▲ **Photo 6.2** Peer relationships are a fertile testing ground for youth and their emerging identities.

Peer relationships are a fertile testing ground for youth and their emerging identities (Brown, 2004). Many adolescents seek out a peer group with compatible members, and inclusion or exclusion from certain groups can affect their identity and overall development. David Costa's peer groups include the baseball team and a group of gay males from school. Carl Fleischer seems to be gravitating toward the "heads" for his peer group—although this choice appears to be related to a perception of rejection by other groups. Monica Golden enjoys easy acceptance by several peer groups: the peer counselors at high school, the senior class officers, the Young Republicans, and the track team.

For some adolescents, participation in certain peer groups influences their behavior negatively. Peer influence may not be strong enough to undo protective factors, but if the youth is already at risk, the influence of peers becomes that much stronger (Rew, 2005). Sexual behaviors and pregnancy status are often the same for same-sexed best friends (Cavanaugh, 2004). Substance use is also a behavior that most often occurs in groups of adolescents. The same is true for violent and delinquent behaviors (Garbarino, 1999; Klein, 1995).

Romantic Relationships

Adolescents in many cultures become involved in romantic relationships during middle school and high school. By late adolescence, the quality of these relationships becomes more intimate. Furrow and Wehner (1997, cited in Newman & Newman, 2009, p. 343) suggest that romantic relationships meet four needs: affiliation, attachment, caregiving, and sexual gratification. The timing and rituals for forming romantic relationships vary from culture to culture and from one age cohort to another. In some cultures, the romantic relationship develops in the context of an arranged marriage. In the United States and many other societies, romantic relationships develop through a dance of flirtation and dating. Children who have close friendships in middle school have been found to be more likely to have romantic relationships in adolescence (Newman & Newman).

▲ **Photo 6.3** Adolescents in many cultures become involved in romantic relationships during middle school and high school.

Relationships With Organizations, Communities, and Institutions

As adolescents loosen their ties to parents, they develop more direct relationships in other arenas such as school, the broader community, employment, leisure, and the mass media, including cell phones and the Internet.

School

In the United States, as well as other wealthy nations, youth are required to stay in school through a large portion of adolescence. The situation is quite different in many poor nations, however, where children may not even receive a primary school education (United Nations Development Program, 2005).

In their time that is spent at school, adolescents are gaining skills and knowledge for their next step in life, either moving into the workforce or continuing their education. In school, they also have the opportunity to evolve socially and emotionally; school is a fertile ground for practicing future orientation, role experimentation, exploration, and self-evaluation.

Middle schools have a very structured format and a very structured environment; high schools are less structured in both format and environment, allowing a gradual transition to greater autonomy. The school experience changes radically, however, at the college level. Many college students are away from home for the first time and are in very unstructured environments. David Costa, Carl Fleischer, and Monica Golden have had different experiences with structure in their environments to date. David's environment has required him to move flexibly between two cultures. That experience may help to prepare him for the unstructured college environment. Carl has had the least structured home life. It remains to be seen whether that has helped him to develop skills in structuring his own environment, or left him with insufficient models for doing so. Monica is accustomed to juggling multiple commitments and should have little trouble with the competing attractions and demands of college.

School is also an institutional context where cultures intersect, which may create difficulties for students who are not familiar or comfortable with mainstream culture. That is most likely an important contributing factor to the low high school graduation rates of youth of color. Recent research by the Civil Rights Project at Harvard University indicates that 75% of White students graduate from high school compared with approximately half of Black, Hispanic, and Native American youth (Orfield, Losen, Wald, & Swanson, 2004). You may not realize how Eurocentric the educational model in the United States is until you view it through a different cultural lens. We can use a Native American lens as an example. Michael Walkingstick Garrett (1995) uses the experiences of the boy Wind-Wolf as an example of the incongruence between Native American culture and the typical education model:

Wind-Wolf is required by law to attend public school. . . . He speaks softly, does not maintain eye contact with the teacher as a sign of respect, and rarely responds immediately to questions, knowing that it is good to reflect on what has been said. He may be looking out the window during class, as if daydreaming, because he has been taught to always be aware of changes in the natural world. These behaviors are interpreted by his teacher as either lack of interest or dumbness. (p. 204)

Children in the United States spend less time in school-related activities than do Chinese or Japanese children and have been noted to put less emphasis on scholastic achievement. Some researchers attribute oft-noted cross-cultural differences in mathematics achievement to these national differences in emphasis on scholastics (Newman, 2008). For adolescents, scholastic interest, expectations, and achievements may also vary, based not only on nationality but also on gender, race, ethnicity, economic status, and expectations for the future. Girls have been found to be more invested in school activities than boys (Shanahan & Flaherty, 2001). In a study of students in 33 middle and high schools, African American and Hispanic students were found to be more disengaged from school than Asian and White students, and economically disadvantaged teenagers were found to be more disengaged than more economically advantaged students (Csikszentmihalyi & Schneider, 2000). Recent longitudinal research found that adolescents with a future orientation and expectations of further schooling, marriage, and good citizenship devote a greater percentage of their time to school-related activities (Shanahan & Flaherty).

> What are some ways that different cultural expectations regarding education affect adolescent development?

The American Youth Policy Forum reexamined a 1988 report called *The Forgotten Half* by the William T. Grant Foundation in its study *Forgotten Half Revisited: American Youth and Young Families, 1988–2008* and found that "the nearly ten million 18–24 year-old Americans who don't go on to college after high school aren't doing as well at the end of the 1990's as they were a decade ago" (American Youth Policy Forum, 2009, para. 1). Through the early 1990s, vocational education in the United States was stigmatized as the high school track for students with poor academic capabilities, special needs, or behavioral problems (Gamoran & Himmelfarb, 1994). Congress and most educators, however, believe that broadening the segment of the student population that participates in vocational education and adding academic achievement and postsecondary enrollment to the traditional objectives of technical competency, labor market outcomes, and general employability skills will improve the quality of these programs (Lynch, 2000). Moreover, the National Women's Law Center has reported that there is pervasive sex segregation in high school vocational programs in the United States, with girls clustered in programs that train them for lower-paying jobs ("Sex Bias Cited in Vocational Ed.," 2002).

The Broader Community

In the United States, the participation of high school students in volunteer work in the community is becoming common, much more so than in Europe. Indeed, community service is required in many U.S. high schools. Flanagan (2004) argues that community volunteer service provides structured outlets for adolescents to meet a wider circle of community people and to experiment with new roles. The community youth development movement is based on the belief that such community service provides an opportunity to focus on the strengths and competencies of youth rather than on youth problems (see Villarruel, Perkins, Borden, & Keith, 2003). One research team found that participation in community service and volunteerism assisted in identity clarification and in the development of political and moral interests (McIntosh, Metz, & Youniss, 2005).

Another way that adolescents can have contact with the broader community is through a mentoring relationship with a community adult. The mentoring relationship may be either formal or informal. The mentor becomes a role model and trusted advisor. Mentors can be found in many places, in part-time work settings, in youth serving organizations, in religious organizations, at school, in the neighborhood, and so on. There is unusually strong evidence for the positive value of mentoring for youth (Hamilton & Hamilton, 2004). One recent study found that perceived mentoring from an unrelated adult in the work setting was associated with psychosocial competencies and adjustment in both U.S. and European samples (Vazsonyi & Snider, 2008). Longitudinal research with foster care youth has found that youth who had been mentored had better overall health, less suicidal ideation, fewer sexually transmitted infections (STIs), and less aggression in young adulthood than foster care youth who had not been mentored (Ahrens, DuBois, Richardson, Fan, & Lozano, 2008).

Work

Like many adolescents, Carl and Monica also play the role of worker in the labor market. Work can provide an opportunity for social interaction and greater financial independence. It may also lead to personal growth by promoting notions of contribution, responsibility, egalitarianism, and self-efficacy and by helping the adolescent to develop values and preferences for future jobs—answers to questions like "What kind of job would I like to have in the future?" and "What am I good at?" (Mortimer & Finch, 1996, p. 4). For example, Monica tried many jobs before deciding that she loves working with children and wants to become a pediatrician. In addition, employment may also offer the opportunity to develop job skills, time management skills, customer relation skills, money management skills, market knowledge, and other skills of value to future employers.

In July 2006, 21.9 million U.S. youth ages 16 to 24 were employed for an employment rate of 59.2% of the civilian noninstitutional population (U.S. Bureau of Labor Statistics, 2006). The rate fell almost 11 points between July 1989 and July 2003 but has remained fairly constant from 2003 to 2006. Being in the labor force means the individual is working either full time or part time as a paid employee in an ongoing relationship with a particular employer, such as working in a supermarket. Individuals are not considered to be in the labor force if they work in "freelance jobs" that involve doing tasks without a specific employer, such as babysitting or mowing lawns. Broken down by gender and race, the employment rate for July 2006 was 61.9% for young men, 56.5% for young women, 63.3% for Whites, 43.5% for Blacks, 42.8% for Asians, and 55.2% for Latinos (U.S. Bureau of Labor Statistics).

The U.S. Department of Labor has launched a new initiative called YouthRules! that seeks to promote positive and safe work experiences for young workers. Their guidelines may be the social policy result of research that suggests that for youth, work, in spite of some positive benefits, may also detract from development by cutting into time needed for sleep, exercise, maintenance of overall health, school, family relations, and peer relations. Unfortunately, the types of work that are available to adolescents are usually low-skill jobs that offer little opportunity for skill development. Adolescents who work more than 10 hours per week have been found to be at increased risk for poor academic performance, psychological problems such as depression, anxiety, fatigue, and sleep difficulties, as well as physical problems such as headaches, stomachaches, and colds. They are also more likely to use cigarettes, alcohol, or other drugs, regardless of ethnicity, socioeconomic status (SES), or age (Entwisle, Alexander, & Olson, 2005; Marsh & Kleitman, 2005). Although we cannot draw causal conclusions, Carl Fleischer is a good example of this linkage: he works more than 10 hours a week and also has declining grades and uses tobacco and marijuana.

Leisure

In wealthy nations, a sizable portion of an adolescent's life is spent in leisure pursuits. These activities often have great influence on various aspects of the individual's development, such as identity formation, and psychological and behavioral functioning (Bartko & Eccles, 2003). Cross-national research indicates that there are national differences in the way adolescents use nonschool time (Verma & Larson, 2003). For example, Korean and Japanese youth spend more time on homework and preparation for college entrance exams than U.S. or European youth (Lee, 2003). Compared with European teens from 12 countries, U.S. teens spend less time on schoolwork, less time in reading for leisure, more time in paid employment, and more time hanging out with friends (Flammer & Schaffner, 2003; Larson & Seepersad, 2003). Japanese and U.S. youth spend a great deal of time on extracurricular activity, particularly organized sports, based on a cultural belief that these activities build character (Larson & Seepersad; Nishino & Larson, 2003). Across national lines, girls tend to have more chores and spend more time in the arts than boys, and boys spend more time in sports and with electronic media than girls (Silbereisen, 2003).

One research team (Bartko & Eccles, 2003) examined the nonschool activity profiles of 918 adolescents from Washington, D.C., across 11 different activity domains. Using cluster analysis, they identified a typology of six unique activity profiles:

Sports Cluster: highly involved in sports and also in spending time with friends

School Cluster: highly involved in school-based clubs, homework, and reading for pleasure

Uninvolved Cluster: activity levels below the mean in all 11 activity domains

Volunteer Cluster: highly involved in volunteer activities

High-Involved Cluster: highly involved in a range of activities, including community-based clubs, sports, homework, reading, chores, volunteering, and religious activities; low involvement in unstructured activities

Working Cluster: highly involved in paid work, and low levels of involvement in other activity domains

There were no race differences in activity choices, but there were gender differences. Males were overrepresented in the Sports Cluster and Uninvolved Cluster. Females were overrepresented in the School Cluster, Volunteer Cluster, and High-Involved Cluster. The parents of the High-Involved Cluster had higher educational attainment than students in

▲ **Photo 6.4** In wealthy nations, a sizable portion of an adolescent's life is spent in leisure pursuits.

the other clusters. Psychological and behavioral functioning was associated with the activity profiles of the respondents. Respondents in the School and High-Involved Clusters had the highest grade point averages, and Uninvolved respondents had the lowest grade point averages. Behavior problems were more often reported by respondents in the Sports, Uninvolved, and Work Clusters. The highest rates of depression were found in the Uninvolved Cluster.

Another study examining the relationship between leisure and identity formation for adolescents found that the patterns of influence are different for girls and boys (Shaw, Kleiber, & Caldwell, 1995). Participation in sports and physical activities has a positive effect on identity development for female adolescents but shows no effect for males. Watching television has a negative effect on identity development for male adolescents but shows no effect for females. And involvement in social activities and other leisure activities was not significantly correlated with identity development for either gender.

Access to leisure activities varies. Leisure activities for rural adolescents are different from leisure activities for urban youth, for example. Adolescents living in urban areas have greater access to transportation and to public recreational activities and programs. Rural youth lack this access and thus rely more heavily on school-related leisure activities (Garton & Pratt, 1991). Access to leisure activities also increases with SES.

Cell Phones and the Internet

Nationally, the use of cell phones is not only big business, but it is also a cultural phenomenon whose impact remains to be seen. According to an article in the *Washington Post,* more than 75 billion text messages are sent each month, with the most prolific texters in the 13 to 17 age range (St. George, 2009). Adolescents average 2,272 text messages a month versus 203 calls from their cell phones. This phenomenon brings another level of connectedness—with potential benefits, such as maintaining distant relationships, keeping parents updated on their child's whereabouts or needs, broader social networks; but also potential risks—driving while texting, mental and physical (primarily thumbs) fatigue, social disconnectedness, instant gratification.

The Internet is also a relatively new vehicle for connectedness, and increasingly, teens are using the web to complete schoolwork, obtain general information, play games, and socialize. In 2004, it was estimated that two thirds of households in the United States had access to the Internet (Croteau & Hoynes, 2006). And with children and teenagers comprising one of the fastest growing groups of Internet users, researchers estimate that almost 25 million youth in the United States between the ages of 10 and 17 are regular Internet users today (Wolak, Mitchell, & Finkelhor, 2006). Nationwide, 24.9% of high school students said they played video or computer games or used a computer for something

▲ **Photo 6.5**   Adolescents are prolific users of text messaging, bringing a high level of connectedness.

other than schoolwork for more than three hours on an average school day (CDC, 2008d).

Empirical evidence indicates that the Internet fosters social connections and identity development, is an important source for adolescent health information, and provides opportunities for practicing leadership skills (Borzekowski, Fobil, & Asante, 2006; Greenfield & Zheng, 2006; Gross, 2004). Internet social networking programs such as Facebook, allow adolescents to try on various identities and create various relationships. As Bakardjieva states in the book, *Community in the Digital Age: Philosophy and Practice,* social networking sites allow individuals "to traverse the social world, penetrate previously unattainable regions of anonymity" (Bakardjieva, 2004, p. 122). Conversely, parents, school officials, and legislators have become increasingly concerned that adolescents will see sexually explicit material on the Internet and may be sexually exploited or otherwise harassed via the Internet. The Internet Crimes Against Children Task Forces (ICAC) are comprised of 61 federal, state, and local task forces. Since 1998, this ICAC network of task forces has reviewed more than 180,000 complaints of alleged child sexual victimization and arrested more than 16,5000 individuals (ICAC, 2010). Moreover, the U.S. Department of Justice increased funding for the ICAC program from $2.4 million in 1998 to $75 million in 2009 (ICAC, 2010).

In 1999 and 2000, researchers Wolak, Mitchell, and Finkelhor conducted the first Youth Internet Safety Survey (YISS-1) with a national sample of more than 1,500 youth ages 10 to 17 who used the Internet at least once a month for the past 6 months. A second Youth Internet Safety Survey (YISS-2) was conducted in 2005 by the same researchers, again using a sample of more than 1,500 youth ages 10 to 17 (Wolak et al., 2006). Some of the main findings of YISS-2 are presented below:

- 91% of the youth had home Internet access, compared with 74% in YISS-1

- 74% had access in three or more places, compared with 51% in YISS-1

- 86% of the youth had used the Internet in the past week, compared with 76% in YISS-1

- 23% reported using the Internet more than two hours at a time, compared with 13% in YISS-1

- 49% used the Internet five to seven days a week, compared with 31% in YISS-1

- 30% visited online chat rooms, compared with 56% in YISS-1

- 34% saw sexual material online that they did want to see in the past year, up from 25% in YISS-1, despite the increased use of filtering, blocking, and monitoring software

- 34% communicated online with people they did not know in person, compared with 40% in YISS-1

- One in seven youth received unwanted sexual solicitation, compared with 1 in 5 in YISS-1

- 4% received aggressive sexual solicitations, which attempted offline contact, compared with 3% in YISS-1

- 4% reported that online solicitors asked them for nude or sexually explicit photographs of themselves; this information was not collected in YISS-1

- 9% were the victims of online harassment and/or bullying, compared with 6% in YISS-1

- 28% had made rude or nasty comments to someone on the Internet, compared with 14% in YISS-1

YISS-2 also found a large increase in the posting or sending of personal information or pictures between 2000 and 2005. In 2005, 34% had posted their real names, home addresses, telephone number, or their school names; 45% had posted their date of birth or age; and 18% had posted pictures of themselves. In 2000, only 11% had posted personal information, and only 5% had posted pictures of themselves. This increase reflects the rise of personal profile sites such as Facebook, MySpace, Friendster, and Xanga. Wolak, Mitchell, and Finkelhor (2003) surmise that "adolescents may be especially drawn to online relationships because of their intense interest in forming relationships, and because the expansiveness of cyberspace frees them from some of the constraints of adolescence by giving them easy access to a world beyond that of their families, schools and communities" (p. 106). Unfortunately, adolescents are also vulnerable to unethical marketers who engage in such tactics as bundling digital pornography material with game demos and other products that youth are likely to download (Wolak et al., 2006). Researchers have also found that sex offenders target young teenagers by playing on their desire for romance and interest in sex (Wolak et al., 2006). The adolescents who are most vulnerable to these advances are girls who have high levels of conflict with their parents or who are highly troubled and boys with low levels of communication with their parents or who are highly troubled (Wolak et al., 2003).

ADOLESCENT SPIRITUALITY

Another potential facet of adolescent development is spirituality or religiosity. As adolescents become capable of advanced thinking and begin to contemplate their existence, identity, and future, many also undertake spiritual exploration. Sociology of religion researchers suggest that adolescents are a population that many religious organizations particularly target in order to exert influence in their lives, and adolescence and young adulthood are the life stages when religious conversion is most likely to take place (Smith, Denton, Faris, & Regnerus, 2002, p. 597).

The National Study of Youth and Religion (NSYR) is the most comprehensive study of spirituality and religion among U.S. adolescents to date. Supported by the Lilly Endowment, this study began in August 2001 and was funded through December 2007. The first wave of data collection was conducted from July 2002 to April 2003. It was a nationally representative, random-digit-dial method, telephone survey of 3,290 English- and Spanish-speaking teenagers ages 13 to 17 and of their parents living in all 50 states. It also included more than 250 in-depth, face-to-face interviews of a subsample of survey respondents. The second wave included 78% of the original respondents and was conducted from June 2005 to November 2005.

> How important is it for social workers to assess the spirituality of adolescents with whom they work?

The NSYR found that the vast majority of U.S. teenagers identify themselves as Christian (52% Protestant, various denominations, and 23% Catholic). Sixteen percent are not religious. In addition, 2.8% identify themselves with two different faiths, 2.5% are Mormon, 1.5% are Jewish, and other minority faiths (Jehovah's Witness, Muslim, Eastern Orthodox, Buddhist, Pagan or Wiccan, Hindu, Christian Science, Native American, Unitarian Universalist) each comprised less than 1% of the representative sample. Four out of 10 U.S. adolescents say they attend religious services once a week or more, pray daily or more, and are currently involved in a religious youth group. Eighty-four percent of the surveyed youth believe in God whereas 12% are unsure about belief about God, and 3% do not believe in God.

The bulk of the NSYR data are analyzed in the book *Soul Searching: The Religious and Spiritual Lives of American Teenagers* by Smith and Denton (2005), who reached these empirical conclusions:

Religion is a significant presence in the lives of many U.S. teens today.

Teenage religiosity in the United States is extraordinarily conventional and very few youth appear to be pursuing 'spiritual but no religious' personal quests.

The religious diversity represented by U.S. adolescents is no more varied today than it has been for a very long time.

The single most important social influence on the religious and spiritual lives of adolescents is their parents.

The greater the supply of religiously grounded relationships, activities, programs, opportunities, and challenges available to teenagers the more likely teenagers will be religiously engaged and invested.

At the level of subjective consciousness, adolescent religious and spiritual understanding and concern seem to be generally very weak.

It is impossible to adequately understand the religious and spiritual lives of U.S. teenagers without framing that understanding to include the larger social and institutional contexts that form their lives.

Significant differences [exist] in a variety of important life outcomes between more and less religious teenagers in the United States. (pp. 260–263)

A growing volume of research is finding religion to be a positive force in adolescent development (King, 2007). Here are some of the themes found in that research. Religious participation has been found to promote civic engagement and altruism (Donnelly, Atkins, & Hart, 2005; Kerestes, Youoniss, & Metz, 2004). Religion and spirituality have been found to contribute to positive identity development (Templeton & Eccles, 2006). Religion has been found to be a coping resource for adolescents in both good and ill health (Mahoney, Pendleton, & Ihrke, 2005). Attendance at religious services has been found to serve as a protective mechanism in high-risk neighborhoods, providing supportive relationships, moral values, and positive rituals and routines (Regenerus & Elder, 2003). Active religious participation provides adolescents with the opportunity to interact with nonparental adults (King & Furrow, 2004). Religious youth are less likely to engage in risky sexual behavior (Adamczyk & Felson, 2006) and to engage in other high-risk behaviors such as substance abuse and violence (Wagener, Furrow, King, Leffert, & Benson, 2003).

For many youth, spirituality may be closely connected to culture. Interventions with adolescents and their families should be consistent with their spirituality, but knowing someone's cultural heritage will not always provide understanding of their religious or spiritual beliefs. For example, it is no longer safe to assume that all Latino Americans are Catholic. Today, there is much religious diversity among Latino Americans who increasingly have membership in Protestant denominations such as Methodist, Baptist, Presbyterian, and Lutheran, as well as in such religious groups as Mormon, Seventh-Day Adventist, and Jehovah's Witness. And, the fastest growing religions among Latino Americans are the Pentecostal and evangelical denominations (Garcia & Zunuiga, 2007). Many Latino Americans, particularly Puerto Ricans, combine traditional religious beliefs with a belief in spiritualism, which is a belief that the visible world is surrounded by an invisible world made up of good and evil spirits who influence human behavior. Some Latino Americans practice Indigenous healing rituals, such as *Santeria* (Cuban American) and *curanderismo* (Mexican American). In these later situations, it is important to know whether adolescents and their families are working with an Indigenous folk healer (Ho, Rasheed, & Rasheed, 2004).

Although adolescents may not seem to be guided by their spirituality or religiosity, they may have underlying spiritual factors at work. As with any biological, psychological, or social aspect of the individual, the spiritual aspect of youth must be considered to gain the best understanding of the whole person.

Critical Thinking Questions 6.2

Children and adolescents in the United States spend less time on school-related activities than students in most other industrialized countries. Do you think children and adolescents in the United States should spend more time in school? How would you support your argument on this issue? How could high schools in the United States do a better job of supporting the cognitive development of adolescents? Should the high schools be concerned about supporting emotional and social development of adolescents? Why or why not?

ADOLESCENT SEXUALITY

With the changes of puberty, adolescents begin to have sexual fantasies, sexual feelings, and sexual attractions. They must come to an understanding of what it means to be a sexual being, and make some decisions about which, if any, sexual behaviors to engage in. They also begin to understand the kinds of people they find sexually attractive. In their experimentation, some adolescents will contact STIs and some will become pregnant. Unfortunately, some will experience unwanted sexual attention and be victims of sexual aggression.

Sexual Decision Making

Transition into sexualized behavior is partly a result of biological changes. The amount of the sex hormone DHEA in the blood peaks between the ages of 10 and 12, a time when both boys and girls become aware of sexual feelings. The way that sexual feelings get expressed depends largely on sociocultural factors, however. Youth are influenced by the attitudes toward sexual activity that they encounter in the environment, at school; among peers, siblings, and family; in their clubs/organizations; in the media; and so on. When and how they begin to engage in sexual activity is closely linked to what they perceive to be the activities of their peers (Henderson, Butcher, Wight, Williamson, & Raab, 2008; Ponton & Judice, 2004; Rew, 2005). Research also suggests that youth who are not performing well in school are more likely to engage in sexual activity than are those who are doing well (Rew). Finally, beliefs and behaviors regarding sexuality are also shaped by one's culture, religion/spirituality, and value system. Ponton and Judice suggest that "a nation's attitude about adolescent sexuality plays an important role in the adolescent's sexual development and affects the laws, sexual media, sexual services, and the interaction of religion and state as well as the type of education that they receive in their schools" (p. 7). Adolescents report a variety of social motivations for engaging in sexual intercourse, including developing new levels of intimacy, pleasing a partner, impressing peers, and gaining sexual experience (Impett & Tolman, 2006).

As the pubertal hormones cause changes throughout the body, most adolescents spend time becoming familiar with those changes. For many, exploration includes **masturbation,** the self-stimulation of the genitals for sexual pleasure. Almost 50% of boys and 30% of girls report masturbating by age 13; boys masturbate earlier and more often than girls (Leitenberg, Detzer, & Srebnik, 1993). The gender difference has been found to be even greater in Bangkok, Thailand, where 79% of male secondary students report masturbating, compared with 9% of females (O-Prasetsawat

& Petchum, 2004). Masturbation has negative associations for some adolescents. Thus, masturbation may have psychological implications for adolescents, depending on the way they feel about masturbation and on how they think significant others feel about it. Female college students who are high in religiosity report more guilt about masturbation than female college students who are low in religiosity (Davidson, Moore, & Ullstrup, 2004).

The U.S. Youth Risk Behavior Survey suggests that, nationwide, 47.8% of high school students reported having had sexual intercourse during their life, 7.1% had sexual intercourse for the first time before age 13, 14.9% have had sexual intercourse with four or more persons during their life, and 35.0% are sexually active during the last three months (CDC, 2008d). Of the 35% of high school students who indicated that they are currently sexually active, 61.5% report that either they or their partner used a condom during last sexual intercourse, 16% reported that either they or their partner had used birth control pills to prevent pregnancy before last intercourse, and 22.5% had drunk alcohol or used drugs before their last sexual intercourse (CDC, 2008d).

Data suggest that, on average, adolescents in the United States experience first sexual intercourse slightly earlier than adolescents in other industrialized countries; the average age of first intercourse in the United States was found to be 15.8 years, compared with 16.2 in Germany, 16.8 in France, and 17.7 in the Netherlands (Berne & Huberman, 1999). In the United States, 70% of females who had sex before age 13 did so nonvoluntarily (Alan Guttmacher Institute, 1999). One study found that the majority of teens in the United States who are sexually active wish they had waited until they were older to begin to have sexual intercourse (National Campaign to Prevent Teen Pregnancy, 2002).

As compared with the already high rates of adolescent sexual involvement in North America and Europe, there is recent research to suggest that rates of adolescent sexual involvement have been increasing in Latin America, sub-Saharan Africa, and East and Southeast Asia (Larson et al., 2002). And although sexual relationships remain heavily sanctioned for adolescents, primarily girls, in the Middle East and South Asia, research also points to increased cross-gender interaction among urban youth in these regions (Larson et al.).

Regardless of nation or milieu, there is most certainly a need for adolescents to develop skills for healthy management of sexual relationships. Early engagement in sexual intercourse has some negative consequences. The earlier a youth begins engaging in sexual intercourse, the more likely he or she is to become involved in delinquent behavior, problem drinking, and marijuana use (Armour & Haynie, 2007; Costa, Jessor, Donovan, & Fortenberry, 1995). One researcher found that while some adolescents experience mental health disruptions after first sexual intercourse, the majority do not (Meier, 2007).

Rates of sexual activity among teens in the United States are fairly comparable with those in Western Europe, yet the incidence of adolescent pregnancy, childbearing, and STIs in the United States far exceeds the level of most other industrialized nations (Feijoo, 2001). For instance, the Netherlands, France, and Germany have far better sexual outcomes for teens than the United States. Teens in those countries begin sexual activity at slightly later ages and have fewer sexual partners than teens in the United States. The teen pregnancy rate in the United States is eight times greater than the pregnancy rate in the Netherlands and Japan, nearly five times greater than the rate in Germany, nearly four times greater than the rate in France, and twice as high as in England, Wales, or Canada. The teenage abortion rate in the United States is nearly seven times the rate in the Netherlands, nearly three times the rate in France, and nearly eight times the rate in Germany. There are similar differences in rates of STIs among teens when comparing the United States with European countries (Advocates for Youth, 2002; Alan Guttmacher Institute, 2006a). This discrepancy is probably related to three factors: Teenagers in the United States make less use of contraception than teens in European countries, reproductive health services are more available in European countries, and sexuality education is more comprehensively integrated into all levels of education in most of Europe than in the United States (Feijoo, 2001; Huberman, 2001). It should be noted, however, that between 1995 and 2002, there was a decline in the percentage of U.S. teens having sexual intercourse before age 15, down from 19% to 13% for females and from 21% to 15% for males (Alan Guttmacher Institute, 2006a).

The popular press, including *The New York Times* and *The Washington Post,* has reported that oral sex has gained popularity among adolescents (Jarrell, 2000; Stepp, 1999). This information has, for the most part, been anecdotal, because as adolescent sexuality researcher Lisa Remez contends, obtaining parent consent to surveys about the sexual activity of their minor children can be difficult. There is a generalized fear that asking young people about sex will somehow lead them to choose to have sex, and the federal government has been reluctant to sponsor controversial research about the noncoital sexual behaviors of adolescents (Remez, 2000).

However, the 2002 National Survey of Family Growth (NSFG) was able to collect data on oral sex among people ages 15 to 44, and the data have been analyzed and reanalyzed by several organizations. The consensus is that the data show that 22% of females and 24% of males ages 15 to 19 who haven't had sexual intercourse have engaged in heterosexual oral sex. In addition, 83% of females and 88% of males who have had sexual intercourse have also engaged in heterosexual oral sex. It was also found that fewer than 1 in 10 adolescents who engaged in oral sex used condoms to protect against STIs (Mosher, Chandra, & Jones, 2005).

These findings raise some important questions for social workers who work with adolescents. Do adolescents think oral sex is less intimate—reserving sexual intercourse for that special person but engaging in fellatio and cunnilingus more casually? Adolescents know that oral sex prevents pregnancy, but are they aware that most STIs can also be contracted orally? What are the psychosocial effects of rape via coerced oral sex—do adolescents consider this rape if they don't consider oral sex as sex?

Sexual Orientation

As they develop as sexual beings, adolescents begin to discover the types of people that they find sexually attractive. **Sexual orientation** refers to erotic, romantic, and affectionate attraction to people of the same sex, the opposite sex, or both sexes. It can be understood along a continuum from completely heterosexual to bisexual to completely homosexual attractions. There are also questioning adolescents who are less certain of their sexual orientation than those who label themselves as heterosexual, bisexual, or gay/lesbian (Poteat, Aragon, Espelage, & Koenig, 2009). About 6.8% of youth responding to the U.S. National Health Survey reported having experienced same-sex attractions or same-sex relationships, but only a small group reported same-sex sexual behaviors, and even fewer identified themselves as gay, lesbian, or bisexual (cited in Savin-Williams & Diamond, 2004). Glover, Galliher, and Lamere (2009, pp. 92–93) suggest that sexual orientation should be conceptualized as a "complex configuration of identity, attractions, behaviors, disclosure, and interpersonal explorations."

Still, adolescence is the time when most people develop some awareness of their sexual orientation. In their comprehensive investigation of gay and lesbian sexuality, Marcel Saghir and Eli Robins (1973) found that most adult gay men and lesbians reported the onset of homosexual arousal, homosexual erotic imagery, and homosexual romantic attachment during early adolescence before age 15. More recent research has produced similar findings (Diamond, 2000). Recent studies indicate, however, that gay and lesbian youth may be "coming out" and accepting the homosexual identity at earlier ages than in prior eras (Saltzburg, 2004; Taylor, 2000).

> How does sexual orientation affect development during adolescence?

Gay and lesbian youth typically suffer from the awareness that they are different from most of their peers in an aspect of identity that receives a great deal of attention in our culture (Glover et al., 2009). Consider David Costa's conflict over his homosexuality. Dennis Anderson (1994) suggests that a "crisis of self-concept occurs because the gay adolescent senses a sudden involuntary joining to a stigmatized group" (p. 15). He goes on to elaborate:

To some gay and lesbian adolescents the experience of watching boys and girls in school walk hand-in-hand down the hallway, while their own desires must be kept secret, produces feelings of rage and sadness that are difficult to resolve. In addition to having no opportunity to experience social interactions with gay or lesbian peers, there is little likelihood that they will see gay or lesbian adult role models in their day-to-day lives. (p. 18)

Given the societal assumption of heterosexuality, many LGBQ (lesbian, gay, bisexual, questioning) youth are "creating, questioning, and sometimes even fighting their sexual identity" (Bond, Hefner, & Drogos, 2009, p. 35). In the process, they seek out information about sexual attraction, alternative sexual orientations, and the coming-out process. Research is indicating that the current generation of LGBQ youth uses the Internet to get this information and to begin the coming-out process. This provides a safe and anonymous venue for exploration and questioning as well as for initiating the coming out process; it can lead to greater self-acceptance before coming out to family and friends (Bond et al., 2009).

There is some question about whether research has captured the diversity within the sexual minority youth community. One research team focused on the psychosocial concerns of questioning youth and racial minority LGB youth. All LGB youth have been found to face increased victimization, but questioning youth have been found to face higher levels of victimization, substance abuse, and suicidal thoughts than other sexual minority youth (Poteat et al., 2009). It is possible that questioning youth are marginalized by both heterosexual and LGB peers. Bisexual youth also may be marginalized by the LG community. Although LGB youth of color experience discrimination based on sexual orientation, they may experience more discrimination based on race than on sexual orientation.

LGB adolescents who have disclosed their sexual orientation to parents have been found to have less internalized homophobia than those who have not disclosed to their parents. However, adolescents who have disclosed to their parents report that they had to undergo a period of verbal victimization from parents before they reached a point where parents were supportive (D'Augelli, Grossman, & Starks, 2005). One research team found that higher rates of family rejection are associated with poorer health outcomes. LGB young adults who reported high levels of family rejection during adolescence were 8.4 times more likely to report suicide attempt, 5.9 times more likely to report serious depression, 3.4 times more likely to use illegal drugs, and 3.4 times more likely to report unprotected sexual intercourse than LGB young adults who reported little or no family rejection. Latino men reported the highest level of family rejection related to sexual orientation in adolescence (Ryan, Huebner, Diaz, & Sanchez, 2009).

To forestall potential rejection from family and friends, the Parents, Families and Friends of Lesbians and Gays (PFLAG) (2001), a social movement with the goal of promoting a more supportive environment for gay males and lesbians, produced a brochure titled *Read This Before Coming Out to Your Parents*. This brochure lists 12 questions to ponder prior to coming out, reproduced in Exhibit 6.5. These are heavy questions for any adolescent, and there are still too few nonfamilial supports available to assist adolescents in resolving their questions related to sexual orientation or easing the process of coming out.

---

1. Are you sure about your sexual orientation?
2. Are you comfortable with your gay sexuality?
3. Do you have support?
4. Are you knowledgeable about homosexuality?
5. What's the emotional climate at home?
6. Can you be patient?
7. What's your motive for coming out now?
8. Do you have available resources?
9. Are you financially dependent on your parents?
10. What is your general relationship with your parents?
11. What is their moral societal view?
12. Is this your decision?

▲ **Exhibit 6.5**   Questions to Ponder Prior to Coming Out

SOURCE: Parents, Families and Friends of Lesbians and Gays, 2001.

Pregnancy and Childbearing

Approximately 750,000 adolescent girls ages 15 to 19 become pregnant each year in the United States (Guttmacher Institute, 2010). This is a pregnancy rate of 71.5 per 1,000 15- to 19-year-old women. The teen pregnancy rate declined 41% between 1990 and 2005. The majority of the decline was the result of more consistent use of contraceptives, but some of the decline was the result of teens delaying sexual activity. However, the teen pregnancy rate rose in 2006, with a 3% increase over 2005. It is too early to tell if this increase will begin a new trend upward. The teen pregnancy rate varies by race and ethnicity, with the pregnancy rate of Hispanic (127 per 1,000) and Black (126 per 1,000) females being almost three times that of non-Hispanic White females (44 per 1,000). The pregnancy rate among Black teens decreased 45% between 1990 and 2005, however. Of teen pregnancies, 57% end in birth, 29% end in abortion, and 14% end in miscarriage (Alan Guttmacher Institute, 2006a). Two thirds of teen pregnancies occur among 18- to 19-year-olds, an age by which many adolescents are taking on adult roles (Guttmacher Institute, 2010).

> What factors might be producing the recent fluctuations in the teen birthrate?

As discussed in Chapter 2, adolescent pregnancies carry increased physical risks to mother and infant, including less prenatal care and higher rates of miscarriage, anemia, toxemia, prolonged labor, premature delivery, and low birth weight. In many Asian, Eastern Mediterranean, African, and Latin American countries, the physical risks of adolescent pregnancy are mitigated by social and economic support (Hao & Cherlin, 2004). In the United States, however, adolescent mothers are more likely than their counterparts elsewhere to drop out of school, to be unemployed or underemployed, to receive public assistance, and to have subsequent pregnancies and lower educational and financial attainment. Teenage fathers may also experience lower educational and financial attainment (Bunting & McAuley, 2004).

The developmental tasks of adolescence are typically accomplished in this culture by going to school, socializing with peers, and exploring various roles. For the teenage mother, these avenues to development may be radically curtailed. The result may be long-lasting disadvantage. Consider Monica Golden's path. She obviously loves children and would like to have her own some day, but she would also like to become a pediatrician. If Monica were to become pregnant unexpectedly, an abortion would challenge her religious values and a baby would challenge her future goals.

Sexually Transmitted Infections

Youth have always faced pregnancy as a consequence of their sexual activity, but other consequences now include infertility and death as a result of **sexually transmitted infections (STIs).** The majority of sexually active adolescents used contraception the first time they had sexual intercourse, 74% of females and 82% of males, and even more at the most recent sexual intercourse, 83% of females of 91% of males (Alan Guttmacher Institute, 2006a). The condom is the most common form of contraception used. However, as discussed earlier, the NSFG study found that only 1 in 10 adolescents use protection when engaging in oral sex (Mosher et al., 2005). Health and sex education at home and in the schools often does not prepare adolescents for the difficult sexual decisions they must make, and they may be particularly ill-informed about STIs (Berne & Huberman, 2000). Recent research has found several contextual and personal factors to be associated with STIs, including housing insecurity, exposure to crime, childhood sexual abuse, gang participation, frequent alcohol use, and depression. These factors all appear to increase risky sexual behaviors (Buffardi, Thomas, Holmes, & Manhart, 2008).

Data collection on STIs is complicated for several reasons. Only five STIs—chlamydia, gonorrhea, syphilis, hepatitis A, and hepatitis B—are required to be reported to state health departments and the CDC, and these conditions are not always detected and reported. Some STIs, such as chlamydia and human papillomavirus (HPV), are often asymptomatic and go undetected. In addition, many surveys are not based on representative samples (Alan Guttmacher Institute, 2006b; Weinstock, Berman, & Cates, 2004). Therefore, the data presented in this discussion are the best estimates available. And, the best estimates available indicate that adolescents and young adults ages 15 to 24 constitute 25% of the sexually active population but account for almost half of the STI diagnoses each year (Guttmacher Institute, 2010; Weinstock et al.). Although rates of gonorrhea, chlamydia, and syphilis are above average in this age group, three STIs together account for nearly 90% of the new STIs among 15- to 24-year-olds each year; they are HPV, trichomoniasis, and chlamydia (Weinstock et al.). We discuss these three here as well as HIV, which is on the rise among adolescents.

- *Chlamydia.* Chlamydia trachomatis, or T-strain Mycoplasma, is the most commonly reported infectious disease in the United States. In 2007, approximately 1.1 million cases were reported to the CDC with more than half of these in females between the ages of 15 to 25 years (CDC, 2009f) (see Exhibit 6.6). Although the CDC recommends annual Chlamydia screening for all sexually active women under the age of 26, recent data show that less than half of these women are screened (NCQA, 2008). Chlamydia is typically transmitted through sexual contact but can also be spread nonsexually, through contact with the mucus or feces of an infected person. The symptoms of chlamydia include vaginal itching and discharge in women (although most women remain asymptomatic) or a thin, whitish discharge in men (approximately 40% remain asymptomatic). These symptoms appear one to three weeks after contact. Chlamydia is most often treated with antibiotics like azithromycin or doxycycline, but if left untreated can result in pelvic inflammatory disease (PID) and infertility.

- *HPV.* Human papillomavirus actually refers to a group of viruses, which has more than 100 different strains, more than 40 of which are genital. Approximately 6.2 million Americans get a new genital HPV infection each year. The CDC reports that at least 50% of sexually active men and women acquire genital HPV infection at some point in their lives and by age 50, at least 80% of women will have had a genital HPV infection (CDC, n.d.a). Estimating adolescent rates of HPV infection is difficult, but it has been estimated that approximately 30% of sexually active female adolescents are infected with HPV (Weinstock et al., 2004) and that HPV accounts for nearly half of the diagnosed STIs among 15–24-year-olds

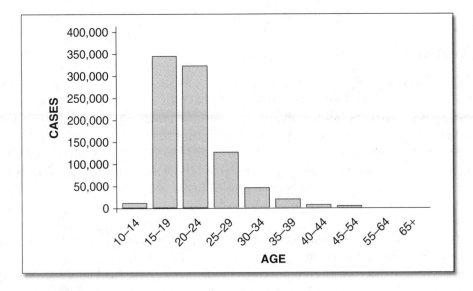

▲ **Exhibit 6.6**   Reported Cases of Chlamydia by Age, 2008

SOURCE: CDC, 2009f (http://www.cdc.gov/std/stats08/trends/htm).

each year (Guttmacher Institute, 2010). Genital HPV infection may be contracted during vaginal or anal intercourse or during childbirth. Most people who have a genital HPV infection do not show any signs or symptoms and therefore can unknowingly transmit the disease to sexual partners. Some people get visible genital warts. The warts usually begin as flesh-colored, painless bumps in the genital area that may then resemble tiny cauliflower florets. After sexual contact with an infected person, warts may appear within weeks or months or most often—not at all (CDC, n.d.a). Pap tests may reveal precancerous circumstances caused by HPV in women, but currently there are no tests to detect HPV in men. HPV has no cure. The warts, however, can be treated with imiquimod cream, podophyllin, podofilox, fluorouracil cream, trichloroacetic acid or with surgical, laser, or freezing treatments. Because the virus is always present in the body of someone who is infected, however, the warts often come back after treatment. Early treatment may prevent cancer of the cervix, vulva, or penis. In June of 2006, the U.S. Food and Drug Administration (FDA) approved the use of the vaccine Gardasil for females ages 9 to 26, which may prevent four strains of the human papillomavirus, which together cause 70% of cervical cancers and 90% of genital warts (FDA, 2006).

- *Trichomoniasis.* It is estimated that there were 7.4 million new cases of trichomoniasis in the United States in 2000, and that 25% of those cases occurred in 15- to 24-year-olds (Weinstock et al., 2004). Trichomoniasis is caused by Trichomonas vaginalis, a single-celled protozoan parasite. The parasite is transmitted by penis-to-vagina intercourse or vulva-to-vulva contact with an infected partner. Women can be infected by either men or women, but men are only infected by women. The vagina is the most common site of the infection in women, and the urethra is the most common site of infection in men (CDC, n.d.b). Most men with trichomoniasis do not have symptoms, but some men may have a temporary irritation inside the penis, mild discharge, or burning after urination or ejaculation. Symptoms are more common in women who may have a yellow-green vaginal discharge with a strong odor, discomfort during intercourse and urination, or irritation and itching in the vaginal area. In order to detect a trichomoniasis infection in men and women, a health care provider must conduct a physical examination and a laboratory test to diagnose the disease. Trichomoniasis can usually be cured with metronidazole, and both partners should be treated at the same time to eliminate the parasite (CDC, n.d.b).

- *HIV/AIDS.* Individuals infected with STIs are two to five times more likely than individuals not infected with STIs to acquire HIV infection transmitted through sexual contact (CDC, n.d.a). HIV attacks the immune system and is the virus that causes AIDS. HIV also reduces the body's ability to combat other diseases. Transmission of the virus can occur through unprotected sexual contact, shared drug paraphernalia, perinatal transmission from an HIV-infected mother to fetus or to newborn during childbirth, and through breastfeeding. Early in the HIV/AIDS epidemic, blood transfusions were another significant method of transmission, but safety measures have almost eliminated this as a method of transmission in the United States (Hutchison & Kovacs, 2007). In 2004, 50% of all newly diagnosed HIV/AIDS cases globally occurred in persons between the ages of 15 and 24 (UNAIDS, 2005). In the United States in that same year, 14% of all persons with newly diagnosed infections were under 25, but the number of people living with HIV/AIDS increased for the age group 15 to 19 between 2001 and 2004 (CDC, 2006b). Refer to Exhibit 6.7 to see the racial disparity in the U.S. AIDS infection rates for youth ages 13 to 19. Although White non-Hispanic youth comprise 63% of the U.S. adolescent population, they only make up 13% of the adolescent AIDS cases, whereas Black non-Hispanic youth only comprise 15% of the adolescent population but make up 73% of the adolescent AIDS cases. In 2006, a little less than 1 million persons were living with HIV/AIDS in the United States, an estimated 252,000 to 312,000 HIV-infected persons in the United States were unaware of their HIV infection, and an estimated 40,000 new HIV infections were expected to occur that year (CDC, 2006b). The CDC's latest HIV/AIDS Surveillance Report suggests that HIV diagnoses increased 15% from 2004 to 2007 in the 34 states that maintain long-term, name-based HIV reporting (CDC, 2008d). Most people infected with HIV carry the virus for years before it destroys enough CD4+ T cells for AIDS to develop. Symptoms of HIV infection may include swollen lymph nodes, unexplained weight loss, loss of appetite, persistent fevers, night sweats, chronic fatigue, unexplained diarrhea, bloody stools, skin rashes, easy bruising, persistent and severe headaches, and unexplained chronic dry cough, all of which can result from opportunistic infections. As of 2010, there is no cure for AIDS. Several anti-HIV drugs can slow the immune system destruction, but these have not been tested extensively with children or adolescents. HIV/AIDS education efforts continue to be paramount. The CDC reports that in the United States in 2007, 89.5% of high school students reported having been taught in school about HIV/AIDS, and 12.9% of high school students had been tested for HIV (not counting tests done when donating blood) (CDC, 2008d).

Some social workers who work with adolescents may encounter STI issues, but all social workers who work with adolescents should discuss STI prevention. Teaching communication skills to youth will probably benefit them the most, but in addition, they should be educated to:

- Recognize the signs and symptoms of STIs

- Refrain from sexual contact if they suspect themselves or a partner of having any of these signs or symptoms and instead get medical attention as soon as possible

- Use a latex condom correctly during sexual activity

- Have regular checkups that include STI testing

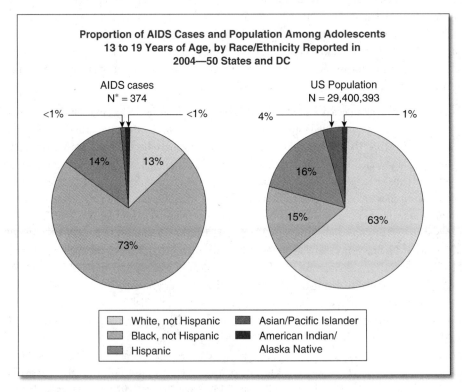

▲ **Exhibit 6.7**   Facts About AIDS and Adolescents

SOURCE: Centers for Disease Control and Prevention (http://www.cdc.gov/hiv/topics /surveillance/resources/slides/ adolescents/index.htm).

For AIDS information, the CDC has a confidential toll-free hotline in English and in Spanish (800-CDC-INFO or 800-232-4636). The American Social Health Association also provides an STI resource center at 919-361-8488 or www.ashastd.org.

POTENTIAL CHALLENGES TO ADOLESCENT DEVELOPMENT

Many adjustments have to be made during adolescence in all areas of life: physical, family relationships, school transitions, and career planning. Adjustments to biological changes are a major developmental task of young adulthood, family relationships are continuously renegotiated across the adolescent phase, and career planning begins in earnest for most youth in to mid- to late adolescence. Most adolescents have the resources to meet these new challenges and adapt. But, many adolescents engage in risky behaviors or experience other threats to physical and mental health. We have already looked at risky sexual behavior. Seven other threats to physical and mental health are discussed here: substance use and abuse, juvenile delinquency, bullying and other school and community violence, dating violence and statutory rape, poverty and low educational attainment, obesity and eating disorders, and depression and suicide.

Substance Use and Abuse

In adolescence, many youth experiment with the use of nicotine, alcohol, and other psychoactive substances, with the motivation to be accepted by peers or to cope with life stresses (Weichold, 2007). For example, Carl Fleischer's use of tobacco and marijuana has several likely effects on his general behavior. Tobacco may make him feel tense, excitable, or anxious, and these feelings may amplify his concern about his weight, his grades, and his family relationships. Conversely, the marijuana may make Carl feel relaxed, and he may use it to counteract or escape from his concerns.

High school students in the United States have a higher rate of illicit drug use than youth in other industrialized countries (Johnston, O'Malley, Bachman, & Schulenberg, 2004, 2005). However, between 2002 and 2008, rates of current use for youth aged 12 to 17 declined significantly for marijuana (from 8.2% to 6.7%), cocaine (from 0.6% to 0.4%), prescription-type drugs used for nonmedical purposes (from 4.0% to 2.9%), pain relievers (from 3.2% to 2.3%), stimulants (from 0.8% to 0.5%), and methamphetamine (from 0.3% to 0.1%) (SAMHSA, 2009a). Overall, in 2008, 9.3% of adolescents aged 12 to 17 were current illicit drug users: 6.7% used marijuana, 2.9% used prescription-type drugs for nonmedical purposes, 1.1% used inhalants, 1.0% used hallucinogens, and 0.04% used cocaine (SAMHSA, 2009a). Oxycontin (a narcotic) use, however, increased from 1.3% to 2.6% of eighth-graders. Also, 9.7% of 12th-graders abuse vicodin (another narcotic), and 7% of 12th-graders abuse cold medicines (National Institute on Drug Abuse, 2006). Alcohol continues to be the most widely used of all the drugs for adolescents. More than 10 million people aged 12 to 20 (26.4% of this age group) reported drinking alcohol in the past month according to 2008 statistics (SAMHSA, 2009a). Furthermore, approximately 6.6 million (17.4%) considered themselves binge drinkers, and 2.1 million stated they were heavy drinkers. Rates of current, binge, and heavy alcohol consumption for youth declined between 2002 and 2008; current use declined from 28.8% to 26.4% ; binge use from 19.3% to 17.4% ; and heavy use from 6.2% to 5.5% (SAMHSA, 2009a). Tobacco is considered a gateway drug to further substance use and abuse. According to the *National Survey on Drug Use and Health* (SAMHSA, 2009b), for youth aged 12 to 17, their past month use of any tobacco product declined between 2002 to 2008, going from 15.2% to 11.4%.

Despite industry claims that alcohol is not marketed to children, animation, adolescent humor, and rock music are prevalent in alcoholic beverage advertising. Moreover, in the first six months of 2001, 217 varieties of "malternatives" (such as Rick's Spiked Lemonade, Tequiza, Hooper's Hooch, Smirnoff Ice, Skyy Blue) were approved by the Bureau of Alcohol, Tobacco, and Firearms (CASA, 2002). Forty-one percent of youth ages 14 to 18 have tried these sweet-tasting and colorfully packaged alcoholic beverages (CASA, 2002).

Decision Making About Substance Use

When asked why youth choose to use alcohol, adolescents cite the following reasons: to have a good time with friends, to appear adultlike, to relieve tension and anxiety, to deal with the opposite sex, to get high, to cheer up, and to alleviate boredom. When asked why youth use cocaine, the additional responses were to get more energy and to get away from problems. Overall drug use at a party is also cited quite often as a reason (Engels & Knibbe, 2000). The following factors appear to be involved in adolescents' choice of drugs: the individual characteristics of the drug, the individual characteristics of the user, the availability of the drug, the current popularity of the drug, and the sociocultural traditions and sanctions regarding the drug (Segal & Stewart, 1996).

Adolescents who choose to abuse substances seem to differ from those who do not. In a 12-year longitudinal study, Richard Jessor (1987) found that adolescent problem drinkers differ from other adolescents in their personal qualities, their social environment, and their other patterns of behavior. Problem drinkers are less likely to hold traditional values about education, religion, or conformity. They perceive large differences between their family's values and their peers' values, are more influenced by their peers, and have peers who are also engaged in problem drinking. Finally, problem drinkers are also more likely to participate in other risk-taking behaviors, such as sexual activity and delinquency (Jessor). More recently, Jessor and colleagues have tested the stability of these findings using six adolescent samples that range the years from 1974 to 1992, two national samples and four local community samples. Even though there were significant changes in the sociohistorical context over the years of the six samples, the researchers found that the personal and environmental correlates of problem drinking remained the same across all samples and were the same correlates as summarized above from Jessor's longitudinal study (Donovan, Jessor, & Costa, 1999).

> What are the risk factors for substance abuse in adolescence?

Moreover, some adolescents are clearly more at risk for substance abuse than others. American Indian youth and Alaska Native youth begin using alcohol and other drugs at a younger age than other youth, use them more frequently, use a greater amount, and use more different substances in combination with each other (Cameron, 1999; Novins, Beals, Shore, & Manson, 1996). The death rate caused by substance abuse among American Indian youth is twice that of other youth (Pothoff et al., 1998). In response to this social need, drug treatment to Native American teens is undergoing a rapid change, with direct service provided by the tribes, employing mainly Native American staff, and using traditional Native American healing approaches in combination with standard addiction treatment approaches (Novins et al., 1996; Novins, Fleming, Beals, & Manson, 2000). It is too early to know how successful these new approaches will be.

Consequences of Substance Use and Abuse

Chemical substances pose a threat to the health of adolescents, because substance abuse affects metabolism, internal organs, the central nervous system, emotional functioning, and cognitive functioning (Segal & Stewart, 1996; Weichold, 2007). Alcohol and opiates can cause severe intoxication, coma, and withdrawal symptoms. Sedative drugs can depress the nervous and respiratory systems; withdrawal may lead to disturbances in breathing, heart function, and other basic body functions. Intravenous use of cocaine has been linked to adolescent cases of hepatitis, HIV, heart inflammation, loss of brain tissue, and abnormally high fever. Extended use of inhalants can cause irreparable neuropsychological damage. And finally, substances can weaken the immune system and increase a youth's likelihood of disease or general poor health. Preliminary evidence suggests that exposure to alcohol and other substances during adolescence, a time of rapid brain development, may alter neurocognitive functioning and lead to later misuse of substances. Indeed, most adults who are addicted to substances developed the substance abuse problem before age 25 (Spear, 2002; Weichold, Emans, Woods, & DuRant, 2007).

As mentioned earlier, substance use can also affect the decision to engage in sexual activity. After substance use, youth are more likely to engage in sexual activity and are less likely to use protection; thus, they are more likely to become pregnant or impregnate and to contract a STI (Brooks-Gunn & Furstenberg, 1989; Segal & Stewart, 1996; Shrier et al., 1996). In general, adolescents who use tobacco products, alcohol, marijuana, and other substances are more likely to be sexually active and to have more sexual partners (CASA, 2002; Lowry et al., 1994).

Juvenile Delinquency

Almost every adolescent breaks the rules at some time—disobeying parents or teachers, lying, cheating, and perhaps even stealing or vandalizing. As we've seen, many adolescents smoke cigarettes and drink alcohol and some skip school or stay out past curfew. For some adolescents, this behavior is a phase, passing as quickly as it appeared. Yet for others, it becomes a pattern and a probability game. Although most juvenile delinquency never meets up with law enforcement, the more times young people offend, the more likely they are to come into contact with the juvenile justice system.

In the United States, persons older than 5 but younger than 18 can be arrested for anything for which an adult can be arrested. (Children under 6 are said not to possess *mens rea,* which means "guilty mind," and thus are not considered capable of criminal intent.) In addition, they can be arrested for what are called **status offenses,** such as running away from home, skipping school, violating curfew, and possessing tobacco or alcohol—behaviors not considered crimes when engaged in by adults. When adolescents are found guilty of committing either a crime (by adult standards) or a status offense, we refer to their behavior as **juvenile delinquency.**

The Office of Juvenile Justice and Delinquency Prevention reports that the number of delinquency cases, at approximately 1.7 million, has stayed approximately the same from 2000 to 2005 (Sickmund, 2009). Although the number of delinquency cases for females has increased (from 19% in 1985 to 27% in 2005), it is still a relatively small proportion of the overall delinquency caseload at 464,700 in 2005 (as compared with 1,233,200 for males in that same year). Meanwhile, of the total U.S. population in 2005, White youth comprised 78%, Black youth comprised 17%, Asian youth (including Native Hawaiian and other Pacific Islander) comprised 4%, and Native American (including Alaska Native) comprised 1%; but 64% of the delinquency cases handled in 2005 were for White youth, 33% were for Black youth, 1% for Asian American youth, and 1% for Native American youth. The rate at which petitioned cases were waived to criminal court was 10% greater for Black youth than the rate for White youth, and the rate at which youth in adjudicated cases were ordered to residential placement was 24% greater for Black youth than for White youth (Sickmund).

According to the 2006 National Report for Juvenile Offenders and Victims by the U.S. Department of Justice and the Office of Juvenile Justice and Delinquency Prevention (OJJDP):

- By age 17, 33% of all youth said they had been suspended from school at least once, 18% had run away from home (i.e., had at least once left home and stayed away overnight without a parent's prior knowledge or permission), and 8% had belonged to a gang.

- By age 17, a greater proportion of juveniles reported that they had committed an assault with the intent of seriously hurting the person than reported ever having run away from home, sold drugs, carried a handgun, stolen something worth more than $50, or belonged to a gang.

- Males were significantly more likely than females to report ever being suspended from school (42% vs. 24%) or ever belonging to a gang (11% vs. 6%) and were four times more likely to report ever carrying a handgun (25% vs. 6%).

- White youth were significantly less likely than Black or Hispanic youth to report ever belonging to a gang.

- With the exception of selling drugs, the proportions of youth who reported committing the above behaviors at age 17 are either the same or less than the proportions reporting the same behaviors at earlier ages (Snyder & Sickmund, 2006).

In 2008, U.S. law enforcement agencies made 2.11 million arrest of persons younger than 18, at a rate of 3.8 arrests per 100,000 juveniles ages 10 to 17 (Puzzanchera, 2009). Also in 2008, juveniles comprised 16% of all violent crime arrests and 26% of all property crime arrests. In addition, 11% of all murder victims were younger than 18. And, although African American youth comprised 16% of the juvenile population aged 10 to 17, Black youth were involved in 52% of the Violent Crime Index arrests and 33% of the Property Crime Index arrests in 2008 (Puzzanchera).

In October of 2009, the National Youth Gang Center (OJJDP) merged with the National Gang Center (BJA) and is now recognized as the National Gang Center (2010). In 2007, the National Youth Gang Survey estimated that more than 27,000 gangs are active in the United States: 40.7% are in larger cities, 33.5% in smaller cities, 19.9% in suburban counties, and 5.9% in rural counties (National Youth Gang Center, 2009). Demographically, 49% of gang members in the United States are Hispanic/Latino, 35% are African American/Black, 9% are Caucasian/White, 7% are "other." In 2006, 36.5% of gang members were juveniles (under 18) and 63.5% were adults (18 and over). OJJDP researchers Snyder and Sickmund (2006) found that some problem behaviors cluster—or are likely to contribute to other problem behaviors. They contend that juveniles who reported belonging to a gang were twice as likely as other juveniles to have committed a major theft, three times more likely to have sold drugs, four times more likely to have committed a serious assault, and five times more likely to have carried a handgun (p. 72).

Other Threats to Physical and Mental Health

Several other threats to physical and mental health may come to the attention of social workers, including bullying and other school and community violence, dating violence and statutory rape, poverty and low educational attainment, and obesity and eating disorders.

Bullying and Other School and Community Violence

School bullying has come to the attention of social workers because of its short- and long-term effects on children's physical and mental health. School bullying can be defined as physical or verbal attack or intimidation with the purpose of causing fear, distress, or harm to the victim (Farrington & Ttofi, 2009). The Department of Health and Human Services, through the Health Resources and Services Administration (HRSA), has created a website with resources for youth and adults regarding bullying and cyberbullying (www.stopybullyingnow.hrsa.gov). The most comprehensive U.S. study of bullying reports that 13% of sixth- to tenth-grade students bully, 10% are victims, and 6% are both victims and bullies (Nansel et al., 2001). Further research suggests that bullying can be a first step to additional aggressive acts such as assault or even murder (Sampson, 2009).

In 2002, on average, four juveniles were murdered daily in the United States. That was the third leading cause of death for juvenile ages 12 to 17, with only unintentional injury and suicide more common among young people

(Snyder & Sickmund, 2006). An estimated 1,600 persons under age 18 were murdered in the United States in 2002— 10% of all persons murdered that year. About one third (36%) of these juvenile murder victims were female. About 1 in 10 (8%) were ages 12 to 14, and 4 in 10 (43%) were ages 15 to 17. More than half (51%) of juvenile murder victims in 2002 were White, 45% were Black, and 4% were either Native American or Asian. With White youth comprising 78% of the U.S. resident juvenile population in 2002 and Black youth comprising 16%, the murder rate for Black youth in 2002 was more than four times the White murder rate (see Exhibit 6.8). This disparity was seen across victim age groups and increased with victim age. More than three quarters of juvenile homicides are committed with firearms (Snyder & Sickmund, 2006).

These murders are not happening at schools, however, so although school shootings have received media attention and have thus increased public concern for student safety, school-related violent deaths account for less than 1% of homicides among school-aged children and youth (Anderson et al., 2001). In fact, in 2001, students were safer in school and on their way to and from school than they were in 1992 because crimes against juveniles fell substantially between 1992 and 2001 both in and out of school (Snyder & Sickmund, 2006).

Juveniles are, however, more likely than adults to be both victims and perpetrators of violence. A 2005 Bureau of Justice Statistics (BJS) report (Baum, 2005) summarized National Crime Victimization Survey data for the years 1993 to 2003 to document the trends in nonfatal violent victimizations of youth ages 12 to 17. On average from 1993 through 2003, juveniles ages 12 to 17 were about 2.5 times more likely than adults (i.e., ages 18 and older) to be the victim of a nonfatal violent crime. That means that in a typical group of 1,000 youth ages 12 to 17, 84 experienced nonfatal violent victimizations, compared with 32 per 1,000 persons ages 18 and older (Baum).

Data collected in 2007 as part of the Youth Risk Behavior Survey (YRBS) reveal that on at least one of the 30 days preceding the survey, 18% of high school students had carried a weapon and 5.2% had carried a gun. And during the 12 months that preceded the survey, 4.2% had been in a physical fight for which they had to be treated by a doctor or nurse (CDC, 2008d).

Even if they are not perpetrators or direct victims of violence, many U.S. adolescents witness violence. One study of 935 urban and suburban youth found that more than 45% had witnessed a shooting or stabbing or other serious act of violence during the previous year (O'Keefe, 1997). Moreover, participating in violence and/or witnessing violence can be a significant predictor of aggressive acting-out behavior for both male and female adolescents (O'Keefe) as well as a

Victim Age	2002 Homicide Rate*		
	White	Black	Black to White Ratios
0–17	1.4	6.0	4.2
0–5	1.9	6.5	3.4
6–11	0.4	1.6	3.6
12–14	0.7	2.8	4.4
15–17	3.3	18.1	5.5

▲ **Exhibit 6.8**   Homicide Rates for Black and White Youth, 2002

SOURCE: Snyder & Sickmund, 2006, p. 22

*Homicide rates are the number of homicides per 100,000 juveniles in the age group.

significant source of depression, anger, anxiety, dissociation, posttraumatic stress, and total trauma symptoms (Fitzpatrick & Boldizar, 1993; Singer, Anglin, Song, & Lunghofer, 1995).

Dating Violence and Statutory Rape

Acquaintance rape can be defined as forced, manipulated, or coerced sexual contact by someone known to the victim. Women between 16 and 24 are the primary victims of acquaintance rape, but junior high school girls are also at great risk (U.S. Department of Justice Bureau of Justice Statistics, 2000).

Nationwide in 2007, 9.9% of high school students responded to the YRBS that they had been hit, slapped, or physically hurt on purpose by their boyfriend or girlfriend at least once over the course of the 12 months that preceded the survey (CDC, 2008d). Young women, ages 16 to 24, experience the highest rates of relationship violence (Rennison & Welchans, 2000). One study found that approximately one in five female high school students reported being physically and/or sexually abused by a dating partner (Silverman, Raj, Mucci, & Hathaway, 2001).

The YRBS data reveal that 7.8% of the students stated that they had been physically forced to have sexual intercourse when they did not want to. Overall, the prevalence of having been forced to have sexual intercourse was higher among Black (10.5%) and Hispanic (8.8%) than White (7%) students. The prevalence of having been forced to have sexual intercourse was higher among 11th-grade (8.5%) and 12th-grade (8.3%) than among 9th-grade (6.6%) students (CDC, 2008d).

Because of their underreporting, date rape and dating violence may be even more prevalent among adolescents than we have data to suggest. And, unfortunately, researchers have found that adolescent girls who report a history of experiencing dating violence are more likely to exhibit other serious health-risk behaviors (Silverman et al., 2001).

Statutory rape occurs when individuals have voluntary and consensual sexual relations and one individual is either too young or otherwise unable (e.g., mentally retarded) to legally consent to the behavior. The majority of victims of statutory rape are females ages 14 to 15 whereas 82% of the rape perpetrators of female victims were adults ages 18 and older (Snyder & Sickmund, 2006). Not only were most offenders adults, but most were also substantially older than their victims. About half of the male offenders of female victims in statutory rapes reported to law enforcement were at least six years older than their victims. For male victims, the difference was even greater; in these incidents, half of the female offenders were at least nine years older than their victims (Snyder & Sickmund).

Poverty and Low Educational Attainment

Additional threats to physical and mental health may also stem from poverty and low educational attainment, both of which are rampant in the nonindustrialized world. In the United States, 12% of all persons lived at or below their poverty thresholds in 2002. This proportion was far greater for persons under age 18 (18%) than for those ages 18 to 64 (11%) and those above age 64 (10%) (Snyder & Sickmund, 2006).

The education institution is becoming a prime force in perpetuating, if not exacerbating, economic inequalities. A 2006 report by the Education Trust indicates that current trends in the education institution are the principle reason that there is less upward mobility in the social class structure in the United States today than there was 20 years ago, and less mobility in the United States than in any European nation except England (Haycock, 2006). High school graduation rates are a key measure of whether schools are making adequate yearly progress under the provisions of the No Child Left Behind (NCLB) legislation (see Chapter 5 for a fuller discussion of NCLB). As it turns out, most school districts do not have a system for calculating graduation rates, and there are major holes in their reported data. Furthermore, researchers have analyzed the reported state data and found that all states inflated their graduation rates, ranging from a 1% to a 33% inflation rate (see Hall, 2005). These researchers estimate that graduation rates for students who entered high school in 2000 ranged from 51% in South Carolina to 86% in New Jersey. More than half of nongraduates were African American, Latino, or Native American, indicating an overrepresentation because these groups together comprise about one third of students in public school nationally. Even when students in impoverished rural and urban neighborhoods graduate, their high schools may not have offered the types of courses that college admissions departments require. There is also a critical shortage of teachers who are trained to teach English language learners who often must navigate very large high school settings (Hood, 2003).

Obesity and Eating Disorders

As suggested earlier, the dietary practices of some adolescents put them at risk for overall health problems. These practices include skipping meals, usually breakfast or lunch; snacking, especially on high-calorie, high-fat, low-nutrition snacks; eating fast foods; and dieting. Poor nutrition can affect a youth's growth and development, sleep, weight, cognition, mental health, and overall physical health.

An increasing minority of adolescents in the United States is obese, and the risks and consequences can be profound (Hedley et al., 2005; James, 2006). As demonstrated in Exhibit 6.9, the 2003 to 2004 National Health and Nutrition Examination Survey (NHANES) found that an estimated 17% of children and adolescents (ages 2 to 19), more than 12.5 million, are overweight (defined as BMI-for-age at or above the 95th percentile of the 2000 CDC BMI-for-age growth charts for the United States) (Ogden, Carroll, Curtin, Lamb, & Flegal, 2010; Ogden et al., 2006). This represents an increase from 7.2% to 13.9% among 2- to 5-year-olds, from 11% to 19% among 6- to 11-year-olds, and from 11% to 17% among 12- to 19-year-olds since the NHANES III 1988–1994 statistics (Ogden et al., 2006, 2010).

It is important to note that this is a worldwide trend. According to one report (James, 2006), almost half of the children in North and South America, about 38% of children in the European Union, and about 20% of children in China, were expected to be overweight by 2010. Significant increases were also expected in the Middle East and Southeast Asia. Mexico, Brazil, Chile, and Egypt have rates comparable with fully industrialized countries.

This chapter has emphasized how tenuous self-esteem can be during adolescence, but the challenges are even greater for profoundly overweight or underweight youth. Overweight adolescents may suffer exclusion from peer groups and discrimination in education, employment, marriage, housing, and health care (DeJong, 1993). Carl Fleischer has already begun to face some of these challenges. He thinks of himself as a "fat, slow geek" and assumes females would not be interested in him because of his weight.

Age (years)[1]	NHANES 1963–65 1966–70[2]	NHANES 1971–74	NHANES 1976–80	NHANES 1988–94	NHANES 1999–2000	NHANES 2001–02	NHANES 2003–04
2–5	–	5	5	7.2	10.3	10.6	13.9
6–11	4.2	4	6.5	11.3	15.1	16.3	18.8
12–19	4.6	6.1	5	10.5	14.8	16.7	17.4

▲ **Exhibit 6.9** Prevalence of Overweight Among Children and Adolescents Ages 2 to 19 Years, for Selected Years (1963–2004)

SOURCE: National Center for Health Statistics, 2006 (http://www.cdc.gov/nchs/data/hestat/overweight/overwght_child_03.htm).

[1]Excludes pregnant women starting with 1971–1974. Pregnancy status not available for 1963–1965 and 1966–1970.

[2]Data for 1963–1965 are for children 6 to 11 years of age; data for 1966–1970 are for adolescents 12 to 17 years of age, not 12 to 19 years.

Research is exposing the breadth of the problem. Almost 16% of the high school students in the nationwide sample of the YRBS are overweight (CDC, 2008d). Yet, 29.3% of that same sample described themselves as slightly or very overweight, and 45.2% were trying to lose weight. Moreover, within the 30 days preceding the survey, 11.8% of the high schools students had gone without eating for 24 hours or more, 5.9% had taken diet pills, powders, or liquids, and 4.3% had vomited or taken laxatives to lose weight or to keep from gaining weight (CDC, 2008d).

Girls' body dissatisfaction reflects the incongruence between the societal ideal of thinness and the beginning of normal fat deposits in pubescent girls. Joan Brumberg (1997) used unpublished diaries to do a historical analysis of femaleness in adolescence. Her analysis suggests a strong trend for girls in the United States to define themselves more and more through their appearance. She suggests that we now have a situation in which girls are reaching sexual maturity at a younger age in a highly sexualized culture that exploits girls' normal sensitivity to their changing bodies, often using the prepubescent female body as a sexual symbol. And using that prepubescent female as the ideal may be why the American Psychiatric Association (APA) suggests that most eating disorders like **anorexia nervosa** and **bulimia nervosa** begin in adolescence (APA, 2000b).

- Anorexia nervosa means literally "loss of appetite due to nerves," but the disorder is actually characterized by a dysfunctional body image and voluntary starvation in the pursuit of weight loss. According to the *Diagnostic and Statistical Manual of Mental Disorders (DSM-IV-TR)* (APA, 2000a), the essential features of anorexia nervosa are refusal to maintain minimally normal weight, fear of gaining weight, and disturbance in body image.

- Bulimia nervosa is characterized by a cycle of binge eating; feelings of guilt, depression, or self-disgust; and purging (producing vomiting or evacuation of the bowels). The *DSM-IV-TR* (APA, 2000a) suggests that individuals with bulimia nervosa are also excessively influenced by body shape and weight, and exhibit binge eating followed by purging at least twice a week for at least 3 months.

The American Psychiatric Association (2000b) estimates that 0.5% to 3.7% of women suffer from anorexia nervosa in their lifetime and about 1% of female adolescents have anorexia nervosa. An estimated 1.1% to 4.2% of women have bulimia nervosa in their lifetime. And 50% of people who have had anorexia nervosa develop bulimia or bulimic patterns (APA, 2000b).

Depression and Suicide

Epidemiological studies suggest that as many as 8.3% of adolescents in the United States may have a major depressive disorder, with early adolescents particularly vulnerable to depression. Parents are less likely to recognize depression in their adolescents than the adolescents themselves. Although there are no gender differences in depression prior to adolescence, during adolescence, girls are about twice as likely as boys to have a major depressive disorder (Sadock & Sadock, 2007). Research suggests that African American and Mexican American youth may be at increased risk for depression (Roberts, Roberts, & Chen, 1997).

Adolescent depression may also be underdiagnosed, among males and females alike, because it is difficult to detect. Many parents and professionals expect adolescence to be a time of ups and downs, moodiness, melodrama, anger, rebellion, and increased sensitivity. There are, however, some reliable outward signs of depression in adolescents: poor academic performance, truancy, social withdrawal, antisocial behavior, changes in eating or sleeping patterns, changes in physical appearance, excessive boredom or activity, low self-esteem, sexual promiscuity, substance use, propensity to run away from home, and excessive family conflict. Additional symptoms of depression not unique to adolescence include pervasive inability to experience pleasure, severe psychomotor retardation, delusions, and a sense of hopelessness (Sadock & Sadock, 2007).

The many challenges of adolescence sometimes prove overwhelming. We have already discussed the risk of suicide among gay male and lesbian adolescents. Nationwide, during the 12 months preceding the 2007 YRBS survey, 28.5%

of high school students reported having felt so sad or hopeless almost every day for 2 weeks or more that they stopped doing some usual activities (CDC, 2008d). Furthermore, 14.5% had seriously considered attempting suicide, 11.3% had made a suicide plan, 6.9% had actually attempted suicide, and 2.0% had made a suicide attempt that resulted in an injury, poisoning, or overdose that had to be treated by a doctor or nurse (CDC, 2008d). Overall, suicide is the third leading cause of death for adolescents in the United States (NIMH, 2000). In 2001, 3,971 youth ages 15 to 24 took their own lives (Anderson & Smith, 2003). Of those 3,971 deaths, 86% were male and 14% were female, and 54% used firearms. During that same year, American Indian and Alaskan Natives had the highest rate of suicides (Anderson & Smith). Cheryl King and Christopher Merchant (2008) have analyzed the research on factors associated with adolescent suicidal thinking and behavior. They identified a number of risk factors found in the research: social isolation, low levels of perceived support, childhood abuse and neglect, and peer abuse.

RISK FACTORS AND PROTECTIVE FACTORS IN ADOLESCENCE

The U.S. Department of Health and Human Services has proposed 12 adolescent health objectives for its Healthy People 2020 campaign (Office of Disease Prevention & Health Promotion, 2009), which attempt to minimize risk factors and maximize protective factors in adolescence. They are as follows:

1. Increase educational achievement of adolescents and young adults.

2. Increase the percentage of adolescents who participate in extracurricular and out-of-school activities.

3. Increase the percentage of adolescents who have been tested for HIV.

4. Increase the proportion of adolescents who have a wellness checkup in the past 12 months.

5. Increase the percentage of middle and high schools that prohibit harassment based on a student's sexual orientation or gender identity.

6. Decrease the percentage of adolescents who did not go to school at least once in the past month because of safety concerns.

7. Decrease the percentage of public middle and high schools with a violent incident.

8. Increase the percentage of adolescents who are connected to a parent or other positive adult caregiver.

9. Decrease the percentage of adolescents who have been offered, sold, or given an illegal drug on school property.

10. Increase the percentage of vulnerable adolescents who are equipped with the services and skills necessary to transition into an independent and self-sufficient adulthood.

11. Decrease the proportion of adolescents and young adults who are involved with criminal activity.

12. Increase the percentage of schools with a school breakfast program.

There are many pathways through adolescence; both individual and group-based differences result in much variability. Some of the variability is related to the types of risk factors and protective factors that have accumulated prior to adolescence. Emmy Werner and Ruth Smith (2001) have found, in their longitudinal research on risk and protection, that females have a better balance of risk and protection in childhood, but the advantage goes to males during adolescence. Their research indicates that the earlier risk factors that most predict poor adolescent adjustment are a childhood spent in chronic poverty, alcoholic and psychotic parents, moderate to severe physical disability, developmentally disabled siblings, school problems in middle childhood, conflicted relationships with peers, and family disruptions. The most important earlier protective factors are easy temperament, positive social orientation in early childhood, positive peer relationships in middle childhood, nonsex-typed extracurricular interests and hobbies in middle childhood, and nurturing from nonparental figures.

Much attention has also been paid to the increase in risk behaviors during adolescence (Silbereisen & Lerner, 2007b). In the United States, attention has been called to a set of factors that are risky to adolescent well-being and serve as risk factors for adjustment in adulthood as well. These factors include use and abuse of alcohol and other drugs; unsafe sex, teen pregnancy, and teen parenting; school underachievement, failure, and dropout; delinquency, crime, and violence; and youth poverty. The risk and resilience research indicates, however, that many youth with several of these risk factors overcome the odds. Protective factors that have been found to contribute to resilience in adolescence include family creativity in coping with adversity, good family relationships, faith and attachment to religious institutions, social support in the school setting, and school-based health services. As social workers, we will want to promote these protective factors while, at the same time, working to prevent or diminish risk factors.

> What are the implications of research on risk and protection for social work program development?

Critical Thinking Questions 6.3

Adolescence is a time of rapid transition in all dimensions of life, physical, emotional, cognitive, social, and spiritual. What personal, family, cultural, and other social factors help adolescents cope with all of this change? What factors lead to dissatisfaction with body image and harmful or unhealthy behaviors? How well does contemporary society support adolescent development?

IMPLICATIONS FOR SOCIAL WORK PRACTICE

Adolescence is a vulnerable period. Adolescents' bodies and psyches are changing rapidly in transition from childhood to adulthood. Youth are making some very profound decisions during this life course period. Thus, the implications for social work practice are wide ranging.

- When working with adolescents, meet clients where they are physically, psychologically, and socially—because that place may change frequently.

- Be familiar with typical adolescent development and with the possible consequences of deviations from developmental timelines.

- Be aware of, and respond to, the adolescent's level of cognition and comprehension. Assess the individual adolescent's ability to contemplate the future, to comprehend the nature of human relationships, to consolidate specific knowledge into a coherent system, and to envision possible consequences from a hypothetical list of actions.

- Recognize that the adolescent may see you as an authority figure who is not an ally. Develop skills in building rapport with adolescents.

- Assess the positive and negative effects of the school environment on the adolescent in relation to such issues as early or late maturation, popularity/sociability, culture, and sexual orientation.

- Where appropriate, advocate for change in maladaptive school settings, such as those with Eurocentric models or homophobic environments.

- Provide information, support, or other interventions to assist adolescents in resolving questions of sexual identity and sexual decision making.

- Where appropriate, link youth to existing resources, such as extracurricular activities, education on STIs, prenatal care, and gay and lesbian support groups.

- Provide information, support, or other interventions to assist adolescents in making decisions regarding use of tobacco, alcohol, or other drugs.

- Develop skills to assist adolescents with physical and mental health issues, such as nutritional problems, obesity, eating disorders, depression, and suicide.

- Participate in research, policy, and advocacy on behalf of adolescents.

- Work at the community level to develop and sustain recreational and social programs and places for young people.

KEY TERMS

acquaintance rape

anorexia nervosa

bulimia nervosa

gender identity

generalized other

gonads

individuation

juvenile delinquency

masturbation

menarche

postconventional moral reasoning

primary sex characteristic

psychological identity

puberty

rites of passage

secondary sex characteristic

sex hormones

sexual orientation

sexually transmitted infections

 (STIs)

social identity

spermarche

status offenses

statutory rape

ACTIVE LEARNING

1. Recalling your own high school experiences, which case study individual would you most identify with—David, Carl, or Monica? For what reasons? How could a social worker have affected your experiences?

2. Visit a public library and check out some preteen and teen popular fiction or magazines. Which topics from this chapter are discussed, and how are they dealt with?

3. Have lunch at a local high school cafeteria. Be sure to go through the line, eat the food, and enjoy conversation with some students. What are their concerns? What are their notions about social work?

WEB RESOURCES

ABA Juvenile Justice Center
www.abc-directory.com/site/2790593

Site presented by the American Bar Association Juvenile Justice Center contains links to juvenile justice-related sites.

Add Health
www.cpc.unc.edu/projects/addhealth/pubs/published

Site presented by the Carolina Population Center contains a reference list of published reports of The National

Longitudinal Study of Adolescent Health (Add Health), which includes measures of social, economic, psychological, and physical well-being.

Adolescent Health
www.cdc.gov/healthyyouth/az/index/htm

Site maintained by the Centers for Disease Control and Prevention contains links to a variety of health topics related to adolescents, including alcohol and drug use, sexual behavior, nutrition, youth suicide, and youth violence.

DukeLEARN
http://dukebrainworks.com

Site presented by DukeLEARN, an interdisciplinary team of neuroscientists, psychologists, physicians, and social scientists at Duke University contains links to research and publication directed to public understanding of the brain.

Sexually Transmitted Infections Information
www.ashastd.org

Site maintained by the American Social Health Association, which is dedicated to improving the health of individuals, families, and communities, with an emphasis on sexual health and a focus on preventing sexually transmitted diseases.

Youth Risk Behavior Surveillance System (YRBSS)
www.cdc.gov/HealthyYouth/yrbs/index.htm

Site presented by the National Center for Chronic Disease Prevention and Health Promotion contains latest research on adolescent risk behavior.

CHAPTER

7

Young Adulthood

Holly C. Matto

OPENING QUESTIONS

- Why is it important for social workers to understand transitional markers associated with young adulthood from a multidimensional perspective, recognizing systemic-structural impacts on development as well as the psychosocial factors that are traditionally studied?

- How do social class, culture, and gender affect the transition to adulthood?

- Given that our educational institution serves as gatekeeper to economic opportunities, what are the ways in which our educational system identifies and responds to the changing labor market trends in order to create viable long-term opportunities for all of society's young adults?

KEY IDEAS

As you read this chapter, take note of these central ideas:

1. A new phase called "emerging adulthood" (ages 18 to 25) has been proposed as a time when individuals explore and experiment with different life roles, occupational interests, educational pursuits, religious beliefs, and relationships—with more focus than in adolescence but without the full commitment of young adulthood.

2. Traditional transitional markers associated with young adulthood have included obtaining independent housing, establishing a career, developing significant partnerships that lead to marriage, and becoming a parent; current research suggests that financial independence and authority in decision making are the markers considered important by emerging adults.

3. In young adulthood, cognitive capacities become more flexible; "moral conscience" expands in social awareness, responsibility, and obligation; and religious beliefs are often reexamined.

4. Identity development continues into adulthood and is not static, but is dynamic and ever evolving through significant interpersonal relationships.

5. Young adults struggle with the Eriksonian psychosocial crisis of intimacy versus isolation—the challenge of finding meaningful connections to others without losing oneself in the process.

6. Labor force experience and connection in young adulthood is associated with psychological and social well-being; advanced education is increasingly important in attaining quality jobs.

7. Discrimination and multilevel racism-related stressors can directly and indirectly affect entry into young adulthood.

Case Study 7.1

Johnny Nunez's Parenting Role and Newly Jobless Status

Johnny Nunez is a 20-year-old male living in a predominately mixed ethnicity working-class community in a medium-sized Midwestern town. Johnny's paternal grandfather emigrated from Mexico, originally settling in the southwestern United States. As a child, Johnny's father migrated north to the upper Midwestern states with his family during the summers to work in the migrant beet fields. When Johnny was in late adolescence, his father, tired of migrating by seasons, ultimately decided to stay in the upper Midwest and married a Midwestern farm girl from town. Two years after they married, Johnny was born. Johnny's early years were pleasantly unremarkable, and he seemed to be a genuinely curious and "good" boy. Despite attending an underresourced semirural high school with a fairly high dropout rate, Johnny completed his high school degree, with the encouragement and support of a devoted school social worker who recognized Johnny's intellectual capacity and motivation. The social worker was able to successfully link Johnny to the high school classes that maximally engaged his interests and kept him in school, at a time when so many of his friends were dropping out to pursue employment opportunities. Now at age 20, Johnny is the primary caretaker of his biological 18-month-old son and his girlfriend's 3-year-old son and 6-year-old daughter. Johnny, his 22-year old girlfriend, and their three children all live with Johnny's father in a modest brick rambler that is typical of the housing stock in their working-class neighborhood.

Johnny's girlfriend, Samantha, works full time at a nearby sandwich shop located in a gas station food mart. Johnny, too, wants to be working full time but is currently unemployed, after recently losing his full-time job at a big-box store on the outskirts of town. Although the store told him they had to "employ cost-cutting measures to respond to the economic recession," Johnny believes he was targeted for the layoff because he had missed a number of days from work to take his 18-month old son to the doctor for recurrent ear infections. Shortly after Johnny lost his full-time job, he was able to pick up some part-time work at a nearby auto repair shop, utilizing the mechanical skills developed at age 11 when he watched his uncles work on their own trucks and neighbors' cars. Johnny enjoyed the work, but even at part-time status the shop continued to cut his hours more and more each week, until he was down to only about 15 hours per week, with those hours never guaranteed. With inconsistent income, Johnny and his girlfriend could not justify paying for the in-home child care they were using for their two young boys. Even at the "family friend" reduced rate (the in-home daycare provider is a friend of the family's), they decided it made better financial sense for Johnny to stay home with the two young children while continuing to look for full-time employment. Johnny is in relatively good health, though he does use an inhaler for the chronic asthma problem that he developed during his elementary school years.

Case Study 7.2

Sheila Henderson's Long-Awaited Family Reunification

Sheila Henderson, 25 years old, her boyfriend, David, 27 years old, and her 4-year-old daughter, Johanna, from a previous relationship, all said goodbye at the family readiness center at Fort Bragg, North Carolina, 18 months ago, as Sheila departed for her second tour to Afghanistan as a lieutenant in the infantry division of the United States Army. The family hasn't seen each other since, although they have participated in weekly family video calls. While Sheila was on tour, she sustained a minor closed head injury when she was participating in a training exercise with her unit in Afghanistan. Her injury was deemed "minor" and not likely to cause significant or long-term impairment, but Sheila can't help but notice a change in her ability to handle

(Continued)

(Continued)

emotions. She notices new limitations in her ability to concentrate and says she becomes easily agitated or "set off" over minor inconveniences, which is "not like her." And she cries more than she used to. She is opposed to calling her injury a disability and can't help but think that maybe it's just all in her mind anyway. She regularly experiences a variety of emotions, from frustration, anger, resentment at her time spent away from family and friends, to loyalty and pride in serving her country. She occasionally feels guilty for taking so much time to "dwell" on her own challenges when she knows so many others have died or have been more seriously incapacitated while serving their country in Afghanistan and Iraq.

Sheila knows she is going to struggle with transitioning back to life with her family but is giddy with excitement to be reunited with her daughter, who will be turning 5 shortly and entering kindergarten in the fall, and to rejoin her boyfriend whom she says has had the most difficulty with her absence. Her boyfriend, though officially a civilian working as an accountant, considers the military community where they live to be family. There is an informal ethos in their community that military families care for each other's children when one or more parents are deployed, and David has benefited from this support while Sheila's been away. What concerns him most is Sheila's transition back into their family life. He can't help but wonder how she will respond to the year and a half of developmental changes Johanna has gone through, and how she will jump back into the role of disciplining her behavior and facilitating the family routines and schedule that David has worked so hard to establish. In fact, of Johanna's 4.5 years, Sheila has really only been physically present for about a year and half of that time. David wonders how the routine will play itself out now and how the family will reunite together. There is also the lingering anticipation and unpredictability of the next possible deployment, and that keeps him up at night. He wonders why Sheila seems so at ease with the uncertainty, and he hopes he will be able to gain her strength in negotiating the ambiguity of their family's shared life space in the future. But for now, he's overjoyed that she's home. They have a lot of catching up to do.

Case Study 7.3

Carla Aquino's Transition to Parenthood

Carla Aquino is a 30-year-old Latina living in a large West Coast city. She graduated from the local college with a degree in business and is currently employed as an accountant. She has been married for 4 years to a man she met through her church and is 4 month's pregnant with her first child.

In the midst of her excitement about the new baby, Carla is anxious about how she will juggle the new caregiving responsibilities with her career aspirations. She knows she wants to have a meaningful career and to be a good mother but is very concerned about managing multiple demanding roles. Her husband, a consultant, works long hours and travels frequently for his job. Carla has discussed with the social worker at the company Employee Assistance Program the disruption, strain, and lack of continuity she feels in their marriage as a result of her husband's intense work schedule, but she also knows that he makes good money and she respects the fact that he enjoys his work.

Carla and her husband are actively involved in their church group, where they meet monthly with other young adults for spirituality discussions. They also participate in the church's various outreach projects, and

Carla volunteers 2 hours each week with Streetwise Partners. However, they live in a very transient part of the city, and she is struggling to develop more meaningful connections with neighbors.

One of Carla's close friends, Marissa, was just diagnosed with breast cancer, which came as a shock to family and friends, because Marissa is only in her late 20s and does not have a family history of cancer. Carla has had a lot of difficulty dealing with her friend's diagnosis and worries about her own risks for breast cancer, as she remembers her aunt had a malignant tumor removed 2 years ago.

Carla's mother died of liver failure the year before Carla graduated from high school, but Carla's father is still alive and is a significant support in her life. Most of Carla's extended family live nearby or in towns outside the central city, although some relatives still live in the Dominican Republic. Carla's mother-in-law, Jan, lives close by and just recently got divorced after 27 years of marriage. Jan relies heavily on her son and daughter-in-law for emotional (and some financial) support during this life transition.

Carla and her husband both say that they are having trouble dealing with the myriad roles they are faced with (such as young professionals, marriage partners, supportive family members), and are considering how the new role of first-time parents will affect their current lives and future life choices.

A DEFINITION OF YOUNG ADULTHOOD

Defining young adulthood and the transitional markers that distinguish this period from adolescence and middle adulthood has been the challenge and life's work of a number of developmental scholars. A broad challenge has been to determine a framework for identifying the developmental characteristics of young adulthood. For example, is a young adult one who has reached a certain biological or legal age? One who has achieved specific physiological and psychological milestones? Or perhaps one who performs certain social roles? Research, theory, and scholarly thinking about young adulthood present a variety of perspectives related to each of these dimensions. Current research suggests that the transitional markers that have traditionally defined adulthood in decades past, such as marriage and childbearing, are no longer the most salient markers characterizing the young adult in today's soci-

> Is it biological age, psychological age, social age, or spiritual age that best defines young adulthood?

ety (e.g., see Settersten, Furstenberg, & Rumbaut, 2005). For example, in 1960, three fourths (77%) of women and 65% of men left home, completed school, became financially independent, got married, and had at least one child by age 30. In 2000, not even half (46%) of women and 31% of men had done so by age 30 (Furstenberg, Kennedy, McCloyd, Rumbaut, & Settersten, 2003, cited in Draut, 2005, p. 6).

Typical chronological ages associated with young adulthood are 22 to 34 (Ashford, LeCroy, & Lortie, 2006) or 18 to 34 (Settersten et al., 2005), and the international chronological standard for defining adulthood is age 18 (Lloyd, Behrman, Stromquist, & Cohen, 2006). Researchers estimate that the 18- to 24-year-old cohort will increase by 21% by 2010 (Sum, Fogg, & Mangum, 2000). Some scholars define young adulthood even more broadly, from the age of 17 to about 40 (Levinson, 1978). Other scholars assert that such broad ranges encompass too much variety of experience:

If ages 18 [to] 25 are young adulthood, what would that make the thirties? Young adulthood is a term better applied to the thirties, which are still young but are definitely adult in a way that the years 18 [to] 25 are not. It makes little sense to lump late teens, twenties, and thirties together and call the entire period young adulthood. The period from ages 18 to 25 could hardly be more distinct from the thirties. (Arnett, 2000, p. 479)

Grossman (2005) calls those persons who are no longer adolescents and yet not adults by conventional standards "twixters" and suggests that this period can extend to age 29; Gordon and Shaffer (2004) call this developmental transition "adultscence." Similarly, "freeters," in Japan, are those individuals aged 15 to 34 who are typically unattached to the full-time labor market and are not enrolled in higher education, often working in part-time, temporary positions (K. Newman, 2008).

In this book, however, we are using a broad range of approximately 18 to 40. Although a wide chronological age range can be useful in providing some chronological boundaries around this developmental period, from a life course perspective it is more useful to examine the social role transitions, important life events, and significant turning points associated with young adulthood. The major challenges facing young adults are attaining independent financial stability and establishing autonomy in decision making, although attaining financial independence is becoming more delayed as advanced educational credentials are increasingly necessary to secure quality employment (Arnett, 2004). Young adults ages 18 to 25 agree when asked about what they see as markers of entry into young adulthood (Arnett, 1998). Young persons who do not attend college are as likely as college students to say that making independent decisions based on their own values and belief systems is important for defining adult status (Arnett, 2000). And, there are international differences in home-leaving timing. For example, in Japan 64% of unmarried emerging adult men aged 25 to 29 reside with their parents, and 80% of unmarried emerging adult women reside with their parents (K. Newman, 2008). Social role changes young people face during the transition from adolescence to adulthood include the following:

- Leaving home and becoming responsible for housing

- Taking on work and/or education tasks

- Marrying or committing to a significant partnership

- Raising children and caring for others

- Starting a career

- Making time commitments to their families of origin and to their newly created families

Some scholars also define young adulthood as the point at which young persons become functioning members of the community, demonstrated by obtaining gainful employment, developing their own social networks, and establishing independent housing (Halpern, 1996). From a psychosocial perspective, this period is seen as a time of progressive movement out of an individualized and egocentric sense of self and into greater connection with significant others. Social role transitions in young adulthood are summarized in Exhibit 7.1.

Timing of these transitions and psychological readiness for adopting adult roles are important factors in the individual's life course trajectory. However, research indicates that individual variation in the timing and sequence of transitions—when and in what order the individual leaves home, starts a career, and forms a family, for example—does not have large-scale effects on the individual's eventual socioeconomic status (Marini, 1989). These findings contradict the popular notion that people who don't "grow up" on schedule will never "amount to much." However, the timing and sequencing of child-bearing, entry into postsecondary educational institutions, and labor market attachment may have wide-ranging effects on economic viability and security over the long-term. For example, very young single-parents employed in full-time, low-wage work without adequate access to affordable quality child care or health care will be faced with difficulty in affording and finding time for the additional higher education necessary to obtain employment with better wages, better benefits, and better work schedules (e.g., see Edin & Lein, 1997). However, it is important to consider that other macro context variables may be interacting with individuals' planned sequences to influence life chances. We can see this in the dynamic and nonlinear nature of Johnny Nunez's labor market attachment, illustrating that neither occupational skill set nor personal desire necessarily contributed to sustained

- Leaving home
- Gaining financial independence
- Gaining independence in decision making
- Pursuing an education or vocational skills
- Making a partnership commitment
- Becoming a parent
- Renegotiating relationships with parents
- Engaging with the community and the wider social world

▲ **Exhibit 7.1**   Social Role Transitions in Young Adulthood

employment, rather the larger economic environment of a national recession seems to be interacting with what Johnny suspects to be negative perception of his commitment to the workplace because of his family demands, adversely affecting his labor market opportunities.

Nevertheless, young adulthood is a challenging and exciting time in life. Young people are confronted with new opportunities and the accompanying stressors associated with finances, occupational planning, educational pursuits, development of significant relationships, and new family roles (Newman & Newman, 2009). Kenneth Keniston, an eminent developmental scholar writing in the late 1960s, during an era of student activism and bold social expression, described young adulthood as a time of struggle and alienation between an individual and society (Keniston, 1966). Young adulthood remains a period of intrapersonal and interpersonal questing as well as a period of critiquing and questioning of social

▲ **Photo 7.1**   Young adulthood is a challenging and exciting time in life, bringing new opportunities and new challenges.

norms. Young persons grapple with decisions across several polarities: independence versus relatedness, family versus work, care for self versus care for others, and individual pursuits versus social obligations.

THEORETICAL APPROACHES TO YOUNG ADULTHOOD

Two prominent developmental theories, promulgated by Erik Erikson and Daniel Levinson, specifically address this life course phase.

Erikson's Psychosocial Theory

Erik Erikson's psychosocial theoretical framework is probably one of the most universally known approaches to understanding life course development. Young adulthood is one of Erikson's original eight stages of psychosocial development (refer back to Exhibit 3.7). Erikson described it as the time when individuals move from the identity fragmentation, confusion, and exploration of adolescence into more intimate engagement with significant others (Erikson, 1968, 1978).

Individuals who successfully resolve the crisis of **intimacy versus isolation** are able to achieve the virtue of love. An unsuccessful effort at this stage may lead the young adult to feel alienated, disconnected, and alone. A fear

> How is the capacity for intimacy affected by earlier social relationships?

that exists at the core of this crisis is that giving of oneself through a significant, committed relationship will result in a loss of self and diminution of one's constructed identity. To pass through this stage successfully, young adults must try out new relationships and attempt to find a way to connect with others in new ways while preserving their individuality (Erikson, 1978; Fowler, 1981).

For example, we might wonder about the relational context of Sheila's family of origin and how it might be influencing her current relationships. What were the relationship templates that were established when she was zero to 5 years old? How are these relationships being replicated in her current family, particularly in her daughter? How are Sheila's own intimacy needs being addressed with so many geographic disruptions and work that is engaging but intense, and at times unpredictable and physically and emotionally risky?

Levinson's Theory of Life Structure

Daniel Levinson (1978) describes adulthood as a period of undulating stability and stress, signified by transitions that occur at specific chronological times during the life course. He initially developed his theory based on interviews with men about their adult experiences; later he included women in the research (1996). From his research he developed the concept of **life structure,** which he described as the outcome resulting from specific decisions and choices made along the life course in such areas as relationships, occupation, and childbearing. He considered the ages of 17 to 33 to be the **novice phase** of adulthood. The transition into young adulthood, which occurs during the ages of 17 to 22, includes the tasks of leaving adolescence and making preliminary decisions about relationships, career, and belief systems; the transition out of this phase, which occurs about the age of 30, marks significant changes in life structure and life course trajectory.

During the novice phase, young persons' personalities continue to develop, and they prepare to differentiate (emotionally, geographically, financially) from their families of origin (Levinson, 1978). The transition to adulthood takes hold primarily in two domains: work and relationships. Levinson suggested that it may take up to 15 years for some individuals to resolve the transition to adulthood and to construct a stable adult life structure.

Building on Levinson's concepts, others have noted that cultural and societal factors affect life structure choices during young adulthood by constraining or facilitating opportunities (Newman & Newman, 2009). For example, socioeconomic status, parental expectations, availability of and interactions with adult role models, neighborhood conditions, and community and peer group pressures may all contribute to a young person's decisions about whether to marry early, get a job or join the military before pursuing a college education or advanced training, or delay childbearing. Social and economic factors may directly or indirectly limit a young person's access to alternative choices, thereby rigidifying a young person's life structure. Along these lines, many researchers discuss the strong link between social capital and human capital, suggesting that a family's "wealth transfer" or extent of familial assets, such as the ability to pay for children's college education, is influential in opening up or limiting young adults' opportunities for advanced education and viable employment (Lui, Robles, Leonard-Wright, Brewer, & Adamson, 2006; Rank, 2005).

Johnny Nunez's father chose to opt out of the migratory lifestyle that he experienced growing up, risking the established livelihood of his family's migrant farm work to preserve stability and rootedness in community for his own family. That served his son, Johnny, well. In his Midwestern community Johnny was able to build a social network that helped him to do well through elementary school, graduate from high school, and develop vocational skills (e.g., auto-mechanic skills). Carla Aquino may find herself making decisions to curtail some of her career aspirations in order to fulfill her familial obligations and responsibilities as a new parent. Especially in young adulthood, life structures are in constant motion, changing with time and evolving as new life circumstances unfold.

Decisions made during the young adulthood transition, such as joining the military, forgoing postsecondary education, or delaying childbearing, may not accurately or completely represent a young person's desired life structure or goals. Social workers need to explore goal priorities and the resources and obstacles that will help or hinder the individual in achieving these goals. Social workers are also often called on to help young adults negotiate conflicting, incompatible, or competing life roles throughout this novice phase, such as renegotiating family and work responsibilities as parenthood approaches.

Arnett's "Emerging" Adulthood

A number of prominent developmental scholars who have written about the stages of adolescence and young adulthood in advanced industrial countries have described phenomena called "prolonged adolescence," "youthhood," or "psychosocial moratorium," which represent an experimentation phase of young adulthood (Arnett, 2000; Erikson, 1968; Settersten et al., 2005; Sheehy, 1995). Jeffrey Jensen Arnett has gone one step further, defining a phase he terms **emerging adulthood** in some detail (Arnett, 2000, 2004; Arnett & Tanner, 2005). He describes emerging adulthood as a developmental phase distinct from both adolescence and young adulthood, occurring between the ages of 18 and 25 in industrialized societies (Arnett, 2000, p. 470). There is considerable variation in personal journeys from emerging adulthood into young adulthood, but most individuals make the transition by age 30 (Arnett, 2000). Arnett conceptualized this new phase of life based on research showing that a majority of young persons ages 18 to 25 believe they have not yet reached adulthood and that a majority of people in their 30s do agree they have reached adulthood.

> What historical trends are producing "emerging adulthood"?

According to Arnett, identity exploration has become the central focus of emerging adulthood, not of adolescence (Arnett, 2006, 2007). Emerging adulthood is a period of prolonged exploration of social and economic roles where young people try out new experiences related to love, work, financial responsibilities, and educational interests without committing to any specific lasting plan. The social role experimentation of adolescence becomes further refined, more focused, and more intense, although commitment to adult roles is not yet solidified. Arnett explains this adulthood transition using an organizing framework that includes cognitive, emotional, behavioral, and role transition elements (Arnett & Taber, 1994).

Most young persons in emerging adulthood are in education, training, or apprenticeship programs working toward an occupation; most individuals in their 30s have established a more solid career path and are moving through occupational transitions (e.g., promotion to leadership positions and recognition for significant accomplishments). Studies do show more occupational instability during the ages 18 to 25 as compared with age 30 (Rindfuss, Cooksey, & Sutterlin, 1999). Indeed, Arnett (2007) suggests that emerging adulthood can be an "unstructured time" characterized by a lack of attachment to social institutions, where young people are moving out from their families of origin, have not yet formed new families of their own, and are moving out of prior educational systems and into new vocational, educational, or employment sectors (p. 25).

Although marriage has traditionally been cited as a salient marker in the adulthood transition, current research shows that marriage has not retained its high status as the critical benchmark of adulthood. Today, independent responsibility for decision making and finances seems to be more significant in marking this transition than marriage is (Arnett, 1998). Overall, the emphasis in emerging adulthood is on trying out new roles without the pressure of making any particular commitment (Schwartz, Cote, & Arnett, 2005). The transition, then, from *emerging* adulthood into *young* adulthood is marked by solidifying role commitments. Newer research shows that, across race and ethnicity, the difference between those who follow a **default individualization** pathway (adulthood transitions defined by circumstance and situation, rather than individual agency) versus a **developmental individualization** pathway (adulthood transitions defined by personal agency and deliberately charted growth opportunities in intellectual, occupational, and psychosocial domains) is a firmer commitment to goals, values, and beliefs for those in the developmental individuation pathway (Schwartz et al., p. 204). In addition, these researchers found that personal agency, across race and ethnicity, is associated with a more flexible and exploratory orientation to adulthood commitments, and is less associated with premature closure and circumscribed commitment.

Residential stability and mobility is another theme of this transition. Emerging adults in their early 20s may find themselves at various times living with family, living on their own in independent housing arrangements yet relying on parents for instrumental support, and living with a significant partner or friends. Indeed, residential instability and mobility is typically at its height in the mid-20s (Rindfuss et al., 1999). In our case examples, Johnny Nunez, although he most likely considers himself an adult, is a parent still living with his own father to get by. Sheila, too, experiences residential instability and considers the military a primary residence when deployed for months at a time. Thus, a traditional definition of the separation-individuation process may not be appropriately applied to emerging adulthood. True "separation" from the family of origin may appear only toward the end of young adulthood or, perhaps for some, during the transition to middle adulthood.

Demographic changes over the past several decades, such as delayed marriage and childbearing, have made young adulthood a significant developmental period filled with complex changes and possibilities (Arnett, 2000; Sheehy, 1995). Current global demographic trends suggest a similar picture. Overall, globally, family size has decreased, the timing of first marriage is being delayed, including a decrease in teenage marriages, and there are overall decreases in adolescent labor accompanied by increases in educational attainment. However, in some countries like Pakistan, the delay in first marriage has been attributed to a rise in the rate of adolescent girls in the labor market (see Lloyd et al., 2006; White, 2003). In addition, there is similarity in adulthood transitioning trends between developing countries and more economically developed countries, with East Asian countries showing the highest trend similarities and sub-Saharan African countries showing the least similarities (Behrman & Sengupta, 2006). Specifically, there has been an increased reliance on finding employment outside the family, an emphasis on more formal schooling, rather than family-based learning, a decreased gender gap, and greater transiency in young adulthood (Behrman & Sengupta).

Recent fertility data reported in *The Economist* ("Go Forth and Multiply a Lot Less," 2009) suggest a worldwide trend in declining fertility rates (the number of children a woman is projected to have during her lifetime), even in poor and developing countries, which have typically yielded larger fertility rates. Scholars believe that the disparity between women's desired and actual number of children has decreased in recent years in part because of increased access to family planning and literacy programs that have remarkably grown in countries such as Iran, where such education for women just decades ago was negligible (i.e., in 1976, 10% of rural Iranian women aged 20 to 24 were literate; today it is 91%) (p. 30). These changing demographic trends have other societal ramifications, one of which is the potential to make it easier for women across the globe to transition to the formal workplace. A chart in *The Economist* ("Go Forth and Multiply a Lot Less") article from 2007 data shows a clear association between countries' fertility rates and the economy. Countries with fertility rates above the replacement rate of 2.1 (such as Ghana and India) have lower income per person, while countries that have maintained fertility rate stability at or below the replacement rate of 2.1 (such as China, Brazil, Iran, South Korea, United States) have higher income per person.

Cultural Variations

Another advantage of the theory of emerging adulthood is that it recognizes diversity. Individual routes of development (the timing and sequence of transitions) are contingent on socialization processes experienced within family, peer groups, school, and community. Specifically, environmental opportunities, expressed community attitudes, and family expectations may all influence the timing and sequencing of transitions during emerging adulthood. Socially constructed gauges of adulthood—such as stable and independent residence, completion of education, entry into a career path, and marriage or significant partnership—hold varying importance across families and cultures.

> How do culture and socioeconomic status affect the transition to adulthood?

For some young persons, decisions may be heavily weighted toward maintaining family equilibrium. For example, some may choose not to move out of the family home and establish their own residence in order to honor the family's expectation that children will continue to live with their parents, perhaps even into their 30s. For others, successful adult development may be defined through the lens of pragmatism; a young person may be expected to make decisions based on immediate, short-term, utilitarian outcomes. For example, they may be expected to enter the labor force and establish a career in order to care for a new family and release the family of origin from burden. Carla Aquino seems to be struggling to uphold several Latina social norms, as seen through her emotional and financial commitments to her immediate and extended family, efforts to maintain a meaningful connection to her church, and creation of a family of her own. However, the multiple role demands experienced are considerable, as her own personal goals of maintaining a professional identity, being a good wife, and giving back to the community compete for Carla's time and emotional energy.

One recent study examined the home-leaving behavior of poor and nonpoor emerging adults in the United States. Using a longitudinal data set and a family economic status measure that included a federal poverty line indicator and childhood public assistance receipt, the authors found significant home-leaving and returning differences between poor and nonpoor emerging adults (De Marco & Cosner Berzin, 2008). Specifically, having a family history of public welfare assistance, dropping out of high school, and becoming a teen parent were the characteristics most likely to predict leaving the family home before age 18 years old. Repeated home-leaving (leaving, returning, leaving again) was more frequent for nonpoor as compared with poor emerging adults. And when they left home, nonpoor emerging adults were more likely than poor emerging adults to transition to postsecondary educational opportunities (De Marco & Cosner Berzin).

International research that has focused specifically on foster youth aging out of care suggests that such youth face significant transitioning risks, such as homelessness, substance abuse, and involvement with the criminal justice system (Tweddle, 2007, p.16). More successful transitioning outcomes for former foster youth, such as finding stable housing and employment, are associated with having had a strong social support system and problem-solving skill development before leaving care (Stein, 2005; Tweddle).

Culture and gender also have significant influence on young adult roles and expectations (Arnett & Taber, 1994). Social norms may sanction the postponement of traditional adult roles (such as marriage) or may promote marriage and childbearing in adolescence. There may be different family expectations about what it means to be a "good daughter" or "good son," and these expectations may be consistent or inconsistent with socially prescribed gender roles, potentially creating competing role demands. For example, a young woman may internalize her family's expectations of going to college and having a career while at the same time being aware of her family's expectations that her brothers will go directly into a job to help support the family and her college expenses. In addition, this woman may internalize society's message that women can "do it all"—have a family and career and yet see her friends putting priority on having a family and raising children. As a result, she may feel compelled to succeed in college and a career to make good on the privilege that her brothers did not have while at the same time feeling anxious about putting a career over creating a new family of her own.

For example, in examining the life course priorities of Appalachian emerging adults aged 19 to 24, Brown, Rehkopf, Copeland, Costello, and Worthman (2009) found that high family poverty, and particularly the combination of poverty and parental neglect, was associated with emerging adults' lower educational goals. In addition, the experience of traumatic stressors was associated with lowered economic attainment priorities among Appalachian emerging adults.

Some environments may offer limited education and occupational opportunities. Economic structures, environmental opportunities, family characteristics, and individual abilities also contribute to variations in transitioning during emerging adulthood. Young adults with developmental disabilities tend to remain in high school during the adulthood transitioning years of 18 to 21, as compared with their peers without such disabilities who are more likely to continue on to college or enter the workforce. Research suggests that more inclusive postsecondary environments that offer higher education opportunities for young adults with developmental disabilities, and the necessary accommodations for such adults to succeed, can increase their social and academic skills as well as facilitate productive interactions between young adults with and without disabilities (Casale-Giannola & Kamens, 2006). Some studies have shown that Latina mothers of young adults with developmental disabilities encourage family-centered adulthood transitioning, with less emphasis on traditional markers of independence and more emphasis on the family's role in the young adults' ongoing decision making, with such mothers reporting that their young adults' social interactions were more important to them than traditional measures of productivity (Rueda, Monzo, Shapiro, Gomez, & Blacher, 2005).

Individuals who grow up in families with limited financial resources or who are making important transitions during an economic downturn, have less time for lengthy exploration than others do and may be encouraged to make occupational commitments as soon as possible. Certainly Johnny Nunez is struggling with the financial pressure of the current economic recession and would like to quickly become re-employed. Although he enjoys caring for his children, he feels that he *should* be the breadwinner in the family.

Indeed, research shows that childhood socioeconomic status is an important mediating factor in young adult transitions (Smyer, Gatz, Simi, & Pedersen, 1998). For example, Astone, Schoen, Ensminger, and Rothert (2000) examined the differences between "condensed" (or time-restricted) and "diffuse" (or time-open) human capital development, with findings suggesting that a diffuse educational system offers opportunities for school reentry across the life course, which may be beneficial to young people who do not immediately enter higher education because of family or economic reasons, such as going into the military or entering the labor force. And, more specifically, they found that military service after high school increased the probability of returning to higher education for men, but not for women.

A family's economic background and resources are strongly associated with the adult status of the family's children; high correlations exist between parents' income and occupational status and that of their children (Rank, 2005). For example, about one third (34%) of youth from low-income families go on to college with 83% of youth from high-income families (Hair, Ling, & Cochran, 2003). Individuals with greater financial stability often have more paths to choose from and may have more resources to negotiate the stressors associated with this developmental period.

Multigenerational Concerns

In today's society, young persons are increasingly becoming primary caretakers for elderly family members. Such responsibilities can dramatically affect a young adult's developing life structure. Family life, relationships, and career may all be affected (Dellmann-Jenkins & Blankemeyer, 2009; Dellmann-Jenkins, Blankemeyer, & Pinkard, 2001). The demographic trend of delaying childbearing, with an increase of first births for women in their 30s and 40s and a decrease of first births to women in their 20s (Ashford et al., 2006), suggests that young adults are also likely to face new and significant role challenges as primary caretakers for their own aging parents. This can result in young adults caring for the generation ahead of them as well as the generation behind them. A recent Associated Press article ("Premature Births Worsen U.S. Infant Death Rates," 2009) cited a report from the U.S. Centers for Disease Control and Prevention on the link between premature births and infant mortality in the United States, with 1 in 8 premature births (defined as birth before 37 weeks' gestation) contributing to the United States' 30th ranking worldwide in infant death. Causes of premature birth are thought to be related to maternal risk factors, such as smoking, obesity, infection, and health care industry practices, such as early caesarian section delivery, induced labor, fertility treatments, and lack of access to prenatal care for some segments of the pregnant populations (e.g., poor, low-income women). In addition to the special, intensive care premature babies need in the immediate year postbirth, such infants are also at risk for cognitive delays, vision, hearing and learning disorders, which are often detected when children enter formal schooling. Therefore, for sandwich-generation families with children who have special physical, emotional, and/or learning needs, the challenge of providing the necessary care for their children while simultaneously providing care for their parents can be overwhelming.

The concern is that young adults will face a substantial caregiving burden, trying to help their aging parents with later-in-life struggles while nurturing their own children. We might see a shorter period of "emerging adulthood" for many people, which would mean that they have less opportunity to explore, to gain a sense of independence, and to form new families themselves. There may be less support for the notion of giving young people time to get on their feet and establish a satisfactory independent adulthood. In addition, young adults may increasingly experience the emotional responsibilities of supporting late-in-life divorcing parents or parents deciding to go back to school at the same time these young adults may be considering advanced educational opportunities themselves.

Carla Aquino and her husband are clearly facing these multigenerational role demands as they become the main social support for Jan at the same time that they are trying to get ahead in their careers and prepare for their new baby. Luckily, Carla and her husband have the financial resources and an adequate support network themselves (Carla's father, some extended family, and their church) to help with logistical problem solving, such as finding day care, and to help them deal effectively with the emotional stressors of these role demands.

Critical Thinking Questions 7.1

Which transitional markers do you see as the best indicators that one has become an adult? Why did you choose these particular markers? How do the stories of Johnny Nunez, Sheila Henderson, and Carla Aquino fit with the developmental markers you have chosen?

PHYSICAL FUNCTIONING IN YOUNG ADULTHOOD

Physical functioning is typically at its height during early adulthood. But as young adults enter their 30s, an increased awareness of physical changes—changes in vision, endurance, metabolism, and muscle strength—is common (e.g., Bjorklund & Bee, 2008). With new role responsibilities in family, parenting, and career, young adults may also spend less time in exercise and sports activities than during adolescence and pay less attention to their physical health. And at the same time, young adults ages 18 to 34 are the least insured when it comes to health care coverage as compared with any other age cohort (Draut, 2005). However, many young adults make an effort to maintain or improve their physical health, committing to exercise regimens and participating in wellness classes (such as yoga or meditation). They may choose to get more actively involved in community recreational leagues in such sports as hockey, soccer, racquetball, and Ultimate Frisbee. Sometimes physical activities are combined with participation in social causes, such as Race for the Cure runs, AIDS walks, or organized bike rides.

Behavioral risks to health in emerging and young adulthood may include unprotected sex. The potential for sexually transmitted infections, including HIV, is related to frequent sexual experimentation, substance use (particularly binge drinking), and smoking or use of other tobacco products.

According to the Substance Abuse and Mental Health Administration's most recent data from the National Survey on Drug Use and Health, one fifth (19.6%) of young adults aged 18 to 25 years old used illicit drugs in 2008, which was

▲ **Photo 7.2** Young adults may choose to get more actively involved in community recreational leagues.

higher than the rate for youth ages 12 to 17 (9.3%) and for adults over the age of 26 (5.9%). The nonmedical use of pain medications for this age group during 2008 was 4.6%, up from 4.1% in 2002. Illicit drug use for adults aged 18 years and older showed highest rates for the unemployed (19.6%) and lower rates for part-time (10.2%) and full-time (8.0%) employment status (SAMHSA, 2009a).

Data from the Drug Abuse Warning Network (DAWN) showed that 2 million drug-related emergency department (ED) visits occurred in 2004. Cocaine, then marijuana, heroin, stimulants, and other drugs represent an ordered account of the drug-prevalence linked to these ED visits (DHHS, 2006a). The National Hospital Ambulatory Medical Care Survey showed an increase from 1993 to 2003 of 19% in ED visits by adults ages 22 to 49, with 11.4% of alcohol-related ED visits accounted for by adolescents and young adults under age 21 and half (53.2%) occurring by adults ages 21 to 44. Young adults ages 15 to 24 had the highest injury-related emergency ED visits, with two thirds (66.7%) of alcohol-related visits characterized by injury. In addition, African Americans, across age cohorts, had an 86% higher rate of ED utilization compared with that of Whites (McCaig & Burt, 2005). Combined, the data seem to indicate that young adults are at high risk for accidents and related health injuries associated with drug use.

Other health concerns include type 1 diabetes ("juvenile diabetes"), typically diagnosed in children and young adults. Although this type of diabetes is less prevalent than type 2 (diagnosed in older adults), young adults do have a risk of getting type 1 diabetes in their 20s. Adults who are diagnosed with diabetes will have to adjust to lifestyle changes, such as more consistent exercise, modified diets, and monitoring of blood sugar levels.

Research has shown physical and psychosocial interactions. For example, obesity in adolescence leads to depression and lower social attainment (i.e., educational, economic, work satisfaction) in young adulthood for females but not males (Merten et al., 2008). Important associations exist between being overweight and having depression in adolescence and young adulthood for African American and White females (Franko et al., 2005). And, Geronimus and colleagues' (2006) decades of research on the physical weathering hypothesis suggests that accelerated aging characterized by early onset of chronic disease may disproportionately affect African Americans as compared with Whites and may be linked to an environmental impact on the body, such as stress exposure, racial discrimination, and economic hardship. Newer research by Geronimus, Hicken, Keene, & Bound is examining biomarkers such as telomeres, indicators associated with the physical aging process, and their differential expression in African American and White populations.

The changing economic environment, particularly the recent economic volatility experienced nationally, has also been found to affect physical health. According to a 2008 National Study of the Changing Workplace (Aumann & Galinsky, 2009), workers' overall health has declined from 2002 levels, with an increase in frequency of minor health problems (such as headaches), rising obesity rates, and rising stress levels (41% reported significant stress). Of those workers who experience chronic health problems, most report high blood pressure (21%), high cholesterol (14%), diabetes (7%), heart condition (3%), or a mental health disorder (4%).

Data from the American Cancer Society show that breast cancer rates for women ages 20 to 39 have not changed significantly over the past decade. Although women under age 40 are not usually at high risk for breast cancer, young women should have an understanding of the signs, symptoms, and risk factors associated with breast cancer and be vigilant of their own health as they age into middle adulthood.

In working with young adults who do have a health-related illness, social workers will want to assess the client's relationship to the illness and evaluate how the treatments are affecting the psychosocial developmental tasks of young adulthood (Dunbar, Mueller, Medina, & Wolf, 1998). For example, an illness may increase a young person's dependence on others at a time when independence from parents is valued, and individuals may have concerns about finding a mate. Societal stigma associated with the illness may be intense at a time when the individual is seeking more meaningful community engagements, and adjustment to the possibilities of career or parenthood delays may be difficult. Increasingly, social networking sites such as Patients Like Me (www.patientslikeme.com) are being used by young adults with chronic health conditions to create online communities to promote social interaction and information exchange. Users can create a shared health profile and find other users who have the same health condition to share treatment experiences. Examples of current disease communities include HIV/AIDS, fibromyalgia, mood conditions, and multiple sclerosis. Currently, about one third (34%) of the Patients Like Me member base is under age 39, with the majority (72%) women.

> How does infertility alter the young adult's phase of the life course?

In addition, young adult partners who struggle with infertility problems may have to confront disappointment from family members and adjust to feelings of unfulfilled social and family expectations. Costs of treatment may be prohibitive, and couples may experience a sense of alienation from peers who are moving rapidly into parenthood and child rearing. See Chapter 2 in this book for further discussion of infertility.

THE PSYCHOLOGICAL SELF

Young adulthood is a time when an individual continues to explore personal identity and his or her relationship to the world. Cognition, spirituality, and identity are intertwined aspects of this process.

Cognitive Development

Psychosocial development will depend on cognitive and moral development, which are parallel processes (Fowler, 1981). Young adulthood is a time when individuals expand, refine, and challenge existing belief systems, and the college environment is especially fertile ground for such broadening experiences. Late adolescents and young adults are also entering Piaget's formal operations stage, during which they begin to develop the cognitive ability to apply abstract principles to enhance problem solving and to reflect on thought processes (refer back to Exhibit 3.5 for an overview of Piaget's stages of cognitive development). These more complex cognitive capabilities, combined with a greater awareness of personal feelings, characterize cognitive development in young adulthood (Gardiner & Kosmitzki, 2008).

The abstract reasoning capabilities of adulthood and the awareness of subjective feelings can be applied to life experiences in ways that help individuals negotiate life transitions, new roles, stressors, and challenges (Labouvie-Vief, 1990, 2005). You might think of the development in cognitive processing from adolescence to young adulthood as a gradual switch from obtaining information to using that information in more applied ways (Arnett & Taber, 1994). Young adults are better able to see things from multiple viewpoints and from various perspectives than adolescents are.

With increasing cognitive flexibility, young adults begin to solidify their own values and beliefs. They may opt to retain certain traditions and values from their family of origin while letting go of others in order to make room for new ones. During this sorting out process, young adults are also defining what community means to them and what their place in the larger societal context might be like. Individuals begin establishing memberships in, and attachments to, selected social, service, recreational, and faith communities. Research indicates that religious beliefs, in particular, are reevaluated and critically examined in young adulthood, with individuals sorting out beliefs and values they desire to hold onto and those they choose to discard (Arnett & Jensen, 2002; Hodge, Johnson, & Luidens, 1993). However, there is a danger that discarded family beliefs may not be replaced with new meaningful beliefs (Arnett,

2000). Many emerging adults view the world as cold and disheartening and are somewhat cynical about the future. With this common pitfall in mind, we can take comfort from Arnett's finding that nearly all the 18- to 24-year-olds who participated in his study believed that they would ultimately achieve their goals at some point in the future (Arnett, 2000).

In terms of moral development, Lawrence Kohlberg (1976) categorized individuals ages 16 and older as fitting into the postconventional stage, which has these characteristics (refer back to Exhibit 4.2 for an overview of Kohlberg's stages of moral reasoning):

- Greater independence in moral decision making

- More complex contemplation of ethical principles

- Development of a "moral conscience"

- Move from seeking social approval through conformity to redefining and revising values and selecting behaviors that match those values

- Recognition of larger systems and appreciation for community

- Understanding that social rules are relativistic, rather than rigid and prescribed

> How does continued moral development affect the capacity for human agency in making choices?

Young adults begin to combine the principle of utility and production with the principle of equality, coming to the realization that individual or group gain should not be at the detriment of other individuals or social groups.

Kohlberg's research indicates that people do not progress in a straight line through the stages of moral development. Late adolescents and young adults may regress to conventional moral reasoning as they begin the process of critical reflection. In any case, successful resolution of the adolescent identity crisis, separation from home, and the willingness and ability to take responsibility for others are necessary, but not sufficient, conditions for postconventional moral development (Kohlberg, 1976).

Spiritual Development

As mentioned earlier, young adulthood is a time when individuals explore and refine their belief systems. Part of that process is development of **spirituality,** a focus on that which gives meaning, purpose, and direction to one's life. Spirituality manifests itself through one's ethical obligations and behavioral commitment to values and ideologies. It is a way of integrating values relating to self, other people, the community, and a "higher being" or "ultimate reality" (Hodge, 2001). Spirituality has been found to be associated with successful marriage (Kaslow & Robison, 1996), considerate and responsible interpersonal relations (Ellison, 1992), positive self-esteem (Ellison, 1993), more adaptive approaches to coping with stress (Tartaro, Lueken, & Gunn, 2005), and general well-being (George, Larson, Koenig, & McCullough, 2000).

Spirituality develops in three dimensions related to one's connection with a higher power (George et al., 2000; Hodge, 2001):

1. *Cognition.* Beliefs, values, perceptions, and meaning related to work, love, and life

2. *Affect.* Sense of connection and support; attachment and bonding experiences; psychological attachment to work, love, and life

3. *Behavior.* Practices, rituals, and behavioral experiences

Generally, consistency across all three dimensions is necessary for a vigorous spiritual life. For Carla Aquino, for example, it is not enough just to attend church (behavior) or just to subscribe to a defined belief set (cognition); she also needs to feel that she is "making a difference" through her church service projects (affect).

Research has shown that religious behavioral practices are correlated with life course stages. One study found that religiosity scores (reflecting beliefs, practices, and personal meaning) were higher for a group of young adults (ages 18 to 25) than for a group of adolescents (ages 14 to 17) (Glover, 1996), suggesting a growing spiritual belief system with age. Individuals making the transition from adolescence into young adulthood seem to place a particularly high value on spirituality. In addition, religious participation has been found to increase with age, even within the young adulthood stage (Gallup & Lindsay, 1999; Stolzenberg, Blair-Loy, & Waite, 1995; Wink & Dillon, 2002).

In an attempt to understand the development of spirituality, James W. Fowler (1981) articulated a theory of six stages of faith development. Fowler's research suggested that two of these stages occur primarily in childhood and two others occur primarily during late adolescence and young adulthood. Fowler's stages are very closely linked with the cognitive and moral development paradigms of Piaget and Kohlberg. Adolescents are typically in a stage characterized by **synthetic-conventional faith,** during which faith is rooted in external authority. Individuals ages 17 to 22 usually begin the transition to **individuative-reflective faith,** a stage when the person begins to let go of the idea of external authority and looks for authority within the self (Fowler). During this time, young adults establish their own belief system and evaluate personal values, exploring how those values fit with the various social institutions, groups, and individuals with whom they interact.

The transition from synthetic-conventional faith to individuative-reflective faith usually occurs in the early to mid-20s, although it may occur in the 30s and 40s, or may never occur at all (Fowler, 1981). An individual's faith development depends on his or her early attachments to other people, which serve as templates for understanding one's connection to more abstract relationships and which help shape these relationships. Faith growth, therefore, is heavily related to cognitive, interpersonal, and identity development.

The process also depends on crises confronted in the 20s and 30s; challenges and conflict are critical for change and growth in faith. In one study, young adult women who were HIV-positive were interviewed in order to explore coping strategies, women's experiences of living with the diagnosis, and life transformations or changes (Dunbar et al., 1998). The majority of women discussed the spiritual dimensions activated by their illness, such as renewing relationships, developing a new understanding of the self, experiencing heightened connections with nature and higher powers, and finding new meaning in the mundane. The interviews revealed several themes related to spiritual growth, including "reckoning with death," which led to the will to continue living and renewed "life affirmation"; finding new meaning in life; developing a positive sense of self; and achieving a "redefinition of relationships." These young women found new meaning and purpose in their lives, which gave them renewed opportunities for social connection (Dunbar et al.).

Identity Development

Identity development is generally associated with adolescence and is often seen as a discrete developmental marker, rather than as a process spanning all stages of the life course. However, identity development—how one thinks about and relates to oneself in the realms of love, work, and ideologies—continues well into adulthood. Ongoing identity development is necessary to make adult commitments possible, to allow individuals to abandon the insular self, and to embrace connection with important others. In addition, continuing identity development is an important part of young adults' efforts to define their life's direction (Glover, 1996; Kroger, 2007).

The classic work of James Marcia (1966) defined stages of identity formation in terms of level of exploration and commitment to life values, beliefs, and goals (as discussed in Chapter 6) as follows:

- Diffused (no exploration; no commitment)

- Foreclosed (no exploration; commitment)

- Moratorium (exploration; no commitment)

- Achievement (exploration; commitment)

Marcia (1993) has stated that people revisit and redefine their commitments as they age. As a result, identity is not static, but dynamic, open, and flexible. More recently, he has suggested that during times of great upheaval and transition in young adulthood, people are likely to regress to earlier identity modes (Marcia, 2002).

Research exploring this notion that identity formation is a process that continues deep into adulthood shows several interesting outcomes. In one study the researchers interviewed women and men between the ages of 27 and 36 to explore the process of commitment in five domains of identity: religious beliefs, political ideology, occupational career, intimate relationships, and lifestyle (Pulkkinen & Kokko, 2000). Results showed that men and women differed in their overall commitment to an identity at age 27. Women were more likely to be classified in Marcia's "foreclosed" identity status, and men were more likely to be classified in the "diffused" identity status. However, these gender differences diminished with age, and by age 36, foreclosed and achieved identity statuses were more prevalent than diffused or moratorium statuses for both men and women. This trend of increasing commitment with age held constant across all domains except political ideology, which showed increased diffusion with age. Also, across ages, women were more likely than men to be classified in the achieved identity status for intimate relationships; for men, the diffused identity status for intimate relationships was more prevalent at age 27 as compared with age 36.

The young adult who is exploring and expanding identity experiences tension between independence and self-sufficiency on one hand and a need for connection with others and reliance on a greater whole on the other. Young adults are often challenged to find comfort in connections that require a loosening of self-reliant tendencies. Some suggest that the transition into adulthood is signified by increased self-control while simultaneously submitting to the social conventions, structure, and order of the larger community.

Another study of the development of identity well into adulthood used a sample of women in their 20s (Elliott, 1996). The researchers found that the transition into young adulthood excites new definitions of identity and one's place in society, leading to potential changes in self-esteem and psychological self-evaluations. Although self-esteem tends to remain stable in young adulthood, several factors appeared to influence self-esteem in a positive or negative direction:

- Marriage may have a positive effect on self-esteem if it strengthens a young adult's economic stability and social connectedness.

- Parenthood is likely to have a negative effect if the role change associated with this life event significantly increases stresses and compromises financial stability.

- Receiving welfare is likely to decrease a young woman's self-esteem over time.

- Employment may mitigate the negative effects brought about by the transition into parenthood.

Employment tends to expand one's self-construct and identity and can offer a new parent additional social support as well as a supplemental source of validation. However, the extent to which employment will operate as a stress buffer is contingent on the occupational context and conditions. Certainly, good-quality jobs with benefits may enhance, and are unlikely to harm, a woman's psychological well-being (Elliott, 1996). However, dead-end, low-paying jobs do not help with the stresses of parenthood and have the potential to undermine a young woman's self-esteem.

Some scholars suggest that identity development for African American emerging adults may be significantly influenced by "stereotype threat" whereby there is a collective internalization that society expects African American emerging adults to fail. Identity development, then, for some emerging adults may require confrontation with held stereotypes at a collective level that serve to inform how they are expected to perform as a group (Arnett & Brody, 2008).

Newer research shows that social networking media sites, such as Facebook, that allow the development of and participation in Internet communities, have significant impact on emerging adults' identity and social development (Pempek, Yermolayeva, & Calvert, 2009). One study reported that college students' average use was 30 minutes per day with 80% using Facebook to communicate with existing friends. Such social networking technology offers young adults the opportunity to create personal identity profiles that can be shared and responded to in a public forum.

Social workers need to be aware of how peoples' work life impinges on their development of identity. In our case example, Johnny Nunez believes that he was targeted for dismissal at work because of his family demands, which led to a significant change in role from full-time employee to full-time child care provider. Carla Aquino is beginning the process of exploring family benefits provided by her place of employment as she prepares for the new baby. She knows that some of her friends work in environments that have on-site day care, but she does not think her company has that service. She is aware that her work is central to her identity, but she also recognizes that she and her husband must find a way to balance their commitments to work and family.

Critical Thinking Questions 7.2

Erik Erikson suggested that identity development occurred in adolescence, but recent theory and research suggest that identity is open and flexible and continues to develop across adulthood. What do you think about this recent suggestion that identity development is an ongoing process? What types of experiences in young adulthood might affect identity development? Do you think that your identity has changed since late adolescence? If so, which aspects of your identity have changed? What role do you think that the new technologies, particularly cell phones and the Internet, have on young adult identity development?

SOCIAL DEVELOPMENT AND SOCIAL FUNCTIONING

There are, of course, many paths to early adulthood, and not all arrive at this phase of the life course with equal resources for further social role development. This section looks at some of the special challenges faced by young adults as they negotiate new social roles, and the impact on social functioning in young adulthood—particularly in regard to interpersonal relationships and work attachment.

Research has shown that problem behavior in young adults is linked to challenges experienced in negotiating new social roles (see Kroger, 2007). However, it is oftentimes difficult to definitively capture the direction of influence. For example, does prior "deviant" behavior create difficulties in committing to work, or does a failure in finding a good job lead to problematic behaviors?

> What factors put individuals at risk when making the transition to adulthood?

The Child Trends study (Hair et al., 2003) on educationally disadvantaged youth identifies six categories of vulnerable youth making the transition to adulthood: out-of-school youth, youth with incarcerated parents, young welfare recipients, youth transitioning out of incarceration, runaway/homeless youth, and youth leaving foster care (p. 15). The largest group was out-of-school youth, although there is considerable overlap among these vulnerable categories. Many of these educationally disadvantaged youth lack parental monitoring, supervision, and support that would help facilitate the transition into adulthood. Along these lines, poor social functioning in young adulthood appears to be linked to a variety of difficulties in making the transition to new roles (Ronka & Pulkkinen, 1995):

- Problems in school and family in adolescence lead to social functioning problems in young adulthood.

- Unstable employment for males is associated with strained relationships, criminality, and substance abuse.

- Men who have many behavioral problems in young adulthood can be differentiated from young adult males who do not exhibit behavioral problems by several childhood factors, such as aggressive history, problems in school and family, and lack of formal educational attainment.

It is estimated that approximately half of educationally disadvantaged 18- to 24-year-olds have not completed a high school education, have not moved on to college, or moved on to more advanced vocational training (Hair et al., 2003). The transition to young adulthood from the secondary school environment can be challenging, particularly for students with learning disabilities. They drop out of high school at a higher rate than students without these challenges. Results from a qualitative study suggest some reasons why (Lichtenstein, 1993), one being that many students with learning disabilities worked while in high school, often because employment provided an environment where they could gain control over decision making, exercise authority, garner support, and increase self-esteem—outcomes that such students were not able to experience in the traditional educational system. In this study, working during the high school years was related to later employment but was also related to the risk of dropping out of high school altogether before graduation. These findings suggest a need for a well-tailored individual education plan (IEP) for each learning-disabled youth that outlines how that person can best make the transition out of high school and which postschool opportunities might be appropriate as well as a need for better transitioning services and active follow-up. In addition, the parents of students with learning disabilities need to be educated on their rights, and parent advocacy efforts within the school need to be strengthened (Lichtenstein).

The Child Trends study (Hair et al., 2003) cites 12 empirically evaluated programs that operate to facilitate adulthood transitioning for youth: Alcohol Skills Training Program; Job Corps; JOBSTART; Job Training Partnership Act; New Chance; Nurse Home Visitation Program; Ohio Learning, Earning and Parenting Program; School Attendance Demonstration Project; Youth Corps; AmeriCorps; Skill-Based Intervention on Condom Use; and Teenage Parent Demonstration. These programs primarily focus on educational and employment gains, and most showed solid gains in employment and improvement in school attendance and completion of a general equivalency diploma or gaining of a high school diploma, but not definitive gains in increasing earnings or job retention. Specifically, the Youth Corps program showed the most significant outcomes for African American males who earned higher incomes from their employment, had better employment relationships, and were more likely to have attained advanced education than those who did not participate in the program. Latino males who participated in the program also showed increased employment and work promotions as compared with those who did not participate, while White males actually showed negative effects from participation as they were less likely to be employed and received lower earnings from their work. African American, Latina, and White females all benefited from participation, showing increased work hours and higher educational aspirations (Hair et al.).

A summary of empirically tested programs that have been found to positively influence young adulthood transitioning include the following: Alcohol Skills Training geared to college students; AmeriCorps for youth ages 17 and older; Job Corps; JOBSTART for 16- to 24-year-old disadvantaged youth; and the Job Training Partnership Act, aimed at increasing educational and occupational advancement of adults and out-of-school youth (Bronte-Tinkew, Brown, Carrano, & Shwalb, 2005, p. 32).

Another special population that is likely to face challenges in making the transition into young adulthood is young persons with more severe emotional difficulties. Approximately three quarters of adults with psychiatric diagnoses experienced symptoms before the age of 24, with symptom expression peaking in the early 20s (McGorry & Purcell, 2009). These young adults often have trouble forming meaningful interpersonal relationships, maintaining employment, managing physical health needs, and gaining financial independence. Research shows that disability diagnosis and severity may influence social outcomes. For example, young adults with severe cognitive disability and coexisting impairments tend to show the most limited leisure involvement and date less frequently than those young adults with cerebral palsy, hearing loss, or epilepsy (Van Naarden Braun, Yeargin-Allsopp, & Lollar, 2006).

Many young adults with developmental and/or emotional disabilities may have tenuous experience with the labor market and weakened connections to work. Often their families do not have sufficient resources to help them make the transition from high school, potentially delaying the youth's opportunity to live independently. Many of these young persons do not have a stable support network, and as a result, they are at higher than usual risk for homelessness (Davis & Vander Stoep, 1997). In a 20-year longitudinal study following a cohort of individuals with developmental delays who were first diagnosed at age 3, both parents and their young adult children expressed concern about the young adults' social isolation and inability to find gainful employment. Many of the young adults were concerned about not having enough peer involvement and too much parental involvement in their lives. Three types of parent-young adult relationships tended to emerge: (1) *dependent* relationships, which were comfortable to the young adults in that parents responded to needs in appropriate quality and quantity; (2) *independent* relationships, which were comfortable to the young adults in that parents responded to young adult needs only in times of crisis; and (3) *interdependent* relationships, which was the most conflictual of the three types and was characterized by young adult resentment of parental involvement (Keogh, Bernheimer & Guthrie, 2004).

Another group of youth at risk in the transition from late adolescence to early adulthood are those with poor relationships with their parents. Emotional intimacy in the parent-child relationship has been found to be important in the development of self-esteem, with the benefits lasting into adulthood. However, engaging and satisfying employment seems to mediate a poor parent-child relationship, increasing the youth's well-being (Roberts & Bengston, 1993).

Youth with unstable attachments to adult caregivers, like many foster care youth who are transitioning out of the foster care system, have a great need for developmentally appropriate and culturally sensitive supportive services as they make the transition into young adulthood. Social workers should examine the ways in which formal services facilitate the transition to adulthood for youths who have no informal supports. Certainly, terminating services to these youths at the age of majority, without making arrangements for them to receive adult services, will undermine the efforts made during the youth's adolescence and put these individuals at a disadvantage as young adults (Davis & Vander Stoep, 1997). Particularly for individuals with developmental disabilities, there may be a strong need for services to continue on into young adulthood (Keogh et al., 2004).

Finally, the immigration experience for youth may pose a risk during the adulthood transition. Research shows that more than one third (38.2%) of young adult Latinos do not have a high school degree, and immigration transition and associated stressors as well as socioeconomic barriers may be contributing factors. As social workers, we must ask about the context of the immigration experience and examine how it influences young adult development. For example: Was immigration a choice? Were there family separations along the way, and what was the nature of such separations? What motivated the immigration experience? Was there a change in the family's socioeconomic and/or role statuses? What are the hardships encountered in the new country? Are these hardships experienced differently by different members of the same family? What is the level of the family's and individual members' acculturation (Chapman & Perreira, 2005)? It is important to assess for the extent of intergenerational stress that may have developed from the immigration experience as studies show that both high and low levels of acculturation are associated with risk behaviors such as substance abuse and mental health problems (Chapman & Perreira).

Relationship Development in Young Adulthood

Erikson's concept of intimacy, which relies on connection with a significant partner, is at the core of relationship development during early adulthood. Typically, young adults develop sustained commitments to others and come to recognize a responsibility for others' well-being. This developmental process may manifest as thoughtful awareness in the early years, changing to more active behavioral commitment in later years—for example, caring for children or aging parents, getting involved in the community, and taking on social obligations.

Intimacy, which can be defined as a sense of warmth or closeness, has three components: interdependence with another person, self-disclosure, and affection (Perlman & Fehr, 1987). Intimacy may take the form of cognitive/intellectual intimacy, emotional intimacy, sexual intimacy, physical intimacy apart from a sexual relationship, and spiritual intimacy. When reflecting on intimate relations, some people talk about finding a "soul mate"; feeling intensely connected; sharing values, beliefs, and philosophical inquiries; and feeling as though the relationship has strong direction and purpose.

Establishing intimacy is a multifaceted process. Exhibit 7.2 lists some of the tasks involved in fostering an intimate relationship with someone. The ability to perform these tasks depends not only on personal abilities but also on external factors, such as the individual's family background. Research has found several family factors in adolescence to be important in the ability to develop intimate relationships during young adulthood: (1) a positive relationship with the mother (e.g., effective, clear communication with her, as well as mutual respect and empathy), and (2) adaptability of the family unit (e.g., good habits of conflict resolution and appropriate discipline) (Robinson, 2000). The young adult's ability to develop intimate relationships also depends on favorable environmental conditions, such as having adequate resources to accommodate stressors, handle life responsibilities, and deal effectively with the multiple life transitions of this developmental stage.

An individual's family relationships and attachment to the family unit as a whole are transformed during young adulthood. The family's life cycle stage and the psychosocial development of individual members will influence the nature of family relationships in young adulthood. Generally, though, young adults may see parents, siblings, and relatives less frequently as work, romantic attachments, and new family responsibilities take precedence. With greater independence, geographic distance may also preclude more visits. Thus, time spent together may center around holiday celebrations. As traditional family roles evolve, young adults may take more active responsibility for holiday preparations. They may find themselves wanting to spend less time with old friends and more time with family. As young adults have children, holiday activities and family interactions may increasingly focus on the new generation.

- Effectively negotiating expectations for the relationship
- Negotiating roles and responsibilities
- Making compromises
- Prioritizing and upholding values
- Deciding how much to share of oneself
- Identifying and meeting individual needs
- Identifying and meeting partnership needs
- Renegotiating identity
- Developing trust and security
- Allowing for reciprocal communication
- Making time commitments to partner
- Effectively resolving conflict and solving problems
- Demonstrating respect, support, and care

▲ **Exhibit 7.2**   Tasks in Fostering Intimacy

Romantic Relationships

Romantic relationships are a key element in the development of intimacy during early adulthood. **Romantic love** has been described as a relationship that is sexually oriented, is "spontaneous and voluntary," and occurs between equal partners (Solomon, 1988). Satisfaction in romantic partnerships depends on finding a delicate balance between positive and negative interactions across time (Gottman, 1994).

Anthropologist Helen Fisher (2004) suggests that the choice of romantic partners is based on three distinct emotional systems: lust, attraction, and attachment. *Lust* is sexual attraction and is associated with androgen hormones. *Attraction* involves feeling great pleasure in the presence of the romantic interest and thinking of the other person all the time. Fisher suggests that attraction is associated with increased levels of dopamine and norepinephrine and decreased levels of serotonin, which are neurotransmitters in the brain. Fisher's description of *attachment* is similar to Bowlby's concept described in Chapter 3 of this book. It involves a sense of security when in the presence of the attachment figure, which is the romantic partner in this discussion. Attachment has been associated with the hormone oxytocin.

▲ **Photo 7.3** The transition from emerging adulthood to young adulthood is marked by solidifying role commitments, such as marriage.

In the United States, heterosexual romantic love has traditionally been considered a precursor to marriage. However, a recent trend in romantic relationships is to have sex earlier but marry later. For the past decade, more than half of all marriages occurred after a period of cohabitation (Heuveline & Timberlake, 2004). It is important to remember, however, that in many parts of the world and among many recent immigrant groups to the United States, marriage is arranged and not based on romantic courtship. Many other variations in relationship development exist as well, represented by single-parent families, childless couples, gay/lesbian partnerships, couples who marry and choose to live apart to establish individual career tracks, and couples where partners are in different life stages (e.g., early adulthood and middle adulthood).

In the past, increasing education decreased women's likelihood of marrying, but recent data suggest a reversal of that trend. The cohort of women who recently graduated from college, both Black and White, are likely to marry later than women of their cohort without a college education, but their rate of eventual marriage will be higher (Goldstein & Kenney, 2001). The researchers interpret this trend to indicate that marriage is increasingly becoming a choice only for the most educated members of society. Given the advantages of a two-earner family, this trend may contribute toward the widening economic gap in our society.

An increasing awareness of variation in relationships has prompted research into all sorts of romantic attachments. One focus is homosexual relationships. One study that identified three "scripts" in lesbian relationships helps to differentiate romantic attachment from other kinds of intimacy (Rose & Zand, 2000): (1) the "romance" script combines emotional intimacy and sexual attraction. It is characterized by an attenuated dating period and quick commitment to a relationship; (2) "friendship" is a script in which individuals fall in love and are emotionally committed, though sexual behaviors are not necessarily a part of the relationship. Research shows that this is the most common script among lesbians, emphasizing

How does sexual orientation affect young adult development?

emotional intimacy over sexuality. Women have suggested that the ambiguity implicit in this script often makes defining the relationship difficult; (3) "sexually explicit" focuses on sexual attraction and leaves emotional intimacy at the periphery. This script is void of any direct expression of future commitment. These scripts are summarized in Exhibit 7.3.

Lesbian and gay partnering becomes more complex if the coming-out process begins in early adulthood. The individuals involved have to negotiate through their parents' emotional reactions and responses at the same time as the new relationship is developing. One study found that lesbian and gay partners are less likely to identify family as a significant social support as compared with heterosexual couples (Kurdek, 2004). One possible reason is that siblings and other relatives may be forced to confront their own comfort, biases, and values associated with the young adult's relationship. If gay and lesbian couples decide to have children, their own parents will inevitably be forced to confront the homosexual identity in order to develop their grandparent role with the new child.

Even in families where "acceptance" has taken root, people in the family's social network may have limited understanding that is difficult to work through. Family members who thought they had come to terms with the young adult's homosexual identity may find themselves harboring anger, hurt, disappointment, or confusion about how the young person's life trajectory is affecting their own life trajectories.

Other complicating factors related to gay and lesbian relationship development can be connections with the larger community and with the gay and lesbian community itself. Current legal inequities—such as the lack of legal sanction for marriage-like partnerships, the associated lack of benefits (e.g., survivorship and inheritance rights and housing loans), and the lack of authority in decision making for gay and lesbian partners (in such matters as child custody and health care/medical procedures)—can cause additional external strain on new couples.

Currently, only five states—Connecticut, Iowa, Massachusetts, New Hampshire, and Vermont—plus the District of Columbia in the United States have legalized gay marriage. New York recognizes gay marriages of residents who obtained legal marriages in other states but does not perform same-sex marriages.

The legal impact of these political wranglings on gay and lesbian adults' rights has been described, but how a young adult's family status is defined in legal terms by society may also influence other decision-making processes, such as choice of community or residential neighborhood, childbearing decisions, employment choices, and options during times of unemployment (e.g., if one partner's benefits, such as health insurance, are not legally available to the other partner when one young adult loses a job). In addition, impact may be experienced via various systems' (e.g., school, health care, child care centers) interactions with same-sex parents if there is a lack of recognition of the rights of both parents in decision making for their child.

Regardless of the sexuality of young adult clients, social workers need to consider the client's partner when exploring intimacy issues (LaSala, 2001). These partners may be a valuable resource in matters relating to the partnership itself as well as relations with the family of origin. Social workers also need to assess the adequacy of a young adult's

Script	Descriptor
Romance	Emotional and sexual attraction; quick commitment
Friendship	Emotional commitment; sexual behavior may or may not be part of relationship
Sexually Explicit	Sexual attraction is focal point; emotional intimacy secondary

▲ **Exhibit 7.3** Lesbian Relationship Development

SOURCE: Adapted from Rose & Zand, 2000.

support system across multiple dimensions and to identify and respond to any perceived gaps. Although marriages and partnerships typically expand a young adult's social support network, this might not be the case for all individuals, and social workers should be cautious about making such assumptions.

Parenthood

Parenting is an interactive process, with reciprocal parent-child and child-parent influences (Maccoby, 2002b). The multiple role transitions that mark entry into parenthood during young adulthood can be both exciting and challenging, as new familial interdependencies evolve. New social obligations and responsibilities associated with caregiving affect the relationship between the young adult partners and between the young adults and their parents.

Often, the nature of the partners' relationship before parenthood will determine how partners will manage the demands of these changing roles (Durkin, 1995). Adjustment to parenthood, and successful role reorganization, depends on five dimensions (Cowan, 1991):

1. Individual factors, such as how role changes affect one's sense of self

2. Quality of the partners' relationship (e.g., how the couple negotiates responsibilities and their decision-making capabilities)

3. Quality of the relationship between the young adults and their children

4. Quality of each partner's relationships with his/her family of origin

5. Quality of external relationships (e.g., school, work, community)

How partners negotiate the division of labor along gender lines also influences parenting and marital satisfaction. Much of the parenting literature has focused on the role strain mothers face in maintaining work commitments alongside new parenting responsibilities. Some new literature has focused on the more positive aspects of mothers' participation in the workforce (Gürsory & Bicakci, 2007; Losoncz & Bortolotto, 2009; Zaslow & Emig, 1997). However, fatherhood and the positive impact of paternal parenting on both child well-being and on the father's own successful male adult development need further exploration.

According to the most recent statistics from the National Survey of Family Growth, about two thirds (64%) of men ages 15 to 44 had a first child in their 20s. One quarter of Black fathers had a first child before age 20 compared with one fifth of Latino fathers and 11% of White males. One fifth of children in two-parent families have their father as their primary caregiver (Halle, 2002). Just over one third (37%) of Black fathers were married when they had their first child, as compared with three quarters (77%) of White fathers and half (52%) of Latino fathers (Department of Health and Human Services [DHHS], 2006b). The Rochester Youth Development Study (Thornberry, Smith, & Howard, 1997) estimated that more than one quarter (28%) of public school males become fathers by the age of 19, and other studies show that adolescent fatherhood is a risk factor for delinquency (Stouthamer-Loeber & Wei, 1998) and is associated with weakened school attachment and lower wages (Pirog-Good, 1996). In addition, lower socioeconomic status, aggressive behavior, and low academic achievement are antecedents to teen fatherhood (Xie, Cairns, & Cairns, 2001). Weinman, Buzi, and Smith (2005) found that young fathers have significant mental health needs and address the importance of fatherhood education, advocating for a "social marketing" approach that delivers educational messages to male youth indigenously within targeted communities.

Research on tasks associated with responsible fathering identify the provision of economic and emotional support to children, basic caregiving, offering guidance and control, and "being there" (or being present) as most important to the fathering role as defined by young fathers and linked to successful fathering (Peart, Pungello, Campbell, & Richey, 2006). Fathers who are highly involved with their children often describe their peers' parents as being influential in their own development as a father (Masciadrelli, Pleck, & Stueve, 2006). Further research needs to account for the presence of male **fictive kin** (nonrelatives that are considered family) and their role in helping young adults develop as fathers, and to document the strengths of special populations of fathers, such as young African American fathers (see Connor & White, 2006).

Some evidence of paternal parenting styles was provided in a longitudinal study of father-child relationships based on interviews with 240 working-class families (Snarey, 1993). Results showed that 35% of fathers in the study were "not very active," 41% reported being "substantially involved," and 24% were "highly involved" in fatherhood activities. Data showed that fathers were more involved during childhood as compared with adolescence or infancy. Socioemotional support was the most common support that fathers provided during activities shared with their children, followed by physical/athletic support and intellectual/ academic support.

As for mothers, the evidence suggests that maternal employment may have a positive influence on her sense of self, leading to better outcomes for her children. However, Pamela Stone's book *Opting Out?* (2007) reminds us that the decision to opt out of careers, even after intensive postsecondary advanced education and career success, may be related to institutional barriers experienced in the employment sector rather than an indicator of personal choice or family preference. For example, workplace environments that require long work hours or that may have inflexible family policies that compete with family demands may pose barriers to choosing full-time work for some families.

With these findings in mind, it becomes necessary to identify groups for whom employment opportunities may be limited. Parents of children with disabilities fall into this category. Research shows that 12% of children in the United States have at least one developmentally related functional limitation that requires special attention and care (Hogan & Msall, 2002). Parenting a child with a functional disability demands extra care, which may decrease a parent's opportunity to enter or continue participation in the labor market. One study suggested that two thirds of families with a child who has a functional limitation will experience significant changes in labor force participation (Hogan & Msall).

Low-income mothers are another group for whom maternal employment is significantly related to child well-being (Zaslow & Emig, 1997). Employment often creates child care difficulties. However, characteristics associated with positive parenting (e.g., the mother's ability to express warmth to the child, her lack of depressive symptoms, and the quality of her verbal interaction with the child) have been found to mediate the ill effects on child well-being that may arise in welfare-to-work programs, which sometimes leave low-income mothers with poor child care options (McGroder, Zaslow, Moore, Hair, & Ahluwalia, 2002). Other studies have found that parents who have more social support are better at parenting (Marshall, Noonan, McCartney, Marx, & Keefe, 2001).

Helping young adults to develop parenting efficacy may help them overcome environmental conditions and improve their children's well-being. Unfortunately, research shows that one of the biggest gaps in independent living services for young adults transitioning out of foster care is in parenting skills development (the other was housing preparation) (Georgiades, 2005). Another study compared the effects of increasing the mother's parenting efficacy in White and Black families characterized by a weak marriage and living in economically disadvantaged neighborhoods (Ardelt & Eccles, 2001). The Black families showed greater benefits in the form of increased academic success for their children. Parenting efficacy also contributed more to positive child outcomes in Black families with a compromised marriage than in Black families where the marriage was strong and secure. Parenting-related protective factors in Latino families include respect, familism, and biculturalism (Chapman & Perreira, 2005).

Mentoring/Volunteering

Although young adults seek out older adult mentors in work as they begin establishing themselves in new careers, young persons also often serve as mentors themselves. Serving as a mentor can help young adults move through the adulthood transition by facilitating new experiences and helping them to develop new roles that require "taking care of others" as opposed to "being taken care of" themselves. As young adults refine their ideologies, beliefs, and values, they form group affiliations consistent with their emerging identity, career, relationships, community, and religious and political views.

With the newly signed Edward M. Kennedy Serve America Act (signed April 21, 2009), President Obama reauthorized and expanded the service opportunities funded by the Corporation for National and Community Service, such as initiating the Summer of Service programs aimed at engaging youth in tutoring, recreation, and service opportunities.

Some examples of current groups and mentoring programs young adults might get involved in include 20 Something, a gay/lesbian young adult social group; Young Democrats/Young Republicans political groups; YMCA/YWCA; and Big Brothers/Big Sisters youth mentoring programs. Service-related groups young adults may choose to become involved with include Junior Achievement, a nonprofit organization that brings young adults together with elementary school students to teach children economic principles, and Streetwise Partners, where young adults help low-income and unemployed persons with job skills training. College students may also get actively involved in Habitat for Humanity projects or student associations such as the College Hispanic American Society, Campus Crusaders for Christ, and Association of Black Students, which spearhead philanthropic and community-integration activities.

Work and the Labor Market

Statistics reported that, as of November 2009, the unemployment rate was at 10.2% nationally, the highest since 1983 (U.S. Department of Labor, 2009). And, actually, the jobless rate rises to 17.5% if individuals working part time (who wish to be working full time), and those who have abandoned looking for a job because of lack of success are included. The largest labor market losses have been in manufacturing, construction, and retail, with more men losing jobs than women. The recent economic recession has produced significant stress on young adults and young families who may have lost jobs, are currently underemployed, or who have had difficulties obtaining initial entry-level positions because of employers' cost-cutting measures. Recent research shows that 77% of employers surveyed have had to implement cost-saving measures during 2008–2009, with 69% of those employers laying off employees (Galinsky & Bond, 2009).

The transition into the world of work is an important element of social development during early adulthood. A young adult's opportunity for successful adulthood transitioning into the labor market depends on a variety of dimensions, to include **human capital** (talents, skills, intellectual capacity, social development, emotional regulatory capacity) as well as **community assets** such as public infrastructure (e.g., adequate transportation to get to work), community networks, and educational opportunities. In addition, family capital is important. "Transformative assets," or those family contributions that aid in deferring the immediate economic costs of long-term investments such as a college education or the down payment for a house, are differentially spread across race, with half of White families giving young adults this investment edge, while data show that only 20% of Black families are able to do so (Lui et al., 2006). This coupled with the fact that, in some states, children of undocumented immigrants do not receive in-state tuition for higher education, makes the prospects of getting into and affording a college education out of reach for many young adults and erodes their longer-term access to asset growth and economic stability. One report (Draut & Silva, 2004) indicates that young adults face daunting economic challenges characterized by underemployment, high cost of purchasing a first home, and rising debt from student loans and credit cards. According to another report, adults aged 18 to 24 spend close to two times the amount on debt expenditures as they did in 1992, with approximately 30% of income going to paying off their debt (Mintel Report, 2004).

Given that our educational institution operates as society's gatekeeper to economic opportunities, we need to examine how our educational system is preparing our youth for future employment as well as how and to whom such opportunities are afforded. For example, what kind of jobs are our youth getting and what educational and vocational paths lead to these jobs? Are we effectively and appropriately matching educational and vocational opportunities to the current economic landscape so that all youth transitioning into the adult world of work can benefit? Does our educational system effectively track and keep pulse on changing labor market trends, identify careers with long-term gains (e.g., with benefits and growth potential), and then create the appropriate education and training experiences necessary to be attractive in competing for these jobs? In other words, if education provides opportunities to gain assets such as jobs, promotions, credit, and safety net/benefits such as health care (Lui et al., 2006, p. 229), and asset accumulation leads to prosperity and economic stability (Rank, 2005), we need to examine how differential education and training tracks might be influencing lifelong economic and labor market trajectories, keeping certain groups entrenched in poverty.

Indeed, as important as individual factors are in the transition to work, the changing labor market and structural shifts in the economy may have an even greater influence by shaping a young person's opportunities for finding and maintaining productive work. Work in industry and manufacturing has been diminishing for four decades now, and the number of jobs in the service sector has increased (Portes & Rumbaut, 2001). Manufacturing jobs once offered unskilled youth with relatively little education an opportunity for good wages, employment benefits, and job security. However, the service sector is divided between low-wage, temporary or part-time service jobs, and work opportunities that call for advanced, technical skills. Today there is a high labor market demand for low-wage, low-skill jobs as well as a high demand among employers for workers with more specialized and technical skills (Portes & Rumbaut).

Data suggest that youth with disabilities are at higher risk for dropping out of high school compared with youth who do not have a disability; and, more specifically, African American and Latino youth with disabilities are at significantly

> How do factors such as gender, race, ethnicity, and disability affect transitions into the labor market?

higher risk than their White counterparts (Trainor, 2008). Although approximately three quarters of White youth with disabilities entered paid employment after high school, only 61.7% of African American and 65.4% of Latino youth with disabilities obtained employment after high school. Only one fifth of youth with disabilities go on to higher education opportunities (Wagner, Newman, Cameto, & Levine, 2005). Other vulnerable youth populations, such as youth transitioning out of state care, face challenges in moving to paid employment in young adulthood. Reid (2007) suggests that "seven pillars" serve as a foundation for success for youth transitioning out of state care at age of majority, which include the following: relationships, education, housing, life skills, identity, youth engagement (ownership over the transitioning plan), and emotional healing (p. 35). A recent Child Trends report summarized specific empirically validated competencies that have been shown to increase high school students' success in the labor market: second language competency; ability to interact with others to problem-solve and work through conflict; critical thinking skills; planfulness; good judgment; strong work ethic such as reliability and professionalism in the work environment; having had internship experience; and general self-management skills such as responsibility, initiative, and time-management skills (Lippman & Keith, 2009, pp. 1–2). Policies and programs such as the Foster Care Independence Act (PL 106–169) and John H. Chafee Foster Care Independence Program (1999) provide additional support for postsecondary education, vocational training, housing, health care, and counseling until age 21, and are a good start in responding to these specific needs.

Incarcerated youth who are discharged from the juvenile justice system as emerging adults also face significant labor attachment challenges. Many face uncertain outcomes upon discharge back into their preinstitutionalized communities that can include rearrest for new crimes (about one third will be rearrested) or violence from peers who vow revenge for wrongs committed before the youth were institutionalized (Inderbitzin, 2009). Difficulty in obtaining gainful employment upon release can be complicated because of deficient legitimate job skills, stigma of institutionalization, and lack of prosocial community and economic capital (Inderbitzin). Job training, transitioning to new neighborhoods, and engaging in a safety net of continuing care services are critical predictors for successful release back into the community.

The dilemma facing disadvantaged youth entering adulthood is vexing. Labor market attachment is not only the surest route to material well-being (for example, according to Shapiro [2004] once basic living expenses are accounted for, each additional dollar of annual income generates $3.26 in net worth over a person's lifetime), but labor market attachment also has been found to be significantly related to mental health and psychosocial well-being. One study looked at factors associated with well-being and adjustment between ages 16 and 21. The study found that experiences of unemployment were significantly associated with thoughts of suicide, substance abuse, and crime (Fergusson,

Horwood, & Woodward, 2001). Benefits of work include increased self-esteem, increased social interaction, and external validation through social recognition. Increasingly, therefore, youths' life trajectories will be determined by access to advanced education and then good jobs.

Immigration and Work

Alejandro Portes and Ruben G. Rumbaut (2001), in their timely book *Legacies: The Story of the Immigrant Second Generation,* based on results from the Children of Immigrants Longitudinal Study (CILS), note that the structural labor market change of the past few decades disproportionately affects immigrants, particularly youth in late adolescence who will be emerging into this new occupational landscape. "Increasing labor market inequality implies that to succeed socially and economically, children of immigrants today must cross, in the span of a few years, the educational gap that took descendents of Europeans several generations to bridge" (p. 58). An important finding from the CILS is the contrast in job selection between older and younger generations of immigrants. Today's young people are more likely to turn down "traditional immigrant jobs" that are seen

▲ **Photo 7.4** A major challenge facing young adults is attaining independent financial stability and establishing autonomy and decision making.

as unfulfilling, in contrast to older immigrants who often felt compelled to take any job available in their youth without such questioning (Portes & Rumbaut).

Another study investigated how migration affects the earnings prospects of Latino men making the transition into young adulthood (Padilla & Jordan, 1997). Specifically, seeking work opportunities in more favorable socioeconomic environments during early adulthood was found to be associated with decreased likelihood of poverty in adulthood. Increased education and cognitive ability were also associated with a decreased likelihood of being in poverty during the transition into adulthood.

It is important for social workers to understand the social and economic conditions that immigrant youth face. This large and growing group, born from the surge in immigration of recent decades, faces special challenges as young adults under recent economic conditions.

Role Changes and Work

A number of other factors are related to the type of work young adults secure, and thus their occupational prestige and income earned later in life. Across race and gender, educational attainment has a strong effect. Marriage itself is not a significant predictor of occupational prestige or earnings for males or females. Analysis of data from the National Survey of Families found that men were more likely to be employed if they were fathers and their work hours increased as the number of children in the family increased. Conversely, women were less likely to work if they had children and their work hours decreased as the number of children in the family increased (Kaufman & Uhlenberg, 2000).

For the social worker, it would be important to examine to what extent culture affects educational and work-related opportunities and timing sequences. Social workers also need to explore with individuals the extent of role overload that may exist. For example, an additional effect of employment on low-income earners may be the added expense that occurs when work and family pressures collide. Exploring the unique costs and benefits of employment decisions for each individual, recognizing the larger family context, can be helpful. Social workers should also assess clients' coping strategies and ask clients for their perceptions about how identified stressors are affecting the individual and family.

Race, Ethnicity, and Work

The associations among race, ethnicity, and work attachment have received some attention. Although first-generation Mexican immigrants earn incomes that are half that of White males, second generation immigrants typically earn three quarters that of White men and more than Black men. About 40% of first-generation Mexican immigrants ages 16 to 20 are in school or college as compared with two thirds of second-generation immigrants in this age cohort ("Of Meat, Mexicans and Social Mobility," 2006).

Unfortunately, the labor force participation among young Black men has declined since 1980. Labor force connection tends to be weakest for Black males who have little formal education and who lack work experience (Holzer, 2009). Of course, the economic restructuring of past decades has made good-quality jobs for young adults without specialized skills hard to come by. Other barriers for young Black men include discrimination in hiring, absence of adult mentors in the community who might help socialize youth toward work roles, a disconnect from a good-paying job with benefits, diminished self-efficacy related to perceptions of constricted economic opportunities, hopelessness about finding quality jobs, and the presence of alternative informal and more prosperous economic options (e.g., drug dealing, gambling). All may decrease the youth's ability or motivation to pursue formal work opportunities. But that is not to say that young Black men do not want to succeed in the world of work:

> Young black men want jobs and wages comparable to white young men, and their reluctance to take inferior jobs, despite less experience, lengthens their period of unemployment. They share middle-class values and aspirations. The problem is how to achieve those aspirations. (Laseter, 1997, p. 74)

Racism may be a factor in job prospects for young Black males as well. Sociological studies have shown that White men with a prison record are more likely to be hired for a job than Black men without a prison record (Lui et al., 2006). Racism can directly tax individuals and families and can indirectly deplete their buffering resources and weaken solutions to managing direct stressors (Harrell, 2000). Stressors and resources change over the life course, however, and social workers need to be able to assess the ways in which individuals and families are able to adapt to such changes.

Although social workers need to understand the effects of oppressive living conditions and environmental stressors on all groups, they should be aware of the disproportionate number of African Americans living in such conditions. Regardless of socioeconomic status (SES), African American males have the lowest well-being scores of any group studied (White women and men, African American women and men) (Woody & Green, 2001). Their low scores are potentially explained by social conditions such as stigma, constrained economic opportunities, health-related discrepancies, and a perception of lack of control over their lives. It is dually important, however, for social workers to understand the range of diversity within the African American community along many social dimensions, including SES, in order to avoid perpetuating the stereotypes that further stigmatize this diverse group.

In addition, social workers should be aware of how social assistance is unequally distributed and should work toward eliminating such disparities. For example, of those exiting welfare, Whites are twice as likely as Blacks or Latinas to receive child care or transportation transitional assistance. In addition, the median wage for a White welfare exiter between 1997–1999 was $7.31/hour compared with $6.88 and $6.71 for African American and Latina exiters, respectively (Lui et al., 2006). Other research shows that when women who leave Temporary Assistance to Needy Families (TANF) are employed in steady jobs and remain employed over time, their wages increase with this longevity in the work world (Corcoran, Danziger, Kalil, & Seefeldt, 2000). However, the reality is that many young women leaving TANF do not enter long-term continuous employment because of a variety of barriers, such as maternal and child physical and/or mental health problems; unaffordable/inaccessible/or poor-quality child care; or unreliable transportation (Corcoran et al.). Without addressing these problems, the *long-term* wage stability and economic viability of these families remain in question. The living wage social movement that continues to gain momentum will help bring more public awareness and hopefully policy change to these issues.

RISK FACTORS AND PROTECTIVE FACTORS IN YOUNG ADULTHOOD

A longitudinal study that followed a cohort of individuals born in 1955 from infancy to age 40 identified clusters of protective factors at significant points across the life course (see Exhibit 7.4) that are associated with successfully making the transition to adulthood (Werner & Smith, 2001). The researchers identified high-risk individuals and then determined the specific factors that influenced their positive adaptation to adulthood at age 32. The protective factors included successful early social, language, and physical development; good problem-solving skills in middle childhood; educational and work expectations and plans by age 18; and social maturity and a sense of mastery and control in late adolescence. Family factors included stable maternal employment when the child was 2 to 10 years old, access to a variety of social support sources, and the child's sense of belonging within the family unit at age 18. Community factors included having access to nurturing, caring adults in one's community, including the presence of adult mentors, and having access to "enabling," as opposed to "entrapping," community niches (see Saleeby, 1996).

How can social workers help to provide protective factors for the adult transition?

Other researchers have identified similar protective factors associated with successful developmental transitions into emerging adulthood and young adulthood, to include childhood IQ, parenting quality, and socioeconomic status. Adaptation in emerging adulthood, specifically, is associated with an individual's planning capacity, future motivation, autonomy, social support, and coping skills (Masten et al., 2004).

	Individual Characteristics	Caregiving Context
Infancy	Autonomy; social competence Health status	Maternal competence Emotional support Number of stressful events
Middle childhood	Academic proficiency Health status	Emotional support to child (extended family; mentor) Number of stressful events
Adolescence	Self-efficacy Health status	Emotional support to child (peer relations; feelings about family) Number of stressful events
Young adulthood	Temperament Health status	Emotional support (quality of partner, work, & community relationships) Number of stressful events

▲ **Exhibit 7.4**   *Common Core Protective Factors Predicting Adult Adaptation*

SOURCE: Adapted from Werner & Smith, 2001, pp. 161–163.

Risk factors that researchers found to be associated with the transition to adulthood included low family income during infancy, poor reading achievement by age 10, problematic school behavior during adolescence, and adolescent health problems (Werner & Smith, 2001). For men, an excessive number of stressful events, living with an alcoholic or mentally ill father, and substance abuse contributed to problematic coping in early adulthood. Other studies have found that adolescent fatherhood can be a risk factor for delinquency, which, in turn, can lead to problematic entry into adulthood (Stouthamer-Loeber & Wei, 1998). For women, a sibling death in early childhood, living with an alcoholic or mentally ill father, and a conflicted relationship with the mother were significant risk factors for successful coping at age 32 (Werner & Smith).

A recent study (Ringeisen, Casaneuva, Urato, & Stambaugh, 2009) found that although about half (48%) of young adults with a maltreatment history had mental health problems, only 25% of these young adults received treatment services for their problems. In particular, there was a significant decline in those receiving services in adolescence (47.6%) to those continuing to receive such services in adulthood (14.3%). Data suggest that there is a significant risk of losing continuity of mental health services when making the move out of adolescence and into young adulthood, with data showing particularly high risk for non-Whites and those without Medicaid assistance (Ringeisen et al.).

Other studies of youth aging out of the foster care system have found similar declining trends in mental health service utilization during the adolescent-adult transition. A study by McMillan and Raghavan (2009) found that 60% of 19-year-old foster youth dropped out of services during the transition from pediatric system care to the adult service system. This is significant given that 20,000 youth age out of foster care each year (U. S. DHHS, 2005) and that former foster youth (ages 19 to 30) have twice the rate of posttraumatic stress disorder as U.S. war veterans (Pecora et al., 2005) and more severe mental health and behavioral problems than the general population and than children who have a maltreatment history but not foster care placement (Lawrence, Carlson, & Egeland, 2006).

A recent study of the effects of war on adult mental health reveals other risk factors that social workers should be aware of. Although some researchers have found that military service often provides youth a positive opportunity in transitioning into adulthood (Werner & Smith, 2001) and frequently leads to facilitating a young adult's return to higher education (Astone et al., 2000), the ravages of war experienced during military service can pose significant mental health risk. For example, Hoge, Auchterlonie, and Milliken (2006) examined the prevalence of mental health problems and service utilization among military personnel who recently returned from service in Iraq and found that one fifth (19.1%) of those returning from Iraq had at least one mental health problem, with about one third (35%) of those adults accessing mental health services during their first year back home. In addition, those personnel who were assessed as having a mental health condition were more likely to subsequently leave the military as compared with those personnel who returned home without a mental health condition. Therefore, it appears that although military service can be a positive path for many transitioning youth, the nature and quality of a youth's military experience may influence later physical and mental health outcomes as well as work trajectory decisions (e.g., to leave the military early). It appears that military service in a time of war may be a risk factor rather than protective factor. In addition, the availability of, access to, and quality of mental health care for military personnel upon their return home may also contribute to the severity of wartime service as a risk factor. We see Sheila's struggle with her own military deployments—the time away from family, the physical risks, and the reliance on community to provide family support in her absence. Sheila's story helps us to see that it may be difficult to disentangle the emotional and physical sequelae related to a traumatic brain injury and illustrates the challenges in family reintegration.

Knowledge of risk and protective factors related to the adulthood transition can help social workers assess young adult clients' current challenges, vulnerabilities, strengths, and potentials. Gaining an accurate understanding of the client's developmental history provides guidance to the social worker in formulating appropriate goals and intervention strategies. It is important to remember to check out your own assumptions of "risk" with clients in order to clarify the unique impact such experiences have on individual clients.

> ## Critical Thinking Questions 7.3
>
> How do you think that cumulative advantage/cumulative disadvantage affect human behavior during young adulthood? What personal, family, cultural, and other social factors during childhood and adolescence have an impact on the transition into young adulthood?

IMPLICATIONS FOR SOCIAL WORK PRACTICE

This discussion of young adulthood suggests several practice principles for social workers:

- Recognize that social roles during emerging adulthood may be different from those later in young adulthood.

- Explore cultural values, family expectations, attitudes toward gender roles, and environmental constraints/resources that may influence life structure decisions and opportunities when working with young adult clients.

- Assess specific work, family, and community conditions as they pertain to young adult clients' psychological and social well-being; be aware of any caregiving roles young adults may be playing.

- Where appropriate, help young adults to master the tasks involved in developing intimate relationships.

- Where appropriate, assist young adults with concerns about differentiating from family of origin and do so in a culturally sensitive manner.

- Work with other professionals to advocate for policies that promote transitional planning and connect youth to the labor market, particularly for youth aging out of foster care placements, correction facilities, group home environments, or other formal residential mental health settings.

- Take the initiative to develop mentoring programs that build relations between young adults and younger or older generations.

- Take the initiative to develop parenting classes for first-time parents, and recognize and develop the unique strengths of fathers, especially in mentoring teen fathers' to increase parenting skills.

- Understand the ways that social systems promote or deter people from maintaining or achieving health and well-being.

- Discover, appraise, and attend to changing locales, populations, scientific and technological developments, and emerging societal trends.

KEY TERMS

community assets	human capital	novice phase
default individualization	individuative-reflective faith	romantic love
developmental individualization	intimacy	spirituality
emerging adulthood	intimacy versus isolation	synthetic-conventional faith
fictive kin	life structure	

ACTIVE LEARNING

1. Identify one current social issue as portrayed in the media (e.g., housing, immigration policies, health care access or coverage or affordability, living wage) and explore how this social issue uniquely affects young adults.

2. Create your own theory of young adulthood. What are some of the important characteristics? What makes someone a young adult? What differentiates this stage from adolescence and middle adulthood? Start the process by answering the following question: "Do you consider yourself to be an adult?"

3. Choose one of the case studies at the beginning of the chapter (Johnny Nunez, Sheila Henderson, or Carla Aquino). Change the gender for that case without changing any other major demographic variable. Explore how your assumptions change about the individual's problems, challenges, and potential. Now choose a different case. Change the race or ethnicity for that case and again explore your assumptions. Finally, using the remaining case, change the SES and again explore how your assumptions change.

WEB RESOURCES

AmeriCorps NCCC (National Civilian Community Corps)
www.americorps.gov/about/programs/nccc.asp

Site details AmeriCorps' programs for young adults ages 18 to 24, offering full-time residential community service opportunities. Target goals include developing youths' leadership capacity through intensive and directed community service.

Child Trends
www.childtrends.org

Site of Child Trends, a nonprofit research organization located in Washington, D.C., provides data and reports focused on child well-being and marriage/family, to include fatherhood and parenting.

High School and Beyond Survey
http://nces.ed.gov/surveys/hsb

Site of the National Education Longitudinal Studies program of the National Center for Education Statistics, provides data and reports from their longitudinal projects that have tracked the educational and personal development of youth transitioning into adulthood.

National Fatherhood Initiative
www.fatherhood.org/default.asp

Site of the National Fatherhood Initiative, provides numerous resources and links to other fatherhood sites; discusses educational and outreach campaigns underway to promote involved fathering and family well-being.

National Gay and Lesbian Task Force
www.thetaskforce.org

Site presented by the National Gay and Lesbian Task Force contains information about the task force, news and views, special issues, state and local organizations, and special events.

National Guard Youth Challe*NG*e Program
www.ngycp.org

Site that reports on success stories of a multistate program that targets youth who have dropped out of high school to provide them with a 5-month residential program and ongoing mentoring services to facilitate their entry into employment, higher education/training, or the military.

National Survey of Family Growth
www.cdc.gov/nchs/nsfg.htm

Site of the National Center for Health Statistics offers reports, other publications, and data from their CDC-sponsored survey documenting family formation issues in adulthood, such as fertility and family planning, sexual behavior and health.

Network on Transitions to Adulthood
www.transad.pop.upenn.edu

Site presented by the Network on Transitions to Adulthood, examines the policies, programs, and institutions influencing the adulthood transition; contains fast facts and information on research initiatives. The Network is funded by the John D. and Catherine T. MacArthur Foundation and focuses on six areas: education, labor economics, social history, changing attitudes and norms, developmental changes, and ethnography.

Sloan Work and Family Research Network
http://wfnetwork.bc.edu

Site presented by the Sloan Work and Family Research Network of Boston College contains a literature database, research newsletter, resources for teaching, research profiles, and work and family links. Part of the Network's mission is to inform policymakers on key family-work issues.

CHAPTER

Middle Adulthood

Elizabeth D. Hutchison

OPENING QUESTIONS

- How are increased longevity, coupled with a post-World War II baby boom, altering the life course phase of middle adulthood in affluent societies?

- What do social workers need to know about biological, psychological, social, and spiritual changes in middle adulthood?

- What are the antecedent risk factors and protective factors that affect resilience in middle adulthood as well as the effects of midlife behavior on subsequent health and well-being?

KEY IDEAS

As you read this chapter, take note of these central ideas:

1. Increased life expectancy and a post-World War II baby boom in the United States and other industrial countries are leading to a trend of "mass longevity" and a large cohort of adults in midlife; very recently, this trend has led to an intense research interest in middle adulthood.

2. Theories about middle adulthood propose that midlife adults are deeply involved in care and concern for the generations to come and that midlife is a time when individuals attempt to find balance in opposing aspects of their lives.

3. Most biological systems reach their peak in the mid-20s, and gradual declines begin after that; by age 50, biological change becomes physically noticeable in most people, particularly changes in physical appearance, mobility, the reproductive system, and in vulnerability to chronic disease.

4. Middle adulthood is the period of peak performance of four mental abilities: inductive reasoning, spatial orientation, vocabulary, and verbal memory. Perceptual speed and numerical ability decline in middle adulthood.

5. There is good evidence of both stability and change in personality in middle adulthood; one often-noted personality change during middle adulthood is a gender-role expansion.

6. Theory and research suggest that humans have the potential for continuous spiritual growth across the life course, with midlife adults having the capacity to recognize many truths and become more oriented to service to others.

7. The most central roles in middle adulthood are related to family and paid work.

Case Study 8.1

Viktor Spiro, Assuming New Responsibilities as He Turns 40

Viktor Spiro was born in a village outside of Tirana, Albania, and lived most of his life, as did many Albanians in the Stalinist state, amid very impoverished conditions. He was the youngest of four children, with two sisters and a brother 12 years his senior. Viktor describes his childhood as "normal," until he sustained a serious head injury after falling from a tractor when he was 13. He experienced an increasing depression following

(Continued)

(Continued)

his hospitalization; his school performance declined and he withdrew from his friends. When Viktor was 20, his older brother died from a rare gastrointestinal illness, another traumatic event that exacerbated Viktor's depression and substance abuse. He subsequently went absent without leave (AWOL) from his military post and fled to Greece, where he continued to drink heavily and was reportedly hospitalized at a psychiatric facility.

Because his father was a U.S. citizen, Viktor was able to immigrate to the United States in his late 20s after the dissolution of Albania's repressive communist regime. He secured a job as a painter, but the language barrier and fast-paced life left him feeling vulnerable. Struggling to cope, Viktor made a series of suicide attempts and was arrested after lunging for the gun of a police officer who was trying to help him. Viktor claims that he did not intend to harm the officer, but that he saw the gun as a quick means to end his own life. Viktor's suicide attempts and arrest led to the beginning of a long relationship with mental health services (MHS). He was diagnosed with bipolar disorder with psychotic features, made more suicide attempts, was hospitalized, and lived in a group home.

After a few years, Viktor's father and mother, Petro and Adriana, moved to the United States to reunite with Viktor and his sister Maria. Viktor moved into an apartment with his parents and showed some signs of improved adjustment, including advances in his use of English and steady employment secured through the MHS job service program. However, his first-hand exposure to the worsening state of Petro's vascular dementia proved very traumatic. Then, Petro broke his hip and was in a nursing home briefly. He may have benefited from more advanced care and rehabilitation in a nursing facility, but his family could not wait to get him home. Supporting an elderly family member at an institution was culturally unacceptable.

Viktor and his father were both referred to a residential program to obtain counseling and case management services. The family was transferred here approximately 8 months after Viktor's most recent suicide attempt. His social worker learned that Viktor had accrued more than $140,000 in hospital bills and was still on "medical leave" from his job. The family had no significant income other than Petro's monthly $400 social security check and Adriana's stipend from Social Services to "take care" of her husband. Viktor shared that he had deep regrets about his latest suicide attempt and could not put himself or his family through this again. He felt that he was at a turning point and needed to take on more responsibility as he approached 40, especially with caring for his ailing parents. Viktor and Adriana were thankful for the agency's help and insisted on "payment" in the form of having his social worker break bread with the family and lighting incense in prayer for the agency workers.

It soon became clear that Adriana is the backbone of this family. The social worker tried to find ways to help Adriana lighten her load, but Adriana let him know that caring for the family is her role. Although the family is quite dependent on the agency to navigate their social environment, the home is Adriana's environment, and she finds purpose and a clearly defined role as keeper of the house as she acclimates to life in the United States.

As Viktor and his social worker met regularly, Viktor became more aware of his mother's struggles to fulfill family needs and began to do more in the house. Adriana began to trust the social worker's commitment to her family, and with Viktor translating, the social worker learned that Adriana wears her black dress and gold crucifix on a daily basis in mourning for her deceased son. Adriana called her life "unlucky," as she recounted the death of her first born, the chronic depression and strokes that have afflicted her husband over the past 40 years, and Viktor's ongoing struggles with his mental illness. Although the Spiro family clearly has experienced much suffering and trauma, their incredible strength and resolve are impressive. They are very affectionate and exhibit an enduring love for one another, demonstrating much resiliency in the laughter that often fills the apartment during mealtimes and in the family's optimism that their "luck" will change.

Viktor began to reveal a more reflective, insightful side during his recovery. He confided to his treatment team that he was hearing voices for nearly 6 months prior to his last suicide attempt but didn't tell anyone. He hoped the voices would just "go away." Viktor was able to communicate more freely about his emotions and no longer seemed preoccupied with past anxiety about being discovered by the military or with guilt regarding his brother's premature passing. His social worker and job coach assisted him with transition back into the work force, and he eventually obtained the medical clearance to return to his dishwashing job, resuming the role as the primary breadwinner for the family. This was a real lift to Viktor's self-esteem. The Spiro family experienced another financial lift with the news of a total forgiveness of Viktor's outstanding hospital bills.

While the Spiro family was enjoying their improving situation, the treatment team worked with Viktor to expand his social network outside the family. Viktor had been spending all of his time with his parents in their apartment when he was not working. As his confidence grew with his psychiatric improvement, however, he became more receptive to suggestions about weekend social activities coordinated by the agency. Viktor tried out a couple of the groups and enjoyed the activities and chance to form new relationships. He quickly immersed himself in a variety of weekend activities that involved shopping, movies, athletics, and cultural events.

The social worker assisted Viktor with the long process of reapplying for naturalization, after learning that he did not provide INS with the required documents on his previous application. With his improved mental state, Viktor was able to concentrate on studying for the citizenship test, which he passed. His citizenship ceremony was a wonderful day for Viktor and his family, and he made a poignant speech about dreaming of this day as a teenager watching CHIPS reruns in Albania.

The Spiro family clearly enjoyed the series of positive events for Viktor, but soon they faced another change of events. Petro developed pneumonia and respiratory failure and was placed on a respirator. He was eventually taken off the respirator successfully, but his physician indicated that he may not have long to live. The Spiros were grief stricken and wanted to take Petro home immediately. They struggled to understand the medical issues and needed assistance to interpret such figurative language as "the end is near," and to grasp the concept of a Do Not Resuscitate Order. Petro has held on through several medical crises, but his health remains quite tenuous. Viktor grieves for his father, but his handling of his health crises is a remarkable change from the impulsive and often dangerous behavior he had previously exhibited when responding to stressful situations. However, Viktor and his family will need help to deal with end-of-life issues, in the context of his mental illness and the ongoing cultural barriers. Adriana and Viktor draw on Greek Orthodox faith and rituals during this difficult time.

—Derek Morch

Case Study 8.2

Helen Tyson, Struggling to Be a "Good Mother" at 42

Helen Tyson was the youngest of four girls. She lived with her parents and sisters in a low socioeconomic area in a northeast suburb of Melbourne, Australia. Helen's family was of Anglo-Australian origin and she describes them as "battlers" and says "Mum and Dad did it tough, but always loved us and did the best they could."

(Continued)

(Continued)

Helen describes herself as "wild" as an adolescent, "out partying instead of studying." About 9 p.m. one Thursday evening when she was 16, she was traveling to a friend's place on the train when she was forced into a car by a number of men, driven to an empty factory, and repeatedly raped and bashed over a period of 6 hours. The men then dumped her at the railway station. A taxi driver found her and drove her to a hospital, and the police were called. Helen says that her parents were "fantastic," but she believed the attack was "karma for being wild." She knew the identity of "a couple of the men"—she had seen them at parties and was aware that they had been involved in similar incidents with other young women. Although she was fearful about possible repercussions, she cooperated with the police. The police investigations found evidence that these young men were involved in a consistent pattern of rape and intimidation of young women in the area. The men were charged with sexual offences against Helen and three other young women. During the period leading up to the trial, Helen's friends and family received a number of warnings advising her not to continue to cooperate with the police. The men were subsequently convicted and jailed.

Helen received counseling at a sexual assault service for 6 months after the rape. She said "it helped" and she felt "okay" with the support of her family and friends. Initially she was terrified and frightened to be on her own and needed someone to remain with her at all times. The counseling focused on this, and she felt that she had achieved something when she was able to go to a job interview on her own. She ceased counseling at this stage. Her schoolwork was affected, however, and she left school after completing Year 11. She had a couple of short-term jobs but was always anxious about people's intentions. She stopped work when she married Jim at age 20. She met Jim at a cousin's wedding and says that because he was older, she "felt safe with him." She told him about the rape and then they agreed not to refer to it again. Helen says that she always wanted to be a "good mother" and felt that this would prove that she was "okay" and not "damaged goods." She felt that to be a "good mother" would ameliorate some of the "badness" of being raped. She describes her pregnancies as fine, noting that she was relieved to be advised to have caesarean births; she felt uncomfortable about a vaginal birth because her vagina seemed "damaged."

Helen and Jim have been married for 22 years, and they own their own home. Jim is the owner and operator of a small courier business that he operates with one van. Helen has not worked outside the home but volunteered at her children's schools and worked at the various clubs in which her children were involved. This gave her satisfaction and made her feel that she was a "good mother." Helen says her marriage with Jim is "good" and thinks that he has been a good provider and father to the children. She has never enjoyed their sexual relationship but likes the fact that they are "good friends."

Helen and Jim have three children, Samantha, age 20, Will, age 18, and Sarah, age 16. Samantha recently moved out of home to live with her boyfriend, Joe. Will left school after completing Year 12. He did not apply for any tertiary (college-bound) courses and has had intermittent employment since. He had learning difficulties at school and currently has symptoms of depression. He has lost confidence and spends lots of time in his room. Jim and Helen have tried to help him find work through their friends and contacts but nothing has been successful. Sarah works part time in a sandwich bar and is still at secondary school. She has recently started going out at night with friends. Helen describes Sarah as "bright," and, "she's the one most like me."

Helen's parents provided a great deal of emotional, financial, and practical support to her and Jim, and Helen was devastated when her mother died of breast cancer 12 months ago. Her father has since become physically frail and has shown some loss of cognitive function. He still lives close to Helen, and she and her three sisters provide support for him—taking turns to clean, provide food, and so forth. Helen has no close friends and says she finds it difficult to trust people. She relies on her sisters for support.

Helen has had great difficulty accepting Samantha's boyfriend. He is from the same ethnic background as the men who raped her and while she can say "I know he's not like that," she is still concerned about cultural attitudes to women and about her emotional response to him. Helen feels that she cannot talk to Samantha about this because she does not want Samantha to know that she had been raped, saying, "Children should be protected from things like that." Helen is also frightened that knowledge of the rape would change how Samantha sees her. Helen missed Samantha when she moved out, she is worried about Will, concerned that he has lost direction, and she is terrified that the same thing will happen to Sarah that happened to her when she was 16. The issues in her children's lives are causing her to question whether or not she is a "good mother." Jim says he "loves" her but he has recently started to question the point of their relationship.

Helen had never been back to the railway station where she was abducted until very recently. She had avoided traveling in that area, but one night Sarah phoned for a lift from the train station and Jim was busy. Helen tried to find someone else to pick Sarah up, but eventually went herself. This precipitated a crisis. Helen started having flashbacks to the rapes, insomnia, and panic attacks. Her general physician has diagnosed depression and suggested that she contact the sexual assault service from which she received counseling at age 16.

—Lesley Hewitt

Case Study 8.3

Phoung Le, Serving Family and Community at 57

Le Thi Phoung, or Phoung Le as she is officially known in the United States, grew up in Saigon, South Vietnam, in the midst of war and upheaval. She has some fond memories of her first few years when Saigon was beautiful and peaceful. She loves to remember riding on her father's shoulders down the streets of Saigon on a warm day and shopping with her grandmother in the herb shops. But, she also has chilling memories of the military presence on the streets, the devastation caused by war, and the persistent fear that pervaded her home.

Phoung was married when she was 17 to a man chosen by her father. She smiles when she recounts the story of her future groom and his family coming to visit with the lacquered boxes full of betrothal gifts of nuts, teas, cake, and fruit. She admits that, at the time, she was not eager to marry and wondered why her father was doing this to her. But, she is quick to add that her father made a wise choice, and her husband Hien is her best friend, and is, as his name suggests, "nice, kind, and gentle." Their first child, a son, was born just before Phoung's 20th birthday, and Phoung reveled in being a mother.

Unfortunately, on Phoung's 20th birthday, April 30, 1975, life in Saigon turned horrific; that is the day that the North Vietnamese army overran Saigon. For Phoung and Hien, as well as for most people living in South Vietnam, just surviving became a daily struggle. Both Phoung's father and her father-in-law were in the South Vietnamese military and both were imprisoned by the Viet Cong for a few years. Both managed to escape and moved their families around until they were able to plan an escape from Vietnam by boat. Family members got separated during the escape, and others were lost when pirates attacked their boats. Phoung's father and

(Continued)

one brother have never been heard from since the pirate attack. Phoung and Hien and their son spent more than 2 years in a refugee camp in Thailand before being resettled in southern California. Their second child, a daughter, was born in the camp and a second daughter was born 1 year after they resettled in California. Over time, other family members were able to join them in the large Vietnamese community where they live.

Phoung's and Hien's opportunities for education were limited during the war years, but both came from families that valued education, and both managed to receive several years of schooling. Luckily, because they were living in a large Vietnamese community, language did not serve as a major barrier to employment in the United States. Phoung found a job working evenings as a waitress at a restaurant in Little Saigon, and Hien worked two jobs, by day as dishwasher in a restaurant, and by night cleaning office buildings in Little Saigon. Phoung's mother lived with Phoung and Hien and watched after the children while Phoung and Hien worked. Hien's parents lived a few blocks away, and several siblings and cousins of both Phoung and Hien were in the neighborhood. The Vietnamese community provided much social support and cultural connection. Phoung loved taking the children to visit the shops in Little Saigon and found special pleasure in visiting the herb shops where the old men sat around and spoke animatedly in Vietnamese.

Phoung grieved the loss of her beloved father and brother, but she wanted to create a positive life for her children. She was happy that she was able to stay connected to her cultural roots and happy that her children lived in a neighborhood where they did not feel like outsiders. But, she also wanted her children to be able to be successful outside the Vietnamese community as well as a resource for the community. She was determined that her children would have the education that she and Hien had been denied. Although she could have gotten by well in her neighborhood without English, she studied English along with her children because she wanted to model for the children how to live a bilingual, bicultural life. She was pleased that the children did well in school and was not surprised at how quickly the older two adapted to life in their adopted country. Sometimes there was tension in the multigenerational family about how the children were acculturating, and Phoung often served as the mediator in these tensions. She understood the desire of the older generation to keep cultural traditions, and she herself loved traditions such as the celebration of the Chinese New Year, with the colorful dresses and the little red *lai-see* envelopes of good luck money that were given to the children. She wanted her children to have these traditional experiences. But, she also was tuned in to the children's desire to be connected with some aspects of the dominant culture, such as the music and other popular media. She was also aware of how hard it was for the family elders to enforce the traditional family hierarchy when they were dependent on younger family members to help them navigate life in the English-speaking world outside their cultural enclave.

When her children reached adolescence, Phoung herself was uncomfortable with the Western cultural ideal for adolescent independence from the family, but she found ways to give her children some space while also holding them close and keeping them connected to their cultural roots. Other mothers in the neighborhood began to seek her advice about how to handle the challenging adolescent years. When her own adolescent children began to be impatient with the pervasive sadness they saw in their grandparents, Phoung suggested that they do some oral history with their grandparents. This turned out to be a therapeutic experience for all involved. The grandparents were able to sift through their lives in Vietnam and the years since, give voice to all that had been lost, but also begin to recognize the strength it took to survive and their good fortune to be able to live among family and a community where much was familiar. The grandchildren were able to hear a part of their family narrative that they did not know because the family had preferred not to talk about it. Phoung was so pleased with this outcome that she asked to start a program of intergenerational dialog at the

Vietnamese Community Service Center. She thought that this might be one way to begin to heal the trauma in her community while also giving the younger generation a strong cultural identity as they struggled to live in a multicultural world. She continues to be an active force in that program, even though her own children are grown.

Their 40s and early 50s brought both great sorrow and great joy to Phoung and Hien. Within a 2-year period, Phoung's mother and Hien's mother and father died. Phoung and Hien became the family elders. They provided both economic and emotional support during times of family crisis, such as a sibling's cancer, a niece's untimely pregnancy, and a nephew's involvement with a neighborhood gang. But there was also great joy. Phoung was very good at her job and became the supervisor of the wait staff at the best restaurant in Little Saigon. Hien was able to buy his own herb shop. After attending the local community college, the children were all able to go on to university and do well. Their son became an engineer, the older daughter became a physician, and the younger daughter recently finished law school. Their son is now father to two young children, and Phoung finds great joy in being a grandmother. She is playing an important role in keeping the grandchildren connected to some Vietnamese traditions. Phoung finds this phase of life to be a time of balance in all areas of her life, and she is surprised and pleased to find renewed interest in spiritual growth through her Buddhist practices.

Phoung has come to talk to the social worker at the Vietnamese Community Services Center. Her younger daughter has recently informed Phoung that she is lesbian. Phoung says that she has struggled with this news and has not yet told Hien. She knows that the Vietnamese community does not engage in "gay bashing" the way some communities do, but she also knows that homosexuality carries some stigma in her Vietnamese community. She has done much soul searching as she tries to integrate what her daughter has told her. But, she knows one thing: she loves her daughter very much and she wants her daughter to feel loved and supported by her family and her community. Her daughter plans to march with a Vietnamese gay rights group in the upcoming Tet Celebration march and she has asked Phoung to march with her. Phoung is trying to decide what to do. She has come to ask the social worker if the Community Services Center runs any groups for parents of gays and lesbians. If not, she would like to start one.

THE CHANGING SOCIAL CONSTRUCTION OF MIDDLE ADULTHOOD

Although their life paths have been very different, Viktor Spiro, Helen Tyson, and Phoung Le are all in the life course phase of middle adulthood. Not so long ago, middle adulthood was nearly an unstudied terrain. Recently, however, because of a confluence of demographic trends and research accomplishments, there has been intense interest in the middle adult years in affluent societies. Although we still have only a hazy picture of middle adulthood, that picture is coming into better focus.

Changing Age Demographics

Adults in the middle adult years currently constitute approximately one third of the U.S. population (Whitbourne & Willis, 2006). That is an astounding statistic, and given this situation, it is not surprising that researchers have begun to take serious interest in the middle adult phase of the life course. Beginning in the 1990s, an interdisciplinary group of researchers in North America and Europe launched several large research projects to move our understanding of middle adulthood from mythology to science (see Brim, Ryff, & Kessler, 2004; Willis & Martin, 2005). These researchers span the fields of anthropology, economics, genetics, neurology, psychology, and sociology. From a life course perspective, it is important to note that most of what we "know" about middle adulthood is based on research on the current cohort of midlife adults, a cohort known as the baby boom generation. Therefore, it is important to remember that this cohort is the result of a singular demographic event, a "fifteen-year splurge of births" (Eggebeen & Sturgeon, 2006, p. 3) that occurred after World War II. This splurge of births was a departure from a long-term trend of declining births, a trend that was resumed in the 1960s when fertility began to decline again.

The current large cohort of middle adults, the largest middle-aged cohort ever alive (Wahl & Kruse, 2005), was created by 15 years of high fertility, but increasing life expectancy is another contributing factor. In 1900, the median age of the U.S. population was 23 and the average life expectancy was 47.3 years (U.S. Census Bureau, 1999). By 1950, the median age was 30.2 years and average life expectancy was 68.2 years (National Center for Health Statistics, 2001). By 2000, the median age was 35.3 and the average life expectancy was 76.9. And by 2009, the estimated median age was 36.7 years and the estimated average life expectancy at birth was 78.1 years (Central Intelligence Agency, 2009). These changing demographics are presented visually in Exhibit 8.1. These data do not mean that no one lived past what we now consider middle age in 1900. The average life expectancy in 1900 was deflated by high rates of infant mortality. Indeed, in 1900, 18% of the population of the United States was 45 years old or older. This compares with 28% in 1950 and 34% in 2000. Living past age 45 is not new, but more people are doing it. This trend has an enormous impact on our understanding of the adult life course (Wahl & Kruse, 2005).

> How might these changing demographics affect the midlife phase of the life course?

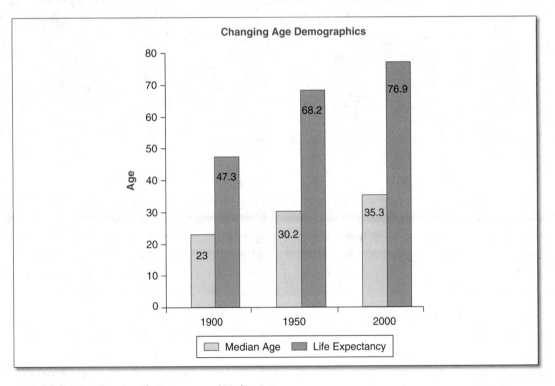

▲ **Exhibit 8.1**   Changing Life Expectancy and Median Age

SOURCES: Based on U.S. Bureau of the Census, 1999, and the National Center for Health Statistics, 2001.

Longevity and birthrates vary across global populations. Mass longevity and declining birthrates hold true in advanced industrial societies, but in poor and less-developed societies, the trends are radically different. International data show a high life expectancy of 84.6 years in Macau (special administrative region in China) and a low of 31.9 years in Swaziland in 2009 estimates (Central Intelligence Agency, 2009). In that same year, the average life expectancy was less than 50 years in no fewer than 17 countries, including Afghanistan, where the average life expectancy is 44.6. Social workers who work in the international arena or with immigrant families will need to develop appropriate understanding of how the life course varies across world populations.

A Definition of Middle Adulthood

Before we go further, we need to pause and consider *who* is included in middle adulthood. In the most general sense, we are talking about people who are in midlife, or the central part of the life course. Beyond that, we do not have generally agreed upon ages to include in middle adulthood. The most frequently used definition of middle adulthood includes those persons who are between the ages of 40 and 64 (Bjorklund & Bee, 2008), but some scholars use a lower limit as young as age 30 and an upper limit as late as age 70 (Dittmann-Kohli, 2005). The National Council on the Aging (2000) found that one third of its sample in their 70s thought of themselves as middle-aged, and other researchers have found that the older one is, the later the reported age of middle adulthood (Lachman & Bertrand, 2001).

> Is biological age, psychological age, social age, or spiritual age the best marker for middle adulthood?

Some authors argue that middle adulthood should not be thought of in terms of chronological age, but instead in terms of achieving certain developmental tasks. Generally, midlife adults have established a family, settled into and peaked in a career, and taken responsibility for their children, their parents, and their community (Staudinger & Bluck, 2001). Any definition of middle adulthood must also include biological aging processes, subjective perceptions, and social roles as well as historical and generational contexts (Moen & Wethington, 1999). This suggestion is consistent with the major themes of a life course perspective discussed in Chapter 1 of this book. Dittman-Kohli (2005) suggests that middle adulthood is "a friendly expression for not being young anymore but not really very old yet" (p. 323).

Some authors have been critical of any approach to defining middle adulthood that includes such a wide age range as 40 to 60 or older (e.g., Staudinger & Bluck, 2001). They suggest that the beginning of midlife is very different from the latter part of midlife, and that lumping these parts of the life course together may lead to contradictory findings. They call for a division of middle adulthood into early midlife and late midlife (Kohli & Künemund, 2005; Lachman, 2004). You may recall a similar concern about the boundaries of young adulthood noted in Chapter 7. Late adulthood, which is divided into late adulthood and very late adulthood in this book, encompasses an even larger age span, potentially from 65 to 100-plus. As longevity increases, the adult portion of life is likely to be divided into finer and finer phases.

Culture and the Construction of Middle Adulthood

With the identification of a middlehood, societies must construct roles for, and make meaning of, middle adulthood. Wahl and Kruse (2005) argue that middle adulthood was created by the increase of life expectancy in modern society. Evidence, indicates, however, that middle adulthood has been incorporated into views of the life course since at least the early Middle Ages (Dittmann-Kohli, 2005). In his book *Welcome to Middle Age! (And Other Cultural Fictions)*, Richard Shweder (1998) suggests that middle age is a "cultural fiction" and the fiction does not play out the same way in all cultures. He does not use "fiction" to mean false, but to mean, instead, that ideas about middle age are culturally created. Shweder suggests that the European American cultural construction of middle adulthood casts it primarily in terms of chronology (middle age), biology, and medicine. He argues that this cultural construction is a story of mental and physical decline. Other cultures, he suggests, organize the life course, including middle adulthood, in terms of "a social history of role transitions" (p. xi), focusing particularly on family roles.

Consider how middle adulthood is defined and understood in three cultures: upper-caste Hindu in rural India, middle-class Japanese, and middle-class Anglo American (Menon, 2001):

- Asian Indian Hindu beliefs and practices differ greatly according to region and caste, but middle adulthood is not defined as a separate, clearly distinguished life phase as it is in the United States. To the extent that it is recognized, it is thought of as "maturity" and seen in relation to transitions in family roles. Women become senior wives, and men replace their fathers as head of the family, responsible for family decision making and for the family's interaction with the community. Maturity is considered to be the best time in the life course.

- In Japan, aging is associated with power and creativity. This view of aging is tied to two central beliefs. First, life is about becoming, not being, and all phases of the life course offer opportunities for personal growth, to reach for human perfection. A second central belief is that aging is a natural process. Although the Japanese recognize some loss and decline with the passing of years, the general view of middle adulthood is that it is the "prime of life," a time of fullness, activity, and spiritual growth.

- Empirical research about the meaning of midlife in the United States suggests two divergent cultural beliefs: One view sees middle adulthood as a positive time of having accumulated resources for coping; the other view sees middle adulthood as a negative time of decline and loss. This latter view of decline and loss (of being "over the hill") often seems to permeate popular culture. However, much of the recent research on middle adulthood reveals an attempt to recast middlehood as the "prime of life." What images come to mind when you think of middle adulthood? Do you think first of sagging chins, wrinkles, reading glasses, thinning or graying hair, hot flashes, loss of sex drive, and so on, or do you think first of emotional and spiritual maturity that gives power and creativity? What images do you think Viktor Spiro, Helen Tyson, and Phoung Le hold of middle adulthood?

Comparing views of middlehood in these three cultures helps us recognize that our taken-for-granted views of this life course phase are, indeed, highly influenced by culture. It also alerts us to the possibility that our clients from different cultural groups may have different expectations for midlife roles. However, it is important to note that the above descriptions cover relatively privileged groups within wider cultures. Evidence suggests that conceptions of the adult life course vary across social class lines within a given society. Clearly, location in the global economy, war, and the HIV pandemic are factors that have different impacts on different groups of people around the globe and can lead to very different constructions of middle adulthood.

THEORIES OF MIDDLE ADULTHOOD

Few theories focus directly on middle adulthood, but a number of theories address middle adulthood as a part of a larger developmental framework. Themes from three of those theories are presented here.

Erikson's Theory of Generativity

According to Erik Erikson's (1950) life span theory, the psychosocial struggle of middle adulthood is generativity versus stagnation (refer back to Exhibit 3.7 for an overview of Erikson's psychosocial stage theory). **Generativity** is the ability to transcend personal interests to provide care and concern for younger and older generations; it encompasses "procreation, productivity, and creativity, and thus the generation of new beings, as well as of new products and new ideas, including a kind of self-generation concerned with further identity development" (Erikson, 1982, p. 67). Generative adults provide "care, guidance, inspiration, instruction, and leadership" (McAdams, 2001, p. 395) for future generations. Failure to find a way to con-

> How does generativity affect the capacity for interdependence?

tribute to future generations, or to make a contribution to the general well-being, results in self-absorption and a sense of stagnation. Erikson saw generativity as an instinct that works to perpetuate society. With some help, Viktor Spiro is beginning to practice generativity in his relationship with his parents. For Helen Tyson, generativity is expressed in care of her father and her children. Phoung Le is finding a variety of ways to enact generativity in both her family and her community. As a social worker, however, you will most likely encounter people who struggle with a sense of stagnation in middle adulthood.

Dan McAdams and Ed de St. Aubin (de St. Aubin, McAdams, & Kim, 2004; McAdams, 2006; McAdams & de St. Aubin, 1992, 1998) have presented a model of generativity that includes the seven components found in Exhibit 8.2. McAdams and de St. Aubin (1992, 1998) see generativity coming from both the person (personal desire) and the social and cultural environment (social roles and cultural demand).

Even though Erikson outlined middlehood generativity in 1950, generativity was not a subject of empirical investigation until the 1980s (Peterson & Duncan, 2007). There is limited longitudinal research to answer the question, are midlife adults more generative than people in other life course phases? Most of the cross-sectional research on generativity reports greater generativity during middle adulthood than in young adulthood or late adulthood (An & Cooney, 2006; McAdams, 2001; Zucker, Ostrove, & Stewart, 2002), but other researchers have found that generativity continues to grow past middle adulthood (Sheldon & Kasser, 2001). Some researchers have identified three components of generativity: generative desire, generative felt capacity, and generative accomplishment, noting that some research indicates that young adults may be high in generative motivation but not have the resources for generative accomplishments (Zucker, Ostrove, & Stewart).

Research also finds that generativity is associated with gender, class, and race, but the findings are inconsistent. Several researchers (Marks, Bumpass, & Jun, 2004; McAdams & de St. Aubin, 1992; McKeering & Pakenham, 2000) have found that men who had never been fathers scored particularly low on measures of generativity, but not being a mother did not have the same effect for women. However, An and Cooney (2006) did not find parenting to be more associated with generativity for men than women, but did find that midlife women are more involved in both private and public caring than midlife men. Phoung Le is certainly more involved in providing more private and public caring than Hien, who is nevertheless active in his family and community. When Phoung sees a need in her own family, she also wants to address the need at the community level. Another recent research project found that as generativity increases for adults ages 35 to 74, so does psychological well-being, and this association between generativity and well-being is equally strong for childless adults as for parents (Rothrauff & Cooney, 2008). Generativity has been found to increase with educational level (Keyes & Ryff, 1998). Black adults have been found to score higher on some measures of generativity than White adults (Hart, McAdams, Hirsch, & Bauer, 2001).

1. Inner desire for immortality and to be needed
2. Cultural demand for productivity
3. Concern for the next generation
4. Belief in the species
5. Commitment
6. Action: creating, maintaining, or offering
7. Development of a generative life story

▲ **Exhibit 8.2**   McAdams and de St. Aubin's Seven Components of Generativity

SOURCE: Adapted from McAdams, Hart, & Maruna, 1998.

Jung's and Levinson's Theories of Finding Balance

Both Carl Jung and Daniel Levinson suggest that middle adulthood is a time when individuals attempt to find balance in their lives in several ways. Jung (1971) sees middle adulthood as a time when we discover and reclaim parts of the self that were repressed in the search for conformity in the first half of life. He emphasizes the importance of gender identity in middle adulthood. Adults begin to move from the stereotyped gender-role behavior of young adulthood to a more androgynous behavioral repertoire at this age. Jung also suggested that **extroversion,** or orientation to the external world, and **introversion,** or orientation to the internal world, come into greater balance in middle adulthood. He suggested that the challenges of establishing family and work roles demand extroversion in young adulthood, but in middle adulthood individuals tend to turn inward and explore their own subjective experience. Viktor Spiro is beginning to show a more reflective side in therapy. Perhaps the same will happen for Helen Tyson. Phoung Le is using Buddhist practices to engage in deeper internal exploration.

Daniel Levinson (Levinson, 1986, 1990; Levinson & Levinson, 1996; Levinson, Darrow, Klein, Levinson, & McKee, 1978) conceptualizes the life course as a sequence of eras, each with its own biopsychosocial character (Levinson & Levinson, 1996) with major changes from one era to the next. Changes do occur within eras, but these changes are small and do not involve major revision of the life structure. Adult life is composed of alternating periods of relative stability and periods of transition. As mentioned in Chapter 7, a key concept of Levinson's theory is life structure, by which he means "the underlying pattern or design of a person's life at a given time" (Levinson & Levinson, p. 22). In most cases, family and occupation are the central components in the life structure, but people vary widely in how much weight they assign to each. During the transition to middle adulthood, individuals often try to give greater attention to previously neglected components. Levinson sees this transition in terms of balancing four opposing aspects of identity: young versus old, creation versus destruction, feminine versus masculine, and attachment versus separation (Levinson, 1977).

Life-Span Theory and the Gain-Loss Balance

Life-span theory has much in common with the life course perspective introduced in Chapter 1 of this book. It is more firmly rooted in psychology, however, whereas the life course perspective has more multidisciplinary roots and emphasizes the historical and cultural context of life course development. Life-span theory is based in ongoing transactions between persons and environments and begins with the premise that development is lifelong. Six central propositions of the life-span theory as they relate to middle adulthood are summarized in Exhibit 8.3.

- Human development is lifelong and no age period is supreme in the developmental trajectory. Midlife cannot be studied in isolation; it must be studied in terms of both its antecedents and its consequences.

- Development involves both gains and losses. In midlife, there is a tie in the relationship between gains and losses.

- Biological influences on development become more negative, and cultural support becomes more important, with increasing age in adulthood. A distinction can be made between early and late midlife.

- With increasing age in adulthood, there is an overall reduction in resources. At midlife, adults must put a major effort into managing resources.

- Even though challenges increase and biological resources decrease in midlife, there is still possibility for change.

- The experience of midlife adults may depend on cultural and historical contexts.

▲ **Exhibit 8.3**   Central Propositions of Life-Span Theory as They Relate to Middle Adulthood

SOURCE: Adapted from Staudinger & Bluck, 2001, pp. 17–18.

We focus here particularly on the proposition that in midlife there is a tie in the balance of gains and losses (Staudinger & Bluck, 2001). Life-span researchers have raised the question, what is the balance of gains and losses in midlife (Baltes, Lindenberger, & Staudinger, 1998)? For example, there is good evidence of gains in self-esteem and emotional maturity and of losses in biological functioning. Some researchers are finding that the balance shifts from a dominance of developmental gains in early midlife to a dominance of developmental losses in late midlife (e.g., Heckhausen, 2001; Staudinger & Bluck, 2001). It is important to note, however, that gains or losses are defined and given meaning in cultural contexts and are influenced by both group-based and individual-based attributes. For example, there is evidence that in Samoa, middle adulthood is associated with political power and physical activity, and "aging as a loss of youth is not given any importance" (p. 327) in the story told about midlife (Dittmann-Kohli, 2005). One might wonder how Viktor Spiro, Helen Tyson, and Phoung Le see the gain-loss balance in early midlife.

With professional help, Viktor Spiro seems to be making some gains in emotion regulation, economic security, relationships, and comfort in his adopted country but is facing loss in the form of the rapidly declining health of his father. Helen Tyson sees gain in the stability of her marriage, but she seems more focused on losses, the loss of her mother and declining control over her children. It is quite possible that the reactivation of an earlier traumatic experience and the accompanying depression is contributing to her focus on losses. Phoung Le, who is in late midlife, has many social, emotional, and spiritual resources for coping with challenges and seems to be focused on gains rather than losses in several spheres. She takes special pleasure in being a grandmother and in serving her community. She has suffered the losses of her mother and her parents-in-law in recent years, however.

As we review the research on changes in middle adulthood in the remaining sections of this chapter, it is important to note that it is hard to know whether what we are learning about midlife is tied to a specific cohort, the baby boomers. Research on middle adulthood is quite new, and there are no long-term longitudinal studies available of earlier cohorts of midlife adults. Among the factors to keep in mind as you read research results is that the baby boomers (born 1946–1964) represent a very large cohort, and have, throughout their adulthood, faced more competition for jobs and other resources than earlier cohorts.

> ### Critical Thinking Questions 8.1
>
> What do you think is the balance of gains and losses in Viktor Spiro's early phase of middle adulthood compared with his experience with young adulthood? What are the gains and what are the losses? What about Helen Tyson; what is the balance of gains and losses for her in the early phase of middle adulthood compared with young adulthood? What are the gains and what are the losses? And what about Phoung Le in the late phase of middle adulthood; what is the balance of gains and losses for her in this phase of life compared with earlier phases? What are the gains and what are the losses?

BIOLOGICAL CHANGES AND PHYSICAL AND MENTAL HEALTH IN MIDDLE ADULTHOOD

There have been dramatic changes in the last few decades in the numbers of adults who enjoy healthy and active lives in the years between 45 and 65 and beyond. However, some physical and mental decline does begin to occur. Most biological systems reach their peak performance in the mid-20s. Age-related changes over the next 20 to 30 years are usually gradual, accumulating at different rates in different body systems. The changes are the result of interactions of biology with psychological, sociocultural, and spiritual factors, and individuals play a very active role in the aging process throughout adulthood, as we can see in the life trajectories of Viktor Spiro, Helen Tyson, and Phoung Le. However, by the age of 50, the accumulation of biological change becomes physically noticeable in most people.

> What factors have led to changes in biological age in middle adulthood?

The biggest stories in biological functioning and physical and mental health in middle adulthood are changes in physical appearance; changes in mobility; changes in the reproductive system; and changes in health, more specifically the beginnings of chronic disease. Enormous individual differences exist in the timing and intensity of these changes, but some changes affect almost everyone, such as presbyopia for both men and women and menopause for women.

Changes in Physical Appearance

Probably the most visible signs of physiological changes in middle adulthood are changes in physical appearance (Bjorklund & Bee, 2008). The skin begins to sag and wrinkle as it loses its firmness and elasticity. Small, localized areas of brown pigmentation, often called aging spots, may appear in parts of the body exposed to sunlight. As the sebaceous glands that secrete oils become less active, the skin becomes drier. Hair on the head often becomes thinner and grayer, and hair may appear in places where it is not wanted, such as ears, thicker clumps around the eyebrows, and the chin on women. Many midlife adults wear glasses for the first time because of the decreased ability to focus on near objects (presbyopia) that occurs in most adults between the ages of 45 and 55.

There are significant changes in body build as midlife adults begin to lose height and gain weight. Beginning in their 40s, people lose about one half inch in height per decade as a result of loss of bone material in the vertebrae. Starting about age 20, there is a tendency to gain weight until about the mid-50s. Body fat begins to accumulate in the torso and accounts for a greater percentage of weight in middle adulthood than in adolescence and early adulthood. In the late 50s, people tend to begin to lose weight, but this weight loss comes from loss of lean body mass (bone and muscle) rather than from loss of fat.

Changes in skin can be minimized by using sunscreen, skin emollients, applications of vitamin E, facial massages, and by smoking cessation. Increasingly, affluent baby boomers are using procedures such as plastic surgery and Botox to maintain a youthful appearance. Changes in body build can be minimized by involvement in aerobic exercise and resistance training to improve muscle tone, reduce fat, and offset bone loss. The current recommendation is 30 to 60 minutes of exercise 3 to 4 days per week.

Changes in Mobility

Beginning in the 40s, losses in muscles, bones, and joints start to have an impact on mobility. A progressive loss of muscle mass leads to loss of strength beginning at about age 45, and muscle strength continues to decline at the rate of 12% to 15% per decade thereafter (Whitbourne, 2001). The most apparent loss of muscle strength occurs in the legs and back (Merrill & Verbrugge, 1999). By engaging in strength training, midlife adults can minimize the loss of muscle mass. An effective strength-training program involves two to three workouts per week.

Maximum bone density is reached in early adulthood, and there is a progressive loss of bone mineral after that. The rate of bone loss accelerates in the 50s. Microcracks begin to develop in the bones in response to stress, and bones also begin to lose their elasticity. By the end of middle adulthood, bones are less strong and more brittle. The rate of bone loss is about two times greater in women than in men, linked to the loss of estrogens after menopause. Bone loss tends to be greater in people with fair skin, and Black women have higher bone mineral than White women or Hispanic women. Bone loss is accelerated by smoking, alcohol use, and poor diet. It is slowed by aerobic activity, resistance training, increased calcium intake in young adulthood, and use of vitamin D (Whitbourne, 2001).

Changes in the joints begin to occur before skeletal maturity, but without injury, no obvious symptoms appear until the 40s. The cartilage that protects joints begins to degenerate, and an outgrowth of cartilage starts to develop and interfere with ease of movement. Unlike muscles, joints do not benefit from constant use. To prevent unnecessary wear and tear on joints, it is important to wear the proper footwear when engaging in exercise activities and to avoid repetitive movements of the wrists. Flexibility exercises help to expand the range of motion for stiff joints. Exercises to strengthen the muscles that support joints also help to minimize the mobility problems associated with changes in joints.

Changes in the Reproductive System and Sexuality

Perhaps the most often noted biological change in middle adulthood is the lost or diminished reproductive capacity (see, e.g., Avis & Crawford, 2006; Marshall, 2007; Rossi, 2004a). Although both men and women experience reproductive changes during adulthood, changes in women have received much more attention from researchers and the popular media than changes in men. For this reason, the following discussion begins with what is known about women's reproductive changes during middle adulthood.

In middle adulthood, women's capacity to conceive and bear children gradually declines until menopause, when the capacity for conceiving children ends (although reproductive technology to extend a woman's reproductive life may eventually become more generally available). **Menopause** is the permanent cessation of menstruation, and for research purposes is usually defined as 12 consecutive months with absence of menstruation (Avis & Crawford, 2006). The median age of menopause is 50 or 51 years; it occurs between the ages of 45 and 55 in 90% of women in the United States.

> What effect do these sex differences in changes in the reproductive system have on middle adulthood?

Although female menopause is often described as a less gradual process than occurs in men, it is a more gradual process than often recognized (Avis & Crawford, 2006; Rossi, 2004a). The menopause process begins when the woman is in her 30s. At this time, called **premenopause,** the woman begins to have occasional menstrual cycles without ovulation, or the production of eggs. This change usually goes without notice.

By the mid- to late 40s, the supply of egg cells is depleted, ovarian production of hormone slows, and more and more menstrual cycles occur without ovulation. The menstrual cycle becomes irregular, some menstrual periods are skipped, and the production of estrogen drops. In this period, known as *perimenopause,* changes in the reproductive system begin to be noticed (Gyllstrom, Schreiner, & Harlow, 2007). **Perimenopause** is defined as the period of time that begins immediately prior to menopause, when there are biological and clinical indicators that reproductive capacity is reaching exhaustion, and continues through the first year after the last menstrual period. Symptoms that are often proposed to be associated with perimenopause include hot flashes, night sweats, vaginal dryness, headaches, insomnia, fatigue, anxiety, depression, irritability, memory loss, difficulty concentrating, and weight gain.

In popular culture, menopause is seen as a major milestone, a prominent biological marker, for women; it is popularly called the "change of life." Cross-cultural studies suggest widely differing experiences with menopause, with many non-Western cultures viewing it as a positive change, ushering in a time of greater freedom for women, a time when they are allowed greater participation in the world beyond the family (Rossi, 2004a). In the past, the Euro-American perspective focused on menopause as a deficiency disease, but this view appears to be losing dominance (Avis & Crawford, 2006).

Although perimenopause, and purported associated symptoms and discomforts, has received much attention in the popular media in recent years, it has not been the subject of intensive scientific study. Menopause did not receive much attention either until the 1980s. This increased interest seems to come from a confluence of factors. Chief among those factors is that the current baby boom generation of women, who are now in middlehood, have, as a cohort, asserted their control over their reproductive lives and challenged taboos about sexuality. Two other influential factors include epidemiological studies that identified estrogen decline in menopause as a risk factor for osteoporosis and cardiovascular disease, and the development of medications for the "treatment" of menopause. To date, however, research on the connection between menopause and many of the symptoms believed to be a consequence is far from conclusive.

Existing research suggests considerable variation in signs and symptoms of menopause. Gail Robinson (2002) reviewed studies from Israel, North America, Japan, Peru, the Yucatan, and the Greek island of Evia and found enormous differences in the experiences of menopause among women in the same culture as well as among women in different cultures. One recent large national research project compared menopausal symptoms across racial and ethnic groups in the United States, including Caucasian, African American, Chinese, Japanese, and Hispanic women (Avis et al., 2001; Bromberger et al., 2001). The researchers found that the Caucasian women reported significantly more psychosomatic symptoms than women from the other racial and ethnic groups. African American women were significantly more likely and Asian women were less likely to report hot flashes or night sweats than Caucasian women. It is hard to tease out the relative contribution of cultural beliefs about menopause from different patterns of diet and exercise. For example, Japanese diets are lower in fat and higher in phytoestrogens than diets in Canada and the United States (Avis & Crawford, 2006). Existing research also reports considerable individual variation in the signs and symptoms of menopause in the United States.

Numerous studies have explored the connection between depression and menopause and although there is inconsistency in the findings, there is a fairly consistent finding that depression is more common among women in early perimenopause than among women in either premenopause or menopause. One longitudinal study found a moderate increase in depression during perimenopause, but most women who became depressed during perimenopause had prior episodes of depression (Avis, Brambilla, McKinlay, & Vass, 1994). Two recent cross-sectional research projects found that middle-aged women with depressive symptoms are more likely to report hot flashes, night sweats, and trouble sleeping (Brown, Gallicchio, Flaws, & Tracy, 2009; Reed et al., 2009). Given the cross-sectional nature of their study, which does not allow the researchers to know which came first, depression or menopausal symptoms,

Reed et al. conclude that either depressive symptoms amplify menopausal symptoms or severe hot flashes exacerbate depression symptoms. Brown et al. suggest that sleep disturbance may be exacerbated by hot flashes, and sleep disturbance may contribute to depression. Women with a history of schizophrenia have also been found to be vulnerable to relapse during perimenopause (Kulkarni, 2005).

Research does indicate that vaginal lubrication decreases as women age (Laumann, Paik, & Rosen, 1999). With lower estrogen levels, the blood supply to the vagina and surrounding nerves and glands is reduced. The tissues become thinner and drier and cannot produce sufficient lubrication for comfortable intercourse. There is also increased risk of infection unless estrogen replacement or an artificial lubricant is used. Longer periods of foreplay can also help with this situation.

Menopause is big business in the United States, but perhaps not as big as it once was. Starting in the 1940s, menopause was constructed as a deficiency disease, a disease that could be treated pharmaceutically with hormone-replacement therapy. The purpose of the treatment was not to prolong reproductive capacity, but rather to treat the symptoms thought to be associated with menopause. There are two primary types of hormone therapy for menopause: estrogen alone (ERT) or estrogen combined with progestin (hormone-replacement therapy, or HRT). ERT was introduced first in the 1940s and was promoted widely by pharmaceutical companies and by popular books such as *Feminine Forever* (Wilson, 1966) in the 1960s. In the 1970s, several research studies reported that ERT increased women's risk for endometrial cancer (Mack et al., 1976; Smith, Prentice, Thompson, & Hermann, 1975; Ziel & Finkle, 1975). In response to these studies, pharmaceutical companies discovered that combining estrogen with progestin could prevent the excessive buildup of estrogen that increased the risk for endometrial cancer. HRT then became the recommended treatment for menopausal women who still have an intact uterus, and use of HRT more than doubled between 1982 and 1992 and continued to increase at the beginning of the 21st century (Rossi, 2004a).

Although manufacturers of hormone products had advertised the benefits to physical and mental health from HRT, recent research has found a much more complex story (Bouchez, 2007). In the United States, the Women's Health Initiative (WHI) was involved in a large, ongoing study, scheduled to last for 8.5 years, comparing hormone therapy with a placebo. But in a surprising move, they called a halt to their study after 5.2 years in the summer of 2002 because the health risks exceeded the health benefits. HRT was found to increase the risks of coronary heart disease, breast cancer, stroke, and pulmonary embolism. These risks were weighed against the slight positive effects on colorectoral cancer, endometrial cancer, and hip fracture (Hlatky, Boothrody, Vittinghoff, Sharp, & Whooley, 2002; Okie, 2002; Rossi, 2004a).

More recent analysis of international data sets tells an even more complicated story. Here are some of the most recent findings:

- If a woman begins HRT between the ages of 50 and 55 or less than 10 years after she started menopause, she has less heart disease and less death than a woman taking a placebo—if HRT is used on a short-term basis (Bouchez, 2007).

- Using HRT, no matter the age started, increases the risk of stroke by 32% (Bouchez, 2007).

- For most women taking hormones on a short-term basis (2 to 3 years), there is no increase in breast cancer in the short term, but long-term risk cannot be ruled out. Breast cancer risk increases the longer a woman stays on HRT (Bouchez, 2007).

- HRT reduces hip fractures (Bouchez, 2007).

- HRT increases the risk of ovarian cancer by 38%, regardless of the duration of use or the dose (Mørch, Løkkegaard, Andreasen, Krüger-Kiaer, & Lidegaard, 2009).

Based on these research findings, there has been a large reduction in the number of HRT users since 2002 (Avis & Crawford, 2006). The current recommendation is that middle-aged women and their medical advisors must make individual decisions that take into consideration the woman's own unique configuration of risk and protective factors. Recently, some researchers have begun to explore another alternative to HRT, selective estrogen replacement modulators (SERMs), such as raloxifene and tamoxifen. These newer alternatives are thought to have a more targeted effect on bone loss (Johnson, 2006). It is important to note that lifestyle changes have also been shown to reduce the risks related to hormonal changes during menopause: quitting smoking, exercising, reducing cholesterol intake, taking calcium supplements, and losing weight.

For men, the quantity of viable sperm begins to decrease in the late 40s or 50s, and most births are fathered by men younger than 60 years, but men in their 80s have been known to father children. The testes shrink gradually and the volume of seminal fluid begins to decline after about age 60. There is a gradual decline in testosterone beginning in early adulthood and continuing throughout life, but many men stay in the "normal" range for younger men throughout middle adulthood (Bjorklund & Bee, 2008; Marshall, 2007). Although little research has been done on the topic, recent interest has led to speculation that the decline in testosterone is often associated with low energy, decreased sexual desire and performance, muscle and bone loss, sleep disturbance, hot flashes, decreased cognitive function, and depression (see health-cares.net, 2005). This condition is called male menopause, climacteric, or andropause (Marshall, 2007).

Some argue that the recent interest in creating a theory of "a reversible state of testosterone deficiency" (Marshall, 2007, p. 510) is stimulated by the hope that pharmaceutical companies can benefit by treating this deficiency with hormonal therapy. You probably have noticed that the suggested symptoms of testosterone deficiency are very similar to the symptoms often proposed for female menopause. The evidence for the association between these symptoms and testosterone deficiency is even sparser than the evidence for symptoms of female menopause, however. Nevertheless, reminiscent of the earlier promise of "feminine forever" with hormone replacement for women, both medical science and the popular media have become interested in the past two decades in finding a hormonal treatment that ensures "masculine forever." According to one report, prescriptions for testosterone supplements increased by 400% between 1997 and 2002 (Marshall, 2007). Given the still unfolding history of the benefits and risks of HRT for women, it seems wise to proceed with caution with testosterone therapy. The very limited research suggests that testosterone can make prostate cancers grow, cause sleep apnea, and cause the body to make too many red blood cells, which can increase the risk of heart disease (Mayo Clinic Staff, 2008; Nilsen, 2008).

The physical changes in middle adulthood require some adjustments in the sexual lives of midlife men and women. Beginning in their late 50s, men begin to experience a gradual slowdown in sexual responses. This includes decreased frequency and intensity of orgasms, increased difficulty in achieving erection, and longer time needed before achieving subsequent erection. For women, the vaginal dryness that often occurs during menopause may cause painful intercourse. Many couples adjust well to these changes, however, and with children out of the home, may find that their sexual lives become less inhibited and more passionate. The sex lives of midlife adults may benefit from improved self-esteem that typifies middle adulthood and, in relationships of some longevity, from better understanding of the desires and responses of the sexual partner. Currently, besides testosterone supplements, there are a number of treatments available to assist with deficient sexual responses in men, including Viagra as well as a number of products being developed (Lux, Reyes, Morgentaler, & Levine, 2007; Stroberg, Hedelin, & Ljunggren, 2006).

Changes in Health Status

As we can see in the stories of Viktor Spiro and Helen Tyson, who are both in early midlife, and Phoung Le who is in late midlife, health during middle adulthood is highly variable. There are some positive changes: The frequency of accidents declines, as does susceptibility to colds and allergies. Conversely, although many people live through middle adulthood with little disease or disability, the frequency of chronic illness, persistent symptoms, and functional disability begins to rise in middlehood. And the death rate increases continuously over the adult years, as demonstrated by death rates in the United States reported in Exhibit 8.4. You will also note that there are significant gender and race/ethnicity differences in the death rates in middle adulthood, with men having higher death rates than women in Black, White, and Hispanic populations, and Blacks of both genders having alarmingly higher death rates than their White and Hispanic counterparts.

> What might be some reasons for these race and gender differences in health in middle adulthood?

In the past century, there has been a change in the types of diseases that are likely to affect health across the life course in affluent countries. In the early 1900s, when life expectancy was in the mid-40s, most deaths were caused by infectious diseases, such as pneumonia, tuberculosis, and influenza (Sapolsky, 2004). With the increase in life expectancy, chronic disease plays a more important role in the great stretch of middle adulthood and beyond. People are now living long enough to experience a chronic illness: "We are now living well enough and long enough to slowly fall apart. . . . [T]he diseases that plague us now are ones of slow accumulation of damage—heart disease, cancer, cerebrovascular disorders" (Sapolsky, p. 3).

The prevalence of chronic conditions increases with each decade from middle adulthood on. (Note: *Prevalence* measures the proportion of a population that has a disease at a point in time. *Incidence* measures the number of new cases of a disease or condition over a period of time, such as 1 year.) There is an increase in potentially fatal chronic conditions as well as nonfatal chronic conditions. The important role of chronic illness as cause of death is demonstrated in Exhibit 8.5, which reports the five leading causes of death for selected age groups in the United States. Except for accident, suicide, and homicide, all the leading causes of death are chronic diseases: heart disease, cancer,

Age Group	Both Sexes All Origins	Male				Female			
		All Origins	Black	Hispanic	Non-Hispanic White	All Origins	Black	Hispanic	Non-Hispanic White
35–39 Years	148.7	189.0	336.8	142.4	183.0	107.9	196.5	69.0	103.7
40–44 Years	229.3	285.8	471.1	215.6	278.0	173.1	308.4	107.0	165.1
45–49 Years	347.7	435.3	732.9	326.7	417.1	262.2	467.0	177.0	246.7
50–54 Years	516.4	659.7	1199.1	507.1	621.0	378.9	673.7	263.9	356.7
55–59 Years	730.1	920.0	1662.0	718.7	869.7	551.0	928.8	389.3	528.4
60–64 Years	1110.2	1373.6	2355.8	1030.0	1327.5	869.7	1348.2	622.4	851.6
65–69 Years	1656.6	2040.2	3190.8	1553.4	2000.1	1321.4	1911.3	957.8	1306.2

▲ **Exhibit 8.4**   Death Rate (per 100,000 Persons) in Selected Age Groups in 2006

SOURCE: Based on Heron et al., 2009.

HIV/AIDS, cerebrovascular disease (stroke), diabetes, and chronic obstructive pulmonary disease (COPD, includes chronic bronchitis and emphysema). With advancing age, chronic conditions replace accidents, suicide, and homicide as primary causes of death.

15–24 Years	Accidents (46.5%)
	Homicide (16.4%)
	Suicide (12.0%)
	Cancer (4.7%)
	Heart Disease (3.9%)
25–34 Years	Accidents (34.8%)
	Suicide (11.6%)
	Homicide (11.0%)
	Cancer (8.5%)
	HIV/AIDS (2.8%)
35–44 Years	Accidents (21.1%)
	Heart Disease (18.6%)
	Cancer (16.8%)
	Suicide (7.9%)
	HIV (4.3%)
45–54 Years	Cancer (27.2%)
	Heart Disease (25.4%)
	Accidents (10.6%)
	Chronic Liver Disease and Cirrhosis (4.2%)
	Suicide (4.0%)
55–64 Years	Cancer (36.0%)
	Heart Disease (28.7%)
	COPD (4.4%)
	Accidents (4.1%)
	Diabetes (4.1%)
65–74 Years	Cancer (35.3%)
	Heart Disease (30.5%)
	COPD (7.2%)
	Stroke (4.7%)
	Diabetes (4.0%)

▲ **Exhibit 8.5**   Five Leading Causes of Death and Percentage of Total Deaths in Age Groups in United States, 2006

COPD, chronic obstructive pulmonary disease (includes chronic bronchitis and emphysema).

SOURCE: Based on Heron et al., 2009.

It is important to note that there are some global differences in causes of death. The World Health Organization (WHO, 2008) reports on the leading causes of death in low-income, middle-income, and high-income countries. In high-income countries, heart disease is the number-one cause of death, and cerebrovascular disease (stroke) is the number-two cause of death. In middle-income countries, the situation is reversed, with stroke the number-one cause and heart disease the number-two cause. In low-income countries, however, lower respiratory infection (pneumonia) is the number-one cause, followed by heart disease. In low-income countries, diarrheal disease is the number three cause of death, and HIV/AIDS is the number four cause. Neither of these conditions is included in the top 10 causes of death in middle-income and high-income countries. Tuberculosis, neonatal infections, and malaria are also among the top 10 causes of death in low-income countries. None of these conditions are included in the top 10 in high-income countries, and only tuberculosis is among the top 10 in middle-income countries, where it is the ninth cause. These data indicate that chronic illness is the major cause of death in high-income and middle-income countries, but infectious diseases continue to be a major challenge in less affluent nations that lack access to safe water and adequate sanitation.

Death is not the only outcome of chronic illness. As Sapolsky (2004) suggests: Chronic disease often has a slow course and involves some level of disability over a number of years. The WHO uses the concept of Disability Adjusted Life Year (DALY) to measure the sum of the years lost because of premature death *plus* the number of years spent in states of poor health or disability. There is much international evidence that socioeconomic position is a powerful predictor of both mortality and poor health (morbidity) (Marmot & Fuhrer, 2004). The WHO has calculated the worldwide leading causes of DALYs for males and females 15 years old and older; these are reported in Exhibit 8.6. It is important to note that the WHO data include mental health as well as physical health conditions whereas health statistics in the United States do not. Therefore, the WHO data are useful because they give a better picture of the impact of unipolar depressive disorders and alcohol use disorders on global health. The stories of Viktor Spiro and Helen Tyson demonstrate the important impact that mental health conditions can have on life trajectories. It is important to note, however, that the data in Exhibit 8.6 are for ages 15 years and older, and not just for middle adulthood. For example, road traffic accidents and violence are much more common causes of death in adolescent and young adult males than in middle adult males. There is evidence that baby boomers in the United States and Europe have higher rates of depression and substance abuse than previous generations (Piazza & Charles, 2006). A longitudinal study in the Netherlands found that mental health tends to improve across the life course, but a minority of midlife adults shows persistently high levels of depressive symptoms and loneliness across the middle adult years (Deeg, 2005). These researchers, like many other researchers of middle adulthood, emphasize that reporting average results can mask the great variability in middle adult trajectories.

Viktor Spiro struggled with depression and substance abuse before he immigrated to the United States, and, as happens with many immigrants, the multiple losses and demands associated with the immigration experience exacerbated his mental health problems. As Karen Aroian and Anne E. Norris (2003) note, "Depression significantly impairs immigrants' ability to adapt to the new country and has serious emotional and economic consequences for immigrants and their families" (p. 420). Aroian and Norris found high levels of depression in a sample of immigrants from the former Soviet Union; they also found that the severity and longevity of depressive symptoms were correlated with the level of immigration-related stressors. They concluded that mental health interventions with depressed immigrants should focus on relieving these stressors by focusing on such practical issues as learning English and obtaining employment as well as on emotional issues such as loss, trauma, and feeling at home in the new country. Viktor was lucky to find mental health professionals who did just this, assisting him to get debt forgiveness and attain citizenship while also working on issues of emotion regulation and expanding his social network.

Helen Tyson survived a traumatic experience at age 16 and seems to have gotten through young adulthood without the flashbacks and panic attacks she has recently experienced. It does appear, however, that since her attack she has reduced her involvement with the external world, which is another symptom of posttraumatic stress disorder (PTSD). Researchers have found that "midlife is a particularly high-risk period for either delayed onset or reactivated PTSD" (Solomon & Mikulincer, 2006, p. 664). Helen is facing an impending change in her life structure, which has been

Males	Females
1. HIV/AIDS	1. Unipolar depressive disorders
2. Ischemic heart disease	2. HIV/AIDS
3. Cerebrovascular disease	3. Ischemic heart disease
4. Unipolar depressive disorders	4. Cerebrovascular disease
5. Road traffic injuries	5. Cataracts
6. Tuberculosis	6. Hearing loss, adult onset
7. Alcohol use disorders	7. COPD
8. Violence	8. Tuberculosis
9. COPD	9. Osteoarthritis
10. Hearing loss, adult onset	10. Diabetes mellitus

▲ **Exhibit 8.6**   Leading Causes of Disease Burden (DALYs) for Males and Females Ages 15 Years and Older, Worldwide, 2002

COPD, chronic obstructive pulmonary disease (includes chronic bronchitis and emphysema).

SOURCE: World Health Organization, 2003.

focused on active mothering. Such transitions often invite a period of reminiscence and review of one's life. This review may bring suppressed traumatic memories to the surface. In addition, Helen's recent loss of her mother, the declining health of her father, and the sense of loss of control over her children may be breaking through the defenses that have helped her avoid painful memories. In addition, she may have been triggered by having Sarah arrive at the age of her attack, especially given that she sees much of herself in Sarah. A recent longitudinal investigation of PTSD symptoms among combat veterans found that the symptoms decreased by the third year following combat trauma but had been reactivated in many veterans in the 20-year follow-up. It is important for social workers to recognize the possibility of delayed and reactivated PTSD in their midlife clients. This will be particularly important in the years ahead as veterans of the Iraq and Afghanistan wars become clients in every social service sector.

Phoung Le and her family saw many horrors in Saigon, both during war and after. They suffered the loss of family members as well as a homeland. Phoung knows that many Vietnamese refugees did not fare well when they reached the United States, some falling prey to substance abuse, family violence, and suicide; others living lives of quiet desperation. She feels lucky to have been able to settle among so many other Vietnamese people and feels that their support has been invaluable to her own well-being. She also feels that her children have given her hope and belief in the future. She has painful memories but she feels lucky that they have not overpowered her.

INTELLECTUAL CHANGES IN MIDDLE ADULTHOOD

Perhaps no domain of human behavior in middle adulthood arouses more concern about the balance of gains and losses than intellectual functioning. A trip to your local pharmacy will confront you with the variety of supplements and herbal remedies that are marketed to midlife adults with promises of maintaining mental alertness and mental acuity. And yet, middle-aged adults are often at the peak of their careers and filling leadership roles. Most of the recent presidents of the United States were men older than 50. Most multinational corporations are run by midlife adults.

Research on cognitive changes in middle adulthood is recent, but there is growing and clear evidence that cognitive performance remains stable for the majority of midlife adults (Martin & Zimprich, 2005; Willis & Schaie, 2005). However, a significant subset of midlife adults shows important gain in cognitive functioning, and another significant subset shows important decline (Willis & Schaie). The amount of gain and decline varies across different types of cognitive functioning. For example, one study found that depending on the specific cognitive skill, the proportion of midlife adults who were stable in performance ranged from 53% to 69%, the proportion who gained ranged from 6% to 16%, and the proportion who declined ranged from 15% to 31% (Willis & Schaie).

Researchers are finding that individual differences in intellectual performance increase throughout middle adulthood (Martin & Zimprich, 2005). These increasing variations are related to both biological factors and environmental factors. Several biological risk factors have been identified for cognitive decline in midlife—including hypertension, diabetes, high cholesterol, and the APOE gene (a gene that has been associated with one type of Alzheimer's disease). Several protective factors have also been identified, most of them social in nature, including education, work or other environments that demand complex cognitive work, and physical exercise (Willis & Schaie, 2005). These findings are consistent with increasing evidence of brain plasticity throughout the life course, and suggest that cognitive decline can be slowed by engaging in activities that train the brain.

The Seattle Longitudinal Study (SLS) is studying intellectual changes from the early 20s to very old age by following the same individuals over time as well as drawing new samples at each test cycle. Willis and Schaie (2006) summarize the findings about changes for selected mental abilities across the life course, paying attention to gender differences. By incorporating data on new participants as the survey progresses, they are also able to study generational (cohort) differences, addressing the question, is the current baby boom midlife cohort functioning at a higher intellectual level than their parent's generation?

Willis and Schaie (2005, 2006) summarize the findings for six mental abilities:

1. *Vocabulary:* ability to understand ideas expressed in words

2. *Verbal Memory:* ability to encode and recall language units, such as word lists

3. *Number:* ability to perform simple mathematical computations quickly and accurately

4. *Spatial Orientation:* ability to visualize stimuli in two- and three-dimensional space

5. *Inductive Reasoning:* ability to recognize and understand patterns in and relationships among variables to analyze and solve logical problems

6. *Perceptual Speed:* ability to quickly make discriminations in visual stimuli

The research shows that middle adulthood is the period of peak performance of four of the six mental abilities: inductive reasoning, spatial orientation, vocabulary, and verbal memory. Two of the six mental abilities, perceptual speed and numerical ability, show decline in middle adulthood, but the decline in perceptual speed is much more dramatic than the decline in numerical ability. The question is "How much does the culture value speed?" In the United States, speed is highly valued, and quick thinking is typically seen as an indication of high intelligence. In many non-Western countries, perceptual speed is not so highly valued (Gardiner & Kosmitzki, 2008). Willis and Schaie (2005) note that the mental abilities that improve in middle adulthood—inductive reasoning, spatial orientation, vocabulary, and verbal memory—are among the more complex, higher-order mental abilities.

There are gender differences in the changes in mental abilities during middle adulthood. On average, men reach peak performance somewhat earlier than women. Men reach peak performance on spatial orientation, vocabulary, and verbal memory in their 50s, and women reach peak performance on these same mental abilities in their early 60s.

Conversely, on average, women begin to decline in perceptual speed somewhat earlier than men, in their 20s compared with the 30s for men. The improvement in mental abilities in middle adulthood is more dramatic for women than for men. Across the adult life course, women score higher than men on vocabulary, verbal memory, perceptual speed, and inductive reasoning. Men, conversely, score higher than women across the adult life course on spatial orientation. Some evidence indicates that cognitive decline in middle adulthood is predictive of cognitive impairment in late adulthood (Willis & Schaie, 2005).

Willis and Schaie (2006) also report on cohort differences in the selected mental abilities. They found that the baby boom cohort scored higher on two of the abilities, verbal memory and inductive reasoning, than their parents' gener-

> What factors might be producing this historical trend toward declines in numerical ability?

ation did at the same chronological age. The baby boomers also scored higher than their parents did on spatial orientation, but these differences were smaller than those for verbal memory and inductive reasoning. There were virtually no cohort differences on vocabulary and perceptual speed. The boomers did not score as well as their parents' generation on numerical ability, and the authors note that this is a continuation of a negative trend in numerical ability since the early 1900s found in other studies.

Currently, intense research efforts are exploring what is happening in the middle-aged brain (see Strauch [2010] for a summary of the research). It is clear that some brains age better than others, resulting in much variability in middle-aged brains. Researchers are finding evidence of both loss and gain, but, on balance, the news is good. Parts of memory wane, most notably the part that remembers names. But, the ability to make accurate judgments about people and situations gets stronger. In summarizing this situation, Barbara Strauch notes that "this middle-aged brain, which just as it's forgetting what it had for breakfast can still go to work and run a multinational bank or school or city . . . then return home to deal with . . . teenagers, neighbors, parents" (pp. xvi–xvii). Neuroscientists are suggesting that as we reach midlife, our brains begin to reorganize and behave in a different way. Most notably, people in middle age begin to use both sides of their brains to solve problems for which only one side was used in the past, a process called bilateralization. The two hemispheres of the brain become better integrated. Research also indicates that starting in middle age, the brain's ability to tune out irrelevant material wanes, leading to more time in daydream mode but also greater capacity to capture "the big picture." Researchers are not certain about the most protective things that can be done for the aging brain, but the best evidence to date indicates that education buffers the brain and physical exercise is a "potent producer of new neurons" (Strauch, p. 128). The ideal dosage of physical exercise is not yet known.

PERSONALITY CHANGES IN MIDDLE ADULTHOOD

Does it appear to you that Viktor Spiro, Helen Tyson, and Phoung Le have grown "more like themselves" over their life course trajectories, or do you see changes in their personalities as they travel the life course? Little attention has been paid to the issue of personality in middle adulthood until quite recently. The literature that does exist on the topic consists largely of an argument about whether personality is stable or dynamic during middle adulthood. One theoretician (Whitbourne, 1986) has focused on identity processes in middle adulthood.

The Argument for Personality Stability

The idea that personality is stable in middle adulthood is an old one, rooted in Freud's psychoanalytic theory that saw personality as determined sometime in middle childhood. In this view, personality change past the age of 50 was practically impossible. The idea that personality is stable throughout adulthood comes from another very different approach to personality, commonly known as **trait theory.** According to this view, personality traits are enduring characteristics that are rooted in early temperament and are influenced by genetic and organic factors. Recent empirical studies have focused on the degree to which individuals exhibit five broad personality traits, often referred to as the Big Five personality traits (Dörner, Mickler, & Studinger, 2005; Gardiner & Kosmitzki, 2008; Roberts, Robins, Trzesniewski, & Caspi, 2003):

1. *Neuroticism:* tendency to be moody, anxious, hostile, self-conscious, and vulnerable

2. *Extroversion:* tendency to be energetic, outgoing, friendly, lively, talkative, and active

3. *Conscientiousness:* tendency to be organized, reliable, responsible, hardworking, persistent, and careful

4. *Agreeableness:* tendency to be cooperative, generous, cheerful, warm, caring, trusting, and gentle

5. *Openness to experience:* tendency to be curious, imaginative, creative, intelligent, adventurous, and nonconforming

Avshalom Caspi's **contextual model** also proposes personality stability across the life course, but it presents a different explanation for that stability (Caspi, 1987; Caspi & Roberts, 1999). Caspi and colleagues assert that personality influences both the environments we select for ourselves and how we respond to those environments. Personality leads us to choose similar environments over time, and these similar environments reinforce our personal styles.

The Argument for Personality Change

Some psychoanalysts have broken with Freud and proposed that personality continues to change across adulthood. More specifically, they propose that middle adulthood is a time when the personality ripens and matures. Most notable of these are Carl Jung, Erik Erikson, and George Vaillant. All three are consistent with humanistic models of personality that see middle adulthood as an opportunity for continued growth. Jung conceptualizes middle adulthood as a time of balance in the personality. Although Erikson sees early life as important, he suggests that societal and cultural influences call for different personal adaptations over the life course. Vaillant (1977, 2002) suggests that with age and experience, **coping mechanisms,** or the strategies we use to master the demands of life, mature. He divides coping mechanisms into *immature mechanisms* (denial, projection, passive aggression, dissociation, acting out, and fantasy) and *mature mechanisms* (sublimation, humor, altruism, and suppression). He proposes that as we age across adulthood, we make more use of mature coping mechanisms such as altruism, sublimation, and humor and less use of immature coping mechanisms such as denial and projection. Definitions for both the immature and mature coping mechanisms are found in Exhibit 8.7.

As you might imagine, life course theorists see possibilities for personality change in middle adulthood, as individuals experience life events and culturally influenced role changes. In fact, Daniel Levinson (Levinson, 1977, 1986; Levinson & Levinson, 1996), influenced by both Erikson and Jung, proposed that many adults experience a life event he called a "midlife crisis" in the transition to middle adulthood.

Evidence for Stability and Change in Midlife Personality

What can we conclude about personality in middle adulthood? Is it marked by stability or change? The available research suggests that we should think of the midlife personality in terms of both stability and change.

Research on the Big Five personality traits suggests that there is long-term stability in terms of the ranking of traits. For example, a person who is high in agreeableness at one point in adulthood will continue to be high in agreeableness across the life course (Dörner et al., 2005; Gardiner & Kosmitzki, 2008; Roberts et al., 2003). However, there

Immature Coping Mechanisms
Acting out. Ideas and feelings are acted on impulsively rather than reflectively.
Denial. Awareness of painful aspects of reality are avoided by negating sensory information about them.
Dissociation. Painful emotions are handled by compartmentalizing perceptions and memories, and detaching from the full impact.
Fantasy. Real human relationships are replaced with imaginary friends.
Passive-aggression. Anger toward others is turned inward against the self through passivity, failure, procrastination, or masochism.
Projection. Unacknowledged feelings are attributed to others.

Mature Coping Mechanisms
Altruism. Pleasure is attained by giving pleasure to others.
Mature humor. An emotion or thought is expressed through comedy, allowing a painful situation to be faced without individual pain or social discomfort.
Sublimation. An unacceptable impulse or unattainable aim is transformed into a more acceptable or attainable aim.
Suppression. Attention to a desire or impulse is postponed.

▲ **Exhibit 8.7**   Coping Mechanisms

SOURCE: Vaillant, 1977, 2002.

is some evidence that there is a slight drop in consistency during early midlife, suggesting that this might be a period of the life course that is more conducive to personality change than other adult phases (Dörner et al.). Researchers have studied the genetic basis of the Big Five traits and found a small genetic contribution, particularly for neuroticism and agreeableness (Jang et al., 2001). In addition, a 40-year longitudinal study drawn from the Berkeley Guidance Study—which collected data during late childhood and again during young adulthood and middle adulthood—found a great deal of personality consistency over time (Caspi, 1987).

Nevertheless, a number of both cross-sectional and longitudinal studies report age-related changes in personality traits in middle and late adulthood (Dörner et al., 2005; McCrae et al., 1999; Roberts et al., 2003). Extroversion (activity and thrill seeking), neuroticism (anxiety and self-consciousness), and openness to experience have been found to decline with age starting in middle adulthood. Conversely, agreeableness has been found to increase with age, and conscientiousness and emotional stability have been found to peak in middle adulthood (Dörner et al.; Lachman & Bertrand, 2001). What's more, these patterns of age-related changes in personality have been found in cross-cultural research that included samples from Germany, Italy, Portugal, Croatia, and South Korea (Gardiner & Kosmitzki, 2008). Although the research found much individual stability in aspects of personality over adulthood, one longitudinal study of a group of college-educated women found them, as a group, to become "less compulsive, more considerate of others, more organized, and better able to adapt to institutional settings" in middle adulthood (Roberts, Helson, & Klohnen, 2002, p. 96). They also became more tolerant of human diversity. This greater openness to human diversity appears to be occurring in Phoung Le in late midlife.

Some researchers have found gender differences in personality traits to be greater than age-related differences (Lachman & Bertrand, 2001). Women score higher than men in agreeableness, conscientiousness, extroversion, and neuroticism. Men, conversely, score higher than women on openness to experience. These gender differences in personality have been found in 26 cultures, but the magnitude of differences varied across cultures. The researchers were surprised to find that the biggest gender differences occurred in European and North American cultures, where traditional gender roles are less pronounced than in many other countries (Costa, Terracciano, & McCrae, 2001).

In spite of these gender differences, a number of researchers have found evidence for a gender-role shift during middle adulthood, as hypothesized by Jung, who suggested that in midlife both men and women become more androgynous. In fact, one research team found that scales measuring femininity and masculinity were among the scales that revealed the most change between the ages of 43 and 52 (Helson & Wink, 1992). Women were found by these and other researchers to increase in decisiveness, action orientation, and assertiveness during midlife (Roberts, Helson, & Klohnen, 2002). Men have been found to increase in nurturance and affiliation by some researchers (Havighurst, Neugarten, & Tobin, 1968; Neugarten & Gutmann, 1968). Recent support for this idea was reported by one research team that found that in late midlife, women's emotional satisfaction was correlated with bodily sexual practices, and men's physical pleasure was associated with relationship factors, a finding that contradicts gender stereotypes (Carpenter, Nathanson, & Kim, 2009). Joan Borysenko (1996), a cellular biologist, provides evidence for a gender crossover in personality in midlife that she attributes to changes in levels of sex hormones. Conversely, some researchers have found no gender role crossover for men (Lowenthal, Thurnher, & Chiriboga, 1975), and recent research suggests that it is motherhood and not age that promotes femininity in women (Roberts, Helson, & Klohnen, 2002). Bjoklund and Bee (2008) suggest that it is more accurate to talk about "expansion of gender roles" rather than "gender role crossover," as midlife adults become more open to unexpressed aspects of the self. This is consistent with Jung's theory of increased androgyny in middle adulthood.

Although there is evidence that midlife adults often engage in review and reappraisal, there is much disagreement about whether that review and reappraisal is serious enough to constitute the midlife crisis proposed by Levinson and others. Most researchers who have studied this issue take a middle ground, suggesting that some midlife adults do reach crisis level in midlife, but in general, the idea of midlife crisis has been greatly overstated (see, e.g., Sterns & Huyck, 2001). One research team found that turning points in adulthood suggest that they are most likely to occur in young adulthood (Wethington, Kessler, & Pixley, 2004), but another research team found that when older adults were asked to identify turning points in their lives, there was some clustering of situations in their middle adulthood (Cappeliez et al., 2008). It appears that Viktor Spiro, Helen Tyson, and Phoung Le all had turning points in either adolescence or young adulthood, and it is unclear whether the events they are facing now will become turning points for their future life course trajectories.

Whitbourne's Identity Process Model

Susan Whitbourne and colleagues (Jones, Whitbourne, & Skultety, 2006; Whitbourne, 1986; Whitbourne & Connolly, 1999) propose that identity plays a central role in adult personality stability and change. Drawing on Piaget's theory of cognitive development, they suggest that identity continues to develop throughout adulthood through the processes of assimilation and accommodation. **Assimilation** is the process through which individuals incorporate new experiences into their existing identity. **Accommodation,** conversely, is the process through which an individual changes some aspect of identity in response to new experiences. Three identity styles are identified, based on the way that midlife individuals respond to new experiences:

1. *Assimilative identity style.* Midlife individuals see themselves as unchanging and may either deny the physical and other changes they are experiencing or rationalize them as something else.

2. *Accommodative identity style.* Midlife individuals overreact to physical and other changes, and this undermines their identity and leaves it weak and incoherent.

3. *Balanced identity style.* Midlife individuals, combining goals and inner purpose with the flexibility to adapt to new experiences, recognize the physical and other changes of aging, engage in good health maintenance to minimize risk and enhance protection, and accept what cannot be changed.

> How does a balanced identity style relate to human agency in making choices?

It appears that earlier losses and trauma may have predisposed Viktor Spiro and Helen Tyson to an accommodative identity style. As he enters middle adulthood, with professional help, Viktor appears to be making some movement toward a more balanced identity style. It seems quite likely that Helen Tyson's counselor will be attempting to help her do the same. Conversely, Phoung Le appears to have a balanced identity style in spite of early experiences with war and resettlement. She moved with both purpose and flexibility to help her multigenerational family adapt to resettlement in the United States, and she remains open to new ways to express generativity.

SPIRITUAL DEVELOPMENT IN MIDDLE ADULTHOOD

Religion and a search for connectedness play a major role in Phoung Le's life. Religion is also very important in the life of Viktor Spiro's mother, and both he and his mother are drawing strength from their Greek Orthodox faith as they deal with Petro's declining health. The same is true of many midlife adults. The major world religions associate spiritual growth with advancing age (see, e.g., Biggs, 1999; Wink & Dillon, 2002). And yet, until very recently, the burgeoning U.S. literature on middle adulthood had almost entirely overlooked the issue of spiritual development; this continues to be the case in the European literature. The primary effort has been models of spiritual development that propose that humans have the potential for continuous spiritual growth across the life course.

For example, James Fowler's Theory of Faith Development (1981) proposes six stages of faith. The first two stages occur primarily in childhood. These are the four stages that can occur in adulthood:

1. *Synthetic-conventional faith.* The basic worldview of this faith stage is that spiritual authority is found outside the individual. In this faith stage, the individual relies on a pastor or rabbi or other spiritual leader to define morality. Many people remain in this faith stage throughout their lives and never progress to the other stages.

2. *Individuative-reflective faith.* The adult no longer relies on outside authority and begins to look for authority within the self, based on moral reasoning. The individual also takes responsibility for examining the assumptions of his or her faith.

3. *Conjunctive faith.* In this stage, the individual looks for balance in such polarities as independence and connection, recognizes that there are many truths, and opens out beyond the self in service to others. Fowler proposes that many people never reach the stage of **conjunctive faith,** and if they do, they almost never reach it before middle adulthood.

4. *Universalizing faith.* In Fowler's final stage, **universalizing faith,** individuals lead selfless lives based on principles of absolute love and justice. Fowler notes that only rare individuals reach this stage.

Fowler's theory has received support in cross-sectional research but has not yet been put to test in longitudinal research. Therefore, it should be applied with caution, recognizing that it may reflect the influences of historical time on faith development.

Interestingly, Fowler's description of conjunctive faith overlaps with theories of middle adulthood previously discussed in this chapter. For example, the reference to balance calls to mind the theories of Jung and Levinson, who saw middle adulthood as a time of bringing balance to personality and life structure. In addition, the idea of opening oneself in service to others is consistent with Erikson's idea of generativity as the psychosocial struggle of middle adulthood (Biggs, 1999; Dollahite, Slife, & Hawkins, 1998). It appears that Phoung Le is entering Fowler's stage of conjunctive faith, as she searches for balance and seeks opportunities to serve others. Drawing on Jung, one theorist proposes that late midlife is "a time when our energy naturally moves beyond the concerns of our nuclear family into a concern with the world family" (Borysenko, 1996, p. 185). The emphasis is on spirituality as a state of "being connected." Using data from a national survey of midlife adults in the United States, one researcher has found a strong correlation between regular participation in religious activities and community volunteer service, particularly in terms of making financial contributions to community organizations and charities (Rossi, 2004b).

Actually, there are two different models of spiritual development in adulthood (Wink & Dillon, 2002). Fowler's theory can be called a growth model, an approach that sees spiritual growth as a positive outcome of a maturation process. The other model sees increased spirituality across the adult life course as an outcome of adversity (Wink and Dillon call it an adversity model) rather than as a natural maturation process; in this view spirituality becomes a way to cope with losses, disappointments, and difficulties. One rare longitudinal study of spiritual development across the adult life course found evidence for both of these models (Wink & Dillon). The researchers found a strong tendency for increased spirituality beginning in late middle adulthood, something that occurred among all research participants but was more pronounced among women than men. They also found that experiencing negative life events in early adulthood was associated with higher levels of spirituality in middle and late adulthood. Phoung Le reports a renewed intensity to her spiritual quest, which seems to include both a drive for spiritual growth and a resource for coping with loss and difficulty.

One of the few studies of spiritual development in middle adulthood was described in Wade Clark Roof's *A Generation of Seekers* (1993), which reported on the "spiritual journeys of the baby boom generation" in the United

States. Roof emphasizes the likelihood of cohort effects in this study, and some critics have suggested that the study is best seen as a study of culture and spirituality (Wink & Dillon, 2002). Drawing on survey data and interview responses, Roof suggested that the baby boom generation was "changing America's spiritual landscape" (Roof, p. 50). He reported that most baby boomers grew up in religious households, but 58% of his sample dropped their relationships with religious institutions for at least two years during their adolescence or young adulthood. Roof acknowledges that earlier generations have also dropped out of religion during early adulthood, but not in the numbers found in his sample of baby boomers. He suggests that the turmoil of the 1960s and 1970s, with a youth culture that questioned authority, is probably largely responsible for the high rate of dropout among baby boomers. Roof found that about one fourth of his sample that had dropped

▲ **Photo 8.1**   Religion and spiritual connectedness often play a major role in the lives of midlife adults.

out had returned to religious activities by the end of the 1980s. For many of them, their return seemed to be related to having children at home.

Roof found that religious affiliation and activity did not tell the whole story about the spiritual lives of baby boomers, however. Regardless of religious affiliation, baby boomers were involved in an intense search for personal meaning (Roof, 1993). But for many of Roof's sample, the current spiritual quest was a very personal, introspective quest—one that embraced a wide range of nontraditional as well as traditional beliefs.

In a follow-up study with the same sample from 1995 to 1997, Roof (1999) found that many boomers had shifted in their religious affiliation again. More than half of the earlier dropouts who had returned to religious activities by the late 1980s had dropped out again. But, conversely, one half of those who had dropped out in the 1980s had returned to religious activities by the mid-1990s. Presence of children in the home again seemed to be the factor that motivated a return to religion.

> What does Roof's research suggest about spiritual age in middle adulthood?

Roof suggests that the baby boomers are leading a shift in U.S. religious life away from an unquestioning belief to a questioning approach, and toward a belief that no single religious institution has a monopoly on truth. That shift is certainly not total at this point, however. Roof identifies five types of contemporary believers from his sample: 33% are born-again or Evangelical Christians, 25% are old-line mainstream believers, 15% are dogmatists who see one truth in the doctrine and form of their religious tradition, 15% are metaphysical seekers, and 12% are nonreligious secularists. Thus, almost three quarters of his sample could be classified as more or less unquestioning adherents of a particular system of beliefs but with an increasing trend toward recognition of the legitimacy of multiple spiritual paths. It is important to note that religion plays a much more central role in the lives of adults in the United States than it does in European countries (Reid, 2004).

Unfortunately, Roof does not analyze racial and ethnic differences in religious and spiritual expression for his baby boom sample. Others have found evidence, however, of strong racial and ethnic differences (Gallup & Lindsay, 1999). Black baby boomers have been much more constant in their religious beliefs and participation than White baby boomers and are far more likely to consider religion very important in their lives. Although not as steadfast as their Black cohorts, Hispanic baby boomers have also been less fluid in their religious activity than their non-Hispanic White cohorts.

Critical Thinking Questions 8.1

How does culture influence the reactions of midlife adults to the biological changes that occur in this life phase? How are the reactions to these changes affected by socioeconomic status? What images of these changes are presented in the popular media in the United States? How have your ideas about middle adulthood been influenced by the popular media?

RELATIONSHIPS IN MIDDLE ADULTHOOD

Social relationships play a major role in life satisfaction and physical well-being across the life course. In contemporary life, both women and men fulfill multiple social roles in midlife (Antonucci, Akiyama, & Merline, 2001). The most central roles are related to family and paid work. Relationships with family, friends, and coworkers are an important part of life in middle adulthood, and some scholars argue that the current generation of midlife adults are experiencing unprecedented complexity in their configurations of relationships (Blieszner & Roberto, 2006). The life course perspective reminds us that relationships in middle adulthood have been shaped by relationships in earlier life phases, in the attachment process in infancy as well as in family and peer relationships in childhood, adolescence, and young adulthood (Blieszner & Roberto; Möller & Stattin, 2001). Although current relationships are shaped by our experiences with earlier relationships, longitudinal research indicates that it is never too late to develop new relationships that can become turning points in the life course (Vaillant, 2002; Werner & Smith, 2001).

Toni Antonucci and colleagues (Antonucci & Akiyama, 1987, 1997; Antonucci, Akiyama, & Takahashi, 2004) suggest that we each travel through life with a **convoy,** or a network of social relationships that protect, defend, aid, and socialize us. They also acknowledge that the convoy can have damaging effects on individuals, contributing more stress than support, and creating problems rather than solving them. In one study, the researchers asked respondents in representative samples of people ages 8 to 93 from both the United States and Japan to map their convoys of support, using three concentric circles surrounding the individual respondent (Antonucci et al.). In the inner circle, the respondents were asked to identify people who were so close and important to them that they could not imagine living without them (very close). In the middle circle, respondents were asked to name people who were not quite that close but still very close and important to them (still close). In the outer circle, respondents were asked to name people who were not as close as those in the two inner circles but who were still important enough that they came to mind as members of the support network (less close).

They found no differences in the composition of the convoys between the U.S. and Japanese participants. They found that the convoys of the midlife adults ages 40 to 59 were slightly smaller than among young adults ages 20 to 39 and slightly larger than the convoys of late life adults. Women reported more very close relationships (inner circle) than men. On average, midlife adults reported eight members in their convoys: mother, spouse, daughter, and son in the inner circle (very close); sister, brother, and female friend in the middle circle (still close); and female friend in the outer circle (less close). It is important to note that the size of convoy does not necessarily indicate how much support is available (Chen, 2006a).

Other research has found racial and ethnic differences as well as social class differences in reported convoys in the United States. Whites have been found to have larger convoys than African Americans, and the convoys of African American adults as well as other adults with low incomes have a higher proportion of kin in them than the convoys of higher income White adults (Ajrouch, Antonucci, & Janevic, 2001; Antonucci et al., 2001; Montague, Magai, Consedine, & Gillespie, 2003). A study conducted in Taiwan suggests that in our very mobile times, when younger generations leave home to follow jobs in global cities, some people may have only one or two circles in their convoys (Chen, 2006b). Certainly, it is important to understand the very dynamic nature of convoys in the lives of many people in a globalized world.

Most of the other research that has been done on midlife adult relationships is based on the premise that the marital or partner relationship is the focal relationship in middle adulthood. Consequently, too little is known about other familial and nonfamilial relationships. Recently, however, gerontologists have suggested that a variety of relationships are important to adults in late adulthood, and this hypothesis has led to preliminary investigations of a variety of relationships in middle adulthood. In the following sections, we look first at multigenerational family relationships and then review the limited research on friendship and community and organizational relationships.

Middle Adulthood in the Context of the Multigenerational Family

Because of increasing longevity, multigenerational families are becoming more common. By the early 1990s, three quarters of adults ages 50 to 54 in the United States had a family with at least three generations; about 40% had families with four generations (Sweet & Bumpass, 1996). Similarly, in Germany, 80% of adults ages 40 to 54, and 76% of adults 55 to 69, have three-generation families (Kohli & Künemund, 2005). With a declining birthrate, the multigenerational family becomes increasingly vertical, with more generations but fewer people in each generation. This is the picture in all industrialized countries; the historical pyramid shape of the family has been replaced by a beanpole shape (tall and thin) (Putney & Bengtson, 2003). There is also increasing complexity in the multigenerational family, with divorces and remarriages adding a variety of step-relationships to the mix.

There is much popular speculation that family ties are weakening as geographic mobility increases. Research in the United States and Germany suggests, however, that there is more intergenerational solidarity than we may think (Bengtson, 2001; Putney & Bengtson, 2001; Kohli & Künemund, 2005). Certainly, we see much intergenerational solidarity in the families of Viktor Spiro, Helen Tyson, and Phoung Le. Using a national representative sample in the United States, Bengtson and colleagues have identified five types of extended family relationships. About one quarter (25.5%) of the families are classified as *tightly knit,* and another quarter (25.5%) are classified as *sociable,* meaning that family members are engaged with each other but do not provide for, and receive concrete assistance from, each other. The remaining families are about evenly split among the *intimate-but-distant* (16%); *obligatory,* or those who have contact but no emotional closeness or shared belief system (16%); and *detached* (17%) classifications. It is important to note that no one type of extended family relationship was found to be dominant, suggesting much diversity in intergenerational relationships in the United States. Ethnicity is one source of that variation. For example, Black and Hispanic families report stronger maternal attachments than are reported in White families, and they are also more likely to reside in multigenerational households (Putney & Bengtson, 2003). One researcher has also found much diversity in intergenerational relationships in Taiwan (Chen, 2006b).

Another way of categorizing extended families is as collectivist oriented or individualistic (Pyke & Bengtson, 1996). In families with a strong collectivist orientation, kinship ties and family responsibilities take precedence over nonfamily roles. In families with a strong individualistic orientation, personal achievement and independence take precedence over family ties. The researchers found that most families were some mix of collectivist and individualistic.

▲ **Photo 8.2**   Research finds that there is a lot of intergenerational solidarity in contemporary families.

Despite the evidence that intergenerational family relationships are alive and well, there is also evidence that many family relationships include some degree of conflict. One longitudinal study concluded that about 1 in 8 adult intergenerational relationships can be described as "long-term lousy relationships" (Bengtson, 1996).

After studying multigenerational family relationships for several decades, Bengtson (2001) suggests that, with increased marital instability and a declining birthrate, multigenerational family relationships are once again becoming more important in the United States and may replace some nuclear family functions. We should perhaps think of the multigenerational family as a "latent kin network" (Bengtson, 2001, p. 12) that may be activated only at times of crisis. Of course, strong multigenerational families are still the norm in many parts of the world, and many immigrant groups bring that approach to family life with them to the United States, as did Phoung Le's family.

The trend toward multiple generations in extended families has particular relevance for midlife adults, who make up the generation in the middle. Several researchers (see, e.g., Sotirin & Ellingson, 2006) have found that midlife adults are the kinkeepers in multigenerational families and that this holds true across cultures. **Kinkeepers** are family members who work at keeping family members across the generations in touch with one another and who make sure that both emotional and practical needs of family members are met. Historically, when nuclear families were larger, kinkeepers played an important role in working to maintain ties among large sibling groups. With increased longevity and multiple generations of families, kinkeepers play an important role in the multigenerational family, working to maintain ties across the generations, ties among grandparents, parents, children, grandchildren, siblings, aunts, uncles, nieces, nephews, and cousins.

Researchers have found that most kinkeepers are middle-aged women (Sotirin & Ellingson, 2006). Women help larger numbers of kin than men and spend three times as many hours helping kin. Because of this kinkeeping role, midlife women have been described as the "sandwich generation." This term was originally used to suggest that midlife women are simultaneously caring for their own children as well as their parents. Recent research suggests that with demographic changes, few women still have children at home when they begin to care for parents, but midlife women continue to be "sandwiched" with competing demands of paid work roles and intergenerational kinkeeping (Kohli & Künemund, 2005; Putney & Bengtson, 2001).

Helen Tyson and her sisters are all middle-aged women who play important kinkeeping roles in their extended family. They provide increasing assistance to their frail father and guidance and assistance of various kinds to their children. In addition, they take the initiative to plan extended family holiday get-togethers. The sisters are lucky to be able to share these kinkeeping roles because they now must balance assistance to their father with the needs of their own children. Phoung Le also plays an important kinkeeping role in her large multigenerational family. She provides both emotional and practical support to her own children and grandchildren as well as to a large number of siblings and nieces and nephews. But, she also thinks that her husband, Nien, is a kinkeeper, because he provides much practical assistance to these same family members.

Relationships With Spouse or Partner

In recent decades, there has been an increased diversity of marital statuses at midlife. Some men and women have been married for some time, some are getting married for the first time, some are not yet married, some will never marry, some were once married but now are divorced, some are in a second or third marriage, and some are not married but are living in a long-term committed relationship with someone of the same or opposite sex (Antonucci et al., 2001). Only 1 in 20 adults ages 40 to 59 in the United States has never been married (Marks et al., 2004). Adults such as Viktor Spiro who have struggled with mental health issues are more likely than other adults to be single.

The 2000 U.S. census reported that 5.5 million couples were living together but not married, up from 3.2 million in 1990 (Simmons & O'Connell, 2003). The majority of these couples were opposite-sex partners, but 1 in 9 (594,000) were same-sex couples. It is hard to interpret the data on same-sex couples, since some gay and lesbian couples choose not to reveal their relationships. The opposite-sex unmarried couples were, on average, younger than the same-sex couples who were in their early 40s. Many of the cohabiting opposite-sex couples will marry each other at some point, but that option is still not available to same-sex couples in most states in the United States. As of May 2010, same-sex couples are allowed to marry in Massachusetts, Connecticut, Iowa, New Hampshire, Vermont, and Washington, D.C. Maryland and New York recognize same-sex marriages performed in other states. Seven countries recognize same-sex marriage: Canada, Sweden, the Netherlands, Belgium, Spain, and South Africa (Human Rights Campaign, 2010).

We know very little about the different midlife experiences of partners of different marital statuses, but there is evidence that each person brings prior relationship experiences to partner relationships of all types. Möller and Stattin (2001) reviewed the empirical literature on these relationships and identified a number of characteristics of prior relationships that have been found to influence partner relationships in adulthood. For example, affection and warmth in the household during the preschool years has been associated with long and happy partnerships in adulthood. Interactions with peers during adolescence help to build the social skills necessary to sustain partner relationships. Based on these findings, Möller and Stattin (2001) engaged in longitudinal research with a Swedish sample to investigate the links between early relationships and later partner relationships. They found that warm relationships with parents during adolescence are associated with later satisfaction in the partner relationship. Relationships with fathers were more strongly related to partner satisfaction for males than for females. Contrary to previous research, Möller and Stattin found that the quality of parents' marital relationship was not associated with the quality of later partner relationships. The parent-child relationship was a better predictor of later partner relationships than the quality of the parents' marital relationships.

For heterosexual marriages, there is a long line of research that indicates a U-shaped curve in marital happiness, with high marital satisfaction in the early years of marriage, followed by a decline that hits bottom in early midlife, but begins to rise again in the postparental years. However, one longitudinal research project, one of the few studies to use a national representative sample, found no upturn in marital satisfaction in later life. As found in other studies, satisfaction took a steep decline over the first 5 years of marriage. This was followed by a gradual decline during the next 20 years, after which marital satisfaction leveled off for a few years, but declined again beginning at 40 years of marriage (VanLaningham, Johnson, & Amato, 2001). The researchers also found that for most marital cohorts, there was a steeper decline in marital satisfaction in the 1980s than in the 1990s, which seems to indicate an impact of some societal changes. There was also some indication that more recent cohorts have lower marital satisfaction than earlier cohorts.

The current generation of midlife adults is balancing a variety of roles, family roles, work roles, and community roles, and this requires partners to coordinate their role enactments. In one study of African American midlife baby boomers, couples described how they share responsibilities; stay engaged with work, family, and faith; and make time for each other to keep their relationship alive (Carolan & Allen, 1999). There is evidence that unmarried partners tend to be more egalitarian in the division of household activities than married couples (Simmons & O'Connell, 2003), but considerable evidence that African American married couples engage in more egalitarian role sharing than White married couples (Coltrane, 2000).

Likewise, midlife gay and lesbian partnerships have been found to be more egalitarian than married heterosexual couples. Kurdek (2004) compared gay, lesbian, and married heterosexual couples in long-term relationships. In this study, the gay and lesbian couples lived without children and the married heterosexual couples lived with children. For 50% of the comparisons, gay and lesbian couples did not differ from married heterosexual couples with children. Three major differences between gay/lesbian couples and married heterosexual couples were found: (1) gay and lesbian couples reported more autonomy and more equality; (2) gay and lesbian couples were better at conflict resolution; and (3) heterosexual married couples had more support from their families. In a later project, Kurdek (2008) followed four groups of couples—gay couples without children, lesbian couples without children, heterosexual married couples without children, and heterosexual married couples with children—for the first 10 years they cohabited. Lesbian partners reported the highest relationship quality at all points of assessment and showed no change in relationship quality over time. Gay partners reported the second highest relationship quality and also showed no change over time. Both groups of heterosexual couples reported lower levels of relationship quality than both gay and lesbian partners, and both groups also reported change over time. Heterosexual couples without children reported a steep decline in relationship quality in the early years followed by stability. In contrast, heterosexual couples with children reported a steep decline in the early years, followed by a gradual decline until year 8 when another period of steep decline began. This research begins to clarify some different experiences in partner relationships of various types, but only covers relationships through the young adult period. Hopefully, further longitudinal research will continue into middle adulthood and will also investigate relationships of gay and lesbian couples with children. At any rate, Phoung Le should be encouraged by the implications of this research for her younger daughter's relationship future.

Weinberg, Williams, and Pryor (2001) followed 56 people who identify as bisexual from young adulthood to middle adulthood. They found that the participants continue to report a bisexual identity and attraction to members of both sexes in middle adulthood. However, they also report less involvement in the bisexual community and more investment in work or a partner, and a move toward activity with just one sex. In other words, there is no change in bisexual attraction, but growing commitment to work and partnerships.

Baby boomers are more likely to be divorced than midlife adults in earlier cohorts (Fingerman & Dolbin-MacNab, 2006); this is not surprising given the finding of a drop in marital satisfaction among baby boomers compared with the earlier cohort (VanLaningham et al., 2001). Although many marriages flourish once the children have been launched, some marriages cannot survive without the presence of children to buffer conflicts in the marriage. Men report more marital satisfaction than women in the United States and Chinese Malaysia (Mickelson, Claffey, & Williams, 2006; Ny, Loy, Gudmunson, & Cheong, 2009), and most divorces are initiated by women (Carter & McGoldrick, 2005a). Longitudinal research has found that baby boom women are less satisfied with their marriages than their mothers were at midlife, reminding us of the importance of considering cohort effects when reporting life course trends (Putney & Bengtson, 2003).

Although there is a period of adjustment to divorce, midlife adults cope better with divorce than young adults (Greene, Anderson, Hetherington, Forgatch, & DeGarmo, 2003). Some individuals actually report improved well-being after divorce (Antonucci et al., 2001). Women have been found to be more adversely affected by a distressed marriage and men more adversely affected by being divorced (Hetherington & Kelly, 2002). However, the financial consequences of divorce for women are negative. After divorce, men are more likely to remarry than women, and Whites are more likely to remarry than African Americans.

Relationships With Children

Although a growing number of midlife adults are parenting young or school age children, most midlife adults are parents of adolescents or young adults. Parenting adolescents can be a challenge, and launching young adult offspring from the nest is a happy experience for most families. It is a family transition that has been undergoing changes in the past 20 years, however, coming at a later age for the parents and becoming more fluid in its timing and progress (K. Newman, 2008).

In the United States and the industrialized European countries, it became common for young adults to live outside the family prior to marriage in the 1960s. Then, in the United States, in the 1980s, two trends became evident: increased age at first leaving home and increased incidence of returning home. Popular culture has used phrases such as "prolonged parenting," "cluttered nest," "boomerang generation," and "adultolescents" to describe these trends (Putney & Bengtson, 2001, 2003). Recent data indicate that 30% to 40% of parents between the ages of 40 and 60 in the United States live with their adult children. Approximately half of these young adult children have never left home, and the other half have left home but returned one

> What factors are producing these trends in family life?

or more times. About 40% of recent cohorts of young adults have returned home at least once after leaving home (Putney & Bengtson, 2001). A very similar trend exists in Northern Europe; of parents ages 50 to 59, 28% in Denmark, 36% in Sweden, and 48% in Germany and Austria live with adult children. In contrast, 79% of parents in the same age group live with adult children in Spain and 82% in Italy (Kohli & Künemund, 2005). In general, parents are more positive than their young adult children about living together (Blieszner & Roberto, 2006).

Blieszner and Roberto (2006) argue that "lifestyles of midlife baby-boom parents revolve around their children" (p. 270). Providing support to children is associated with better psychological well-being in midlife adults. In general, mothers have closer relationships with their young adult children than fathers, and divorced fathers have been found to have weaker emotional attachments with their adult children than either married fathers or divorced mothers (Putney & Bengtson, 2003).

It is also important to note the common exchange of material resources between generations. Viktor Spiro and his parents are pooling resources to stay afloat economically. Helen Tyson and her husband received financial assistance from her midlife parents during the early years of their marriage. Phuong Le and her husband provided as much financial assistance as they could afford for their children to attend community college and university. Recent research in Germany suggests that intergenerational financial transfers are common and often sizable, with midlife and late life adults particularly providing financial assistance to adult children with poor economic position (Kohli & Künemund, 2005).

Research also indicates that midlife adults can be negatively affected by their relationships with their adult children. Greenfield and Marks (2006) found that midlife adults whose adult children have problems such as chronic disease or disability, emotional problems, problems with alcohol or other substances, financial problems, work-related problems, partner relationship problems, and so on report lower levels of well-being than midlife adults who do not report such problems in their adult children. Ha, Hong, Setlzer, and Greenberg (2008) found that midlife parents of adult children with developmental disabilities or mental health problems were more likely than parents of nondisabled children to report higher levels of negative emotions, decreased psychological well-being, and somatic symptoms. Seltzer et al. (2009) found that midlife adults had more negative emotions, more disruption in cortisol, and more physical symptoms on the days that they spent more time with their disabled children. These findings suggest a need for social service support for midlife parents whose adult children are facing ongoing challenges.

Relationships With Parents

Most research shows that middle-aged adults are deeply involved with their aging parents (Kohli & Künemund, 2005; Marks et al., 2004). As suggested in the stories of Viktor Spiro, Helen Tyson, and Phoung Le, the nature of the relationship with aging parents changes over time. A cross-national study of adults in Norway, England, Germany, Spain, and Israel found that across countries, support was bidirectional, with aging parents providing emotional and financial support to their midlife adult children and also receiving support from them (Lowenstein & Daatland, 2006). Viktor Spiro lives with his parents and receives much emotional support from his mother. Helen Tyson feels lost without the emotional support of her mother who died a year ago. Phoung Le's mother monitored the after-school activities of Phoung's adolescent children. As the parents' health begins to deteriorate, they turn more to their midlife children for help, as is currently the case for Viktor and Helen and was the situation for Phoung a few years ago. In the United States, a national survey by AARP (2001) found that about 78% of baby boomers age 45 to 55 provide some caregiving services to their own parents or to other older adults, but only 22% identify themselves as caregivers. A German study found that caring for elderly family members peaks between the ages of 50 to 54 (Kohli & Künemund, 2005).

Traditionally, and typically still, caregivers to aging parents are daughters or daughters-in-law (Blacker, 2005). This continues to be the case, even though a great majority of midlife women are employed full-time (Czaja, 2006). This does not tell the whole story, however. The baby boom cohort has more siblings than earlier and later cohorts, and there is some evidence that caregiving is often shared among siblings, with sisters serving as coordinators of the care (Hequembourg & Brallier, 2005). In spite of competing demands from spouses and children, providing limited care to aging parents seems to cause little psychological distress (AARP, 2001). Extended caregiving, conversely, has been found to have some negative effects as midlife adults try to balance a complex mix of roles (Putney & Bengtson, 2001; Savia, Almeida, Davey, & Zant, 2008), but there is also some evidence of rewards of caregiving (Robertson, Zarit, Duncan, Rovine, & Femia, 2007).

Most of the research on caregiving focuses on *caregiver burden,* or the negative effects on mental and physical health caused by caregiver stress. Compared with matched comparison groups who do not have caregiving responsibilities, caregivers of elderly parents report more depressive symptoms, taking more antidepressant and anti-anxiety medication, poorer physical health, and lower marital satisfaction (Martire & Schulz, 2000; Sherwood, Given, Given, & Von Eye, 2005). Savia et al. (2008) found that psychological distress was greater on days that adult children provided assistance to aging parents, but they also found more distressed mood among caregivers with higher caregiving demands and lower resources.

Although this research is not as prevalent, some researchers have been interested in a phenomenon they call *caregiver gain* or *caregiver reward.* One early proponent of this line of inquiry found that the majority of caregivers have something positive to say about their caregiving experiences (Kramer, 1997). One group of researchers was interested in the balance of positive and negative emotions in family caregivers of older adults with dementia (Robertson et al., 2007). They found considerable variation in the responses of caregivers in terms of the balance of stressful and positive experiences of caregiving. The stressful experiences included behavior problems of the care receiver; need to provide personal assistance with activities such as eating, dressing, grooming, bathing, toileting, and transferring into bed; role overload; and role captivity (feeling trapped in caregiver role). The positive experiences of caregiving included caregiving rewards such as growing personally, repaying care receiver, fulfilling duty, and getting perspective on what is important in life; sense of competence; and positive behaviors in care receiver. The researchers identified different groups of caregivers in terms of their levels of distress. The most well-adjusted group had more resources in terms of health, education, and so on and reported fewer behavior problems and fewer needs for personal assistance of the care recipients.

Culture appears to play a role in whether providing care to aging parents is experienced as burden or gain. For example, Lowenstein and Daatland (2006) found a strong expectation of providing care for parents in Spain and Israel, but a more negotiable obligation in northern Europe. In countries where caregiving is normalized, caregiving is often provided out of affection, not obligation, may be shared among family members, and may be less likely to be experienced as burden. This seems to be the situation for Helen Tyson and her sisters, and for Phoung Le. Evans et al. (2009) report that Hispanic caregivers have been found to have slightly less caregiver burden than Anglos. Very individualistic families value individual independence and may find elder care particularly troublesome to both caregiver and care recipient. However, there is evidence that both individualistically oriented families and collectivist-oriented families experience negative effects of long-term, intensive caregiving, especially those families with few economic and social resources (Robertson et al., 2007).

Other Family Relationships

Midlife is typically a time of launching children and a time when parents die. It is also a time when new family members get added by marriage and the birth of grandchildren. However, family relationships other than marital relationships and parent-child relationships have received little research attention. The grandparent-grandchild relationship has received the greatest amount of research attention, followed by a growing body of research on sibling relationships.

In the United States, about three fourths of adults become grandparents by the time they are 65 (Bjorklund & Bee, 2008). For those adults who become grandparents, the onset of the grandparent role typically occurs in their 40s or 50s, or increasingly in their 60s. Grandparenthood has been reported to be among the top three most important roles among middle-aged men and women in the United States (Reitzes & Mutran, 2002). Baby boom grandparents are likely to have fewer grandchildren than their parents had, spend more years in the grandparent role, and share that role with more people, including step-grandparents (Blieszner & Roberto, 2006). Vern Bengtson (2001) asserts that grandparents play an important socializing role in families, and that this role is likely to grow in importance in the near future.

There are many styles of grandparenting and many cultures of grandparenting. In cultures with large extended families and reverence for elders—such as in China, Mexico, and many Asian and African countries—grandparents often live with the family, as was the case with Phoung Le's mother. In the United States, Asian American, African American, Hispanic American, and Italian American grandparents are more likely to play an active role in the lives of grandchildren than other ethnic groups (Gardiner & Kosmitzki, 2008). Research has indicated gender differences in enactment of the grandparent role as well, with most research suggesting that grandmothers, particularly maternal grandmothers, play more intimate roles in their grandchildren's lives than grandfathers (Bjorklund & Bee, 2008). However, James Bates (2009) argues that grandfathers have been underrepresented in research on grandparenting and recommends a more focused research effort to examine these relationships.

Researchers have noted two potential problems for grandparents. First, if adult children divorce, custody agreements may fail to attend to the rights of grandparents for visitation (Blieszner & Roberto, 2006). And, baby boom adults are often serving as step-grandparents, a role that can be quite ambiguous. Second, if adult children become incapacitated by substance abuse, illness, disability, or incarceration, grandparents may be recruited to step in to raise the grandchildren. The number of children cared for by grandparents in the United States has risen dramatically in the past 30 years. About 2.4 million baby boom grandparents are serving as the primary caregiver to grandchildren. Racial and ethnic minority grandparents are two to three times more likely than European American grandparents to be serving in this role (Blieszner & Roberto, 2006). Unfortunately, grandparents with the least resources are often the ones called upon to become primary caregivers to their grandchildren (Fields, 2004).

Baby boomers have more siblings than earlier and later cohorts, and most midlife adults today have at least one sibling. Sibling relationships have been found to be important for the well-being of both men and women in midlife. Siblings often drift apart in young adulthood, but contact between siblings increases in late midlife (McGoldrick, Watson, & Benton, 2005). They are often brought together around the care and death of aging parents, and recent research indicates that sibling contact decreases again after the death of the last parent (Khodyakov & Carr, 2009). Sibling collaboration in the care of aging parents may bring them closer together or may stir new as well as unresolved resentments. Although step- and half-siblings tend to stay connected to each other, their contact is less frequent than the contact between full siblings.

Research in the Netherlands found that brothers provide more practical support to siblings and sisters provide more emotional support (Voorpostel & van der Lippe, 2007). In Taiwan, however, brother-brother dyads were found to provide the most companionship and emotional support of any dyad type (Lu, 2007). In the Netherlands, siblings seemed to overcome geographic distance to provide emotional support more easily than friends, but relationship quality was an important predictor of which sibling groups would offer emotional support (Voorpostel & van der Lippe).

Viktor Spiro's sister was an important lifeline for him when he immigrated to the United States, but tensions developed during the time when Viktor was suicidal. Their mutual concern about their father's health is drawing them closer again. Helen Tyson and her sisters have remained close over the years, and, indeed, Helen's sisters have been her major source of support. Currently, their collaboration around the care of their father is an important point of mutual interest. Phoung Le has close relationships with her siblings, and these relationships have remained close since her mother died.

Relationships With Friends

Midlife adults have more family members in their social convoys than do younger and older adults, but they also continue to report at least a few important friendships (Antonucci et al., 2004). Baby boom midlife adults are good friends with about seven people on average; these friends are usually of the same age, sex, race/ethnicity, social class, education, and employment status (Blieszner & Roberto, 2006). Some boomers also maintain cross-sex friendships, and these are particularly valued by men who are more likely than women to see a sexual dimension to these relationships (Monsour, 2002). It has been suggested that midlife adults have less time than other adult age groups for friendships (Antonucci et al., 2001).

Friendships appear to have an impact on midlife well-being for both men and women, although they do not seem to be as important as close familial relationships. For instance, the adequacy of social support, particularly from friends, at age 50 predicts physical health for men at age 70 (Vaillant, 2002). Likewise, midlife women who have a confidant or a close group of female friends report greater well-being than midlife women without such interpersonal resources (McQuaide, 1998). Women who report positive feelings toward their women friends also have fewer depressive symptoms and higher morale than women who report less positive feelings toward female friends (Paul, 1997). Whether good feelings toward friends protect against depression or depression impairs the quality of friendships remains to be determined, however.

Given this research, it appears that Phoung Le's wide circle of friends, as well as family, bode well for her continuing good health. Conversely, the research indicates that Helen Tyson's lack of friends, and inability to trust others enough to develop friendships, may be a risk factor for continued depression. This is an issue that she and her counselor may want to address. Viktor Spiro's recent participation in social events is providing him an opportunity to expand his social convoy and appears to be adding an important dimension to his life circumstances.

> Why is it important for social workers to recognize the role of chosen family in the lives of their clients?

It appears that the importance of friends in the social convoy varies by sexual orientation, race, and marital status. Friends are important sources of support in the social convoys of gay and lesbian midlife adults, often serving as an accepting "chosen family" for those who have traveled the life course in a homophobic society (Johnson & Colucci, 2005). These chosen families provide much care and support to each other, as evidenced by the primary caregiving they have provided in times of serious illness such as AIDS and breast cancer (McGoldrick, 2005). Friends also become family in many African American families. The literature on African American families often calls attention to the "nonblood" family members as a strength for these families (Boyd-Franklin, 2003). Friendships also serve an important role in the social convoys of single midlife adults, serving as a chosen family rather than a "poor substitute" for family (Berliner, Jacob, & Schwartzberg, 2005).

Community/Organizational Relationships

Phoung Le is known in her tight-knit Vietnamese community for her community service. Little information is available about midlife relationships in the community and within organizations, but it is increasingly recognized that these relationships are important in the lives of midlife adults (Antonucci et al., 2001). The two most frequently cited places for forming friendships are workplace and neighborhood. Mentoring younger employees at work has been found to provide a good forum for the expression of generativity (McDermid, Heilbrun, & DeHaan, 1997). Contacts with neighbors and with volunteer associations are positively correlated with health and well-being in middle adulthood, as in other periods of the adult life course. Black midlife women have been found to score higher on political participation than White middle-aged women in one cross-sectional study. The relationship between this participation and well-being deserves further study (Cole & Stewart, 1996). Participation in a religious community is consistently found to be associated with health and well-being (Antonucci et al., 2001). Participation in voluntary associations becomes a more important part of the social convoy after retirement (Moen, 1997). Alice Rossi (2004b) found that social class makes a difference in the nature of relationships in middle adulthood. Lower income persons are more likely than more affluent persons to be involved in hands-on caregiving to family and friends, and affluent persons are more likely than their lower income peers to be involved in contributing time and money to the larger community.

WORK IN MIDDLE ADULTHOOD

Like Viktor Spiro and Phoung Le, the majority of midlife adults engage in paid labor, but the first decade of the 21st century has been a precarious time for middle-aged workers. The national unemployment rate in the United States in 2004 was 4.4%, but it had risen to 10% in December 2009 (U.S. Bureau of Labor Statistics, 2009a). In the deep economic recession that began in December 2007, workers age 45 had a lower unemployment rate than younger workers, but they were disproportionately represented among the long-term unemployed, out of work for an average of 22.2 weeks, compared with 16.2 weeks for younger workers (Luo, 2009). These midlife baby boomers are too young to draw a pension or to have medical coverage through Medicare.

Work and retirement have different meanings for different people. Among the meanings work can have are the following (Friedmann & Havighurst, 1954):

- A source of income

- A life routine and way of structuring time

- A source of status and identity

- A context for social interaction

- A meaningful experience that provides a sense of accomplishment

Given these meanings, employment is an important role for midlife adults in many parts of the world, for men and women alike (Dittmann-Kohli, 2005; Kim & Moen, 2001). Helen Tyson and her counselor might want to consider whether returning to paid work would benefit Helen at this time, perhaps providing a source of status and identity, a context for social interaction, and a sense of accomplishment. These possible benefits would have to be weighed against the stress of balancing work and family.

In affluent societies, the last few decades have seen a continuing decline in the average age of retirement, particularly for men (Kim & Moen, 2001; Moen, 2004). This trend exists alongside trends of lengthening of years of both midlife and late adulthood and the fact that adults are entering midlife healthier and better educated than in previous eras. Improved pension plans are at least partially responsible for this trend, but in the United States, there is a growing gap in pension coverage. Between 1979 and 1993, the gap in pension coverage between workers with less than 12 years of education and workers with 16 years or more of education more than quadrupled (O'Rand, 2003). Governmental policies minimize the pension gap in European countries (Heinz, 2003).

Overall, the work patterns of middle-aged workers in the United States have changed considerably in the past three decades. Four trends stand out:

1. *Greater job mobility among middle-aged workers.* Changes in the global economy have produced job instability for middle-aged workers. In the late 20th century, corporate restructuring, mergers, and downsizing revolutionized the previous lockstep career trajectories and produced much instability in midcareer employment (Moen, 2003). Midlife white-collar workers who had attained midlevel management positions in organizations have been vulnerable to downsizing and reorganization efforts aimed at flattening organizational hierarchies. Midlife blue-collar workers have been vulnerable to changes in job skill requirements as the global economy shifts from an industrial base to a service base. Within these broad trends, gender, class, and race have all made a difference in the work patterns of midlife adults (D. Newman, 2008). Women are more likely than men to have job disruption throughout the adult life course, although those with higher education and higher income are less vulnerable to job disruption. In the recent recession, however, men have been more vulnerable to job loss than women. Race is a factor in the midlife employment disruption for men but not for women. Although Black men have more job disruptions than White men, there are no race differences for women when other variables are controlled. Research indicates that loss of work in middle adulthood is a very critical life event that has negative consequences for emotional well-being (Dittmann-Kohli, 2005).

2. *Greater variability in the timing of retirement.* Some midlife workers retire in their late 50s. Today, many other midlife adults anticipate working into their late 60s or early 70s. The decision to retire is driven by both health and financial status (more particularly, the availability of pension benefits) (Han & Moen, 1999; Moen, 2003).

The National Academy on an Aging Society (Sterns & Huyck, 2001) found that 55% of persons in the United States who retired between the ages of 51 and 59 reported a health condition as a major reason for retirement. Although availability of a pension serves as inducement for retirement, men and women who work in physically demanding jobs often seek early retirement whether or not they have access to a pension. Some leave the workforce as a result of disability and become eligible for Social Security disability benefits.

▲ **Photo 8.3** Changes in the global economy have produced job instability for middle-aged workers and job retraining often becomes essential.

3. *Blurring of the lines between working and retirement.* Many people now phase into retirement. Some middle-aged retirees return to work in different occupational fields than those from which they retired. Others leave a career at some point in middle adulthood for a part-time or temporary job. Increasing numbers of middle-aged workers leave a career position because of downsizing and reorganization and

find reemployment in a job with less financial reward, a "bridge job" that carries them into retirement (Moen, 2003; Sterns & Huyck, 2001).

4. *Increasing educational reentry of midlife workers.* This trend has received little research attention. However, workers with high levels of educational attainment prior to middle adulthood are more likely than their less-educated peers to retrain in middle adulthood (Luo, 2009). This difference is consistent with the theory of cumulative advantage; those who have accumulated resources over the life course are more likely to have the resources for retraining in middle adulthood. But in this era of high job obsolescence, relatively few middle-aged adults will have the luxury of choosing to do one thing at a time; to remain marketable, many middle-aged adults will have to combine work and school.

These trends aside, there is both good news and bad news for the middle-aged worker in the beginning of the 21st century. Research indicates that middle-aged workers have greater work satisfaction, organizational commitment, and self-esteem than younger workers (Dittmann-Kohli, 2005). Phoung Le appears to be a good example of this finding. However, with the current changes in the labor market, employers are ambivalent about middle-aged employees. Employers may see middle-aged workers as "hard-working, reliable, and motivated" (Sterns & Huyck, 2001, p. 476). But they also often cut higher-wage older workers from the payroll as a short-range solution for reducing operating costs and staying competitive.

For some midlife adults, such as Viktor Spiro, the issue is not how they will cope with loss of a good job but rather how they can become established in the labor market. In the previous industrial phase, poverty was caused by unemployment. In the current era, the major issue is the growing proportion of low-wage, no-benefit jobs. Black men with a high school education or less have been particularly disadvantaged in the current phase of industrialization, largely because of the declining numbers of routine production jobs. Adults such as Viktor, with disabilities, have an even harder time finding work that can support them. In July 2009, the unemployment rate for persons with a disability was 15.1% compared with 9.5% for persons with no disability (U.S. Bureau of Labor Statistics, 2009b). Even with legislation of the past two decades, much remains to be done to open educational and work opportunities to persons with disabilities. In addition, Viktor has had to contend with language and cultural barriers.

Thus, middle-aged workers, like younger workers, are deeply affected by a changing labor market. Like younger workers, they must understand the patterns in those changes and be proactive in maintaining and updating their skills. As researchers are finding, however, that task is easier for middle-aged workers

▲ **Photo 8.4** Research indicates that middle-aged workers often have greater work satisfaction, organizational commitment, and self-esteem than younger workers.

who arrive in middle adulthood with accumulated resources (Moen, 2003). Marginalization in the labor market in adulthood is the result of "cumulative disadvantage" over the life course. Unfortunately, adults such as Viktor Spiro who have employment disruptions early in the adult life course tend to have more job disruption in middle adulthood as well.

RISK FACTORS AND PROTECTIVE FACTORS IN MIDDLE ADULTHOOD

From a life course perspective, midlife behavior has both antecedents and consequences. Earlier life experiences can serve either as risk factors or as protective factors for health and well-being during middle adulthood. And midlife behaviors can serve either as risk factors or as protective factors for future health and well-being. The rapidly growing body of literature on risk, protection, and resilience based on longitudinal research has recently begun to add to our understanding of the antecedents of midlife behavior.

One of the best-known programs of research is a study begun by Emmy Werner and associates with a cohort born in 1955 on the island of Kauai, Hawaii. The research participants turned 40 in 1995, and Werner and Ruth Smith (2001) capture their risk factors, protective factors, and resilience in *Journeys From Childhood to Midlife*. They summarize their findings by suggesting that they "taught us a great deal of respect for the self-righting tendencies in human nature and for the capacity of *most* individuals who grew up in adverse circumstances to make a successful adaptation in adulthood" (p. 166). At age 40, compared with previous decades, the overwhelming majority of the participants reported "significant improvements" in work accomplishments, interpersonal relationships, contributions to community, and life satisfaction. Most adults who had a troubled adolescence had recovered by midlife.

> Why is it important for social workers to understand both antecedents and consequences of midlife behavior?

Many of these adults who had been troubled as youth reported that the "opening of opportunities" (p. 168) in their 20s and 30s had led to major *turning points*. Such turning points included continuing education at community college, military service, marriage to a stable partner, religious conversion, and survival despite a life-threatening illness or accident. At midlife, participants were still benefiting from the presence of a competent, nurturing caregiver in infancy, as well as from the emotional support along the way of extended family, peers, and caring adults outside the family.

Although this research is hopeful, Werner and Smith (2001) also found that 1 out of 6 of the study cohort was doing poorly at work and in relationships. The earlier risk factors associated with poor midlife adjustment include severe perinatal trauma, small for gestational age birth weight, early childhood poverty, serious health problems in early childhood, problems in early schooling, parental alcoholism and/or serious mental illness, health problems in adolescence, and health problems in the 30s. Viktor Spiro's early life produced several of these risk factors: early childhood poverty, health problems in adolescence, and his father's chronic depression. For men, the most powerful risk factor was parental alcoholism from birth to age 18. Women were especially negatively affected by paternal alcoholism during their adolescence. It is interesting to note that the long-term negative effects of serious health problems in early childhood and adolescence were just beginning to show up at age 40. We are also learning, as we see with Helen Tyson, that some negative effects of childhood and adolescent trauma may not present until early midlife.

Studies have also examined the effects of midlife behavior, specifically the effects on subsequent health (see Dioussé, Driver, & Gaziano, 2009). They have found a number of health behaviors that are risk factors for more severe and prolonged health and disability problems in late adulthood. These include smoking, heavy alcohol use, diet high in fats, overeating, and sedentary lifestyle. Economic deprivation and high levels of stress have also been found to be risk factors throughout the life course (Auerbach & Krimgold, 2001; Spiro, 2001). A health behavior that is receiving much research attention as a protective factor for health and well-being in late adulthood is a physical fitness program that includes stretching exercises, weight training, and aerobic exercise (Whitbourne, 2001).

Critical Thinking Questions 8.2

The research indicates that family ties remain strong in societies around the world. What do you think about this? Do you think that the family ties are strong in your multigenerational families? Are there kinkeepers in your multigenerational family? If so, who are they, and why do you think they play this role? What have you observed about the work life of the midlife adults in your family? How has the work life of the midlife adults in your family been affected by growing insecurity in the labor market, if at all? How are the midlife adults in your family working to balance family and work? How well are their efforts working?

IMPLICATIONS FOR SOCIAL WORK PRACTICE

This discussion has several implications for social work practice with midlife adults:

- Be familiar with the unique pathways your clients have traveled to reach middle adulthood.

- Recognize the role that culture plays in constructing beliefs about appropriate midlife roles and assist clients to explore their beliefs.

- Help clients to think about their own involvement in generative activity and the meaning that this involvement has for their lives.

- Become familiar with biological changes and special health issues in middle adulthood. Engage midlife clients in assessing their own health behaviors.

- Be aware of your own beliefs about intellectual changes in middle adulthood and evaluate those against the available research evidence.

- Be aware of both stability and the capacity for change in personality in middle adulthood.

- Help clients assess the role that spirituality plays in their adjustments in middle adulthood and, where appropriate, to make use of their spiritual resources to solve current problems.

- Engage midlife clients in a mutual assessment of their involvement in a variety of relationships, including romantic relationships, relationships with parents, relationships with children, other family relationships, relationships with friends, and community/organizational relationships.

- Collaborate with social workers and other disciplines to advocate for governmental and corporate solutions to work and family life conflicts.

KEY TERMS

accommodation (identity)	extroversion	perimenopause
assimilation (identity)	generativity	premenopause
conjunctive faith	introversion	trait theory
contextual model	kinkeepers	universalizing faith
convoy	life-span theory	
coping mechanism	menopause	

ACTIVE LEARNING

1. Think about how you understand the balance of gains and losses in middle adulthood. Interview three midlife adults ranging in ages from 40 to 60 and ask them whether they see the current phase of their lives as having more gains or more losses over the previous phase.

2. Draw your social convoy as it currently exists with three concentric circles:

   - Inner circle of people who are so close and important to you that you could not do without them

   - Middle circle of people who are not quite that close but are still very close and important to you

- Outer circle of people who are not as close and important as those in the two inner circles but still close enough to be considered part of your support system

- What did you learn from engaging in this exercise? Do you see any changes you would like to make in your social convoy?

3. What evidence do you see of antecedent risk factors and protective factors that are affecting the midlife experiences of Viktor Spiro, Helen Tyson, and Phoung Le? What evidence do you see of current behaviors that might have consequences, either positive or negative, for their experiences with late adulthood?

WEB RESOURCES

Boomers International
boomersint.org

Site presented by Boomers International: World Wide Community for the Baby Boomer Generation contains information from the trivial to the serious on the popular culture of the baby boomer generation.

Families and Work Institute
www.familiesandwork.org

Site presented by the Families and Work Institute contains information on work-life research, community mobilization forums, information on the Fatherhood Project, and frequently asked questions.

Max Planck Institute for Human Development
www.mpib-berlin.mpg.de/index_js.en.htm

Site presented by the Max Planck Institute for Human Development, Berlin, Germany, contains news and research about life course development.

Network on Successful Midlife Development
www.midmac.medharvard.edu

Site presented by the John D. and Catherine T. MacArthur Foundation Research Network on Successful Midlife Development (MIDMAC) contains an overview of recent research on midlife development and links to other human development research projects.

Seattle Longitudinal Study
http://geron.psu.edu/sls

Site at Pennsylvania State University presents information on the Seattle Longitudinal Study and publications from the study.

Late Adulthood

Matthias J. Naleppa and Rosa Schnitzenbaumer

Acknowledgment: The authors wish to thank Mariette Klein, Dr. Peter Maramaldi, and Dr. Michael Melendez for contributions to this chapter.

OPENING QUESTIONS

- How will the trend toward increased longevity affect family life and social work practice?

- What do social workers need to understand about the biological, psychological, social, and spiritual changes in late adulthood and the coping mechanisms used to adapt to these changes?

- What formal and informal resources are available for meeting the needs of elderly persons?

KEY IDEAS

As you read this chapter, take note of these central ideas:

1. Unlike in earlier historical eras, many people in the United States and other industrialized countries today reach the life phase of late adulthood, and the older population is a very heterogeneous group, including the young-old (65 to 74 years), the middle-old (75 to 84 years), and the oldest-old (85 and above). In this chapter, we consider the young-old and the middle-old.

2. The cumulative effect of health disparities based on race, ethnicity, gender, and socioeconomic status impacts the quality of aging for significant subpopulations of older people in the United States and around the world.

3. The most commonly discussed psychosocial theories of social gerontology are disengagement, activity, continuity, social construction, feminist, social exchange, life course, and age stratification theories; the most common theories of biological aging are the genetic theories, molecular/cellular theories, and system theories.

4. All systems of the body appear to be affected during the aging process.

5. It has been difficult to understand psychological changes in late adulthood without long-term longitudinal research, but recent longitudinal research suggests that with age and experience, individuals tend to use more adaptive coping mechanisms.

6. Families play an important role in late adulthood, and as a result of increased longevity, multi-generational families are more common than ever.

7. Although most persons enter retirement in late adulthood, some individuals continue to work even after they are eligible to retire, either out of financial necessity or by choice.

8. Older adults rely on a number of both informal and formal resources to meet their changing needs.

Case Study 9.1

The Smiths in Early Retirement

The Smiths are a Caucasian couple in their early retirement years who have sought out couples counseling. Lois Smith is 66 and Gene Smith is 68 years of age. They have lived in the same quiet suburban neighborhood since they married 20 years ago. When they met, Gene was a widower and Lois had been divorced for 3 years. They have no children from this marriage but three children from Lois's first marriage. The Smiths are grandparents to the three children of their married daughter, who lives 4 hours away. Their two sons are both single and also live in a different city. The Smiths visit their children frequently, but family and holiday gatherings usually take place at the Smiths' house.

The Smiths live in a comfortable home, but their neighborhood has changed over the years. When they bought the house, many other families were in the same life stage, raising adolescent children and seeing them move out as young adults. Many of the neighbors from that time have since moved, and the neighborhood has undergone a change to young families with children. Although the Smiths feel connected to the community, they do not have much interaction with the people in their immediate neighborhood. Only one other neighbor, a woman in her mid-80s, is an older adult. This neighbor has difficulty walking and no longer drives a car. The Smiths help her with chores around the house and often take her shopping.

Until her divorce, Lois had focused primarily on raising her children. After the divorce at age 43, she needed to enter the job market. Without formal education beyond high school, she had difficulty finding employment. She worked in a number of low-paying short-term jobs before finding a permanent position as a secretary at a small local company. She has only a small retirement benefit from her 12 years on that job. Gene had worked as bookkeeper and later assistant manager with a local hardware store for more than 30 years. Although their combined retirement benefits enable them to lead a comfortable retirement, Gene continues to work at the hardware store on a part-time basis.

The transition into retirement has not been easy for the Smiths. Both Gene and Lois retired last year, which required them to adjust all at once to a decrease in income. Much more difficult, however, has been the loss of status and feeling of void that they are experiencing. Both were accustomed to the structure that was provided by work. Gene gladly assists in his former company on a part-time basis, but he worries that his employer will think he's getting too old. Lois has no plans to reenter the workforce. She would like her daughter to live closer so she could spend more time with the grandchildren. Although the infrequency of the visits with the grandchildren has placed some strain on Lois's relationship with her daughter, especially in the period following her retirement, Lois has now begun to enjoy the trips to visit with her daughter as a welcome change in her daily routine. But those visits are relatively infrequent, and Lois often wishes she had more to do.

Case Study 9.2

Ms. Ruby Johnson, Caretaker for Three Generations

Ms. Ruby Johnson is a handsome woman who describes herself as a "hard-boiled, 71-year-old African American" who spent the first 30 years of her life in Harlem, until she settled in the Bronx, New York. She married at 19 and lived with her husband until her 30th birthday. During her initial assessment for case management services, she explained her divorce with what appeared to be great pride. On her 29th birthday, Ruby told her husband that he had one more year to choose between "me and the bottle." She tolerated his daily drinking for another year, but when he came home drunk on her 30th birthday, she took their 6-year-old daughter and left him and, she explained, "never looked back."

Ruby immediately got a relatively high-paying—albeit tedious—job working for the postal service. At the same time, she found the Bronx apartment, in which she has resided for the past 41 years. Ruby lived there with her daughter, Darlene, for 18 years until she "put that girl out" on what she describes as the saddest day of her life.

(Continued)

(Continued)

Darlene was 21 when she made Ruby the grandmother of Tiffany, a vivacious little girl in good health. A year later, Darlene began using drugs when Tiffany's father abandoned them. By the time Darlene was 24, she had a series of warnings and arrests for drug possession and prostitution. Ruby explained that it "broke my heart that my little girl was out there sellin' herself for drug money." Continuing the story in an unusually angry tone, she explained that "I wasn't gonna have no 'ho' live in my house."

During her initial interview, Ruby's anger was betrayed by a flicker of pride when she explained that Darlene, now 46, has been drug free for more than 20 years. Tiffany is 25 and lives with her husband and two children. They have taken Darlene into their home to help Ruby. Ruby flashed a big smile when she shared that "Tiffany and Carl [her husband] made me a great-grandma twice, and they are taking care of Darlene for me now." Darlene also has a younger daughter—Rebecca—from what Ruby describes as another "bad" relationship with a "no good man." Rebecca, age 16, has been living with Ruby for the past two years since she started having difficulty in school and needed more supervision than Darlene was able to provide.

In addition, about a year ago, Ruby became the care provider for her father, George. He is 89 and moved into Ruby's apartment because he was no longer able to live independently after his brother's death. On most weeknights, Ruby cooks for her father, her granddaughter, and everyone at Tiffany's house as well. Ruby says she loves having her family around, but she just doesn't have half the energy she used to have.

Ruby retired 5 years ago from the postal service, where she worked for 36 years. In addition to her pension and Social Security, she now earns a small amount for working part-time providing child care for a former coworker's daughter. Ruby explains that she has to take the extra work in order to cover her father's prescription expenses not covered by his Medicare benefits and to help pay medical/prescription bills for Tiffany's household. Tiffany and Carl receive no medical benefits from their employers and are considering lowering their income in order to qualify for Medicaid benefits. Ruby wants them to keep working, so she has been trying to use her connections to get them jobs with the postal service. Ruby reports this to be her greatest frustration, because her best postal service contacts are "either retired or dead."

Although Ruby's health is currently stable, she is particularly concerned that it may worsen. She is diabetic and insulin dependent and worries about all the family members for whom she feels responsible. During the initial interview, Ruby confided that she thinks that her physical demise has begun. Her greatest fear is death; not for herself, she says, but for the effect it would have on her family. She then asked her social worker to help her find a way to ensure their well-being after her death.

—*Peter Maramaldi*

Case Study 9.3

Joseph and Elizabeth Menzel, a German Couple

Christine, the 51-year-old daughter of Joseph and Elizabeth Menzel, came to the geriatric counseling center in a small town in Bavaria, Germany. She indicated that she could no longer provide adequate care to her parents and requested assistance from the geriatric social work team. Christine described the family situation as follows.

Her parents, Joseph and Elizabeth, live in a small house about 4 miles away from her apartment. Her brother Thomas also lives close by, but he can only provide help on the weekends because of his employment situation. The 79-year old mother has been diagnosed with dementia of the Alzheimer's type. Her increasing forgetfulness is beginning to interfere with her mastery of the household and some other activities of daily living. Her 84-year-old father's behavior is also adding to the mother's difficulties. Joseph Menzel is described as an authoritarian and very dominant person. For example, Christine says that he does not allow his wife to select which television shows she can watch or what music she can to listen to, even though she would like to make such choices by herself. According to the daughter, his behavior seems to add to Elizabeth Menzel's confusion and lack of personal confidence. At the same time, however, Joseph Menzel spends a lot of his time in bed. During those times he does not interact much with Elizabeth Menzel. Sometimes he would not get up all day and neglected his own personal care. It was not clear how much his staying in bed was related to his general health condition; he has silicosis and congestive heart failure.

The couple lives a fairly isolated life and has no friends. Family members, the son Thomas, the daughter Christine and her partner, four grandchildren, and a brother of Elizabeth Menzel, are the only occasional visitors. Christine's primary concern was with her mother's well-being. The mother needs assistance with the instrumental activities of daily living as well as with her health care. Having full-time employment, the daughter indicated that she has a hard time providing the assistance and care that she thinks would be needed. Chores such as doctors visits, shopping, cleaning, and regular checking in with the parents could be done by her and her brother. However, additional care responsibilities seem to be beyond the daughter's capacity at this time. During the initial contact with the daughter, the following services were discussed:

- An application for additional funding through the long-term care insurance (German Pflegeversicherung) will be completed. Because Elizabeth Menzel suffers from dementia, she would be eligible for higher levels of support. The additional funding would enable her to access the services she requires.

- A local care provider will be hired to help with managing medications. It is expected that this may help the parents get used to receiving outside assistance, in case they require higher levels of support with physical care and hygiene down the road. Having someone stop by on a daily basis will also provide an added measure of security and social contact.

- The Menzels will apply for daily lunch delivery through the local meals-on-wheels service.

- A volunteer will be found through the local volunteer network. This person should stop by one to two times per week to engage the mother in activities such as music, walks, playing games, or memory training.

- Elizabeth Menzel will be asked whether she would like to attend the weekly Erzählcafé meetings, a local group for persons with dementia.

- Joseph Menzel will receive information from the geriatric counseling center regarding how to attend to his wife's dementia. Furthermore, an assessment will be completed to establish whether he has depression and, if needed, he will be connected to relevant medical services.

- In addition to receiving assistance from the geriatric counseling center, the daughter is invited to participate in a support group for relatives and caregivers of persons with dementia.

(Continued)

(Continued)

All of the described services and programs were secured within a short succession. After three initial visits, Elizabeth Menzel had established a good relationship with the volunteer helper and indicates that she likes attending the Erzählcafé meetings. After the assistance for his wife started, Joseph Menzel opened up to having a conversation with the geriatric social worker. He indicated that he was thinking a lot lately about his own personal biography. He and his wife were displaced after the war. They grew up as neighbors in Silesia (today part of Poland). Both of their families had to leave everything behind and flee overnight in October of 1946. After staying in various refugee camps, their families finally ended up in Bavaria. This is where they started dating and finally married. Having lost everything, they had to start all over again. They had to work hard for everything they have today. Joseph Menzel worked his entire live as a miner, supplementing his income through a second job painting houses. His wife was employed as a seamstress. Respected for their hard work and engagement, they were soon accepted as members of their new community. However, Joseph Menzel says that he has never come to terms with his postwar displacement and the loss of his homeland. He started a community group and organized regular meetings for displaced persons. Together with his daughter, he also wrote a book about his homeland. Now he only feels too weak and ill to do anything. He just wants to stay at home and sit in his recliner all day. After talking with the geriatric social worker, Joseph Menzel overcame his initial reluctance and agreed to have additional contacts with the geriatric counseling center.

Soon after connecting with the geriatric counseling center, the daughter unexpectedly died during a routine surgery. After the initial shock and grieving of the unexpected loss, the family began adjusting to the new situation. The brother assumed the overall coordination and management of his mother's care. Other family members took on more responsibilities and increased the frequency of visiting their grandmother. The contacts with the volunteer proved to be a valuable support for Elizabeth Menzel's work around the loss and grief issues. In spite of her dementia, she had experienced her daughter's death very intensively.

While this all was occurring, Joseph Menzel's health declined rapidly. He has been hospitalized twice for longer periods over the past few months. During this time, more intensive assistance had to be provided to his wife.

Students in the United States are probably not familiar with the Bavarian Geriatric Counseling Centers. So some description is in order. The regional funding providers in Bavaria realized that older adults have a higher unmet need for social-psychiatric assistance than younger adults. These differing needs are related to the specific developmental tasks of late adulthood, such as morbidity, grieving the decline of one's own physical and mental abilities, grieving the loss of close persons, search for meaning and personal biographical work, and reconciliation with one's life story. In an effort to address this need, geriatric counseling centers were created. In urban settings, the work is accomplished through interdisciplinary teams consisting of social workers, psychiatric nurses, psychologist, and occupational therapists. The task of the counseling center is to coordinate and provide geriatric services to older adults in the community and to create service provider networks. In rural areas, such as the area in which the Menzels live, geriatric counseling centers assume additional provision-related tasks, including direct practice, home visiting, caregiver support and counseling, case management, developing senior groups (groups focusing on dementia, life review/biographical work, grief, or depression), creation of volunteer networks and training of volunteers, and psycho-educational work.

DEMOGRAPHICS OF THE OLDER POPULATION

Older adults do not live primarily in the past. Like all other individuals, their day-to-day life incorporates past, present, and future orientations. In terms of their life span, they have more time past them and less time ahead, but research regularly shows that the overemphasis on the past is a myth (Mayer et al., 1999). Research from the longitudinal Berlin Aging Study has been able to dispel some of the commonly held beliefs about older adults. According to their research as well as findings from other studies, older adults:

- Are not preoccupied with death and dying

- Are able and willing to learn new things

- Still feel that they can and want to be in control of their life

- Still have life goals

- Do not live primarily in the past

- Still live an active life, their health permitting

The term late adulthood covers about one quarter to one third of a person's life and includes active and less active, healthy and less healthy, working and nonworking persons. Late adulthood encompasses a wide range of age-related life experiences. Someone retiring today and having lived in the United States has experienced school segregation and busing for the purposes of school integration, Martin Luther King's "I have a dream" speech, but also the election of the first African American president and the first Latina Supreme Court Justice. He or she may have experienced the Dust Bowl, two world wars, and would have grown up listening to radio shows before TV existed. The person may have been at Woodstock and could be the in the age cohort of Mick Jagger and Bob Dylan. Every client in the stories above could be considered old, and yet, they are functioning in different ways and at different levels. In the context of U.S. society, the term *old* can have many meanings. These meanings reflect attitudes, assumptions, biases, and cultural interpretations of what it means to grow older. In discussing life course trajectories, we commonly use the terms *older population* or *elderly persons* to refer to those over 65 years of age. But an Olympic gymnast is "old" at age 25, a president of the United States is "young" at age 50, and a 70-year-old may not consider herself "old" at all.

Late adulthood is perhaps a more precise term than *old,* but it can still be confusing because of the 50-year range of ages it may include. *Late adulthood* is considered to start at 65 and continue through the 85 and older range. Considering age 65 as the starting point for late adulthood is somewhat arbitrary, since there is no sudden change to our physiology, biology, or personality. Rather, it can be traced back to Bismarck's social insurance schemes in Germany more than 100 years ago and the introduction of the Social Security Act in the United States in 1935. In both cases, 65 years was selected for retirement based on population statistics and expected survival rates. Many people today reach the life stage of late adulthood. In 2008, there were approximately 508 million people 65 years or older in the world, and by 2040 this number will increase to 1.3 billion (National Institute of Aging, National Institute of Health [NIA/NIH], 2009). Globally, the United States is fairly young as wealthy nations go, with slightly more than 12% of its population 65 and older. Most European countries average 15% of their population as 65 or older. Japan and Italy's older population stands at 20% of the total population (Federal Interagency Forum on Aging Related Statistics, 2008). The enormous increase in life expectancy is not unique to the United States. Nor is it occurring only in the developed world. Most nations of the world have a growing older population. Currently, 62% of the population over 65 lives in nonindustrialized or newly industrializing countries, and the population growth in these countries is twice that of developed countries (NIA/NIH, 2009). Because of this trend, it is expected that 1 billion people over 65, that is, 76% of the projected world total, will live in today's developing countries (NIA/NIH, 2009). Disability rates are declining among the older population in the United States, Japan, and a number of European nations, contributing to an extended life expectancy rate internationally (American Association of Retired Persons, 2003).

According to the U.S. Census, the 85 and older population is the fastest growing segment of the aging population, projected to increase from 4.2 million in 2000 to 8.7 million in 2030 (U.S. Bureau of the Census, 2008b). There are increasing numbers of people 100 years and older, a staggering 117% increase from 1990 figures (Administration on Aging, 2008). As of 2006, persons reaching age 65 have an average life expectancy of an additional 19 years (20.3 years for females and 17.4 for males). A child born in 2006 could expect to live 78.1 years, about 30 years longer than a child born in 1900 (Administration on Aging).

Increased life expectancy is a product of a number of factors: decrease in mortality of children and young adults, decreased mortality among the aging, improved health technology, and other factors. Life expectancy also varies by race, gender, and socioeconomic status. On average, Whites can expect to live 5½ years longer than minority groups in the United States. The gap is anticipated to narrow to a point where life expectancy for Whites is 1.6 years longer than for Blacks (Administration on Aging, 2008; George, 2005; Rieker & Bird, 2005; Williams, 2005).

Just a century ago, it was uncommon to reach 65. The first population census of the United States, conducted in 1870, estimated about 3% of the population to be more than 65 years of age. Today, more than three fourths of all persons in the United States live to be 65 (Walker, Manoogian-O'Dell, McGraw, & White, 2001). The U.S. Census Bureau estimates that in the next 25 years, the elderly population will double to 72 million. By 2030, 1 in 5 people in the United States will be 65 or older. People in the United States are living longer, are more racially diverse, have lower rates of disability, are less likely to live in poverty, and on average have higher levels of education than in the past (Administration on Aging, 2008; U.S. Bureau of the Census, 2004). These salutary developments are not without social and economic implications for both the aging and general population.

> What factors are leading to this trend toward increased longevity?

Age structure, the segmentation of society by age, will affect the economic and social condition of the nation, especially as it regards dependence. An interesting side effect of the growing elderly population is a shifting **dependency ratio**—a demographic indicator that expresses the degree of demand placed on society by the young and the aged combined. There are three dependency ratios: the elderly dependency ratio, the number of elders 65 and older per 100 people ages 18 to 64; the child dependency ratio, the number of children under 18 per 100 persons ages 18 to 64; and the total dependency ratio, the combination of both of these categories (U.S. Bureau of the Census, 2008b).

The nature of the U.S. dependency ratio has changed gradually over the past century, as the percentage of children in the population has decreased and the percentage of dependent older adults has increased. As Exhibit 9.1 demonstrates, the elderly dependency ratio is predicted to continue to increase at a fairly rapid pace in the near future. U.S. Census projections indicate small increases of elderly dependency from 20.9 per 100 persons age 18 to 64 in 1995 to 21.2 per 100 in 2010. Steep increases are projected from 2010 to 2030, with stability occurring at the level of 36 per 100 by 2050. The child dependency ratio has shown a modest "U" trend. There were about 43 persons under 18 per 100 persons ages 18 to 64 in 1995, with an anticipated drop to 39 per 100 by 2010 and expected increase to 43 by 2030. The overall dependency ratio is expected to stabilize to about 80 per 100 persons ages 18 to 64 between 2030 and 2050 (Administration on Aging, 2008). The social and economic implications of this increase in the dependency ratio are the focus and concern of many scholars and policymakers.

The older population encompasses a broad age range and is often categorized into subgroups: the young-old (age 65 to 74), the middle-old (age 75 to 84), and the oldest-old (over 85). The Smiths and Ruby Johnson exemplify the

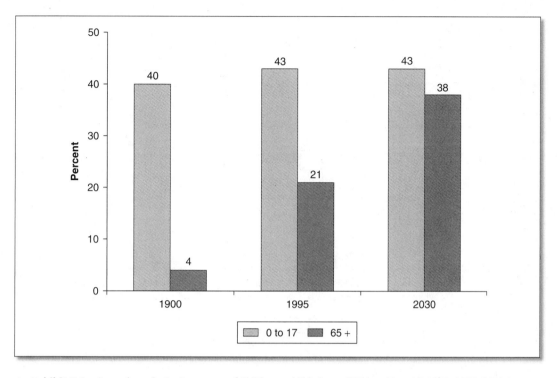

young-old, the Menzels the middle-old. In this chapter, we discuss those persons in the young-old and middle-old categories, ages approximately 65 to 84. Very late adulthood is discussed in Chapter 10, covering ages 85 and over.

The U.S. society is one of the most racially and ethnically diverse societies in the world. By 2050 it has been predicted that 48% of the general population will be minorities, with approximately one third of the older adults reflecting minority communities. The aging population reflects these shifting trends in the general population. The data available from 2007 indicate that 19.3% of adults over age 65 are non-White, with 8.3% non-Hispanic Black, 6.6% Hispanic, 3.2% Asian and Pacific Islander, and less than 1% indigenous Americans (Administration on Aging, 2008). As demonstrated in Exhibit 9.2, racial and ethnic composition of older adults is projected to change profoundly by 2050. This change reflects the decline in the White elderly (from 83% of older Americans in 2004 to 72% in the year 2030 and 66% by 2050), as well as dramatic increases in all other categories. The U.S. Census Bureau estimates that between 2000 and 2050, the Hispanic population will be the fastest growing subpopulation, accounting for 19.8% of older adults by 2050. Hispanics will be a larger and older group than the Black non-Hispanic population of elders that is projected to be 11%, while 7.8% of elders will be non-Hispanic (Asian and Pacific Island persons), and 1% indigenous/Native Americans (Administration on Aging). Proportionally, 6.8% of the populations of minorities are older as compared with 15% of the White population. In 2007, 9.7% of the elderly population was living in poverty. A significant difference exists, when looking at poverty rates of different racial groups among older adults. Although 7.4% of White elderly lived in poverty, this was the case for 23.2% of African Americans, 11.3% of Asians, and 17.1% of Hispanics (Administration on Aging).

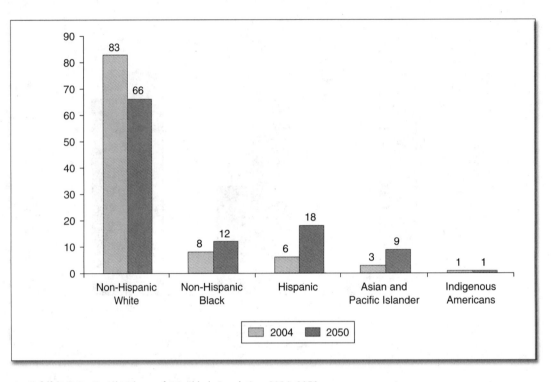

▲ **Exhibit 9.2**   Racial Makeup of U.S. Elderly Population, 2004, 2050

SOURCE: Administration on Aging, 2006a, 2006b, 2006c.

A number of factors account for this ethnic and racial shift in the U.S. aging population. They include high fertility rates among Black, Hispanic, and Asian populations; low mortality rates among Asians and Hispanics; and the influence of immigration rates on Asian and Hispanic populations (Administration on Aging, 2008). The number of immigrants age 60 and older has risen over the past 30 years; approximately 70,000 immigrants in 2001 were elderly compared with 20,000 in 1969. In 2001, upon arrival in the United States, nearly 7% of immigrants were age 60 or older. Additionally, the number of immigrants admitted as parents of U.S. citizens increased from 45,000 in 1986 to more than 80,000 in 2001 (Wilmoth & Longino, 2006).

Among the older population in the United States, women—especially those in very late adulthood (85 and older)—continue to outnumber men across all racial and ethnic groups. Census data analyzed in 2004 indicate that older women (21.1 million) outnumber older men (15.2 million). In 2007, the sex ratio among older adults stood at 137 females per 100 males. The female to male ratio increases with age, ranging from 114 females per 100 males for the 65 to 69 age group to a high of 210 females per 100 males for those 85 and older (Administration on Aging, 2008). As long as men exceed women in mortality rates, women will outnumber men among the elderly, especially in the oldest-old group of 85 years or more (Administration on Aging; U.S. Bureau of the Census, 2004).

One of the biggest gender differences in life circumstances of older adults relates to marital status. Older men are more likely to be married than older women. According to data from 2008, 78% of men 65 to 74 were married as compared with 57% of women in the same age group (Federal Interagency Forum on Aging-Related Statistics, 2008). This is an important consideration, because marital status influences a person's emotional and economic status, living arrangement, and caregiving needs. As of 2007, the rate of divorce and separation for older Americans was 10.6%. This figure has doubled since 1980, when it stood at 5.3%. Approximately 18% of women and 10% of men age 65 or older were divorced in 2007 (Administration on Aging, 2008).

Gender, race, and ethnicity have a significant effect on the economic status of elderly individuals. As of 2007, 9.7% of elderly persons were below the poverty level. An additional 6.4% of elderly persons were classified as "near poor" (income levels between poverty level and 125% of that level). The poverty rate increases with age from 9% for persons 65 to 74, to 12% for the population between the ages of 65 to 74, and 14% for those ages 85 and older. However, elderly men have a significantly lower poverty rate than elderly women (6.6% vs. 12%).

> How are gender, race, ethnicity, and social class related in late adulthood?

As described above, the poverty rates also differ for racial groups. Almost 40% of those older adults with the highest poverty levels were older African American and Hispanic women living alone (Administration on Aging, 2008). Although it was initially thought that trends indicated that the poverty rate was declining for all racial and ethnic groups of older adults, there is mounting evidence of increasing economic disparities across groups (Schoeni, Martin, Andreski, & Freedman, 2005; Wilmoth & Longino, 2006).

The geographic distribution of the elderly population varies considerably by states across the United States. In 2007, about half (52%) of older U.S. adults were concentrated in nine states: California, Florida, New York, Texas, Pennsylvania, Ohio, Illinois, Michigan, and New Jersey (Administration on Aging, 2008). Between 1990 and 2000, every state experienced population increases in the proportion of age 65 and older, ranging from a 1% increase in Rhode Island to a 79% increase in Nevada. Only the District of Columbia showed a decrease in the proportion of people age 65 and older. The greatest regional increases in percentages of older people occurred in the West (20%) and the South (16%). Increases occurred at significantly lower rates in the Midwest (7%) and the Northeast (5%). Between 1997 and 2007, 10 states had a 20% or more increase in their 65 and older population: Nevada, Alaska, Arizona, New Mexico, Colorado, Delaware, Utah, Georgia, South Carolina, and Idaho (Administration on Aging).

Residential mobility has a significant impact on the distribution of the elderly population. However, older adults are less likely to change residence than any other age group. From 2006 to 2007, only 4.2% of older persons moved as opposed to 17.0% of the population under 65. More than half (57.9%) of older adults who moved stayed within the same county, and 78.9% remained in the same state (Administration on Aging, 2008). Nevertheless, migration of older persons to states such as Florida after retirement contributes to its high percentage of elderly residents. Conversely, high percentages of elderly residents in some other regions are the result of outward migration by younger people (Franklin, 2003).

Residential mobility can also lead to changing age structures within neighborhoods and thus affect the elderly person's life. A recent study noted that the role of neighborhood structural context, as measured by poverty, residential stability, and aged-based demographic concentration, was predictive of the health and well-being of elders (Subramanian, Kubzansky, Berman, Fay, & Kawachi, 2006). For example, the Smiths used to be a "typical" family in their neighborhood. Now, as one of only two households with elderly occupants, they are the exception.

CULTURAL CONSTRUCTION OF LATE ADULTHOOD

The ethnic/racial diversity of the older population in the United States underscores the complexity and importance of taking cultural differences in perceptions of aging into account. A salient example of cultural differences in approaches to aging is the contrasts between traditional Chinese and mainstream U.S. beliefs and values. China has been described in anthropological literature as a "gerontocracy," wherein older people are venerated, given deference, and valued in nearly every task. Benefiting from the Confucian values of filial piety, older people hold a revered position in the family and society.

> How important is social age in defining late adulthood?

▲ **Photos 9.1a & b** The ethnic/racial diversity of the older population in the United States underscores the importance of taking cultural differences in perceptions of aging into account.

By contrast, consider the traditional cultural influences in the United States, where individualism, independence, and self-reliance are core values that inherently conflict with the aging process. In the United States, older people have traditionally been collectively regarded as dependent, and cultural values dictate that older people living independently are given higher regard than those requiring assistance. As people age, they strive to maintain the independence and avoid—at all costs—becoming a burden to their family. Older people in the United States typically resort to intervention from private or social programs to maintain their independence rather than turning to family. By contrast, Chinese elders traditionally looked forward to the day when they would become part of their children's household, to live out their days being venerated by their families (Gardiner & Kosmitzki, 2008).

No discussion of comparisons between cultures would be complete without mention of differences that occur within groups. An individual Chinese person might value independence. And an individual in the United States might be closer to the Confucian value of filial piety than traditional U.S. values. Additionally, processes such as acculturation, assimilation, and bicultural socialization further influence the norms, values, expectations, and beliefs of all cultural groups, including that which is considered the dominate cultural norm. Globalization of economics and information exchange also impact and change the cultural norms of all countries so that culture must be construed as something that is dynamic, fluid, emergent, improvisational, and enacted (Gardiner & Kosmitzki, 2008). In fact, U.S. values of aging appear to be shifting, influenced in part by political and market forces. In the United States, we are now bombarded with contradictory information about aging—media presentations of long-lived, vibrant older adults are juxtaposed with media presentations of nursing home horror stories (Vaillant, 2002).

In his book, *Aging Well*, George Vaillant (2002) raises the question, "Will the longevity granted to us by modern medicine be a curse or a blessing?" (p. 3). The answer, he suggests, is influenced by individual, societal, and cultural values, but his research makes him optimistic. Vaillant reports on the most long-term longitudinal research available, the Study of Adult Development. The study includes three separate cohorts of 824 persons, all of whom have been studied since adolescence:

1. *268 socially advantaged graduates of Harvard University born about 1920.* These research participants were selected for their physical and psychological health as they began college.

2. *456 socially disadvantaged inner-city men born in 1930.* These research participants were selected because they were nondelinquent at age 14. Half of their families were known to five or more social agencies, and more than two thirds of their families had been recent public welfare recipients.

3. *90 middle-class intellectually gifted women born about 1910.* These participants were selected for their high IQs when they were in California elementary schools.

A significant limitation of the study is the lack of racial and ethnic diversity among the participants, who are almost exclusively White. The great strength of the study is its ability to control cohort effects by following the same participants over such a long period of time.

Much of the news from the Study of Adult Development is good news. Vaillant reminds us that Immanuel Kant wrote his first book of philosophy at 57, Titian created many art works after 76, Ben Franklin invented bifocals at 78, and Will Durant won a Pulitzer Prize for history at 83. Unless they develop a brain disease, the majority of older adults maintain a "modest sense of well-being" (2002, p. 5) until a few months before they die. Older adults are also less depressed than the general population. Many older adults acknowledge hardships of aging but also see a reason to continue to live. Vaillant concludes that "positive aging means to love, to work, to learn something we did not know yesterday, and to enjoy the remaining precious moments with loved ones" (p. 16). Although he found many paths to successful aging, Vaillant identifies six traits for "growing old with grace," found in Exhibit 9.3.

> How much choice do we have over the six traits for "growing old with grace"?

Vaillant reports that he had originally planned to study only the rate of physical deterioration as individuals age. He had absorbed the cultural bias that aging was only about decay. He recounts a letter he received from one study participant, who wrote, "You ask us what we can no longer do . . . but I detect little curiosity about our adaptability, our zest for life, how our old age is, or isn't, predictable from what went before" (2002, p. 36). This feedback influenced Vaillant to pursue the possibilities in late adulthood, without denying the special hardships of this life phase. Note that this study participant and other members of the current generation of older adults are exercising human agency and, in the process, producing changes in some of the culture of aging in the United States.

A more recent study using longitudinal data from the Americans' Changing Lives (ACL) study continues to examine the question of the impact of life expectancy and quality of life as a person ages. This is a nationally representative sample of adults age 25 years and older, first interviewed in 1986 and re-interviewed in 1989, 1994, and 2001/2002 (House, Lantz, & Herd, 2005). The ACL was designed to address one central dilemma of research on aging and health: whether increased life expectancy in the United States and other developed nations foreshadowed a scenario of longer life but worsening health with the result of increasing chronically ill and functionally limited and disabled people requiring expensive medical and long-term care—or whether, through increased understanding of psychosocial as well as biomedical risk factors, the onset of serious morbidity and attendant functional limitation and disability could be potentially postponed or "compressed."

These authors focused on socioeconomic disparities in health changes through the middle and later years. They represent a set of scholars who are examining a theoretical concept of cumulative advantage and disadvantage and its role in understanding differential aging among various populations (Hatch, 2005; Wickrama, Conger, & Abraham, 2005). (See Chapter 1 for a discussion of these concepts.) They argue that multiple interacting factors throughout the life course impact the quality of the health of older individuals. For example, early poverty, lifetime of poverty, poor environmental conditions, poor education, race, and gender have a direct impact on how a person will age. It is not a simple linear causal track, but instead reflects the complexity of interacting risk and protective factors.

Reviewing research findings from the ACL study, House et al. (2005) examined the impact of two factors related to socioeconomic status (SES), education and income, on poor health. They found that overall socioeconomic disparities do impact health outcomes rather than the reverse. Additionally, they found that education has a greater impact

1. Caring about others and remaining open to new ideas

2. Showing cheerful tolerance of the indignities of old age

3. Maintaining hope

4. Maintaining a sense of humor and capacity for play

5. Taking sustenance from past accomplishments while remaining curious and continuing to learn from the next generation

6. Maintaining contact and intimacy with old friends

▲ **Exhibit 9.3**   Six Traits for Growing Old With Grace

SOURCE: Vaillant, 2002, pp. 310–311.

than income on the onset of functional limitations/disabilities. Income, however, has a greater impact on the progression of functional limitations. Finally, the impact of educational disparities on the onset of functional limitations increased strikingly in later middle and early old age, with more highly educated individuals postponing limitations and thus compressing the number of years spent with limitations (House et al.).

Other authors (George, 2005; Rieker & Bird, 2005; Williams, 2005) argue that SES is not the sole explanatory factor for the quality of aging. George argues that SES is only one form of social stratification, arguing that gender and race/ethnicity are other important forms of stratification. Although they are significantly related to SES, their associations with health extend beyond SES in complex ways. Race and gender are partial determinants of SES. However they are "ascribed statuses" that involve basic obstacles and barriers to opportunities and resources associated with better aging. Additionally, these ascribed statuses contend with overt forms of microaggressions associated with racism and sexism. For these authors, this raises the question as to whether race and gender are more fundamentally associated with illness and poor quality of aging than the more general category of SES.

PSYCHOSOCIAL THEORETICAL PERSPECTIVES ON SOCIAL GERONTOLOGY

How social workers see and interpret aging will inspire our interventions with older adults. **Social gerontology**—the social science that studies human aging—offers several theoretical perspectives that can explain the process of growing old. Eight predominant theories of social gerontology are introduced here. An overview of the primary concepts of each theory is presented in Exhibit 9.4.

1. *Disengagement theory.* **Disengagement theory** suggests that as elderly individuals grow older, they gradually decrease their social interactions and ties and become increasingly self-preoccupied (Cumming & Henry, 1961). This is sometimes seen as a coping mechanism in the face of ongoing deterioration and loss (Tobin, 1988). In addition, society disengages itself from older adults. Although disengagement is seen as a normative and functional process of transferring power within society, the theory does not explain, for example, the fact that a growing number of older persons, such as Gene and Lois Smith and Ruby Johnson, continue to assume active roles in society (Hendricks & Hatch, 2006). Although it was the first comprehensive theory trying to explain the aging process (Achenbaum & Bengston 1994), disengagement theory has received much criticism and little research support. To the contrary, research conducted through the National Social Life Health and Aging Project shows that older Americans are generally well-connected and engaged in community life according to their abilities (Cornwell, Laumann, & Schumm, 2008). Disengagement theory is now widely discounted by gerontologists (Hooyman, 2008).

Theory	Primary Theme
Disengagement theory	Elderly persons gradually disengage from society.
Activity theory	Level of life satisfaction is related to level of activity.
Continuity theory	Elderly persons continue to adapt and continue their interaction patterns.
Social construction theory	Self-concepts arise through interaction with the environment.
Feminist theory	Gender is an important organizing factor in the aging experience.
Social exchange theory	Resource exchanges in interpersonal interactions change with age.
Life course perspective/Life course capital perspective	Aging is a dynamic, lifelong process characterized by many transitions. People accumulate human capital during the life course to address their needs.
Age stratification perspective	Society is stratified by age, which determines people's roles and rights.

▲ **Exhibit 9.4**   Psychosocial Theoretical Perspectives on Social Gerontology

2. *Activity theory.* **Activity theory** states that higher levels of activity and involvement are directly related to higher levels of life satisfaction in elderly people (Havighurst, 1968). If they can, individuals stay active and involved, and carry on as many activities of middle adulthood as possible. There is growing evidence that examining and promoting physical activity is associated with postponing functional limitation and disability (Benjamin, Edwards, & Bharti, 2005). Activity theory has received some criticism for not addressing relatively high levels of satisfaction for individuals such as Ms. Johnson, whose level of activity is declining. It also does not address the choice made by many older individuals to adopt a more relaxed lifestyle. Some argue that the theory does not adequately address factors such as ethnicity, life style, gender, and socioeconomic status (Eliopoulus, 2010; Moody, 2010). Activity theory also does not sufficiently take into account individual life circumstances and loses sight of personhood in order to satisfy society's view of how people should age (Moody).

An alternative construct for measuring quality of aging is the concept of self-efficacy. Self-efficacy is the perception, or belief, that one has the ability to produce and to regulate events in one's life and achieve desired goals. Having a sense of mastery and competence can be associated with a whole range of activities, not just physical activity. Brandtstadter (2006) argues that self-efficacy is more predictive of positive aging than life satisfaction.

▲ **Photo 9.2**   Variables that often predict healthy aging include practicing healthy habits such as exercising, eating well, maintaining a healthy weight, and not smoking or abusing alcohol.

3. *Continuity theory.* **Continuity theory** was developed in response to critiques of the disengagement and activity theories. According to continuity theory, individuals adapt to changes by using the same coping styles they have used throughout the life course, and they adopt new roles that substitute for roles lost because of age (Neugarten, Havighurst, & Tobin, 1968). Individual personality differences are seen as a major influence in adaptation to old age. Those individuals who were active earlier in life stay active in later life, whereas those who adopted a more passive lifestyle continue to do so in old age. Older adults also typically retain the same stance concerning religion and sex as they always did. Current scholarship considers the interaction between personal and contextual factors that promote or impede the accomplishment of desired goals and new roles, recognizing that individuals have control over some contextual factors but not others (Brandtstadter, 2006). Continuity theory might help counsel someone such as Lois Smith. Just as she adapted actively to her divorce by reentering the job market later in life, she might actively seek new roles in retirement. She might find great satisfaction in volunteering in her church and in being a grandmother. Continuity theory is difficult to empirically test (Hooyman & Kiyak, 2008). There is also criticism regarding the definition of "normal aging." The theory distinguishes normal aging from pathological aging and does not sufficiently address older persons with chronic health conditions (Quadagno, 2007).

4. *Social construction theory.* **Social construction theory** aims to understand and explain the influence of social definitions, social interactions, and social structures on the individual elderly person. This theoretical framework suggests that ways of understanding are shaped by the cultural, social, historical, political, and economic conditions in which knowledge is developed; thus, values are associated with various ways of understanding (Dean, 1993). Conceptions about aging arise through interactions of an individual with the social environment (Dannefer & Perlmutter, 1990). For instance, George Vaillant's conceptions of aging changed as he followed research participants into late adulthood. His emphasis on the negative aspects of aging was counterbalanced by a respondents' own sense of a fulfilling life. The recent conceptualization of "gerotranscendence" is an example of the application of social constructionist theory to aging. The idea of gerotranscendence holds that human development extends into old age and does not simply end or diminish with aging (Hooyman & Kiyak, 2008; Tornstam 2005). According to this theory, aging persons evaluate their lives in terms of the time they have ahead and try to derive a sense of identity, self, and place in the world and universe (Degges-White, 2005; Tornstam, 2005). Using focus group methodology, Wadensten (2005) found that participants identified the concept of gerotranscendence as salient and beneficial to them because it gave them a more positive view of aging, allowing them to affirm themselves as they are.

5. *Feminist theory.* Proponents of **feminist theories** of aging suggest that gender is a key factor in understanding a person's aging experience. They contend that because gender is a critical social stratification factor with attendant power, privilege, and status that produces inequalities and disparities throughout the life course, we can only understand aging by taking gender into account (Arber & Ginn, 1995). Gender is viewed as influencing the life course trajectory by impacting access and opportunity, health disparities, and disparities in socioeconomic opportunities and by creating a lifelong condition of "constrained choice" (Rieker & Bird, 2005). Gabriela Spector-Mersel (2006) argues that in Western societies, older persons have been portrayed as "ungendered." Older men are in a paradoxical position because the metaphors for old age are the opposite of the metaphors for masculinity in these societies. Think, for example, about Joseph Menzel's experience as a caregiver to his wife and how some of his role obligations differ from his lifelong role expectations as a man. Also, consider Ms. Johnson's experience as a single older woman. How might her personal situation differ if she were a man?

6. *Social exchange theory.* **Social exchange theory** is built on the notion that an exchange of resources takes place in all interpersonal interactions (Blau, 1964; Homans, 1961). This theory is rooted in an analysis of values developed from a market-driven capitalist society. Individuals will only engage in an exchange if they perceive a favorable cost/benefit ratio or if they see no better alternatives (Hendricks, 1987). As individuals become older, the resources they are able to bring to the exchange begin to shift. Exchange theory bases its explanation of the realignment of roles, values, and contributions of older adults on this assumption. For example, many older persons get involved in volunteer activities; this seemingly altruistic activity may also be seen as fulfilling an emotional need that provides a personal gain. Thus, they are able to adjust and adapt to the altered exchange equation. Older individuals who withdraw from social activities may perceive their personal resources as diminished to the point where they have little left to bring to an exchange, thus leading to their increasing seclusion from social interactions. As social workers, then, it is important to explore how older couples such as Joseph and Elizabeth Menzel are dealing with the shift in resources within their relationship. Several studies indicate that maintaining reciprocity is important for older individuals (Fiori, Consedine, & Magai, 2008). For example, a recent study of reciprocity among residents of assisted living looked at the positive contributions of aging care recipients to their social relationships, including their interactions with caregivers (Beel-Bates, Ingersoll-Dayton, & Nelson, 2007).

7. *Life course perspective.* From the life course perspective, the conceptual framework for this book, aging is a dynamic, lifelong process. Human development is characterized by multidirectionality, multifunctionality, plasticity, and continuity in the person's experiences of gains and losses over the life course (Greve & Staudinger, 2006). Individuals go through many transitions in the course of their life span. Human development continues through aging and involves the interaction of person-specific factors, social structures, and personal agency (Hendricks & Hatch, 2006). The era they live in, the cohort they belong to, and personal and environmental factors influence individuals during these transitions. "Life course capital" is a contemporary addition to the life course perspective. The theory states that people, over the course of their life, accumulate human capital, that is, resources that they can use to address their needs. This capital can take on various forms; for example, it may be social, biological, psychological, or developmental human capital (Hooyman & Kiyak, 2008). This accumulation of life course capital has an impact on a person's aging, for example, on his or her health (e.g., morbidity, mortality) or wealth (e.g., standard of living in retirement).

8. *Age stratification perspective.* The **age stratification perspective** falls into the tradition of the life course perspective (Foner, 1995; Riley, 1971). Stratification is a sociological concept that describes a given hierarchy that exists in a given society. Social stratification is both multidimensional and interactive as individuals occupy multiple social locations with varying amounts of power, privilege, and status. The age stratification perspective suggests that, similar to the way society is structured by socioeconomic class, it is also stratified by age. Roles and rights of individuals are assigned based on their membership in an age group or cohort. Individuals proceed through their life course as part of that cohort. The experience of aging differs across cohorts because cohorts differ in size, composition, and experience with an ever-changing society. Current scholarship argues that social stratifications of gender, race/ethnicity, and socioeconomic status are pertinent stratifications to consider in aging, given the cumulative effect of disparities that are the result of such stratification (George, 2005). Hooyman and Kiyak suggest that the size of the baby boomer generation entering old age will have a significant impact on the age stratification system. For example, they will "view retirement and leisure more positively, be physically active and healthier, be more likely to challenge restrictions on their roles as workers and community participants, live long enough to be great grandparents, be more planful and proactive about aging and dying processes" (2008, p. 316).

> **Critical Thinking Questions 9.1**
>
> At what age will you consider yourself old? What do you think your favorite activity will be when you are "old?" What do you think your biggest challenge will be when you are "old?" What do you think will be important to you when you are "old?" Where do you get your ideas about old age?

BIOLOGICAL CHANGES IN LATE ADULTHOOD

Every day, our bodies are changing. In a sense, then, our bodies are constantly aging. As social workers, however, we need not be concerned with the body's aging until it begins to affect the person's ability to function in her or his world, which typically begins to occur in late adulthood. There are more than a dozen biological theories of why our bodies age. In this discussion, we follow Carolyn Aldwin and Diane Gilmer's (2004) lead and consider three categories of theories: genetic theories, molecular/cellular theories, and system-level theories. We also discuss developmental biocultural co-constructivism, a newer theoretical approach to aging in the human environment.

> How important is the impact of biological age on the experience of the late adult phase of the life course?

Genetic theories of biological aging propose that there are genetically determined differences between species in the maximum life span, for example a maximum life span of about 120 years for humans and about 30 days for a fruit fly (Aldwin & Gilmer, 2004, p. 46). It is not yet clear what mechanisms are involved in regulating aging and death, but several possibilities are being forwarded. **Programmed aging theories** propose that cells cannot replicate themselves indefinitely. A slowing down in the replication of cells occurs as we become older. Hayflick (1994) has proven that some human cells can only divide a limited number of times, approximately 50 times. **Random error theories** propose that physiological aging occurs because of damaging processes that become more frequent in late adulthood but are not a part of a genetic unfolding process.

Molecular/cellular theories of biological aging, as the name suggests, propose that biological aging is caused by molecular or cellular processes. One of the most popular theories in this category is the *free radical theory.* Free radicals are reactive oxygen species (ROS) that are created during the oxidation process in cells. ROS are unstable and highly chemically reactive and they cause damage when they attach to other molecules. The free radical theory proposes that there is an increased concentration of free radicals with age, because aging cells create more free radicals, aging cells have less ability to generate antioxidants, and cellular repair is less efficient in aging cells. There is some experimental support for the free radical theory (Cristafalo, Tresini, Francis, & Volker, 1999). Another theory in this category is *waste product accumulation theory,* which proposes that as we age, waste products build up in the body's cells and interfere with bodily functioning and sometimes lead to cell death (Moody, 2010). A third theory in this category is *autoimmune theory,* which proposes that the aging body loses some of its ability to recognize foreign bacteria, viruses, and other invaders. The body also starts to attack some of its own healthy cells by producing antibodies against itself, thus possibly producing autoimmune diseases.

System-level theories of biological aging propose that aging is caused by processes operating across biological systems. The *homeostasis approach* operates on the premise that to be stable, organisms must maintain good communication among the various organ systems. This communication is largely organized by the autonomic nervous system through the neuroendocrine system. With age, a number of systems may show slower responses and, over time, may begin to show exaggerated responses and take longer to return to baseline. Target organs may become less responsive to neuroendocrine signals (Taffett, 1996). One of the earliest theories of biological aging was the *wear and tear theory,* which proposes that with continual use our organs and joints simply wear out. This theory was once in great favor but has not held up well in empirical research. If this were the whole story, athletes would have shorter lives than sedentary individuals. What research does show is that abuse of a system will shorten its life span. Consequently, *stress theory,* which has good empirical support, has replaced wear and tear theory. Stress theory proposes that prolonged exposure to both physiological and psychosocial stress hastens aging in many organ systems as a result of the toxic effects of stress-related hormones (Sapolsky, 2004).

Developmental biocultural co-constructivism is a recent theoretical orientation to human development. Although not a theory of aging per se, it adds important concepts for understanding the process of human aging. Theorists following this perspective claim that "brain and culture are in a continuous, interdependent, co-productive transaction and reciprocal determination" (Baltes, Rösler, & Reuter-Lorenz, 2006, p. 3). With this definition, they go beyond the nature and nurture debate, which focuses on whether nature or nurture makes the greater contribution to human behavior. In their view, this does not sufficiently address the *active* and *multidirectional* nature of this process. Developmental biocultural co-constructivism "gives equal standing to both the brain and the environment" (Baltes et al., p. 8). The perspective presumes dynamic reciprocal interactions of culture and human environment with the biology of a person. The brain is considered a dependent variable, that is, being co-shaped by experiences and culture and human behavior is "inherently the outcome of a 'dialogue' among and 'co-production' of genes, brain, and culture" (Baltes et al., p. 6). This is not a passive process. Rather, it can be described as a "shared and *collaborative production,* including *reciprocal modifications* and which under some conditions involves qualitatively new states whose emergence cannot be fully predicted from either of the two sources alone" (Baltes et al., p. 8). Longitudinal research seems to provide support to this theory. For example, Schooler and Mulatu (2004) found that reciprocal effects exist between the intellectual functioning and the complexity of tasks older adults had to fulfill during their employment years.

Health and Longevity

Mortality rates—the frequency at which death occurs within a population—have declined significantly for all segments of the population in the United States during the last century. Between 1981 and 2001, the overall age-adjusted death rates for all causes of death for individuals 65 years and older declined by 18%. In this age bracket, death rates from heart disease and stroke declined by approximately 44%. However, the death rates for some diseases increased, such as diabetes mellitus by 38% and chronic lower respiratory diseases by 53%. In 2008, the leading causes of death for people 65 and older were, in descending order, heart disease, cancer, stroke, chronic lower respiratory diseases, Alzheimer's disease, influenza/pneumonia, and diabetes. Overall death rates in 2001 were higher for older men than for older women (Federal Interagency Forum on Aging-Related Statistics, 2008; National Health Statistics, 2005).

As mortality has decreased, **morbidity**—the incidence of disease—has increased. In other words, the proportion of the population suffering from age-related chronic conditions has increased in tandem with the population of elderly persons. In 2006, for people 65 years or older, the most prevalent and debilitating chronic conditions in descending order were arthritis (54% of men, 43% of women), hypertension (52% of men, 54% of women), heart disease (37% of men, 26% of women), cancer (24% of men, 19% of women), and diabetes (19% of men, 17% of women). Chronic illnesses are long-term, rarely cured, and costly health conditions (Federal Interagency Forum on Aging Related Statistics, 2008; National Health Statistics, 2005).

The prevalence of chronic conditions varies significantly by gender, race, and ethnicity. For example, older women report higher levels of hypertension, asthma, chronic bronchitis, and arthritic symptoms than older men. Older men are more likely to identify heart disease, cancer, diabetes, and emphysema. Racial and ethnic differences also exist. Non-Hispanic Blacks report higher levels of hypertension (70% compared with 51%) and diabetes (29% compared with 16%) than non-Hispanic Whites. Hispanics (25%) report higher levels of diabetes than Whites (16%). Between 1992 and 2002, the prevalence of certain conditions among ethnic/racial minorities increased, including a 50% increase in hypertension and a 16% increase in diabetes (Federal Interagency Forum on Aging-Related Statistics,

2008). As of 2002, arthritis was reported by 68% of non-Hispanic African Americans, 58% of non-Hispanic Whites, and 50% of Hispanics. Interestingly, cancer is more prevalent among Whites, reported by 21% of non-Hispanic Whites, 11% of Hispanics, and 9% of non-Hispanic African Americans (Federal Interagency Forum on Aging-Related Statistics, 2004). Physical decline is also associated with SES, but it is difficult to separate SES from race and ethnicity because minority groups tend to be overrepresented in lower SES groups (Wilmoth & Longino, 2006; George, 2005). Vaillant (2002) found the physical conditions of his inner-city men ages 68 to 70 to be similar to the physical conditions of the women and the Harvard men ages 78 to 80.

A chronic condition can have considerable impact on a family system. In Ms. Johnson's case, the seven people for whom she cares—including two toddlers, an adolescent, an adult daughter who is functionally impaired, a granddaughter and her husband who both are at risk of leaving the workforce, and an aging father—are all affected by her chronic diabetes. This case illustrates the untold impact of chronic conditions in aging populations that are rarely described by national trend reports.

▲ **Photo 9.3**   Social workers need to be concerned with aging if and when it affects a person's ability to function in his or her world.

For many people, illness and death can be postponed through lifestyle changes. In recent years, the importance of preventing illness by promoting good health has received considerable attention (Agency for Healthcare Research and Quality [AHRQ], 2006). The goals of health promotion for older adults include preventing or delaying the onset of chronic disease and disability; reducing the severity of chronic diseases; and maintaining mental health, physical health, and physical functioning as long as possible (Greve & Staudinger, 2006; Hendricks & Hatch, 2006; McAuley et al., 2006). Ways to promote health in old age include improving dietary habits, increasing activity levels and physical exercise, stopping smoking, and obtaining regular health screenings (blood sampling, blood pressure measurement, cancer screening, glaucoma screening). An important finding has been the roles of self-efficacy, sense of mastery, positive attitude, and social supports in improving the quality of life and delaying functional limitation and disability (Brandtstadter, 2006; Collins & Smyer, 2005; Fiksenbaum, Greenglass, & Eaton, 2006; McAuley et al., 2006).

Age-Related Changes in Physiology

All systems of the body appear to be affected during the aging process. Consider the *nervous system.* In the brain, neurons and synapses are the transmitters of information throughout the nervous system. The number of neurons decreases throughout the life span (NIA/NIH, 2009); the result is a slow decrease of brain mass after age 30. Because we are born with many more neurons and synapses than we need to function, problems usually do not arise, however. Also, if the older adult develops brain deficits in one area of the brain, he or she may make up for these deficits by increasing activity in other brain regions (Whitbourne, 2001). However, a neurological injury or disease may result in more permanent and serious consequences for an older person. This is just one of the changes that may affect the brain, spinal cord, nerves, and mechanisms controlling other organs in the body. There is also evidence of stress-related increases in norepinephrine in the aging brain, resulting in difficulty returning to baseline after stressful events (Aldwin & Gilmer, 2004). We will look more closely at changes in the brain and neurodegenerative diseases in the next section.

Our *cardiovascular system* also changes in several ways as we become older. The cardiac output—the amount of blood pumped per minute—decreases throughout adult life, and the pulse slows with age (Bjorklund & Bee, 2008). The arteries become less elastic and harden, which can result in arteriosclerosis. Fatty lipids accumulate in the walls of the blood vessels and make them narrower, which can cause atherosclerosis. As a result of these changes, less oxygen is available for muscular activities (Whitbourne, 2001). With advancing age, it takes longer for the blood pressure and heart rate to return to normal resting levels after stressful events (Aldwin & Gilmer, 2004).

The *respiratory system* too changes with age. Beginning at about 20 years of age, a person's lung capacity decreases throughout the life span (Whitbourne, 2001). The typical decrease from age 20 to age 80 is about 40% for a healthy person. But, in healthy older adults who do not smoke, respiratory function is quite good enough for daily activities (Bjorklund & Bee, 2008).

The most important age-related change in our *skeletal system* occurs after age 30, when the destruction of bones begins to outpace the reformation of bones. The gradual decrease in bone mass and bone density can cause osteoporosis. Osteoporosis occurs in 20% of women over 50 and half of women over 80 (Bjorklund & Bee, 2008). It is estimated that bone mineral content decreases by 5% to 12% per decade from the 20s through the 90s. One result is that we get shorter as we age. As the cartilage between the joints wears thin, arthritis, a chronic inflammation of the joints, begins to develop. Although many individuals suffer from some form of arthritis in their 40s, the symptoms are often not painful until late adulthood. Some of these changes can be ameliorated by diet and exercise and by avoiding smoking and alcohol (Aldwin & Gilmer, 2004).

With increasing age, the *muscular system* declines in mass, strength, and endurance. As a consequence, an elderly person may become fatigued more easily. In addition, muscle contractions begin to slow down, which contributes to deteriorating reflexes and incontinence. However, the muscular system of older individuals can be successfully strengthened through weight training and changes in diet and lifestyle (Bjorklund & Bee, 2008).

Changes in the neurological, muscular, and skeletal systems have an impact on the *sensory system* and the sense of balance, which contributes to the increase in accidental falls and bone fractures in late adulthood. Vision decreases with age, and older persons need more light to reach the retina in order to see. The eye's adaptation to the dark slows with age, as does visual acuity, the ability to detect details (Aldwin & Gilmer, 2004). Age-related decreases in hearing are caused by degenerative changes in the spiral organ of the ear and the associated nerve cells. Many older adults have a reduced ability to hear high-pitched sounds (Aldwin & Gilmer). By age 65, about one third of adults have significant hearing loss, with men being more likely than women to suffer hearing loss (Bjorklund & Bee, 2008). Age-related changes in taste appear to be minimal. Differences may reflect individual factors, such as exposure to environmental conditions like smoking, periodontal disease, or use of medications, rather than general processes of aging. The smell receptors in the nose can decrease with age, however, and become less sensitive (Aldwin & Gilmer).

The *integumentary system* includes the skin, hair, and nails. The skin comprises an outer layer (epidermis) and an inner layer (dermis). With age, the epidermis becomes thinner and pigment cells grow and cluster, creating age spots on the skin (Aldwin & Gilmer, 2004). The sweat and oil-secreting glands decrease, leaving the skin drier and more vulnerable to injury. Much of the fat stored in the hypodermis, the tissue beneath the skin, is lost in age, causing wrinkles. The skin of an older person often feels cool because the blood flow to the skin is reduced (Aldwin & Gilmer).

Sexual potency begins to decline at age 20, but without disease, sexual desire and capacity continue in late adulthood. According to a 1998 survey, half of all persons in the United States age 60 or older are sexually active. Among those who are sexually active, 74% of the men and 70% of the women report that they are as satisfied or more satisfied with their sex lives now than they were in their 40s (National Council on the Aging, n.d.). Vaillant (2002) reports that *frequency* of sexual activity decreases, however. He found that partners in good health at 75 to 80 often continue to have sexual relations, but that the average frequency is approximately once in every 10 weeks. Interestingly, Vaillant also found that among the women in his study, mastering the life task of generativity, rather than mastering the task of intimacy, was the predictor of regular attainment of orgasm.

Contemporary views on the physiology of aging focus on longevity. Anti-aging medicine focuses on developing interventions that will delay age-related pathology or other changes that are not officially listed as disease or decreases in bone and muscle mass. Science and technology are achieving gains that show great promise for the future. However, to date, there is no evidence that these gains have increased the maximum life span of humans (International Longevity Center-USA, 2002). Some of the more promising gains in this area include the following:

- Supernutrition is the only technique that has extended life in humans with consistency. Supernutrition involves properly dosed dietary supplements of multivitamins and multiminerals, along with restricted fats and fresh, whole, unprocessed foods. The convergence of nutritional sciences and the emphasis on preventive medicine is likely to yield a new generation of supernutritional foods in the not-so-distant future (Dychtwald, 1999). Reservatol, an ingredient in red wine and red grapes, has demonstrated antiplatelet, anti-inflammatory, anticancer, antimutagenic, and antifungal properties. It thus shows prospect in reducing many age-related diseases, including arthritis, cancer, cardiovascular disease, diabetes, pancreatitis, and kidney disease (Faloon, 2008; Olas & Wachowicz, 2005). Vitamin K keeps calcium in the bones and out of the arteries. New research shows that Vitamin K may reverse arterial calcification, protect against cancer, suppress chronic inflammatory disorders, and extend the human life span (Faloon, 2009).

- Calorie restricted diet has been shown to extend the maximum life span in laboratory organisms of various species. When caloric intake is reduced, age-related decline slows and age-related diseases are reduced. Increases in longevity do not occur because of a reduction in a particular part of the diet, but because of caloric reduction in the whole. Based on the findings in other species, it is theorized that a reduction to 1,400 calories per day in the human diet could lead to a gain of 30 years of life (Barzilai & Bartke, 2009; Moody, 2010)

- Hormone therapy is already used in some medical conditions today. Further breakthroughs with the use of estrogen, testosterone, melatonin, dehydroepiandrosterone (DHEA), and human growth hormone (HGH) are currently investigated but are wrought with potentially dangerous side effects to date (Dychtwald, 1999). DHEA increases the production of immune cells and helps fight bacteria and viruses. It may enhance longevity as it increases strength and muscle mass, raises testosterone productions, and increases sexual energy (Khorram, 1997; Singh, 2009).

- Gene manipulation will potentially have the greatest impact of all interventions on human aging. But despite recent advances in gene mapping, the technology is not yet developed enough for large-scale human applications. Recent research has found a way to double the life of skin cells by switching off the gene that regulates production of a protein responsible for aging. Research now focuses on the "mortality genes," which determine the number of times cells divide. If successful, this could have significant impact and application for persons with Alzheimer's disease, Parkinson's disease, or cancer (Moody, 2010).

- Bionics and organ or tissue cloning would have seemed like science fiction a generation ago, but the convergence of biological science and engineering may produce limbs and organs to replace those worn out or deteriorated with age. Currently, laboratories and biotechnology researchers can grow skin (used for burn victims) and cartilage (used for joint surgery). Bone substitutes are already being artificially produced. Drugs are currently being tested that stimulate nerve growth and techniques may soon be available to implant cells that reverse damage to the central nervous system (Moody, 2010). Tissue and cell cloning have particular appeal for brain diseases such as Parkinson's or Alzheimer's, because it could provide patients with healthy neural tissue identical to their own. In each of these areas, significant research efforts are being conducted the world over. How many of these technologies will come into widespread use is uncertain. It is clear, however, that economic and ethical considerations and debates will be as unprecedented as the technologies themselves.

The Aging Brain and Neurodegenerative Diseases

Before discussing the most common neurodegenerative diseases, dementia, Alzheimer's, and Parkinson's disease, we would like to provide a brief overview of the brain and how it functions. The brain is probably the most complex and least well-understood part of the human body. It weighs about 3 pounds or about 2% of a person's weight and is made up of various types of cells. The most essential brain cells are the neurons. They are the "communicators," responsible for most of the information processing in our brain. Human brains consist of 100 billion neurons that on average make 10,000 links with other cells (Whalley, 2001). Between the neurons are synaptic gaps. Our brain has more than 100 trillion of the so-called synapses (NIA/NIH, 2009). Information flows from a neuron through the synapses to neuroreceptors, which are the receiver of the next neuron. More than 50 different types of such neuro- transmitters exist, including dopamine, serotonin, acetylcholine, and norepinephrine. Glial cells are the second major type of brain cells. They are the "housekeepers," providing neurons with nutrition, insulating them, and helping trans- port damaged cells and debris (NIA/NIH). Capillaries are tiny blood vessels that provide the brain with oxygen, energy, nutrition, and hormones, and transport waste. The brain has 400 billion such capillaries. Twenty percent of a person's blood flows through these capillaries to the brain (NIA/NIH).

The brain consists of two cerebral hemispheres. Current science believes that the difference is less in what infor- mation the two hemispheres process, but in how they process it (NIA/NIH, 2009). It seems that the left hemisphere works on the details, while the right hemisphere processes the broader picture. Each brain hemisphere consists of four different lobes.

The frontal lobe is the "organizer." This is where thinking, planning, memory, problem solving, and movement are processed. The parietal lobe deals with perceptions and inputs from our senses. It sits right behind the frontal lobe. The occipital lobe processes vision and sits at the back of the cerebral hemisphere. Finally, the tem- poral lobe focuses on taste, smell, sound, and memory storage. It sits at the side of the brain and below the frontal lobe. At the back bottom of the brain is the cerebellum. This is where balance, coordination, and motor coordi- nation occur. Located below it is the brain stem, connecting the brain with the spinal cord. It manages the body functions that are immediately responsible for our survival such as breathing, heart rate, and blood pressure (NIA/NIH, 2009).

Several changes occur to the brain as we age. Between ages 20 and 90, the brain loses 5% to 10% of its weight (Palmer & Francis, 2006). The areas most affected by this decrease are the frontal lobe and the hippocampus. A gen- eral loss of neurons also occurs. At the same time, the normal aging brain does not appear to lose synapses (Palmer & Francis, 2006). The transmission of information between neurons through the neurotransmitters can also decrease in some brain regions as we age. Furthermore, there is less growth of new capillaries and a reduced blood flow caused by narrowing arteries in the brain. Plaques and tangles develop in and around the neurons (see discussion of Alzheimer's disease below) and inflammation and damage by free radicals increase (NIA/NIH, 2009). At the same time, the effects of these changes on performing tasks and memory are generally fairly small. Scores for task perfor- mance, for example, are similar for younger and older adults, when the older group is provided with additional time. Older adults can compensate and adapt well to many age-related brain changes. Part of this adaptation occurs through changes in the brain. Neuroimaging shows that some brain functions seem to get reorganized as the brain ages (Reuter-Lorenz, 2002). Imaging results point to a process in which the aging brain starts using areas of the two hemi- spheres that were previously not focusing on performing those tasks to compensate for age-related loss (Li, 2006). Negative changes can also be offset by age-related overall improvements in some cognitive areas such as verbal knowl- edge or vocabulary (NIA/NIH). Other brain changes, however, can become more challenging. We will now turn to some of these neurodegenerative diseases.

Dementia

Dementia is the term for brain disease in which memory and cognitive abilities deteriorate over time. It may be significantly unrecognized and undiagnosed in many older adults. One research team found that in Canada as many as 64% of community-dwelling older adults with dementia are not diagnosed as such (Sternberg, Wolfson, & Baumgarten, 2000). The estimates available suggest that the incidence of dementia is between 0.7 and 3.5 per 1,000 per year for persons ages 65 to 69, and doubles about every 5 years (Joshi & Morley, 2006). The risk of a person over 90 years to show signs of severe mental decline caused by some form of dementia is around 60% (Helmchen et al. 1999). Reversible dementia is caused by factors such as drug and alcohol use, a brain tumor, hypothyroid, syphilis or AIDS, or severe depression, and the cognitive decline is reversible if identified and treated early enough (Joshi & Morley, 2006). Irreversible dementia is not curable. In the advanced stages, the person may repeat the same words over and over again, may have problems using appropriate words, and may not recognize a spouse or other family members. At the same time, the person may still be able to recall and vividly describe events that happened many years ago. Epidemiological studies indicate that Alzheimer's disease is the most common form of dementia, responsible for 60% to 80% of cases (Alzheimer's Association, 2009; Nourhashemi, Sinclair, & Vellas, 2006).

The initial stage of cognitive dysfunction is called *age-associated memory impairment* (AAMI). It is followed by even greater memory loss and diagnosed as *mild cognitive impairment* (MCI), which may progress to dementia. The rate of decline in cognitive and functional skills is predictive of mortality among nondemented older adults (Schupf et al., 2006). AAMI and MCI involve primarily memory loss, whereas dementia results in disruption of daily living and difficulty or inability to function normally. MCIs have been thought not to constitute dementia, but to be a transitional stage between normal cognitive functioning and Alzheimer's disease. Studies have identified a subset of amnesic MCI as evidence of early stage Alzheimer's disease (Morris, 2006).

Risk factors for cognitive decline and dementia include genetic factors; female gender; medical conditions, including but not limited to hypertension, heart disease, and diabetes; lifestyle choices such as smoking or substance abuse; psychological and psychosocial factors such as low educational achievement, lack of physical activity, lack of social interaction and leisure activities, and excessive response to stress (Institute for the Study of Aging, 2001).

The case study of Elizabeth Menzel refers to her attendance at an Erzählcafé. We thought you might like to know more about Erzählcafé. Exhibit 9.5 provides a description of the Erzählcafé and Mrs. Menzel's participation in it.

Alzheimer's Disease

Alzheimer's disease is the most common type of dementia, accounting for 60% to 80% of cases and is estimated to cost up to 148 billion dollars annually (Alzheimer's Association, 2009). It is considered the third most expensive illness in the United States (Joshi & Morley, 2006). The numbers of death caused by heart disease, stroke, and many forms of cancer have seen significant reductions during the first half decade of this century. During the same time, deaths caused by Alzheimer's disease have increased by 47% (Alzheimer's Association). As populations around the world age, this is a trend that can be seen on the global level as well. Alzheimer's disease is characterized by a progression of stages that a person goes through. A general distinction is made between mild, moderate, and severe stages of Alzheimer's disease, although the description of the symptoms show that the stages are not completely distinct. Exhibit 9.6 provides an overview of the three stages of Alzheimer's disease and the related symptoms.

Early detection and diagnosis of Alzheimer's disease is still difficult. The time period from the diagnosis of Alzheimer's disease to death ranges between 3 to 4 years to up to 10 years, depending on the person's age. However, it is believed that the changes in the brain that cause Alzheimer's disease begin 10 or even 20 years before its onset. Consequently, there is a strong focus on trying to find biomarkers in cerebrospinal fluids, blood, or urine that may help to detect the presence of developing Alzheimer's disease.

Erzählcafé (coffee house chat) is a group work concept for persons with dementia that takes into account the cultural tradition of going to social clubs to meet and chat with friends. The target group includes persons with mild to moderate dementia. Persons with dementia often retreat from social activities. By offering them an environment in which they can meet and interact with other persons in a safe small group setting, they receive the reassurance and appreciation that are important for persons with dementia. To provide continuity and structure, the meetings occur on a weekly basis. They are organized around the ritual of having coffee with friends. This is integrated with senior group work activities like mobility exercises and dance circles, reminiscing and life review, singing and listening to music, and celebrating holidays. The mix of activities and methods tries to help participants tap into their personal resources, including the hidden ones. Group leaders carefully plan the exercise to stimulate participants while not overwhelming them. For example, a clear separation exists between the physical activities, having coffee, and doing craft work. An intended corollary of the coffee house chat is to provide caregivers with respite and help them experience that it is O.K. to let someone else take care of their relative for a while. The latter can be difficult for caregivers and may contribute to burnout and failure to access available services in a timely manner. The interaction with group coordinators also is an opportunity to exchange information and reduce service barriers. German social work has a service concept called "niederschwellig" (the low doorstep when entering the house), meaning that the process of accessing service is particularly important, has to be carefully planned, and needs to be as easy as possible. Coffee house chats are coordinated by a geriatric social worker and led by trained volunteers from the local senior volunteer network.

Elizabeth Menzel in our case example is a regular visitor of an Erzählcafé. Her husband Joseph reminds her about the group in the morning, but usually she remembers herself, since it is listed on her weekly calendar and she looks forward to attending it. Before going to the Café, she changes and puts on nicer clothes. She still gets a little excited when the volunteer driver comes to pick her up. Her husband tells her to have a wonderful afternoon and gives her money for coffee and cake. Joseph also enjoys having some time to himself. In addition, it provides the couple an opportunity to share what each of them did that afternoon, which they like, since they otherwise do everything together. In the bus, the participants have a game: trying to remember who else will be picked up. At times they share with each other how it feels to forget things, for example when one of the participants checks for the fifth time whether she brought her keys. On sunny days, the van often gets stuck in traffic jams, caused by younger retirees flocking to the mountains.

Once the bus arrives, the participants greet each other and the group leader starts the afternoon with a sitting gymnastic and breathing exercise. Participants like doing the physical exercise. It loosens the entire body and deepens breathing, which helps their overall well-being. Over time, the group leaders see improvements in the lateral and cross-body coordination, which research shows can have a positive impact on the mental abilities of persons with dementia. Like most participants, Elizabeth Menzel enjoys the more playful activities, such as throwing a softball back and forth. All of these physical efforts have to be rewarded. After half an hour of exercising, it is time for coffee and cake and participants move to the already set tables. As a conversation piece and to get the chat going, tables are decorated in a different way each time. Today bouquets of herbal flowers are the centerpiece, since the church will have its annual blessing of the herbs the following Sunday. Elizabeth Menzel shares how it was celebrated where she grew up, and a woman from Romania notices parallels to her childhood memories. Together, participants start identifying the assortment of herbs and flowers and talk about the history of this religious tradition. Suddenly Elizabeth Menzel becomes very sad. For the past years, her daughter has taken care of the herbal bouquet, but now she is dead. Her neighbor spontaneously gives her a hug and after a while Elizabeth Menzel feels ready to continue. Today the third part of the group schedule, doing crafts or something creative, focuses on creating paper flowers. Everyone is cutting, gluing, and folding flowers. Participants help each other according to their skills. They just about get their craft work done, when it is time to leave again. After singing their farewell song, a ritual that the group has come up with, they are brought back home again. Elizabeth Menzel takes some of the left over plum cake for her husband—his favorite cake. She also wants to give him the sunflower she crafted, so he has something to look at when he stays back home during the coffee chats. She already is looking forward to next week's Erzählcafe.

▲ **Exhibit 9.5**   Erzählcafé—A Coffee House Chat Group for Persons With Dementia

Stage of Alzheimer's Disease	Typical Symptoms
Mild or Early Stage	■ Memory loss ■ Confusion about location of familiar places ■ Taking longer for routine daily tasks ■ Trouble handling money and bills ■ Loss of spontaneity ■ Mood and personality changes ■ Increased anxiety and aggression
Moderate Stage	■ Increased memory loss and confusion ■ Decreased attention span ■ Inappropriate outbursts of anger and irritability ■ Problems recognizing friends and family members ■ Language problems ■ Difficulty reading, writing, working with numbers ■ Difficulty organizing thoughts ■ Inability to cope with new or unexpected situations ■ Restlessness, agitation, anxiety ■ Wandering, especially in late afternoon and at night ■ Repetitive statements or movements ■ Hallucinations, delusions, suspiciousness, paranoia ■ Loss of impulse control ■ Inability to carry out complex tasks requiring multiple steps
Severe or Late Stage	■ Weight loss ■ Seizures ■ Skin infections ■ Difficulty swallowing ■ Groaning, moaning, grunting ■ Increased sleeping ■ Lack of bladder and bowel control

▲ **Exhibit 9.6**   Symptoms of Alzheimer's Disease

SOURCE: Based on NIA/NIH, 2009, pp. 30–32.

In the mild or early stage, the first signs of the disease such as forgetfulness, confusion, and mood and personality changes appear. This stage may be the most stressful for many persons afflicted with Alzheimer's disease, since they often are very aware of the changes happening to their mind. Fluctuations in the severity of symptoms are common, both within a day and between days. Oftentimes the person will start to experience significant anxiety related to these changes.

Moderate stage Alzheimer's disease is characterized by increased memory loss, problems organizing thoughts and language, difficulty recognizing friends and family members, and restlessness. As the disease progresses the person may exhibit reduced impulse control, repetitive behavior and speech, hallucinations, delusion, and suspiciousness.

In late stage Alzheimer's disease, a person is often bed-ridden and has increasing health difficulties. The most common reason for death in the late stage is aspiration pneumonia, when the person can no longer swallow properly and fluids and food end up in the lungs (NIA/NIH, 2009). Mrs. Menzel would fall into the earlier phases of the disease and would be considered to have mild to moderate stage dementia.

Despite significant progress in researching the disease and trying to find possible cures, much is still unknown. Research shows that brains of persons with Alzheimer's disease have an unusual accumulation of two substances: neurofibrillary tangles and amyloidal plaques. Amyloidal plaques are a substance building up *outside* the neuron cells. The plaques develop when amyloidal peptides, proteins associated with the cell membrane of neurons, divide improperly and turn into beta amyloid, which in turn is toxic to neurons. The neurons die and together with the proteins create these lumps (NIA/NIH, 2009). Neurofibrillary tangles are an "abnormal collection of twisted protein threads found inside a nerve cell" (NIA/NIH, p. 25). These tangles are caused by a protein (tau) breaking down and sticking together with other tau proteins to create tangled clumps *inside* the neuron cells. When these tangles develop, they reduce the neurons' ability to communicate with other neurons. The neuron cells eventually die, which over time leads to brain atrophy. The role of the plaques is still not well understood. For example, it is not clear whether these plaques are a cause or a consequence of Alzheimer's disease. Some researchers believe that the plaques are an effort to get harmful proteins away from the neurons (NIA/NIH). Scans can clearly show the progression of brain atrophy in persons with Alzheimer's disease. As the disease progresses, the fluid-filled gaps in the brain called ventricles become increasingly larger.

Several medications are available for persons with Alzheimer's disease, including donepezil (Aricept), galantamine (Razadyne), and rivastigmine (Exelon). All of these medications can slow the progression of the disease, but none can reverse or cure it. Currently no cure for the disease is on the horizon.

Parkinson's Disease

Parkinson disease is a chronic and progressive movement disorder that primarily affects older adults over the age of 70 years. However, as in the case of movie star Michael J. Fox, it can afflict persons earlier in life as well. It is estimated that at least 500,000 persons in the United States have Parkinson's disease, but since it is hard to diagnose, the actual number may be significantly higher (National Institute of Neurological Disorders and Stroke [NINDS], 2009).

Symptoms of Parkinson's include tremors, (arms, legs, head), rigidity (stiffness of limbs), bradykinesia (trouble with and slowness of movement), and postural instability (insecure gait and balance). It can also cause language problems, cognitive difficulties, and in extreme cases lead to a complete loss of movement. The disease is difficult to accurately diagnose, because some features of the normal aging process can be mistaken for Parkinson's disease. Tremors, slower movements, or insecure ways of walking all may be part of normal aging, symptoms of depression, or medication-induced side effects. Consequently, Hughes et al. (2002) found a significant error rate with the diagnosis of Parkinson's disease. Even though Parkinson's disease is a neurodegenerative movement disorder, it often has mental health consequences. For example, cognitive impairment, dementia, depression, and sleep disorders may be associated with or co-occur with Parkinson's disease.

Parkinson's disease is caused by a gradual loss of cells that produce dopamine in a part of the brain called basal ganglia, which is located at the base of the frontal brain area and is involved in coordinating a body's movements. The chemical dopamine is a neurotransmitter that transmits information about movement in the brain. A decrease in neurons that transmit information with the help of dopamine alters the processing of information related to physical movement (Playfer, 2006). Losing neurons in the substantia nigra, which is a part of the basal ganglia, is part of normal aging. We are born with 400,000 neurons in this part of the brain, at age 60 we have about 250,000 neurons left. However, research indicates that persons afflicted with Parkinson's disease may have as little as 60,000 to 120,000 neurons present in this part of the brain (Palmer & Francis, 2006). Research has also found decrease in the nerve endings that produce norepinephrine, a neurotransmitter responsible for some of the body's automatic functions like blood pressure and pulse (NINDS, 2009). The brain cells of a person with Parkinson's disease also include clumps of a protein (synuclein) called Lewis body. It is not clear whether this contributes to the disease by preventing the cells from working correctly or whether it is an attempt of the body to bind these harmful proteins to keep other cells working (NINDS, 2009).

Several drugs are available to address Parkinson's disease. A combination of these drugs with physical rehabilitation has shown great success in reducing the symptoms of the disease (Playfer, 2006). One group of medications works on increasing the dopamine levels in the brain. Levodopa is an example of such a drug. It is the most common medication for treating Parkinson's disease and has been used with success for more than 40 years (Playfer). A second type of drug mimics dopamine (dopamine antagonists) or inhibits dopamine breakdown (NINDS, 2009). A more recent approach to treating the effects of Parkinson's disease is deep brain stimulation. Using this method, a tiny electrode is surgically implanted into the brain. Through a pulse generator this implant then stimulates the brain and stops many of the symptoms (NINDS, 2009). Results of deep brain simulation show a positive effect on cognitive functions (Zangaglia et al. 2009).

PSYCHOLOGICAL CHANGES IN LATE ADULTHOOD

Without good longitudinal research, it has been difficult to understand psychological changes in late adulthood. Because cross-sectional research cannot control for cohort effects, we need to exercise great caution in interpreting findings of age differences in human psychology. Three areas that have received a lot of attention are changes in personality, changes in intellectual functioning, and mental health and mental disorders in late adulthood. The Berlin Aging Study, one of the largest studies of older adults, included numerous measures of psychological aging. Findings suggest that one should not think about a uniform process of psychological aging (Baltes & Mayer, 1999). Rather, changes in areas such a cognition, social relationships, self, and personality occur to a large extent independent of each other.

Personality Changes

A couple of theorists have addressed the issue of how personality changes as individuals age. As noted in Chapter 8, Erik Erikson's (1950) life-span theory proposes that the struggle of middle adulthood is generativity versus stagnation (refer back to Exhibit 3.7 for an overview of Erikson's stages of psychosocial development). You may recall that generativity is the ability to transcend personal interests to guide the next generation. The struggle of late adulthood, according to Erikson, is **ego integrity versus ego despair.** *Integrity* involves the ability to make peace with one's "one and only life cycle" and to find unity with the world. Erikson (1950) also noted that from middle adulthood on, adults participate in a "wider social radius," with an increasing sense of social responsibility and interconnectedness. Some support was found for this notion in a 50-year follow-up of adult personality development (Haan, Millsap, & Hartka, 1986). The researchers found that in late adulthood, three aspects of personality increased significantly: outgoingness, self-confidence, and warmth. A recent study examining the association of chronological aging with positive psychological change supported the idea that some forms of positive psychological change are normative across the life span and that older people know clearly what values are most important and that they pursue these objectives with a more mature sense of purpose and ownership (Sheldon, 2006).

Vaillant (2002) has also considered the personality changes of late adulthood. He found that for all three of the cohorts in the Study of Adult Development, mastery of generativity tripled the likelihood that men and women would find their 70s to be a time of joy instead of despair. He also proposed that another life task, Keeper of the Meaning, comes between generativity and integrity. The **Keeper of the Meaning** takes on the task of passing on the traditions of the past to the next generation. In addition, Vaillant suggests that humans have "elegant unconscious coping mechanisms that make lemonade out of lemons" (2002, p. 91). As discussed in Chapter 8, Vaillant reports that with age and experience, individuals tend to use more adaptive

> Do you have any "keepers of the meaning" in your multigenerational family?

coping mechanisms. This idea is supported by Fiksenbaum et al. (2006), who see successful coping as an essential aspect of aging.

Vaillant finds support for the proposition that coping mechanisms mature with age. He found that over a 25-year period, the Harvard men made significant increases in their use of altruism and humor and significant decreases in their use of projection and passive aggression. Overall, he found that 19 of 67 Harvard men made significant gains in use of mature coping mechanisms between the ages of 50 and 75, 28 men were already making strong use of mature mechanisms at age 50, use of mature mechanisms stayed the same for 17 men, and only 4 out of the 67 men used less mature coping mechanisms with advancing age. Vaillant (1993) in part attributed this maturation in coping to the presence of positive social support and the quality of their marriages. These findings are consistent with findings from another longitudinal study of aging that found that in late adulthood, participants became more forgiving, more able to meet adversity cheerfully, less prone to take offense, and less prone to venting frustrations on others (McCrae & Costa, 1990). Langle and Probst (2004) suggest that this might be the result of older adults being required to face fundamental questions of existence because coping with the vicissitudes of life loom ever larger during aging.

In Chapter 8, we read that there are controversies about whether personality changes or remains stable in middle adulthood. There are similar controversies in the literature on late adulthood. Findings from the large scale Berlin Aging Study indicate that, on the whole, self and personality change only little with age (Staudinger, Freund, Linden, & Maas, 1999). Vaillant (2002), conversely, found evidence for both change and continuity. He suggests that personality has two components: temperament and character. Temperament, he concludes, does not change, and adaptation in adolescence is one of the best predictors of adaptation in late adulthood. Studies on depression, anxiety, and suicidal ideation in late adulthood support this idea that coping and adaptation in adolescence is a good predictor of later life temperament (Lynch, Cheavens, Morse, & Rosenthal, 2004; Cheung & Todd-Oldehaver, 2006; Wickrama et al., 2005). Conversely, character, or adaptive style, does change, influenced both by experiences with the environment and the maturation process. Vaillant (2002) attributes this change in adaptive style over time to the fact that many genes are "programmed to promote plasticity," or the capacity to be shaped by experience. One personality change that was noted in Chapter 8 to occur in middle age is gender role reversal, with women becoming more dominant and men becoming more passive. This pattern has also been noted in late adulthood.

Intellectual Changes, Learning, and Memory

Answering the question about how our intellectual capabilities change in late adulthood is a complex and difficult task. One often-cited study on age-related intellectual changes found that fluid intelligence declines with age, but crystallized intelligence increases (Horn, 1982). **Fluid intelligence** is the capacity for abstract reasoning and involves such things as the ability to "respond quickly, to memorize quickly, to compute quickly with no error, and to draw rapid inferences from visual relationships" (Vaillant, 2002, p. 238). **Crystallized intelligence** is based on accumulated learning and includes the ability to reflect and recognize (e.g., similarities and differences, vocabulary) rather than to recall and remember. This theory has received much criticism, however, because it was based on a cross-sectional comparison of two different age groups. Researchers who followed a single cohort over time found no general decline of intellectual abilities in late adulthood (Schaie, 1984). Rather, they found considerable individual variation. Other longitudinal research has found that fluid intelligence declines earlier than crystallized intelligence, which has been found to remain the same at 80 as at 30 in most healthy older adults (Vaillant, 2002).

Learning and memory are closely related; we must first learn before we can retain and recall. Memory performance, like the impact of aging on intelligence, demonstrates a wide degree of variability. One study suggests that the effects of aging on the underlying brain processes related to retention and recall are dependent on individual memory performance, and the researchers call for further investigation of performance variability in normal aging (Duarte,

Ranganath, Trujillo, & Knight, 2006). When we process information, it moves through several stages of memory (Bjorklund & Bee, 2008; Palsson, Johansson, Berg, & Skoog, 2000; Winkler & Cowan, 2005):

- *Sensory memory.* New information is initially recorded in sensory memory. Unless the person deliberately pays attention to the information, it is lost within less than a second. There seems to be little age-related change in this type of memory.

- *Primary memory.* If the information is retained in sensory memory, it is passed on to the primary memory, also called recent or short-term memory. Primary memory has only limited capacity; it is used to organize and temporarily hold information. *Working memory* refers to the process of actively reorganizing and manipulating information that is still in primary memory. Although there are some age-related declines in working memory, there seems to be little age-related decline in primary memory.

- *Secondary memory.* Information is permanently stored in secondary memory. This is the memory we use daily when we remember an event or memorize facts for an exam. The ability to recall seems to decline with age, but recognition capabilities stay consistent.

- *Tertiary memory.* Information is stored for extended periods, several weeks or months, in tertiary memory, also called remote memory. This type of memory experiences little age-related changes.

Another way to distinguish memory is between intentional and incidental memory. **Intentional memory** relates to events that you plan to remember. **Incidental memory** relates to facts you have learned without the intention to retain and recall. Research suggests that incidental memory declines with old age, but intentional memory does not (Direnfeld & Roberts, 2006).

Another element of intellectual functioning studied in relation to aging is *brain plasticity,* the ability of the brain to change in response to stimuli. Research indicates that even older people's brains can rewire themselves to compensate for lost functioning in particular regions, and in some instances, may even be able to generate new cells. As a result, people are capable of lifelong learning, despite myths to the contrary. Typically researchers have used years of education as the proxy and predictor of decline in cognitive ability, memory, and executive function. Manly, Schupf, Tang, and Stern (2005) found that literacy was a better predictor of learning, memory, retention, and cognitive decline than educational years. This is especially salient for minority ethnic groups whose access to formal education may be limited. However, adult education and intellectual stimulation in later life may actually help maintain cognitive health. Not only are humans capable of lifelong learning, but the stimulation associated with learning new things may reduce the risk of impairments (Institute for the Study of Aging, 2001).

Mental Health and Mental Disorders

A number of longitudinal studies indicate that, without brain disease, mental health improves with age (Vaillant, 2002). Older adults have a lower prevalence of mental disorders than adults in young and middle age. This finding is supported by virtually all epidemiological studies ever conducted (Bengtson, Gans, Putney, & Silverstein, 2009). Although older adults are more predisposed to certain brain diseases such as dementia, these disorders are not a part of the normal aging process. The prevalence of mental disorders in residents of long-term care facilities is high (Conn, 2001) and many institutionalized individuals with mental disorders may not receive all the needed care from mental health professionals. However, many of the more common mental disorders associated with older age can be diagnosed and treated in elderly persons much as they would be in earlier adulthood (Aldwin & Gilmer, 2004). Given the aging of the population, the need for gero-psychiatric research and clinical practice is likely to increase.

Some of the more commonly diagnosed mental disorders in late adulthood include the following:

- *Anxiety.* Anxiety in older adults is similar to that in the younger population. Diagnosis and treatment, however, are often more complex and difficult, because anxiety in older adults often does not follow any direct stimulus. Rather, anxiety is frequently an indication of an underlying mental or physical disorder (Tueth, 1993). Situational stressors that may trigger anxiety in older adults include financial concerns, physical stressors, and loss and loneliness. Symptoms of anxiety include tension, worry, apprehension, and physiological symptoms such as dizziness, gastrointestinal distress, palpitations, urinary disturbance, sweating, and tremors. One recent study found that non-Hispanic Whites had twice the rate of anxiety symptoms as either non-Hispanic Blacks or Hispanics (Ostir & Goodwin, 2006). About 9% of the general older adult population experiences considerable anxiety levels (Bengtson et al., 2009). Anxiety has not received the same attention in geriatric practice and research as some of the other mental health problems such as depression. As with other adult populations, anxiety often occurs concurrently with depression (Beck & Averill, 2004). For older adults, anxiety is frequently connected with chronic conditions and co-occurs with neurodegenerative diseases such as Alzheimer's and Parkinson's disease.

- *Depression.* The most common mental health problem in older adults is depression (NIMH/NIH, 2009), and major depression is the leading cause of suicide in late adulthood (Blazer, 1995). Symptoms of depression include sadness and depressed mood, loss of interest, weight loss, insomnia, and fatigue. To be diagnosed, the depressive episode has to persist for at least 2 weeks. Many depressive episodes in older adults are associated with problems in coping with difficult life events, such as death of a loved person or physical illness. Treatment with antidepressive medication, especially in combination with psychotherapy, significantly improves depressive symptoms in most older adults (NIMH/NIH, 2009). Comparison of White and Black older persons found that lower education and functional disability were common risk factors for severe depressive symptoms for both groups, and sense of mastery and satisfaction with support were common protective factors. Advanced age was a risk factor for Caucasians but not for African American persons, and being female and being less religious were risk factors for African Americans but not for Caucasians (Jang, Borenstein, Chiriboga & Mortimer, 2005). This is yet another reminder of the important role of religious coping among many African Americans. Comparison of older adults in the United States and Japan found that multiple roles were more detrimental to the mental health of the Japanese elders than to U.S. elders (Kikuzawa, 2006). It should be noted that depression is not a normal part of aging (NIMH/NIH, 2009). Moreover, longitudinal research found no increase in clinical levels of depression with age (Helmchen et al. 2006).

- *Delirium.* One of the two most prevalent cognitive disorders in the elderly population (Sadock & Sadock, 2007), **delirium,** is characterized by an impairment of consciousness. The syndrome has a sudden onset (a few hours or days), then follows a brief and fluctuating course that includes impairment of consciousness, and has the potential for improvement when the causes are treated. Prevalent causative factors include not only central nervous system disturbances but also outside factors such as toxicity from medications, low oxygen states, infection, retention of urine and feces, undernutrition and dehydration, and metabolic conditions (Joshi & Morley, 2006). The prevalence of delirium is high among hospitalized elderly persons, with approximately 50% of hospital patients over age 65 experiencing an episode postsurgery during their hospital stay compared with 15% 25% of other patients (Berthold, 2009). Delirium is very common for older persons admitted to intensive care and those transferred to nursing facilities (AGS Foundation for Health in Aging, 2009). It accounts for almost half of the hospital days for older adults (Inouye, 2006).

- *Dementia.* The other most prevalent cognitive disorder among older adults is dementia, which was discussed earlier in the context of neurodegenerative disease. Dementia has a slower onset than delirium and is not characterized by an impairment of consciousness. Rather, dementia is characterized by multiple impairments of the person's cognitive functioning.

- *Substance abuse.* Alcohol continues to be the drug of choice among today's older adults. It is estimated that about 3.6% of older adults (3.2 million) have a substance abuse problem with alcohol; however, less than 17% of these persons were abusing other illegal drugs (Blank, 2009). Elders with severe dependency are less likely than younger people to seek treatment from a specialty clinic (National Institute of Alcohol Abuse and Alcoholism [NIAAA], 2005). Substance abuse is the second most frequent reason (after depression) for admitting older adults to an inpatient psychiatric facility (Moss, Mortens, & Brennan, 1993). The general consumption of alcohol is lower for older adults than for younger adults, but many heavy drinkers do not reach old age, and alcohol abuse is often more hidden among older adults. The consequence of alcoholism for older adults is higher risk of stroke, injury, falls, suicide, and potential interactions with the development of dementia (NIAAA). There is a tendency for families and society to minimize the seriousness of the problem and to convey such notions as "He's too old to change," "If I were old I would drink too," or "Don't take away her last pleasure." These attitudes often prevent efforts to intervene. Contrary to these common attitudes, however, many older persons respond as well to treatment as younger adults do.

Critical Thinking Questions 9.2

George Vaillant suggests that his longitudinal research indicates that humans have "elegant unconscious coping mechanisms that make lemonade out of lemons." Think of a late life adult whom you know that has or is making lemonade out of lemons. What challenges has this person faced in earlier life or in late adulthood? What is it about this late life adult that makes you think of her or him as making lemonade out of lemons? What types of coping mechanisms do you think this person uses to deal with adversities?

SOCIAL ROLE TRANSITIONS AND LIFE EVENTS OF LATE ADULTHOOD

Transitions are at the center of the life course perspective, and people experience many transitions, some of them very abrupt, in late adulthood. Retirement, death of a spouse or partner, institutionalization, and one's own death are among the most stressful events in human existence, and they are clustered in late adulthood. Several other events are more benign but may still enter into the social worker's analysis of the changing configuration of person and environment represented by each case. Despite the concern of the impact of the loss of social roles, studies have demonstrated that older adults generally adapt to late life role transitions and maintain emotional well-being (Hinrichsen & Clougherty, 2006).

Families in Later Life

As you saw with the Smiths, the Menzels, and Ms. Johnson, families continue to play an important role in the life of an older person. With increased longevity, however, the post–empty nest and postretirement period lengthens (Walsh, 2005). Thus, the significance of the marital or partner relationship increases in late adulthood. As older individuals are released from their responsibilities as parents and members of the workforce, they are able to spend more time together. Some studies have suggested a U-shaped curve of marital satisfaction, with the highest levels during the first period of the marital relationship and in late adulthood, and lower levels during the childbearing years (Bjorklund & Bee, 2008). Moreover, overall satisfaction with the quality of life seems to be higher for married elderly individuals than for the widowed or never married. For married couples, the spouse is the most important source of emotional, social, and personal support in times of illness and need of care.

Thirty percent (9.7 million) of noninstitutionalized U.S. older adults live alone. The most common living arrangement for men over 65 is with their wife; in 2003, 73% of men over 65 lived with their spouse (Administration on Aging, 2005). The picture is different for older women, who are twice as likely as older men to be living alone. By age 75, more than one half of women are living alone.

Living arrangements for older adults vary by race and ethnicity. In 2004, the proportion of White and Black women living alone was similar, about 41%. Fewer older Hispanic women lived alone (25%) and even fewer Asian and Pacific Island women lived alone (21%) (Administration on Aging, 2005). Older Black and Hispanic women are less likely than White women to live with a spouse (Himes, 2001). Older Asian women are more likely to live with relatives than women of other races. Black men are three times more likely to live alone than Asian men, who are three times more likely to live with relatives than men from other races (Federal Interagency Forum on Aging-Related Statistics, 2004). A complex relationship between culture, socioeconomic status, and individual personality has to be considered in accounting for the ethnic and racial differences in living arrangements. Drawing inferences based solely on cultural differences is overly simplistic given the use of racial categories devised by the General Accounting Office as proxies for cultural identity.

▲ **Photo 9.4** As older adults are released from responsibilities as parents and members of the workforce, they are able to spend more time together.

Family relationships have been found to be closer and more central for older women than for older men. Mother-daughter relationships have been found to be particularly strong (Silverstein & Bengtson, 2001). Additionally, friendship appears to be a more important protective factor for older women than for older men. Friendships have been associated with lower levels of cognitive impairment and increased quality-of-life satisfaction (Beland, Zunzunegui, Alvarado, Otero, & del Ser, 2005).

The never married constitute a very small group of the current elderly population. It will further decrease for some time as the cohort of baby boomers, with its unusually high rate of marriage, enters late adulthood (Bjorklund & Bee, 2008). However, the proportion of elderly singles and never married will probably increase toward the middle of the next century, because the cohort that follows the baby boomers has had an increase in the number of individuals remaining single.

Singlehood caused by divorce in late adulthood is increasing, however, as divorce is becoming more socially accepted in all population groups. As in all stages of life, divorce in later life may entail financial problems, especially for older women, and it may be especially difficult to recuperate financially in postretirement. Divorce also results in a change of kinship ties and social networks, which are important sources of support in later life. The incidence of remarriage after divorce or widowhood is significantly higher for older men than for older women. The fact that there are more elderly women than men contributes to this trend. Even if older adults are not themselves divorced, they may need to adjust to the enlarged and complicated family networks that come from the divorces and remarriages of their children and grandchildren (Walsh, 2005).

One group of older adults that has often been neglected in the discussion of late adulthood is elderly gay men and lesbians. Estimates of the proportion of gay men and lesbians among elderly persons are similar to those for younger age groups (Teitelman, 1995). Being faced not only with ageist but also with homophobic attitudes, elderly gay men and lesbians may be confronted by a double jeopardy. Eligibility requirements for many services to elderly adults continue to be based on a norm of heterosexuality. Although growing in number, services catering directly to older gay or lesbian persons are still few and far between in many parts of the country. But the most problematic aspect of being an elderly homosexual may be the lack of societal sanction to grieve openly when the partner dies (Barranti & Cohen, 2001; Humphreys & Quam, 1998; Teitelman).

Sibling relationships play a special role in the life of older adults. Siblings share childhood experiences and are often the personal tie with the longest duration. Siblings are typically not the primary source of personal care, but they often play a role in providing emotional support. Sibling relationships often change over the life course, with closer ties in preadulthood and later life and less involvement in early and middle adulthood. Women's ties with siblings have been found to be more involved than those of men (Bjorklund & Bee, 2008).

Relationships with children and grandchildren are also significant in late adulthood. The "myth of the golden age" in the United States suggests that in the past, older people were more likely to live in a multigenerational family, be well taken care of, and have valued emotional and economic roles. This heartwarming picture is a myth, however, because people died earlier and multigenerational families were less prevalent than they are in our era of increased longevity (Hareven, 2000). Furthermore, even in the past, elderly individuals valued independent living, and they typically resided in separate households from their adult children, although they usually lived in close proximity.

In fact, multigenerational families have become more common in recent years, resulting in more interactions and exchanges across generations. Contrary to common belief, intergenerational exchanges between adult children and elderly parents are not one-directional. Children often take care of their elderly parents, but healthy elderly persons also provide significant assistance to their adult children, as is the case with Ms. Johnson. Research on elderly parents living with their adult children suggests that for the young-old, more assistance flows from the elderly parents to the adult children than the other way around (Speare & Avery, 1993). In another study (Ward, Logan, & Spitze, 1992), older parents living with their adult children reported doing more than three quarters of the housework. Patterns of coresidence between parents and adult children vary by race. Non-Hispanic White elderly are the least likely to coreside with their children; Asian elderly are the most likely to live with their children (Speare & Avery).

Grandparenthood

In some cases, older people such as Ms. Johnson are assuming full responsibility for parenting their grandchildren, because their children have problems with drugs, HIV infection, or crime. Beginning in the early 1990s, the U.S. Census Bureau began to note an increasing number of children under 18 living with grandparents, rising from 3% of children under age 18 in 1970 to 5.5% in 1997 (Bryson & Casper, 1999). About 1.53 million older people in the United States live in a household in which a grandchild is present. Approximately 50% of this number resides in parent-maintained households (Administration on Aging, 2005). A little more than one quarter are primary caregivers for their grandchildren (U.S. Bureau of the Census, 2004). This has been viewed by some as a negative trend, but there is no inherent reason why grandchildren receiving care from grandparents is problematic, and, indeed, across time and place, grandparents have sometimes been seen as appropriate caregivers. Many cultural groups often have multigenerational households that are not predicated on dysfunction within the family. Recall that large percentages of Asian, Hispanic, and Black elders live with family members, not their spouse. It does appear, however, that the current trend is influenced by the growth of drug use among parents, teen pregnancy, and the rapid rise of single-parent families (Bryson & Casper, 1999). As a result, new physical, emotional, and financial demands are placed on grandparents with already limited resources. Some speculate that custodial grandparents may also be caring for their own impaired adult child, because two thirds of grandparent-headed households have a member of the "skipped generation" in residence (Burnette, 1999).

> How do culture, social class, and gender affect grandparenting styles?

Grandparenthood is a normative part of the family life cycle, but the majority of grandparents do not coreside with their grandchildren. The timing of grandparenthood influences the way it is experienced and the roles and responsibilities that a grandparent will take on. Predominately, many first-time grandparents are middle-aged adults in their early 50s.

However, the census data from 2004 indicate that grandparenthood has been documented as beginning as young as age 30 (U.S. Bureau of the Census, 2004). Yet, others do not become grandparents until they are 70 or 80 years old. Because individuals are enjoying longer lives, more and more assume the role of grandparent, and they assume it for more years. Many spend the same number of years being a grandparent as being a parent of a child under the age of 18. As life expectancy has continued to increase, the number of great-grandparents is also expected to grow over the next decades.

In general, being a grandparent is a welcome and gratifying role for most individuals, but it may increase in significance and meaning for an older person. The Smiths, for example, both enjoy being grandparents, and Lois Smith especially gains pleasure and satisfaction from her role as grandmother to her daughter's children.

Family researchers have begun to take a strong interest in the grandparenting role, but little is actually known about grandparent-grandchild relationships. A classic study of middle-class grandparents in the early 1960s identified several styles of grandparents: formal grandparents, fun seekers, distant figures, surrogate parents, and mentors (Neugarten & Weinstein, 1964).

A more recent study by Margaret Mueller and her associates has focused particularly on the relationships between grandparents and adolescent grandchildren; the average age of grandparents in this study was 69 years old (Mueller, Wilhelm, & Elder, 2002). This study identified five dimensions of the grandparenting role in 451 families: face-to-face contact, activities done together, intimacy, assistance, and authority/discipline. Each of these grandparenting dimensions is defined in Exhibit 9.7. Using a statistical clustering method, the researchers identified five styles of grandparenting:

1. *Influential grandparents* are highly involved in all aspects of grandparenting, scoring high on all five dimensions. These grandparents constituted 17% of the sample. Ms. Johnson is grandparenting Rebecca in this manner.

2. *Supportive grandparents* are highly involved in the lives of their grandchildren but do not see themselves in a role of disciplinarian or authority figure. About a quarter of the sample fit this pattern.

3. *Passive grandparents* are moderately involved in their grandchildren's lives, but they do not provide instrumental assistance and do not see themselves as discipline/authority figures. About 19% of the sample fit this pattern. Lois and Gene Smith seem to be following this pattern of grandparenting.

4. *Authority-oriented grandparents* see their role as authority figures as the central component in their grandparenting, and they are relatively inactive in their grandchildren's lives compared with both influential and supportive grandparents. These grandparents constitute about 13% of the sample.

5. *Detached grandparents* are the least involved of the grandparents, scoring lowest on all the dimensions of grandparenting. This was the largest group, comprising about 28% of the sample.

This research is helpful because it demonstrates that the grandparent role may be played in many different ways. A number of factors may influence the style of grandparenting, including geographic proximity, ages of grandparents and grandchildren, number of grandchildren, and family rituals. There is a major drawback to the sample, however; it is entirely White and Midwestern. It does not, therefore, address the possibility of cultural variations in grandparenting roles. For example, Caribbean immigrants' grandparents are the primary attachment figures in many families.

A smaller scale study of grandparenting in 17 Native American families, including Sioux, Creek, Seminole, Choctaw, and Chickasaw, partially addresses the issue of cultural variation (Weibel-Orlando, 2001). Like the research of Mueller and her associates, this study identified five styles of grandparenting:

1. *The distanced grandparent* lives at considerable geographic distance from grandchildren but also has psychological and cultural distance. This type of grandparenting is not common among Native Americans. It is most likely to occur if the family has migrated to an urban area and the grandparents return to their ancestral homeland after retirement.

Dimension	Definition
Face-to-face contact	How often grandparents see their grandchildren
Activities done together	Participation in shared activities, such as shopping, working on projects together, attending grandchildren's events, teaching the grandchild a skill
Intimacy	Serving as confidant, companion, or friend; discussing grandparent's childhood
Assistance	Providing instrumental assistance, such as financial aid and/or interpersonal support
Discipline and authority	Disciplining the grandchild or otherwise serving as an authority figure

▲ **Exhibit 9.7**   Dimensions of Grandparenting Role

SOURCE: Based on Mueller et al., 2002.

2. *The ceremonial grandparent* also lives at considerable geographic distance from grandchildren but visits regularly. Intergenerational visits are times for ethnic ceremonial gatherings, and grandparents model appropriate ceremonial behavior.

3. *The fictive grandparent* assumes the elder role with children who are not biologically related. These grandparents may have no grandchildren of their own or may live at a great distance from their biological grandchildren.

4. *The custodial grandparent* lives with the grandchildren and is responsible for their care. This style of grandparenting is usually the result of parental death, incapacitation, or abandonment, and is based on necessity rather than choice.

5. *The cultural conservator grandparent* actively pursues the opportunity to have grandchildren live with her (all such grandparents were women in this study) so that she might teach them the Native American way of life.

Think about your relationships with your grandparents. How would you characterize their grandparenting styles? Did you have different types of relationships with different grandparents? Did your grandparents have different types of relationships with different grandchildren? What might explain any differences?

Work and Retirement

Until the 20th century, the average worker retired about 3 years before death. In 1890, 90% of men in the United States over age 70 were still in the workforce. Increased worker productivity, mass longevity, and Social Security legislation changed that situation, however, and by 1986, only 31% of 65-year-old men were in the workforce. As of 2004, only 14.4 % of U.S. adults 65 and older were still in the workforce—18% of men and 10% of women. However, in the age group 65 to 74, 25% of men and 15% of women were still in the labor force (U.S. Bureau of the Census, 2004). In the past century, with the combined impact of increased longevity and earlier retirement, the average number of years spent in retirement before death is almost 15 years (Vaillant, 2002).

How do these social trends affect the late adult phase of the life course?

Retirement patterns vary with social class. Vaillant found that only 20% of his sample of surviving inner-city men were still in the workforce at age 65, but half of the sample of Harvard men were still working full time at 65. The inner-city men retired, on average, 5 years earlier than the Harvard men. Poor health often leads to earlier retirement among less advantaged adults (Sterns & Huyck, 2001). In addition, higher levels of education make workers eligible for more sedentary jobs, which are a better fit with the declining energy levels in late adulthood (Vaillant, 2002).

Data about retirement have been based on the work patterns of men, probably because women's labor force involvement has been less uniform. Current trends reflect the history of women's involvement in the workforce, with many "baby boomers" having never worked or worked intermittently. A trend was noted in the early 1990s, however, in which labor force participation rates for men over 50 were falling while labor force participation rates of women over 50 were increasing. The greatest increase of women workers in the 55 to 61 age range occurred between 1963 and 2003, up from 44% to 63%. During the same period, the labor force participation of women increased from 29% to 39% among women ages 62 to 64 and from 17% to 23% for women ages 65 to 69. The gap between male and female labor participation has narrowed from 46% in 1963 to 12% in 2003 (Federal Interagency Forum on Aging-Related Statistics, 2004). The decline in labor force participation of men can be accounted for by a number of factors, including eligibility for retirement at age 62 and greater wealth generated by workers, consequently permitting retirement (Federal Interagency Forum on Aging-Related Statistics).

The "appropriate" age for retirement in the United States is currently understood to be age 65. This cultural understanding has been shaped by Social Security legislation enacted in 1935. However, the 1983 Social Security Amendments included a provision for a gradual increase in the age at which a retired person could begin receiving Social Security retirement benefits. Exhibit 9.8 shows the schedule for increasing the age for receiving full benefits. In arguing for this legislative change, members of Congress noted increased longevity and improved health among older adults (Federal Interagency Forum on Aging-Related Statistics, 2004).

Certainly, some older individuals continue to work for many years after they reach age 65. Labor statistics indicate that a little over 20% of adults between the ages of 65 and 74 are working, and a little more than 5% of adults over 75 are in the labor force (Bjorklund & Bee, 2008). Individuals who continue to work fall into two groups: those who could afford to retire but choose to continue working and those who continue to work because of a financial need. Older adults of the first group usually receive great satisfaction in sharing their knowledge and expertise, and gain a feeling of purpose from being productive. Members of the second group continue to work out of necessity. Because economic status in old age is influenced by past employment patterns and the resultant retirement benefits, this second group consists of individuals who had lower-paying employment throughout their lives. This group also includes elderly divorced or widowed women who depended on their husband's retirement income and are now faced with poverty or near poverty. Lifelong gender inequality in wages contributes to inequality in pension and retirement funds (Wilmoth & Longino, 2006). Gene Smith falls into the first category, because he continued working even though he and his wife had sufficient combined benefits to retire. However, Lois Smith's own benefits would not have enabled her to lead a financially comfortable retirement if she were not married, and she would probably face some financial hardship if she were to become a widow. Ruby Johnson continues to be employed on a part-time basis out of financial necessity.

When we think about retirement, we often picture individuals cleaning up their desks to stop working completely and sit in a rocking chair on the front porch. Yet, there are many ways of retiring from the workforce. Some individuals do cease work completely, but others continue with part-time or part-year employment. Others may retire for a period and then reenter the labor market, as Gene Smith did when his former employer offered him a part-time position. Retirement is a socially accepted way to end an active role in the workforce. Most persons retire because of advancing age, mandatory retirement policies, health problems, a desire to pursue other interests, or simply a wish to relax and lead the life of a retiree.

Individuals vary in whether they view retirement as something to dread or something to look forward to. Most often, however, retirement is a positive experience. Vaillant (2002) found no evidence in his longitudinal research that

Year of Birth	Full Retirement Age
1937 and earlier	65
1938	65 and 2 months
1939	65 and 4 months
1940	65 and 6 months
1941	65 and 8 months
1942	65 and 10 month
1943–1954	66
1955	66 and 2 months
1956	66 and 4 months
1957	66 and 6 months
1958	66 and 8 months
1959	66 and 10 month
1960 and later	67

▲ **Exhibit 9.8**   Amended Age to Receive Full Social Security Benefits (1983)

SOURCE: Social Security Administration, 2009.

retirement is bad for physical health. For every person who indicated that retirement was bad for her or his health, four retirees indicated that retirement had improved their health. Vaillant noted four conditions under which retirement is perceived as stressful (p. 221):

1. Retirement was involuntary or unplanned.

2. There are no other means of financial support besides salary.

3. Work provided an escape from an unhappy home life.

4. Retirement was precipitated by preexisting bad health.

These conditions are present among only a fraction of retirees, but those are the retirees with whom social workers are likely to come into contact.

Vaillant found that retirement has generally been rewarding for many of the participants of his study. Four basic activities appear to make retirement rewarding:

1. Replacing work mates with another social network

2. Rediscovering how to play

3. Engaging in creative endeavors

4. Continuing lifelong learning

Vaillant also suggests that retirement would be less stressful if the culture provided rituals for the transition, as it does for other life transitions. Although some people with a long tenure in a job are given retirement parties by their employers, he found little evidence of significant rituals in his research.

Caregiving and Care Receiving

As retirement unfolds, declining health may usher in a period of intensive need for care. The majority of older adults with disabilities lives in the community and receives predominately informal care from spouses, children, and extended family. The percentage of older adults receiving informal or formal caregiving actually declined from 15% in 1984 to 11% in 1999. More than 90% of those older adults with disabilities who received care between 1984 and 1999 received primarily informal caregiving in combination with some formal caregiving. Two thirds of this group received only informal caregiving (Federal Interagency Forum on Aging-Related Statistics, 2004). Eighty percent of older adults who need long-term care receive that care in the community rather than in an institution. Women are the primary source of caregiving in old age (Walsh, 2005). Daughters are more likely than sons to take care of elderly parents. Moreover, elderly men tend to be married and thus are more likely to have a wife available as caregiver.

Caregiving can be an around-the-clock task and often leaves caregivers overwhelmed and exhausted. Mr. Menzel is a good example of the burden that can be experienced by an elderly spouse. Programs that can assist caregivers such as he in reducing their exceptional levels of stress have received much attention. Many programs combine educational components—for example, information about and training in adaptive coping skills—with ongoing support through the opportunity to share personal feelings and experiences. Respite programs for caregivers are also available. In-home respite programs provide assistance through a home health aide or a visiting nurse. Community-based respite is often provided through adult day care and similar programs.

Based on their research on the topic, Rhonda Montgomery and Kosloski (2000, 2009) developed a caregiver identity theory. Their framework consists of seven "career markers," stages that individuals typically move through in their career as caregivers. The first marker signifies the time when the dependency situation begins. One person needs assistance with routine activities and another person starts performing caregiving tasks. The second marker is reached when the self-definition as a caregiver begins; that is, the person incorporates the role of caregiver into his or her personal and social identity. Marker three is characterized by the performance of personal care tasks. At this time, caregiving family members begin to evaluate whether to continue as caregivers or seek alternatives. Although spousal caregivers may already

> How can such programs buffer the stress of caregiving and care receiving?

see themselves as such after reaching marker two, they now begin to unambiguously identify with their new role. The next marker is reached when outside assistance is sought and formal service use is considered. Whether outside help is requested depends on factors such as seeing one's personal situation as deficient, recognizing the potential service as addressing that deficiency, and the psychological and monetary cost-benefit of using the service (Montgomery & Kosloski, 1994). Considering nursing home placement is the fifth marker. Although the institutional placement is considered at earlier phases, the decision now is more imminent. Nursing home placement is the sixth marker. When caregiving becomes too overwhelming, a nursing home placement may be pursued. Caregiving often continues after a family member enters a nursing home. Although caregivers are relieved from direct care, they continue to be involved in the emotional and social aspects of care in the nursing home (Naleppa, 1996). Although many individuals will spend some time in a nursing home, others never enter such an institution and die at home. The final marker in Montgomery and Kosloski's caregiver identity theory is the termination of the caregiver role (2000). This may occur because of recovery or death of the care recipient or through "quitting" as a caregiver.

Stress and burden are not experienced only by the caregiver. The care recipient also experiences significant strain. Requiring care is a double loss: The person has lost the capability to perform the tasks for which he or she needs assistance and the person has also lost independence. Having to rely on others for activities that one has carried out independently throughout one's adult life can be the source of tremendous emotional and psychological stress. Some individuals respond by emotional withdrawal, others become agitated and start blaming others for their situation. The levels of stress that an elderly care recipient may experience depend on "(1) personal and situational characteristics of the elderly recipient; (2) characteristics of the caregiver; (3) social support provided to caregiver and recipient; (4) aspects of the relationship between family caregiver and recipient; and (5) characteristics of caregiving" (Brubaker, Gorman, & Hiestand, 1990, p. 268).

Think of Joseph Menzel. His stress as a caregiver was probably amplified by culturally defined norms promoting independence, individuality, and pride. Helping someone like him to overcome his uneasiness about receiving assistance may include asking him to verbalize his worries, listening to him express his feelings, and looking together at ways that he could overcome his uneasiness in small steps.

Widowhood

Widowhood is more common among women than men. Almost half (43%) of all older women in 2004 were widows. This was four times the rate of widowers (2 million widowers compared with 8.4 million widows) (Administration on Aging, 2005). The death of a spouse has been found to be the most stressful event in a person's life. In most cases, it is the loss of someone with whom the individual has shared a major part of life. Moreover, the marital relationship is one of the most important relationships for a person in later life. Because they have a longer life expectancy, more women than men face this life event.

Losing a spouse signifies the end of one phase in a person's life course and the beginning of a new phase called widowhood. It requires the individual to readjust to a new social role and a new way of relating to others. Those who saw the world through the eyes of a spouse have to learn to see everything from a new perspective. Widowhood also confronts the person with his or her own mortality. There is evidence that the loss of a spouse is associated with subsequent illness and earlier mortality (Martikainen & Valkonen, 1996), but a recent Finnish study found this to be true for women but not for men (Vahtera et al., 2006). Loss, grief, and bereavement are discussed in greater detail in Chapter 10.

Adjustment to widowhood is facilitated by a person's own inner strength, family support, a strong network of friends and neighbors, and membership in a church or an active community. The family is the most important source of emotional, social, and financial support during this time.

Widowhood may be especially difficult if the surviving spouse provided intensive caregiving for a prolonged period. In this case, the partner's death may be a relief from the burdensome caregiving task, but it may also mean the loss of a role and sense of purpose. In addition, during the period of intensive caregiving, the survivor may have had to give up many social interactions and thus have a shrunken social support network.

Institutionalization

Another myth of aging is that older individuals are being abandoned and neglected by their families and being pushed into nursing homes to get them out of the way. Fewer elderly persons are institutionalized than we generally assume, but the risk for entering a nursing home increases significantly with age. During the past decade, the percentages of older people living in nursing homes actually declined from 5.1% in 1990 to 4.5% in 2000, but the total number has increased because of the rapid growth in the aged population (Federal Interagency Forum on Aging-Related Statistics, 2004). However, the risk of entering a nursing home does continue to increase with age. Only 1.1% of older adults between the age of 65 and 74, compared with 18.2% of those 85 and older, live in nursing homes. Additionally 5% of older adults live in self-described senior housing, many of which have supportive services

(Administration on Aging, 2005). There have been many efforts to reduce disability that can result in nursing home placement (Agency for Healthcare Research and Quality, 2006). It remains to be seen whether Gene Smith, Lois Smith, Ms. Johnson, or Mr. or Mrs. Menzel will spend some time before death in a nursing home.

Most children and spouses do not use nursing homes as a dumping ground for their elderly relatives. They turn to nursing homes only after they have exhausted all other alternatives. Nor is institutionalization a single, sudden event. It is a process that starts with the need to make a decision, continues through the placement itself, and ends in the adjustment to the placement (Naleppa, 1996).

Researchers have taken a close look at the factors that predict a person's entry into a nursing home. Among the most important are the condition and needs of the elderly individual. Functional and behavioral deficits, declining health, previous institutionalization, and advanced age all contribute to the decision to enter a nursing home. Family characteristics that are good predictors of institutionalization include the need for 24-hour caregiving, caregiver feelings of distress, caregiver health and mental status, and caregiving environment (Naleppa, 1996). Marital status is a strong predictor of institutionalization for elderly men. Unmarried and never married men have the highest risk of entering a nursing home (Dolinsky & Rosenwaike, 1988; Hanley, Alecxih, Wiener, & Kennell, 1990). Individuals without a spouse who live alone in the community are at a higher risk of entering a nursing home than those living with spouses, family members, or friends (Montgomery & Kosloski, 1994).

The placement decision itself is emotionally stressful for all involved and can be viewed as a family crisis. Yet, it can be considered a normative part of the family life cycle. The process of making a placement decision itself unfolds in four stages: "the recognition of the potential for institutionalization; discussion of the institutionalization option; implementation of action steps toward institutionalization; and placement of the relative in the institutional setting" (Gonyea, 1987, p. 63). Because many nursing home placements are arranged from the hospital for an elderly individual who entered the hospital expecting to return home, many people may not have time to progress well through these stages. For those who unexpectedly enter a nursing home from the hospital, it may be advisable to arrange a brief visit home to say farewell to their familiar environment. Although society has developed rituals for many occasions, unfortunately no rituals exist for this difficult life transition.

Entering a nursing home means losing control and adjusting to a new environment. How well a person adjusts depends on many factors. If the elderly individual sees entering the nursing home in a favorable light and feels in control, adjustment may proceed well. Frequent visits by relatives and friends also help in the adaptation to the new living arrangement. Despite the commonly held belief that families do not visit their relatives, continued family involvement seems to be the norm. About two thirds of nursing home residents receive one or more visitors a week, and only a very small group is never visited (Bitzan & Kruzich, 1990).

THE SEARCH FOR PERSONAL MEANING

As adults become older, they spend more time reviewing their life achievements and searching for personal meaning. In gerontology, the concept of **life review** as a developmental task of late adulthood was introduced by Robert Butler (1963). He theorized that this self-reflective review of one's life is not a sign of losing short-term memory, as had been assumed. Rather, life review is a process of evaluating and making sense of one's life. It includes a reinterpretation of past experiences and unresolved conflicts. Newer forms of clinical interventions rooted in narrative theory underscore the importance of providing structure, coherence, and opportunity for meaning making of one's experience that "storying" provides (Morgan, 2000). Social workers can influence a more positive outcome of a life review through relationship, empathic listening and reflection, witness to the story, and providing alternative reframes and interpretations of past events. For example, promoting a story of resiliency as a lifelong process helps to reframe stories that support successful mastery of challenges and compensatory recovery in the face of adversity (O'Leary & Bhaju, 2006; Wadensten, 2005).

The life review can lead to diverse outcomes, including depression, acceptance, or satisfaction (Butler, 1987). If the life review is successful, it leads the individual to personal wisdom and inner peace. But the reassessment of one's life may also lead to despair and depression. This idea that the process of life review may lead to either acceptance or depression is similar to the eighth stage of Erikson's theory of adult development; through the life review, the individual tries to work through the conflict between ego integrity (accepting oneself and seeing one's life as meaningful) and despair (rejecting oneself and one's life).

The ways in which individuals review their lives differ considerably. Some undertake a very conscious effort of assessing and reevaluating their achievements; for others, the effort may be subtle and not very conscious. Regardless of how they pursue it, life review is believed to be a common activity for older adults that occurs across cultures and time.

The concept of **reminiscence** is closely related to life review. Most older persons have a remarkable ability to recall past events. They reminisce about the past and tell their stories to anyone who is willing to listen, but they also reminisce when they are on their own. This reminiscing can serve several functions (Sherman, 1991):

- Reminiscing may be an enjoyable activity that can lift the spirits of the listener and of the person telling the story.

- Some forms of reminiscing are directed at enhancing a person's image of self, as when individuals focus on their accomplishments.

- Reminiscing may help the person cope with current or future problems, letting her or him retreat to the safe place of a comfortable memory or recall ways of coping with past stressors.

- Reminiscing can assist in the life review, as a way to achieve ego integrity.

Reminiscing combines past, present, and future orientations (Sherman, 1991). It includes the past, which is when the reviewed events occurred. However, the construction of personal meaning is an activity that is also oriented to the present and the future, providing purpose and meaning to life. A recent study examined the association between reminiscence frequency, reminiscence enjoyment or regret, and psychological health outcomes. The study found that high frequency of reminiscence and having regret were associated with poor psychological health. Reminiscence enjoyment, conversely, was positively associated with psychological health outcomes (Mckee et al., 2005). The Erzählcafé that Elizabeth Menzel visits tries to incorporate this by regularly including group activities that foster reminiscing in a safe, positive, and fun environment.

Another factor in the search for personal meaning is religious or spiritual activity. Cross-sectional research has consistently found that humans become more religious or spiritual in late adulthood (Gallup & Lindsay, 1999). Vaillant's (2002) longitudinal research did not find support for this idea, however. He found that the importance of religion and spirituality, on average, did not change in the lives of his study participants over time. He suggests that the cross-sectional finding may be picking up a cohort effect, and that subsequent cohorts of older adults may be less religious or spiritual in adolescence and young adulthood than the current cohort of older adults was. What Vaillant fails to address is whether his cohort reaches a higher faith stage in late adulthood, as developmental theorists would suggest.

RESOURCES FOR MEETING THE NEEDS OF ELDERLY PERSONS

The persons in the case studies at the beginning of this chapter needed several kinds of assistance. Lois and Gene Smith, for example, needed some counseling to help them settle comfortably into retirement together. Gene went back to work to fill some of his leisure hours, but Lois needed some suggestions about the volunteer opportunities that could give meaning to her life. Ms. Johnson requires a level of assistance most practically provided by effective and comprehensive case management. The Menzels' needs were quite different. Elizabeth Menzel is confronted with Alzheimer's related care and assistance needs. Much of this assistance has been provided by her daughter Christine and her husband Joseph. Joseph Menzel, in turn, needs some respite services to prevent him from being overwhelmed by the demands of giving care. This respite is being provided by his wife's weekly attendance in an Alzheimer's social group meeting.

The types of support and assistance that elderly persons receive can be categorized as either formal or informal resources. Formal resources are those provided by formal service providers. They typically have eligibility requirements that a person has to meet in order to qualify. Some formal resources are free, but others are provided on a fee-for-service basis, meaning that anyone who is able to pay can request the service. Informal resources are those provided through families, friends, neighbors, churches, and so forth. Elderly persons receive a considerable amount of support through these informal support networks. As the society ages, more attention will need to be paid to the interaction between the informal and formal support systems (Wacker & Roberto, 2008).

Informal Resources

The family is the most important provider of informal resources for many older individuals. It is estimated that 80% to 90% of the care provided to elderly persons living in the community is provided by family members (Allen, Blieszner, & Roberto, 2001). Usually family members can provide better emotional and social support than other providers of services. Family members know the person better and are more available for around-the-clock support. Different family members tend to provide different types of assistance. Daughters tend to provide most of the caregiving and are more involved in housekeeping and household chores. Sons are more likely to provide assistance with household repairs and financial matters.

> What types of social service programs can enhance informal supports for older adults?

However, the family should not be considered a uniformly available resource or support. Not all family networks are functional and able to provide needed support. As Ms. Johnson's story illustrates, even when family members are involved in the elderly person's life, they may place additional demands on the older person instead of relieving the burden. The increased presence of women in the labor market places them in a particularly difficult position—trying to balance the demands of raising children, taking care of their parents, and being part of the workforce. Furthermore, the size of the family network available to support elderly persons is decreasing as a consequence of the decreasing average number of children in a family (Walsh, 2005).

A second source of informal resources is friends and neighbors, who often provide a significant amount of care and assistance. Although they may be less inclined than family members would be to provide personal care, friends and neighbors like Gene and Lois Smith often offer other forms of assistance, such as running errands or performing household chores. Sometimes a system of informal exchanges evolves—for example, an elderly woman invites her elderly neighbor over for meals while he mows her lawn and drives her to medical appointments.

Finally, informal resources are also provided by religious and community groups. Religious-related resources include social and emotional support through group activities and community events. It is this form of support that an active retired person such as Lois Smith finds most helpful. In addition, some religious groups are involved in providing more formal resources, such as transportation or meal services.

Formal Resources

The second type of support for older adults is the formal service delivery system, which offers a wide range of services. Four different Social Security trust funds are the backbone of formal resources to older people in the United States:

1. *Old-Age and Survivors Insurance (OASI).* The retirement and survivors' component of the U.S. Social Security system is a federally administered program that covers almost all workers. To qualify, a person must have worked at least 10 years in employment covered by the program. The benefit is based on the individual's earnings and is subject to a maximum benefit amount. Through cost-of-living adjustments, the amount is adjusted annually for inflation. Many older individuals are able to supplement this benefit with private pension benefits.

2. *Hospital Insurance Trust Fund (Medicare Part A).* This fund covers a major part of the cost of hospitalization as well as a significant part of the costs of skilled nursing facility care, approved home health care, and under certain conditions, hospice care. Depending on the type of service needed, beneficiaries pay a one-time copayment or a percentage of the actual costs. Most beneficiaries do not need to pay a monthly premium (Kingson & Berkowitz, 1993).

3. *Supplementary Medical Insurance. Medicare Part B* covers medical costs such as physicians' services, inpatient and outpatient surgery, and ambulance services, as well as laboratory services, medically necessary home health care, and outpatient hospital treatment. It may also cover physical therapy and prosthetic services. Beneficiaries pay a small monthly premium (Kingson & Berkowitz, 1993). Some services require a copayment or a deductible. *Medicare Part D,* a result of the Medication Prescription Drug Improvement and Modernization Act of 2003, became effective on January 1, 2006. It was designed to provide older adults and people with disabilities access to prescription drug coverage. Rather than being administered by the federal government, as in the case of Part A and Part B, Part D is being administered by private insurance plans that are then reimbursed by the Centers for Medicare and Medicaid Services (CMS) (U.S. Department of Health and Human Services, 2006). Participants have choices of a number of private insurance plans, but the choices, to date, are not straightforward. Plans with the lowest premiums may not cover the drugs needed by a particular participant. In addition, plans may change their drug prices frequently. The initial coverage was limited to drug costs of $2,400, and catastrophic coverage did not pick up until drug costs reached $3,850, placing considerable financial burden on many older beneficiaries (Medicare Advocacy, 2007). This problem with Medicare part D was termed the "doughnut hole." The health reform bill passed in March 2010 attempts to close the "doughnut hole."

4. *Disability insurance.* This component provides benefits for workers younger than 62 with a severe long-term disability. There is a 5-month waiting period, but the benefits continue as long as the disability exists.

> How do these federal programs serve as protective factors in late adulthood?

In addition, Supplemental Social Security Income (SSI) is a financial need-based program that provides cash benefits to low-income, aged, blind, and disabled persons. It is not part of the Social Security trust funds but is a federal welfare program.

Other formal services are available regionally. Here is an overview of some of the most important ones:

- *Adult day care.* Some elderly individuals have conditions that prevent them from staying at home while their caregiver is at work, or the caregiver may benefit from respite. Two forms of adult day care exist for such situations. *The social adult day care model* provides meals, medication, and socialization, but no personal care. *The medical adult day care model* is for individuals who need medical care, nursing services, physical or occupational therapy, and more intensive personal care.

- *Senior centers.* Community forums for social activities, educational programs, and resource information are available even in small communities.

- *Home health care services.* Several types of home health care are available, varying greatly in level of assistance and cost. They range from homemakers who assist with household chores, cleaning, and errands to registered nurses who provide skilled nursing service, use medical equipment, and provide intravenous therapy.

- *Hospice programs.* The purpose of a hospice program is to provide care to the terminally ill. Through inpatient or outpatient hospice, patients typically receive treatment by a team of doctors, nurses, social workers, and care staff.

- *Senior housing.* An elderly person may require a change in his or her living arrangement for a number of reasons, and several alternative living arrangements are available. Senior apartments and retirement communities are for persons who can live independently. They typically offer meals and housekeeping services, but no direct care. Many offer transportation, community rooms, and senior programs.

- *Adult homes.* For seniors in need of more assistance, adult homes usually have rooms, rather than apartments, and provide meals, medication management, and supervision.

- *Health-related senior facilities.* For those in need of nursing care and intensive assistance with activities of daily living, residents live in private or semiprivate rooms, and share living and dining rooms. Medications, meals, personal care, and some therapeutic services are provided. Included in this category is the growing number of a*ssisted living facilities,* which may provide small apartments as well as single rooms. The skilled nursing facility provides the highest level of care, including nursing and personal care and an array of therapeutic services. Several noninstitutional alternatives to the nursing home exist, including *adult foster care* programs that operate in a similar way to foster care programs for children and adolescents.

- *Nutrition programs.* Deficits in nutrition can affect a person's health and the aging process. Nutritional services are provided through a number of programs, the best known being Meals on Wheels (Wacker & Roberto, 2008).

- *Transportation services.* Public and private providers offer transportation for elderly persons with mobility problems.

- *Power of attorney.* Some elderly persons have difficulty managing their legal and financial affairs. A **power of attorney (POA)** is a legal arrangement by which a person appoints another individual to manage his or her financial and legal affairs. The person given the POA should be a person the client knows and trusts. Standard POA forms are available at stationery stores, but the POA can be tailored to the individual's situation. It then needs to be notarized, a service provided by attorneys and some banks. A POA can be limited (for a limited time period), general (no restrictions), or durable (begins after the client reaches a specified level of disability) (Wacker & Roberto, 2008).

With so many types of services available, the social worker's most daunting task is often assessing the elderly person's needs. It may also be a challenge, however, to find quality services that are affordable. Thus, advocacy on behalf of older adults remains a concern of the social work profession.

Naturally, the ways formal and informal resources are offered differ among countries and even regions of a country. As can be deduced from our discussion of the problems older adults face, many are neither unique to an individual nor are they country specific. Rather, they are occurring as part of the aging process for older adults around the globe. We already described some of the programs as they pertain to older adults in the United States. To illustrate different approaches taken to address similar problems, we are including a brief comparison of the retirement benefits, health care, and long-term care in the United States, the environment of the Smiths and Mrs. Johnson, and in Germany, the Menzels' home environment (see Exhibit 9.9). As you can see, there are similarities in some areas and significant differences in others. The United States often uses a more incremental approach to policy changes. In Germany, policy change usually takes a longer time, but when it occurs, the new policies are often very comprehensive and far-reaching in their application.

Germany	United States
Retirement Benefits	Retirement Benefits
Current retirees receive a guaranteed income through a range of pension schemes. Social assistance kicks in if pensions are inadequate. Most retirement benefits are through the statutory pension systems, which provides a monthly pension based on a formula that takes into consideration factors such as years or employment and income. Government employees and civil servants are part of a government retirement system, providing a slightly better level of benefits. Recent changes to statutory pension schemes require current members of the workforce to purchase additional private pension saving plans to supplement their future retirement benefits. In the future, statutory pensions will only provide a basic financial security, not considered high enough to continue with a similar standard of living in retirement. The current retirement age of 65 is increasing incrementally to 67 years. Since the German job market discriminates against older workers, it is expected that this will cause problems for some retiring baby boomers.	Social Security is the foundation of the benefits for older individuals, including retirement benefits, disability benefits, and dependent's and survivor's benefits. Social Security provides a guaranteed retirement benefit to almost all citizens. The benefit level is based on a formula taking into consideration factors such as years of employment and income. Social Security is only considered to be a basic retirement benefit. Individuals are expected to supplement their Social Security income through private savings, individual retirement plans, or other retirement investments. Significant variation exists in retirement planning. Many in the current workforce are not able to contribute to private retirement savings, since their employment status does not come with retirement benefits. The current retirement age of 65 is increasing incrementally to 67 years. Aside from economic cycles and related unemployment, it can be expected that the job market in the United States will be able to adapt to this change.
Health Care	Health Care
German older adults continue to receive the same health care coverage and remain with their providers after reaching retirement age. No differences exist between pre- and postretirement health care coverage. Health care insurance is universal, but not socialized. Almost all citizens are required to have health insurance. The premiums are shared with the employer. If someone is unemployed, the government covers costs. People select their own insurance plan from private insurance companies that are regulated by government. The system consists primarily of private players, i.e., health insurance companies, physicians, pharmacies, and many hospitals are for-profit businesses. In general, premiums for retirees remain at about the same levels; however, they have to pay the entire costs.	Health care for those over 65 years is provided almost exclusively through Medicare, making it a near universal health care plan for older adults. Eligibility includes U.S. citizens 65 years or older that have contributed Medicare taxes for at least 10 years. Medicare is considered a single payer health care plan that covers most health care of older adults. It consists of four parts: Part A—hospital insurance, Part B—medical insurance, Part C—Medicare advantage plans, and Part D—drug prescription plans. Medicare is financed in part through a 2.9% payroll tax. Recipients may be required to pay additional fees; for example Medicare Part B requires enrollees to pay a premium. "Medigap" insurances are available to purchase protection against costs that are not covered through Medicare.
Long-Term Care	Long-Term Care
The German long-term care insurance (LTCI; Pflegeversicherung) is the youngest of the German social welfare programs. It was introduced in 1994 after two decades of political discussion (Scharf, 1998). The LTCI is formally attached to health insurance and is financed through a 1.7% payroll tax. LTCI is a needs-based program. In order to receive coverage, a person completes an application, a medical assessment is conducted, and the person is given a needs level score (Pflegestufe) of 1–3. The amount and type of care giving services is based on this score. The care recipient is in control of the services, i.e., she decides which provider to hire from a menu of local for-profit and non-profit service providers. Family members may be hired as well, but reimbursement rates are slightly lower. Recently an additional needs category has been added to include persons with dementia, who may not qualify in terms of their medical care needs, but may require extensive other assistance by their caregivers.	No comprehensive long-term care insurance exists. Recipients of Medicaid and VA benefits may receive some long-term care coverage. Individuals enrolled in Medicare Part A are covered for short-term stays in a skilled nursing facility (full coverage for the first 20 days, another 80 days with co-pay). Various options exist to purchase private long-term care insurance, albeit at rather high premiums. For example, Federal employees can enroll in a Federal Long-Term Care Insurance program.

▲ **Exhibit 9.9** Some Comparisons of Aging Policy in Germany and the United States

RISK FACTORS AND PROTECTIVE FACTORS IN LATE ADULTHOOD

Chapter 8 suggests that midlife behavior has both antecedents and consequences. The same can be said for late adulthood. Early life experiences can serve either as risk factors or as protective factors for health and well-being during late adulthood. And late adult behaviors can serve either as risk factors or as protective factors for future health and well-being.

As the longest-term longitudinal research available on late adult behavior, Vaillant's Study of Adult Development (2002) provides the clearest understanding of the antecedents of late adult well-being. Like Emmy Werner, who has studied a cohort until midlife (see Chapter 8), Vaillant is impressed with the self-righting tendencies in human nature. He summarizes the antecedent risk factors and protective factors for late adulthood in this way: "What goes right in childhood predicts the future far better than what goes wrong" (p. 95). He also suggests that unhappy childhoods become less important over the stages of adulthood. Consequently, Vaillant suggests that it is more important to count up the protective factors than to count up the risk factors. Although he found childhood experiences to diminish in importance over time, Vaillant also found that much of the resilience, or lack thereof, in late adulthood is predicted by factors that were established by age 50. He suggests that risk factors and protective factors change over the life course.

Exhibit 9.10 lists six variables that Vaillant was surprised to find did not predict healthy aging and seven factors that he did find to predict healthy aging. Some of the factors that did not predict healthy aging did predict good adjustment at earlier adult stages. In terms of stress, Vaillant found that if we wait a few decades, many people recover from psychosomatic illness. In terms of parental characteristics, he found that they are still important for predicting adaptation at age 40 but not by age 70. In terms of both childhood temperament and general ease in social relationships, he found that they are strong predictors of adjustment in young adulthood but no longer important at age 70.

Conversely, Vaillant found that the seven factors on the right side of Exhibit 9.7, collectively, are strong predictors of health 30 years in the future. He also found that each variable, individually, predicted healthy aging, even when the other six variables were statistically controlled. Vaillant has chosen to frame each of these predictive factors in terms of protection; he sees risk as the flip side of protection. He notes the danger of such a list of protective factors: that it be used to "blame the victim" rather than provide guidance for aging well. He sees the list of predictors as "good news," however, because they all represent something that can be controlled to some extent.

Variables That Do Not Predict Healthy Aging	Variables That Do Predict Healthy Aging
Ancestral longevity	Not smoking, or stopping young
Cholesterol	Using mature coping mechanisms
Stress	Not abusing alcohol
Parental characteristics	Healthy weight
Childhood temperament	Stable marriage
General ease in social relationships	Some exercise
	Years of education

▲ **Exhibit 9.10**   Variables That Affect Healthy Aging

SOURCE: Vaillant, 2002.

By following cohorts across the period of young-old and middle-old, Vaillant (2002) also has some suggestions about the consequences of late adult behavior. We have already taken a look at his prescription for growing old gracefully. In addition, he notes the following personal qualities in late adulthood to bode well for continued well-being:

- Good self-care
- Future orientation, ability to anticipate, plan, and hope
- Capacity for gratitude and forgiveness
- Capacity for empathy, to imagine the world as the other sees it
- Desire to do things with people rather than to them

Critical Thinking Questions 9.3

At what age do you expect to retire? If you were promised a full pension that would allow you to stop working now, would you want to continue to work? Why or why not? What does work mean to you? Do you work to live or live to work? What factors do you think a person should consider when making decisions about retirement?

IMPLICATIONS FOR SOCIAL WORK PRACTICE

Several practice principles for social work with older adults can be recommended:

- When working with an older adult, take into account the person's life history.
- Develop self-awareness of your views on aging and how different theoretical perspectives may influence your practice.
- Be conscious that age-related social roles change over time and that they vary for different cohorts.
- Identify areas in which you can assist an elderly client in preventing future problems, such as health-related difficulties.
- Develop an understanding of and skills to assess the difference between the physical, biological, psychological, and socioemotional changes that are part of normal aging and those that are indicative of a problematic process. Develop an understanding of how such factors may affect the intervention process.
- Develop an understanding of the different types of families in later life. Because older adults continue to be part of their families, it may be beneficial to work with the entire family system.
- Develop an understanding of the retirement process and how individuals adjust differently to this new life stage.
- Carefully assess an elderly person's caregiving network. Be conscious of the difficulties that the caregiving situation poses for both the caregiver and the care recipient. Be conscious of the potential for caregiver burnout, and familiarize yourself with local caregiver support options.
- Develop an understanding of the process of institutionalizing an older adult. Be careful not to label it as an act of abandonment. Rather, be aware that institutionalization is stressful for all involved and is typically done only as a last resort. Develop an understanding of the process of adaptation to nursing home placement and skills to assist an older adult and his or her family with that adaptation.

- When assessing the need for service, be conscious of the availability of formal and informal support systems. Develop an understanding and knowledge of the formal service delivery system.

- Avoid treating older persons as if they were incapable of making decisions simply because they may not be able to carry out the decision. Rather, involve them to the maximum extent possible in any decisions relating to their personal life and care, even if they are not able to carry out the related actions.

KEY TERMS

activity theory (of aging)
age stratification perspective
Alzheimer's disease
continuity theory (of aging)
crystallized intelligence
delirium
dementia
dependency ratio
developmental biocultural
    co-constructivism
disengagement theory (of aging)

ego integrity versus ego despair
feminist theories (of aging)
fluid intelligence
genetic theories of biological aging
incidental memory
intentional memory
keeper of the meaning
life review
molecular/cellular theories of
    biological aging
morbidity

mortality rate
power of attorney (POA)
programmed aging theories
random error theories
reminiscence
social construction theory
    (of aging)
social exchange theory (of aging)
social gerontology
system-level theories of biological
    aging

ACTIVE LEARNING

1. Think about the three case studies presented at the outset of this chapter (Smith, Johnson, and Menzel). Which theory/theories of social gerontology seems to be the best fit with each of these individuals?

2. Think of examples of how older adults are presented in the media (TV, movies, advertisements). How are they typically characterized? What does this say about our society's views on aging? Think of examples of how older adults could be presented in an age-appropriate way in the media. Develop a short script for an advertisement that features older adults.

3. Think about your own extended family. What roles do the members of the oldest generation play in the family? How do the different generations interact, exchange resources, and influence each other? How do the different generations deal with their role changes and life transitions as they age? In what ways do the different generations support and hinder each other in life transitions?

WEB RESOURCES

Agency for Health Care Research and Quality
www.ahrq.gov

Site provides consumer, patient, and clinical practice information focused on specific populations: aging, women, and rural health.

AgingStats.Gov
www.agingstats.gov

Site presented by the Federal Interagency Forum on Aging-Related Statistics covers 31 key indicators of the lives of older people in the United States and their families.

American Association of Retired Persons
www.aarp.org

Organizational site provides a wide range of resources from health technology, travel, legal, and policy and advocacy.

Center on Aging Society—Older Hispanic Americans
http://ihcrp.georgetown.edu/agingsociety/pubhtml /hispanics/hispanics.html

Site that presents research results on chronic conditions of older Latino Americans.

National Academy on an Aging Society
www.agingsociety.org

Organization provides clear unbiased research and analysis focused on public policy issues arising from the aging of America's and world population.

National Center and Caucus on Black Aged
www.ncba-aged.org

Site contains aging news for policymakers, legislators, advocacy groups, minority professionals, and consumers addressing finances, caregiving, intergenerational issues, and governmental programs.

National Council on the Aging
www.ncoa.org

Site presented by the National Council on the Aging (NCOA) contains information on advocacy, programs, publications, and a number of good links to other aging resources.

National Institute on Aging
www.nia.nih.gov

Site presented by the National Institute on Aging (NIA) contains information about the NIA, news and events, health information, research programs, funding and training, and National Advisory Council on Aging.

Social Security Online
www.ssa.gov

Site maintained by the U.S. Social Security Administration contains benefits information and online direct services.

U.S. Administration on Aging
www.aoa.gov

Site accesses information about Older Americans Act, federal legislation, and range of programs and statistics.

CHAPTER

10

Very Late Adulthood

Pamela J. Kovacs

CHAPTER OUTLINE

OPENING QUESTIONS

- What are some of the reasons for the fast growth and increased diversity among very late-life adults, and what are some of the main challenges associated with increased longevity?

- What are some of the implications for intimacy among very late-life adults as their families and peers die and they become less mobile and independent?

- When working with clients in very late adulthood, what do social workers need to know about how people respond to crises such as severe illness, acquired disability, and loss?

KEY IDEAS

As you read this chapter, take note of these central ideas:

1. People 85 and older are the fastest growing segment of the older adult population. Never have so many people lived so long.

2. Among very late-life adults, women outnumber men 5 to 2, and 4 out of 5 centenarians are women.

3. Because the more frail individuals die sooner, those surviving to very late adulthood tend to be a relatively robust group, but they face an increased incidence of chronic disease and disability.

4. In very late adulthood, individuals continue to desire and need connections to other people.

5. In very late adulthood, spirituality is often associated with making meaning of loss and finding a way to stay connected to others.

6. Very late adulthood is the one life course phase when dying is considered "on time," and very late-life adults seem to have less denial about the reality of death than those in other age groups.

7. Theoreticians and researchers continue to try to understand the multidimensional process of grief.

Case Study 10.1

Margaret Davis Stays at Home

Margaret Davis has lived in her small, rural community in southern West Virginia for all of her 85 years. It is in this Appalachian mountain town that she married her grade-school sweetheart, packed his pail for long shifts in the mine, and raised their four children. It has been more than 30 years since she answered the door to receive the news that her husband had perished in an accident at the mine. She remains in that same house by herself, with her daughter living in a trailer on the same property and one of her sons living just down the road. Her other son recently moved to Cleveland to find work and her other daughter lives in the same town but has been estranged from the family for several years.

Mrs. Davis has hypertension and was recently diagnosed with type 2 diabetes. The nurse from the home health agency is assisting her and her daughter with learning to give insulin injections. It is the nurse who asks for a social work consult for Mrs. Davis. The nurse and Mrs. Davis's daughter are concerned that she is becoming increasingly forgetful with her medications and often neglects her insulin regime. They also suspect that she is experiencing some incontinence, as her living room couch and carpet smell of urine.

Mrs. Davis and her daughter Judy greet the social worker at her home. They have been baking this morning and offer a slice of peanut butter pie. Judy excuses herself to go to her trailer to make a phone call. The social worker asks Mrs. Davis about how her insulin regime has been going and if she feels that she could keep up with the injections. She responds that she has learned to give herself the shots and "feels pretty fair." The social worker conveys the concern that she may be missing some of the injections and other medications as well. To this she replies, "Oh, don't worry about me, I'm fine." The social worker proceeds to ask the sensitive question as to whether she has been having trouble with her bladder or getting to the bathroom. This causes Mrs. Davis to become very quiet. Looking up at the social worker she shares that witches have been visiting her house late at night and have been urinating in her living room. The witches are very "devious" but because she is a very religious person, she does not feel that they will harm her.

Judy returns to the home and joins her mother and the social worker. Judy voices her concern about her mother's safety, noting the problems with medications and with general forgetfulness. Judy is able to prepare meals, dispense the medications, and give insulin injections in the morning because she works evenings at a factory. Judy's daughter, Tiffany, has been staying overnight in the home but complains of her grandmother's wandering and confusion late at night. As a result, she is often exhausted during her day shifts at a nursing home in the next county and in caring for her small children. When asked about Mrs. Davis's son's involvement in her care, Judy responds, "He works and is in the Guard some weekends. He handles mom's money mostly and his wife, well, she has her own problems." Judy also reported that her mother has Medicare but she was not sure if that would be sufficient to pay for all her mother's care long-term. Judy is also worried because her old car has been giving her problems lately, and the repairs are becoming expensive. She concludes by stating, "We promised mom that she would never go to a home . . . we take care of our own."

—*Kristina Hash*
—*Meenakshi Venkataraman*

Case Study 10.2

Bina Patel Outlives Her Son

Bina Patel is a 90-year-old immigrant who moved to the United States 25 years ago from India with her son and his family. Like many other South Asian older adults, Bina prefers to reside with her adult children and values the mutual interdependency among generations common in their culture. Upon arriving in this country at age 65, Bina, a widow, played a critical role in the family, providing child care, assisting with meals and various household tasks, and offering companionship and support for her adult children. True to her cultural tradition, Bina expects adult children—especially sons—to provide for parents in their old age, and believes that

(Continued)

(Continued)

the role of the elder is to provide crucial functions such as passing on wisdom and guidance to children and grandchildren, and being constantly available to them.

Bina had been in remarkably good health until she had a mild stroke last year. She was managing well at home with weekly physical therapy and her family's assistance with bathing. She and her family have been unprepared for her longevity; and in fact it appears that she will outlive her son, who at age 69 was recently diagnosed with pancreatic cancer with a prognosis of 6 to 12 months to live. Her daughter-in-law is home full-time with Bina but does not drive and currently is emotionally distraught over her husband's rapid decline. Bina's two grandchildren, who are in their 30s, have relocated with their own families because of employment. They are in frequent telephone contact, but they live a 2-hour plane ride away and are busy with work and children's school and activities. Although this family has traditionally handled their family needs on their own or with the help of a small South Asian network, the son's decline in health has caused tremendous concern regarding Bina's future well-being.

The hospital social worker has been asked to meet with the son and daughter-in-law during his hospitalization to explore possible sources of assistance during the son's pending decline as well as to help strategize for Bina's anticipated increased need of physical care, given her recent decline in cognitive and physical capacity.

Case Study 10.3

Pete Mullin Loses His Sister's Support

Pete Mullin and Lucy Rauso, brother and sister, ages 96 and 92, have lived together since the death of Lucy's husband, Tony, 25 years ago. Pete and Lucy are second-generation Irish Catholic Americans and Tony Rauso was Italian American. Pete was married in his 30s, but had lived alone since his divorce at age 55. Pete and Lucy were both in their early 70s when they decided to pool their limited savings and retirement income to buy a small home in a rural retirement community in central Florida. The promise of lower cost of living and milder winters, and the fact that many of their friends had moved or died, made it easier for Lucy and Pete to leave the community in Massachusetts where they had spent their entire lives.

Pete has been estranged from his one daughter since his divorce but is in touch with a granddaughter who "found" him when she moved to Florida a few years ago. Lucy has one surviving son in New Jersey and several grandchildren who provide limited financial support and some social support via phone calls and an occasional visit. Pete has enjoyed his life and, despite some difficulty with his vision and hearing, manages to get around well in his familiar surroundings. He is especially fond of tending his orchids in the back porch.

Lucy has just been hospitalized with chronic heart failure and is not expected to make it through the night. A neighbor has brought Pete to the intensive care unit to be with Lucy. Pete states that together he and Lucy managed to provide for each other and served as each other's durable power of attorney, health care surrogate, and in general made it possible for each of them to remain in their home. He wonders what will happen to him after Lucy's death. He knows that many people his age live in nursing homes, but he prefers to stay in his own home. He wonders if the Meals on Wheels will still come to the home, because their eligibility was based on Lucy's diagnosis of chronic heart failure. He hopes he will die soon and quickly like Lucy.

The social worker employed for the Meals on Wheels program has been asked to make a home visit within the week following Lucy's death to reassess Pete's eligibility for services. The social worker had not realized how much her job would involve working with people who have experienced a major loss, whether death of a loved one as in Pete's case, or the accompanying losses that come with illness, disability, and aging.

VERY LATE ADULTHOOD: CHARTING NEW TERRITORY

At 85, 90, 92, and 96, Margaret Davis, Bina Patel, Lucy Rauso, and Pete Mullin are charting new territory. They are a part of the rapidly growing population over age 85. Bina Patel—and perhaps Margaret Davis, Pete Mullin, and Lucy Rauso as well—has surprised herself, as well as her family, by living so long. Never have so many people lived to be so old.

> How does the fact that the current cohort of very late-life adults are charting new territory affect their experience with this life course phase?

In the first edition of this book (1999), the chapter on late adulthood covered all persons 65 and older. The fact that subsequent editions present this content in two chapters ("Late Adulthood" and "Very Late Adulthood") indicates the scope and rapidity of the demographic changes taking place in the United States and other late industrial societies. Within the past 15 to 20 years some researchers have begun to more methodically consider age distinctions after age 65 or 75 given the population growth in this age group.

This chapter summarizes some of the emerging literature on very late adulthood, including those who reach 100—our centenarians. (Much of what appears in the previous chapter on late adulthood applies as well.) However, current knowledge about very late adulthood is still somewhat limited, but growing as the population and related interest grows each year. Given the scarcity of longitudinal studies that have followed a cohort from early adulthood deep into very late adulthood, it is difficult to tease out the cohort effects in the available cross-sectional research.

One issue that comes up at all adult stages is what ages are you including? As you have seen throughout this book, chronological markers of age are arbitrary at best and influenced by biological age, psychological age, social age, and spiritual age. But it is fairly standard to think of 85 and older as old old, oldest old, or very late adulthood. In this chapter, we use "very late adulthood" to describe this life course phase. For the most part, we use "very late-life adults" to describe people in this life course phase, but we also use "old old" and "oldest old" when citing work where those terms are used. However, keep in mind that chronological age may not be the best marker for categorizing very late-life adults (Pipher, 1999). Loss of health might be a better criterion for categorization as very late adulthood or old old. Nevertheless, in keeping with the other chapters in the book, this chapter uses a chronological distinction.

The drawback to using a chronological marker for entry into very late adulthood is that the path through very late adulthood is quite diverse, and for many people over 85, ill health is not a central theme of their lives. In his book *Aging Well*, George Vaillant (2002) reminds us that:

- Frank Lloyd Wright designed the Guggenheim Museum at age 90.

- Dr. Michael DeBakey obtained a patent for a surgical innovation when he was 90.

- Pablo Casals was still practicing cello daily at 91.

- Leopold Stokowski signed a 6-year recording contract at 94.

- Grandma Moses was still painting at 100.

In addition, we would add that:

- Sarah and Elizabeth Delany (1993) published their book *Having Our Say: Our First 100 Years* when Sarah (Sadie) was 103 and Elizabeth (Bessie) was 101.

- Sadie Delany (1997) published *On My Own at 107: Reflections on Life Without Bessie* at the age of 107.

- Daniel Schorr was heard weekly on National Public Radio as the Senior News Analyst until the age of 93, having served as a news journalist for more than 60 years.

So, there is much variation in the age at which health issues take on great importance. Margaret Davis has reached this stage in her mid-80s, Bina Patel reached this stage in her late 80s, Lucy Rauso reached it in her early 90s, and it does not yet seem to have overtaken Pete Mullin in his mid-90s. But sooner or later in very late adulthood, health issues and impending death become paramount.

With our current ways of living, such as busy and pressured work schedules and families geographically scattered, late industrial societies are not organized to make aging easy. That portion of the physical environment attributable solely to human efforts was designed, in the main, by and for those in young and middle adulthood, not for children, persons with various types of disabilities, or older adults. Not only is the current cohort of very late-life adults charting new territory, but as a society we are also charting new territory that will become more and more familiar when the large baby boom generation reaches very late adulthood. What can we learn from people who reach 85 and beyond, and what do social work practitioners need to know to provide meaningful interventions?

As Erik Erikson suggested, we have one and only one life cycle (at least in this incarnation). Sooner or later, each of us will complete that life cycle and die. For some of us, that death will come quickly, but for others, death will come after a protracted period of disease and disability. One of the life tasks of late adulthood is to come to terms with that one and only life cycle, and the evidence suggests that most very late-life adults do that remarkably well. We began this book with a discussion of conception and birth, the starting line of the life course, and in this chapter we end the book with a discussion of death and dying, the finish line of the life course.

VERY LATE ADULTHOOD IN HISTORICAL AND CULTURAL PERSPECTIVE

There have always been those who outlive their cohort group, but greater numbers of people are surpassing the average life expectancy and more are becoming centenarians. Although very few 100-year-old people were known to exist in the United States in 1900, this population increased from 37,306 in 1990 to 65,658 in 2004, a 73% increase (Federal Interagency Forum on Aging-Related Statistics, 2008). Overall, the 85 and older population is the fastest growing segment of the aging population (Hall, 2008), projected to grow from 4.2 million in 2000 to nearly 21 million by 2050, due in part to the baby boomers moving into this category after 2030 (U.S. Bureau of the Census, 2008c).

The phenomenon of the baby boom generation helps explains the current growth in the midlife age groups as well as these projections for future growth in the over 85 population. But what else accounts for the fact that persons 85 and older are the fastest growing segment of the older adult population? Several contributing factors include the following: better health care in early and middle years; earlier diagnosis and improved technology for treatment and overall health care; improved health habits, including less smoking, less consumption of alcohol and saturated fats; and increased exercise in some groups. In addition, fewer people die of infectious diseases. Although increasing numbers of older adults are living with chronic illnesses, fewer have debilitating illnesses (Hooyman & Kiyak, 2008).

Because both group-based and individual differences within this age group are great, one is cautioned against stereotyping very late-life adults in an attempt to describe them (Field & Gueldner, 2001; Innes, 2009). For instance, gender and racial/ethnic differences are embedded within these overall statistics. Life expectancy at birth in the United States in 2006 was about 80.6 years for White females, 76.5 years for Black females, 75.7 years for White males, and 69.7 years for Black males. Life expectancy has not been uniformly calculated for other ethnic groups, but estimates do exist. According to these estimates, an American Indian/Alaska Native (Census Bureau language) born in 1999 to 2001 has a life expectancy of 74.5 years (no gender breakdown available). Hispanic females born in that same period have an estimated life expectancy of 83.7 years and Hispanic males an estimated life expectancy of 77.2 years. The estimated life expectancy of Asian females born in that period is 86.5 years and for Asian males it is 80.9 years (U.S. Department of Health and Human Services, Health Resources and Services Administration, 2009c). Among very late-life adults, women outnumber men 5 to 2, and 4 out of 5 centenarians are women (Federal Interagency Forum on Aging-Related Statistics, 2008). At this point, very late adulthood is largely a woman's territory. Pete Mullin is an exception to this trend. Culturally, the most significant fact is that very late-life adults, like other age groups, are becoming more diverse. The percent by racial category for 2006 and the projected percentage for 2050 are as follows for the population age 65 and over: non-Hispanic White 83%/61%; Black 8%/12%; Hispanic 6%/18%; Asian 3%/8%; and all other races 1%/3% (Federal Interagency Forum on Aging-Related Statistics). These trends should eventually lead to more diversity among the old old.

Census data such as these are of interest to researchers studying *ethnogerontology,* the study of the causes, processes, and consequences of race, national origin, and culture on individual and population aging (Hooyman & Kiyak, 2008). Innes (2009) refers to the cross-cutting interplay of gender, class, and age on aging experiences. Poverty is another indicator of interest with the older population, given decreased earning power and increased health-related expenses. In terms of gender, older women (13%) were almost twice as likely to be poor as older men (7%) in 2004. Overall, the poverty rate increased with age, with 9% of people 65 to 74 and 10% of those over 75 years of age living in poverty. In addition to gender, race and ethnicity are related to poverty among older adults, with non-Hispanic Whites far less likely (7%) than older Blacks (23%) and older Hispanics (19%) to live in poverty (Federal Interagency Forum on Aging-Related Statistics, 2008).

Chapter 1 suggests that one of the themes of the life course perspective is that individual and family development must be understood in historical context. It is particularly important when we interact with very late-life adults to be aware of the historical worlds in which their life journeys have taken place. To help us to keep this in mind, Exhibit 10.1 captures some historical events faced by the current cohort of 92-year-olds (as of 2009). Of course, many of these events have also been shared by young adults, midlife adults, and late-life adults, but at different life phases.

Chapter 1 also discusses the concept of *cohort effects,* which suggests that a historical event affects one cohort differently than it affects subsequent cohorts because of the life phase in which it occurred. Let's look, for example, at the wide use of the computerized worldwide network (the Internet). It was experienced:

- By the current cohort of 85-year-olds when they were in their 70s

- By the current cohort of 65-year-olds when they were in their 50s

- By the current cohort of 45-year-olds when they were in their 30s

- By the current cohort of 25-year-olds when they were in their teens

- By the current cohort of 10-year-olds as a staple of life from infancy

What differences do you think this cohort effect makes for cognitive and social development?

Individuals' cultural backgrounds also play a role in their perceptions of very late adulthood. Margaret Davis has spent her entire life in an impoverished small Appalachian town where families are expected to "take care of their own." Bina Patel lived the first 65 years of her life in India where the very old are expected to live out their lives under the care of their extended families and where traditionally elders are regarded with more respect than in this country.

When He or She Was...	Historical Event
An infant	The United States enters World War I.
3	Women win the right to vote in the United States.
6	The National Woman's Party launches a campaign for an equal rights amendment. First shopping center opens in Kansas City.
11	First color motion picture is demonstrated.
A teenager	Mount Rushmore is completed. "Star Spangled Banner" is adopted as national anthem. The Great Depression becomes a worldwide phenomenon. Social Security legislation is passed.
20-something	American Medical Association approves birth control. U.S. Supreme Court rules Blacks are entitled to first class services on railroad trains. United States enters World War II after the attack at Pearl Harbor. GI Bill is signed, giving broad benefits to returned servicemen.
30-something	Minimum wage is raised from 40 to 75 cents. U.S. Supreme Court outlaws racial segregation in public schools. Rosa Parks refuses to relinquish her seat to a White man on a bus in Montgomery, Alabama. Jonas Salk develops polio vaccine.
40-something	Russia sends first satellite into space, and the United States follows soon behind. The computer microchip is invented. BankAmericard and American Express issue credit cards. Alaska and Hawaii become the 49th and 50th states. President Kennedy becomes the first Catholic president of the United States. John Glenn becomes the first American to orbit Earth. Black Civil Rights Movement reaches its peak. National Organization for Women (NOW) is formed. United States involvement in Vietnam deepens. Lyndon Johnson begins a War on Poverty.
50-something	First human heart transplant takes place. Antiwar sentiment against U.S. involvement in Vietnam intensifies. Student protest movement against war and racism spreads. Neil Armstrong walks on the moon. Thousands flock to music festival at Woodstock, New York. Computerized axial tomography (CAT) scan is developed. Watergate break-in ultimately causes Richard Nixon to resign. OPEC imposes a 6-month oil embargo on the United States. *Roe v. Wade* imposes constitutional protections on abortion. *Saturday Night Live* television show debuts.

When He or She Was . . .	Historical Event
60-something	First "test-tube baby" is born.
	The World Health Organization announces that smallpox has been eradicated worldwide.
	CNN, the first 24-hour TV news channel, is launched.
	IBM introduces the first generation of personal computers.
	MTV is created.
	Sandra Day O'Connor becomes the first woman on the U.S. Supreme Court.
	Astronaut Sally Ride is the first U.S. woman to travel in space.
	Crack cocaine addiction becomes a serious problem.
	Terrorism becomes a fact of life.
	The space shuttle *Challenger* explodes immediately after takeoff.
70-something	Communism loses its hold in Eastern Europe, and the Soviet Union disintegrates.
	The Americans with Disabilities Act recognizes the civil rights of persons with disabilities.
	The U.S. wages Operation Desert Storm to liberate Kuwait from Iraq.
	Basketball star "Magic" Johnson announces on TV that he had contracted HIV.
	Islamic terrorists bomb New York's World Trade Center (the first time) killing five people.
	The computer-based worldwide network (Internet) revolutionizes communications.
	Former President Ronald Reagan reveals he is suffering from Alzheimer's disease.
	War veteran Timothy McVeigh bombs the Alfred P. Murrah Federal Building in Oklahoma City.
	President Bill Clinton signs legislation that ends "welfare as we knew it."
	The Taliban gains control in Afghanistan.
80-something	Researchers in Great Britain clone a sheep.
	The stock market hits unprecedented highs, before deflating.
	On September 11, 2001, terrorists fly hijacked airplanes into the World Trade Center in New York City and the Pentagon.
	Scandals at major big businesses in the United States reveal accounting fraud and greed.
	President George W. Bush wages war on Iraq despite worldwide protests.
	Hurricane Katrina devastates New Orleans and much of the Gulf Coast.
90-something	Internet-based social networking sites, such as Facebook, became popular means of communicating worldwide.
	The biggest economic recession since the Great Depression leads to high unemployment and home foreclosures.
	President Barack Obama becomes the first African American president of the United States.

▲ **Exhibit 10.1**   Historical Events Witnessed by a 92-Year-Old Born in 1917 (as of 2009)

SOURCE: Based on National Geographic Society, 1998; and updated by author.

In contrast, Pete Mullin and Lucy Rauso relocated from Massachusetts to Florida in their 70s, moving away from family and friends. Social workers need to try to understand clients' years in their previous homes and any important historical markers in those settings. They also need to know something about migration experiences as well.

WHAT WE CAN LEARN FROM CENTENARIANS

"Forget about Generation X and Generation Y. Today, the nation's most intriguing demographic is Generation Roman numeral C—folks age 100 and over" (Harvard Health Letter, 2002, p. 1). Phrases such as "special and vibrant" and "expert agers" (Poon et al., 1992, p. 7) have been used to describe centenarians in a variety of studies in the United States, Italy, Sweden, and Denmark.

In the United States, the number of centenarians doubled in the 1980s and again in the 1990s, with approximately 84,330 estimated in 2007 (Hall, 2008). In the next 50 years, midrange projections anticipate that more than 800,000 people in the United States could reach the century mark. The number is expected to grow to 834,000 by 2050 and double every 10 years thereafter (Coles, 2004). Other industrialized countries report similar trends. Future editions of human behavior textbooks might in fact report on another group that demographers are now counting—supercentenarians, people age 110 and over (Coles).

> How will this longevity trend alter our views on appropriate roles for other adult phases?

More than counting numbers, researchers want to know the answers to fundamental questions about human health and longevity, such as:

What does it take to live a long life?

- How much do diet, exercise, and other lifestyle factors matter compared with "good" genes and other genetic factors?

- What is the quality of life among very late-life adults?

- What role do individual characteristics such as gender, race and ethnicity, personality, and socioeconomic status play in longevity?

- What is the role of social support, religion and spirituality, and social environment in longevity?

- Basically, what is the secret?

Much of what is known about centenarians in the United States comes from the work of Leonard Poon and his colleagues in the Georgia Centenarian Study (1992, 2007) and from the New England Centenarian Study (Terry, Sebastiani, Andersen, & Perls, 2008). These and other centenarian studies are trying to understand the interrelationship between multiple variables such as family longevity, gender, personality, environmental support, adaptational skills, individual traits, life satisfaction, and health.

These studies reveal that because the more frail individuals die sooner, those remaining are a relatively robust group. Although these "extra" years are for the most part healthy years, several studies report high levels of dementia (66% in one study and 51% in another) and cardiovascular disease (72%), urinary incontinence (60%), and osteoarthritis (54%) (Hall, 2008). What is

▲ **Photo 10.1**   Fred Hale Sr. smiles as his great-great-granddaughters arrive to celebrate his 113th birthday. In the United States, the number of centenarians doubled in the 1980s and again in the 1990s, totaling more than 80,000 in 2007.

more notable, however, is that the period of serious illness and disability for those who make it to 100 tends to be brief. Some factors thought to contribute to centenarians' robustness in U.S. studies are physical activity such as walking, biking, golfing, and swimming, as well as mental exercise such as reading, painting, and playing a musical instrument. The Okinawa Centenarian Study notes the importance of the traditional lifestyle that includes high physical activity, social integration at all ages, a deep spirituality, adaptability, and optimistic attitudes (cited in Hooyman & Kiyak, 2008). A cluster of personality traits—low neuroticism (reflecting emotional stability), high competence, and high extroversion—were found among centenarians in the Georgia Study (Martin et al., 2006).

However, 100 is still old and life expectancy is short at 100, with most only living one to two more years. In the New England Study, 75% of the people were still living at home and taking care of themselves at 95. By age 102, this number had dropped to 30%—which is still quite remarkable (Terry et al., 2008).

The gender gap in very late adulthood widens further past the age of 100, with female centenarians outnumbering males nine to one. However, men who reach their 100th birthday are, on the whole, more healthy than their female counterparts, reporting lower incidence of dementia and other serious medical problems. Estrogen may give women an edge in longevity. Another possibility is that there may be some protective genes in the X chromosome, of which women have two but men only one. Others theorize that menstruation and systems related to childbirth better equip women to eliminate toxins from the body. Another hypothesis is that genetics are relatively neutral, but women tend to be more social, and these connections are thought to be critical in weathering old age (Harvard Health Letter, 2002).

> How does the gender gap affect the experience of very late adulthood?

In general, findings point to a life course of healthy lifestyles among centenarians: they didn't smoke, or if they did, not for long; didn't overeat, and their diet included many fruits and vegetables; didn't drink heavily; got regular physical exercise for as long as they were able; challenged their minds; had a positive outlook and were able to "shed stress easily"; and maintained close ties with family and friends (Harvard Health Letter). Future cross-cultural studies in which differences in diet, physical activity, and other lifestyle factors can be compared will be important in helping researchers better understand the influence of these multiple contributing variables.

FUNCTIONAL CAPACITY IN VERY LATE ADULTHOOD

Although persons who reach 85 years of age and older demonstrate resilience in the simple fact of their longevity, they continue to face an increased incidence of chronic illness and debilitation with age. Chapter 9 provides a good overview of changes in physiology and mental functioning that begin to occur in late adulthood and only become more prevalent with advancing age. Unfortunately, much of the available information does not distinguish the 85 and older cohort group from the larger 65 and older group. We do know that the likelihood of living in a nursing home increases with age. Among nursing home residents, about 12% are between 65- and 74-years-old, 32% are between 75 and 84, and 45% are 85 and older (Federal Interagency Forum on Aging-Related Statistics, 2008). Many late-life adults enter a nursing home for a period of convalescence after hospitalization and then return to home or another setting.

Although trend data from a four wave National Long Term Care Survey indicated a high level of disability among older adults 85 and over, the rate of disability declined over a 15-year period from 62.0% in 1984 to 55.5% in 1999 (Spillman, 2003). There was no decline in limitations in **activities of daily living (ADLs),** or basic self-care activities, but declines did occur in limitations in **instrumental activities of daily living (IADLs),** which are more complex everyday tasks. (Exhibit 10.2 lists common ADLs and IADLs.) About the same percentage of 85 and older adults received human assistance with at least one ADL in 1984 (19.9%) and 1999 (18.5%). However, the percentage using

ADL equipment increased from 1.9% in 1984 to 5.7% in 1999. The percentage receiving human assistance with IADLs declined from 16.6% in 1984 to 9.8% in 1999. There was no change in the use of community IADL equipment, which occurred in about 1% of the 85 and over population. The percentage of this population in institutions remained at about 20% during this 15-year period.

In general, all persons experience **primary aging,** or changes that are a normal part of the aging process. There is a recognized slowing with age—slowing of motor responses, sensory responses, and intellectual functioning. "Older individuals can do what younger ones can, but it takes more time. The causes of the slowing are not fully understood, although animals of all species become slower as they age" (Seifert, Hoffnung, & Hoffnung, 1997, p. 589). For example, the percentage of older adults in the United States with significant visual loss increases during late and very late adulthood: 9% among the 65- to 75-year-olds, 16% among the 75- to 84-year-olds, and 28% among those over 85. Similarly, in terms of hearing, 23% of 65- to 74-year-olds, 34% of 75- to 84-year-olds, and 51% of persons 85 and older experience significant hearing loss.

How much control do we have over secondary aging?

In addition, many experience **secondary aging** caused by health-compromising behaviors such as smoking or environmental factors such as pollution (Bjorklund & Bee, 2008). Access to health care, ample and nutritious food, safe and affordable housing, safe working conditions, and other factors that influence the quality of life also affect longevity.

Although late adulthood is a time of loss of efficiency in body systems and functioning, the body is an organism that repairs and restores itself as damage occurs. Those persons who live to be 85 and older may be blessed with a favorable genetic makeup. But they may also have found ways to compensate, to prevent, to restore, and to maintain other health-promoting behaviors. One cross-sectional study of individuals age 85 and over found that most report well-being despite their physical and social losses (Johnson & Barer, 1997). Most very late-life adults come to think of themselves in ways that fit their circumstances.

Activities of Daily Living
Bathing
Dressing
Walking a short distance
Shifting from a bed to a chair
Using the toilet
Eating
Instrumental Activities of Daily Living
Doing light housework
Doing the laundry
Using transportation
Handling finances
Using the telephone
Taking medications

▲ **Exhibit 10.2** Common Activities of Daily Living (ADLs) and Instrumental Activities of Daily Living (IADLs)

They narrow the scope of their activities to those that are most cherished, and they carefully schedule their activities to make the best use of their energy and talents.

Sooner or later, however, most very late-life adults come to need some assistance with ADLs and IADLs. As a society, we have to grapple with the question of who will provide that assistance. Currently, most of the assistance is provided by family members. But as families grow smaller, fewer adult children exist to provide such care. A number of family theorists have begun to wonder how multigenerational families might adjust their relationships and better meet long-distance caregiving needs (Cagle, 2008; Harrigan & Koerin, 2007; MetLife/National Alliance for Caregiving, 2004).

Chapter 9 provides an overview of dementia and more specifically Alzheimer's disease (AD). Additional content here emphasizes the importance of ongoing and longitudinal research, needs of families and other caregivers, and also some interesting perspectives about the medicalization of dementia.

To better understand the progression of AD in the oldest old and compare it with the progression among younger older adults, functional (ADLs) and cognitive Mini Mental Status Evaluations, or MMSE, were studied in a cohort of adults who were older than 85 and a cohort of adults who were younger than 85, all living in the community in France (Nourhashemi et al., 2009). The progression of cognitive impairment was the same across groups; however, after adjusting for age and dependency (help with ADLs), the progression of dependence occurred more quickly for the older group. In sum, dementia shortened life, especially among women. Studies such as this have important public health consequences, helping us better prepare for the type of care some of our oldest citizens, and our most rapidly growing age group, may need. Additional studies that follow cohorts over time are needed to learn more about the progression of AD.

Innes (2009) summarizes some thought-provoking theories and commentaries about our current approach to understanding dementia, suggesting that we tend to medicalize dementia so as to then seek a cure for aging and death. Vincent (2006, cited in Innes, p. 22) writes of an antiaging science that tends to perceive "old age as a problem to be resolved rather than a stage of life to be embraced and accepted."

Critical Thinking Questions 10.1

Imagine that you are having lunch with Fred Hale Sr. (from Photo 10.1). How do you imagine the conversation going? What questions would you like to ask him? How do you think life will be different for centenarians in 2050?

RELATIONSHIPS IN VERY LATE ADULTHOOD

Much of what is presented in Chapter 9 under the section called Families in Later Life applies also to very late adulthood. Research that looks specifically at relationship patterns among very late-life adults is limited, but two themes are clear (Carstensen, 2001):

1. Individuals continue to desire and need connections to other people throughout life.

2. In very late adulthood, people interact with others less frequently, but old-old adults make thoughtful selections about the persons with whom they will interact.

> How do current social arrangements threaten and/or support the desire for social connections among very late-life adults?

After intensive interviews with groups that she labeled as young-old and old-old, Mary Pipher (1999) concluded that "the situations that work for people in the young-old stage are not feasible for the old-old. Young-old people may love their mountain cabin or Manhattan townhouse, but old-old people need relatives nearby" (p. 32). That is one of the issues that will need to be explored as our society charts the new demographic territory.

Relationships With Family and Friends

Social isolation is considered to be a powerful risk factor not only for the development of cognitive and intellectual decline in very late adulthood but also for physical illness (McInnis-Dittrich, 2009). A sense of connectedness with family and friends can be achieved in person, on the phone, and more recently via e-mail, chat rooms, blogs, social networking sites, and Skype. The focus in this section is on relationships with people; however, remember that pets, plants, and other connections with nature bring comfort to any age group, including older adults.

Pertinent to very late-life adults is the increased likelihood that one will have lost a spouse/partner, friends, and other family members to death, illness, debilitation, or relocation. Loss is more prevalent during this stage than at other times of life, but there is also greater opportunity for intergenerational family contact as four-, five- and six-generation families become more common.

Siblings often provide companionship and caregiving for each other, as Pete Mullin and Lucy Rauso did in the case study. Siblings are comforting because they are part of one's cohort and also have experienced many of the same family events. In addition, siblings tend to be the most long-standing relationships in a person's life (Hooyman & Kiyak, 2008). Obviously, sibling relationships may range from loving and close to ambivalent, distant, or even hostile. Sharing responsibility for aging parents may create greater closeness between siblings or increase tension. There is some evidence that sibling relationships are especially important sources of support among members of lower socioeconomic groups. Close relationships with sisters in very late adulthood have been found to be positively related to positive mental health, but close relationships with brothers have not been found to have the same benefit (Cicerelli, 1995).

▲ **Photo 10.2**   Loss is more prevalent during this stage than at other times of life, but there is also greater opportunity for intergenerational family contact as four-, five-, and six-generation families become more common.

Relationships with adult children are another important part of the social networks of very late-life adults, as is the case with Margaret Davis. However, one study of a predominantly White sample in San Francisco found that older people prefer to be independent from their children when possible, with adult children serving more as managers of social supports than providing direct care (Johnson & Barer, 1997). Very late-life adults in the United States are in fact institutionalized more often for social reasons than for medical reasons (Hooyman & Kiyak, 2008). One reason for this is that approximately 1 in 5 women 80 and older has been childless throughout her life or has outlived her children. In addition, baby boomers and their children tended to have more divorces and fewer children, decreasing the caregiving options for their parents and grandparents (Hooyman & Kiyak). Racial and ethnic variations exist, however. The proportion of multigenerational relationships that involve parents living with adult children tends to be higher among some families of color, especially African Americans (Hooyman & Kiyak) as well as there being more grandparents raising grandchildren, especially in African American and Latino families (Richardson & Barusch, 2006). Also, as in Bina Patel's case, families with a collectivist heritage prefer to have elderly parents reside with their grown children. It is important to understand and honor historical and cultural expectations of each family when addressing the caregiving and health care needs of aging members. Geographic separation, most often because of the adult child's mobility, tends to interfere with intergenerational interaction among family members, although many manage "intimacy at a distance" (Hooyman & Kiyak, 2008, p. 370) or strong emotional ties despite the separation.

Agencies serving older adults and children often seek opportunities for contact across generations. Whether referred to as inter-, multi-, or cross-generational, many programs recognize the benefits of activities that bring older adults, young parents, teens, and /or children and infants together. Each has something to offer and something to receive. Some examples include elders providing tutoring, telephone support, assistance in day care and school settings or serving as surrogate grandparents; adolescents providing assistance around the yards and homes of older adults, helping to write life reviews, being pen or computer pals; and children and elders interacting around crafts, music, gardening, storytelling, and other activities that create ways of being together (Hooyman & Kiyak, 2008; Slaught & Stampley, 2006).

Relationships with friends remain important in very late adulthood. In general, women have fewer economic resources but more social resources, and richer, more intimate relationships than do older men (Hooyman & Kiyak, 2008). But over time, women tend to outlive partners, friends, and other key members of their social support system, often being left to deal with end-of-life decisions at an advanced age, without the social and perhaps financial support of earlier life.

Relationships with a domestic partner become much less likely in very late adulthood than in earlier phases of life. Very late-life adults have the potential to have shared 60 to 70 years with a spouse or partner. Such long-term relationships, where they do exist, present the risk of tremendous loss when one member of the relationship dies. (Widowhood is presented in more detail in Chapter 9.) Because women outnumber men 5 to 2 over the age of 85, heterosexual men stand a greater chance of starting a new relationship than heterosexual women. With the current gender demographics, lesbian domestic partnerships may have the greatest opportunity for continued long-term relationships in very late adulthood.

Intimacy and Sexuality in Very Late Adulthood

Given the scarcity of men and the fact that many partners and friends have died, many persons 85 and older, especially women, are more alone in this life stage than at other times in their lives. The implications for intimacy and sexuality for heterosexual women are significant. Although minimal research has been conducted specifically about intimacy and sexuality with this age group, some tentative conclusions can be drawn from literature on aging. In particular, a summer 2001 issue of *Generations* focused on "Intimacy and Aging," including the expressions of intimacy in a variety of relationships, challenges related to physical and mental illness, gay and lesbian relationships, and separation of couples because of institutionalization.

Intimacy can be seen as much broader than sexuality, which has been identified as only one of five major components of intimacy (Moss & Schwebel, cited in Blieszner & deVries, 2001). The five major components of intimacy in this view are:

1. *Commitment.* Feeling of cohesion and connection

2. *Affective intimacy.* A deep sense of caring, compassion, and positive regard and the opportunities to express the same

3. *Cognitive intimacy.* Thinking about and awareness of another, sharing values and goals

4. *Physical intimacy.* Sharing physical encounters ranging from proximity to sexuality

5. *Mutuality.* A process of exchange or interdependence

Closeness is inherent in cognitive, affective, and physical intimacy. Communication, or self-disclosure, facilitates intimacy.

Although sexuality is only one aspect of intimacy, it deserves additional attention; it should not be neglected, as it often is in our interaction with older adults. "Research clearly documents that older adults continue to experience significant desire and express overall positive attitudes toward sexuality" (Skultety, 2007, p. 33). The lack of a sexual partner because of divorce, death, or illness is one of the most common reasons for an older adult reporting low interest in sex and little sexual activity. However, there are other physical and psychosocial conditions that impact the sexual interest level, satisfaction, and performance of older adults and social workers need to be comfortable addressing this important aspect of quality of life. Medical conditions such as heart disease, diabetes, arthritis, chronic pain, depression, and medications prescribed to address these and other conditions may reduce or restrict movement or sexual function as well as impact pleasure (Hooyman & Kiyak, 2008; Skultety). Because of these conditions, some very late-life adults are relieved to move into a less sexualized type of intimacy (Pipher, 1999).

Some of the more common psychosocial factors associated with reduced sexual desire or sexual dysfunction include restrictive beliefs about sexuality and aging, role changes because of illness or disability in one or both of the partners, anxiety about sexual function, and psychological disorders. Depression and substance abuse are especially prevalent in older adults with sexual dysfunction. Also, cultural ideals about body image and perceived sexual attractiveness make it more difficult for some older adults to embrace age-related changes (Zeiss & Kasl-Godley, 2001). Many older adults grew up in a time when older people were generally expected to be asexual or not interested in forming new romantic attachments. This cultural conditioning may make it difficult to accept today's greater openness about sexual and romantic relationships, sexual orientation, and varying partnership choices at all ages (Huyck, 2001).

Relationships With Organizations and Community

Relationships with the wider world peak in young and middle adulthood. They grow more constricted as access to social, occupational, recreational, and religious activities becomes more difficult due to decreased mobility and independence, and as the physical and cognitive impairments associated with age increase. As mobility declines, community-based programs such as Meals on Wheels can become important resources to people like Pete Mullin and Lucy Rauso, providing them not only with essential resources such as food but serving also as a connection to the community.

One organizational relationship becomes more likely with advancing age, however. As people live longer and need greater assistance, many move into some form of institutional care. When reading the following discussion about the housing continuum, consider the benefits and the challenges each option presents.

THE HOUSING CONTINUUM

As people live longer, the likelihood of illness and disability increases; spouses, partners, and friends die, and the chance of needing more support than is available to the very late-life adults in their own home increases. Review the section on informal and formal resources in Chapter 9 for a description of the variety of options along the continuum as needs for assistance increase.

How do gender, race, ethnicity, and social class affect access to physical assistance in very late adulthood?

Other than skilled nursing care reimbursed by Medicare and other health insurance, the majority of assistance that people need must be paid for privately. Financing is a major problem for low-income and even many middle-income people. Women, especially women of color, are overrepresented in lower socioeconomic categories, and in very late adulthood, safe, affordable housing options are a serious concern for them.

But even Pete Mullin and Lucy Rauso found housing a problem until they moved in together and pooled their resources. Margaret Davis's daughter, Judy, is determined that Margaret won't go "to a home," but she is also worried about how costly Margaret's care will become in the future.

Current trends indicate that in the future, the following housing options will be in greater demand and hopefully more readily available (Hogstel, 2001):

- Shared housing, shared expenses, and support by family members and friends

- Options for care and assistance in the home with education and support available to family and other informal caregivers

- Housing options such as assisted living facilities, which provide 24-hour assistance, and continuing care retirement communities, which offer a range of services and options for aging in place, without a large initial investment

- Inner-city high-rise retirement communities close to medical, cultural, and recreational activities

- Governmental benefits for home health skilled care services

At the same time, the number of skilled nursing facilities that provide custodial care is likely to decrease, with their role taken over by assisted-living facilities.

Access and receptivity to this continuum of options are influenced by several factors: geographic location, including urban and rural location; socioeconomic status; race; ethnicity; gender; family support; and health care status. In particular, African American and Latino women historically have been admitted to nursing homes at less than one half the rate of Caucasian women, because of access barriers such as location, cost, language, and acceptability (Johnson & Tripp-Reimer, 2001). This underrepresentation may also reflect greater availability of family support, less willingness to institutionalize older family members, or institutionalized discrimination implicit in admission policies (Hooyman & Kiyak, 2008). As social workers, we must recognize the unfortunate reality that, as Mary Pipher (1999) suggests, "being old-old costs a lot of money" (p. 50). Many of the current cohort of very late-life adults have arrived at that stage without any expectation that they would live so long, or any preparation for such a prolonged life. And some arrive there after a full life course of limited resources, as is the situation with Margaret Davis.

▲ **Photo 10.3**   Although those who reach 85 and older demonstrate resilience by surviving, they continue to face increased incidence of chronic illness and debilitation with increased age.

SPIRITUALITY IN VERY LATE ADULTHOOD

When I called my 85-year-old aunt to wish her a happy birthday, my uncle said, "She has been thinking a lot more about the hereafter." Curious about what sounded like a connection to aging and spirituality, I asked her to tell me more. She added with a chuckle, "Yes, I go into a room and I wonder 'What am I here after?'" On one hand, she was trying to make light of some short-term memory loss. But I also know that increasingly she had been questioning the meaning of her life and wondering about her own death, especially since the recent death of her 58-year-old son to cancer.

The following discussion about spirituality refers to aging in general, not specifically to the very late-life adults, but is included in this chapter because of the connection between aging, loss, spirituality, and meaning making. It is when faced by crises—particularly those of severe illness, disability, and/or loss—that one tends to reexamine the meaning of life (Ai, 2000). And although illness, disability, and loss occur throughout life, these challenges tend to accumulate and come at a faster pace during very late adulthood.

Many definitions of spirituality exist. Some social work educators suggest that spirituality refers to the way in which persons seek, find, create, use, and expand personal meaning in the context of their universe, with each person having a unique spiritual style (Ellor, Netting, & Thibault, 1999). More simply, spirituality represents the way in which people seek meaning and purpose in their lives (Nelson-Becker & Canda, 2008; MacKinlay, 2006; Sheridan, 2008). Simmons (2005) reminds us to find a definition or association with the word "spirituality" that fits for each person, given that for some older adults the term may have negative connotations. Based on qualitative interviews with older women, Moremen (2004–2005) concluded that "spiritual questioning—independent of organized religion, significant loss, or impending death—is a natural part of the aging process as one approaches the end of the life span" (p. 309). Dalby (2006) notes that some aspects of spirituality pertain across the life course; however, the following tasks, needs, or changes become more relevant with aging: integrity, humanistic concern, changing relationships with others and greater concern for younger generations, relationship with a transcendent being or power, self-transcendence, and coming to terms with death.

Spirituality late in life is often associated with loss (Armatowski, 2001, p. 75). Over time, losses accumulate in the following areas:

- Relationships: to children, spouses and partners, friends, and others

- Status and role: in family, work, and society

- Health: stamina, mobility, hearing, vision, and other physical and cognitive functions

- Control and independence: finances, housing, health care, and other decision-making arenas

Whether incremental or sudden, these losses can be difficult for members of a society where personal autonomy, independence, and sense of control are highly valued. Ironically, this increased focus on spirituality often coincides with decreased mobility and independence and diminishing social contact, limiting access to religious services and other opportunities for spiritual fulfillment and social support (Harrigan & Farmer, 2000; Watkins, 2001). Spirituality that develops over a lifetime is most responsive to the challenges and the immediacies of old age (Koenig & Brooks, 2002).

This search for meaning is a central element of Erik Erikson's (1963) eighth and final developmental task, referred to as maturity. It involves the challenge of *ego integrity versus ego despair* and centers on one's ability to process what has happened in life and accept these experiences as integral to the meaning of life. Other important spiritual challenges facing elders include transcendence beyond oneself and a sense of connectedness to others (McInnis-Dittrich, 2009). An elderly person's struggle to maintain independence and the ability to make choices in the face of multiple challenges, versus becoming dependent on others, is both psychosocial and spiritual, calling for a social work response addressing both. It is important to remember that culture, race, religious upbringing, and other life experiences may influence each person's spiritual journey.

Fischer (1993) suggests that for older adults, the meaning of spirituality often takes the form of these five themes of advice:

1. Embrace the moment.

2. Find meaning in past memories as part of constructing meaning in your life.

3. Confront your own limitations.

4. Seek reconciliation and forgiveness.

5. Reach out to others through prayer or service.

These themes suggest a process of slowing down, looking back, and reaching out—steps that make sense developmentally as one nears the end of life. Over time, people tend to review their lives, some informally, and others more formally. The more formal life review involves helping people shape their memories and experiences for others, usually family and loved ones. Whether shared orally or in writing, social workers, family members, or others who share a closeness with a person often help facilitate this process of reflection and meaning making (Hooyman & Kiyak, 2008).

The subject of spirituality is separated in this chapter from the subject of dying to emphasize the point that spirituality is not just about preparing for death. Rather, it is about finding meaning in life, transcending oneself, and remaining connected to others (McInnis-Dittrich, 2009).

Critical Thinking Questions 10.2

How do you think very old adults cope with the reality that many of their relatives and friends die while they still live? How have you observed very old adults in your own family cope with the accumulation of loss? Why do you think it is important to people like Margaret Davis to stay in their own homes? The majority of very old adults today are women. What are the implications of this for social policy and programs?

THE DYING PROCESS

The topic of death and dying is almost always in the last chapter of a human behavior textbook, reflecting the hope that death will come as late as possible in life. Obviously, people die in all stages of life, but very late adulthood is the time when dying is considered "on time."

Despite our strong cultural predisposition toward denial of the topic, and perhaps in response to this, there have been a plethora of efforts to talk about death, starting most notably with Elisabeth Kübler-Ross's book *On Death and Dying* in 1969. In recent years, efforts like the Project on Death in America (PDIA) funded by the Soros Foundation and end-of-life initiatives funded by the Robert Wood Johnson Foundation have set out to change mainstream attitudes. The mission of PDIA was to understand and transform the culture and experience of dying and bereavement. It promoted initiatives in research, scholarship, the humanities, and the arts, and fostered innovations in the provision of care, education, and policy. Television programs such as the Public Broadcasting Service's *On Our Own Terms: Moyers on Dying* have facilitated public education and community dialogue.

On a more individual level, many factors influence the ways in which a person adjusts to death and dying, including one's religion and philosophy of life, personality, culture, and other personal traits. Adjustment may also be affected by the conditions of dying. A person with a prolonged terminal illness has more time and opportunity to accept and prepare for his or her own death, or that of a loved one, than someone with an acute and fatal illness or sudden death.

The following adjectives used to describe death are found in both the professional and popular literature: good, meaningful, appropriate, timely, peaceful, sudden, and natural. One can be said to die well, on time, before one's time, and in a variety of ways and places. This terminology reflects an attempt to embrace, acknowledge, tame, and integrate death into one's life. Other language is more indirect, using euphemisms, metaphors, medical terms, and slang, reflecting a need to avoid directly talking about death—suggesting the person is "lost," has "passed away," or has "expired" (DeSpelder & Strickland, 2005). It is important for a social worker to be attentive to words that individuals and families choose because they often reflect one's culture and/or religious background, and comfort level.

As with life, the richness and complexity of death are best understood from a multidimensional framework involving the biological, psychological, social, and spiritual dimensions (Bern-Klug, 2004; Bern-Klug, Gessert, & Forbes, 2001). The following conceptualizations of the dying process help capture the notion that dying and other losses, and the accompanying bereavement, are processes that differ for each unique situation, yet share some common aspects.

In *On Death and Dying,* Kübler-Ross (1969) described stages that people tend to go through in accepting their own inevitable death or that of others, summarized in Exhibit 10.3. Although these stages were written with death in mind, they have application to other loss-related experiences, including the aging process. Given time, most individuals experience these five reactions, although not necessarily in this order. People often shift back and forth between the reactions rather than experience them in a linear way, get stuck in a stage, and/or skip over others. Kübler-Ross suggests that, on some level, hope of survival persists through all stages.

Although these reactions may fit people in general, very late-life adults appear to experience far less denial about the reality of death than other age groups (McInnis-Dittrich, 2009). As they confront their limitations of physical health and become socialized to death with each passing friend and family member, most very late-life adults become less fearful of death. Unfortunately, some professionals and family members may not be as comfortable expressing their feelings related to death and dying, which may leave the elder feeling isolated.

In addition to expressing feelings about death, some very late-life adults have other needs related to dying. A fear of prolonged physical pain or discomfort, as well as fear of losing a sense of control and mastery, trouble very late-life adults most. Some have suggested that older adults who are dying need a safe and accepting relationship in which to express the fear, sadness, anger, resentment, or other feelings related to the pending loss of life and opportunity, especially separation from loved ones (Bowlby, 1980).

Ira Byock (1997, 2004) writes about the importance of certain tasks when facing death, as well as in everyday life given that we never know how much time we have. These tasks address affirmation (I love you; do you love me?); reconciliation (I forgive you; do you forgive me?); and saying goodbye. Farber, Egnew, and Farber (2004) prefer the notion of a

---

Denial: The person denies that death will occur: "This is not true. It can't be me." This denial is succeeded by temporary isolation from social interactions.

Anger: The individual asks, "Why me?" The person projects his or her resentment and envy onto others and often directs the anger toward a supreme being, medical caregivers, family members, and friends.

Bargaining: The individual starts bargaining in an attempt to postpone death, proposing a series of deals with God, self, or others: "Yes, me, but I will do . . . in exchange for a few more months."

Depression: A sense of loss follows. Individuals grieve about their own end of life and about the ones that will be left behind. A frequent reaction is withdrawal from close and loved persons: "I just want to be left alone."

Acceptance: The person accepts that the end is near and the struggle is over: "It's okay. My life has been . . . ."

▲ **Exhibit 10.3** Stages of Accepting Impending Death

SOURCE: Based on Kübler-Ross, 1969.

"respectful death" over a "good death," proposing a process of respectful exploration of the goals and values of individuals and families rather than a prescription for successfully achieving a "good death." This approach reminds us of the importance of a social worker's nonjudgmental relationship that recognizes the uniqueness of each person's situation.

Advance Directives

On a more concrete level, social workers can help patients and families discuss, prepare, and enact health care **advance directives,** or documents that give instructions about desired health care if, in the future, individuals cannot speak for themselves. Such discussions can provide an opportunity to clarify values and wishes regarding end-of-life treatment. Ideally, this conversation has been started prior to very late adulthood (see Chapter 9 regarding a power of attorney and other health care decision-making processes). If not, helping people to communicate their wishes regarding life-sustaining measures, who they want to act on their behalf when they are no longer competent to make these decisions, and other end-of-life concerns helps some people feel empowered.

> How do advance directives promote a continued sense of human agency in making choices?

Since the passage of the Patient Self-Determination Act in 1990, hospitals and other health care institutions receiving Medicare or Medical Assistance funds are required to inform patients that should their condition become life-threatening, they have a right to make decisions about what medical care they would wish to receive (McInnis-Dittrich, 2009). The two primary forms of advance directives are the living will and the durable power of attorney for health care.

A **living will** describes the medical procedures, drugs, and types of treatment that one would choose for oneself if able to do so in certain situations. It also describes the situations for which the patient would want treatment withheld. For example, one may instruct medical personnel not to use any artificial means or heroic measures to keep one alive if the condition is such that there is no hope for recovery. Although a living will allows an individual to speak for oneself in advance, a durable power of attorney designates someone else to speak for the individual.

The promotion of patient rights as described above has helped many patients feel empowered and comforted some family members, but this topic is not without controversy. Because the laws vary from state to state, laypersons and professionals must inquire about the process if one relocates. Also, rather than feeling comforted by knowing a dying person's wishes, some family members experience the burden of difficult decision making that once was handled by the physician. Advance directives are not accepted or considered moral by some ethnic, racial, and religious groups. Because of historical distrust of the White medical establishment, some African American and Hispanic families have preferred life-sustaining treatment to the refusal of treatment inherent in advance directives. Among some religious groups, the personal control represented in advance directives is seen to interfere with a divine plan and is considered a form of passive suicide. As discussed below, social workers must approach each patient and family with an openness to learn about their values and wishes. Volker (2005) cautions health care providers to consider the relevancy of Western values, such as personal control over one's future, in the lives of non-Western patient groups.

Care of People Who Are Dying

Although some associate hospice and palliative care with "giving up" and there being "nothing left to do," in fact hospices provide **palliative care**—a form of care focusing on pain and symptom management as opposed to curing disease. The focus is on "caring, not curing" (National Hospice and Palliative Care Organization [NHPCO], 2008), when curative focused treatment is no longer available or desired. Palliative care attends to the psychological, social, and spiritual issues in addition to the physical needs. The goal of palliative care is achievement of the best possible quality of life for patients and their families.

Hospice is one model of palliative care, borrowed from the British, which began in the United States in the mid-1970s to address the needs of dying persons and their loved ones. It is more a philosophy of care than a place, with the majority of persons receiving hospice services where they live, whether that is their private residence (42%), or a nursing or residential facility (38.3%) (NHPCO, 2008). Hospice services are typically available to persons who have received a prognosis of 6 months or less and who are no longer receiving care directed toward a cure. For instance, the hospital social worker may want to give Bina Patel and her daughter-in-law information about hospice care, as an additional support during her son's illness. Exhibit 10.4 summarizes the key ideas that distinguish hospice care from more traditional care of the dying.

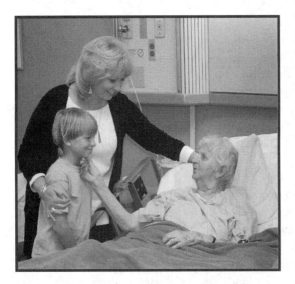

▲ **Photo 10.4** Palliative care focuses on providing pain and symptom management when cure of disease is no longer an option. The patient and the family is the unit of care.

The National Hospice and Palliative Care Organization (NHPCO, 2008) estimates that the United States had 4,700 hospice programs in 2007 serving most rural, suburban, and urban communities in all 50 states. In 2007, approximately 1.4 million patients, representing approximately 38.8% of all deaths in the United States, received hospice services. Four out of five hospice patients are 65 years of age or older and about 37% are 85 and older. When hospice care was first established in the United States in the 1970s, cancer patients accounted for the majority of hospice admissions. Over time, hospices responded to the needs of others with end-stage disease (i.e., renal, lung, kidney, and heart disease, AIDS, and dementia), and in 2006, cancer accounted for less than half of all admissions (41.3%).

Health disparities have been noted in hospice care, as in other health care settings, with persons of color historically being underserved. Initiatives through NHPCO, the Soros Foundation's Faculty Scholar program, as well as the Robert Wood Johnson Foundation's Promoting Excellence in End-of-Life Care have focused on program development specific to the needs of patients and families in African American, Hispanic, Native American, and other communities that have been underserved by more traditional hospice programs (Crawley et al., 2000; NHPCO, 2008).

The patient and the family (as defined by the patient) are the unit of care.

Care is provided by an interdisciplinary team composed of physician, nurse, nurse's aide, social worker, clergy, volunteer, and other support staff who attend to the spectrum of biopsychosocial and spiritual needs of the patient and family.

The patient and family have chosen hospice services and are no longer pursuing aggressive, curative care, but selecting palliative care for symptom management.

Bereavement follow-up is part of the continuum of care available to family members after the patient's death.

▲ **Exhibit 10.4** Key Ideas of Hospice Care

SOURCES: McInnis-Dittrich, 2009; NHPCO, 2008.

Palliative care programs are emerging in hospital settings to address pain and symptom management in patients who might not fit the hospice criteria. Some hospitals have palliative care units specializing in management of short-term, acute symptoms; others have palliative care consultative services that bring their expertise to medical, oncology, pediatric, and other units throughout the hospital (Reith & Payne, 2009).

End-of-Life Signs and Symptoms

Family members and others caring for a person who is dying often experience a great deal of anxiety when they do not have adequate information about the dying process. Most families appreciate knowing what to expect, and honest, factual information can help allay their fears of the unknown (Cagle & Kovacs, 2009; Proot et al., 2004). Pete Mullin, for instance, might benefit by knowing what to expect as his sister was dying. Many hospice services provide written information about symptoms of death for those families anticipating the death of a loved one at home. Exploring how much information people have and want is an important part of the social worker's assessment.

Obviously, each individual situation will differ, but the following general information about symptoms of impending death, summarized in Exhibit 10.5, helps people prepare (Foley, 2005; Reith & Payne, 2009):

- *Temperature and circulation changes.* The patient's arms and legs may become cool to the touch, and the underside of the body may darken in color as peripheral circulation slows down. Despite feeling cool to touch, the patient is usually not aware of feeling cold and light bed coverings usually provide sufficient warmth.

- *Sleeping.* The dying patient will gradually spend more time sleeping and at times may be difficult to arouse as metabolism decreases. The patient will gradually retreat from the surroundings. It is best to spend more time with the patient during the most alert times.

- *Vision and hearing.* Clarity of vision and hearing may decrease. The patient may want the lights on as vision decreases. Hearing is the last of the five senses to be lost, so it should not be assumed that an unresponsive patient cannot hear. Speech should be soft and clear, but not louder than necessary. Many patients talk until minutes before death and are reassured by the exchange of words between loved ones.

- *Secretions in the mouth and congestion.* Oral secretions may become more profuse and collect in the back of the throat. Most people are familiar with the term *death rattle,* a result of a decrease in the body's intake of fluids and inability to cough up normal saliva. Tilting the head to the side and elevating the head of the bed will ease breathing. Swabbing the mouth and lips also provides comfort.

- *Incontinence.* Loss of bowel and bladder function may occur around the time of death or as death is imminent, as the muscles begin to relax. The urine will become very dark in color. If needed, pads should be used to keep skin clean and dry.

- *Restlessness and confusion.* The patient may become restless or have visions of people or things that do not exist. These symptoms may be a result of a decrease in the oxygen circulation to the brain and a change in the body's metabolism. Someone should stay with the patient, reassuring the person in a calm voice, telling the person it is okay to let go, and using oxygen as instructed. Soft music, back rubs, and gentle touch may help soothe the patient. The patient should not be interfered with or restrained, yet prevented from falling.

- *Eating, drinking, and swallowing.* Patients will have decreased need for food and drink. It may be helpful to explain that feeding will not improve the condition, and in fact may exacerbate symptoms. Slight dehydration may be beneficial in reducing pulmonary secretions and easing breathing. Dehydration also generally results in mild renal insufficiency that is mildly sedating. To withhold food and water feels counterintuitive, however, because food and water are usually equated with comfort and sustaining life. Ice chips, small sips of water, and small amounts of food that have meaning to the patient and family are more helpful than forcing food or liquids.

- *Breathing changes.* Breathing may become irregular, with periods of 10 to 30 seconds of no breathing. This symptom is very common and indicates a decrease in circulation and buildup of body waste products. Elevating the head of the bed and turning the patient on his or her side often helps relieve irregular breathing patterns.

- *Pain.* Frequent observation will help determine if the patient is experiencing pain. Signs of discomfort include moaning, restlessness, and a furrowed brow. Medication should be given as instructed or the nurse or physician should be contacted if pain persists.

Dying may take hours or days; no one can predict the time of death even when the person is exhibiting signs and symptoms of dying. The following are signs that death has occurred:

- Breathing stops

- Heart stops beating

- Bowel or bladder control is lost

- No response to verbal commands or shaking

- Eyelids may be slightly open with eyes fixed on a certain spot

- Mouth may fall open slightly as the jaw relaxes

Such explicit discussion of death with those attending a dying family member or close friend may seem upsetting, but this knowledge is also comforting and can help ease the anxiety related to the fear of the unknown. Dying persons are also comforted knowing that their family members have the informational, medical, and social support they need to help them in their caregiving role. It is also helpful to have funeral plans in place so that one phone call to the mortuary facilitates the process, rather than facing difficult and emotional decision making at the time of death.

Lowered temperature and slowed circulation

Deeper and longer periods of sleep

Decreased acuity of vision and hearing

Increased secretions in the mouth and congestion

Incontinence

Restlessness and confusion

Reduced need for eating and drinking and difficulty swallowing

Irregular and interrupted breathing

Increased signs of pain

▲ **Exhibit 10.5**   Signs and Symptoms of Impending Death

SOURCES: Foley, 2005; Reith & Payne, 2009.

LOSS, GRIEF, AND BEREAVEMENT

Loss is a common human experience. There is a great deal of evidence that people of all cultures have strong, painful reactions to the death of the people to whom they are emotionally attached (Doka & Tucci, 2009). Sadness, loneliness, disbelief, and anxiety are only a few of the feelings a person may experience in times of bereavement. The challenge is to refrain from making grief the problem, thereby pathologizing someone's experience; to understand the complexities related to death in a society that has grown increasingly old age and death avoidant (McKnight, 1995). So, we offer the following, cautioning against turning someone's grief into a problem, and encouraging readers to help others understand grief as a normal part of life.

Grief, bereavement, and mourning are words that are often used interchangeably, perhaps because no one word "reflects the fullness of what a death introduces into the life of an individual, family or community" (Silverman, 2004, p. 226). The following definitions help distinguish the various aspects of this process:

- **Loss.** The severing of an attachment an individual has with a loved one, a loved object (such as a pet, home, or country), or an aspect of one's self or identity (such as a body part or function, physical or mental capacity, or role or position in family, society, or other context) (Stroebe, Stroebe, & Hansson, 1993). Silverman (2004) suggests that loss doesn't happen to us; rather it is "something we must make sense out of, give meaning to, and respond to" (p. 226).

- **Bereavement.** The state of having suffered a loss.

- **Grief.** The normal internal reaction of an individual experiencing a loss. Grief is a complex coping process, is highly individualized (Stroebe et al., 1993), and is an expected period of transition (Silverman, 2004).

- **Mourning.** The external expression of grief (Stroebe et al., 1993); the "mental work following the loss of a loved one . . . social process including the cultural traditions and rituals that guide behavior after a death" (Silverman, 2004, p. 226).

The rituals associated with death vary in historical and cross-cultural context (Counts & Counts, 1991; Doka & Tucci, 2009). In some cultures, the dead are buried; in other cultures, the dead are burned and the ashes are spread. In some places and times, a surviving wife might have been burned together with her husband. In the United States, death rituals can be as different as a traditional New Orleans funeral, with street music and mourners dressed in white, or a somber and serene funeral with hushed mourners dressed in black. Some cultures prescribe more emotional expression than others. Some cultures build ritual for expression of anger, and some do not. However, the death rituals in most cultures include the following (Counts & Counts):

- Social support provided to grievers

- Ritual and ceremony used to give meaning to death

- Visual confrontation of the dead body

- A procession

▲ **Photo 10.5** Many factors influence the way in which a person adjusts to death and dying, including one's religion and philosophy of life, personality, and other traits.

Throughout life, we are faced with many losses, some that occur by death but many that occur in other ways as well. For example, Margaret Davis lost her husband to death, but she has also lost a daughter through estrangement and faced much loss of independence and privacy as she increasingly needed assistance from her children and grandchildren. Bina Patel lost a homeland when she immigrated to be near her children, and she lost some physical functioning after her stroke. Pete Mullin lived through the losses related to divorce and retirement. Recently, the burgeoning literature on loss, grief, and bereavement has recognized that there may be similar processes for grieving all losses, including those that occur for reasons other than death. Loss is one of the most important themes in our work as social workers. For example, we encounter loss caused by foster care placement, divorce, disease and disability, migration and immigration, forced retirement, and so on.

> Did these earlier experiences with loss serve as either risk factors or protective factors for coping with current losses?

Theories and Models of Loss

A variety of theorists have sought to make sense of the complex experience of loss. Much of the literature on grief and bereavement for the past century has been influenced by Sigmund Freud's (1917/1957) classic article "Mourning and Melancholia." Freud described the "work of mourning" as a process of severing a relationship with a lost person, object, or ideal. He suggested that this happens over time as the bereaved person is repeatedly faced with situations that remind him or her that the loved person (object or ideal) has, indeed, been lost. From this classic work came the idea of a necessary period of **grief work** to sever the attachment bond, an idea that has been the cornerstone of a number of stage models of the grief process.

In the United States, Erich Lindemann (1944) was a pioneer in grief research. Through his classic study of survivors of a fire at the Cocoanut Grove Lounge in Boston, he conceptualized grief work as both a biological and psychological necessity. The common reactions to loss that he identified included the following:

- Somatic distress, occurring in waves lasting from 20 minutes to an hour, including tightness in throat, choking and shortness of breath, need for sighing, empty feeling in abdomen, lack of muscular power, and intense subjective distress

- Preoccupation with image of deceased, yearning for the lost one to return, wanting to see pictures of the deceased or touch items that are associated with the deceased

- Guilt

- Hostile reactions, toward the deceased as well as toward others

- Loss of patterns of conduct, where the ability to carry out routine behaviors is lost

Lindemann proposed that grief work occurs in stages, an idea that has been popular with other theorists and researchers since the 1960s. A number of stage models of grief have been proposed, and four are presented in Exhibit 10.6. As you can see, although the number and names of stages vary somewhat among theorists and researchers, in general the stage models all agree that grief work progresses from disbelief and feelings of unreality, to painful and disorganizing reactions, to a kind of "coming to terms" with the loss. Parkes (2002) notes that stages or phases run the risk of being misused when taken too literally; however, they have served to remind us that grief is a process that people "need to pass through on the way to a new view of the world" (p. 380).

Typical Stages of Stage Models of Grief	Erich Lindemann (1944)	Elisabeth Kübler-Ross (1969)	John Bowlby (1980)	Therese Rando (1993)
Disbelief and feelings of unreality	Shock and disbelief	Denial and isolation	Numbness	Avoidance
Painful and disorganizing reactions	Acute mourning	Anger Bargaining Depression	Yearning Disorganization Despair	Confrontation
A kind of "getting over" the loss	Resolution	Acceptance	Reorganization	Accommodation

▲ **Exhibit 10.6**   Four Stage Models of Grief

J. William Worden (2009) took a somewhat different approach, writing about the "tasks of mourning" rather than stages of mourning. He considered *task* to be more consistent with Freud's concept of grief work given that the mourner needs to take action and do something rather than passively move through grief. Worden suggests that the following four tasks of mourning are important when a person is adapting to a loss:

Task I: To accept the reality of the loss. Working through denial takes time, because this involves both an intellectual and an emotional acceptance. Some people have traditional rituals that help with this process.

Task II: To work through to the pain of grief. Because people are often uncomfortable with the outward displays of grief, our society often interferes with this task. People often seek a geographic cure or quickly replace the lost person in a new relationship but often still have this task to complete.

Task III: To adjust to an environment in which the deceased is missing. This includes filling roles previously filled by the deceased and making appropriate adjustments in daily activities. In terms of roles, many widows report being thrown the first time they have to cope with a major home repair. Regarding adjustments in daily activities, many bereaved persons report that they find themselves automatically putting the favorite foods of the deceased in their grocery carts.

Task IV: To emotionally relocate the deceased and move on with life. This task was best described by Sadie Delany after the loss of her beloved sister, Bessie, "I don't want to get over you. I just want to find a way to live without you" (Delany with Hearth, 1997).

In the past couple of decades, there has been a critique of the idea of grief work. A highly influential article, "The Myths of Coping With Loss" (Wortman & Silver, 1989), disputed two major themes of the traditional view of grief work: distress is an inevitable response to loss, and the failure to experience distress is a sign of improper grieving. In fact, a number of researchers have found that those who show the highest levels of distress immediately following a loss are more likely than those who show little distress to be depressed several years later. In another vein, Silverman (2004) challenges the notion of "tasks," which suggests something can be completed, recommending that we focus instead on "issues and processes" (p. 237).

Given the tremendous diversity among individuals based on gender, culture, personality style, and life experience, as well as the various circumstances surrounding a loss, the grieving process is not easily defined, but theorists and practitioners continue to try and provide some framework for understanding the process. Camille Wortman and Roxanne Silver (1990) proposed that at least four different patterns of grieving are possible: normal, chronic, delayed, and absent. Worden (2009) elaborated on these patterns:

1. *Normal or uncomplicated grief.* Relatively high level of distress soon after the loss encompassing a broad range of feelings and behaviors, followed by a relatively rapid recovery.

2. *Chronic or prolonged grief.* High level of distress continuing over a number of years without coming to a satisfactory conclusion.

3. *Delayed grief (or inhibited, suppressed, or postponed grief).* Little distress in the first few months after the loss, but high levels of distress at some later point.

4. *Absent grief.* No notable level of distress either soon after the loss or at some later time. Some question this notion and wonder if it is not absent, but masked or delayed; observation over time is important.

In their research, Wortman and Silver (1990) found absent grief in 26% of their bereaved participants, and other researchers have had similar findings (Levy, Martinkowski, & Derby, 1994). These same researchers have found a high rate (more than 30%) of chronic grief.

Given these critiques of traditional models of grief, theorists and researchers have looked for other ways to understand the complex reactions to loss. Recently, the study of bereavement has been influenced by developments in the study of stress and trauma reactions. Research on loss and grief has produced the following findings (Bonanno & Kaltman, 1999):

- It is the evaluation of the nature of the loss by the bereaved survivor that determines how stressful the loss is.

- How well a coping strategy works for dealing with loss depends on the context and the nature of the person-environment encounter.

- Maintaining some type of continued bond with the deceased, a strong sense of the continued presence of the deceased, may be adaptive.

- The capacity to minimize negative emotions after a loss allows the bereaved to continue to function in areas of personal importance.

- Humor can aid in the grief process by allowing the bereaved to approach the enormity of the loss without maximizing psychic pain or alienating social support.

- In situations of traumatic loss, there is a need to talk about the loss, but not all interpersonal relationships can tolerate such talk.

Martin and Doka's (2000) model of adult bereavement explores the role of gender, culture, and other characteristics that influence a person's grieving style. This model includes two adaptive grieving styles that they theorize to be at two ends of a continuum: the internal experience of loss and the outward expression relating to the loss. Doughty (2009) surveyed 20 experts in the field of thanatology to examine their opinions about this model. Consensus was found on the following items: the uniqueness of the griever; recognition of multiple factors influencing the grief process; the use of both cognitive and affective strategies in adapting to bereavement; and most people experience both internal and external pressures to grieve in certain ways.

In summary, grief is a multidimensional process—a normal life experience—that theorists and practitioners continue to try to understand. There seems to be general agreement that culture, past experience, gender, age, and other personal characteristics influence how one copes with loss.

Culture and Bereavement

It is important to be informed about the impact of each individual's culture and how religious and spiritual practices affect the individual bereavement process. Historically, because of sensitivity about racial issues, there has been some hesitancy to address issues of race and ethnicity in the health care arena. Unfortunately, when ethnic differences are not taken into consideration, too often it is assumed that the norm is White and middle class. As the United States becomes increasingly multiracial and ethnically diverse, you will need to continually inform yourself about cultural, ethnic, and religious traditions of individuals and families with whom you work so as to avoid becoming unintentionally ethnocentric. Del Rio (2004) reminds us that our own view of reality is "always socially constructed, does not account for all the phenomena of life, and should not take precedence over a client's view of reality" (p. 441). Given the tremendous diversity within groups as well as among them, the individual and the family are your best teachers. Ask them, "What do I need to know about you (your family, cultural, or religious and spiritual traditions) so that I can be of help to you?"

> Why is it important for social workers to learn about cultural variations in grief and bereavement?

Some suggest that all people feel the same pain with grief, but that cultural differences shape our mourning rituals, traditions, and behavioral expresses of grief (Cowles, 1996). In the United States, we tend to psychologize grief, understanding it in terms of sadness, depression, anger, and other emotions (McKnight, 1995). There may be a cohort divide in the United States on this issue, however, and the current generation of very late-life adults are often much more matter-of-fact about death than younger adults are (Pipher, 1999). In China and other Eastern societies, grief is more often somatized, or expressed in terms of physical pain, weakness, and other physical discomfort (Irish, Lundquist, & Nelsen, 1993). We need to be aware of the possibility of somatization when working with many clients from different cultures as well as with some older adults of Anglo heritage.

Cultural variation also exists regarding the acceptable degree of emotional expression of grief, from "muted" to "excessive" grief, with many variations between these two ends of the continuum. Gender differences exist in many cultures, including the dominant U.S. culture, where men have learned to be less demonstrative with emotions of grief and sadness than women (Murray, 2001).

Mourning and funeral customs also differ a great deal. For example, among African Americans, customs vary depending on whether the family is Southern Baptist, Black Catholic, northern Unitarian, Black Muslim, or Pentecostal (Perry, 1993); in fact "religion may be a stronger determining factor than race alone" (Barrett, 2009, p. 85). Perhaps because of some vestiges of traditional African culture and slavery, a strong desire to celebrate the person's life and build up a sense of community, funerals are important external expressions of mourning in many Black communities.

The complex, and at times impersonal, health care system in the United States often is insensitive to cultural traditions. In some cultures, proper handling of the body, time to sit with the deceased, and other traditions are important. For example, the Hmong believe that proper burial and worship of ancestors directly influence the safety and health of the surviving family members. They believe that the spiritual world coexists with the physical world. Because they believe that each person has several souls, it is important that the souls be "sent back appropriately" (Bliatout, 1993, p. 83).

Tremendous diversity exists within the Latino cultures in the United States, depending upon country of origin and degree of acculturation; however, for the most part these subgroups share several common Latino values, language, religion, and traditional family structure. Some Latino cultural themes that can influence care at the end of life include: *familismo* (emphasis of family over individual); *personalismo* (trustbuilding over time based on mutual respect); *jerarquismo* (respect for authority and hierarchy); *presentismo* (focus on present more than past or future); *espiritismo* (belief that good and evil spirits can impact health); and *fatalism* (fate determines life outcomes) (Sandoval-Cros, 2009).

Given approximately 350 distinct Native American tribes in the United States and more than 596 different bands among the First Nations in Canada, and because of the differing degrees of acculturation and religious practices from one group to another, it is difficult to provide useful generalizations about this cultural group (Brokenleg & Middleton, 1993). However, honoring cultural norms of each person will help health care professionals learn about ceremonies and customs a Native American may find comforting when facing death or when grieving. Most understand death as a natural end of life, not fearing it, and although it may be a painful separation for the living who are left behind, rituals exist to help with the transition (Cox, 2009).

These are only a few examples of the rich diversity among some of the peoples in our increasingly multiethnic society. You cannot possibly know all the specific traditions, but it is important to assume that you do not know, and therefore to inquire of the family how you can assist them.

THE LIFE COURSE COMPLETED

In this book, we have explored the seasons of the life course. These seasons have been and will be altered by changing demographics. Current demographic trends have led to the following predictions about the future of the life course (Hogstel, 2001):

- The size and inevitable aging of the baby boom generation will continue to drive public policy debate and improve services for very late-life adults.

- Women will continue to live longer than men.

- Educational attainment levels of the very late-life adult will increase, with more women having been in the labor force long enough to have their own retirement income.

- Six-generation families will be common, although the generations will live in geographically dispersed settings, making care for very late-life adults difficult.

- Fewer family caregivers will be available for very late-life adults because the baby boomers and their children tended to marry later and have fewer children. At the same time, the need for informal or family caregiving to supplement formal care will be increasing.

- Assessment and management of health care, as well as health care education, will increasingly be available via telephone, computer/Internet, and television, providing greater access in remote areas but running the risk of rendering the service more impersonal.

As a society, we have a challenge ahead of us, to see that newborns begin the life course on a positive foot and that everyone reaches the end of life with the opportunity to see his or her life course as a meaningful whole. As social workers, we have a responsibility to take a look at our social institutions and evaluate how well they guarantee the opportunity for each individual to meet basic needs during each season of life, as well as whether they guarantee the opportunity for interdependence and connectedness appropriate to the season of life.

Critical Thinking Questions 10.3

What does death mean to you? Is it the final process of life, the beginning of life after death, a joining of the spirit with a cosmic consciousness, rest and peace, a continuation of the spirit, etc.? How has culture influenced your understanding of the meaning of death? How has religion influenced your understanding of the meaning of death? How might your understanding of the meaning of death affect your work with someone who is dying? What does it mean to live a good life?

IMPLICATIONS FOR SOCIAL WORK PRACTICE

All the implications for practice listed in Chapter 9 on late adulthood apply in very late adulthood as well. See the following resources for additional information about social work practice and end-of-life related patient and family care (Csikai & Jones, 2007; Hooyman & Kramer, 2006; Kashushin, & Egan, 2008; Kovacs, Bellin, & Fauri, 2006). In addition, the following practice principles focus on the topics of spirituality, relationships, the dying process, and loss, grief, and bereavement:

- Given the link between aging, disability, loss, and spirituality, consider doing a spiritual assessment to find ways to help very late-life adults address increasing spiritual concerns.

- Assess the impact of loss in the lives of your very late-life clients—loss of partners, friends, children, and other relationships, but also loss of role, status, and physical and mental capacities.

- Recognize and be delighted when very late-life adults are grateful for their "extra time."

- Assess the loneliness and isolation that may result from cumulative loss.

- Be informed about available formal and informal resources to help minimize isolation for older adults.

- Be aware of your own feelings about death and dying so that you may become more comfortable being physically and emotionally present with clients and their loved ones.

- Identify literature, cultural experiences, key informants, and other vehicles for ongoing education about your clients' cultural, ethnic, and religious practices that are different from your own. Remember, the client may be your best teacher.

- Assume that the very late-life adult continues to have needs for intimacy. Stretch your conceptualization of intimacy to include any relationship the person might have, wish for, or grieve, including a spouse or partner, friends, children, self, and community.

KEY TERMS

activities of daily living (ADLs)	hospice	mourning
advance directives	instrumental activities of daily	palliative care
bereavement	living (IADL)	primary aging
grief	living will	secondary aging
grief work	loss	

ACTIVE LEARNING

1. Take an inventory of your assumptions about what it is like to be 85 and older. What are your biggest fears? What do you think would be the best part of reaching that age? Think about how these assumptions might influence your feelings about working with clients in very late adulthood.

2. You have recently been hired as the social worker at an assisted living facility, and Margaret Davis, Bina Patel, and Pete Mullin have all recently moved in. All three are unhappy to be there, preferring their prior living arrangements. Bina's son and Pete's sister recently died. You want to help them share some of their recent experiences related to loss but want to be sensitive to the diversity in life experience that they bring with them. What barriers might you face in accomplishing your goal? What are some ways that you might begin to help them?

3. Think about possible relationships between poverty, gender, sexual orientation, and race as one ages in the United States today. Identify ways that social workers can influence policies that affect housing, health care, and other essential services directly related to quality of life in very late-life adulthood.

WEB RESOURCES

AARP
www.aarp.org

Site maintained by American Association of Retired Persons contains health and wellness information, information on legislative issues, and links to online resources regarding aging.

American Society on Aging
www.asaging.org

Site provides general information about aging-related services, including: a link to LGBT Aging Issues Network (LAIN) and LGBT Aging Resources Clearinghouse (LARC); information on older adults, alcohol, medication, and other drugs.

Duke Institute on Care at the End of Life
www.iceol.duke.edu

Site provides information on spirituality, cultural diversity, and end-of-life care.

Generations United
www.gu.org

Generations United (GU) is the national membership organization focused solely on improving the lives of children, youth, and older people through intergenerational strategies, programs, and public policies. See site for links to resources, bibliographies, and so on.

Hospice Foundation of America
www.hospicefoundation.org

Site contains information on locating hospice programs, a newsletter, and links to resources.

National Association of Social Workers
www.naswdc.org/aging.asp

Site provides access to resources related to aging and social work practice, including some online courses.

National Hospice and Palliative Care Organization
www.nhpco.org

Site maintained by the National Hospice and Palliative Care Organization contains information on the history and current development of hospice and palliative care programs, advance directives, grief and bereavement, caregiving, and other related topics.

National Caregivers Library
www.caregiverslibrary.org

National Caregivers Library was created by FamilyCare America, Inc. and makes resources available to caregivers through alliances with professionals, businesses and other organizations serving seniors and caregivers.

National Center for Gerontological Social Work Education
www.cswe.org/CenterInitiatives/GeroEdCenter.aspx

Site maintained by the Council on Social Work Education Gero-Ed Center (National Center for Gerontological Social Work Education) provides resources for aging and end-of-life care.

Office on Aging
www.apa.org/pi/aging

Site presented by the Office of Aging of the American Psychological Association contains news briefs, publications, and links to aging organizations.

References

Aarnoudse-Moens, C. S., Weisglas-Kuperus, N., van Goudoever, J. B., & Oosterlaan, J. (2009). Meta-analysis of neurobehavioral outcomes in very premature and/or very low birth weight children. *Pediatrics, 124*(2), 717–728.

AARP. (2001). *In the middle: A report on multicultural boomers coping with family and aging issues.* Washington, DC: Author.

Abdel-Latif, M. E., Bajuk, B., Oel, J., Vincent, T., Sutton, L., & Liu, K. (2006). Does rural or urban residence make a difference to neonatal outcome in premature birth? A regional study in Australia. *Archives of Disease in Childhood: Fetal and Neonatal Edition, 91*(4), F251–F256.

Achenbaum, W. A., & Bengtson, V. C. (1994). Re-engaging the disengagement theory of aging: Or the history and assessment of theory development in gerontology. *The Gerontologist, 34*, 756–763.

Achievements in Public Health: 1900–1999. (1999). Healthier mothers and babies. *Morbidity and Mortality Weekly, 49*(38), 849–858.

Adair, L. S., & Gordon-Larsen, P. (2001). Maturational timing and overweight prevalence in US adolescent girls. *American Journal of Public Health, 9*(4), 642–644.

Adam, E. K., & Chase-Lansdale, L. P. (2002). Home sweet home(s): Parental separations, residential moves, and adjustment problems in low-income adolescent girls. *Developmental Psychology, 38*(5), 792–805.

Adamczyk, A., & Felson, J. (2006). Friends' religiosity and first sex. *Social Science Research, 35*(4), 924–947.

Adams, G. R., & Marshall, S. K. (1996). A developmental social psychology of identity: Understanding the person-in-context. *Journal of Adolescence, 19*, 429–442.

Adler, L. (1993). Introduction and overview. *Journal of Education Policy, 8*(5–6), 1–16.

Administration on Aging. (2005). *A profile of older Americans: 2005.* Washington, DC: U.S. Department of Health and Human Services.

Administration on Aging. (2006a). *Aging in the 21st century—Demography.* Washington, DC: U.S. Department of Health and Human Services. Retrieved July 7, 2006, from http://www/aoa/gov/prof/Statistics/future_growth/aging21/demography.asp

Administration on Aging. (2006b). *A statistical profile of Hispanic older Americans aged 65+.* Washington, DC: U.S. Department of Health and Human Services. Retrieved July 7, 2006, from http://www/aoa/gov/prof/Statistics.

Administration on Aging. (2006c). *A statistical profile of black older Americans aged 65+.* Washington, DC: U.S. Department of Health and Human Services. Retrieved July 7, 2006, from http://www/aoa/gov/prof/Statistics.

Administration on Aging, U.S. Department of Health and Human Services. (2008). *A profile of older Americans: 2008.* Retrieved May 19, 2010, from http://www.csrees.usda.gov/new/economics/pdfs/profile_older_americans_2008.pdf.

Advanced Fertility Center of Chicago. (2009). *Cost of IVF at the advanced fertility clinic of Chicago.* Retrieved December 27, 2009, from http://www.advancedfertility.com/ivfprice.htm.

Advocates for Youth. (2002). *Adolescent sexual health in Europe and the U.S.: Why the difference?* Retrieved June 6, 2002, from http://www.advocatesforyouth.org.

Afable-Munsuz, A., & Braveman, P. (2008). Pregnancy intention and preterm birth: Differential associations among a diverse population of women. *Perspectives on Sexual and Reproductive Health, 40*(2), 66–73.

Agency for Healthcare Research and Quality. (2006). Preventing disability in the elderly with chronic disease. *Research in Action, 3.* Retrieved July 7, 2006, from http://www.ahrq.gov/research/elderis.htmAging.

The AGS Foundation for Health in Aging. (2009). *Aging in the know: Delirium (sudden confusion).* Retrieved March 3, 2010, from http://www.healthinaging.org/agingintheknow/chapters_print_ch_trial.asp?ch=57.

Ahman, E. L., & Shah, I. H. (2006). Contraceptive use, fertility, and unsafe abortion in developing countries. *The European Journal of Contraception and Reproductive Health Care: The Official Journal of the European Society of Contraception, 11*(2), 126–131.

Ahrens, K., DuBois, D., Richardson, L., Fan, M., & Lozano, P. (2008). Youth in foster care with adult mentors during adolescence have improved adult outcomes. *Pediatrics, 121*(2), 246–252.

Ai, A. L. (2000). Spiritual well-being, spiritual growth, and spiritual care for the aged: A cross-faith and interdisciplinary effort. *Journal of Religious Gerontology, 11*(2), 3–28.

Ainsworth, M., Blehar, M., Waters, E., & Wall, S. (1978). *Patterns of attachment: A psychological study of the strange situation.* Hillsdale, NJ: Lawrence Erlbaum.

Aitken, R. J., Baker, M. A., Doncel, G. F., Matzuk, M. M., Mauck, C. K., & Harper, M. J. K. (2008). As the world grows: Contraception in the 21st century. *Journal of Clinical Investigation, 118*(4), 1330–1343.

Aitken, R. J., Skakkebaek, N. E., & Roman, S. D. (2006). Male reproductive health and the environment. *Medical Journal of Australia, 185*(8), 414–416.

Ajrouch, K., Antonucci, T., & Janevic, M. (2001). Social networks among blacks and whites: The interaction between race and age. *Journal of Gerontology: Social Sciences, 56,* S112-S118.

Akbulut, Y. (2007). Bilingual acquisition and cognitive development in early childhood: Challenges to the research paradigm. *Elementary Education Online, 6*(3), 422–429. Retrieved January 19, 2010, from http://ilko-gretim-online .org.tr/vol6say3/v6s3m32.pdf.

Alan Guttmacher Institute. (1999). *Teen sex and pregnancy.* Retrieved June 6, 2006, from http://www.agi-usa.org/pubs/ fb_teen_sex.html.

Alan Guttmacher Institute. (2005). *Facts in brief: Contraceptive use.* Retrieved December 13, 2006, from http://www.guttmacher .org/pubs/fb_const_use.html.

Alan Guttmacher Institute. (2006a). *Facts on American teens' sexual and reproductive health.* Retrieved November 29, 2006, from http://www.guttmacher.org/pub/fb_ATSRH.html.

Alan Guttmacher Institute. (2006b). *Facts on sexually transmitted infections in the United States.* Retrieved November 20, 2006, from http://www.guttmacher.org/pbus/fb_sti.html.

Aldwin, C., & Gilmer, D. (2004). *Health, illness, and optimal aging: Biological and psychosocial perspectives.* Thousand Oaks, CA: Sage.

Alexander, H. A., & Carr, D. (2006). Philosophical issues in spiritual education and development. In E. C. Roehlkepartain, P. E. King, L. Wagener, & P. L. Benson (Eds.), *The handbook of spiritual development in children and adolescence* (pp. 34–45). Thousand Oaks, CA: Sage.

Al-Hasani, S., & Zohni, K. (2008). The overlooked role of obesity in infertility. *Journal of Family and Reproductive Health, 2*(3), 115–122.

Alink, L., Mesmon, J., & van Zeijl, J. (2006). The early childhood aggression curve: Development of physical aggression in 10- to 50-month-old children. *Child Development, 77*(4), 954–966.

Allen, E. K., & Marotz, L. R. (2003). *Developmental profiles: Pre-birth through twelve* (4th ed.). Canada: Delmar Learning/Thomson.

Allen, K., Blieszner, R., & Roberto, K. (2001). Families in the middle and later years: A review and critique of the research in the 1990s. *Journal of Marriage and the Family, 62,* 911–926.

Allen, R. H., & Goldberg, A. B. (2007). Emergency contraception: A clinical review. *Clinical Obstetrics & Gynecology, 50*(4), 927–936.

Allen, V. M., Wilson, R. D., & Cheung, A. (2006). Pregnancy outcomes after assisted reproductive technology. *Journal of Obstetrics and Gynaecology Canada, 28*(3), 220–250.

Allen-Meares, P., Washington, R. O., & Walsh, B. (1996). *Social work services in schools* (2nd ed.). Englewood Cliffs, NJ: Prentice Hall.

Allison, B., & Schultz, J. (2004). Parent-adolescent conflict in early adolescence. *Adolescence, 39,* 101–119.

Allison, K., Lavery, M., & Sarwer, D. (2009). Obesity and reproductive functioning: Psychiatric considerations. *Primary Psychiatry, 16*(3), 35–40.

Als, H., Heidelise, A., & Butler, S. (2008). Newborn individualized developmental care assessment program: Changing the future for infants and families in intensive care and special care nurseries. *Early Childhood Services: An Interdisciplinary Journal of Effectiveness, 2*(1), 1–19.

Al-Saleh, I., Coskun, S., Mashhour, A., Shinwari, N., El-Doush, I., Billedo, G., et al. (2008). Exposure to heavy metals (lead, cadmium and mercury) and its effects on the outcome of in-vitro fertilization treatment. *International Journal of Hygiene and Environmental Health, 211*(5–6), 560–579.

Altken, R. J., Wingate, J. K., De Iullis, G. N., Koppers, A. J., & McLaughlin, E. A. (2006). Cis-unsaturated fatty acids stimulate reactive oxygen species generation and lipid peroxidation in human spermatozoa. *The Journal of Clinical Endocrinology and Metabolism, 91*(10), 4154–4163.

Alviggi, C., Humaidan, P., Howles, C. M., Tredway, D., & Hillier, S. G. (2009). Biological versus chronological ovarian age: Implications for assisted reproductive technology. *Reproductive Biology and Endocrinology, 7,* 101.

Alwin, D., & McCammon, R. (2003). Generations, cohorts, and social change. In J. Mortimer & M. Shanahan (Eds.), *Handbook of the life course* (pp. 23–49). New York: Kluwer Academic/Plenum Publishers.

Alwin, D., McCammon, R., & Hofer, S. (2006). Studying baby boom cohorts within a demographic and developmental context: Conceptual and methodological issues. In S. Whitbourne & S. Willis (Eds.), *The baby boomers grow up: Contemporary perspectives on midlife* (pp. 45–71). Mahwah, NJ: Lawrence Erlbaum.

Alzheimer's Association (2009). *2009 Alzheimer's disease facts and figures.* Chicago: Author.

Amato, P. R. (2003). Family functioning and child development: The case of divorce. In R. M. Lerner, F. Jacobs, & D. Wertlieb (Eds.), *Handbook of applied developmental science, Vol. 1* (pp. 319–338). Thousand Oaks, CA: Sage.

American Academy of Family Physicians. (2005). *Natural family planning.* Retrieved August 5, 2006, from http://familydoc-tor.org/126.xml?printxml.

American Academy of Pediatrics. (1999). *Caring for your baby and young child.* New York: Bantam.

American Academy of Pediatrics-Committee on Adolescence. (2005). Emergency contraception: Policy statement. *Pediatrics, 116*(4), 1026–1035.

American Association of Birth Centers. (2007). *Birth centers lead cost containment efforts while providing quality care.* Retrieved August 9, 2009, from http://www.birthcenters .org/pdf/bcexp.pdf.

American Association of Retired Persons. (2003). *Global aging: Achieving its potential.* Washington, DC: Author.

American Association of University Women. (1995). *How schools shortchange girls.* New York: Marlowe.

American College of Nurse-Midwives (2005). *Position statement on home birth.* Retrieved May 19, 2010, from http://mid-wife.org.siteFiles/position/homeBirth.pdf.

American College of Nurse-Midwives. (2008). *Midterm Annual Report 2008.* Retrieved August 9, 2009, from http://www .midwife.org/annualreport2008.pdf.

American College of Nurse-Midwives. (2009). *American College of Nurse-Midwives responds to AMA resolutions on homebirth and physician oversight of midwives.* Retrieved August 9, 2009, from http://www.midwife.org/ACNM_Response_to_ AMA.cfm.

The American Congress of Obstetricians and Gynecologists. (2008). *ACOG statement on home births* [ACOG news release]. Retrieved May 19, 2010, from http://www.acog.org/ from_home/publications/press_releases/nr02–06–08–2.cfm.

American Medical Association House of Delegates. (2008). *Resolution 205(A-08). Home deliveries.* Retrieved May 19, 2010, from http://www.aolcdn.com/tmz_documents/0617_ ricki_lake_wm.pdf.

American Medical Association. (2002). *Emergency contraception.* Retrieved September 9, 2002, from http://www .ama-assn.org/special/contrmergenca/support/ppfa/ emergenc.htm.

American Pregnancy Association. (2009). *Preimplantation genetic diagnosis: PGD.* Retrieved January 3, 2010, from http://www .americanpregnancy.org/infertility/preimplantiongenetic diagnosis.htm.

American Pregnancy Association. (2010). *Fetal alcohol spectrum disorders (FASD); fetal alcohol syndrome (FAS).* Retrieved January 3, 2010, from http://www.americanpregnancy.org/ pregnancycomplications/fetalalcohol.html.

American Psychiatric Association. (2000a). *Diagnostic and statistical manual of mental disorders* (4th ed. Text rev.). Washington, DC: American Psychiatric Association.

American Psychiatric Association Work Group on Eating Disorders. (2000b). Practice guidelines for the treatment of patients with eating disorders (revision). *American Journal of Psychiatry, 157*(1 Suppl), 1–39.

American Psychological Association. (1996). *Violence and the family: Report of the APA President Task Force on Violence and the Family.* Washington, DC: Author.

American Public Health Association. (2001). *Increasing access to out-of-hospital maternity services through state-regulated and nationally-certified direct-entry midwives. APHA Public Policy Statements, 1948-present, cumulative.* Washington, DC: APHA. Retrieved May 19, 2010, from http://www.cfwid-wifery.org/pdf/apha.pdfhttp://www.uptodate.com/patients/ content/topic.do?topicKey=~1010wKntyU7Dhn1.

American Society for Reproductive Medicine. (2002). Human immunodeficiency virus and infertility treatment. *Fertility and Sterility, 77*(2), 218–222.

American Youth Policy Forum. (2009). *The forgotten half revisited: American youth and young families, 1988–2008.* Retrieved February 8, 2010, from http://www.aypf.org/pressreleases/ pr18.htm.

Ameta, E. S., & Sherrard, P. A. (1995). Inquiring into children's social worlds: A choice of lenses. In B. A. Ryan, G. R. Adams, T. P. Gullotta, R. P. Weissberg, & R. L. Hampton (Eds.), *The family-school connection: Theory, research, and practice* (pp. 29–74). Thousand Oaks, CA: Sage.

An, J., & Cooney, T. (2006). Psychological well-being in mid to late life: The roles of generativity development and parent-child relationships across the lifespan. *International Journal of Behavioral Development, 30*(5), 410–421.

Ananth, C. V., Liu, S., Joseph, K. S., Kramer, M. S., & Fetal and Infant Health Study Group of the Canadian Perinatal Surveillance System. (2008). A comparison of foetal and infant mortality in the United States and Canada. *International Journal of Epidemiology, 38*(2), 480–489.

Anderson, C. (2005). Single-parent families: Strengths, vulnerabilities, and interventions. In B. Carter & M. McGoldrick, *The expanded family life cycle: Individual, family, and social perspectives* (3rd ed., pp. 399–416). Boston: Allyn & Bacon.

Anderson, D. A. (1994). Lesbian and gay adolescents: Social and developmental considerations. *High School Journal, 77* (1–2), 13–19.

Anderson, L. (2008, June 29). Teen pregnancies at 30-year-low: Recent rise could be anomaly or sign of bigger problem. *Chicago Tribune*, p. 3.

Anderson, M., Kaufman, J., Simon, T. R., Barrios, L., Paulozzi, L., Ryan, G., et al. and the School-Associated Violent Deaths Study Group. (2001). School-associated violent deaths in the United States, 1994–1999. *Journal of American Medical Association, 286*, 2695–2702.

Anderson, R. E., & Anderson, D. A. (1999). The cost-effectiveness of home birth. *Journal of Nurse Midwifery, 44*(1), 30–35.

Anderson, R. N., & Smith, B. L. (2003). Deaths: Leading causes for 2001. *National Vital Statistics Report, 52*(9), 1–86.

Andrews, L. B. (1994). *Assessing genetic risks: Implications for health and social policy.* Washington, DC: National Academy Press.

Ankum, W. M. (2000). Diagnosing suspected ectopic pregnancy. *British Medical Journal, 321*(7271), 1235–1237.

Antonucci, T., & Akiyama, H. (1987). Social networks in adult life and a preliminary examination of the convoy model. *Journal of Gerontology: Social Sciences, 42,* S519–S527.

Antonucci, T., & Akiyama, H. (1997). Concern with others at midlife: Care, comfort, or compromise? In M. Lachman & J. James (Eds.), *Multiple paths of midlife development* (pp. 145–169). Chicago: University of Chicago Press.

Antonucci, T., Akiyama, H., & Merline, A. (2001). Dynamics of social relationships in midlife. In M. Lachman (Ed.), *Handbook of midlife development* (pp. 571–598). New York: Wiley.

Antonucci, T., Akiyama, H., & Takahashi, K. (2004). Attachment and close relationships across the life span. *Attachment & Human Development, 6*(4), 353–370.

Api, O., Unal, O., Api, M., Ergin, B., Alkan, N., Kars, B., et al. (2006). Ultrasonograpic appearance of cervical pregnancy following successful treatment with methotrexate. *Ultrasound in Obstetrics and Gynecology, 28*(6), 845–848.

Applegate, J. S., & Shapiro, J. R. (2005). *Neurobiology for clinical social work: Theory and practice.* New York: W. W. Norton.

Arber, S., & Ginn, J. (1995). *Connecting gender and aging: A sociological approach.* Philadelphia: Open University Press.

Archer, J. (1992). Childhood gender roles: Social content and organization. In H. McGurk (Ed.), *Childhood social development* (pp. 31–62). Hillsdale, NJ: Lawrence Erlbaum.

Archibald, A., Graber, J., & Brooks-Gunn, J. (2003). Pubertal processes and physiological growth in adolescence. In G. Adams & M. Berzonsky (Eds.), *Blackwell handbook of adolescence* (pp. 27–47). Oxford, UK: Blackwell.

Ardelt, M., & Eccles, J. S. (2001). Effects of mothers' parental efficacy beliefs and promotive parenting strategies on inner-city youth. *Journal of Family Issues, 22*(8), 944.

Argetsinger, A. (2001, August 27). An oversupply of undergrads. *Washington Post,* pp. A1, A5.

Armatowski, J. (2001). Attitudes toward death and dying among persons in the fourth quarter of life. In D. O. Moberg (Ed.), *Aging and spirituality: Spiritual dimensions of aging theory, research, practice, and policy* (pp. 71–83). New York: Haworth Pastoral Press.

Armour, S., & Haynie, D. (2007). Adolescent sexual debut and later delinquency. *Journal of Youth and Adolescence, 36*(2), 141–152.

Armstrong, E. M. (2000). Lessons in control: Prenatal education in the hospital. *Social Problems, 47*(4), 583-611.

Arnett, J. J. (1998). Learning to stand alone: The contemporary American transition to adulthood in cultural and historical context. *Human Development, 41*(5), 295–297.

Arnett, J. J. (2000). Emerging adulthood: A theory of development from the late teens through the twenties. *American Psychologist, 55*(5), 469–480.

Arnett, J. J. (2004). *Emerging adulthood: The winding road from the late teens through the twenties.* New York: Oxford University Press.

Arnett, J. J. (2006). G. Stanley Hall's Adolescence: Brilliance and nonsense. *History of Psychology, 9,* 186–197.

Arnett, J. J. (2007). Suffering, selfish, slackers? Myths and reality about emerging adults. *Journal of Youth and Adolescence, 36,* 23–29.

Arnett, J. J., & Brody, G. H. (2008). A fraught passage: The identity challenges of African-American emerging adults. *Human Development, 51,* 291–293.

Arnett, J., & Jensen, L. (2002). A congregation of one. *Journal of Adolescent Research, 17*(5), 451–467.

Arnett, J. J., & Taber, S. (1994). Adolescence terminable and interminable: When does adolescence end? *Journal of Youth & Adolescence, 23*(5), 517–538.

Arnett, J. J., & Tanner, J. L. (2005). *Emerging adults in America: Coming of age in the 21st century.* Washington, DC: American Psychological Association.

Aroian, K., & Norris, A. (2003). Depression trajectories in relatively recent immigrants. *Comprehensive Psychiatry, 44*(5), 420–427.

Arsenio, W., & Gold, J. (2006). The effects of social injustice and inequality on children's moral judgments and behavior: Towards a theoretical model. *Cognitive Development, 21,* 388–400.

Asher, S., & Paquette, J. (2003). Loneliness and peer relations in childhood. *Current Directions in Psychological Science, 12,* 75–78.

Ashford, J. B., LeCroy, C. W., & Lortie, K. L. (2001). *Human behavior in the social environment* (2nd ed.). Belmont, CA: Wadsworth.

Ashford, J. B., LeCroy, C. W., & Lortie, K. L. (2006). *Human behavior in the social environment: A multidimensional perspective* (3rd ed.). Pacific Grove, CA: Brooks/Cole.

Astone, N. M., Schoen, R., Ensminger, M., & Rothert, K. (2000). School reentry in early adulthood: The case of inner-city African Americans. *Sociology of Education, 73,* 133–154.

Astor, R. A., Benbenishty, R., Pitner, R. O., & Meyer, H. A. (2004). Bullying and peer victimization in the schools. In P. Allen-Meares & M. W. Fraser (Eds.), *Intervention with children and adolescents: An interdisciplinary perspective* (pp. 417–448). Boston: Allyn & Bacon.

Auerbach, J., & Krimgold, B. (Eds.). (2001). *Income, socioeconomic status, and health.* Washington, DC: National Policy Association.

Aumann, K., & Galinsky, E. (2009). *The state of health in the American workforce: Does having an effective workplace matter?* New York: Families and Work Institute. Retrieved January 10, 2010, from http://www.familiesandwork.org/site/research/reports/HealthReport.pdf.

Australian Government: Department of Family and Community Services: Office for Women. (2006). *What the Australian government is doing for women.* Retrieved November 2, 2006, from http://www.ofw.facs.gov.au/publications/budget2005/booklet.pdf.

Avis, N., Brambilla, D., McKinlay, S., & Vass, K. (1994). A longitudinal analysis of the association between menopause and depression: Results from the Massachusetts Women's Health Study. *Annals of Epidemiology, 4,* 214–220.

Avis, N., & Crawford, S. (2006). Menopause: Recent research. In S. Whitbourne & S. Willis (Eds.), *The baby boomers grow up: Contemporary perspectives on midlife* (pp. 3–21). Mahwah, NJ: Lawrence Erlbaum.

Avis, N., Stellato, R., Crawford, S., Bromberger, Ganz, P., Cain, V., & Kagawa-Singer, M. (2001). Is there a menopausal syndrome? Menopausal status and symptoms across racial/ethnic groups. *Social Science & Medicine, 52*(3), 345.

Awsare, N. S., Krishnan, J., Boustead, G. B., Hanbury, D. C., & McNicholas, T. A. (2005). Complications of vasectomy. *Annals of the Royal College of Surgeons of England, 87*(6), 406–410.

Aziz, N., Agarwal, A., Nallella, K. P., & Thomas, A. J. (2006). Relationship between epidemiological features and aetiology of male infertility as diagnosed by a comprehensive infertility service provider. *Reproductive BioMedicine Online, 12*(2), 209–214.

Bachmann, G. A. (2007). Preventing pregnancy without hormones. *Cortlandt Forum, 20*(2), 55–56.

Bada, H. S., Das, A., Bauer, C. R., Shankaran, S., Lester, B. M., Gard, C. C., et al. (2005). Low birth weight and preterm births: Etiological fraction attributable to prenatal drug exposure. *Journal of Perinatology, 25*(10), 631–637.

Bahrick, L., Lickliter, R., & Flom, R. (2006). Up versus down: The role of intersensory redundancy in the devvelopmnet of infants'sensitivity to the orientation of moving objects. *Infancy, 9,* 73–96.

Bailey, S. M. (2002). Foreword. In *The Jossey-Bass reader on gender and education* (pp. xxi–xxiv). San Francisco: Jossey-Bass.

Baillargeon, R. (1987). Object permanence in 3½ and 4½ month old infants. *Developmental Psychology, 23,* 655–664.

Baillargeon, R. (2004). Infants' physical world. *Current Directions in Psychological Science, 13,* 89–94.

Bain, M. D., Gau, D., & Reed, G. B. (1995). An introduction to antenatal and neonatal medicine, the fetal period and perinatal ethics. In G. B. Reed, A. E. Claireaux, & F. Cockburn (Eds.), *Diseases of the fetus and newborn* (2nd ed., pp. 3–23). London: Chapman & Hall.

Bak, C. (2004). Cultural lack of birth experience empowers media representations, not women. *Midwifery Today, 72,* 44–65.

Bak, C. (2009). The conscious choice to culturally reframe birth. *Midwifery Today, 90,* 39–41.

Bakardjieva, M. (2004) Virtual togetherness: An everyday life perspective. In A. Feenberg & D. Barney (Eds.), *Community in the digital age: Philosophy and practice* (pp. 121–142). Lanham, Md.: Rowman & Littlefield.

Baker, A. (1990). The psychological impact of the Intifada on Palestinian children in the occupied West Bank and Gaza: An exploratory study. *American Journal of Orthopsychiatry, 60,* 496–505.

Baker, L. (2006). Are we transferring women into the community too quickly? *British Journal of Midwifery, 14*(3), 148–149.

Bakhru, A., & Stanwood, N. (2006). Performance of contraceptive patch compared with oral contraceptive pill in a high-risk population. *Obstetrics and Gynecology, 108*(2), 378–386.

Balaban, V. (2008). Assessment of children. In E. B. Foa, T. M. Keane, M. J. Friedman, & J. A. Cohen (Eds.), *Effective treatments for PTSD: Practice guidelines from the International Society for Traumatic Stress Studies* (2nd ed., pp. 62–82). New York: Guilford Press.

Baler, R. D., Vakow, N. D., Fowler, J. S., & Benveniste, H. (2008). Is fetal brain monoamine oxidase inhibition the missing link between maternal smoking and conduct disorders? *Journal of Psychiatry and Neuroscience, 33*(3), 187–198.

Baltes, P., Lindenberger, U., & Staudinger, U. (1998). Life-span theory in developmental psychology. In R. Lerner (Ed.), *Handbook of child psychology* (5th ed., pp. 1029–1143). New York: Wiley.

Baltes, P. B., & Mayer, K. U. (Eds.) (1999). *The Berlin Aging Study: Aging from 70 to 100.* Cambridge: Cambridge University Press.

Baltes, P. B., Rösler, F., & Reuter-Lorenz, P. A. (2006). Prologue: Biocultural co-constructivism as a theoretical metascript. In Baltes, P. B., Reuter-Lorenz, P. A., & Rössler, F. (Eds.), *Life span development and the brain: The perspective of biocultural co-constructivism* (pp. 3–39). Cambridge: Cambridge University Press.

Bandura, A. (1977). Self-efficacy: Toward a unifying theory of behavioral change. *Psychological Review, 84,* 191–215.

Bandura, A. (1977). *Social learning theory.* Englewood Cliffs, NJ: Prentice Hall.

Bandura, A. (2002). Social cognitive theory in cultural context. *Applied Psychology: An International Review, 51*(2), 269–290.

Bandura, A. (2006). Toward a psychology of human agency. *Perspectives on Psychological Science, 1*(2), 164–180.

Barajas. R., Philipsen, N., & Brooks-Gunn, J. (2008). Cognitive and emotional outcomes for children in poverty. In D. Crane & T. Heaton (Eds.), *Handbook of families & poverty* (pp. 311–333). Thousand Oaks, CA: Sage.

Baranowski, T. (1983). Social support, social influence, ethnicity, and the breastfeeding decision. *Social Science & Medicine, 17,* 1599–1611.

Barbarin, O., McCandies, T., Coleman, C., & Atkinson, T. (2004). Ethnicity and culture. In P. Allen-Meares and M. W. Fraser (Eds.), *Intervention with children and adolescents: An interdisciplinary perspective* (pp. 27–53). Boston: Allyn & Bacon.

Barber, B., & Demo, D. (2006). The kids are alright (at least, most of them): Links between divorce and dissolution and child well-being. In M. Fine & J. Harvey (Eds.), *Handbook of divorce and relationship dissolution* (pp. 289–311). Mahwah, NJ: Lawrence Erlbaum.

Barbu, S., Le Maner-Idrissi, G., & Jouanjean, A. (2000). The emergence of gender segregation: Towards an integrative perspective. *Current Psychology of Letters: Behavior, Brain, and Cognition, 3,* 7–18.

Barclay, L. (2009). ACOG issues guidelines for stillbirth management. *Obstetrics & Gynecology, 113,* 748–761.

Barker, K. K. (1998). "A ship upon a stormy sea": The medicalization of pregnancy. *Social Science & Medicine, 47*(8), 1067–1076.

Barr, R. D., & Parrett, W. H. (1995). *Hope at last for at-risk youth.* Boston: Allyn & Bacon.

Barranti, C., & Cohen, H. (2001). Lesbian and gay elders: An invisible minority. In R. Schneider, N. Kropf, & A. Kisor (Eds.), *Gerontological social work: Knowledge, service setting, and special populations* (pp. 343–368). Belmont, CA: Brooks/Cole.

Barrett, R. (2009). Sociolcultural considerations: African Americans, grief, and loss. In D. J. Doka & A. S. Tucci, (Eds.), *Living with grief: Diversity and end-of-life care* (pp. 79–91). Washington, DC: Hospice Foundation of America.

Barry, T. D., Lyman, R. D., & Klinger, L. G. (2002). Academic underachievement and Attention-Deficit/Hyperactivity Disorder: The negative impact of symptom severity on school performance. *Journal of School Psychology, 40*(3), 259–283.

Bartholomae, S., & Fox, J. (2010). Economic stress and families. In S. Price, C. Price, & P. McKenry (Eds.), *Families & change: Coping with stressful events and transitions* (pp. 185–209). Thousand Oaks, CA: Sage.

Bartko, W. T., & Eccles, J. (2003). Adolescent participation in structured and unstructured activities: A person-oriented analysis. *Journal of Youth and Adolescence, 32*(4), 233–241.

Bartley, M., Blane, D., & Montgomery, S. (1997). Health and the life course: Why safety nets matter. *British Medical Journal, 314*(7088), 1194–1196.

Barzilai, N., & Bartke, A. (2009). Biological approaches to mechanistically understand the healthy life span extension achieved by calorie restriction and modulation of hormones. *Journals of Gerontology Series A: Biological Sciences & Medical Sciences, 64A*(2), 187–191.

Bassali, R., & Benjamin, J. (2002, July 12). Failure to thrive. *EMedicine Journal, 3*(7). Retrieved August 21, 2002, from http://www.emedicine.com/PED/topic738.htm.

Bassuk, E. L., & Friedman, S. M. (2005). *Facts on trauma and homeless children.* Durham, NC: National Child Traumatic Stress Network. Retrieved January 19, 2010, http://www.nctsnet.org/nctsn_assets/pdfs/promising_practices/Facts_on_Trauma_and_Homeless_Children.pdf.

Bates, J. (2009). Generative grandfathering: A conceptual framework for nurturing grandchildren. *Marriage & Family Review, 45,* 331–352.

Baum, K. (2005, August). *Juvenile victimization and offending. 1993–2003* (Special Report. National Crime Victimization Survey. NCJ 209468). Washington, DC: U.S. Department of Justice, Office of Justice Programs, Bureau of Justice Statistics.

Baumrind, D. (1971). Current patterns of parental authority. *Developmental Psychology Monographs, 41*(1, Pt. 2).

Bausch, R. S. (2006). Predicting willingness to adopt a child: A consideration of demographic and attitudinal factors. *Sociological Perspectives, 49*(1), 47–56.

Baxter, C., & Warnock, J. K. (2007). Psychiatric issues of infertility and infertility treatments. *Primary Psychiatry, 14*(5), 59–65.

Beatson, J., & Taryan, S. (2003). Predisposition to depression: The role of attachment. *Australian and New Zealand Journal of Psychiatry, 37,* 219–225.

Beaudoin, M., & Taylor, M. (2004). *Breaking the culture of bullying and disrespect, grades K–8: Best practices and successful strategies.* Thousand Oaks, CA: Corwin.

Beck, J. G., & Averill, P. M. (2004). Older adults. In D. Mennon, R. Heimberg, & C. Turk (Eds.), *Generalized Anxiety Disorder: Advances in research and practice* (pp. 409–433). New York: Guilford Press.

Beel-Bates, C. A., Ingersoll-Dayton, B., & Nelson, E. (2007). Deference as a form of reciprocity on aging, *Research on Aging, 29,* 626–643.

Behrman, J., & Sengupta, P. (2006). Documenting the changing contexts within which young people are transitioning to adulthood in developing countries: Convergence toward developed economies? In C. B. Lloyd, J. R. Behrman, N. Stromquist, & B. Cohen (Eds.), *The changing transitions to adulthood in developing countries: Selected studies* (pp. 13–55). Washington, DC: National Research Council.

Beland, F., Zunzunegui, M., Alvardo, B. Otero, A., & del Ser, T. (2005). Trajectories of cognitive decline and social relations. *Journals of Gerontology: Series B: Psychological Sciences and Social Sciences, 60*(6), 320–330.

Belden, A., Thompson, N., & Luby, J. (2008). Temper tantrums in healthy versus DSM-IV depressed and disruptive preschoolers: Defining tantrum behaviors associated with clinical problems. *Journal of Pedatrics, 152,* 117–122.

Belizan, J.M. (2008). Women deliver. *Current Women's Health Reviews, 4*(1), 1–2.

Bellamy, C. (2004). *The state of the world's children 2005.* New York: The United Nations Children's Fund.

Belsky, J. (1987). Infant day care and socioemotional development: The United States. *Journal of Child Psychology and Psychiatry, 29,* 397–406.

Belsky, J., & Braungart, J. M. (1991). Are insecure-avoidant infants with extensive day care experience less stressed by and more independent in the strange situation? *Child Development, 62,* 567–571.

Belsky, J., Campbell, S., Cohn, J., & Moore, G. (1996). Instability of infant-parent attachment security. *Developmental Psychology, 32,* 921–924.

Bem, S. L. (1993). *The lenses of gender: Transforming the debate on sexual inequality.* New Haven, CT: Yale University Press.

Bem, S. L. (1998). Gender schema theory and its implications for child development: Raising gender-aschematic children in a gender-schematic society. In D. L. Anselmi & A. L. Law (Eds.), *Questions of gender: Perspectives and paradoxes.* Boston: McGraw Hill.

Benasich, A., & Leevers, H. (2003). Processing of rapidly presented auditory cues in infancy: Implications for later language development. In H. Hayne & J. Fagen (Eds.), *Progress in infancy research* (Vol. 3, pp. 245–288). Mahwah, NJ: Lawrence Erlbaum.

Benefice, E., Caius, N., & Garnier, D. (2004). Cross-cultural comparison of growth, maturation, and adiposity. *Public Health Nutrition, 74*(4), 479–485.

Benenson, J. (1993). Greater preference among females than males for dyadic interaction in early childhood. *Child Development, 64,* 544–555.

Bengtson, V. (1996). Continuities and discontinuities in intergenerational relationships over time. In V. Bengtson & K. Schaie (Eds.), *Adulthood and aging* (pp. 246–268). New York: Springer.

Bengtson, V. (2001). Beyond the nuclear family: The increasing importance of multigenerational bonds. *Journal of Marriage and Family, 63,* 1–16.

Bengtson, V. L., Gans, D., Putney, N. M., & Silverstein, M. (2009). *Handbook of theories of aging* (2nd ed.). New York: Springer.

Benjamin, K., Edwards, N. C., & Bharti, V. K. (2005). Attitudinal, perceptual, and normative beliefs influencing the exercise decisions of community-dwelling physically frail seniors. *Journal of Aging and Physical Activity, 13*(3), 276–293.

Benjet, C., & Hernandez-Guzman, I. (2002). A short-term longitudinal study of pubertal change, gender, and psychological wellbeing of Mexican early adolescents. *Journal of Youth and Adolescence, 31,* 923–931.

Benson, P. L. (1990). *The troubled journey: A portrait of 6th-12th grade youth.* Minneapolis, MN: Search Institute.

Benson, P. L., Yeager, R. J., Wood, P. K., Guerra, M. J., & Manno, B. V. (1986). *Catholic high schools: Their impact on low-income students.* Washington, DC: National Catholic Educational Association.

Bergen, D., & Coscia, J. (2001). *Brain research and childhood education: Implications for educators.* Olney, MD: Association for Childhood Education International.

Berk, L. E. (2002a). *Infants and children: Prenatal through middle childhood* (4th ed.). Boston: Allyn & Bacon.

Berk, L. E. (2002b). *Infants, children, & adolescents* (4th ed.). Boston: Allyn & Bacon.

Berk, L. E. (2005). *Infants, children, & adolescents* (5th ed.). Boston: Pearson.

Berkeley Planning Associates. (1996). *Priorities for future research: Results of BAs' Delphi survey of disabled women.* Retrieved November 6, 2002, from http://www.ncddr.org/rr/ women/ priorities.html.

Berliner, K., Jacob, D., & Schwartzberg, N. (2005). The single adult and the family life cycle. In B. Carter & M. McGoldrick (Eds.), *The expanded family life cycle: Individual, family, and social perspectives* (3rd ed., pp. 362–372). Boston: Allyn & Bacon.

Berman, R.O. (2006). Perceived learning needs of minority expectant women and barriers to prenatal education. *The Journal of Perinatal Education, 15*(2), 36–42.

Berndt, T. J. (1988). Friendships in childhood and adolescence. In W. Damon (Ed.), *Childhood development today and tomorrow* (pp. 332–348.). San Francisco: Jossey-Bass.

Berne, L., & Huberman, B. (1999). *European approaches to adolescent sexual behavior & responsibility.* Washington, DC: Advocates for Youth.

Berne, L., & Huberman, B. (2000). Lessons learned: European approaches to adolescent sexual behavior and responsibility. *Journal of Sex Education & Therapy, 25*(2–3), 189–199.

Bern-Klug, M. (2004). The ambiguous dying syndrome. *Health and Social Work, 29*(1), 55–65.

Bern-Klug, M., Gessert, C., & Forbes, S. (2001). The need to revise assumptions about the end of life: Implications for social work practice. *Health and Social Work, 26*(1), 38–48.

Berthold, J. (2009). *Dealing with delirium in older hospitalized adults. ACP Hospitalist.* Retrieved May 16, 2010, from http://www.acphospitalist.org/archives/2009/06/delirium.htm.

Bertrand, J., Floyd, R. L., & Weber, M. K. (2005, October 28). Guidelines for identifying and referring persons with Fetal Alcohol Syndrome. *Centers for Disease Control, 54*(RR11), 1–10.

Best, K. (2002). Medical barriers often unnecessary: Barriers with no scientific basis can limit choice and endanger health (facilitating contraception choice). *Network, 21*(3), 4–14.

Bhathena, R. K., & Guillebaud, J. (2006). Contraception for the older woman: An update. *Climacteric: The Journal of the International Menopause Society, 9*(4), 264–276.

Bhattacharya, G. (2000). The school adjustment of South Asian immigrant children in the United States. *Adolescence, 35,* 77–85.

Biehl, M., Natsuaki, M., & Ge, X. (2007). The influence of pubertal timing on alcohol use and heavy drinking trajectories. *Journal of Youth & Adolescence, 36*(2), 153–167.

Biggs, S. (1999). *The mature imagination: Dynamics of identity in midlife and beyond.* Philadelphia: Open University Press.

Billingsley, A. (1999). *Mighty like a river: The black church and social reform.* New York: Oxford University Press.

Bishop, K. (1993). Psychosocial aspects of genetic disorders: Implications for practice. *Families in Society, 74,* 207–212.

Bitzan, J. E., & Kruzich, J. M. (1990). Interpersonal relationships of nursing home residents. *The Gerontologist, 30,* 385–390.

Bjorklund, B., & Bee, H. (2008). *The journey of adulthood* (6th ed.). Upper Saddle River, NJ: Pearson Prentice Hall.

Blacker, L. (2005). The launching phase of the life cycle. In B. Carter & M. McGoldrick (Eds.), *The expanded family life cycle: Individual, family, and social perspectives* (3rd ed., pp. 287–306). Boston: Allyn & Bacon.

Blackmon, S., & Vera, E. (2008). Ethnic and racial identity development in children of color. In J. Asamen, M. Ellis, & G. Berry (Eds.), *The Sage handbook of child development, multiculturalism, and the media* (pp. 47–61). Thousand Oaks, CA: Sage.

Blandford, J. M., & Gift, T. L. (2006). Productivity losses attributable to untreated chlamydial infection and associated pelvic inflammatory disease in reproductive-aged women. *Sexually Transmitted Diseases, 33*(10), S117–S121.

Blass, E., & Ciaramitaro, V. (1994). A new look at some old mechanisms in human newborns: Taste and tactile determinants of state, affect, and action. *Monographs of the Society for Research in Child Development, 59*(1), v–81.

Blau, P. M. (1964). *Exchange and power in social life.* New York: Wiley.

Blazer, D. G. (1995). Depression. In G. L. Maddox (Ed.), *The encyclopedia of aging: A comprehensive resource in gerontology and geriatrics* (2nd ed., pp. 265–266). New York: Springer.

Bliatout, B. (1993). Hmong death customs: Traditional and acculturated. In D. Irish, K. Lundquist, & V. Nelsen (Eds.), *Ethnic variations in dying, death, and grief: Diversity in universality* (pp. 77–99). Washington, DC: Taylor & Francis.

Blieszner, R., & deVries, B. (2001). Perspectives on intimacy. *Generations, 25*(2), 7–8.

Blieszner, R., & Roberto, K. (2006). Perspectives on close relationships among the baby boomers. In S. Whitbourne & S. Willis (Eds.), *The baby boomers grow up: Contemporary perspectives on midlife* (pp. 261–281). Mahwah, NJ: Lawrence Erlbaum.

Blinn, C. (1997). *Maternal ties: A selection of programs for female offenders.* Lanham, MD: American Correctional Association.

Bloom, B. (1995). Imprisoned mothers. In K. Gabel & D. Johnson (Eds.), *Children of incarcerated parents* (pp. 21–30). New York: Lexington Press.

Bloom, B., & Steinhart, D. (1993). *Why punish the children? A reappraisal of the children of incarcerated mothers in America.* San Francisco: National Council on Crime and Delinquency.

Bloom, D. A., Yinghao, S., Sabanegh, E., De Almeida, J. C., Miner, J., & Gopalakrishan, G. (2009). Take home messages. *American Urological Association News (AUANews), 14*(5), 4–9.

Bloom, L. (1998a). Language development: Emotional expression. *Pediatrics, 102,* 1272–1277.

Bloom, L. (1998b). Language acquisition in its developmental context. In W. Damon, D. Kuhn, & R. Siegler (Eds.), *Handbook of child psychology: Cognition, perception, and language* (5th ed., Vol. 2., pp. 309–370). New York: Wiley.

Blyth, D. A., & Roehlkepartian, E. C. (1993). *Healthy communities, healthy youth.* Minneapolis, MN: Search Institute.

Boger, J., & Orfield, G. (2005). *School resegregation: Must the south turn back?* Chapel Hill, NC: University of North Carolina.

Boggia, B., Carbone, U., Farinari, E., Zarrilli, S., Lombardi, G., Colao, A., et al. (2009). Effects of working posture and exposure to traffic pollutants on sperm quality. *Journal of Endocrinological Investigation, 32*(5), 430–434.

Boldizar, J. P. (1991). Assessing sex typing and androgyny in children: The children's sex role inventory. *Developmental Psychology, 27,* 505–515.

Bonanno, G., & Kaltman, S. (1999). Toward an integrative perspective on bereavement. *Psychological Bulletin, 125*(6), 760–776.

Bond, B., Hefner, V., & Drogos, K. (2009). Information-seeking practices during the sexual development of lesbian, gay, and bisexual individuals: The influence and effects of coming out in a mediated environment. *Sexuality & Culture, 13,* 32–50.

Bonne, O. B., Rubinoff, B., & Berry, E. M. (1996). Delayed detection of pregnancy in patients with anorexia nervosa: Two case reports. *International Journal of Eating Disorders, 20,* 423–425.

Borke, H. (1975). Piaget's mountains revisited: Changes in the egocentric landscape. *Developmental Psychology, 11,* 240–243.

Borse, N. N., Gilchrist, J., Dellinger, A. M., Rudd, R. A., Ballesteros, M. F., & Sleet, D. A. (2008). *CDC childhood injury report.* Washington, DC: Centers for Disease Control and Prevention. Retrieved January 19, 2010, http://www.cdc.gov/safechild/images/CDC-ChildhoodInjury.pdf.

Borysenko, J. (1996). *A woman's book of life: The biology, psychology, and spirituality of the feminine life cycle.* New York: Riverhead Books.

Borzekowski, D., Fobil, J., & Asante, O. (2006). Online access by adolescents in Accra: Ghanian teens' use of the Internet for health information. *Developmental Psychology, 42*(3), 450–458.

Bos, H., van Balan, F., & Visser, A. (2005). Social and cultural factors in infertility and childlessness. *Patient Education and Counseling, 59*(3), 223–225.

Bostan, A., Vannin. A.S., Emiliani, S., Debaisieux, L., Liesnard, C., & Englert, Y. (2008). Development and evaluation of single sperm washing for the risk reduction in artificial reproductive technology (ART) for extreme oligospermic HIV positive patients. *Current HIV Research, 6*(5), 461–465.

Boucher, D., Bennett, D., McFarlin, B., & Freeze, R. (2009). Staying home to give birth: Why women in the United States choose home birth. *Journal of Midwifery and Women's Health, 54*(2), 119–126.

Bouchez, C. (2007). *HRT: Revisiting the hormone decision.* WebMD. Retrieved May 19, 2010, from http://www.webmd.com/menopause/features/hrt-revisitng-the-hormone-decision.

Bourne, K. E. (2009). Diagnosis of ectopic pregnancy with ultrasound. *Best Practices Research in Clinical Obstetrical Gynaecology, 23*(4), 501–506.

Boushey, A. (2001). The grief cycle—one parent's trip around. *Focus on Autism and Other Developmental Disabilities, 16*(1), 27–30.

Bowlby, J. (1969). *Attachment and loss.* New York: Basic Books.

Bowlby, J. (1980). *Attachment and loss: Loss, sadness, and depression* (Vol. 3). New York: Basic Books.

Bowlby, J. (1982). *Attachment and loss* (Vol. 1). New York: Basic Books.

Bowles, S., & Gintis, H. (1976). *Schooling in capitalist America: Educational reform and the contradictions of economic life.* New York: Basic Books.

Bowling, A., See-Tai, S., Ebrahim, S., Gabriel, Z., & Solanki, P. (2005). Attributes of age-identity. *Aging & Society, 25,* 479–500.

Boyd-Franklin, N. (2003). Race, class, and poverty. In F. Walsh (Ed.), *Normal family processes: Growing diversity and complexity* (3rd ed., pp. 260–279). New York: Guilford.

Bradley, L. A. (1995). Changing American birth through childbirth education. *Patient Education and Counseling, 25*(1), 75–82.

Bradley, R., Whiteside, L., Mundfrom, D., Casey, P., Kelleher, K., & Pope, S. (1994). Early indications of resilience and their relation to experiences in the home environments of low birthweight, premature children living in poverty. *Child Development, 65,* 346–360.

Bradley, S. (2000). *Affect regulation and the development of psychopathology.* New York: Guilford Press.

Bramlett, M. D., & Mosher W. D. (2002). *Cohabitation, marriage, divorce, and remarriage in the United States.* (CDC National Center for Health Statistics and Vital Health Stat Series 23 Number 22). Retrieved January 19, 2010, from http://www.cdc.gov/nchs/data/series/sr_23/sr23_022.pdf.

Branch, C., Tayal, P., & Triplett, C. (2000). The relationship of ethnic identity and ego identity status among adolescents and young adults. *International Journal of Intercultural Relations, 23,* 777–790.

Brandon, D. H., Ryan, D. J., & Barnes, A. H. (2008). Effect on environmental changes on noise in the NICU. *Advances in Neonatal Care: Official Journal of the National Association of Neonatal Nurses, 8*(5 suppl), S5–10.

Brandon, G. D., Adeniyl-Jones, S., Kirkby, S., Webb, D., Culhane, J., & Greenspan, J. S. (2009). Are outcomes and care processes for preterm neonates influenced by health insurance status? *Pediatrics, 124*(1), 122–127.

Brandtstadter, J. (2006). Adaptive resources in later life: Tenacious goal pursuits and flexible role adjustment. In M. Csikszentmihalyi & I. Csikszentmihalyi (Eds.), *A life worth living: Contributions to positive psychology* (pp. 143–164). New York: Oxford Press.

Brauner, C. B., & Stephens, C. B. (2006). Estimating the prevalence of early childhood serious emotional/behavioral disorders: Challenges and recommendations. *Public Health Reports, 121*(3), 303–310.

Brazelton, T. B. (1983). *Infants and mothers: Differences in development.* New York: Delta/Seymour Lawrence.

Brennan, D., & Spencer, A. (2009). Life events and oral-health-related quality of life among young adults. *Quality of Life Research, 18*(5), 557–565.

Bridgett, D., Gartstein, M., Putnam, S., McKay, T., Iddins, E., Robertson, C., et al. (2009). Maternal and contextual influences and the effect of temperament development during infancy on parenting in toddlerhood. *Infant Behavior & Development, 32,* 103–116.

Brim, O., Ryff, C., & Kessler, R. (Eds.). (2004). *How healthy are we? A national study of well-being at midlife.* Chicago: University of Chicago Press.

Brinch, M., Isager, T., & Tolstrup, K. (1988). Anorexia nervosa and motherhood: Reproduction pattern and mothering behavior of 50 women. *Acta Psychiatrica Scandinavica, 77,* 611–617.

Brockington, I. F., Aucamp, H. M., & Fraser, C. (2006). Severe disorders of the mother-infant relationship: Definitions and frequency. *Archives of Women's Mental Health, 9*(5), 243–251.

Broderick, P. C., & Blewitt, P. (2006). *The life span: Human development for helping professionals* (2nd ed.). Upper Saddle River, NJ: Pearson.

Brokenleg, M., & Middleton, D. (1993). Native Americans: Adapting, yet retaining. In D. Irish, K. Lundquist, & V. Nelsen (Eds.), *Ethnic variations in dying, death, and grief: Diversity in universality* (pp. 101–112). Washington, DC: Taylor & Francis.

Bromberger, J., Meyer, P., Kravitz, H., Sommer, B., Cordal, A., Powell, L., et al. (2001). Psychological distress and natural menopause: A multiethnic community study. *American Journal of Public Health, 91*(9), 1435.

Bronfenbrenner, U. (1979). *The ecology of human development: Experiments by nature and design.* Cambridge, MA: Harvard University Press.

Bronfenbrenner, U. (1993). The ecology of cognitive development: Research models and fugitive findings. In R. Wozniak & K. Fischer (Eds.), *Development in context: Acting and thinking in specific environments* (pp. 3–44). Hillsdale, NJ: Lawrence Erlbaum.

Bronte-Tinkew, J., Brown, B., Carrano, J. & Shwalb, R. (2005). *Logic models and outcomes for youth in the transition to adulthood.* Washington, DC: Child Trends. Retrieved January 5, 2010, from http://www.childtrends.org/Files/Child_Trends-2005_04_19_FR_logicModel.pdf.

Brooks, P., Jia., X, Braine, M., & DaGraca Dias, M. (1998). A cross-linguistic study of children's comprehension of universal quantifiers: A comparison of Mandarin Chinese, Portuguese, and English. *First Language, 18,* 33–79.

Brooks-Gunn, J., & Furstenberg, F. (1989). Adolescent sexual behavior. *American Psychologist, 44,* 249–257.

Brooks-Gunn, J., & Paikoff, R. (1993). Sex is a gamble, kissing is a game: Adolescent sexuality and health promotion. In S. Millstein, A. Peteresen, & E. Nightingale (Eds.), *Promoting the health of adolescents* (pp. 180–208). New York: Oxford University Press.

Brown, B., & Klute, C. (2003). Friendships, cliques, and crowds. In G. Adams & M. Berzonsky (Eds.), *Blackwell handbook of adolescence* (pp. 330–345). Oxford, UK: Blackwell.

Brown, B. B. (2004). Adolescent's relationships with peers. In R. M. Lerner & L. Steinberg (Eds.), *Handbook of adolescent psychology* (2nd ed., pp. 363–394). New York: Wiley.

Brown, J. (2003). The self-enhancement motive in collectivistic cultures: The rumors of my death have been greatly exaggerated. *Journal of Cross-Cultural Psychology, 34,* 603–605.

Brown, J., Dutton, K., & Cook, K. (2001). From the top down: Self-esteem and self-evaluation. *Cognition and Emotion, 15,* 615–631.

Brown, J., Gallicchio, L., Flaws, J., & Tracy, J. (2009). Relations among menopausal symptoms, sleep disturbance and depressive symptoms in midlife. *Maturitas, 62*(2), 184–189.

Brown, R. A., Rehkopf, D. H., Copeland, W. E., Costello, E. J., & Worthman, C. M. (2009). Lifecourse priorities among Appalachian emerging adults: Revisiting Wallace's organization of diversity. *ETHOS, 37*(2), 225–242.

Brown, S. G., Morrison, L. A., Larkspur, L. M., Marsh, A. L., & Nicolaisen, N. (2008). Well-being, sleep, exercise patterns, and the menstrual cycle: A comparison of natural hormones, oral contraceptive and depo-provera. *Women's Health, 47*(1), 105–121.

Brown-Guttovz, H. (2006). Myths and facts about ectopic pregnancy. *Nursing, 36*(8), 70.

Browne, C., Mokuau, N., & Braun, K. (2009). Adversity and resiliency in lives of Native Hawaiian elders. *Social Work, 54*(3), 253–261.

Brubaker, E., Gorman, M. A., & Hiestand, M. (1990). Stress perceived by elderly recipients of family care. In T. H. Brubaker (Ed.), *Family relationships in later life* (2nd ed., pp. 267–281). Newbury Park, CA: Sage.

Bruce, E., & Schultz, C. (2002). Non-finite loss and challenges to communication between parents and professionals. *British Journal of Special Education, 29*(1), 9–14.

Bruce, S., & Muhammad, Z. (2009). The development of object permanence in children with intellectual diability, physical disability, autism, and blindness. *International Journal of Disability, Development & Education, 56*(3), 229–246.

Brückner, H., & Mayer, K. (2005). De-standardization of the life course: What it might mean? And if it means anything, whether it actually took place? In R. MacMillan (Ed.), *The structure of the life course: Standardized? Individualized? Differentiated?* (pp. 27–53). New York: Elsevier.

Brumberg, J. (1997). *The body project: An intimate history of American girls.* New York: Random House.

Brunello, G., & Checchi, D. (2007). Does school tracking affect equality of opportunity? New evidence. *Economic Policy, 22,* 781–861.

Brunner, H., Larissa, R., & Huber, K. R. (2009). Contraceptive choices of women 35–44 years of age: Findings the behavioral risk factor surveillance system. *Annals of Epidemiology, 19*(11), 823–831.

Bryson, K., & Casper, L. (1999). *Coresident grandparents and grandchildren.* Washington, DC: U.S. Census Bureau.

Buekens, P., Xiong, X., & Harville, E. W. (2006). Hurricanes and pregnancy. *Birth, 22,* 91–93.

Buffardi, A., Thomas, K., Holmes, K., & Manhart, L. (2008). Moving upstream: Ecosocial and psychosocial correlates of sexually transmitted infections among young adults in the United States. *American Journal of Public Health, 98*(6), 1128–1136.

Bulik, C., Von Holle, A., Siega-Riz, A., Torgenson, L., Lie, K., Hamer, R., Berg, C., Sullivan, P., & Reichborn-Kjennerud, T. (2009). Birth outcomes in women with eating disorders in the Norwegian Mother and Child Cohort Study (MoBa). *International Journal of Eating Disorders, 42*(1), 9–18.

Bullis, R. K., & Harrigan, M. (1992). Religious denominational policies on sexuality. *Families in Society, 73,* 304–312.

Bullough, V. L. (2005). Artificial insemination. *GLBTQ Social Sciences,* 1–3.

Bunting, L., & McAuley, C. (2004). Teenage pregnancy and motherhood: The contribution of child support. *Child and Family Social Work, 9,* 201–215.

Burchinal, M. R., Peisner-Feinberg, E. S., Bryant, D. M., & Clifford, R. M. (2000). Children's social and cognitive development and child care quality: Testing for differential associations related to poverty, gender, or ethnicity. *Applied Developmental Science, 4,* 149–165.

Bureau of Justice Statistics. (2009). *Prisoners in 2008.* Retrieved December 30, 2009, from http://bjs.oip.usdoj.gov/index .cfm?ty=pbdetail&iid=1763.

Burnette, D. (1999). Custodial grandparents in Latino families: Patterns of service use and predictors of unmet needs. *Social Work, 44*(1), 22–34.

Busato, J., & Wilson, F.S. (2009). Vasectomy reversal: A seven-year experience. *Urologia Internationalis, 82*(2),170–174.

Buss, L., Tolstrup, J., Munk, C., Bergholt, T., Ottesen, B., Gronbaek, M., et al. (2006). Spontaneous abortion: A prospective cohort study of younger women from the general population in Denmark: Validation, occurrence and risk determinants. *Acta Obstetricia et Gynaecologica Scandinavica, 85*(4), 467–475.

Butler, R. N. (1963). The life review: An interpretation of reminiscence in the aged. *Psychiatry, 26,* 65–70.

Butler, R. N. (1987). Life review. In G. L. Maddox (Ed.), *The encyclopedia of aging: A comprehensive resource in gerontology and geriatrics* (2nd ed., pp. 397–398). New York: Springer.

Byock, I. (1997). *Dying well: Peace and possibilities at the end of life.* New York: Riverhead Books.

Byock, R. (2004). *The four things that matter most: A book about living.* New York: Free Press.

Cagle, J. G. (2008). *Informal caregivers of advanced cancer patients: The impact of geographic proximity on social support and bereavement adjustment.* Unpublished doctoral dissertation, Virginia Commonwealth University. Retrieved January 8, 2010, from https://digarchive.library.vcu.edu/bitstream/ 10156/1974/1/caglejg_phd.pdf.

Cagle, J. G., & Kovacs, P. J. (2009). Education: A complex and empowering social work intervention at the end of life. *Health & Social Work, 34*(1), 17–27.

Cain, A. C. (2006). Parent suicide: Pathways of effects into the third generation. *Psychiatry, 69*(3), 204–227.

Calkins, S. (2004). Early attachment processes and the development of emotional self-regulation. In R. Baumeister & K. Vohs (Eds.), *Handbook of self-regulation: Research, theory, and application* (pp. 324–339). New York: Guilford Press.

Calkins, S., & Hill, A. (2007). Caregiver influences on emerging emotion regulation: Biological and environmental transactions in early development. In J. Gross (Ed.), *Handbook of emotion regulation* (pp. 229–248). New York: Guilford.

Callaghan, W. M., MacDorman, M. F., Rasmussen, S. A., Cheng, Q., & Lackritz, E. M. (2006). The contribution of preterm birth to infant mortality rates in the United States. *Pediatrics, 118*(4), 1566–1573.

Calman, L., & Tarr-Whelan, L. (2005). *Early childhood education for all: A wise investment.* Retrieved May 3, 2007, from http://web.mit.edu/workplacecenter/docs/Full%Report.pdf.

Cameron, L. (1999). Understanding alcohol abuse in American Indian/Alaskan native youth. *Pediatric Nursing, 25*(3), 297.

Campbell, L., Campbell, B., & Dickinson, D. (1999). *Teaching and learning through multiple intelligences* (2nd ed.). Needham Heights, MA: Allyn & Bacon.

Campbell, R., & MacFarlane, A. (1986). Place of delivery: A review. *British Journal of Obstetrics and Gynaecology, 93*(7), 675–683.

Campbell, R., & Sais, E. (1995). Accelerated metalinguistic (phonological) awareness in bilingual children. *British Journal of Developmental Psychology, 13,* 61–68.

Campbell, S. (2002). *Behavioral problems in preschool children* (2nd ed.). New York: Guilford Press.

Canadian Council on Learning. (2006). *Why is high-quality child care essential?* Retrieved February 13, 2010, from http:// www.ccl-cca.ca.

Cannella, B. L. (2006). Mediators of the relationship between social support and positive health practices in pregnant women. *Nursing Research, 55*(6), 437–445.

Cantor, K. (2007). PREEMIE act passes Congress: Funding still needed to reduce preterm births. *Nursing for Women's Health, 11*(2), 129–132.

Cappeliez, P., Beaupré, M, & Robitaille, A. (2008). Characteristics and impact of life turning points for older adults. *Ageing Internaltional, 32,* 54–64.

Cappello, F., de Macario. E. C., Di Felice, V., Zummo, G., & Macario. A. J. L. (2009). Chlamydia trachomatis infection and anti-Hsp60 immunity: The two sides of the coin. *PLoS Pathogens, 6*(8), 1–9.

Carey, T. A. (1994). "Spare the rod and spoil the child." Is this a sensible justification for the use of punishment in child rearing? *Child Abuse and Neglect, 18,* 1005–1010.

Carolan, M., & Allen, K. (1999). Commitments and constraints to intimacy for African American couples at midlife. *Journal of Family Issues, 20,* 3–4.

Carpenter, L., Nathanson, C., & Kim, Y. (2009). Physical women, emotional men: Gender and sexual satisfaction in midlife. *Archives of Sexual Behavior, 38*(1), 21–26.

Carstensen, L. (2001). Selectivity theory: Social activity in lifespan context. In A. Walker, M. Manoogian-O'Dell, L. McGraw, & D. White (Eds.), *Families in later life: Connections and transitions* (pp. 265–275). Thousand Oaks, CA: Pine Forge.

Carter, B., & McGoldrick, M. (2005a). *The expanded family life cycle: Individual, family and social perspectives* (3rd ed.). Boston: Allyn & Bacon.

Carter, B., & McGoldrick, M. (2005b). The divorce cycle: A major variation in the American family life cycle. In B. Carter & M. McGoldrick (Eds.), *The expanded family life cycle: Individual, family, and social perspectives* (3rd ed., pp. 373–380). Boston: Allyn & Bacon.

Carter, D. B., & Patterson, C. J. (1982). Sex roles as social conventions: The development of children's conceptions of sex-role stereotypes. *Developmental Psychology, 18,* 812–824.

Carter, S. (2000). *No excuses: Lessons from 21 high-performing, high poverty schools.* Washington, DC: The Heritage Foundation.

Carvalho, A. E., Linhares. M. B., Padovani, F. H., & Martinez, F. E. (2009). Anxiety and depression in mothers of preterm infants and psychological intervention during hospitalization in neonatal ICU. *The Spanish Journal of Psychology, 12*(1), 161–170.

CASA. (2002). *CASA 2002 teen survey.* New York: National Center on Addiction and Substance Abuse at Columbia University (CASA).

Casale-Giannola, D., & Kamens, M. W. (2006). Inclusion at a university: Experiences of a young woman with Down Syndrome. *Mental Retardation, 44*(5), 344–352.

Case, R. (1998). The development of conceptual structures. In D. Kuhn & R. Siegler (Eds.), *Handbook of child psychology: Vol. 2. Cognition, perception, and language* (5th ed., pp. 745–800). New York: Wiley.

Caspi, A. (1987). Personality in the life course. *Journal of Personality and Social Psychology, 53*(6), 1203–1213.

Caspi, A., & Roberts, B. (1999). Personality continuity and change across the life course. In L. A. Pervin & O. P. John (Eds.), *Handbook of personality: Theory and research* (2nd ed., pp. 300–326). New York: Guilford Press.

Catlin, A. J., & Volat, D. (2009). When the fetus is alive but the mother is not: Critical care somatic support as an accepted model of care in the twenty-first century? *Critical Care Nursing Clinics of North America, 21*(2), 267–276.

Cavanagh, S. (2004). The sexual debut of girls in early adolescence: The intersection of race, pubertal timing, and friendship group characteristics. *Journal of Research on Adolescence, 14,* 285–312.

Ceelen, M., van Weissenbruch, M. M., Vermeiden, J. P. W., van Leeuwen, F. E., & Delemarre-van de Waal, H. A. (2008). Growth and development of children born after in vitro fertilization. *Fertility and Sterility, 90*(5), 1662–1673.

Centers for Disease Control and Prevention. (2000). *Abortion surveillance: Preliminary analysis: United States, 1997.* Retrieved November 6, 2002, from http://www.infoplease.com/ipa/A0764203.html.

Centers for Disease Control and Prevention, National Center for Injury and Prevention and Control. (2005a). *Child maltreatment: Fact sheet.* Retrieved May 2, 2005, from http://www.cdc.gov/ncipc/factsheets/cmfacts.htm.

Centers for Disease Control and Prevention. (2005b). *Trends in reportable sexually transmitted diseases in the United States, 2004. National Surveillance Data for Chlamydia, Gonorrhea, and Syphillis. Sexually Transmitted Disease Surveillance, 2004.* Atlanta: U.S. Department of Health and Human Services, Centers for Disease Control and Prevention.

Centers for Disease Control and Prevention. (2006a). *Breastfeeding: Data and statistics: Breastfeeding practices—Results from the 2005 National Immunization Survey.* Retrieved December 11, 2006, from http://www.cdc.gov/breastfeedomgdat/NIS_data/data_2005.htm.

Centers for Disease Control and Prevention. (2006b). *Cases of HIV infection and AIDS in the United States, 2004. HIV/AIDS surveillance report* (Vol. 16). Atlanta, GA: U.S. Department of Health and Human Services, Centers for Disease Control and Prevention.

Centers for Disease Control and Prevention. (2008a). *Teen pregnancy and birth rates: Birth rates in teen girls ages 15–19, 2006.* CDC/National Center for Health Statistics. Retrieved November 1, 2009, http://www.cdc.gov/featerues/dsteenpregnancy.

Centers for Disease Control and Prevention. (2008b). *NCHS Data on teenage pregnancy.* CDC/National Center for Health Statistics. Retrieved November 1, 2009, from http://www.cdc.gov/nchs/data/infosheets/infosheet_teen_preg.htm.

Centers for Disease Control and Prevention. (2008c). *Sexual violence: Facts at a glance.* Washington, DC: Author. Retrieved January 19, 2010, from http://www.cdc.gov/violenceprevention/pdf/SV-DataSheet-a.pdf.

Centers for Disease Control and Prevention. (2008d). *Youth risk behavior surveillance—United States, 2007.* Retrieved May 19, 2010, from http://cdc.gov/mmwr/preview/mmwrtml/ss5704a1.htm.

Centers for Disease Control and Prevention. (2009a). *Assisted reproduction technology (ART) report: National summary and fertility clinic reports.* Retrieved January 8, 2010, from http://apps.nccd.cdc.gov/ART/Marquee.aspx.

Centers for Disease Control and Prevention. (2009b). *Teen births.* CDC/National Center for Health Statistics. Retrieved October 31, 2009, from http://www.cdc.gov/nchs/fastats/beenbrth.htm.

Centers for Disease Control and Prevention. (2009c). *Teen birth rates up again in 2007.* CDC/National Center for Health Statistics. Retrieved November 8, 2009, from http://www.cdc.gov/nchs/pressroom/09newsreleases/teenbirth2007.htm.

Centers for Disease Control and Prevention. (2009d). *FastStats: Birthweight and gestation.* Retrieved January 17, 2010, from http://www.cdc.gov/nchs/fastats/birthwt.htm.

Centers for Disease Control & Prevention. (2009e). *Autism spectrum disorders*. Retrieved February 22, 2010, from http://www.cdc.gov/ncbddd/autism/screening.html.

Centers for Disease Control and Prevention. (2009f). *Sexually transmitted diseases surveillance, 2007*. Retrieved February 9, 2010, from http://www.cdc.gov/std/stats07/natoverview.htm.

Centers for Disease Control and Prevention. (n.d.a). *Sexually transmitted diseases. Genital HPV infection—CDC fact sheet*. Retrieved January 5, 2007, from http://www.cdc.gov/std/HPV/STDFact-HPV.htm.

Centers for Disease Control and Prevention. (n.d.b). *Sexually transmitted diseases. Trichomoniasis—CDC Fact Sheet*. Retrieved January 5, 2007, from http://www.cdc.gov/std/trichomonas/STDFact-Trichomoniasis.htm.

Central Intellegence Agency. (2009). *The world fact book*. Retrieved August 24, 2009, from https://www.cia.gov/library/publications/the-world-factbook/.

Chadwick, R., Levitt, M., & Shickle, D. (1997). *The right to know and the right not to know*. Brookfield, VT: Avebury.

Chambliss, L. R. (2008). Intimate partner violence and its implications for pregnancy. *Clinical Obstetrics and Gynecology, 51*(2), 385–397.

Champagne, E. (2001). Listening to . . . listening for . . . : A theological reflection on spirituality in early childhood. In J. Erriker, C. Ota, & C. Erricker (Eds.), *Spiritual education: Cultural, religious, and social differences: New perspectives for the 21st century*. Brighton, England: Sussex Academic.

Champion, J. D., Piper, J., Holden, A., Korte, J., & Shain, R. N. (2004). Abused women and risk for pelvic inflammatory disease. *Western Journal of Nursing Research, 26*(2), 176–195.

Champion, J. D., Piper, J., Holden, A., Shain, R. N., Perdue, S., & Dorte, J. E. (2005). Relationship of abuse and pelvic inflammatory disease risk behavior in minority adolescents. *Journal of the American Academy of Nurse Practitioners, 17*(6), 234–241.

Chan, B. C., & Lao, T. H. (2008). Effect of parity and advanced maternal age on obstetric outcome. *International Journal of Gynecology and Obstetrics, 102*(3), 237–241.

Chang, G., McNamara, T., Orav, E., & Wilkins-Haug, L. (2006). Alcohol use by pregnant women: Partners, knowledge and other predictors. *Journal of Studies of Alcoholism, 67*(20), 245–251.

Chang, L. (2001). The development of racial attitudes and self concepts of Taiwanese preschoolers (China). *Dissertation Abstracts International: Section A: Humanities & Social Sciences, 61*(8-A), 3045.

Chang, S. H., Cheng, B. H., Lee, S. L., Chuang, H. Y., Yang, C. Y., Sung, F. C., et al. (2005). Low blood lead concentration in association with infertility in women. *Environmental Research 101*(3), 380–386.

Chapman, M. V., & Perreira, K. M. (2005). The well-being of immigrant Latino youth: A framework to inform practice. *Families in Society, 86*, 104–111.

Charles, P., & Perreira, K. (2007). Intimate partner violence during pregnancy and 1-year post-partum. *Journal of Family Violence, 22*(7), 609–619.

Charles, V. E., Polis, C. B., Sridhara, S. K. & Blum, R. W. (2008). Abortion and long-term mental health outcomes: A systematic review of the evidence. *Contraception, 79*(6), 436–450.

Charlesworth, L. (2007). Child maltreatment. In E. Hutchison, H. Matto, M. Harrigan, L. Charlesworth, & P. Viggiani (Eds.), *Challenges of living: A multidimensional working model for social workers* (pp. 105–139). Thousand Oaks, CA: Sage.

Chase-Lansdale, P. L., & Vinovskis, M. A. (1995). Whose responsibility? An historical analysis of the changing roles of mothers, fathers, and society. In P. L. Chase-Lansdale & J. Brooks-Gunn (Eds.), *Escape from poverty: What makes a difference for children?* (pp. 11–37). New York: Cambridge University Press.

Chavarro, J. E., Rich-Edwards, J. W., Rosner, B. A., & Willett, W. C. (2007). Diet and lifestyle in the prevention of ovulatory disorder fertility. *Obstetrics and Gynecology, 110*(5), 1050–1058.

Chavarro, J. E., Rich-Edwards, J. W., Rosner, B. A., & Willett, W. C. (2009). Caffeine and alcohol do not affect ovulation to the point of reducing fertility. *Epidemiology, 20*(3), 374–381.

Cheap IVF Needed: Editorial. (2006, August). *Nature, 442*(31), 958. Retrieved October 28, 2006, from http://www.nature.com.proxy.lib.odu.edu/nature/journal/v442/n7106/pdf/442958a.pdf.

Check, J. H. (2007). Treatment of male infertility. *Clinical and Experimental Obstetrics and Gynecology, 34*(4), 201–207.

Chedraui, P. (2008). Pregnancy among young adolescents: Trends, risk factors, and maternal-perinatal outcome. *Journal of Perinatal Medicine, 36*(3), 256–259.

Chen, C. (2006a). Does the completeness of a household-based convoy matter in intergenerational support exchanges? *Social Indicators Research, 79*, 117–142.

Chen, C. (2006b). A household-based convoy and the reciprocity of support exchange between adult children and noncoresiding parents. *Journal of Family Issues, 27*(8), 1100–1136.

Chen, X. (2009). The linkage between deviant lifestyles and victimization: An examination from a life course perspective. *Journal of Interpersonal Violence, 24*(7), 1083–1110.

Chestang, L. (1972). *Character development in a hostile environment*. Chicago: University of Chicago Press.

Chethik, M. (2000). *Techniques of child therapy: Psychodynamic approaches* (2nd ed.). New York: Guilford Press.

Cheung, G., & Todd-Oldehaver, C. (2006). Personality trait of harm avoidance in late-life depression. *International Journal of Geriatric Psychiatry, 21*(2), 192–193.

Child Welfare League of America. (2005). *Statement of the Child Welfare League of America for House Subcommittee on Human Resources of the Committee on Ways and Means for the hearing on federal foster care financing.* Retrieved December 27, 2006, from http://www.cwla.org/advocacy/fostercare050609.htm.

Children's Defense Fund. (2000). *Yearbook 2000: The state of America's children.* Washington, DC: Author.

Children's Defense Fund. (2008). *The state of America's children, 2008.* Washington, DC: Author.

Chodorow, N. (1978). *The reproduction of mothering: Psychoanalysis and the sociology of gender.* Berkeley: University of California Press.

Chodorow, N. (1989). *Feminism and psychoanalytic theory.* New Haven, CT: Yale University Press.

Choi, S., & Tittle, G. (2002). *Parental substance abuse and child maltreatment literature review.* Retrieved January 19, 2010, from http://www.cfrc.illinois.edu/LRpdfs/ParentalSAMaltx.LR.pdf.

Chomsky, N. (1968). *Language and mind.* New York: Harcourt Brace Jovanovich.

Chowdhury, F. (2004). The socio-cultural context of child marriage in a Bangladeshi village. *International Journal of Social Welfare, 13,* 244–253.

Christiansen, O. B., Nielsen, H. S., & Kolte, A. M. (2006). Future directions of failed implantation and recurrent miscarriage research. *Reproductive Biomedicine Online, 13.*

Chugani, H., Behen, M., Muzik, O., Juhasz, C., Nagy, F., & Chugani, D. (2001). Local brain functional activity following early deprivation: A study of post-institutional Romanian orphans. *Neuroimage, 14,* 1290–1301.

Chumlea, W. C., Schubert, C. M., Roche, A. F., Kulin, H. E., Lee, P. A., Himes, J. H., et al. (2003). Age at menarche and racial comparisons in US girls. *Pediatrics, 111*(1), 110–113.

Clare, R., Mazzucchelli, T., Studman, L., & Sanders, M. (2006). Behavioral family intervention for children with developmental disabilities and behavioral problems. *Journal of Clinical Child and Adolescent Psychology, 35*(2), 180–193.

Clark, K., & Clark, M. (1939). The development of consciousness of self and the emergence of racial identification in Negro preschool children. *Journal of Social Psychology, 10,* 591–599.

Clark, M. K., Dillon, J. Sowers, M., & Nichols, S. (2005). Weight, fat mass, and central distribution of fat increase when women use depotmedroxprogesterone acetate for contraception. *International Journal of Obesity, 29*(10), 1252–1258.

Clark, P. A. (2009). Embryo donation/adoption: Medical, legal, and ethical perspectives. *The Internet Journal of Law, Healthcare, and Ethics, 5*(2), 1–12. Retrieved May 19, 2010, from http://www.ispub.journal/the_internet_journal_of_law_he althcare_and_ethics.volume_5_number_1_45/article/emb ryo_donation_adoption_medical_legal_and_ethical_perspectives.htm.

Clark, R., Glick, J. Bures, R. (2009). Immigrant families over the life course. *Journal of Family Issues, 30*(6), 852–872.

Clarke, J., & Craven, A. (2005). The gender balance. *Geography Review, 19*(1), 2–5.

Clarke-Stewart, K. A. (1988). "The 'effects' of infant day care reconsidered" reconsidered: Risks for parents, children, and researchers. *Early Childhood Research Quarterly, 3*(3), 293–318.

Clarke, L. (2008). Grandparents: A family resource? In D. R. Crane & T. Heaton (Eds.), *Handbook of families & poverty* (pp. 365–380). Thousand Oaks, CA: Sage.

Clarke-Stewart, K. A. (1989). Infant day care: Maligned or malignant? *American Psychologist, 17,* 454–462.

Clayton, A. (2004). Mental health concerns with infertility. *Primary Psychiatry, 11*(5), 17–18.

Clearfield, M., & Nelson, N. (2006). Sex differences in mothers' speech and play behavior with 6-, 9-, and 14-month-old infants. *Sex Roles, 54*(1/2), 127–137.

Clearinghouse on International Developments in Child, Youth and Family Policies at Columbia University. (2002). *Child policy international.* Retrieved June 7, 2002, from http://www.childpolicyintl.org.

Cohen, J., & Sandy, S. (2007). The social, emotional and academic education of children: Theories, goals, methods and assessments. In R. Bar-On, J. Maree, & M. Elias (Eds.), *Educating people to be emotionally intelligent* (pp. 63–77). Wesport, CT: Praeger.

Coid, J., Petruckevitch, A., Feder, G., Chung, W. S., Richardson, J., & Moorey, S. (2001). Relation between childhood sexual and physical abuse and risk of revictimisation in women: A cross-sectional survey. *The Lancet, 358,* 450–454.

Coie, J. D., Dodge, K. A., & Coppotelli, H. (1982). Dimensions and types of social status: A cross age perspective. *Developmental Psychology, 18,* 557–570.

Cole, P., Luby, J., & Sullivan, M. (2008). Emotions and the development of childhood depression: Bridging the gap. *Child Development Perspectives, 2*(3), 141–148.

Cole, S. S., & Cole, T. M. (1993). Sexuality, disability, and reproductive issues through the lifespan. In F. P. Haseltine, S. S. Cole, & D. B. Gray (Eds.), *Reproductive issues for persons with physical disabilities* (pp. 3–21). Baltimore: Brookes.

Coles, L. S. (2004). Demography of human supercentenarians. *Journal of Gerontology: Biological Sciences, 59*(6), 579–586.

Coles, R. (1987). *The moral life of children.* Boston: Houghton Mifflin.

Coles, R. (1990). *The spiritual life of children.* Boston, MA.

Coles, R. (1997). *The moral intelligence of children.* New York: Random House.

Collins, A. L., & Smyer, M. A. (2005). The resilience of self-esteem in late adulthood. *Journal of Aging and Health, 17*(4), 471–489.

Coltrane, S. (2000). Research on household labor: Modeling and measuring the social embeddedness of routine family work. *Journal of Marriage and the Family, 62,* 1208–1233.

Comer, J. P. (1994). Home, school, and academic learning. In K. I. Goodland & P. Keating (Eds.), *Access to knowledge: The continuing agenda for our nation's schools.* New York: College Board.

Comprehensive School Reform Quality Center and American Institutes for Research. (2006). *CSRQ Center report on middle and high school comprehensive school reform models.* Retrieved December 30, 2006, from http://www.csrq.org/documents/MSHS2006Report_FinalFullVersion11-16-06.pdf.

Condon, J. (2006). What about dad? Psychosocial and mental health issues for new fathers. *Australian Family Physician, 35*(9), 690–692.

Conger, R., & Conger, K. (2008). Understanding the processes through which economic hardship influences families and children. In D. Crane & T. Heaton (Eds.), *Handbook of families & poverty* (pp. 64–81). Thousand Oaks, CA: Sage.

Conn, D. K. (2001). Mental health issues in long-term care facilities. In D. Conn, N. Herrmann, A. Kaye, D. Rewilak, & B. Schogt (Eds.), *Practical psychiatry in the long-term care facility: A handbook for staff* (pp. 1–16). Seattle, WA: Hogrefe & Huber.

Connie, T. A. (1988). *Aids and adaptations for disabled parents: An illustrated manual for service providers and parents with physical or sensory disabilities* (2nd ed.). Vancouver: University of British Columbia, School of Rehabilitation Medicine.

Connor, D., Gabel, S., Gallagher, D., & Morton, M. (2008). Disability studies and inclusive education: Implications for theory, research and practice. *International Journal of Inclusive Education, 12*(5–6), 441–457.

Connor, M. E., & White, J. L. (2006). *Black fathers: An invisible presence in America.* Mahwah, NJ: Lawrence Erlbaum.

Constable, R., & Walberg, H. (1996). School social work: Facilitating home-school partnerships in the 1990s. In R. Constable, J. P. Flynn, & S. McDonald (Eds.), *School social work: Practice and research perspectives* (3rd ed., pp. 182–196). Chicago: Lyceum Books.

Contraceptive Technology Update. (2005). Teens improve contraceptive use, but more women at risk for pregnancy. *Author, 26*(3), 29–32.

Contraceptive Technology Update. (2007). U.S. teen pregnancy rates decline due to improved contraceptive use. *Author, 28*(3), 25–36.

Coohey, C. (1996). Child maltreatment: Testing the isolation hypothesis. *Child Abuse and Neglect, 20*(3), 241–254.

Cooper, P. G. (2000). Ectopic pregnancy. *Clinical Reference Systems, Annual, 2000,* 565.

Cooper, T. (2004). Changing the culture, normalizing birth. *British Journal of Midwifery, 12*(4), 45–49.

Corbin, J. M. (1987). Women's perceptions and management of pregnancy complicated by chronic illness. *Health Care Women International, 8*(5–6), 317–337.

Corcoran, M., Danziger, S. K., Kalil, A., & Seefeldt, K. S. (2000). How welfare reform is affecting women's work. *Annual Review of Sociology, 26,* 241–269.

Cordero, L., Hines, S., Shibley, K. A., & Landon, M. B. (1992). Perinatal outcome for women in prison. *Journal of Perinatology, 12,* 205–209.

Cornish, J. A., Tan, E., Simillis, C., Clark, S. K., Teare, J., & Tekkis, P. P. (2008). The risk of oral contraceptives in the etiology of inflammatory bowel disease: A meta analysis. *American Jouranl of Gastroenterology, 103*(9), 2394–2400.

Cornwell, B., Laumann, E.O., & Schumm, L.P. (2008). The social connectedness of older adults: A national profile. *American Sociological Review, 73*(2), 185–203.

Corsaro, W. (2005). *The sociology of childhood* (2nd ed.). Thousand Oaks, CA: Pine Forge.

Costa, F. M., Jessor, R., Donovan, J. E., & Fortenberry, J. D. (1995). Early initiation of sexual intercourse: The influence of psychosocial unconventionality. *Journal of Research on Adolescents, 5,* 93–121.

Costa, P., Terracciano, A., & McCrae, R. (2001). Gender differences in personality traits across cultures: Robust and surprising findings. *Journal of Personality and Social Psychology, 81*(2), 322.

Costigan, C., & Dokis, D. (2006). Similarities and differences in acculturation among mothers, fathers, and children in immigrant Chinese families. *Journal of Cross-Cultural Psychology, 37,* 723–741.

Costigan, C., Su, T., & Hua, J. (2009). Ethnic identity among Chinese Canadian youth: A review of the Canadian literature. *Canadian Psychology, 50*(4), 261–272.

Cota-Robles, S., Neiss, M., & Rowe, D. C. (2002). The role of puberty in violent and nonviolent delinquency among Anglo American, Mexican American, and African American boys. *Journal of Adolescent Research, 17,* 364–376.

Cotter, A., & O'Sullivan, M. (2004). Update on managing HIV in pregnancy: It's imperative to identify more HIV-infected women earlier in pregnancy through HIV testing and to reduce mother-to-child transmission of the virus that causes AIDS. *Contemporary OB/GYN, 49*(11), 57–66.

Coughlan, R., & Owens-Manley, J. (2006). *Bosnian refugees in America: New communities, new cultures.* New York: Springer Science and Business Media, Inc.

Council on Social Work Education. (2008). *Educational policy and accreditation standards.* Alexandria, VA: Author.

Counts, D. R., & Counts, D. A. (1991). *Coping with the final tragedy: Cultural variation in dying and grieving.* Amityville, NY: Baywood.

Cousins, E. (2000). *Roots: From outward bound to expeditionary learning.* Dubuque, IA: Kendall Hunt Publishing.

Cowan, P. A. (1991). Individual and family life transitions: A proposal for a new definition. In P. A. Cowan & M. Hetherington (Eds.), *Family transitions* (pp. 3–30). Hillsdale, NJ: Lawrence Erlbaum.

Cowles, K. V. (1996). Cultural perspectives of grief: An expanded concept analysis. *Journal of Advanced Nursing, 23,* 287–294.

Cox, G. R. (2009). Death, dying, and end of life in American-Indian communities. In D. J. Doka & A. S. Tucci, *Living with grief: Diversity and end-of-life care.* (pp. 107–115). Washington, DC: Hospice Foundation of America.

Cox, S. J., Glazebrook, C., Sheard, C., Ndukwe, G., & Oates, M. (2006). Maternal self-esteem after successful treatment for infertility. *Fertility and Sterility, 85*(1), 84–89.

Craig, G. J., &. Baucum, D. (2002). *Human development* (9th ed.). Upper Saddle River, NJ: Prentice Hall.

Crain, R. (1996). The influences of age, race, and gender on child and adolescent multidimensional self-concept. In B. Bracken (Ed.), *Handbook of self-concept* (pp. 395–420). New York: Wiley.

Crane, J. & Winsler, A. (2008). Early autism detection: implications for pediatric practice and public policy. *Journal of Disability Policy Studies, 18*(4), 245–253.

Crawford, J. J., Nobles, W. W., & Leary, J. D. (2003). Reparations and healthcare for African Americans: Repairing the damage from the legacy of slavery. In R. Winbush (Ed.), *Should America pay? Slavery and the raging debate on reparations* (pp. 251–281). New York: Harper Collins Publishing.

Crawley, L., Payne, R., Bolden, J., Payne, T., Washington, P., & Williams, S. (2000). Palliative and end-of-life care in the African American community. *Journal of the American Medical Association, 284*(19), 2518–2521.

Cristafalo, V., Tresini, M., Francis, M., & Volker, C. (1999). Biological theories of senescence. In V. L. Bengston & K. W. Schaie (Eds.), *Handbook of theories of aging* (pp. 98–112). New York: Springer.

Critchley, H. O., & Wallace, W. H. (2005). Impact of cancer treatment on uterine function. *Journal of the National Cancer Institute, 34,* 64–68.

Croteau, A., Marcoux, S., & Brisson, C. (2007). Work activity in pregnancy, preventative measures, and the risk of preterm delivery. *American Journal of Epidemiology, 166*(8), 951–966.

Croteau, D., & Hoynes, W. (2006). *The business of media: Corporate media and the public interest* (2nd ed.). Thousand Oaks, CA: Pine Forge Press.

Croxatto, H. B., Brache, V., Massai, R., Ivarez, F., Forcelledo, M. L., Pavez, M., et al. (2005). Feasibility study of Nestorone-ethinylestradiol vaginal contraceptive ring for emergency contraception. *Contraception, 73*(1), 46–52.

Crozier, J. C., & Barth, R. P. (2005). Cognitive and academic functioning in maltreated children. *Children & Schools, 27*(4), 197–206.

Csikai, E. L., & Jones, B. (2007). *Teaching resources for end of life and palliative care courses.* Chicago: Lyceum Books, Inc.

Csikszentmihalyi, M., & Schneider, B. (2000). *Becoming adult: How teenagers prepare for the world of work.* New York: Basic Books.

Culp, R., McDonald Culp, A., Dengler, B., & Maisano, P. (1999). First-time young mothers living in rural communities use of corporal punishment with their toddlers. *Journal of Community Psychology, 27*(4), 503–509.

Cumming, E., & Henry, W. (1961). *Growing old.* New York: Basic Books.

Cwikel, J., Gidron, Y., & Sheiner, E. (2004). Psychological interactions with infertility among women. *European Journal of Obstetrics and Gynecology and Reproductive Biology, 117,* 126–131.

Czaja, S. (2006). Employment and the baby boomers: What can we expect in the future? In S. Whitbourne & S. Willis (Eds.), *The baby boomers grow up: Contemporary perspectives on midlife* (pp. 283–298). Mahway, NJ: Lawrence Erlbaum Associates.

Dahlberg, G., Moss, P., & Pence, A. (2007). *Beyond quality in early childhood education and care: Postmodern perspectives* (2nd ed.). New York: Routledge Falmer.

Dalby, P. (2006). Is there a process of spiritual change or development associated with ageing? A critical review of research. *Aging and Mental Health, 10*(1), 4–12.

Dallas, C. M. (2009). Interactions between adolescent fathers and health care professionals during pregnancy, labor, and early postpartum. *Journal of Obstetric, Gynecologic & Neonatal Nursing, 38*(3), 290–299.

Damus, K. (2008). Prevention of premature births: A renewed national priority. *Current Opinions in Obstetrics and Gynecology, 20,* 590–596.

Dannefer, D. (2003a). Whose life course is it, anyway? Diversity and "linked lives" in global perspective. In R. Settersten, Jr. (Ed.), *Invitation to the life course: Toward new understandings of later life* (pp. 259–268). Amityville, NY: Baywood Publishing Co., Inc.

Dannefer, D. (2003b). Toward a global geography of the life course: Challenges of late modernity for life course theory. In J. Mortimer & M. Shanahan (Eds.), *Handbook of the life course* (pp. 647–659). New York: Kluwer Academic/Plenum Publishers.

Dannefer, D., & Perlmutter, M. (1990). Development as a multidimensional process: Individuals and social constituents. *Human Development, 33,* 108–137.

Darcy, A. E. (2009). Complications of the late preterm infant. *The Journal of Perinatal and Neonatal Nursing, 23*(1), 78–86.

Darling-Hammond, L. (2007). The flat earth and education: How America's commitment to equity will determine our future. *Educational Researcher, 36*(6), 318–334.

Datar, A., & Jacknowitz, A. (2009). Birth weight effects on children's mental, motor, and physical development. *Maternal and Child Health Journal, 13*(6), 780–794.

D'Augelli, A., Grossman, A., & Starks, M. (2005). Parents' awareness of lesbian, gay, and bisexual youths' sexual orientation. *Journal of Marriage and Family, 67,* 474–482.

David, H. P. (1996). Induced abortion: Psychosocial aspects. In J. J. Sciarra (Ed.), *Gynecology and obstetrics* (Vol. 6, pp. 1–8). Philadelphia: Lippincott-Raven.

Davidson, J., Moore, N., & Ullstrup, L. (2004). Religiosity and sexual responsibilities: Relationships of choice. *Journal of Health Behavior, 28*(4), 335–346.

Davies, D. (2004) *Child development: A practitioner's guide* (2nd ed.). New York: Guilford Press.

Davis, B., & Jocoy, S. (2008). *In vitro fertilization for infertility.* WebMD. Retrieved December 27, 2009, from http://www.webmd.com/infertility-and-reproduction/in-vitro-fertilization-for-infertility.

Davis, D., Webster, P., Stainthrope, H., Chilton, J., Jones, L., & Doi, R. (2007). Declines in sex ratio at birth and fetal deaths in Japan, and in U.S. whites but not African Americans. *Environmental Health Perspectives, 115*(6), 941–946.

Davis, M., & Vander Stoep, A. (1997). The transition to adulthood for youth who have serious emotional disturbance: Developmental transition and young adult outcomes. *Journal of Mental Health Administration, 24*(4), 400–427.

Davis, R. (2001). The postpartum experience for southeastern Asian women in United States. *MCN: The American Journal of Maternal/Child Nursing, 26*(4), 208–213.

Dean, R. G. (1993). Teaching a constructivist approach to clinical practice. In J. Laird (Ed.), *Revisioning social work education: A social constructionist approach* (pp. 55–75). New York: Haworth Press.

De Brucker, M., Haentjens, P., Evenepoel, J., Devroey, P., Collins, J., & Tournaye, H. (2009). Cumulative delivery rates in different age groups after artificial insemination with donor sperm. *Human Reproduction, 24*(8), 1891–1899.

Declercq, E. R., Paine, L. L., & Winter, M. R. (1995). Home birth in the United States, 1989–1992. A longitudinal descriptive report of national birth certificate data. *Journal of Nurse-Midwifery, 40*(6), 474–482.

de Escobar, G. M. (2004). Maternal thyroid hormones early in pregnancy and fetal brain. *Clinical Endocrinology and Metabolism, 18*(2), 225–248.

de Escobar, G. M., Ares, S., Berbel, P., Obregon, M. J., & del rey, F. E. (2008). The changing role of maternal thyroid hormone in fetal brain development. *Seminars in Perinatology, 32*(6), 380–386.

Deeg, D. (2005). The development of physical and mental health from late midlife to early old age. In S. Willis & M. Martin (Eds.), *Middle adulthood: A lifespan perspective* (pp. 209–241). Thousand Oaks, CA: Sage.

Degges-White, S. (2005). Understanding gerotranscendence in older adults: A new perspective for counselors. *Adultspan Journal, 4*(1), 36–48.

DeHart, G. B., Sroufe, L. A., & Cooper, R. G. (2000). *Child development: Its nature and course* (4th ed.). Boston: McGraw-Hill.

DeJong, W. (1993). Obesity as a characterological stigma: The issue of responsibility and judgments of task performance. *Psychological Reports, 73,* 963–970.

de Jonge, A., van der Goes, B. Y. Ravelli, A. C. J., Amelink-Verbury, M. P., Mol, B. W., Nijhuis, J. G., et al. (2009). Prenatal mortality and morbidity in a nationwide cohort of 529,688 low-risk, planned home and hospital births. *BJOG: An Internatnional Journal of Obstetrics and Gynaecology, 116*(9), 1177–1184.

Delany, S., & Delany, E., with Hearth, A. (1993). *Having our say: The Delany sisters' first 100 years.* New York: Kodansha International.

Delany, S., with Hearth, A. (1997). *On my own at 107: Reflections on life without Bessie.* New York: HarperCollins.

Delaunay-El Allam, M., Marlier, L., & Schaal, B. (2006). Learning at the breast: Preference formation for the artificial scent and its attraction against the odor of maternal milk. *Infant Behavior and Development, 29*(3), 308–321.

Delgado, C. E. F., Vagi, S. J., & Scott, K. G. (2007). Identification of early risk factors for developmental delay. *Exceptionality, 15*(2), 119–136.

Della Porta, D., & Diani, M. (2006). *Social movements: An introduction* (2nd ed.). Malden, MA: Blackwell.

Dellmann-Jenkins, M. & Blankemeyer, M. (2009). Emerging and young adulthood and caregiving. In K. Shifren (Ed.), *How caregiving affects development: Psychological implications for child, adolescent, and adult caregivers* (pp. 93–117). Washington, DC: American Psychological Association.

Dellmann-Jenkins, M., Blankemeyer, M., & Pinkard, O. (2001). Incorporating the elder caregiving role into the developmental tasks of young adulthood. *International Journal of Aging and Human Development, 52*(1), 1.

Del Rio, N. (2004). A framework for multicultural end-of-life care: Enhancing social work practice. In J. Berzoff & P. R. Silverman

(Eds.), *Living with dying: A handbook for end-of-life healthcare practitioners* (pp. 439–461). New York: Columbia University Press.

De Marco, A. C., & Cosner Berzin, S. (2008). The influence of family economic status on home-leaving patterns during emerging adulthood. *Families in Society, 89*(2), 208–218.

Denner, J., & Dunbar, N. (2004). Negotiating femininity: Power and strategies of Mexican American girls. *Sex Roles, 50, 301–314.*

Dennis, C., & Chung-Lee, L. (2006). Postpartum depression help-seeking barriers and maternal treatment preferences: A qualitative systematic review. *Birth, 33*(4), 323–331.

Dennison, B., Edmunds, J., & Stratton, H. (2006). Rapid infant weight gain predicts childhood overweight. *Obesity, 14*(3), 491–499.

Department of Health and Human Services (DHHS). (2006a). *Drug Abuse Warning Network, 2004: National estimates of drug-related emergency department visits* (DAWN Series D-28, DHHS Publication No. (SMA) 06–4143). Rockville, MD: Author.

Department of Health and Human Services (DHHS). (2006b). *Fertility, contraception, and fatherhood: Data on men and women from cycle 6 of the 2002 National Survey of Family Growth* (DHHS Publication No. (PHS) 2006–1978). Hyattsville, MD: Author.

Derbyshire, E., & Abdula, S. (2008). Habitual caffeine intake in women of childbearing age. *Journal of Human Nutrition and Dietetics: The Official Journal of the British Dietetic Association, 21*(2), 159–164.

Derman, S. G., & Seifer, D. B. (2003). In vitro fertilization in the older patient. *Current Women's Health Reports, 3*(5), 275–283.

DeRosier, M. E., Kupersmidt, J. B., & Patterson, C. J. (1994). Children's academic and behavioral adjustment as a function of the chronicity and proximity of peer rejection. *Child Development, 65,* 1799–1813.

De Schipper, J., Tavecchio, L., & Van IJzendoorn, M. (2008). Children's attachment relationship with day care caregivers: Associations with positive caregiving and the child's temperament. *Social Development, 17*(3), 454–470.

DeSpelder, L. A., & Strickland, A. L. (2005). *The last dance: Encountering death and dying* (7th ed.). Boston: McGraw-Hill.

de St. Aubin, E., McAdams, D., & Kim, T. (2004). *The generative society: Caring for future generations.* Washington, DC: American Psychological Association.

Devitt, N. (1977). The transition from home to hospital births in the United States. *Birth and Family Journal, 4,* 47–58.

de Vries, B., & Watt, D. (1996). A lifetime of events: Age and gender variations in the life story. *International Journal of Aging and Human Development, 42*(2), 81–102.

Diamond, L. (2000). Passionate friendships among adolescent sexual-minority women. *Journal of Research on Adolescence, 10,* 191–209.

Diamond, L. M., & Savin-Williams, R. C. (2003). Gender and sexual identity. In R. M. Lerner, F. Jacobs, & D. Wertlieb (Eds.), *Handbook of applied developmental science* (Vol. 1, pp. 101–121). Thousand Oaks, CA: Sage.

Dickason, E. J., Schult, M., & Silverman, B. L. (1990). *Maternal-infant nursing care.* St. Louis, MO: Mosby.

Dickason, E., Silverman, B., & Kaplan, J. (1998). *Maternal-infant nursing care* (3rd ed.). St. Louis, MO: Mosby.

Dick-Read, G. (1944). *Childbirth without fear: Principles and practices of natural childbirth.* New York: Harper & Row.

Diekema, D. S. (2003). Involuntary sterilization of persons with mental retardation: An ethical analysis. *Mental Retardation and Developmental Disabilities Research Reviews, 9*(1), 21–26.

Dinitto, D. M., & Cummings, L. K. (2006). *Social welfare: Politics and public policy* (6th ed.). Boston: Allyn & Bacon.

Dioussé, L., Driver, J., & Gaziano, J. (2009). Relation between modifiable lifestyle factors and lifetime risk of heart failure. *Journal of American Medical Association, 302*(4), 394–400.

Direnfeld, D., & Roberts, J. (2006). Mood congruent memory in dysphoria: The roles of state affect and cognitive style. *Behavior Research and Therapy, 44*(9), 1275–1285.

Dirubbo, N. E. (2006). Counsel your patients about contraceptive options. *The Nurse Practitioner, 31*(4), 40–44.

Disabled Women's Network Ontario. (2006). *Forced sterilization & women with disabilities.* Retrieved February 10, 2010, from http://dawn.thot.net/forced_sterilization.html.

Dittmann-Kohli, F. (2005). Middle age and identity in a cultural and lifespan perspective. In S. Willis & M. Martin (Eds.), *Middle adulthood: A lifespan perspective* (pp. 319–353). Thousand Oaks, CA: Sage.

Doka, K. J., & Tucci, A. S. (2009). *Living with grief: Diversity and end-of-life care.* Washington, DC: Hospice Foundation of America.

Dolinsky, A. L., & Rosenwaike, I. (1988). The role of demographic factors in the institutionalization of the elderly. *Research on Aging, 10,* 235–257.

Dollahite, D., Slife, B., & Hawkins, A. (1998). Family generativity and generative counseling: Helping families keep faith with the next generation. In D. McAdams & E. de St. Aubin (Eds.), *Generativity and adult development: How and why we care for the next generation* (pp. 449–481). Washington, DC: American Psychological Association.

Domenech Rodriguez, M., Donovick, M., & Crowley, S. (2009). Parenting styles in a cultural context: Observations of "protective parenting" in first-generation Latinos. *Family Process, 48*(2), 195–210.

Domina, T. (2005). Leveling the home advantage: Assessing the effectiveness of parental involvement in elementary school. *Sociology of Education, 78*(3), 233–249.

DONA International. (n.d.). *For mothers & families s.* Retrieved May 20, 2010, from http://www.dona.org/mothers/index.php.

Donleavy, G. (2008). No man's land: Exploring the space between Gilligan and Kohlberg. *Journal of Business Ethics, 80,* 807–822.

Donnelly, T., Atkins, R., Hart, D. (2005). The relationship between spiritual development and civic engagement. In P. Benson, E. Roehlkepartain, P. King, & L. Wagener (Eds.), *The handbook of spiritual development in childhood and adolescence.* Thousand Oaks, CA: Sage.

Donovan, J., Jessor, R., & Costa, F. (1999). Adolescent problem drinking: Stability of psychosocial and behavioral correlates across a generation. *Journal of Studies on Alcohol, 60*(3), 352–361.

Dörner, J., Mickler, C., & Studinger, U. (2005). Self-development at midlife: Lifespan perspectives on adjustment and growth. In S. Willis & M. Martin (Eds.), *Middle adulthood: A lifespan perspective* (pp. 277–317). Thousand Oaks, CA: Sage.

Doughty, E. A. (2009). Investigating adaptive grieving styles: A delphi study. *Death Studies, 33,* 462–480.

Downs, A. C., & Langlois, J. H. (1988). Sex typing: Construct and measurement issues. *Sex Roles, 18*(1–2), 87–100.

Downs, S. W., Moore, E., McFadden, E. J., Michaud, S. M., & Costin, L. B. (2004). *Child welfare and family services: Policies and practice* (7th ed.). Boston: Pearson.

Draut, T. (2005). *Strapped: Why America's 20- and 30-somethings can't get ahead.* New York: Doubleday.

Draut, T., & Silva, J. (2004). *Generation broke: The growth of debt among young Americans. Borrowing to make ends meet series.* Retrieved January 5, 2010, from http://archive.demos .org/Pubs/Generation_Broke.pdf.

Dryfoos, J. G. (1994). *Full-service schools: A revolution in health and social services for children, youth, and families.* San Francisco: Jossey-Bass.

Duarte, A., Ranganath, C., Trujillo, C., & Knight, R. T. (2006). Intact recollection memory in high-performing older-adults: RP and behavioral evidence. *Journal of Cognitive Neuroscience, 18*(1), 33–47.

Dubrow, N., & Garbarino, J. (1989). Living in the war zone: Mothers and young children in a public housing development. *Child Welfare, 68,* 3–20.

Dunbar, H. T., Mueller, C. W., Medina, C., & Wolf, T. (1998). Psychological and spiritual growth in women living with HIV. *Social Work, 43,* 144–154.

Duncan, G., Kalil, A., & Ziol-Guest, K. (2008). *Economic costs of early childhood poverty* (Issue Paper #4). Retrieved January 19, 2010, from http://www.partnershipforsuccess.org/docs/ researchproject_duncan_200802_paper.pdf.

Dundas, S., & Kaufman, M. (2000). The Toronto lesbian family study. *Journal of Homosexuality, 34*(2), 65–79.

DuPlessis, H. M., Bell, R., & Richards, T. (1997). Adolescent pregnancy: Understanding the impact of age and race on outcomes. *Journal of Adolescent Health, 20*(3), 187–197.

Dupper, D. R., & Poertner, J. (1997). Public schools and the revitalization of impoverished communities: School-linked, family resource centers. *Social Work, 42,* 415–422.

Durkin, K. (1995). *Developmental social psychology.* Malden, MA: Blackwell.

Dychtwald, K. (1999). *Age power: How the 21st century will be ruled by the new old.* New York: Jeremy P. Tarcher/Putnam.

Early Intervention Support. (2009). *Child development.* Retrieved February 15, 2010, from http://www.earlyinterventionsupport.com/development/.

East, P. L. (1996). The younger sisters of childbearing adolescents: Their attitudes, expectations, and behaviors. *Child Development, 67,* 267–282.

East, P. L., Khoo, S. T., & Reyes, B. T. (2006). Risk and protective factors predictive of adolescent pregnancy: A longitudinal, prospective study. *Applied Developmental Science, 10*(4), 188–199.

East, P. L., & Shi, C. R. (1997). Pregnant and parenting adolescents and their younger sisters: The influence of relationship qualities and younger sister outcomes. *Journal of Developmental and Behavioral Pediatrics, 18*(2), 84–90.

Edin, K., & Lein, L. (1997). *Making ends meet.* New York: Russell Sage Foundation.

Edlich, R. F., Winters, K. L., Long, W. B., III, & Gubler, K. D. (2005). Rubella and congenital rubella. *Journal of Long-Term Effects of Medical Implants, 15*(3), 319–328.

Education Daily. (2008). Study: U.S. teen birth, unmarried childbearing rates rise. *Education Daily, 41*(2), 6.

Education Trust. (2006). *Yes we can: Telling truths and dispelling myths about race and education in America.* Retrieved November 7, 2006, from http://www2.edutrust.org/edtrust.

Edwards, C. (1992). Normal development in the preschool years. In E. V. Nuttall, I. Romero, & J. Kalesnik (Eds.), *Assessing and screening preschoolers* (pp. 9–22). Boston: Allyn & Bacon.

Edwards, E., Eiden, R., & Leonard, K. (2006). Behavior problems in 18–36-month-old children of alcoholic fathers: Secure mother-father attachment as a protective factor. *Developmental and Psychopathology, 18*(2), 395–407.

Egeland, B., Carlson, E., & Sroufe, L. A. (1993). Resilience as process. *Development and Psychopathology, 5,* 517–528.

Eggebeen, D., & Sturgeon, S. (2006). Demography of the baby boomers. In S. Whitbourne & S. Willis (Eds.), *The baby boomers grow up: Contemporary perspectives on midlife* (pp. 3–21). Mahwah, NJ: Lawrence Erlbaum.

Ego, A. (2001). Survival analysis of fertility after ectopic pregnancy. *JAMA, The Journal of the American Medical Association, 285*(23), 2955.

Ehrenberg-Buchner, S., Sandadi, S., Moawad, N.S., Pinkerton, J., & Hurd, W. W. (2009). Ectopic pregnancy: Role of laparoscopic treatment. *Clinical Obstetrical Gynecology, 42*(3), 372–379.

Eisenberg, M., & Resnick, M. (2006). Suicidality among gay, lesbian and bisexual youth: The role of protective factors. *Journal of Adolescent Health, 39,* 662–668.

Eisenberg, N. (2000). Emotion, regulation, and moral development. *Annual Review of Psychology, 51,* 665–697.

Eisenberg, N. Guthrie, I., Murphy, B., Shepard, S., Cumberland, A., & Carlo, G. (1999). Consistency and development of prosocial dispositions: A longitudinal study. *Child Development, 70,* 1360–1372.

Elder, G., Jr. (1974). *Children of the Great Depression.* Chicago: University of Chicago Press.

Elder, G., Jr. (1986). Military times and turning points in men's lives. *Developmental Psychology, 22,* 233–245.

Elder, G., Jr. (1992). Life course. In E. Borgatta & M. Borgatta (Eds.), *Encyclopedia of sociology* (pp. 1120–1130). New York: Macmillan.

Elder, G., Jr. (1994). Time, human agency, and social change: Perspectives on the life course. *Social Psychology Quarterly, 57*(1), 4–15.

Elder, G., Jr. (1998). The life course as developmental theory. *Child Development, 69*(1), 1–12.

Elder, G., & Giele, J. (2009). Life course studies: An evolving field. In G. Edler & J. Giele (Eds.), *The craft of life course research* (pp. 1–24). New York: Guilford.

Elder, G., Jr., & Kirkpatrick Johnson, M. (2003). The life course and aging: Challenges, lessons, and new directions. In R. Settersten, Jr. (Ed.), *Invitation to the life course: Toward new understandings of later life* (pp. 49–81). Amityville, NY: Baywood Publishing Co.

Eliason, M., & Arndt, S. (2004). Pregnant inmates: A growing concern. *Journal of Addictions Nursing, 15*(4), 163–170.

Eliopoulus, C. (2010). *Gerontological nursing* (7th Ed.). Philadelphia: Lippincott, Williams & Wilkins.

Elkind, D. (2001). *The hurried child: Growing up too fast too soon* (3rd ed.). Reading, MA: Addison-Wesley.

Elley, N. (2001). Early birds, too early: Prematurity may mean poor performance. *Psychology Today, 34*(15), 28.

Elliott, M. (1996). Impact of work, family, and welfare receipt on women's self-esteem in young adulthood. *Social Psychology Quarterly, 59*(1), 80–95.

Ellis, B. J., & Garber, J. (2000). Psychosocial antecedents of pubertal maturation in girls: Parental psychopathology, stepfather presence, and family and marital stress. *Child Development, 71,* 485–501.

Ellison, C. G. (1992). Are religious people nice? Evidence from a national survey of Black Americans. *Social Forces, 71*(2), 411–430.

Ellison, C. G. (1993). Religious involvement and self-perception among Black Americans. *Social Forces, 71*(4), 1027–1055.

Ellison, N. B., Steinfield, C., & Lampe, C. (2007). The benefits of Facebook 'friends': Social capital and college students' use of online social network sites. *Journal of Computer-Mediated Communication, 12*(4), 1143–1168.

Ellor, J. W., Netting, F. E., & Thibault, J. M. (1999). *Understanding religious and spiritual aspects of human service practice.* Columbia, SC: University of South Carolina Press.

Emery, R. (1999). *Marriage, divorce, and children's adjustment* (2nd ed.). Thousand Oaks, CA: Sage.

Emmett, T., & Alant, E. (2006). Women & disability: Exploring the interface of multiple disadvantage. *Development of Southern Africa, 23*(4), 455–460.

Emmons, P. G. (2005). *Understanding sensory dysfunction: Learning, development and sensory dysfunction in autism spectrum disorders, ADHD, learning disabilities and bipolar disorder.* London: Jessica Kingsley Publishers.

Engels, R., & Knibbe, R. (2000). Alcohol use and intimate relationships in adolescence: When love comes to town. *Addictive Behavior, 25,* 435–439.

Entwisle, D., Alexander, K., & Olson, L. (2005). Urban teenagers: Work and dropout. *Youth and Society, 37,* 3–32.

Epps, S., & Jackson, B. J. (2000). *Empowered families, successful children: Early intervention programs that work.* Washington, DC: American Psychological Association.

Epstein, J. L., & Lee, S. (1995). National patterns of school and family connections in the middle grades. In B. A. Ryan, G. R. Adams, T. P. Gullotta, R. P. Weissberg, & R. L. Hampton (Eds.), *The family-school connection: Theory, research, and practice* (pp. 108–154). Thousand Oaks, CA: Sage.

Epstein, S. (1973). The self-concept revisited: Or, a theory of a theory. *American Psychologist, 28,* 404–416.

Epstein, S. (1991). Cognitive-experiential self-theory: An integrative theory of personality. In R. Cutis (Ed.), *The self with others: Convergences in psychoanalytic, social, and personality psychology* (pp. 111–137). New York: Guilford.

Epstein, S. (1998). Cognitive-experiential self-theory. In D. Barone & M. Hersen (Eds.), *Advanced personality* (pp. 211–238). New York: Plenum Press.

Epstein, S., Lipson, A., Holstein, C., & Huh, E. (1993). Irrational reactions to negative outcomes: Evidence for two conceptual systems. *Journal of Personality and Social Psychology, 62,* 328–339.

Erikson, E. H. (1950). *Childhood and society.* New York: Norton.

Erikson, E. H. (1959). The problem of ego identity. *Psychological Issues, 1,* 101–164.

Erikson, E. H. (1963). *Childhood and society* (2nd ed.). New York: Norton.

Erikson, E. H. (1968). *Identity: Youth and crisis.* New York: Norton.

Erikson, E. H. (Ed.). (1978). *Adulthood.* New York: Norton.

Erikson, E. H. (1982). *The life cycle completed.* New York: Norton.

Espelage, D. L., & Swearer, S. M. (2003). (Ed.). *Bullying in American schools: A social-ecological perspective on prevention and intervention.* Mahwah, NJ: Lawrence Erlbaum.

The Ethics Committee of the American Society for Reproductive Medicine (2006). Access to fertility treatment by gays, lesbians and unmarried persons. *Fertility and Sterility, 92*(4), 1190–1193.

Evans, B., Crogan, N., Belyea, M., & Coon, D. (2009). Utility of the life course perspective in research with Mexican American caregivers of older adults. *Journal of Transcultural Nursing, 20*(1), 5–14.

Evans, G. W., & English, K. (2002). The environment of poverty: Multiple stressor exposure, psychophysiological stress and socioemotional adjustment. *Child Development, 73*(4), 1238–1248.

Fabelo-Alcover, H. (2001). *Black beans and chopsticks: A refugee Latino social worker collaborates with Vietnamese survivors of reeducation camps.* Unpublished manuscript, Virginia Commonwealth University.

Fagan, J. (2008). Randomized study of prebirth coparenting intervention with adolescent and young fathers. *Family Relations, 57*(3), 309–323.

Falicov, C. (2005). The Latino family life cycle. In B. Carter & M. McGoldrick (Eds.), *The expanded family life cycle: Individual, family, and social perspectives* (3rd ed., pp. 141–152). Boston: Allyn & Bacon.

Faloon, W. (2008). Extreme life extension. *Life Extension, 14*(2), 9–18.

Faloon, W. (2009). Protection against arterial calcification, bone loss, cancer and aging. *Life Extension, 15*(1), 62–75.

Family Health International. (2006). *FHI research briefs on the female condom. No. 2: Effectiveness for preventing pregnancy and sexually transmitted infections.* Retrieved November 12, 2006, from http://www.fhi.org/en/RH/Pubs/Briefs/fcbriefs/ EffectiveSTIs.htm.

Fan, X. (2001). Parental involvement and students' academic achievement: A growth modeling analysis. *Journal of Experimental Education, 70,* 27–61.

Fan, X., & Chen, M. (2001). Parental involvement and students' academic achievement: A meta-analysis. *Educational Psychology Review, 13*(1), 1–22.

Fantuzzo, J. W., Mohr, W. K., & Noone, M. J. (2000). Making the invisible victims of violence against women visible through university/community partnerships. In R. A. Geffner, P. G. Jaffe, & M. Suderman (Eds.), *Children exposed to domestic violence: Current issues in research, intervention, prevention, and policy development* (pp. 9–24). New York: Haworth Press.

Farber, S., Egnew, T., & Farber, A. (2004). What is a respectful death? In J. Berzoff & P. R. Silverman (Eds.), *Living with dying: A handbook for end-of-life healthcare professionals* (pp. 102–127). New York: Columbia University Press.

Farkas, B. (2004). Etiology and pathogenesis of PTSD in children and adolescents. In R. R. Silva (Ed.), *Postraumatic stress disorders in children and adolescents* (pp. 123–140). New York: W. W. Norton and Company.

Farmer, R. (2009). *Neuroscience and social work practice: The missing link.* Thousand Oaks, CA: Sage.

Farrington, D. P., & Ttofi, M. M. (2009). *School-based programs to reduce bullying and victimization.* Rockville, MD: Campbell Collaboration Crime and Justice Group and the U.S. Department of Justice. NCJ 229377. Retrieved February 9, 2010, from http://www.ncjrs.gov/pdffiles1/nij/grants/ 229377.pdf.

Fass, P., & Mason, M. (Eds.). (2000). *Childhood in America.* New York: New York University Press.

Fawcett, M. (2000). Historical views of childhood. In M. Boushel, M. Fawcett, & J. Selwyn (Eds.), *Focus on early childhood: Principles and realties* (pp. 7–20). Oxford: Blackwell.

Federal Interagency Forum on Aging-Related Statistics. (2004). *Older Americans 2004: Key indicators of well-being.* Washington, DC: U.S. Government Printing Office.

Federal Interagency Forum on Aging-Related Statistics. (2008). *Older Americans 2008: Key indicators of well-being.* Retrieved May 20, 2010, from http://www.agingstats.gov/agingstats dotnet/NMain_Site/Data/2008_Documents/OA_2008.

Feijoo, A. (2001). Adolescent pregnancy, birth, and abortion rates in Western Europe far outshine U.S. rates. *Transitions, 14*(2), 4–5.

Feldman, R. (2004). Mother infant skin-to-skin contact and the development of emotion regulation. In S. Shohov (Ed.), *Advances in psychology research* (Vol. 27, pp. 113–131). Hauppauge, NY: Nova Science.

Feldman, R., & Edelman, A. (2003). Mother-infant skin-to-skin contact (Kangaroo Care) accelerates autonomic and neurobehavioral maturation in premature infants. *Developmental Medicine and Child Neurology, 45*(4), 274–281.

Felitti, V., Anda, R., Nordenburg, D., Williamson, D., Spitz, A., Edwards, V., et. al. (1998). Relationship of childhood abuse and household dysfunction to many of the leading causes of death in adults: The adverse childhood experiences (ACE) study. *American Journal of Preventive Medicine, 14*(4), 245–258.

Felson, R. B. (2002). Pubertal development, social factors, and delinquency among adolescent boys. *Criminology, 40*(4), 967–988.

Fergusson, D. M., Horwood, L. J., & Woodward, L. J. (2001). Unemployment and psychosocial adjustment in young adults: Causation or selection? *Social Science & Medicine, 53*(3), 305.

Ferlin, A., Arredi, B., & Foresta, C. (2006). Genetic causes of male infertility. *Reproductive Technology, 22*(2), 133–141.

Ferraro, K., & Shippee, T. (2009). Aging and cumulative inequality: How does inequality get under the skin? *The Gerontologist, 49*(3), 333–343.

Fertility Plus. (n.d.). *Frequently asked questions about intrauterine insemination (IUI)*. Retrieved November 6, 2002, from http://www.fertilityplus.org/faq/iui.html.

Field, T., Woodson, R., Greenberg, R., & Cohen, C. (1982). Discrimination and imitation of facial expressions by neonates. *Science, 218*, 179–181.

Fields, J. (2003). *Children's living arrangements and characteristics: March 2002. Current Population Reports*. Retrieved January 14, 2007, from http://www.census.gov/prod/2003 pubs/p20–547.pdf.

Fields, J. (2004). *America's families and living arrangements: 2003. U.S. Census Bureau Current Population Reports*. Retrieved December 3, 2006, from http://www.census.gov/prod/2004pubs/p20–553.pdf.

Figa-Talamanca, I., Cini, C., Varricchio, G. C., Dondero, F., Gandini, L., Lenzi, A., et al. (1996). Effects of prolonged auto vehicle driving on male reproduction: A study among taxi drivers. *American Journal of Industrial Medicine, 30*(6), 750–758.

Figueira-McDonough, J. (1990). Abortion: Ambiguous criteria and confusing policies. *Affilia, 5*(4), 27–54.

Fiksenbaum, L. M., Greenglass, E. R., & Eaton, J. (2006). Perceived social support, hassles, and coping among the elderly. *Journal of Applied Gerontology, 25*(1), 17–30.

Findlay, L., Girardi, A., & Coplan, R. (2006). Links between empathy, social behavior, and social understanding in early childhood. *Early Childhood Research Quarterly, 21*(3), 347–359.

Fine, M., Ganong, L., & Demo, D. (2010). Divorce: A risk and resilience perspective. In S. Price, C. Price, & P. McKenry (Eds.), *Families & change: Coping with stressful events and transitions* (4th ed., pp. 211–233). Thousand Oaks, CA: Sage.

Finer, L., & Henshaw, S. (2006). Disparities in rates of unintended pregnancy in the United States, 1994 and 2001. *Perspectives on Sexual and Reproductive Health, 38*(2), 90–96.

Fingerman, K., & Dolbin-MacNab, M. (2006). The baby boomers and their parents: Cohort influences and intergenerational ties. In S. Whitbourne & S. Willis (Eds.), *The baby boomers grow up: Contemporary perspectives on midlife* (pp. 237–259). Mahwah, NJ: Lawrence Erlbaum.

Finn, J. (2009). Making trouble. In L. Nybell, J. Shook, & J. Finn (Eds.), *Childhood, youth, & social work in transformation: Implications for policy & practice* (pp. 37–66). New York: Columbia University Press.

Finn, J. D. (1989). Withdrawing from school. *Review of Educational Research, 59*, 117–142.

Fiori, J. L., Consedine, N. S., & Magai, C. (2008). Ethnic differences in patterns of social exchange among older adults: The role of resource context. *Ageing & Society, 28*, 495–524.

Fischer, K. (1993). Aging. In M. Downey (Ed.), *The new dictionary of Catholic spirituality* (pp. 31–33). Collegeville, MN: Liturgical Press.

Fisher, H. (2004). Why we love: The nature and chemistry of romantic love. New York: Holt.

Fitzgerald, H. E., & McKelvey, L. (2005). Low-income adolescent fathers: Risk for parenthood and risky parenting. *Zero to Three, 25*(4), 35–41.

Fitzpatrick, K. M., & Boldizar, J. P. (1993). The prevalence and consequences of exposure to violence among African American youth. *Journal of the American Academy of Child and Adolescent Psychiatry, 56*, 22–34.

Fjerstad, M., Truissell, J., Sivin, I., Lichtenberg, S. & Cullins, V. (2009). Rates of Servoious infection after changes in regimens for medical abortion. *New England Journal of Medicine, 361*(2), 145–151.

Flammer, A., & Schaffner, B. (2003). Adolescent leisure across European nations. In S. Verma & R. Larson (Eds.), *Examining adolescent leisure time across culture: New directions for child and adolescent development, No. 99* (pp. 65–77). San Francisco: Jossey-Bass.

Flanagan, C. (2004). Institutional support for morality: Community-based and neighborhood organizations. In T. A. Thorkildsen & H. Walberg (Eds.), *Nurturing morality* (pp. 173–183). New York: Kluwer Academic/Plenum.

Fogarty, R. (2009). *Brain compatible classrooms* (3rd ed.). Thousand Oaks, CA: Corwin.

Foley, K. M. (Ed.). (2005). *When the focus is on care: Palliative care and cancer*. Atlanta, GA: American Cancer Society.

Fonagy, P. (2003). The development of psychopathology from infancy to adulthood: The mysterious unfolding of disturbance in time. *Infant, Mental Health Journal, 24*, 212–239.

Foner, A. (1995). Social stratification. In G. L. Maddox (Ed.), *The encyclopedia of aging: A comprehensive resource in gerontology and geriatrics* (2nd ed., pp. 887–890). New York: Springer.

Fong, R. (Ed.). (2003). *Culturally competent practice with immigrant and refugee children and families*. New York: Guilford Press.

Food and Drug Administration (FDA). (2006, June 8). *FDA licenses new vaccine for prevention of cervical cancer and other diseases in females caused by human papillomavirus* (FDA News P06-7). Retrieved November 29, 2006, from http://www.fda.gov/bb/topics/NEWS/2006/NEW01385.html.

Fost, N. (1981). Counseling families who have a child with severe congenital anomaly. *Pediatrics, 67,* 321–323.

Foster, D. G., Rostovtseva, D. P., Brindis, C. D., Biggs, M. A., Hulett, D., & Darney, P. D. (2009). Cost savings from the provision of specific methods of contraception in a publically funded program. *American Journal of Public Health, 99*(3), 446–451.

Fowler, J. (1981). *Stages of faith: The psychology of human development and the quest for meaning.* San Francisco: Harper.

Fowler, J. W., & Dell, M. L. (2006). Stages of faith from infancy through adolescence: Reflections on three decades of faith development theory. In E. C. Roehlkepartain, P. E. King, L. Wagener, & P. L. Benson (Eds.), *The handbook of spiritual development in children and adolescence* (pp. 34–45). Thousand Oaks, CA: Sage.

Francisco, M. A., Hicks, K., Powell, J., Styles, K., Tabor, J. L., & Hulton, L. J. (2008). The effect of childhood sexual abuse on adolescent pregnancy: An intergrative research review. *Journal for Specialists in Pediatric Nursing, 13*(4), 237–248.

Franklin, R. (2003). *Migration of the young, single, and college educated: 1995 to 2000.* Washington, DC: U.S. Census Bureau. Retrieved November 19, 2009, from http://www.census.gov/prod/2003pubs/censr-12.pdf.

Franko, D., & Striegel-Moore, R. (2002). The role of body dissatisfaction as a risk factor for depression in adolescent girls: Are the differences Black and White? *Journal of Psychosomatic Research, 53,* 975–983.

Franko, D. L., Striegel-Moore, R. H., Thompson, D., Schreiber, G. B., & Daniels, S. R. (2005). Does adolescent depression predict obesity in black and white young adult women? *Psychological Medicine, 35,* 1505–1513.

Fraser, M. (2004). *Risk and resilience in childhood: An ecological perspective* (2nd ed.). Washington, DC: NASW Press.

Fraser, M., Kirby, L., & Smokowski, P. (2004). Risk and resilience in childhood. In M. Fraser (Ed.), *Risk and resilience in childhood: An ecological perspective* (2nd ed., pp. 13–66). Washington, DC: NASW Press.

Freeman, S. (2004). Nondaily hormonal contraception: Considerations in contraceptive choice and patient counseling. *Journal of the American Academy of Nurse Practitioners, 16*(6), 226–238.

Freeman, E., & Dyer, L. (1993). High risk children and adolescents: Family and community environments. *Families in Society, 74,* 422–431.

Freeman, L., Shaffer, D., & Smith, H. (1996). Neglected victims of homicide: The needs of young siblings of murder victims. *American Journal of Orthopsychiatry, 66,* 337–345.

Freisthler, B., Merritt, D. H., & LaScala, E. A. (2006). Understanding the ecology of child maltreatment: A review of the literature and directions for future research. *Child Maltreatment, 11*(3), 263–280.

French, S., Seidman, E., Allen, L., & Aber, J. (2006). The development of ethnic identity during adolescence. *Developmental Psychology, 42,* 1–10.

Freud, S. (1905/1953). Three essays on the theory of sexuality. In J. Strachey (Ed. & Trans.), *The standard edition of the complete works of Sigmund Freud* (Vol. 7, pp. 135–245). London: Hogarth.

Freud, S. (1917/1957). Mourning and melancholia. In J. Strachey (Ed. & Trans.), *The standard edition of the complete psychological works of Sigmund Freud* (Vol. 14, pp. 237–258). London: Hogarth.

Freud, S. (1927). Some psychological consequences of the anatomical distinction between the sexes. *International Journal of Psycho-Analysis, 8,* 133–142.

Freud, S. (1938/1973). *An outline of psychoanalysis.* London: Hogarth Press.

Freundl, G., Sivin, I., & Batár, I. (2010). State of the art of nonhormonal methods of contraception: IV. Natural family planning. *European Journal of Contraceptive and Reproductive Health Care, 15*(2), 113–123.

Friedman, S. H., Kessler, A. R., & Martin, R. (2009). Psychiatric help for caregivers of infants in neonatal intensive care. *Psychiatric Services, 60*(4), 554.

Friedmann, E., & Havighurst, R. (1954). *The meaning of work and retirement.* Chicago: University of Chicago Press.

Fry, C. (2003). The life course as a cultural construct. In R. Settersten, Jr. (Ed.), *Invitation to the life course: Toward new understandings of later life* (pp. 269–294). Amityville, NY: Baywood Publishing Co.

Fu, H., Darroch, J., Haas, T., & Ranjit, N. (1999). Contraceptive failure rats: New estimates from the 1995 National Survey of Family Growth. *Family Planning Perspectives, 31*(2), 52–58.

Fuligni, A. (1997). The academic achievement of adolescents from immigrant families: The roles of family background, attitudes, and behavior. *Child Development, 68*(2), 351–363.

Gabel, K., & Johnston, D. (Eds.). (1995). *Children of incarcerated parents.* New York: Lexington Books.

Gable, I, Gostin, L., & Hodge, J. (2008). HIV/AIDS, reproductive and sexual health, and the law. *American Journal of Public Health, 98*(10), 1779–86.

Gagnon, A., Dougherty, G., Platt, R., Wohoush, O., Stewart, D., George, A., et al. (2004). Needs of refugee mothers after pregnancy–early response services (normap-ers): An example of scientific challenges in studies of migration. *Journal of Epidemiology & Community Health, 58*(1), A23–A24.

Galambos, N., Albrecht, A., & Jansson, S. (2009). Dating, sex, and substance use predict increases in adolescents' subjective age across two years. *International Journal of Behavioral Development, 33,* 32–41.

Galinsky, E., & Bond, J. T. (2009). The impact of the recession on employers. New York: Families and Work Institute. Retrieved

January 5, 2010, from http://www.familiesandwork.org/site/research/reports/Recession2009.pdf.

Gallup, G., Jr., & Lindsay, D. M. (1999). *Surveying the religious landscape: Trends in U.S. beliefs.* Harrisburg, PA: Morehouse.

Gamoran, A., & Himmelfarb, H. (1994). *The quality of vocational education.* Washington, DC: U.S. Department of Education.

Garbarino, J. (1995). *Raising children in a socially toxic environment.* San Francisco: Jossey-Bass.

Garbarino, J. (1999). *Lost boys: Why our sons turn violent and how we can save them.* New York: Free Press.

Garbarino, J. (2006). *See Jane hit: Why girls are growing more violent and what we can do about it.* New York: Penguin.

Garcia, B., & Zuniga, M. (2007). Cultural competence with Latino Americans. In D. Lum (Ed.), *Culturally competent practice: A framework for understanding diverse groups and justice issues* (3rd ed., pp. 299–327). Belmont, CA: Thomson Brooks/Cole.

Garcia, D., & Siddiqui, A. (2009). Adolescents' psychological well-being and memory for life events: Influences on life satisfaction with respect of temperamental dispositions. *Journal of Happiness Studies, 10*(4), 407–419.

Garcia, E. (2001). Parenting in Mexican American families. In N. Boyd Webb (Ed.), *Culturally diverse parent-child and family relationships: A guide for social workers and other practitioners* (pp. 157–179). New York: Columbia University Press.

Gardiner, H., & Kosmitzki, C. (2008). *Lives across cultures: Cross-cultural human development* (4th ed.). Boston: Pearson.

Gardner, H. E. (1993). *Multiple intelligences: The theory in practice.* New York: Basic Books.

Gardner, H. (2006). *Multiple intelligences: New horizons.* New York: Basic Books.

Gargiulo, R. M. (2005). *Young children with special needs.* Albany, NY: Thomson/Delmar Learning.

Gargus, R. A., Vohr, B. R., Tyson, J. E., High, P., Higgins, R. D., Wrage, L. A., & Poole, K. (2009). Unimpaired outcomes for extremely low birth weight infants at 18 and 22 months. *Pediatrics, 124*(1), 112–121.

Garmezy, N. (1993). Vulnerability and resilience. In D. C. Funder, R. D. Parke, C. Tomlinson-Keasey, & K. Widaman (Eds.), *Studying lives through time* (pp. 377–398). Washington, DC: American Psychological Association.

Garmezy, N. (1994). Reflections and commentary on risk, resilience, and development. In R. J. Haggerty, L. R. Sherrod, N. Garmezy, & M. Rutter (Eds.), *Stress, risk, and resilience in children and adolescents: Processes, mechanisms, and interventions* (pp. 1–18). New York: Cambridge University Press.

Garrett, B. (2009). *Brain & behavior: An introduction to biological psychology* (2nd ed.). Thousand Oaks, CA: Sage.

Garrett, J. L. (2006). Educating the whole child. *Kappa Delta Pi Record, 42*(4), 154–155.

Garrett, M. W. (1995). Between two worlds: Cultural discontinuity in the dropout of Native American youth. *The School Counselor, 10,* 199–208.

Garton, A. F., & Pratt, C. (1991). Leisure activities of adolescent school students: Predictors of participation and interest. *Journal of Adolescence, 14,* 305–321.

Gartrell, N., Hamilton, J., Banks, A., Mosbacher, D., Reed, N., Sparks, C., & Bishop, H. (1996). The national lesbian family study: 1. Interviews with prospective mothers. *American Journal of Orthopsychiatry, 66,* 272–281.

Gartstein, M., Gonzales, C., Carranza, J., Adaho, S., Rothbart, M., & Yang, S. (2006). Studying cross-cultural differences in the development of infant temperament: People's Republic of China, the Unites States of America, and Spain. *Child Psychiatry and Human Development, 37,* 145–161.

Gartstein, M., Knyazev, G., & Slobodskaya, H. (2005). Cross-cultural differences in the structure of temperament: United States of America (U.S.) and Russia. *Infant Behavior and Development, 28,* 54–61.

Gartstein, M., Peleg, Y., Young, B., & Slobodskaya, H. (2009). Infant temperament in Russia, United States of America, and Israel: Differences and similarities between Russian-speaking families. *Child Psychiatry and Human Development, 40,* 241–256.

Garver, K. L. (1995). Genetic counseling. In G. B. Reed, A. E. Claireaux, & F. Cockburn (Eds.), *Diseases of the fetus and newborn* (2nd ed., pp. 1007–1012). London: Chapman & Hall.

Garvey, C. (1984). *Children's talk.* Cambridge, MA: Harvard University Press.

Garvin, V., Kalter, N., & Hansell, J. (1993). Divorced women: Factors contributing to resiliency and vulnerability. *Journal of Divorce and Remarriage, 21*(1/2), 21–39.

Gaur, D. S., Talekar, M., & Pathak, V. P. (2007). Effect of cigarette smoking on semen quality of infertile men. *Singapore Medical Journal, 48*(20), 119–123.

Gavin, N. I., Kuo, M., Adams, E. K., Ayadi, M. F., & Gilbert, B. C. (2005). Medicaid service use and program costs for pregnant teens. *Expert Review of Pharmacoeconomics and Outcomes Research, 5*(6), 683–694.

Gaylord, M., Greer, M., & Botti, J. (2008). Improving perinatal health: A novel approach to improve community and adult health. *Journal of Perinatology, 28,* 91–96.

Ge, X., Conger, R. D., & Elder, G. H., Jr. (2001). The relation between puberty and psychological distress in adolescent boys. *Journal of Research on Adolescence, 11,* 49–70.

Geary, S., & Moon, Y. S. (2006). The human embryo in vitro: Recent progress. *Journal of Reproductive Medicine, 51*(4), 293–302.

Gee, J. P. (1996). *Social linguistics and literacies: Ideology in discourses* (2nd ed.). London: Falmer.

Gehlbach, H. (2006). How changes in students' goal orientations relate to outcomes in social studies. *Journal of Education Research, 99,* 358–370.

Geiger, B. (1996). *Fathers as primary caregivers.* Westport, CT: Greenwood Publishing.

Gelles, R. (1989). Child abuse and violence in single-parent families: Parent absence and economic deprivation. *American Journal of Orthopsychiatry, 59,* 492–501.

Gelles, R. (2010). Violence, abuse, and neglect in families and intimate relationships. In S. Price, C. Price, & P. McKenry (Eds.), *Families & change: Coping with stressful events and transitions* (4th ed., pp. 119–139). Thousand Oaks, CA: Sage.

Gelles, R., & Hargreaves, E. (1981). Maternal employment and violence toward children. *Journal of Family Issues, 2,* 509–530.

Generations. (2001, Summer), *25*(2).

George, L. (2003). What life-course perspective offers the study of aging and health. In R. Settersten, Jr. (Ed.), *Invitation to the life course: Toward new understandings of later life* (pp. 161–188). Amityville, NY: Baywood Publishing Co., Inc.

George, L. K. (2005). Socioeconomic status and health across the life course: Progress and prospects. *The Journal of Gerontology: Series B: Psychological Sciences and Social Sciences, 60B,* 135–139.

George, L. K., Larson, D. B., Koenig, H. G., & McCullough, M. E. (2000). Spirituality and health: What we know, what we need to know. *Journal of Social & Clinical Psychology, 19,* 102–116.

Georgiades, S. D. (2005). Emancipated young adults' perspectives on independent living programs. *Families in Society, 86*(4), 503–510.

Georgieff, M. K. (2007). Nutrition and the developing brain: Nutrient priorities and measurement. *American Journal of Clinical Nutrition, 85*(2), 614S–620S.

Gerhardt, S. (2004). *Why love matters: How affection shapes a baby's brain.* New York: Brunner-Routledge.

Geronimus, A. T., Hicken, M., Keene, D., & Bound, J. (2006). 'Weathering' and age patterns of allostatic load scores among blacks and whites in the United States. *American Journal of Public Health, 96,* 826–833.

Gibbs, J. T., & Huang, L. N. (1989). A conceptual framework for assessing and treating minority youth. In J. T. Gibbs & L. N. Huang (Eds.), *Children of color: Psychological interventions with minority youth* (pp. 1–29). San Francisco: Jossey-Bass.

Gibson, D. M., & Myers, J. E. (2002). The effect of social coping resources and growth-fostering relationships on infertility stress in women. *Journal of Mental Health Counseling, 24*(1), 68–81.

Giedd, J. (2008). The teen brain: Insights from neuroimaging. *Journal of Adolescent Health, 42,* 335–343.

Giedd, J. (2009). Editorial: Linking adolescent sleep, brain maturation, and behavior. *Journal of Adolescent Health, 45,* 319–320.

Gielen, U., & Markoulis, D. (2001). Preference for principled moral reasoning: A developmental and cross-cultural perspective. In L. Adler & U. Gielen (Eds.), *Cross-cultural topics in psychology* (2nd ed., pp. 81–101). Westport, CT: Praeger/Greenwood.

Gilbert, W. M., Jandial, D., Field, N. T., Bigelow, P., & Danielsen, B. (2004). Birth outcomes in teenage pregnancies. *The Journal of Maternal-Fetal and Neonatal Medicine, 16,* 265–270.

Gilligan, C. (1982). *In a different voice: Psychological theory and women's development.* Cambridge, MA: Harvard University Press.

Gilman, S. E., Kawachi, I., & Fitzmaurice, G. M. (2003). Family disruption in childhood and risk of adult depression. *American Journal of Psychiatry, 160*(5), 939–946.

Giudice, L. C. (2006). Infertility and the environment: The medical context. *Seminars in Reproductive Medicine, 24*(5), 1039–1048.

Giurgescu, C., Penckofer, S., Maurer, M.C., & Bryant, F.B. (2006). Impact of uncertainty, social support, and prenatal coping on the psychological well-being of high-risk pregnant women. *Nursing Research, 55*(5), 356–365.

Glaser, D. (2000). Child abuse and neglect and the brain—A review. *Journal of Child Psychology and Psychiatry, 41*(1), 97–116.

Glass, C. S., & Wegar, K. (2000). Teacher perceptions of the incidence and management of Attention Deficit Hyperactivity Disorder. *Education, 121*(2), 412–420.

Glover, J., Galliher, R., & Lamere, T. (2009). Identity development and exploration among sexual minority adolescents: Examination of a multidimensional model. *Journal of Homosexuality, 56,* 77–101.

Glover, R. (1996). Religiosity in adolescence and young adulthood: Implications for identity formation. *Psychological Reports, 78,* 427–431.

Go Forth and Multiply a Lot Less. (2009, October 29). *The Economist.* Retrieved May 20, 2010, from http://www.econo.hit-u.ac.jp/~makoto/education/economist_fertility_20091031.pdf.

Gogtay, N., Giedd, J., Lusk, L., Hyashi, K., Greenstein, D., Vaituzis, A. C., et al. (2004). Dynamic mapping of human cortical development during childhood through early adulthood.

The Proceedings of the National Academy of Science, 101(21), 8174–8179.

Gold, K. J., Dalton, V. K., Schwenk, T. L., & Hayward, R. A., (2007). What causes pregnancy loss? Preexisting mental illness as an independent risk factor. *General Hospital Psychiatry, 29*(3), 207–213.

Goldberg, A. B., Cohen, A., & Lieberman, E. (1999). Nulliparas' preference for Epidural analgesia: Their effects on actual use in labor. *Birth: Issues In Perinatal Care, 26*(3), 139–143.

Goldberg, W., Clarke-Stewart, K., Rice, J., & Dellis, E. (2002). Emotional energy as an explanatory construct for fathers' engagement with their infants. *Parenting: Science & Practice, 2,* 379–408.

Goldenberg, R. L., & Jobe, A. H. (2001). Prospects for research in reproductive health and birth outcomes. *Journal of the American Medical Association, 285*(5), 633–642.

Goldenberg, R. L., Hauth, J. C., & Andrews, W. W. (2000). Intrauterine infection and premature delivery. *New England Journal of Medicine, 342*(20), 1500–1508.

Goldstein, H., Kaczmarek, L. A., & English, K. M. (2002). *Promoting social communication: Children with developmental disabilities from birth to adolescence.* Baltimore, MD: Paul H. Brookes Publishing Co.

Goldstein, J., & Kenney, C. (2001). Marriage delayed or marriage forgone? New cohort forecasts of first marriage for U.S. women. *American Sociological Review, 66*(4), 506–519.

Goldstein, S., & Brooks, R. B. (2005). Why study resilience? In S. Goldstein & R. B. Brooks (Eds.), Handbook of resilience in children (pp. 3–15). New York: Kluwer Academic/Plenum Publishers.

Goleman, D. (1995). *Emotional intelligence.* New York: Bantam.

Goleman, D. (2006). *Social intelligence: The new science of human relationships.* New York: Bantam.

Gomez, N. (2001). EEG during different emotions in 10 month old infants of depressed mothers. *Journal of Reproductive and Infant Psychology, 19*(4), 295–313.

Gonyea, J. G. (1987). The family and dependency: Factors associated with institutional decision-making. *Journal of Gerontological Social Work, 10,* 61–77.

Gonzalez-Quintero, V., Tolaymat, L., Luke, B., Gonzalez-Garcia, A. Duthely, L., & O'Sullivan, M. (2006). Outcomes of pregnancies among Hispanics: Revisiting the epidemiologic paradox. *Journal of Reproductive Medicine, 51*(1), 10–14.

Good, T., & Nichols, S. (2001). Expectancy effects in the classroom: A special focus on improving the reading performance of minority students in first-grade classrooms. *Educational Psychologist, 36,* 113–126.

Gopaul-McNicol, S. (1988). Racial identification and racial preference of Black preschool children in New York and Trinidad. *Journal of Black Psychology, 14*(2), 65–68.

Gordon, L., & Shaffer, S. (2004). *Mom, can I move back in with you? A survival guide for parents of twentysomethings.* New York: Tarcher.

Gordon, D., Nandy, S., Pantazis, C., Pemberton, S., & Townsend, P. (2003). *Child poverty in the developing world.* Bristol, UK: The Policy Press. Retrieved January 19, 2010, from http://www.undp.org/povertycentre/.

Gordon L., Thakur, M., & Altas, M. (2007). What hormonal contraception is most effective for obese women? *Journal of Family Practice, 56*(6), 471–475.

Gosten, L. O. (2007). Abortion politics: Clinical freedom, trust in the Judiciary, and the autonomy of women, *Journal of American Medical Association, 298*(13), 1562–1564.

Gottman, J. M. (1994, May/June). Why marriages fail. *Family Therapy Networker,* 41–48.

GovTrack.us. (2006). *S707: PREEMIE Act.* Retrieved January 17, 2010, from http://www.govtrack.us/congress/bill.xpd?bill=s109-707.

Grady, D. (2009, November 3). Premature rates are fueling higher rate of infant mortality in U.S: Report says. *New York Times, A15.* Retrieved January 17, 2010, from http://www.nytimes.com/2009/11/04/health/04infant.html.

Graff, H. (1995). *Conflicting paths: Growing up in America.* Cambridge, MA: Harvard University Press.

Grainger, D. A., Frazier, L. M., & Rowland, C. A. (2006). Preconception care and treatment with assisted reproductive technologies. *Maternal and Child Health Journal, 10* (Suppl 7), 161–164.

Granic, I., Dishion, T., & Hollenstein, T. (2003). The family ecology of adolescence: A dynamic systems perspective on normative development. In G. Adams & M. Berzonsky (Eds.), *Blackwell handbook of adolescence* (pp. 60–91). Oxford, UK: Blackwell.

Greene, S., Anderson, E., Hetherington, E. Forgatch, M., & DeGarmo,D. (2003). Risk and resilience after divorce. In F. Walsh (Ed.), *Normal family processes: Growing diversity and complexity* (3rd ed., pp. 96–120). New York: Guilford.

Greenfield, E., & Marks, N. (2006). Linked lives: Adult children's problems and their parents' psychological and relational well-being. *Journal of Marriage and Family, 68,* 442–454.

Greenfield, P., Keller, H., Fuglini, A., & Maynard, A. (2003). Cultural pathways through universal development. *Annual Review of Psychology, 54,* 461–490.

Greenfield, P., & Zheng, Y. (2006). Children, adolescents, and the Internet: A new field of inquiry in developmental psychology. *Developmental Psychology, 42*(3), 391–394.

Greenman, P., & Schneider, B. (2009). Stability and change in patterns of peer rejection: Implications for children's academic performance over time. *School Psychology International, 30*(2), 163–183.

Greenspan, S. (2006). Rethinking "harmonious parenting" using a three-factor discipline model. *Child Care in Practice, 12*(1), 5–12.

Greve, W., & Staudinger, U. M. (2006). Resilience in later adulthood and old age: Resources and potentials for successful aging. In D. Cicchetti & D. J. Cohen (Eds.), *Developmental psychopathology, Vol. 3: Risk, disorder and adaptation* (pp. 796–840). Hoboken, NJ: John Wiley & Sons.

Griffith, S. (1996). *Amending attachment theory: Ambiguities among maternal care, day care peer group experience, general security and altruistic prosocial proclivities in 3, 4 & 5 year old children.* Unpublished doctoral dissertation, Adelphi University, New York.

Grimes, D. A., Lopez, L., Raymond, E. G., Halpern, V., Nanda, K., & Schulz, K. F. (2005). Spermicide used alone for contraception. *Cochrane Database of Systematic Review, 19*(4), CD005218.

Grinspun, A. (2004, March). From the editor. *In Focus.* Retrieved January 19, 2010, from http://www.undp.org/poverty centre/.

Gromley, W., Gayer, T., Phillips, D., & Dawson, B. (2004). *The effects of universal pre-k on cognitive development.* Retrieved May 21, 2010, from http://www.crocus.georgetwon.edu/reports/ oklahoma9z.pdf.

Gross, E. (2004). Adolescent Internet use: What we expect, what teens report. *Applied Developmental Psychology, 25*, 633–649.

Grossman, L. (2005, January 24). Grow up? Not so fast. *Time, 165*(4), 42–48, 50, 52.

Groves, B. M. (1997). Growing up in a violent world: The impact of family and community violence on young children and their families. *Topics in Early Childhood Special Education, 17*(1), 74–102.

Guarnaccia, P., & Lopez, S. (1998). The mental health and adjustment of immigrant and refugee children. *Child and Adolescent Psychiatric Clinic of North America, 7*(3), 537–553.

Guidozzi, F., & Black, V. (2009). The obstetric face and challenge of HIV/AIDS. *Clinical Obstetrics & Gynecology, 52*(2), 270–284.

Guillory, V. J., Cai, J., & Hoff, G. L. (2008). Secular trends in excess fetal and infant mortality using perinatal periods of risk analysis. *Journal of the National Medical Association, 100*(12), 1450–1456.

Guisbond, L., & Neill, M. (Sept/Oct 2004). Failing our children: No Child Left Behind undermines quality and equity in education. *Clearing House, 78*(1), 12.

Gunnar, M., & Quevedo, K. (2007). The neurobiology of stress and development. *Annual Review of Psychology, 58*, 145–173.

Guralnick, M., Neville, B., Hammond, M., & Connor, R. (2008). Continuity and change from full-inclusion early childhood programs through the early elementary period. *Journal of Early Intervention, 30*(3), 237–250.

Gurgan, T., & Demiro, A. (2007). Unresolved issues regarding assisted reproductive technology. *Reproductive BioMedicine Online, Supp 1*(14), 40–43.

Gurian, M. (2001). *Boys and girls learn differently! A guide for teachers and parents.* San Francisco: Jossey-Bass.

Gürsory, F., & Bicakci, M. (2007). A comparison of parental attitude perceptions in children of working and nonworking mothers. *Social Behavior & Personality: An International Journal, 35*(5), 693–706.

Guterman, N., & Embry, R. (2004). Prevention and treatment strategies targeting physical child abuse and neglect. In P. Allen-Meares & M. Fraser (Eds.), *Intervention with children and adolescents: An interdisciplinary perspective* (pp. 130–158). Boston: Allyn & Bacon.

Gutiérrez, K. (2008). Developing a sociocritical literacy in the third space. *Reading Research Quarterly, 43*(2), 148–164.

Gutierrez, R. A. (2004). Internal colonialism: An American theory of race. *Social Science Research on Race, 1*(2), 281–295.

Gutman, H. (1976). *The Black family in slavery and freedom, 1750–1925.* New York: Pantheon.

Guttmacher Institute. (2009a). *Facts on induced abortion worldwide.* Retrieved November 20, 2009, from http://www .guttmacher.org/pubs/fb_IAW.pdf.

Guttmacher Institue. (2009b). *1.94 million unintended pregnancies and 810,000 abortions are prevented each year by publically funded family planning services.* Retrieved January 14, 2010, from http://www.guttmacher.org/media/nr/2009/ 02/23/index .html.

Guttmacher Institute. (2010). *Facts on American teens' sexual and reproductive health.* Retrieved February 2, 2010, from http://www.guttmacher.org/pubs/FB-ATSRH.html.

Guvendag, E. S. (2006). Serum biochemistry correlates with the size of tubal ectopic pregnancy on sonography. *Ultrasound in Obstetrics and Gynecology, 28*(6), 826–891.

Gyllstrom, M. E., Schreiner, P., & Harlow, B. (2007). Perimenopause and depression: Strength of association, causal mechanisms and treatment recommendations. *Best Practice & Research Clinical Obstetrics & Gynaecology, 21*(2), 275–292.

Ha, J., Hong, J., Seltzer, M., & Greenberg, J. (2008). Age and gender differences in the well-being of midlife and aging parents with children with mental health or developmental problems: Report of a national study. *Journal of Health and Social Behavior, 49*, 3010–316

Haan, N., Millsap, R., & Hartka, E. (1986). As time goes by: Change and stability in personality over fifty years. *Psychology and Aging, 1*, 220–232.

Habig, J. E. (2008). Defining the protected class: Who qualifies for protection under the pregnancy discrimination act? *The Yale Law Journal, 117*(6), 1215–1224.

Haden, C., Haine, R., & Fivush, R. (1997). Developing narrative structure in parent-child reminiscing across the preschool years. *Developmental Psychology, 33,* 295–307.

Hagestad, G. (2003). Interdependent lives and relationships in changing times: A life-course view of families and aging. In R. Settersten, Jr. (Ed.), *Invitation to the life course: Toward new understandings of later life* (pp. 135–159). Amityville, NY: Baywood Publishing Co., Inc.

Hahn, S., Haselhorst, U., Quadbeck, B., Tan, S., Kimming, R., Mann, K., et al. (2006). Decreased soluble leptin receptor levels in women with polycystic ovarian syndrome. *European Journal of Endocrinology, 154*(2), 287–294.

Haider, A. (2006). Roper v. Simmons: The role of the science brief. *Ohio State Journal of Criminal Law, 375,* 369–377.

Haider, S., & Darney. P. D., (2007). Injectable contraception. *Clinical Obstetrics and Gynecology, 50*(4), 898–906.

Haidt, J. (2007). The new synthesis in moral psychology. *Science, 316,* 998–1002.

Hair, E., Ling, T., & Cochran, S. W. (2003). *Youth development programs and educationally disadvantaged older youths: A synthesis.* Washington, DC: Child Trends.

Hakuta, K., Ferdman, B. M., & Diaz, R. M. (1987). Bilingualism and cognitive development: Three perspectives. In S. Rosenberg (Ed.), *Advances in applied psycholinguistics: Vol. 2. Reading, writing, and language learning* (pp. 284–319). New York: Cambridge University Press.

Hale, R. (2007). Choices in contraception. *British Journal of Midwifery, 15*(5), 305–309.

Hall, D. (2005). *Getting honest about grad rates: How states play the numbers and students lose.* Retrieved November 7, 2006, from http://www2.edtrust.org/edtrust.

Hall, G. (1904). *Adolescence: Its psychology and its relations to physiology, anthropology, sociology, sex, crime, religion, and education.* New York: Appleton.

Hall, W. J. (2008). Centenarians: Metaphor becomes reality. *Archives of Internal Medicine, 168* (3), 262–263.

Halle, T. (2002). *Charting parenthood: A statistical portrait of fathers and mothers in America.* Washington, DC: Child Trends.

Halpern, A. (1996). Transition: A look at foundations. *Exceptional Children, 51,* 479–486.

Hamblen, J. (2002). *Terrorism and children.* Retrieved January 23, 2002, from http://www .ncptsd.org/facts/disasters/fs_children_disaster.html.

Hamilton, B. E., Martin, J. A., & Ventura, S. J. (2007). Preliminary data for 2006. *National Vital Statistics Reports, 56*(7). Hyattsville, MD: National Center for Health Statistics.

Hamilton, S., & Hamilton, M. (2004). Implications for youth development practices. In S. Hamilton & M. Hamilton (Eds.), *The youth development handbook: Coming of age in American communities* (pp. 351–371). Thousand Oaks, CA: Sage.

Hammarberg, K., & Clarke, V. E. (2005). Reasons for delaying childbearing—A survey of women aged 35 years seeking assisted reproductive technology. *Australian Family Physician, 34*(3), 187–188.

Han, S., & Moen, P. (1999). Clocking out: Temporal patterning of retirement. *American Journal of Sociology, 105,* 191–236.

Hanley, R. J., Alecxih, L. M., Wiener, J. M., & Kennell, D. L. (1990). Predicting elderly nursing home admissions: Results from the 1982–1984 National Long-Term Care Survey. *Research on Aging, 12,* 199–227.

Hansen, C., & Zambo, D. (2007). Loving and learning with Wemberly and David: Fostering emotional development in early childhood education. *Early Childhood Education Journal, 34*(4), 273–278.

Hansen, L. B., Saseen, J. J., & Teal, S. B. (2007) Levonorgestrel-only dosing strategies for emergency contraception. *Pharmacotherapy, 27*(2), 278–284.

Hao, L., & Cherlin, A. J. (2004). Welfare reform and teenage pregnancy, childbirth, and school dropout. *Journal of Marriage and Family, 66,* 179–184.

Hareven, T. (Ed.). (1978). *Transitions: The family and the life course in historical perspective.* New York: Academic Press.

Hareven, T. (1982a). American families in transition: Historical perspectives on change. In F. Walsh (Ed.), *Normal family processes* (pp. 446–466). New York: Guilford.

Hareven, T. (1982b). *Family time and industrial time: The relationship between the family and work in a New England industrial community.* New York: Cambridge University Press.

Hareven, T. (Ed.). (1996). *Aging and generation relations over the life course: A historical and cross-cultural perspective.* New York: Walter de Gruyter.

Hareven, T. (2000). *Families, history, and social change.* Boulder, CO: Westview.

Harkness, S., & Super, C. (2003). Culture and parenting. In M. Bornstein (Ed.), *Handbook of parenting* (2nd ed., Vol. 2, pp. 253–280). Mahwah, NJ: Lawrence Erlbaum.

Harkness, S., & Super, C. (2006). Themes and variations: Parental ethnotheories in Western cultures. In K. Rubin (Ed.), *Parental beliefs, parenting, and child development in cross-cultural perspectives* (pp. 61–80). New York: Psychology Press.

Harper, C. (2004, March). Escaping poverty cycles. *In Focus.* Retrieved January 19, 2010, from http://www.undp.org/.

Harps, S. N. (2005). Race-related stress, racial socialization, and African American adolescent adjustment: Examining the mediating role of racial identity. *Dissertation Abstracts International: The Humanities and Social Sciences, 66*(5), November 1975-A.

Harrell, S. P. (2000). A multidimensional conceptualization of racism-related stress: Implications for the well-being of people of color. *American Journal of Orthopsychiatry, 70*(1), 42–57.

Harrigan, M. P., & Farmer, R. L. (2000). The myths and facts of aging. In R. L. Schneider, N. P. Kropf, & A. J. Kisor (Eds.), *Gerontological social work: Knowledge, service settings, and special populations* (2nd ed., pp. 26–64). Belmont, CA: Wadsworth.

Harrigan, M. P., & Koerin, B. B. (2007). Long distance caregiving: Personal realities and practice implications. *Reflections, 13(2), 5–16.*

Harris, J. (1998). *The nurture assumption: Why children turn out the way they do.* New York: Touchstone.

Harry, B. (2006). *Why are so many minority students in special education?: Understanding race & disability in schools.* New York: Teachers College Press.

Hart, B., & Risley, T. (1995). *Meaningful differences in the everyday experiences of young American children.* Baltimore: Brookes.

Hart, H., McAdams, D., Hirsch, B., & Bauer, J. (2001). Generativity and social involvements among African-American and among Euro-American adults. *Journal of Research in Personality, 3*(2), 208–230.

Hart, T. (2006). Spirituality experiences and capacities of children and youth. In E. C. Roehlkepartain, P. E. King, L. Wagener, & P. L. Benson (Eds.), *The handbook of spiritual development in children and adolescence* (pp. 34–45). Thousand Oaks, CA: Sage.

Hart, V. A. (2002). Infertility and the role of psychotherapy. *Issues in Mental Health Nursing, 23*(1), 31–41.

Harter, S. (1988). Developmental processes in the construction of self. In T. D. Yawkey & J. E. Johnson (Eds.), *Integrative processes and socialization: Early to middle childhood* (pp. 45–78). Hillsdale, NJ: Lawrence Erlbaum.

Harter, S. (1998). The development of self-representations. In W. Damon & N. Eisenberg (Eds.), *Handbook of social development: Vol. 3. Social, emotional and personality development* (pp. 553–618). New York: Wiley.

Harvard Health Letter (2002). Aging—living to 100: What's the secret? *Harvard Health Letter, 27*(3), 1–3.

Harvey, S. M., Beckman, L. J., Sherman, C., & Petitti, D. (1999). Women's experience and satisfaction with emergency contraception. *Family Planning Perspectives, 31,* 237–240, 260.

Harwood, R. (1992). The influence of culturally derived values on Anglo and Puerto Rican mothers' perceptions of attachment behavior. *Child Development, 63,* 822–839.

Hatch, S. L. (2005). Conceptualizing and identifying: Cumulative adversity and protective resources: Implications for understanding health inequalities. *The Journal of Gerontology: Series B: Psychological Sciences and Social Sciences, 60B,* 130–135.

Hatecher, R. A., Trussel, J., Stewart, F., Stewart, G. K., Kowal, D., Guest, F., Cates, W., & Policar, M. S. (1994). *Contraception technology, 16th edition.* New York: Irvington.

Hauser-Cram, P., & Howell, A. (2003). The development of young children with disabilities and their families: Implications for policies and programs. In R. M. Lerner, F. Jacobs, & D. Wertlieb (Eds.), *Handbook of applied developmental science, Vol. 1* (pp. 259–279). Thousand Oaks, CA: Sage.

Havighurst, R. J. (1968). Personality and patterns of aging. *The Gerontologist, 8,* 20–23.

Havighurst, R., Neugarten, B., & Tobin, S. (1968). Personality and patterns of aging. In B. L. Neugarten (Ed.), *Middle age and aging* (pp. 173–177). Chicago: University of Chicago Press.

Hay, D., & Nye, R. (2006). *The spirit of the child* (Rev. ed.). London: Jessica Kingsley Publishers.

Haycock, K. (2006). *Promise abandoned: How policy choices and institutional practices restrict college opportunities.* Retrieved November 3, 2006, from http://www2.edtrust.org/EdTrust/Promise+Abondoned+Report.htm.

Hayflick, L. (1994). *How and why we age.* New York: Ballantine Books.

Haynie, D., Petts, R., Maimon, D., & Piquero, A. (2009). Exposure to violence in adolescence and precocious role exits. *Journal of Youth and Adolescence, 38,* 269–286.

health-cares.net. (2005). *What're the symptoms of andropause?* Retrieved August 24, 2009, from http://mens-health.health-cares.net/andropause-symptoms.php.

Healthy People 2010. (2000). Retrieved April 6, 2002, from http://www.health.gov/healthypeople/default.htm.

Heck, K. E., Schoendorf, K. C., & Chavez, G. F. (2002). The influence of proximity of prenatal services on small-for-gestational age birth. *Journal of Community Health, 27*(1), 15–27.

Heckhausen, J. (2001). Adaptation and resilience in midlife. In M. Lachman (Ed.), *Handbook of midlife development* (pp. 345–394). New York: Wiley.

Hedley, A. A., Ogden, C. L., Johnson, C. L., Carroll, M. D., Curtin, L. R., & Flegal, K. M. (2004). Overweight and obesity among U.S. children, adolescents, and adults, 1999–2002. *Journal of American Medical Association, 291,* 2847–2850.

Hehir, T. (2003). Beyond inclusion. *School Administrator, 60*(3), 36–40.

Heimpel, S., Wood, J., Marshall, J., & Brown, J. (2002). Do people with low self-esteem really feel better? Self-esteem differences in motivation to repair negative moods. *Journal of Personality and Social Psychology, 82,* 128–147.

Heinz, W. (2003). From work trajectories to negotiated careers: The contingent work life course. In J. Mortimer & M. Shanahan (Eds.), *Handbook of the life course* (pp. 185–204). New York: Kluwer Academic/Plenum Publishers.

Helburn, S., & Bergmann, B. (2002). *America's child care problem: The way out.* New York: Palgrave Macmillan.

Helmchen, H., Baltes, M. M., Geiselmann, S., Kanowski, S., Linden, M., Reischies, F. M., et al. (1999). Psychiatric illness in old age. In P. B. Baltes & K. U. Mayer, (Eds.), *The Berlin Aging Study: Aging from 70 to 100* (pp. 167–196). Cambridge: Cambridge University Press.

Helson, R., & Wink, P. (1992). Personality change in women from the early 40s to the early 50s. *Psychology and Aging, 7,* 46–55.

Henderson, J., & Petrou, S. (2008). Economic implications of home births and birth centers: A structured review. *Birth, 35*(2), 136–146.

Henderson, M., Butcher, I., Wight, D., Williamson, L., & Raab, G. (2008). What explains between-school differences in rates of sexual experience? *BMC Public Health, 8*(8), 53.

Hendrick, J. (1990). Early childhood. In R. Thomas (Ed.), *The encyclopedia of human development and education: Theory, research, and studies.* Oxford, UK: Pergamon.

Hendricks, J. (1987). Exchange theory in aging. In G. L. Maddox (Ed.), *The encyclopedia of aging* (pp. 238–239). New York: Springer.

Hendricks, J., & Hatch, L. R. (2006). Lifestyle and aging. In R. H. Binstock & L. K. George (Eds.), *Handbook of aging and the social sciences* (pp. 301–319). Amsterdam: Elsevier.

Hepp, S. M., & Meuleman, E. J. (2006). Vasectomy: Indications and implementation in historic perspective. *Nederlands Tijdschrift Voor Geneeskunde, 150*(11), 611–614.

Hequembourg, A., & Brallier, S. (2005). Gendered stories of parental caregiving among siblings. *Journal of Aging Studies, 19,* 53–71.

Herberth, G., Weber, A., Röder, S., Elvers, H-E., Krämer, U., Schins, R. et al. (2008). Relation between stressful life events, neuropeptides and cytokines: Results from the LISA birth cohort study. *Pediatric Allergy & Immunology, 19*(8), 722–729.

Herdiman, J., Nakash, A., & Beedham, T. (2006). Male contraception: Past, present and future. *Journal of Obstetrics and Gynaecology, 26*(8), 721–727.

Heron, M., Hoyert, D., Murphy, S., Xu, J., Kochanek, K., & Tejada-Vera, B. (2009, April 17). Deaths: Final data for 2006. *National Vital Statistics Reports, 57*(14). Retrieved August 24, 2009, from http://www.cdc.gov/nchs/data/nvsr/nvsr57/nvsr57_14.pdf.

Herrenkohl, T. I., Mason, W. A., Kosterman, R., Lengua, L. J., Hawkins, J. D., & Abbott, R. D. (2004). Pathways from physical childhood abuse to partner violence in young adulthood. *Violence and Victims, 19*(2), 123–145.

Herring, R. D. (1995). Developing biracial ethnic identity: A review of the increasing dilemma. *Journal of Multicultural Counseling and Development, 23*(1), 29–38.

Hessol, N., & Fuentes-Afflick, E. (2005). Ethnic differences in neonatal and postneonatal mortality. *Pediatrics, 115*(1), 164.

Hetherington, E. M., & Jodl, K. M. (1994). Stepfamilies as settings for child development. In A. Booth & J. Dunn (Eds.), *Stepfamilies: Who benefits? Who does not?* (pp. 55–79). Hillsdale, NJ: Lawrence Erlbaum.

Hetherington, E. M., & Kelly, J. (2002). *For better or for worse: Divorce reconsidered.* New York: W.W. Norton.

Heuveline, P., & Timberlake, J. (2004). The role of cohabitation in family formation: The United States in comparative perspective. *Journal of Marriage and Family, 66,* 1214–1230.

Heyman, R. E., & Smith Slep, A. M. (2002). Do child abuse and interparental violence lead to adulthood violence? *Journal of Marriage and Family, 64*(4), 864–871.

Hillis, S. D., Andra, R. F., Dube, S. R., Felitti, V. J., Marchbanks, P. A., & Marks, J. S. (2004). The association between adverse childhood experiences and adolescent pregnancy, long-term psychosocial consequences, and fetal death. *Pediatrics, 113*(2), 320–327.

Himes, C. (2001). Social demography of contemporary families and aging. In A. Walker, M. Manoogian-O'Dell, L. McGraw, & D. L. White (Eds.), *Families in later life: Connections and transitions* (pp. 47–50). Thousand Oaks, CA: Pine Forge Press.

Hines, P. M. (2005). The family life cycle of African American families living in poverty. In B. Carter & M. McGoldrick (Eds.), *The expanded family life cycle: Individual, family and social perspectives* (3rd ed., pp. 327–345). Boston: Allyn & Bacon.

Hines, P., Preto, N., McGoldrick, M., Almeida, R., & Weltman, S. (2005). Culture and the family life cycle. In B. Carter & M. McGoldrick (Eds.), *The expanded family life cycle: Individual, family, and social perspectives* (3rd ed., pp. 69–87). Boston: Allyn & Bacon.

Hinrichsen, G. A., & Clougherty, K. F. (2006). Role transitions. In *Interpersonal psychotherapy for depressed older adults* (pp. 133–152). Washington, DC: American Psychological Association.

Hitlin, S., & Elder, G., Jr. (2007). Time, self, and the curiously abstract concept of agency. *Sociological Theory, 25*(2), 170–191.

Hitti, M. (2009, May 28). *Pregnancy weight gain: New guidelines.* Health and Pregnancy, WebMD. Retrieved January 19, 2010, from http://www.webmd.com/baby/news/20090528/pregnancy-weight-gain-new-guidelines.

Hlatky, M., Boothrody, D., Vittinghoff, E., Sharp, P., & Whooley, M. (2002). Quality-of-life and depressive symptoms in postmenopausal women after receiving hormone therapy:

Results from heart and estrogen/progestin replacement study (HERS) trial. *JAMA, The Journal of the American Medical Association, 287*(5), 591–597.

Ho, M., Rasheed, J., & Rasheed, M. (2004). *Family therapy with ethnic minorities* (2nd ed.). Thousand Oaks, CA: Sage.

Hodge, D. R. (2001). Spiritual assessment: A review of major qualitative methods and a new framework for assessing spirituality. *Social Work, 46*(3), 203–214.

Hodge, D., Johnson, B., & Luidens, D. (1993). Determinants of church involvement of young adults who grew up in Presbyterian churches. *Journal for the Scientific Study of Religion, 32*(3), 242–255.

Hodnett, E. D., Downe, S., Edwards, N., & Walsh, D. (2005, January 25). Home-like versus conventional institutional settings for birth (Cochrane Review). *The Cochrane Database of Systematic Reviews,* Issue 1, CD000012.

Hoek, H. (2006). Incidence, prevalence and mortality of anorexia nervosa and other eating disorders. *Current Opinion in Psychiatry, 19,* 389–394.

Hoff, E. (2009). *Language development* (4th ed.). Pacific Grove, CA: Cengage.

Hogan, D. P., & Msall, M. E. (2002). Family structure and resources and the parenting of children with disabilities and functional limitations. In J. G. Borkowski, S. Landesman Ramey, & M. Bristol-Power (Eds.), *Parenting and the child's world* (pp. 311–344). Mahwah, NJ: Lawrence Erlbaum.

Hoge, C. W., Auchterlonie, J. L., & Milliken, C. S. (2006). Mental health problems, use of mental health services, and attrition from military service after returning from deployment to Iraq or Afghanistan. *Journal of the American Medical Association, 295*(9), 1023–1032.

Hogstel, M. (2001). *Gerontology: Nursing care of the older adult.* Albany, NY: Delma-Thompson Learning.

Hollander, D. (2008). FYI. *Perspectives on Sexual & Reproductive Health, 40*(3), 128–129.

Hollman, D., & Alderman, E. (2008). Fatherhood in adolescence. *Pediatrics in Review, 29,* 364–369.

Holm, S. M., Forbes, E. E., Ryan, N. D., Phillips, M. L., Tarr, J. A., & Dahl, R. E. (2009). Reward-related brain function and sleep in pre/early pubertal and mid/late pubertal adolescents. *The Journal of Adolescent Health, 45*(4), 326–334.

Holmes, T. (1978). Life situations, emotions, and disease. *Psychosomatic Medicine, 19,* 747–754.

Holmes, T., & Rahe, R. (1967). The social readjustment rating scale. *Journal of Psychosomatic Research, 11,* 213–218.

Holter, M. C. (2004). Autistic spectrum disorders: Assessment and intervention. In P. Allen-Meares & M. W. Fraser (Eds.), *Intervention with children and adolescents: An interdisciplinary perspective* (pp. 205–228). Boston: Allyn & Bacon.

Holzer, H. (2009). The labor market and young black men: Updating Moynihan's perspective. *Annals of the American Academy of Political and Social Science, 621,* 47–69.

Homans, G. C. (1961). *Social behavior: Its elementary forms.* New York: Harcourt Brace Jovanovich.

Hong-zheng, L., Zue-rong, L., & Mei-ying, L. (2004). Development of Life Events Inventory for Compulsory Servicemen of Land Army. *Chinese Journal of Clinical Psychology, 12*(3), 234–236.

Hood, L. (2003). *Immigrant students, urban high schools: The challenge continues.* Retrieved November 7, 2006, from http://www.carnegie.org/pdf/immigrantstudents.pdf.

Hooyman, N. R., & Kiyak, H. A. (2008*). Social gerontology: A multidisciplinary perspective.* Boston: Allyn & Bacon.

Hooyman, N. R., & Kramer, B. J. (2006). *Living through loss: Interventions across the life span.* New York: Columbia University Press.

Hope, R. M., & Hodge, D. M. (2006). Factors affecting children's adjustment to the death of a parent: The social work professional's point of view. *Child and Adolescent Social Work Journal, 23*(1), 107–126.

Horn, A. W., & Alexander, C. I. (2005). Recurrent miscarriage. *Journal of Family Planning and Reproductive Health Care, 31*(2), 103–107.

Horn, J. L. (1982). The theory of fluid and crystallized intelligence in relation to concepts of cognitive psychology and aging in adulthood. In F. I. M. Craik & S. Trehub (Eds.), *Aging and cognitive processes* (pp. 237–278). New York: Plenum.

Hosmer, L. (2001). Home birth, alternative medicine, and obstetrics. *Clinical Obstetrics and Gynecology, 44*(4), 671–680.

Hosp, J. L., & Reschly, D. J. (2003). Referral rates for intervention or assessment: A meta-analysis of racial differences. *Journal of Special Education, 37*(2), 67–80.

House, J. S., Lantz, P. M., & Herd, P. (2005). Continuity and change in the social stratification of aging and health over the life course: Evidence from a nationally representative longitudinal study from 1986 to 2001/2002 (Americans' Changing Lives Study). *The Journal of Gerontology: Series B: Psychological Sciences and Social Sciences, 60B,* 15–26.

Houtenville, A., & Conway, K. (2008). Parental effort, school resources, and student achievement. *Journal of Human Resources, 43*(2), 437–453.

Howard, D., Strobino, D., Sherman, S., & Crum, R (2008). Within prisons, is there an association between the quantity of prenatal care and infant birthweight? *Paediatric & Perinatal Epidemiology, 22*(4), 369–378.

Howard, D., Strobino, D., Sherman, S., Crum, R (2009). Timing of incarceration during pregnancy and birth outcomes: Exploring racial differences. *Maternal & Child Health Journal, 13*(4), 457–466.

Howard, D. E., Wang, M. Q., & Yan, F. (2007). Prevalence and psychosocial correlates of forced sexual intercourse among U.S. high school adolescents. *Adolescence, 42*(168), 629–643.

Hoyert, D. L. (2007). Maternal mortality and related Concerns. *National Center for Health Statistics—Vital Health Stat, 3*(33).

Hoyert, D. L., Matthews, T. J., Menacker, F., Strobino, D. M., & Guyer, B. (2006). Annual summary of vital statistics: 2004. *Pediatrics, 117*(10), 168–183.

HR Specialist. (2009, July). How to legally manage pregnancy and maternity leaves. *HR Specialist: The New York Employment Law, 4*(7), 4.

Hser, Y., Longshore, D., & Anglin, M. (2007). The life course perspective on drug use. *Evaluation Review, 31*(6), 515–547.

Huang, L. Z., & Winzer-Serhan, U. H. (2006). Chronic neonatal upregulates heteromeric nicotinic acetylcholine receptor binding without change in subunit mRNA expression. *Brain Research, 1113* (1), 94–109.

Huberman, B. (2001). The lessons learned: A model to improve adolescent sexual health in the United States. *Transitions, 14*(2), 6.

Hubley, A., & Russell, L. (2009). Prediction of subjective age, desired age, and age satisfaction in older adults: Do some health dimensions contribute more than others? *International Journal of Behavioral Development, 33*(1), 12–21.

Huebner, A., & Garrod, A. (1993). Moral reasoning among Tibetan monks. A study of Buddhist adolescents and young adults in Nepal. *Journal of Croos-Cultural Psychology, 24*, 167–185.

Hueston, W. J., Geesey, M. E., & Diaz, V. (2008). Prenatal care initiation among pregnant teens in the United States: An analysis over 25 years. *Journal of Adolescent Health, 42*(3), 243–248.

Hueston, W. J., Quattlebaum, R. G., & Benich, J. J. (2008). How much money can early prenatal care for teen pregnancies save? A cost-benefit analysis. *Journal of American Board of Family Medicine, 21*(3), 184–190.

Hughes, D., Hagelskamp, C., Way, N., & Foust, M. (2009). The role of mothers' and adolescents' perceptions of ethnic-racial socialization in shaping ethnic-racial identity among early adolescent boys and girls. *Journal of Youth and Adolescence, 38*, 605–626.

Hughes, F. (2010). *Children, play, and development* (4th ed.). Los Thousand Oaks, CA: Sage.

Hughes, H. (1988). Psychological and behavioral correlates of family violence in child witnesses and victims. *American Journal of Orthopsychiatry, 58*, 77–90.

Huinink, J., & Feldhaus, M. (2009). Family research from the life course perspective. *International Sociology, 24*(3), 299–324.

Human Genome Project. (2009a). *Human Genome project legislation.* Retrieved December 2, 2009, from http://www.ornl.gov/hgmis.

Human Genome Project. (2009b). *Genetics privacy and legislation.* Retrieved December 2, 2009, from http://www.ornl.gov/sci/techresources/ Human_Genome/elsi/legislat.shtml.

Human Rights Campaign. (2010). *Marriage equality & other relationship recognition laws.* Retrieved May 12, 2010, from http://www.hrc.org/statelaws.

Human Rights Watch. (2006). *Child labor.* Retrieved January 13, 2007, from http://hrw.org/children/labor.htm.

Humphreys, N. A., & Quam, J. K. (1998). Middle-aged and old gay, lesbian, and bisexual adults. In G. A. Appleby & J. W. Anastas (Eds.), *Not just a passing phase: Social work with gay, lesbian, bisexual people* (pp. 243–267). New York: Columbia University Press.

Hunger Notes. (2009). *World hunger facts 2009.* Retrieved May 21, 2010, from http://www.endhunger.org/ham/WorldHunger%20Facts2009.pdf.

Hussein, I. (2004). Prolongation of pregnancy in a woman who has sustained brain death at 26 weeks gestation. *British Journal of Obstetrics and Gynaecology: An International Journal of Obstetrics and Gynaecology, 113*(1), 120–122.

Hussein, I., Govenden, V., Grant, J., & Said, M. (2006). Prolongation of pregnancy in a woman who sustained brain death at 26 weeks of gestation. *BJOG: An International Journal of Obstetrics and Gynaecology, 113*(1), 130–133.

Hutchinson, K. C., Moore, G. A., Propper, C., & Mariaskin, A. (2008). Incarcerated women's psychological functioning during pregnancy. *Psychology of Women Quarterly, 32*, 440–453.

Hutchison, E. (2007). Community violence. In E. Hutchison, H. Matto, M. Harrigan, L. Charlesworth, & P. Viggiani (Eds.), *Challenges of living: A multidimensional working model for social workers* (pp. 71–104). Thousand Oaks, CA: Sage.

Hutchison, E., & Kovacs, P. (2007). HIV/AIDS. In E. Hutchison, H. Matto, M. Harrigan, L. Charlesworth, & P. Viggiani (Eds.), *Challenges of living: A multidimensional working model for social workers* (pp. 233–266). Thousand Oaks, CA: Sage.

Hutchison, E., Matto, H., Harrigan, M., Charlesworth, L., & Viggiani, P. (2007). *Challenges of living: A multidimensional working model for social workers.* Thousand Oaks, CA: Sage.

Huttenlocher, P., & Kabholkar, A. (1997). Regional differences in synaptogenesis in human cerebral cortex. *Journal of Comparative Neurology, 387*, 167–178.

Huyck, M. H. (2001). Romantic relationships in later life. *Generations, 25*(2), 9–17.

Hyde, B. (2008a). *Children and spirituality: Searching for meaning and connectedness.* Philadelphia, PA: Jessica Kingsley Publishers.

Hyde, B. (2008b). Weaving the threads of meaning: A characteristic of children's spirituality and its implications for religious education. *British Journal of Religious Education, 30(3)*, 235–245.

Hyde, J. (2005). The gender similarities hypothesis. *American Psychologist, 60*, 581–592.

Hyson, M. (2004). *The emotional development of young children: Building an emotion-centered curriculum.* New York: Teachers College Press.

Iannotti, R. (1985). Naturalistic and structured assessments of prosocial behavior in preschool children: The influence of empathy and perspective taking. *Developmental Psychology, 21*, 46–55.

Impett, E. & Tolman, D. (2006). Late adolescent girls' sexual experiences and sexual satisfaction. *Journal of Adolescent Research, 21, 628–646.*

Inderbitzin, M. (2009). Reentry of emerging adults: Adolescent inmates' transition back into the community. *Journal of Adolescent Research, 24*, 453–476.

Inhorn, M. C. (2003). Global infertility and the globalization of the new reproductive technologies: Illustrations from Egypt. *Social Science and Medicine, 56*(9), 1837–1852.

Innes, A. (2009). *Dementia studies.* Washington, DC: Sage.

Institute for the Study of Aging. (2001). *Achieving and maintaining cognitive vitality with aging* (International Longevity Center Workshop Report). New York: Author.

Institute of Medicine. (2009). *Weight gain during pregnancy: Reexamining the guidelines.* Retrieved January 19, 2010, from http://www.iom.edu/Reports/2009/Weight-Gain-During-Pregnancy-Reexamining-the-Guidelines.aspx.

Institute of Medicine of the National Academies. (2006). *Preterm birth: Causes, consequences and prevention.* Washington, DC: National Academies Press.

International Federation of Persons with Physical Disability. (2008). *Violence against women: Forced sterilization of women with disabilities is a reality in Europe.* Retrieved February 10, 2010, from http://www.fimitic.org/node/314.

International Longevity Center-USA. (2002). *Is there an "anti-aging" medicine?* (Workshop Report D17692). New York: Author.

Internet Crimes Against Children Task Force Program. (2010). *Program summary.* U.S. Department of Justice, Office of Justice Programs, Office of Juvenile Justice and Delinquency Prevention. Retrieved January 11, 2010, from http://www.ojjdp.ncjrs.gov/Programs/ProgSummary.asp?pi=3.

Irish, D., Lundquist, K., & Nelsen, V. (1993). *Ethnic variations in dying, death, and grief: Diversity in universality.* Washington, DC: Taylor & Francis.

Ito, M., & Sharts-Hopko, C. (2002). The Japanese women's experience of childbirth in the United States. *Health Care for Women International, 23*(6–7), 666–677.

Jackson, A., & Mott, P. (2007). Reproductive health care for women with spinal bifida. *Scientific World Journal, 7*, 1875–1883.

Jackson, K. M., & Nazar, A. M. (2006). Breastfeeding, the immune response, and long-term health. *Journal of the American Osteopathic Association, 106*, 203–207.

Jaddoe, V. W., Troe, E. J., Hofman, A., Mackenbach, J. P., Moll, H. A., Steegers, E. A., et al. (2008). Active and passive maternal smoking during pregnancy and the risks of low birthweight and preterm birth: The generation R study. *Paediatric and Perinatal Epidemiology, 22*(2), 162–171.

Jaffe, R. B. (2006). Risk factors for ectopic pregnancy in women with symptomatic first-trimester pregnancies. *Obstetrical & Gynecological Survey, 61*(12), 780–782.

Jahromi, L., Putnam, S., & Stifter, C. (2004). Maternal regulation of infant reactivity from 2 to 6 months. *Developmental Psychology, 40*, 477–487.

Jain, T. (2006). Socioeconomic and racial disparities among infertility patients seeking care. *Fertility and Sterility, 85*(4), 876–881.

Jain, T., & Gupta, R. S. (2007). Trends in the use of intracyctoplasmic sperm injection in the United States. *New England Journal of Medicine, 357*(3), 251–257.

James, W. P. T. (2006). The challenge of childhood obesity. *The International Journal of Pediatric Obesity, 1*(1), 7–10.

Jang, K., Liveseley, J., Riemann, R., Vernon, P., Hu, S., Angleirner, A., et al. (2001). Covariance structure of neuroticism and agreeableness: A twin and molecular genetic analysis of the role of the serotonin transporter gene. *Journal of Personality and Social Psychology, 81*(2), 295.

Jang, Y., Borenstein, A. R., Chiriboga, D. A., & Mortimer, J. A. (2005). Depressive symptoms among African American and white older adults. *Journals of Gerontology: Series B: Psychological Sciences and Social Sciences, 6*(6), 313–319.

Jans, L., & Stoddard, S. (1999). *Chartbook on woman and disability in the United States. An InfoUse Report.* Washington, DC: U.S. Department of Education. National Institute on Disability and Rehabilitation Research.

Jansen, P., Raat, H., Mackenbach, J., Jaddoe, V., Hofman, A., Verhulst, F., et al. (2009). Socioecnonomic inequalities in infant temperament. *Social Psychiatry and Psychiatric Epidemiology, 44*, 87–95.

Janssen, R., Saxell, L., Page, L.A., Klein, M.C., Liston, R.M., & Lee, S.K. (2009). Outcomes of planned home birth with registered midwife versus planned hospital birth with midwife or physician. *Canadian Medical Association Journal, 191*(6–7), 377–383.

Jarrell, A. (2000, April 2). The face of teenage sex grows younger. *The New York Times,* Section 9, p. 1, Column 1.

Jasso, G. (2003). Migration, human development, and the life course. In J. Mortimer & M. Shanahan (Eds.), *Handbook of the life course* (pp. 331–364). New York: Kluwer Academic/Plenum Publishers.

Jensen, L. A. (2003). Coming of age in a multicultural world: Globalization and adolescent cultural identity formation. *Applied Developmental Science, 7*, 188–195.

Jessor, R. (1987). Problem-behavior theory, psychosocial development, and adolescent problem drinking. *British Journal of Addiction, 82,* 331–342.

Johanson, R., Newburn, M., & Macfarlane, A. (2002). Has the medicalisation of childbirth gone too far? *British Medical Journal, 324*(7342), 892–895.

Johnson, A. (2005). *Privilege, power and difference.* New York: McGraw-Hill.

Johnson, A. N. (2008). Engaging fathers in the NICU: Taking down the barriers to the baby. *The Journal of Perinatal and Neonatal Nursing, 22*(4), 302–306.

Johnson, B., & Chavkin, W. (2007). Policy efforts to prevent ART-related preterm Birth. *Maternal Child Health Journal, 11,* 219–225.

Johnson, C., Ironsmith, M., Snow C., & Poteat, M. (2000). Peer acceptance and social adjustment in preschool and kindergarten. *Early Childhood Education Journal, 27*(4), 207–212.

Johnson, K. (2006). The SERM of my dream. *The Journal of Clinical Endocrinology & Metabolism, 91*(10), 3754–3756.

Johnson, K. C., & Davis, B. (2005). Outcomes of planned homebirths with certified professional midwives: Large prospective study in North America. *British Medical Journal, 330*(7505), 1416.

Johnson, M. P. (2002). An exploration of men's experience and role at childbirth. *The Journal of Men's Studies, 10*(12), 165–183.

Johnson, M. P., & Baker, S. R. (2004). Implications of coping repertoire as predictors of men's stress, anxiety, and depression following pregnancy, childbirth, and miscarriage: A longitudinal study. *Journal of Psychosomatic Obstetrics and Gynecology, 25*(2), 87–98.

Johnson, R., Browne, K., & Hamilton-Giachritsis, C. (2006). Young children in institutional care at risk of harm. *Trauma, Violence & Abuse, 7*(1), 34–60.

Johnson, R. S., & Tripp-Reimer, T. (2001). Aging, ethnicity, and social support: A review. *Journal of Gerontological Nursing, 27*(6), 15–21.

Johnson, S., Blum, R., & Giedd, J. (2009). Adolescent maturity and the brain: The promise and pitfalls of neuroscience research in adolescent health policy. *Journal of Adolescent Health, 45,* 216–221.

Johnson, T., & Colucci, P. (2005). Lesbians, gay men, and the family life cycle. In B. Carter & M. McGoldrick (Eds.), *The expanded family life cycle: Individual, family, and social perspectives* (3rd ed., pp. 346–361). Boston: Allyn & Bacon.

Johnston, L., O'Malley, P., Bachman, J., & Schulenberg, J. (2004). *Monitoring the future national results on adolescent drug use: Overview of key findings, 2003* (NIH Publication No. 04–5506). Bethesda, MD: National Institute of Drug Abuse.

Johnston, L., O'Malley, P., Bachman, J., & Schulenberg, J. (2005). *Monitoring the future national results on adolescent drug use: Overview of key findings, 2004* (NIH Publication No. 04–5506). Bethesda, MD: National Institute of Drug Abuse.

Johnston, L., O'Malley, P., Bachman, J., & Schulenberg, J. (2006). *Monitoring the future national results on drug use: Overview of key findings, 2005* (NIH Publication No. 06–5882). Bethesda, MD: National Institute on Drug Abuse.

Jones, A. (1992). Self-esteem and identity in psychotherapy with adolescents from upwardly mobile middle-class African American families. In L. Vargas & J. Koss-Chioino (Eds.), *Working with culture: Psychotherapeutic interventions with ethnic minority children and adolescents.* San Francisco: Jossey-Bass.

Jones, J. (2009). Who adopts? Characteristics of women and men who have adopted children. *NCHS Data Brief, 12,* 1–8.

Jones, K., Whitbourne, S., & Skultety, K. (2006). Identity processes and the transition to midlife among baby boomers. In S. Whitbourne & S. Willis (Eds.), *The baby boomers grow up: Contemporary perspectives on midlife* (pp. 149–164). Mahwah, NJ: Lawrence Erlbaum.

Jones, R. (2001). How parents can support learning: Not all parent involvement programs are equal, but research shows what works. *American School Board Journal, 188*(9), 18–22.

Jones, R. K., Zolna, M. R., Henshaw, S. K., & Finer, L. B. (2008). Abortion in the United States: Incidence and access to services, 2005. *Perspectives on Sexual and Reproductive Health, 40*(1), 6–16.

Jordan, J. V. (2005). Relational resilience in girls. In S. Goldstein & R. B. Brooks (Eds.), *Handbook of resilience in children* (pp. 79–90). New York: Kluwer Academic/Plenum Publishers.

Jordon, C. B., & Ferguson, R. J. (2006). Infertility-related concerns in two family practice sites. *Family, Systems, and Health, 24*(1), 28–32.

Joseph, K. S., Allen, A. C., Dodd, S. C., Turner, L. A., Scott, H., & Liston, R. (2005). The perinatal effects of delayed childbearing. *Obstetrics and Gynecology, 105*(6), 1410–1418.

Joshi, S., & Morley, J. (2006). Cognitive impairment. *Medical Clinics of North America, 90*(5), 769–787.

Joss-Moore, L., & Lane, R. (2009). The developmental origins of adult diseases. *Current Opinions in Pediatrics, 21*(2), 230–234.

Jung, C. (1971). *The portable Jung.* New York: Viking Press.

Kagan, S., & Kagan, M. (1998). *Multiple intelligences: The complete multiple intelligences book.* San Clemente, CA: Kagan Cooperative Learning.

Kaiser Family Foundation. (2008). *Fact sheet: Abortion in the U.S.: Utilization, financing, and access (#3269–02).* Retrieved November 20, 2009, from http://www.kff.org.

Kakouros, E., Maniadaki, K., & Papaeliou, C. (2004). How Greek teachers perceive functioning of pupils with ADHD. *Emotional and Behavioural Difficulties, 9*(1), 41–53.

Kalia, J. L., Visintainer, P., Brumberg, H. L., Pici, M., & Kase, J. (2009). Comparison of enrollment in interventional therapies between late-preterm and very preterm infants at 12 months corrected age. *Pediatrics, 123*(3), 804–809.

Kaltiala-Heino, R., Kosunen, E., & Rimpela, M. (2003). Pubertal timing, sexual behaviour and self-reported depression in middle adolescence. *Journal of Adolescence, 26*(5), 531–454.

Kalyani, R., Basavaraj, P. B., & Kumar, M. L. (2007). Factors influencing quality of semen: A two year prospective study. *Indian Journal of Pathology and Microbiology, 50*(4), 890–895.

Kamerman, S. (1996). Child and family policies: An international overview. In E. Zigler, S. Kagan, & N. Hall (Eds.), *Children, families, & government: Preparing for the twenty-first century* (pp. 31–48). New York: Cambridge University Press.

Kamerman, S., & Kahn, A. (1995). Innovations in toddler day care and family support services: An international overview. *Child Welfare, 74*(6), 1281–1300.

Kanabus, A. (2006, September 5). *HIV AIDS & pregnancy.* Retrieved October 1, 2006, from http://www.avert.org/pregnancy.htm.

Kandakai, T. L., & Smith, L. C. R. (2007). Denormalizing a historical problem: Teen pregnancy, policy, and public health action. *American Journal of Health Behavior, 31*(2), 170–180.

Kaplan, B., Nahum, R., Yairi, Y., Hirsch, M., Pardo, J., & Orvieto, R. (2005). Use of various contraceptive methods and time of contraception in a community-based population. *European Journal of Obstetrics, Gynecology, and Reproductive Biology, 123*(1), 72–76.

Kaplan, C. (2006). Special issues in contraception: caring for women with disabilities. *Journal of Midwifery & Women's Health, 51*(6), 450–457.

Kaplan, D. W., Feinstein, R. A., Fisher, M. M., Klein, J., Olmedo, L. F., Rome, E. S., et al. (2001). Condom use by adolescents. *Pediatrics, 107*(6), 1463–1469.

Kaplan, J., Aziz-Zadeh, L., Uddin, L., & Iacoboni, M. (2008). The self across the sense: An fMRI study of self-face and self-voice recognition. *Social Cognitive & Affective Neuroscience, 3,* 218–223.

Kaplan, M. S., & Sasser, J. E. (1996). Women behind bars: Trends and policy issues. *Journal of Sociology and Social Welfare, 23*(4), 43–56.

Kaplowitz, P. (2006). Pubertal development in girls: Secular trends. *Current Opinions in Obstetrics and Gynecology, 18,* 487–491.

Karjane, N. W., Stovall, D. W., Berger, N. G., & Svikis, D. S. (2008). Alcohol abuse risk factors and psychiatric disorders in pregnant women with a history of infertility. *Journal of Women's Health, 17*(10), 1623–1627.

Karpa, K. D. (2006). Pharmacist critique was ill-informed. *The Annals of Pharmacotherapy, 40*(7–8), 1441–1444.

Kashushin, G., & Egan, M. (2008). *Gerontological home health care: A guide for the social work practitioner.* New York: Columbia University Press.

Kaslow, F., & Robison, J. A. (1996). Long-term satisfying marriages: Perceptions of contributing factors. *The American Journal of Family Therapy, 24*(2), 153–170.

Katz, P. (1976). *Toward the elimination of racism.* New York: Pergamon Press.

Kaufman, G., & Uhlenberg, P. (2000). The influence of parenthood on the work effort of married men and women. *Social Forces, 78,* 931–949.

Kavanaugh, M. L., & Schwarz, E. B. (2008). Counseling about and use of emergency contraception in the United States. *Perspectives on Sexual and Reproductive Health, 40*(2), 81–86.

Kayne, M., Greulich, M., & Albers, L. (2001). Doulas: An alternative yet complementary addition to care during childbirth. *Clinical Obstetrics and Gynecology, 44*(4), 692–703.

Kdous, M. (2006). Nonsurgical management of ectopic pregnancy. La *Tunis Medicale, 84*(6), 331–339.

Kdous, M., Fadhlaoui, A., Boubaker, M., Youssef, A., Chaker, A., Ferchious, M., Zhioua, F., & Meriah, S. (2007). Intrauterine insemination with conjoint semen: How to increase the success rate? *La Tunisie Medicale, 85*(9), 781–787.

Keating, D. (2004). Cognitive and brain development. In R. M. Learner & L. Steinberg (Eds.), *Handbook of adolescent psychology* (2nd ed., pp. 45–84). New York: Wiley.

Keating, P. (1994). Striving for sex equity in schools. In K. I. Goodland & P. Keating (Eds.), *Access to knowledge: The continuing agenda for our nation's schools* (pp. 91–106). New York: The College Board.

Keenan, T., & Evans, S. (2009). *An introduction to child development* (2nd ed.). Thousand Oaks, CA: Sage.

Kefer, J. C., Agarwal, A., & Sabenegh, E. (2009). Role of antioxidants in the treatment of male infertility. *International Journal of Urology, 16*(5), 449–457.

Kegan, R. (1982). *The evolving self: Problem and process in human development.* Cambridge, MA: Harvard University Press.

Kegan, R. (1994). *In over our heads: The mental demands of modern life.* Cambridge, MA: Harvard University Press.

Kellaghan, T., Sloane, K., Alvarez, B., & Bloom, B. S. (1993). *The home environment and school learning: Promoting parental involvement in the education of children.* San Francisco: Jossey-Bass.

Kelly, Y., Sacker, A., Schoon, I., & Nazroo, J. (2006). Ethnic differences in achievement of developmental milestones by 9 months of age: The Millenium Cohort Study. *Developmental Medicine & Child Neurology, 48,* 825–830.

Kelly-Weeder, S., & O'Connor, A. (2006). Modifiable risk factors for impaired fertility in women: What nurse practitioners need to know. *Journal of the American Academy of Nurse Practitioners, 18,* 268–276.

Kendall-Tackett, K. A. (2007). Violence against women and the perinatal period: The impact of lifetime violence and abuse on pregnancy, postpartum, and breastfeeding. *Trauma, Violence, and Abuse, 8*(3), 344–353.

Keniston, K. (1966). *The uncommitted: Alienated youth in American society.* New York: Harcourt, Brace, & World.

Kent, G. (2002). Breastfeeding vs formula-feeding among HIV-infected women in resource-poor areas. *Journal of the American Medical Association, 287*(9), 1110–1114.

Kent, M. M. (2009). *Premature births help explain higher U.S. infant mortality.* Retrieved January 17, 2010, from http://www.prb.org/Articles/2009/prematurebirths.aspx.

Keogh, B. K., Bernheimer, L. P., & Guthrie, D. (2004). Children with developmental delays twenty years later: Where are they? How are they? *American Journal on Mental Retardation, 109*(3), 219–230.

Kerestes, M., Youniss, J., & Metz, E. (2004). Longitudinal patterns of religious perspective and civic integration. *Applied Developmental Science, 8*(1), 39–46.

Kesmodel, U., Wisborg, K., Olsen, J., Hendriksen, T., & Secher, N. (2002). Moderate alcohol intake in pregnancy and the risk of spontaneous abortion. *Alcohol and Alcoholism, 37*(1), 87–92.

Keyes, C., & Ryff, C. (1998). Generativity in adult lives: Social structural contours and quality of life consequences. In D. McAdams & E. de St. Aubin (Eds.), *Generativity and adult development: How and why we care for the next generation* (pp. 227–263). Washington, DC: American Psychological Association.

Khaw, L., & Hardesty, J. (2007). Theorizing the process of leaving: Turning points and trajectories in the stages of change. *Family Relations, 56,* 413–425.

Khawaja, U. B., Khawaja, A. A., Gowani, S. A., Shoukat, S., Ejaz, S., Ali, F. N., Rizvi, J., & Nawaz, F. H. (2009). Frequency of endometriosis among infertile women and association of clinical signs and symptoms with the laparoscopic staging of endometriosis. *The Journal of Pakistan Medical Association, 59*(1), 30–34.

Khodyakov, D., & Carr, D. (2009). The impact of late-life parental death on adult sibling relationships. *Research on Aging, 31*(5), 495–519.

Khorram, O. (1997). Activation of immune function by dehydroepiandrosterone DHEA in age-advanced men. *Journal of Gerontology Series A Biological Sciences & Medical Sciences, 52*(1), M1–7.

Khoshnood, B., Wall, S., & Lee, K. (2005). Risk of low birth weight associated with advanced maternal age among four ethnic groups in the United States. *Maternal and Child Health Journal, 9*(1), 3–9.

Kikuzawa, S. (2006). Multiple roles and mental health in cross-cultural perspective; The elderly in the United States and Japan. *Journal of Health and Social Behavior, 47*(1), 62–76.

Kim, J., & Moen, P. (2001). Moving into retirement: Preparation and transitions in late midlife. In M. Lachman (Ed.), *Handbook of midlife development* (pp. 487–527). New York: Wiley.

Kimball, C. (2004). Teen fathers: An introduction. *Prevention Researcher, 11*(4), 3–5.

Kindlon, D. J. (2003). *Too much of a good thing: Raising children of character in an indulgent age.* New York: Miramax Books.

Kindlon, D., & Thompson, M. (1999). *Raising Cain: Protecting the emotional life of boys.* New York: Random House.

King, B. R. (2001). Ranking of stigmatization toward lesbians and their children and the influence of perceptions of controllability of homosexuality. *Journal of Homosexuality, 41*(2), 77–97.

King, C., & Merchant, C. (2008). Social and interpersonal factors relating to adolescent suicidality: A review of the literature. *Archives of Suicide Research, 12,* 181–196.

King, K., & Gurain, M. (2006). With boys in mind: Teaching to the minds of boys. *Educational Leadership, 64*(1), 56–61.

King, P. (2007). Adolescent spirituality and positive youth development: A look at religion, social capital, and moral functioning. In R. Silbereisen & R. Lerner (Eds.), *Approaches to positive youth development* (pp. 227–242). Thousand Oaks, CA: Sage.

King, P., & Furrow, J. (2004). Religion as a resource for positive youth development: Religion, social capital, and moral outcomes. *Developmental Psychology, 40*(5), 703–713.

King, W. (2009). Toward a life-course perspective of police organizations. *Journal of Research in Crime and Delinquency, 46*(2), 213–244.

Kingson, E. R., & Berkowitz, E. D. (1993). *Social Security and Medicare: A policy primer.* Westport, CT: Auburn House.

Kissin, D. M., Anderson, J. E., Kraft, J. M., Warner, L., & Jamison, D. J. (2008). Is there a trend of increased unwanted childbearing among young women in the United States? *Journal of Adolescent Medicine, 43*(4), 364–371.

Kitayama, S., Karasawa, M., & Mesquita, B. (2004). Collective and personal processes in regulating emotions: Emotion and self in Japan and the United States. In P. Philippot & R. Feldman (Eds.), *The regulation of emotion* (pp. 251–276). Mahwah, NJ: Lawrence Erlbaum.

Kiwi, R. (2006). Recurrent pregnancy loss: Evaluation and discussion of the causes and their management. *Cleveland Clinic Journal of Medicine, 73*(10), 913–991.

Klaczynski, P. (2000). Motivated scientific reasoning biases, epistemological beliefs, and theory polarization: A two-process approach to adolescent cognition. *Child Development, 71*(5).

Klaczynski, P., & Fauth, J. (1997). Developmental differences in memory-based intrusions and self-serving statistical reasoning biases. *Merrill-Palmer Quarterly, 43,* 539–566.

Klein, J. D. (2005). Adolescent pregnancy: Current trends and issues. *Pediatrics, 116*(1), 281–286.

Klein, M. (1995). *The American street gang: Its nature, prevalence, and control.* New York: Oxford University Press.

Kliman, J., & Madsen, W. (2005). Social class and the family life cycle. In B. Carter & M. McGoldrick (Eds.), *The expanded family life cycle: Individual, family, and social perspectives* (3rd ed., pp. 88–105). Boston: Allyn & Bacon.

Knapp, M. S. (1995). *Teaching for meaning in high-poverty classrooms.* New York: Teachers College Press.

Knight, M., & Plugge, E. (2005).The outcomes of pregnancy among imprisoned women: A systematic review. *An International Journal of Obstetrics & Gynaecology, 112,* 1467–1474.

Knitzer, J. (2007). Putting knowledge into policy: Toward an infant-toddler policy agenda. *Infant Mental Health Journal, 28*(2), 237–245.

Koball, H., & Douglas-Hall, A. (2006). *The new poor: Regional trends in child poverty since 2000.* Retrieved November 13, 2006, from http://www.nccp.org/pub_npr06.html.

Koch, W. (2006, October 30). Fewer teens are giving birth, but the cost to taxpayers still steep. *USA Today.* Retrieved November 3, 2009, from http://www.usatoday.com/news/health/2006–10-29-teen-births_x.htm.

Kochanska, G. (1997). Multiple pathways to conscience for children with different temperaments: From toddlerhood to age 5. *Developmental Psychology, 33,* 228–240.

Kochanska, G., Aksan, N., & Joy, M. (2007). Children's fearfulness as a moderator of parenting in early socialization: Two longitudinal studies. *Developmental Psychology, 43,* 222–237.

Kochanska, G., Forman, D., Aksan, N., & Dunbar, S. (2005). Pathways to conscience: Early mother-child mutually responsive orientation and children's moral emotion, conduct, and cognition. *Journal of Child Psychology and Psychiatry, 46,* 19–34.

Koehn M. (2008). Contemporary women's perceptions of childbirth education. *Journal of Perinatal Education, 17*(1), 11–18.

Koenig, H. G., & Brooks, R. G. (2002). Religion, health, and aging: Implications for practice and public policy. *Public Policy and Aging Report, 12,* 13–19.

Kohlberg, L. (1969). Stage and sequence: The cognitive developmental approach to socialization. In D. A. Goslin (Ed.), *Handbook of socialization theory and research* (pp. 347–480). Chicago: Rand McNally.

Kohlberg, L. (1976). Moral stages and moralization: The cognitive-developmental approach. In T. Lickona (Ed.), *Moral development and behavior: Theory, research, and social issues* (pp. 31–53). New York: Holt.

Kohlberg, L. (1984). *Essays on moral development: Vol. 2. The psychology of moral development.* San Francisco: Harper & Row.

Kohler, P. K., Manhart, L. E., & Lafferty, W. E. (2008). Abstinence-only and comprehensive sex education and the initiation of sexual activity and teen pregnancy. *Journal of Adolescent Health, 42*(4), 344–351.

Kohli, M., & Künemund, H. (2005). The midlife generation in the family: Patterns of exchange and support. In S. Willis & M. Martin (Eds.), *Middle adulthood: A lifespan perspective* (pp. 35–61). Thousand Oaks, CA: Sage.

Kohut, H. (1971). *The analysis of the self.* New York: International Universities Press.

Kominski, R., Shin, H., & Marotz, K. (2008*). Language needs of school-age children.* Paper presented at the Annual Meeting of the Population Association of America. New Orleans, Louisiana. April 16–19, 2008. Retrieved January 19, 2010, from http://www.census.gov/population/www/socdemo/lang_use.html.

Koppel, G., & Kaiser, D. (2001). Fathers at the end of their rope: A brief report on fathers abandoned in the perinatal situation. *Journal of Reproductive and Infant Psychology, 19*(3), 249–251.

Kopola, M., Esquivel, G., & Baptiste, L. (1994). Counseling approaches for immigrant children: Facilitating the acculturative process. *The School Counselor, 41,* 352–359.

Kornelsen, J. (2005). Essences and imperatives: An investigation of technology in childbirth. *Social Science & Medicine, 61*(7), 1495–1504.

Koshar, J. H. (2001). Teen pregnancy 2001—Still no easy answers. *Pediatric Nursing, 25*(5), 505–512.

Kotch, J., Browne, D., Ringwalt, C., Dufort, V., Ruina, E., Stewart, P., et al. (1997). Stress, social support, and substantiated maltreatment in the second and third years of life. *Child Abuse and Neglect, 21*(11), 1026–1037.

Kovács, Á., & Mehler, J. (2009). Flexible learning of multiple speech structures in bilingual infants. *Science, 325,* 611–612,

Kovacs, P. J., Bellin, M. H., & Fauri, D. F. (2006). Family-centered care: A resource for social work in end-of-life and palliative care. *Journal of Social Work in End-of-Life & Palliative Care, 2*(1), 13–27.

Kowalik, S. C. (2004). Neurobiology of PTSD in children and adolescents. In R. Silva (Ed.). *Posttraumatic stress disorders in children and adolescents* (pp. 83–122). New York: W. W. Norton.

Kowalski, K. (1996). The emergence of ethnic/racial attitudes in preschool-age children. *Dissertation Abstracts International: Section B: The Sciences & Engineering, 56*(8-B), 4604.

Kozol, J. (1991). *Savage inequalities: Children in America's schools.* New York: HarperPerennial.

Kozol, J. (2005). *The shame of the nation: The restoration of apartheid schooling in America.* New York: Crown.

Kramer, B. (1997). Gain in the caregiving experience: Where are we? What next? *The Gerontologist, 37,* 218–232.

Kramer, M. R., & Hogue, C. R. (2009). What causes racial disparities in very preterm birth? A biosocial perspective. *Epidemiological Reviews, 31,* 84–98.

Kramer, M. R., Rowland Hogue, C. J., & Gaydos, L. (2007). Noncontracepting behavior in women at risk for unintended pregnancy: What's religion got to do with it? *Annals of Epidemiology, 17*(5), 327–334.

Kreider, R. M., & Fields, J. (2005). Living arrangements of children 2001. *Current Population Reports,* pp. 70–104. Retrieved January 19, 2010, from http://www.census.gov/prod/2005pubs/p70–104.pdf.

Kreider, R. M. & Elliott, D. B. (2009). *America's families and living arrangements: 2007.* Washington, DC: U.S. Census Bureau. Retrieved May 21, 2010, from http://www.census.gov/prod/2009pubs/p20-561.pdf.

Kremer, H., Ironson, G., & Kaplan, L. (2009). The fork in the road: HIV as a potential positive turning point and the role of spirituality. *AIDS Care, 21*(3), 368–377.

Krisberg, K. (2006). Emergency contraception now available prescription-free. *Nation's Health, 36*(8), 6–8.

Kroger, J. (2007). *Identity development: Adolescence through adulthood* (2nd ed.). Thousand Oaks, CA: Sage.

Kroon, L. A. (2007). Drug interactions with smoking. *American Journal of Health-System Pharmacy, 64*(18), 1917–1921.

Krug, E., Dahlberg, L., Mercy, J., Zwi, A., & Lozano, R. (2002). *World report on violence and health.* Geneva, Switzerland: World Health Organization.

Kübler-Ross, E. (1969). *On death and dying.* New York: Macmillan.

Kuh, D., & Ben-Sholomo, Y. (2004). *A life course approach to chronic disease epidemiology* (2nd ed.). New York: Oxford University Press.

Kulkarni, J. (2005). Psychotic illness in women at perimenopause and menopause. In D. Stewart (Ed.), *Menopause: A mental health practitioner's guide* (pp. 85–133). Washington, DC: American Psychiatric Publishing.

Kurdek, L. (2004). Are gay and lesbian cohabiting couples *really* different from heterosexual married couples? *Journal of Marriage and the Family, 66,* 880–900.

Kurdek, L. (2008). Change in relationship quality for partners from lesbian, gay male, and heterosexual couples. *Journal of Family Psychology, 22*(5), 701–711.

Kurjak, A., Pooh, R. K., Merce, L. T., Carrera, J. M., Salihagic-Kadic, A., & Andonotopo, W. (2005). Structural and functional early human development assessed by three-dimensional and four-dimensional sonography. *Fertility and Sterility, 84*(5), 1285–1299.

Kwok, O., Haine, R. A., Sandler, I. N., Ayers, T. S., Wolchik, S. A., & Tein, J. Y. (2005). Positive parenting as a mediator of the relations between parental psychological distress and mental health problems of parentally bereaved children. *Journal of Clinical Child and Adolescent Psychology, 34*(2), 260–271.

Kyei-Aboagye, K., Vragovic. O., & Chong, D. (2000). Birth outcome in incarcerated, high-risk pregnant women. *Obstetrics: Ethics, Medico-Legal Issues, and Public Policy, 55*(11), 682–684.

Labouvie-Vief, G. (1990). Modes of knowledge and the organization of development. In M. Commons, L. Kohlberg, R. Richards, & S. Sinnott (Eds.), *Beyond formal operations: Vol. 2. Models and methods in the study of adult and adolescent thought* (pp. 43–62). New York: Praeger.

Labouvie-Vief, G. (2005). Self-with-other representations and the organization of the self. *Journal of Research in Personality 39,* 185–205.

Lachman, M. (2004). Development in midlife. *Annual Review of Psychology, 55,* 305–331.

Lachman, M., & Bertrand, R. (2001). Personality and the self in midlife. In M. Lachman (Ed.), *Handbook of midlife development* (pp. 279–309). New York: Wiley.

Ladd, H. (2007). Teacher labor markets in developed countries. *The Future of Children: Excellence in the Classroom, 17*(1), 201–217.

Ladson-Billings, G. (2004). Landing on the wrong note: The price we paid for Brown. *Educational Researcher, 33*(7), 3–13.

Ladson-Billings, G. (2006). From the achievement gap to educational debt: Understanding achievement in U.S. schools. *Educational Researcher, 35*(7), 3–12.

Laflamme, D., Pomerleau, A., & Malcuit, G. (2002). A comparison of fathers' and mothers' involvement in childcare and stimulation behaviors during free play with their infants at 9 and 15 months. *Sex Roles, 47,* 507–518.

Laird, J., & Green, R. (Eds.). (1996). *Lesbian and gays in couples and families: A handbook for therapists.* San Francisco: Jossey-Bass.

Lam, V., & Smith, G. (2009). African and Caribbean adolescents in Britain: Ethnic identity and Britishness. *Ethnic and Racial Studies, 32*(7), 1248–1270.

Lamaze, F. (1958). *Painless childbirth: Psychoprophylactic method* (L. R. Celestin, Trans.). London: Burke.

Landau, E. (2008). *Report: Teen pregnancies up for first time in 15 years.* Atlanta, GA: CNN. Retrieved October 31, 2009, from http://www.cnn.com/2008/HEALTH/07/10/teen.pregnancy/index.html.

Lane, A., Westbrook, A., Grady, D., O'Connor, R., Counihan, T. J., Marsh, B., et al. (2004). Maternal brain death: Medical, ethical, and legal issues. *Intensive Care Medicine, 30*(7), 1484–1486.

Lang, A. J., Stein, M. B., Kennedy, C. M., & Foy, D. W. (2004). Adult psychopathology and intimate partner violence among survivors of childhood maltreatment. *Journal of Interpersonal Violence, 19*(10), 1102–1118.

Langle, A., & Probst, C. (2004). Existential questions of the elderly. *Archives of Psychiatry and Psychotherapy, 6*(2), 15–20.

Lansford, J., Deater-Deckard, K., Dodge, K., Bates, J., & Petttit, G. (2004). Ethnic differences in the link between physical discipline and later adolescent externalizing behaviors. *Journal of Child Psychology and Psychiatry, 45,* 801–812.

Larson, E. J. (1995). The effects of maternal substance abuse on the placenta and fetus. In G. B. Reed, A. E. Claireaux, & F. Cockburn (Eds.), *Diseases of the fetus and newborn* (2nd ed., pp. 353–361). London: Chapman & Hall.

Larson, R., & Seepersad, S. (2003). Adolescents' leisure time in the United States: Partying, sports, and the American experiment. In S. Verma & R. Larson (Eds.), *Examining adolescent leisure time across culture: New directions for child and adolescent development, No. 99* (pp. 53–64). San Francisco: Jossey-Bass.

Larson, R. W., Wilson, S., & Mortimer, J. T. (2002). Adolescence in the 21st century: An international perspective—Adolescents' preparation for the future. *Journal of Research on Adolescence, 12*(1), 159–166.

LaSala, M. C. (2001). The importance of partners to lesbians' intergenerational relationships. *Social Work Research, 25*(1), 27–40.

Laseter, R. (1997). The labor force participation of young black men: A qualitative examination. *Social Service Review, 71,* 72–88.

Latva, R., Lehtonen, L., Salmelin, R. K., & Tamminen, T. (2007). Visits by the family to the neonatal intensive care. *Acta Paediatricia, 96*(2), 215–220.

Lau, A., Litrownik, A., Newton, R., Black, M., & Everson, M. (2006). Factors affecting the link between physical discipline and child externalizing problems in Black and White families. *Journal of Community Psychology, 34*(1), 89–103.

Laumann, E., Paik, A., & Rosen, R. (1999). Sexual dysfunction in the United States: Prevalence and predictors. *Journal of the American Medical Association, 279,* 537–544.

Laurino, M. Y., Bennett, R. L., Sariya, D. S., Baumeister, L., Doyle, D. L., Leppig, K., et al. (2005). Genetic evaluation and counseling of couples with recurrent miscarriage: Recommendations of the National Society of Genetic Counselors. *Journal of Genetic Counseling, 14*(3), 165–181.

Lawrence, C. R., Carlson, E. A., & Egeland, B. (2006). The impact of foster care on development. *Development and Psychopathology, 18*(1), 57–76.

Leddy, M., Jones, C., Morgan, M., & Schulkin, J. (2009). Eating disorders and obstetric-gynecologic care. *Journal of Women's Health, 18*(9), 1395–401.

Lederberg, J. (2001). The meaning of epigenetics. *The Scientist, 15*(18), 6.

Lee, E., Menkart, D., & Okazawa-Rae, M. (1998). *Beyond holidays and heroes: A practical guide to K–12 anti-racist multicultural education and staff development.* Washington, DC: Network of Educators in the Americas.

Lee, K. (2009). *Infant reflexes.* MedlinePlus medical encyclopedia. Retrieved February 12, 2010, from http://www.nlm.nih.gov/medlineplus/ency/article/003292.htm.

Lee, M. (2003). Korean adolescents' "examination hell" and their use of free time. In S. Verma & R. Larson (Eds.), *Examining adolescent leisure time across culture: New directions for child and adolescent development, No. 99* (pp. 9–21). San Francisco: Jossey-Bass.

Lee, M., Whitehead, J., & Ntoumanis, N. (2007). The measurement of the attitudes to moral decision-making in youth sport questionnaire. *Psychology of Sport and Exercise, 8,* 369–392.

Lee, V., & Hoaken, P.N.S. (2007). Cognitive, emotion, and neurobiological development: Mediating the relation between maltreatment and aggression. *Child Maltreatment, 12*(3), 281–298.

Leeder, E. (2004). *The family in global perspective: A gendered journey.* Thousand Oaks, CA: Sage.

LeFever, G. B., Villers, M. S., Morrow, A. L., & Vaughn, E. S. (2002). Parental perceptions of adverse educational outcomes among children diagnosed and treated for ADHD: A call for improved school/provider collaboration. *Psychology in the Schools, 39*(1), 63–71.

Leisering, L. (2003). Government and the life course. In J. Mortimer & M. Shanahan (Eds.), *Handbook of the life course* (pp. 205–225). New York: Kluwer Academic/Plenum Publishers.

Leitenberg, H., Detzer, M. J., & Srebnik, D. (1993). Gender differences in masturbation and the relationship of masturbation experience in preadolescence and/or early adolescence and sexual behavior and sexual adjustment in young adulthood. *Archives of Sexual Behavior, 22,* 299–313.

Leonard, R. (2006). Turning points in the lives of midlife and older women: Five-year follow-up. *Australian Psychologist, 41*(1), 28–36.

LePoire, B. (2006). *Family communication: Nurturing and control in a changing world.* Thousand Oaks, CA: Sage.

Lerner, J. V., Castellino, D. R., Lolli, E., & Wan, S. (2003). Children, families, and work: Research findings and implications for policies and programs. In R. M. Lerner, F. Jacobs, & D. Wertlieb (Eds.), *Handbook of applied developmental science, Vol. 1* (pp. 281–304). Thousand Oaks, CA: Sage.

Levinson, D. (1977). The mid-life transition. *Psychiatry, 40, 99–112.*

Levinson, D. (1978). *The seasons of a man's life.* New York: Knopf.

Levinson, D. (1980). Toward a conception of the adult life course. In N. J. Smelser & E. H. Erikson (Eds.), *Themes of work and love in adulthood* (pp. 265–290). Cambridge, MA: Harvard University Press.

Levinson, D. (1986). A conception of adult development. *American Psychologist, 41*(1), 3–13.

Levinson, D. (1990). A theory of life structure development in adulthood. In C. N. Alexander & E. J. Langer (Eds.), *Higher stages of human development* (pp. 35–54). New York: Oxford University Press.

Levinson, D., Darrow, C., Klein, E., Levinson, M., & McKee, B. (1978). *The seasons of a man's life.* New York: Knopf.

Levinson, D., & Levinson, J. (1996). *The seasons of a woman's life.* New York: Ballantine Books.

Levy, G. D., Taylor, M. G., & Gelman, S. A. (1995). Traditional and evaluative aspects of flexibility in gender roles, social conventions, moral rules and physical laws. *Child Development, 66,* 515–531.

Levy, L., Martinkowski, K., & Derby, J. (1994). Differences in patterns of adaptation in conjugal bereavement: Their sources and potential significance. *Omega, 29,* 71–87.

Levy, S. (2000). Still confused after all these years. *Fieldwork, 13*(2). Retrieved December 30, 2006, from http://www.elschools.org/publications/webarchive/v018n02.html.

Lewis, M. (2005). The child and its family: The social network model. *Human Development, 48,* 8–27.

Lewis, T. (1994). A comparative analysis of the effects of social skills training and teacher directed contingencies on social behavior of preschool children with disabilities. *Journal of Behavioral Education, 4,* 267–281.

Li, S.-C. (2006). Biocultural co-construction of life span development. In P. B. Baltes, P. A. Reuter-Lorenz, & F. Rössler (Eds.), *Life span development and the brain: The perspective of biocultural co-constructivism* (pp. 40–60). Cambridge: Cambridge University Press.

Lichtenstein, S. (1993). Transition from school to adulthood: Case studies of adults with learning disabilities who dropped out of school. *Exceptional Children, 59*(4), 336–347.

Limber, S. P., & Small, M. A. (2003). State laws and policies to address bullying in schools. *School Psychology Review, 32*(3), 445–455.

Lindell, S. G. (1988). Education for childbirth: A time for change. *Journal of Gynecologic and Neonatal Nursing, 17*(2), 108–112.

Lindemann, E. (1944). Symptomatology and management of acute grief. *American Journal of Psychiatry, 101,* 141–148.

Ling, Z. J., Lian, W. B., Ho, S. K., & Yeo, C. L. (2009). Parental knowledge of prematurity and related issues. *Singapore Medical Journal, 50*(3), 270–277.

Linver, M. R., Fuligni, A. S., Hernandez, M., & Brooks-Gunn, J. (2004). Poverty and child development. In P. Allen-Meares & M. W. Fraser (Eds.), *Intervention with children and adolescents: An interdisciplinary perspective* (pp. 106–129). Boston: Allyn & Bacon.

Lippman, L., & Keith, J. (2009). *A developmental perspective on workplace readiness: Preparing high school students for success.* Washington, DC: Child Trends. Retrieved January 5, 2009, from http://www.childtrends.org/Files//Child_Trends-2009_04_28_RB_WorkReady.pdf.

Littky, D., & Grabelle, S. (2004) *The big picture: Education is everyone's business.* Alexandria, VA: Association for Supervision and Curriculum Development.

Litty, C., & Hatch, J. A. (2006). Hurry up and wait: Rethinking special education identification in kindergarten. *Early Childhood Education Journal, 33*(4), 203–208.

Liu, S., Hearman, M., Kramer, M. S., Demissie, K., Wen, S. W., & Marcoux, S. (2002). Length of hospital stay, obstetric conditions at childbirth, and maternal admission: A population-based cohort study. *American Journal of Obstetrics and Gynecology, 187*(3), 681–687.

Liu, Z., Liu., L., Owens, J., & Kaplan, D. (2005). Sleep patterns and sleep problems among school children in the United States and China. *Pediatrics, 115,* 241–249.

Lloyd, C. B., Behrman, J. R., Stromquist, N. P., & Cohen, B. (2006). *The changing transitions to adulthood in developing countries: Selected studies.* Washington, DC: National Research Council.

Lochman, J. E., Coie, J. D., Underwood, M. K., & Terry, R. (1993). Effectiveness of a social relationship intervention program for aggressive and nonaggressive, rejected children. *Journal of Consulting and Clinical Psychology, 61,* 1053–1058.

Locke, A., Ginsborg, J., & Peers, I. (2002). Development and disadvantage: Implications for the early years and beyond. *International Journal of Language & Communication Disorders, 37*(1), 3–15.

Lodhi, F., Fattah, A., Abozaid, T., Murphy, J., Formantini, E., Sasy, M., et al. (2004). Gamete intra-fallopian transfer or intrauterine insemination after controlled ovarian hyperstimulation for treatment of infertility due to endometriosis. *Gynecological Endocrinology, 152*(8), 152–160.

Lomsky-Feder, E., & Leibovitz, T. (2010). Inter-ethnic encounters within the family: Competing cultural models and social exchange. *Journal of Ethnic & Migration Studies, 36*(1), 107–124.

Lonzano, H., & Ballesteros, F. (2006). A study on breakfast and school performance in a group of adolescents. *Nutrition Hospital, 21*(3), 346–352.

Losoncz, I., & Bortolotto, N. (2009). Work-life balance: The experience of Australian working mothers. *Journal of Family Studies, 15*(2), 122–138.

Loveless, T. (1999). *The tracking wars: State reform meets school policy.* Washington, DC: Brookings Institution Press.

Lowe, J., Erickson, S., MacLean, P., & Duvall, S. (2009). Early working memory and maternal communication in toddlers born very low birth weight. *Acta Paediatrica, 98,* 660–663.

Lowenstein, A., & Daatland, S. (2006). Filial norms and family support in a comparative cross-national context: Evidence from the OASIS study. *Ageing and Society, 26,* 203–223.

Lowenthal, M., Thurnher, M., & Chiriboga, D. (1975). *Four stages of life: A comparative study of women and men facing transition.* San Francisco: Jossey-Bass.

Lowry, R., Holtzman, D., Truman, B. I., Kann, L., Collins, J. L., & Kolbe, L. J. (1994). Substance use and HIV-related sexual behaviors among U.S. high school students: Are they related? *American Journal of Public Health, 84,* 1116–1120.

Lu, M. C., Prentice, J., Yu, S. M., Inkelas, M., Lange, L. O., & Halfon, N. (2003). Childbirth education classes: Sociodemographic disparities in attendance and the association of attendance with breastfeeding initiation. *Maternal and Child Health Journal, 7*(2), 87–93.

Lu, P. (2007). Sibling relationships in adulthood and old age: A case study in Taiwan. *Current Sociology, 55*(4), 621–637.

Lucille Packard Children's Hospital. (2010). *Very low birthweight.* Retrieved January 17, 2010, from http://www.lpch.org/DiseaseHealthInfo/HealthLibrary/hrnewborn/vlbw.html.

Lui, M., Robles, B., Leondar-Wright, B., Brewer, R., & Adamson, R. (2006). *The color of wealth.* New York: The New Press.

Lum, D. (2004). *Social work practice and people of color: A process state approach* (5th ed.). Belmont, CA: Wadsworth.

Lum, D. (2007). *Culturally competent practice: A framework for understanding diverse groups and justice issues* (3rd ed.). Belmont, CA: Thomson.

Luo, M. (2009, April 12). Longer unemployment for those 45 and older. *The New York Times.* Retrieved September 3, 2009, from http://www.nytimes.com/2009/04/13/us/13age.html.

Luthar, S. (Ed.). (2003). *Resilience and vulnerability: Adaptation in the context of childhood adversities.* New York: Cambridge University Press.

Lux, M., Reyes, V., Morgentaler, A., & Levine, L. (2007). Outcomes and satisfaction rates for the redesigned 2-piece penile prosthesis. *Journal of Urology, 177*(1), 262–266.

Lykeridou, K., Gourounti, K., Deltsidou, A., Loutradis, D., & Vaslamatzis, G. (2009). The impact of infertility diagnosis on psychological status of women undergoing fertility treatment. *Journal of Reproductive and Infant Psychology, 27*(3), 223–237.

Lynch, R. (2000). *New directions for high school career and technical education in the 21st century.* Washington, DC: U.S. Department of Education.

Lynch, T. R., Cheavens, J. S., Morse, J. Q., & Rosenthal, M. Z. (2004). A model predicting suicidal ideation and hopelessness in depressed older adults: The impact of emotion inhibition and affect intensity. *Aging and Mental Health, 8*(6), 486–497.

Lyons-Ruth, K., Lyubchik, A., Wolfe, R., & Bronfman, E. (2002). Parental depression and child attachment: Hostile and helpless profiles of parent and child behavior among families at risk. In S. Goodman & I. Gotlib (Eds.), *Children of depressed parents: Mechanisms of risk and implications for treatment* (pp. 89–120). Washington, DC: American Psychological Association.

Maccoby E. (2002a). Gender and group processes: A developmental perspective. *Current Directions in Psychological Science, 11,* 55–58.

Maccoby, E. E. (2002b). Parenting effects: Issues and controversies. In J. G. Borkowski, S. Landesman Ramey, & M. Bristol-Power (Eds.), *Parenting and the child's world* (pp. 35–45). Mahwah, NJ: Lawrence Erlbaum.

Maccoby, E., & Jacklin, C. (1974). *The psychology of sex differences.* Stanford, CA: Stanford University Press.

MacDorman, M. F., & Mathews, T. J. (2009). The challenge of infant mortality: Have we reached a plateau? *Public Health Reports, 124*(5), 670–681.

MacDorman, M. F., Menacker, F., & Declercq. E. (2008). Cesarean birth in the United States: Epidemiology, trends, and outcomes. *Clinics in Perinatology, 35*(2), 293–307.

Mack, R., Pike, M., Henderson, M., Pfeffer, R., Gerkins, V., Arthur, M., et al. (1976). Estrogens and endometrial cancer in a retirement community. *The New England Journal of Medicine, 294,* 1262–1267.

Mackey, W. C. (2001). Support for the existence of an independent man-(to)-child afiiliative bond. *Psychology of Men and Masculinity, 2,* 51–66.

MacKinlay, E. (2006). *Spiritual growth and care in the fourth age of life.* London: Jessica Kingsley Publishers.

MacLennan, B. (1994). Groups for poorly socialized children in the elementary school. *Journal of Child and Adolescent Group Therapy, 4,* 243–250.

MacMillan, R., & Copher, R. (2005). Families in the life course: Interdependency of roles, role configurations, and pathways. *Journal of Marriage and Family, 67,* 858–879.

Magill-Cuerden, J. (2006). Nurturing and supporting mothers: A hidden skill in midwifery. *British Journal of Midwifery, 14*(6), 374.

Magwaza, A., Kilian, B., Peterson, I., & Pillay, Y. (1993). The effects of chronic violence on preschool children living in South African townships. *Child Abuse and Neglect, 17,* 795–803.

Mahendru, A., Putran, J., & Khaled, M.A. (2009). Contraceptive methods. *Foundation Years Journal, 3*(3), 9–13.

Mahoney, A., Pendleton, S., & Ihrke, H. (2005). Religious coping by children and adolescents: Unexplored territory in the realm of spiritual development. In G. Roehlkepartain, P. King, L. Wagener, & P. Benson (Eds.), *The handbook of spiritual development in childhood and adolescence* (pp. 341–353). Thousand Oaks, CA: Sage.

Main, M., & Hesse, E. (1990). Parents' unresolved traumatic experiences are related to infant disorganized attachment status: Is frightened and/or frightening parental behavior the linking mechanism? In M. Greenberg, D. Cicchetti, & E. M. Cumming (Eds.), *Attachment in the preschool years: Theory, research and intervention* (pp. 161–182). Chicago: University of Chicago Press.

Malinger, G., Lev, D., & Lerman-Sagie, T. (2006). Normal and abnormal fetal brain development during the third trimester as demonstrated by neurosonography. *European Journal of Radiology, 57*(22), 226–232.

Mallampalli, A., & Guy, E. (2005). Cardiac arrest in pregnancy and somatic support after brain death. *Critical Care Medicine, 33*(10 Suppl.), S325–S331.

Maluccio, A. N. (2006). The nature and scope of the problem. In N. B. Webb (Ed.), *Working with traumatized youth in child welfare* (pp. 3–12). New York: Guilford Press.

Manlove, J., Logan, C., Moore, K. A., & Ikramullah, E. (2008). Pathways from family religiosity to adolescent sexual activity and contraceptive use. *Perspectives on Sexual and Reproductive Health, 40*(2), 105–117.

Manly, J. J., Schupf, N., Tang, M., & Stern, Y. (2005). Cognitive decline and literacy among ethnically diverse elders. *Journal of Geriatric Psychiatry and Neurology, 18*(4), 213–217.

March of Dimes. (2006). *Drinking alcohol during pregnancy.* Retrieved July 19, 2006, from http://www.marchofdimes.com/professionals/681_1170.asp.

March of Dimes. (2009). *Quick reference: Facts sheet.* Retrieved January 17, 2010, from http://www.marchofdimes.com/professionals/14332_1157.asp.

March of Dimes. (2010). *Nation gets a "D" as March of Dimes releases premature birth report card..* Retrieved May 21, 2010, from http://www.marchofdimes.com/aboutus/22684_42538.asp.

Marcia, J. E. (1966). Development and validation of ego-identity status. *Journal of Personality and Social Psychology, 3,* 551–558.

Marcia, J. E. (1980). Identity in adolescence. In J. Adelson (Ed.), *Handbook of adolescent psychology* (pp. 159–187). New York: Wiley.

Marcia, J. E. (1993). The ego identity status approach to ego identity. In J. E. Marcia, A. S. Waterman, D. R. Mattesson, S. L. Arcjer, & J. L. Orlofksy (Eds.), *Ego identity: A handbook for psychosocial research.* New York: Springer.

Marcia, J. E. (2002). Identity and psychosocial development in adulthood. *Identity: An International Journal of Theory and Research, 2,* 7–28.

Marini, M. (1989). Socioeconomic consequences of the process of transition to adulthood. *Social Science Research, 18,* 89–135.

Marino, R., Weinman, M., & Soudelier, K. (2001). Social work intervention and failure to thrive in infants and children. *Health & Social Work, 26*(2), 90–98.

Markovitz, B. P., Cook, R., Flick, L., & Leet, T. L. (2005). Socioeconomic factors and adolescent pregnancy outcomes: Distinctions between neonatal and post-natal deaths? *BioMed Central Public Health, 5,* 1–7.

Marks, A., & Rothbart, B. (2003). *Healthy teens, body and soul: A parent's complete guide.* New York: Simon & Schuster.

Marks, N., Bumpass, L., & Jun, H. (2004). Family roles and well-being during the middle life course. In O. Brim, C. Ryff, & R. Kessler (Eds.), *How healthy are we? A national study of well-being at midlife* (pp. 514–549). Chicago: University of Chicago Press.

Markus, H., & Kitayama, S. (2003). Models of agency: Sociocultural diversity in the construction of action. In G. Berman & J. Berman (Eds.), *Cross-cultural differences in perspectives on the self* (pp. 2–57). Lincoln: University of Nebraska Press.

Marmot, M., & Fuhrer, R. (2004). Socioeconomic position and health across midlife. In O. Brim, C. Ryff, & R. Kessler (Eds.), *How healthy are we? A national study of well-being at midlife* (pp. 64–89). Chicago: University of Chicago Press.

Marsh, H., & Kleitman, S. (2005). Consequences of employment during high school: Character building, subversion of academic goals, or a threshold? *American Educational Research Journal, 42,* 331–370.

Marshall, B. (2007). Climacteric redux? (Re)medicalizing the male menopause. *Men and Masculinities, 9*(4), 509–529.

Marshall, N. L., Noonan, A. E., McCartney, K., Marx, F., & Keefe, N. (2001). It takes an urban village: Parenting networks of urban families. *Journal of Family Issues, 22*(2), 163.

Marshall, V., & Mueller, M. (2003). Theoretical roots of the life-course perspective. In W. Heinz & V. Marshall (Eds.), *Social dynamics of the life course: Transitions, institutions, and interrelations* (pp. 3–32). New York: Aldine de Gruyter.

Marti, E. (2003). Strengths and weaknesses of cognition over preschool years. In J. Valsiner & K. Connolly (Eds.), *Handbook of development psychology* (pp. 257–275). Thousand Oaks, CA: Sage.

Martikainen, P., & Valkonen, T. (1996). Mortality after the death of a spouse: Rates and causes of death in a large Finnish cohort. *American Journal of Public Health, 86,* 1087–1093.

Martin, J. A., Hamilton, B. E., Sutton, P. D., Ventura, S. J., Menacker, F., Kimeyer, S., et al. (2009). Births: Final data for 2006. *National Vital Statistics Reports, 57*(7). Hyattsville, MD: National Center for Health Statistics. Retrieved August 9, 2009, from http://www.cdc.gov/nchs/data/nvsr/nvsr57/nvsr57_07.pdf.

Martin, J. A., Hamilton, B. E., Sutton, P. D., Ventura, S. J., Menacker, F., & Munson, M. L. (2003). Births: Final data for 2002. *National Vital Statistics Reports, 52*(10).

Martin, J. A., Kirmeyer, S., Osterman, M., & Shepherd, R. A. (2009). Born a bit too early: Recent trends in late preterm births. *NCHS Brief, 24,* 1–8.

Martin, M., & Zimprich, D. (2005). Cognitive development in midlife. In S. Willis & M. Martin (Eds.), *Middle adulthood: A lifespan perspective* (pp. 179–206). Thousand Oaks, CA: Sage.

Martin, P., da Rosa, G., Siegler, I. C., Davey, A., MacDonald, M., & Poon, L. W. (2006). Personality and longevity: Findings from the Georgia Centenarian Study. *AGE, 28,* 343–352.

Martin, S. L., Kim, H., Kupper, L. L., Meyer, R. E., & Hays, M. (1997). Is incarceration during pregnancy associated with infant birthweight? *American Journal of Public Health, 87,* 1526–1531.

Martin, T. L., & Doka, K. J. (2000). *Men don't cry . . . women do: Transcending gender stereotypes of grief.* Philadelphia: Brunner/Mazel.

Martire, I., & Schulz, R. (2001). Informal caregiving to older adults: Health effects of providing and receiving care. In A. Baum, T. Revenson, & J. Singer (Eds.), *Handbook of health psychology* (pp. 477–493). Mahwah, NJ: Lawrence Erlbaum.

Maschi, T., Morgen, K., Hatcher, S. S., Rosato, N. S., Violette, N. M. (2009). Maltreated children's thoughts and emotions as behavioral predictors: Evidence for social work action. *Social Work, 54*(2), 135–143.

Masciadrelli, B. P., Pleck, J. H., & Stueve, J. L. (2006). Fathers' role model perceptions: Themes and linkages with involvement. *Men and Masculinities, 9*(1), 23–34.

Massaro, M., Rothbaum, R., & Aly, H. (2006). Fetal brain development: The role of maternal nutrition, exposures, and behaviors. *Journal of Pediatric Neurology, 4*(1),1–9.

Masse, L., & Barnett, W. S. (2002). *A benefit cost analysis of the Abecedarian Early Childhood Intervention.* Retrieved May 3, 2007, from http://niecr.org/resources/research/Abecedarian Study.pdf.

Masten, A. S., Burt, K. B., Roisman, G. I., Obradovic, J., Long, J. D., & Tellegen, A. (2004). Resources and resilience in the transition to adulthood: Continuity and change. *Development and Psychopathology, 16,* 1071–1094.

Mathew, P., & Mathew, J. (2003). Assessment and management of pain in infants. *Postgraduate Medical Journal, 79,* 438–443.

Mathews, T., & Hamilton, B. (2009). *Delayed childbearing: More women are having their first child later in life.* NCHS Data Brief. Retrieved February 14, 2010, from http://www.cdc.gov/nchs/data/databriefs/db21.htm.

Mathews, T., MacDoman, M., & Menacker, F. (2002). Infant mortality statistics from the 1999 period linked birth/infant death data set. *National Vital Statistics, 50*(4), 1–27.

Matteson, K. A., Peipert, J. F., Allsworh, J., Phipps, M. G., & Redding. C. A. (2006). Unplanned pregnancy. *Obstetrics & Gynecology, 107*(1), 121–127.

Matsumoto-Grah, K. (1992). Diversity in the classroom: A checklist. In D. Byrnes & G. Kiger (Eds.), *Common bonds: Antibias teaching in a diverse society* (pp. 105–108). Olney, MD: Association for Childhood Education International.

Mayer, K. U., Baltes, P. B., Baltes, M., Borchelt, M., Delius, J., Helmchen, H., et al. (1999). What do we know about old age and aging? Conclusions from the Berlin Aging Study. In P. B. Baltes & K. U. Mayer (Eds.). *The Berlin Aging Study: Aging from 70 to 100* (pp. 475–519). Cambridge, UK: Cambridge University Press.

Mayes, L., & Cohen, D. (2003). *The Yale child study guide to understanding your child's health and development from birth to adolescence.* New York: Little, Brown.

Mayo Clinic Staff. (2008). *Testosterone therapy: Can it help older men feel young again?* Retrieved August 24, 2009, from http://www.mayoclinic.com/health/testosterone-therapy/ MC00030.

Mbori-Ngacha, D., Nduati, R., John, G., Reilly, M., Richardson, B., Mwatha, A., et al. (2001). Morbidity and mortality in breastfed and formula-fed infants of HIV-1-infected women: A randomized clinical trial. *Journal of American Medical Association, 286*(19), 2413–2420.

McAdams, D. (2001). Generativity in midlife. In M. Lachman (Ed.), *Handbook of midlife development* (pp. 395–443). New York: Wiley.

McAdams, D. (2006). *The redemptive self: Stories Americans live by.* New York: Oxford University Press.

McAdams, D., & de St. Aubin, E. (1992). A theory of generativity and its assessment through self-report, behavioral acts, and narrative themes in autobiography. *Journal of Personality and Social Psychology, 62,* 1003–1015.

McAdams, D., & de St. Aubin, E. (Eds.). (1998). *Generativity and adult development: How and why we care for the next generation.* Washington, DC: American Psychological Association.

McAdams, D., Hart, H., & Maruna, S. (1998). The anatomy of generativity. In D. McAdams & E. de St. Aubin (Eds.), *Generativity and adult development: How and why we care for the next generation* (pp. 7–43). Washington, DC: American Psychological Association.

McAdoo, H. P. (2001). Parent and child relationships in African American families. In N. B. Webb (Ed.), *Culturally diverse parent-child and family relationships: A guide for social workers and other practitioners* (pp. 89–106). New York: Columbia University Press.

McAuley, E., Konopack, J. F., Motl, R. W., Morris, S., Doerksen, S., & Rosengren, K. (2006). Physical activity and quality of life in older adults: Influence of health status and self-efficacy. *Annuals of Behavioral Medicine, 31*(1), 99–103.

McCabe, M. P., & Ricciardelli, L. A. (2003). Sociocultural influences on body image and body changes among adolescent boys and girls. *Journal of Social Psychology, 143*(1), 5–26.

McCaig, L. F., & Burt, C. W. (2005). *National Hospital Ambulatory Medical Care Survey: 2003 Emergency Department Summary* (Advance data from the vital and health statistics, No. 358). Hyattsville, MD: National Center for Health Statistics.

McClure, E. (2000). A meta-analytic review of sex differences in facial expression processing and their development in infants, children and adolescents. *Psychological Bulletin, 126,* 424–453.

McClure, E. M., Nalubamba-Phiri, M., & Goldenberg, R. L. (2006). Stillbirth in developing countries. *International Journal of Gynaecology and Obstetrics: The Official Organ of the International Federation of Gynaecology and Obstetrics, 94*(2), 82–90.

McCrae, R., & Costa, P., Jr. (1990). *Personality in adulthood.* New York: Guilford Press.

McCrae, R., Costa, P., Jr., Ostendorf, F., Angleitner, A., Caprara, G., Barbaranelli, C., et al. (1999). Age differences in personality across the adult life span: Parallels in five cultures. *Developmental Psychology, 35*(2), 466.

McDermid, S., Heilbrun, G., & DeHaan, L. (1997). The generativity of employed mothers in multiple roles: 1979 and 1991. In M. Lachman & J. James (Eds.), *Multiple paths of midlife development* (pp. 207–240). Chicago: University of Chicago Press.

McDiarmid, M. A., Gardiner, P. M., & Jack, B. W. (2008, Supp. B). The clinical content of preconception care: Environmental exposure. *American Journal of Obstetrics and Gynecology, 199*(s6), S357–S361.

McDonnell, J., Thorson, N., Disher, S., Mathot-Buckner, C., Mendel, J., & Ray, L. (2003). The achievement of students with developmental disabilities and their peers without disabilities in inclusive settings: An exploratory study. *Education and Treatment of Children, 26*(3), 224–236.

McElhatton, P. R. (2000). Fetal effects of substances of abuse. *Journal of Toxicology: Clinical Toxicology, 38*(2), 194–195.

McFalls, J., Jr. (1998). Population composition. *Population Bulletin, 53*(3), 26–34.

McFarlane, D.R. (2007). The alchemy of abstinence-only education: Will the new study be sufficient to end it? *Journal of Public Health Policy, 28*(3), 376–378.

McGlade, M., Saha, S., & Dahlstrom, M. (2004). The Latina paradox: An opportunity for restructuring prenatal care delivery. *American Journal of Public Health, 94*(12), 2062–2065.

McGoldrick, M. (2004). Legacies of loss: Multigenerational ripple effects. In F. Walsh & M. McGoldrick (Eds.), *Living beyond loss: Death in the family* (2nd ed., pp. 61–84). New York: W.W. Norton.

McGoldrick, M. (2005). Becoming a couple. In B. Carter & M. McGoldrick (Eds.), *The expanded family life cycle: Individual, family, and social perspectives* (3rd ed., pp. 231–248). Boston: Allyn & Bacon.

McGoldrick, M., Watson, M., & Benton, W. (2005). Siblings through the life cycle. In B. Carter & M. McGoldrick (Eds.), *The expanded family life cycle* (3rd ed., pp. 153–168). Boston: Allyn & Bacon.

McGorry, P., & Purcell, R. (2009). Youth mental health reform and early intervention: Encouraging early signs. *Early Intervention in Psychiatry, 3*(3), 161–162.

McGovern, P. G., Legro, R.,S., Myers, E. R., Bamhart, H. X., Carson, S. A., Diamond, M. P., et al. (2007). Utility of screening for other causes of infertility in women with "known" polycystic ovary syndrome. *Fertility and Sterility, 87*(2), 442–444.

McGroder, S. M., Zaslow, M. J., Moore, K. A., Hair, E. C., & Ahluwalia, S. K. (2002). The role of parenting in shaping the impacts of welfare-to-work programs on children. In J. G. Borkowski, S. Landesman Ramey, & M. Bristol-Power (Eds.), *Parenting and the child's world* (pp. 383–410). Mahwah, NJ: Lawrence Erlbaum.

McHale, S., Crouter, A., & Whiteman, S. (2003). The family contexts of gender development in childhood and adolescence. *Social Development, 12,* 125–148.

McInnis-Dittrich, K. (2009). *Social work with elders: A biopsychosocial approach to assessment and intervention* (2nd ed.). Boston: Allyn & Bacon.

McIntosh, H., Metz, E., & Youniss, J. (2005). Community service and identity formation in adolescence. In J. Mahoney, R. Larson, & J. Eccles (Eds.), *Organized activities as contexts of development: Extracurricular activities, after-school and community programs* (pp. 331–351). Mahwah, NJ: Lawrence Erlbaum.

McIntosh, P. (1988). *White privilege: Unpacking the invisible knapsack.* (Available from Peggy McIntosh, Wellesley College Center for Research on Women, Wellesley, MA 02181.)

McIntyre, J., & Gray, G. (2002). What can we do to reduce mother to child transmission of HIV? (Education and debate). *British Medical Journal, 324*(7331), 218–222.

Mckee, K. J., Wilson, F., Chung, C. M., Hinchliff, S., Goudie, F., Elford, H., et al. (2005). Reminiscence, regrets and activity in older people in residential care: Associations with psychological health. *British Journal of Clinical Psychology, 44*(4), 543–561.

McKenna, J. (2002). Breastfeeding and bedsharing: Still useful (and important) after all these years. *Mothering, 114,* 28–37.

McKeering, H., & Pakenham, K. (2000). Gender and generativity issues in parenting: Do fathers benefit more than mothers from involvement in child care activities? *Sex Roles, 43*(7–8), 459–480.

McKnight, J. (1995). *The careless society.* New York: Basic Books.

McLachlan, H., & Forster, D. (2009). The safety of home birth: Is the evidence good enough? *Canadian Medical Association Journal, 181,* 6–7.

McLaren, J., Burney, R., Milki, A., Westphal, L., Dahan, M., & Lathi, R. (2009). Effect of methotrexate exposure on subsequent fertility in women undergoing controlled ovarian stimulation. *Fertility and Sterility, 92*(2), 515–519.

McLaurin, K. K., Hall, C. B., Jackson, E. A., Owens, O. V., & Mahadevia, P. J. (2009). Persistence of morbidity and cost differences between late-preterm and term infants during the first year of life. *Pediatrics, 123*(2), 653–659.

McLeod, J., & Almazan, E. (2003). Connections between childhood and adulthood. In J. Mortimer & M. Shanahan (Eds.), *Handbook of the life course* (pp. 391–411). New York: Kluwer.

McLeskey, J., Hoppey, D., Williamson, P., & Rentz, T. (2004). Is inclusion an illusion? An examination of national and state trends toward the education of students with learning disabilities in general education classrooms. *Learning Disabilities Research & Practice, 19*(2), 109–115.

McMichael, P. (2008). *Development and social change: A global perspective* (4th ed.). Thousand Oaks, CA: Pine Forge.

McMillan, J. C., & Raghavan, R. (2009). Pediatric to adult mental health service use of young people leaving the foster care system. *Journal of Adolescent Health, 44,* 7–13.

McQuaide, S. (1998). Women at midlife. *Social Work, 43*(1), 21–31.

Meacham, R. B., Joyce, G. F., Wise, M., Kparker, A., & Niederberger, C. (2007). Male infertility. *Journal of Urology, 177*(6), 2058–2067.

Mead, G. H. (1934). *Mind, self and society.* Chicago: University of Chicago Press.

Meade, C. S., Kershaw, T. S., & Ickovis, J. R. (2008). The intergenerational cycle of teenage motherhood: An ecological approach. *Health Psychology: Official Journal of the Division of Health Psychology, American Psychological Association, 27*(4), 419–429.

Mechelli, A., Crinion, J., Noppeney, U., O'Doherty, J., Ashburner, J., Frackowiak, R. S., et al. (2004). Structural plasticity in the bilingual brain. *Science, 431*(7010), 757.

Medical News Today. (2004, March 4). *Woman gives birth to her own grandchildren.* Retrieved February 10, 2010, from http://www.medicalnewstoday.com/articles/6320.php.

Medicare Advocacy. (2007). *Calculating costs to and through the Part D doughnut hole.* Retrieved January 19, 2007, from http://www.medicareadvocacy.org/PartD_Calculating CostsThroughDonutHole.htm.

Meek, M. (2000). Foreword. In K. Roskos & J. Christie (Ed.), *Play and literacy in early childhood: Research from multiple perspectives* (pp. vii–xiii). Mahwah, NJ: Lawrence Erlbaum.

Mehall, K., Spinrad, T., Eisenberg, N., & Gaertner, B. (2009). Examining the relations of infant temperament and couples' marital satisfaction to mother and father involvement: A longitudinal study. *Fathering, 7*(1), 23–48.

Meier, A. (2007). Adolescent first sex and subsequent mental health. *American Journal of Sociology, 112*(6), 1811–1847.

Melby, T. (2009). Emergency contraception: Living up to its promise? *Contemporary Sexuality, 43*(5), 1–6.

Mello, A., Mello, M., Carpenter, L., & Price, L. (2003). Update on stress and depression: The role of the hypothalamic-pituitary-adrenal (HPA) axis. *Reviewe of Brasilian Psychiatry, 25*(4), 231–238.

Meltzoff, A. (2002). Imitation as a mechanism of social cognition: Origins of empathy theory of mind, and the representation of action. In U. Goswami (Ed.), *Blackwell handbook of childhood cognitive development* (pp. 6–25). Malden, MA: Blackwell.

Menacker, F., & Martin, J. (2009). BirthStats: Rates of cesarean delivery, and unassisted, and assisted vaginal delivery, United States, 1996, 2000, and 2006. *Birth, 36*(2),167.

Mendle, J., Turkheimer, E., & Emery, R. E. (2007). Detrimental psychological outcomes associated with early pubertal timing in adolescent girls. *Developmental Review, 27*(2), 151–171.

Mendola, P., Messer, L. C., & Rappazzo, K. (2008). Science linking environmental contaminant exposures with fertility and reproductive health impacts in the adult female. *Fertility and Sterility, 89*(2 Suppl), e81–94.

Menon, U. (2001). Middle adulthood in cultural perspective: The imagined and the experienced in three cultures. In M. Lachman (Ed.), *Handbook of midlife development* (pp. 40–74). New York: Wiley.

Merce, L. T., Barco, M. J. Alcazar, J. L., Sabatel, R., & Trojano, J. (2009). Intervillous and uteroplacental circulation in normal early pregnancy and early pregnancy loss assessed by 3-dimensional power Doppler angiography. *Journal of Obstetrics and Gynecology, 200*(3), 315.e1–8.

Mercer, J. A. (2006). Children as mystics, sages, and holy fools: Understanding the spirituality of children and its significance for clinical work. *Pastoral Psychology, 54(5),* 497–515.

Merrill, S., & Verbrugge, L. (1999). Health and disease in midlife. In S. Willis & J. Reid (Eds.), *Life in the middle: Psychological and social development in middle age* (pp. 78–103). San Diego: Academic Press.

Merten, J., Wickrama, K.A.S., & Williams, A. L. (2008). Adolescent obesity and young adult psychosocial outcomes: Gender and racial differences. *Journal of Youth & Adolescence, 37,* 1111–1122.

Merton, R. (1968). The Matthew Effect in science: The reward and communications systems of science. *Science, 199,* 55–63.

MetLife/National Alliance for Caregiving. (2004). *Miles away: The MetLife study of long-distance caregiving.* West Point, CT: MetLife.

Mickelson, K., Claffey, S., & Williams, S. (2006). The moderating role of gender and gender role attitudes on the link between spousal support and marital quality. *Sex Roles, 55,* 73–82.

Miklowitz, D., & Johnson, B. (2009). Social and familial factors in the course of bipolar disorder: Basic processes and relevant interventions. *Clinical Psychology: Science & Practice, 16*(2), 281–296.

Miller, E., & Marini, I. (2004). Female sexuality and spinal cord injury: Counseling implications. *Journal of Applied Rehabilitation Counseling,35*(4), 17–25.

Miller, J., & Holman, J. R. (2006). Contraception: The state of the art. *Consultant, 46*(4), 28.

Mintel Report. (2004). *Lifestyles of young adults.* Chicago: Mintel International Group, Ltd.

Miyake, K., Campos, J., Kagan, J., & Bradshaw, D. (1986). Issues in socioemotional development in Japan. In H. Azuma, I. Hakuta, & H. Stevenson (Eds.), *Dodoma: Child development and education in Japan* (pp. 239–261). New York: W. H. Freeman.

Moen, P. (1997). Women's roles and resilience: Trajectories of advantage or turning points? In I. H. Gotlib & B. Wheaton (Eds.), *Stress and adversity over the life course: Trajectories and turning points* (pp. 133–156). New York: Cambridge University Press.

Moen, P. (2003). Midcourse: Navigating retirement and a new life stage. In J. Mortimer & M. Shanahan (Eds.), *Handbook of the life course* (pp. 269–291). New York: Kluwer Academic/ Plenum Publishers.

Moen, P., & Wethington, E. (1999). Midlife development in a life course context. In S. Willis & J. Reid (Eds.), *Life in the middle* (pp. 3–24). San Diego, CA: Academic Press.

Mofenson, L. (2006, June 2). Achievements in public health: Reduction in perinatal transmission of HIV infection— United States 1985–2005. *Morbidity and Mortality Weekly Report, 55*(21), 592–597. Retrieved January 13, 2007, from http://www.cdc.gov/mmwr/preview/mwrhtml./mm 5521a3.htm.

Moffett, F. (2007). Studies show fewer black girls are getting pregnant. *Jet, 112*(6), 14.

Mohler, E., Matheis, V., Marysko, M., Finke, P., Kaufmann, C., Cierpka, M., et al. (2008). Complications during pregnancy, peri- and postnatal period in a sample of women with a history of child abuse. *Journal of Psychosomatic Obstetrics and Gynecology, 29*(3), 193–198.

Möller, K., & Stattin, H. (2001). Are close relationships in adolescence linked with partner relationships in midlife? A longitudinal prospective study. *International Journal of Behavioral Development, 25*(1), 69–77.

Monaghan, J., Robinson, J., & Dodge, J. (1979). The children's life events inventory. *Journal of Psychosomatic Research, 23*(1), 63–68.

Mongillo, E., Briggs-Gowan, M., Ford, J., & Carter, A. (2009). Impact of traumatic life events in a community sample of toddlers. *Journal of Abnormal Child Psychology, 37*(4), 455–468.

Monsour, M. (2002). *Women and men as friends: Relationships across the life span in the 21st century.* Mahwah, NJ: Lawrence Erlbaum.

Montague, D., Magai, C., Consedine, N., & Gillespie, M. (2003). Attachment in African American and European American older adults: The roles of early life socialization and religiosity. *Attachment and Human Development, 5,* 188–214.

Montepare, J. (2009). Subjective age: Toward a guiding lifespan framework. *International Journal of Behavioral Development, 33*(1), 42–46.

Montgomery, R. J. V., & Kosloski, K. (1994). A longitudinal analysis of nursing home placement for dependent elders cared for by spouses vs. adult children. *Journal of Gerontology: Social Science, 49,* S62–S74.

Montgomery, R. J. V., & Kosloski, K. D. (2000). Family caregiving: Change, continuity and diversity. In P. Lawton & R. Bubenstein (Eds.). *Alzheimer's disease and related dementias: Strategies in care and research.* New York: Springer.

Montgomery, R. J. V., & Kosloski, K. (2009). Caregiving as a process of changing identity: Implications for caregiver support. *Generations 33,* 47–52.

Moody, H. R. (2010). *Aging: Concepts and controversies* (6th ed.). Thousand Oaks, CA: Pine Pine Forge.

Moon, S., Kang, S., & An, S. (2008). Predictors of immigrant children's school achievement: A comparative study. *Research in Childhood Education, 23*(3), 278–289.

Moore, D. (1987). Parent-adolescent separation: The construction of adulthood by late adolescents. *Developmental Psychology, 23,* 298–307.

Moore, K. (2008, October). *Teen births: Examining the recent increase.* The National Campaign to Prevent Teen and Unplanned Pregnancy. Retrieved February 18, 2010, from http://www.thenationalcampaign.org/resources/pdf/TeenBi rths_ExamIncrease.pdf.

Moore, K. A., Redd, Z., Burkhauser, M, Mbwana, K., & Collins, A. (2009). *Children in poverty: Trends, consequences, and policy options.* Washington, DC: Child Trends. Retrieved January 19, 2010, from http://www.childtrends.org/Files/Child_ Trends-2009_04_07_RB_ChildreninPoverty.pdf.

Moore, K. L., & Persaud, T. V. N. (1998). *Before we are born* (5th ed.). Philadelphia: Saunders.

Mørch, L., Løkkegaard, E., Andreasen, A., Krüger-Kiaer, S., & Lidegaard, O. (2009). Hormone therapy and ovarian cancer. *Journal of American Medical Association, 302*(3), 298–305.

Moreau, C., Cleland, K., & Trussell, J. (2007). Contraceptive discontinuation attributed to method dissatisfaction in the United States. *Contraception, 76*(4), 267–272.

Moremen, R. D. (2004–2005). What is the meaning of life? Women's spirituality at the end of the life span. *Omega: Journal of Death and Dying, 50*(4), 309–330.

Morgan, A. (2000). *What is narrative therapy?* Adelaide, South Australia: Dulwich Centre Publications.

Morris, J. C. (2006). Mild cognitive impairment in early-stage Alzheimer disease. *Archives of Neurology, 63*(1), 15–16.

Morrison, J. W., & Bordere, T. (2001). Supporting biracial children's identity development. *Childhood Education, 77*(3), 134–138.

Mortimer, J. T., & Almazan, E. (2003). Connections between childhood and adulthood. In J. Mortimer & M. Shanahan (Eds.), *Handbook of the life course* (pp. 391–411). New York: Kluwer Academic/Plenum Publishers.

Mortimer, J. T., & Finch, M. D. (1996). *Adolescents, work, and family: An intergenerational developmental analysis.* Thousand Oaks, CA: Sage.

Morton, C. H., & Hsu, C. (2007). Contemporary dilemmas in American childbirth education: Findings from a comparative ethnographic study. *Contemporary Dilemmas, 16*(4), 25–37.

Mosher, W., Chandra, A., & Jones, J. (2005, September 15). Sexual behavior and selected measures. Men and women 15–44 years of age, United States, 2002. *Vital and Health Statistics, 362*, 1–56. Retrieved November 20, 2006, from http://www.cdc.gov/nchs/data/ad/ad362.pdf.

Moshman, D. (1998). Cognitive development beyond childhood. In D. Kuhn & R. Siegler (Eds.), *Handbook of child psychology: Vol. 2. Cognition, perception, and language* (5th ed., pp. 947–978). New York: Wiley.

Moss, R. H., Mortens, M. A., & Brennan, P. L. (1993). Patterns of diagnosis and treatment among late-middle-aged and older substance abuse patients. *Journal of Studies in Alcohol, 54,* 479–487.

Motamedi, G. K., & Meador, K. J. (2006). Antiepileptic drugs and neurodevelopment. *Current neurology and neuroscience reports, 6*(4), 341–346.

Moyer, K. (1974). Discipline. In K. Moyer, *You and your child: A primer for parents* (pp. 40–61). Chicago: Nelson Hall.

Moyers, B. (1993). *Healing and the mind.* New York: Doubleday.

Mueller, M., Wilhelm, B., & Elder, G. (2002). Variations in grandparenting. *Research on Aging, 24*(3), 360–388.

Muir, D., & Lee, K. (2003). The still face effect: Methodological issues and new applications. *Infancy, 4,* 483–491.

Munakata, Y., McClelland, J., Johnson, M., & Siegler, R. (1997). Rethinking infant knowledge: Toward an adaptive process account of successes and failures in object permanence tasks. *Psychological Review, 104*(4), 618–713.

Murano, T., & Cocuzza, T. A. (2009). Ectopic pregnancy. *Emergency Medicine Reports: The Practical Journal for Emergency Physicians, 30*(23), 281–287.

Murphy-Berman, V., & Berman, J. (2002). Cross-cultural differences in perception of distribution of justice: A comparison of Hong Kong and Indonesia. *Journal of Cross-Cultural Psychology, 33,* 1157–1170.

Murray, J. A. (2001). Loss as a universal concept: A review of the literature to identify common aspects of loss in diverse situations. *Journal of Loss and Trauma, 6,* 219–241.

Nair, A., Stega, J., Smith, R. J., & Del Priore, G. (2008). Uterus transplant. *Annals of the New York Academy of Sciences, 1127,* 83–91.

Naleppa, M. J. (1996). Families and the institutionalized elderly: A review. *Journal of Gerontological Social Work, 27,* 87–111.

Nansel, T., Overpeck, M., Pilla, R., Ruan, W., Simons-Morton, B., & Scheidt, P. (2001). Bullying behaviors among U.S. youth: Prevalence and association with psychosocial adjustment. *Journal of the American Medical Association, 285*(16), 2094–2100.

Narberhaus, A., Segarra, D., Caldu, X., Gimenez, M., Junque, C., Pueyo, R., et al. (2007). Gestational age at preterm birth in relation to corpus callosum and general cognitive outcome in adolescents. *Journal of Child Neurology, 22*(6), 761–765.

National Association of Child Care Resource and Referral Agencies. (2006). *Piggy bank: Parents and the high price of child care.* Retrieved December 30, 2006, from http://www.naccrra.org/docs/policy/breaking_the_piggy_bank.pdf.

National Campaign to End Teen Pregnancy. (2002). *General facts and stats.* Retrieved August 26, 2002, from http://www.teen-pregnancy.org/resources/data/genlfact.asp.

National Association of Social Workers. (1999). *Code of ethics* (Rev. ed.). Washington, DC: Author.

National Campaign to Prevent Teen and Unplanned Pregnancy. (2008). *Unplanned pregnancy in the United States.* Washington, DC: Author.

National Center for Children in Poverty. (2008). *Low-income children in the United States.* Retrieved January 19, 2010, from http://www.nccp.org/publications/pub_851.html.

National Center for Clinical Infant Programs. (1992). How community violence affects children, parents, and practitioners. *Public Welfare, 50*(4), 25–35.

National Center for Health Statistics. (2001). *Health, United States, 2001.* Hyattsville, MD: Author.

National Center for Health Statistics (NCHS). (2004, October 6). *Obesity still a major problem, New data show: Prevalence of overweight and obesity among children and adolescents: United States, 1999–2002.* Atlanta: Author.

National Committee for Quality Assurance (NCQA). (2008). *The state of health care quality 2008.* Washington, DC: Author. Retrieved February 9, 2010, from htttp://www.ncqa.org.

National Council on the Aging. (2000, March). *Myths and realities 2000 survey results.* Washington, DC: Author.

National Council on the Aging. (n.d.). *Facts about older Americans.* Retrieved June 29, 2002, from http://www.ncoa.org/press/facts.html.

National Eating Disorders Association. (2005). *Eating disorders & pregnancy: Some facts about the risks.* Retrieved October 9, 2006, from http://www.nationaeatingdisorders.org.

National Gang Center. (2010). *About the National Gang Center.* Retrieved February 8, 2010, from http://www.nationalgangcenter.gov.

National Geographic Society. (1998). *Eyewitness to the 20th century.* Washington, DC: Author.

National Head Start Association. (2010). *National Head Start Association 2010 policy agenda.* Retrieved May 21 2010, from http://www.nhsa.org/files/static_page_files/8AOAE124-1D09-3519-ADD7671F4B28F28D/NHSA2010PolicyAgenda012910.pdf.

National Health Statistics. (2005). *Health United States 2005 with chartbook on trends in the health of Americans.* Hyattsville, MD: U.S. Centers for Disease Control and Prevention.

National Hospice and Palliative Care Organization (2008). *NHPCO facts and figures.* Retrieved July 10, 2009, from http://www.nhpco.org.

National Institute of Aging, National Institute of Health (NIA/NIH). (2009). *An aging world.* Retrieved May 21, 2010, from http://www.nia.nih.gov/ResearchInformation/Extramural Programs/BehavioralAndSocialResearch/an-aging-world.htm.

National Institute of Alcohol Abuse and Alcoholism. (2005, March). *Social work curriculum on alcohol disorders.* Retrieved June 1, 2006, from http://pubs.niaa.hih.gov/publications/Social.main/html.

National Institute of Child Health and Human Development (2007). *What is puberty?* Retrieved January 19, 2010, from http://www.nichd.nih.gov/health/topics/puberty.cfm.

National Institute of Mental Health. (2000). *Depression in children and adolescents.* Bethesda, MD: Author.

National Institute of Mental Health, National Institutes of Health. (2009). *Depression and older adults fact sheet.* Retrieved May 18, 2009, http://www.nimh.nih.gov/health/topics/older-adults-and-mental-health/index.shtml.

National Institute of Neurological Disorders and Stroke (NINDS). (2010). *Parkinson's disease: Hope through research.* Retrieved May 21, 2010, from http://www.ninds.nih.gov/disorders/parkinsons_disease/detail_parkinsons_disease.htm.

National Institute on Drug Abuse. (2006). *Monitoring the Future Survey: Overview of findings 2006.* Retrieved January 14, 2007, from http://www.drugabuse.govnewsroom/06MTF060verview.html.

National Institutes of Health. (2001). *Vital connections: Science of mind-body interactions: A report on the interdisciplinary conference held at NIH March 26–28, 2001.* Bethesda, MD: Author.

National Institutes of Health. (2002). *NHLBI stops trial of estrogen plus progestin due to increased cancer risk, lack of overall benefit.* Retrieved September 3, 2002, from http://www.nhlbi.nih.gov/new/press/02-07-09.htm.

National Research Council. (1990). *Who cares for America's children?* Washington, DC: Author.

National Sleep Foundation. (2005). *Drowsy driving: Facts and stats.* Retrieved November 15, 2006, from http://www.sleepfoundation.org.

National Sleep Foundation. (2006). *2006 sleep in America poll: Highlights and key findings.* Retrieved November 15, 2006, from http://www.sleepfoundation.org.

National Youth Gang Center. (2009). *National Youth Gang Survey analysis.* Retrieved January 21, 2010, from http://www.nationalgangcenter.gov/Survey-Analysis.

Nazzi, T., & Gopnik, A. (2001). Linguistic cognitive abilities in infancy: When does language become a tool for categorization? *Cognition, 80,* B11–B20.

Nduati, R, John, G., Mbori-Ngacha, D., Richardson, B., Overbaugh, J., Mwatha, A., et al. (2000). Effect of breastfeeding and formula feeding on transmission of HIV-1: A randomized clinical trial. *Journal of the American Medical Association 283,* 1167–1174.

Needham, A. (2001). Object recognition and object segregation in 4.5-month-old infants. *Journal of Experimental Child Psychology, 78,* 3–24.

Nelson, C. (2001). The development and neural bases of face recognition. *Infant and Child Development, 10,* 3–18.

Nelson-Becker, H., & Canda, E. R. (2008). Spirituality, religion, and aging research in social work: State of the art and future possibilities. *Journal of Religion, Spirituality and Aging, 20*(3), 177–193.

Nepomnaschy, P., Welch, K., McConnell, D., Low, B., Strassmann, B., & England, B. (2006). Cortisol levels and very early pregnancy loss in humans. *Proceedings of National Academy of Science USA, 103*(10), 3938–3942.

Nettles, S., Mucherah, W., & Jones, D. (2000). Understanding resilience: The role of social resources. *Journal of Education for Students Placed at Risk, 5*(1&2), 47–60.

Neugarten, B. L., & Weinstein, K. K. (1964). The changing American grandparent. *Journal of Marriage and the Family, 26,* 199–204.

Neugarten, B., & Gutmann, D. (1968). Age-sex roles and personality in middle age: A thematic apperception study. In B. L. Neugarten (Ed.), *Middle age and aging* (pp. 58–71). Chicago: University of Chicago Press.

Neugarten, B. L., Havighurst, R. J., & Tobin, S. S. (1968). Personality and patterns of aging. In B. L. Neugarten (Ed.), *Middle age and aging.* Chicago: University of Chicago Press.

Neugebauer, R., Kline, J., Markowitz, J. C., Blelerg, K. L., Baxi, L., Rosing, M. A., et al. (2006). Pilot randomized controlled trial of interpersonal counseling for subsyndromal depression following miscarriage. *The Journal of Clinical Psychiatry, 67*(8), 1299–1304.

New concepts on the causes of recurrent miscarriages. (2006). *Reproductive Biomedicine Online, 12*(3), 291–291. Retrieved November 4, 2006, from http://find.galegroup.com/itx/infomark.do?&contentSet=INGENTA&type=retrieve&tabID=T002&prodId=EAIM&docId=CA14389140&source=gale&srcprod=EAIM&userGroupName=vic_regent&version=1.0.

Newcomb, N., & Dubas, J. S. (1992). A longitudinal study of predictors of spatial ability in adolescent females. *Child Development, 63,* 37–46.

Newman, B., & Newman, P. (2009). *Development through life: A psychosocial approach* (10th ed.). Belmont, CA: Thomson.

Newman, D. (2008). *Sociology: Exploring the architecture of everyday life* (7th ed.). Thousand Oaks, CA: Pine Forge.

Newman, K. (2008). Ties that bind: Cultural interpretations of delayed adulthood in Western Europe and Japan. *Sociological Forum, 23*(4), 645–669.

Newman, R. B. (2005). *Calm birth: New method for conscious childbirth.* Berkeley, CA: North Atlantic Books.

Newton, C., Sherrard, W., & Glavac, I. (1999). The Fertility Problem Inventory: Measuring perceived infertility-related stress. *Fertility and Sterility, 72,* 54–62.

Nguyen, P. (2008). Perceptions of Vietnamese fathers' acculturation levels, parenting styles, and mental health outcome in Vietnamese American adolescent immigrants. *Social Work, 53*(4), 337–346.

Nguyen, P., & Cheung, M. (2009). Parenting styles as perceived by Vietnamese American adolescents. *Child and Adolescent Social Work Journal, 26,* 505–581.

Nhu, T. N., Merialdi, M., Abdel-Aleem, H., Carroli, G., Purwar, M., Zavaleta, N., et al. (2006). Causes of stillbirth and early neonatal deaths: Data from 7993 pregnancies in six developing countries. *Bulletin of the World Health Organization, 84,* 699–705.

Niculescu, M. D., & Lupu, D. S. (2009). High fat diet-induced maternal obesity alters fetal hippocampal development. *International Journal of Developmental Neuroscience, 27*(7), 627–633.

Nield, L. S., Cakan, N., & Kamat, D. (2007). A practical approach to precocious puberty. *Clinical Pediatrics, 46*(4), 299–306.

Nilsen, J. (2008). *Andropause—male menopause and the dangers of testosterone therapy.* Ezine Articles. Retrieved May 21, 2010, from http://ezinearticles.com/?Andropause—Male-Menopause-And-the-Dangers-of-Testosterone-Therapy&id=939817.

Nishino, H., & Larson, R. (2003). Japanese adolescents' free time: Juku, Bakatsu, and government efforts to create more meaningful leisure. In S. Verma & R. Larson (Eds.), *Examining adolescent leisure time across culture: New directions for child and adolescent development, No. 99* (pp. 23–35). San Francisco: Jossey-Bass.

Nishitani, S., Miyamura, T., Tagawa, M., Sumi, M., Takase, R., Doi, H., et al. (2009). The calming effect of a maternal breast milk odor on the human newborn infant. *Neuroscience Research, 63*(1), 66–71.

Noble, R. E. (2005). Depression in women. *Metabolism: Clinical and Experimental, 54* (1), 49–54.

Noddings, N. (1984). *Caring: A feminine approach to ethics and moral education.* Berkeley: University of California Press.

Nojomi, M., Akbarian, A., & Ashory-Moghadam, S. (2006). Burden of abortion: Induced or spontaneous. *Archives of Iranian Medicine, 9*(10), 39–45.

Noll, J. G., Shenk, C. E., & Putnam, K. T. (2009). Childhood sexual abuse and adolescent pregnancy: A meta-analytic update. *Journal of Pediatric Psychology, 34*(4), 366–378.

Nord, M., Andrews, M., & Carlson, S. (2009). *Household food insecurity in the United States, 2008.* Washington, DC: United States Department of Agriculture. Retrieved February 17, 2010, from http://www.thefoodbank.org/documents/usda foodinsecurity08.pdf.

Norton, D. (1993). Diversity, early socialization, and temporal development: The dual perspective revisited. *Social Work, 38*(1), 82–90.

Nosek, M. (1995). Findings on reproductive health and access to health care. *National study of women with physical disabilities.* Houston, TX: Baylor College of Medicine, Department of Physical Medicine and Rehabilitation.

Nosek, M. A., Howland, C. A., Rintal, D. H., Young, M. E., & Chanpong, G. F. (1997). *National study of women with physical disabilities: Final report.* Houston, TX: Center for Research on Women with Disabilities.

Nourhashemi, F., Gillette-Guyonnet, S., Rolland, Y., Cantet, C., Hein, C., & Vellas, B, (2009). Alzheimer's disease progression in the oldest old compared to younger elderly patient: Data from the REAL.FR study. *International Journal of Geriatric Psychiatry, 24,* 149–155.

Nourhashemi, F., Sinclair, A., & Vellas, B. (2006). *Clinical aspects of Alzheimer's disease: Principles and practice of geriatric medicine* (4th ed.). Sussex, UK: John Wiley and Sons Ltd.

Novak, G., & Pelaez, M. (2004). *Child and adolescent development: A behavioral system approach.* Thousand Oaks, CA: Sage.

Novak, J. C., & Broom, B. (1995). *Maternal and child health nursing.* St. Louis, MO: Mosby.

Novins, D., Beals, J., Shore, J., & Manson, S. (1996). Substance abuse treatment of American Indian adolescents: Comorbid symptomatology, gender differences, and treatment patterns. *Child & Adolescent Psychiatry, 35*(12), 1593–1601.

Novins, D., Fleming, C., Beals, J., & Manson, S. (2000). Commentary: Quality of alcohol, drug, and mental health services for American Indian children and adolescents. *American Journal of Medicine Quarterly, 15*(4), 148–156.

Nursing. (2005). Maladies by the numbers. *Nursing, 35*(9), 35.

Ny, K., Loy, J., Gudmunson, C., & Cheong, W. (2009). Gender differences in marital and life satisfaction among Chinese Malaysians. *Sex Roles, 60,* 33–43.

Nybell, L., Shook, J., & Finn, J. (Eds.). (2009). *Childhood, youth, & social work in transformation: Implications for policy & practice.* New York: Columbia University Press.

Oakes, J. (1985). *Keeping track of tracking: How schools structure inequality.* New Haven, CT: Yale University Press.

Oakes, J., & Lipton, M. (1992). Detracking schools: Early lessons from the field. *Phi Delta Kappan, 73,* 448–454.

Obama, B. (2009). *Taking on education.* Retrieved May 21, 2009, from http://www.whitehouse.gov/blog/09/03/10/taking-on-education.

O'Brien, P. A., Kulier, R., Helmerhorst, F. M., Usher-Patel, M., & d'Arcangues, C. (2008). Copper-containing, framed intrauterine devices for contraception: A systematic review of randomized controlled trials. *Contraception, 77*(5), 318–327.

Odent, M. (1998). *Men's role in the labour room.* Conference presentation at the Royal Society of Medicine, London.

Odent, M. (1999). Is the participation of the father at birth dangerous? *Midwifery Today, 51,* 23–24.

OECD. (2008, December 15). *SF6: Share of births outside marriage and teenage births.* Organisation for Economic Co-operation and Development: Social Policy Division Directorate of Employment, Labour, and Social Affairs. Retrieved November 1, 2009, from http://www.oecd.org/dataoecd/38/6/40278615.pdf.

Office of Disease Prevention & Health Promotion. U.S. Department of Health and Human Services. (2009*). Adolescent health.* Retrieved February 8, 2010, from http://www.healthypeople.gov/hp2020/Objectives/TopicArea.aspx?id=11&TopicArea= Adolescence.

Office of the Special Representative of the Secretary-General for Children and Armed Conflict (OSRSG-CAAC) & United Nations Children's Fund. (2009). *Machel study 10-year strategic review: Children and conflict in a changing world.* New York: UNICEF. Retrieved January 19, 2010, from http://www.unicef.org/publications/index_49985.html.

Of Meat, Mexicans and Social Mobility. (2006, June 17). *The Economist, 379*(8482), 31–32.

Office on Smoking and Health. (2000). *Youth tobacco surveillance—United States, 1998–1999.* Washington, DC: Author.

Ogbu, J. U. (1994). Overcoming racial barriers to equal access. In K. I. Goodland & P. Keating (Eds.), *Access to knowledge: The continuing agenda for our nation's schools* (pp. 59–90). New York: The College Board.

Ogden, C., Carroll, M., Curtin, L., Lamb, M., & Flegal, K. (2010). Prevalence of high body mass index in U.S. children and adolescents, 2007-2008. *Journal of American Medical Association, 303*(3), 242–249.

Ogden, C. L., Carroll, M. D., Curtin, L. R., McDowell, M. A., Tabak, C. J., & Flegal, K. M. (2006). Prevalence of overweight and obesity in the United States, 1999–2004. *Journal of American Medical Association, 295,* 1549–1555.

Ogden, J., Stavrinaki, M., & Stubbs, J. (2009). Understanding the role of life events in weight loss and weight gain. *Psychology, Health, & Medicine, 14*(2), 239–249.

O'Hanlon, K. (2009). Why we must make a stronger commitment to lesbian family health. *OBG Management, 21*(11).

O'Hare, W. (2009). *The forgotten fifth: Child poverty in rural America.* Carsey Institute Report, No. 10. University of New Hampshire. Retrieved January 19, 2010, from http://www.carseyinstitute.unh.edu/publications/Report-OHare-ForgottenFifth.pdf.

O'Keefe, M. (1994). Adjustment of children from maritally violent homes. *Families in Society, 75,* 403–415.

O'Keefe, M. (1997). Adolescents' exposure to community and school violence: Prevalence and behavioral correlates. *Journal of Adolescent Health, 20,* 368–376.

Oken, E., Wright, R. O., Kleinman, K. P., Bellinger, D., Amarasiriwardena, H. H., Rich-Edwards, J. W., et al. (2005). Maternal fish consumption, hair mercury, and infant cognition in a U.S. cohort. *Environmental Health Perspectives, 113*(10), 1376–1381.

Okie, S. (2002, February 6). Hormone therapy no panacea: Study tracks menopause treatments' effect on well-being. *Washington Post,* p. A7.

Olas, B., & Wachowicz, B. (2005). Resveratrol: A phenotic antioxidant with effects on blood platelet functions. *Platelets, 16*(5), 251–260.

O'Leary, V. E., & Bhaju, J. (2006). Resilience and empowerment. In J. Worell & C. D. Goodheart (Eds.), *Handbook of girl's and women's psychological health: Gender and well-being across the life span* (pp. 157–165). New York: Oxford Press.

Olds, D., Eckenrode, J., Henderson, C., Kitzman, H., Powers, J., Cole, R., et al. (1997). Long-term effects of home visitation on maternal life course and child abuse and neglect: Fifteen-year follow-up of a randomized trial. *JAMA, 278*(8), 637–643.

Oliver, R. (2005). Birth: Hospital or home: That is the question. *Journal of Prenatal and Perinatal Psychology and Health, 19*(4), 341–348.

Ollendick, T. H., Weist, M. D., Borden, M. C., & Greene, R. W. (1992). Sociometric status and academic, behavioral, and psychological adjustment: A five year longitudinal study. *Journal of Consulting and Clinical Psychology, 60,* 80–87.

Opitz, J. M. (1996). Origins of birth defects. In J. J. Sciarra (Ed.), *Gynecology and obstetrics* (rev. ed., pp. 23–30). Philadelphia: Lippincott-Raven.

O-Prasetsawat, P., & Petchum, S. (2004). Sexual behavior of secondary school students in Bangkok metropolis. *Journal of the Medical Association of Thailand, 87*(7), 755–759.

O'Rand, A. (2003). The future of the life course: Late modernity and life course risks. In J. Mortimer & M. Shanahan (Eds.), *Handbook of the life course* (pp. 693–701). New York: Kluwer Academic/Plenum Publishers.

O'Rand, A. (2009). Cumulative processes in the life course. In G. Elder & J. Giele (Eds.), *The craft of life course research* (pp. 121–140). New York: Guilford.

Orfield, G., Losen, D., Wald, J., & Swanson, C. (2004). *How minority youth are being left behind by the graduation rate crisis.* Cambridge, MA: The Civil Rights Project at Harvard University. Contributors: Advocates for Children of New York, The Civil Society Institute.

Ornoy, A. (2006). Neuroteratogens in man: An overview with special emphasis on the teratogenicity of antiepileptic drugs in pregnancy. *Reproductive Technology, 22*(2), 214–226.

Orr, S. T., James, S. A., & Reiter, J. P. (2008). Unintended pregnancy and prenatal behaviors among urban, black women in Baltimore, Maryland: The Baltimore preterm birth study. *Annals of Epidemiology, 18*(7), 545–551.

Ortiz-Mantilla, S., Choudhury, N., Leevers, H., & Benasich, A. A. (2008). Understanding language and cognitive deficits in very low birth weight children. *Developmental Psychobiology, 50*(2), 107–126.

Osler, M. (2006). The life course perspective: A challenge for public health research and prevention. *European Journal of Public Health, 16*(3), 230.

Ostir, G., & Goodwin, J. (2006). High anxiety is associated with an increased risk of death in an older tri-ethnic population. *Journal of Clinical Epidemiology, 59*(5), 534–540.

Ostrov, J., Crick, N., & Stauffacher, K. (2006). Relational aggression in sibling and peer relationships during early childhood. *Journal of Developmental Psychology, 27*(3), 241–253.

Overpeck, M., Hediger, M., Ruan, W., Davis, W., Maurer, K., Troendle, J., et al. (2000). Stature, weight, and body mass among U.S. children born with appropriate birth weights. *The Journal of Pediatrics, 137*(2), 205–213.

Owens, D. (1985). *None of the above.* New York: Houghton Mifflin.

Oyserman, D., Bybee, D., Mowbray, C., & MacFarlane, P. (2002). Positive parenting among African American mothers with a serious mental illness. *Journal of Marriage and Family, 65,* 65–77.

Padilla, Y. C., & Jordan, M. W. (1997). Determinants of Hispanic poverty in the course of the transition to adulthood. *Hispanic Journal of Behavioral Sciences, 19*(4), 416–433.

Pallas, A. (2003). Educational transitions, trajectories, and pathways. In J. Mortimer & M. Shanahan (Eds.), *Handbook of the life course* (pp. 165–184). New York: Kluwer Academic/Plenum Publishers.

Palmer, A. M., & Francis, P. T. (2006). Neurochemistry of aging. In J. Pathy, A. J. Sinclair, & E. J. Morley, E. J. (Eds.), *Principles and practice of geriatric medicine* (4th ed., pp. 59–67). Chichester, England: John Wiley & Sons.

Palsson, S., Johansson, B., Berg, B., & Skoog, I. (2000). A population study on the influence of depression on neuropsychological functions in 85-year-olds. *Acta Psychiatrica Scandinavica, 101*(3), 185–193.

Pandian, Z., Bhattacharya, S., Vale, L., & Templeton, A. (2005). In vitro fertilization for unexplained subfertilty. *Cochrane Database of Systematic Reviews, 2.*

Papachristou, F., Lialiaris, T., Touloupidis, S., Kalaitzis, C., Simopoulos, C., & Sofiktitis, N. (2006). Evidence of increased chromosomal instability in infertile males after exposure to mitomycin C and caffeine. *Asian Journal of Andrology, 8*(2), 199–204.

Papachristou Ornoy, A. (2006). Neuroteratogens in man: An overview with special emphasis on the teratogenicity of antiepileptic drugs in pregnancy. *Reproductive Technology, 22*(2), 214–226.

Paquette, K., & Bassuk, E. (2009). Parenting and homelessness: Overview and introduction to the special edition. *American Journal of Orthopsychiatry, 79*(3), 292–298.

Pardington, S. (2002, January 13). Multilingual pupils pose a challenge to educators. *Contra Costa Times.* Retrieved January 17, 2002, from http://www.uniontrib.com/news/uniontrib/sun/news/news_0n131ingos.html.

Parham, L., Quadagno, J., Brown, J. (2009). Race, politics, and social policy. In J. Midgley & M. Livermore (Eds.), *The handbook of social policy* (2nd ed., pp. 263–278). Thousand Oaks, CA: Sage.

Parkes, C. M. (2002). Grief: Lessons from the past, visions, for the future. *Death Studies, 26,* 367–385.

Parents, Family and Friends of Lesbians and Gays [PFLAG]. (2001). *Read this before coming out to your parents.* Washington, DC: Sauerman.

Parette, H. (1995, November). *Culturally sensitive family-focused assistive technology assessment strategies.* Paper presented at the DEC Early Childhood Conference on Children with Special Needs, Orlando, FL.

Parke, M. (2003). Are married parents really better for children? What research says about the effects of family structure on well-being, *CLASP Couples and Marriage Series, Brief #2.* Retrieved January 15, 2007, from http://www.clasp.org/publications/marriage_ brief3_annotated.pdf.

Parrenas, R. (2001). *Servants of globalization: Women, migration, and domestic work.* Stanford, CA: Stanford University Press.

Pascoe, J., Pletta, K., Beasley, J., & Schellpfeffer, M. (2002). Best start breastfeeding promotion campaign. *Pediatrics, 109*(1), 170.

Pasquali, R. (2006). Obesity, fat distribution, and infertility. *Maturitas, 54*(4), 363–371.

Pasquali, R., Gambineri, A., & Pagotto, U. (2006). The impact of obesity on reproduction in women with polycystic ovary syndrome. *British Journal of Gynaecology: An International Journal of Obstetrics and Gynaecology, 113*(10), 1148–1159.

Pasqualotto, F. F., Sobreiro, B. F., Hallak, J., Pasqualotto, E. B., & Lucon, A. M. (2006). Cigarette smoking is related to a decrease in semen volume in a population of fertile men. *British Journal of Urology International, 97*(2), 324–326.

Passel, J., & Cohn, D. (2008). *Immigration to play lead role in future U.S. growth.* Retrieved August 3, 2009, from http://pewresearch.org/pubs/729/united-states-population-projections.

Patel, D., Patel, S., Steinkampf, M. P., Whitten, S. J., & Malizia, B. A. (2008). Robotic tubal anastomosis: Surgical technique and cost effectiveness. *Fertility and Sterility, 90*(4), 1175–1179.

Patrikakou, E. N., Weisberg, R. P., Redding, S., & Walberg, H. J. (2005). (Eds.). *School-family partnerships for children's success.* New York: Teachers College Press.

Paul, E. (1997). A longitudinal analysis of midlife interpersonal relationships and well-being. In M. Lachman & J. James (Eds.), *Multiple paths of midlife development* (pp. 171–206). Chicago: University of Chicago Press.

Payne, R. K. (2005). *A framework for understanding poverty* (2nd ed.). Highlands, TX: aha! Process, Inc.

Pearlin, L., & Skaff, M. (1996). Stress and the life course: A paradigmatic alliance. *The Gerontologist, 36*(2), 239–247.

Peart, N. A., Pungello, E. P., Campbell, F. A., & Richey, T. G. (2006). Faces of fatherhood: African-American young adults view the paternal role. *Families in Society, 87*(1), 71–83.

Pecora, P. J., Kessler, R. C., Williams, J., O'Brien, K., Downs, A. C., English, D., et al. (2005). *Improving family foster care: Findings from the Northwest Foster Care Alumni Study.* Seattle, WA: Casey Family Programs.

Pejlert, A. (2001). Being a parent of an adult son or daughter with severe mental illness receiving professional care: Parents' narrative. *Health and Social Care in the Community, 9*(4), 194–204.

Pelligrini, A., & Galda, L. (2000). Cognitive development, play, and literacy: Issues of definition and developmental function. In K. Roskos & J. Christie (Eds.), *Play and literacy in early childhood: Research from multiple perspectives* (pp. 63–76). Mahwah, NJ: Lawrence Erlbaum.

Pempek, T. A., Yermolayeva, Y. A., & Calvert, S. L. (2009). College students' social networking experiences on Facebook. *Journal of Applied Developmental Psychology, 30,* 227–238.

Pena, R., & Wall, S. (2000). Effects of poverty, social inequality and maternal education on infant mortality in Nicaragua, 1988–1993. *American Journal of Public Health, 90*(1), 64–69.

Penn, H. (2005). *Understanding early childhood: Issues and controversies.* Maidenhead, UK: Open University Press and McGraw-Hill Education.

Pennekamp, M. (1995). Response to violence. *Social Work in Education, 17,* 199–200.

Perlman, D., & Fehr, B. (1987). The development of intimate relationships. In D. Perlman & S. Duck (Eds.), *Intimate relationships: Development, dynamics, & deterioration* (pp. 13–42). Newbury Park, CA: Sage.

Perlman, J. M. (2001). Neurobehavioral deficits in premature graduates of intensive care—Potential medical and neonatal environmental risk factors. *Pediatrics, 108*(16), 1339–1449.

Perloff, J., & Buckner, J. (1996). Fathers of children on welfare: Their impact on child well being. *American Journal of Orthopsychiatry, 66,* 557–571.

Perrig-Chiello, P., & Perren, S. (2005). Impact of past transitions on well-being in middle age. In S. Willis & M. Martin (Eds.), *Middle adulthood: A lifespan perspective* (pp. 143–178). Thousand Oaks, CA: Sage.

Perry, B. (2002a). Childhood experience and the expression of genetic potential: What childhood neglect tells us about nature and nurture. *Brain & Mind, 3*(1), 79–100.

Perry, B. (2002b). Helping traumatized children: A brief overview for caregivers. *The Child Trauma Academy.* Retrieved February 12, 2010, from http://www.childtrauma.org.

Perry, H. (1993). Mourning and funeral customs of African Americans. In D. Irish, K. Lundquist, & V. Nelsen (Eds.),

Ethnic variations in dying, death, and grief: Diversity in universality (pp. 51–65). Washington, DC: Taylor & Francis.

Perry, J. (2006). Applying principles of neurodevelopment to clinical work with maltreated and traumatized children: The neurosequential model of therapeutics. In N. B. Webb (Ed.), *Working with traumatized youth in child welfare* (pp. 27–52). New York: Guilford Press.

Pestvenidze, E., & Bohrer, M. (2007). Finally, daddies in the delivery room: Parents' education in Georgia. *Global Public Health, 2*(2), 169–183.

Peterson, B., & Duncan, L. (2007). Midlife women's generativity and authoritarianism: Marriage, motherhood, and 10 years of aging. *Psychology and Aging, 22*(3), 411–419.

Petrini, J. R., Dias, T., McCormick, M. C., Massolo, M. L., Green, N. S., & Escobar, G. J. (2009). Increased risk of adverse neurological development for late preterm infants. *The Journal of Pediatrics, 154*(2), 169–176.

Phillips, K. P., & Tanphaichitr, N. (2008). Human exposure to endocrine disrupters and semen quality. *Journal of Toxicology and Environmental Health: Part B, 11*(3/4), 188–220.

Phillips, S. (2003). Adolescent health. In I. Weiner (Ed.), *Handbook of psychology: Health psychology* (Vol. 9, pp. 465–485). New York: Wiley.

Phinney, J. (2006). Ethnic identity exploration in emerging adulthood. In J. Arnett & J. Tanner (Eds.), *Emerging adults in America: Coming of age in the 21st century* (pp. 117–134). Washington, DC: American Psychological Association.

Piaget, J. (1936/1952). *The origins of intelligence in children.* New York: International Universities Press.

Piaget, J. (1932/1965). *The moral judgment of the child.* New York: Free Press.

Piaget, J. (1972). Intellectual evolution from adolescence to adulthood. *Human Development, 15,* 1–12.

Piazza, J., & Charles, S. (2006). Mental health among baby boomers. In S. Whitbourne & S. Willis (Eds.), *The baby boomers grow up: Contemporary perspectives on midlife* (pp. 111–146). Mahwah, NJ: Lawrence Erlbaum.

Piedra, D. M. (2008). Flirting with the PDA; Congress must give birth to accommodation rights that protect pregnant working women. *Columbia Journal of Gender and the Law, 17*(2), 275–297.

Pinker, S. (2002). *The blank slate: The modern denial of human nature.* New York: Penguin.

Pipher, M. (1994). *Reviving Ophelia: Saving the selves of adolescent girls.* New York: Ballantine Books.

Pipher, M. (1999). *Another country: Navigating the emotional terrain of our elders.* New York: Riverhead Books.

Pirog-Good, M. (1996). The education and labor market outcomes of adolescent fathers. *Youth & Society, 28,* 236–262.

Piwoz, E., Ross, J., & Humphrey, J. (2004). Human immunodeficiency virus transmission during breastfeeding: Knowledge, gaps, and challenges for the future. *Advances in Experimental Medical Biology, 554,* 195–210.

Plaford, G. (2006). *Bullying and the brain: Using cognitive and emotional intelligence to help kids cope.* Lanham, MD: Rowman & Littlefield Education.

Plante, M. (2000). Fertility preservation in the management of gynecological cancers. *Current Opinion in Oncology, 12*(5), 497–507.

Plante, M. (2006). Fertility-preserving options for cervical cancer. *Oncology, 20*(6), 479.

Playfer, J. R. (2006). Parkinson's disease and Parkinsonism in the elderly. In J. Pathy, A. J. Sinclair, & E. J. Morley (Eds.), *Principles and practice of geriatric medicine* (4th ed., pp. 765–776). Chichester, England: John Wiley & Sons.

Pollack, W. (1999). *Real boys: Rescuing our sons from the myths of boyhood.* New York: Henry Holt & Co.

PollingReport.com. (2006). *Abortion and birth control.* Retrieved January 11, 2006, from http://www.pollingreport.com/abortion.htm.

Ponton, L., & Judice, S. (2004). Typical adolescent sexual development. *Child and Adolescent Psychiatric Clinics of North America, 13*(3), 497–511.

Poon, L. W., Clayton, G. M., Martin, P., Johnson, M. A., Courtenay, B. C., Sweaney, A. L.,et al. (1992). The Georgia centenarian study. *International Journal of Aging and Human Development, 34*(1), 1–17.

Poon, L. W., Jazwinski, M., Green, R. C., Woodard, J. L., Martin, P., Rodgers, W. L., et al. (2007). Methodological considerations in studying centenarians: Lessons learned from the Georgia Centenarian Studies. *Annual Review of Gerontology & Geriatrics, 27,* 231–264.

Population Council, Inc. (1999). CDC on infant and maternal mortality in the United States: 1900–1999. *Population and Development Review, 25*(25), 821–824.

Population Reports. (2005, April). *Contraceptive implants.* Baltimore, MD: Johns Hopkins Bloomberg School of Public Health. Retrieved February 17, 2010, from http://info.k4health.org/pr/m19/m19chap4.shtml.

Porcaro, C., Zappasodi, F., Barbati, G., Salustri, C. Pizzella, V., Rossini, P. et al. (2006). Fetal auditory responses to external sounds and mother's heart beat: Detection improved by Independent Component Analysis. *Brain Research, 1101,* 51–58.

Portes, A., & Rumbaut, R. G. (2001). *Legacies.* Berkeley: University of California Press.

Posmontier, B., & Horowitz, J. (2004). Postpartum practices and depression prevalences: Technocentric and ethnokinship cultural perspectives. *Journal of Transcultural Nursing, 15,* 34–43.

Poteat, V. P., Aragon, S., Espelage, D., & Koenig, B. (2009). Psychosocial concerns of sexual minority youth: Complexity and caution in group differences. *Journal of Consulting and Clinical Psychology, 77*(1), 196–201.

Potera, C. (2007). U.S. teen contraceptive use up, pregnancies down. *American Journal of Nursing, 107*(3), 19–24.

Pothoff, S., Bearinger, L., Skay, C., Cassuto, N., Blum, R., & Resnick, M. (1998). Dimensions of risk behaviors among American Indian youth. *Archives of Pediatric & Adolescent Medicine, 152,* 157–163.

Potter, C. C. (2004). Gender differences in childhood and adolescence. In P. Allen-Meares & M. W. Fraser (Eds.), *Intervention with children and adolescents: An interdisciplinary perspective* (pp. 54–79). Boston: Allyn & Bacon.

Prabhakaran, S. (2008). Self-administration of injectable contraceptives. *Contraception, 77*(5), 315–317.

Prata, N. (2009). Making family planning accessible in resource-poor settings. *Philosophical Transactions of the Royal Society of London, Series B, Biological Sciences, 364*(1532), 3093–3099.

Premberg, A., & Lundgren, I. (2006). Fathers' experiences in childbirth education. *Journal of Perinatal Education, 15*(2), 21–28.

Preto, N. (2005). Transformation of the family system during adolescence. In B. Carter & M. McGoldrick (Eds.), *The expanded family life cycle: Individual, family, and social perspectives* (3rd ed., pp. 274–286). Boston: Allyn & Bacon.

Price, S. K. (2006). Prevalence and correlates of pregnancy loss history in a national sample of children and families. *Maternal and Child Health Journal, 10*(6), 489–500.

Proot, I. M., Abu-Saad, H. H., ter Meulen, R. H. J., Goldsteen, M., Spreeuwenberg, C., & Widdershoven, G. A. M. (2004). The needs of terminally ill patients at home: Directing one's life, health and things related to beloved others. *Palliative Medicine, 18,* 53–61.

Pugh, C. (2007). Contraception coverage: Employers may exclude contraception coverage from their health insurance plans-Stanridge v. Union Pacific Railroad Company. *American Journal of Law and Medicine, 33*(2/3), 530–531.

Pulkkinen, L., & Kokko, K. (2000). Identity development in adulthood: A longitudinal study. *Journal of Research in Personality, 34,* 445–470.

Putney, N., & Bengtson, V. (2001). Families, intergenerational relationships, and kinkeeping in midlife. In M. Lachmann (Ed.), *Handbook of midlife development* (pp. 528–570). New York: Wiley.

Putney, N., & Bengtson, V. (2003). Intergenerational relations in changing times. In J. Mortimer & M. Shanahan (Eds.), *Handbook of the life course* (pp. 149–164). New York: Kluwer Academic/Plenum Publishers.

Puzzanchera, C. (2009). Juvenile arrests 2008. *Juvenile Justice Bulletin.* Washington, DC: U.S. Department of Justice, Office of Justice Programs, Office of Juvenile Justice and Delinquency Prevention. Retrieved February 9, 2010, from http://www.ojp.usdoj.gov.

Pyke, D., & Bengtson, V. (1996). Caring more or less: Individualistic and collectivist systems of family eldercare. *Journal of Marriage and the Family, 58,* 379–392.

Pykett, E. (2009, July 16). *Twins are orphaned as oldest mother dies.* Retrieved on February 14, 2010, from http://news.scotsman.com/health/Twins-are-orphaned-as-oldest.5464038.jp.

Quadagno, J. (2007). *Aging and the life course: An introduction to social gerontology* (4th ed.). Hightstown, NJ: McGraw-Hill.

Rabin, R. C. (2009, November 24). Childbirth: Earning a low grade for premature births. *New York Times,* p. 6.

Rabkin, J., Balassone, M., & Bell, M. (1995). The role of social workers in providing comprehensive health care to pregnant women. *Social Work in Health Care, 20*(3), 83–97.

Rakison, D., & Poulin-Dubois, D. (2001). Developmental origin of the animate-inanimate distinction. *Psychological Bulletin, 127,* 209–228.

Ramsey, J., Langlois, J., Hoss, R., Rubenstein, A., & Griffin, A. (2004). Origins of a stereotype: Categorization of facial attractiveness by 6-month-old infants. *Developmental Science, 7,* 201–211.

Rank, M. R. (2005). *One nation, underprivileged: Why American poverty affects us all.* New York: Oxford University Press.

Raphael, J. (2005). Teens having babies: The unexplored role of domestic violence. *Prevention Researcher, 12*(1), 15–17.

Rauch, J. (1988). Social work and the genetics revolution: Genetic services. *Social Work, 9/10,* 389–395.

Reed, G. B. (1996). Introduction to genetic screening and prenatal diagnoses. In J. J. Sciarra (Ed.), *Gynecology and obstetrics* (Rev. ed., pp. 999–1003). Philadelphia: Lippincott-Raven.

Reed, R. K. (2005). *Birthing fathers: The transformation of men in American rites of birth.* New Brunswick. NJ: Rutgers University Press.

Reed. S., Ludman, E., Newton, K., Grothaus, L., LaCroix, A. Nekhyudov, L. et al. (2009). Depressive symptoms and menopausal burden in the midlife. *Maturitas, 62*(3), 306–310.

Reedy, N. J. (2007). Born too soon: The continuing challenge of preterm labor and birth in the United States. *Journal of Midwifery & Women's Health, 52*(3), 281–290.

Reedy, N. J. (2008). The challenge of preterm birth. *Journal of Midwifery & Women's Health, 53*(1), 281–290.

Regenerus, M., & Elder, G. (2003). Staying on track in school: Religious influences in high and low-risk settings. *Journal for the Scientific Study of Religion, 42*(4), 633–649.

Reichman, N. E., & Teitler, J. O. (2006). Paternal age as a risk factor for low birthweight. *American Journal of Public Health, 96*(5), 862–866.

Reid, C. (2007). The transition from state care to adulthood: International examples of best practices. *New Directions for Youth Development, 113,* 33–49.

Reid, T. R. (2004). *The United States of Europe: The new super-power and the end of American supremacy.* New York: Penguin.

Reis, H. (2006). Implications of attachment theory for research on intimacy. In M. Mikulincer & G. Goodman (Eds.), *Dynamics of romantic love: Attachment, caregiving, and sex* (pp. 383–403). New York: Guilford.

Reith, M., & Payne, M. (2009). *Social work in end-of-life and palliative care.* Chicago: Lyceum Books.

Reitzes, D., & Murran, E. (2002). Grandparenthood: Factors influencing frequency of grandparent-grandchildren contact and grandparent role satisfaction. *Journals of Gerontology: Social Sciences, 59B,* S9-S16.

Remez, L. (2000). Oral sex among adolescents: Is it sex or is it abstinence? *Family Planning Perspectives, 32*(6), 298–304.

Rennison, C. M., & Welchans, S. (2000). *Intimate partner violence* (Special Report). Washington, DC: U.S. Bureau of Justice Statistics, National Institute of Justice. (NCJ 178247)

Repetti, R., Taylor, S., & Seeman, T. (2002). Risky families: Family social environments and the mental and physical health of offspring. *Psychological Bulletin , 18,* 330–366.

Reuter-Lorenz, P. A. (2002). New visions of the aging mind and brain. *Trends in Cognitive Sciences, 6,* 394–400.

Rew, L. (2005). *Adolescent health: A multidisciplinary approach to theory, research, and intervention.* Thousand Oaks, CA: Sage.

Richardson, V. E., & Barusch, A. S. (2006). *Gerontological practice for the twenty-first century: A social work perspective.* New York: Columbia University Press.

Richmond, M. (1917). *Social diagnosis.* New York: Russell Sage.

Richter, L. (2006). Studying adolescence. *Science, 312,* 1902–1905.

Riedmann, G. (1996). Preparation for parenthood. In J. J. Sciarra (Ed.), *Gynecology and obstetrics* (2nd ed., Vol. 2, pp. 1–8). Philadelphia: Lippincott-Raven.

Rieker, P. R., & Bird, C. E. (2005). Rethinking gender differences in health: Why we need to integrate social and biological perspectives. *The Journal of Gerontology: Series B: Psychological Sciences and Social Sciences, 60B,* 40–47.

Rieser-Danner, L. (2003). Individual differences in infant fearfulness and cognitive performance: A testing, performance, or competence effect? *Genetic, Social, and General Psychology Monographs, 129*(1), 41–71.

Rifas-Shiman, S. L., Rich-Edwards, J. W., Willett, W. C., Kleinman, K. P., Oken, E., & Gillman, M. W. (2006). Changes in dietary intake from first to second trimester of pregnancy. *Perinatal Epidemiology, 20*(1), 35–42.

Riley, M. W. (1971). Social gerontology and the age stratification of society. *The Gerontologist, 11,* 79–87.

Rimm, S. (1999). *See Jane win.* New York: Three Rivers Press.

Rindfuss, R. R., Cooksey, E. C., & Sutterlin, R. L. (1999). Young adult occupational achievement: Early expectations versus behavioral reality. *Work & Occupations, 26*(2), 220–263.

Rindfuss, R., Swicegood, G., & Rosenfeld, R. (1987). Disorder in the life course: How common and does it matter? *American Sociological Review, 52,* 785–801.

Ringeisen, H., Casanueva, C. E., Urato, M., & Stambaugh, L.F. (2009). Mental health service use during the transition to adulthood for adolescents reported to the child welfare system. *Psychiatric Services, 60*(8), 1084–1091.

Riordan, J., & Auerbach, K. (1999). *Breastfeeding and human lactation* (2nd ed.). Sudbury, MA: Jones & Bartlett.

Rivas-Drake, D. (2008). Perceived opportunity, ethnic identity, and achievement motivation among Latinos at a selective public university. *Journal of Latinos and Education, 7*(2), 113–128.

Roberts, B., Helson, R., & Klohnen, E. (2002). Personality development and growth in women across 30 years: Three perspectives. *Journal of Personality, 70,* 79–102.

Roberts, B., Robins, R., Trzesniewski, K., & Caspi, A. (2003). Personality trait development in adulthood. In J. Mortimer & M. Shanahan (Eds.), *Handbook of the life course* (pp. 579–595). New York: Kluwer Academic/Plenum Publishers.

Roberts, E., Burchinal, M., & Bailey, D. (1994). Communication among preschoolers with and without disabilities in same-age and mixed-age classes. *American Journal on Mental Retardation, 99,* 231–249.

Roberts, R. E. L., & Bengston, V. L. (1993). Relationship with parents, self-esteem, & psychological well-being in young adulthood. *Social Psychology Quarterly, 56*(4), 263–278.

Roberts, R. E., Roberts, C. R., & Chen, Y. R. (1997). Ethnocultural differences in prevalence of adolescent depression. *American Journal of Community Psychology, 25*(1), 95–111.

Robertson, S., Zarit, S., Duncan, L., Rovine, M., & Femia, E. (2007). Family caregivers' patterns of positive and negative affect. *Family Relations, 56,* 12–23.

Robinson, G. (2002). Cross-cultural perspectives on menopause. In A. E. Hunter & C. Forden (Eds.), *Readings in the psychology of gender: Exploring our differences and commonalities* (pp. 140–149). Needham Heights, MA: Allyn & Bacon.

Robinson, G. E., Stotland, N. L., Russo, N. F., Lang, J. A., & Occhiogrosso, M. (2009). Is there an "abortion trauma syndrome"? Critiquing the evidence. *Harvard Review Psychiatry, 17*(4), 266–90.

Robinson, L. C. (2000). Interpersonal relationship quality in young adulthood: A gender analysis. *Adolescence, 35*(140), 775–785.

Roggman, L. (2004). Do fathers just want to have fun? *Human Development, 47,* 228–236.

Roggman, L., Boyce, L., Cook, G., Christiansen, K., & Jones, D. (2004). Playing with daddy: Social toy play, early head start, and developmental outcomes. *Fathering, 2,* 83–108.

Rogoff, B. (2003). *The cultural nature of human development.* New York: Oxford University Press.

Rönkä, A., Oravala, S., & Pulkkinen, L. (2003). Turning points in adults' lives: The effects of gender and amount of choice. *Journal of Adult Development, 10*(3), 203–215.

Ronka, A., & Pulkkinen, L. (1995). Accumulation of problems in social functioning in young adulthood: A developmental approach. *Journal of Personality and Social Psychology, 69*(2), 381–391.

Roof, W. (1993). *A generation of seekers: The spiritual journeys of the baby boom generation.* San Francisco: HarperCollins.

Roof, W. (1999). *Spiritual marketplace: Baby boomers and the remaking of American religion.* Princeton, NJ: Princeton University Press.

Roopnarine, J., Shin, M., Donovan, B., & Suppal, P. (2000). Sociocultural contexts of dramatic play: Implications for early education. In K. Roskos & J. Christie (Eds.), *Play and literacy in early childhood: Research from multiple perspectives* (pp. 205–220). Mahwah, NJ: Lawrence Erlbaum.

Roper v. Simmons, 543 U.S. 551 (2005).

Rose, S., & Zand, D. (2000). Lesbian dating and courtship from young adulthood to midlife. *Journal of Gay & Lesbian Social Services, 11*(2/3), 77–104.

Rosenberg, M. (1986). *Conceiving the self.* Malabar, FL: Robert E. Krieger.

Roskos, K., & Christie, J. (2000). *Play and literacy in early childhood: Research from multiple perspectives.* Mahwah, NJ: Lawrence Erlbaum.

Ross, L. E., Steele, L. S., & Epstein, R. (2006). Lesbian and bisexual women's recommendations for improving the provision of assisted reproductive technology services. *Fertility and Sterility, 86*(3), 735–738.

Ross, L. J. (1992). African-American women and abortion: A neglected history. *Journal of Health Care for the Poor and Underserved, 3,* 274–284.

Ross, M., & Holmberg, D. (1992). Are wives' memories for events in relationships more vivid than their husbands' memories? *Journal of Social and Personal Relationships, 9,* 585–604.

Rossi, A. (2004a). The menopausal transition and aging processes. In O. Brim, C. Ryff, & R. Kessler (Eds.), *How healthy are we? A national study of well-being at midlife* (pp. 153–201). Chicago: University of Chicago Press.

Rossi, A. (2004b). Social responsibility to family and community. In O. Brim, C. Ryff, & R. Kessler (Eds.), *How healthy are we? A national study of well-being at midlife* (pp. 550–585). Chicago: University of Chicago Press.

Rotenberg, K., McDougall, P., Boulton, M., Vaillancourt, T., Fox, C., & Hymel, S. (2004). Cross-sectional and longitudinal relations among peer-reported trustworthiness, social relationships, and psychological adjustment in children and early adolescents from the United Kingdom and Canada. *Journal of Experimental Child Psychology, 88,* 46–67.

Rotheram-Borus, M. J. (1993). Biculturalism among adolescents. In M. Bernal & G. Knight (Eds.), *Ethnic identity* (pp. 81–102). Albany: State University of New York Press.

Rothman, B. K. (1991). *In labor: Women and power in the birthplace* (2nd ed.). New York: W. W. Norton.

Roueche, J. E., & Baker, G. A., III. (1986). *Profiling excellence in America's schools.* Arlington, VA: American Association of School Administrators.

Roumen, F. J., Op Ten Berg, M. M., & Hoomans, E. H. (2006). The combined contraceptive vaginal ring (NuvaRing®): First experience in daily clinical practice in the Netherlands. *The European Journal of Contraception and Reproductive Health: The Official Journal of the European Society of Contraception, 11*(1), 14–22.

Rovee-Collier, C. (1999). The development of infant memory. *Current Directions in Psychological Science, 8*(3), 80–85.

Rowlands, S. (2009). New technologies in contraception. *BJOG: An International Journal of Obstetrics & Gynaecology, 116*(2), 230–239.

Rubenstein, G. (2008). *Full-service schools: Where success is more than academic.* Retrieved May 21, 2010, from http://www.edutopia.org/whats-next-2008-community-services.

Rubin, K. (1986). Play, peer interaction, and social development. In A. Gottfried & C. Brown (Eds.), *Play interactions: The contribution of play materials and parental involvement to children's development* (pp. 163–174). Lexington, MA: Heath.

Rubin, R. (1995). *Maternal identity and the maternal experience: Childbirth educator.* New York: Springer.

Rudacille, D. (2005). *The riddle of gender: Science, activism, and transgender rights.* New York: Pantheon.

Rue, V., Coleman, P., Rue, J., & Reardon, D. (2004). Induced abortion and traumatic stress: A preliminary comparison of American and Russian women. *Medical Science Monitor, 10*(10), SR5–SR16.

Rueda, R., Monzo, L., Shapiro, J., Gomez, J., & Blacher, J. (2005). Cultural models of transition: Latina mothers of young adults with developmental disabilities. *Exceptional Children, 71*(4), 401–414.

Ruffman, T., Slade, L, & Redman, J. (2005). Young infants' expectations about hidden objects. *Cognitive, 97,* B35–B43.

Ruger, J. A., Moser, S. E., & Frisch, L. (2000). Smokers over 35 continue to receive oral contraceptives: Survey of patients in a family practice residency practice. *Scandinavian Journal of Primary Health Care, 18*(2), 113–114.

Rutter, M. (1996). Transitions and turning points in developmental psychopathology: As applied to the age span between childhood and mid-adulthood. *International Journal of Behavioral Development, 19*(3), 603–636.

Ryan, B. A., & Adams, G. R. (1995). The family-school relationships model. In B. A. Ryan, G. R. Adams, T. P. Gullotta, R. P. Weissberg, & R. L. Hampton (Eds.), *The family-school connection: Theory, research, and practice* (pp. 3–28). Thousand Oaks, CA: Sage.

Ryan, C., Huebner, D., Diaz, R., & Sanchez, J. (2009). Family rejection as a predictor of negative health outcomes in White and Latino lesbian, gay, and bisexual young adults. *Pediatrics: Official Journal of the American Academy of Pediatrics, 123,* 346–352.

Ryan, R. (2009). The burden borne late. *Business Review Weekly, 31*(22), 14.

Sabbagh, M., & Baldwin, D. (2001). Learning words from knowledgeable versus ignorant speakers: Links between preschoolers' theory of mind and semantic development. *Child Development, 72,* 1054–1070.

Sadock, B., & Sadock, V. (2007). *Kaplan & Sadock's synopsis of psychiatry: Behavioral sciences/clinical psychiatry* (10th ed.). Baltimore: Wolters Kluwer.

Sagara, J. (2000). Development of attitudes toward gender roles in children: Stereotypes and flexibility. *Japanese Journal of Educational Psychology, 48*(2), 174–181.

Saghir, M. T., & Robins, E. (1973). *Male and female homosexuality: A comprehensive examination.* Baltimore, MD: Williams & Wilkins.

Sagi, A., Koren-Karie, N., Gini, M., Ziv, Y., & Joels, T. (2002). Shedding further light on the effects of various types and quality of early child care on infant-mother attachment relationships: The Haifa study of early child care. *Child Development, 73,* 1166–1186.

Saigal, S., Stoskopf, B., Streiner, D., Boyles, M., Pinelli, J., Paneth, N., et al. (2006). Transition of extremely low birth weight infants from adolescent to young adulthood. *Journal of American Medical Association, 295*(6), 667–675.

St. George, D. (2009, February 22). 6,473 texts a month, but at what cost? Constant cellphone messaging keeps kids connected, parents concerned. *The Washington Post.* Retrieved February 9, 2010, from http://www.washingtonpost.com/wp-dyn/content/article/2009/02/21/AR2009022101863.html.

Saldinger, M. A., Cain, A., Kalter, N., & Lohnes, K. (1999). Anticipating parental death in families with young children. *American Journal of Orthopsychiatry, 69*(1), 39–48.

Saleeby, D. (1996). The strengths perspective in social work practice: Extensions and cautions. *Social Work, 41*(3), 296–304.

Saleeby, D. (2008). *The strengths perspective in social work practice* (5th ed.). Boston: Pearson Education.

Sallmen, M., Sandler, D. P., Hoppin, J. A., Blair, A., & Baird, D. D. (2006). Reduced fertility among overweight and obese men. *Epidemology, 17*(5), 520–523.

Saltzburg, S. (2004). Learning that an adolescent child is gay and lesbian: The parent experience. *Social Work, 49,* 109–119.

Sameroff, A., Bartko, W., Baldwin, A., Baldwin, C., & Seifer, R. (1998). Family and social influences on the development of child competence. In M. Lewis & C. Feiring (Eds.), *Families, risk, and competence* (pp. 161–186). Mahwah, NJ: Lawrence Erlbaum.

Sampson, R. (2009). *Bullying in schools. Problem-oriented guides for police. Problem-specific guides series No. 12.* Washington, DC: U.S. Department of Justice. Office of Community Oriented Policing Services. Retrieved February 9, 2010, from http://www.cops.usdoj.gov/files/RIC/Publications/e070634 14-guide.pdf.

Sandoval-Cros, C. (2009). Hispanic cultural issues in end-of-life care. In D. J. Doka & A. S. Tucci, *Living with grief: Diversity and end-of-life care* (pp. 117–126). Washington, DC: Hospice Foundation of America.

Sands, R., & Goldberg, G. (2000). Factors associated with stress among grandparents raising their grandchildren. *Family Relations, 49*(1), 97–105.

Santelli, J. S., Lindberg, L. D., Finer, L. B., & Singh, S. (2007). Explaining recent declines in adolescent pregnancy in the United States: The contribution of abstinence and improved contraceptive use. *American Journal of Public Health, 97*(1), 150–156.

Santrock, J. (2003). *Life-span development* (8th ed.). New York: McGraw-Hill.

Sapolsky, R. (2004). *Why zebras don't get ulcers* (3rd ed.). New York: Henry Holt and Co.

Sarkar, N. N. (2008). The impact of intimate partner violence on women's reproductive health and pregnancy outcome. *Journal of Obstetrics and Gynaecology, 28*(3), 266–271.

Savia, J., Almeida, D., Davey, A., & Zant, S. (2008). Routine assistance to parents: Effects on daily mood and other stressors. *Journals of Gerontology Series B: Psychological Sciences & Social Sciences, 36B*(3), S154–S161.

Savin-Williams, R., & Diamond, L. (2004). Sex. In R. Lerner & L. Steinberg (Eds.), *Handbook of adolescent psychology* (2nd ed., pp. 189–231). New York: Wiley.

Sawin, K. S. (1998). Health care concerns for women with physical disability and chronic illness. In E. Q. Youngkin & M. S. Davis (Eds.), *Women's health: A primary care clinical guide* (2nd ed., pp. 905–941). Stamford, CT: Appleton & Lange.

Sax, L. (2005). *Why gender matters: What parents and teachers need to know about the emerging science of sex differences.* New York: Random House.

Scarlett, A. G., Naudeau, S., Salonius-Pasternak, D., & Ponte, I. (2005). *Children's play.* Thousand Oaks, CA: Sage.

Schachere, K. (1990). Attachment between working mothers and their infants: The influence of family processes. *American Journal of Orthopsychiatry, 60,* 19–34.

Schafer, J. E., Osborne, L. M., Davis, A. R., & Westhoff, C. (2006). Acceptability and satisfaction using Quick Start with the contraceptive vaginal ring versus an oral contraceptive. *Contraception, 73*(5), 488–492.

Schaie, K. W. (1984). The Seattle Longitudinal Study: A 21-year exploration of psychometric intelligence in adulthood. In K. W. Schaie (Ed.), *Longitudinal studies of adult psychological development* (pp. 64–135). New York: Guilford.

Scharf, T. (1998). *Ageing and ageing policy in Germany.* Oxford: Berg.

Scherger, S. (2009). Social change and the timing of family transitions in West Germany: Evidence from cohort comparisons. *Time & Society, 18*(1), 106–129.

Schild, S., & Black, R. (1984). *Social work and genetics: A guide for practice.* New York: Haworth.

Schmitz, C., & Hilton, A. (1996). Combining mental health treatment with education for preschool children with severe emotional and behavioral problems. *Social Work in Education, 18,* 237–249.

Schneider, H., & Eisenberg, D. (2006). Who receives a diagnosis of Attention Deficit/Hyperactivity Disorder in the United States elementary school population? *Pediatrics, 117*(4), 601–609.

Schoeni, R. F., Martin, L. G., Andreski, P. A., & Freedman, V. A. (2005). Persistent and growing socioeconomic disparities in disability among the elderly: 1982–2002. *American Journal of Public Health, 95*(11), 2065–2072.

Schooler, C., & Mulatu, M. S. (2004). Occupational self-direction, intellectual functioning, and self-directed orientation in older workers: Findings and implications for individuals and societies. *American Journal of Sociology, 110,* 161–197.

Schore, A. N. (2002). Dysregulation of the right brain: A fundamental mechanism of traumatic attachment and the psychopathogenis of post-traumatic stress disorder. *Australian and New Zealand Journal of Psychiatry, 36,* 9–30.

Schuetze, P., Lewis, A., & DiMartino, D. (1999). Relation between time spent in daycare and exploratory behavior. *Infant Behavior & Development Special Issue, 22*(2), 267–276.

Schulte-Day, S. (2006) Pregnant in prison—The incarcerated woman's experience: A preliminary descriptive study. *Journal of Correctional Health Care, 12*(2), 78–88.

Schumm, W. R., Bell, D. B., & Knott, B. (2000). Characteristics of families of soldiers who return prematurely from overseas deployments: An assessment from Operation Restore Hope (Somalia). *Psychological Reports, 86*(3 pt 2), 1267–1272.

Schupf, N., Tang, M., Albert, S., Costa, A. R., Andrews, H., Lee, J., et al. (2005). Decline in cognitive and functional skills increases mortality risk in nondemented elderly. *Neurology, 65*(8), 1218–1226.

Schwartz, S., Cote, J., & Arnett, J. (2005). Identity and agency in emerging adulthood: Two developmental routes in the individualization process. *Youth and Society, 37*(2), 201–229.

Schweinhart, L., Montie, J., Xiang, Z., Barnett, W., Belfield, C., & Nores, M. (2005). *Lifetime effects: The High/Scope Perry preschool study through age 40.* Ypsilanti, MI: High/Scope Educational Research Foundation.

Sclowitz, I. K., & Santos, I. S. (2006). Risk factors for repetition of low birth weight, intrauterine growth retardation, and prematurity in subsequent pregnancies: A systematic review. *Cadernos De Saude Publica, 22*(6), 1129–1136.

Scott, K. D., Klaus, P. H., & Klaus, M. H (1999). The obstetrical and postpartum benefits of continuous support during childbirth. *Journal of Women's Health and Gender Based Medicine, 8*(10), 1257–1264.

Sedikides, C., Gaertner, L., & Toguchi, Y. (2003). Pancultural self-enhancement. *Journal of Personality and Social Psychology, 84,* 60–69.

Sedlak, A., & Broadhurst, D. (1996). *Third national incidence study of child abuse and neglect: Final report.* Washington, DC: U.S. Department of Human Services.

Seefeldt, C. (1993). Educating yourself about diverse cultural groups in our country by reading. *Young Children, 48,* 13–16.

Segal, B. M., & Stewart, J. C. (1996). Substance use and abuse in adolescence: An overview. *Child Psychiatry and Human Development, 26*(4), 193–210.

Segall, M., Dasen, P., Berry, J., & Poortinga, Y. (1999). *Human behavior in global perspective* (2nd ed.). Boston: Allyn & Bacon.

Seifer, D. B., Frazier, L. M., & Grainger, D. A. (2008). Disparity in assisted reproductive technologies outcomes in black women compared to white women. *Fertility and Sterility, 90*(5), 1701–1710.

Seifer, R., & Dickstein, S. (2000). Paternal mental illness and infant development. In C. Zeanah (Ed.), *Handbook of infant mental health* (2nd ed., pp. 145–160). New York: Guilford.

Seifert, K. L., Hoffnung, R. J., & Hoffnung, M. (1997). *Lifespan development.* New York: Houghton Mifflin.

Seigfried, C. (1989). Pragmatism, feminism and sensitivity to context. In M.M. Brabeck (Ed.), *Who cares? Theory, research and educational implications of the ethic of care* (pp. 63–83). New York: Praeger.

Seligman, M., Reivich, K., Jaycox, L., & Gillham, J. (1995). *The optimistic child*. New York: Houghton Mifflin.

Selman, R. L. (1976). Social-cognitive understanding: A guide to educational and clinical practice. In T. Lickona (Ed.), *Moral development and behavior: Theory, research, and social issues* (pp. 219–316). New York: Holt, Rinehart, & Winston.

Seltzer, M., Almeida, D., Greenberg, J., Savla, J., Stawski, R. Hong, J. et al. (2009). Psychosocial and biological markers of daily lives of midlife parents of children with disabilities. *Journal of Health and Social Behavior, 50*, 1–15.

Semprini, A. E., Hollander, L. H., Vucetich, A., & Gilling-Smith, C. (2008). Infertiilty treatment for HIV-positive women. *Women's Health, 4*(4), 369–382.

Sen, A., Partelow, L., & Miller, D. (2005). *Comparative indicators of education in the United States and other G8 countries: 2004* (NCES 2005–021). U.S. Department of Education, National Center for Education Statistics. Washington, DC: U.S. Government Printing Office.

Sepaniak, S., Forges, T., Gerald, H., Foliquet, B., Bene, M. C., & Monnier-Barbarino, P. (2006). The influence of cigarette smoking on human sperm quality and DNA fragmentation. *Toxicology, 223*(1–2), 54–60.

Serbin, L. A., Powlishta, K. K., & Gulko, J. (1993). The development of sex typing in middle childhood. *Monographs of the Society for Research in Child Development, 58*(2), Serial No. 232.

Serrant-Green, L. (2008). Review: Contraceptive patch and vaginal ring are as effective as oral contraceptives. *Evidence-Based Nursing, 11*(4), 108.

Sethi, V. (2004). Iodine deficiency and development of brain. *Indian Journal of Pediatrics, 71*(4), 325–329.

Settersten, R., Jr. (2003a). Introduction: Invitation to the life course: The promise. In R. Settersten, Jr. (Ed.), *Invitation to the life course: Toward new understandings of later life* (pp. 1–12). Amityville, NY: Baywood Publishing Co.

Settersten, R., Jr. (2003b). Age structuring and the rhythm of the life course. In J. Mortimer & M. Shanhan (Eds.), *Handbook of the life course* (pp. 81–98). New York: Kluwer Academic/ Plenum Publishers.

Settersten, R. A., Furstenberg, F. F., & Rumbaut, R. G. (2005). *On the frontier of adulthood: Theory, research, & public policy.* Chicago: University of Chicago Press.

Settersten, R., Jr., & Lovegreen, L. (1998). Educational experiences throughout adult life: New hopes or no hope for life-course flexibility? *Research on Aging, 20*(4), 506–538.

Settersten, R. A., & Mayer, L. U. (1997). The measurement of age, age structuring, and the life course. *Annual Review of Sociology, 23*, 233–261.

Severy, L. J., & Spieler, J. (2000). New methods of family planning: Implications for intimate behavior. *Journal of Sex Research, 37*(3), 258–265.

Sex Bias Cited in Vocational Ed. (2002, June 6). *Washington Post*, pp. 18–19.

Sexton, M. B., Byrd, M. R., & Von Kluge, S. (2010). Measuring resilience in women experiencing infertility using the CD-RISC: Examining infertility-related stress, general distress, and coping styles. *Journal of Psychiatric Research, 44*(4), 236–241.

Shadigian, E., & Bauer, S. (2004). Screening for partner violence during pregnancy. *International Journal of Gynecology & Obstetrics, 84*(3), 273–280.

Shanahan, M. (2000). Pathways to adulthood in changing societies: Variability and mechanisms in life course perspective. *Annual Review of Sociology, 27*, 667–692.

Shanahan, M., & Flaherty, B. (2001). Dynamic patterns of time use in adolescence. *Child Development, 72*(2), 385–401.

Shapiro, T. (2004). *The hidden cost of being African-American: How wealth perpetuates inequality.* New York: Oxford University Press.

Shaw, S., Kleiber, D., & Caldwell, L. (1995). Leisure and identity formation in male and female adolescents: A preliminary examination. *Journal of Leisure Research, 27*, 245–263.

Sheehy, G. (1995). *New passages.* New York: Random House.

Sheiner, E. K., Sheiner, E., Hammei, R. D., Potashnik, G., & Carel, R. (2003). Effect of occupational exposures on male fertility: Literature review. *Industrial Health, 41*(2), 55–62.

Sheldon, K. (2006). Getting older, getting better? Recent psychological evidence. In M. Csikszentmihalyi & I. Csiksezentmihali (Eds.), *A life worth living: Contributions to positive psychology* (pp. 215–229). New York: Oxford University Press.

Sheldon, K., & Kasser, T. (2001). Getting older, getting better? Personal striving and psychological maturity aross the life span. *Developmental Psychology, 37*, 491–501.

Shellenbarger, S. (2008, March 27). Work and family: More women pursue claims of pregnancy discrimination. *Wall Street Journal*, p. D1.

Shepard, M. (1992). Child visiting and domestic abuse. *Child Welfare, 71*, 357–367.

Sheppard-Jones, K., Kleinert, H., Paulding, C., & Espinosa, C. (2008). Family planning for adolescents and young women with disabilities: A primer for practitioners. *International Journal on Disability and Human Development, 7*(3), 343–348.

Sherblom, S. (2008). The legacy of the 'care challenge': Re-envisioning the outcome of the justice-care debate. *Journal of Moral Education, 37*(1), 81–98.

Sherer, M. (2009). *Challenging the whole child: Reflections on best practices in learning, teaching and leadership.* Alexandria, VA: Association for Supervision & Curriculum Development.

Sheridan, M. (2008). The spiritual person. In E. Hutchison (Ed.), *Dimensions of human behavior: Person and environment* (3rd ed.). Thousand Oaks, CA: Sage.

Sherman, E. (1991). *Reminiscence and the self in old age.* New York: Springer.

Sherwood, P., Given, C., Given, B., & Von Eye, A. (2005). Caregiver burden and depressive symptoms: Analysis of common outcomes in caregivers of elderly patients. *Journal of Aging Health, 17,* 125–147.

Shonkoff, J., & Phillips, D. (Eds.). (2000). *From neurons to neighborhoods: The science of early childhood development.* Washington, DC: National Academy Press.

Shonkoff, J., Hauser-Cram, P., Krauss, M., & Upshur, C. (1992). Development of infants with disabilities and their families: Implications for theory and service delivery. *Monographs of the Society for Research in Child Development, 57*(6), 230–239.

Shrier, L., Emans, S., Woods, E., & DuRant, R. (1996). The association of sexual risk behaviors and problem drug behaviors in high school students. *Journal of Adolescent Health, 20,* 377–383.

Shuey, K., & Willson, A. (2008). Cumulative disadvantage and black-white disparities in life-course health trajectories. *Research on Aging,* 30(2), 200–225.

Shweder, R. (Ed.). (1998). *Welcome to middle age! (and other cultural fictions).* Chicago: University of Chicago Press.

Sickmund, M. (2009, June). Delinquency cases in Juvenile Court, 2005. U.S. Department of Justice, Office of Justice Programs, Office of Juvenile Justice and Delinquency Prevention. Retrieved February 9, 2010, from http://www.ncjrs.gov/pdffiles1/ojjdp/224538.pdf.

Siefert, K., & Pimlott, S. (2001). Improving pregnancy outcome during imprisonment: A model residental care program. *Social Work,* 46(2), 125–134.

Siegel, D. (1999). *The developing mind: Toward a neurobiology of interpersonal experience.* New York: Guilford Press.

Silber, J. H., Lorch, S. A., Rosenbaum, P. R., Medoff-Cooper, B., Bakewell-Sachs, S., Millman, A., Mi, L., et al. (2009). Time to send the preemie home? Additional maturity at discharge and subsequent health care costs and outcomes. *Health Services Research, 44* (2p1), 444–463.

Silbereisen, R. (2003). Contextual constraints on adolescents' leisure. In S. Verma & R. Larson (Eds.), *Examining adolescent leisure time across cultures: New directions for child and adolescent development, No. 99* (pp. 95–102). San Francisco: Jossey-Bass.

Silbereisen, R., & Lerner, R. (2007a). Approaches to positive youth development: A view of the issues. In R. Silbereisen & R. Lerner (Eds.), *Approaches to positive youth development* (pp. 3–30). Thousand Oaks, CA: Sage.

Silbereisen, R., & Lerner, R. (2007b). *Approaches to positive youth development.* Thousand Oaks, CA: Sage.

Silveria, M.J., Copeland, L.A., & Feudtner, C. (2006). Likelihood of home death associated with local rates of home birth: Influence of local area healthcare preferences on site of death. *American Journal of Public Health, 96*(7),1243–1248.

Silverman, J., Raj, A., Mucci, L., & Hathaway, J. (2001). Dating violence against adolescent girls and associated substance use, unhealthy weight control, sexual risk behavior, pregnancy, and suicidality. *Journal of American Medical Association, 286*(5), 572–579.

Silverman, P. R. (2004). Bereavement: A time of transition and changing relationships. In J. Berzoff & P. R. Silverman (Eds.), *Living with dying: A handbook for end-of-life healthcare practitioners* (pp. 226–241). New York: Columbia University Press.

Silverstein, M., & Bengtson, V. (2001). Intergenerational solidarity and the structure of adult child-parent relationships in American families. In A. Walker, M. Manoogian-O'Dell, L. McGraw, & D. L. White (Eds.), *Families in later life: Connections and transitions* (pp. 53–61). Thousand Oaks, CA: Pine Forge.

Simmons, H. C. (2005). Religion, spirituality and aging for "The Aging" themselves. *Journal of Gerontological Social Work, 45*(1–2), 41–49.

Simmons, R. (2003). *Odd girl out: The hidden culture of aggression in girls.* Orlando, FL: Harcourt Trade Publishing.

Simmons, T., & O'Connell, M. (2003). *Married-couple and unmarried-partner households: 2000.* Washington, DC: U.S. Census Bureau.

Simon, H., & Zieve, D. (2008). Vasectomy and vasectomy reversal. *Vasectomy and Vasovasostomy (Reversal Surgery),* 1–6.

Singer, M. I., Anglin, T. M., Song, L.Y., & Lunghofer, L. (1995). Adolescents' exposure to violence and associated symptoms of psychological trauma. *Journal of American Medical Association, 273*(6), 477–482.

Singh, B. (2009). Clinical studies demonstrate benefits of life extension DHEA formulation. *Life Extension, 15*(6), 18.

Singh, L., Morgan, J., & Best, C. (2002). Infants' listening preferences: Baby talk or happy talk? *Infancy, 3,* 365–394.

Single-Rod Etonogestrel Implant Safe and Efficacious. (2009, June 15). *Fertility Weekly,* pp. 4–5.

Skaalvik, S., & Skaalvik, E. (2004). Frames of reference for self-evaluation of ability in mathematics. *Psychological Reports, 94,* 619–632.

Skinner, B. F. (1957). *Verbal behavior.* Englewood Cliffs, NJ: Prentice Hall.

Skultety, K. M. (2007). Addressing issues of sexuality with older couples. *Generations,* Fall issue, 31–37.

Slaught E., & Stampley, C. (2006). Promoting intergenerational practice. *Journal of Intergenerational Relationships,* 4(3), 73–86.

Sleeter, C. (1995). White pre-service students and multicultural education coursework. In J. M. Larkin & C. E. Sleeter (Eds.), *Developing multicultural teacher education curricula* (pp. 17–30). Albany, NY: State University of New York Press.

Sloter, E., Schmid, T. E., Marchetti, F., Eskenzai, B., Nath, J., & Wyrobek, A. J. (2006). Quantitative effects of male age on sperm motion. *Human Reproduction, 21*(11), 2868–2875.

Smith, A., Dannison L., & Vach-Hasse, T. (1998). When grandma is mom. *Childhood Education, 75*(1), 12–16.

Smith, B., & Blass, E. (1996). Taste-mediated calming in premature, preterm, and full-term human infants. *Developmental Psychology, 32,* 1084–1089.

Smith, C., & Denton, M. L. (2005). *Soul searching: The religious and spiritual lives of American teenagers.* Oxford: Oxford University Press.

Smith, C., Denton, M. L., Faris, R., & Regnerus, M. (2002). Mapping American adolescent religious participation. *Journal for the Scientific Study of Religion, 41*(4), 597–612.

Smith, D., Prentice, R., Thompson, D., & Hermann, W. (1975). Association of extrogenous estrogen and endometrial carcinoma. *New England Journal of Medicine, 293*(23), 1164–1167.

Smith, D., Stormshak, E., Chamberlain, P., & Whaley, R. (2001). Placement disruption in foster care. *Journal of Emotional and Behavioral Disorders, 9,* 200–211.

Smith, J., O'Connor, I., & Berthelsen, D. (1996). The effects of witnessing domestic violence on young children's psychosocial adjustment. *Australian Social Work, 49*(4), 3–10.

Smith, M., & Brun, C. (2006). An analysis of selected measures of child well-being for use at school- and community-based family resource centers. *Child Welfare, 85*(6), 985–1010.

Smith, M. A., Acheson, L. S., Byrd, J. E., Curtis, P., Day, T. W., Frank, S. H., et al. (1991). A critical review of labor and birth care. *Journal of Family Practice, 33*(3), 281–293.

Smith, Y., van Goozen, S., & Cohen-Kettenis, P. (2001). Adolescents with gender identity disorder who were accepted or rejected for sex assignment surgery: A prospective follow-up study. *Journal of the American Academy of Child and Adolescent Psychiatry, 40,* 472–481.

Smyer, M. A., Gatz, M., Simi, N. L., & Pedersen, N. L. (1998). Childhood adoption: Long-term effects in adulthood. *Psychiatry: Interpersonal and Biological Processes, 61*(3), 191.

Snarey, J. (1993). *How fathers care for the next generation: A four-decade study.* Cambridge, MA: Harvard University Press.

Snyder, H., & Sickmund, M. (2006). *Juvenile offenders and victims: 2006 national report.* Washington, DC: U.S. Department of Justice, Office of Justice Programs, Office of Juvenile Justice and Delinquency Prevention.

Social Security Administration. (n.d.). *Full retirement age goes from 65 to 67.* Retrieved June 25, 2002, from http://www .ssa.gov/pub/retirechart.htm.

Sokol, R. J., Janisse, J. J., Louis, J. M., Bailey, B. N., Ager, J., Jacobson, S. W., et al. (2007). Extreme prematurity: An alcohol-related birth effect. *Alcoholism: Clinical and Experimental Research, 31*(6), 1031–1037.

Solomon, R. C. (1988). *About love: Reinventing romance for modern times.* New York: Simon & Schuster.

Solomon, Z., Helvitz, H., & Zerach, G. (2009). Subjective age, PTSD and physical health among war veterans. *Aging & Mental Health, 13*(3), 405–413.

Solomon, Z., & Mikulincer, M. (2006). Trajectories of PTSD: A 20-year longitudinal study. *American Journal of Psychiatry, 163*(4), 659–666.

Solórzano, R. (2008). High stakes testing: Issues, implications, and remedies for English language learners. *Review of Educational Research, 78*(2), 260–329.

Sonfield, A. (2003). Preventing unintended pregnancy: The need and the means. *The Guttmacher Report on Public Policy, 6*(5), 7–10.

Song, Y., & Lu, H. (2002). *Early childhood poverty: A statistical profile (March 2002).* New York: National Center for Children in Poverty. Retrieved August 21, 2002, from http://cpmcnet .columbia.edu/dept/nccp/ecp302.html.

Sotirin, P., & Ellingson, L. (2006). The "other" women in family life. In K. Floyd & M. Morman (Eds.), *Widening the family circle: New research on family communication* (pp. 81–99). Thousand Oaks, CA: Sage.

Southern California Center for Reproductive Medicine. (2009, December 13). *A woman's age and fertility.* Retrieved December 31, 2009, from http://www.socalfertility.com/age-and-fertility.html.

Souza, J. P., Oliveria-Neto, A., Surita, F. G., Cecatti, J. G., Arnaral, E., & Pinto e Silva, J. L. (2006). The prolongation of somatic support in a pregnant woman with brain-death: A case report. *Reproductive Health, 3,* 3.

Sowell, E. Trauner, D., Gamst, A. & Jernigan, T. (2002). Development of cortical and subcortical brain structures in childhood and adolescence: A structural MRI study. *Developmental Medicine and Child Neurobiology, 44,* 4–16.

Spear, L. (2002). The adolescent brain and the college drinker: Biological basis of propensity to use and misuse alcohol. *Journal of Studies on Alcohol, 63*(Suppl.), 71–81.

Speare, A., Jr., & Avery, R. (1993). Who helps whom in older parent-child families? *Journal of Gerontology, 48,* S64–S73.

Spector-Mersel, G. (2006). Never-aging stories: Western hegemonic masculinity scripts. *Journal of Gender Studies, 15*(1), 67–82.

Speidel, J. J., Harper, C. C., & Shields, W. C. (2008). The potential of long-acting reversible contraceptive to decrease unintended pregnancy. *Contraception Journal, 78,* 197–200.

Spencer, M. (1985). Black children's race awareness, racial attitudes and self concept: A reinterpretation. *Annual Progress in Child Psychiatry & Child Development,* 616–630.

Spencer, M. B., Harpalani, V., Fegley, S., Dell'Angelo, T., & Seaton, G. (2003). Identity, self, and peers in context: A culturally sensitive, developmental framework for analysis. In R. M. Lerner, F. Jacobs, & D. Wertlieb (Eds.), *Handbook of applied developmental science, Vol. 1* (pp. 123–142). Thousand Oaks, CA: Sage.

Spencer, N., & Logan, S. (2002). Social influences on birth weight: Risk factors for low birth weight are strongly influenced by the social environment. *Archives of Disease in Childhood: Fetal and Neonatal Edition, 86*(1), 6–8.

Sperling, D. (2004). The maternal brain death. *American Journal of Law and Medicine, 30*(4), 453–500.

Sperling, D. (2006). *Management of the postmortem pregnancy: Legal and philosophical aspects.* England: Ashgate Publishers.

Spieker, S., Nelson, D., & Petras, A. (2003). Joint influence of child care and infant attachment security for cognitive and language outcomes of low-income toddlers. *Infant Behavior & Development, 26*(3), 326–344.

Spielman, V., & Taubman-Ben-Ari, O. (2009). Parental self-efficacy and personal growth in the transition to parenthood: A comparison between parents of premature and of full-term babies. *Health and Social Work, 34,* 201–222.

Spillman, B. (2003). *Changes in elderly disability rates and the implications for health care utilization and cost.* Washington, DC: Urban Institute.

Spiro, A. (2001). Health in midlife: Toward a life-span view. In M. Lachmann (Ed.), *Handbook of midlife development* (pp. 156–187). New York: Wiley.

Spitz, I. M., Bardin, C. W., Benton, L., & Robbins, A. (1998). Early pregnancy termination with mifepristone and misoprostol in the United States. *The New England Journal of Medicine, 338*(18), 983–987.

Splete, J. (2002). New tool assesses ectopic pregnancy (Microculdoscopy). *OB GYN News, 37*(3), 1–2.

Spong, C. Y. (2009). Preterm birth: An enigma and a priority. *Obstetrics and Gynecology, 113*(4), 770–771.

Spring, J. (2004). *Deculturalization and the struggle for educational equality.* New York: McGraw-Hill.

Sroufe, L. A., Egeland, B. Carlson, E., & Collins, W. A. (2005). *The development of the person: The Minnesota study of risk and adaptation from birth to adulthood.* New York: Guilford.

Staudinger, U., & Bluck, S. (2001). A view on midlife development from life-span theory. In M. Lachman (Ed.), *Handbook of midlife development* (pp. 3–39). New York: Wiley.

Staudinger, U. M., Freund, A. M., Linden, M., & Maas, I. (1999). Self, personality, and life regulation: Facets of psychological resilience in old age. In P. B. Baltes & K. U. Mayer (Eds.), *The Berlin Aging Study: Aging from 70 to 100* (pp. 302–328). Cambridge: Cambridge University Press.

Stein, M. (2005). Resilience and young people leaving care: Implications for child welfare policy and practice in the UK. In R. J. Flynn, P. M. Dudding, & J. G. Barber (Eds.), *Promoting resilience in child welfare* (pp. 264–278). Ottawa: University of Ottawa Press.

Stengel, R. (2005, June 21). The missing-father myth. *Time.* Retrieved September 15, 2009, from http://www.time.com/printout/0,8816,1074862,00.html.

Stepp, L. S. (1999, July 8). Parents are alarmed by an unsettling new fad in middle schools: Oral sex. *The Washington Post,* p. A1.

Stern, J. E., Cedars, M. I., Jaion, T., Klein, N. A., Beaird, C. M., Grainger, D. A., et al. (2007). Assisted reproductive technology practice patterns and the impact of embryo transfer guidelines in the United States. *Fertility and Sterility, 88*(2), 275–282.

Sternberg, S., Wolfson, C., & Baumgarten, M. (2000). Undetected dementia in community-dwelling older people. *Journal of the American Geriatrics Society, 48*(11), 1430–1434.

Sterns, H., & Huyck, M. (2001). The role of work in midlife. In M. Lachman (Ed.), *Handbook of midlife development* (pp. 447–486). New York: Wiley.

Stevens, S. J., & Patton, T. (1998). Residential treatment for drug addicted women and their children: Effective treatment strategies. *Drugs and Society, 13,* 235–249.

Stockard, J., & O'Brien, R. (2002). Cohort effects on suicide rates: International variation. *American Sociological Review, 67,* 854–872.

Stolzenberg, R. M., Blair-Loy, M., & Waite, L. J. (1995). Religious participation in early adulthood: Age and family life cycle effects on church membership. *American Sociological Review, 60*(1), 84–104.

Stone, P. (2007). *Opting out?: Why women really quit careers and head home.* Berkeley, CA: University of California Press.

Stone, P. W., Zwanziger, J., Hinton, W. P., & Buenting, J. (2000). Economic analysis of two models of low-risk maternity care: A freestanding birth center compared to traditional care. *Research in Nursing and Health, 23*(4), 279–289.

Stouthamer-Loeber, M., & Wei, E. H. (1998). The precursors of young fatherhood and its effect on delinquency of teenage males. *Journal of Adolescent Health, 22,* 56–65.

Stovall, K., & Dozier, M. (1998). Infants in foster care: An attachment theory perspective. *Adoption Quarterly, 2*(1), 55–88.

Strasburger, V. C. (2007). *Teen pregnancy rates rise in U.S.* University of New Mexico University School of Medicine. Retrieved October 31, 2009, from http://www.livestrong.com/article/12504-teen-pregnancy-rates-USA.

Strauch, B. (2010). *The secret life of the grown-up brain: The surprising talents of the middle-aged mind.* London: Viking.

Strauss, L. T., Herndon, J., Chang, J., Parker, W. Y., Bowens, S. V., & Berg, C. J. (2002). *Abortion surveillance—United States, 2002.* Retrieved November 15, 2006, from http://www.cdc.gov/mmwr/preview/mmwrhtml/ss5407a1.htm.

Street, J., Harris-Britt, A., & Walker-Barnes, C. (2009). Examining relationships between ethnic identity, family environment, and psychological outcomes for African American adolescents. *Journal of Child and Family Studies, 18,* 412–420.

Streri, A. (2005). Touching for knowing in infancy: The development of manual abilities in very young infants. *European Journal of Developmental Psychology, 2,* 325–343.

Stroberg, P., Hedelin, H., & Ljunggren, C. (2006). Prescribing all phosphodiesterase 5 inhibitors to a patient with erectile dysfunction—a realistic and feasible option in everyday clinical practice—outcome of a simple treatment regime. *European Urology, 49*(5), 900–907.

Strock, M. (2004). *Autism spectrum disorders (pervasive developmental disorders)* (NIH Publication No. NIH-04–5511). Bethesda, MD: National Institute of Mental Health. Retrieved January 15, 2007, from http://www.nimh.nih.gov/publicat/autism.cfm.

Strock, M. (2006). *Attention deficit hyperactivity disorder.* Bethesda, MD: National Institute of Mental Health. Retrieved December 5, 2006, from http://www.nimh.nih.gov/publicat/NIMHadhdpub.pdf.

Stroebe, M., Stroebe, W., & Hansson, R. (1993). *Handbook on bereavement: Theory, research and intervention.* New York: Cambridge University Press.

Subramanian, S. V., Kubzansky, L., Berman, L., Fay, M., & Kawachi, I. (2006) Neighborhood effects on the self-rated health of elders: Uncovering the relative importance of structural and service-related neighborhood environments. *The Journals of Gerontology: Series B: Psychological Sciences and Social Sciences, 61B*(3), 153–161.

Substance Abuse and Mental Health Services Administration (SAMHSA). (2000). *Uniform facility data set (UFDS)* (DHHS: Publication No. (SMA) 00–3463). Rockville, MD: Author.

Substance Abuse and Mental Health Services Administration (SAMHSA). (2005). *Overview of findings from the 2004 National Survey on Drug Use and Health* (Office of Applied Studies, NSDUH Series H-27, DHHS Publication No. SMA 05–4061). Rockville, MD: Author.

Substance Abuse and Mental Health Services Administration (SAMHSA). (2009a). *Results from the 2008 National Survey on Drug Use and Health: National findings* (Office of Applied Studies, NSDUH Series H-36, HHS Publication No. SMA 09–4434). Rockville, MD: Author. Retrieved February 9, 2009, from http://www.oas.samhsa.gov/nsduh/2k7nsduh/2k7 Results.pdf.

Substance Abuse and Mental Health Services Administration (SAMHSA), Office of Applied Studies. (2009b). *The NSDUH Report: Trends in tobacco use among adolescents: 2002 to 2008.* Rockville, MD: Author. Retrieved February 9, 2009, from http://www.oas.samhsa.gov/2k9/152/152 Trends.htm.

Sue, D. W., & McGoldrick, M. (2005). *Multicultural social work practice.* Hoboken, NJ: Wiley.

Suh, E., & Abel, E. (1990). The impact of violence on the children of the abused. *Journal of Independent Social Work, 4*(4), 27–43.

Sukalich, S., Mingione, M. J., & Glantz, J. C. (2006). Obstetric outcomes in overweight and obese adolescents. *American Journal of Obstetrics and Gynecology, 195*(3), 851–855.

Sum, A., Fogg, N., & Mangum, G. (2000). *Confronting the youth demographic challenge: The labor market prospects of out-of-school young adults.* Baltimore, MD: Sar Levitan Center for Social Policy Studies.

Sun, S. S., Schubert, C. M., Chumlea, W. C., Roche, A. F., Kulin, H. E., Lee, P. A., et al. (2002). National estimates of the timing of sexual maturation and racial differences among U.S. children. *Pediatrics, 110*(5), 911–919.

Suzuki, K., Tanaka, T., Kondo, N., Minai, J., Sato, M., & Yamagata, Z., (2008). Is maternal smoking during early pregnancy a risk factor for all low birth weight infants? *Journal of Epidemiology, 18*(3), 89–96.

Swap, S. M. (1993). *Developing home-school partnerships: From concepts to practice.* New York: Teachers College Press.

Sweet, J., & Bumpass, L. (1996). *The national survey of families and households—Waves 1 and 2.* Madison, WI: Center for Demography and Ecology, University of Wisconsin-Madison.

Sword, W., Watt, S., & Krueger, P. (2006). Postpartum health, service needs, and access to care experiences of immigrant and Canadian-born women. *Journal of Obstetric Gynecological and Neonatal Nurses, 35*(6), 717–727.

Taddio, A., Shah, V., Gilbert-Macleod, C., & Katz, J. (2002). Conditioning and hyperalgesia in newborns exposed to repeated heel lances. *Journal of American Medical Association, 288*(7), 857–861.

Taffett, G. (1996). Age-related physiologic changes. In D. Reuben, T. Yoshikawa, & R. Besdine, R. (Eds.), *Geriatric review syllabus* (3rd ed., pp. 11–15). Dubuque, IA: Kendall/Hunt.

Takahashi, K. (1990). Are the key assumptions of the "strange situation" procedure universal? A view from Japanese research. *Human Development, 33,* 23–30.

Takahashi, E. A., & Turnbull, J. E. (1994). New findings in psychiatric genetics: Implications for social work practice. *Social Work in Health Care, 20*(2), 1–21.

Tan, H., & Loth, S. (2010). Microsurgical reversal of sterilization—is this still clinically relevant today? *Annals: Academy of Medicine Singapore, 39*(1), 22–26.

Tang, C., Yeung, D., & Lee, A. (2003). Psychosocial correlates of emotional responses to meanarche among Chinese adolescent girls. *Journal of Adolescent Health, 33,* 193–201.

Tartaro, J., Luecken, L., & Gunn, H. (2005). Exploring heart and soul: Effects of religiosity/spirituality and gender on blood pressure and cortisol stress response. *Journal of Health Psychology, 10,* 753–766.

Tate, A., Dezateux, C., Cole, T., and the Millennium Cohort Study Child Health Group. (2006). Is infant growth changing? *International Journal of Obesity, 30,* 1094–1096.

Tatum, B. (2000). The complexity of identity: Who am I? In M. Adams, W. Blumenfeld, R. Castañeda, H. Hackman, M. Peters, & X. Zúñiga (Eds.), *Readings for diversity and social justice: An anthology on racism, anti-Semitism, sexism, heterosexism, ableism, and classism* (pp. 9–14). New York: Routledge.

Tatum, B. D. (1992). Talking about race, learning about racism: The application of racial identity development in the classroom. *Harvard Educational Review, 62*(1), 1–24.

Tatum, B. D. (2000). *Why are all the Black kids sitting together in the cafeteria? And other conversations about race* (Rev. Ed.). New York: Basic Books.

Tay, J. I., Moore, J., & Walker, J. J. (2000). Ectopic pregnancy. *British Medical Journal, 320*(7239), 916–922.

Taylor, A. (2003). Extent of the problem. *British Medical Journal, 327*(7412), 434–436.

Taylor, H. (2000). Meeting the needs of lesbian and gay young adolescents. *Clearing House, 73*(4), 221–224.

Taylor, J. M., Gilligan, C., & Sullivan, A. M. (1995). *Between voice and silence: Women and girls, race and relationship.* Cambridge, MA: Harvard University Press.

Taylor, M. Y., Wyatt-Asmead, J. W., Gray, J., Bofill, J. A., Martin, R., & Morrison, J. C. (2006). Pregnancy loss after first-trimester viability in women with sickle cell trait: Time for a reappraisal? *American Journal of Obstetrics and Gynecology, 194*(6), 1604–1609.

Taylor, W., Blair, S., Cummings, S., Wun, C., & Malina, R. (1999). Childhood and adolescent physical activity patterns and adult physical activity. *Medicine and Science in Sports and Exercise, 31,* 118–123.

Teicher, M. (2002). Scars that won't heal: The neurobiology of child abuse. *Scientific American, 286*(3), 68–75.

Teitelman, J. L. (1995). Homosexuality. In G. L. Maddox (Ed.), *The encyclopedia of aging: A comprehensive resource in gerontology and geriatrics* (2nd ed., p. 270). New York: Springer.

Templeton, J., & Eccles, J. (2006). The relationship between spiritual development and identity processes. In G. Roelkepartain, P. King, L. Wagener, & P. Benson (Eds.), *The handbook of spiritual development in childhood and adolescence* (pp. 252–265). Thousand Oaks, CA: Sage.

Terry, D. F., Sebastiani, P., Andersen, S. L., & Perls, T. T., (2008). Disentangling the roles of disability and morbidity in survival to exceptional old age. *Archives of Internal Medicine, 168*(3), 277–283.

Thomas, A., & Chess, S. (1986). The New York longitudinal study: From infancy to early adult life. In R. Plomin & J. Dunn (Eds.), *The study of temperament: Changes, continuities, and challenges* (pp. 39–52). Hillside, NJ: Lawrence Erlbaum.

Thomas, A., Chess, S., & Birch, H. G. (1968). *Temperament and behavior disorders in children.* New York: New York University Press.

Thomas, A., Chess, S., & Birch, H. G. (1970). The origin of personality. *Scientific American, 223,* 102–109.

Thomlison, B. (2004). Child maltreatment: A risk and protective factor perspective. In M. F. (Ed.), *Risk and resilience in childhood: An ecological perspective* (2nd ed., pp. 89–131). Washington, DC: NASW.

Thompson, R., & Nelson, C. (2001). Developmental science and the media: Early brain development. *American Psychologist, 56*(1), 5–15.

Thornberry, T. P., Smith, C. A., & Howard, G. J. (1997). Risk factors for teenage fatherhood. *Journal of Marriage & Family, 59,* 505–523.

Tiedje, L. B. (2001). Toward evidence-based practice. Fathers' coping style, antenatal preparation, and experiences of labor and the postpartum. *The American Journal of Maternal Child Nursing, 26*(2), 108–109.

Tiet, A., Bird, H., Hoven, C., Wu, P., Moore, R., & Davies, M. (2001). Resilience in the face of maternal psychopathology and adverse life events. *Journal of Child and Family Studies, 10*(3), 347–365.

Tilley, I. B., Shaaban, O. M., Wilson, M., Glasier, A., & Mishell, D. R. (2009). Breastfeeding and contraception use among women with unplanned pregnancies less than two years after delivery. *International Journal of Gynaecology and Obstetrics: The Official Organ of the International Federation of Gynaecology and Obstetrics, 105*(2), 127–130.

Tiran, D., & Chummun, H. (2004). Complementary therapies to reduce physiologic stress in pregnancy. *Complementary Therapy for Nursing Midwifery, 10*(3), 162–167.

Tobin, S. (1988). Preservation of the self in old age. *Social Casework: The Journal of Contemporary Social Work, 66*(9), 550–555.

Toner, J. P. (2002). Progress we can be proud of: U.S. trends in assisted reproduction over the first 20 years. *Fertility and Sterility, 78,* 943–950.

Tornstam, L. (2005). *Gerotranscendence: A developmental theory of positive aging.* New York: Springer.

Tout, K., & Zaslow, M. (2003). Public investments in child care quality: Needs, challenges, and opportunities. In R. M. Lerner, F. Jacobs, & D. Wertlieb (Eds.), *Handbook of applied developmental science, Vol. 1* (pp. 339–366). Thousand Oaks, CA: Sage.

Trainor, A. A. (2008). Using cultural and social capital to improve postsecondary outcomes and expand transition models for youth with disabilities. *Journal of Special Education, 42*(3), 148–162.

Trattner, W. (1998). *From poor law to welfare state: A history of social welfare in America* (6th ed.). New York: Free Press.

Troccoli, K. (Ed.). (2006). *It's a guy thing: Boys, young men, and teen pregnancy prevention*. National Campaign to Prevent Teen and Unplanned Pregnancy. Retrieved November 4, 2009, from http://www.thenationalcampaign.org/resources/pdf/pubs/Guy_Thing.pdf.

Trussell, J. (2004). Contraceptive failure in the United States. *Contraception, 70*(2), 89–96.

Tueth, M. J. (1993). Anxiety in the older patient: Differential diagnosis and treatment. *Geriatrics, 48,* 51–54.

Turiel, E. (2004). Commentary: Beyond individualism and collectivism: A problem or progress? *New Directions in Child and Adolescent Development, 104,* 91–100.

Turner, H., Finkelhor, D., & Ormord, R. (2006). The effect of lifetime victimization on the mental health of children and adolescents. *Social Science & Medicine, 62*(1), 13–27.

Tutty, L., & Wagar, J. (1994). The evolution of a group for young children who have witnessed family violence. *Social Work With Groups, 17*(1/2), 89–104.

Tweddle, A. (2007). Youth leaving care: How do they fare? *New Directions for Youth Development, 113,* 15–31.

Uddin, L., Iacoboni, M., Lange, C., & Keenan, J. (2007). The self and social cognition: The role of cortical midline structures and mirror neurons. *Trends in Cognitive Sciences, 11*(4), 153–157.

Udry, J. R. (1993). The politics of sex research. *Journal of Sex Research, 30*(2), 103–110.

Uhlenberg, P. (1996). Mutual attraction: Demography and life-course analysis. *The Gerontologist, 36*(2), 226–229.

UNAIDS. (2005). *Global summary of the HIV and AIDS epidemic in 2004.* Retrieved April 24, 2005, from http://www.unaids.org/en/resources/epidemiology.

UNAIDS. (2006). *06 report on the global AIDS epidemic: Executive summary.* Retrieved May 21, 2010, from http://data.unaids.org/pub/Globalreport/2006/2006-GR-ExcutiveSummary-en.pdf.

UNICEF. (2001). A league table of teen births in rich nations. *Innocenti Report Card 3,* 15–19. Retrieved November 1, 2009, from http://www.unicef-irc.org/publications/pdf/repcard3e.pdf.

UNICEF. (2005). *The state of the world's children 2006: Excluded and invisible.* New York: Author.

UNICEF. (2009). *Tracking progress in child and maternal nutrition.* Retrieved February 12, 2010, from http://www.unicef.org/media/files/Tracking_Progress_on_Child_and_Maternal_Nutrition_EN_110309.pdf.

UNICEF. (n.d.). *Facts on children: Early childhood.* Retrieved February 15, 2010, from http://www.unicef.org/earlychildhood/9475.html.

UNICEF Innocenti Research Centre. (2005). *Child poverty in rich countries 2005* (Innocenti Report Card No. 6). Florence, Italy: Author.

Underwood, M. K. (2003). *Social aggression among girls.* New York: Guilford Press.

United Nations Children's Fund. (2000a). *A league table of child poverty in rich nations. Innocenti Report Card (1).* Retrieved December 3, 2006, from http://www.unicef-icdc.org/publications/pdf/repcard1e.pdf.

United Nations Children's Fund. (2000b). *Poverty reduction begins with children.* New York: Author. Retrieved January 15, 2007, from http://www.unicef.org/publications/index_5616.html.

United Nations Children's Fund (2009, July). *Economic update: Countries' evolving vulnerability from a child's perspective.* (Social and Economic Working Brief). New York, NY: Author. Retrieved January 19, 2010, from http://www.unicef.org/socialpolicy/files/Countries_Evolving_Vulnerability_final.pdf.

United Nations Development Program. (2005). *Human development report 2005: International cooperation at the crossroads: Aid, trade, and security in an unequal world.* New York: Oxford University Press.

United States Department of Health and Human Services. (2009). *Healthy people 2010/2020. National Center for Health Statistics.* Retrieved May 21, 2010, from http://www.healthypeople.gov.

Uotinen, V., Rantanen, T., & Suutama, T. (2005). Perceived age as a predictor of old age mortality: A 13-year prospective study. *Age and Ageing, 34,* 368–372.

Upadhyay, U. D. (2005). *New contraceptives choices* [Population Reports, Series M, No. 19]. Baltimore, MD: The John Hopkins Bloomberg School of Public Health.

U.S. Bureau of the Census. (1999). *Statistical abstract of the United States.* Washington, DC: U.S. Government.

U.S. Bureau of the Census. (2004). *We the people: Aging in the United States* (Census 2000 Special Report). Washington, DC: U.S. Department of Commerce.

U.S. Bureau of the Census. (2005). *2005 American community survey.* Retrieved January 14, 2007, from http://www.census.gov/hhes/www/disability/2005acs.html.

U.S. Bureau of the Census. (2008a). *Population estimates.* Retrieved August 3, 2009, from http://www.census.gov/popest/national/asrh/NC-EST2005-asrh.

U.S. Bureau of the Census. (2008b). *Table 2: Projections of population by selected age and sex for groups in the U.S. from 2010 to 2030.* Retrieved March 3, 2010, from http://www.census.gov/population/www/projections.

U.S. Bureau of the Census. (2008c). *Projections of the population by selected age groups and sex for the United States: 2010 to 2050.* Retrieved January 8, 2009, from http://www.census.gov/population/www/projections/files/nation/summary/np2008-t2.xls.

U.S. Bureau of the Census. (2009). *Facts for features.* Retrieved May 21, 2010, from http://www.censusgov.zuom.info/PressRelease/www/releases/archives/facts_for_features_special_editions/013847.html.

U.S. Bureau of the Census. (n.d.). *The living arrangements of children in 2003. Population profile of the United States: Dynamic version.* Washington, DC: Author. Retrieved November 15, 2006, from http://www.census.gov/population/pop-profile/dynamic/LivArrChildren.pdf.

U.S. Bureau of Labor Statistics, U.S. Department of Labor. (2006, August 25). *Bureau of Labor Statistics News: Employment and unemployment among youth summary.* Washington, DC: Author.

U.S. Bureau of Labor Statistics. (2009a). *Economic news release: Metropolitican area employment and unemployment summary.* Retrieved September 3, 2009, from http://www.bls.gov/news.release/metro.nr0.htm.

U.S. Bureau of Labor Statistics. (2009b). *New monthly data series on the employment status of people with a disability.* Retrieved September 3, 2009, from http://www.bls.gov/cps/cpsdisability.htm.

U.S. Department of Health and Human Services. (2000). *Trends in the well-being of America's children and youth.* Washington, DC: U.S. Government Printing Office.

U.S. Department of Health and Human Services. (2006). Center for Medicare and Medicaid Services: *Coordination of benefits Part D: Overview.* Retrieved December 10, 2006, from http://www.cms.hhs.gov/COBPartD/.

U.S. Department of Health and Human Services, Administration on Children, Youth, and Families. (2009a). *Child maltreatment 2007.* Retrieved February 13, 2010, from http://www.acf.hhs.gov/programs/cb/pubs/cm07/cm07.pdf.

U.S. Department of Health and Human Services, Health Resources and Services Administration. (2009b). *Children of foreign-born parents.* Retrieved March 3, 2010, from http://mchb.hrsa.gov/chus08/popchar/pages/102fbp.html.

U.S. Department of Health and Human Services, Administration on Children, Youth, and Families. (2005). *Child maltreatment 2003.* Washington, DC: U.S. Government Printing Office.

U.S. Department of Health and Human Services, Health Resources and Services Administration. (2009c). *Life expectancy.* Retrieved January 8, 2010, from http://mchb.hrsa.gov/whusa09/hstat/hi/pages/2071e.html.

U.S. Department of Health and Human Services/U.S. Department of Agriculture. (2005). *Dietary guidelines for Americans 2005.* Retrieved November 15, 2006, from http://www.healthierus.gov/dietaryguidelines.

U.S. Department of Justice Bureau of Justice Statistics. (2000). *Women ages 16 to 24 experience the highest rates of violence by current or former partners.* Washington, DC: Author.

U.S. Federal Bureau of Prisons. (1998). *A profile of female offenders.* Washington, DC: Author.

U.S. Department of Labor. Bureau of Labor Statistics. (2009). *Labor force statistics from the current population.* Retrieved January 5, 2010, from http://www.bls.gov/cps/.

U.S. Social Security Administration. (2009). *Social security online.* Retrieved March 3, 2010, http://www.ssa.gov/retire2/agereducation.htm.

Vaage, A. B., Garløv, C., Hauff, E., & Thomsen. P. H. (2007). Psychiatric symptoms and service utilization among refugee children referred to a child psychiatry department: A retrospective comparative case note study. *Transcultural Psychiatry, 44*(3), 440–458.

Vahtera, J., Kivimaki, M., Vaananen, A., Linna, A., Pentti, J. L., Helenius, H., et al. (2006). Sex differences in health effects of family death or illness: Are women more vulnerable than men? *Psychosomatic Medicine, 68*(2), 283–289.

Vaillant, G. (1977). *Adaptation to life.* Boston: Little, Brown.

Vaillant, G. (1993). *The wisdom of the ego.* Cambridge, MA: Harvard University Press.

Vaillant, G. (2002). *Aging well: Surprising guideposts to a happier life from the Landmark Harvard Study of Adult Development.* Boston: Little, Brown.

Vallacher, R., & Nowak, A. (1998). *Dynamical social psychology.* New York: Guilford.

Valsiner, J. (1989). *Human development and culture: The social nature of personality and its study.* Lexington, MA: Lexington Books.

Valsiner, J. (2000). *Culture and human development.* Thousand Oaks, CA: Sage.

Van Ausdale, D., & Feagin, J. (1996). Using racial and ethnic concepts: The critical case of very young children. *American Sociological Review, 61,* 119–269.

van de Beek, C., Thijssen J. H., Cohen-Kettenis, P. T., van Goozen, S. H., & Buitelaar, J. K. (2004). Relationships between sex hormones assessed in amniotic fluid, and maternal and umbilical cord serum: What is the best source of information to investigate the effects of fetal hormonal exposure? *Hormones and Behavior, 46*(5), 663–669.

Vandell, D. L., & Wolfe, B. (2000). *Child care quality: Does it matter and does it need to be improved?* (Special Report #78). Madison, WI: Institute for Research on Poverty.

van den Akker, O. B. (2005). Coping, quality of life, and psychological symptoms in three groups of sub-fertile women. *Patient Education and Counseling, 57*(2), 183–189.

van der Hulst, L. A., van Teijlingen, E. R., & Bonsel, G. J. (2004). Does a pregnant woman's intended place of birth influence her attitudes toward and occurrence of obstetric interventions? *Birth: Issues in Perinatal Care, 31*(1), 28–33.

van der Spuy, Z. M., & Dyer, S. J. (2004). The pathogenesis of infertility and early pregnancy loss in polycystic ovary syndrome. *Best Practice and Research: Clinical Obstetrics and Gynaecology, 18*(5), 755–771.

Van der Vegt, G., Eman, B., & Van De Vliert, E. (2001). Patterns of interdependence in work teams: A two-level investigation of the relations with job and team satisfaction. *Personnel Psychology, 54,* 51–69.

Van der Wijden, C. A., Keijnen, J., & Van den Berk, T. (2003). Lactational amenorrhea for family planning. *Cochrane Database Systematic Review,* Issue 3, CD001329.

Vandivere, S., Moore, K. A., & Brown, B. (2000). Child well-being at the outset of welfare reform: An overview of the nation and 13 states. *New Federalism, National Survey of American Families,* Series B, No. B-23. Washington, DC: The Urban Institute.

VanLaningham, J., Johnson, D., & Amato, P. (2001). Marital happiness, marital duration, and the u-shaped curve: Evidence from a five-wave panel study. *Social Forces, 78*(4), 1313–1341.

Van Naarden Braun, K., Yeargin-Allsopp, M., & Lollar, D. (2006). Factors associated with leisure activity among young adults with developmental disabilities. *Research in Developmental Disabilities, 27,* 567–583.

Van Naarden Braun, K., Yeargin-Allsopp, M., & Lollar, D. (2009). Activity limitations among young adults with developmental disabilities: A population-based follow-up study. *Research in Developmental Disabilities, 30,* 179–191.

Van Voorhees, E., & Scarpa, A. (2004). The effects of child maltreatment on the hypothalamic-pituitary-adrenal axis. *Trauma Violence Abuse, 5*(4), 333–352.

Van Voorhis, B. (2006). Outcomes from assisted reproductive technology. *Obstetrics & Gynecology, 107*(1), 183–200.

Varney, D., & van Vliet, W. (2008). Homelessness, children, and youth: Research in the United States and Canada. *American Behavioral Scientist, 51,* 715–720.

Vaughn, B., & Bost, K. (1999). Attachment and temperament. In J. Cassidy & P. Shaver (Eds.), *Handbook of attachment: Theory, research, and clinical applications* (pp. 198–225). New York: Guilford.

Vazsonyi, S., & Snider, J. B. (2008). Mentoring, competencies, and adjustment in adolescents: American part-time employment and European apprenticeships. *International Journal of Behavioral Development, 32*(1), 46–55.

Vekemans, M. (1996). Cytogenetics. In J. J. Sciarra (Ed.), *Gynecology and obstetrics* (Rev. ed., pp. 57–66). Philadelphia: Lippincott-Raven.

Vellery-Rodot, R. T. (1926). *The life of Pasteur.* Garden City, NY: Doubleday.

Veltkamp, L., & Miller, T. (1994). *Clinical handbook of child abuse and neglect.* Madison, CT: International Universities Press.

Ventura, S. J. (2009). *Changing patterns of nonmarital childbearing in the United States.* Centers for Disease Control and Prevention. Retrieved December 5, 2009, from http://www.cdc.gov/nchs/data/databriefs/db18.htm.

Ventura, S. J., Abma, J. C., Mosher, W. D., & Henshaw, S. K. (2008). Estimated pregnancy rates by outcome for the United States, 1990–2004. *National Vital Statistics Reports, 56*(15), Hyattsville, MD: National Center for Health Statistics.

Ventura, S. J., Martin, J. A., Curtin, S. C., & Mathews, T. J. (1998). Report of final natality statistics: 1996. *Monthly Vital Statistics Report, 46*(225), 1–99.

Verhaak, C., Smeenk, J., Evers, A., van Minnen, A., Kremer, J., & Kraaimaat, F. (2005). Predicting emotional response to unsuccessful fertility treatment: A prospective study. *Journal of Behavioral Medicine, 28*(2), 181–190.

Verkuyten, M. (2005). Ethnic group identification and group evaluation among minority and majority groups: Testing the multiculturalism hypothesis. *Journal of Personality and Social Psychology, 88*(1), 121–138.

Verma, S., & Larson, R. (Eds.). (2003). *Examining adolescent leisure time across cultures. New directions for child and adolescent development, No. 99.* San Francisco: Jossey-Bass.

Vikat, A., Speder, Z., Beets, G., Billari, F., & Buhler, C. (2007). Generations and Gender Survey (GGS): Towards a better understanding of relationships and processes in the life course. *Demographic Research Online, 17,* 389–440.

Villarruel, F., Perkins, D., Borden, L., & Keith, J. (2003*). Community youth development: Programs, policies, and practice.* Thousand Oaks, CA: Sage.

Volgt, M., Hermanussen, M., Wittwer-Backofen, U., Fusch, C., & Hesse, V. (2006). Sex-specific differences in birth weight due to maternal smoking during pregnancy. *European Journal of Pediatrics, 165*(110), 757–761.

Volker, D. L. (2005). Control and end-of-life care: Does ethnicity matter? *American Journal of Hospice & Palliative Care, 22*(6), 442–446.

Volkmar, F. R., Paul, R., Klin, A., & Cohen, D. J. (2005). *Handbook of autism and pervasive developmental disorders.* Hoboken, NJ: John Wiley.

Volling, B., Blandon, A., & Kolak, A. (2006). Marriage, parenting, and the emergence of early self-regulation in the family system. *Journal of Child and Family Studies, 15*(4), 493–506.

von Salisch, M. (2001). Children's emotional development: Challenges in their relationships to parents, peers, and friends. *International Journal of Behavioral Development, 25,* 310–319.

Voorpostel, M., & van der Lippe, T. (2007). Support between siblings and between friends: Two worlds apart? *Journal of Marriage and Family, 69,* 1271–1282.

Vuorenkoski, L., Kuure, O., Moilanen, I., Penninkilampi, V., & Myhrman, A. (2000). Bilingualism, school achievement, and mental wellbeing: A follow-up study of return migrant children. *Journal of Child Psychology and Psychiatry and Allied Disciplines, 41*(2), 261–266.

Vygotsky, L. (1986). *Thought and language.* Cambridge, MA: MIT Press.

Wachs, T. D. (2000). *Necessary but not sufficient: The respective roles of single and multiple influences on individual development.* Washington, DC: American Psychological Association.

Wacker, R., & Roberto, K. (2008). *Community resources for older adults: Programs and services in an era of change* (3rd ed.). Thousand Oaks, CA: Sage.

Wadensten, B. (2005). Introducing older people to the theory of gerotranscendence. *Journal of Advanced Nursing, 52*(4), 381–388.

Wagener, L., Furrow, J., King, P., Leffert, N., & Benson, P. (2003). Religion and developmental resources. *Review of Religious Research, 44*(3), 271–284.

Wagner, M., Newman, L., Cameto, R., & Levine, P. (2005). *Changes over time in the early postschool outcomes of youth with disabilities.* Menlo Park, CA: SRI International.

Wahl, H., & Kruse, A. (2005). Historical perspectives of middle age within the life span. In S. Willis & M. Martin (Eds.), *Middle adulthood: A lifespan perspective* (pp. 3–34). Thousand Oaks, CA: Sage.

Waldenstrom, U., Hildingsson, I, Rubertsson, C., & Radestad, I. (2004). A negative birth experience: Prevalence and risk factors in a national sample. *Birth: Issues in Prenatal Care, 31*(4), 17–27.

Walker, A., Manoogian-O'Dell, M., McGraw, L., & White, D. (2001). *Families in later life: Connections and transitions.* Thousand Oaks, CA: Pine Forge.

Walker, L. (1989). A longitudinal study of moral reasoning. *Child Development, 5,* 33–78.

Walker, L., & Taylor, J. (1991). Family interactions and the development of moral reasoning. *Child Development, 62,* 262–283.

Walker, S., Berthelsen, D., & Irving, K. (2001). Temperament and peer acceptance in early childhood: Sex and social status differences. *Child Study Journal, 31*(3), 177–192.

Waller, T. (2009). Modern childhood: Contemporary theories and children's lives. In T. Waller (Ed.), *An introduction to early childhood* (2nd ed., pp. 2–15). Thousand Oaks, CA: Sage.

Wallerstein, I. (1974). *The modern world system: Capitalist agriculture and the origins of the European world economy in the 16th century.* New York: Academic Press.

Wallerstein, I. (1979). *The capitalist world economy.* London: Cambridge University Press.

Wallerstein, J. S., & Blakeslee, S. (1989). *Second chances: Men, women and children a decade after divorce.* New York: Ticknor & Fields.

Wallerstein, J. S., & Corbin, S. (1991). The child and the vicissitudes of divorce. In M. Lewis (Ed.), *Child and adolescent psychiatry: A comprehensive textbook* (pp. 1108–1118). Baltimore, MD: Williams & Wilkins.

Wallerstein, J. S., Corbin, S., & Lewis, J. (1988). Children of divorce: A ten year study. In E. Hetherington & J. Arasteh (Eds.), *Impact of divorce, single-parenting and step-parenting on children* (pp. 198–214). Hillsdale, NJ: Lawrence Erlbaum.

Walling, A. D. (2001). What is optimal strategy in diagnosing ectopic pregnancy? *American Family Physician, 64*(18), 1420–1421.

Walsh, F. (2005). Families in later life: Challenges and opportunities. In B. Carter & M. McGoldrick (Eds.), *The expanded family life style: Individual, family, and social perspectives* (3rd ed., pp. 307–326). Boston: Allyn & Bacon.

Walsh, F. (2006). *Strengthening family resilience* (2nd ed.). New York: Guilford.

Wang, H., Chung, U., Sung, M., & Wu, S. (2006). Development of a web-based childbirth education program for vaginal birth after c-section (vbac) mothers. *Journal of Nursing Research, 14*(1), 1–7.

Wang, H., Parry, S., Macones, G., Sammel, M. D., Kuivaniemi, H., Tromp, G., et al. (2006). A functional SNP in the promoter of the *SERPINH1* gene increases risk of preterm premature rupture of membranes in African Americans. *Proceedings of the National Academy of Sciences of the United States of America (PNMS), 103*(36), 13463–13467.

Wang, M., Walberg, H., & Reynolds, A. (2004). *Can unlike students learn together? Grade retention, tracking, and grouping.* Charlotte, NC: Information Age Publishing.

Wang, R., Needham, L., & Barr, D. (2005). Effects of environmental agents on attainment of puberty: Considerations when assessing exposure to environmental chemicals in the National Children's Study. *Environmental Health Perspectives, 113*(8), 1100–1107.

Wang, Y., & Zhang, Q. (2006). Are American children and adolescents of low socioeconomic status at increased risk of obesity? Changes in the association between overweight and family income between 1971 and 2002. *American Journal of Clinical Nutrition, 84*(4), 707–716.

Ward, R. R., Logan, J., & Spitze, G. (1992). The influence of parent and child needs on coresidence in middle and later life. *Journal of Marriage and the Family, 54,* 209–221.

Watkins, D. R. (2001). Spirituality in social work practice with older persons. In D. O. Moberg (Ed.), *Aging and spirituality: Spiritual dimensions of aging theory, research, practice, and policy* (pp. 133–146). New York: Haworth Pastoral.

Watkins, K. J., & Baldo, T. D. (2004). The infertility experience; Biopsychosocial effects and suggestions for counselors. *Journal of Counseling and Development, 82(*4), 394–409.

Watson, J., & Crick, F. (1953). Molecular structure of nucleic acids. *Nature, 171,* 737–738.

Weaver-Hightower, M. (2003). The "boy turn" in research on gender and education. *Review of Educational Research, 73*(4), 471–498.

Webb. N., & Dumpson, J. (2006). *Working with traumatized youth in child welfare.* New York: Guilford.

Weibel-Orlando, J. (2001). Grandparenting styles: Native American perspectives. In A. Walker, M. Manoogian-O'Dell, L. McGraw, & D. White (Eds.), *Families in later life: Connections and transitions* (pp. 139–145). Thousand Oaks, CA: Pine Forge.

Weichold, K. (2007). Prevention against substance misuse: Life skills and positive youth development. In R. Silbereisen & R. Lerner (Ed.), *Approaches to positive youth development* (pp. 293–310). Thousand Oaks, CA: Sage.

Weinberg, M., Williams, C., & Pryor, D. (2001). Bisexuals at midlife. *Journal of Contemporary Ethnography, 30*(2), 180–208.

Weingartner, N. (2008, October 27). Ohio woman, 56, gives birth to her granddaughters. *Digital Journal.* Retrieved May 19, 2010, from http://www.digitaljournal.com/article/261656.

Weininger, E., & Lareau, A. (2009). Paradoxical pathways: An ethnographic extension of Kohn's findings on class and child-rearing. *Journal of Marriage and Family, 71,* 680–695.

Weinman, M. L., Buzi, R. S., & Smith, P. B. (2005). Addressing risk behaviors, service needs, and mental health issues in programs for young fathers. *Families in Society, 86*(2), 261–266.

Weinstock, H., Berman, S., & Cates, W. (2004). Sexually transmitted diseases among American youth: Incidence and prevalence estimates, 2000. *Perspectives on Sexual and Reproductive Health, 36*(1), 6–10.

Weisglas-Kuperus, N., Hille, E. T., Duivenboorden. H. J., Finken, M. J., Wit, J. M., Van Buuren, S., et al. (2009). Intelligence of very preterm or very low birthweight infants in young adulthood. *Archives of Disease in Childhood, 94*(3), 196–200.

Weisman, C. S., Hillemeier, M. M., Chase, G. A., Dyere, A. M., Baker, S. A., Feinberg, M., et al. (2006). Preconceptual health: Risks of adverse pregnancy outcomes by reproductive live stages in central Pennsylvania. *Women's Health Issues, 16*(4), 216–224.

Weisner, T. (2005). Attachment as cultural and ecological problem with pluralistic solutions. *Human Development, 48,* 89–94.

Weissberg, R., & O'Brien, M. (2004). What works in school-based social and emotional learning programs for positive youth development. *Annals of the American Academy of Political and Social Science, 591,* 86–97.

Wellons, M. F., Lewis, C. E., Schwartz, S. M., Gunderson, E. P., Schreiner, P. J., Sternfeld, B., et al. (2008). Racial differences in self-reported infertility and risk factors for infertility in a cohort of black and white women: The CARDIA women's study. *Fertility and Sterility, 90*(5), 1640–1648.

Welner, S. L. (1997). Gynecologic care and sexuality issues for women with disabilities. *Sexuality and Disability, 15*(10) 33–40

Welsh, R. (1985). Spanking: A grand old American tradition? *Children Today, 14*(1), 25–29.

Wenstrom, K. D. (2009). A randomized, controlled trial of magnesium sulfate for the prevention of cerebral palsy. *Obstetrical and Gynecological Survey, 65*(10), 15–17.

Werner, E. (2000). Protective factors and individual resilience. In J. Shonkoff & S. Meisels (Eds.), *Handbook of early childhood intervention* (2nd ed., pp. 115–132). New York: Cambridge University Press.

Werner, E., Dawson, G., Osterling, J., & Dinno, N. (2000). Brief report: Recognition of autism spectrum disorder before one year of age: A retrospective study based on home videotapes. *Journal of Autism & Developmental Disorders, 30*(2), 157–162.

Werner, E. E., & Smith, R. S. (1992). *Overcoming the odds: High risk children from birth to adulthood.* Ithaca, NY: Cornell University Press.

Werner, E. E., & Smith, R. S. (2001). *Journeys from childhood to midlife.* Ithaca, NY: Cornell University Press.

Wertheimer, R. (2003). *Poor families in 2001: Parents working less and children continue to lag behind.* Washington, DC: Child Trends. Retrieved January 15, 2007, from http://www.childtrends.org/Files/PoorFamiliesRB.pdf.

Wertsch, J. V., del Rio, P., & Alvarez, A. (Eds.). (1995). *Sociocultural studies of the mind.* New York: Cambridge University Press.

Wetherby, A., Woods, J., Allen, L., Cleary, J., Dickinson, H., & Lord, C. (2004). Early indicators of autism spectrum disorders in the second year of life. *Journal of Autism & Developmental Disorders, 34*(5), 473–493.

Wethington, E., Kessler, R., & Pixley, J. (2004). Turning points in adulthood. In O. Brim, C. Ryff, & R. Kessler (Eds.), *How healthy are we? A national study of well-being at midlife* (pp. 586–613). Chicago: University of Chicago Press.

Weyermann, M., Beermann, C., Brenner, H., & Rothenbacher, D. (2006). Adponectin and leptin in maternal serum, cord blood, and breast milk. *Clinical Chemistry, 52*(11), 2095–2102.

Whalley, L. (2001). *The aging brain.* New York: Columbia University Press.

Whitbourne, S. (1986). *The me I know: A study of adult identity.* New York: Springer Verlag.

Whitbourne, S. (2001). The physical aging process in midlife: Interactions with psychological and sociocultural factors. In M. Lachman (Ed.), *Handbook of midlife development* (pp. 109–155). New York: Wiley.

Whitbourne, S., & Connolly, L. (1999). The developing self in midlife. In S. Willis & J. Reid (Eds.), *Life in the middle: Psychological and social development in middle age* (pp. 25–45). San Diego, CA: Academic Press.

Whitbourne, S., & Willis, S. (Eds.), (2006). *The baby boomers grow up: Contemporary perspectives on midlife.* Mahwah, NJ: Lawrence Erlbaum.

White, L., Small, B. J., Petrovitch, H., Ross, G. W., Masaki, K., Abbott, R., et al. (2005). Recent clinical-pathologic research on the causes of dementia in late life: Update from the Honolulu-Asia aging study. *Journal of Geriatric Psychiatry and Neurology, 18*(4), 224–227.

White, N. R. (2003). Changing conceptions: Young people's views of partnering & parenting. *Journal of Sociology, 39*(2), 149–164.

Whiting, E., & Ward, C. (2008). Food insecurity and provisioning. In D. R. Crane & T. Heaton (Eds.), *Handbook of families & poverty* (pp. 198–219). Thousand Oaks, CA: Sage.

Wichstrom, L. (2001). The impact of pubertal timing on adolescents' alcohol use. *Journal of Research on Adolescence, 11,* 130–150.

Wickrama, K. A. S., Conger, R. D., & Abraham, W. T. (2005). Early adversity and later health: The intergenerational transmission of adversity through mental disorder and physical illness. *The Journal of Gerontology: Series B Psychological Sciences and Social Sciences, 60B,* 125–129.

Widmayer, S., Peterson, L., & Larner, M. (1990). Predictors of Haitian-American infant development at twelve months. *Child Development, 61,* 410–415.

Wigert, H., Johannson, R., Berg, M., & Hellstrom, A. L. (2006). Mothers' experiences of having their children in a neonatal intensive care unit. *Scandinavian Journal of Caring Sciences, 20*(10), 35–41.

Wight, V., & Chau, M. (2009a). *Basic facts about low-income children, 2008: Children under age 6.* National Center for Children in Poverty. Retrieved February 17, 2010, from http://www.nccp.org/publications/pdf.text_896.pdf.

Wight, V. R. & Chau, M. (2009b). *Basic facts about low-income children: Children under age 18.* New York: National Center for Children in Poverty. Retrieved February 17, 2010, from http://www.nccp.org/publications/pub_892.html.

Wight, V., Chau, M., & Aratani, Y. (2010). *Who are America's poor children? The official story.* New York: National Center for Children in Poverty. Retrieved February 13, 2010, from http://www.nccp.org/publications/pdf/text_912.pdf.

Wilber, K. (2000). *Integral psychology: Consciousness, spirit, psychology, therapy.* Boston: Shambhala.

Wilber, K. (2001). *A theory of everything: An integral vision for business, politics, science, and spirituality.* Boston: Shambhala.

Wilcox, T., Woods, R., Tuggy, L., & Napoli, R. (2006). Shake, rattle, and . . . one or two objects? Young infants' use of auditory information to individuate objects. *Infancy, 9,* 97–123.

Wilde-Mathews, A. (2009, May 7). Tallying the cost to bring baby home. *Wall Street Journal, 253*(106), pp. D1–D7.

Wilkes, S., & Murdoch, A. (2009). Obesity and female fertility: A primary care perspective. *The Journal of Family Planning and Reproductive Health Care, 35*(5), 181–185.

William T. Grant Foundation, Commission on Work, Family, and Citizenship. (1988). *The forgotten half: Pathways to success for America's youth and young families.* New York: Author.

Williams, D. R. (2005). The health of U.S. racial and ethnic populations. *The Journal of Gerontology: Series B: Psychological Sciences and Social Sciences, 60B,* 53–63.

Williams, J. (2000). *Unbending gender: Why family and work conflict and what to do about it.* New York: Oxford University Press.

Willinger, M., Ko., C., & Reddy, U. (2009). Racial disparities in stillbirth across gestation in the United States. *American Journal of Obstetrics and Gynecology, 201*(5), 469.e1–469.e8.

Willis, S., & Martin, M. (Eds.). (2005). *Middle adulthood: A lifespan perspective.* Thousand Oaks, CA: Sage.

Willis, S., & Schaie, K. W. (2005). Cognitive trajectories in midlife and cognitive functioning in old age. In S. Willis & M. Martin (Eds.), *Middle adulthood: A lifespan perspective* (pp. 243–275). Thousand Oaks, CA: Sage.

Willis, S., & Schaie, K. (2006). Cognitive functioning in the baby boomers: Longitudinal and cohort effects. In S. Whitbourne & S. Willis (Eds.), *The baby boomers grow up: Contemporary perspectives on midlife* (pp. 205–234). Mahwah, NJ: Lawrence Erlbaum.

Wilmoth, J. M., & Longino, C. F. (2006). Demographic trends that will shape U.S. policy in the twenty-first century. *Research on Aging, 28*(3), 269–288.

Wilson, J. F., & Kopitzke, E. J. (2002). Stress and infertility. *Current Women's Health Reports, 2*(3), 194–200.

Wilson, R. (1966). *Feminine forever.* New York: M. Evans.

Wilson, S. (2009). *Fallopian tubes and intrafallopian transfer.* Retrieved May 21, 2010, from http://ezinearticles.com/?Fallopian-Tubes-and-Intrafallopian-Transfer=2875716.

Wimmer, H., & Perner, J. (1983). Beliefs about beliefs: Representation and constraining function of wrong beliefs in young children's understanding of deception. *Cognition, 13,* 104–128.

Wimpory, D., Hobson, R., Williams, J., & Nash, S. (2000). Are infants with autism socially engaged? A study of recent retrospective parental reports. *Journal of Autism & Developmental Disorders, 30,* 525–536.

Wingate, M. S., & Alexander, G. R. (2006). Racial and ethnic differences in perinatal mortality: The role of fetal death. *Annals of Epidemiology, 16*(6), 485–491.

Wink, P., & Dillon, M. (2002). Spiritual development across the adult life course: Findings from a longitudinal study. *Journal of Adult Development, 9*(1), 79–94.

Winkler, I., & Cowan, N. (2005). From sensory to long-term memory: Evidence from auditory memory reactivation studies. *Experimental Psychology, 52*(1), 3–20.

Winters, W. G. (1993). *African American mothers and urban schools: The power of participation.* New York: Lexington Books.

Wischmann, T., Scherg, H., Strowitzki, T., & Verres, R. (2009). Psychosocial characteristics of women and men attending infertility counseling. *Human Reproduction, 24*(2), 378–386.

Wiseman, R. (2002). *Queen bees and wannabes: Helping your daughter survive cliques, gossip, boyfriends, and other realities of adolescence.* New York: Crown Publishers.

Wismont, J. D. (2000). The lived pregnancy experience of women in prison. *Journal of Midwifery and Women's Health, 45*(4), 292–300.

Wisner, K., Chambers, C., & Sit, D. (2006). Postpartum depression: A major public health problem. *Journal of American Medical Association, 296*(21), 2616–2618.

Wockel, A., Shafer, E., Beggel, A., & Abou-Dakn, M. (2007). Getting ready for birth: Impending fatherhood. *British Journal of Midwifery 15*(6), 344–348.

Wojslawowicz Bowker, J., Rubin, K., Burgess, K., Booth-Laforce, C., & Rose-Krasnor, L. (2006). Behavioral characteristics associated with stable and fluid best friendship patterns in middle childhood. *Merrill-Palmer Quarterly, 52*(4), 671–693.

Wolak, J., Mitchell, K. J., & Finkelhor, D. (2003). Escaping or connecting? Characteristics of youth who form close online relationships. *Journal of Adolescence, 26,* 105–119.

Wolak, J., Mitchell, K. J., & Finkelhor, D. (2006). *Online victimization of youth: Five years later.* Retrieved November 15, 2006, from http://www.unh.edu/ccrc/pdf/CV138.pdf.

Wolfner, G., & Gelles, R. (1993). A profile of violence toward children: A national study. *Child Abuse and Neglect, 17,* 197–212.

Woody, D. J., & Green, R. (2001). The influence of race/ethnicity and gender on psychological and social well-being. *Journal of Ethnic & Cultural Diversity in Social Work, 9*(3/4), 151–166.

Wooldredge, J. D., & Masters, K. (1993). Confronting problems faced by pregnant inmates in state prisons. *Crime and Delinquency, 39*(2), 195–203.

Woollett, A., Dosanjh-Matwala, N., Nicolson, P., Marshall, H., Djhanbakhch, O., & Hadlow, J. (1995). The ideas and experiences of pregnancy and childbirth of Asian and non-Asian women in East London. *British Journal of Medical Psychology, 68,* 65–84.

Worden, J. W. (2009). *Grief counseling and grief therapy: A handbook for the mental health practitioner* (4th ed.). New York: Springer Publishing Co.

World Bank. (2009). *Global monitoring report, 2009: A development emergency.* NYC: World Bank. Retrieved January 19, 2010, from http://go.worldbank.org/AR2V89HT70.

World Health Organization. (2003). *The world health report 2003.* Geneva, Switzerland: Author.

World Health Organization. (2004). *Unsafe abortion: Global and regional estimates of unsafe abortion and associated mortality in 2000.* Retrieved January 14, 2006, from http://www.who.int/reproductive-ealth/publications/ unsafe_aboriton_estimates_04/estimates.pdf.

World Health Organization. (2008). *Global burden of disease 2004 update.* Retrieved August 26, 2009, from http://www.who/healthinfo/global_burden_disease/en.

World Health Organization Multicentre Growth Reference Study Group. (2006a). Assessment of differences in linear growth among populations in the WHO Multicentre Growth Reference Study. *Acta Paediatrica, Supplement, 450,* 56–65.

World Health Organization Multicentre Growth Reference Study Group. (2006b). WHO motor development study: Windows of achievement for six gross motor developmental milestones. *Acta Paediatrica, Supplement, 450,* 86–95.

World Health Organization Multicentre Growth Reference Study Group. (2006c). Assessment of sex differences and heterogeneity in motor milestone attainment among populations in the WHO Multicentre Growth Reference Study. *Acta Paediatrica, Supplement, 450,* 66–75.

Wortman, C., & Silver, R. (1989). The myths of coping with loss. *Journal of Consulting and Clinical Psychology, 57,* 349–357.

Wortman, C., & Silver, R. (1990). Successful mastery of bereavement and widowhood. A life course perspective. In P. Baltes & M. Baltes (Eds.), *Successful aging: Perspectives from the behavioral sciences* (pp. 225–264). Cambridge, UK: Cambridge University Press.

Wrigley, E. (1966). Family limitation in pre-industrial England. *Economic History Review, 19,* 82–109.

Wyman, P. A., Cross, W., & Barry, J. (2004). Applying research on resilience to enhance school-based prevention: The promoting resilient children initiative. In C. S. Clauss-Ehlers & M. D. Weist (Eds.), *Community planning to foster resilience in children* (pp. 249–266). New York: Kluwer Academic/Plenum Publishers.

Xie, H., Cairns, B. D., & Cairns, R. B. (2001). Predicting teen motherhood and teen fatherhood: Individual characteristics and peer affiliations. *Social Development, 10,* 488–511.

Yeo, S., & Maeda, Y. (2000). Japanese couples' childbirth experiences in Michigan: Implications for care. *Birth: Issues in Prenatal Care, 27*(3), 191–195.

Young, K. R., Marchant, M., & Wilder, L. K. (2004). School-based interventions for students with emotional and behavioral disorders. In P. Allen-Meares & M. W. Fraser (Eds.), *Intervention with children and adolescents: An interdisciplinary perspective* (pp. 175–204). Boston: Allyn & Bacon.

Yu, C. K., Teoh, T. G., & Robinson, S. (2006). Obesity in pregnancy. *British Journal and Obstetrics and Gynaecology: An International Journal of Obstetrics and Gynaecology, 113*(10), 1117–1125.

Zagorsky, J. (2005). Marriage and divorce's impact on wealth. *Journal of Sociology, 41*(4), 406–424.

Zangaglia, R., Pacchetti, C., Pasotti, C., Mancini, F., Servello, D., Sinforiani, E., et al. (2009). Deep brain stimulation and cognitive functions in Parkinson's disease: A three year controlled study. *Movement Disorder, 11,* 1621–1628.

Zaslow, M. J., & Emig, C. A. (1997). When low-income mothers go to work: Implications for children. *Future of Children, 7*(1), 110–115.

Zeisel, J. (2006). *Inquiry by design: Environment/behavior/neuroscience in architecture, interiors, landscape, and planning* (Rev. ed.). New York: W.W. Norton.

Zeiss, A. M., & Kasl-Godley, J. (2001). Sexuality in older adults' relationships. *Generations, 25*(2), 18–25.

Zellman, G. L., & Waterman, J. M. (1998). Understanding the impact of parent school involvement on children's educational outcomes. *Journal of Educational Research, 91*(6), 370–380.

Zero to Three. (n.d.). *Baby matters: A gateway to state policies and initiatives.* Retrieved May 21, 2010, from http://policy .db/zerotothree.org/policyp/home.aspx.

Ziel, H., & Finkle, W. (1975). Increased risk of endometrial carcinoma among users of conjugated estrogens. *New England Journal of Medicine, 293*(23), 1167–1170.

Zigler, E., Finn-Stevenson, M., & Hall, N. (2002). *The first three years and beyond: Brain development and social policy.* Chicago: R. R. Donnelly & Sons.

Ziolko, M. E. (1993). Counseling parents of children with disabilities: A review of the literature and implications for practice. In M. Nagler (Ed.), *Perspectives on disability* (2nd ed., pp. 185–193). Palo Alto, CA: Health Markets Research.

Zipper, I., & Simeonsson, R. (2004). Developmental vulnerability in young children with disabilities. In M. Fraser (Ed.), *Risk and resilience in childhood: An ecological perspective* (2nd ed., pp. 161–181). Washington, DC: NASW.

Ziv, M., & Frye, D. (2003). The relation between desire and false belief in children's theory of mind: No satisfaction? *Developmental Psychology, 39,* 859–876.

Zucca, P., Milos, N., & Vallortigara, G. (2007). Piagetian object permanence and its development in Eurasian jays. *Animal Cognition, 10*(2), 243–258.

Zucker, A., Ostrove, J., & Stewart, A. (2002). College-educated women's personality development in adulthood: Perceptions and age differences. *Psychology and Aging, 17*(2), 236–244.

Zuniga, M. (1992). Families with Latino roots. In E. Lynch & M. Hanson (Eds.), *Developing cross-cultural competence: A guide for working with young children and their families* (pp. 151–179). Baltimore, MD: Paul H. Brookes.

Zutlevics, T. (2006). Should ART be offered to HIV-serodiscordant and HIV-seroconcordant couples: An ethical discussion. *Human Reproduction, 21*(8), 1956–1960.

Zwelling, E. (1996). Childbirth education in the 1990s and beyond. *Journal of Gynecologic and Neonatal Nursing, 17*(2), 108–112.

Glossary

Accommodation (identity) Process in which an individual changes some aspect of identity in response to new experiences

Acculturation Process by which two or more cultures remain distinct but exchange cultural features (such as foods, music, clothing)

Acquaintance rape Forced, manipulated, or coerced sexual contact by someone you know

Activities of daily living (ADLs) Basic self-care activities, such as bathing, dressing, walking a short distance, shifting from a bed to a chair, using the toilet, and eating

Activity theory (of aging) A theory of aging that proposes that higher levels of activity and involvement are directly related to higher levels of satisfaction in older adults

Advance directives Documents that give instructions about desired health care if, in the future, an individual cannot speak for herself or himself

Age norm The behaviors expected of people of a specific age in a given society at a particular point in time

Age stratification perspective Theory of social gerontology proposed by Riley (1971) and Foner (1995). Similar to the way society is structured by socioeconomic class, it is also stratified by age. Roles and rights of individuals are assigned based on their membership in an age group or cohort. Individuals proceed through their life course as part of that cohort. Theory falls into the tradition of the life course perspective

Age structuring The standardizing of the ages at which social role transitions occur, by developing policies and laws that regulate the timing of these transitions

Alzheimer's disease The most common type of dementia, a progressive and incurable deterioration of key areas of the brain

Anorexia nervosa An eating disorder characterized by a dysfunctional body image and voluntary starvation in the pursuit of weight loss

Assimilation (culture) Process by which the minority culture must adapt and become incorporated into the majority culture

Assimilation (identity) Process by which individuals incorporate new experiences into their existing identity

Assisted reproductive technologies (ART) A range of techniques to help women who are infertile to conceive and give birth

Attachment An enduring emotional bond between two people who are important to each other. Provides affection and a sense of security

Authoritarian parenting A parenting style, identified by Baumrind, that involves unresponsive, inflexible, harsh, and controlling interactions with the child

Authoritative parenting A parenting style, identified by Baumrind, that involves responsive and supportive interactions with the child while also setting firm limits. Thought to be the most effective parenting style

Bereavement The state of having suffered a loss

Biological age A person's level of biological development and physical health, as measured by the functioning of the various organ systems

Blooming A period of overproduction of brain synapses during infancy, followed by a period of synapse pruning

Brain plasticity The ability of the brain to change in response to stimuli

Bulimia nervosa An eating disorder characterized by a cycle of binge eating; feelings of guilt, depression, or self-disgust; and purging

Capital A term used in different ways by different disciplines, but generally refers to having the potential, capacity, and resources to function, produce, or succeed; in the social sciences, refers to possession of attributes associated with civic engagement and economic success

Cerebral cortex The outer layer of gray matter in the human brain thought to be responsible for complex, high-level intellectual functions such as memory, language, and reasoning

Character education The direct teaching and curriculum inclusions of mainstream values thought to be universal by a community (e.g., kindness, respect, tolerance, and honesty)

Child maltreatment Physical, emotional, and sexual abuse and neglect of children, most often by adult caregivers. Definitions vary by culture and professional discipline but typically entail harm, or threatened harm, to the child

Chromosomes Threadlike structures composed of DNA and proteins that carry genes and that are found within each body cell nucleus

Cognition Ability to process and store information and solve problems. Commonly called thinking

Cohort Group of persons who are born in the same time period and who are of the same age group at the time of specific historical events and social changes

Cohort effects The effects of social change on a specific cohort

Community assets Community resources such as public infrastructure (e.g., adequate transportation to get to work), community networks, and educational opportunities

Concrete operations stage The third stage in Piaget's theory of cognitive development. School-age children (ages 7 to 11) begin to use logical reasoning, but their thinking is not yet abstract

Conjunctive faith The fifth faith stage in James Fowler's theory of faith development, a stage when individuals look for balance among competing moral systems, recognize that there are many truths, and open themselves in service to others

Contextual model Avshalom Caspi's model of personality, which proposes that personality is stable across the life course because individuals choose environments that reinforce their personal styles

Continuity theory (of aging) Theory of social gerontology initially proposed by Neugarten, Havighurst, and Tobin (1968) in response to critiques of the disengagement and activity theories. Individuals adapt to changes by using the same coping styles they have used throughout the life course, with new roles serving as substitutes for roles lost because of age

Convoy A person's network of social relationships that protects, defends, aids, and socializes

Coping mechanism Strategy used to master the demands of life

Crystallized intelligence The ability to use knowledge from accumulated learning

Cumulative advantage The accumulation of increasing advantage as early advantage positions an individual for later advantage

Cumulative disadvantage The accumulation of increasing disadvantage as early disadvantage positions an individual for later disadvantage

Deculturalizing The intentional or unintentional process that results in the destruction, or severe limitation, of a culture's ability to sustain itself (language, customs, rituals, and so forth)

Default individualization One possible pathway in young adulthood, which involves making transitions defined by circumstance and situation

Delirium Syndrome characterized by an impairment of consciousness. It has a sudden onset (a few hours or days), follows a brief and fluctuating course that includes impairment of consciousness, and has the potential for improvement when causes are treated. Prevalence of delirium is high among hospitalized elderly persons; toxicity from prescribed medications is a common cause

Dementia Impairment or loss of cognitive functioning caused by damage in the brain tissue. Dementia is not part of the brain's normal aging process, but its prevalence increases with age

Dependency ratio A demographic indicator expressing the degree of demand placed on society by the dependent young and the dependent elderly combined

Developmental biocultural co-constructivism A theory of human development that postulates dynamic reciprocal interactions between the human environment and the biology of the person

Developmental delays Delays in developing skills and abilities in infants and preschoolers

Developmental individualization One possible pathway in young adulthood, which involves making transitions defined by personal agency and deliberately charted growth opportunities in intellectual, occupational, and psychosocial domains

Developmental niche The cultural context into which a particular child is born, guides every aspect of the developmental process

Direct bullying Intentionally inflicting emotional or physical harm on another person through fairly explicit physical or verbal harassment, assault, or injury

Discipline Action taken by a child's caretaker to help the child correct behavioral problems

Disengaged parenting Aloof, withdrawn, and unresponsive parenting

Disengagement theory (of aging) Theory of social gerontology that suggests that as elderly individuals grow older, they gradually decrease their social interactions and ties and become increasingly self-preoccupied

Dominant genes Genes that express themselves if present on one or both chromosomes in a pair

Ego integrity versus ego despair The psychosocial crisis of Erik Erikson's eighth and final stage of development, which centers on one's ability to process what has happened in life and accept these experiences as integral to the meaning of life

Egocentrism The assumption by children in the preoperational stage of cognitive development that others perceive, think, and feel just the way they do. Inability to recognize the possibility of other perspectives

Embryo The stage of prenatal development beginning in the second week and lasting through the eighth week

Emerging adulthood A developmental phase distinct from both adolescence and young adulthood, occurring between the ages of 18 and 25 in industrialized societies

Emotional intelligence The ability to motivate oneself to persist in the face of frustration, to control impulses, to delay gratification, to regulate one's moods, and to empathize with others; theory proposed by Daniel Goleman

Empathy Ability to understand another person's emotional condition

Event history The sequence of significant events, experiences, and transitions in a person's life from birth to death

Extremely low birth weight (ELBW) A newborn weight of less than 1,000 grams (2.2 pounds)

Extroversion Orientation to the external world, in contrast to introversion, which is orientation to the internal world

Family pluralism Recognition of many viable types of family structures

Feminist theories (of aging) Theory of social gerontology suggesting that, because gender is a central organizing principle in our society, we can only understand aging by taking gender into account

Fertilization The penetration of an ovum by a spermatozoon, usually occurring in the fallopian tube

Fertilization age The number of completed weeks of pregnancy counting from 14 days after the beginning of the last menstrual period to the birth of the neonate

Fetal viability The capability to survive outside the womb, typically requiring at least 25 weeks

Fetus The developing organism from the ninth week of pregnancy to birth

Fictive kin Friends who are neither biologically nor romantically related to the family but who are adopted as family and given the same rights and responsibilities as family members

Fine motor skills Skills based on small muscle movements, particularly in the hands, as well as eye-hand coordination

Fluid intelligence Abstract reasoning skills

Formal operations stage The fourth and final stage in Piaget's theory of cognitive development, generally experienced in adolescence. Involves the capacity to apply hypothetical reasoning and to use symbols to solve problems

Gender identity Understanding of oneself as a man or woman

Generalized other A construction that represents how others might view and respond to our behavior

Generativity The ability to transcend personal interests to provide care and concern for generations to come

Genes Basic units of heredity, made of DNA, and found on chromosomes

Genetic liability The state of being prone to hereditary disorders

Genetic theories of biological aging Theories proposing that there are genetically determined differences between species in the maximum life span

Genotype The totality of the hereditary information present in an organism

Germ cell The ova and spermatozoa whose function is to reproduce the organism

Gestation The length of maturation time from conception to birth. In humans it averages 280 days, with a range of 259 to 287 days

Gestational age The number of completed weeks of pregnancy counting from the first day of the last normal menstrual cycle to the birth of the neonate

Gonads Sex glands—ovaries in females and testes in males

Grief The normal internal reaction of an individual experiencing a loss, a complex process that is highly individualized

Grief work A necessary period of working to sever the attachment bond to a lost person or object

Gross motor skills Skills based upon large muscle group movements and most easily observed during whole body movements, such as hopping, skipping, and running

Hospice Program that provides care to the terminally ill. Patients typically receive treatment by a team of doctors, nurses, social workers, and care staff through inpatient or outpatient care

Hostile aggression Aggression that is an attack meant to hurt another individual

Human agency The use of personal power to achieve one's goals

Human capital Individual assets such as talents, skills, intellectual capacity, social development, and emotional regulatory capacity

Incidental memory Memory that relates to facts a person has learned without the intention to retain and recall

Indirect bullying Less explicit and less detectable than direct bullying, including more subtle verbal, psychological, and social or "relational" bullying tactics

Individual education plan (IEP) An individualized, collaboratively developed plan that focuses on facilitating achievement and is designed to respond to the unique needs of a child with a disability in the school setting. Such plans are mandated by the Individuals with Disabilities Education Act of 1990

Individuation The development of a self and identity that are unique and separate

Individuative-reflective faith The fourth stage of James Fowler's six-stage model of faith development, a stage when adults no longer rely on outside authority and look for authority within the self

Infant A young child in the first year of life

Infant mortality The death of a child before his or her first birthday

Infertility The inability to create a viable embryo

Institutional discrimination The systematic denial of access to assets, economic opportunities, associations, and organizations based on minority status

Instrumental activities of daily living (IADLs) More complex everyday tasks such as doing light housework, doing the laundry, using transportation, handling finances, using the telephone, and taking medications

Instrumental aggression Aggression that occurs while fighting over toys and space, etc.

Intentional memory Memory that relates to events that a person plans to remember

Interactive genes Corresponding genes that give separate yet controlling messages

Interrelational intelligence Based on emotional and social intelligence and similar to Howard Gardner's concept of interpersonal intelligence

Intimacy Characteristic of close interpersonal relationships, includes interdependence, self-disclosure, and affection

Intimacy versus isolation Erik Erikson's description of the developmental task of young adulthood, a time when individuals move from the identity fragmentation, confusion, and exploration of adolescence into more intimate engagement with significant others or become isolated

Introversion Orientation to the internal world, in contrast to extroversion, which is orientation to the external world

Juvenile delinquency Acts that, if committed by an adult, would be considered crimes, plus status offenses such as running away from home, skipping school, violating curfew, and possession of tobacco or alcohol

Keeper of the meaning A stage of psychosocial development proposed by George Vaillant to come between Erik Erikson's stages of generativity and integrity, a stage when older adults take on the task of passing on the traditions of the past to the next generation

Kinkeepers Family members who work at keeping family members across the generations in touch with one another and make sure that both emotional and practical needs of family members are met

Late preterm birth Birth that occurs at 34 to 36 weeks' gestation

Lateralization Process in which the two hemispheres of the brain begin to operate slightly differently during early childhood

Learning play Play that is focused on language and thinking skills

Life course perspective An approach to human behavior that recognizes the influence of age but also acknowledges the influences of historical time and culture

Life event Incident or event that is brief in scope but is influential on human behavior

Life review A process of evaluating and making sense of one's life. It includes a reinterpretation of past experiences and unresolved conflicts. The process of life review relates to the eighth stage of Erikson's theory of adult development (ego integrity versus ego despair)

Life-span theory A theory that begins with the premise that development is lifelong and is based in ongoing transactions between persons and environments; based in psychology, whereas the life course perspective has more multidisciplinary roots

Life structure In Levinson's seasons of adulthood theory, the patterns and central components of a person's life at a particular point in time

Living will A document that describes the medical procedures, drugs, and types of treatment that an individual would choose for oneself if able to do so in certain situations. It also describes the situations for which this individual would want treatment withheld

Loss The severing of an attachment an individual has with a loved one, a love object, or an aspect of one's self or identity

Low birth weight (LBW) A newborn weight of less than 2,500 grams (5 pounds, 8 ounces)

Masturbation Self-stimulation of the genitals for sexual pleasure

Menarche The onset of menstruation

Menopause Permanent cessation of menstruation, usually defined as 12 consecutive months with absence of menstruation

Miscarriage Naturally occurring loss of a fetus prior to 20 weeks' gestation; also known as spontaneous abortion

Molecular/cellular theories of biological aging Theories proposing that biological aging is caused by molecular or cellular processes

Morbidity The incidence of disease and illness in a population group

Mortality rate The incidence of death in a population group

Motor skills Control over movements of body parts

Mourning The external expression of grief, also a process, influenced by the customs of one's culture

Multifactorial inheritance Genetic traits that are controlled by multiple genes

Multigravida A pregnant woman who has previously experienced pregnancy

Multipara A mother who has previously given birth

Multiple intelligences Howard Gardner's theory that humans have at least eight critical intelligences: verbal/linguistic, logical/mathematical, visual/spatial, musical/rhythmic, bodily kinesthetic, naturalist, interpersonal, intrapersonal

Neonate Infant up to 1 month of age

Neurons Specialized nerve cells that store and transmit information

Novice phase According to Daniel Levinson, the ages of 17 to 22, in which the transition into young adulthood occurs, including the tasks of leaving adolescence and making preliminary decisions about relationships, career, and belief systems

Object permanence The ability to understand that objects exist even when they cannot be seen

Oppression The intentional or unintentional act or process of placing restrictions on an individual, group, or institution; may include observable actions, but more typically refers to complex, covert, interconnected processes and practices (such as discriminating, devaluing, and exploiting a group of individuals) reflected in and perpetuating exclusion and inequalities over time

Palliative care Active care of patients who have received a diagnosis of a serious, life-threatening illness; a form of care focusing on pain and symptom management as opposed to curing disease

Perimenopause A period of time that begins immediately prior to menopause in women, when there are biological and clinical indicators that a woman's reproductive capacity is reaching exhaustion, and continues through the first year after the last period

Permissive parenting A parenting style, identified by Baumrind, that involves no limit setting on the part of the parent

Perspective taking The ability to see a situation from another person's point of view

Phenotype The expression of genetic traits in an individual

Physical aggression Aggression against another person using physical force

Population pyramid A chart that depicts the proportion of the population in each age group

Postconventional moral reasoning Third and final level of Lawrence Kohlberg's stage theory of moral development; morality based on moral principles that transcend societal rules

Power of attorney (POA) A person appointed by an individual to manage his or her financial and legal affairs. A POA can be limited (for a limited time period), general (no restrictions), or durable (begins after reaching a specified level of disability)

Precociousness Early development; most often refers to a rare level of intelligence at an early age, but may refer to "premature" ability or development in a number of areas

Preconventional level of moral reasoning First level of moral reasoning in Lawrence Kohlberg's stage theory of moral reasoning; morality based on what gets rewarded or punished or what benefits either the child or someone the child cares about

Premenopause The beginning of the menopause process when a woman begins to have occasional menstrual cycles without ovulation

Preoperational stage The second stage in Piaget's theory of cognitive development. Young children (ages 2 to 7) use symbols to represent their earlier sensorimotor experiences. Thinking is not yet logical

Primary aging Changes that are a normal part of the aging process

Primary sex characteristics Physical characteristics that are directly related to maturation of the reproductive organs and external genitalia

Primipara A woman who has delivered only one infant of at least 500 grams (20 weeks' gestation), whether the child is alive or dead at the time of birth

Privilege Unearned advantage that comes from one's position in the social structure

Programmed aging theories Theories of biological aging that start from the assumption that the aging process is genetically determined

Prosocial Behaving in a helpful or empathic manner

Protective factors Personal and societal factors that reduce or protect against risk

Pruning Reduction of brain synapses to improve the efficiency of brain functioning; follows a period of blooming of synapses

Psychological age The capacities that people have and the skills they use to adapt to changing biological and environmental demands, including skills in memory, learning, intelligence, motivation, emotions; also how old people feel

Psychological identity Self-definition as a separate and distinct person

Puberty Stage during which individuals become capable of reproduction

Random error theories Theories of biological aging that propose that physiological aging occurs because of damaging processes that become more frequent in late adulthood but are not a part of a genetic unfolding process

Recessive genes Genes that express themselves only if present on both chromosomes in a pair

Reflex An involuntary response to a simple stimulus

Relational aggression Aggression that involves behaviors that damage relationships without physical force, such as threatening to leave a relationship unless a friend complies with demands, or using social exclusion or the silent treatment to get one's way

Relative poverty A conceptualization of poverty that emphasizes the tendency to define one's poverty status in relation to others within one's social environment

Reminiscence Recalling and recounting past events. Reminiscing serves several functions: It may be an enjoyable activity, it may be directed at enhancing a person's self-image, it may serve as a way to cope with current or future problems, and it may assist in the life review as a way to achieve ego integrity

Resilience Healthy development in the face of risk factors. Thought to be the result of protective factors that shield the individual from the consequences of potential hazards

Risk factors Personal or social factors that increase the likelihood of a problem occurring

Rites of passage Ceremonies that demarcate transition from one role or status to another

Romantic love An intimate relationship that is sexually oriented

Secondary aging Changes caused by health-compromising behaviors such as smoking or environmental factors such as pollution

Secondary sex characteristics Physical characteristics associated with sexual maturation that are not directly related to the reproductive organs and external genitalia

Secondary sexual development Associated with puberty and referring to the development of secondary sex characteristics such as the growth of pubic, chest, and facial hair in males and the growth of pubic hair and breasts in females

Self-esteem The way one evaluates the self in relation to others

Self-theory An organized understanding of the self in relation to others; begins to develop in early childhood

Sensitive period A time in fetal development that is particularly sensitive to exposure to teratogens. Different organs have different sensitive periods. Also called critical period

Sensorimotor stage The first stage in Piaget's theory of cognitive development. Infants (ages 0 to 2 years) learn through sensory awareness and motor activities

Sensory system The system of senses: hearing, sight, taste, smell, touch, responsiveness to the body's position, and sensitivity to pain

Separation anxiety When an infant becomes anxious at the signs of an impending separation from parents, at about 9 months of age

Sex chromosomes Chromosome pair number 23, which determines the sex of the individual

Sex hormones Hormones that affect the development of the gonads, functioning of the gonads, and mating and child-caring behavior; includes androgens, progestins, and estrogens

Sex-linked trait A trait that is controlled by a gene located on one of the sex chromosomes

Sex ratio The number of males per 100 females in a population

Sexual orientation Erotic, romantic, and affectionate attraction to people of the same sex, the opposite sex, or both sexes

Sexually transmitted infections (STIs) Infectious diseases that are most often contracted through oral, anal, or vaginal sexual contact. Also called venereal diseases

Small for gestational age (SGA) Lower than normal birth weight, given the number of weeks of gestation

Social age Age measured in terms of age-graded roles and behaviors expected by society—the socially constructed meanings of various ages

Social competence The ability to engage in sustained, positive, and mutually satisfactory peer interactions

Social construction theory (of aging) A theory that attempts to understand and explain the influence of social definitions, social interactions, and social structures on the aging process

Social exchange theory (of aging) A theory that attempts to understand the realignments of roles and values in late adulthood in light of the shifting resources that older adults bring to social exchanges

Social gerontology The social science that studies human aging

Social identity The part of the self-concept that comes from knowledge of one's membership in a social group and the emotional significance of that membership

Social support Help rendered by others that benefits an individual

Sociodramatic play Fantasy play in a group, with the group coordinating fantasies; important type of play in early childhood

Spermarche Onset of the ability to ejaculate mobile sperm

Spiritual age The position of a person in the ongoing search for meaning and fulfilling relationships

Spirituality That which gives meaning, purpose, and direction to one's life

Spontaneous abortion Naturally occurring loss of a fetus prior to 20 weeks' gestation; also known as miscarriage

Status offenses Behaviors that would not be considered criminal if committed by an adult but are considered delinquent if committed by an adolescent—for example, running away from home, skipping school, violating curfew, and possessing tobacco or alcohol

Statutory rape A criminal offense that involves an adult engaging in sexual activities with a minor or a mentally incapacitated person

Stranger anxiety When an infant reacts with fear and withdrawal to unfamiliar persons, at about 9 months of age

Symbolic functioning The ability to think using symbols to represent what is not present

Symbolic play Fantasy play, begins around the age of 2

Synapses Neural connections

Synthetic-conventional faith The third stage of James Fowler's six-stage model of faith development; faith that is rooted in external authority

System-level theories of biological aging Theories that propose that aging is caused by processes operating across biological systems

Temperament A person's disposition and primary behavioral characteristics in infants and young children

Teratogen Anything present during prenatal life that adversely affects normal cellular development in form or function in the embryo or fetus

Toddler A young child from about 12 to 36 months of age

Trait theory A theory that proposes that personality traits are enduring characteristics rooted in early temperament and influenced by genetic and organic factors

Trajectories Long-term patterns of stability and change based on unique person-environment configurations over time

Transductive reasoning Reasoning from one particular event to another particular event rather than in a logical causal manner

Transitional object Comfort object, such as a favorite blanket or stuffed animal, that toddlers often use to help them cope with separations from parents

Transitions Changes in roles and statuses that represent a distinct departure from prior roles and statuses

Trauma A physical or mental injury generally associated with violence, shock, or an unanticipated situation

Turning point A special event that produces a lasting shift in the life course trajectory

Universalizing faith The final stage of James Fowler's theory of faith development; a stage in which individuals lead selfless lives based on principles of absolute love and justice

Very low birth weight (VLBW) A newborn weight of less than 1,500 grams (3 pounds, 3 ounces)

Working model Model for relationships developed in the earliest attachment relationship

Zone of proximal development According to Vygotsky, the theoretical space between the child's current developmental level (or performance) and the child's potential level (or performance) if given access to appropriate models and developmental experiences in the social environment

Zygote A fertilized ovum cell

Index

About the Author

Elizabeth D. Hutchison, MSW, PhD, received her MSW from the George Warren Brown School of Social Work at Washington University in St. Louis and her PhD from the University at Albany, State University of New York. She was on the faculty in the Social Work Department at Elms College from 1980 to 1987, and as chair of the department from 1982 to 1987. She was on the faculty in the School of Social Work at Virginia Commonwealth University from 1987 to 2009, where she taught courses in human behavior and the social environment, social work and social justice, and child and family policy; she also served as field practicum liaison. She has been a social worker in health, mental health, aging, and child and family welfare settings. She is committed to providing social workers with comprehensive, current, and useful frameworks for thinking about human behavior. Her other research interests focus on child and family welfare. She currently lives in Rancho Mirage, California.

About the Contributors

Suzanne M. Baldwin, PhD, LCSW, MSW, BSN, RN, received her PhD in social work from the School of Social Work at Virginia Commonwealth University. She works as a clinical social worker in private practice with families and spent almost two decades working as a clinical nurse specialist in newborn intensive care. Her major areas of interest are working with families involved with the court system and military family issues. She has taught human behavior, practice, communications, and research courses at Old Dominion University and at the School of Social Work at Virginia Commonwealth University. She is the mother of three adult children. Her oldest daughter was a patient in the neonatal intensive care unit (NICU), and her daughter's son spent a month in the NICU after his birth in 2009.

Nicole Footen Bromfield, MSW, PhD, is Assistant Professor in the Department of Social Work at the United Arab Emirates University. Nicole's research interests include human trafficking and irregular migration, and more recently she has been exploring human trafficking related to international adoption and international surrogacy.

Leanne Charlesworth, LMSW, PhD, is Associate Professor in the Department of Social Work at Nazareth College of Rochester. She has practiced within child welfare systems, and her areas of service and research interest include poverty and child and family well-being. She has taught human behavior and research at the undergraduate and graduate levels.

Marcia P. Harrigan, MSW, PhD, is Associate Professor and Associate Dean of Student and Academic Affairs in the School of Social Work at Virginia Commonwealth University. She has practiced in child welfare, juvenile justice, and mental health. Her major areas of interest are nontraditional family structures, family assessment, multigenerational households, and long-distance family caregiving. She has taught human behavior and practice courses.

Kristina Hash, LICSW, PhD is an Associate Professor in the Division of Social Work at West Virginia University. Her research interests include caregiving, LGBT issues, the use of technology in teaching and research, and geriatric education. Her practice background includes positions in home health care, social work continuing education, and research and program evaluation. Additionally, she has been involved in several volunteer activities with community-based agencies serving older adults. She primarily teaches courses in aging and human behavior in the social environment.

Lesley Hewitt, BSc, BsocWk (Hons), MSW, GCHE, is a lecturer in the Department of Social Work, University of Ballarat, Ballarat, Victoria, Australia, where she was recently inducted onto the Victorian women's Honour Roll. Her practice experience includes working in sexual assault services and child protection. She teaches human development, group work, and aged care at both undergraduate and postgraduate levels. Her research interests include family violence and sexual assault, and social work education.

Pamela J. Kovacs, MSW, PhD, is Associate Professor in the School of Social Work at Virginia Commonwealth University. Her practice experience includes work with individuals, families, and groups in oncology, hospice, and mental health settings. Her major areas of interest are HIV/AIDS, hospice and palliative care, volunteerism, caregiving, and preparing social workers for health care and other settings serving older adults. She teaches clinical practice, social work practice and health care, qualitative research, and additionally serves as a field liaison.

Peter Maramaldi, CSW, MPH, PhD, is Associate Professor at Simmons School of Social Work, Senior Social Work Scientist at the Massachusetts General Hospital in Boston, and a Hartford Faculty Scholar and National Mentor in Gerontology. His current research focuses on behavioral oncology and aging. He worked in a broad range of practice settings for more than 25 years in New York City, and has since taught courses at Simmons in practice, health policy, and research methodology in social work. At Harvard Medical School, he has taught interviewing and interdisciplinary collaboration courses.

Holly C. Matto, MSW, PhD, LCSW-C, is Associate Professor in the School of Social Work at Virginia Commonwealth University. Her research focuses on substance abuse assessment and treatment. She has taught courses in human behavior, social work practice, art therapy in social work practice, and research methodology.

Susan Ainsley McCarter, MS, MSW, PhD, is Assistant Professor in the Department of Social Work at the University of North Carolina at Charlotte. She has worked as a juvenile probation officer; mental health counselor for children, adolescents, and families; social policy advocate; and mother. Her major area of interest is risk and protective factors for adolescents—specifically the overrepresentation of youth of color in the juvenile justice system. She currently teaches research methods and the MSW capstone course and has taught human behavior, social policy, social work and criminal justice, and sociology courses at both the undergraduate and graduate levels.

Derek Morch, MSW, is a recent graduate of the School of Social Work at Virginia Commonwealth University. He has worked in a variety of settings as a clinical case manager for adults with serious mental illness. He has also provided services to children and their families as a home-based counselor and therapeutic mentor. His areas of interest include community-based treatment, mental health parity, and ongoing practice with multicultural populations.

Matthias J. Naleppa, MSW, PhD, is Associate Professor in the School of Social Work at Virginia Commonwealth University and a Hartford Geriatric Social Work Scholar. His research focuses on geriatric social work, short-term treatment, and international social work. He teaches philosophy of science, practice, and research in the MSW and Doctoral Programs at VCU. Over the past years, he has regularly conducted workshops on task-centered practice and geriatric social work in Europe and Asia. He holds an MSW from the Catholic School of Social Work in Munich and a PhD from the University at Albany.

Rosa Schnitzenbaumer is a graduate of the Catholic School of Social Work, Munich, Germany, She works as a geriatric social worker and licensed practical nurse for the Caritas Welfare Organization in Miesbach, Germany. She teaches as adjunct faculty for the School for Care Management at the University of Applied Sciences Innsbruck, Austria, and is a board member of the Adelheid Stein Institute for Therapeutic Roleplay. Throughout her career she has been involved in developing and managing programs for older adults, including a regional outpatient gero-psychiatric counseling center, individualized service systems for older adults, a senior volunteer network, and caregiver training programs. She has also initiated *Erzählcafés,* volunteer-led groups for persons with dementia.

Meenakshi Venkataraman, PhD, is Assistant Professor at the Division of Social Work, West Virginia University. She has taught human behavior and psychopathology courses at the graduate level. Her research interests include psychological, social, and spiritual aspects of adult severe mental illness.

Pamela Viggiani, MSW, PhD, is Assistant Professor in the Department of Social Work Department at Nazareth College of Rochester. Her research focuses on oppression, social justice, and pedagogy. She teaches courses in social justice, social advocacy, diversity, policy, and social work methods. She serves on the New York State Social Work Board. In the past she was an evaluator and consultant for grants funding public child welfare professionalization.

Jim Wood, EdD, is a 33-year veteran in teaching and administration at all levels of public schools and is currently Associate Professor of Childhood Education at the Ralph C. Wilson, Jr. School of Education at St. John Fisher College in

Rochester, New York. His areas of interest include social justice education, integrated school environments, achievement-gap issues, and diverse school cultures.

David Woody III, PhD, LCSW, is currently Director of Program Services at The Salvation Army, DFW Metroplex Command. After several years in academia at the University of Texas at Arlington and Baylor University, Dr. Woody has returned to work in the local community, focused on economic self-sufficiency, clinical counseling for those in poverty, and establishing low-cost medical homes for those without health care insurance. In addition to issues related to poverty, Dr. Woody's major areas of interest include research exploring strengths of African American single mothers, and initiatives enhancing the significance of fatherhood in the African American community.

Debra J. Woody, PhD, LMSW, is Associate Professor in the School of Social Work at the University of Texas at Arlington. Her areas of research and practice interests focus upon child and family issues related to drug and alcohol use. She is the principal investigator for several grants that support a drug and alcohol intervention program called New Connections, providing services to mothers and their drug-exposed infants and toddlers. She currently teaches both undergraduate and graduate research and practice courses.

Maria E. Zuniga, MSW, PhD, is Professor Emeritus from the School of Social Work at San Diego State University, where she taught for 16 years, with an additional 11 years at Sacramento State University. Along with human behavior courses, Dr. Zuniga's areas of focus were direct practice, gerontological practice, and practice with multicultural populations, in particular practice with Latinos. She was also a member of the board of directors of the Council on Social Work Education (CSWE) and helped to develop a CSWE-sponsored conference on Cultural Competence held at the University of Michigan in 1999. She is a consultant on cultural competence for local, state, and national agencies and publishing houses.

Photo Credits

Chapter 1: Photo 1.1, © Kristy-Anne Glubish/Design Pics/Corbis; Photo 1.2. © ComStock/ThinkStock; Photo 1.3, © iStockphoto.com.

Chapter 2: Photo 2.1, © iStockphoto.com; Photo 2.2, © Vernon Wiley/iStockphoto.com; Photo 2.3, © iStockphoto.com.

Chapter 3: Photo 3.1, © iStockphoto.com; Photo 3.2, © iStockphoto.com; Photo 3.3, © Oleg Kozlov/iStockphoto.com.

Chapter 4: Photo 4.1, © iStockphoto.com; Photo 4.2, © iStockphoto.com; Photo 4.3, © Kelly Redinger/Design Pics/Corbis; Photo 4.4, © Erna Vader/iStockphoto.com.

Chapter 5: Photo 5.1, © Bonnie Jacobs/ iStockphoto.com; Photo 5.2, © Josh Hodge/ iStockphoto.com; Photo 5.3, © Brand X Pictures/ ThinkStock.

Chapter 6: Photo 6.1, © Don Hammond/Design Pics/Corbis; Photo 6.2, © Jack Hollingsworth/Digital Vision/ThinkStock; Photo 6.3, © iStockphoto.com; Photo 6.4, © Frank Micelotta/Getty Images Entertainment/Getty Images; Photo 6.5, © Izabela Habur/iStockphoto.com.

Chapter 7: Photo 7.1, © JupiterImages/liquidlibrary/ThinkStock; Photo 7.2, © Tim Pannell/Corbis; Photo 7.3, © Creatas/ThinkStock; Photo 7.4, © Patricia Nelson/iStockphoto.com.

Chapter 8: Photo 8.1, © The Washington Post/Getty Images; Photo 8.2, © Goodshoot/ThinkStock; Photo 8.3, © Bonnie Jacobs/iStockphoto.com; Photo 8.4, © iStockphoto.com.

Chapter 9: Photo 9.1a, © Stockbyte/ThinkStock; Photo 9.1b, © Creatas Images/ThinkStock; Photo 9.2, © iStockphoto.com; Photo 9.3, © iStockphoto.com; Photo 9.4, © Stephen Beaudet/zefa/Corbis.

Chapter 10: Photo 10.1, © Chris Rank/Corbis; Photo 10.2, © Rich Legg/iStockphoto.com; Photo 10.3, © iStockphoto.com; Photo 10.4, © iStockphoto.com; Photo 10.5, © iStockphoto.com.